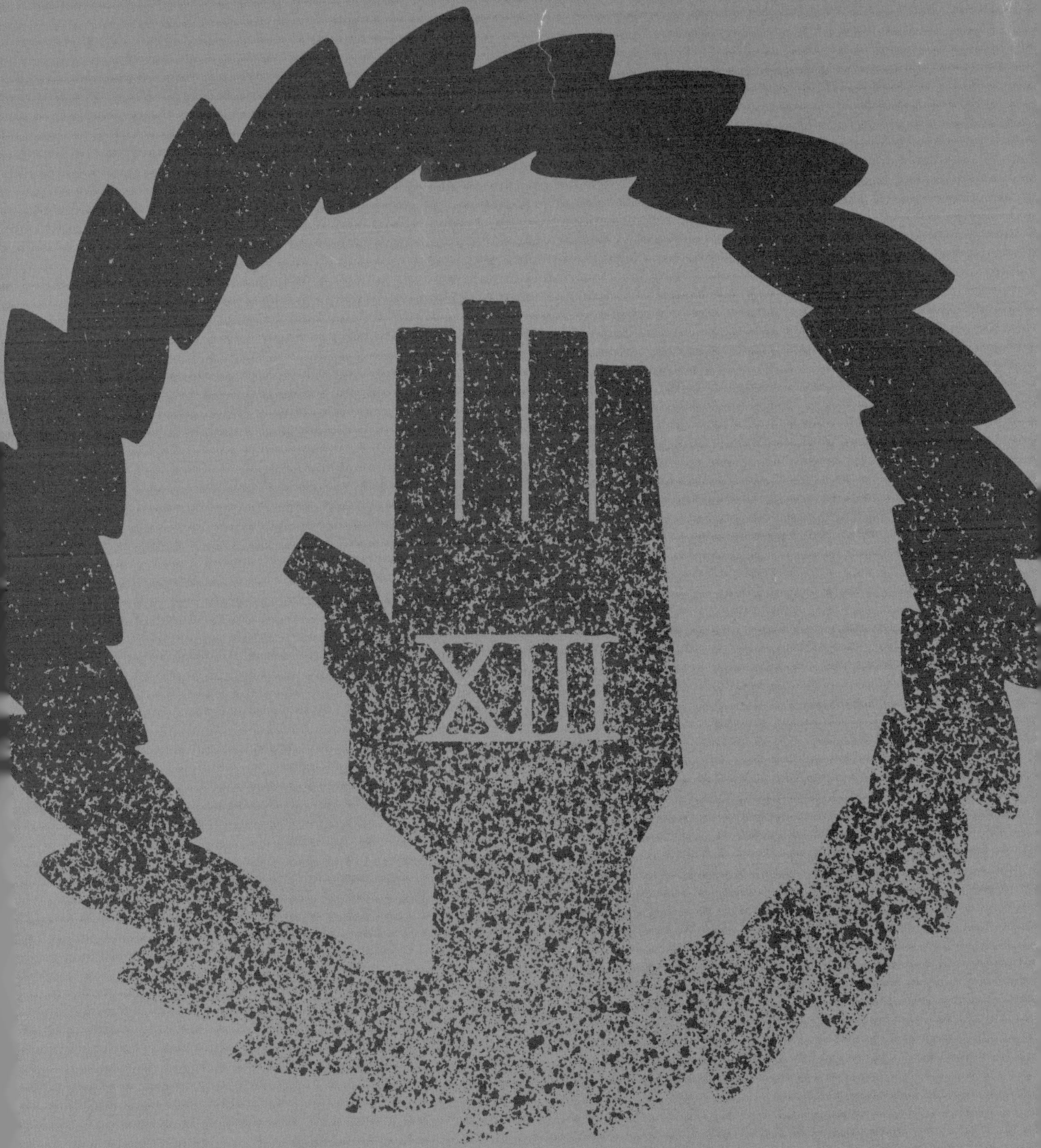
XIII

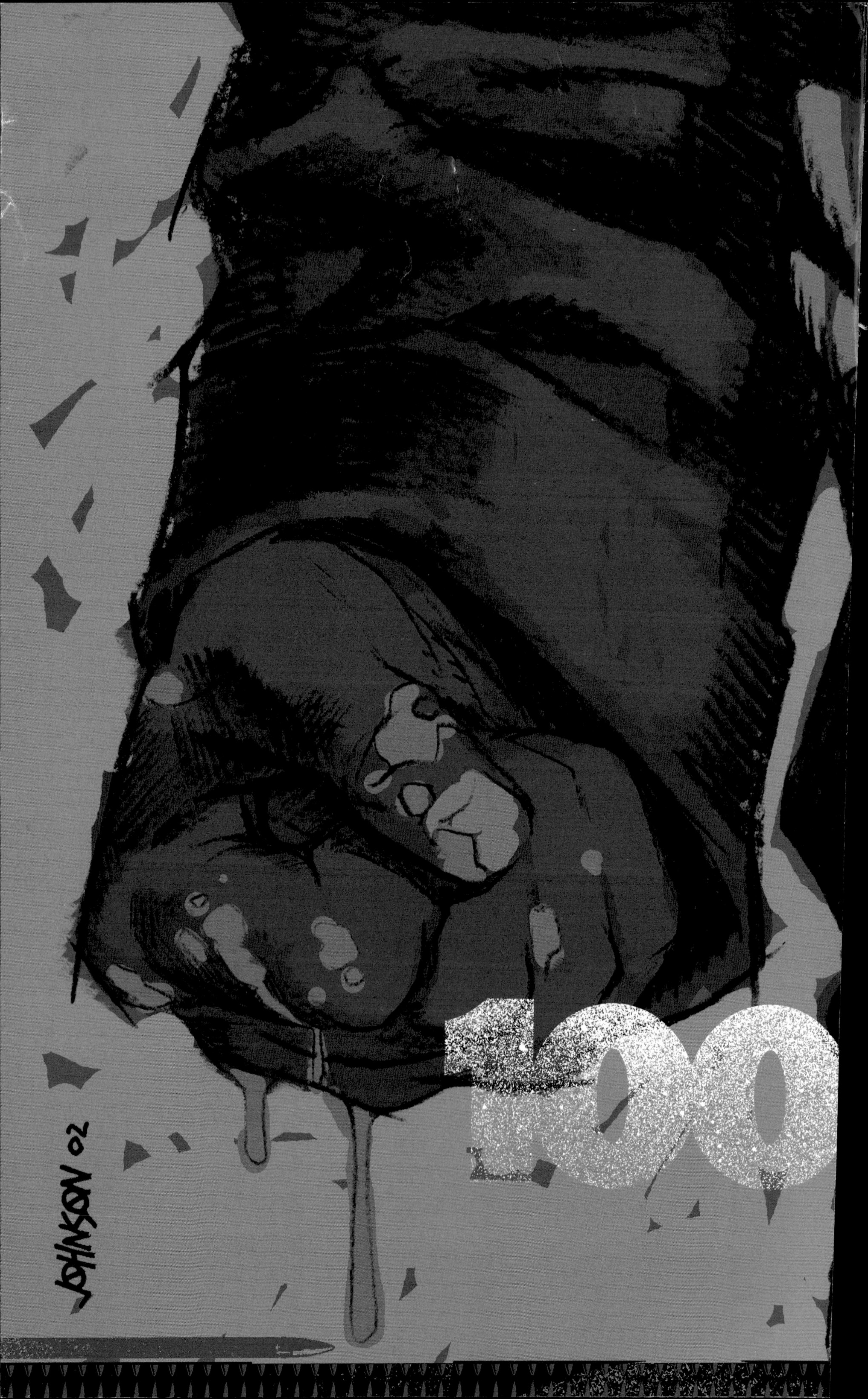
100
JOHNSON 02

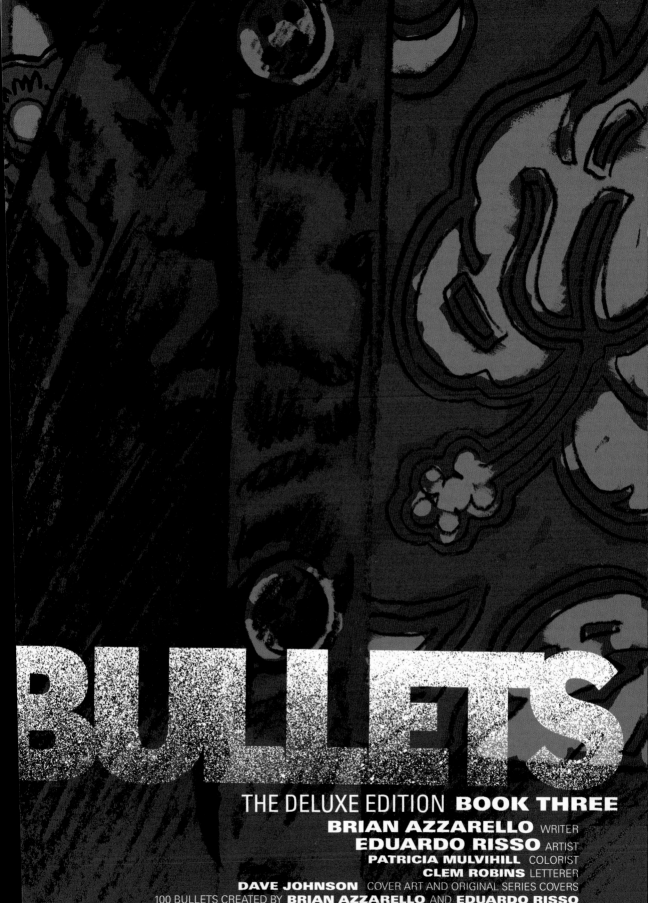

BULLETS

THE DELUXE EDITION **BOOK THREE**

BRIAN AZZARELLO WRITER
EDUARDO RISSO ARTIST
PATRICIA MULVIHILL COLORIST
CLEM ROBINS LETTERER
DAVE JOHNSON COVER ART AND ORIGINAL SERIES COVERS
100 BULLETS CREATED BY **BRIAN AZZARELLO** AND **EDUARDO RISSO**

Will Dennis Editor – Original Series
Zachary Rau Casey Seijas Assistant Editors – Original Series
Scott Nybakken Editor
Robbin Brosterman Design Director – Books
Louis Prandi Publication Design

Karen Berger Senior VP – Executive Editor, Vertigo
Bob Harras VP – Editor-in-Chief

Diane Nelson President
Dan DiDio and **Jim Lee** Co-Publishers
Geoff Johns Chief Creative Officer
John Rood Executive VP – Sales, Marketing and Business Development
Amy Genkins Senior VP – Business and Legal Affairs
Nairi Gardiner Senior VP – Finance
Jeff Boison VP – Publishing Operations
Mark Chiarello VP – Art Direction and Design
John Cunningham VP – Marketing
Terri Cunningham VP – Talent Relations and Services
Alison Gill Senior VP – Manufacturing and Operations
Hank Kanalz Senior VP – Digital
Jay Kogan VP – Business and Legal Affairs, Publishing
Jack Mahan VP – Business Affairs, Talent
Nick Napolitano VP – Manufacturing Administration
Sue Pohja VP – Book Sales
Courtney Simmons Senior VP – Publicity
Bob Wayne Senior VP – Sales

Special thanks to Eduardo A. Santillan Marcus for his translating assistance.

SUSTAINABLE FORESTRY INITIATIVE
Certified Chain of Custody
At Least 25% Certified Forest Content
www.sfiprogram.org
SFI-01042
APPLIES TO TEXT STOCK ONLY

Library of Congress Cataloging-in-Publication Data

Azzarello, Brian.
  100 bullets : the deluxe edition. Book three / Brian Azzarello, Eduardo Risso.
     p. cm.
  "Originally published in single magazine form in 100 Bullets 37-58."
  ISBN 978-1-4012-3729-5 (alk. paper)
  1. Crime--Comic books, strips, etc. 2. Graphic novels. I. Risso, Eduardo. II. Title.
  PN6728.A14A995 2012
  741.5'973--dc23
                          2012021221

Table of Contents

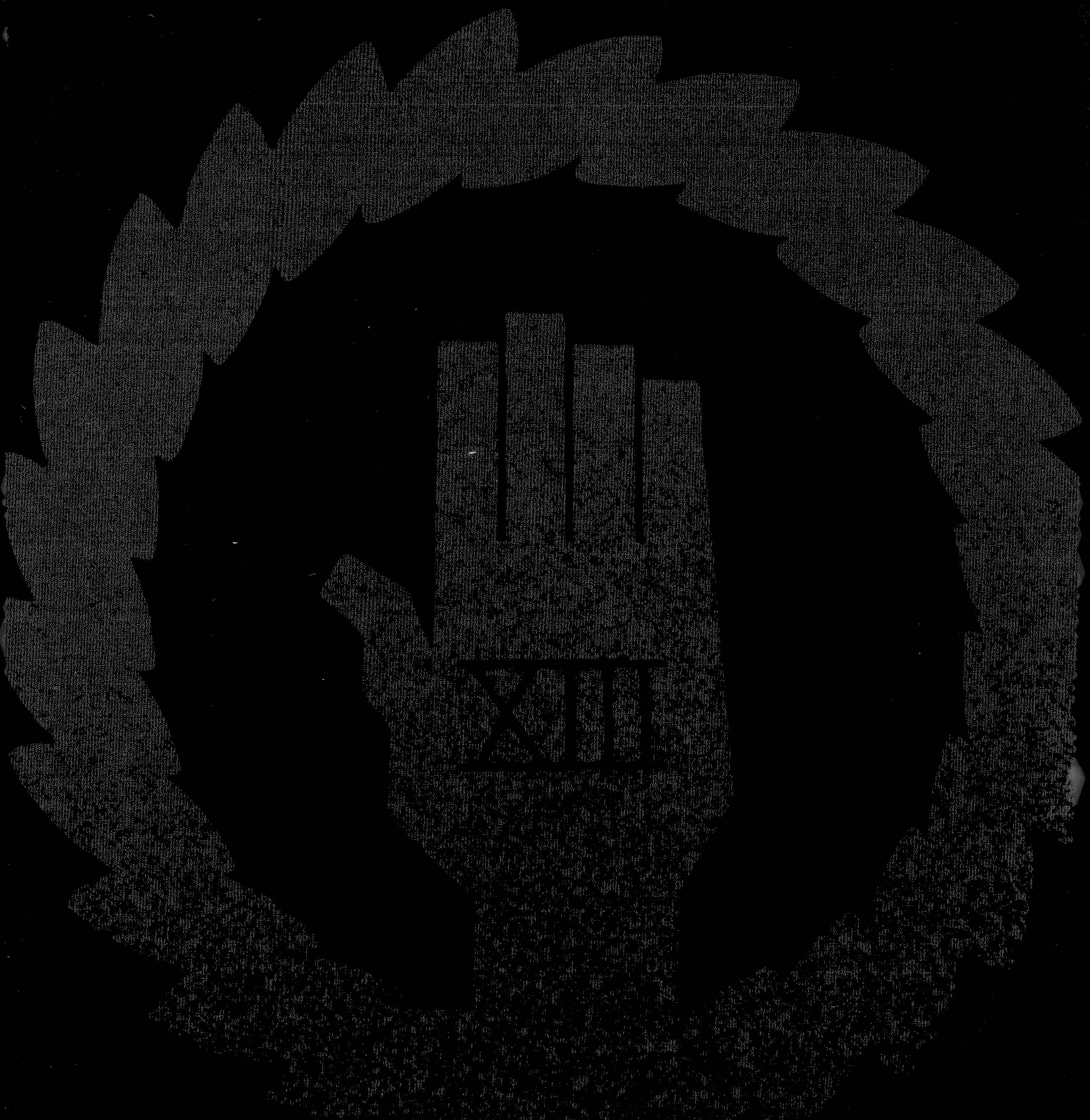
XIII

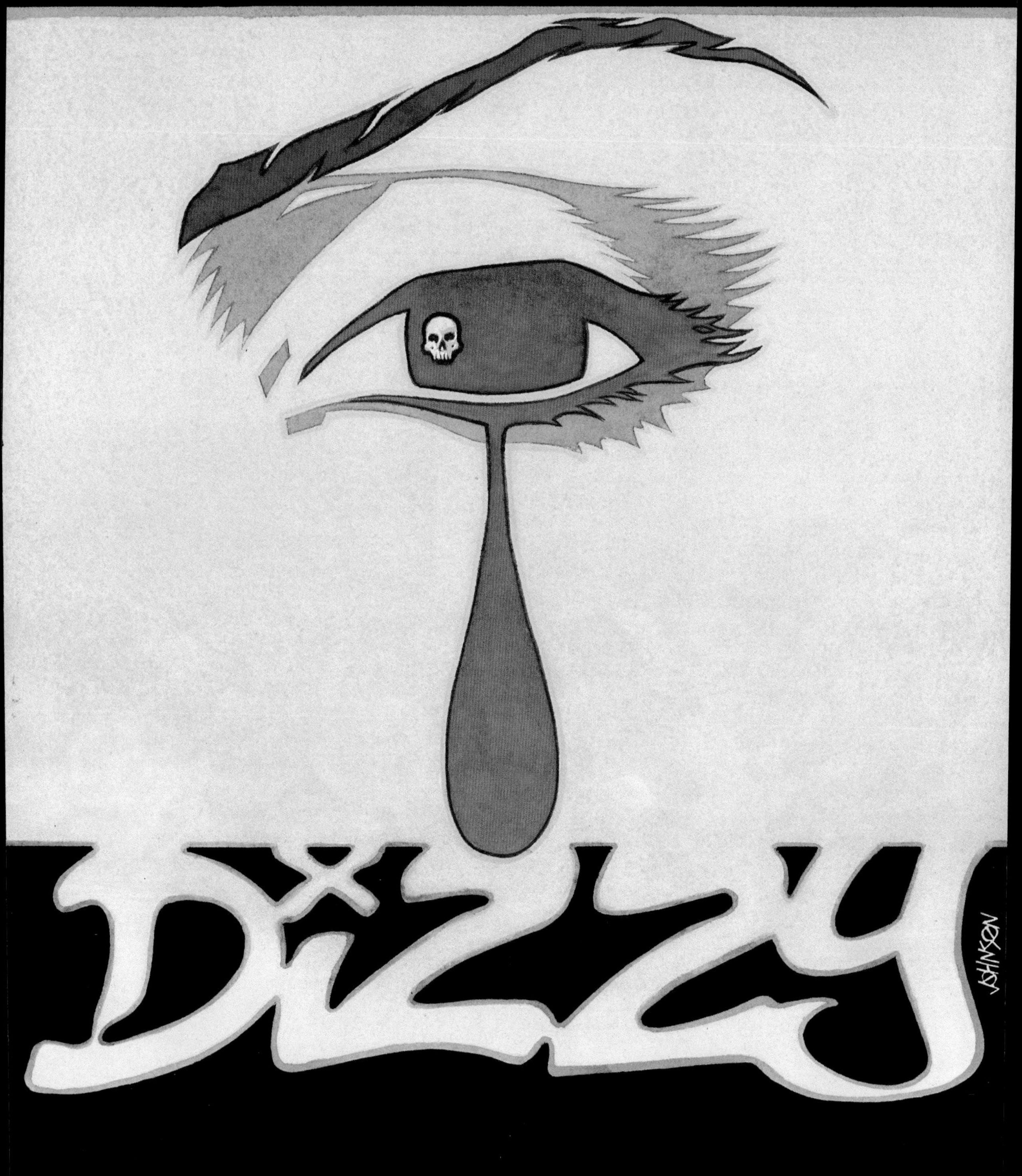
DIZZY
JOHNSON

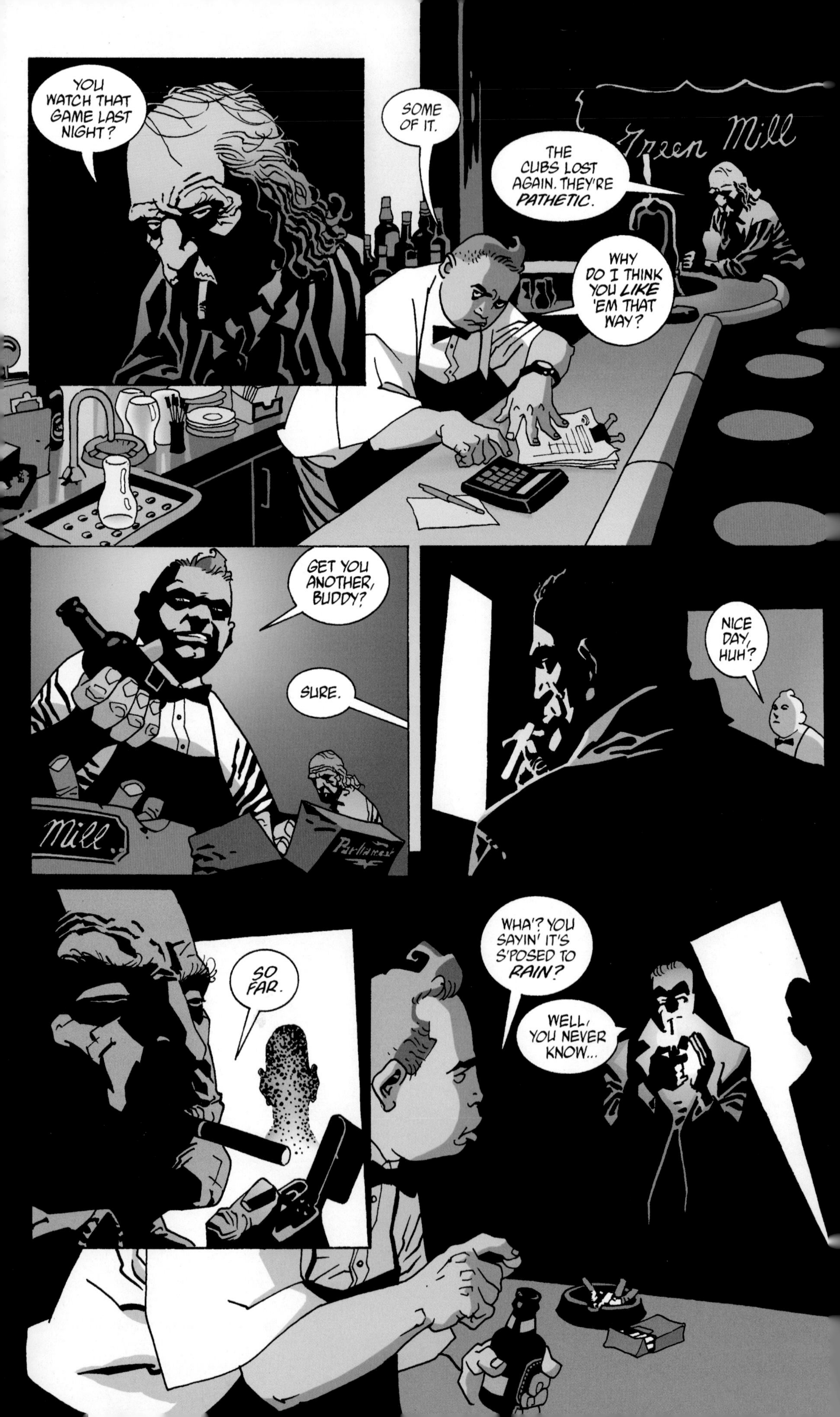

YOU WATCH THAT GAME LAST NIGHT?
SOME OF IT.
Green Mill
THE CUBS LOST AGAIN. THEY'RE PATHETIC.
WHY DO I THINK YOU LIKE 'EM THAT WAY?
GET YOU ANOTHER, BUDDY?
SURE.
Mill
Parliament
NICE DAY, HUH?
SO FAR.
WHA'? YOU SAYIN' IT'S S'POSED TO RAIN?
WELL, YOU NEVER KNOW...

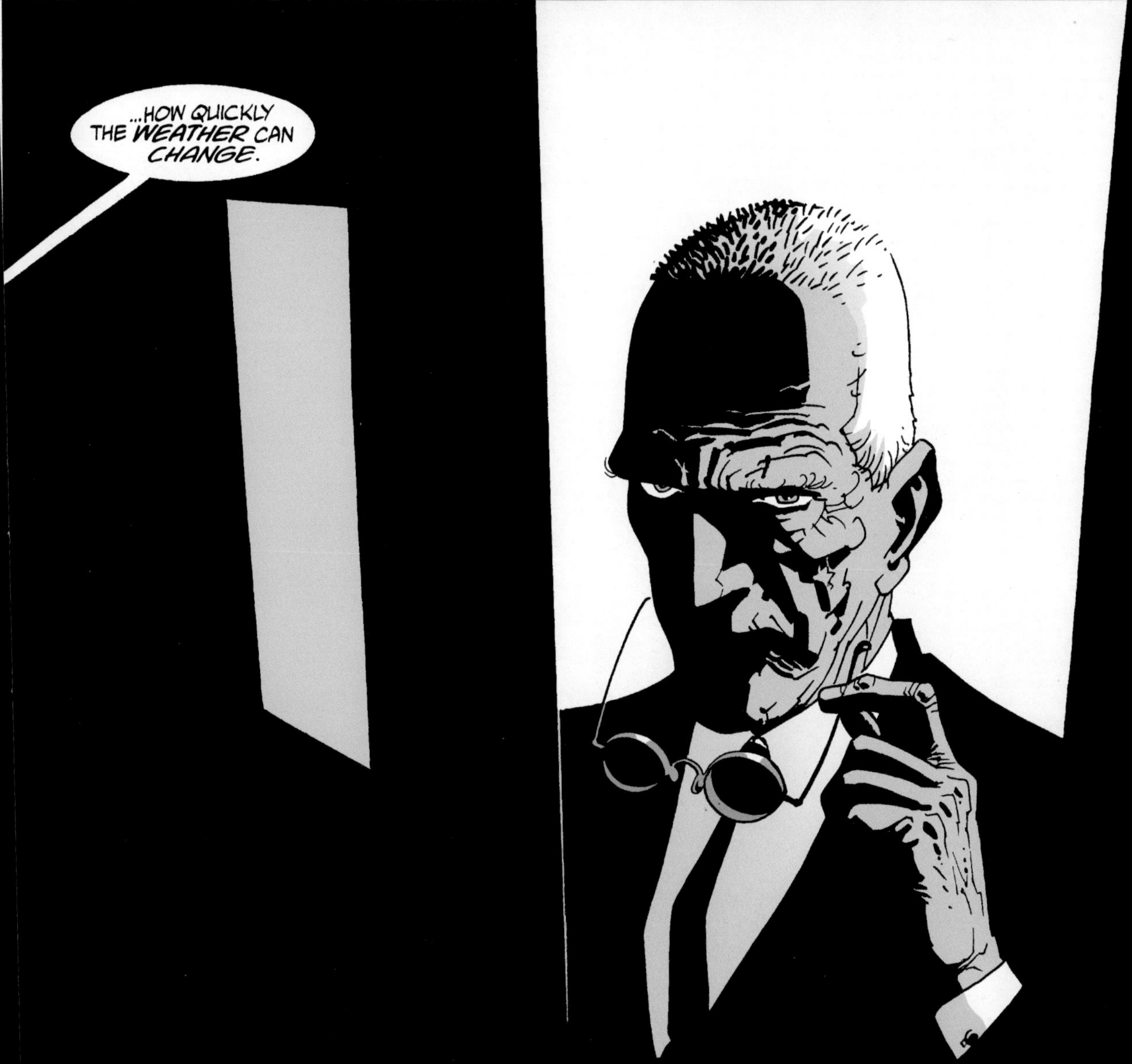
...HOW QUICKLY THE WEATHER CAN CHANGE.

ON ACCIDENTAL PURPOSE

BRIAN AZZARELLO, WRITER **EDUARDO RISSO**, ARTIST

PATRICIA MULVIHILL, COLORIST CLEM ROBINS, LETTERER
DIGITAL CHAMELEON, SEPARATIONS DAVE JOHNSON, COVER ARTIST
ZACHARY RAU, ASSISTANT EDITOR WILL DENNIS, EDITOR

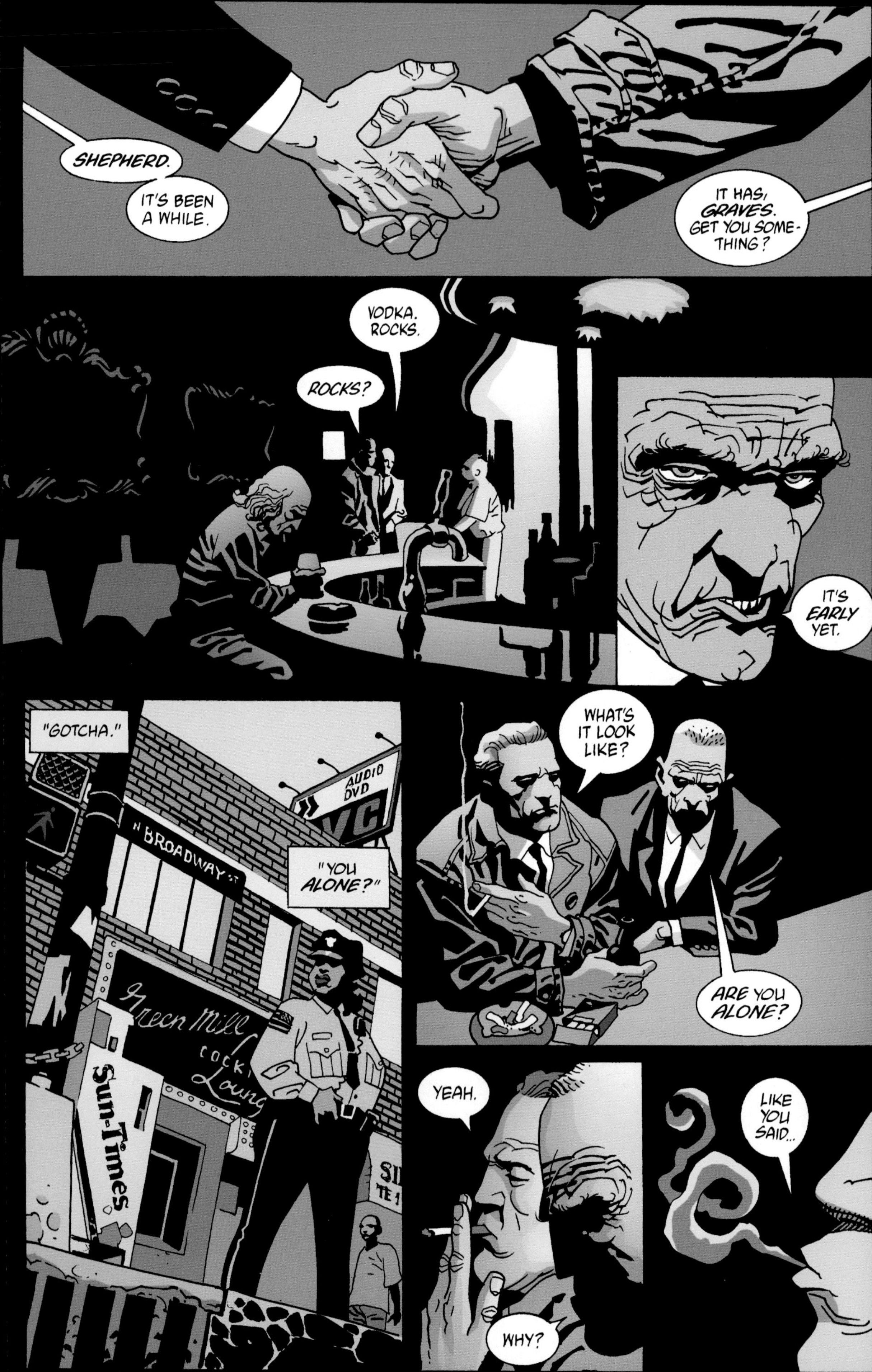
SHEPHERD.
IT'S BEEN A WHILE.
IT HAS, GRAVES. GET YOU SOME-THING?
VODKA. ROCKS.
ROCKS?
IT'S EARLY YET.
"GOTCHA."
AUDIO DVD
N BROADWAY ST
"YOU ALONE?"
Green Mill Cocktail Lounge
Sun-Times
WHAT'S IT LOOK LIKE?
ARE YOU ALONE?
YEAH.
LIKE YOU SAID...
WHY?

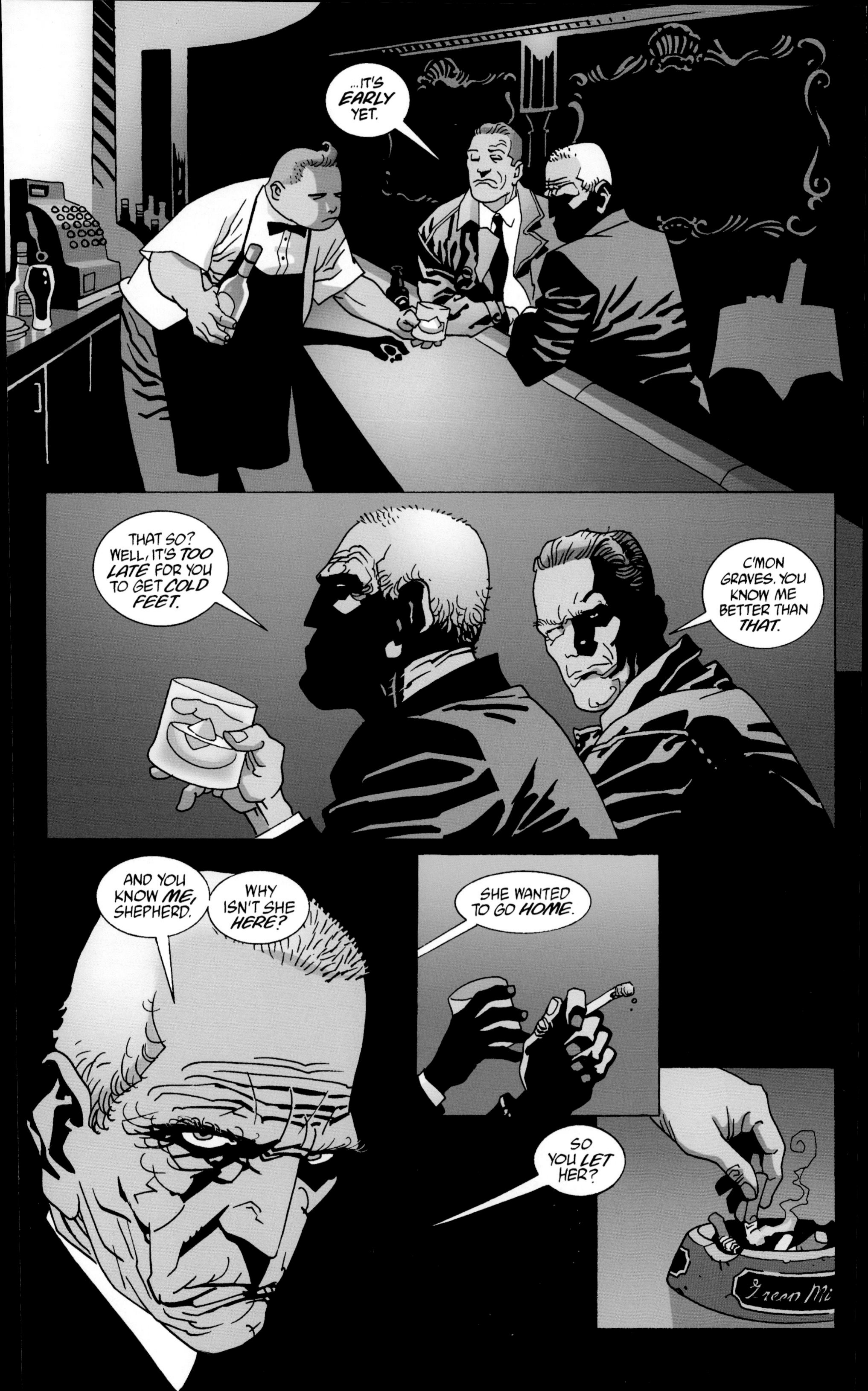

...IT'S *EARLY* YET.
THAT SO? WELL, IT'S *TOO LATE* FOR YOU TO GET *COLD FEET*.
C'MON GRAVES. YOU KNOW ME BETTER THAN *THAT*.
AND YOU KNOW *ME*, SHEPHERD.
WHY ISN'T SHE *HERE*?
SHE WANTED TO GO *HOME*.
SO YOU *LET* HER?

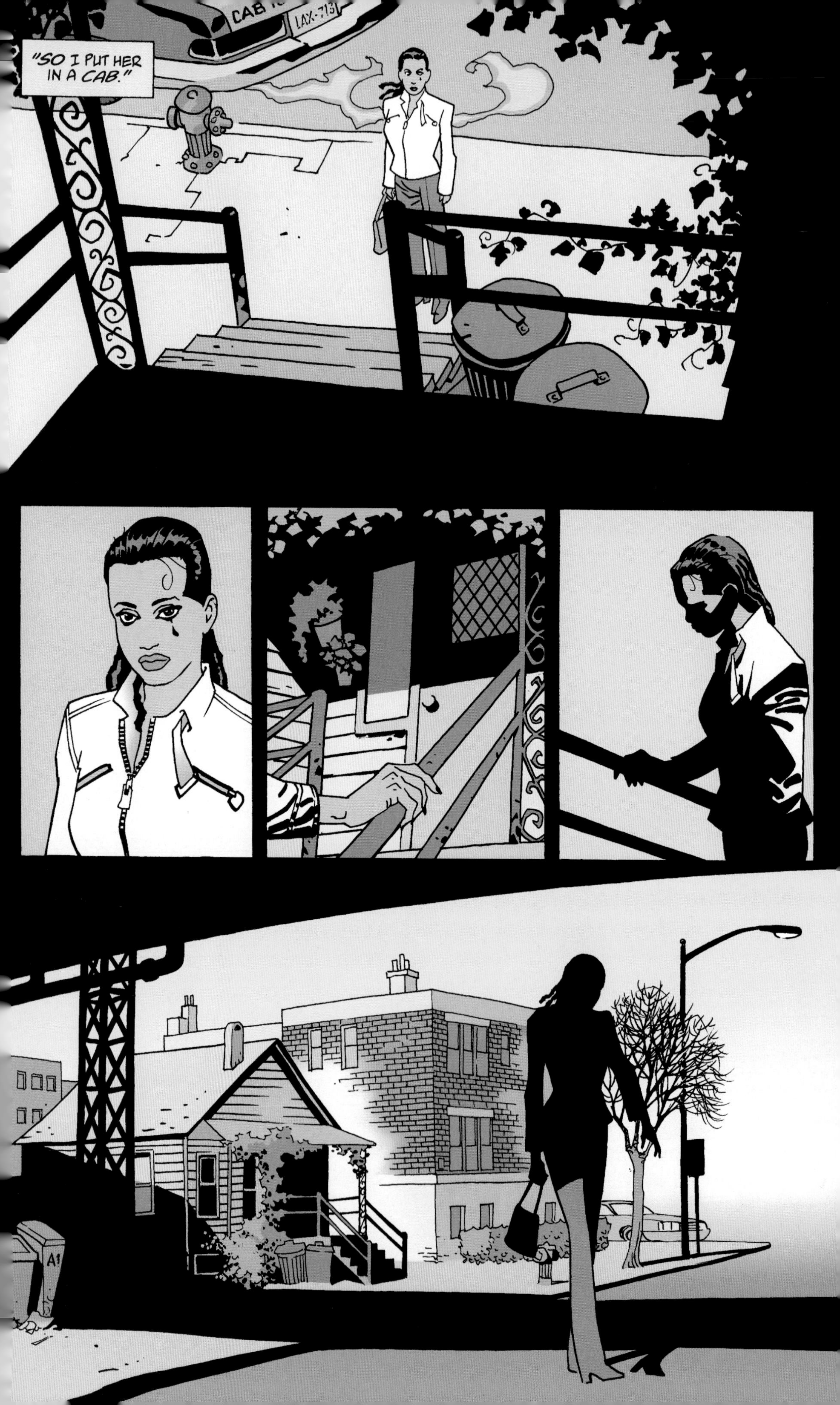
"SO I PUT HER IN A CAB."
CAB
LAX-713
A1

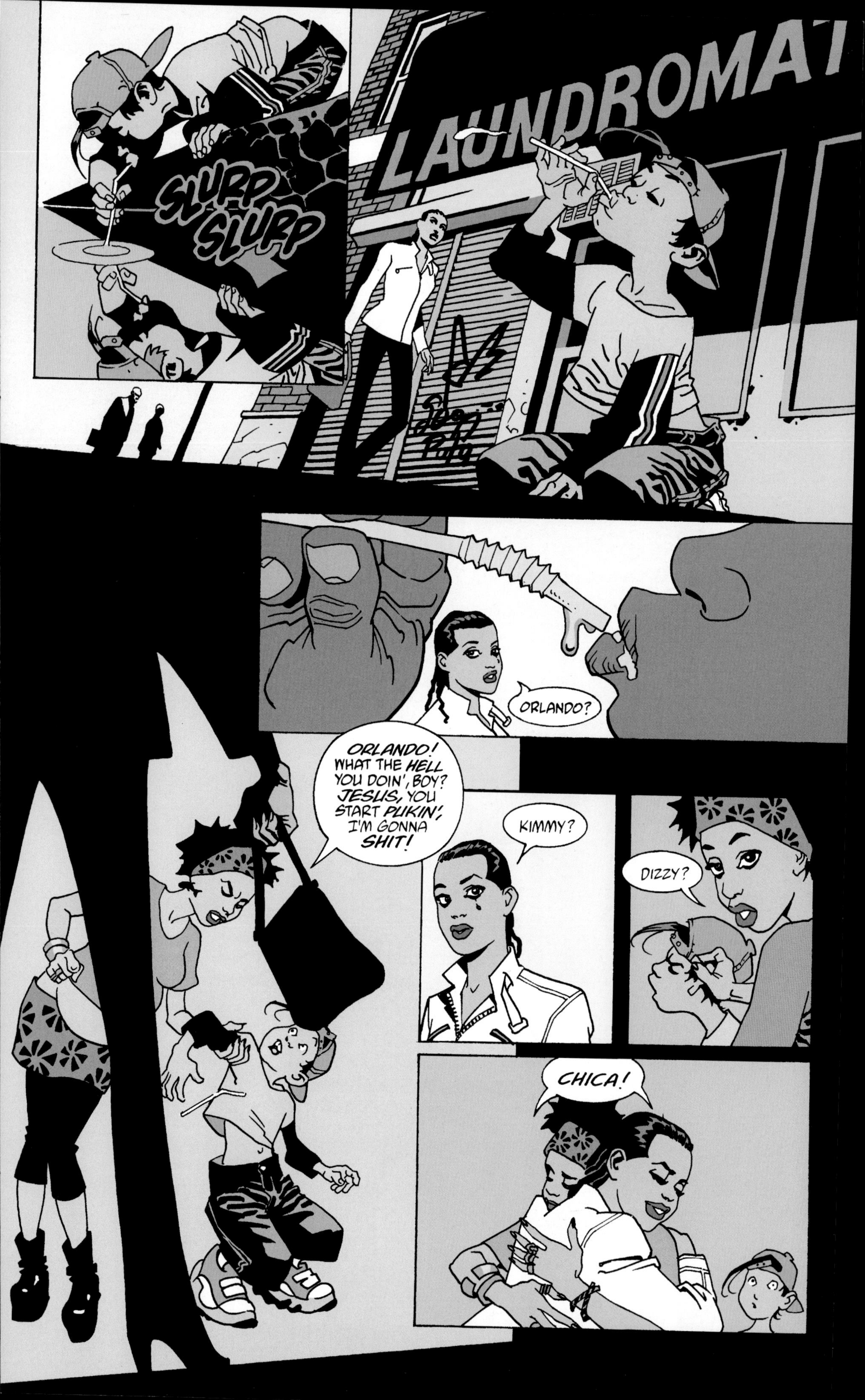
LAUNDROMAT
SLURP SLURP
ORLANDO?
ORLANDO! WHAT THE HELL YOU DOIN', BOY? JESUS, YOU START PUKIN', I'M GONNA SHIT!
KIMMY?
DIZZY?
CHICA!

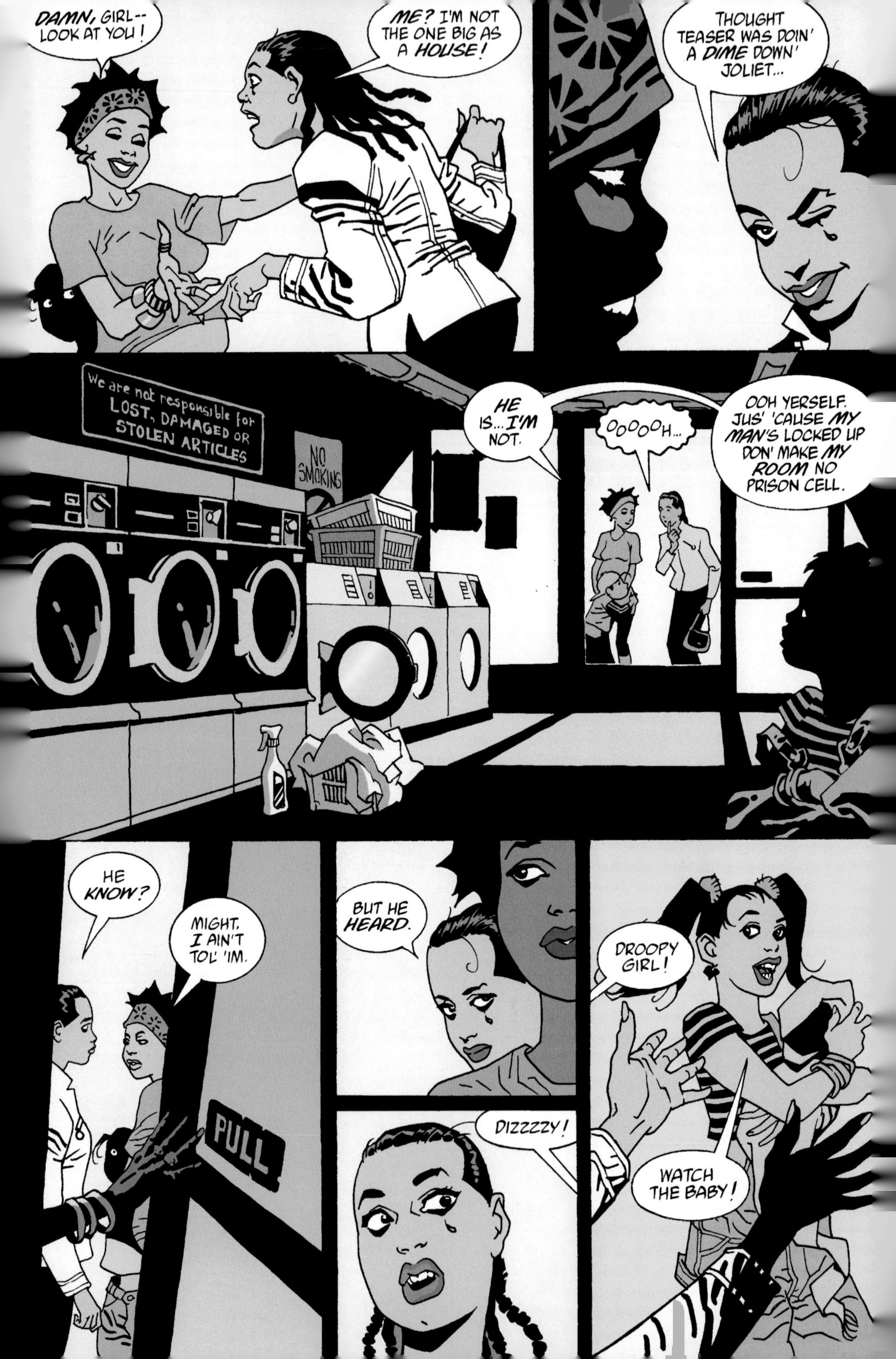
DAMN, GIRL-- LOOK AT YOU!
ME? I'M NOT THE ONE BIG AS A HOUSE!
THOUGHT TEASER WAS DOIN' A DIME DOWN' JOLIET...
We are not responsible for LOST, DAMAGED OR STOLEN ARTICLES
NO SMOKING
HE IS...I'M NOT.
OOOOOH...
OOH YERSELF. JUS' 'CAUSE MY MAN'S LOCKED UP DON' MAKE MY ROOM NO PRISON CELL.
HE KNOW?
MIGHT. I AIN'T TOL' 'IM.
PULL
BUT HE HEARD.
DIZZZZY!
DROOPY GIRL!
WATCH THE BABY!

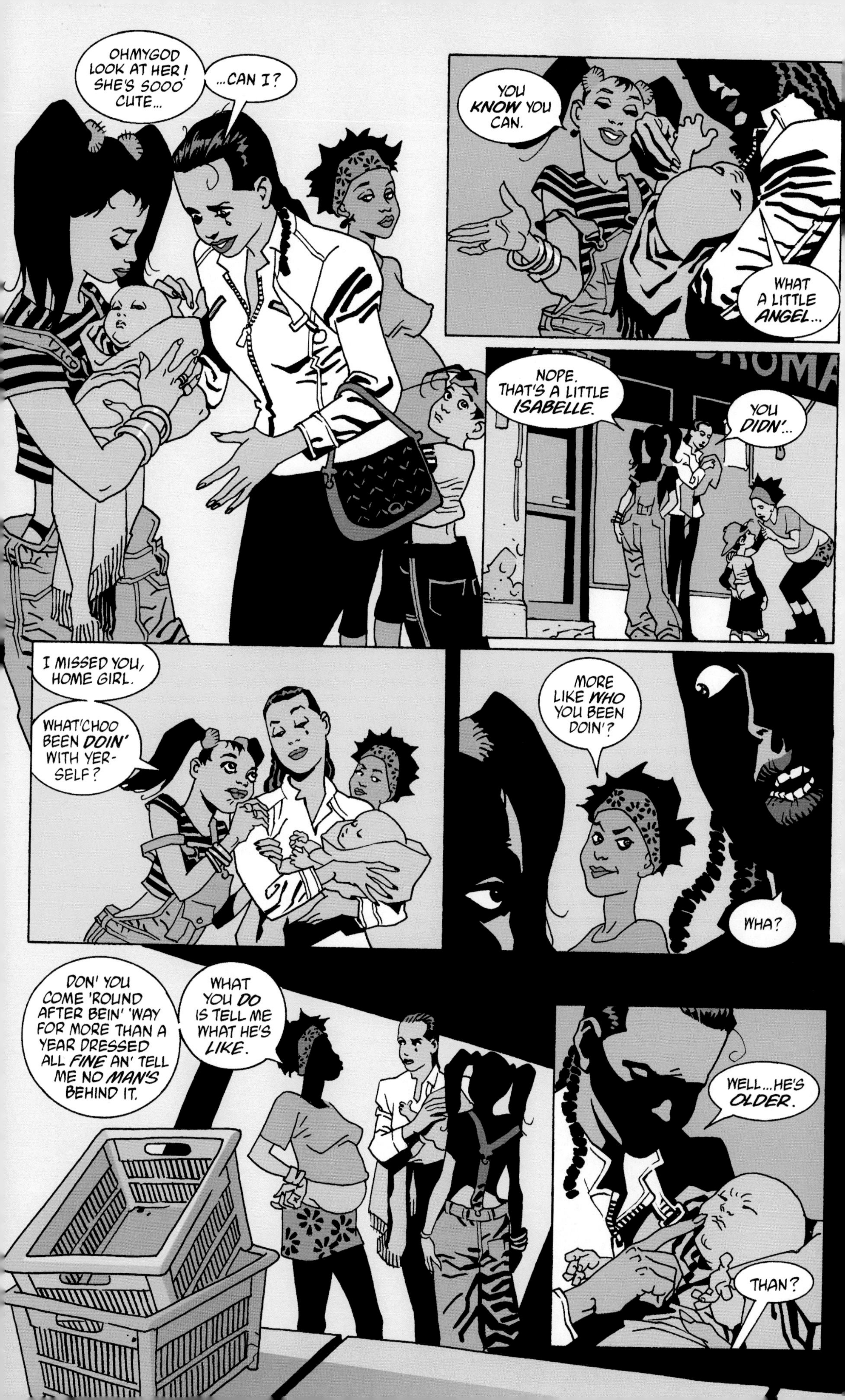
OHMYGOD LOOK AT HER! SHE'S SOOO CUTE...
...CAN I?
YOU KNOW YOU CAN.
WHAT A LITTLE ANGEL...
NOPE. THAT'S A LITTLE ISABELLE.
YOU DIDN'...
I MISSED YOU, HOME GIRL.
WHAT'CHOO BEEN DOIN' WITH YER-SELF?
MORE LIKE WHO YOU BEEN DOIN'?
WHA?
DON' YOU COME 'ROUND AFTER BEIN' 'WAY FOR MORE THAN A YEAR DRESSED ALL FINE AN' TELL ME NO MAN'S BEHIND IT.
WHAT YOU DO IS TELL ME WHAT HE'S LIKE.
WELL...HE'S OLDER.
THAN?

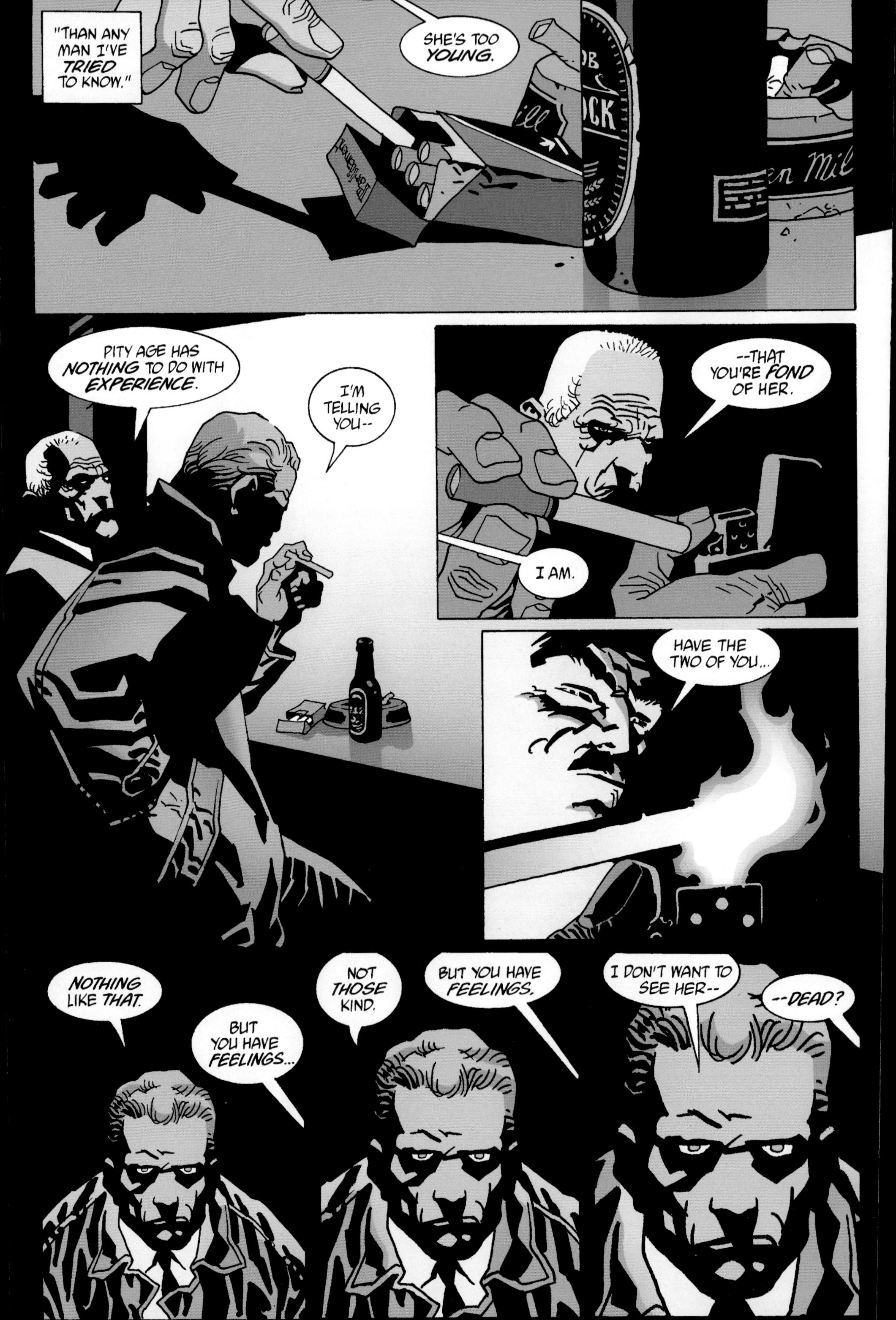
"THAN ANY MAN I'VE TRIED TO KNOW."
SHE'S TOO YOUNG.
PITY AGE HAS NOTHING TO DO WITH EXPERIENCE.
I'M TELLING YOU--
--THAT YOU'RE FOND OF HER.
I AM.
HAVE THE TWO OF YOU...
NOTHING LIKE THAT.
BUT YOU HAVE FEELINGS...
NOT THOSE KIND.
BUT YOU HAVE FEELINGS.
I DON'T WANT TO SEE HER--
--DEAD?

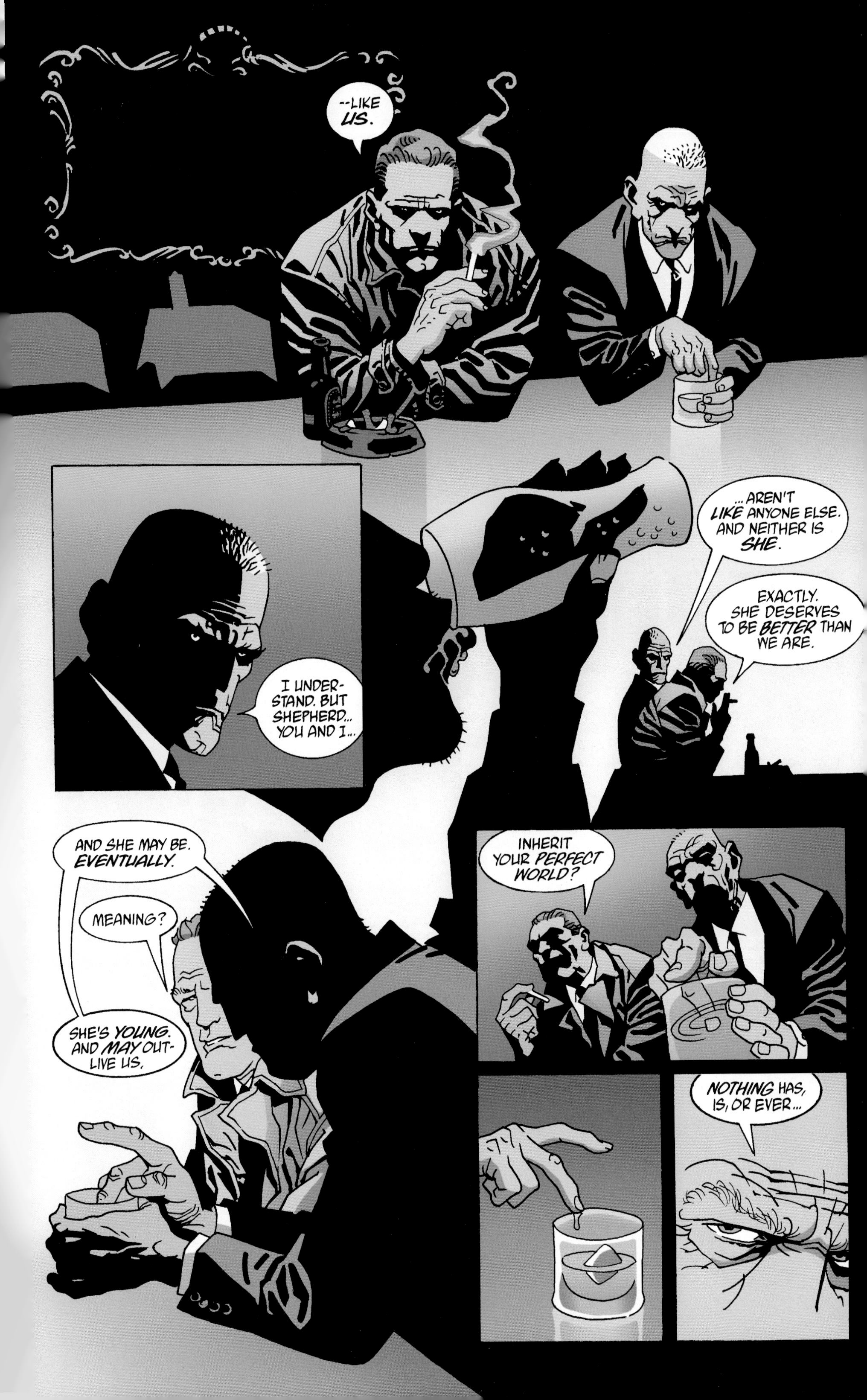
--LIKE US.
I UNDERSTAND. BUT SHEPHERD... YOU AND I...
... AREN'T LIKE ANYONE ELSE. AND NEITHER IS SHE.
EXACTLY. SHE DESERVES TO BE BETTER THAN WE ARE.
AND SHE MAY BE. EVENTUALLY.
MEANING?
SHE'S YOUNG. AND MAY OUTLIVE US.
INHERIT YOUR PERFECT WORLD?
NOTHING HAS, IS, OR EVER...

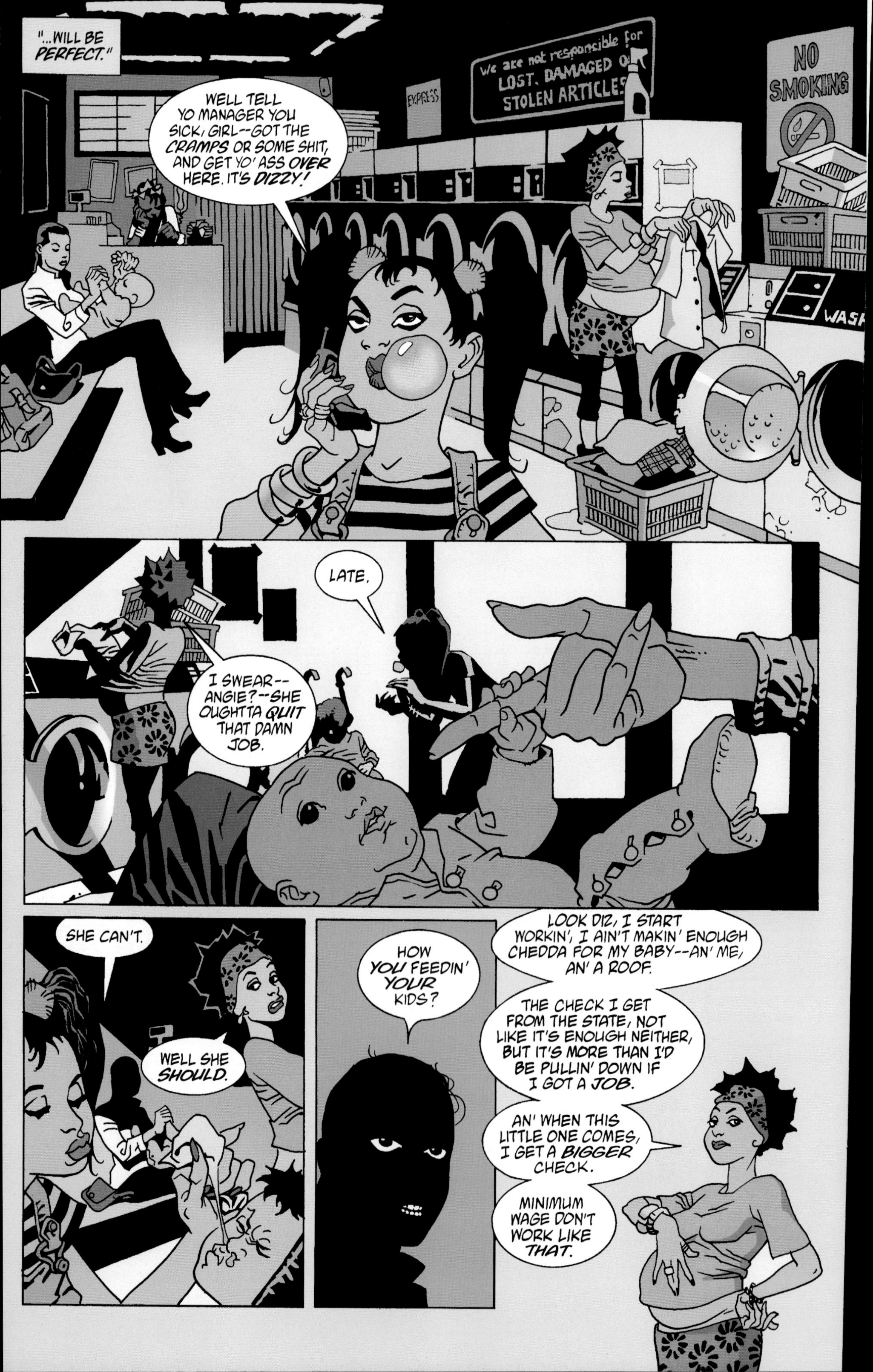
"...WILL BE PERFECT."
We are not responsible for LOST, DAMAGED or STOLEN ARTICLES
EXPRESS
NO SMOKING
WELL TELL YO MANAGER YOU SICK, GIRL--GOT THE CRAMPS OR SOME SHIT, AND GET YO' ASS OVER HERE. IT'S DIZZY!
WASH
LATE.
I SWEAR--ANGIE?--SHE OUGHTTA QUIT THAT DAMN JOB.
SHE CAN'T.
WELL SHE SHOULD.
HOW YOU FEEDIN' YOUR KIDS?
LOOK DIZ, I START WORKIN', I AIN'T MAKIN' ENOUGH CHEDDA FOR MY BABY--AN' ME, AN' A ROOF.
THE CHECK I GET FROM THE STATE, NOT LIKE IT'S ENOUGH NEITHER, BUT IT'S MORE THAN I'D BE PULLIN' DOWN IF I GOT A JOB.
AN' WHEN THIS LITTLE ONE COMES, I GET A BIGGER CHECK.
MINIMUM WAGE DON'T WORK LIKE THAT.

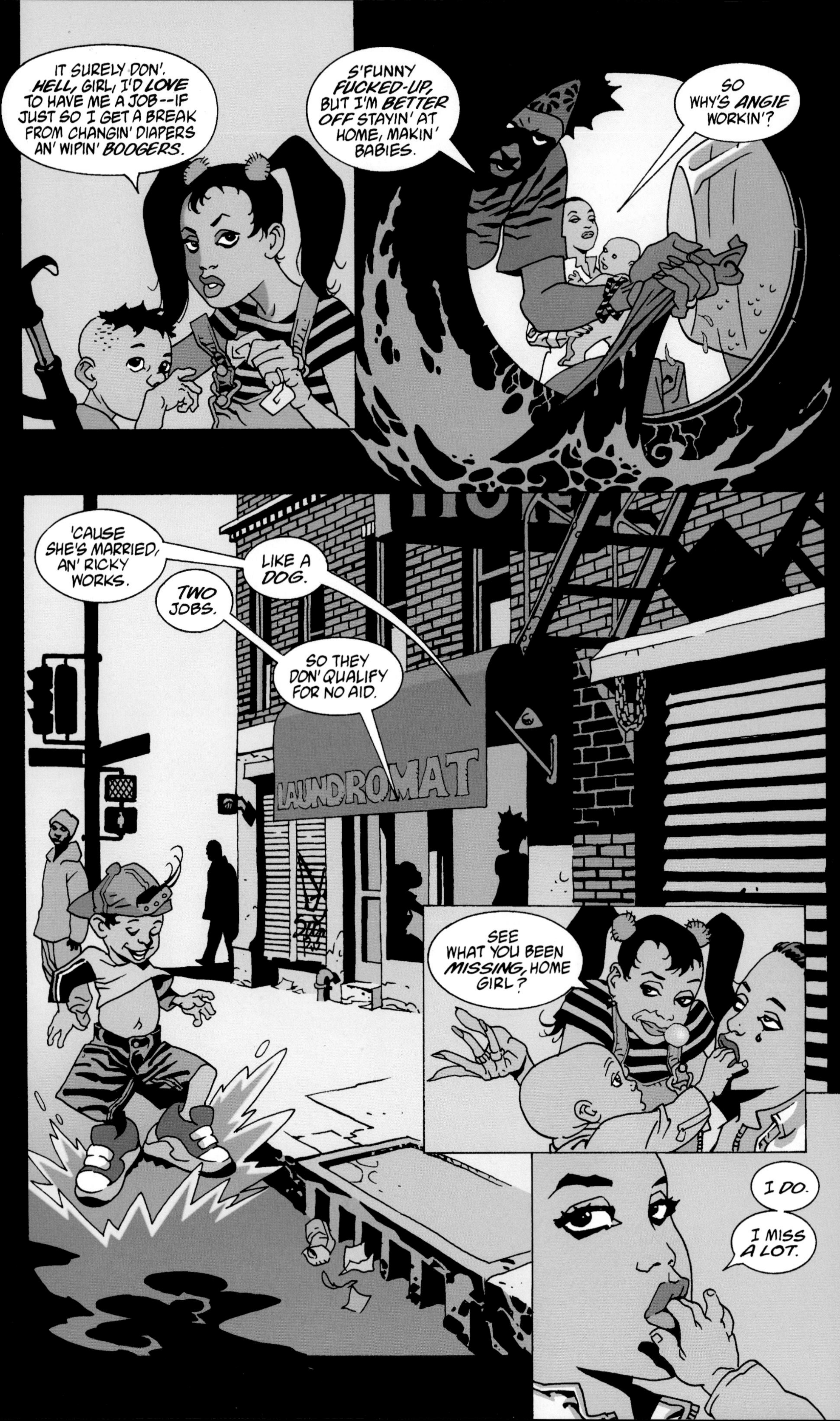
IT SURELY DON'. HELL, GIRL, I'D LOVE TO HAVE ME A JOB--IF JUST SO I GET A BREAK FROM CHANGIN' DIAPERS AN' WIPIN' BOOGERS.
S'FUNNY FUCKED-UP, BUT I'M BETTER OFF STAYIN' AT HOME, MAKIN' BABIES.
SO WHY'S ANGIE WORKIN'?
'CAUSE SHE'S MARRIED, AN' RICKY WORKS.
LIKE A DOG.
TWO JOBS.
SO THEY DON' QUALIFY FOR NO AID.
LAUNDROMAT
SEE WHAT YOU BEEN MISSING, HOME GIRL?
I DO.
I MISS A LOT.

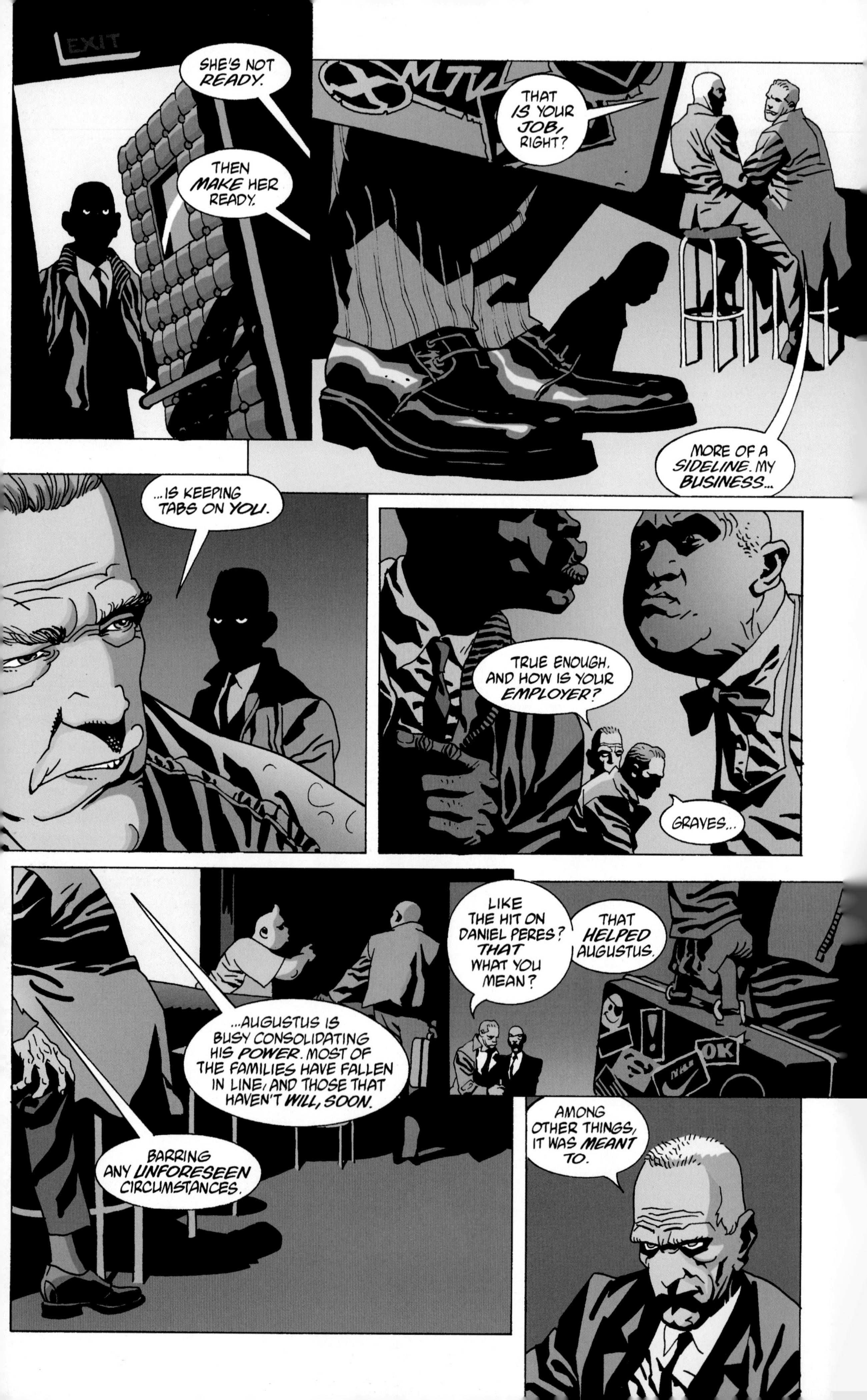

EXIT
SHE'S NOT READY.
THEN MAKE HER READY.
MTV
THAT IS YOUR JOB, RIGHT?
MORE OF A SIDELINE. MY BUSINESS...
...IS KEEPING TABS ON YOU.
TRUE ENOUGH. AND HOW IS YOUR EMPLOYER?
GRAVES...
...AUGUSTUS IS BUSY CONSOLIDATING HIS POWER. MOST OF THE FAMILIES HAVE FALLEN IN LINE, AND THOSE THAT HAVEN'T WILL, SOON.
BARRING ANY UNFORESEEN CIRCUMSTANCES.
LIKE THE HIT ON DANIEL PERES? THAT WHAT YOU MEAN?
THAT HELPED AUGUSTUS.
OK
AMONG OTHER THINGS, IT WAS MEANT TO.

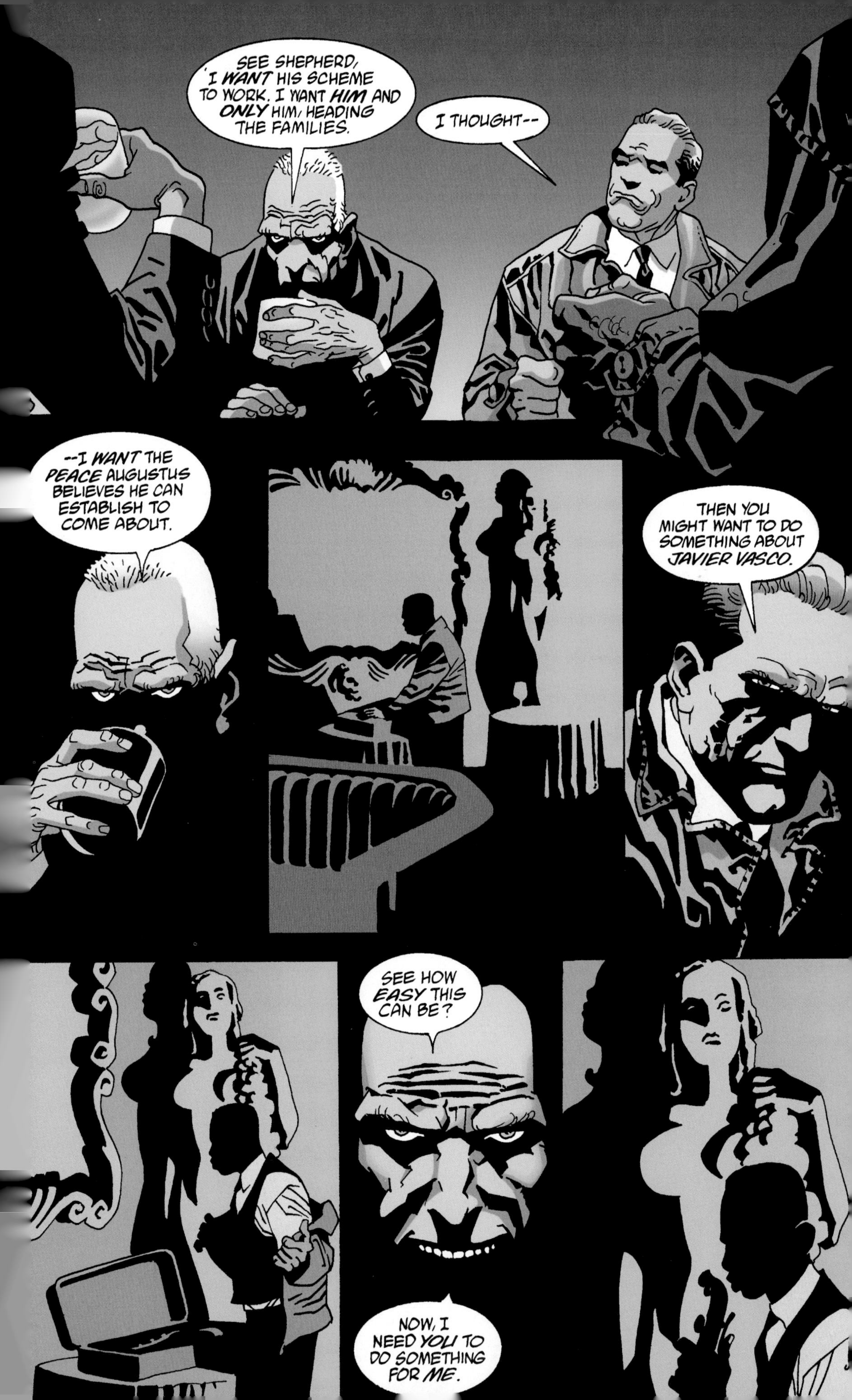
SEE SHEPHERD, I WANT HIS SCHEME TO WORK. I WANT HIM AND ONLY HIM, HEADING THE FAMILIES.
I THOUGHT--
--I WANT THE PEACE AUGUSTUS BELIEVES HE CAN ESTABLISH TO COME ABOUT.
THEN YOU MIGHT WANT TO DO SOMETHING ABOUT JAVIER VASCO.
SEE HOW EASY THIS CAN BE?
NOW, I NEED YOU TO DO SOMETHING FOR ME.

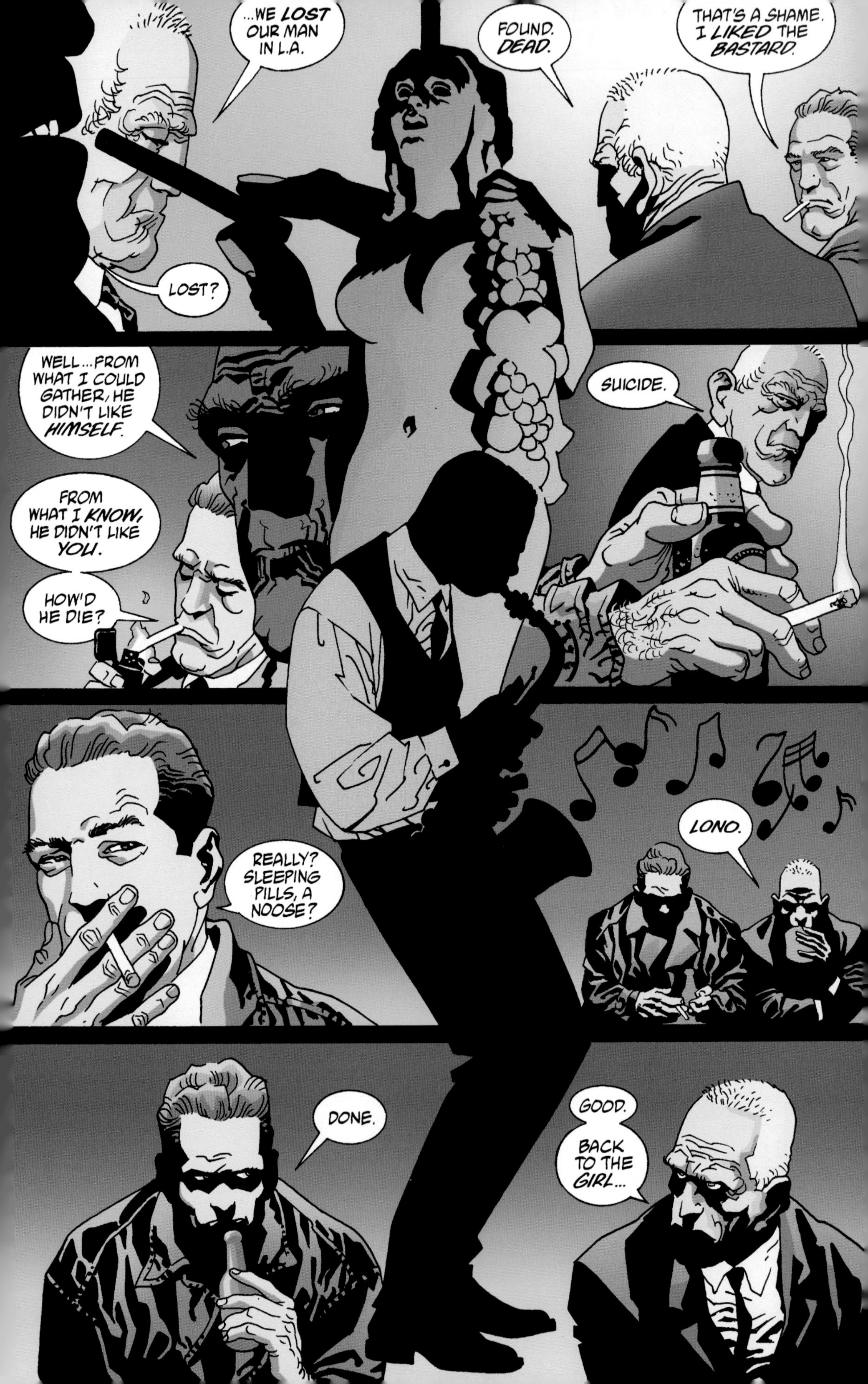
...WE LOST OUR MAN IN L.A.
LOST?
FOUND. DEAD.
THAT'S A SHAME. I LIKED THE BASTARD.
WELL...FROM WHAT I COULD GATHER, HE DIDN'T LIKE HIMSELF.
FROM WHAT I KNOW, HE DIDN'T LIKE YOU.
HOW'D HE DIE?
SUICIDE.
REALLY? SLEEPING PILLS, A NOOSE?
LONO.
DONE.
GOOD.
BACK TO THE GIRL...

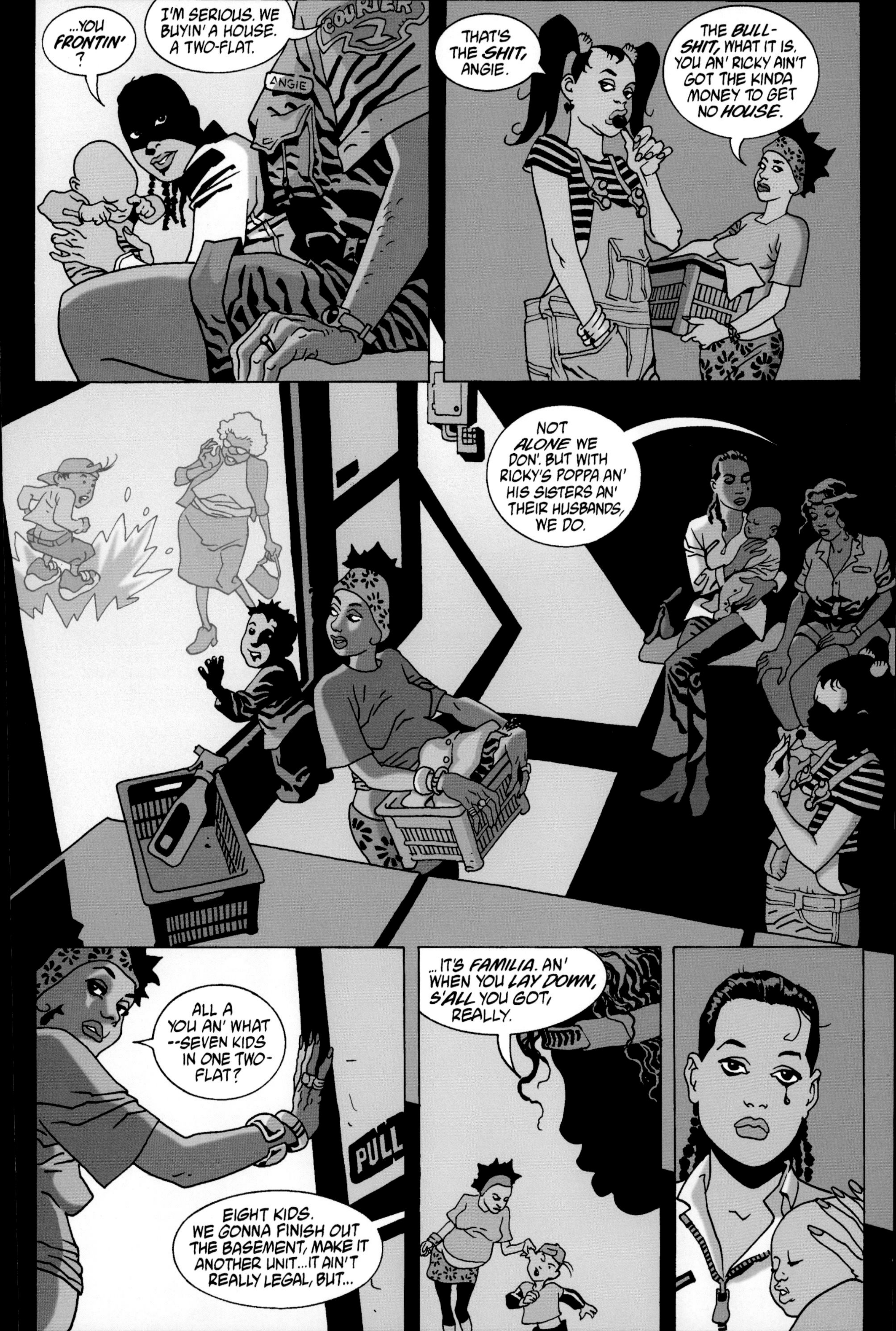

...YOU FRONTIN'?
I'M SERIOUS. WE BUYIN' A HOUSE. A TWO-FLAT.
COURIER
ANGIE
THAT'S THE SHIT, ANGIE.
THE BULL-SHIT, WHAT IT IS. YOU AN' RICKY AIN'T GOT THE KINDA MONEY TO GET NO HOUSE.
NOT ALONE WE DON'. BUT WITH RICKY'S POPPA AN' HIS SISTERS AN' THEIR HUSBANDS, WE DO.
ALL A YOU AN' WHAT --SEVEN KIDS IN ONE TWO-FLAT?
PULL
EIGHT KIDS. WE GONNA FINISH OUT THE BASEMENT, MAKE IT ANOTHER UNIT...IT AIN'T REALLY LEGAL, BUT...
...IT'S FAMILIA. AN' WHEN YOU LAY DOWN, S'ALL YOU GOT, REALLY.

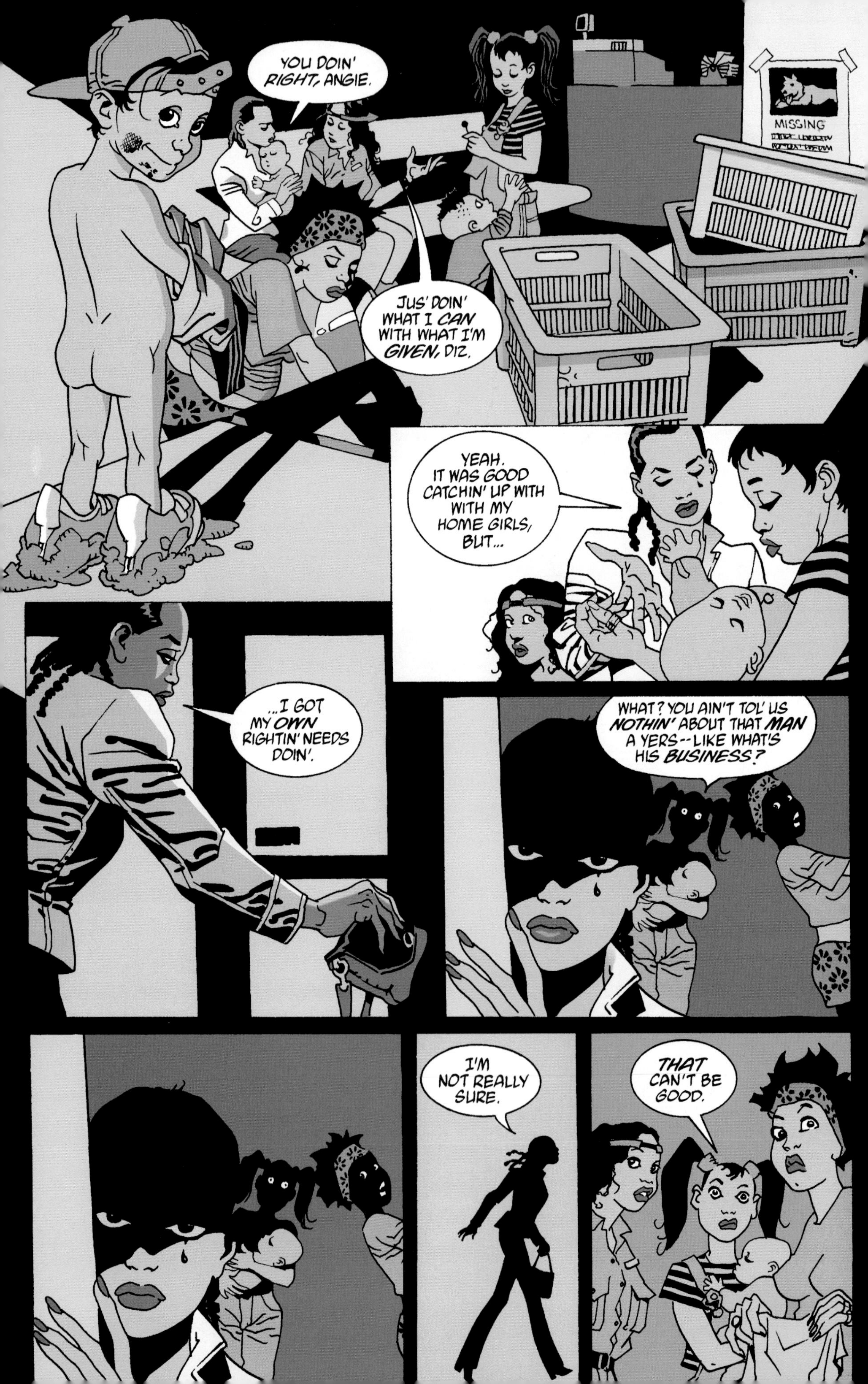

YOU DOIN' RIGHT, ANGIE.
JUS' DOIN' WHAT I CAN WITH WHAT I'M GIVEN, DIZ.
MISSING
YEAH. IT WAS GOOD CATCHIN' UP WITH WITH MY HOME GIRLS, BUT...
...I GOT MY OWN RIGHTIN' NEEDS DOIN'.
WHAT? YOU AIN'T TOL' US NOTHIN' ABOUT THAT MAN A YERS--LIKE WHAT'S HIS BUSINESS?
I'M NOT REALLY SURE.
THAT CAN'T BE GOOD.

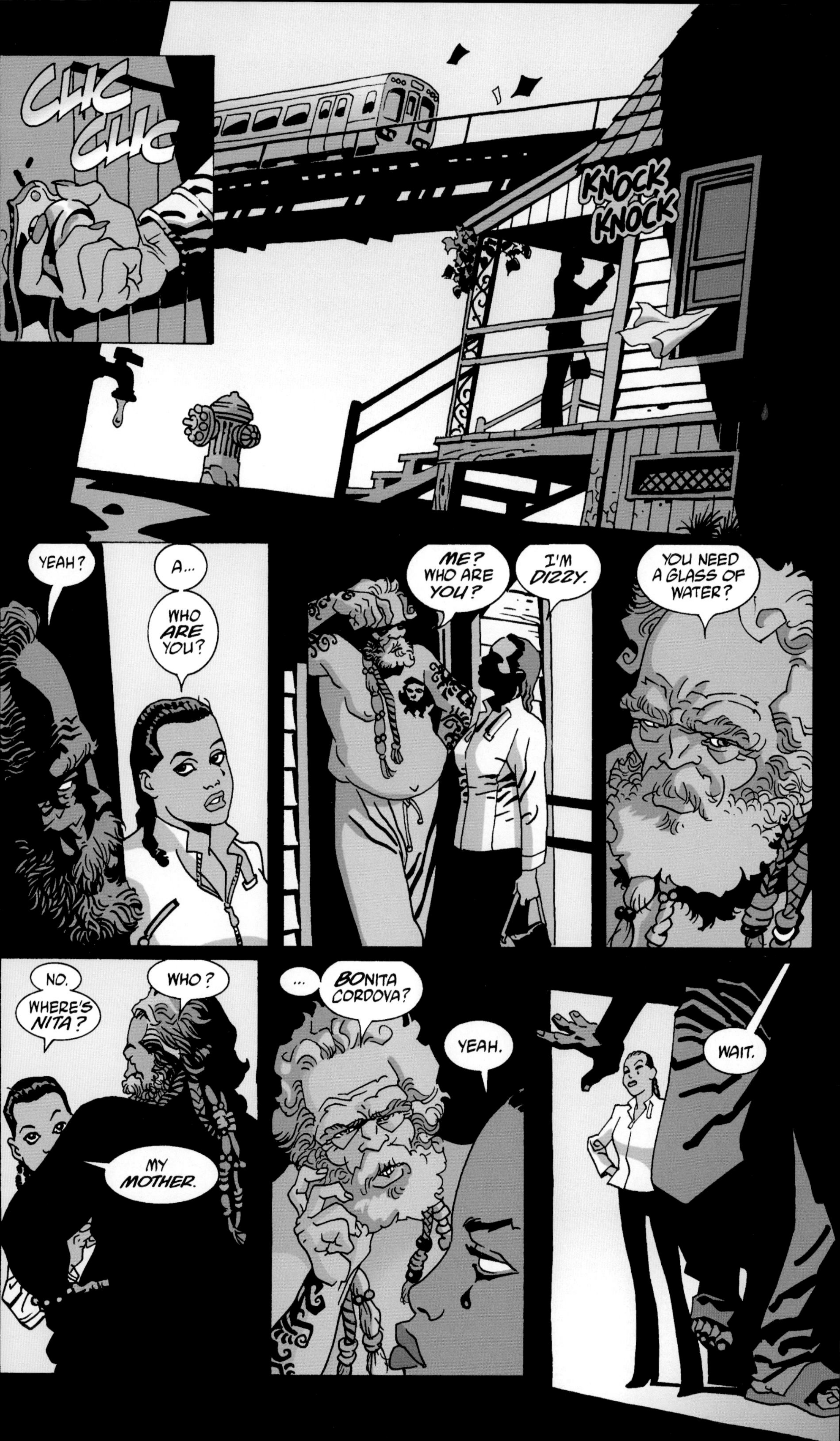
CLIC CLIC
KNOCK KNOCK
YEAH?
A...
WHO ARE YOU?
ME? WHO ARE YOU?
I'M DIZZY.
YOU NEED A GLASS OF WATER?
NO. WHERE'S NITA?
WHO?
MY MOTHER.
... BONITA CORDOVA?
YEAH.
WAIT.

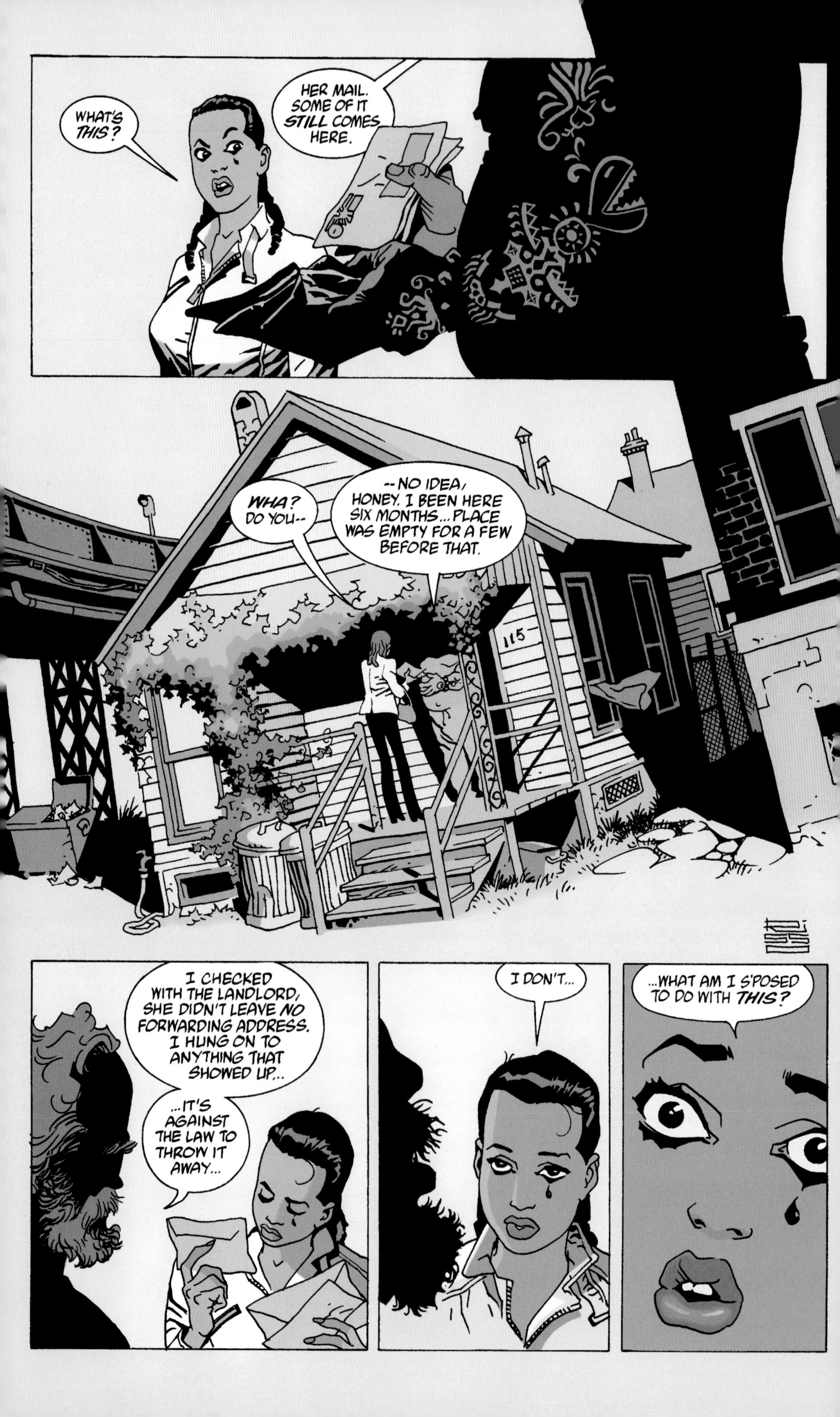
WHAT'S THIS?
HER MAIL. SOME OF IT STILL COMES HERE.
WHA? DO YOU--
--NO IDEA, HONEY. I BEEN HERE SIX MONTHS... PLACE WAS EMPTY FOR A FEW BEFORE THAT.
115
I CHECKED WITH THE LANDLORD, SHE DIDN'T LEAVE NO FORWARDING ADDRESS. I HUNG ON TO ANYTHING THAT SHOWED UP...
...IT'S AGAINST THE LAW TO THROW IT AWAY...
I DON'T...
...WHAT AM I S'POSED TO DO WITH THIS?

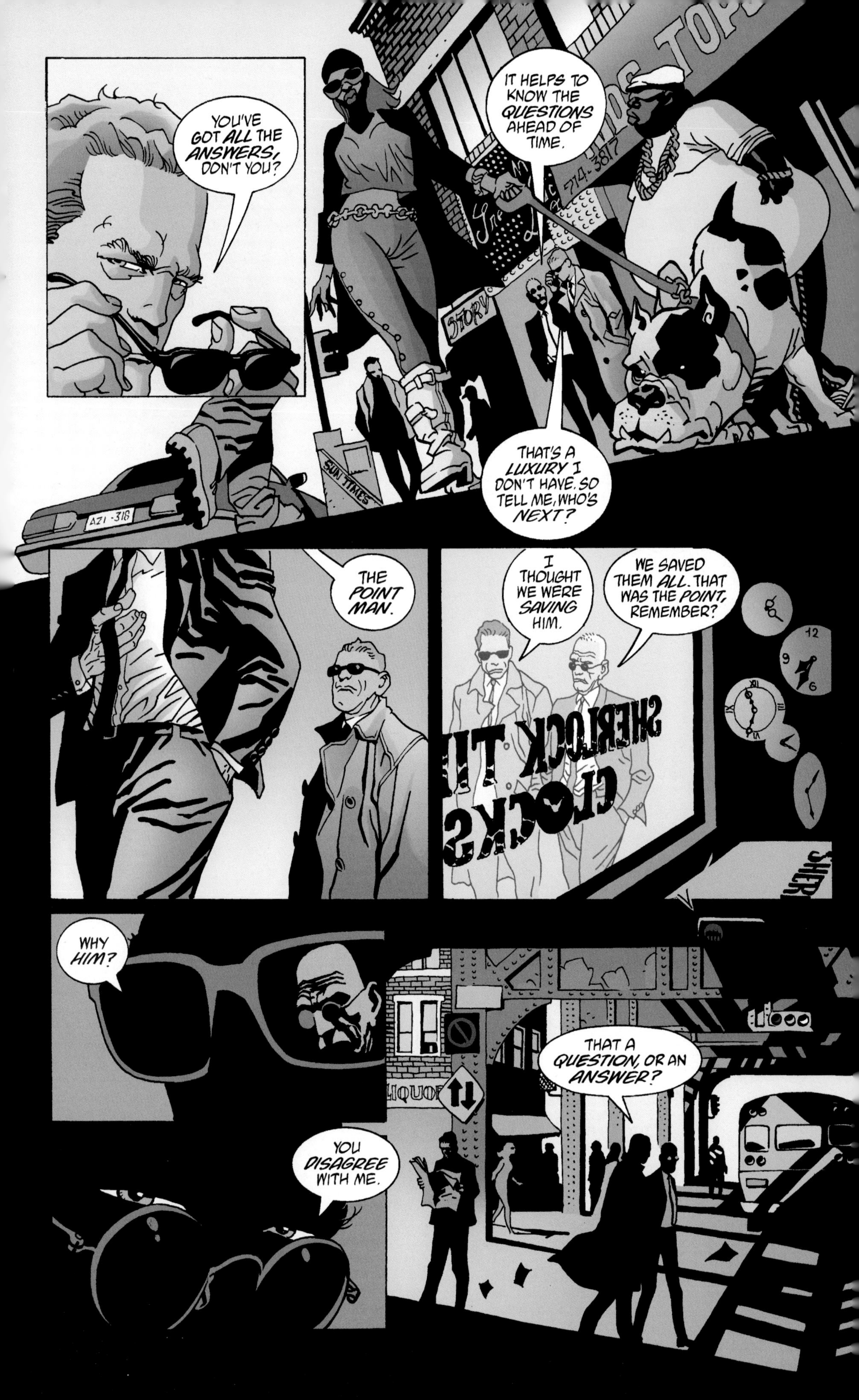
YOU'VE GOT ALL THE ANSWERS, DON'T YOU?
IT HELPS TO KNOW THE QUESTIONS AHEAD OF TIME.
THAT'S A LUXURY I DON'T HAVE. SO TELL ME, WHO'S NEXT?
THE POINT MAN.
I THOUGHT WE WERE SAVING HIM.
WE SAVED THEM ALL. THAT WAS THE POINT, REMEMBER?
SHERLOCK TI
CLOCKS
WHY HIM?
THAT A QUESTION, OR AN ANSWER?
YOU DISAGREE WITH ME.
SUN TIMES
AZI-318
STORY
774-3817

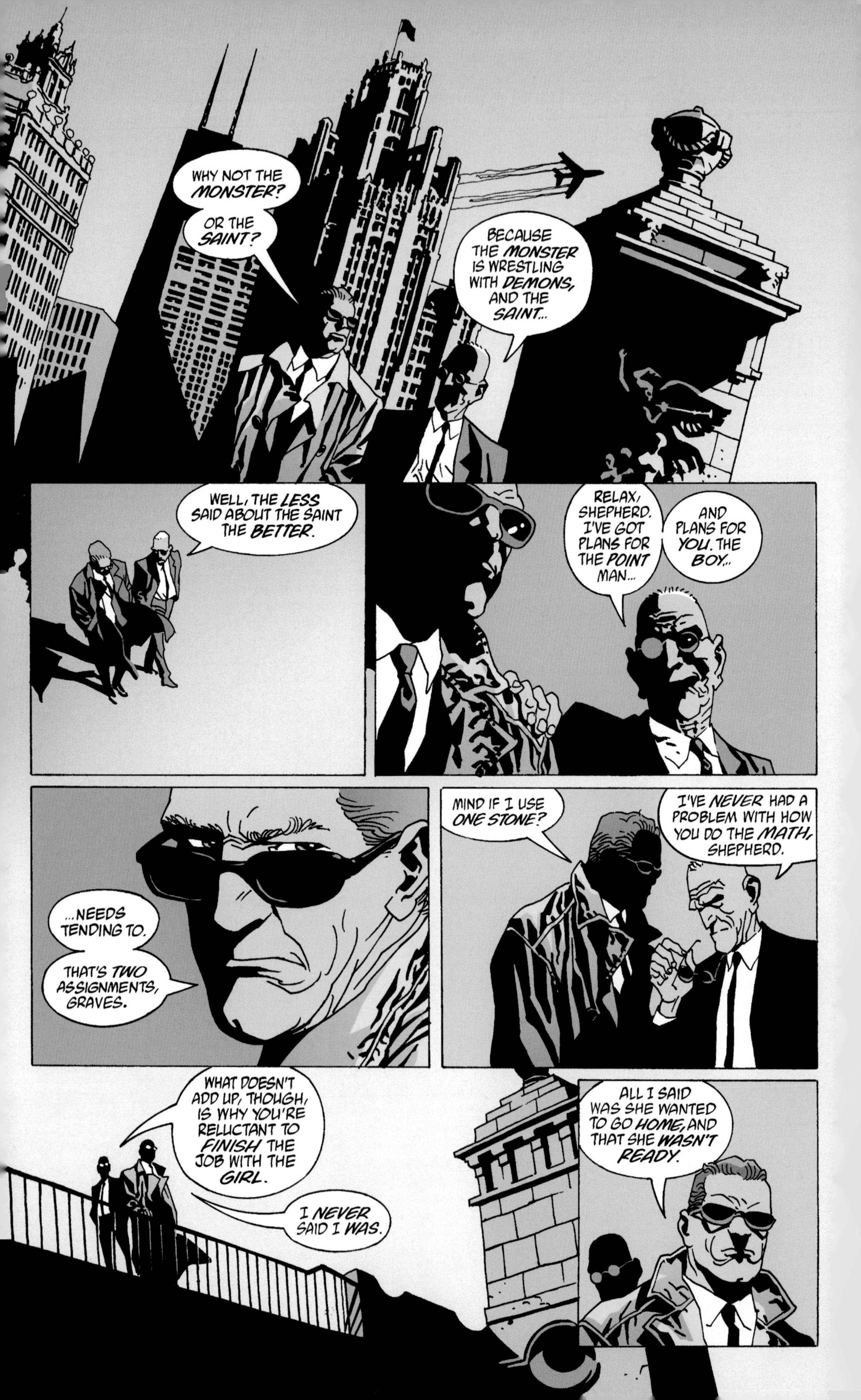
WHY NOT THE MONSTER?
OR THE SAINT?
BECAUSE THE MONSTER IS WRESTLING WITH DEMONS, AND THE SAINT...
WELL, THE LESS SAID ABOUT THE SAINT THE BETTER.
RELAX, SHEPHERD. I'VE GOT PLANS FOR THE POINT MAN...
AND PLANS FOR YOU. THE BOY...
...NEEDS TENDING TO.
THAT'S TWO ASSIGNMENTS, GRAVES.
MIND IF I USE ONE STONE?
I'VE NEVER HAD A PROBLEM WITH HOW YOU DO THE MATH, SHEPHERD.
WHAT DOESN'T ADD UP, THOUGH, IS WHY YOU'RE RELUCTANT TO FINISH THE JOB WITH THE GIRL.
I NEVER SAID I WAS.
ALL I SAID WAS SHE WANTED TO GO HOME, AND THAT SHE WASN'T READY.

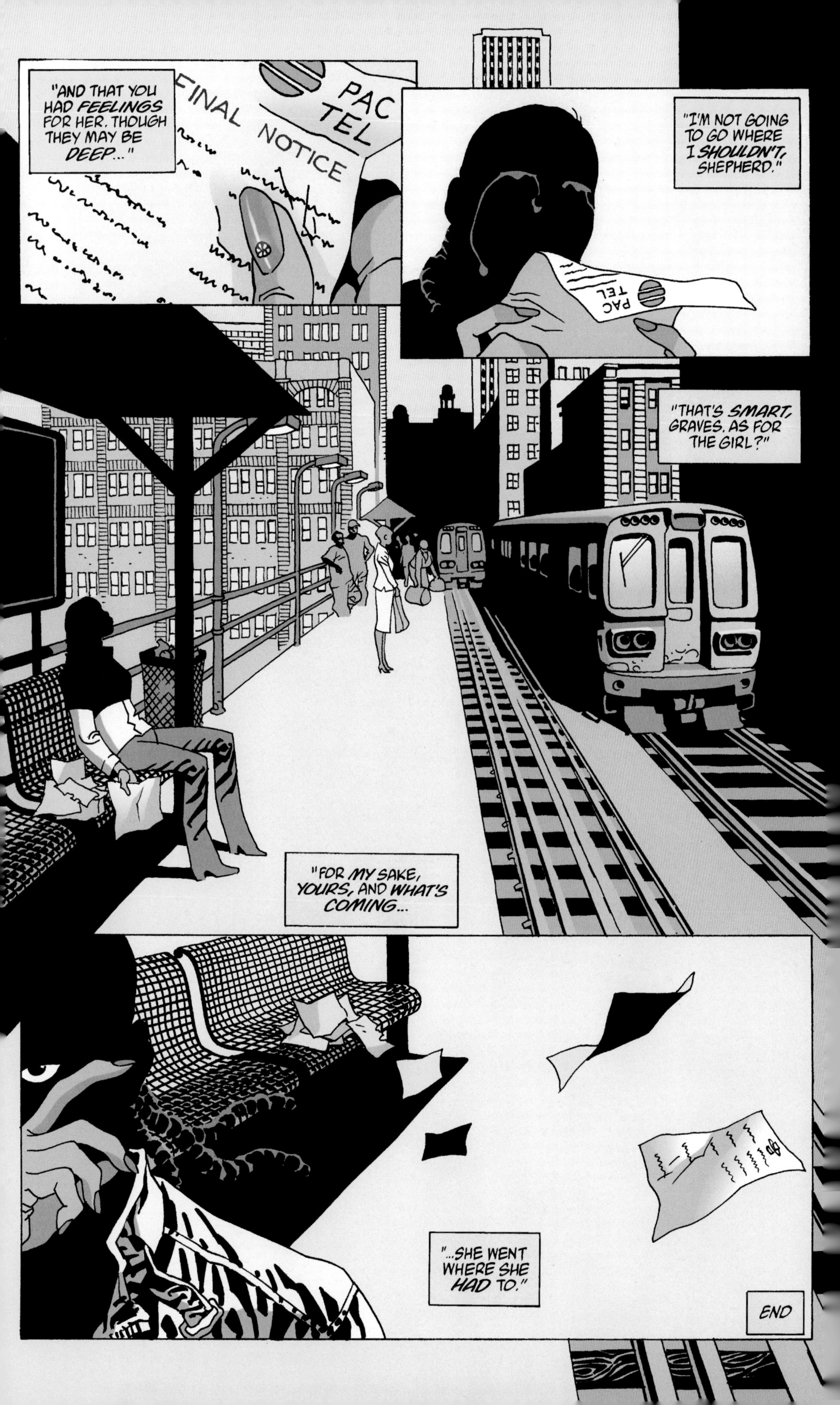
"AND THAT YOU HAD FEELINGS FOR HER. THOUGH THEY MAY BE DEEP..."
FINAL NOTICE
PAC TEL
"I'M NOT GOING TO GO WHERE I SHOULDN'T, SHEPHERD."
PAC TEL
"THAT'S SMART, GRAVES. AS FOR THE GIRL?"
"FOR MY SAKE, YOURS, AND WHAT'S COMING...
"...SHE WENT WHERE SHE HAD TO."
END

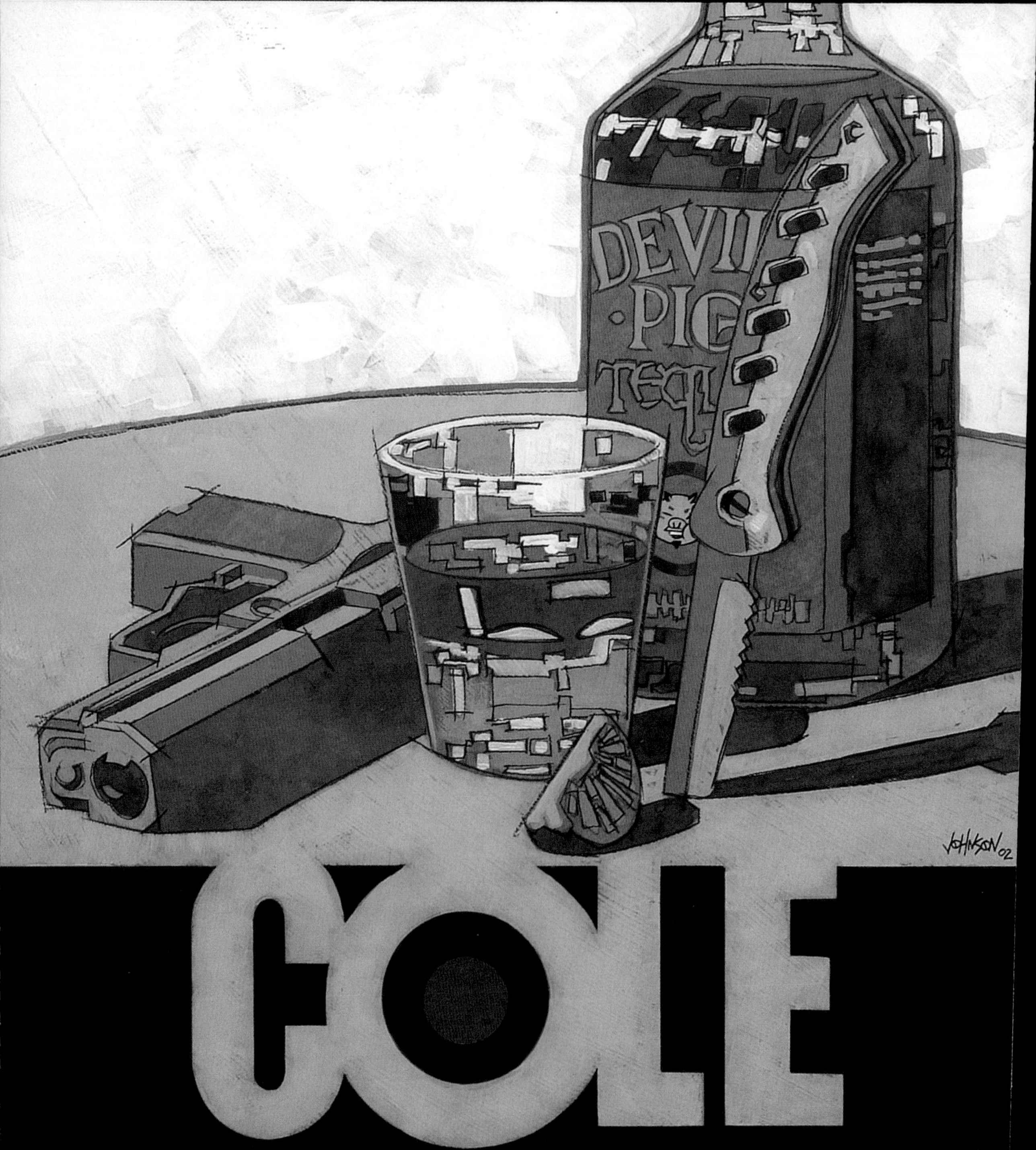
COLE
JOHNSON 02

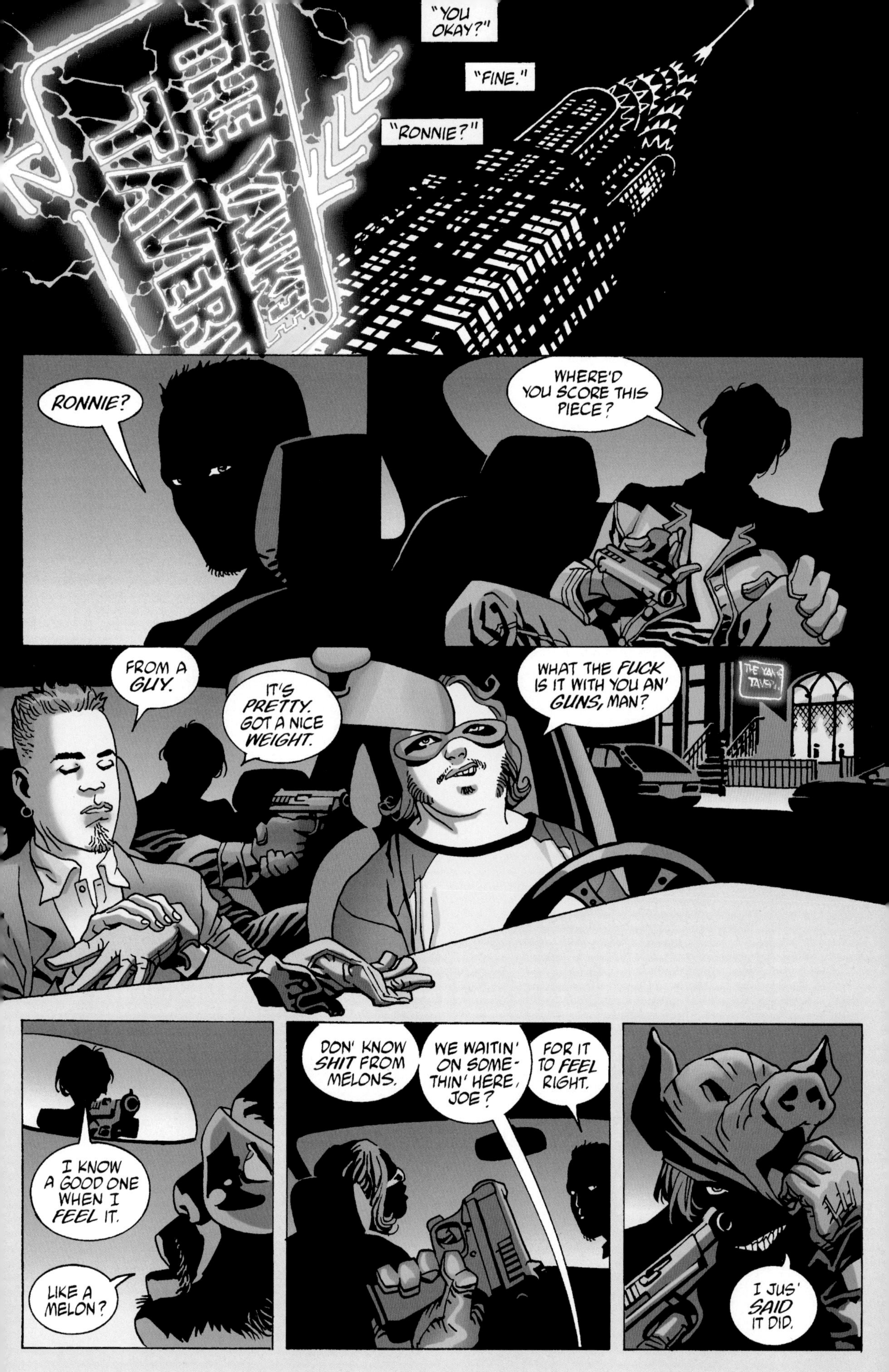

"YOU OKAY?"
"FINE."
"RONNIE?"
THE YANKEE TAVERN
RONNIE?
WHERE'D YOU SCORE THIS PIECE?
FROM A GUY.
IT'S PRETTY. GOT A NICE WEIGHT.
WHAT THE FUCK IS IT WITH YOU AN' GUNS, MAN?
I KNOW A GOOD ONE WHEN I FEEL IT.
LIKE A MELON?
DON' KNOW SHIT FROM MELONS.
WE WAITIN' ON SOME-THIN' HERE, JOE?
FOR IT TO FEEL RIGHT.
I JUS' SAID IT DID.

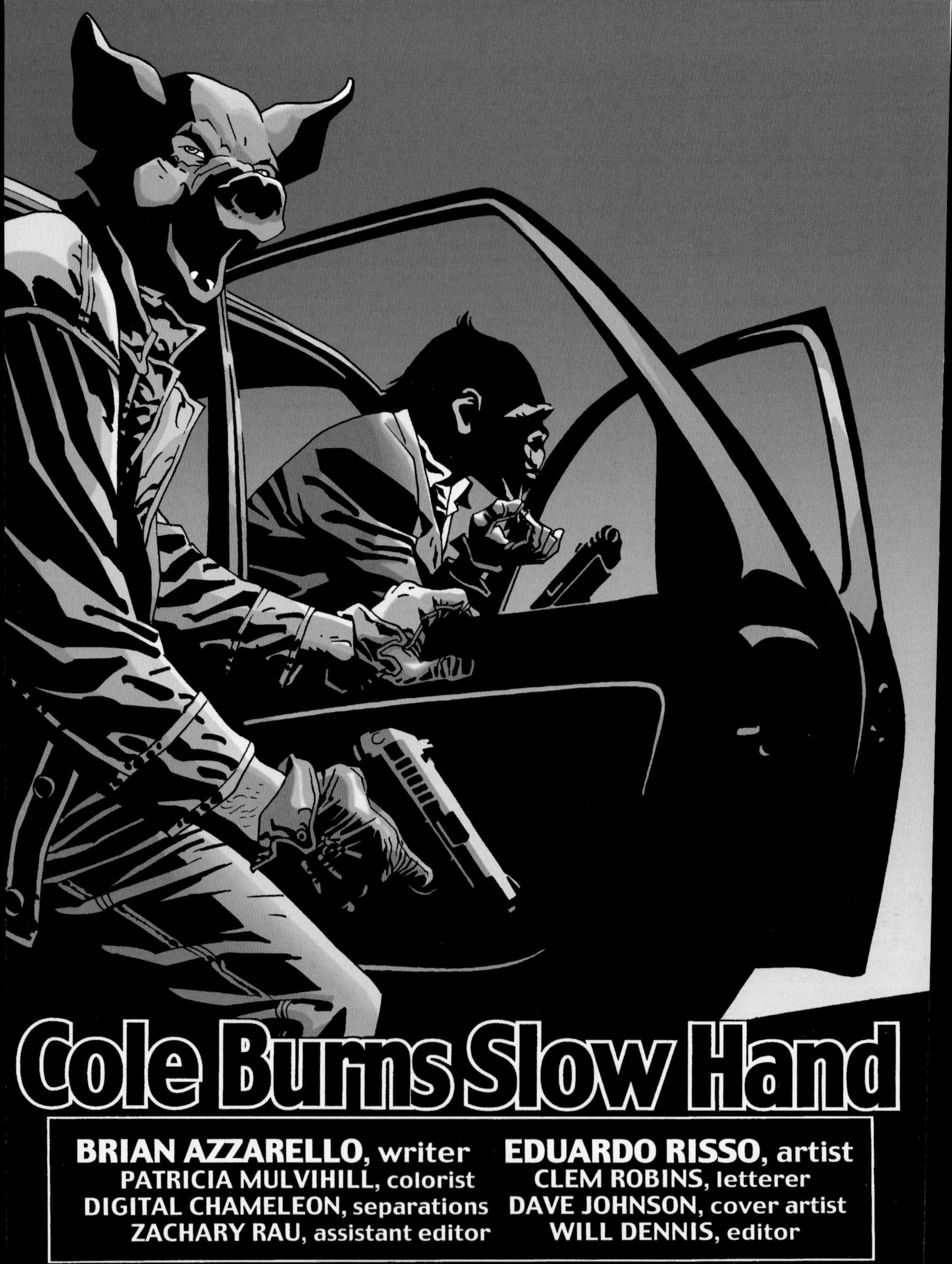

Cole Burns Slow Hand

BRIAN AZZARELLO, writer
PATRICIA MULVIHILL, colorist
DIGITAL CHAMELEON, separations
ZACHARY RAU, assistant editor

EDUARDO RISSO, artist
CLEM ROBINS, letterer
DAVE JOHNSON, cover artist
WILL DENNIS, editor

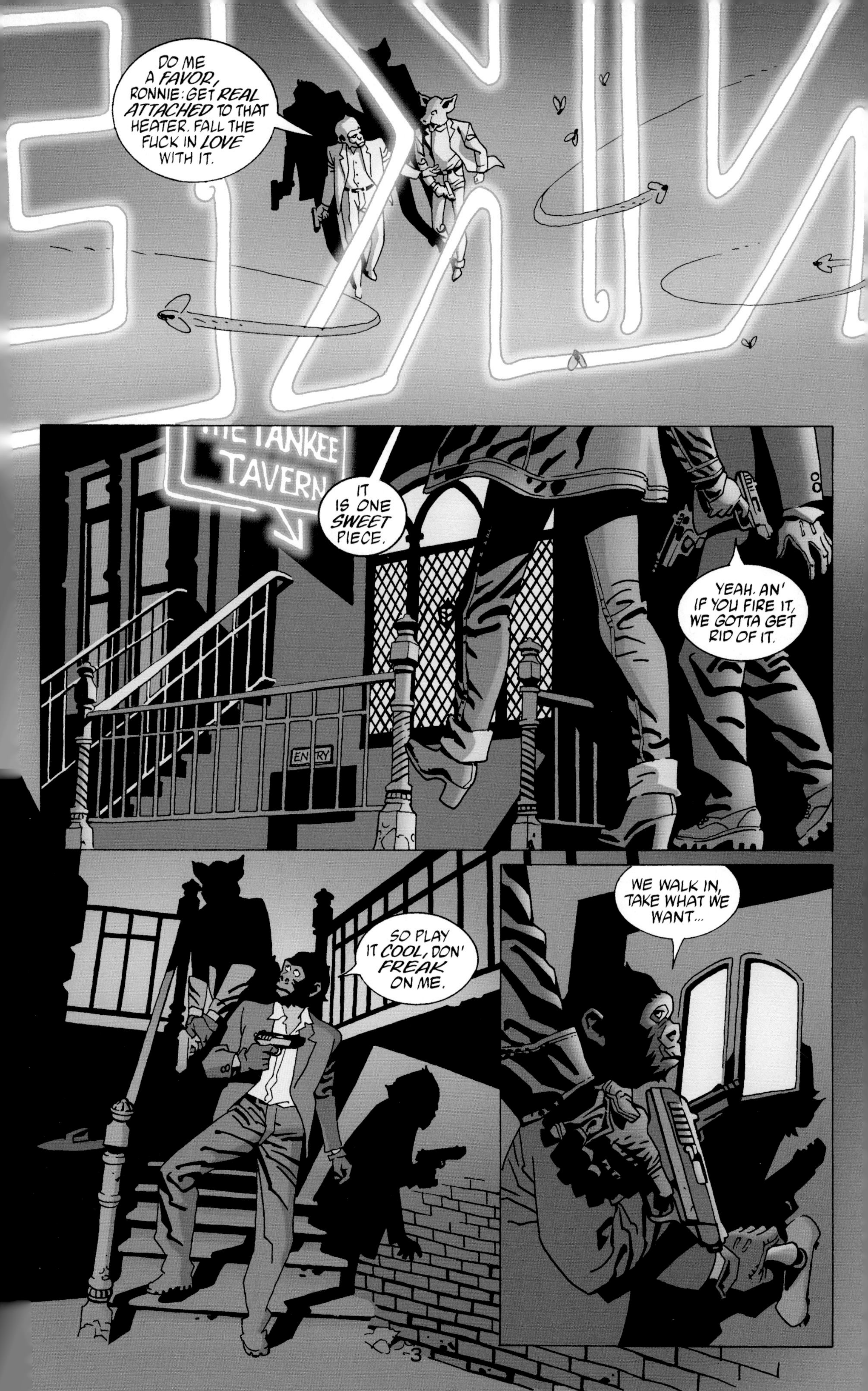
DO ME A FAVOR, RONNIE: GET REAL ATTACHED TO THAT HEATER. FALL THE FUCK IN LOVE WITH IT.
THE YANKEE TAVERN
IT IS ONE SWEET PIECE.
YEAH. AN' IF YOU FIRE IT, WE GOTTA GET RID OF IT.
ENTRY
SO PLAY IT COOL, DON' FREAK ON ME.
WE WALK IN, TAKE WHAT WE WANT...

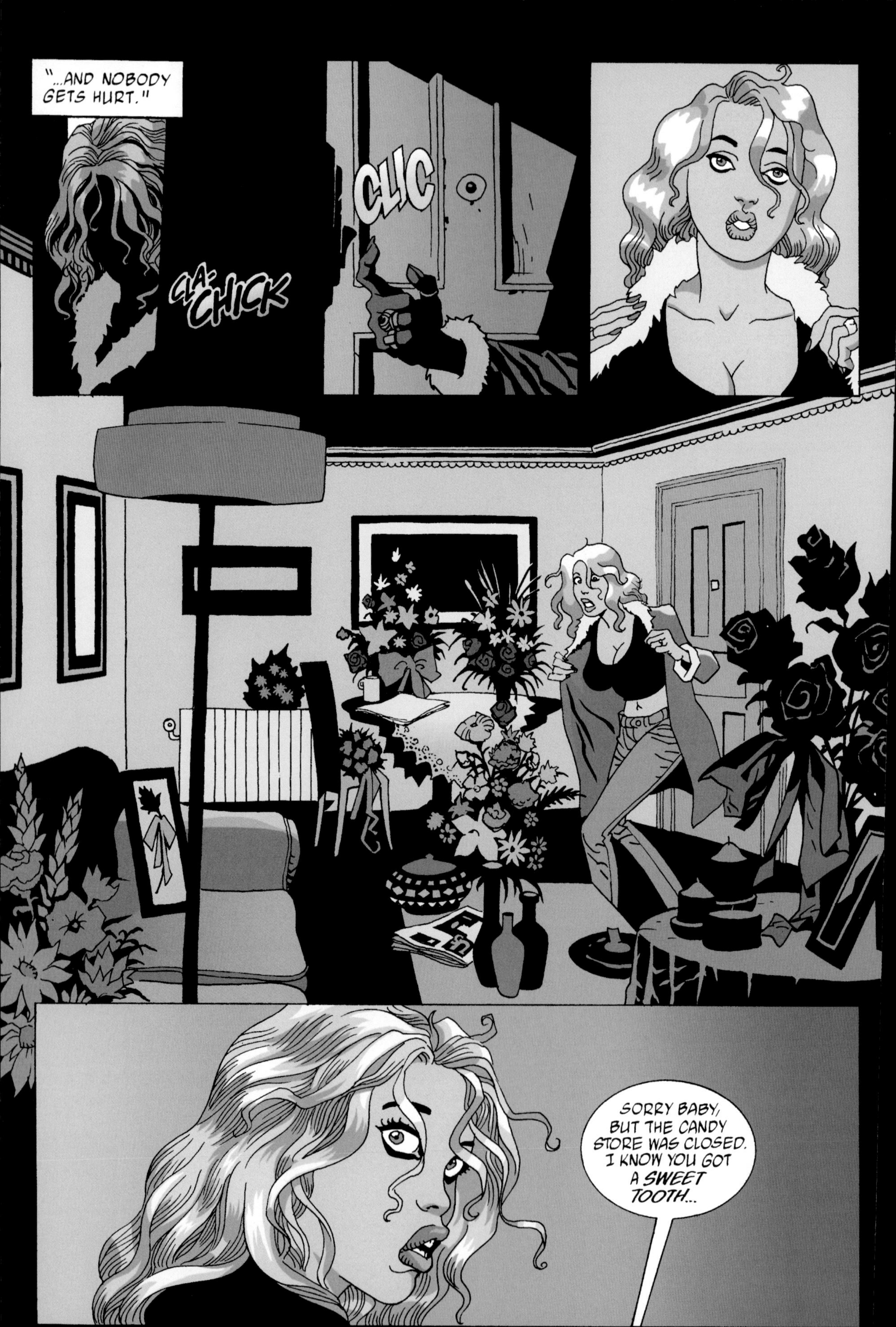
"...AND NOBODY GETS HURT."
CLA-CHICK
CLIC
SORRY BABY, BUT THE CANDY STORE WAS CLOSED. I KNOW YOU GOT A *SWEET TOOTH*...

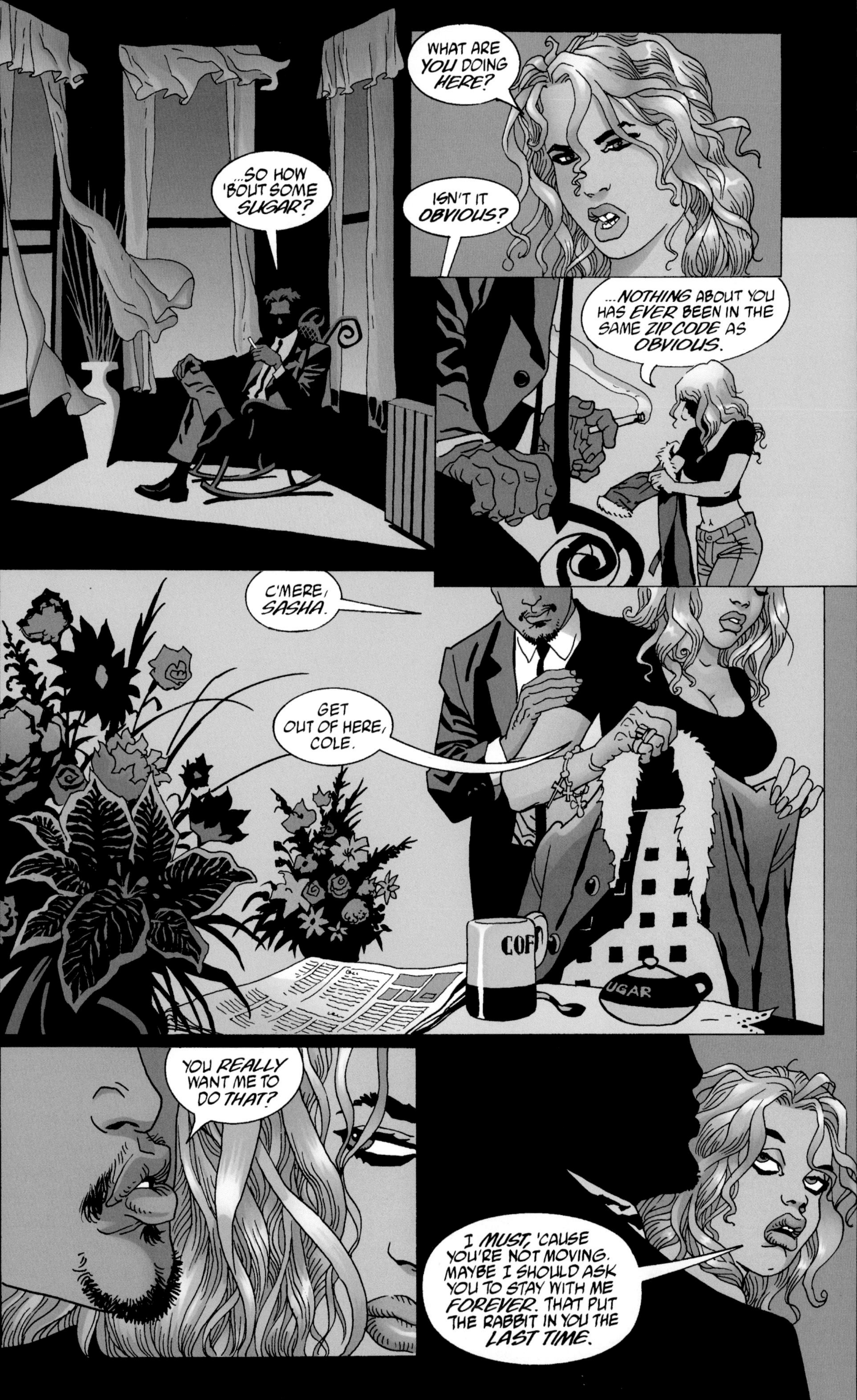
...SO HOW 'BOUT SOME SUGAR?
WHAT ARE YOU DOING HERE?
ISN'T IT OBVIOUS?
...NOTHING ABOUT YOU HAS EVER BEEN IN THE SAME ZIP CODE AS OBVIOUS.
C'MERE, SASHA.
GET OUT OF HERE, COLE.
COF
UGAR
YOU REALLY WANT ME TO DO THAT?
I MUST, 'CAUSE YOU'RE NOT MOVING. MAYBE I SHOULD ASK YOU TO STAY WITH ME FOREVER. THAT PUT THE RABBIT IN YOU THE LAST TIME.

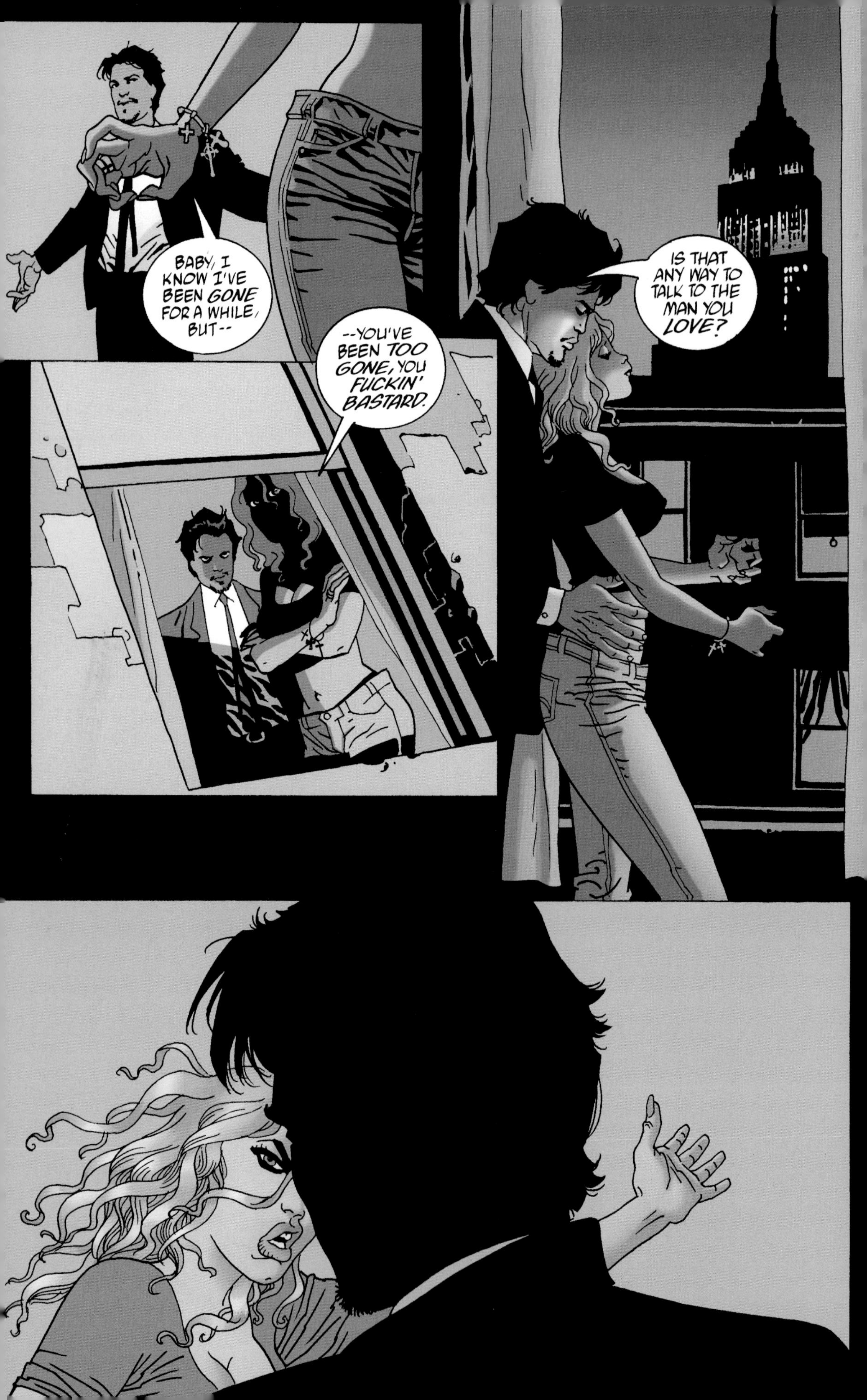

BABY, I KNOW I'VE BEEN GONE FOR A WHILE, BUT--
--YOU'VE BEEN TOO GONE, YOU FUCKIN' BASTARD.
IS THAT ANY WAY TO TALK TO THE MAN YOU LOVE?

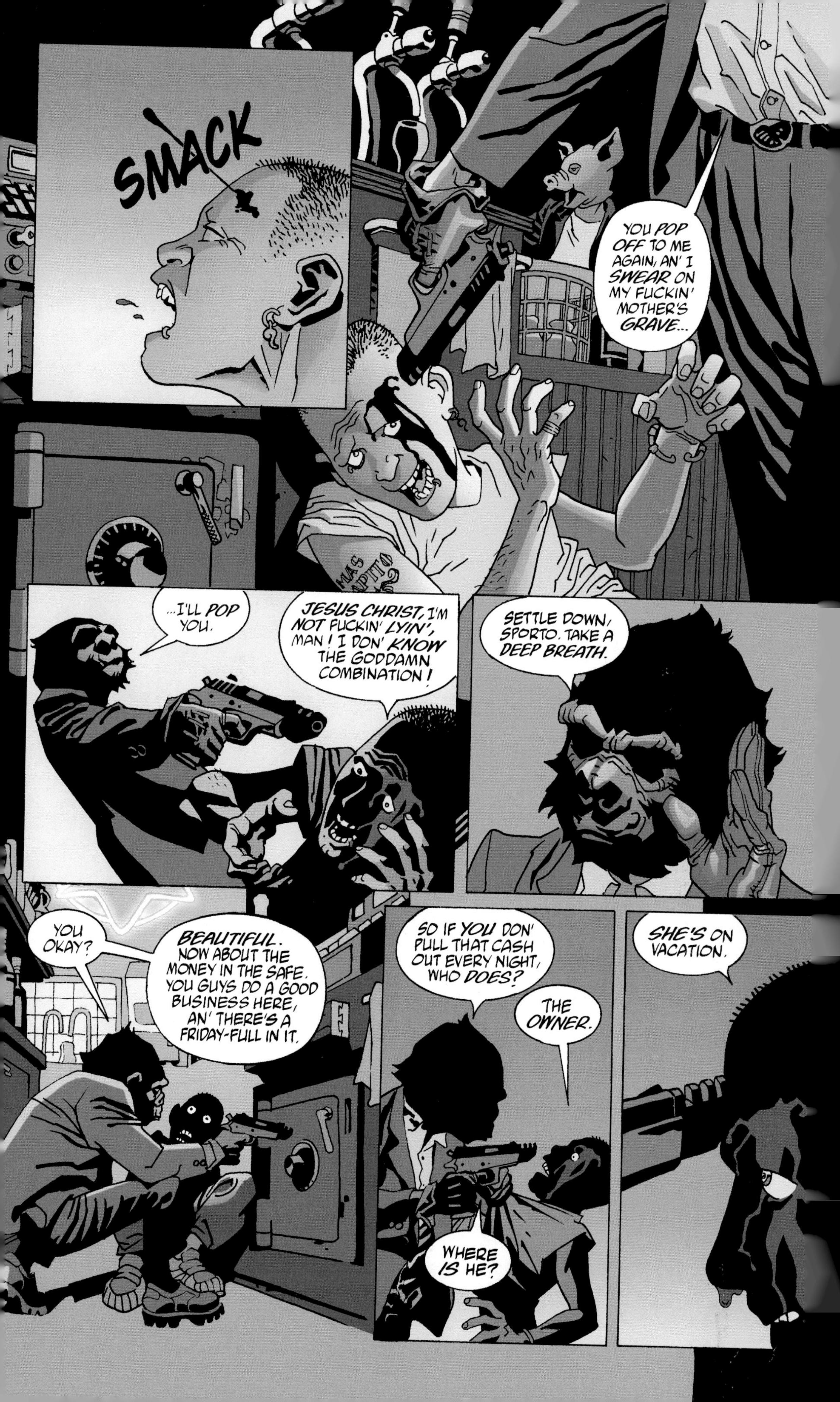
SMACK
YOU POP OFF TO ME AGAIN, AN' I SWEAR ON MY FUCKIN' MOTHER'S GRAVE...
...I'LL POP YOU.
JESUS CHRIST, I'M NOT FUCKIN' LYIN', MAN! I DON' KNOW THE GODDAMN COMBINATION!
SETTLE DOWN, SPORTO. TAKE A DEEP BREATH.
YOU OKAY?
BEAUTIFUL. NOW ABOUT THE MONEY IN THE SAFE. YOU GUYS DO A GOOD BUSINESS HERE, AN' THERE'S A FRIDAY-FULL IN IT.
SO IF YOU DON' PULL THAT CASH OUT EVERY NIGHT, WHO DOES?
THE OWNER.
WHERE IS HE?
SHE'S ON VACATION.

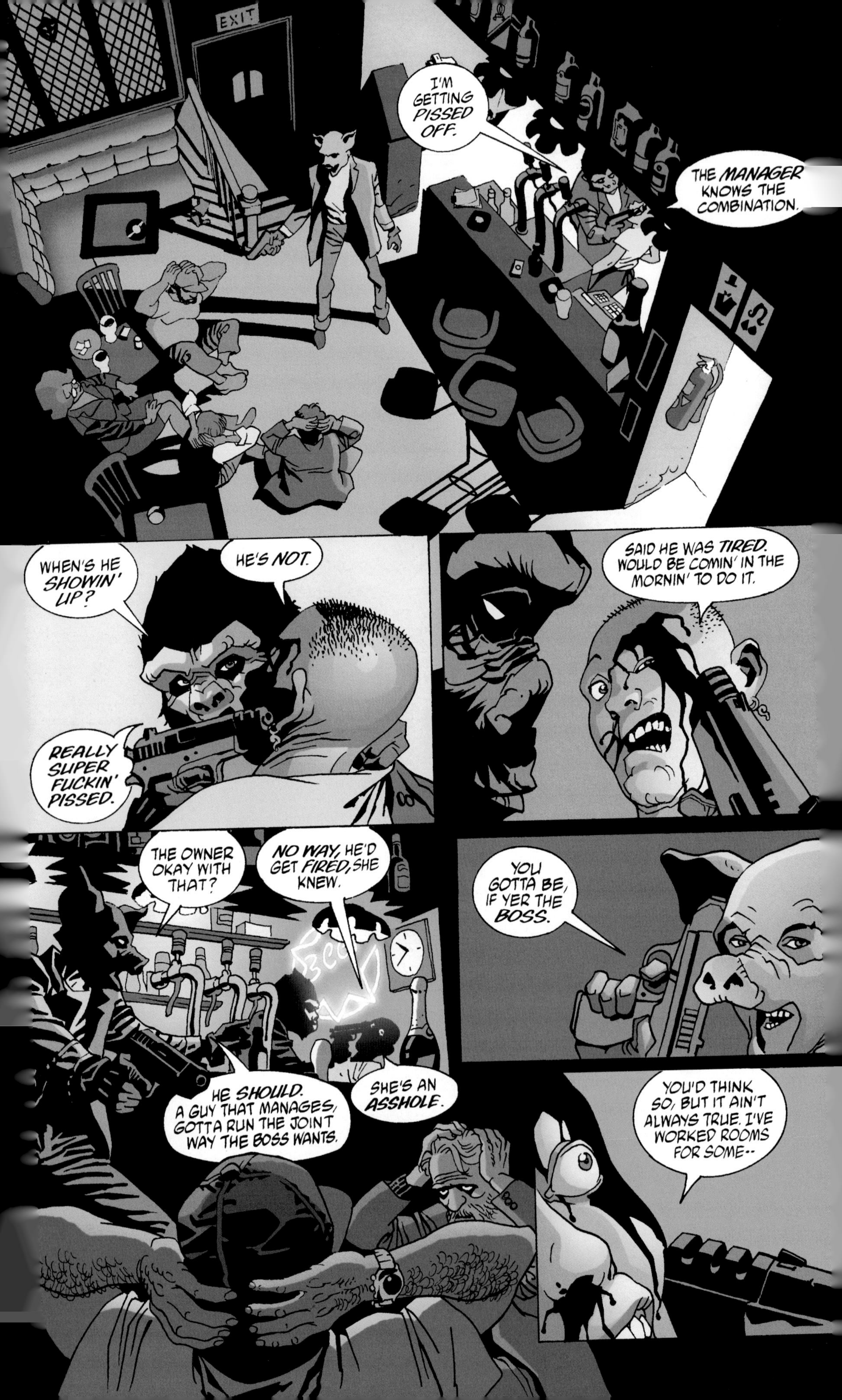
EXIT
I'M GETTING PISSED OFF.
THE MANAGER KNOWS THE COMBINATION.
WHEN'S HE SHOWIN' UP?
HE'S NOT.
REALLY SUPER FUCKIN' PISSED.
SAID HE WAS TIRED. WOULD BE COMIN' IN THE MORNIN' TO DO IT.
THE OWNER OKAY WITH THAT?
NO WAY, HE'D GET FIRED, SHE KNEW.
HE SHOULD. A GUY THAT MANAGES, GOTTA RUN THE JOINT WAY THE BOSS WANTS.
SHE'S AN ASSHOLE.
YOU GOTTA BE, IF YER THE BOSS.
YOU'D THINK SO, BUT IT AIN'T ALWAYS TRUE. I'VE WORKED ROOMS FOR SOME--

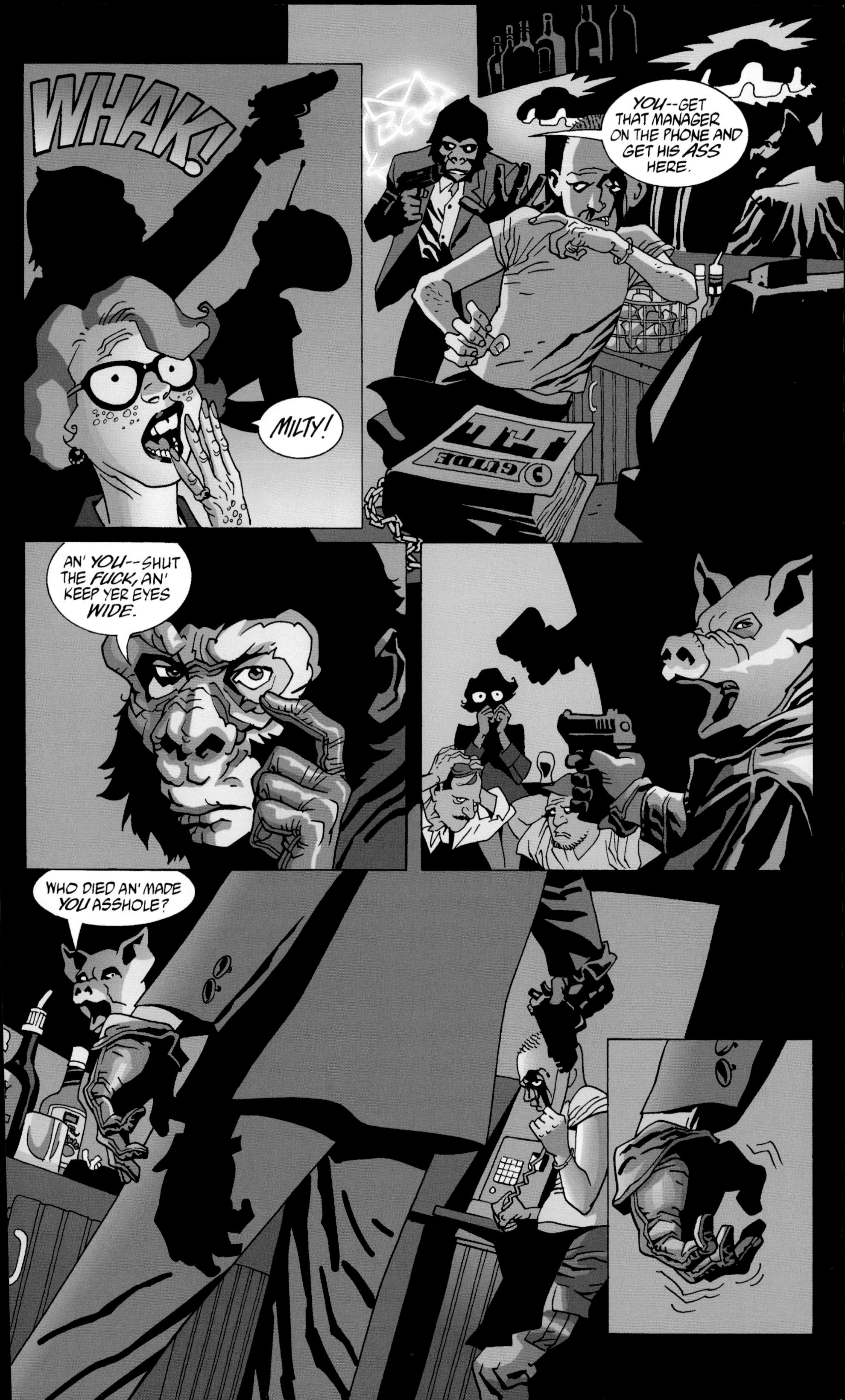
WHAK!
YOU--GET THAT MANAGER ON THE PHONE AND GET HIS ASS HERE.
MILTY!
AN' YOU--SHUT THE FUCK, AN' KEEP YER EYES WIDE.
WHO DIED AN' MADE YOU ASSHOLE?

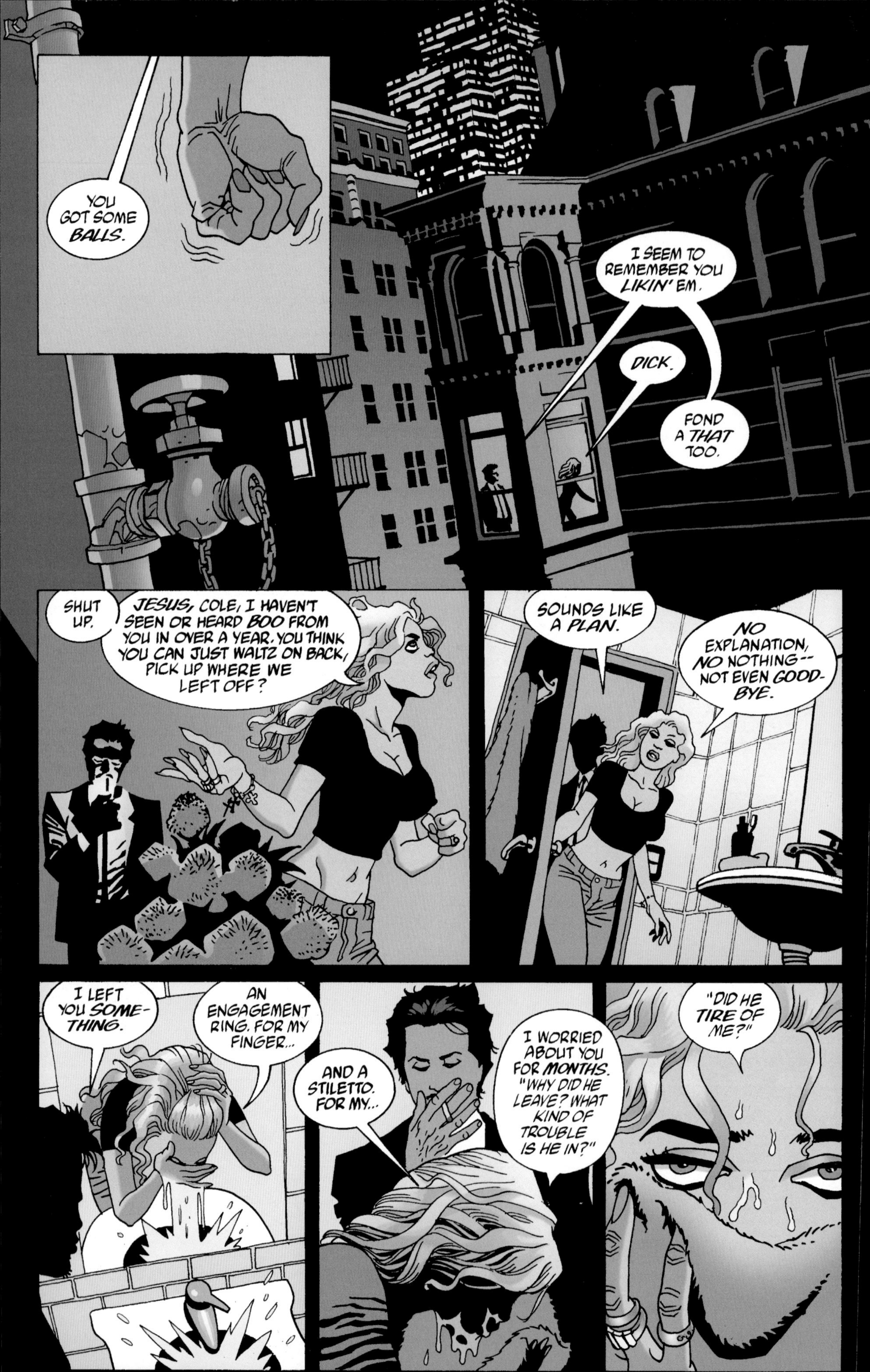
YOU GOT SOME BALLS.
I SEEM TO REMEMBER YOU LIKIN' EM.
DICK.
FOND A THAT TOO.
SHUT UP.
JESUS, COLE, I HAVEN'T SEEN OR HEARD BOO FROM YOU IN OVER A YEAR. YOU THINK YOU CAN JUST WALTZ ON BACK, PICK UP WHERE WE LEFT OFF?
SOUNDS LIKE A PLAN.
NO EXPLANATION, NO NOTHING-- NOT EVEN GOOD-BYE.
I LEFT YOU SOME-THING.
AN ENGAGEMENT RING. FOR MY FINGER...
AND A STILETTO. FOR MY...
I WORRIED ABOUT YOU FOR MONTHS. "WHY DID HE LEAVE? WHAT KIND OF TROUBLE IS HE IN?"
"DID HE TIRE OF ME?"

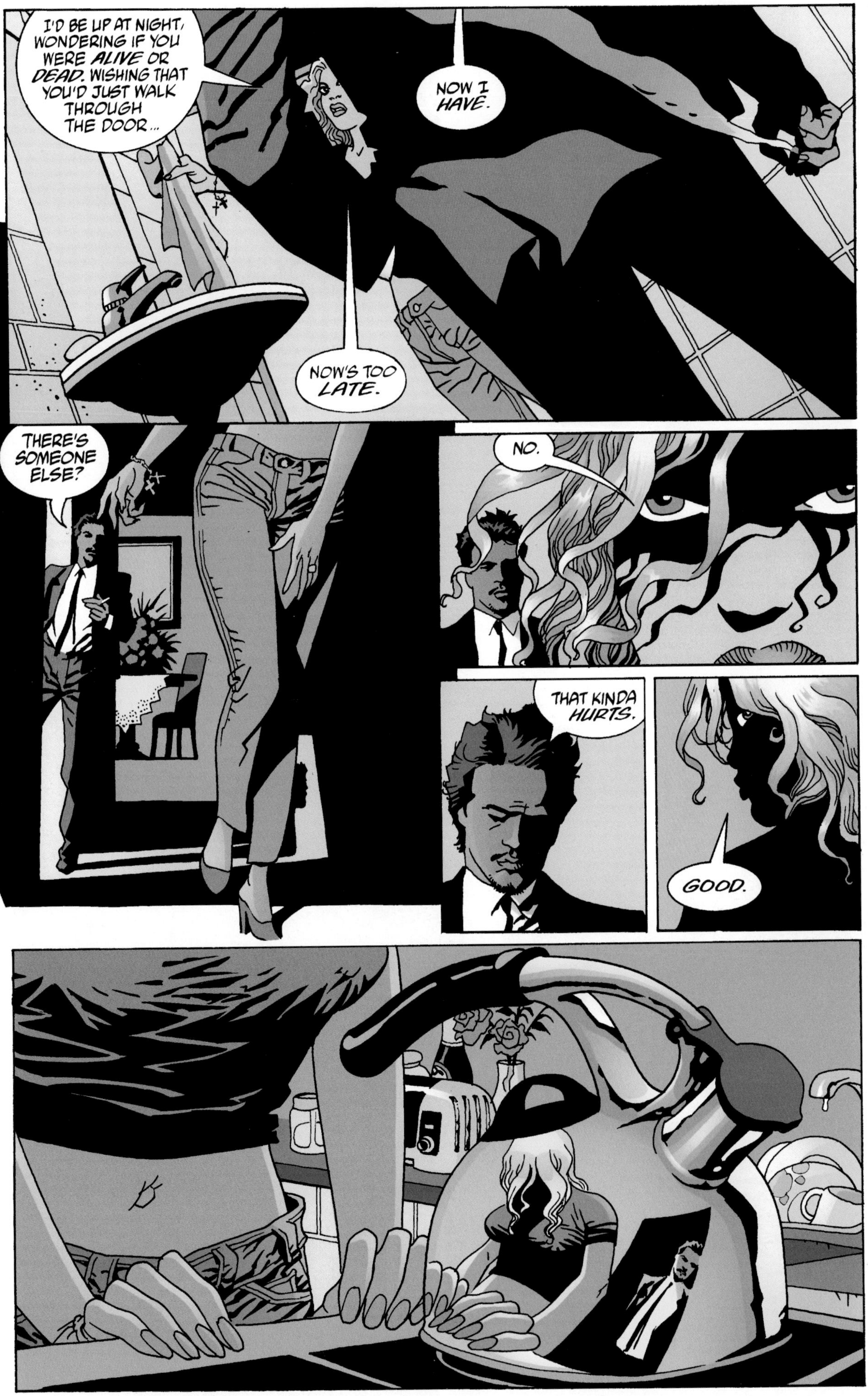
I'D BE UP AT NIGHT, WONDERING IF YOU WERE ALIVE OR DEAD. WISHING THAT YOU'D JUST WALK THROUGH THE DOOR...
NOW I HAVE.
NOW'S TOO LATE.
THERE'S SOMEONE ELSE?
NO.
THAT KINDA HURTS.
GOOD.

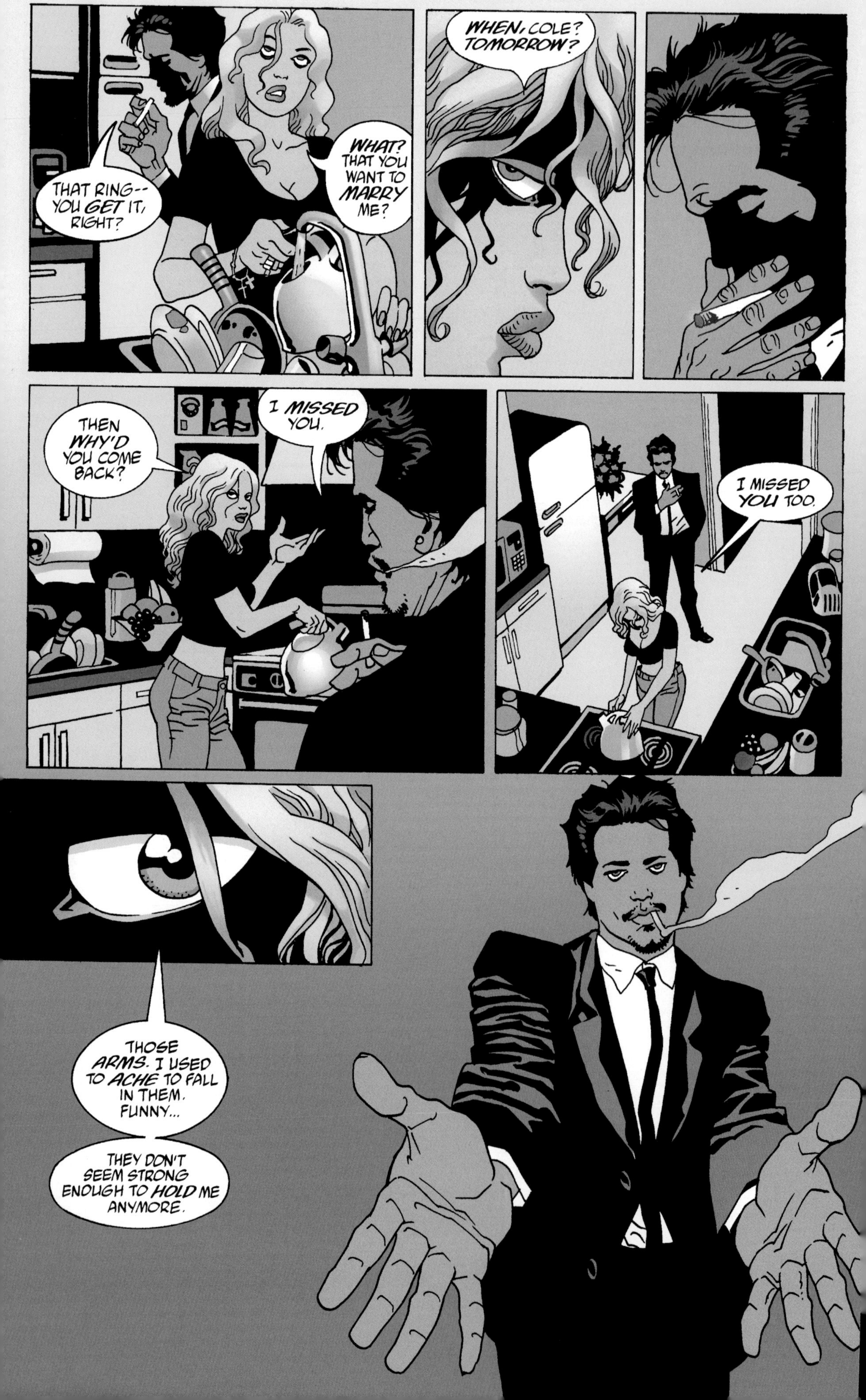
THAT RING-- YOU GET IT, RIGHT?
WHAT? THAT YOU WANT TO MARRY ME?
WHEN, COLE? TOMORROW?
THEN WHY'D YOU COME BACK?
I MISSED YOU.
I MISSED YOU TOO.
THOSE ARMS. I USED TO ACHE TO FALL IN THEM. FUNNY...
THEY DON'T SEEM STRONG ENOUGH TO HOLD ME ANYMORE.

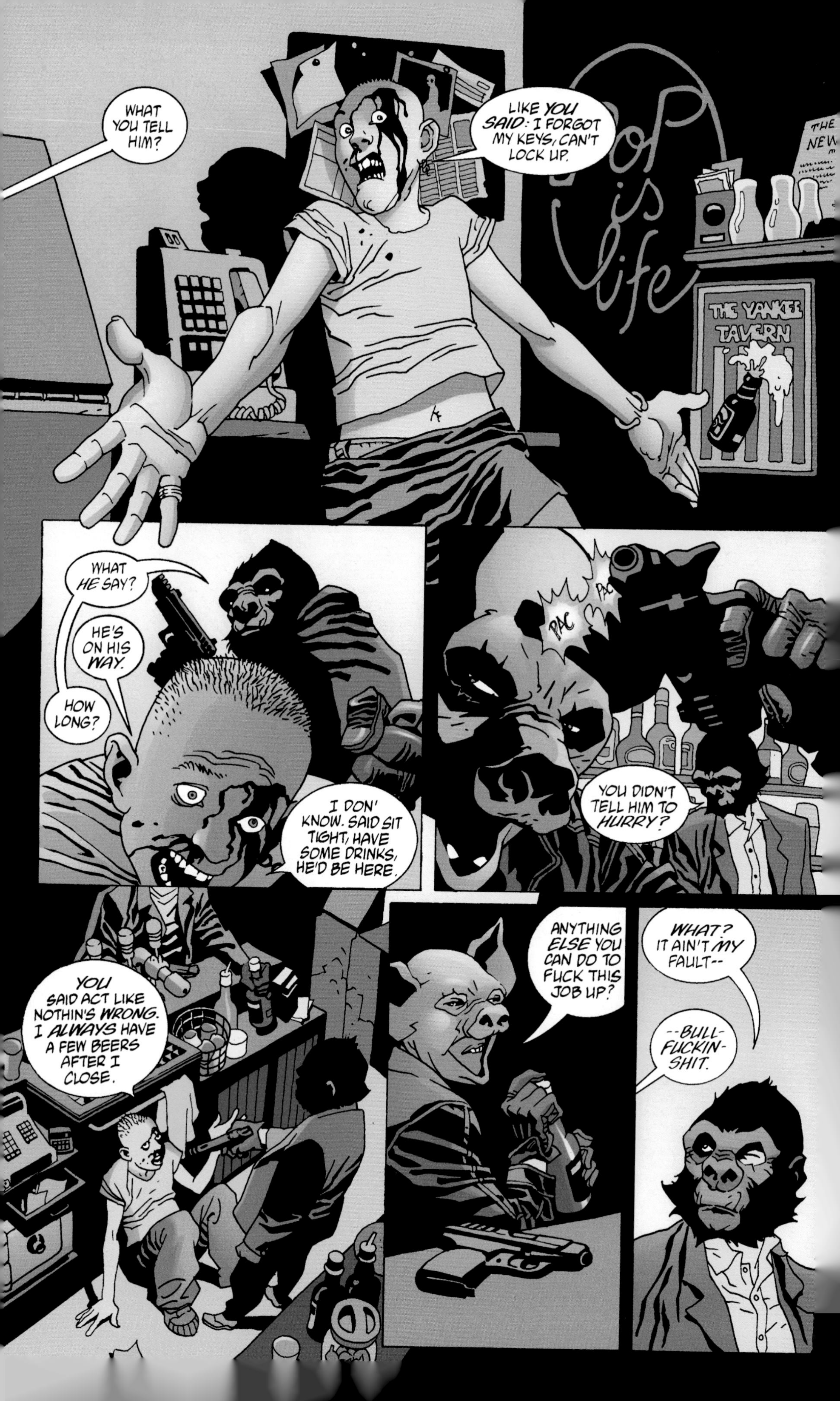
WHAT YOU TELL HIM?
LIKE YOU SAID: I FORGOT MY KEYS, CAN'T LOCK UP.
POP is life
THE YANKEE TAVERN
WHAT HE SAY?
HE'S ON HIS WAY.
HOW LONG?
I DON' KNOW. SAID SIT TIGHT, HAVE SOME DRINKS, HE'D BE HERE.
PAC
PAC
YOU DIDN'T TELL HIM TO HURRY?
YOU SAID ACT LIKE NOTHIN'S WRONG. I ALWAYS HAVE A FEW BEERS AFTER I CLOSE.
ANYTHING ELSE YOU CAN DO TO FUCK THIS JOB UP?
WHAT? IT AIN'T MY FAULT--
--BULL-FUCKIN-SHIT.

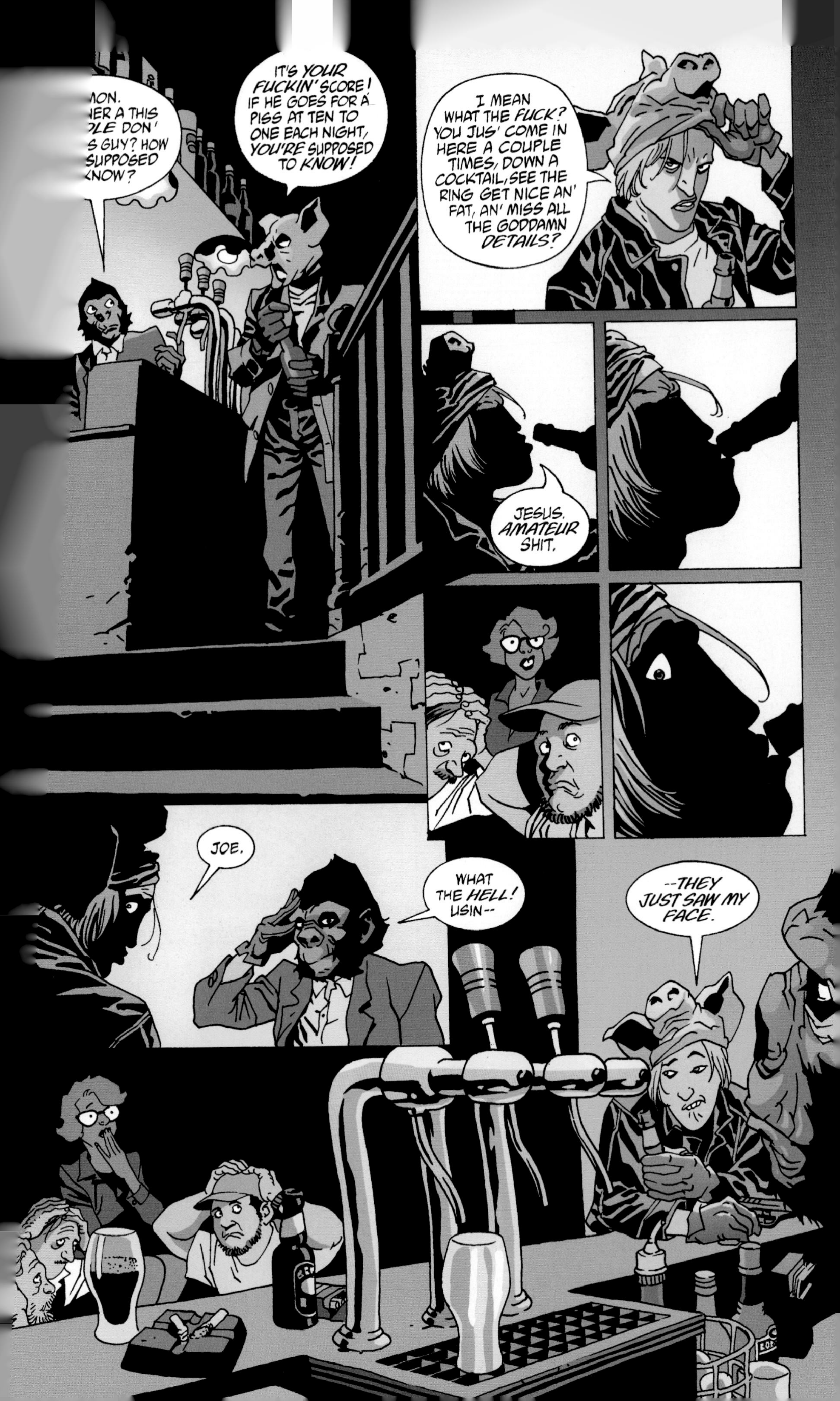

MON.
NER A THIS
PLE DON'
S GUY? HOW
SUPPOSED
KNOW?
IT'S YOUR FUCKIN' SCORE! IF HE GOES FOR A PISS AT TEN TO ONE EACH NIGHT, YOU'RE SUPPOSED TO KNOW!
I MEAN WHAT THE FUCK? YOU JUS' COME IN HERE A COUPLE TIMES, DOWN A COCKTAIL, SEE THE RING GET NICE AN' FAT, AN' MISS ALL THE GODDAMN DETAILS?
JESUS. AMATEUR SHIT.
JOE.
WHAT THE HELL! USIN--
--THEY JUST SAW MY FACE.

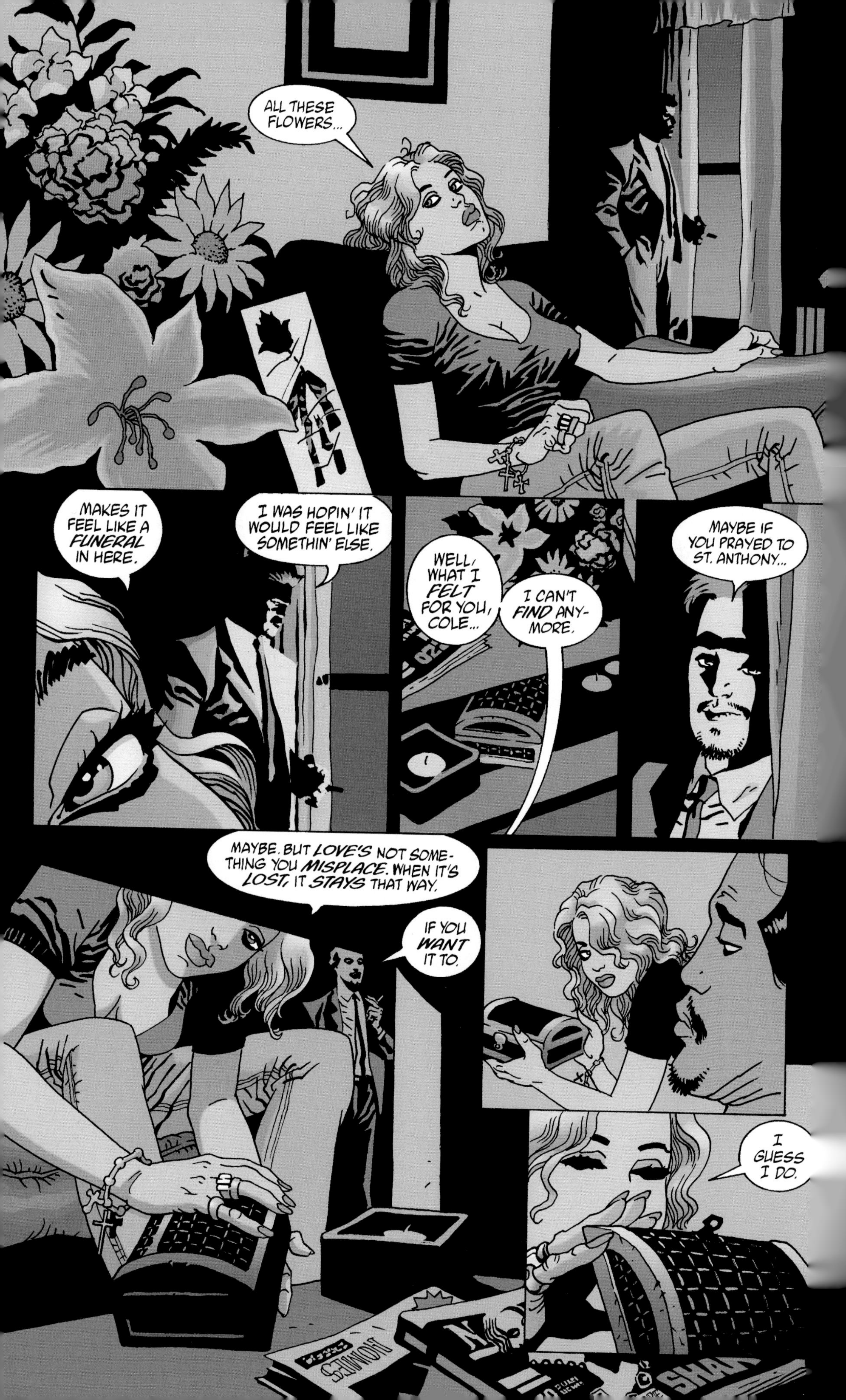

ALL THESE FLOWERS...
MAKES IT FEEL LIKE A FUNERAL IN HERE.
I WAS HOPIN' IT WOULD FEEL LIKE SOMETHIN' ELSE.
WELL, WHAT I FELT FOR YOU, COLE...
I CAN'T FIND ANY-MORE.
MAYBE IF YOU PRAYED TO ST. ANTHONY...
MAYBE. BUT LOVE'S NOT SOME-THING YOU MISPLACE. WHEN IT'S LOST, IT STAYS THAT WAY.
IF YOU WANT IT TO.
I GUESS I DO.

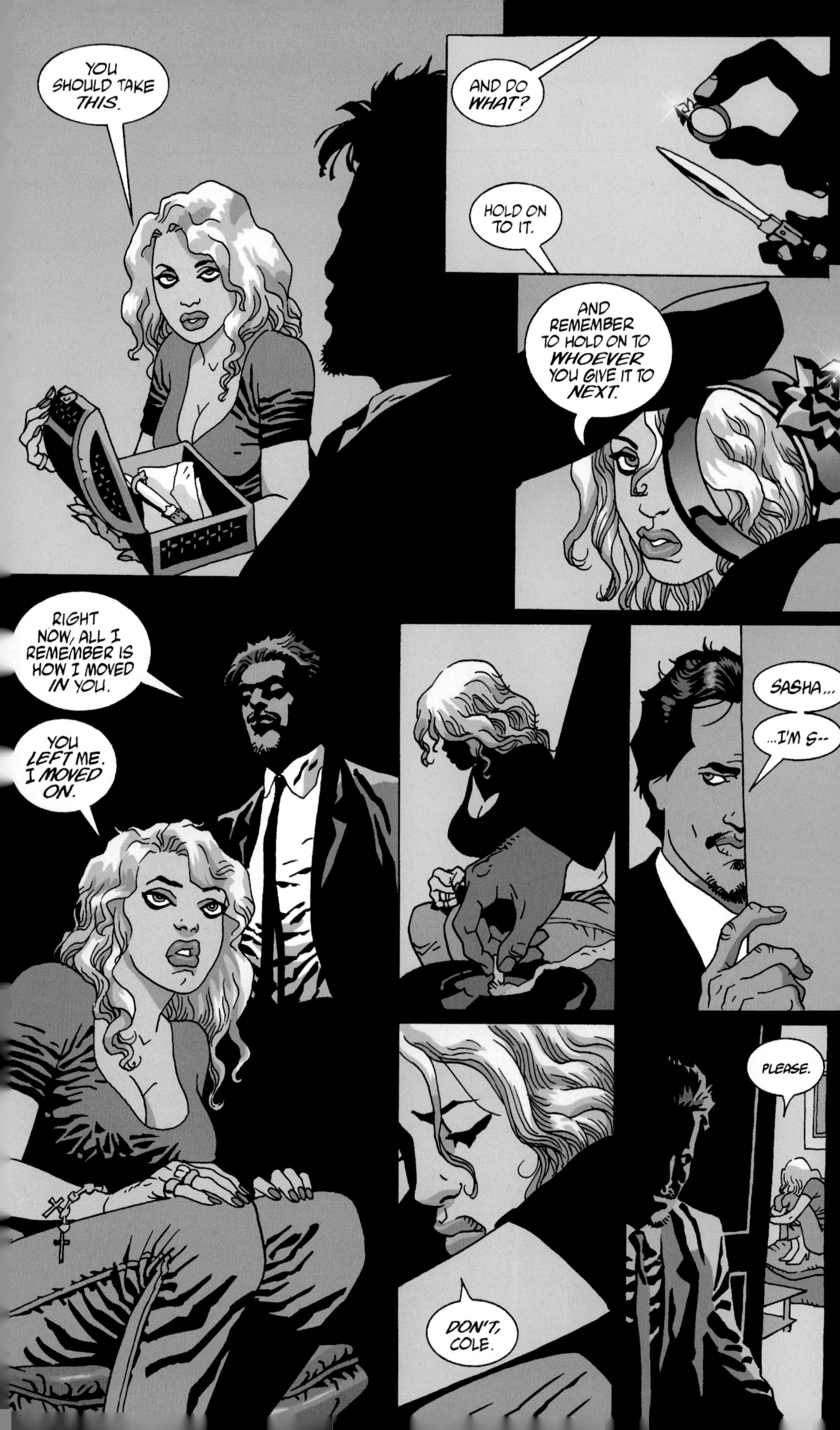
YOU SHOULD TAKE THIS.
AND DO WHAT?
HOLD ON TO IT.
AND REMEMBER TO HOLD ON TO WHOEVER YOU GIVE IT TO NEXT.
RIGHT NOW, ALL I REMEMBER IS HOW I MOVED IN YOU.
YOU LEFT ME. I MOVED ON.
SASHA...
...I'M S--
DON'T, COLE.
PLEASE.

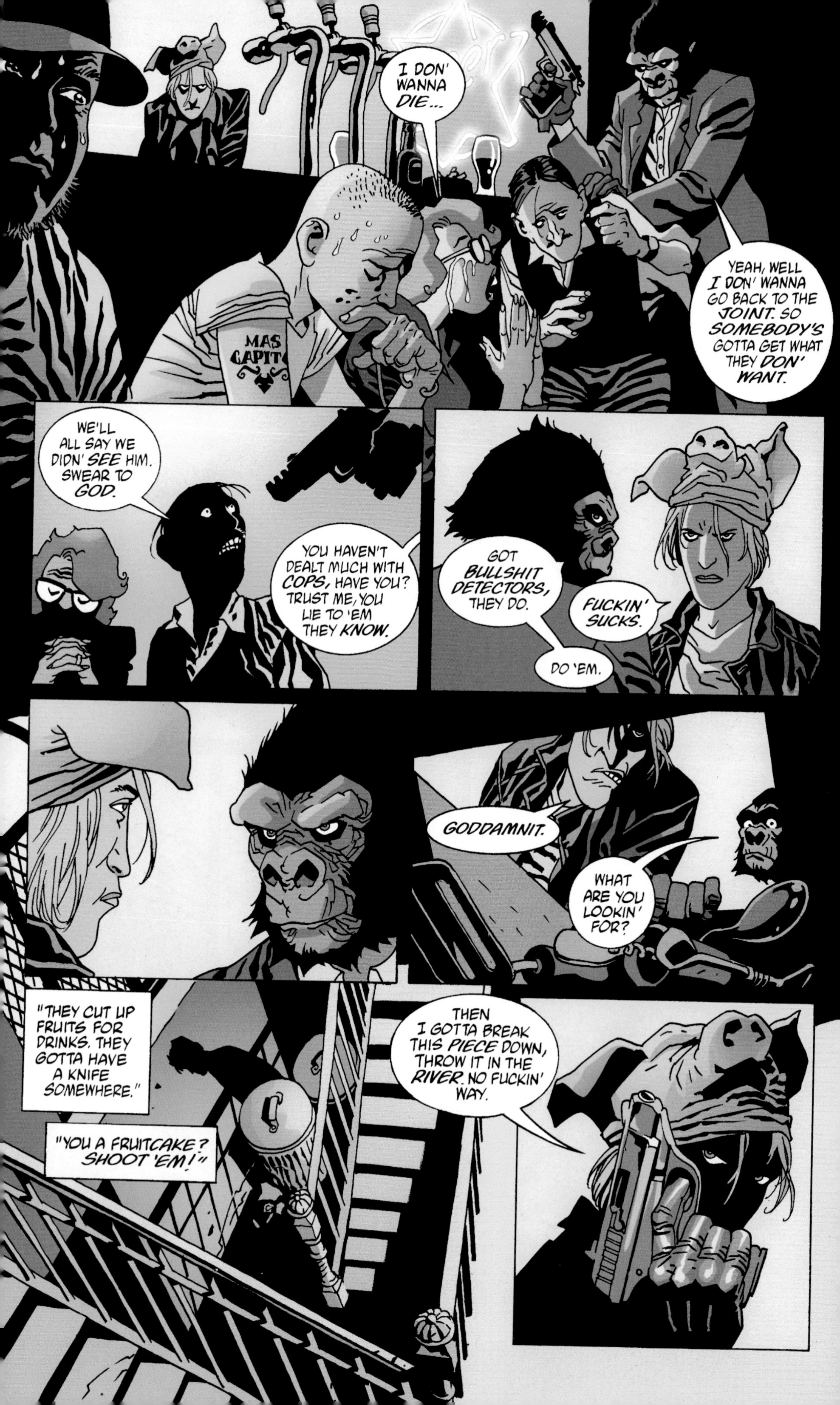

I DON' WANNA DIE...
YEAH, WELL I DON' WANNA GO BACK TO THE JOINT. SO SOMEBODY'S GOTTA GET WHAT THEY DON' WANT.
WE'LL ALL SAY WE DIDN' SEE HIM. SWEAR TO GOD.
YOU HAVEN'T DEALT MUCH WITH COPS, HAVE YOU? TRUST ME, YOU LIE TO 'EM THEY KNOW.
GOT BULLSHIT DETECTORS, THEY DO.
FUCKIN' SUCKS.
DO 'EM.
GODDAMNIT.
WHAT ARE YOU LOOKIN' FOR?
"THEY CUT UP FRUITS FOR DRINKS. THEY GOTTA HAVE A KNIFE SOMEWHERE."
"YOU A FRUITCAKE? SHOOT 'EM!"
THEN I GOTTA BREAK THIS PIECE DOWN, THROW IT IN THE RIVER. NO FUCKIN' WAY.

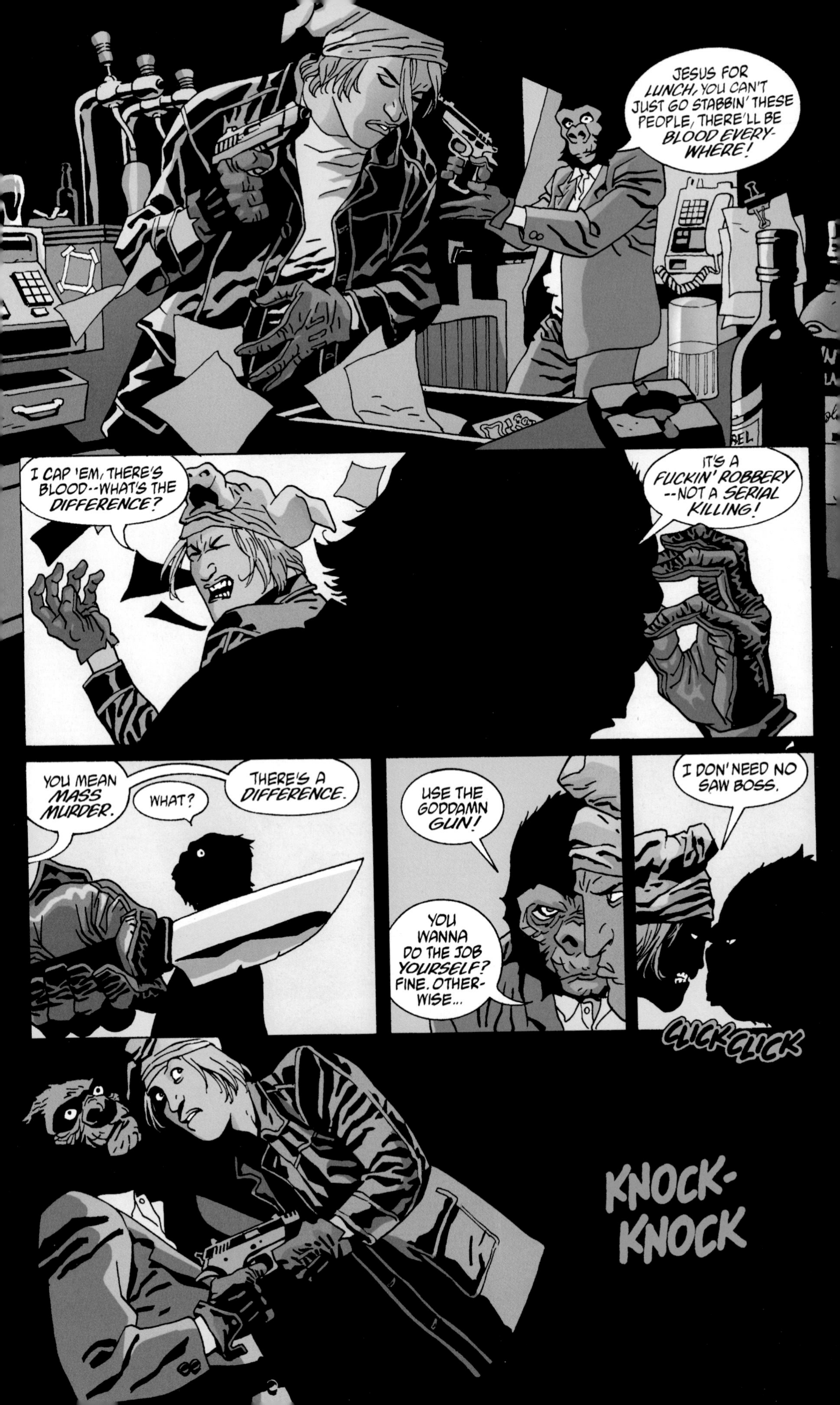
JESUS FOR LUNCH, YOU CAN'T JUST GO STABBIN' THESE PEOPLE, THERE'LL BE BLOOD EVERY-WHERE!
I CAP 'EM, THERE'S BLOOD--WHAT'S THE DIFFERENCE?
IT'S A FUCKIN' ROBBERY --NOT A SERIAL KILLING!
YOU MEAN MASS MURDER.
WHAT?
THERE'S A DIFFERENCE.
USE THE GODDAMN GUN!
YOU WANNA DO THE JOB YOURSELF? FINE. OTHER-WISE...
I DON'NEED NO SAW BOSS.
CLICK CLICK
KNOCK-KNOCK

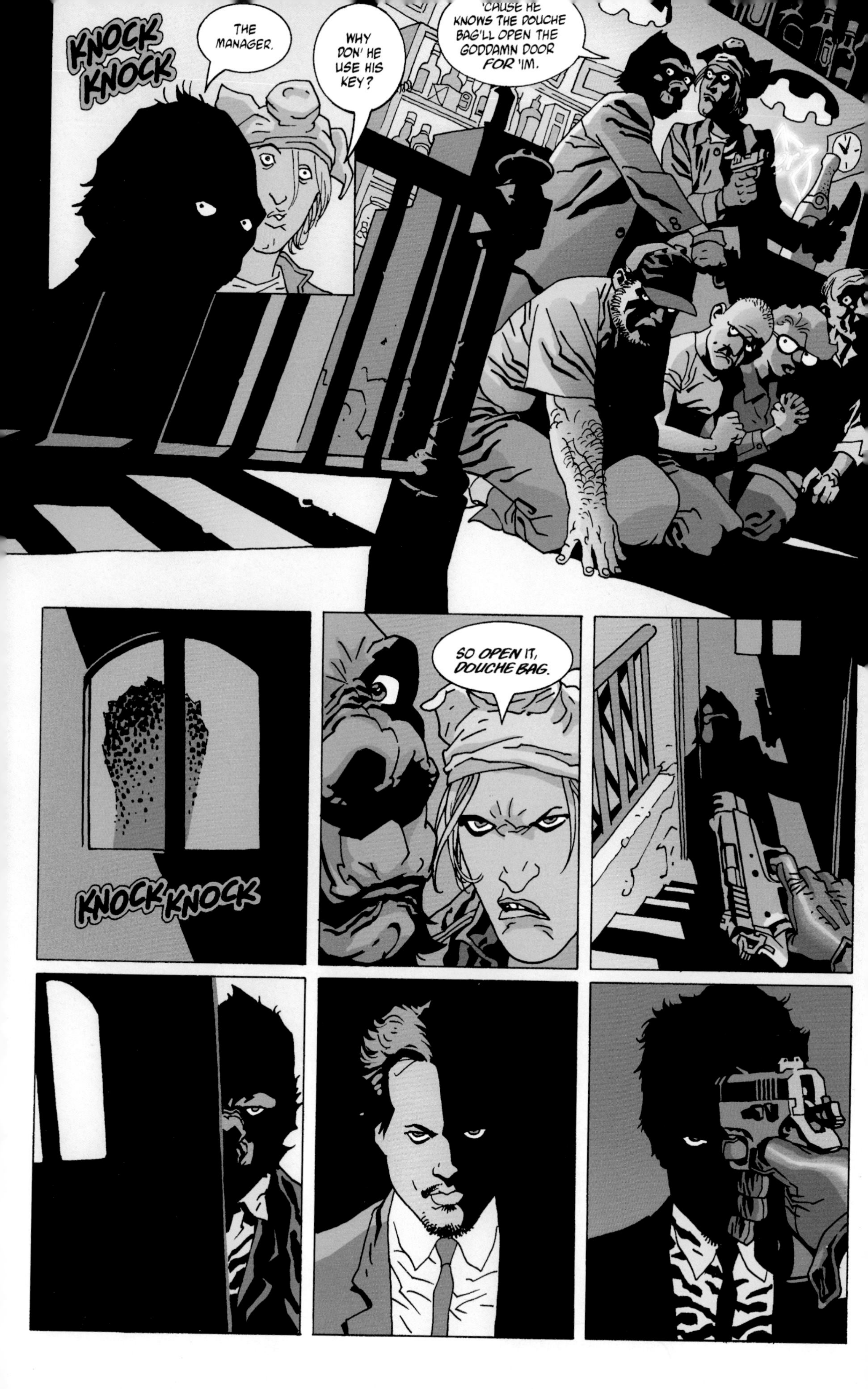
KNOCK KNOCK
THE MANAGER.
WHY DON' HE USE HIS KEY?
'CAUSE HE KNOWS THE DOUCHE BAG'LL OPEN THE GODDAMN DOOR FOR 'IM.
KNOCK KNOCK
SO OPEN IT, DOUCHE BAG.

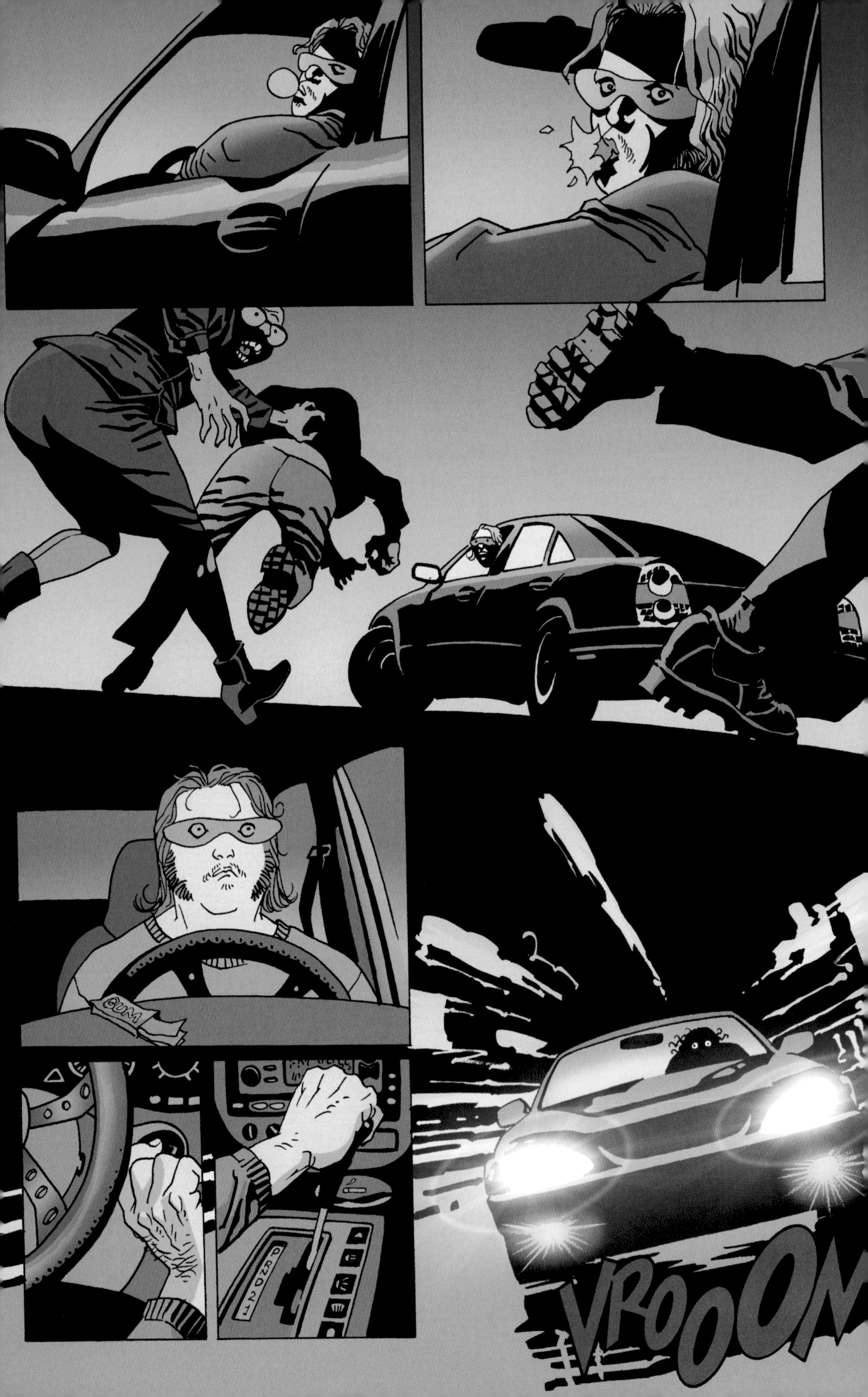
GUM
PRND21
VROOOM

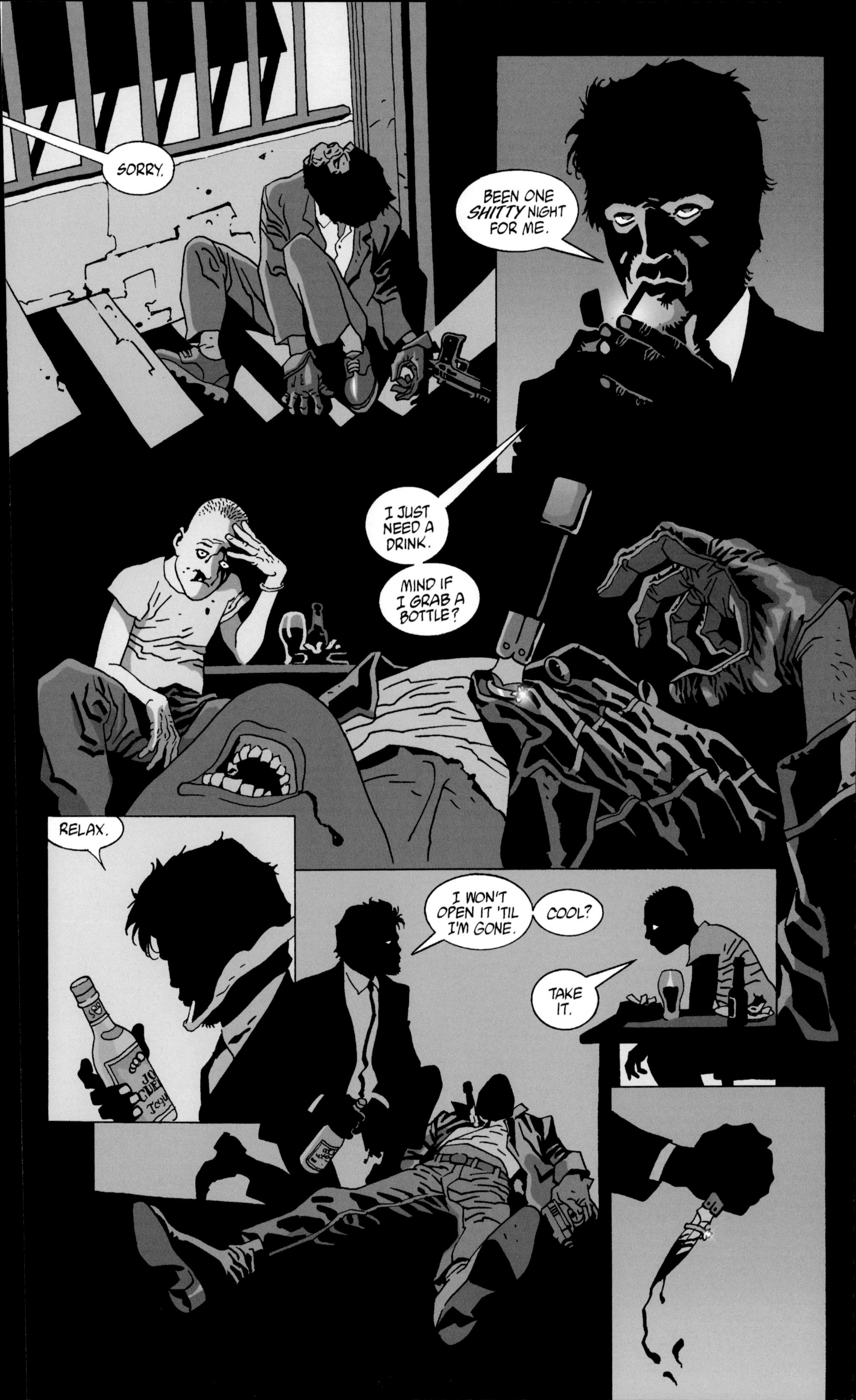
SORRY.
BEEN ONE SHITTY NIGHT FOR ME.
I JUST NEED A DRINK.
MIND IF I GRAB A BOTTLE?
RELAX.
I WON'T OPEN IT 'TIL I'M GONE.
COOL?
TAKE IT.

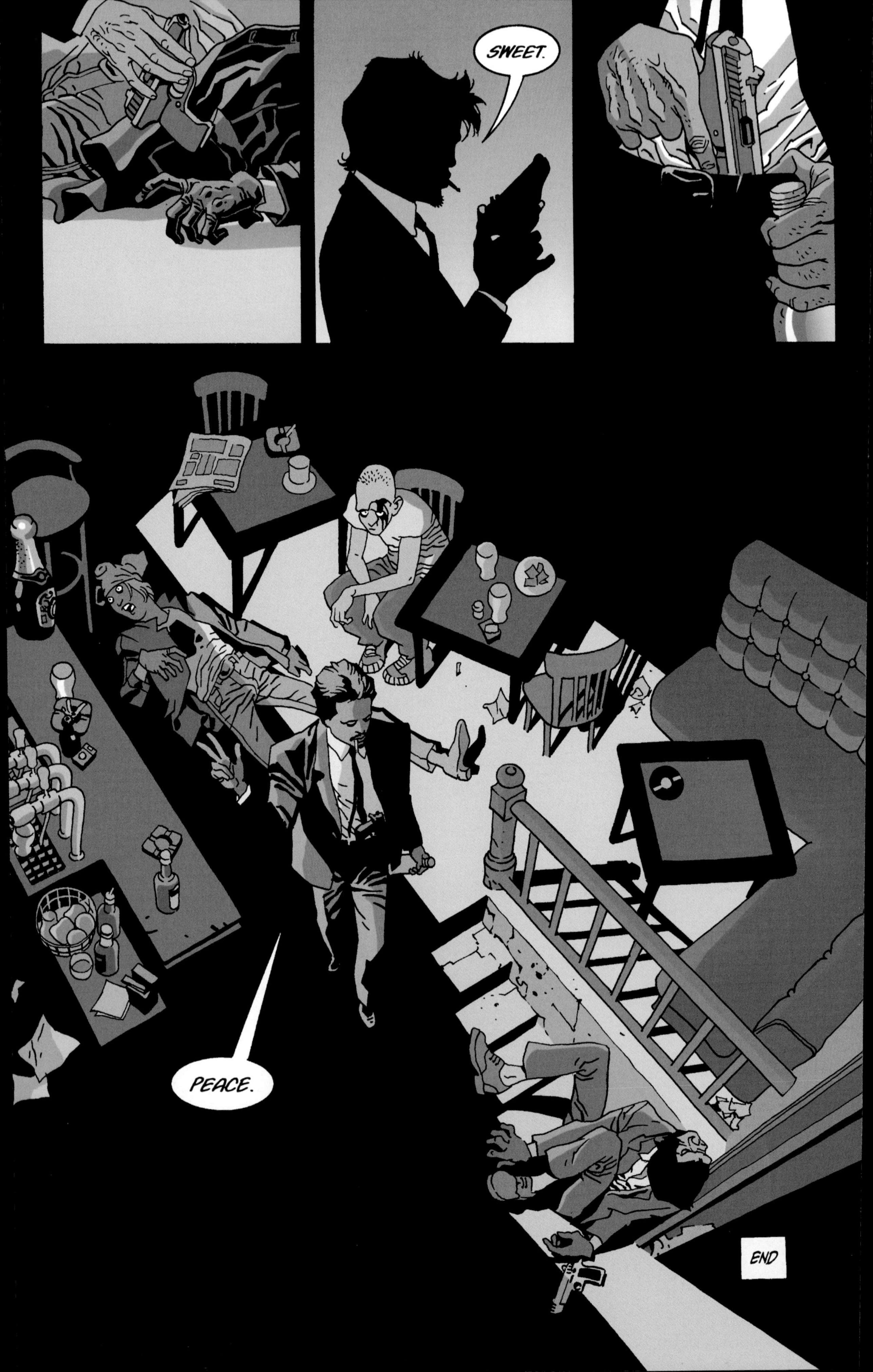
SWEET.
PEACE.
END

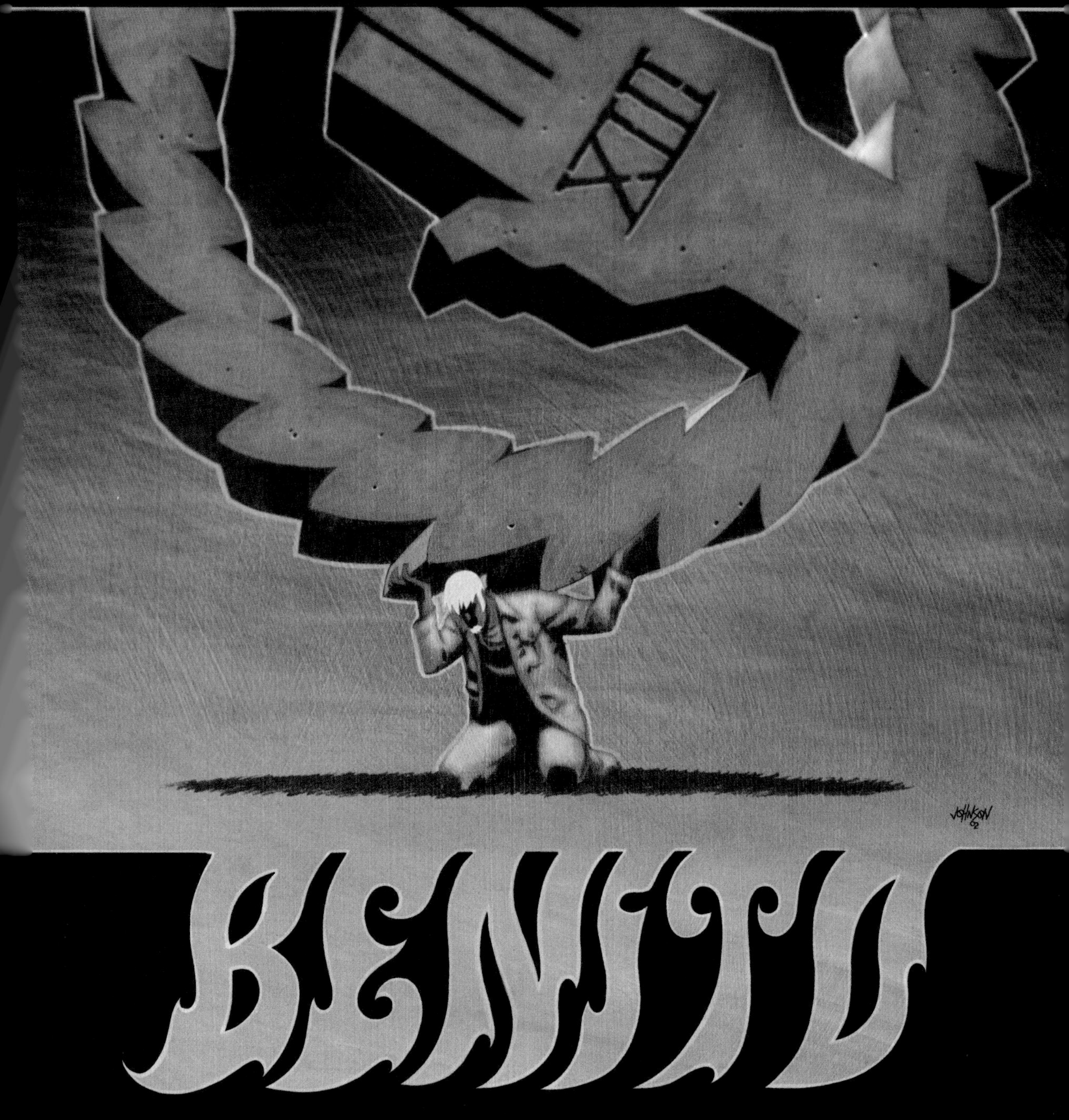
BENITO

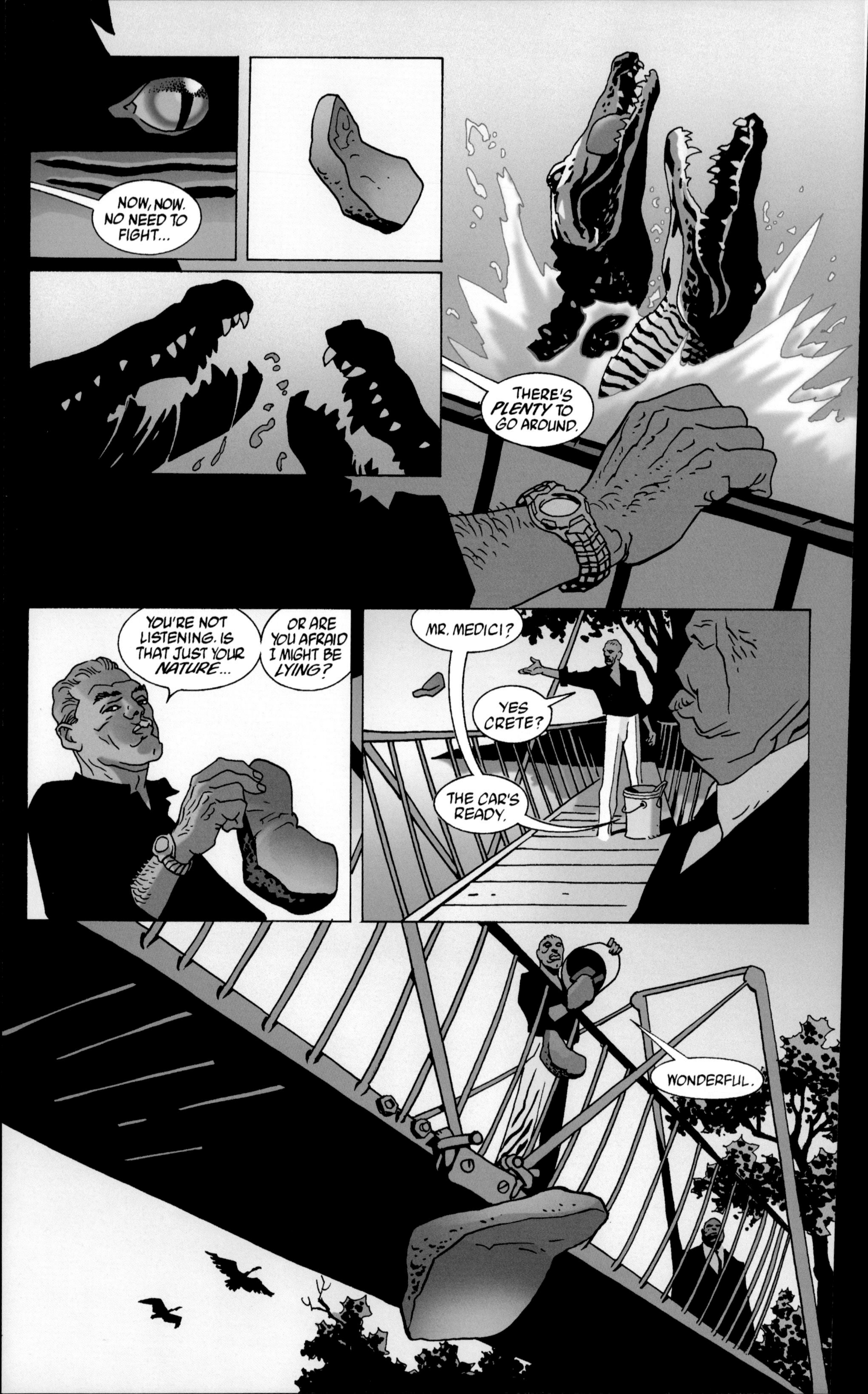
NOW, NOW. NO NEED TO FIGHT...
THERE'S PLENTY TO GO AROUND.
YOU'RE NOT LISTENING. IS THAT JUST YOUR NATURE...
OR ARE YOU AFRAID I MIGHT BE LYING?
MR. MEDICI?
YES CRETE?
THE CAR'S READY.
WONDERFUL.

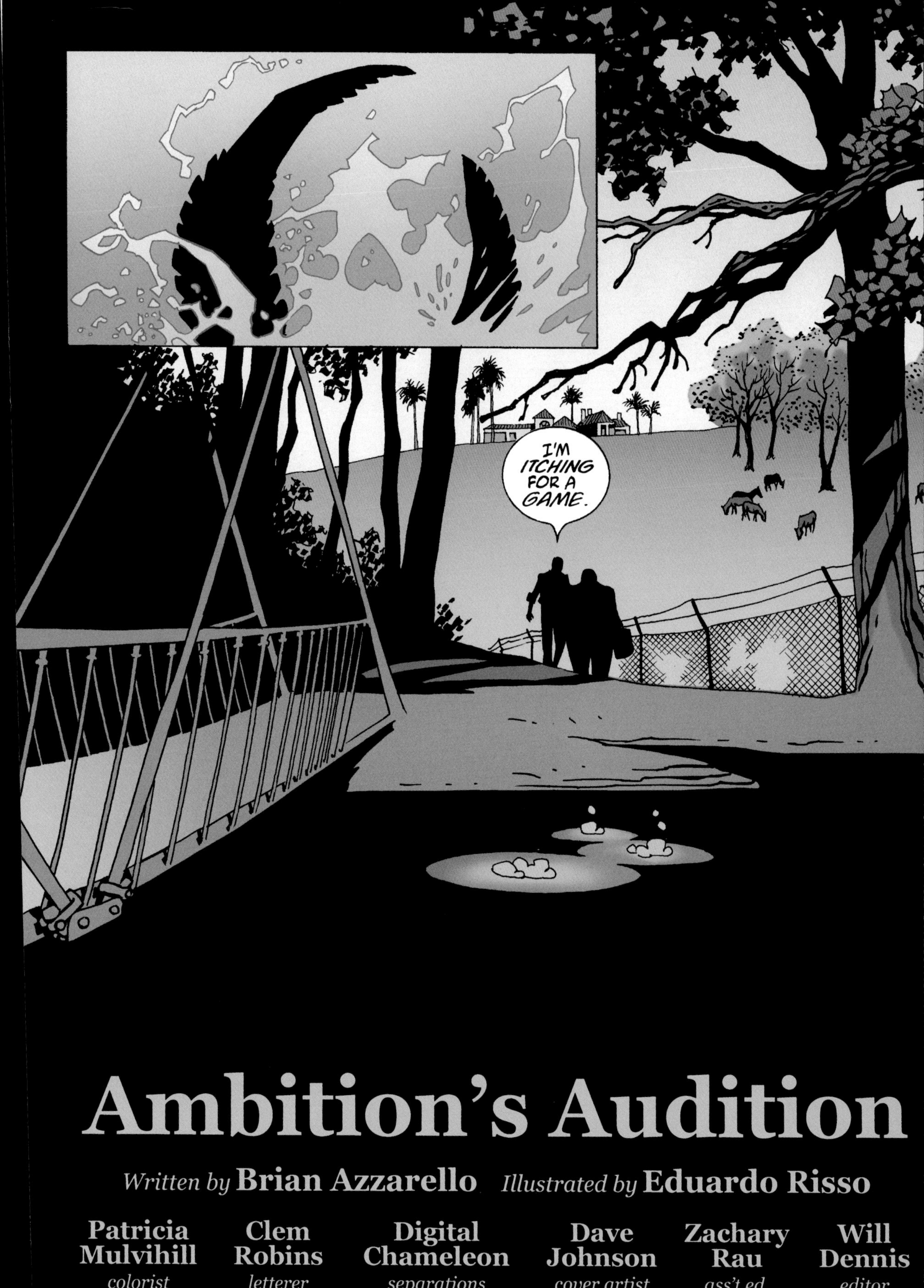
I'M ITCHING FOR A GAME.

Ambition's Audition

Written by **Brian Azzarello** *Illustrated by* **Eduardo Risso**

Patricia Mulvihill *colorist*
Clem Robins *letterer*
Digital Chameleon *separations*
Dave Johnson *cover artist*
Zachary Rau *ass't ed*
Will Dennis *editor*

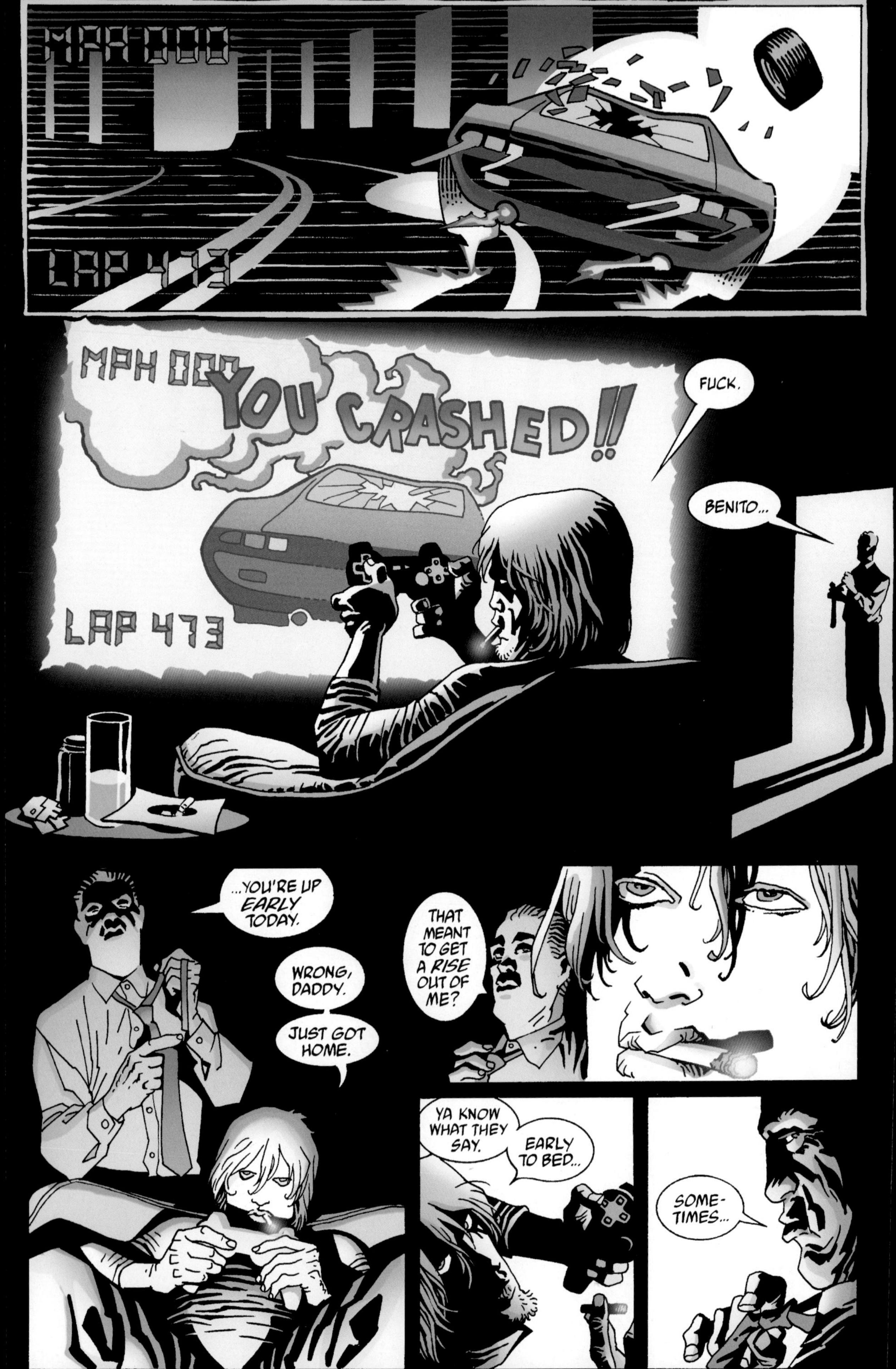
MPH 000
LAP 473
MPH 000
YOU CRASHED!!
LAP 473
FUCK.
BENITO...
...YOU'RE UP EARLY TODAY.
WRONG, DADDY.
JUST GOT HOME.
THAT MEANT TO GET A RISE OUT OF ME?
YA KNOW WHAT THEY SAY.
EARLY TO BED...
SOME-TIMES...

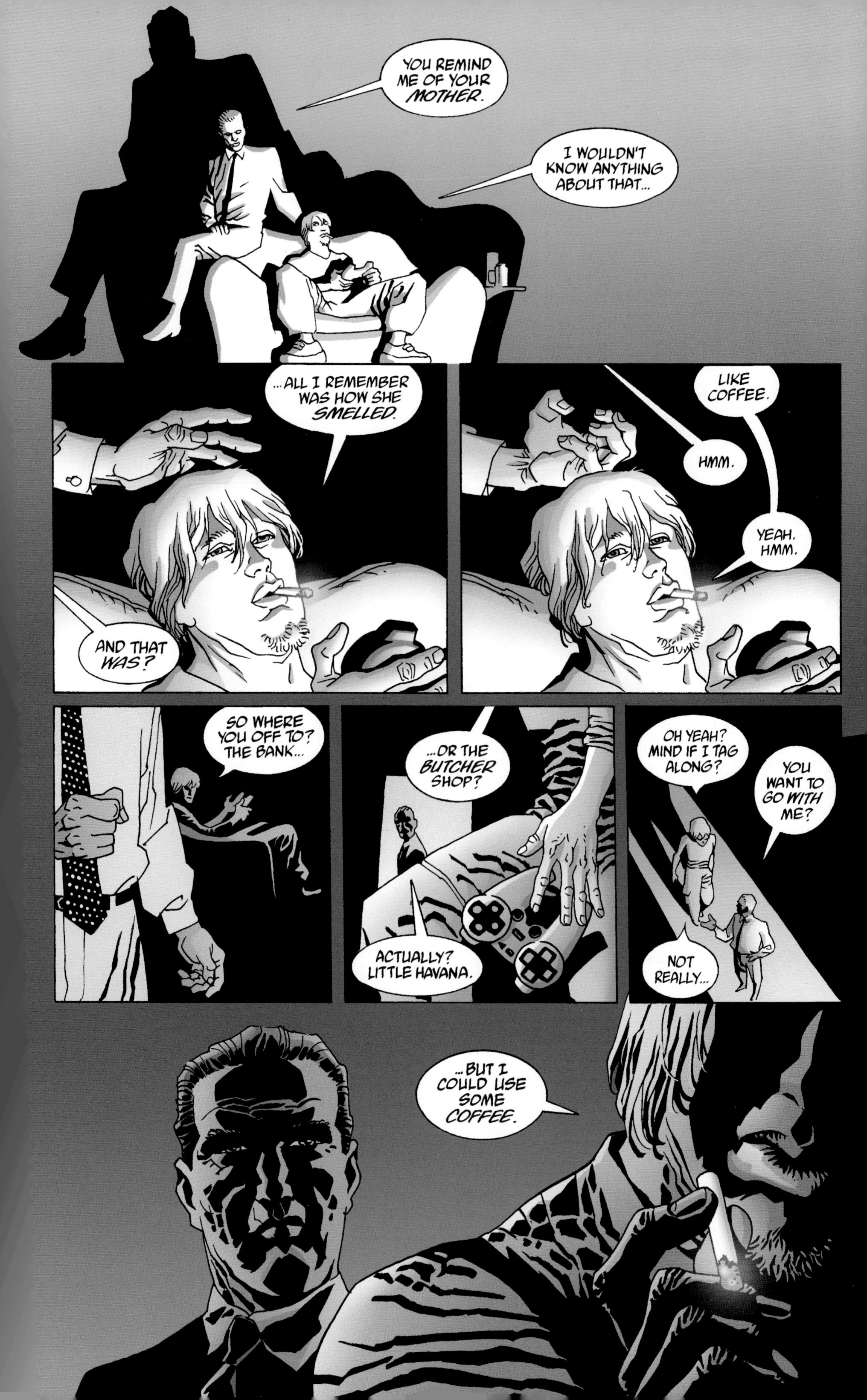
YOU REMIND ME OF YOUR *MOTHER*.
I WOULDN'T KNOW ANYTHING ABOUT THAT...
...ALL I REMEMBER WAS HOW SHE *SMELLED*.
AND THAT *WAS*?
LIKE COFFEE.
HMM.
YEAH. HMM.
SO WHERE YOU OFF TO? THE BANK...
...OR THE *BUTCHER* SHOP?
ACTUALLY? LITTLE HAVANA.
OH YEAH? MIND IF I TAG ALONG?
YOU WANT TO GO *WITH* ME?
NOT REALLY...
...BUT I COULD USE SOME *COFFEE*.

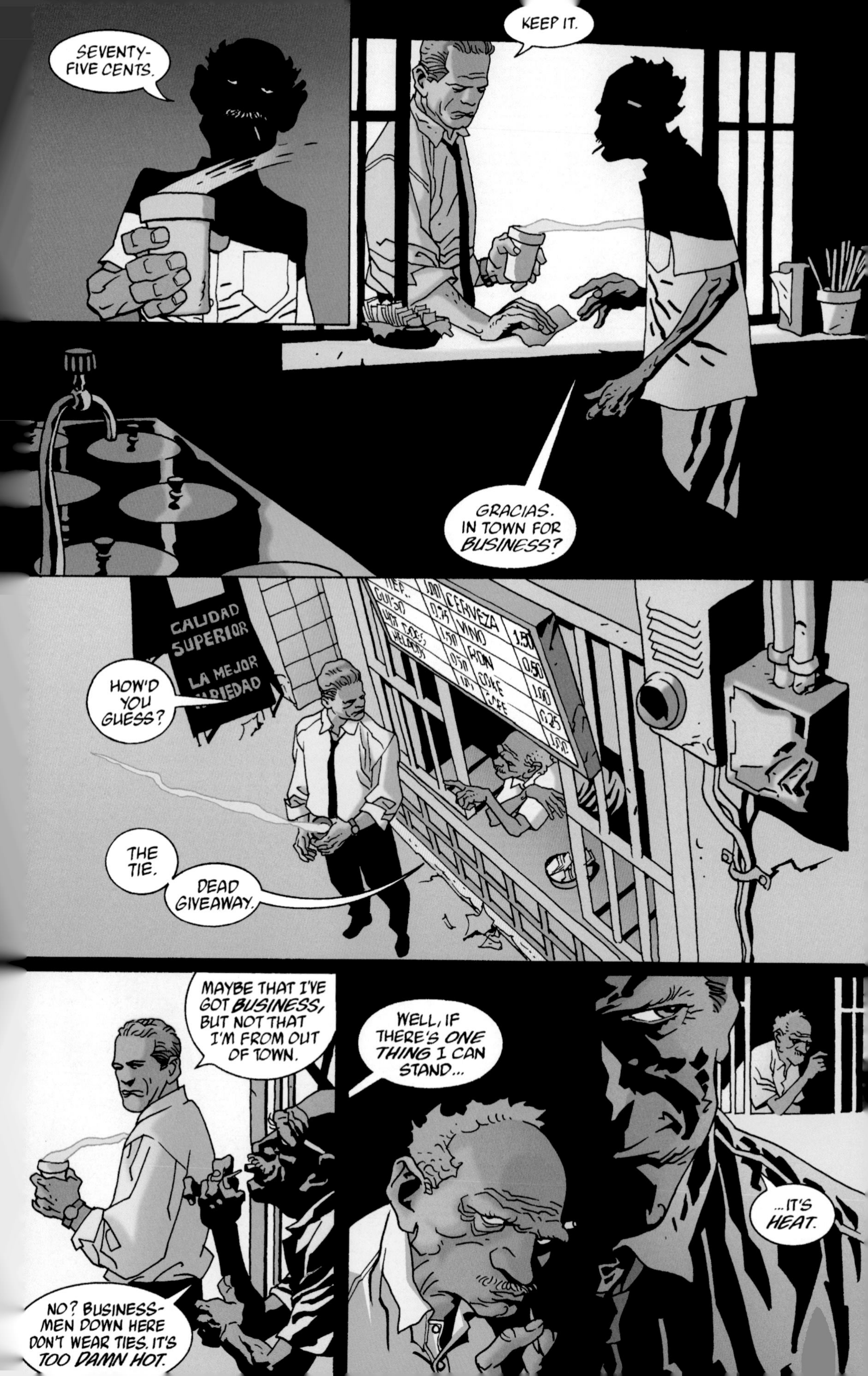
SEVENTY-FIVE CENTS.
KEEP IT.
GRACIAS. IN TOWN FOR *BUSINESS?*
CALIDAD SUPERIOR
LA MEJOR
CERVEZA
VINO
HOW'D YOU GUESS?
THE TIE.
DEAD GIVEAWAY.
MAYBE THAT I'VE GOT *BUSINESS,* BUT NOT THAT I'M FROM OUT OF TOWN.
NO? BUSINESS-MEN DOWN HERE DON'T WEAR TIES. IT'S *TOO DAMN HOT.*
WELL, IF THERE'S *ONE THING* I CAN STAND...
...IT'S *HEAT.*

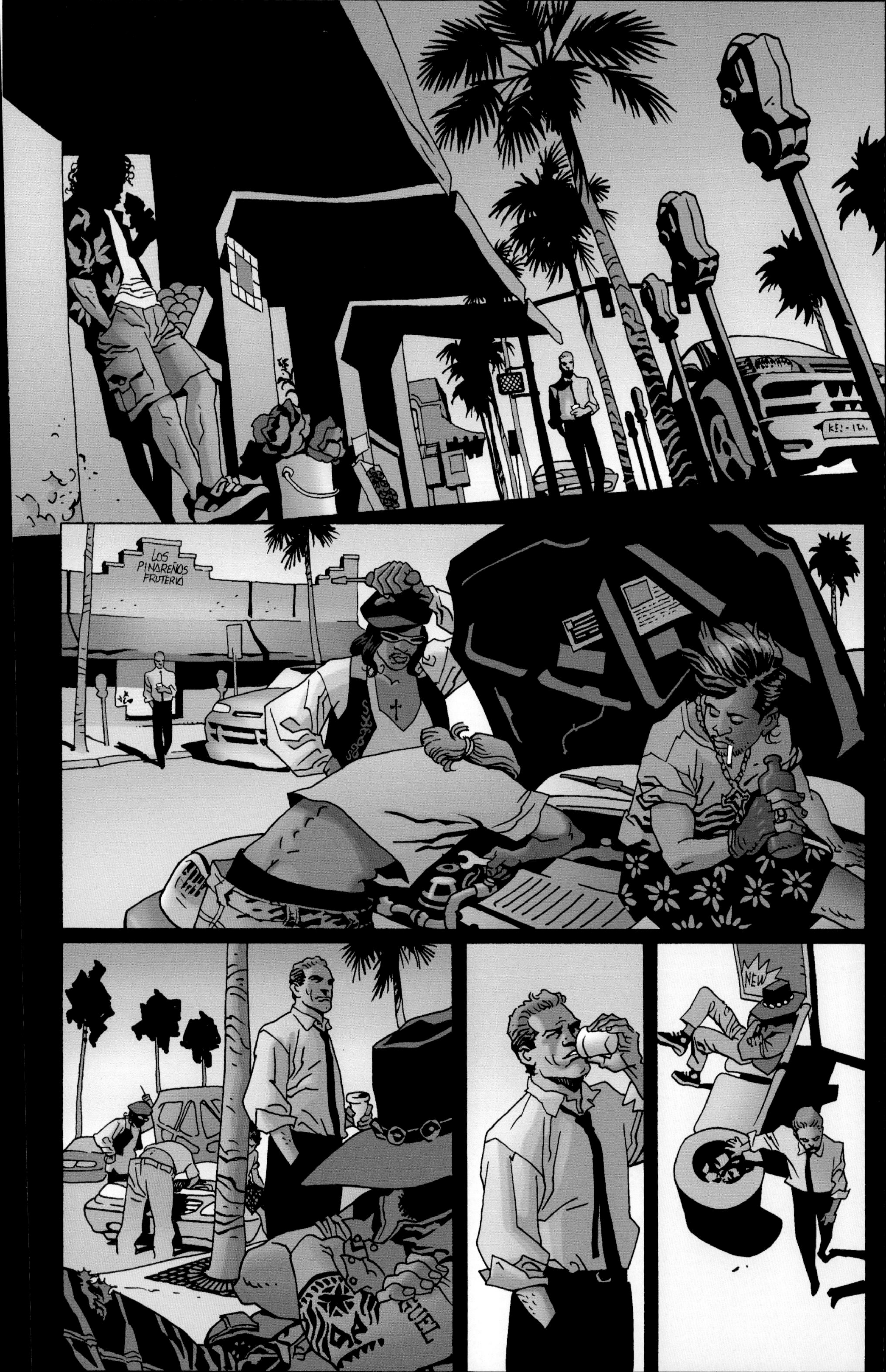
LOS PINAREÑOS FRUTERIA
NEW

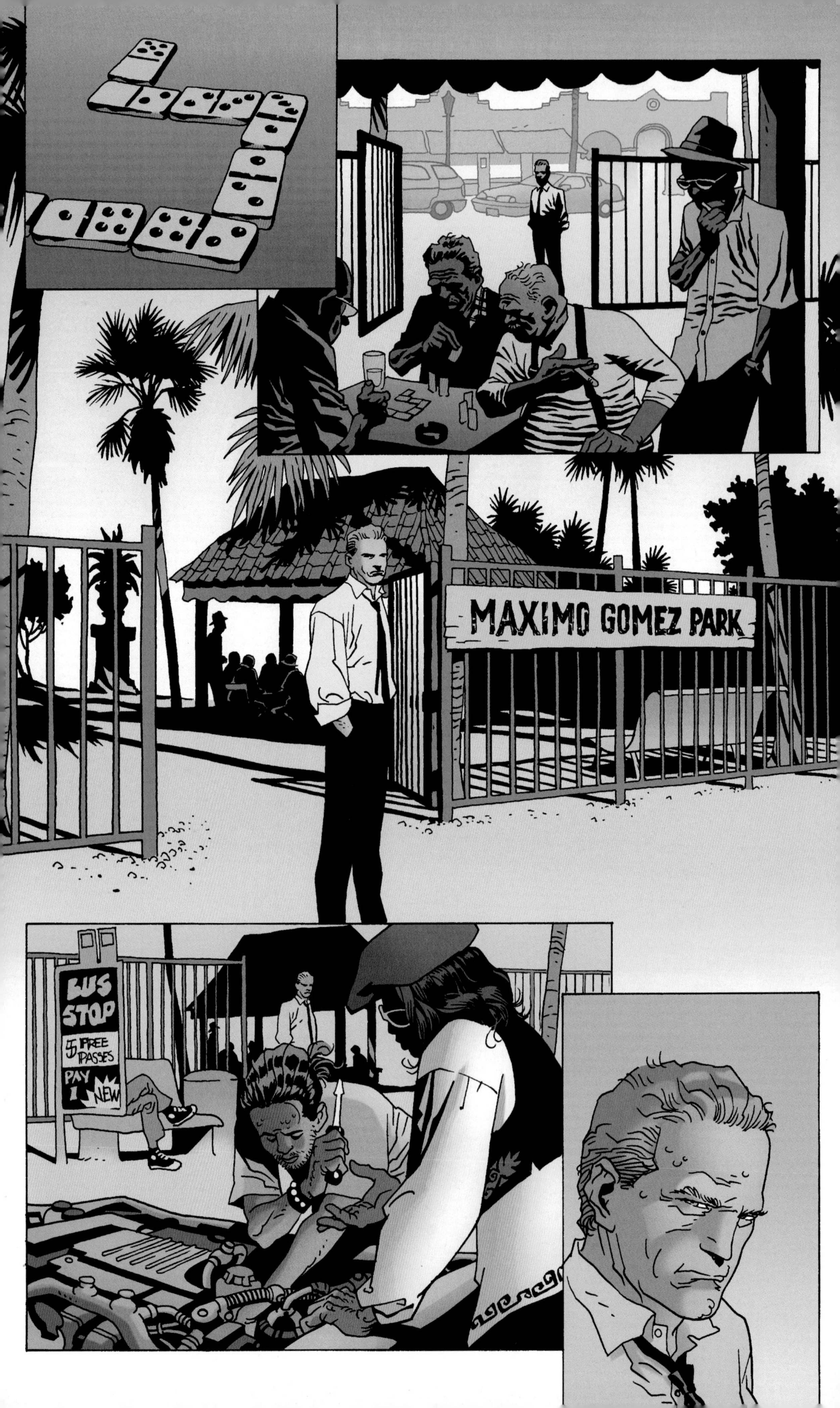

MAXIMO GOMEZ PARK
BUS STOP
5 FREE PASSES
PAY 1 NEW

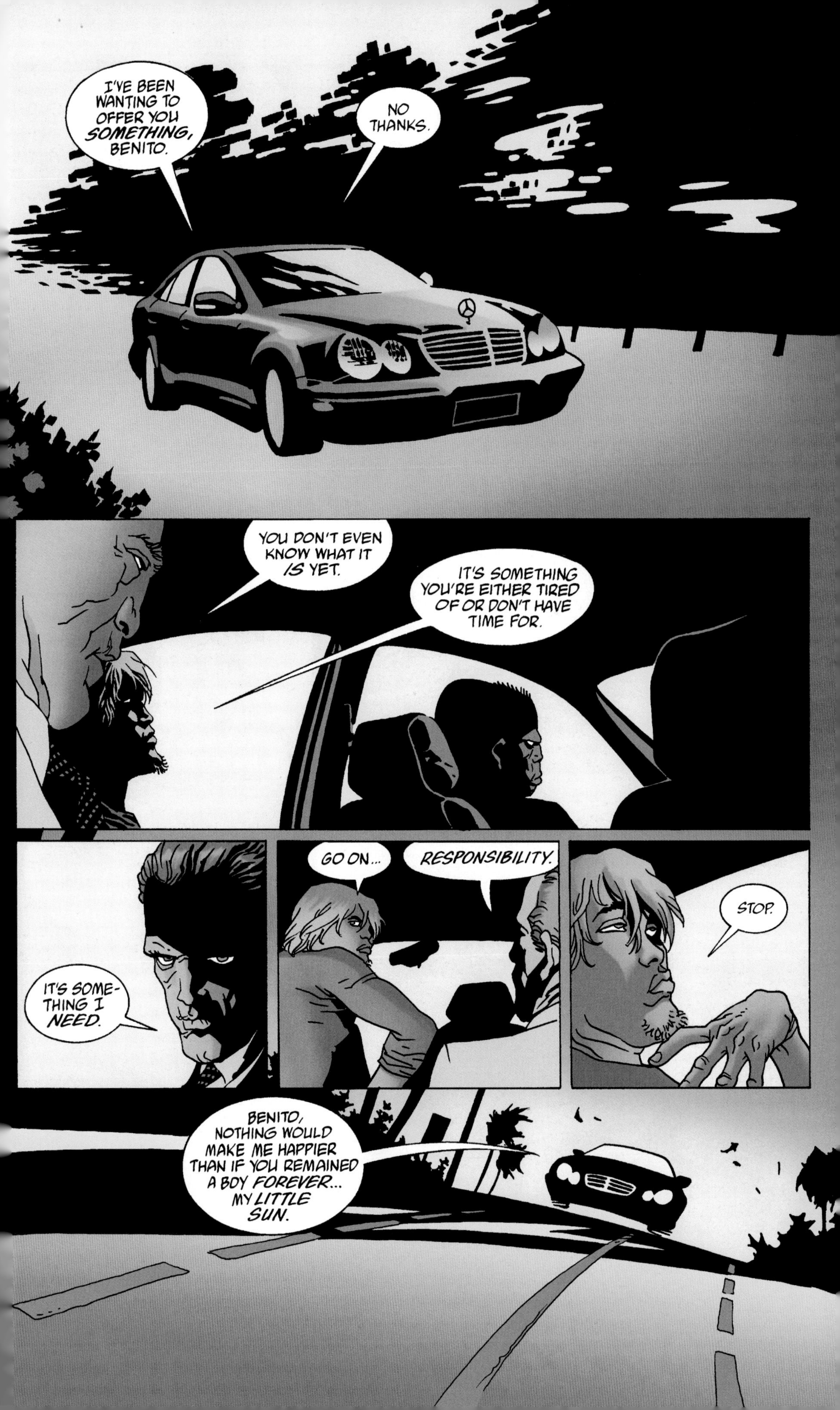
I'VE BEEN WANTING TO OFFER YOU SOMETHING, BENITO.
NO THANKS.
YOU DON'T EVEN KNOW WHAT IT IS YET.
IT'S SOMETHING YOU'RE EITHER TIRED OF OR DON'T HAVE TIME FOR.
IT'S SOME-THING I NEED.
GO ON...
RESPONSIBILITY.
STOP.
BENITO, NOTHING WOULD MAKE ME HAPPIER THAN IF YOU REMAINED A BOY FOREVER... MY LITTLE SUN.

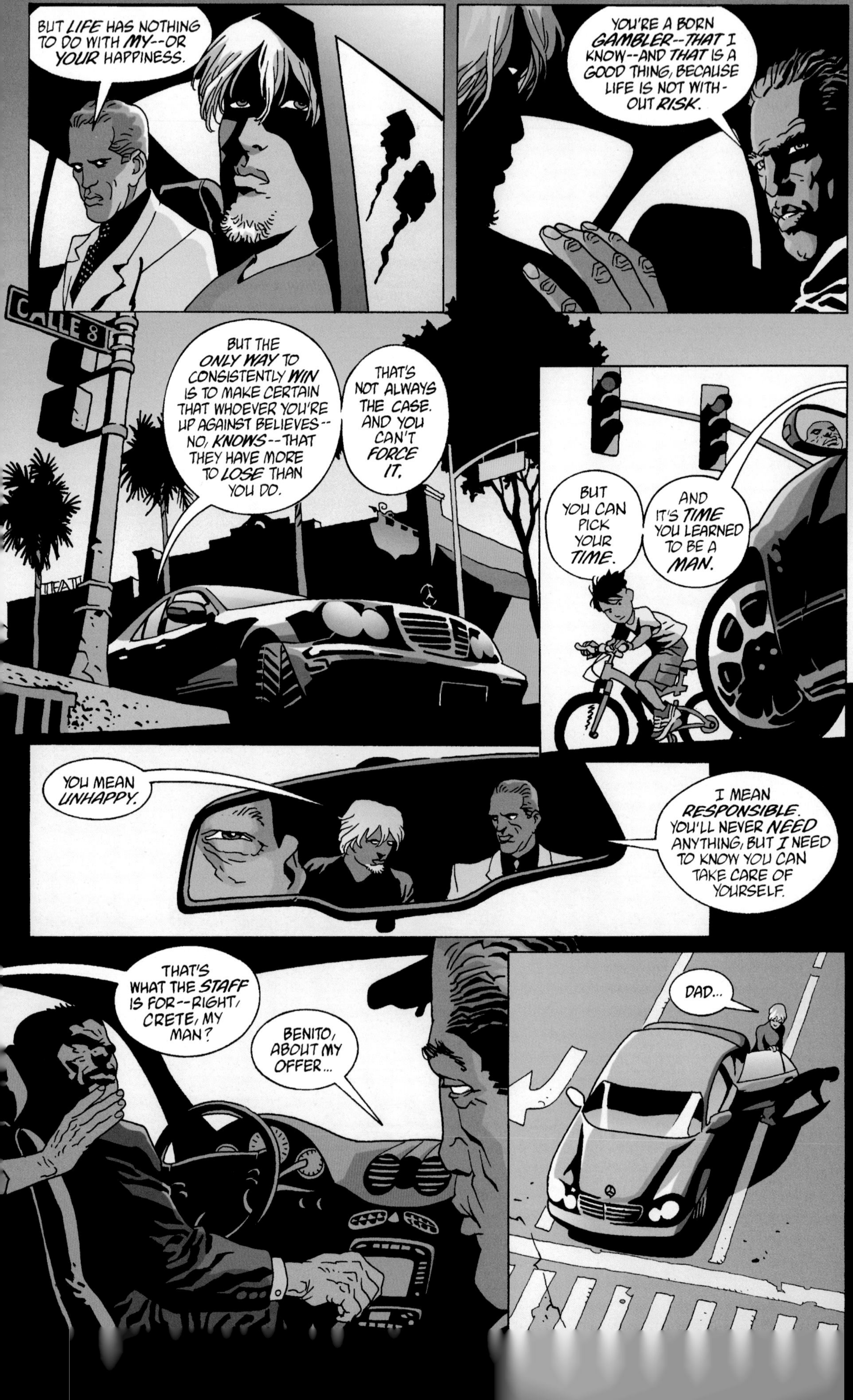

BUT LIFE HAS NOTHING TO DO WITH MY--OR YOUR HAPPINESS.
YOU'RE A BORN GAMBLER--THAT I KNOW--AND THAT IS A GOOD THING, BECAUSE LIFE IS NOT WITH-OUT RISK.
CALLE 8
BUT THE ONLY WAY TO CONSISTENTLY WIN IS TO MAKE CERTAIN THAT WHOEVER YOU'RE UP AGAINST BELIEVES--NO, KNOWS--THAT THEY HAVE MORE TO LOSE THAN YOU DO.
THAT'S NOT ALWAYS THE CASE. AND YOU CAN'T FORCE IT.
BUT YOU CAN PICK YOUR TIME.
AND IT'S TIME YOU LEARNED TO BE A MAN.
YOU MEAN UNHAPPY.
I MEAN RESPONSIBLE. YOU'LL NEVER NEED ANYTHING, BUT I NEED TO KNOW YOU CAN TAKE CARE OF YOURSELF.
THAT'S WHAT THE STAFF IS FOR--RIGHT, CRETE, MY MAN?
BENITO, ABOUT MY OFFER...
DAD...

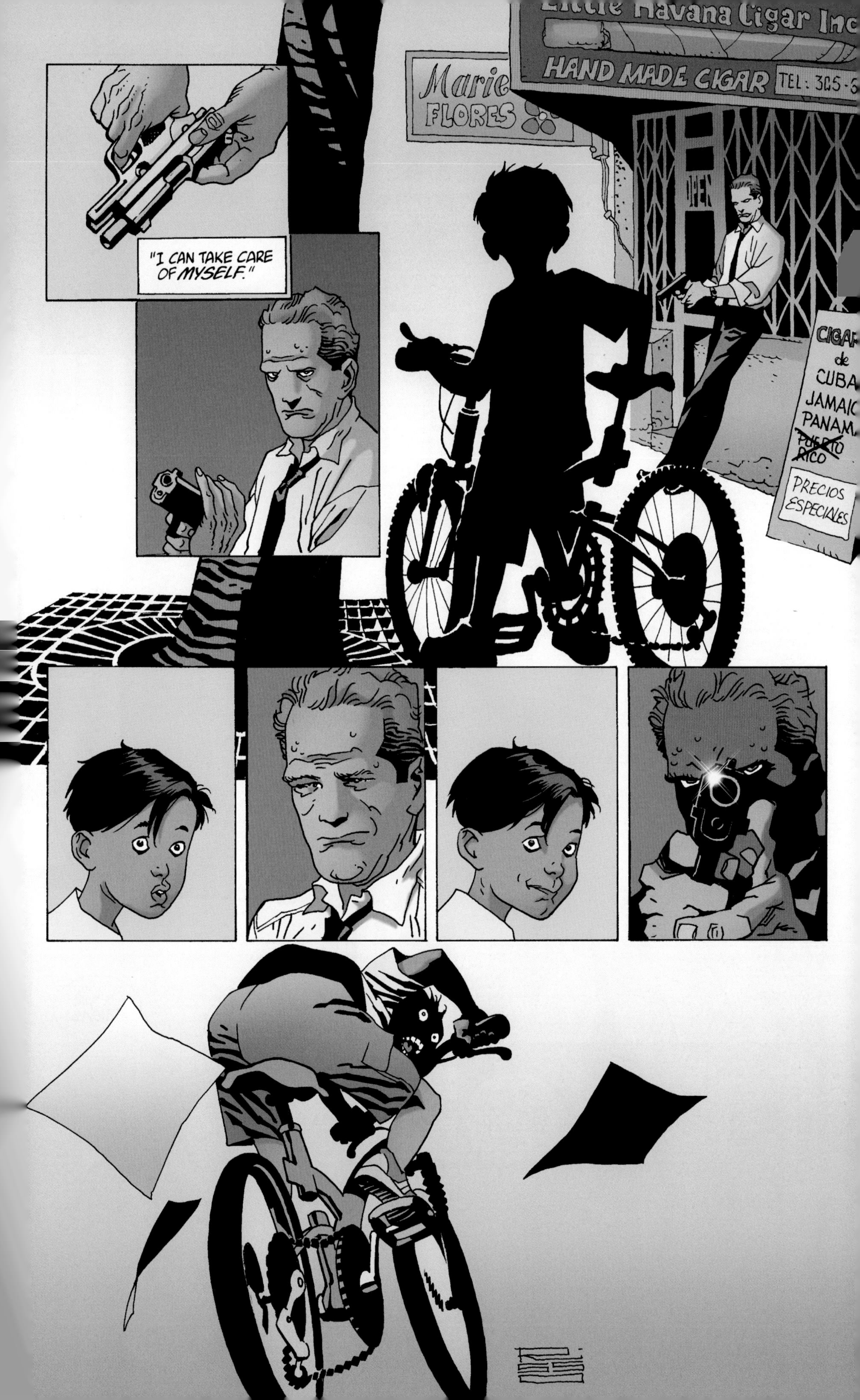
"I CAN TAKE CARE OF MYSELF."
Little Havana Cigar Inc
HAND MADE CIGAR
Marie
FLORES
OPEN
de
CUBA
PRECIOS ESPECIALES

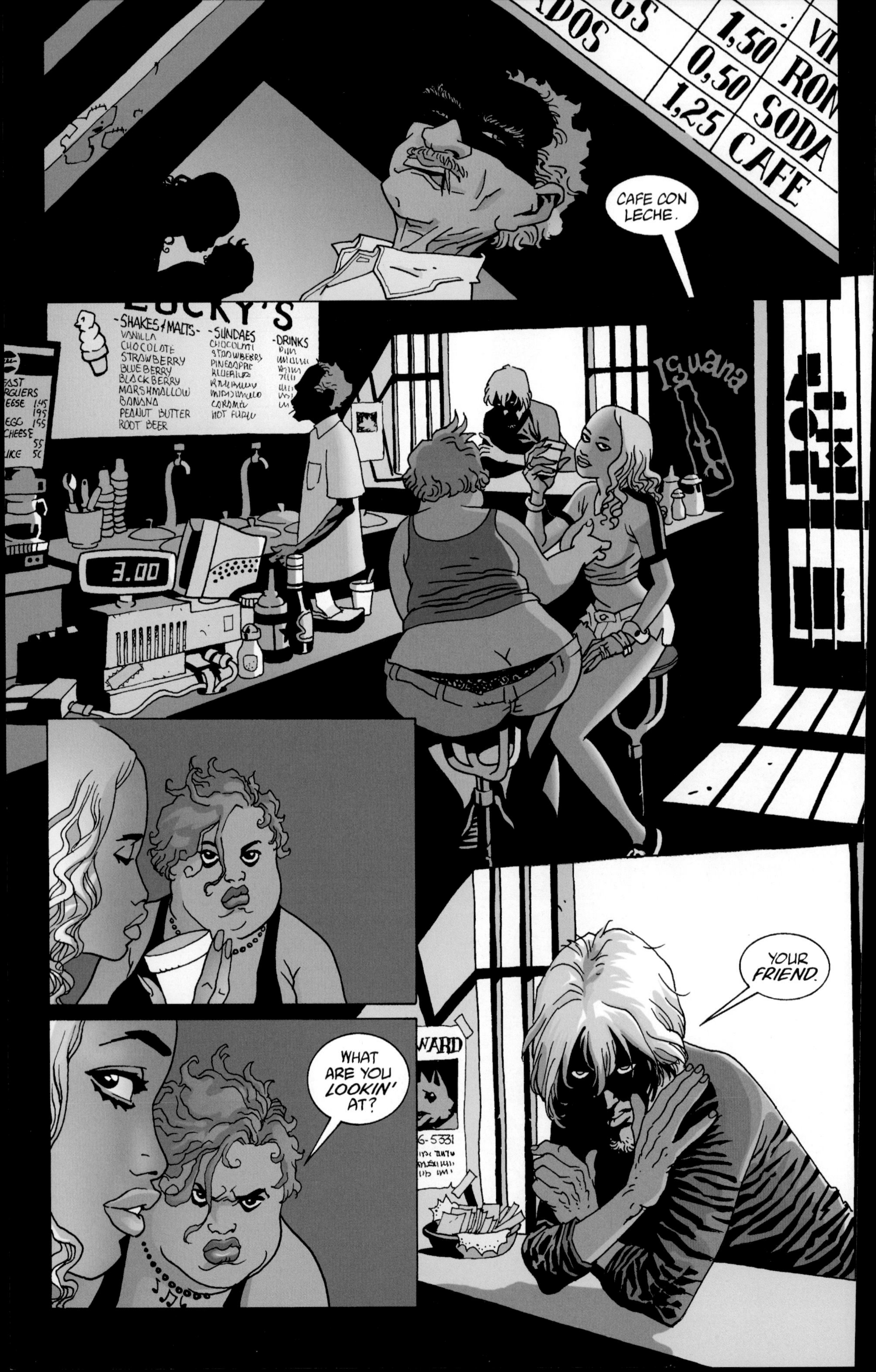
1,50 RON
0,50 SODA
1,25 CAFE
CAFE CON LECHE.
-SHAKES & MALTS-
VANILLA
CHOCOLATE
STRAWBERRY
BLUEBERRY
BLACKBERRY
MARSHMALLOW
BANANA
PEANUT BUTTER
ROOT BEER
-SUNDAES
-DRINKS
3.00
Iguana
YOUR FRIEND.
WHAT ARE YOU LOOKIN' AT?

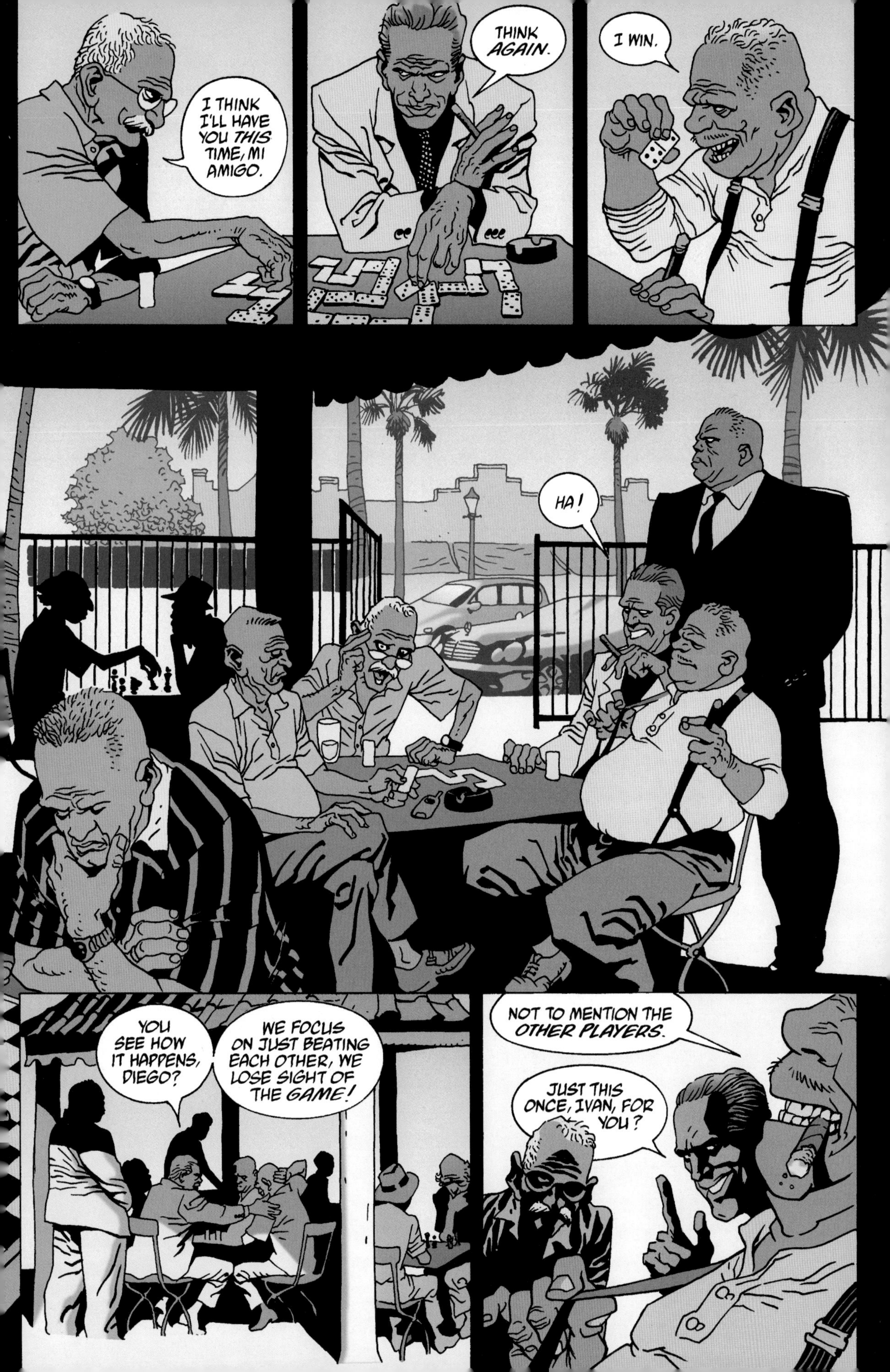
I THINK I'LL HAVE YOU *THIS* TIME, MI AMIGO.
THINK *AGAIN*.
I WIN.
HA!
YOU SEE HOW IT HAPPENS, DIEGO?
WE FOCUS ON JUST BEATING EACH OTHER, WE LOSE SIGHT OF THE *GAME*!
NOT TO MENTION THE *OTHER PLAYERS*.
JUST THIS ONCE, IVAN, FOR YOU?

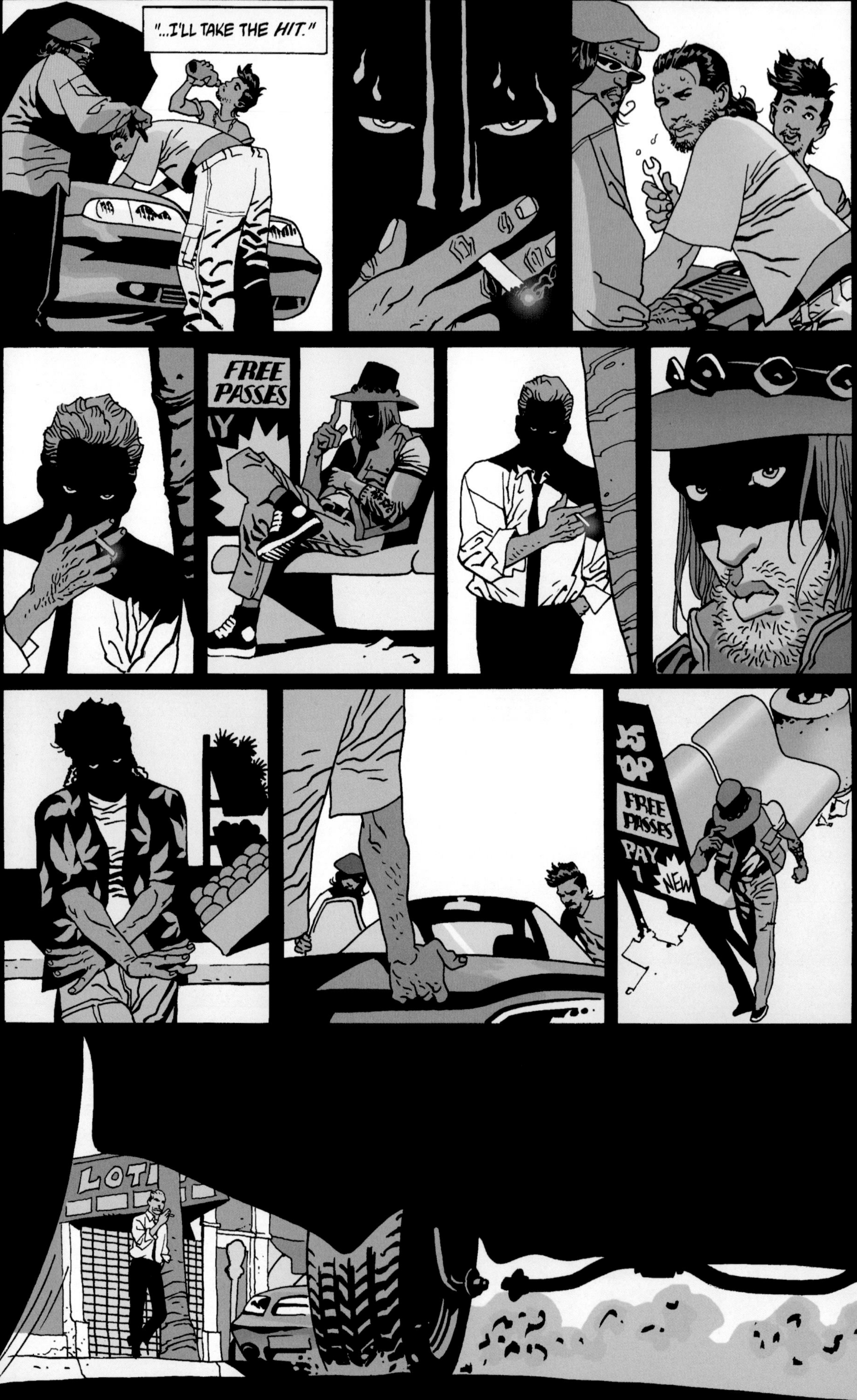
"...I'LL TAKE THE HIT."
FREE PASSES
FREE PASSES
PAY 1
NEW
LOT

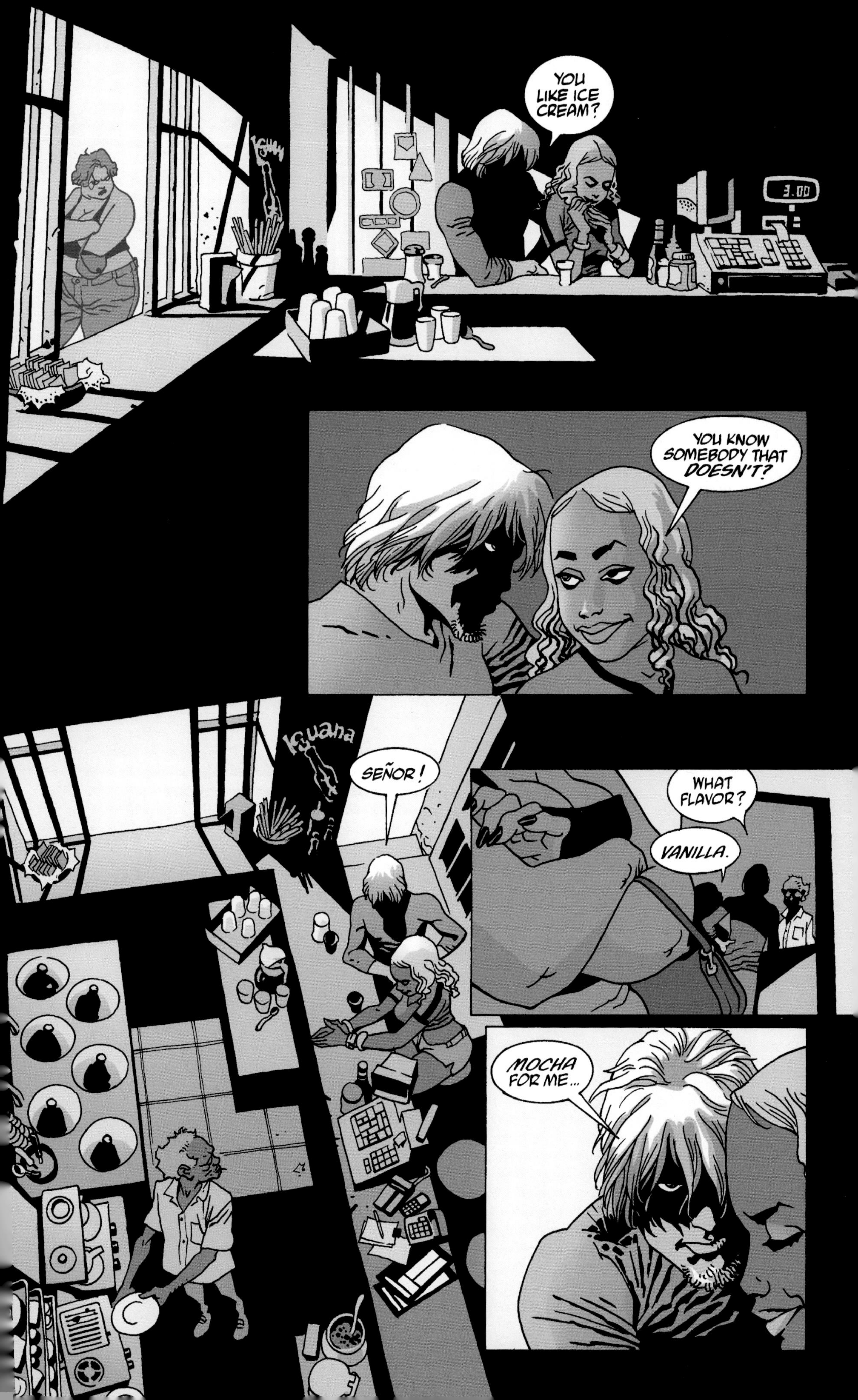
YOU LIKE ICE CREAM?
3.00
YOU KNOW SOMEBODY THAT DOESN'T?
IGUANA
SEÑOR!
WHAT FLAVOR?
VANILLA.
MOCHA FOR ME...

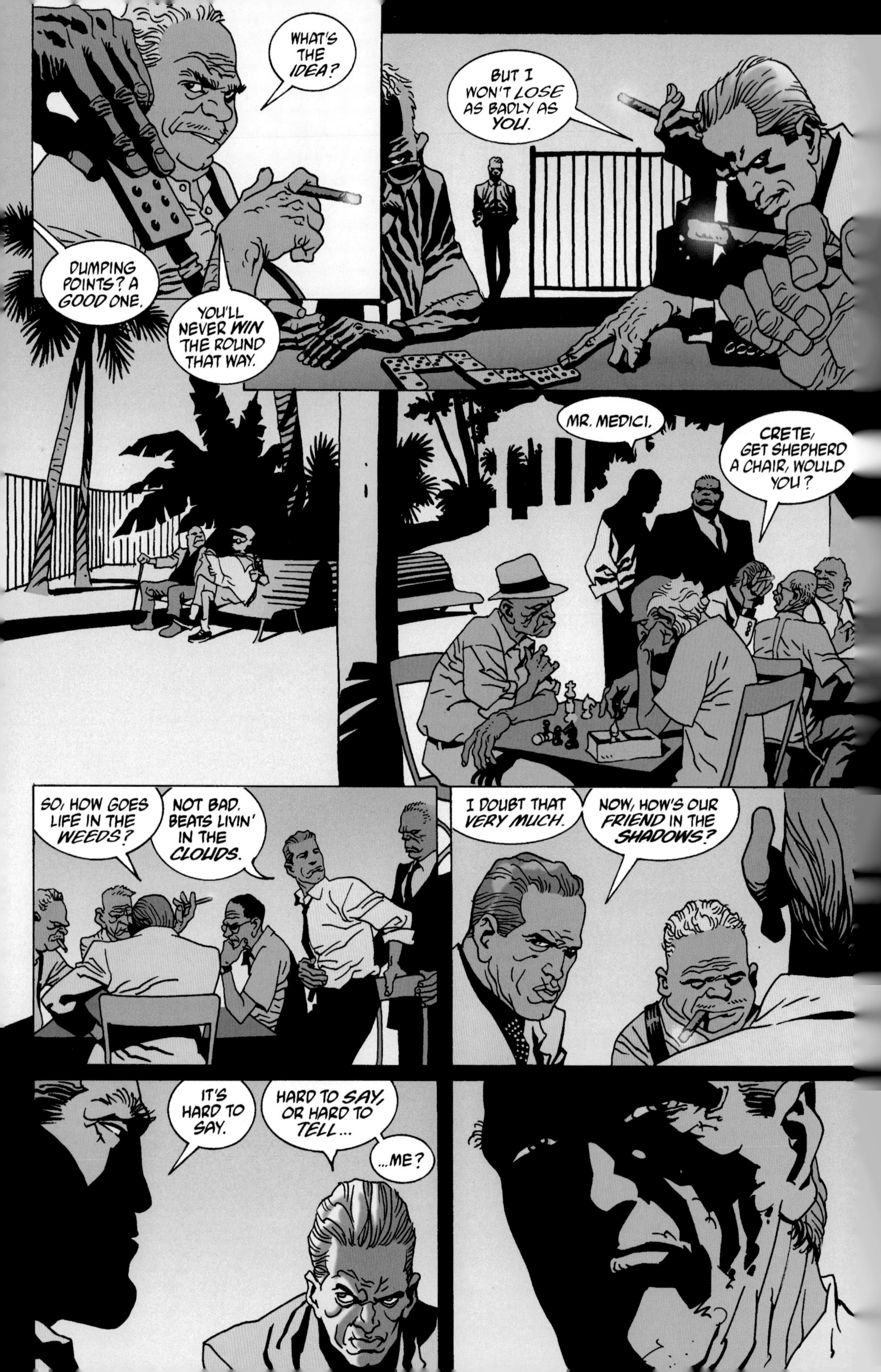
WHAT'S THE IDEA?
DUMPING POINTS? A GOOD ONE.
YOU'LL NEVER WIN THE ROUND THAT WAY.
BUT I WON'T LOSE AS BADLY AS YOU.
MR. MEDICI.
CRETE, GET SHEPHERD A CHAIR, WOULD YOU?
SO, HOW GOES LIFE IN THE WEEDS?
NOT BAD. BEATS LIVIN' IN THE CLOUDS.
I DOUBT THAT VERY MUCH.
NOW, HOW'S OUR FRIEND IN THE SHADOWS?
IT'S HARD TO SAY.
HARD TO SAY, OR HARD TO TELL...
...ME?

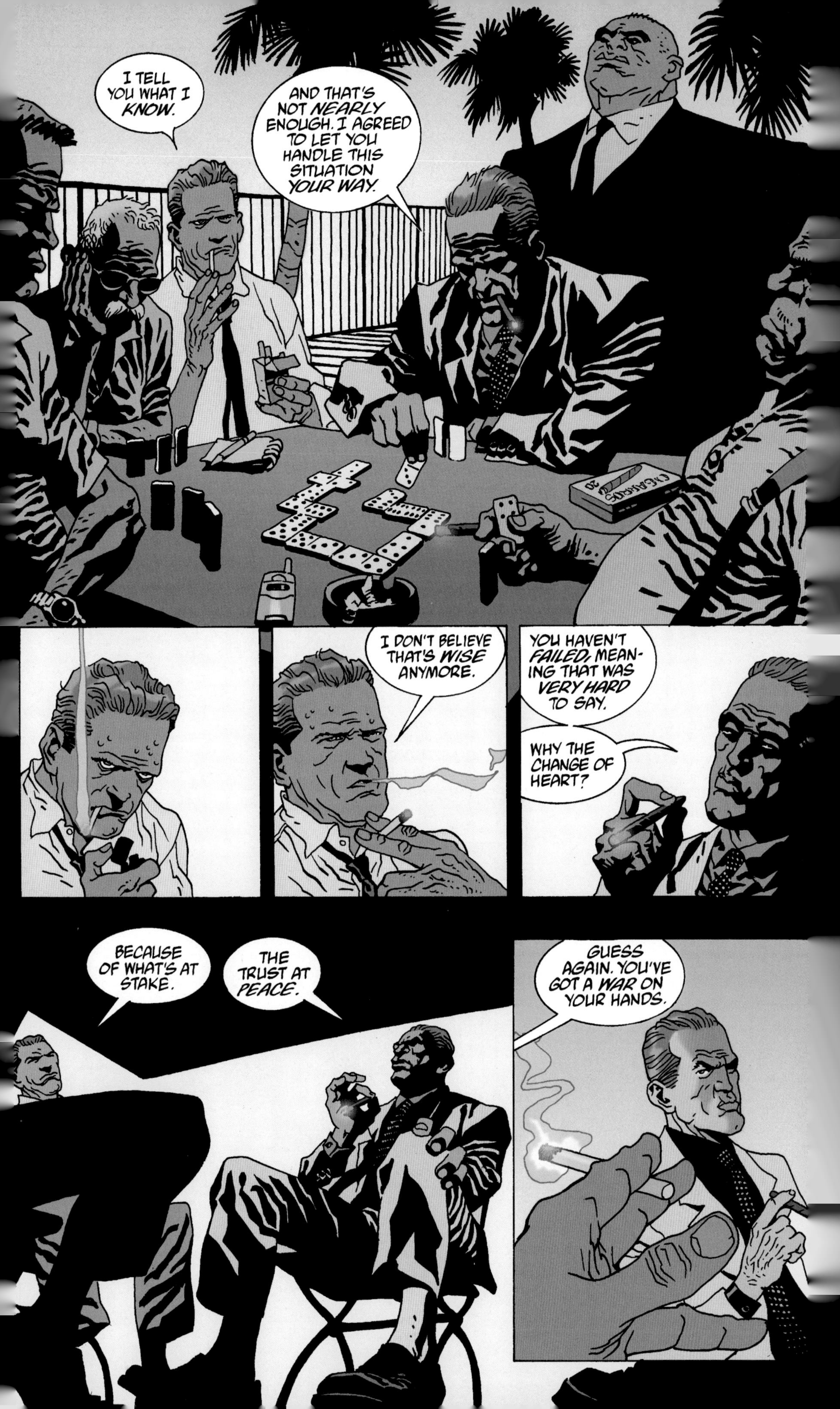

I TELL YOU WHAT I *KNOW*.
AND THAT'S NOT *NEARLY* ENOUGH. I AGREED TO LET YOU HANDLE THIS SITUATION *YOUR WAY*.
I DON'T BELIEVE THAT'S *WISE* ANYMORE.
YOU HAVEN'T *FAILED*, MEANING THAT WAS *VERY HARD* TO SAY.
WHY THE CHANGE OF HEART?
BECAUSE OF WHAT'S AT STAKE.
THE TRUST AT *PEACE*.
GUESS AGAIN. YOU'VE GOT A *WAR* ON YOUR HANDS.

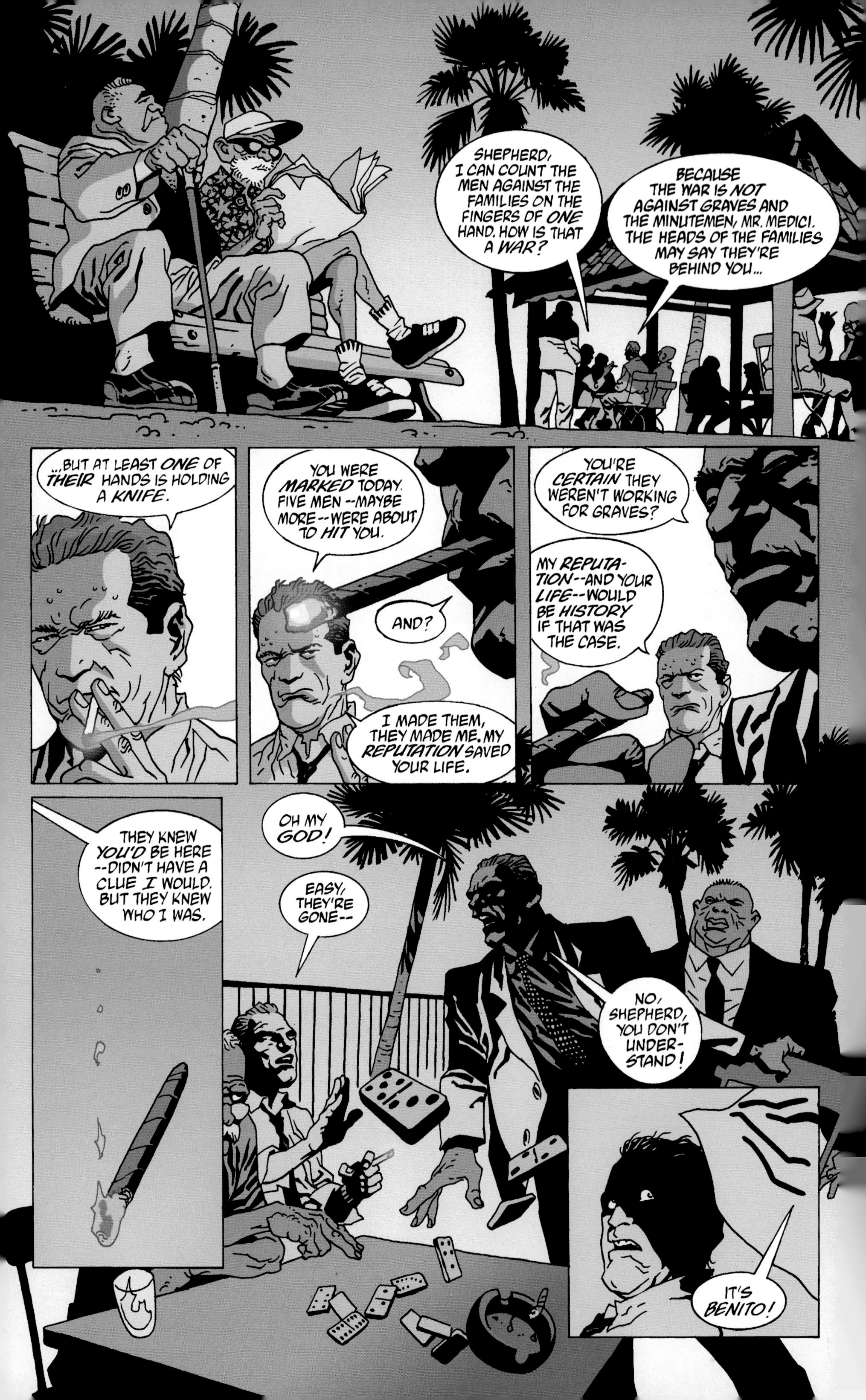
SHEPHERD, I CAN COUNT THE MEN AGAINST THE FAMILIES ON THE FINGERS OF ONE HAND. HOW IS THAT A WAR?
BECAUSE THE WAR IS NOT AGAINST GRAVES AND THE MINUTEMEN, MR. MEDICI. THE HEADS OF THE FAMILIES MAY SAY THEY'RE BEHIND YOU...
...BUT AT LEAST ONE OF THEIR HANDS IS HOLDING A KNIFE.
YOU WERE MARKED TODAY. FIVE MEN --MAYBE MORE--WERE ABOUT TO HIT YOU.
AND?
I MADE THEM, THEY MADE ME. MY REPUTATION SAVED YOUR LIFE.
YOU'RE CERTAIN THEY WEREN'T WORKING FOR GRAVES?
MY REPUTATION--AND YOUR LIFE--WOULD BE HISTORY IF THAT WAS THE CASE.
THEY KNEW YOU'D BE HERE --DIDN'T HAVE A CLUE I WOULD. BUT THEY KNEW WHO I WAS.
OH MY GOD!
EASY, THEY'RE GONE--
NO, SHEPHERD, YOU DON'T UNDERSTAND!
IT'S BENITO!

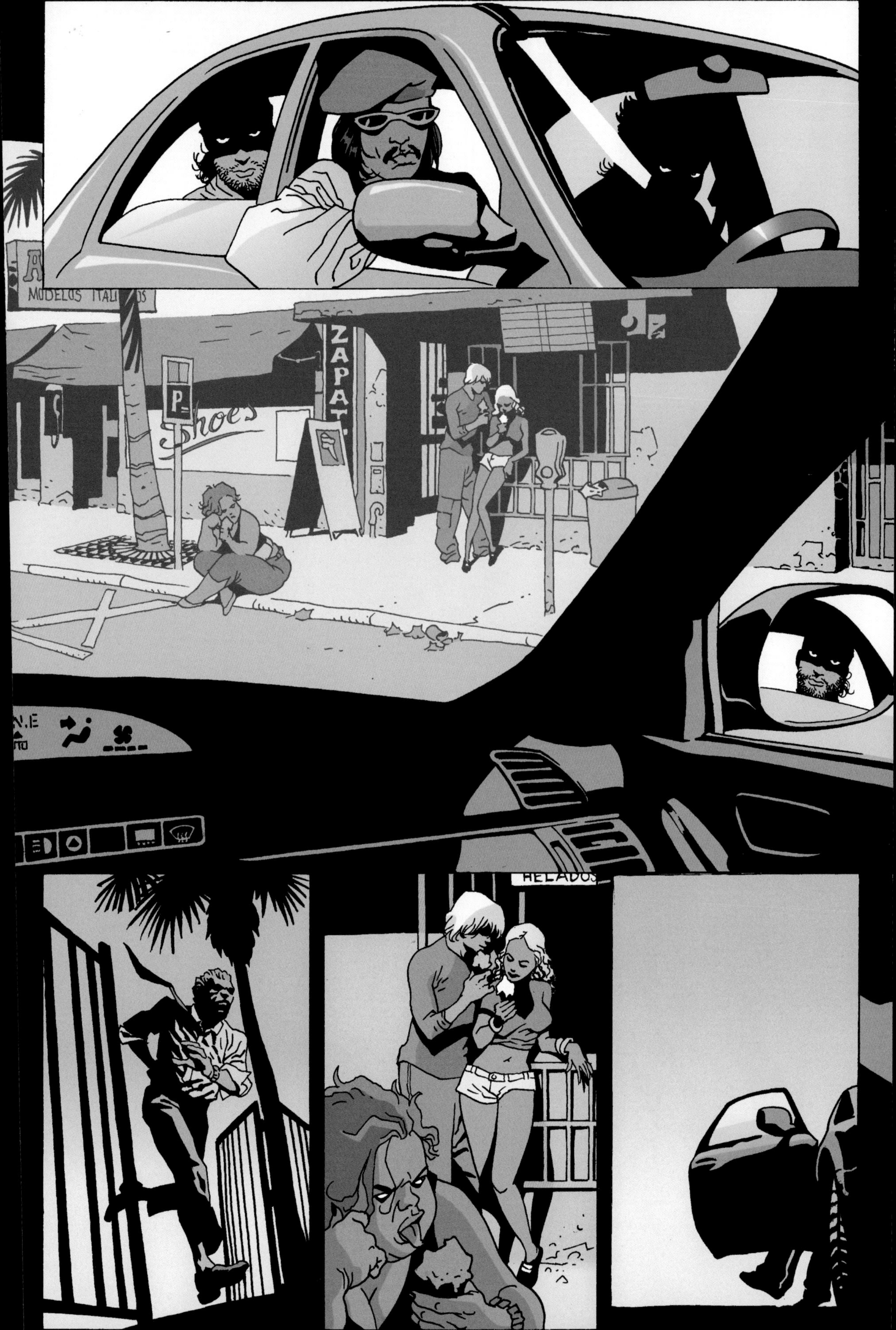
Shoes
HELADOS

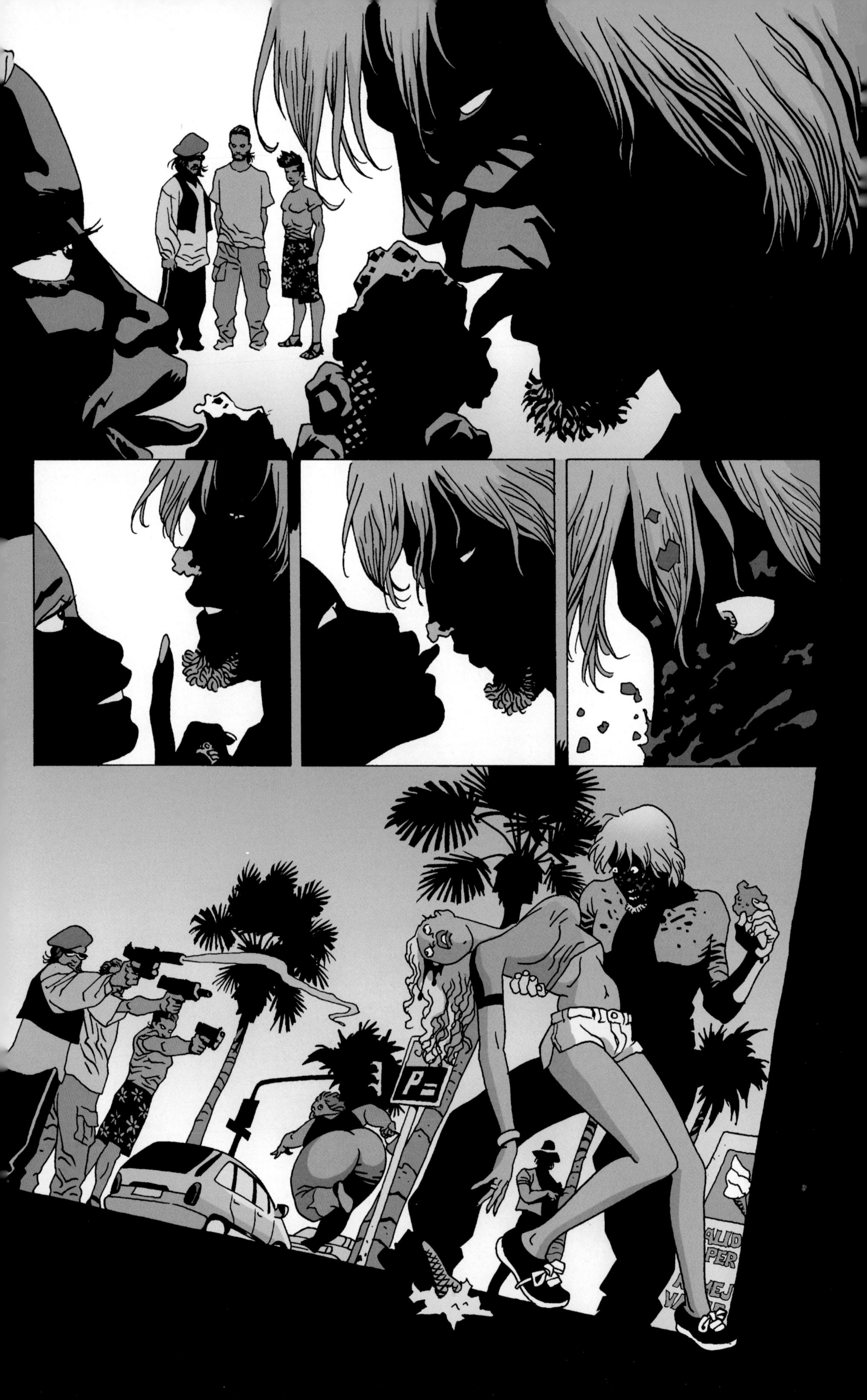

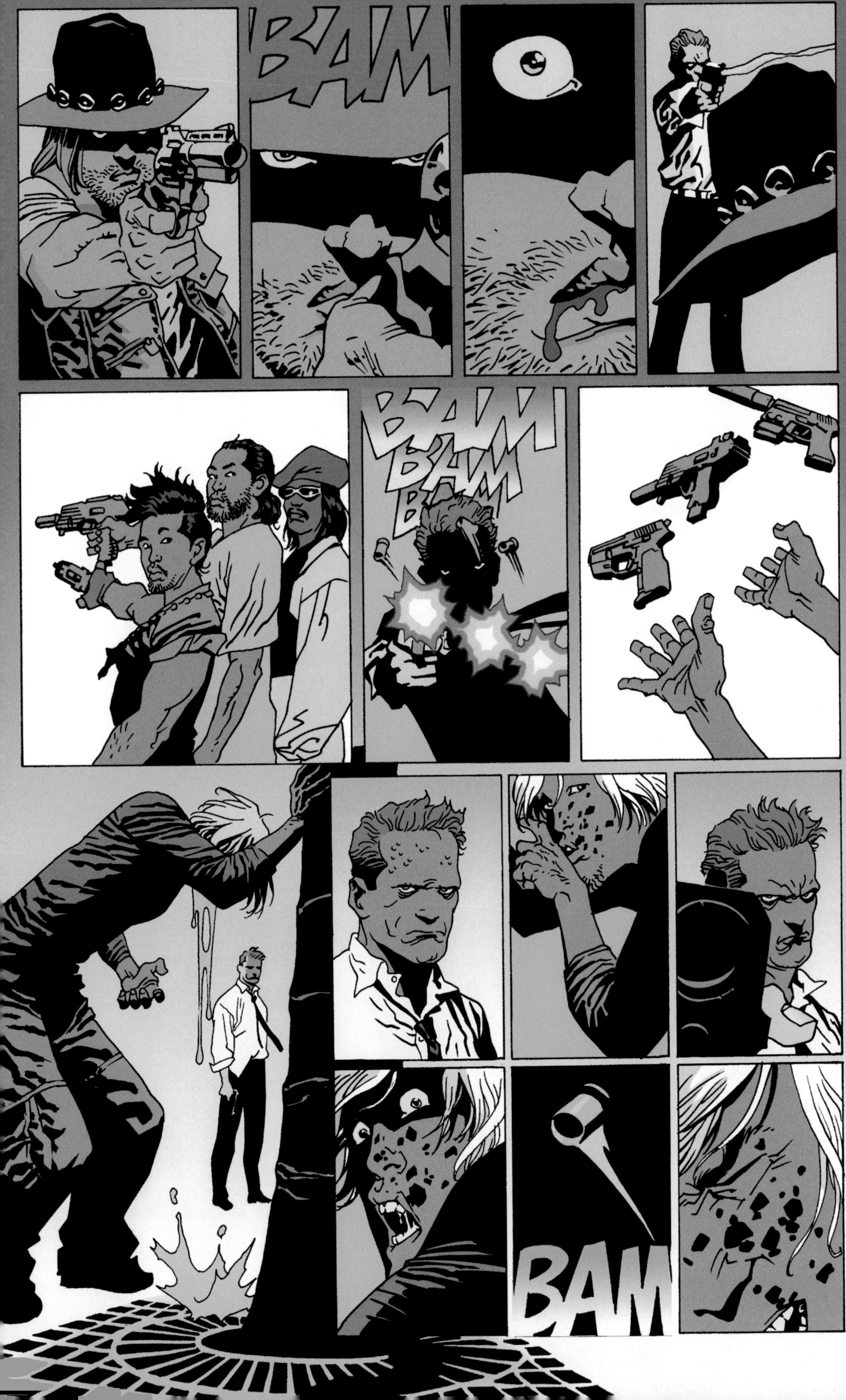
BAM
BAM
BAM
BAM
BAM

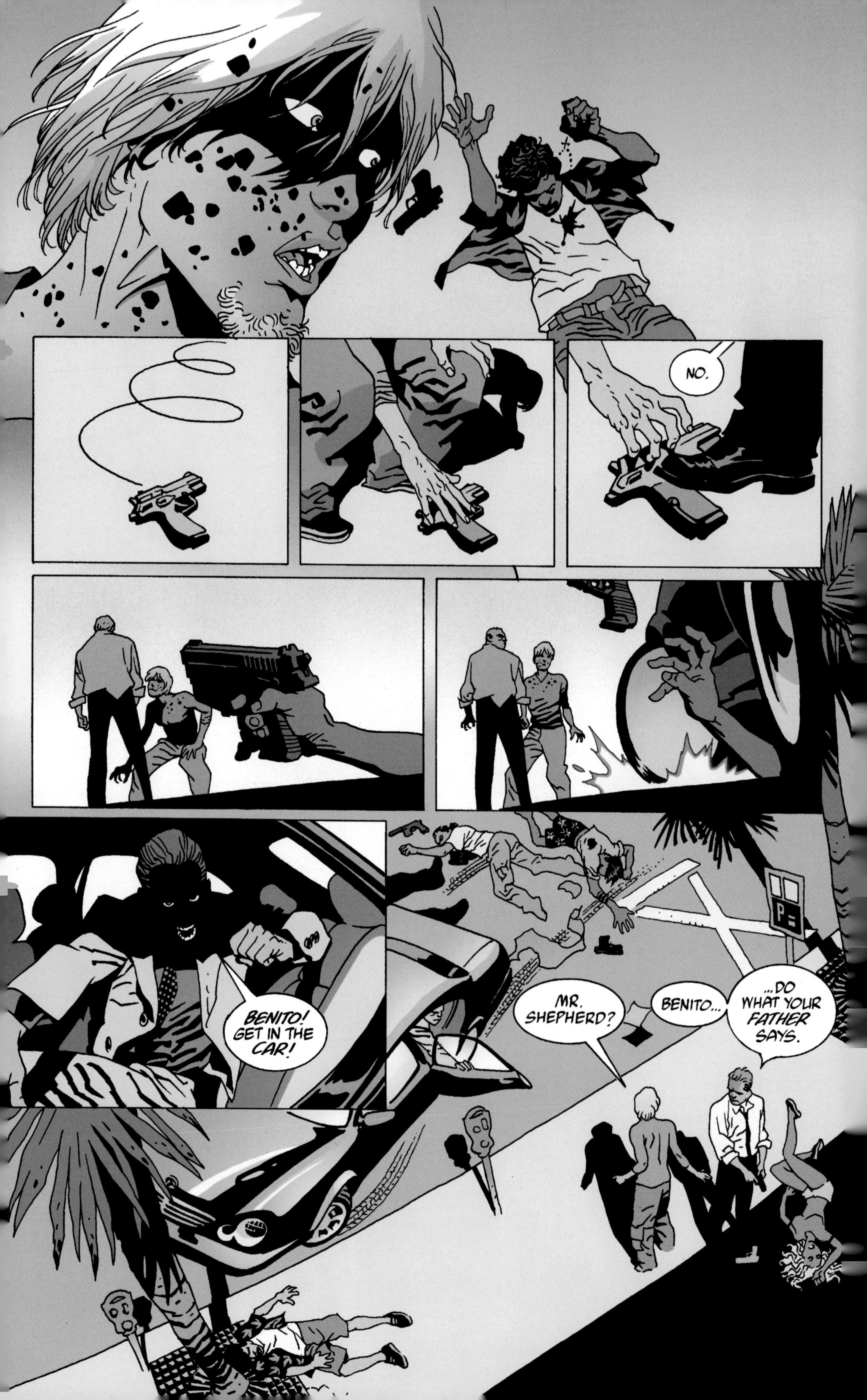
NO.
BENITO! GET IN THE CAR!
MR. SHEPHERD?
BENITO...
...DO WHAT YOUR FATHER SAYS.

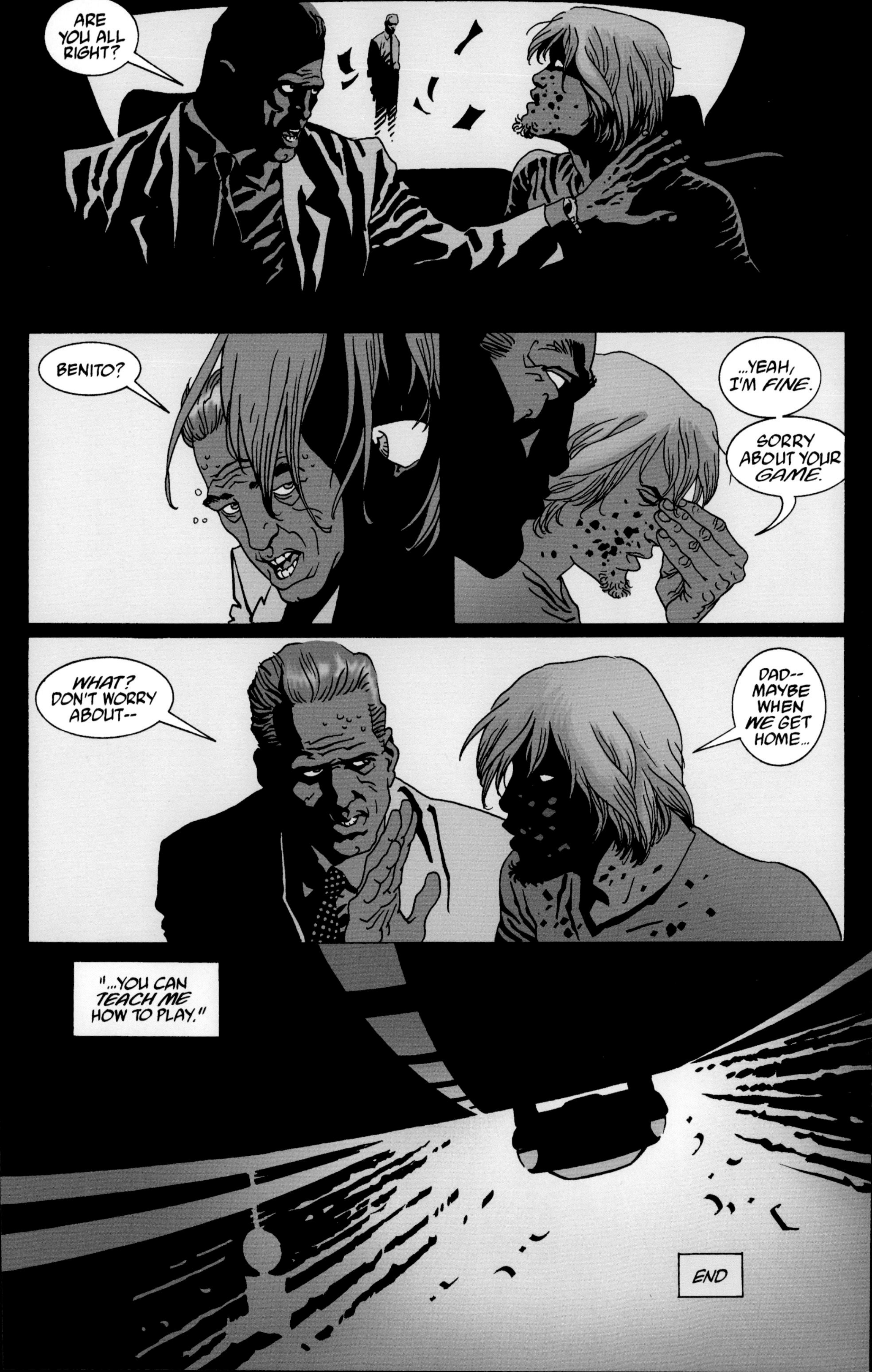
ARE YOU ALL RIGHT?
BENITO?
...YEAH, I'M FINE.
SORRY ABOUT YOUR GAME.
WHAT? DON'T WORRY ABOUT--
DAD-- MAYBE WHEN WE GET HOME...
"...YOU CAN TEACH ME HOW TO PLAY."
END

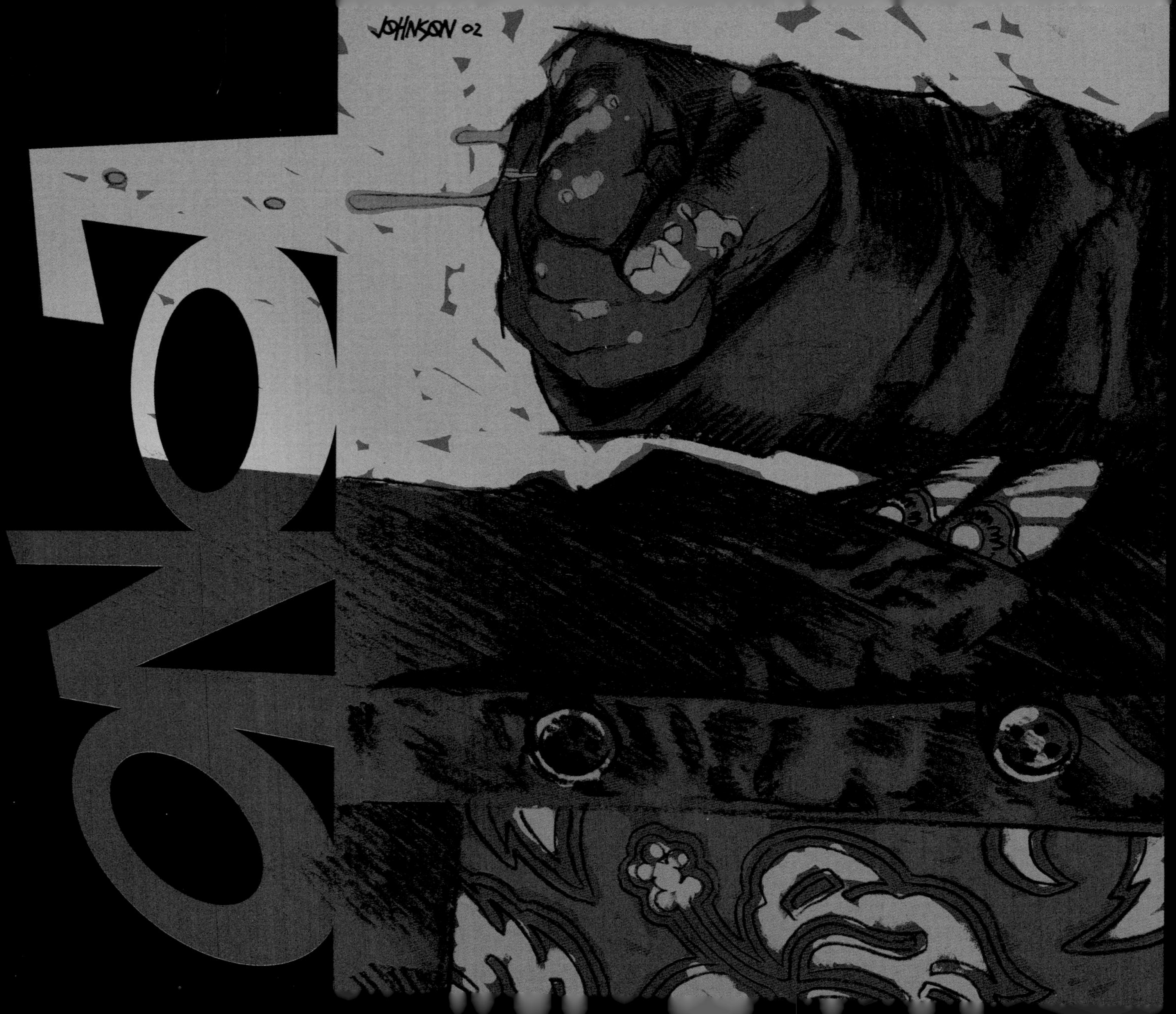

JOHNSON 02
LONO

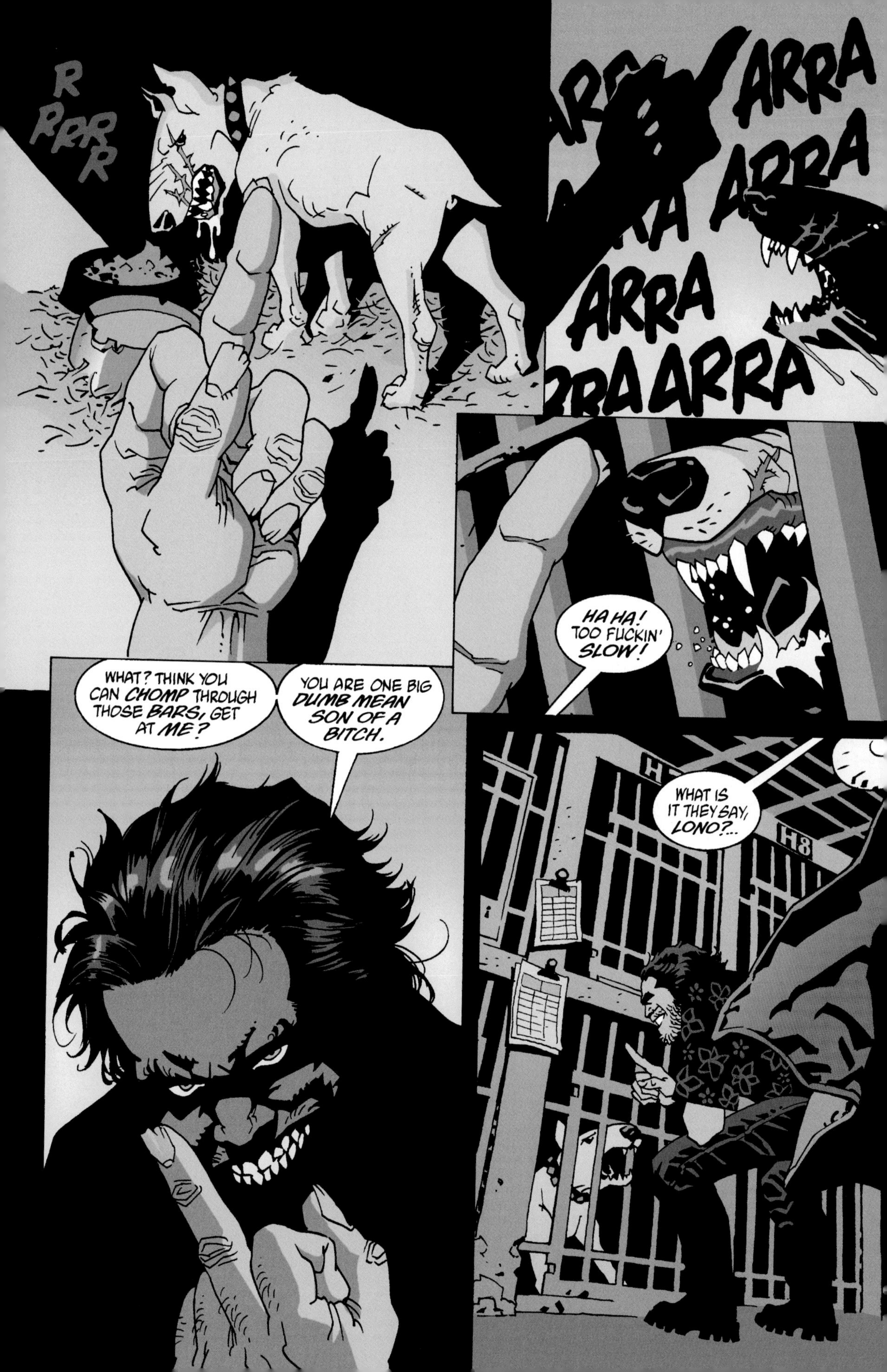
R RRR R
ARRA ARRA ARRA ARRA ARRA ARRA RAARRA
HA HA! TOO FUCKIN' SLOW!
WHAT? THINK YOU CAN CHOMP THROUGH THOSE BARS, GET AT ME?
YOU ARE ONE BIG DUMB MEAN SON OF A BITCH.
WHAT IS IT THEY SAY, LONO?...
H8

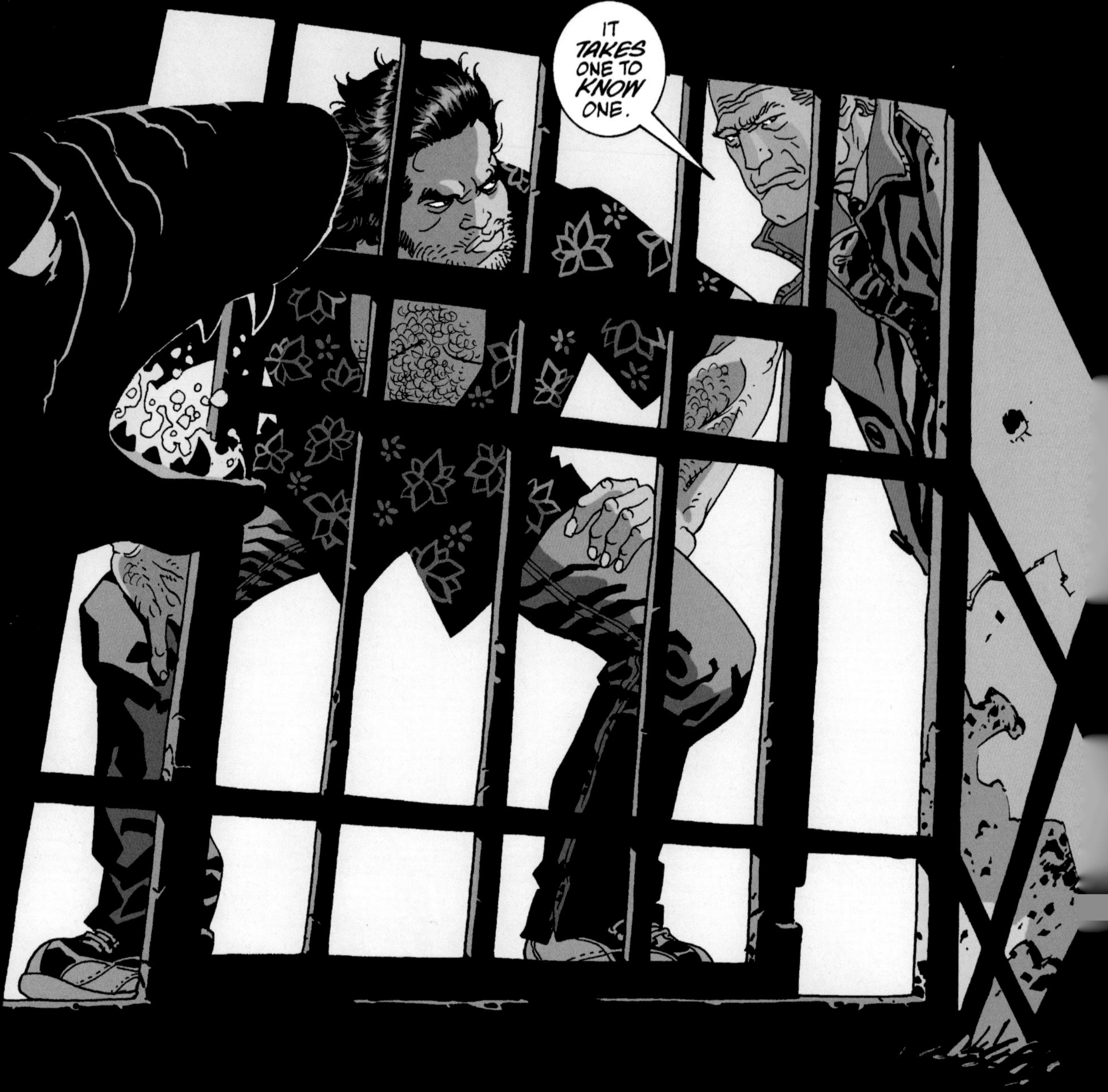
IT TAKES ONE TO KNOW ONE.

NIGHT of the PAYDAY

BRIAN AZZARELLO *writer*
EDUARDO RISSO *artist*
PATRICIA MULVIHILL *colorist*
CLEM ROBINS *letterer*
DIGITAL CHAMELEON *separations*
DAVE JOHNSON *cover*
ZACHARY RAU *ass't ed*
WILL DENNIS *editor*

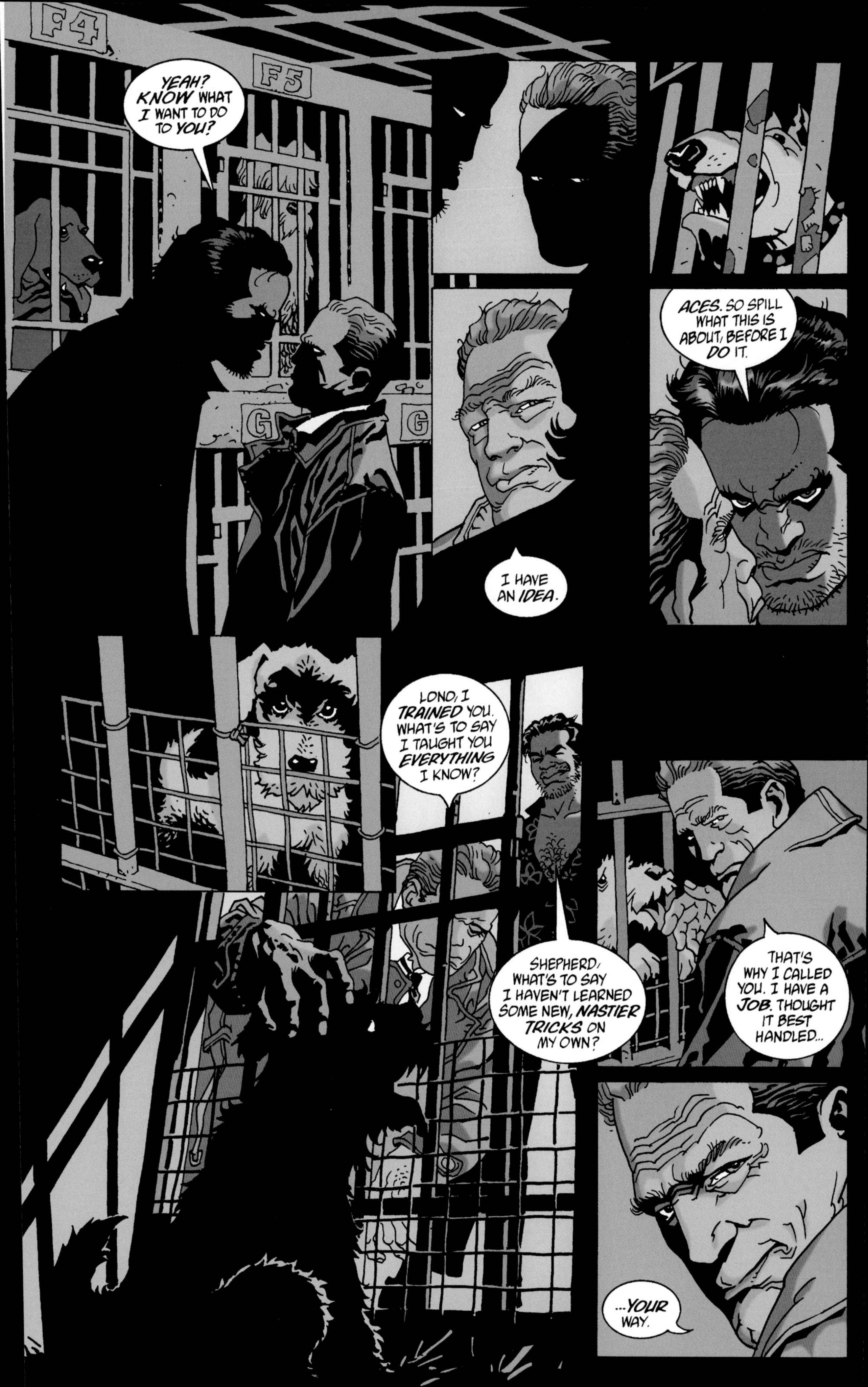
YEAH? KNOW WHAT I WANT TO DO TO YOU?
I HAVE AN IDEA.
ACES. SO SPILL WHAT THIS IS ABOUT, BEFORE I DO IT.
LONO, I TRAINED YOU. WHAT'S TO SAY I TAUGHT YOU EVERYTHING I KNOW?
SHEPHERD, WHAT'S TO SAY I HAVEN'T LEARNED SOME NEW, NASTIER TRICKS ON MY OWN?
THAT'S WHY I CALLED YOU. I HAVE A JOB. THOUGHT IT BEST HANDLED...
...YOUR WAY.

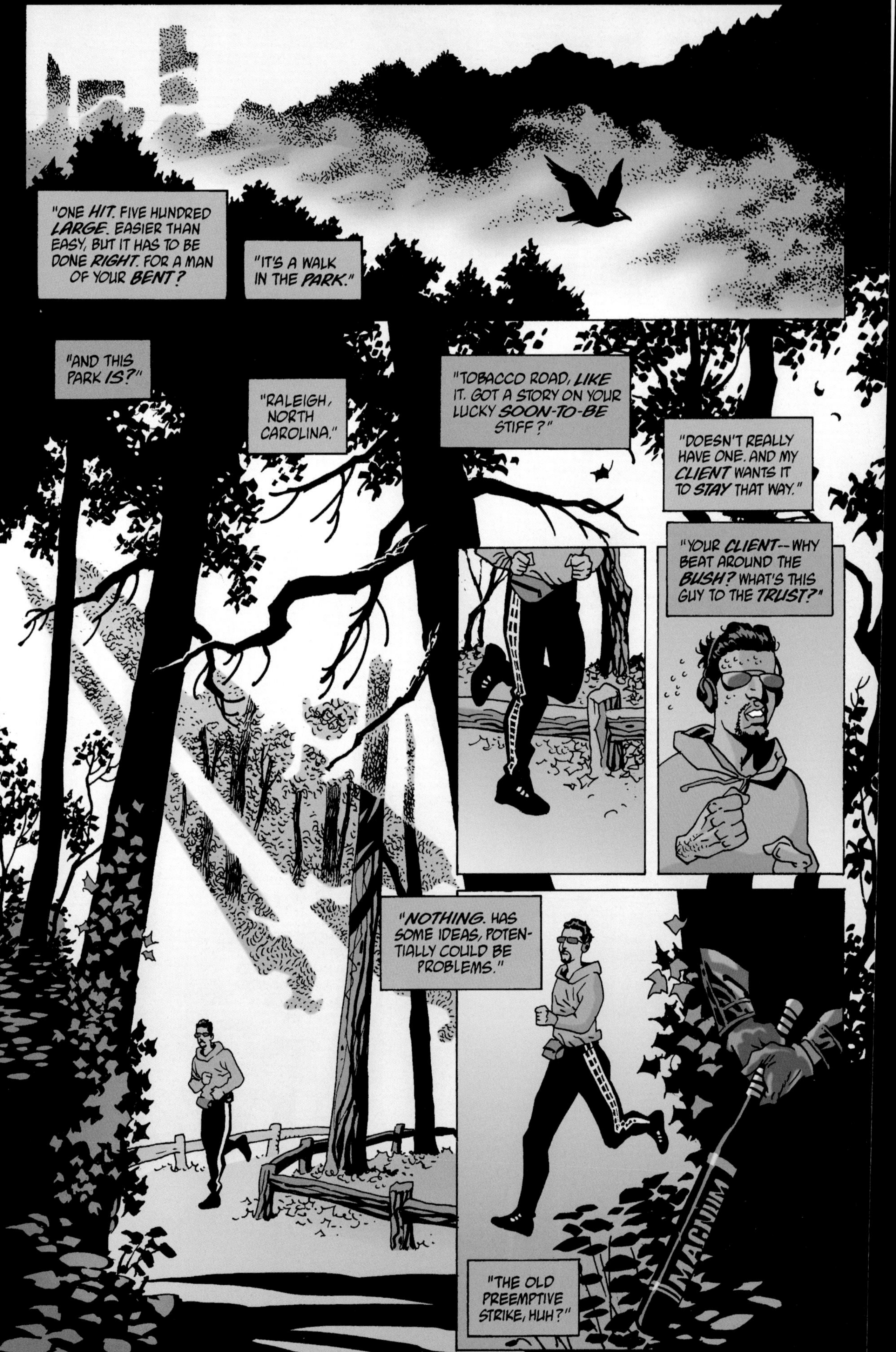
"ONE HIT. FIVE HUNDRED LARGE. EASIER THAN EASY, BUT IT HAS TO BE DONE RIGHT. FOR A MAN OF YOUR BENT?
"IT'S A WALK IN THE PARK."
"AND THIS PARK IS?"
"RALEIGH, NORTH CAROLINA."
"TOBACCO ROAD, LIKE IT. GOT A STORY ON YOUR LUCKY SOON-TO-BE STIFF?"
"DOESN'T REALLY HAVE ONE. AND MY CLIENT WANTS IT TO STAY THAT WAY."
"YOUR CLIENT--WHY BEAT AROUND THE BUSH? WHAT'S THIS GUY TO THE TRUST?"
"NOTHING. HAS SOME IDEAS, POTENTIALLY COULD BE PROBLEMS."
"THE OLD PREEMPTIVE STRIKE, HUH?"
MAGNUM

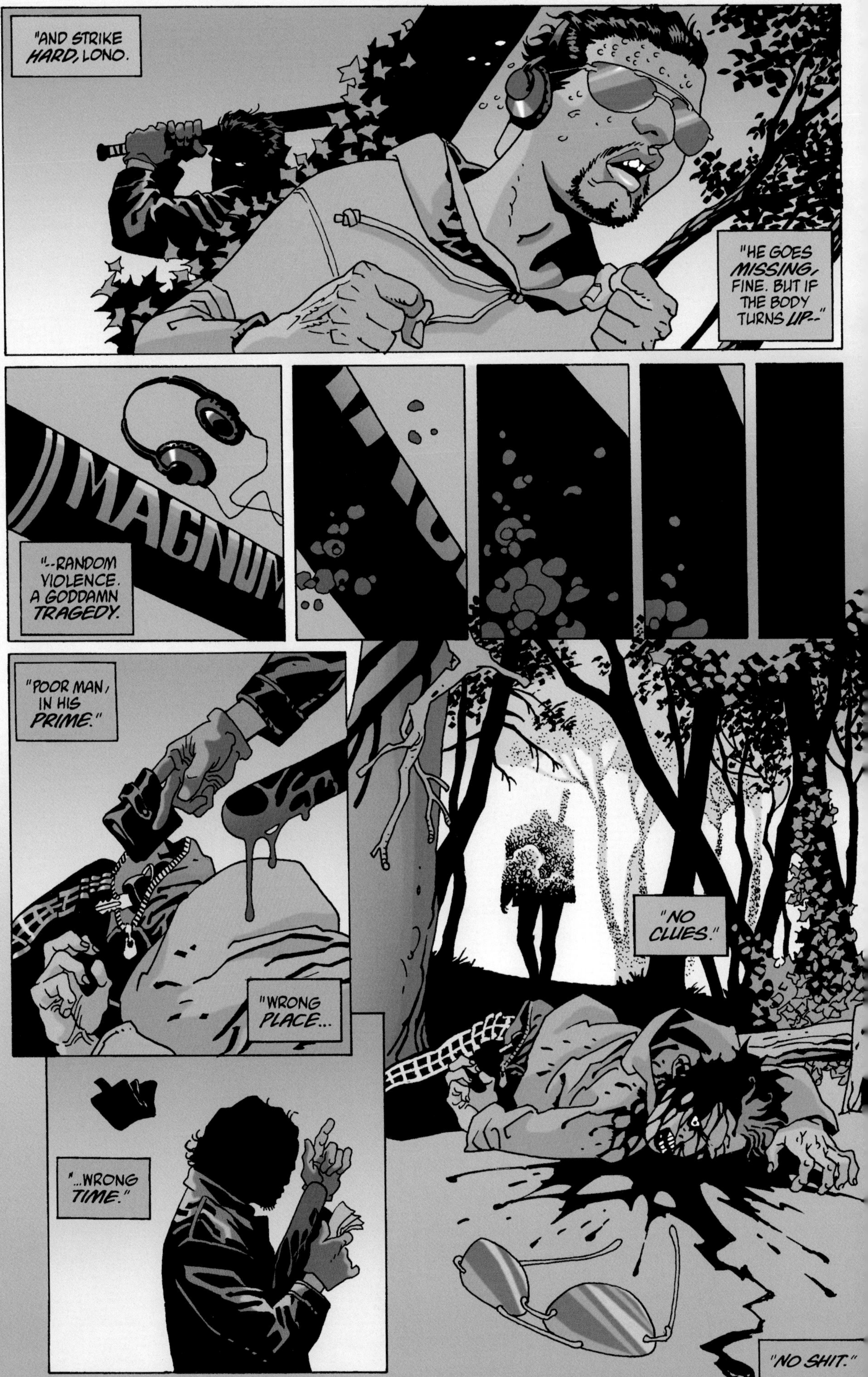
"AND STRIKE HARD, LONO.
"HE GOES MISSING, FINE. BUT IF THE BODY TURNS UP--"
"--RANDOM VIOLENCE. A GODDAMN TRAGEDY.
"POOR MAN, IN HIS PRIME."
"WRONG PLACE...
"...WRONG TIME."
"NO CLUES."
"NO SHIT."

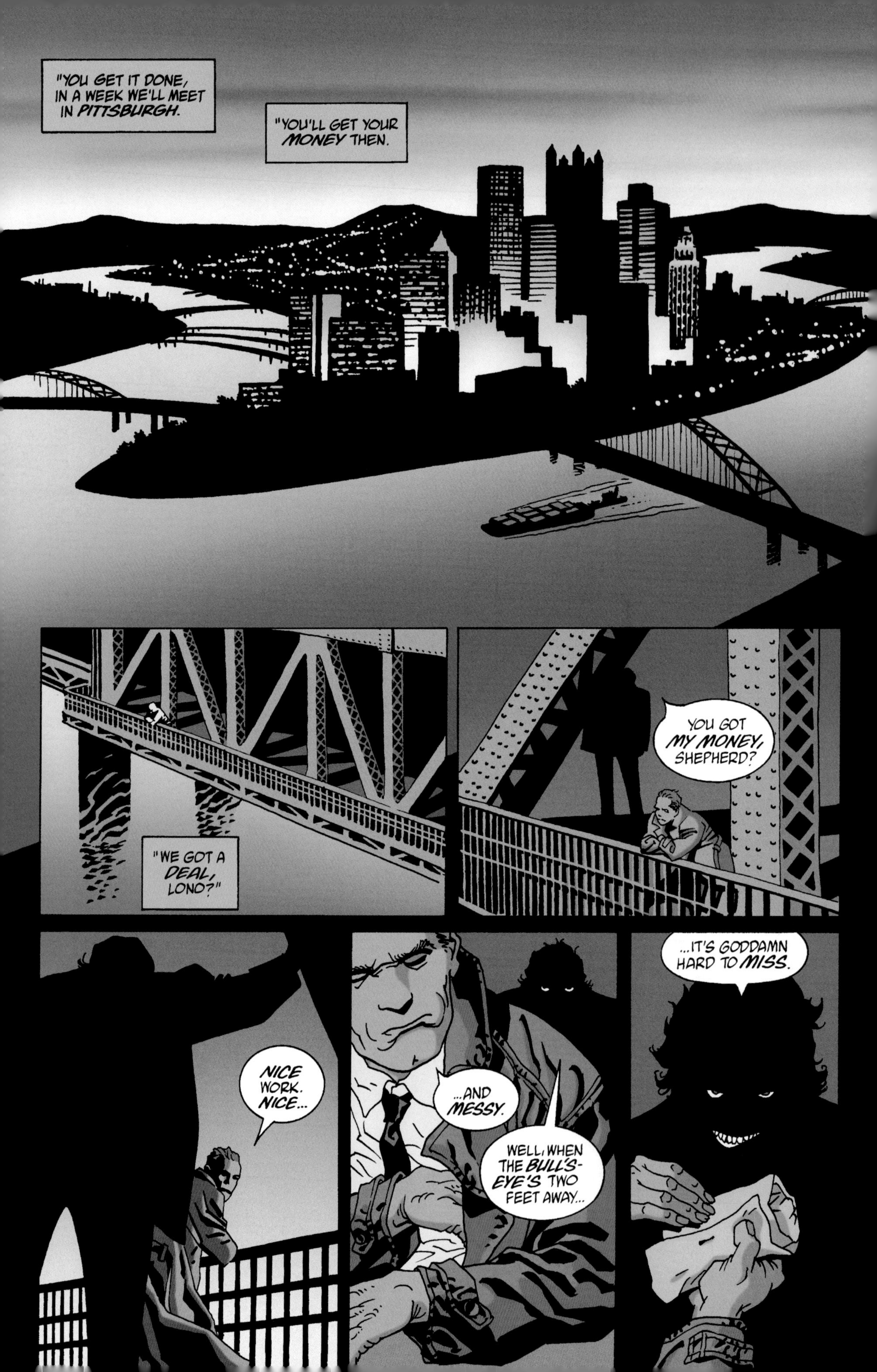

"YOU GET IT DONE, IN A WEEK WE'LL MEET IN PITTSBURGH.
"YOU'LL GET YOUR MONEY THEN.
"WE GOT A DEAL, LONO?"
YOU GOT MY MONEY, SHEPHERD?
NICE WORK. NICE...
...AND MESSY.
WELL, WHEN THE BULL'S-EYE'S TWO FEET AWAY...
...IT'S GODDAMN HARD TO MISS.

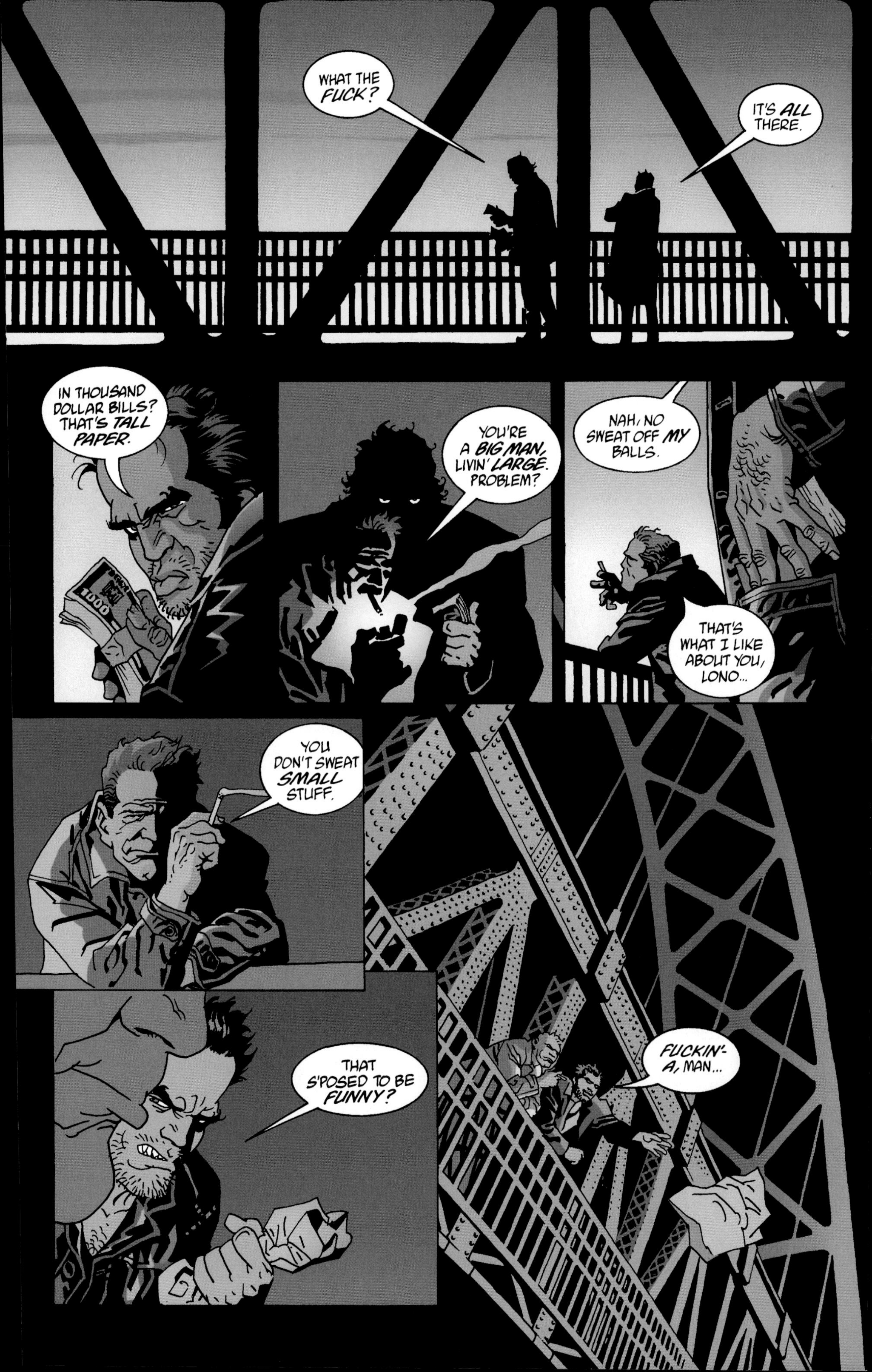
WHAT THE FUCK?
IT'S ALL THERE.
IN THOUSAND DOLLAR BILLS? THAT'S TALL PAPER.
YOU'RE A BIG MAN, LIVIN' LARGE. PROBLEM?
NAH, NO SWEAT OFF MY BALLS.
THAT'S WHAT I LIKE ABOUT YOU, LONO...
YOU DON'T SWEAT SMALL STUFF.
THAT S'POSED TO BE FUNNY?
FUCKIN'-A, MAN...

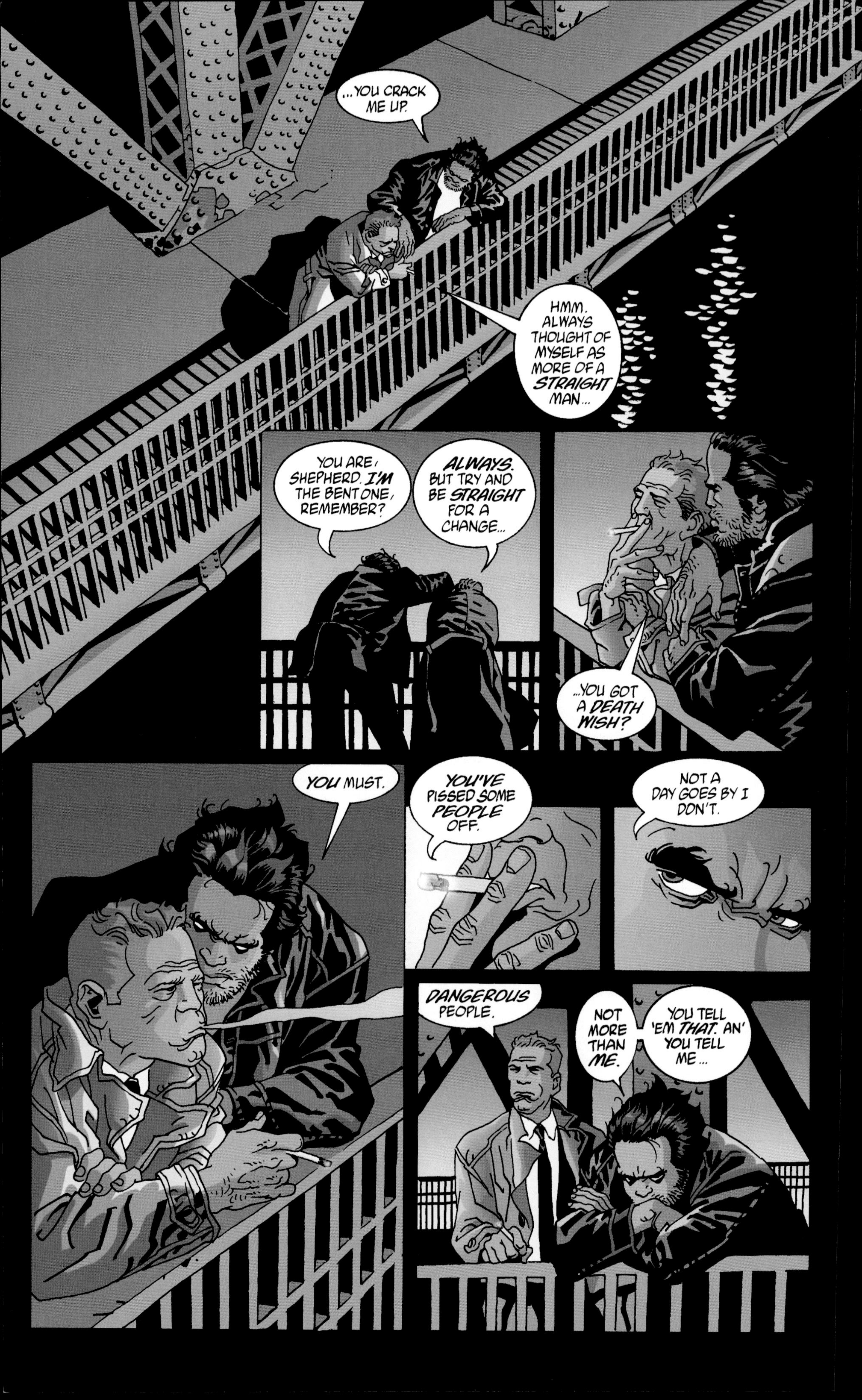
...YOU CRACK ME UP.
HMM. ALWAYS THOUGHT OF MYSELF AS MORE OF A STRAIGHT MAN...
YOU ARE, SHEPHERD. I'M THE BENT ONE, REMEMBER?
ALWAYS. BUT TRY AND BE STRAIGHT FOR A CHANGE...
...YOU GOT A DEATH WISH?
YOU MUST.
YOU'VE PISSED SOME PEOPLE OFF.
NOT A DAY GOES BY I DON'T.
DANGEROUS PEOPLE.
NOT MORE THAN ME.
YOU TELL 'EM THAT. AN' YOU TELL ME...

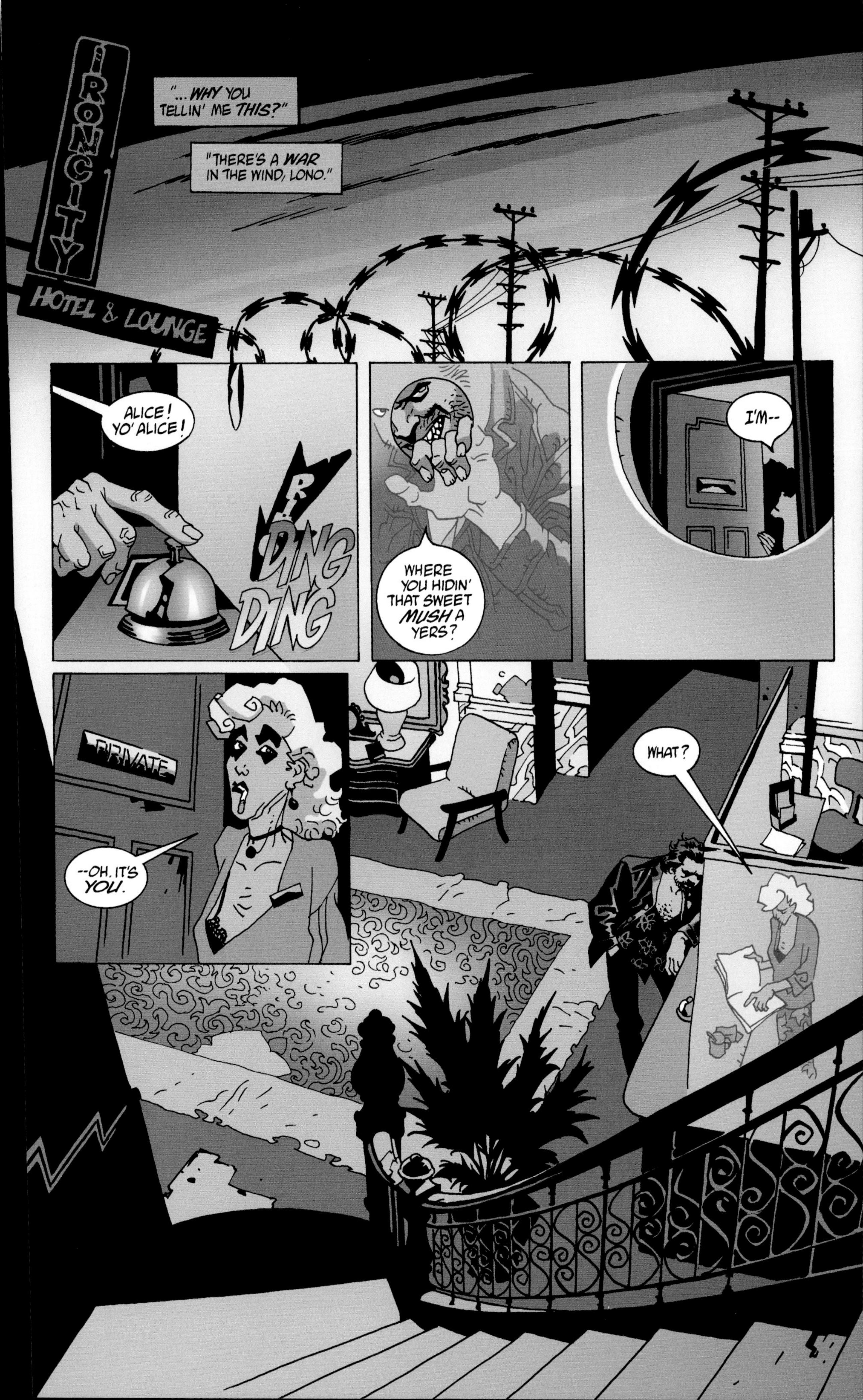
IRONCITY
HOTEL & LOUNGE
"...WHY YOU TELLIN' ME THIS?"
"THERE'S A WAR IN THE WIND, LONO."
ALICE! YO' ALICE!
DING DING
WHERE YOU HIDIN' THAT SWEET MUSH A YERS?
I'M--
PRIVATE
--OH, IT'S YOU.
WHAT?

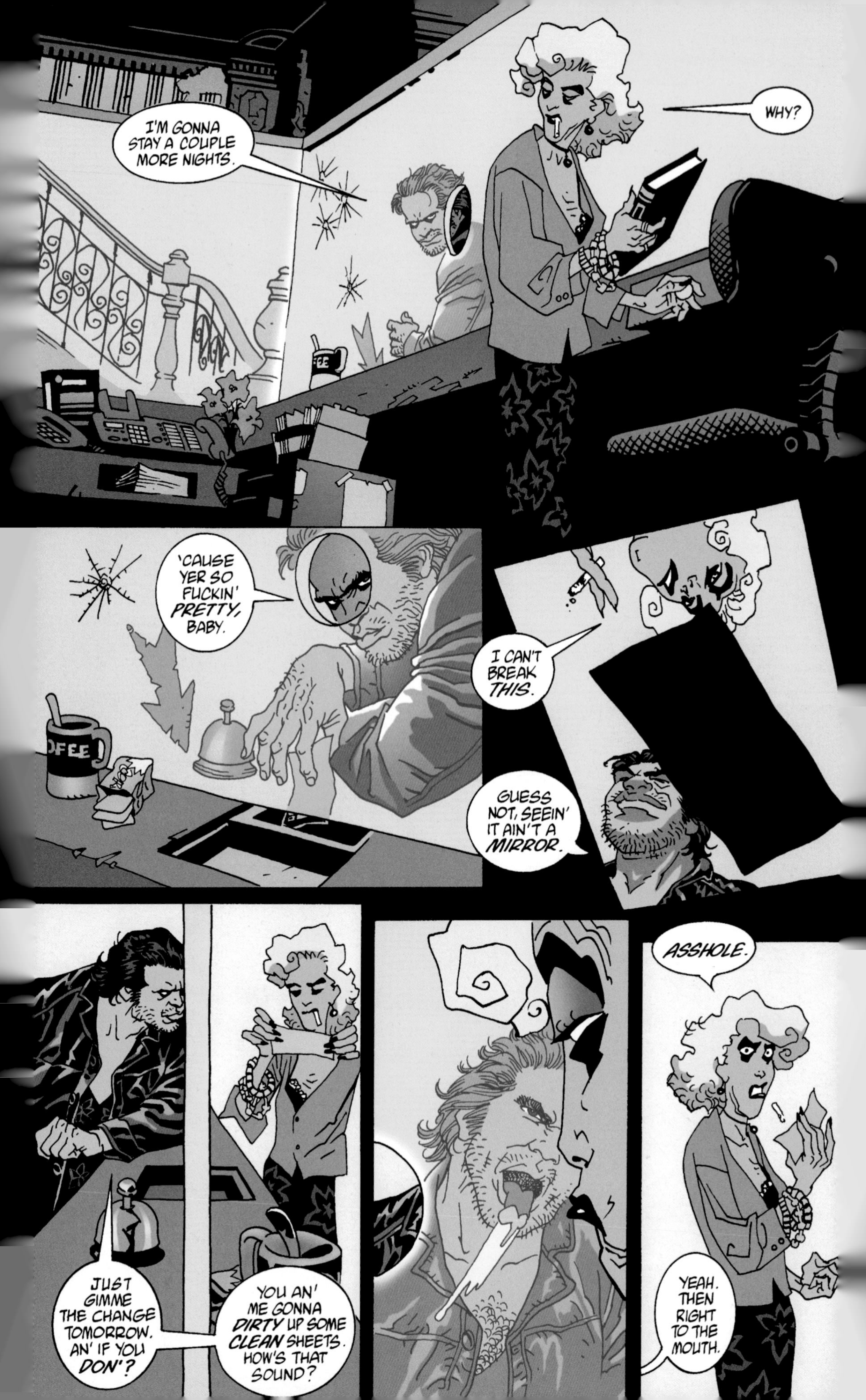
I'M GONNA STAY A COUPLE MORE NIGHTS.
WHY?
'CAUSE YER SO FUCKIN' PRETTY, BABY.
I CAN'T BREAK THIS.
GUESS NOT, SEEIN' IT AIN'T A MIRROR.
JUST GIMME THE CHANGE TOMORROW. AN' IF YOU DON'?
YOU AN' ME GONNA DIRTY UP SOME CLEAN SHEETS. HOW'S THAT SOUND?
ASSHOLE.
YEAH. THEN RIGHT TO THE MOUTH.

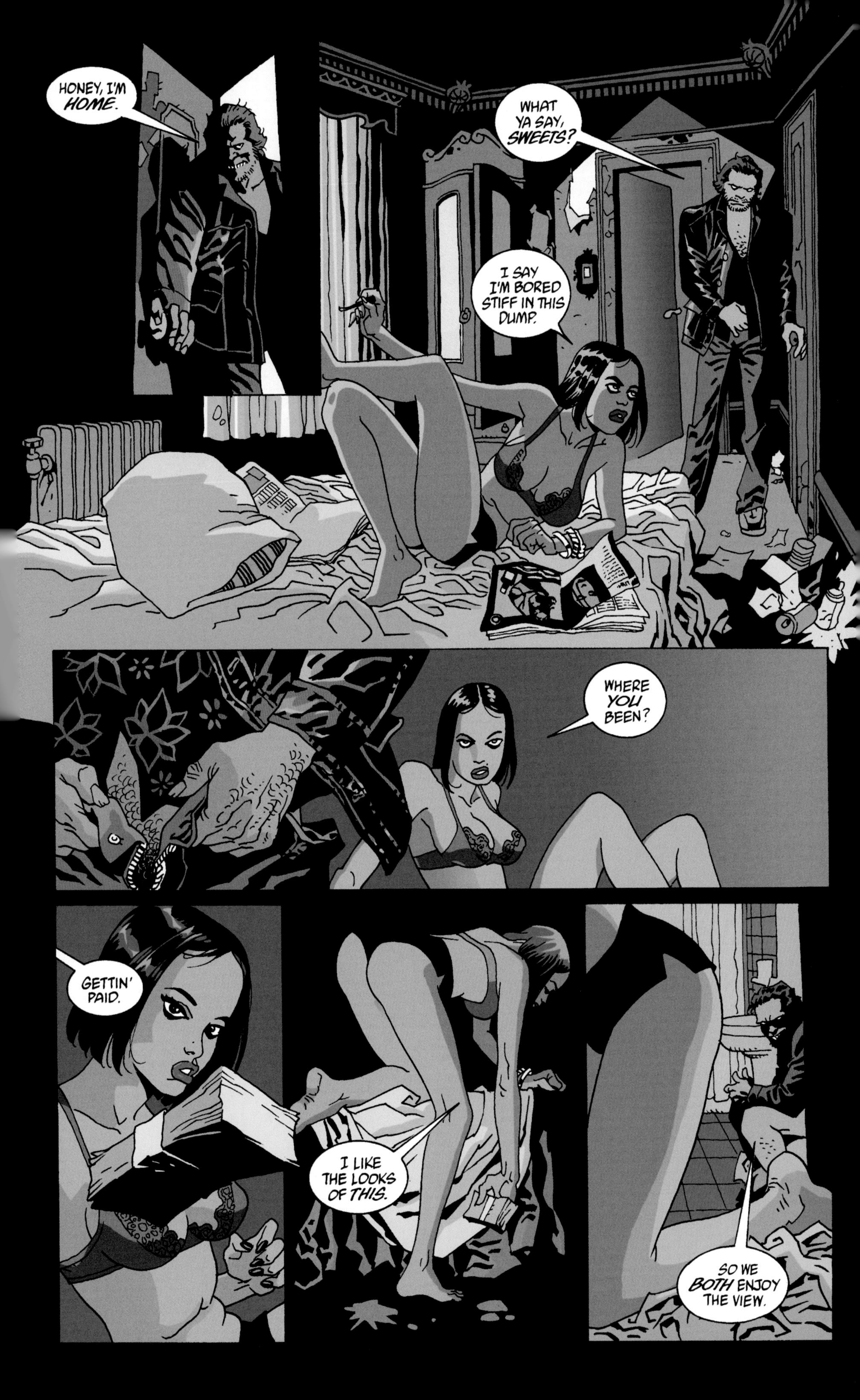
HONEY, I'M HOME.
WHAT YA SAY, SWEETS?
I SAY I'M BORED STIFF IN THIS DUMP.
WHERE YOU BEEN?
GETTIN' PAID.
I LIKE THE LOOKS OF THIS.
SO WE BOTH ENJOY THE VIEW.

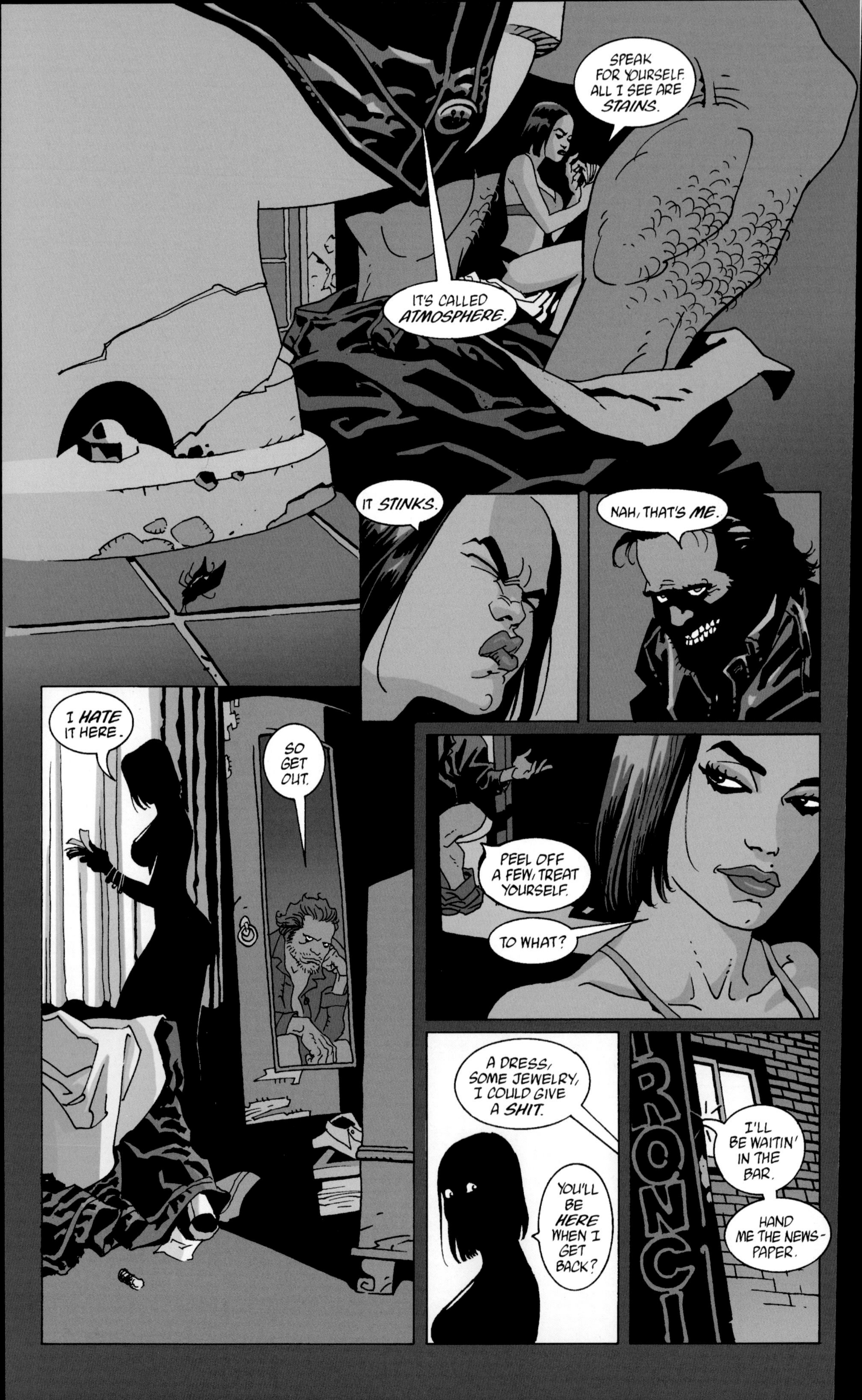
SPEAK FOR YOURSELF. ALL I SEE ARE STAINS.
IT'S CALLED ATMOSPHERE.
IT STINKS.
NAH, THAT'S ME.
I HATE IT HERE.
SO GET OUT.
PEEL OFF A FEW, TREAT YOURSELF.
TO WHAT?
A DRESS, SOME JEWELRY, I COULD GIVE A SHIT.
YOU'LL BE HERE WHEN I GET BACK?
I'LL BE WAITIN' IN THE BAR.
HAND ME THE NEWS-PAPER.
IRONCI

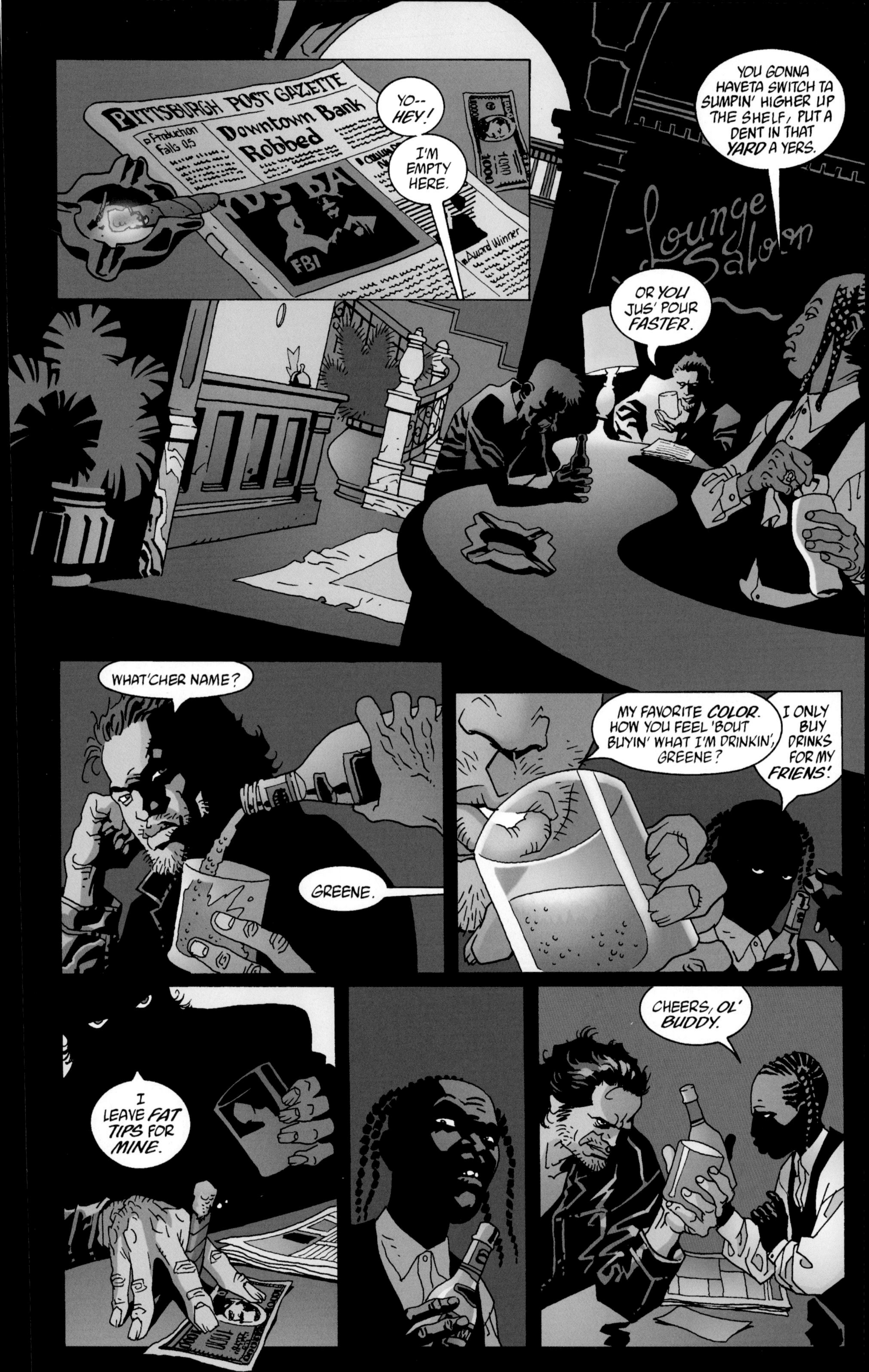
PITTSBURGH POST GAZETTE
Downtown Bank Robbed
FBI
Award Winner
YO-- HEY!
I'M EMPTY HERE.
YOU GONNA HAVETA SWITCH TA SUMPIN' HIGHER UP THE SHELF, PUT A DENT IN THAT YARD A YERS.
Lounge Saloon
OR YOU JUS' POUR FASTER.
WHAT'CHER NAME?
GREENE.
MY FAVORITE COLOR. HOW YOU FEEL 'BOUT BUYIN' WHAT I'M DRINKIN', GREENE?
I ONLY BUY DRINKS FOR MY FRIENS!
I LEAVE FAT TIPS FOR MINE.
CHEERS, OL' BUDDY.

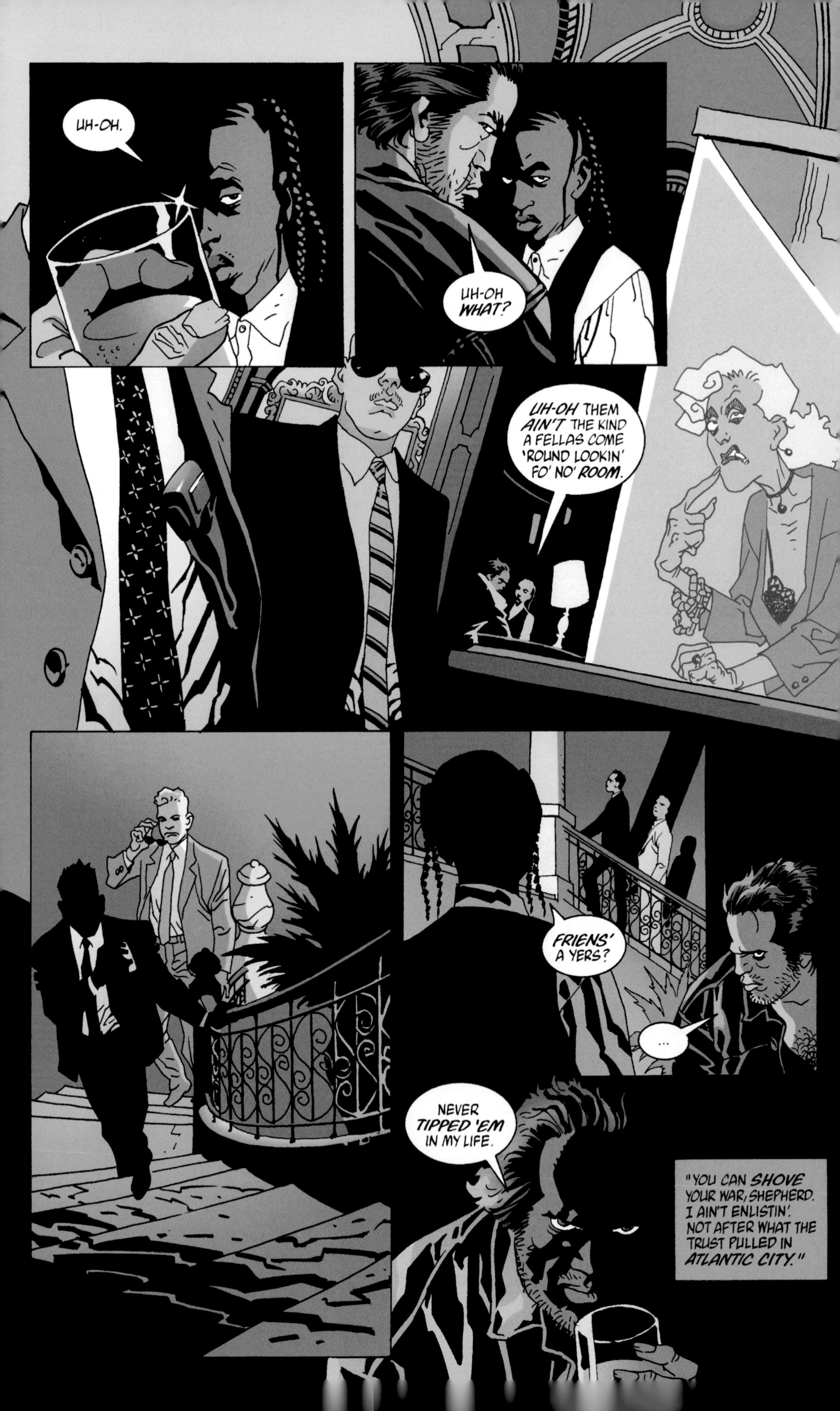
UH-OH.
UH-OH WHAT?
UH-OH THEM AIN'T THE KIND A FELLAS COME 'ROUND LOOKIN' FO' NO' ROOM.
FRIENS' A YERS?
...
NEVER TIPPED 'EM IN MY LIFE.
"YOU CAN SHOVE YOUR WAR, SHEPHERD. I AIN'T ENLISTIN'. NOT AFTER WHAT THE TRUST PULLED IN ATLANTIC CITY."

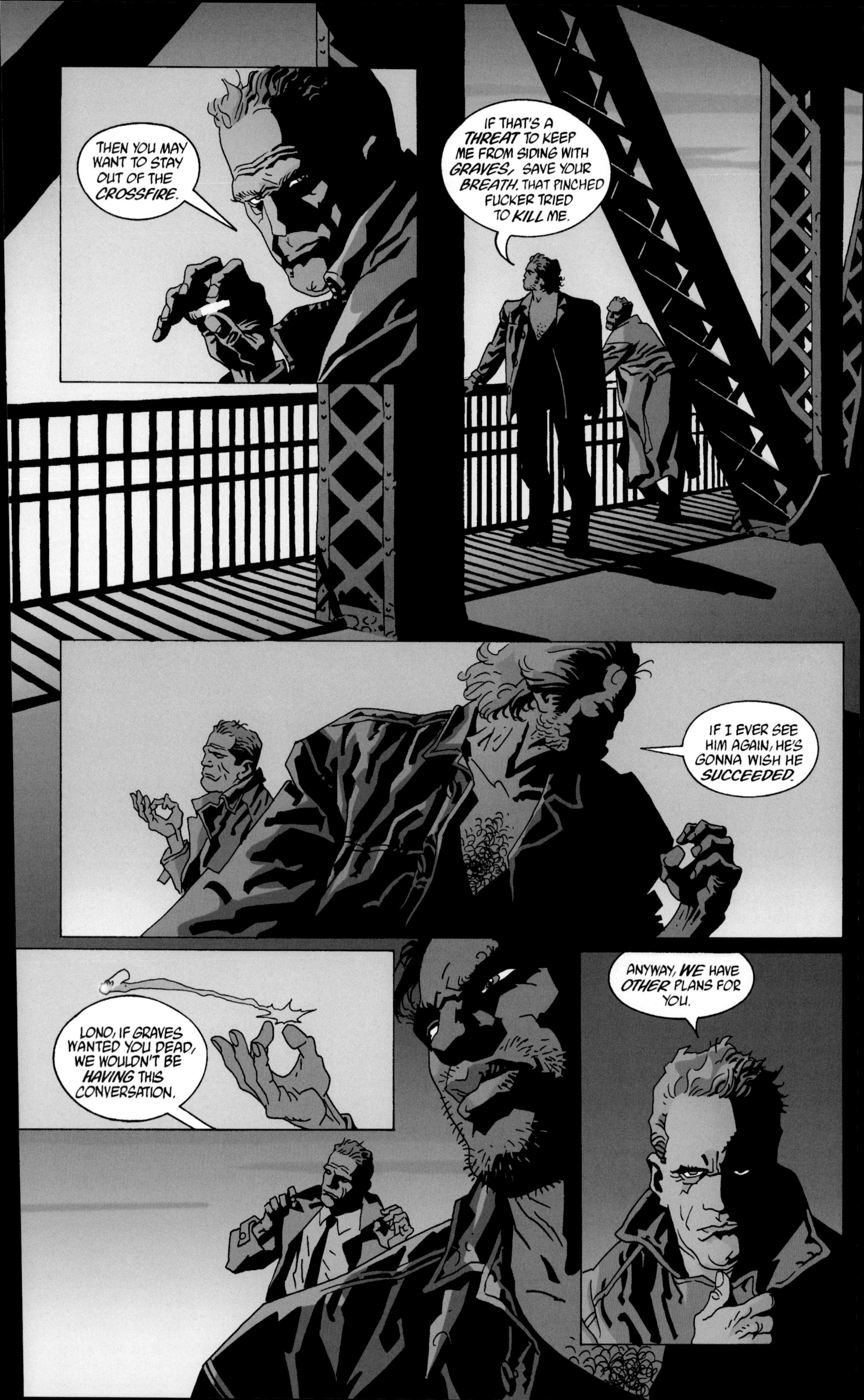
THEN YOU MAY WANT TO STAY OUT OF THE CROSSFIRE.
IF THAT'S A THREAT TO KEEP ME FROM SIDING WITH GRAVES, SAVE YOUR BREATH. THAT PINCHED FUCKER TRIED TO KILL ME.
IF I EVER SEE HIM AGAIN, HE'S GONNA WISH HE SUCCEEDED.
LONO, IF GRAVES WANTED YOU DEAD, WE WOULDN'T BE HAVING THIS CONVERSATION.
ANYWAY, WE HAVE OTHER PLANS FOR YOU.

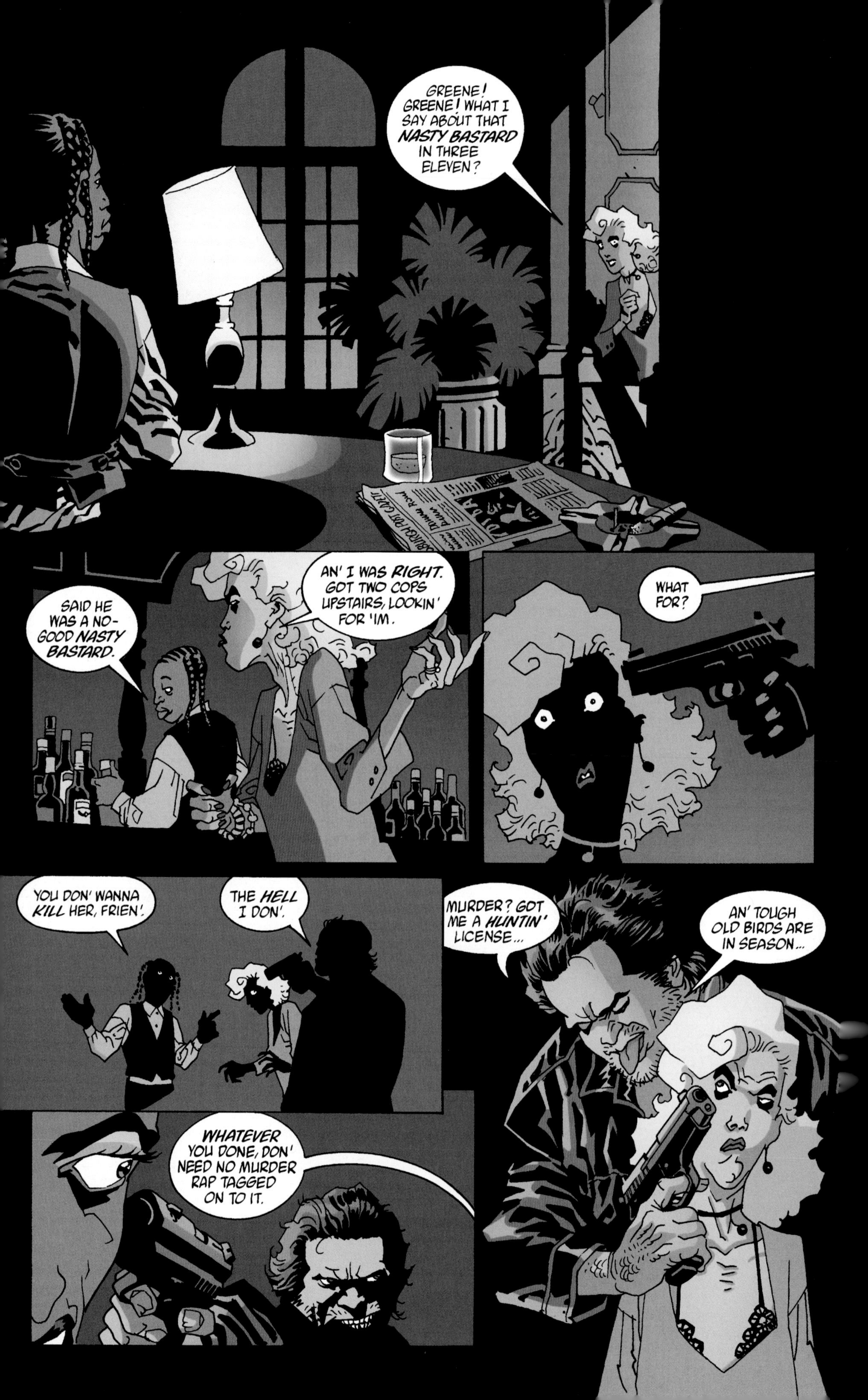
GREENE! GREENE! WHAT I SAY ABOUT THAT NASTY BASTARD IN THREE ELEVEN?
SAID HE WAS A NO-GOOD NASTY BASTARD.
AN' I WAS RIGHT. GOT TWO COPS UPSTAIRS, LOOKIN' FOR 'IM.
WHAT FOR?
YOU DON' WANNA KILL HER, FRIEN'.
THE HELL I DON'.
WHATEVER YOU DONE, DON' NEED NO MURDER RAP TAGGED ON TO IT.
MURDER? GOT ME A HUNTIN' LICENSE...
AN' TOUGH OLD BIRDS ARE IN SEASON...

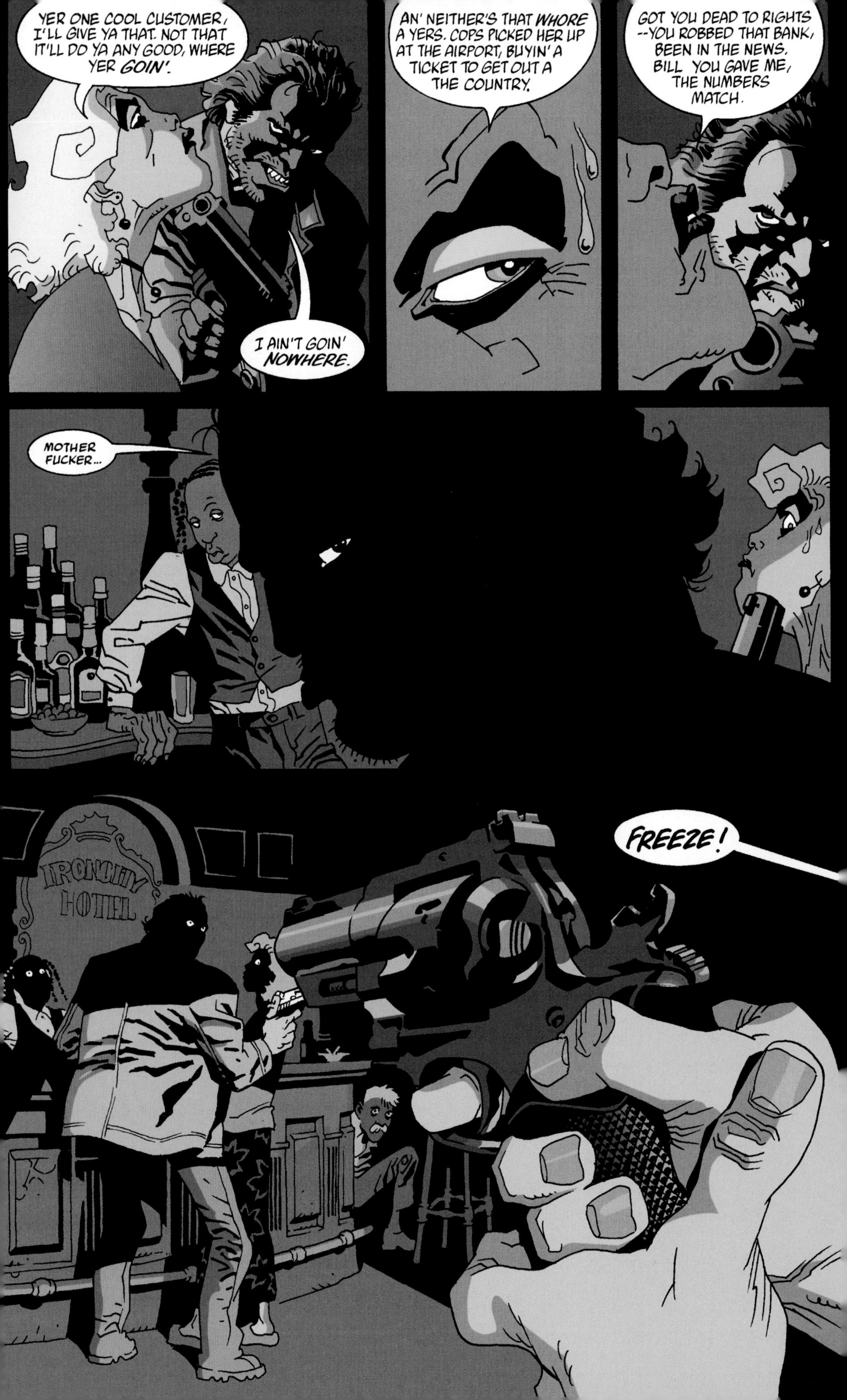
YER ONE COOL CUSTOMER, I'LL GIVE YA THAT. NOT THAT IT'LL DO YA ANY GOOD, WHERE YER GOIN'.
I AIN'T GOIN' NOWHERE.
AN' NEITHER'S THAT WHORE A YERS. COPS PICKED HER UP AT THE AIRPORT, BUYIN' A TICKET TO GET OUT A THE COUNTRY.
GOT YOU DEAD TO RIGHTS --YOU ROBBED THAT BANK, BEEN IN THE NEWS. BILL YOU GAVE ME, THE NUMBERS MATCH.
MOTHER FUCKER...
IRON CITY HOTEL
FREEZE!

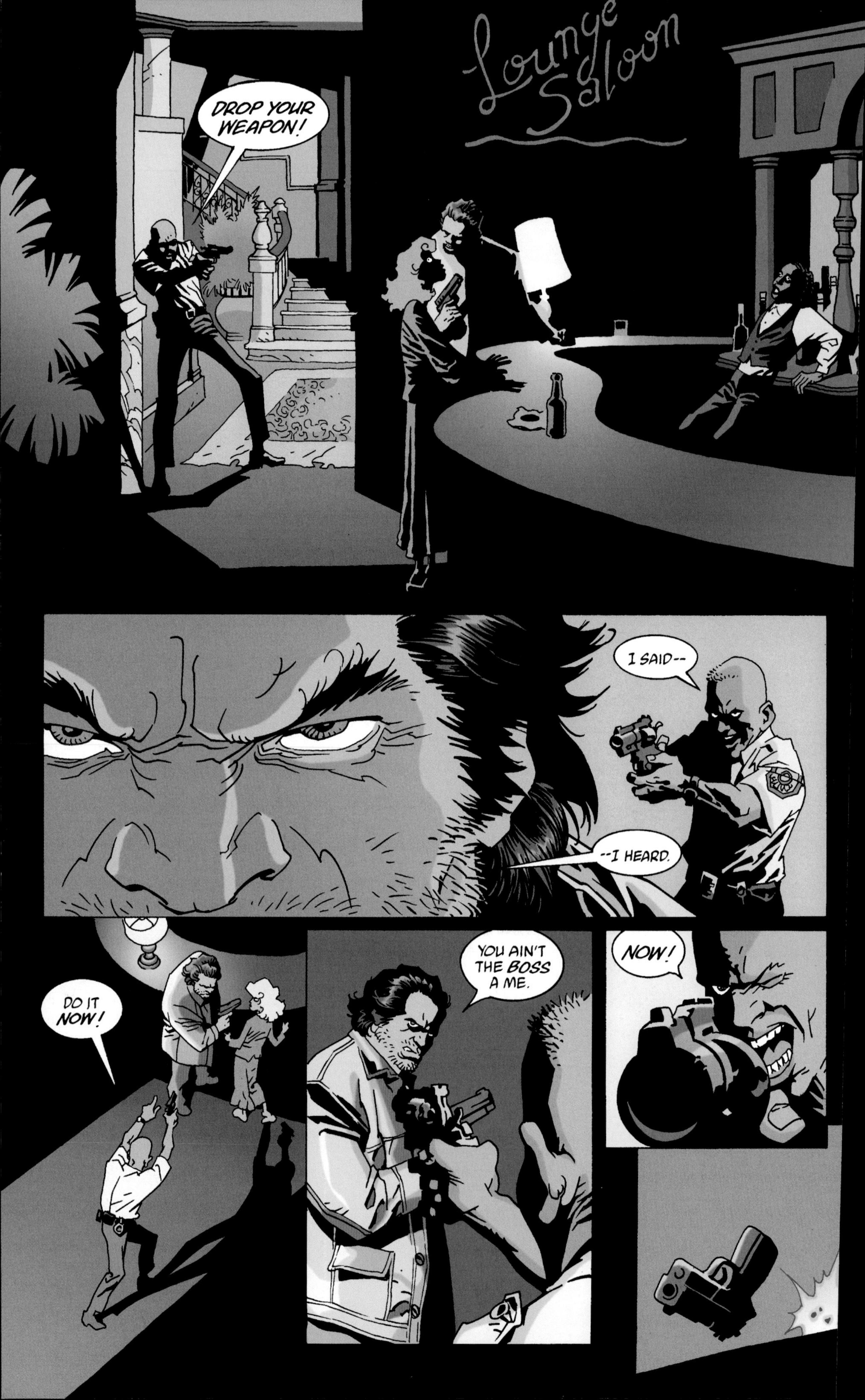
Lounge Saloon
DROP YOUR WEAPON!
I SAID--
--I HEARD.
DO IT NOW!
YOU AIN'T THE BOSS A ME.
NOW!

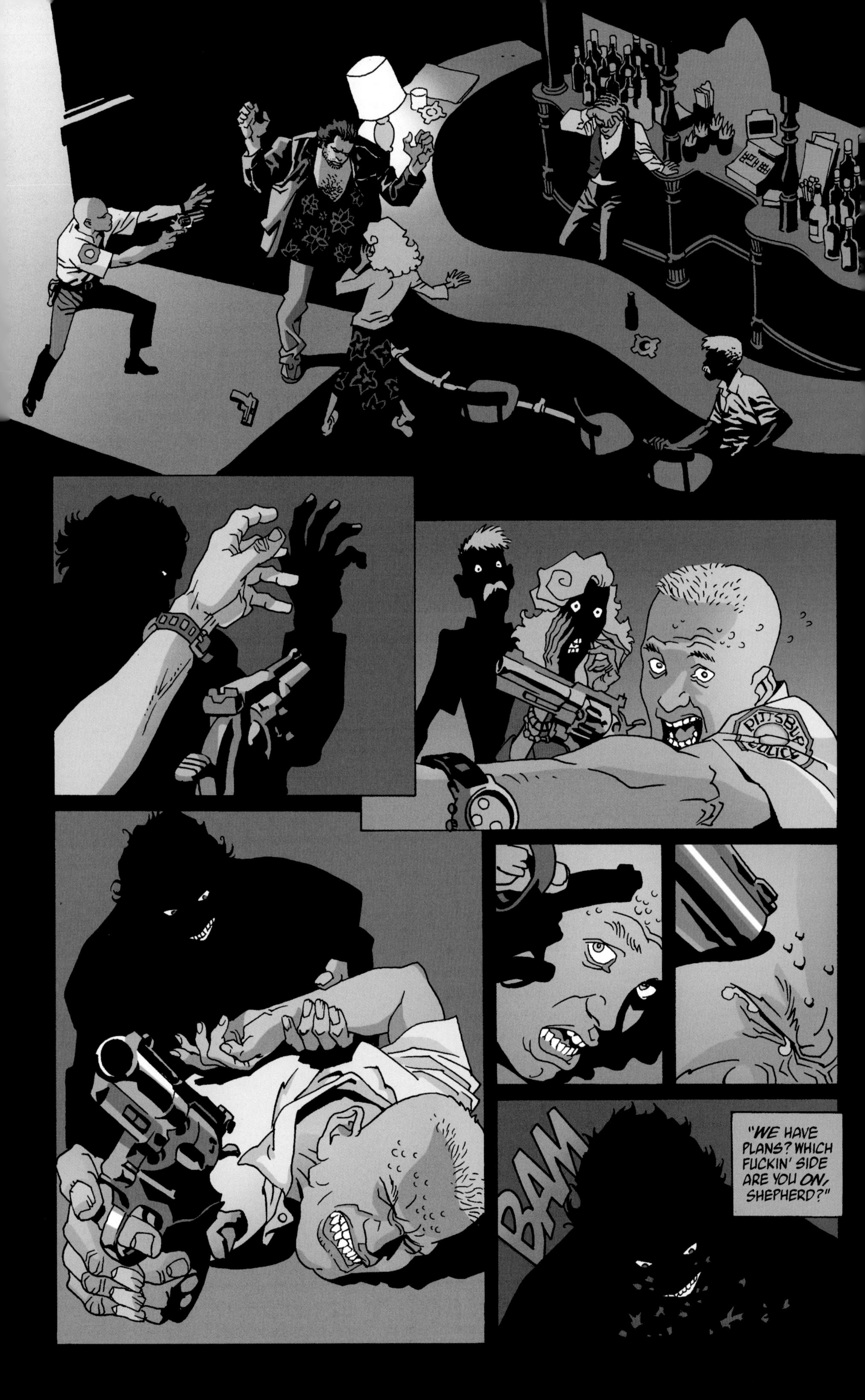
PITTSBURGH POLICE
BAM
"WE HAVE PLANS? WHICH FUCKIN' SIDE ARE YOU ON, SHEPHERD?"

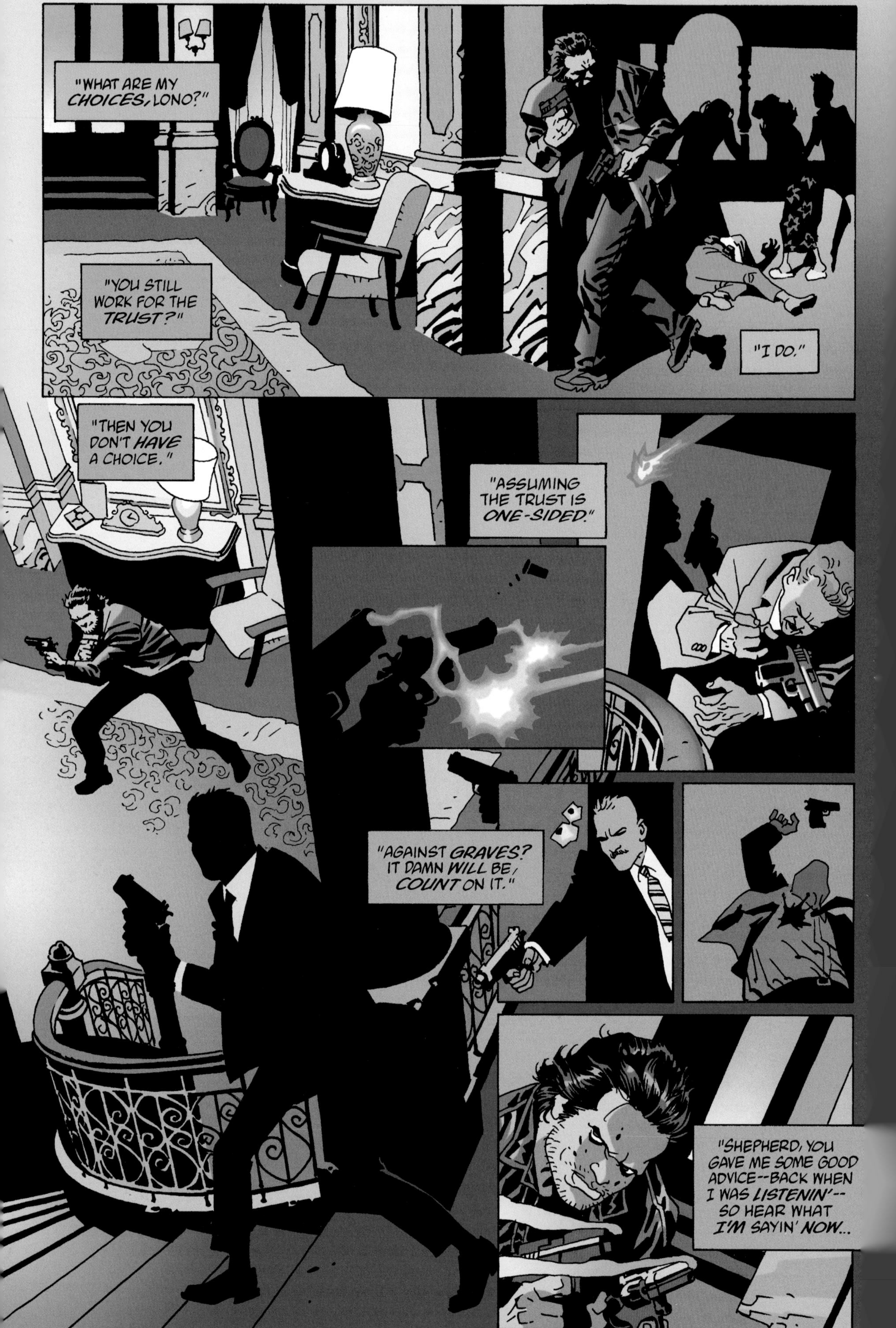
"WHAT ARE MY CHOICES, LONO?"
"YOU STILL WORK FOR THE TRUST?"
"I DO."
"THEN YOU DON'T HAVE A CHOICE."
"ASSUMING THE TRUST IS ONE-SIDED."
"AGAINST GRAVES? IT DAMN WILL BE, COUNT ON IT."
"SHEPHERD, YOU GAVE ME SOME GOOD ADVICE--BACK WHEN I WAS LISTENIN'-- SO HEAR WHAT I'M SAYIN' NOW...

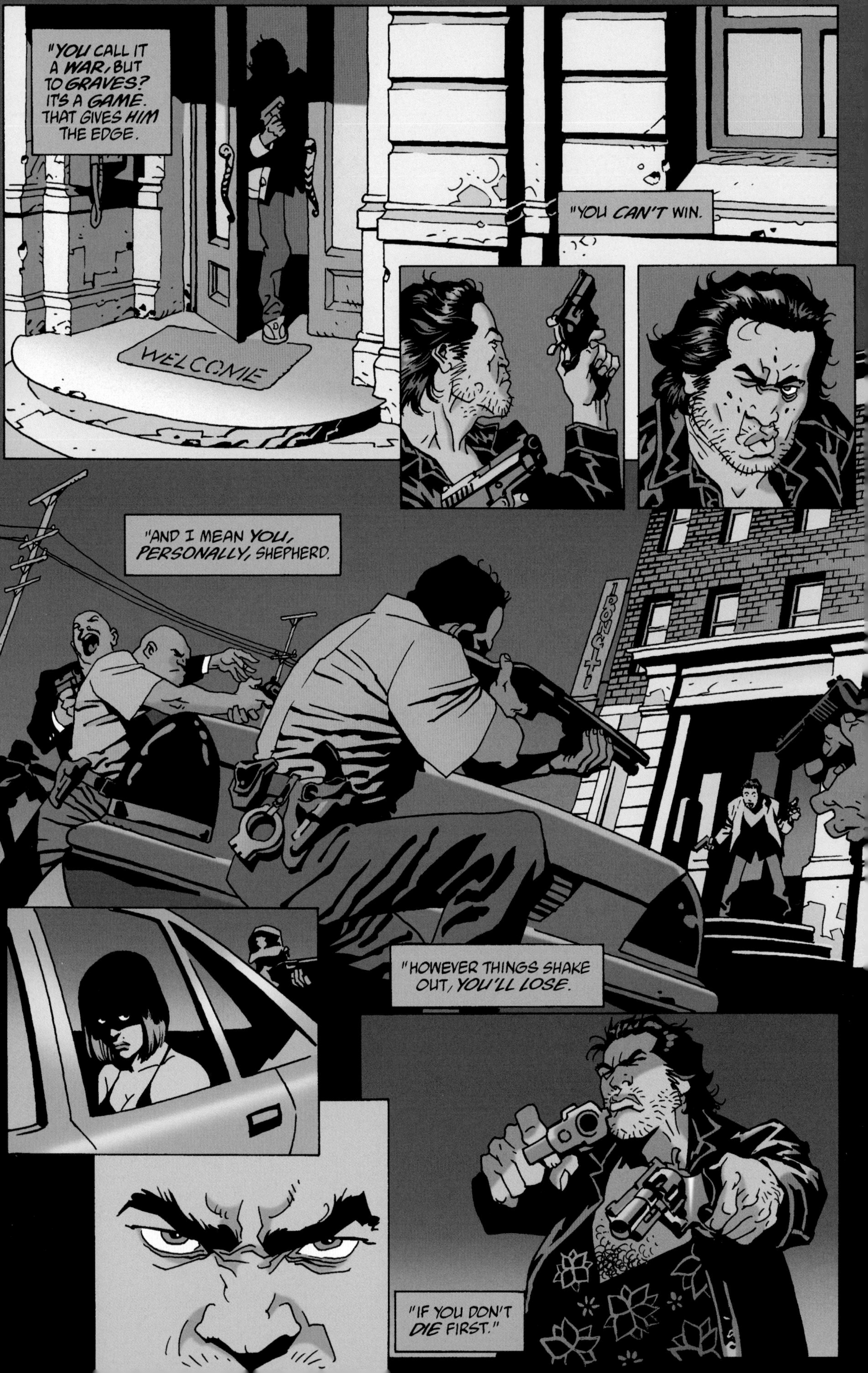

"YOU CALL IT A WAR, BUT TO GRAVES? IT'S A GAME. THAT GIVES HIM THE EDGE.
WELCOME
"YOU CAN'T WIN.
"AND I MEAN YOU, PERSONALLY, SHEPHERD.
"HOWEVER THINGS SHAKE OUT, YOU'LL LOSE.
"IF YOU DON'T DIE FIRST."

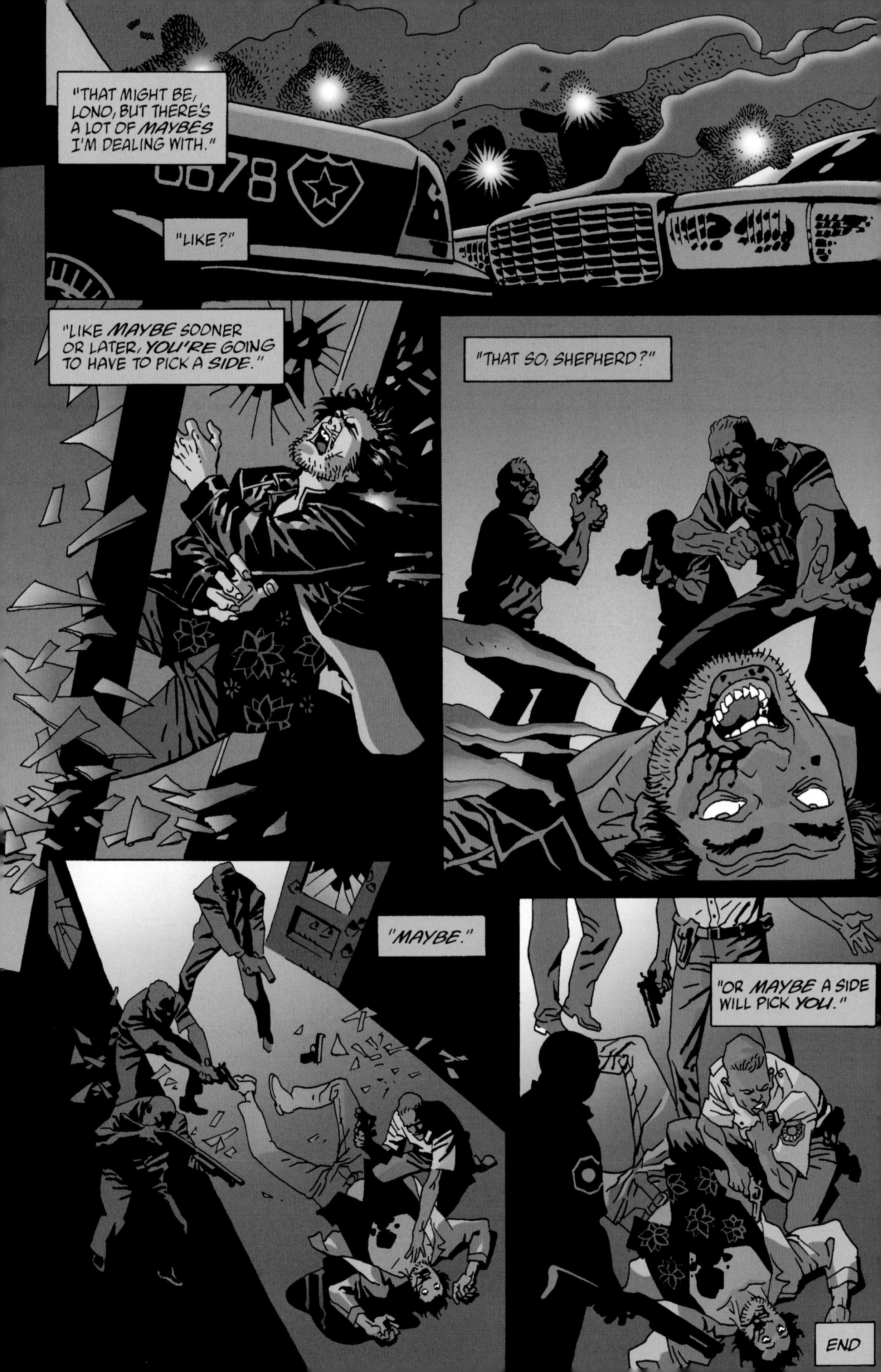
"THAT MIGHT BE, LONO, BUT THERE'S A LOT OF MAYBES I'M DEALING WITH."
"LIKE?"
"LIKE MAYBE SOONER OR LATER, YOU'RE GOING TO HAVE TO PICK A SIDE."
"THAT SO, SHEPHERD?"
"MAYBE."
"OR MAYBE A SIDE WILL PICK YOU."
END

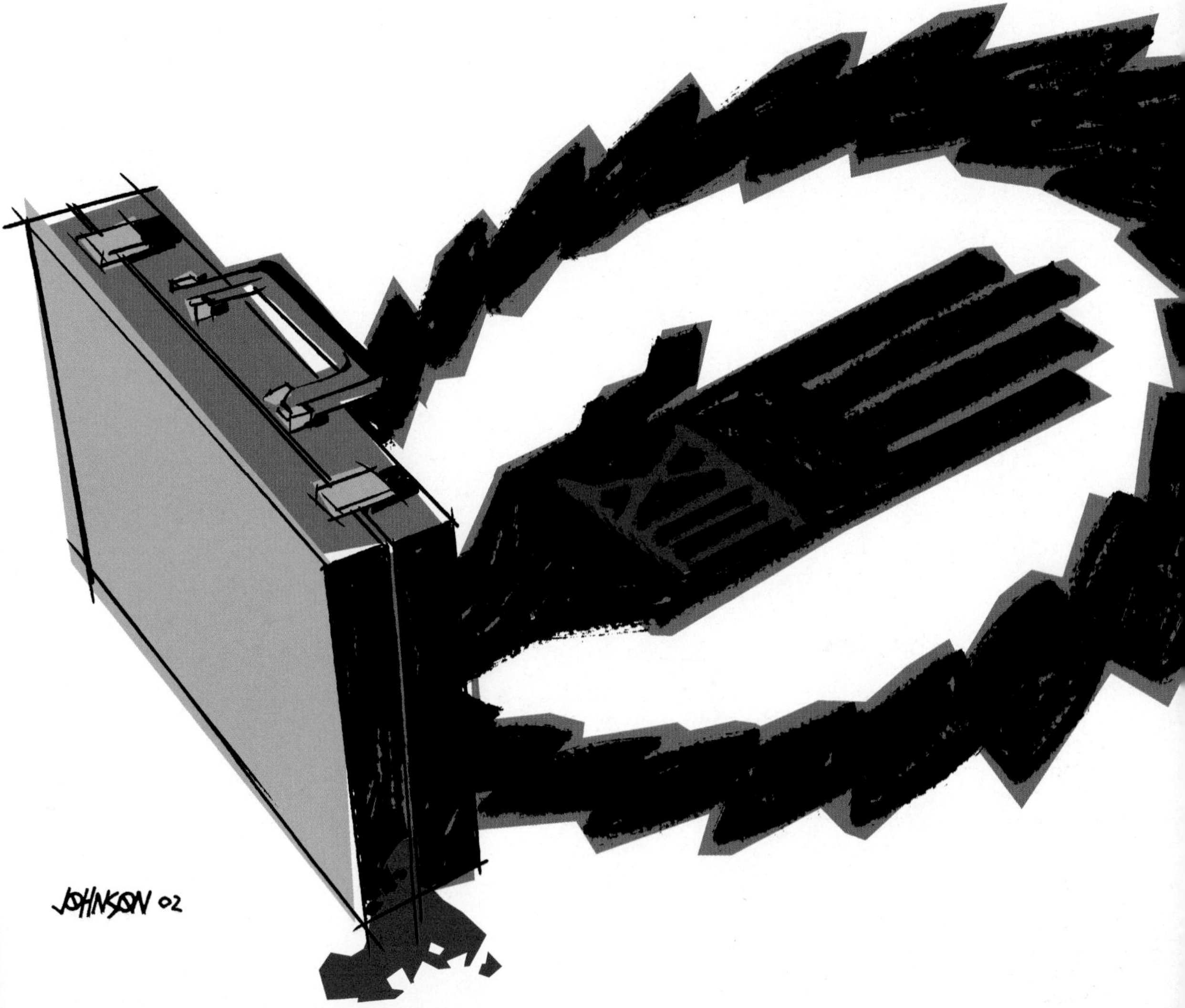
JOHNSON 02

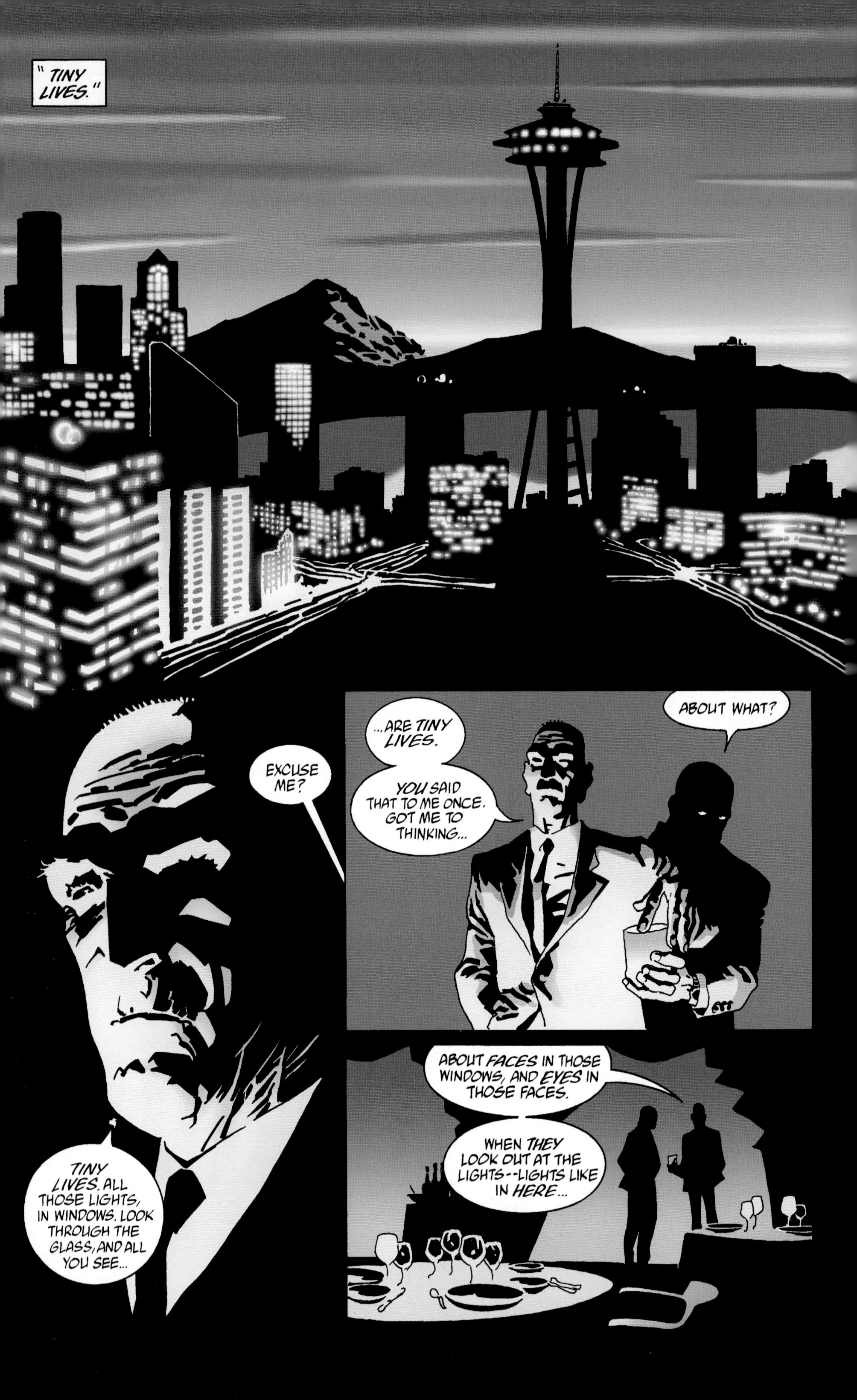
"TINY LIVES."
EXCUSE ME?
...ARE TINY LIVES.
YOU SAID THAT TO ME ONCE. GOT ME TO THINKING...
ABOUT WHAT?
TINY LIVES. ALL THOSE LIGHTS, IN WINDOWS. LOOK THROUGH THE GLASS, AND ALL YOU SEE...
ABOUT FACES IN THOSE WINDOWS, AND EYES IN THOSE FACES.
WHEN THEY LOOK OUT AT THE LIGHTS--LIGHTS LIKE IN HERE...

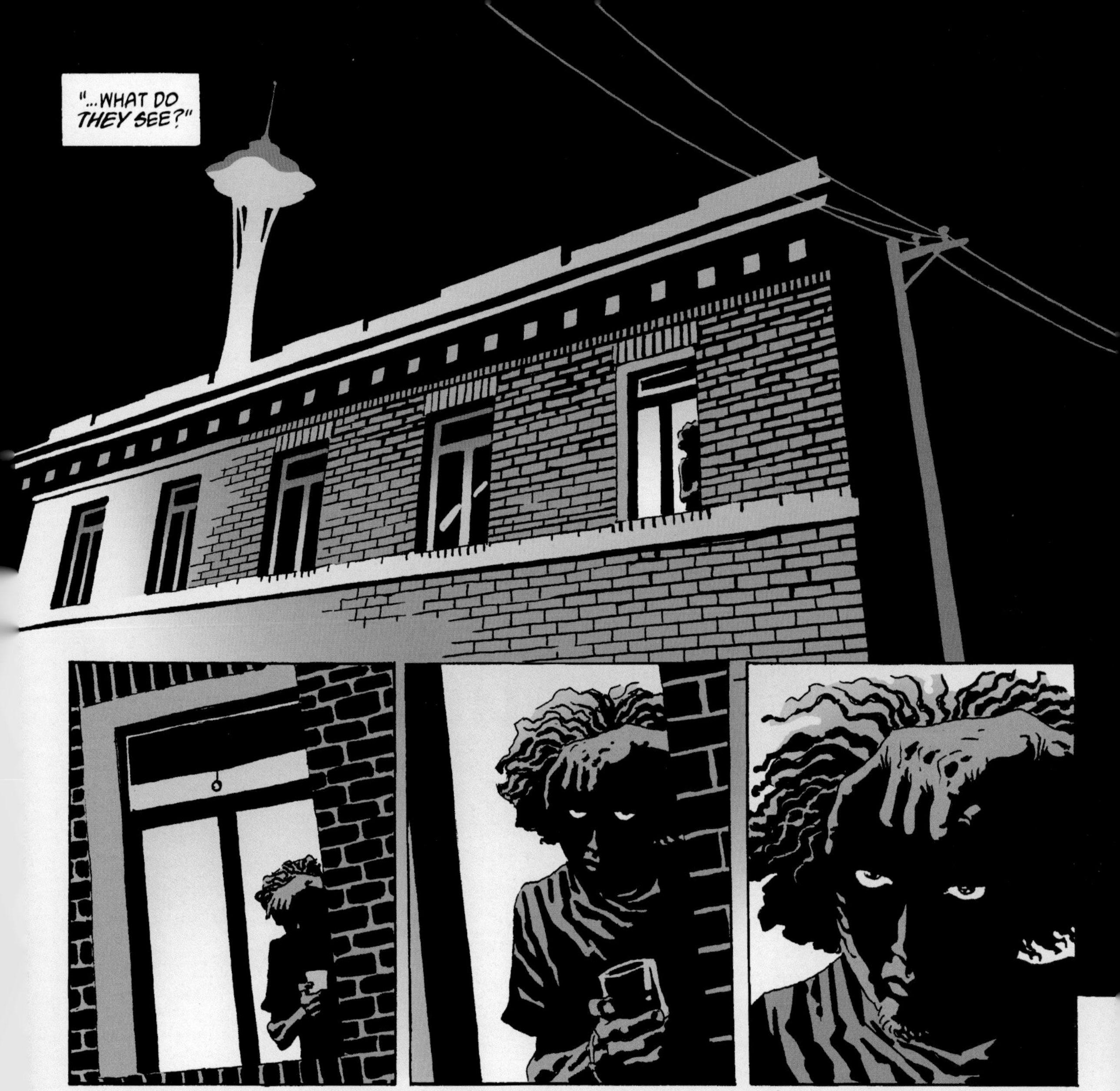
"...WHAT DO THEY SEE?"

a crash

BRIAN AZZARELLO
writer

EDUARDO RISSO
artist

PATRICIA MULVIHILL
colorist

CLEM ROBINS
letterer

DIGITAL CHAMELEON
separations

DAVE JOHNSON
cover

ZACHARY RAU
ass't ed

WILL DENNIS
editor

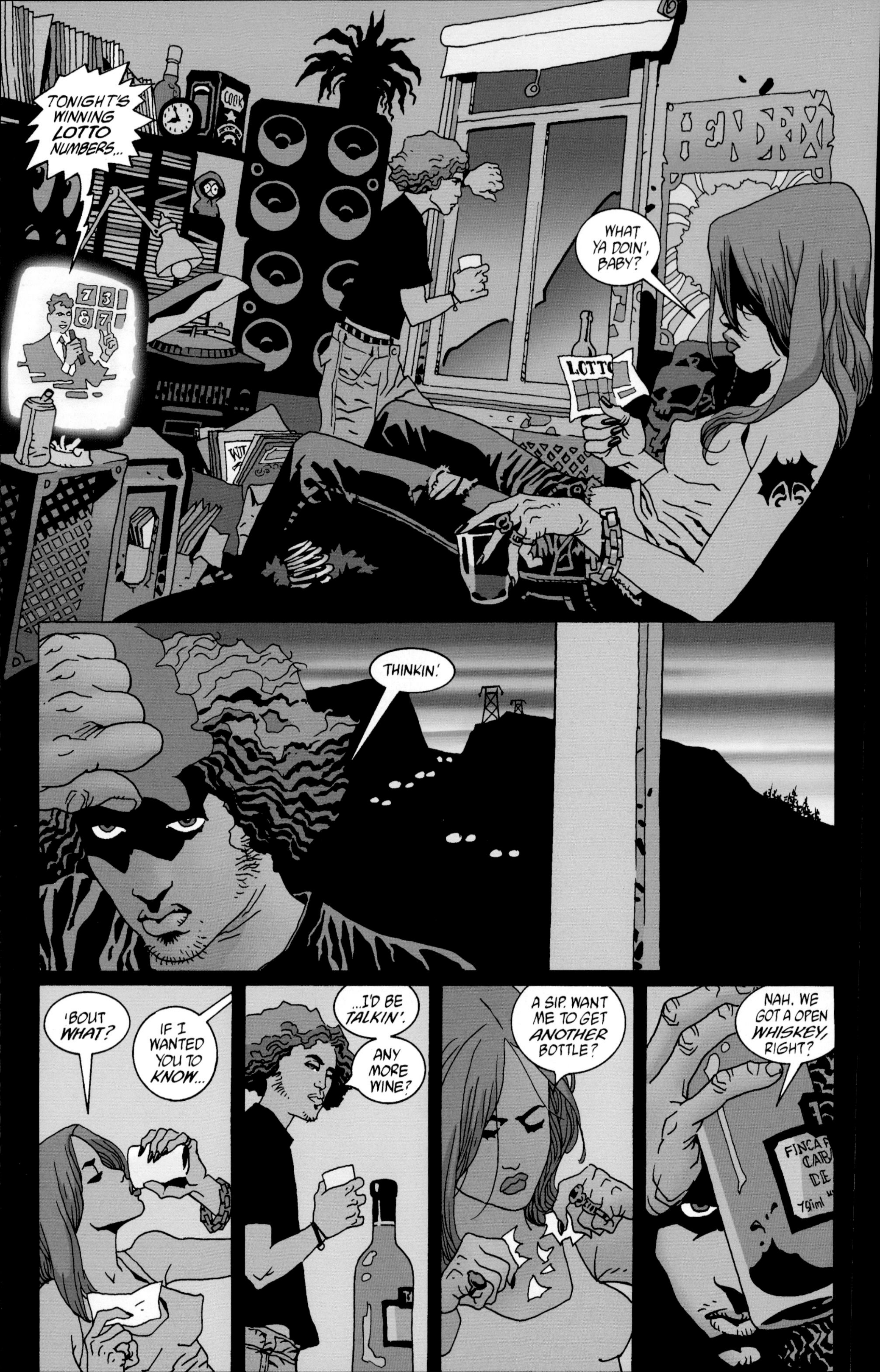
TONIGHT'S WINNING LOTTO NUMBERS...
WHAT YA DOIN', BABY?
LOTTO
THINKIN'.
'BOUT WHAT?
IF I WANTED YOU TO KNOW...
...I'D BE TALKIN'.
ANY MORE WINE?
A SIP. WANT ME TO GET ANOTHER BOTTLE?
NAH. WE GOT A OPEN WHISKEY, RIGHT?

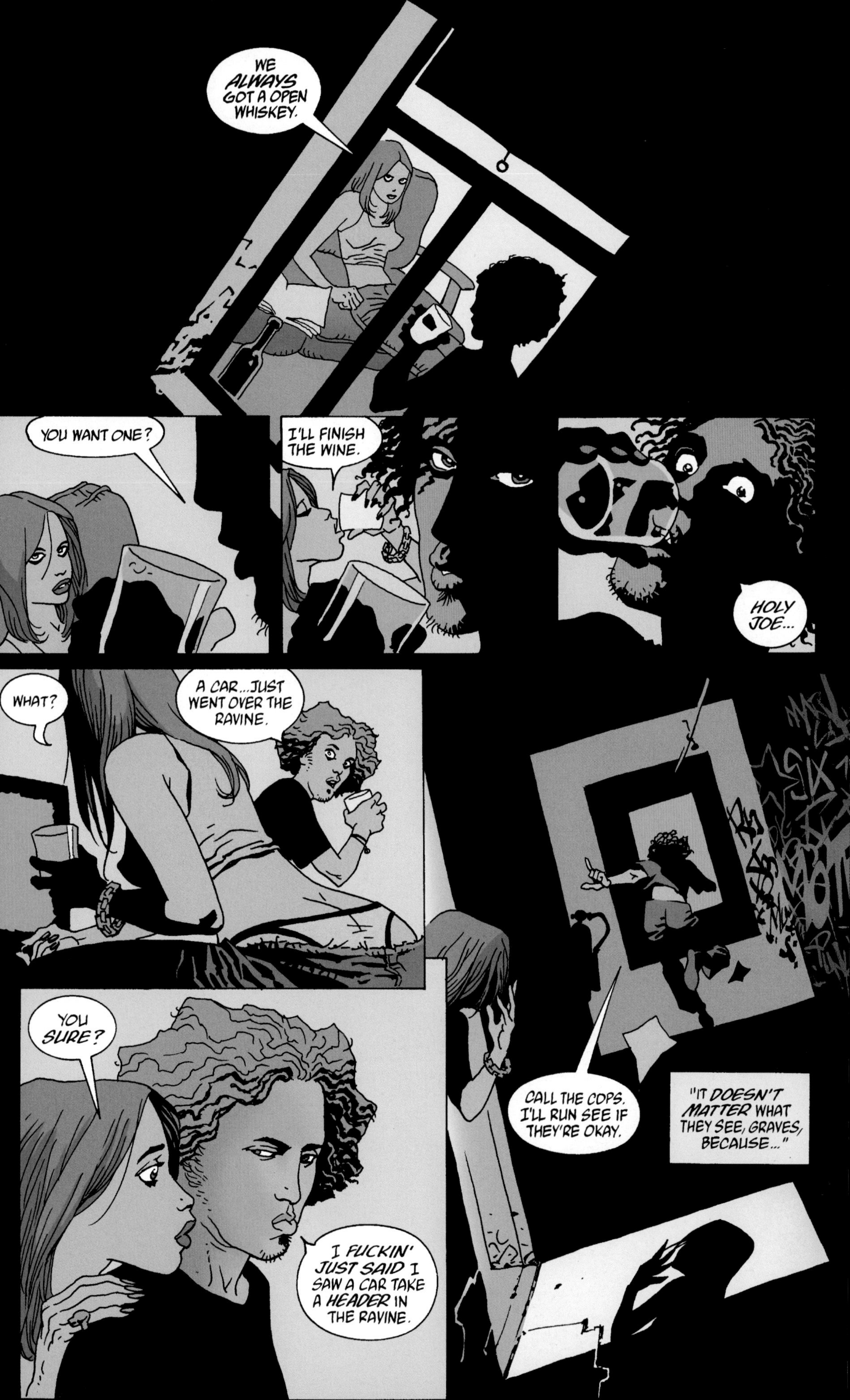
WE ALWAYS GOT A OPEN WHISKEY.
YOU WANT ONE?
I'LL FINISH THE WINE.
HOLY JOE...
WHAT?
A CAR...JUST WENT OVER THE RAVINE.
YOU SURE?
I FUCKIN' JUST SAID I SAW A CAR TAKE A HEADER IN THE RAVINE.
CALL THE COPS. I'LL RUN SEE IF THEY'RE OKAY.
"IT DOESN'T MATTER WHAT THEY SEE, GRAVES, BECAUSE..."

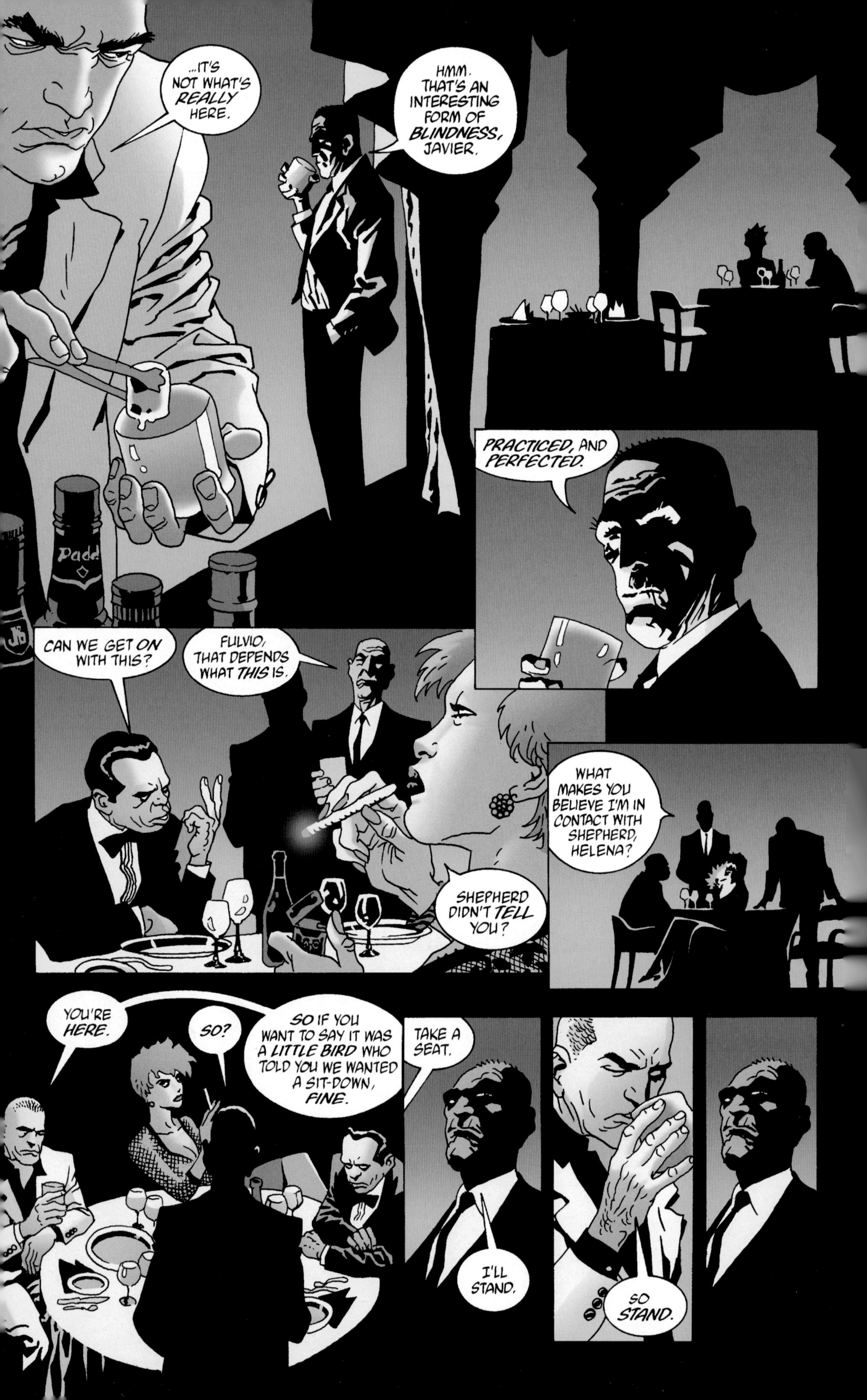
...IT'S NOT WHAT'S REALLY HERE.
HMM. THAT'S AN INTERESTING FORM OF BLINDNESS, JAVIER.
PRACTICED, AND PERFECTED.
CAN WE GET ON WITH THIS?
FULVIO, THAT DEPENDS WHAT THIS IS.
WHAT MAKES YOU BELIEVE I'M IN CONTACT WITH SHEPHERD, HELENA?
SHEPHERD DIDN'T TELL YOU?
YOU'RE HERE.
SO?
SO IF YOU WANT TO SAY IT WAS A LITTLE BIRD WHO TOLD YOU WE WANTED A SIT-DOWN, FINE.
TAKE A SEAT.
I'LL STAND.
SO STAND.

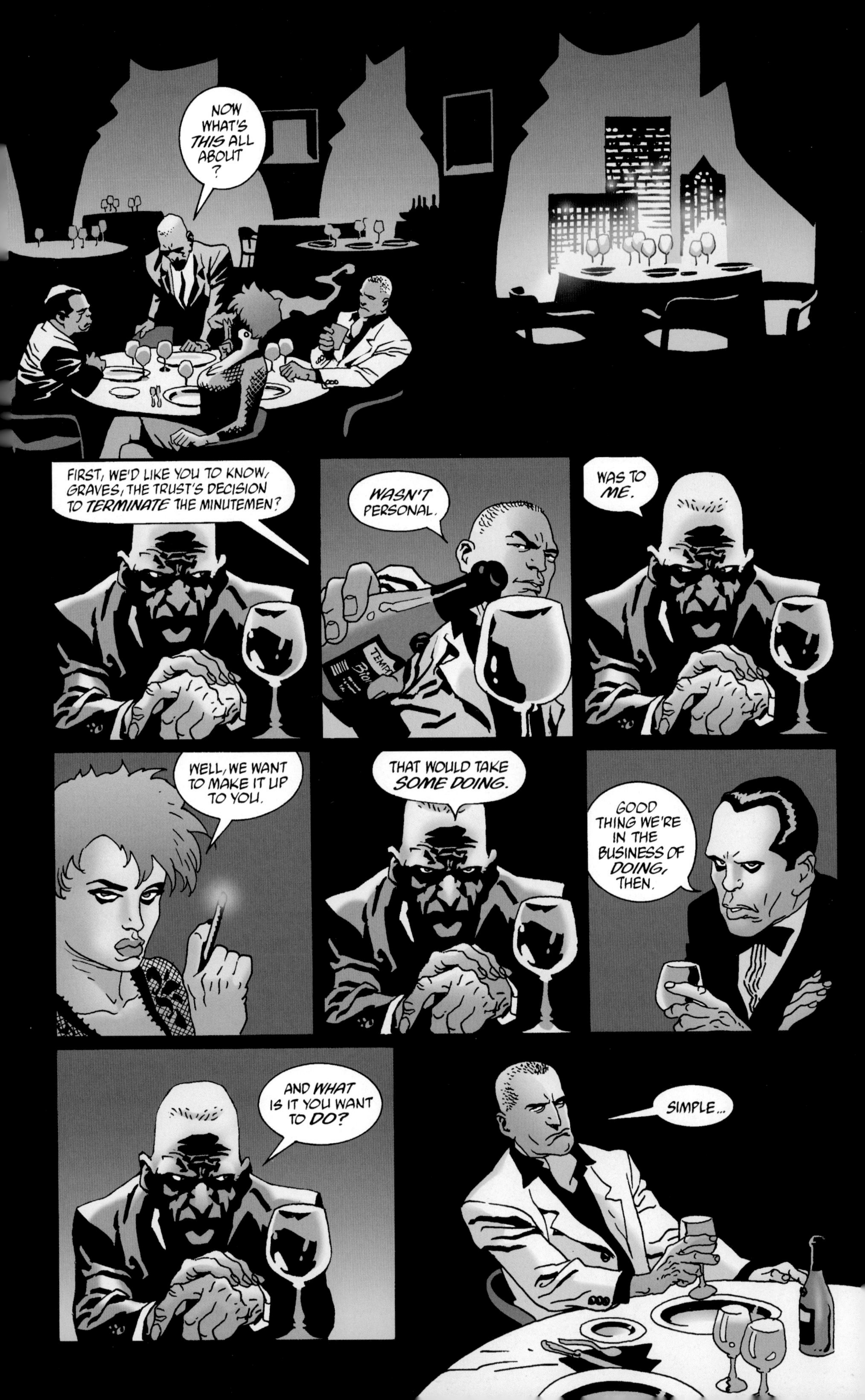
NOW WHAT'S THIS ALL ABOUT?
FIRST, WE'D LIKE YOU TO KNOW, GRAVES, THE TRUST'S DECISION TO TERMINATE THE MINUTEMEN?
WASN'T PERSONAL.
WAS TO ME.
WELL, WE WANT TO MAKE IT UP TO YOU.
THAT WOULD TAKE SOME DOING.
GOOD THING WE'RE IN THE BUSINESS OF DOING, THEN.
AND WHAT IS IT YOU WANT TO DO?
SIMPLE...

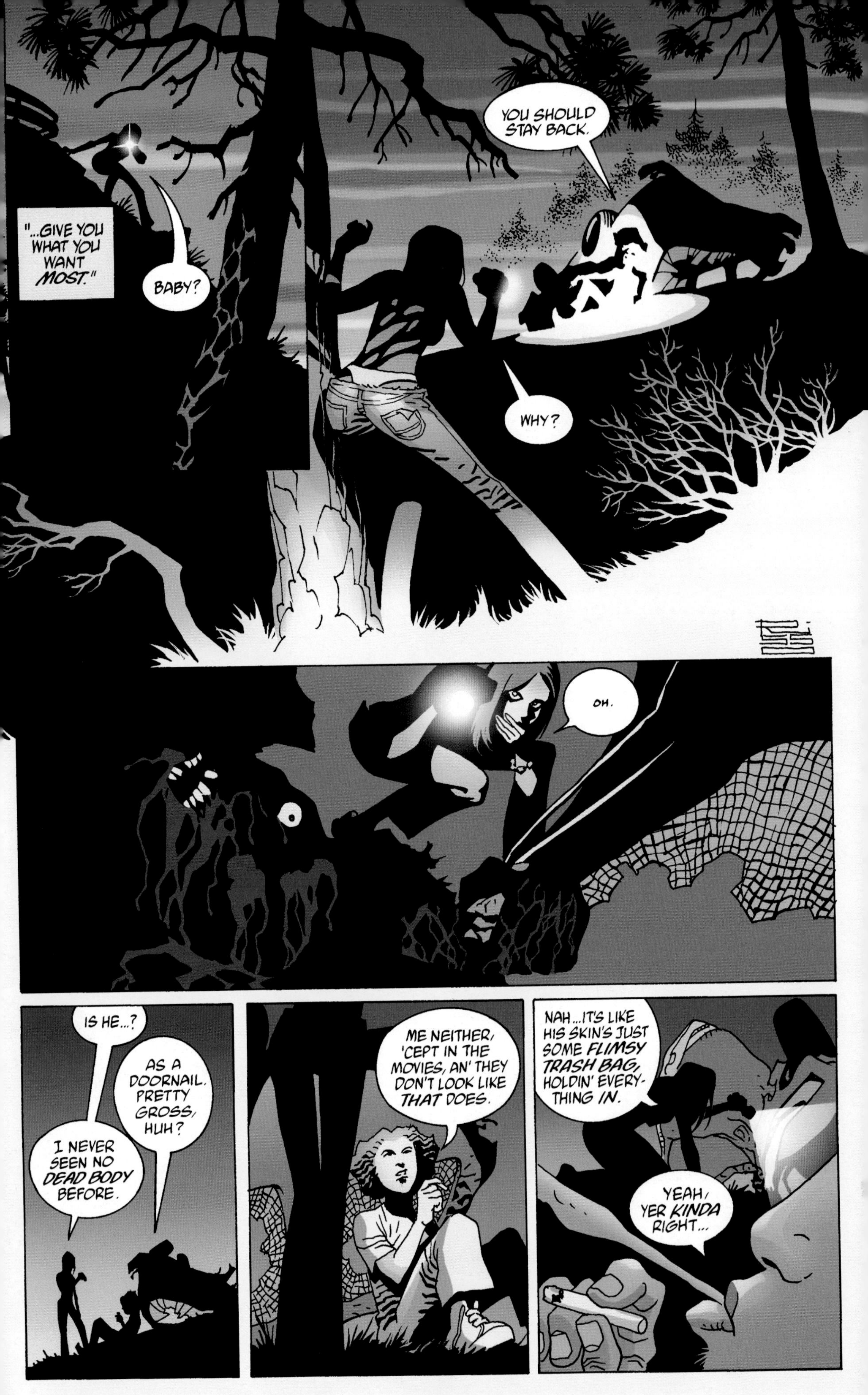
"...GIVE YOU WHAT YOU WANT MOST."
BABY?
YOU SHOULD STAY BACK.
WHY?
OH.
IS HE...?
AS A DOORNAIL. PRETTY GROSS, HUH?
I NEVER SEEN NO DEAD BODY BEFORE.
ME NEITHER, 'CEPT IN THE MOVIES, AN' THEY DON'T LOOK LIKE THAT DOES.
NAH...IT'S LIKE HIS SKIN'S JUST SOME FLIMSY TRASH BAG, HOLDIN' EVERY-THING IN.
YEAH, YER KINDA RIGHT...

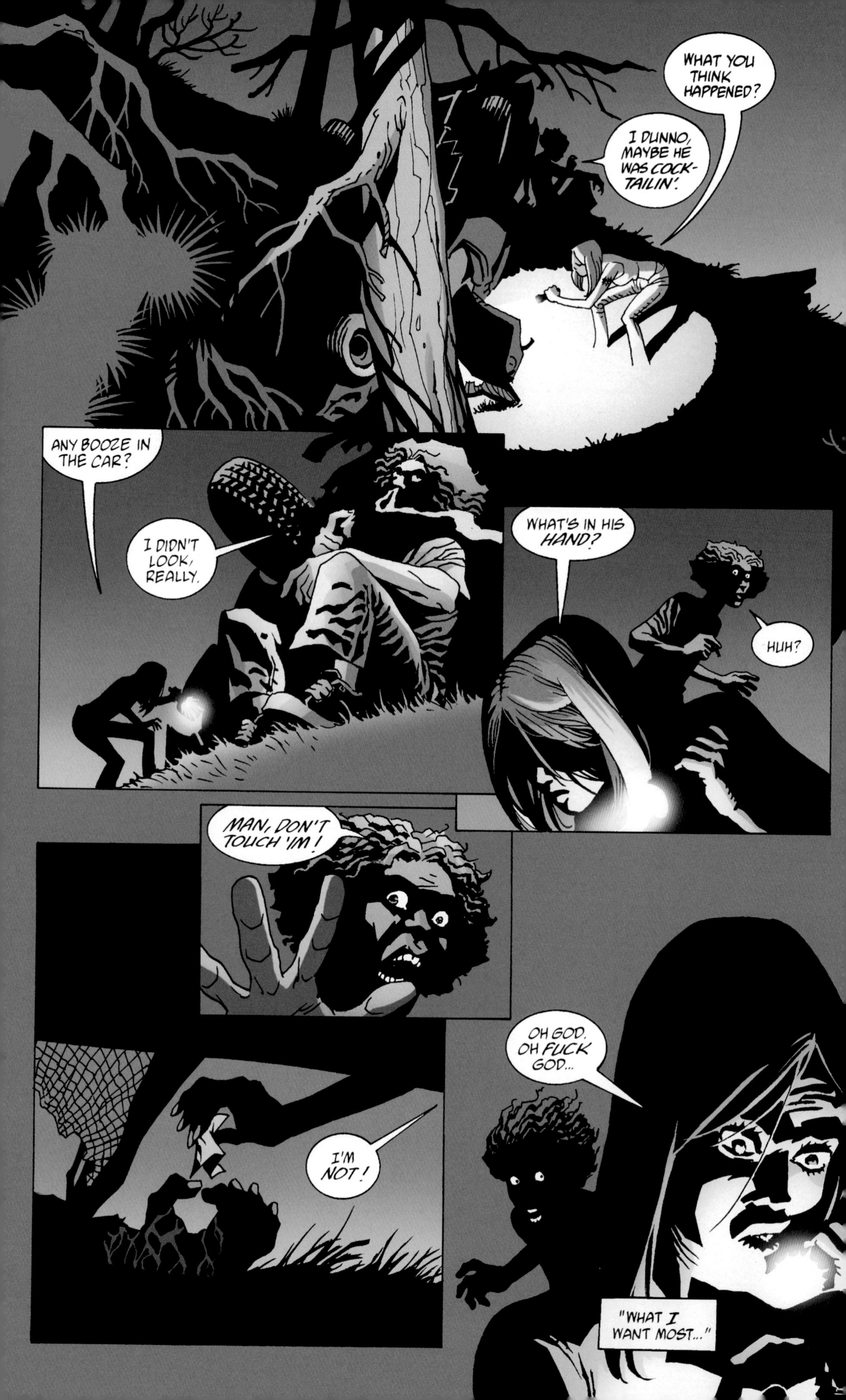
WHAT YOU THINK HAPPENED?
I DUNNO, MAYBE HE WAS COCK-TAILIN'.
ANY BOOZE IN THE CAR?
I DIDN'T LOOK, REALLY.
WHAT'S IN HIS HAND?
HUH?
MAN, DON'T TOUCH 'IM!
I'M NOT!
OH GOD. OH FUCK GOD...
"WHAT I WANT MOST..."

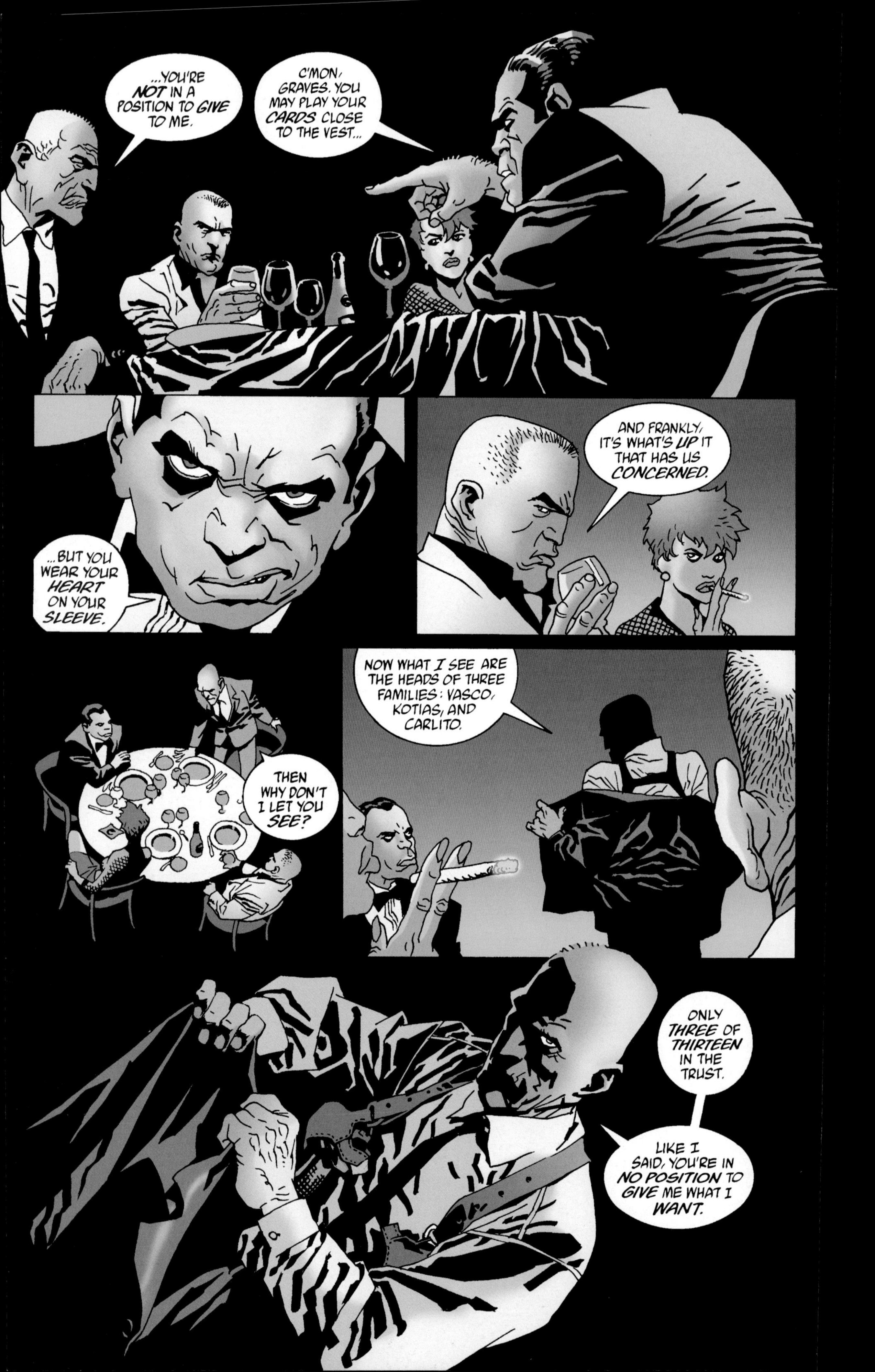
...YOU'RE NOT IN A POSITION TO GIVE TO ME.
C'MON, GRAVES. YOU MAY PLAY YOUR CARDS CLOSE TO THE VEST...
...BUT YOU WEAR YOUR HEART ON YOUR SLEEVE.
AND FRANKLY, IT'S WHAT'S UP IT THAT HAS US CONCERNED.
THEN WHY DON'T I LET YOU SEE?
NOW WHAT I SEE ARE THE HEADS OF THREE FAMILIES: VASCO, KOTIAS, AND CARLITO.
ONLY THREE OF THIRTEEN IN THE TRUST.
LIKE I SAID, YOU'RE IN NO POSITION TO GIVE ME WHAT I WANT.

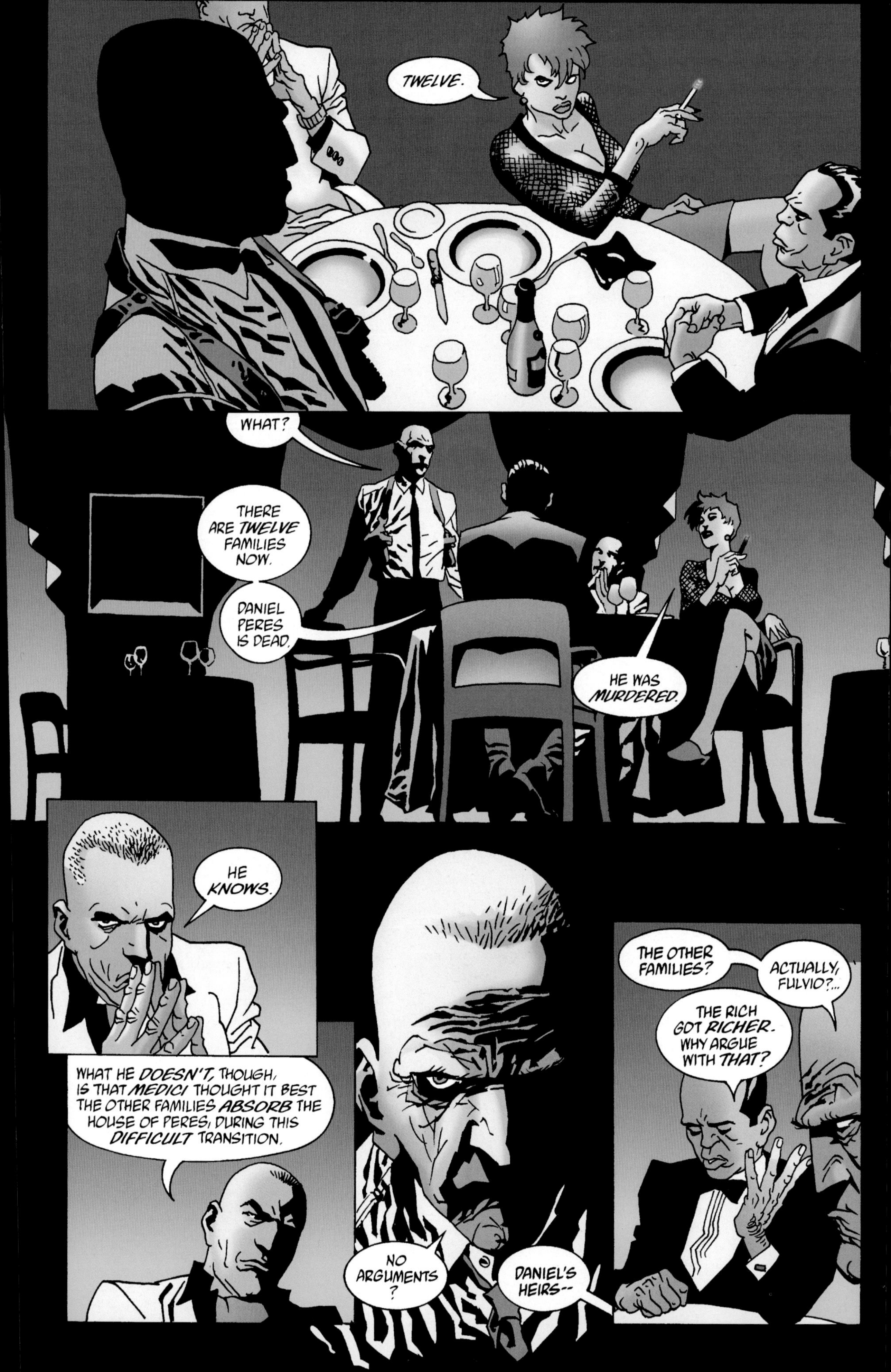
TWELVE.
WHAT?
THERE ARE TWELVE FAMILIES NOW.
DANIEL PERES IS DEAD.
HE WAS MURDERED.
HE KNOWS.
WHAT HE DOESN'T, THOUGH, IS THAT MEDICI THOUGHT IT BEST THE OTHER FAMILIES ABSORB THE HOUSE OF PERES, DURING THIS DIFFICULT TRANSITION.
NO ARGUMENTS?
DANIEL'S HEIRS--
THE OTHER FAMILIES?
ACTUALLY, FULVIO?...
THE RICH GOT RICHER- WHY ARGUE WITH THAT?

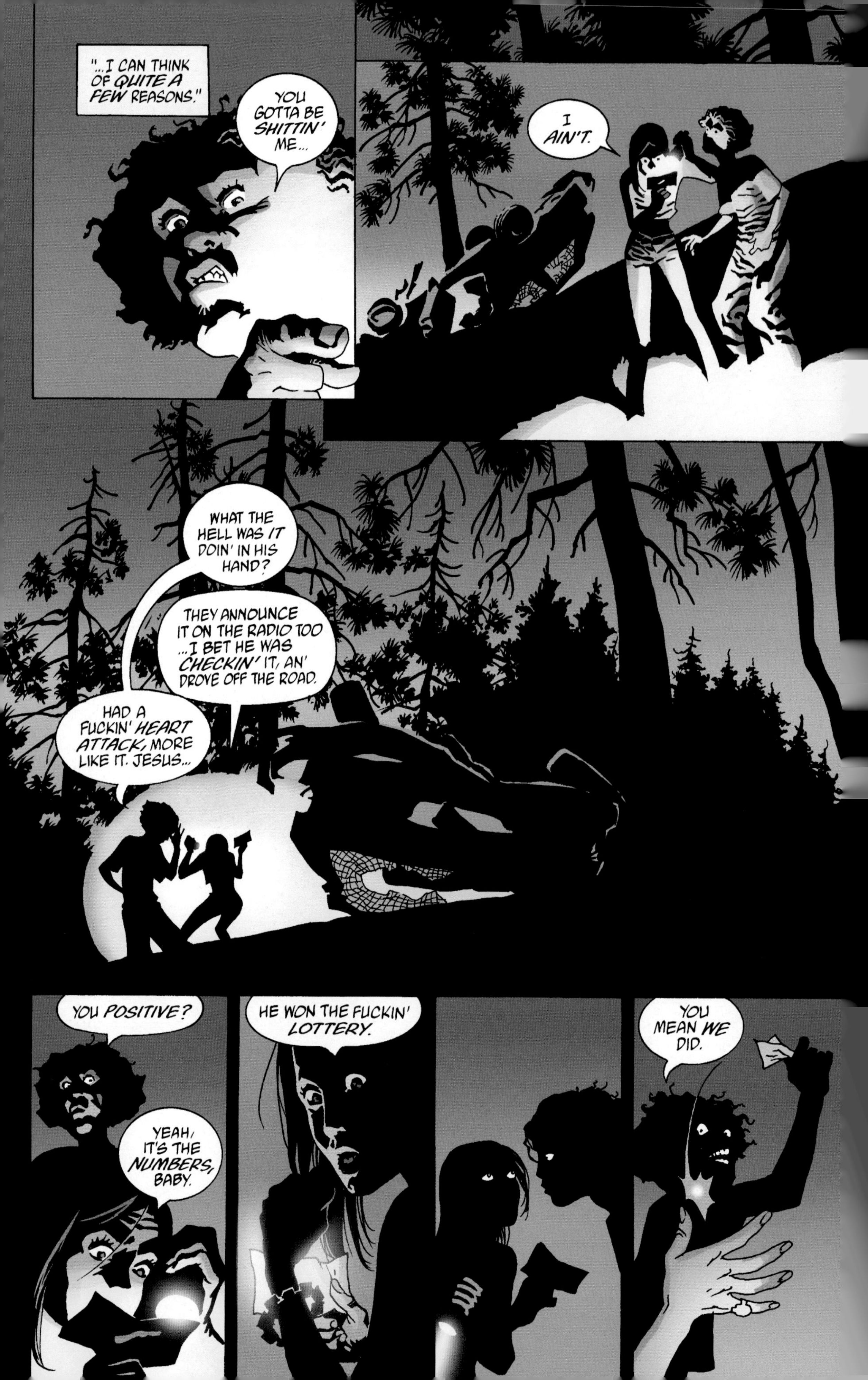

"...I CAN THINK OF QUITE A FEW REASONS."
YOU GOTTA BE SHITTIN' ME...
I AIN'T.
WHAT THE HELL WAS IT DOIN' IN HIS HAND?
THEY ANNOUNCE IT ON THE RADIO TOO ...I BET HE WAS CHECKIN' IT, AN' DROVE OFF THE ROAD.
HAD A FUCKIN' HEART ATTACK, MORE LIKE IT. JESUS...
YOU POSITIVE?
YEAH, IT'S THE NUMBERS, BABY.
HE WON THE FUCKIN' LOTTERY.
YOU MEAN WE DID.

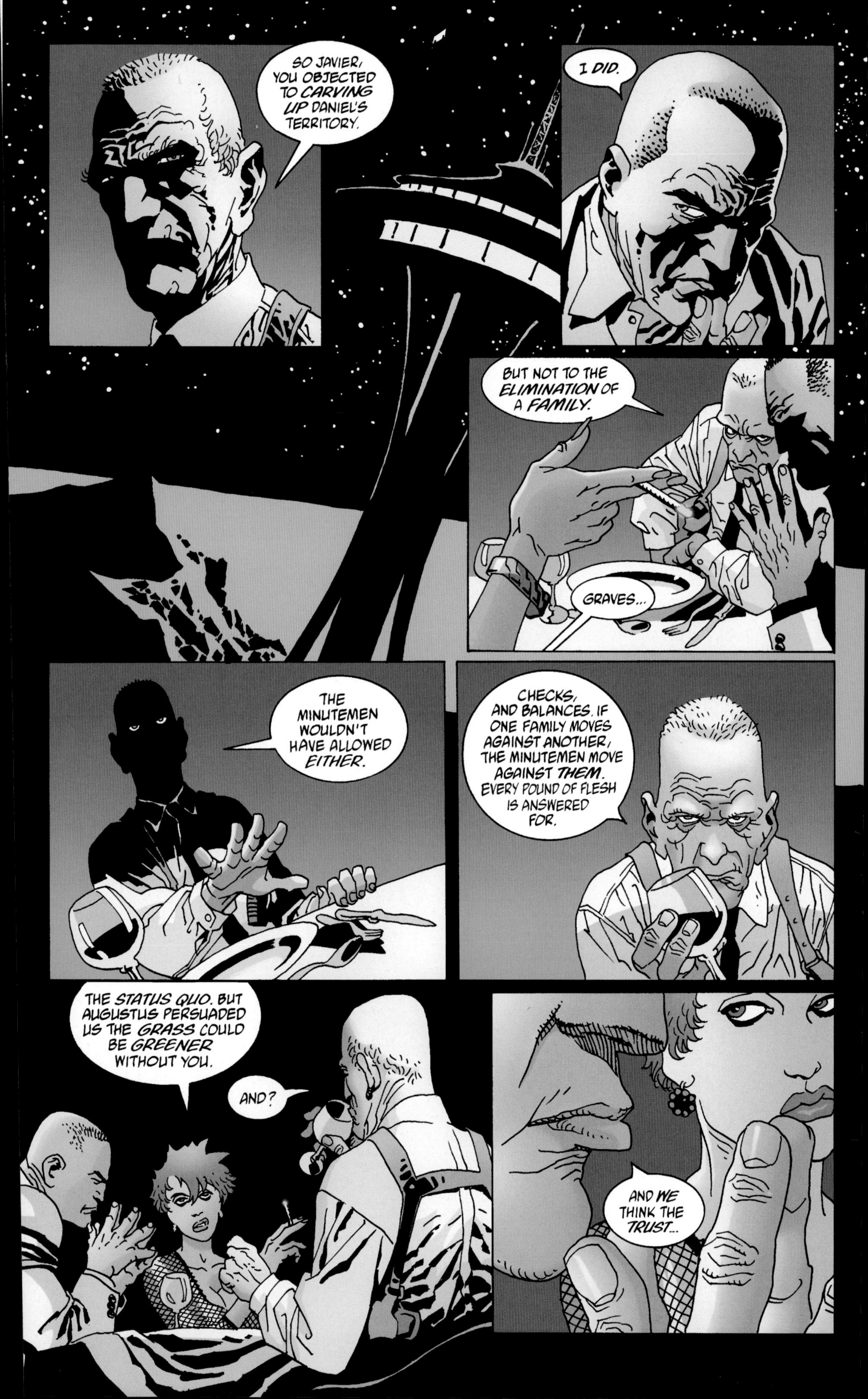
SO JAVIER, YOU OBJECTED TO CARVING UP DANIEL'S TERRITORY.
I DID.
BUT NOT TO THE ELIMINATION OF A FAMILY.
GRAVES...
THE MINUTEMEN WOULDN'T HAVE ALLOWED EITHER.
CHECKS, AND BALANCES. IF ONE FAMILY MOVES AGAINST ANOTHER, THE MINUTEMEN MOVE AGAINST THEM. EVERY POUND OF FLESH IS ANSWERED FOR.
THE STATUS QUO. BUT AUGUSTUS PERSUADED US THE GRASS COULD BE GREENER WITHOUT YOU.
AND?
AND WE THINK THE TRUST...

"...NEEDS SOME YARD WORK."

I CAN'T DO IT.

I CAN.

IT'S STEALING-- IT'S WRONG.

WHAT WRONG? WHAT THE FUCK'S A LOTTERY TICKET WORTH TO A CORPSE?

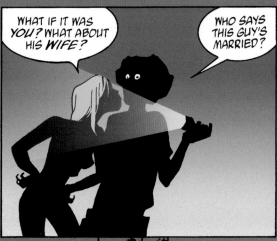

WHAT IF IT WAS YOU? WHAT ABOUT HIS WIFE?

WHO SAYS THIS GUY'S MARRIED?

YOU CARRY MY PICTURE IN YOUR WALLET, DON'CHA?

YEAH, SO?

FUCK.

OKAY.

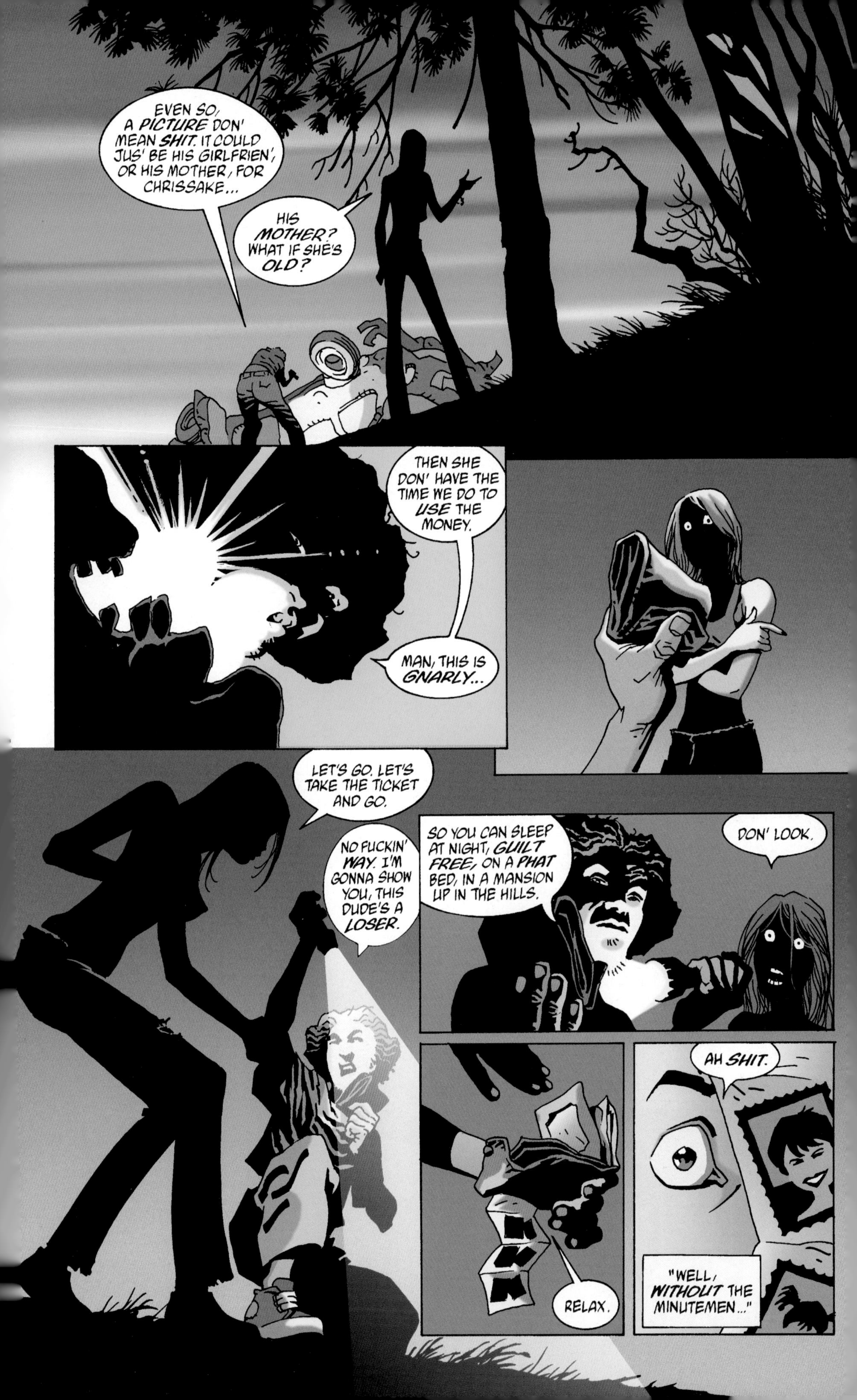
EVEN SO, A PICTURE DON' MEAN SHIT. IT COULD JUS' BE HIS GIRLFRIEN', OR HIS MOTHER, FOR CHRISSAKE...
HIS MOTHER? WHAT IF SHE'S OLD?
THEN SHE DON' HAVE THE TIME WE DO TO USE THE MONEY.
MAN, THIS IS GNARLY...
LET'S GO. LET'S TAKE THE TICKET AND GO.
NO FUCKIN' WAY. I'M GONNA SHOW YOU, THIS DUDE'S A LOSER.
SO YOU CAN SLEEP AT NIGHT, GUILT FREE, ON A PHAT BED, IN A MANSION UP IN THE HILLS.
DON' LOOK.
RELAX.
AH SHIT.
"WELL, WITHOUT THE MINUTEMEN..."

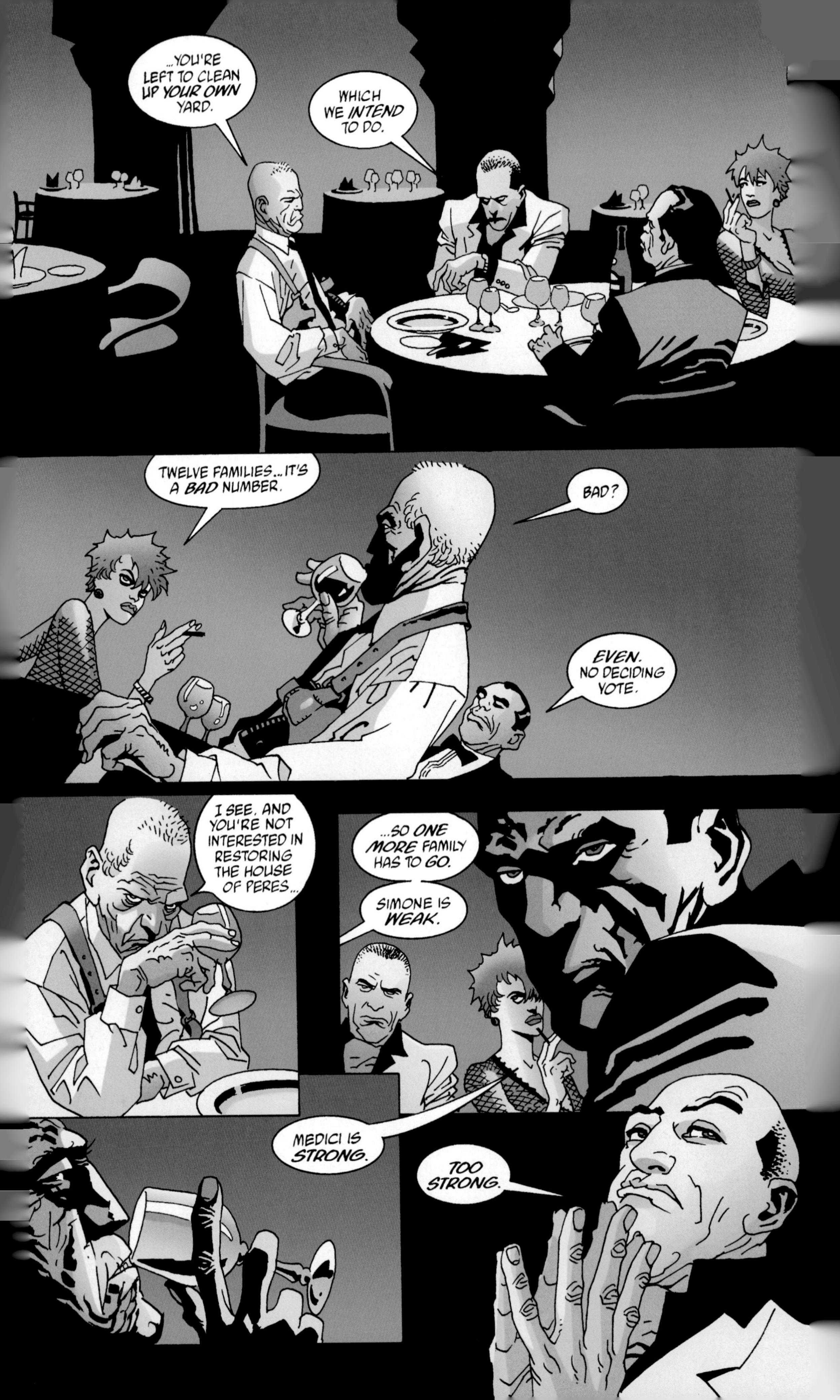
...YOU'RE LEFT TO CLEAN UP YOUR OWN YARD.
WHICH WE INTEND TO DO.
TWELVE FAMILIES... IT'S A BAD NUMBER.
BAD?
EVEN. NO DECIDING VOTE.
I SEE. AND YOU'RE NOT INTERESTED IN RESTORING THE HOUSE OF PERES...
...SO ONE MORE FAMILY HAS TO GO.
SIMONE IS WEAK.
MEDICI IS STRONG.
TOO STRONG.

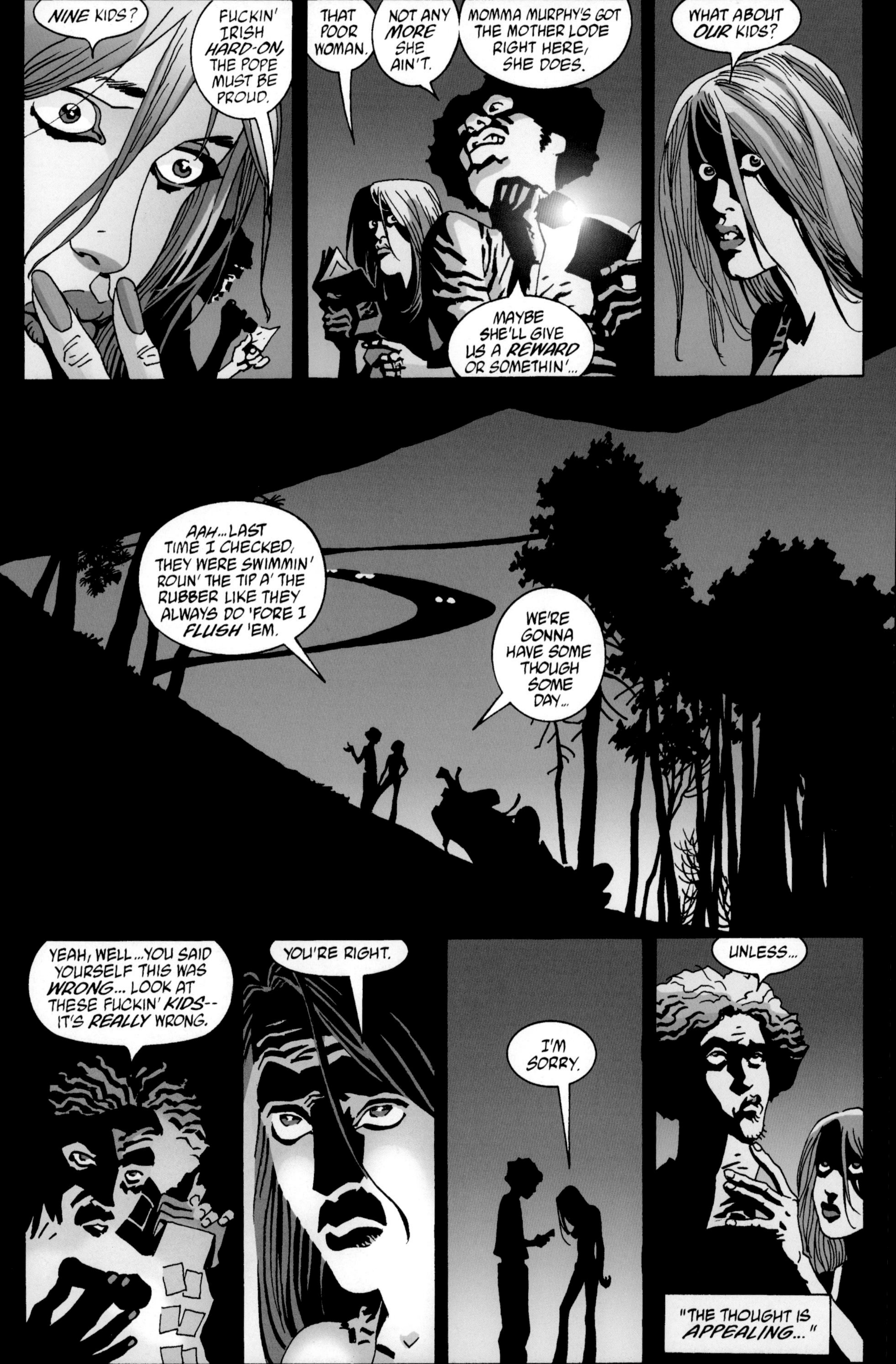

NINE KIDS?
FUCKIN' IRISH HARD-ON, THE POPE MUST BE PROUD.
THAT POOR WOMAN.
NOT ANY MORE SHE AIN'T.
MOMMA MURPHY'S GOT THE MOTHER LODE RIGHT HERE, SHE DOES.
MAYBE SHE'LL GIVE US A REWARD OR SOMETHIN'...
WHAT ABOUT OUR KIDS?
AAH... LAST TIME I CHECKED, THEY WERE SWIMMIN' ROUN' THE TIP A' THE RUBBER LIKE THEY ALWAYS DO 'FORE I FLUSH 'EM.
WE'RE GONNA HAVE SOME THOUGH SOME DAY...
YEAH, WELL... YOU SAID YOURSELF THIS WAS WRONG... LOOK AT THESE FUCKIN' KIDS-- IT'S REALLY WRONG.
YOU'RE RIGHT.
I'M SORRY.
UNLESS...
"THE THOUGHT IS APPEALING..."

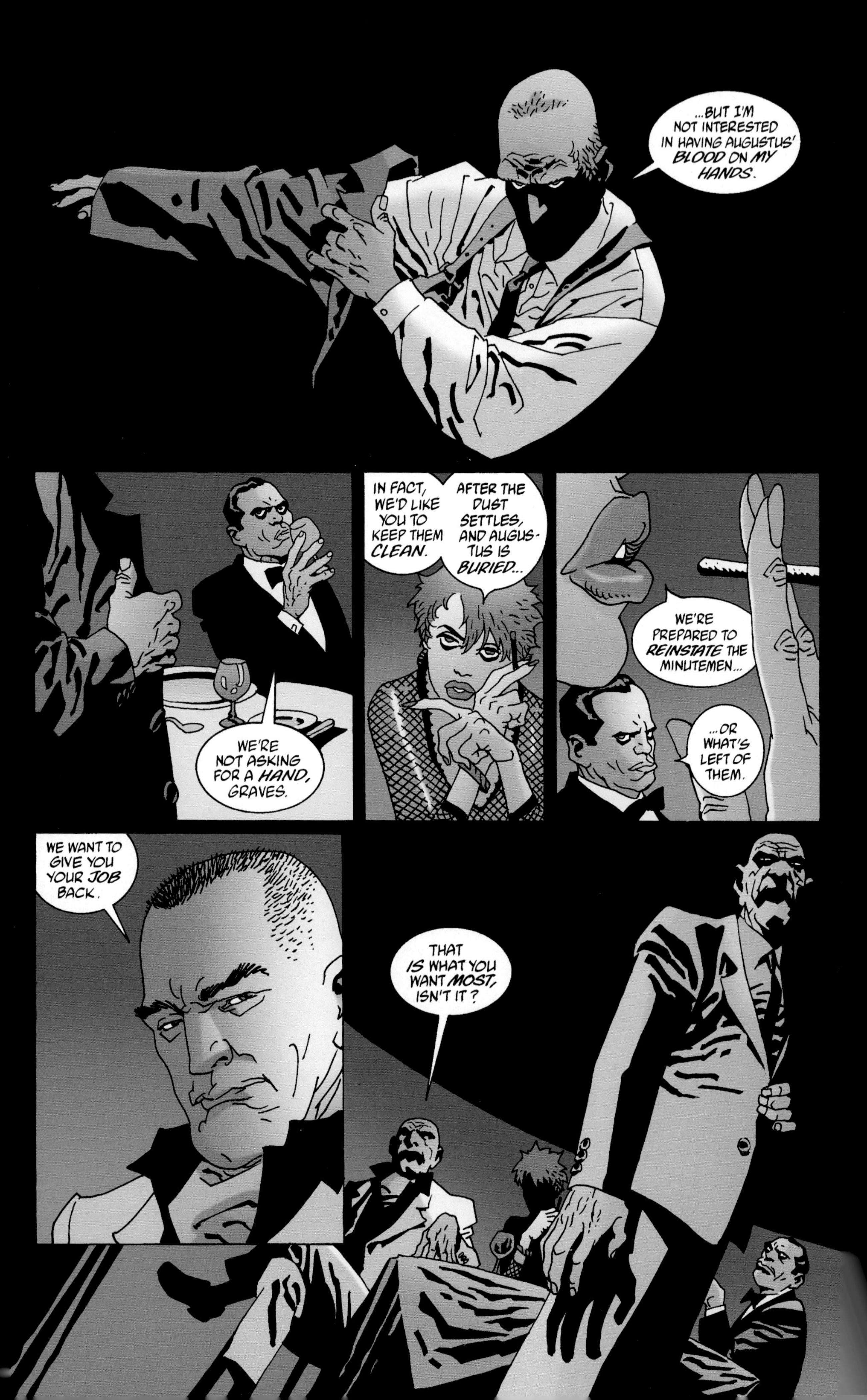
...BUT I'M NOT INTERESTED IN HAVING AUGUSTUS' BLOOD ON MY HANDS.
WE'RE NOT ASKING FOR A HAND, GRAVES.
IN FACT, WE'D LIKE YOU TO KEEP THEM CLEAN.
AFTER THE DUST SETTLES, AND AUGUSTUS IS BURIED...
WE'RE PREPARED TO REINSTATE THE MINUTEMEN...
...OR WHAT'S LEFT OF THEM.
WE WANT TO GIVE YOU YOUR JOB BACK.
THAT IS WHAT YOU WANT MOST, ISN'T IT?

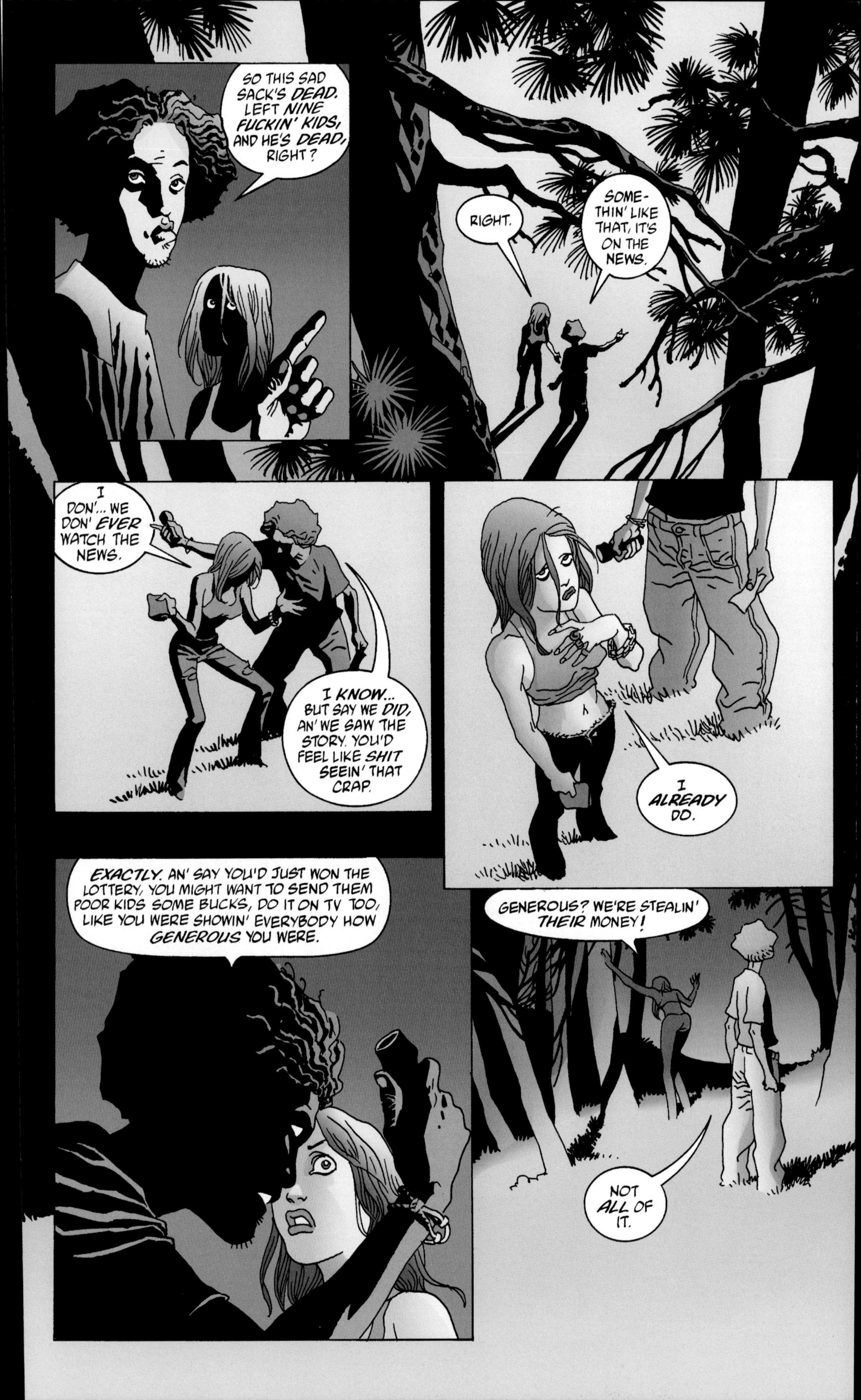
SO THIS SAD SACK'S DEAD. LEFT NINE FUCKIN' KIDS, AND HE'S DEAD, RIGHT?
RIGHT.
SOME-THIN' LIKE THAT, IT'S ON THE NEWS.
I DON'... WE DON' EVER WATCH THE NEWS.
I KNOW... BUT SAY WE DID, AN' WE SAW THE STORY. YOU'D FEEL LIKE SHIT SEEIN' THAT CRAP.
I ALREADY DO.
EXACTLY. AN' SAY YOU'D JUST WON THE LOTTERY, YOU MIGHT WANT TO SEND THEM POOR KIDS SOME BUCKS, DO IT ON TV TOO, LIKE YOU WERE SHOWIN' EVERYBODY HOW GENEROUS YOU WERE.
GENEROUS? WE'RE STEALIN' THEIR MONEY!
NOT ALL OF IT.

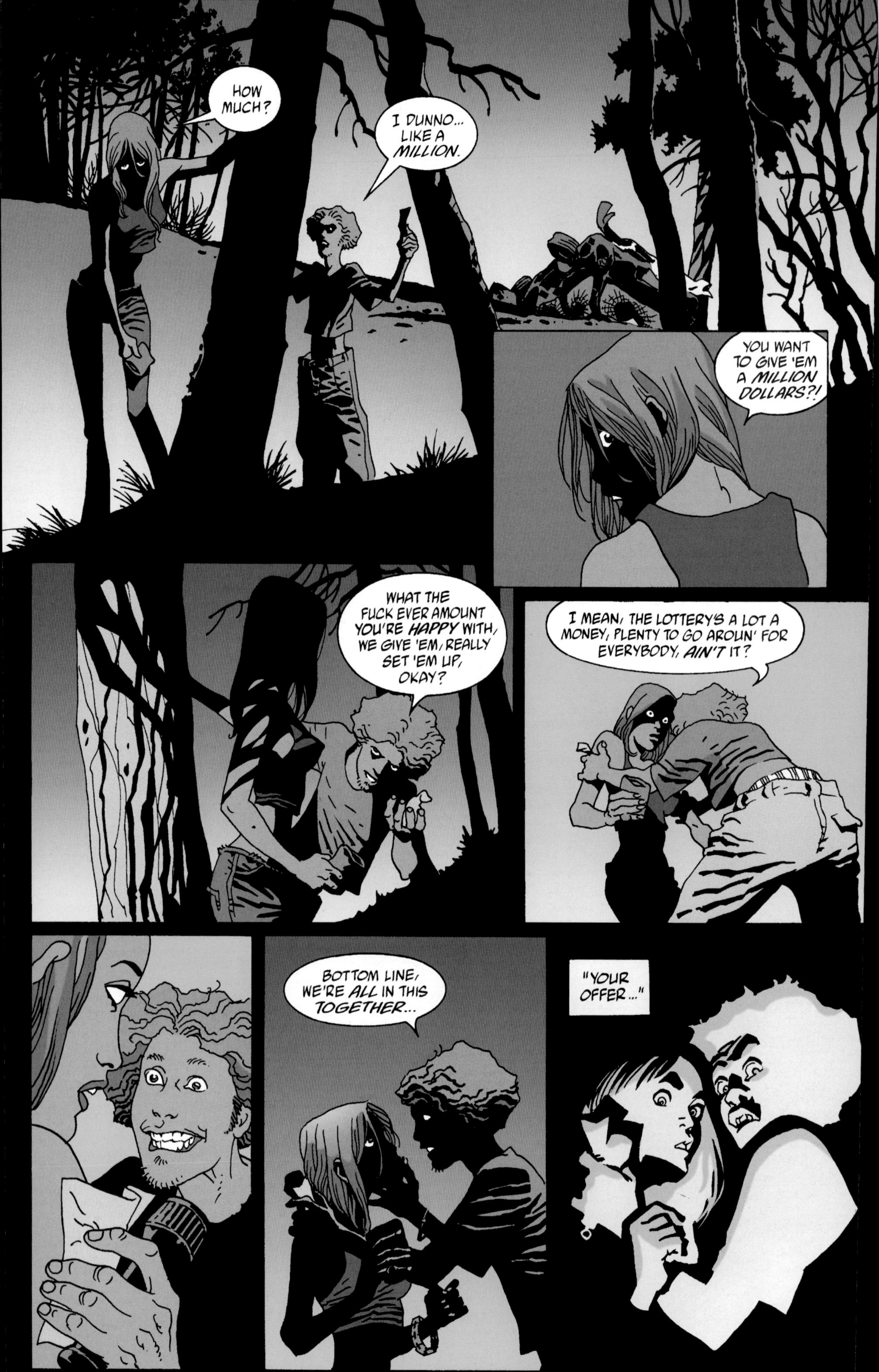
HOW MUCH?
I DUNNO... LIKE A MILLION.
YOU WANT TO GIVE 'EM A MILLION DOLLARS?!
WHAT THE FUCK EVER AMOUNT YOU'RE HAPPY WITH, WE GIVE 'EM, REALLY SET 'EM UP, OKAY?
I MEAN, THE LOTTERY'S A LOT A MONEY, PLENTY TO GO AROUN' FOR EVERYBODY, AIN'T IT?
BOTTOM LINE, WE'RE ALL IN THIS TOGETHER...
"YOUR OFFER..."

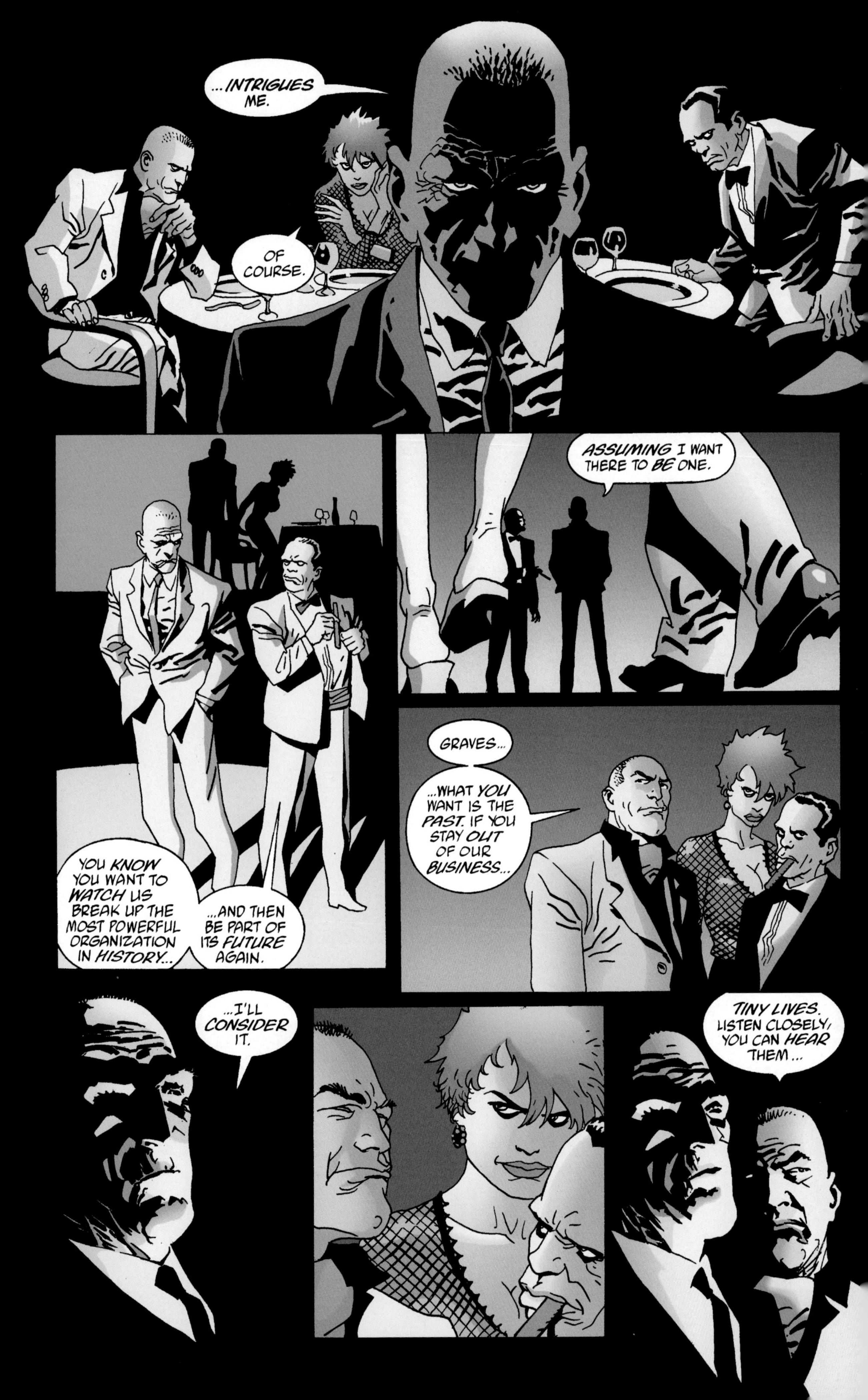
...INTRIGUES ME.
OF COURSE.
YOU KNOW YOU WANT TO WATCH US BREAK UP THE MOST POWERFUL ORGANIZATION IN HISTORY...
...AND THEN BE PART OF ITS FUTURE AGAIN.
ASSUMING I WANT THERE TO BE ONE.
GRAVES...
...WHAT YOU WANT IS THE PAST. IF YOU STAY OUT OF OUR BUSINESS...
...I'LL CONSIDER IT.
TINY LIVES. LISTEN CLOSELY, YOU CAN HEAR THEM ...

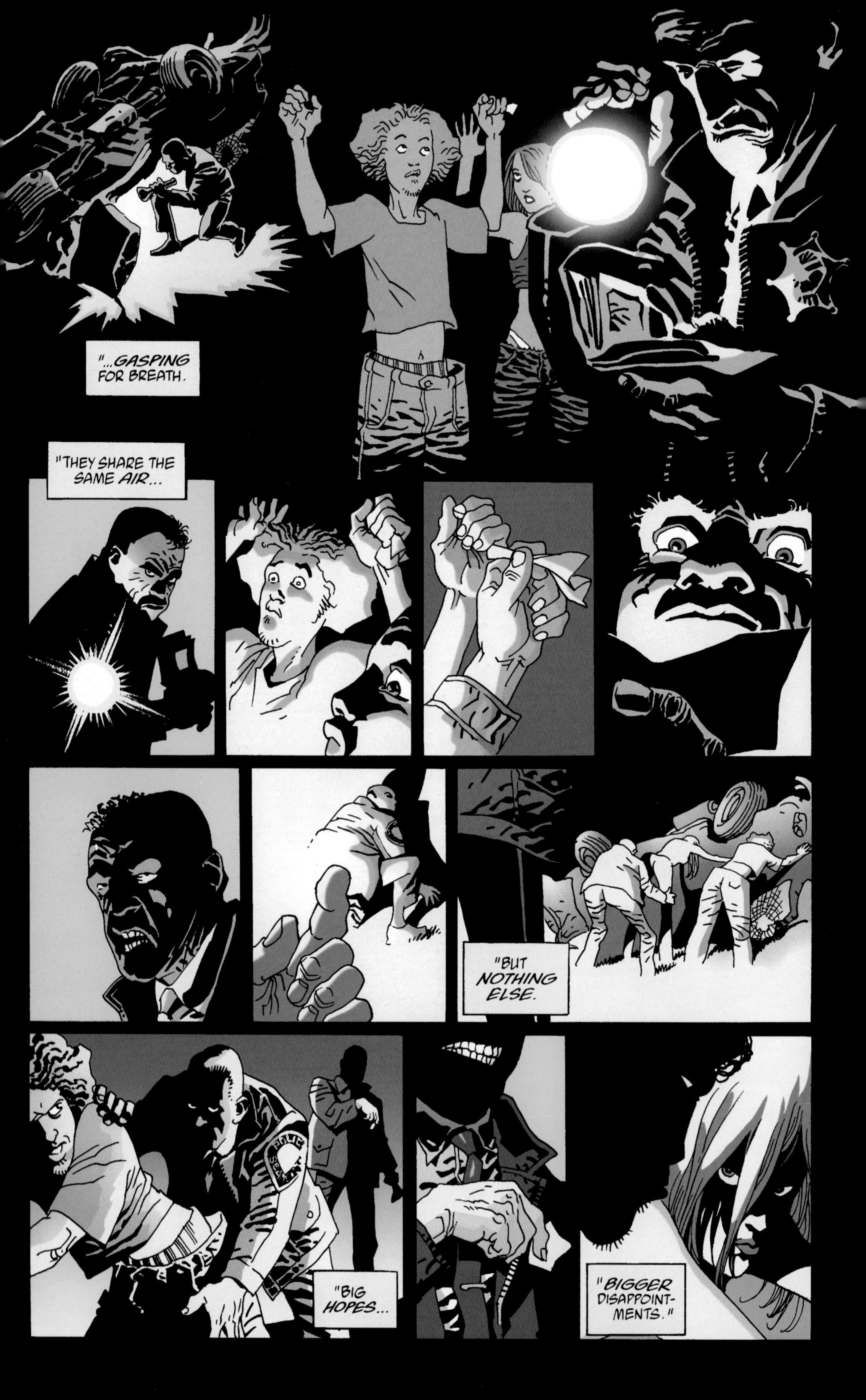
"...GASPING FOR BREATH.
"THEY SHARE THE SAME AIR...
"BUT NOTHING ELSE.
"BIG HOPES...
"BIGGER DISAPPOINT-MENTS."

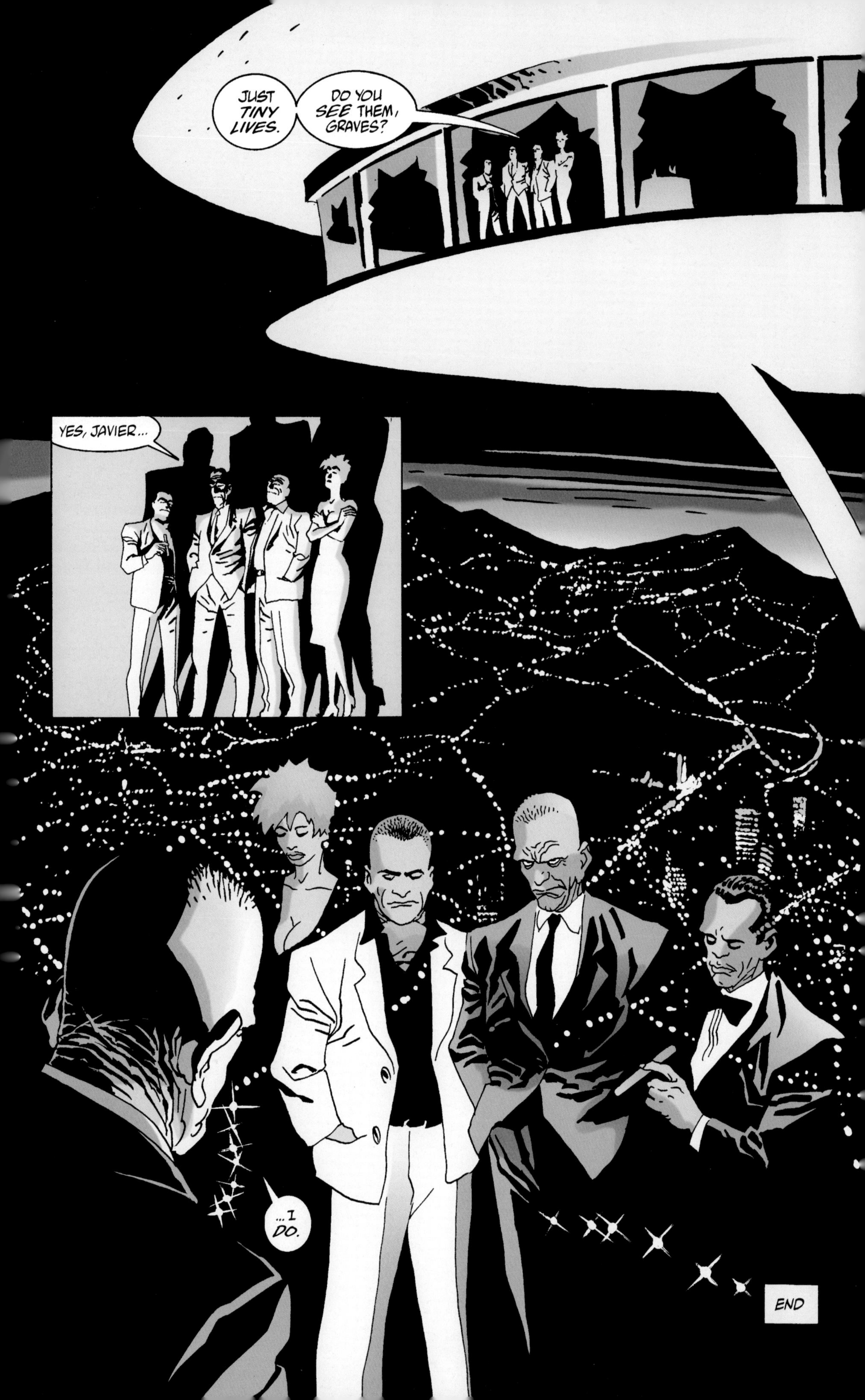
DO YOU SEE THEM, GRAVES?
JUST TINY LIVES.
YES, JAVIER...
...I DO.
END

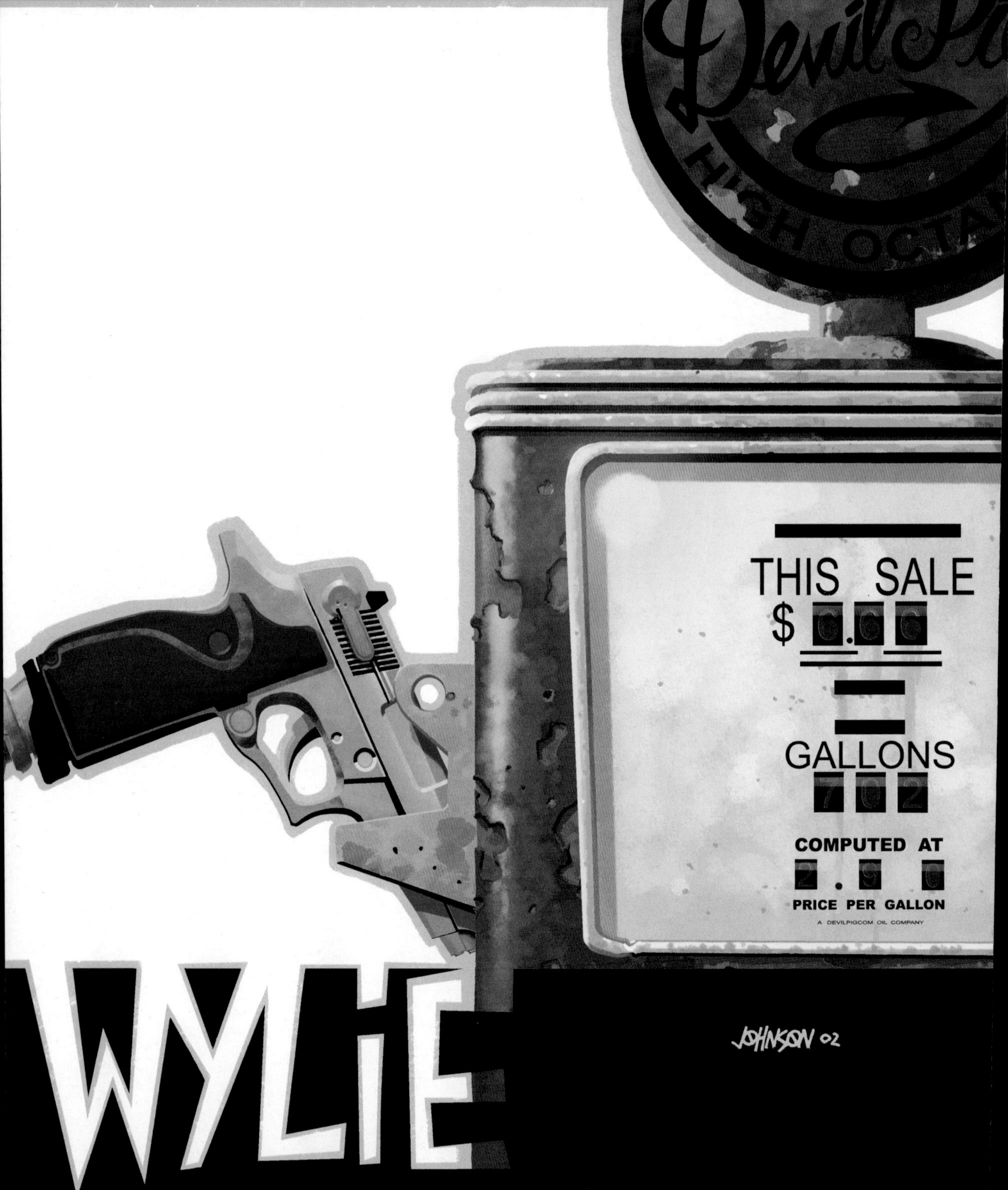
THIS SALE
$
GALLONS
COMPUTED AT
PRICE PER GALLON
A DEVILPIGCOM OIL COMPANY
WYLIE
JOHNSON 02

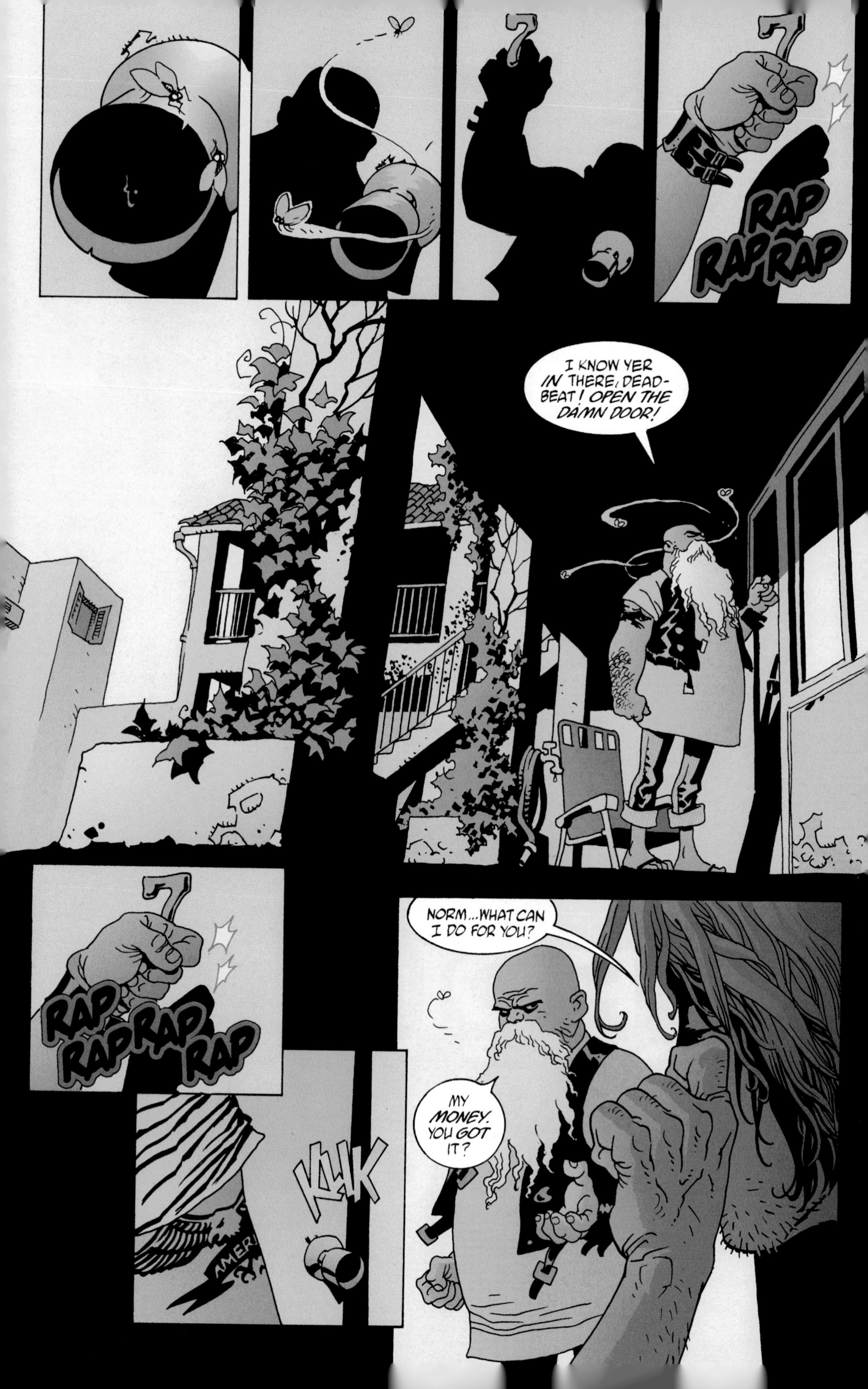
RAP
RAP RAP
I KNOW YER IN THERE, DEAD-BEAT! OPEN THE DAMN DOOR!
RAP RAP RAP RAP
KLIK
NORM...WHAT CAN I DO FOR YOU?
MY MONEY. YOU GOT IT?

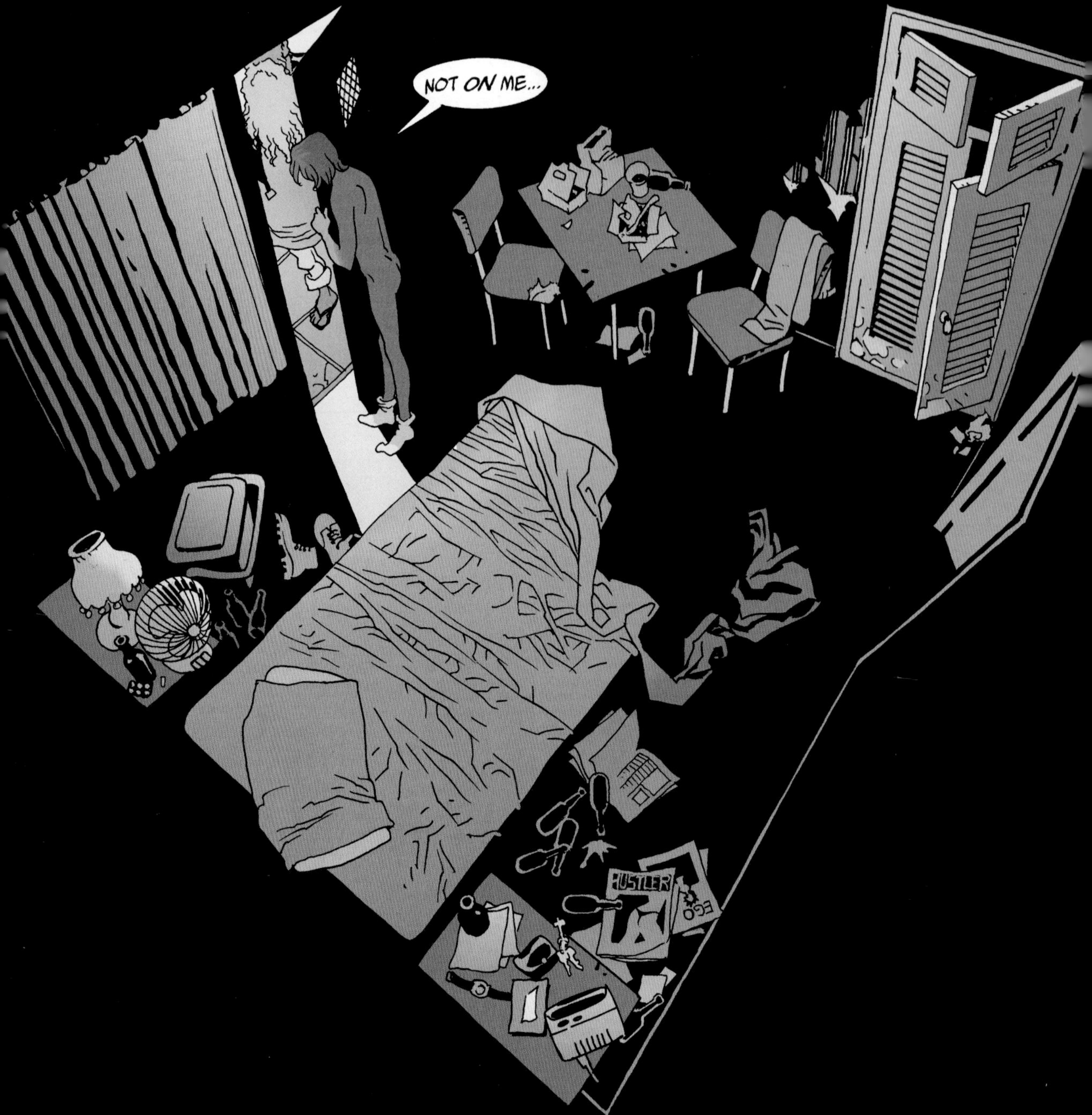
NOT ON ME...
HUSTLER

POINT OFF THE EDGE

BRIAN AZZARELLO
WRITER

EDUARDO RISSO
ARTIST

PATRICIA MULVIHILL
COLORIST

CLEM ROBINS
LETTERER

ZYLONOL
SEPARATIONS

DAVE JOHNSON
COVER

ZACHARY RAU
ASS'T ED

WILL DENNIS
EDITOR

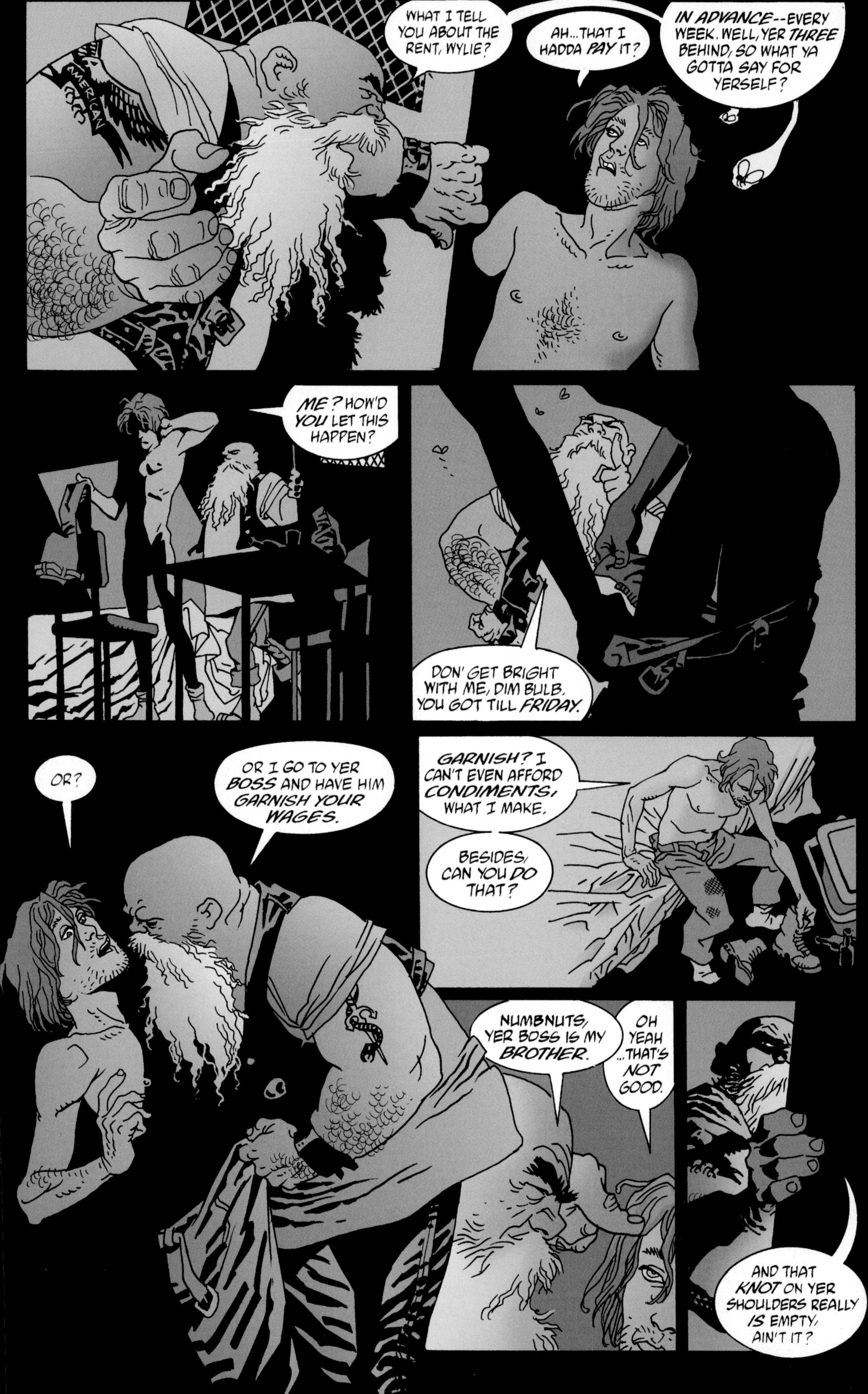

WHAT I TELL YOU ABOUT THE RENT, WYLIE?
AH...THAT I HADDA PAY IT?
IN ADVANCE--EVERY WEEK. WELL, YER THREE BEHIND, SO WHAT YA GOTTA SAY FOR YERSELF?
ME? HOW'D YOU LET THIS HAPPEN?
DON' GET BRIGHT WITH ME, DIM BULB. YOU GOT TILL FRIDAY.
OR?
OR I GO TO YER BOSS AND HAVE HIM GARNISH YOUR WAGES.
GARNISH? I CAN'T EVEN AFFORD CONDIMENTS, WHAT I MAKE.
BESIDES, CAN YOU DO THAT?
NUMBNUTS, YER BOSS IS MY BROTHER.
OH YEAH ...THAT'S NOT GOOD.
AND THAT KNOT ON YER SHOULDERS REALLY IS EMPTY, AIN'T IT?

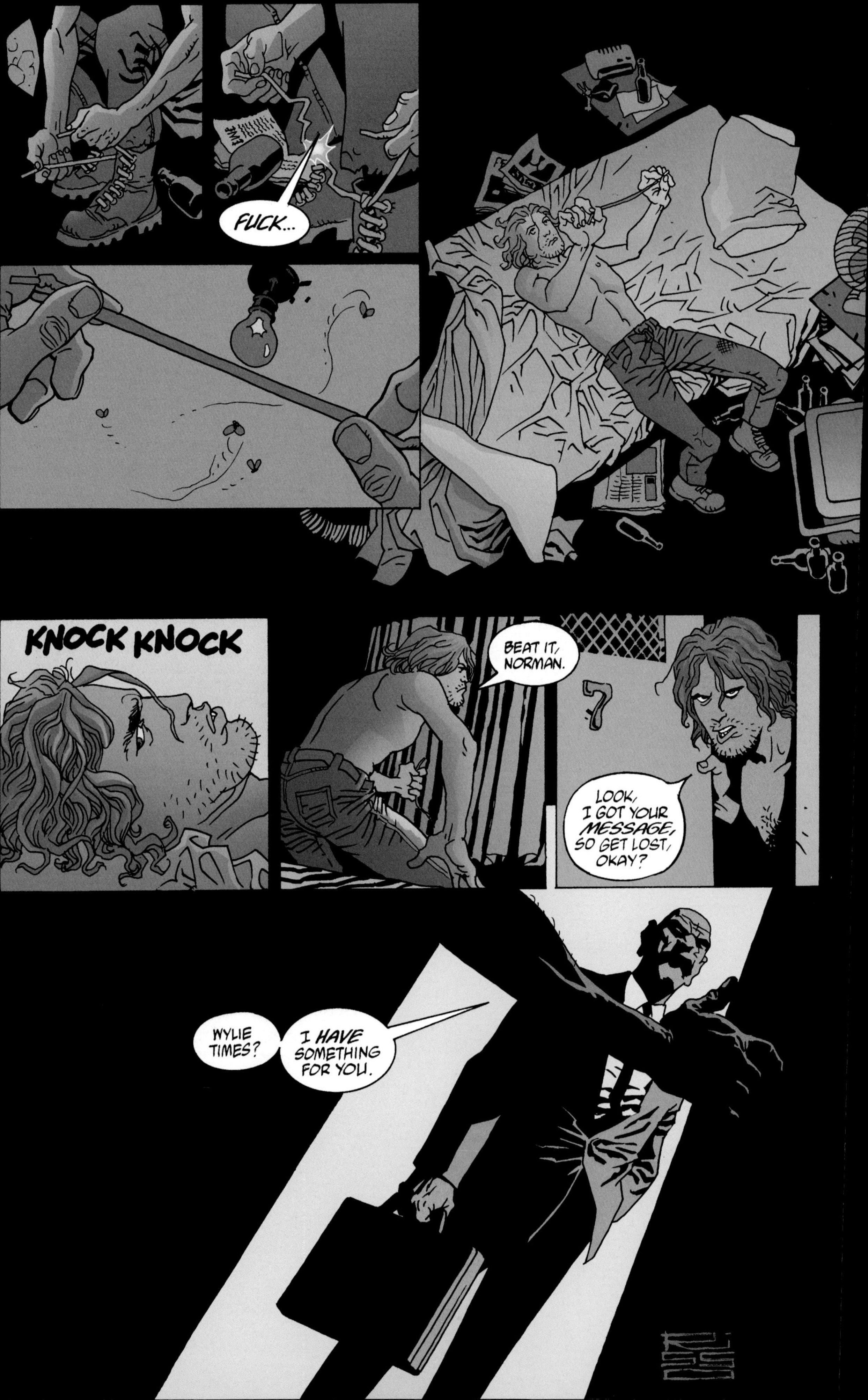
FUCK...
KNOCK KNOCK
BEAT IT, NORMAN.
LOOK, I GOT YOUR MESSAGE, SO GET LOST, OKAY?
WYLIE TIMES?
I HAVE SOMETHING FOR YOU.

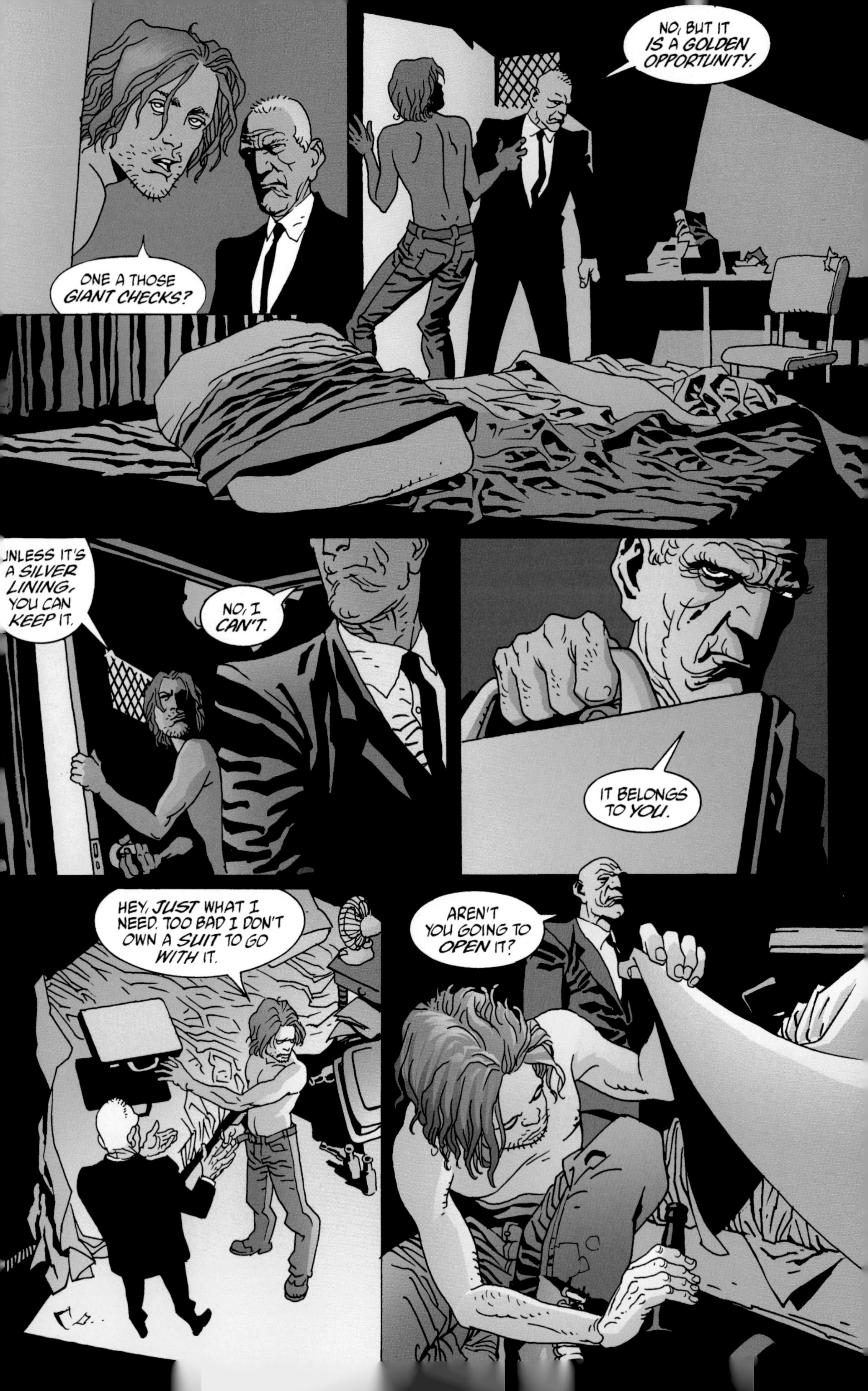
ONE A THOSE GIANT CHECKS?
NO, BUT IT IS A GOLDEN OPPORTUNITY.
UNLESS IT'S A SILVER LINING, YOU CAN KEEP IT.
NO, I CAN'T.
IT BELONGS TO YOU.
HEY, JUST WHAT I NEED. TOO BAD I DON'T OWN A SUIT TO GO WITH IT.
AREN'T YOU GOING TO OPEN IT?

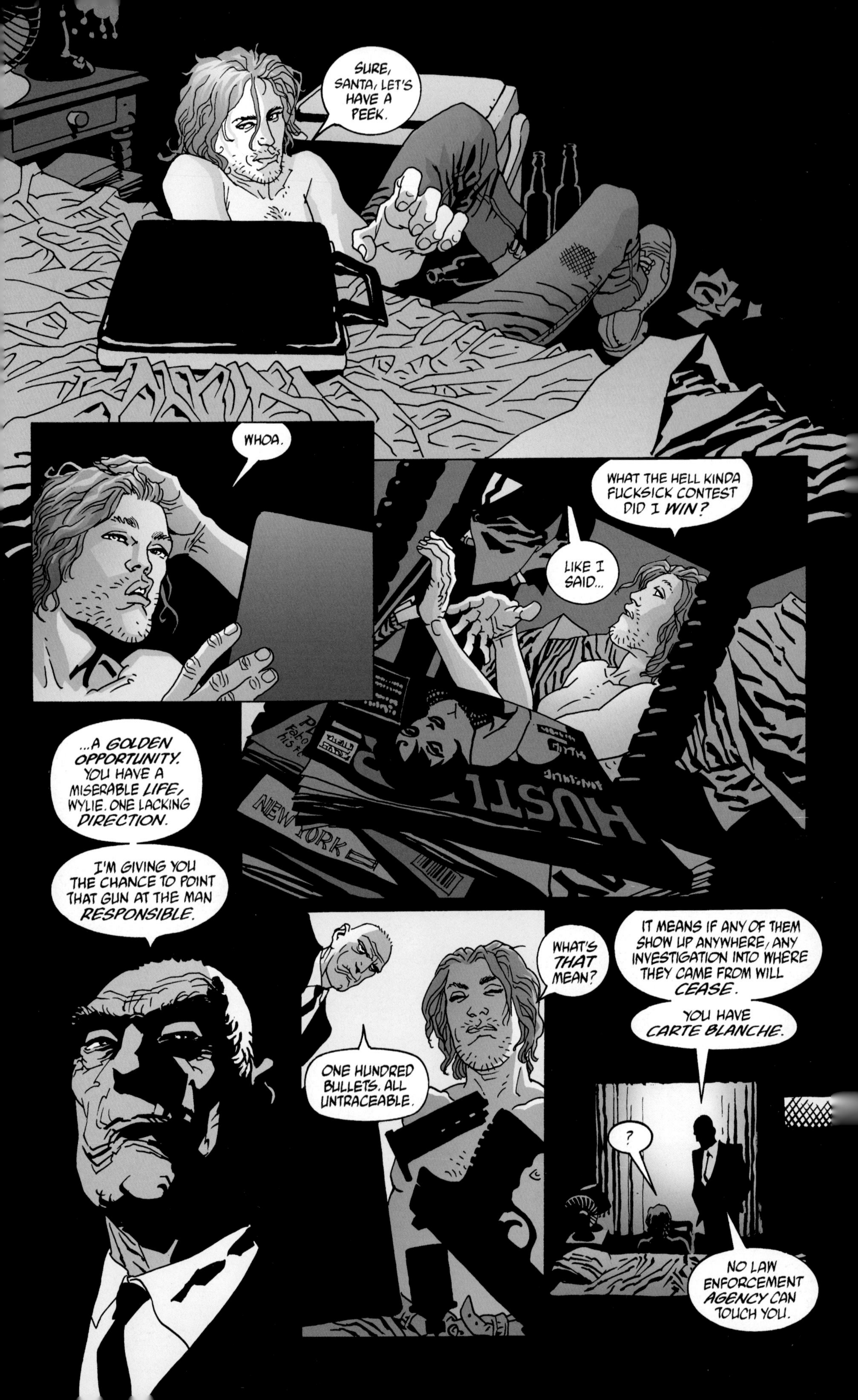
SURE, SANTA, LET'S HAVE A PEEK.
WHOA.
WHAT THE HELL KINDA FUCKSICK CONTEST DID I WIN?
LIKE I SAID...
...A GOLDEN OPPORTUNITY. YOU HAVE A MISERABLE LIFE, WYLIE. ONE LACKING DIRECTION.
I'M GIVING YOU THE CHANCE TO POINT THAT GUN AT THE MAN RESPONSIBLE.
ONE HUNDRED BULLETS. ALL UNTRACEABLE.
WHAT'S THAT MEAN?
IT MEANS IF ANY OF THEM SHOW UP ANYWHERE, ANY INVESTIGATION INTO WHERE THEY CAME FROM WILL CEASE.
YOU HAVE CARTE BLANCHE.
?
NO LAW ENFORCEMENT AGENCY CAN TOUCH YOU.

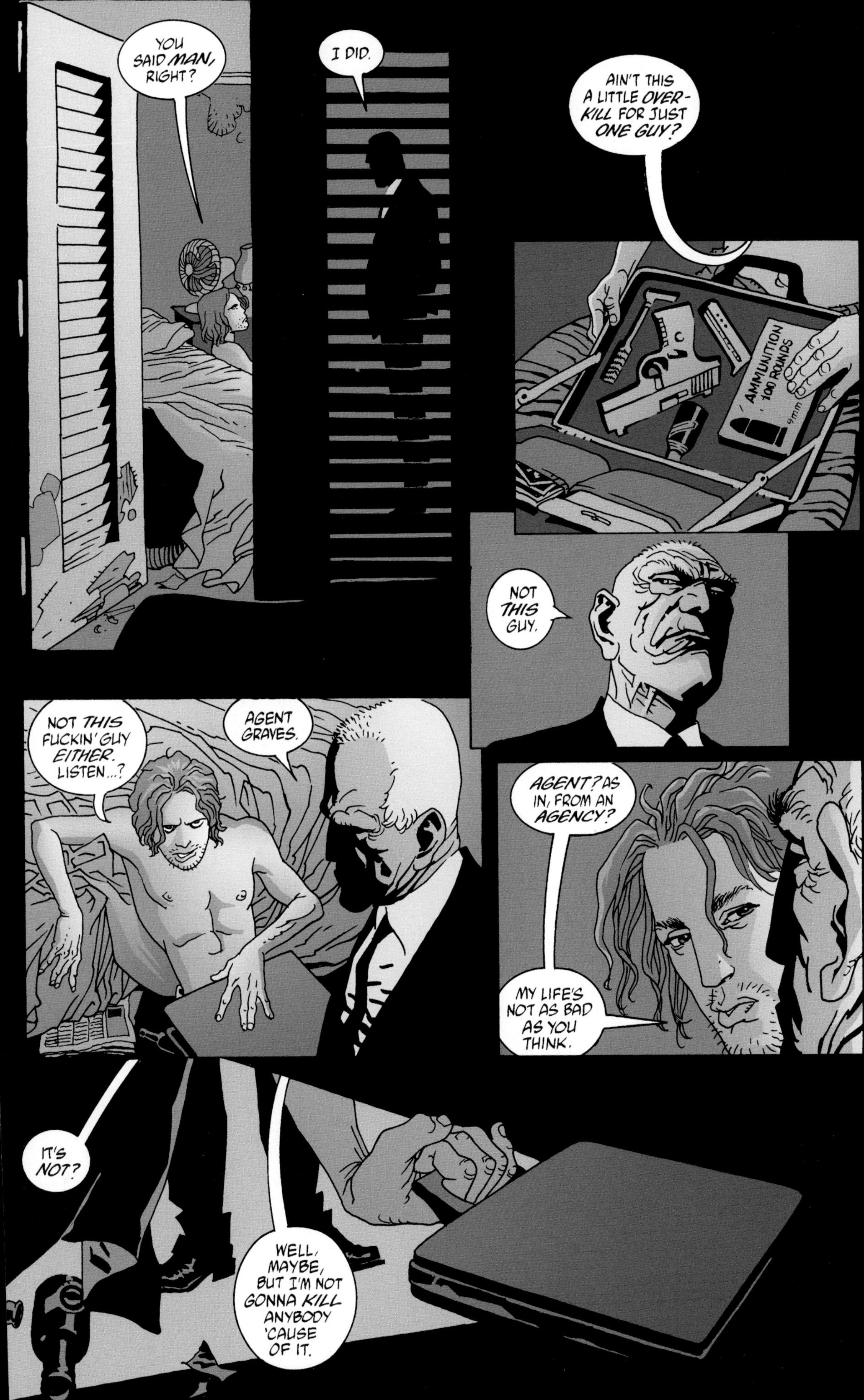
YOU SAID MAN, RIGHT?
I DID.
AIN'T THIS A LITTLE OVER-KILL FOR JUST ONE GUY?
AMMUNITION 100 ROUNDS 9mm
NOT THIS GUY.
NOT THIS FUCKIN' GUY EITHER. LISTEN...?
AGENT GRAVES.
AGENT? AS IN, FROM AN AGENCY?
MY LIFE'S NOT AS BAD AS YOU THINK.
IT'S NOT?
WELL, MAYBE, BUT I'M NOT GONNA KILL ANYBODY 'CAUSE OF IT.

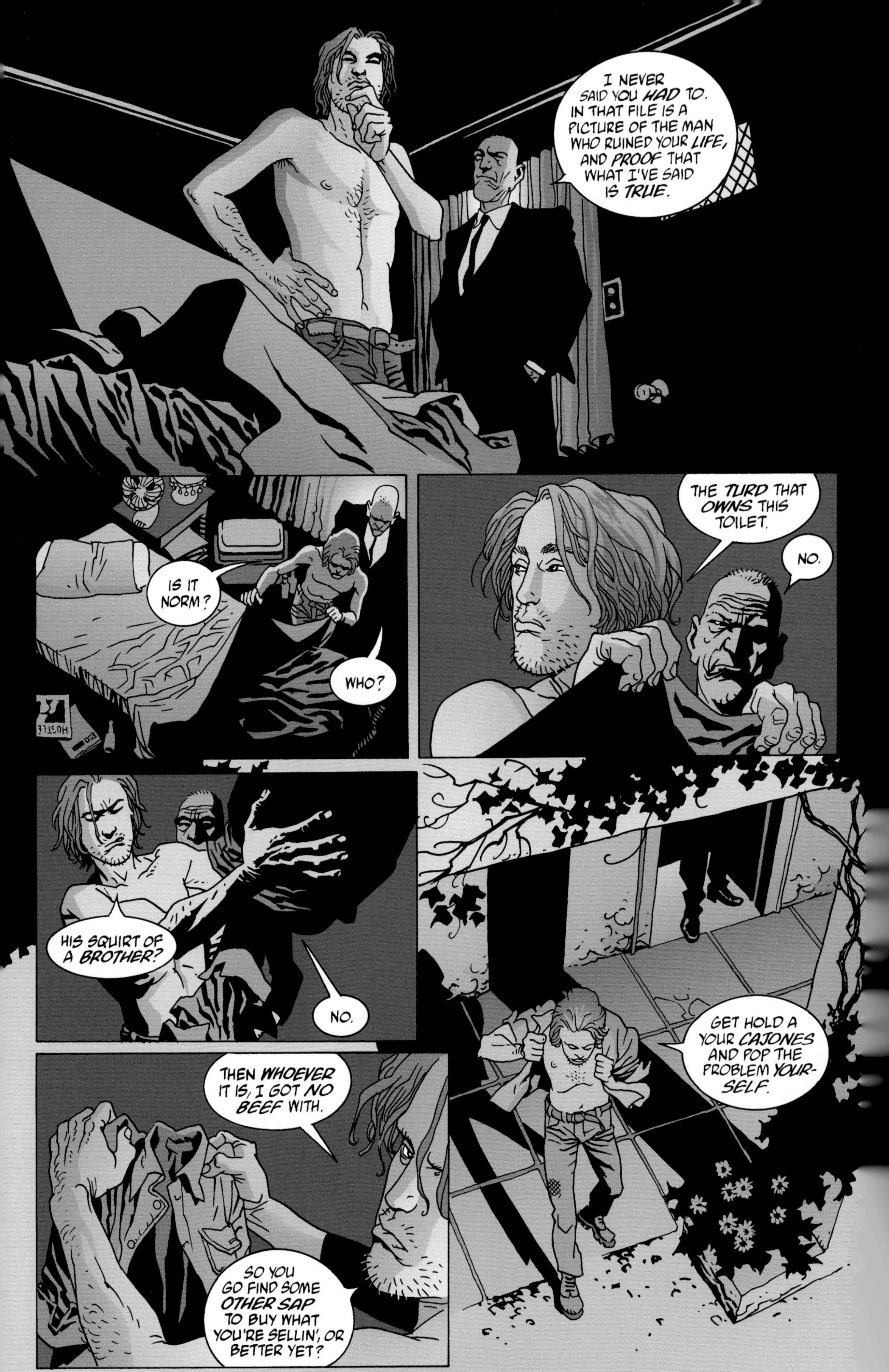
I NEVER SAID YOU HAD TO. IN THAT FILE IS A PICTURE OF THE MAN WHO RUINED YOUR LIFE, AND PROOF THAT WHAT I'VE SAID IS TRUE.
IS IT NORM?
WHO?
THE TURD THAT OWNS THIS TOILET.
NO.
HIS SQUIRT OF A BROTHER?
NO.
THEN WHOEVER IT IS, I GOT NO BEEF WITH.
SO YOU GO FIND SOME OTHER SAP TO BUY WHAT YOU'RE SELLIN', OR BETTER YET?
GET HOLD A YOUR CAJONES AND POP THE PROBLEM YOUR-SELF.
HUSTLE

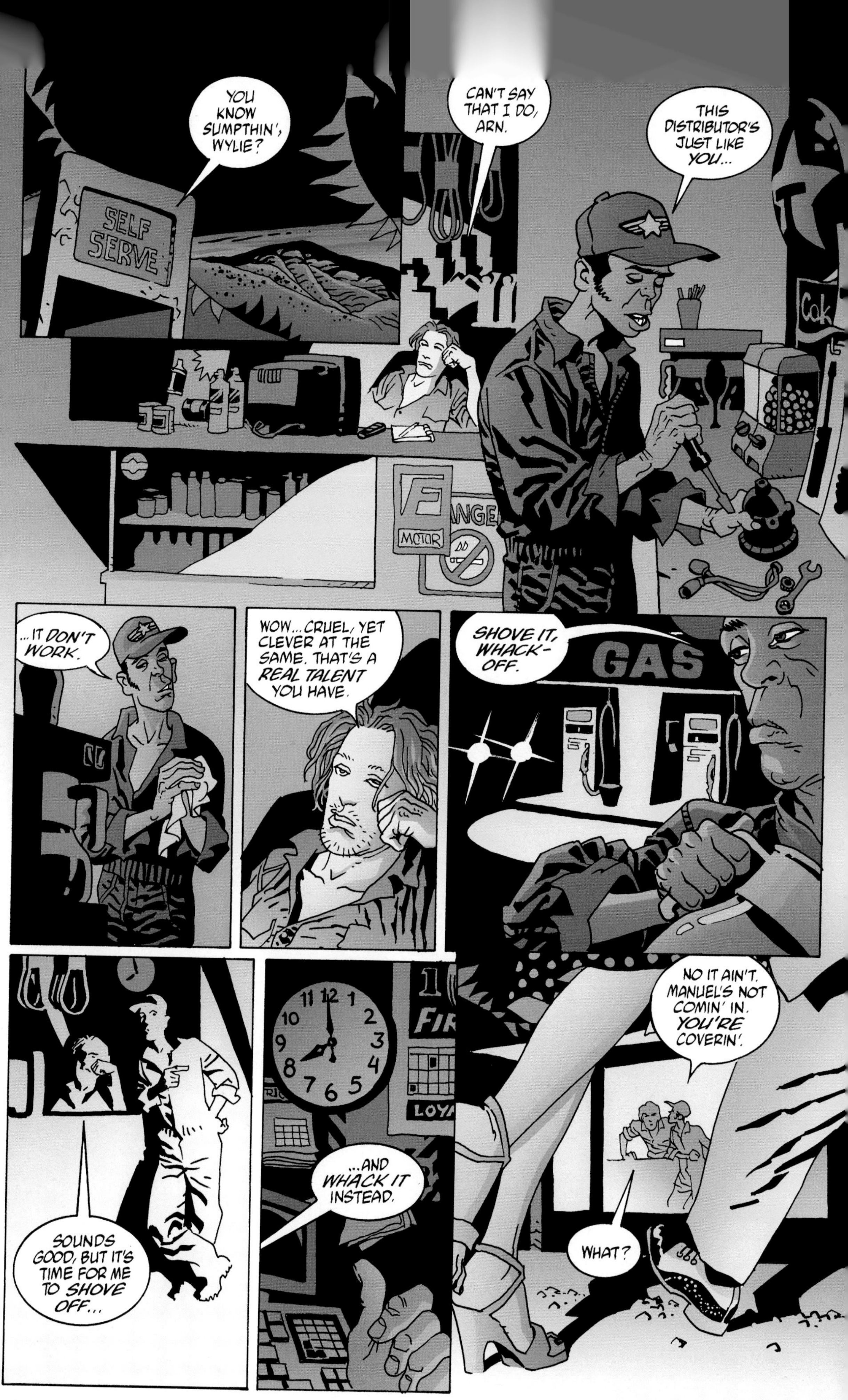
YOU KNOW SUMPTHIN', WYLIE?
CAN'T SAY THAT I DO, ARN.
THIS DISTRIBUTOR'S JUST LIKE YOU...
...IT DON'T WORK.
WOW... CRUEL, YET CLEVER AT THE SAME. THAT'S A REAL TALENT YOU HAVE.
SHOVE IT, WHACK-OFF.
SOUNDS GOOD, BUT IT'S TIME FOR ME TO SHOVE OFF...
...AND WHACK IT INSTEAD.
NO IT AIN'T. MANUEL'S NOT COMIN' IN. YOU'RE COVERIN'.
WHAT?
SELF SERVE
GAS
MOTOR

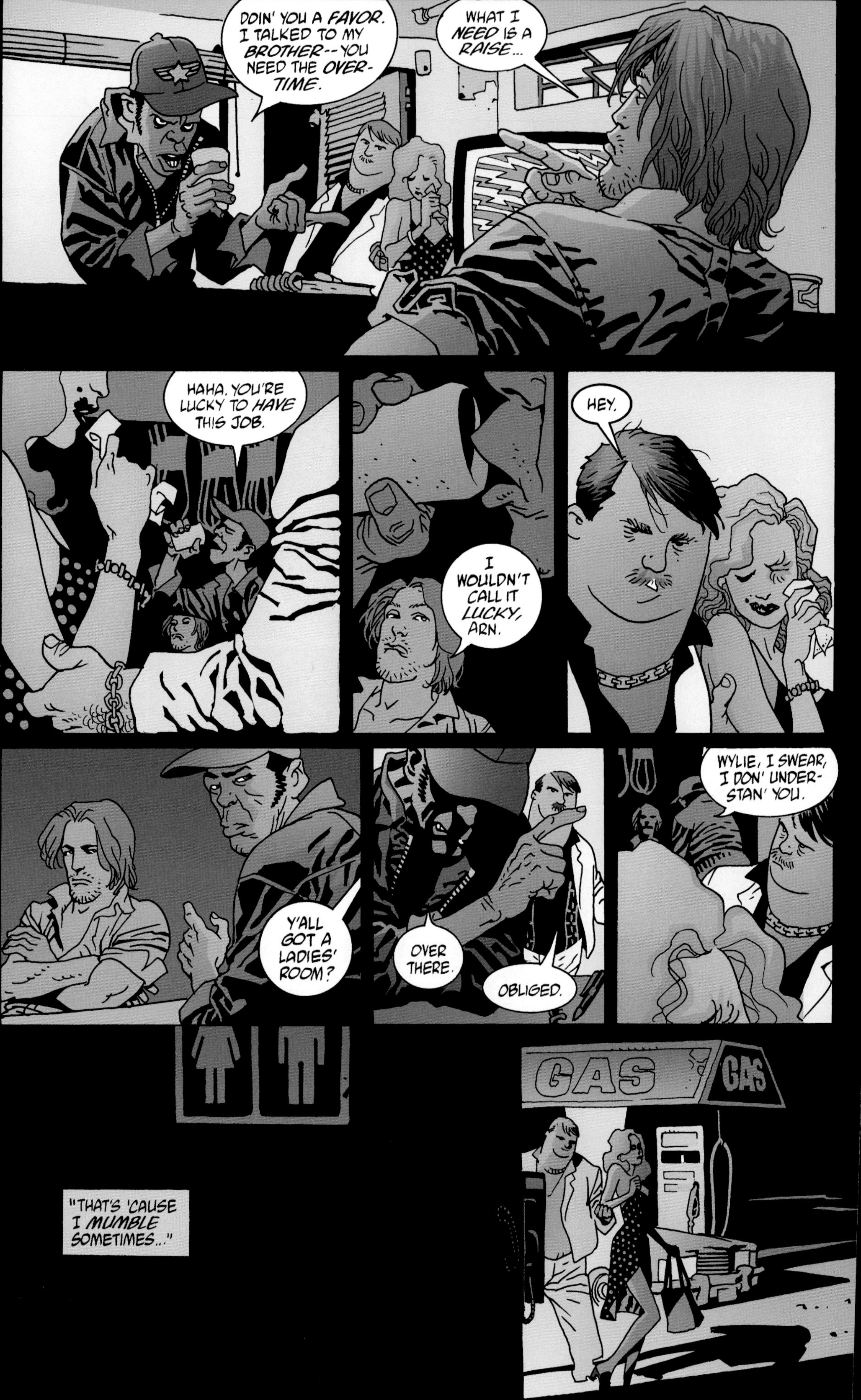
DOIN' YOU A FAVOR. I TALKED TO MY BROTHER--YOU NEED THE OVER-TIME.
WHAT I NEED IS A RAISE...
HAHA. YOU'RE LUCKY TO HAVE THIS JOB.
I WOULDN'T CALL IT LUCKY, ARN.
HEY.
Y'ALL GOT A LADIES' ROOM?
OVER THERE.
OBLIGED.
WYLIE, I SWEAR, I DON' UNDER-STAN' YOU.
"THAT'S 'CAUSE I MUMBLE SOMETIMES..."
GAS
GAS

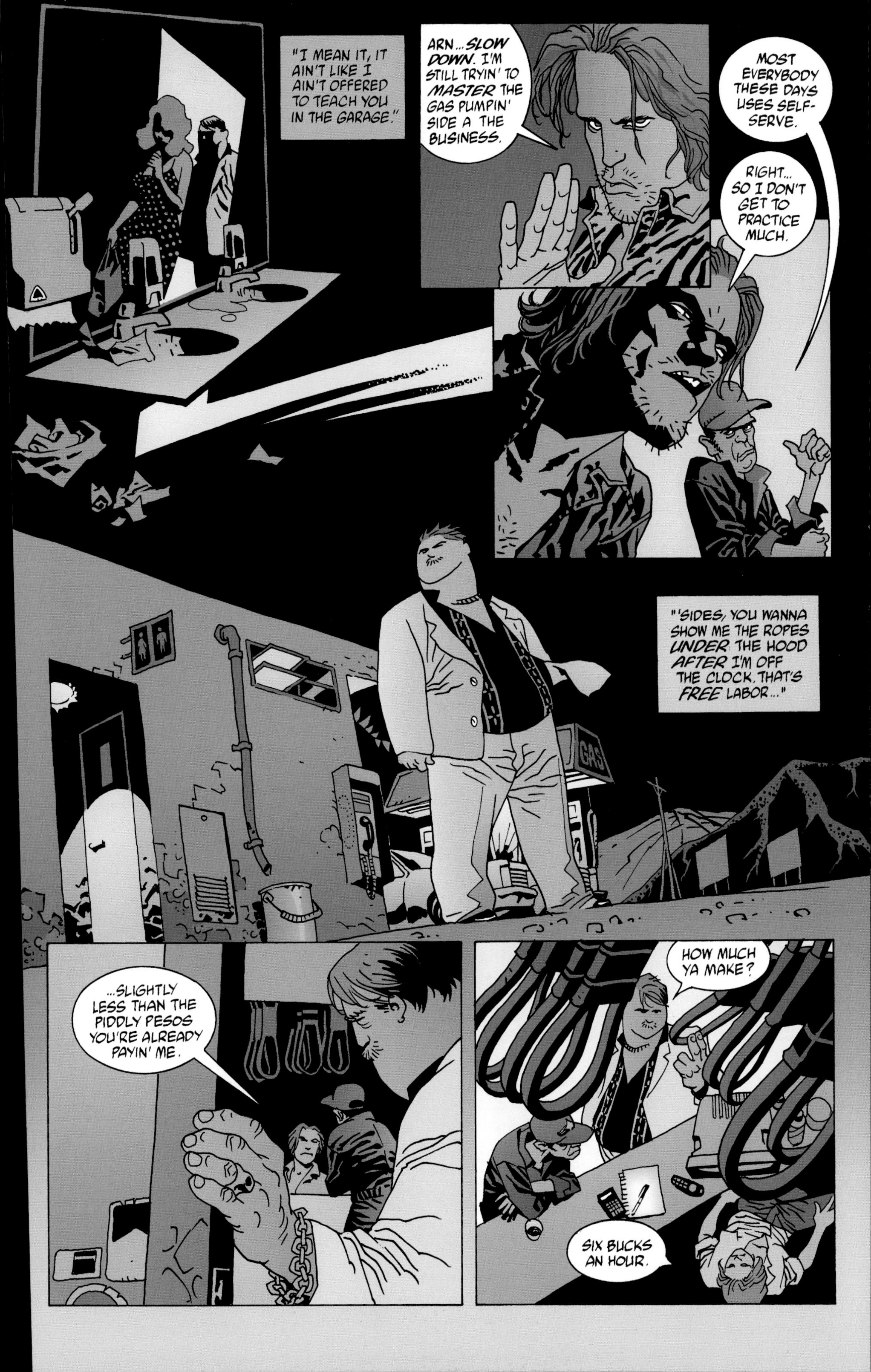
"I MEAN IT, IT AIN'T LIKE I AIN'T OFFERED TO TEACH YOU IN THE GARAGE."
ARN... SLOW DOWN. I'M STILL TRYIN' TO MASTER THE GAS PUMPIN' SIDE A THE BUSINESS.
MOST EVERYBODY THESE DAYS USES SELF-SERVE.
RIGHT... SO I DON'T GET TO PRACTICE MUCH.
"'SIDES, YOU WANNA SHOW ME THE ROPES UNDER THE HOOD AFTER I'M OFF THE CLOCK, THAT'S FREE LABOR..."
GAS
...SLIGHTLY LESS THAN THE PIDDLY PESOS YOU'RE ALREADY PAYIN' ME.
HOW MUCH YA MAKE?
SIX BUCKS AN HOUR.

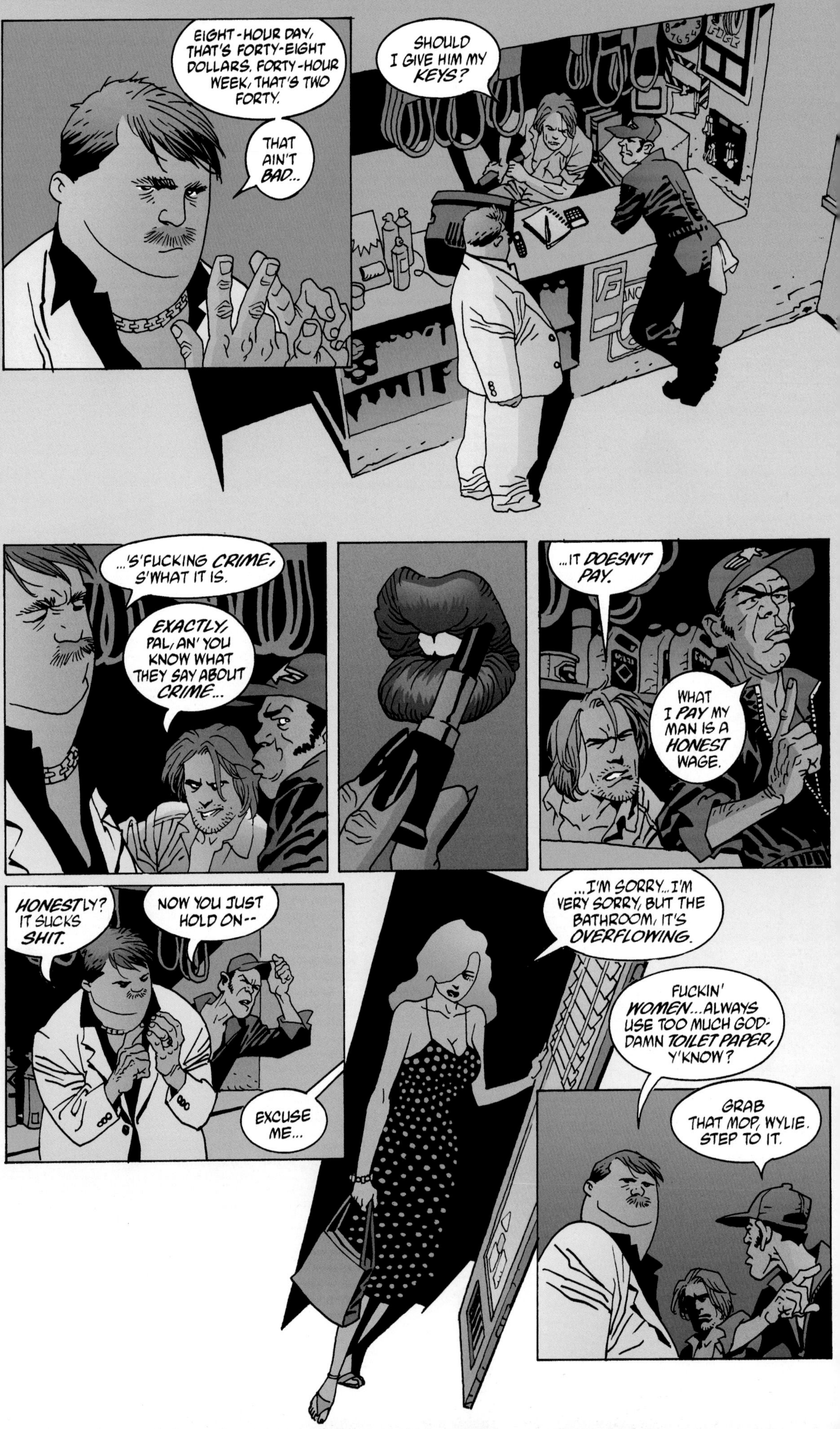
EIGHT-HOUR DAY, THAT'S FORTY-EIGHT DOLLARS. FORTY-HOUR WEEK, THAT'S TWO FORTY.
THAT AIN'T *BAD*...
SHOULD I GIVE HIM MY *KEYS?*
...'S'FUCKING *CRIME*, S'WHAT IT IS.
EXACTLY, PAL, AN' YOU KNOW WHAT THEY SAY ABOUT *CRIME*...
...IT *DOESN'T PAY.*
WHAT I *PAY* MY MAN IS A *HONEST* WAGE.
*HONEST*LY? IT SUCKS *SHIT.*
NOW YOU JUST HOLD ON--
EXCUSE ME...
...I'M SORRY... I'M VERY SORRY, BUT THE BATHROOM, IT'S *OVERFLOWING.*
FUCKIN' *WOMEN*... ALWAYS USE TOO MUCH GOD-DAMN *TOILET PAPER*, Y'KNOW?
GRAB THAT MOP, WYLIE. STEP TO IT.

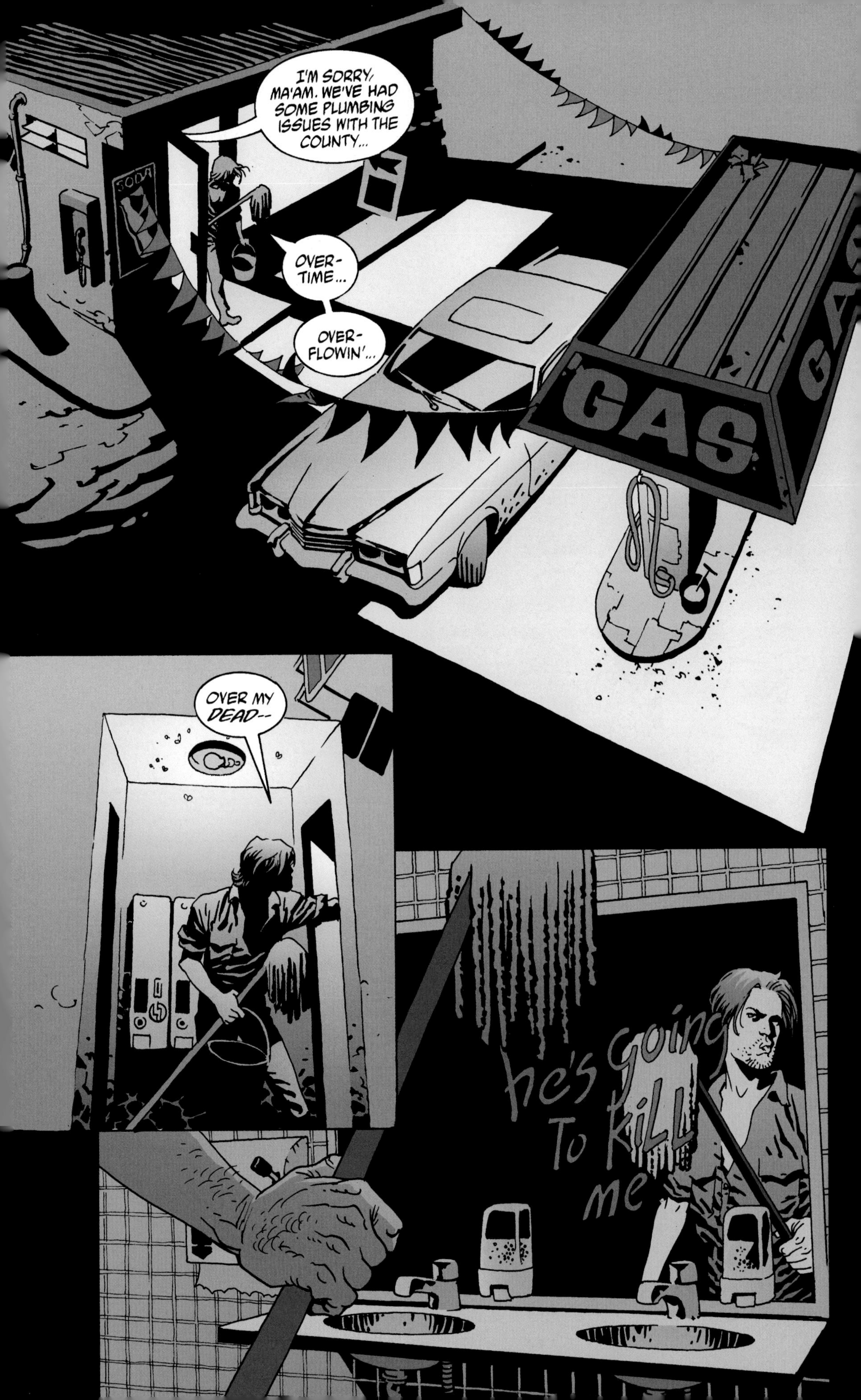
I'M SORRY, MA'AM. WE'VE HAD SOME PLUMBING ISSUES WITH THE COUNTY...
OVER-TIME...
OVER-FLOWIN'...
GAS
GAS
SODA
OVER MY DEAD--
he's going To KiLL me

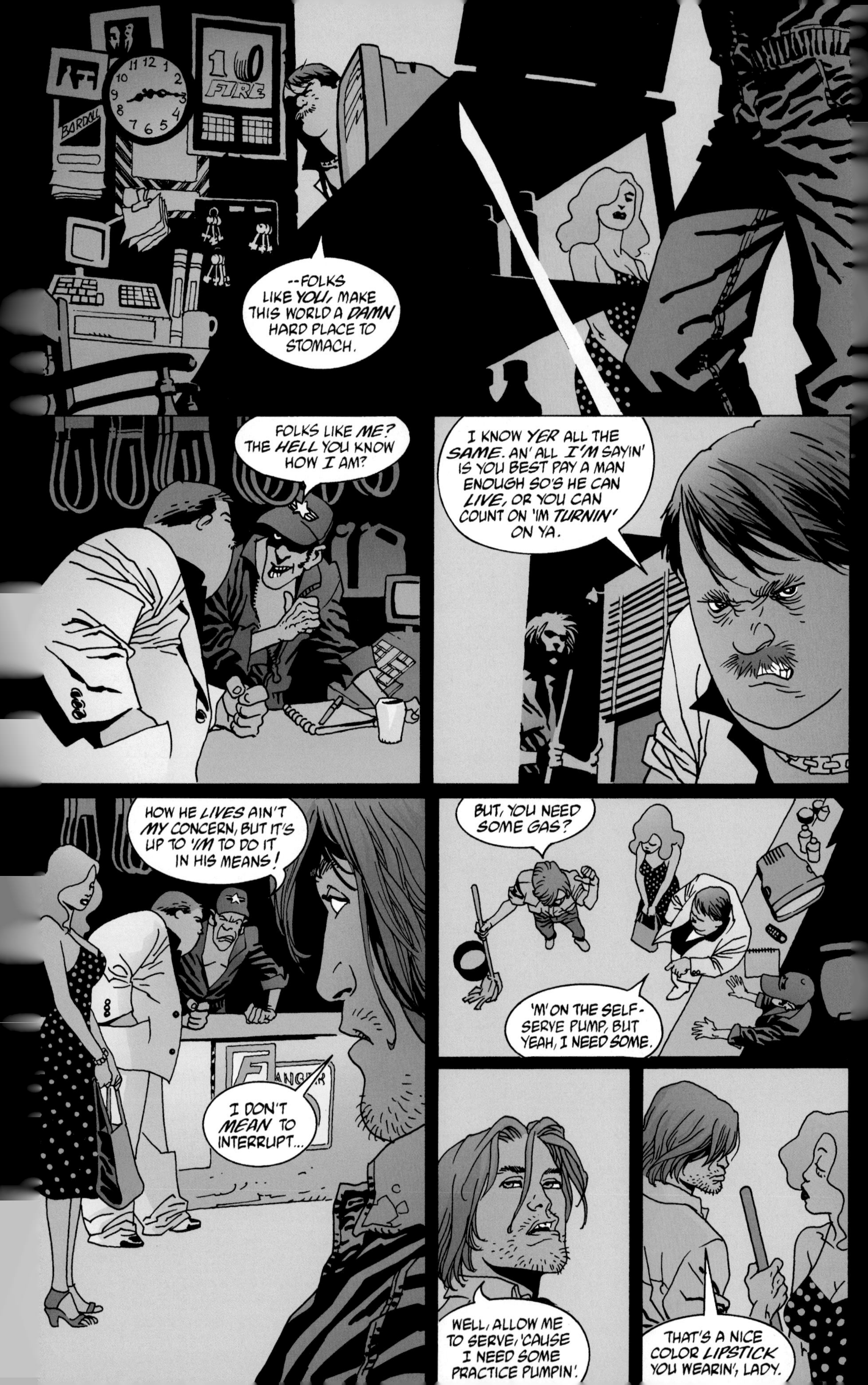
--FOLKS LIKE YOU, MAKE THIS WORLD A DAMN HARD PLACE TO STOMACH.
FOLKS LIKE ME? THE HELL YOU KNOW HOW I AM?
I KNOW YER ALL THE SAME. AN' ALL I'M SAYIN' IS YOU BEST PAY A MAN ENOUGH SO'S HE CAN LIVE, OR YOU CAN COUNT ON 'IM TURNIN' ON YA.
HOW HE LIVES AIN'T MY CONCERN, BUT IT'S UP TO 'IM TO DO IT IN HIS MEANS!
I DON'T MEAN TO INTERRUPT...
BUT, YOU NEED SOME GAS?
'M' ON THE SELF-SERVE PUMP, BUT YEAH, I NEED SOME.
WELL, ALLOW ME TO SERVE, 'CAUSE I NEED SOME PRACTICE PUMPIN'.
THAT'S A NICE COLOR LIPSTICK YOU WEARIN', LADY.

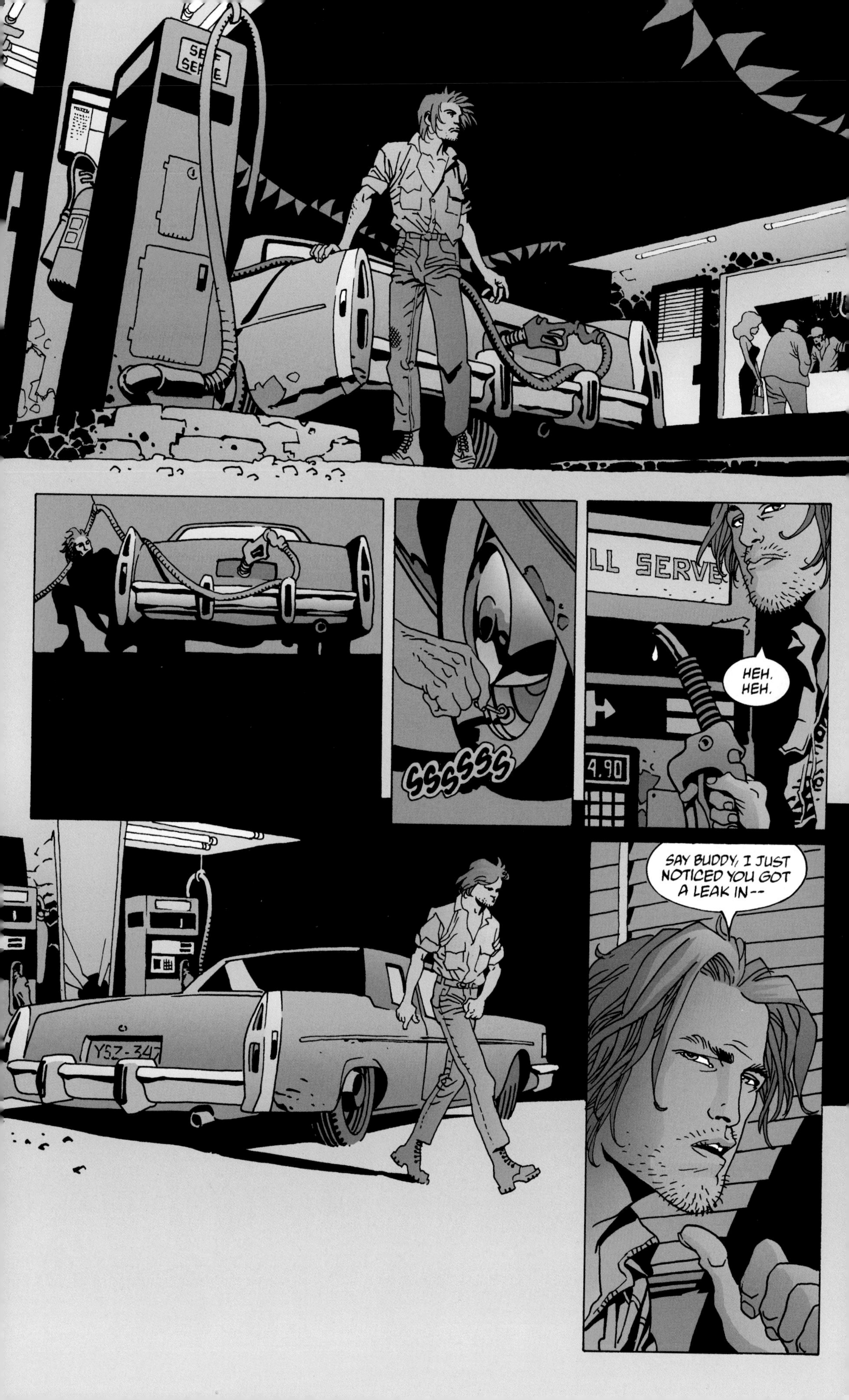
SELF SERVE
LL SERVE
HEH. HEH.
SSSSSS
4.90
YSZ-347
SAY BUDDY, I JUST NOTICED YOU GOT A LEAK IN--

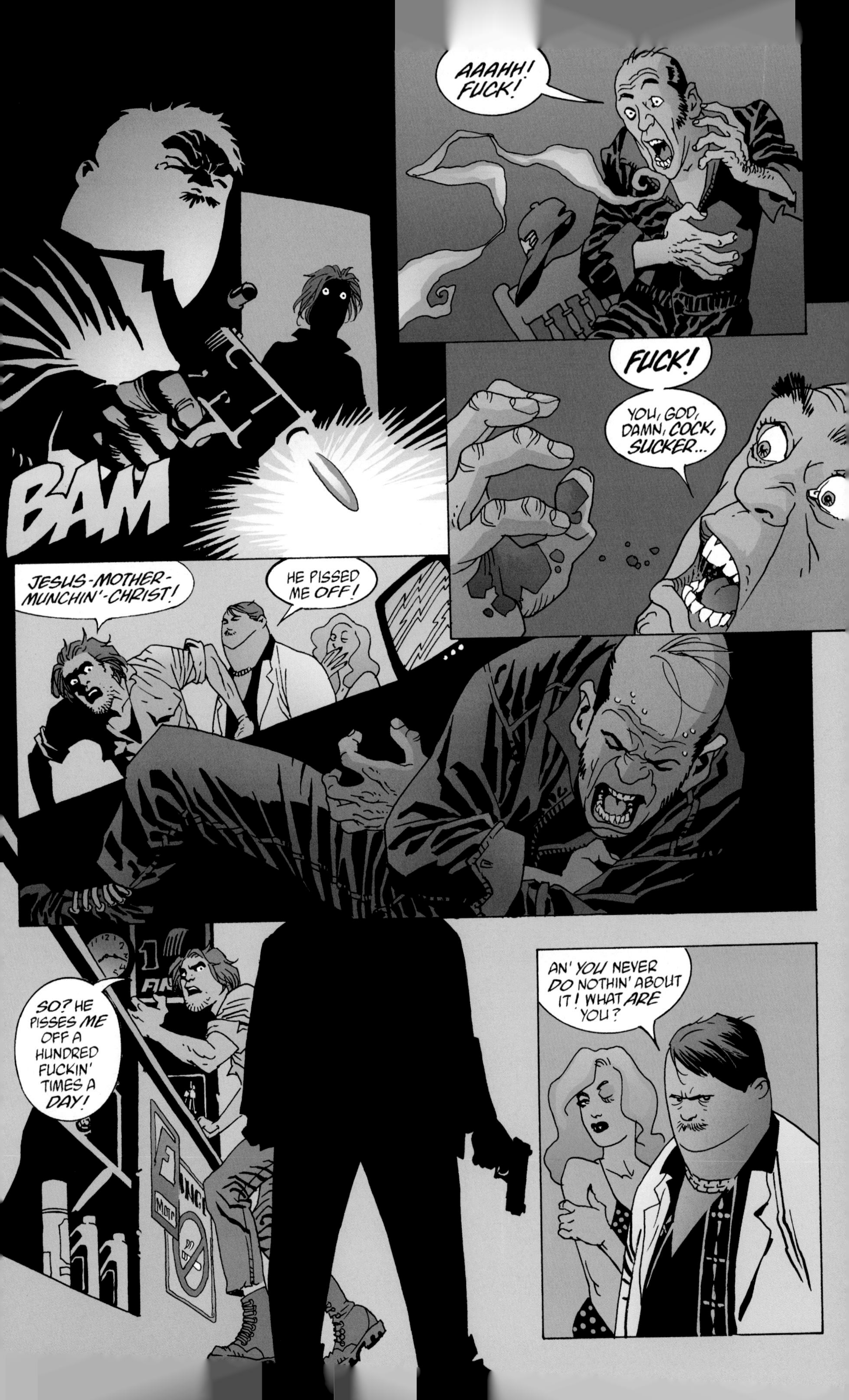
BAM
AAAHH! FUCK!
FUCK!
YOU, GOD, DAMN, COCK, SUCKER...
JESUS-MOTHER-MUNCHIN'-CHRIST!
HE PISSED ME OFF!
SO? HE PISSES ME OFF A HUNDRED FUCKIN' TIMES A DAY!
AN' YOU NEVER DO NOTHIN' ABOUT IT! WHAT ARE YOU?

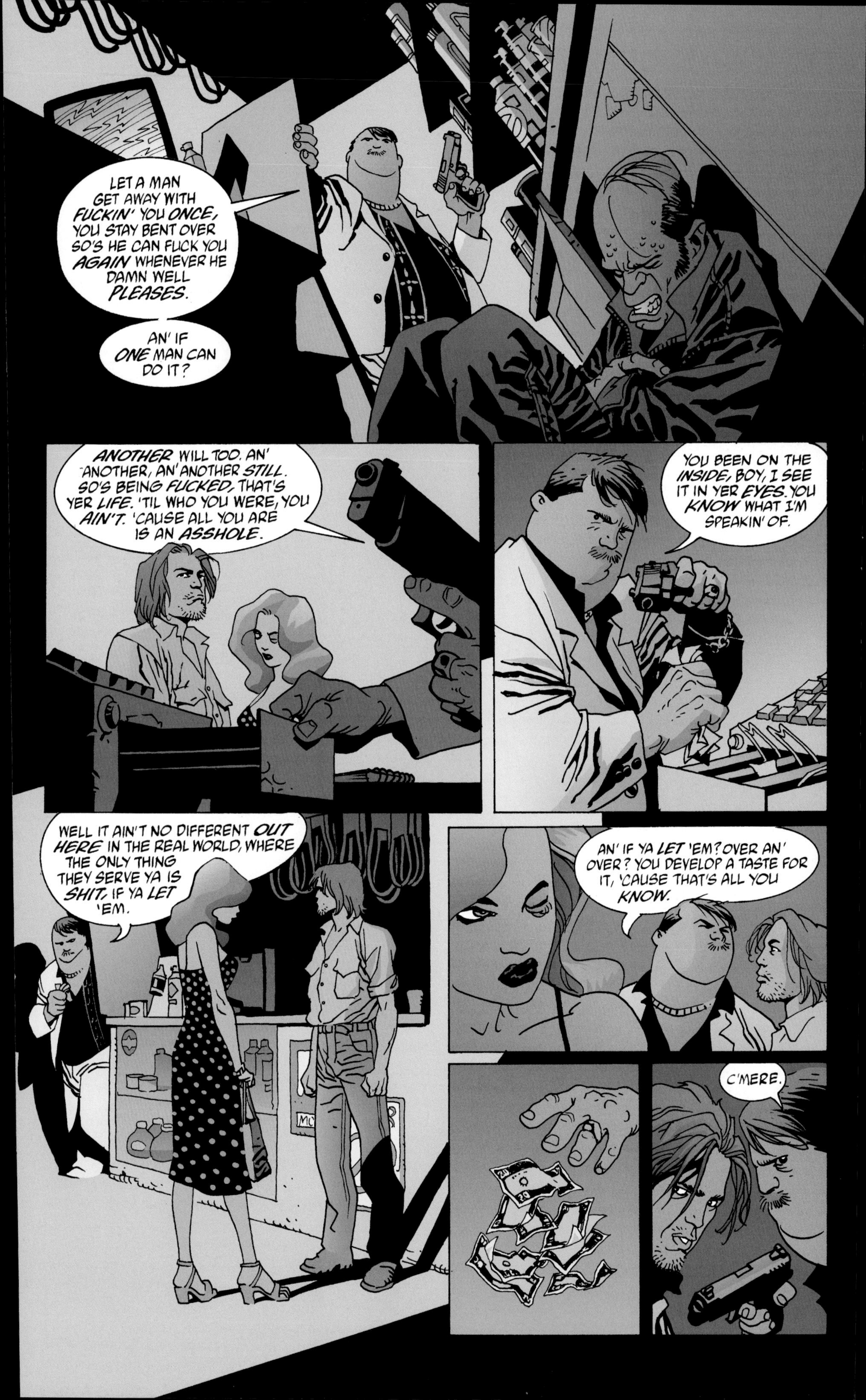
LET A MAN GET AWAY WITH FUCKIN' YOU ONCE, YOU STAY BENT OVER SO'S HE CAN FUCK YOU AGAIN WHENEVER HE DAMN WELL PLEASES.
AN' IF ONE MAN CAN DO IT?
ANOTHER WILL TOO. AN' ANOTHER, AN' ANOTHER STILL. SO'S BEING FUCKED, THAT'S YER LIFE. 'TIL WHO YOU WERE, YOU AIN'T. 'CAUSE ALL YOU ARE IS AN ASSHOLE.
YOU BEEN ON THE INSIDE, BOY, I SEE IT IN YER EYES. YOU KNOW WHAT I'M SPEAKIN' OF.
WELL IT AIN'T NO DIFFERENT OUT HERE IN THE REAL WORLD, WHERE THE ONLY THING THEY SERVE YA IS SHIT, IF YA LET 'EM.
AN' IF YA LET 'EM? OVER AN' OVER? YOU DEVELOP A TASTE FOR IT, 'CAUSE THAT'S ALL YOU KNOW.
C'MERE.

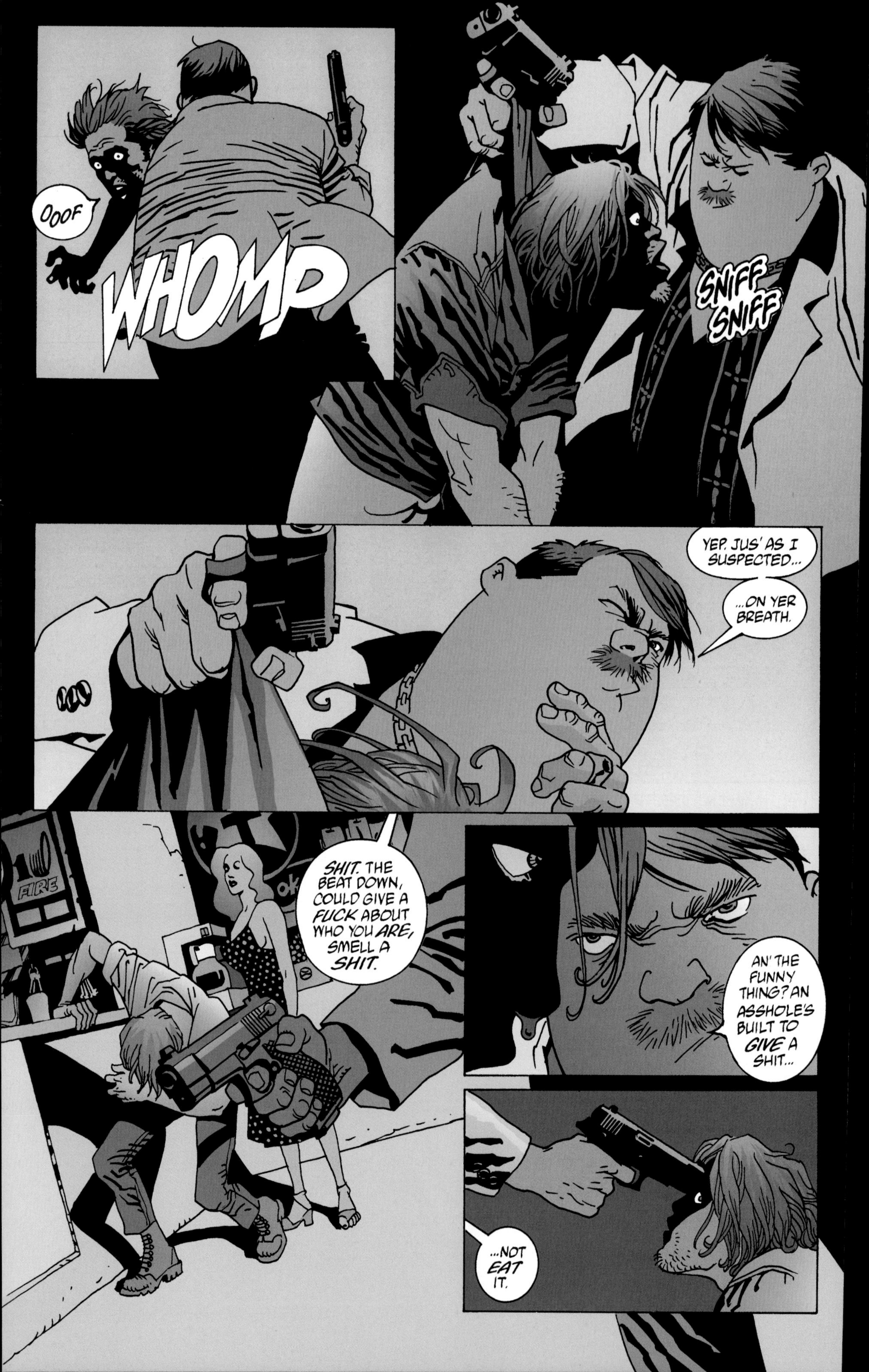

OOOF
WHOMP
SNIFF SNIFF
YEP. JUS' AS I SUSPECTED...
...ON YER BREATH.
SHIT. THE BEAT DOWN, COULD GIVE A FUCK ABOUT WHO YOU ARE, SMELL A SHIT.
AN' THE FUNNY THING? AN ASSHOLE'S BUILT TO GIVE A SHIT...
...NOT EAT IT.
FIRE

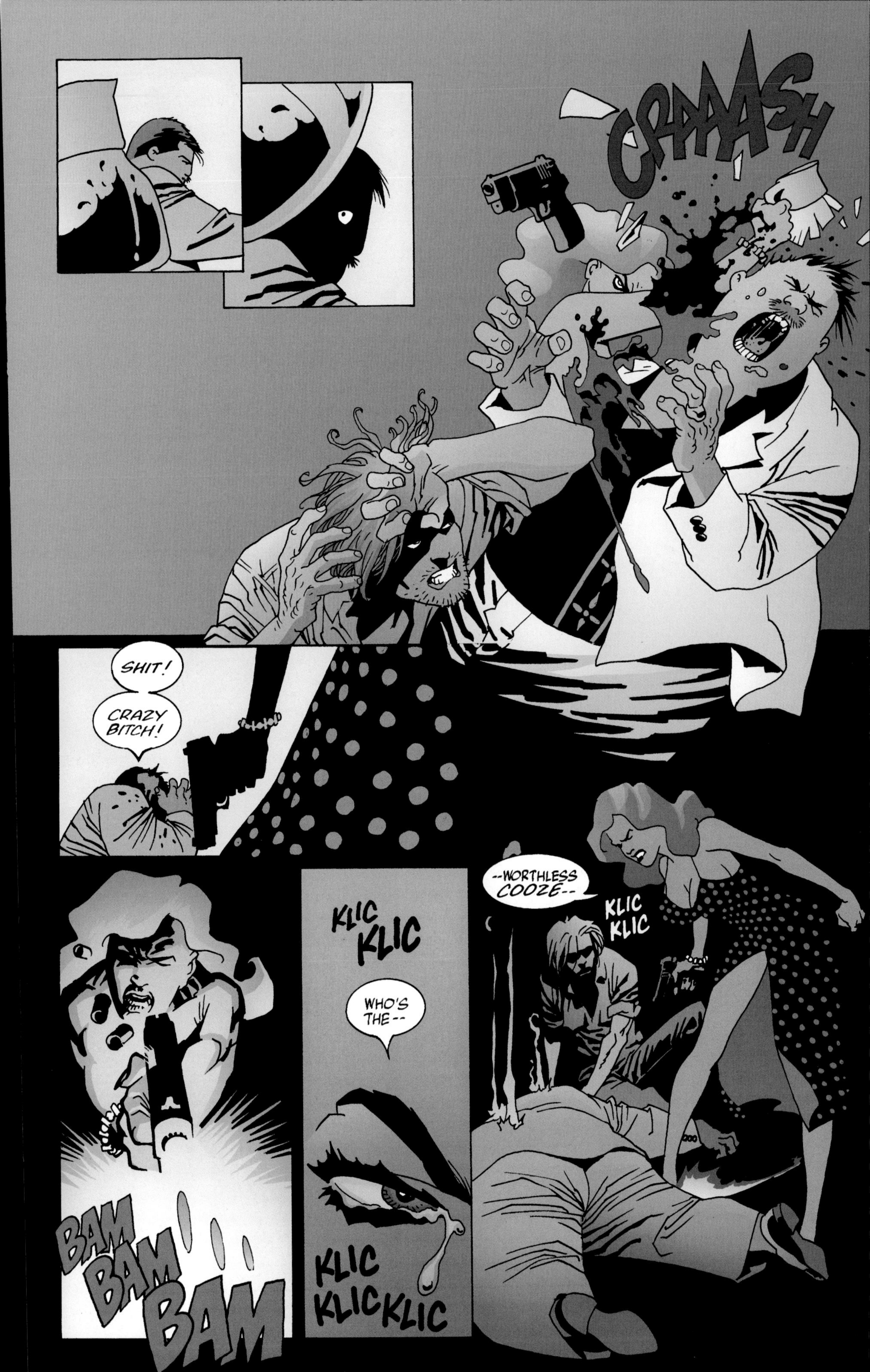
CRRAASH
SHIT!
CRAZY BITCH!
BAM BAM BAM
KLIC KLIC
WHO'S THE--
KLIC KLICKLIC
--WORTHLESS COOZE--
KLIC KLIC

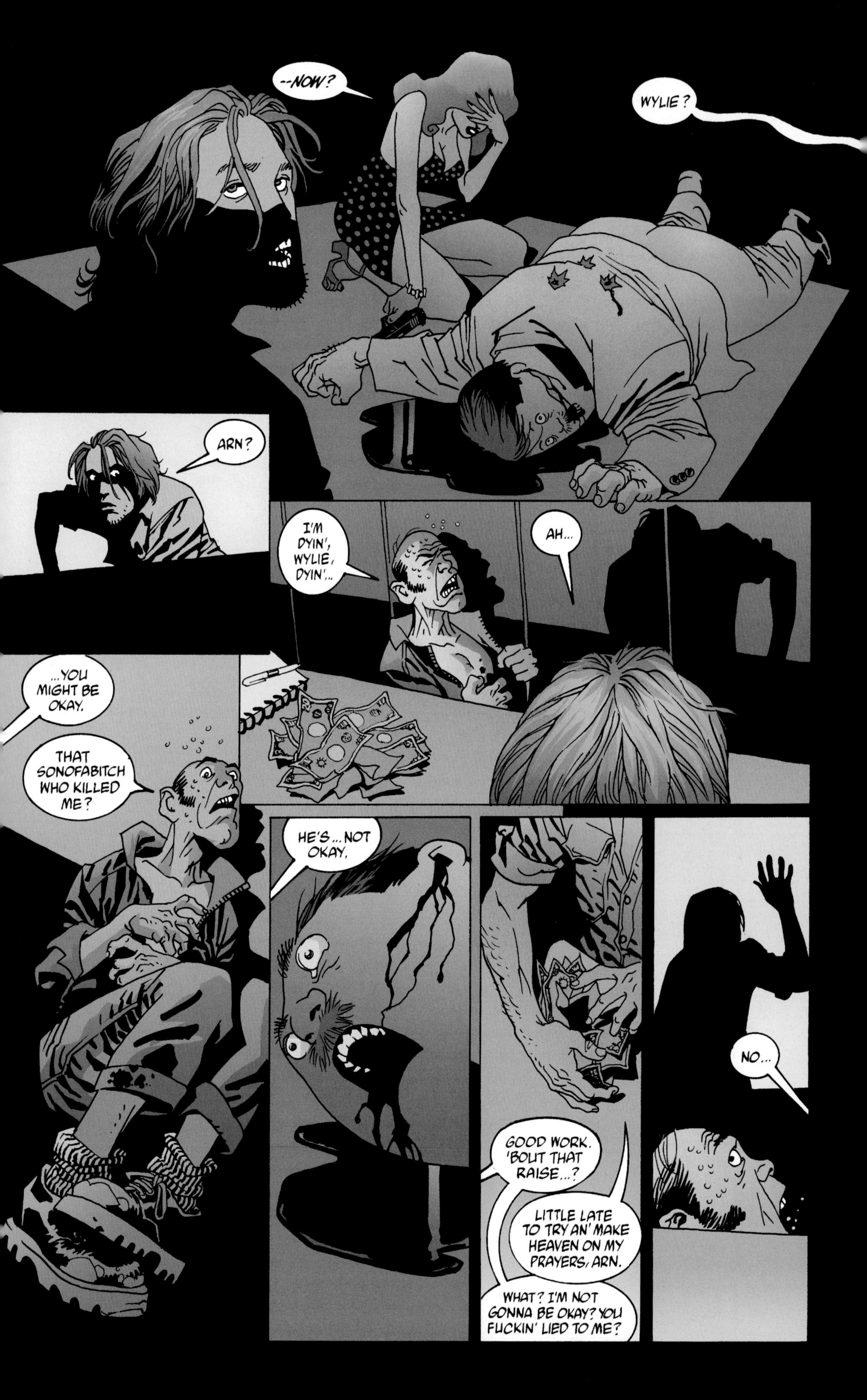
--NOW?
WYLIE?
ARN?
I'M DYIN', WYLIE, DYIN'...
AH...
...YOU MIGHT BE OKAY.
THAT SONOFABITCH WHO KILLED ME?
HE'S...NOT OKAY.
GOOD WORK. 'BOUT THAT RAISE...?
LITTLE LATE TO TRY AN' MAKE HEAVEN ON MY PRAYERS, ARN.
WHAT? I'M NOT GONNA BE OKAY? YOU FUCKIN' LIED TO ME?
NO...

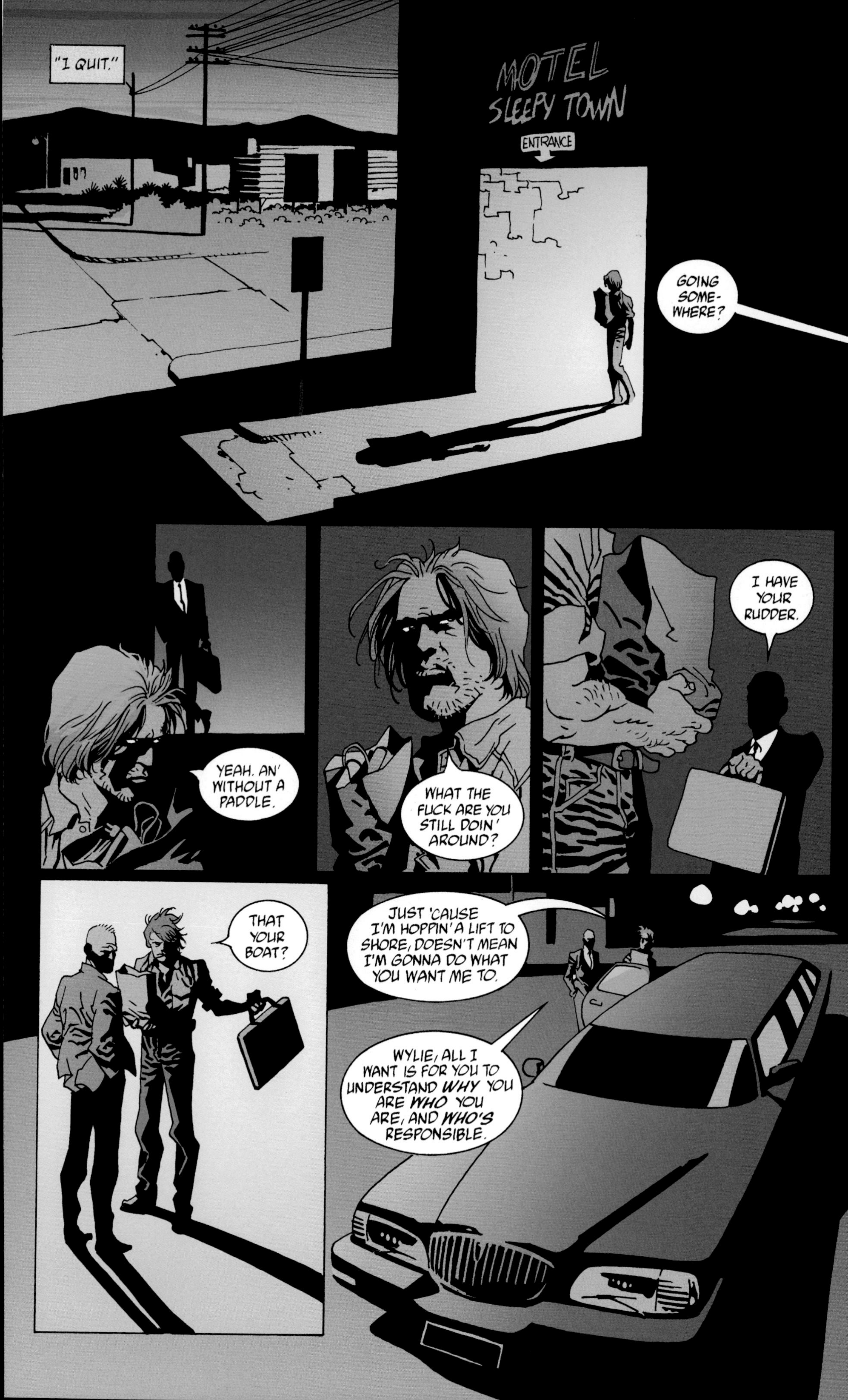
"I QUIT."
MOTEL
SLEEPY TOWN
ENTRANCE
GOING SOME-WHERE?
YEAH. AN' WITHOUT A PADDLE.
WHAT THE FUCK ARE YOU STILL DOIN' AROUND?
I HAVE YOUR RUDDER.
THAT YOUR BOAT?
JUST 'CAUSE I'M HOPPIN' A LIFT TO SHORE, DOESN'T MEAN I'M GONNA DO WHAT YOU WANT ME TO.
WYLIE, ALL I WANT IS FOR YOU TO UNDERSTAND *WHY* YOU ARE *WHO* YOU ARE, AND *WHO'S* RESPONSIBLE.

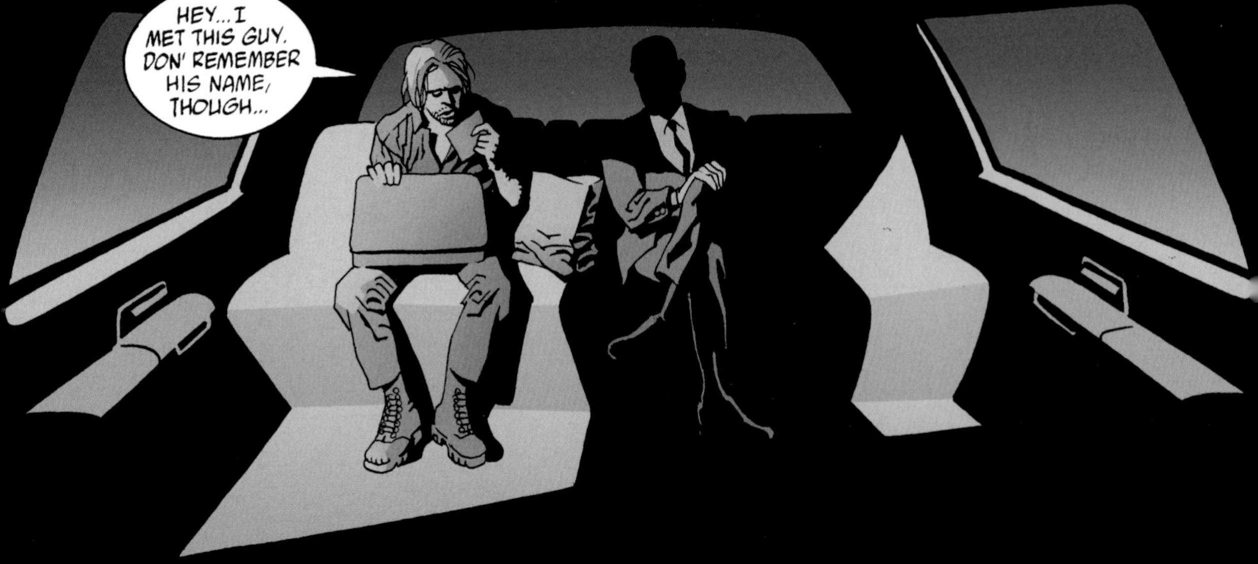
HEY... I MET THIS GUY. DON' REMEMBER HIS NAME, THOUGH...

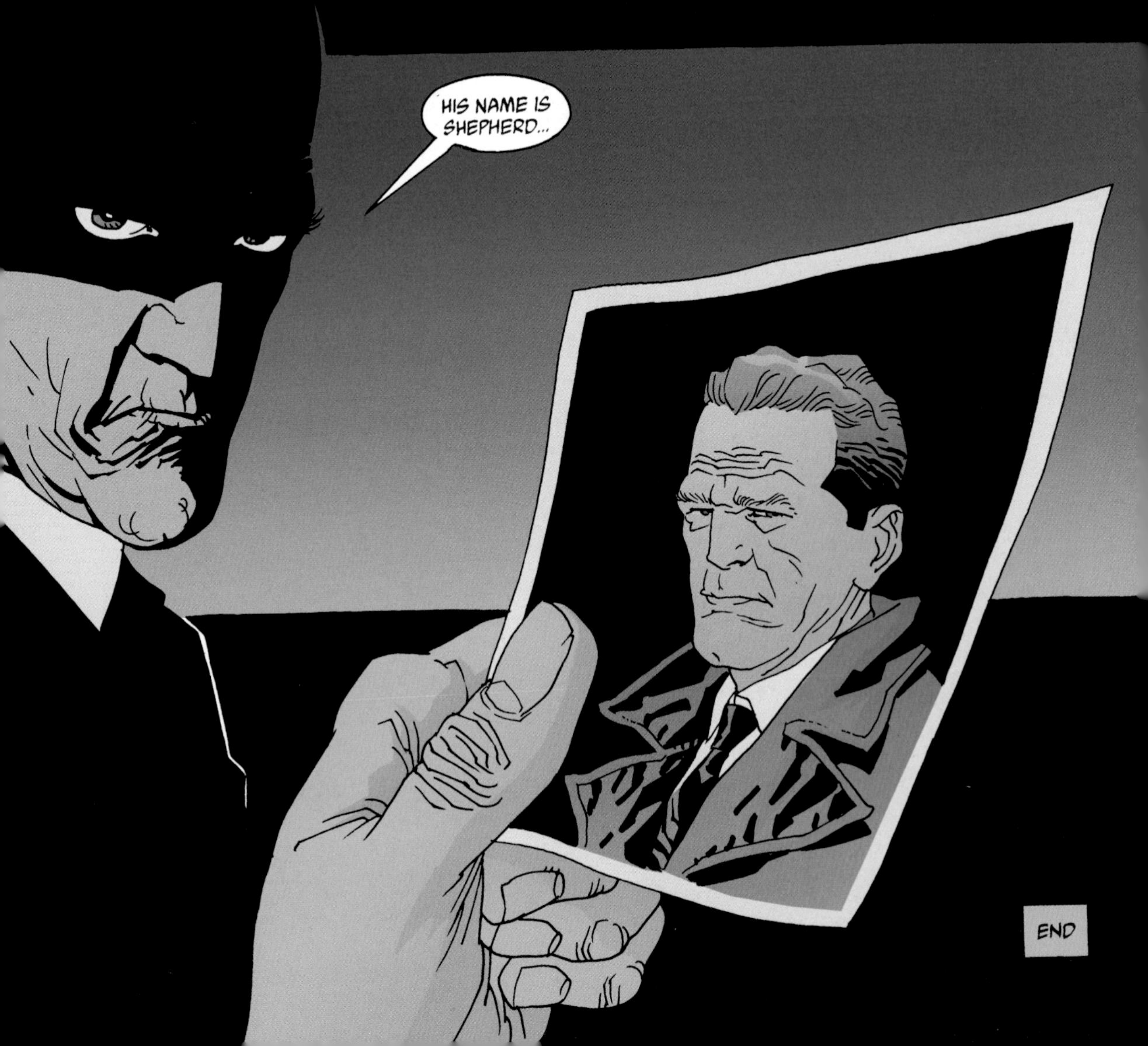
HIS NAME IS SHEPHERD...
END

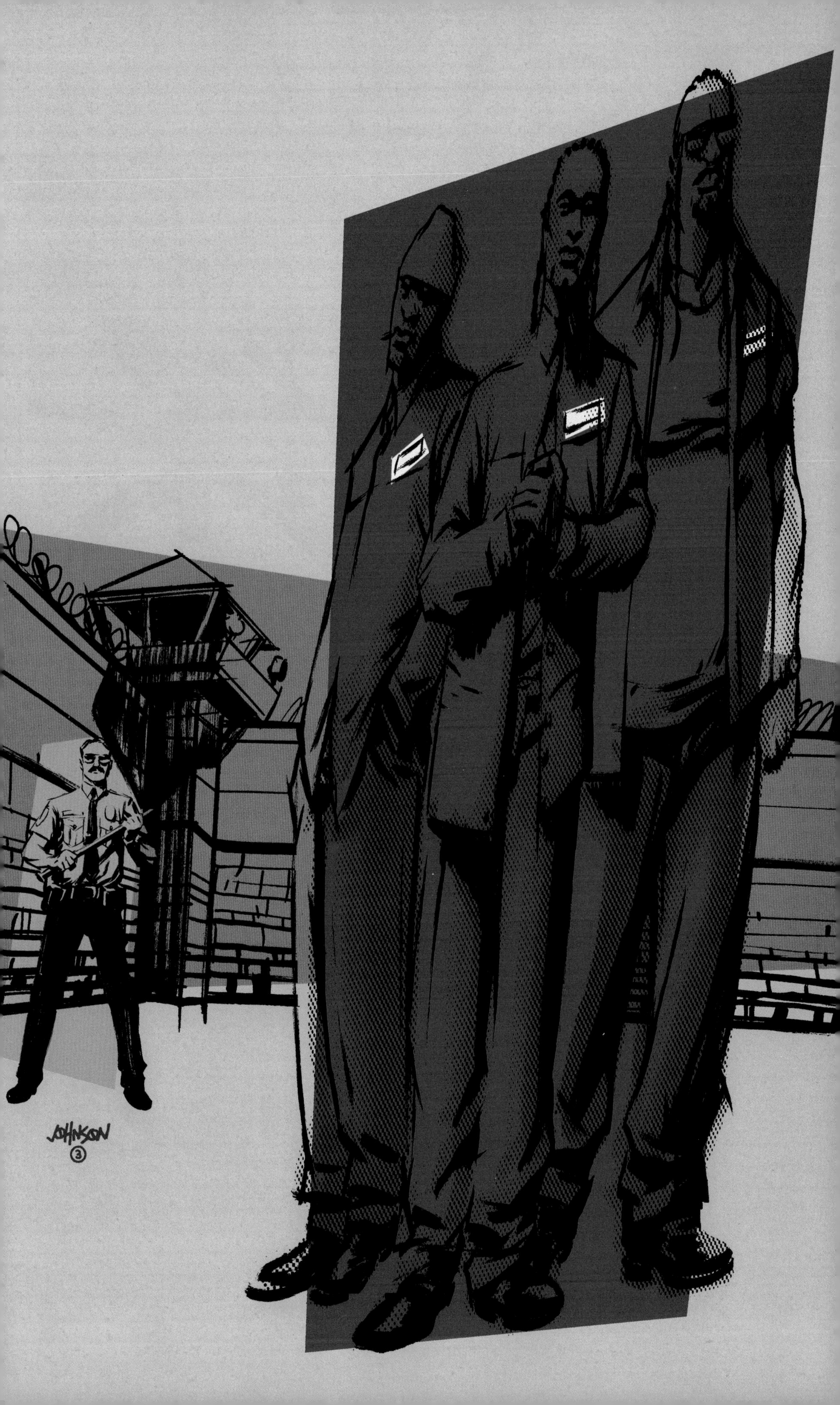
JOHNSON

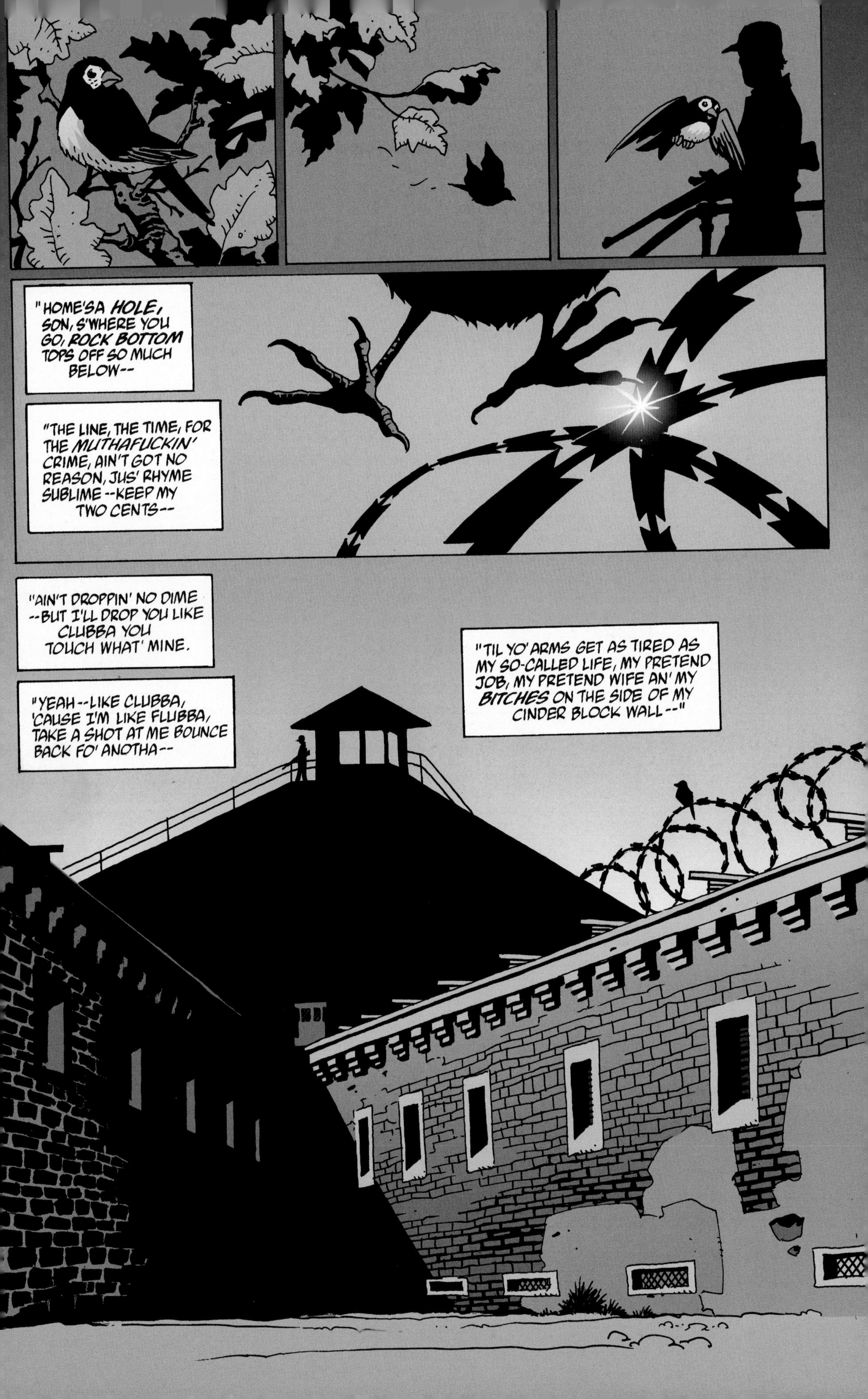
"HOME'SA HOLE, SON, S'WHERE YOU GO, ROCK BOTTOM TOPS OFF SO MUCH BELOW--
"THE LINE, THE TIME, FOR THE MUTHAFUCKIN' CRIME, AIN'T GOT NO REASON, JUS' RHYME SUBLIME--KEEP MY TWO CENTS--
"AIN'T DROPPIN' NO DIME --BUT I'LL DROP YOU LIKE CLUBBA YOU TOUCH WHAT' MINE.
"YEAH--LIKE CLUBBA, 'CAUSE I'M LIKE FLUBBA, TAKE A SHOT AT ME BOUNCE BACK FO' ANOTHA--
"TIL YO' ARMS GET AS TIRED AS MY SO-CALLED LIFE, MY PRETEND JOB, MY PRETEND WIFE AN' MY BITCHES ON THE SIDE OF MY CINDER BLOCK WALL--"

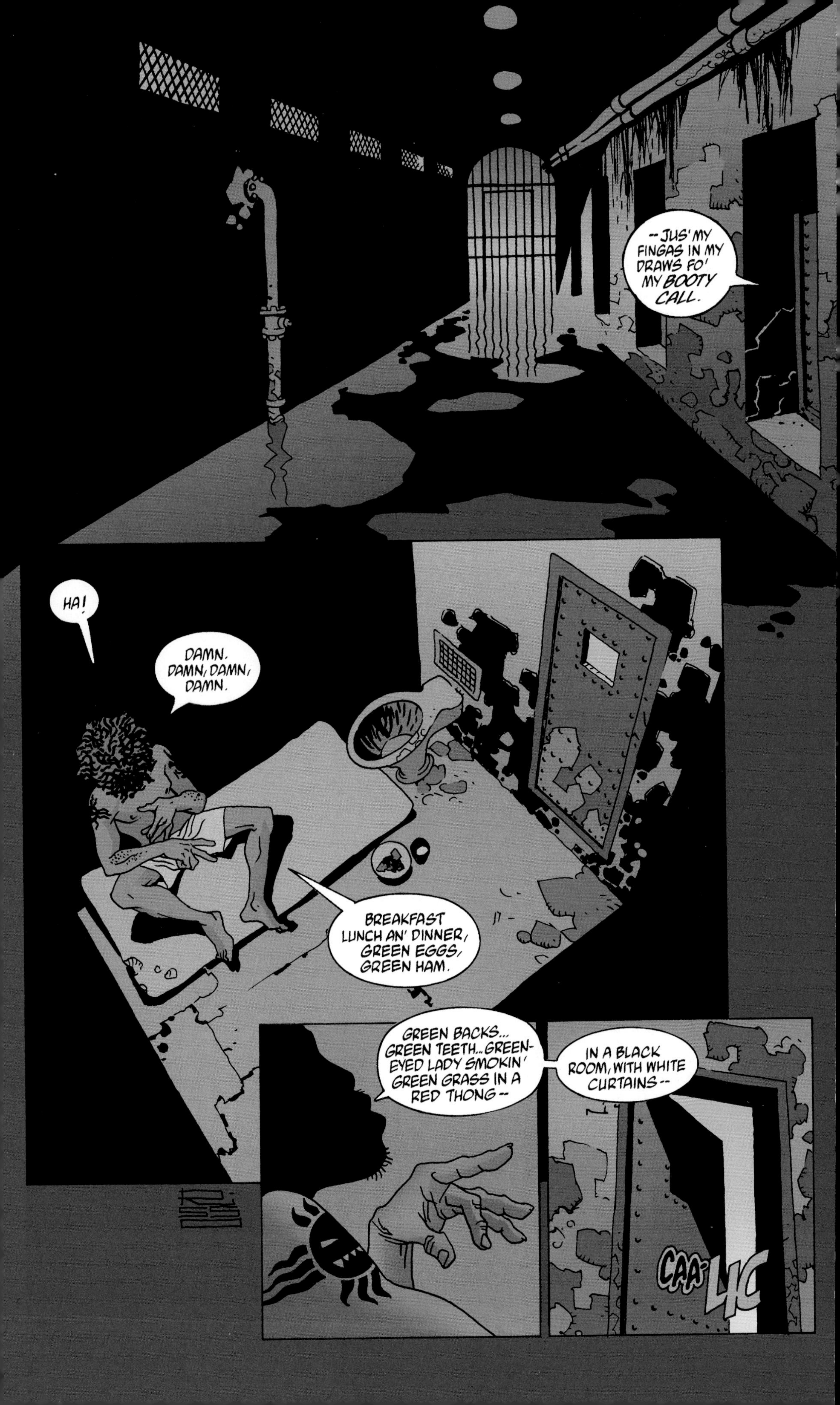

--JUS' MY FINGAS IN MY DRAWS FO' MY BOOTY CALL.
HA!
DAMN. DAMN, DAMN, DAMN.
BREAKFAST LUNCH AN' DINNER, GREEN EGGS, GREEN HAM.
GREEN BACKS... GREEN TEETH...GREEN-EYED LADY SMOKIN' GREEN GRASS IN A RED THONG --
IN A BLACK ROOM, WITH WHITE CURTAINS --
CAA-LIC

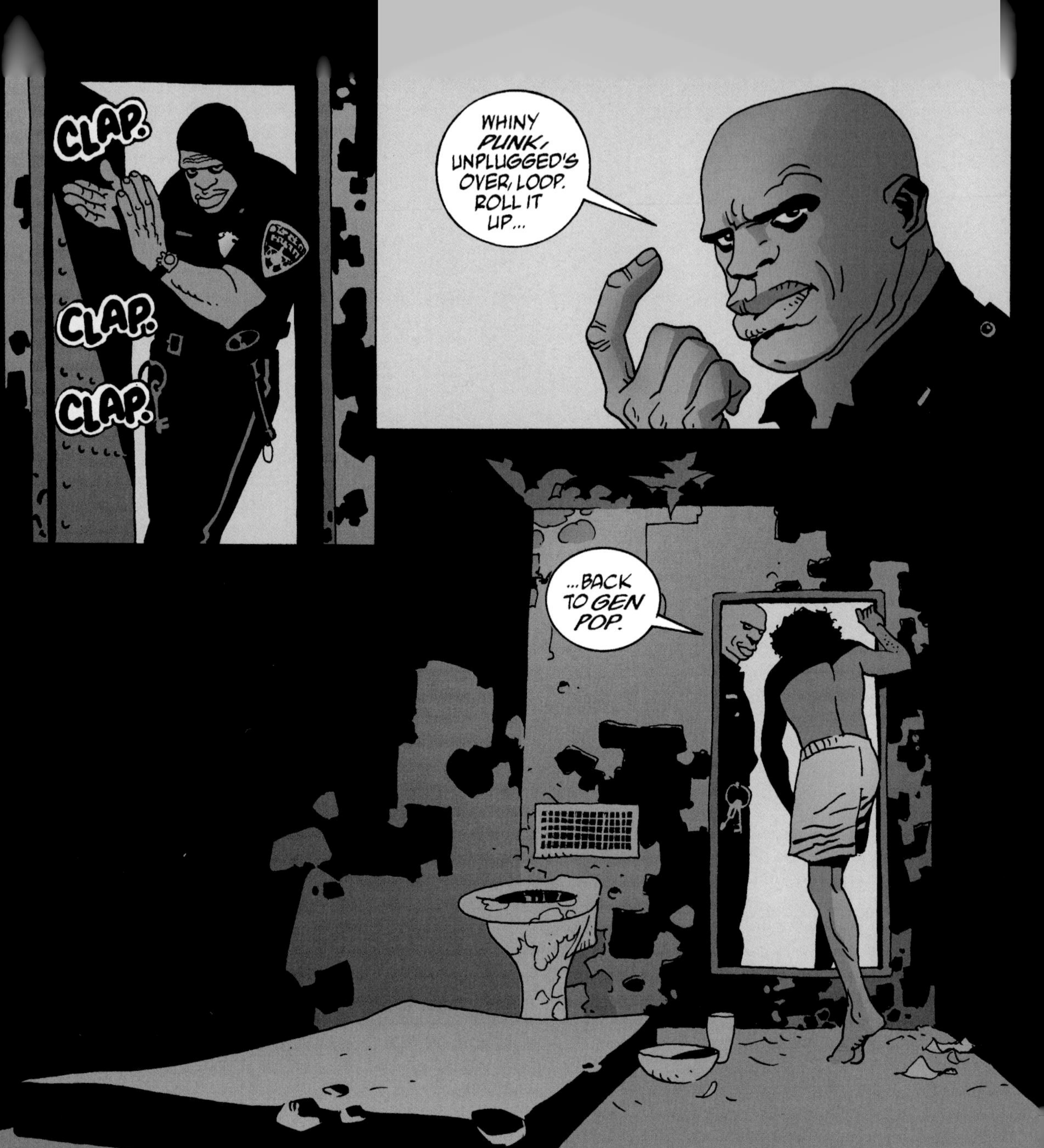
CLAP.
CLAP.
CLAP.
WHINY PUNK, UNPLUGGED'S OVER, LOOP. ROLL IT UP...
...BACK TO GEN POP.

CHILL IN THE OVEN

PART ONE

BRIAN AZZARELLO writer
EDUARDO RISSO artist
PATRICIA MULVIHILL colorist
CLEM ROBINS letterer
ZYLONOL separations
DAVE JOHNSON cover
ZACHARY RAU ass't ed
WILL DENNIS editor

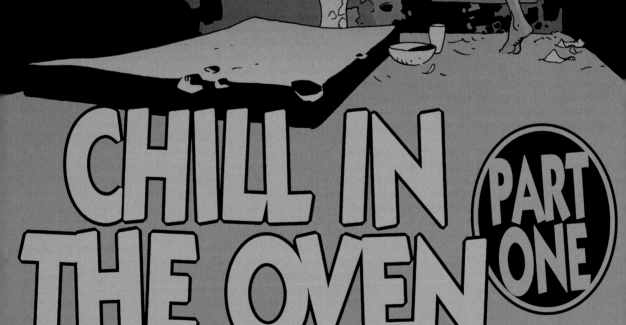

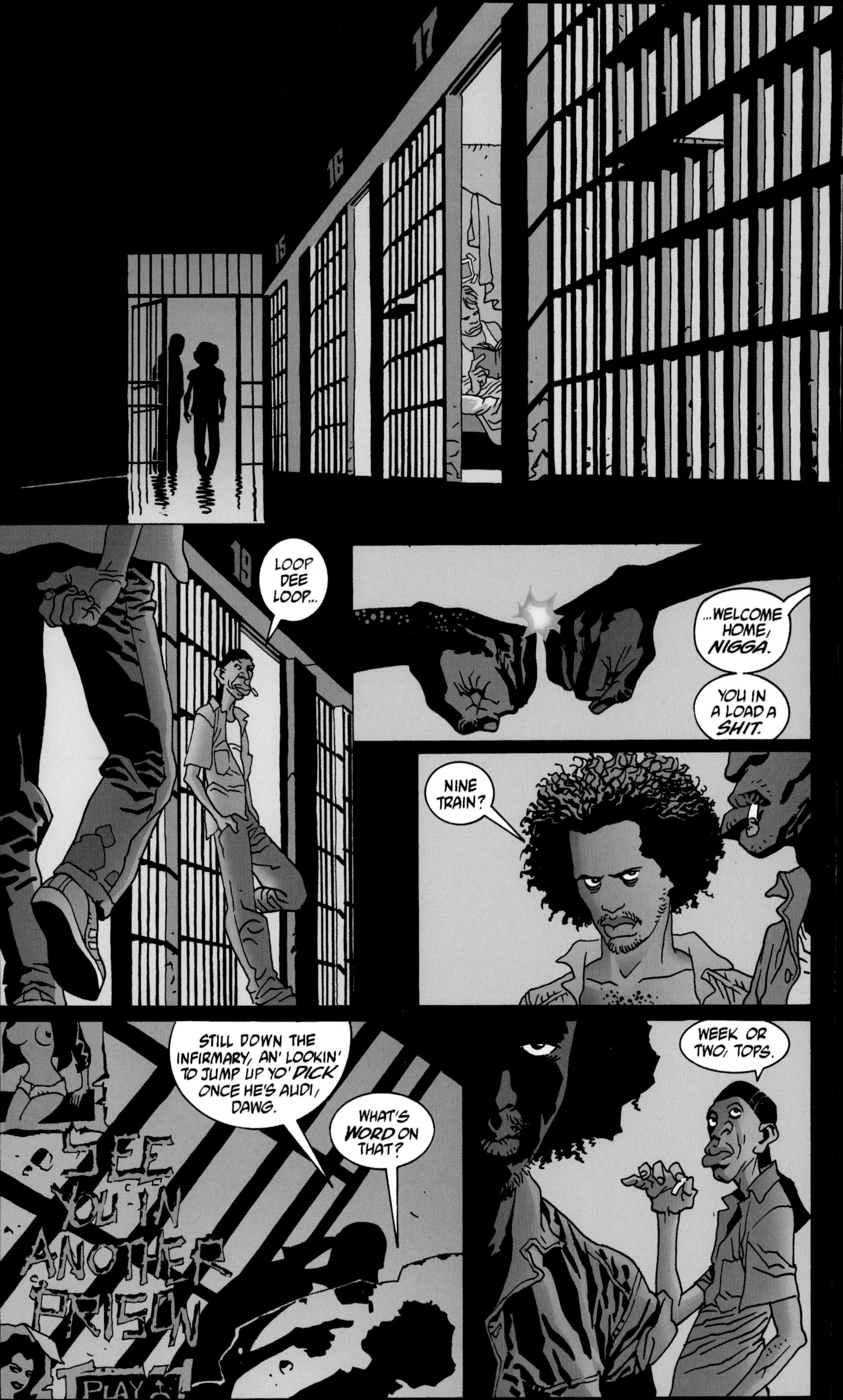

17
16
15
19
LOOP DEE LOOP...
...WELCOME HOME, NIGGA.
YOU IN A LOAD A SHIT.
NINE TRAIN?
STILL DOWN THE INFIRMARY, AN' LOOKIN' TO JUMP UP YO' DICK ONCE HE'S AUDI, DAWG.
WHAT'S WORD ON THAT?
WEEK OR TWO, TOPS.
SEE YOU IN ANOTHER PRISON
PLAY

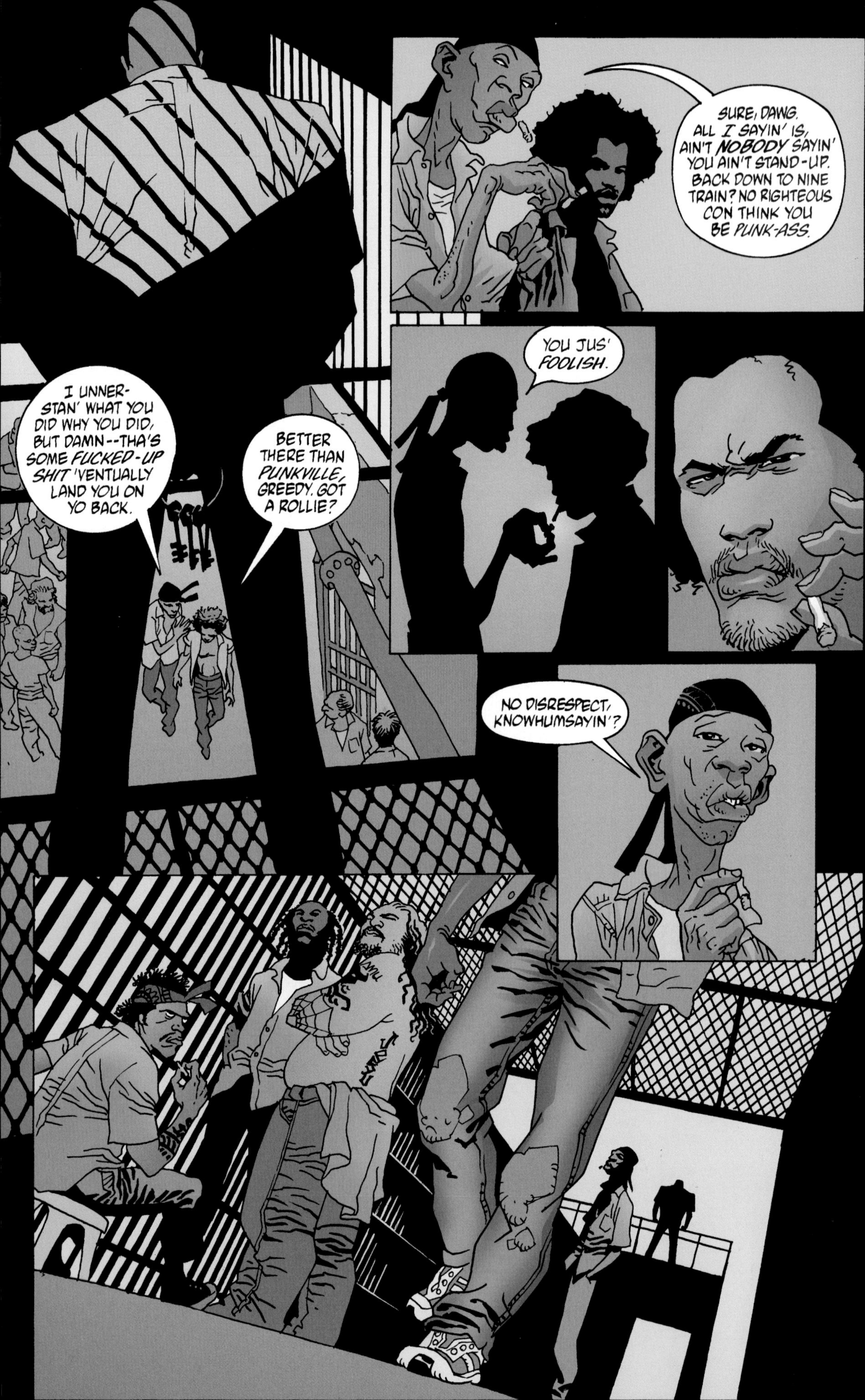
SURE, DAWG. ALL I SAYIN' IS, AIN'T NOBODY SAYIN' YOU AIN'T STAND-UP. BACK DOWN TO NINE TRAIN? NO RIGHTEOUS CON THINK YOU BE PUNK-ASS.
I UNNER-STAN' WHAT YOU DID WHY YOU DID, BUT DAMN--THA'S SOME FUCKED-UP SHIT 'VENTUALLY LAND YOU ON YO BACK.
BETTER THERE THAN PUNKVILLE, GREEDY. GOT A ROLLIE?
YOU JUS' FOOLISH.
NO DISRESPECT, KNOWHUMSAYIN'?

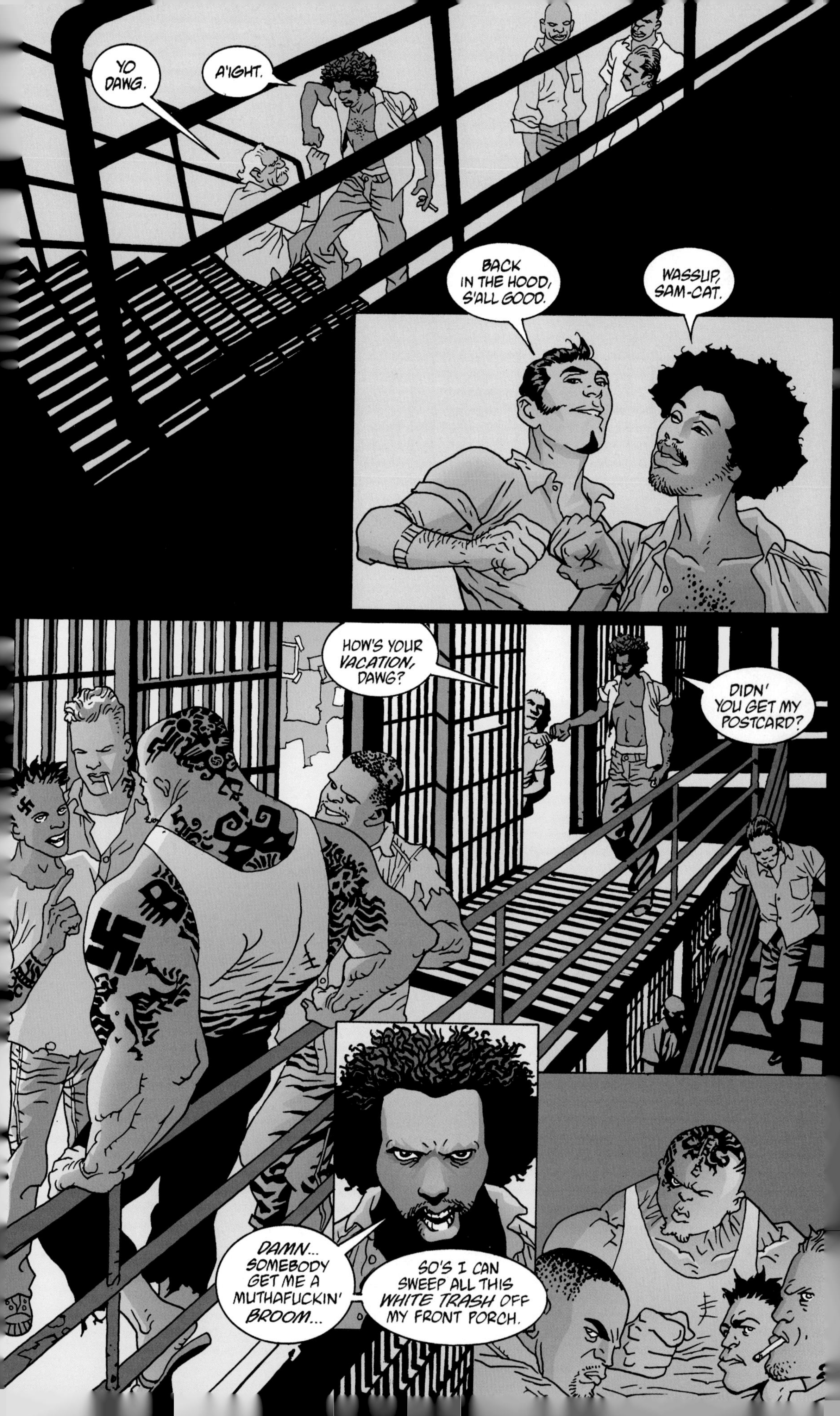
YO DAWG.
A'IGHT.
BACK IN THE HOOD, S'ALL GOOD.
WASSUP, SAM-CAT.
HOW'S YOUR VACATION, DAWG?
DIDN' YOU GET MY POSTCARD?
DAMN... SOMEBODY GET ME A MUTHAFUCKIN' BROOM...
SO'S I CAN SWEEP ALL THIS WHITE TRASH OFF MY FRONT PORCH.

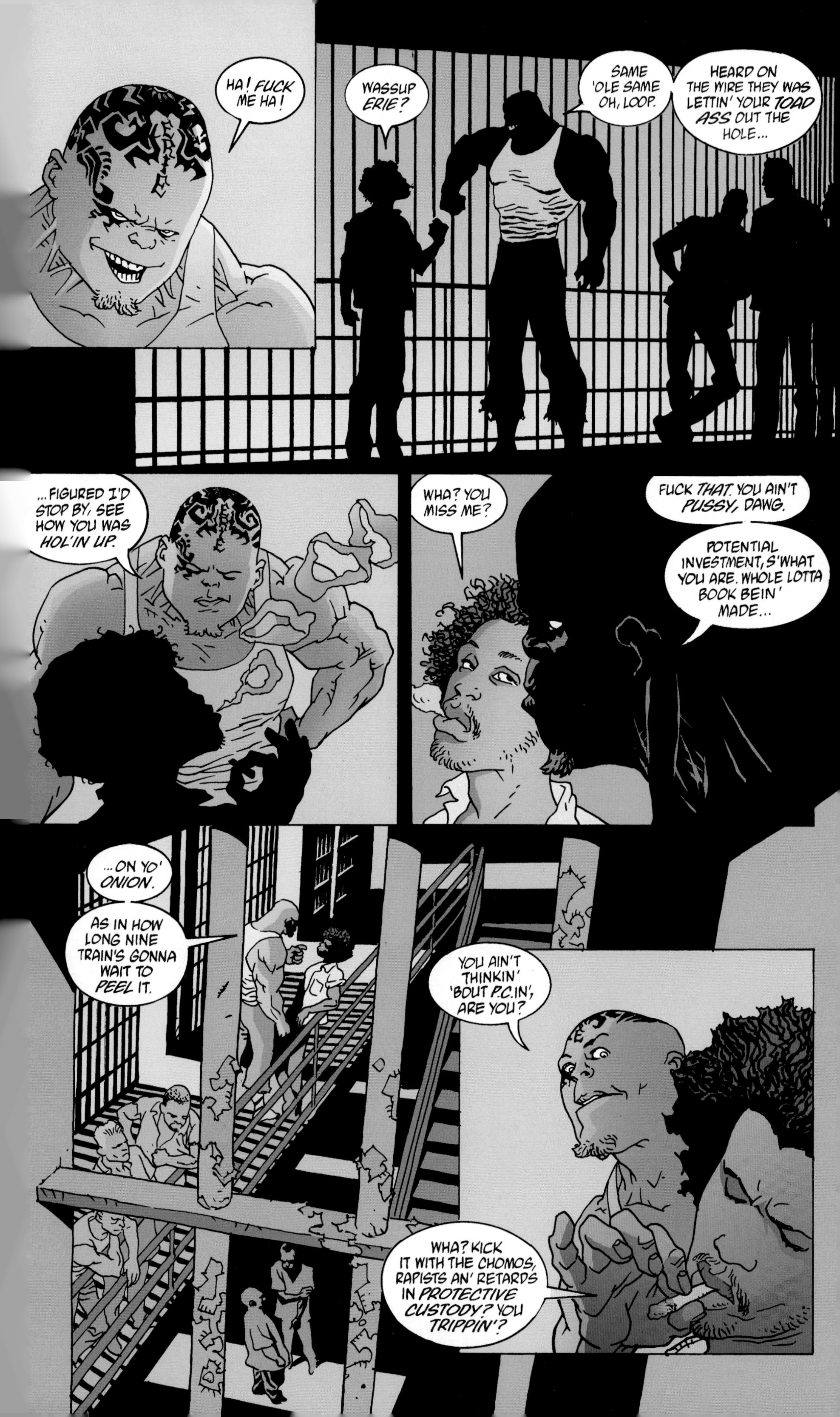
HA! FUCK ME HA!
WASSUP ERIE?
SAME 'OLE SAME OH, LOOP.
HEARD ON THE WIRE THEY WAS LETTIN' YOUR TOAD ASS OUT THE HOLE...
...FIGURED I'D STOP BY, SEE HOW YOU WAS HOL'IN UP.
WHA? YOU MISS ME?
FUCK THAT. YOU AIN'T PUSSY, DAWG.
POTENTIAL INVESTMENT, S'WHAT YOU ARE. WHOLE LOTTA BOOK BEIN' MADE...
...ON YO' ONION.
AS IN HOW LONG NINE TRAIN'S GONNA WAIT TO PEEL IT.
YOU AIN'T THINKIN' 'BOUT P.C.IN', ARE YOU?
WHA? KICK IT WITH THE CHOMOS, RAPISTS AN' RETARDS IN PROTECTIVE CUSTODY? YOU TRIPPIN'?

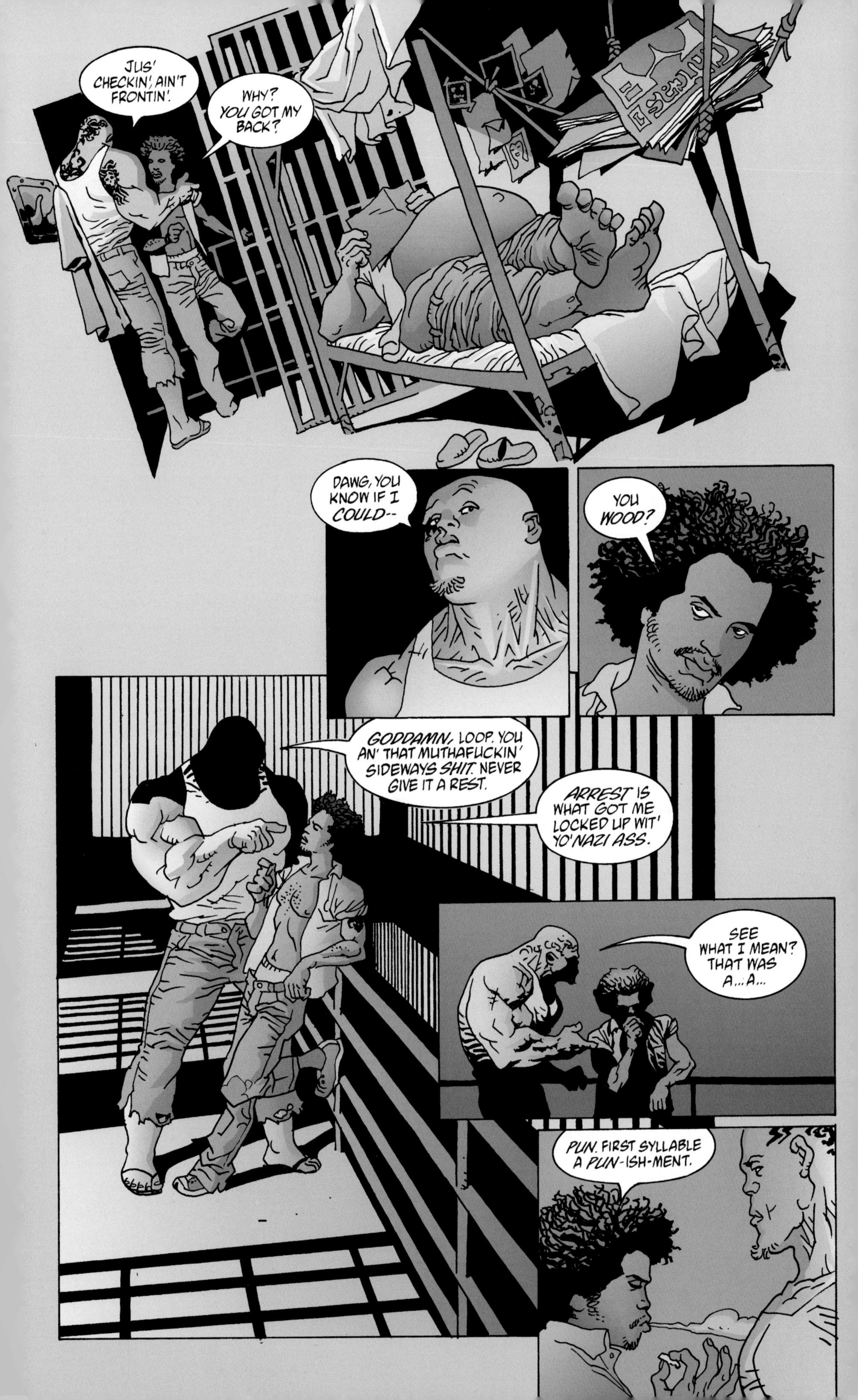
JUS' CHECKIN', AIN'T FRONTIN'.
WHY? YOU GOT MY BACK?
DAWG, YOU KNOW IF I COULD--
YOU WOOD?
GODDAMN, LOOP. YOU AN' THAT MUTHAFUCKIN' SIDEWAYS SHIT. NEVER GIVE IT A REST.
ARREST IS WHAT GOT ME LOCKED UP WIT' YO' NAZI ASS.
SEE WHAT I MEAN? THAT WAS A... A...
PUN. FIRST SYLLABLE A PUN-ISH-MENT.

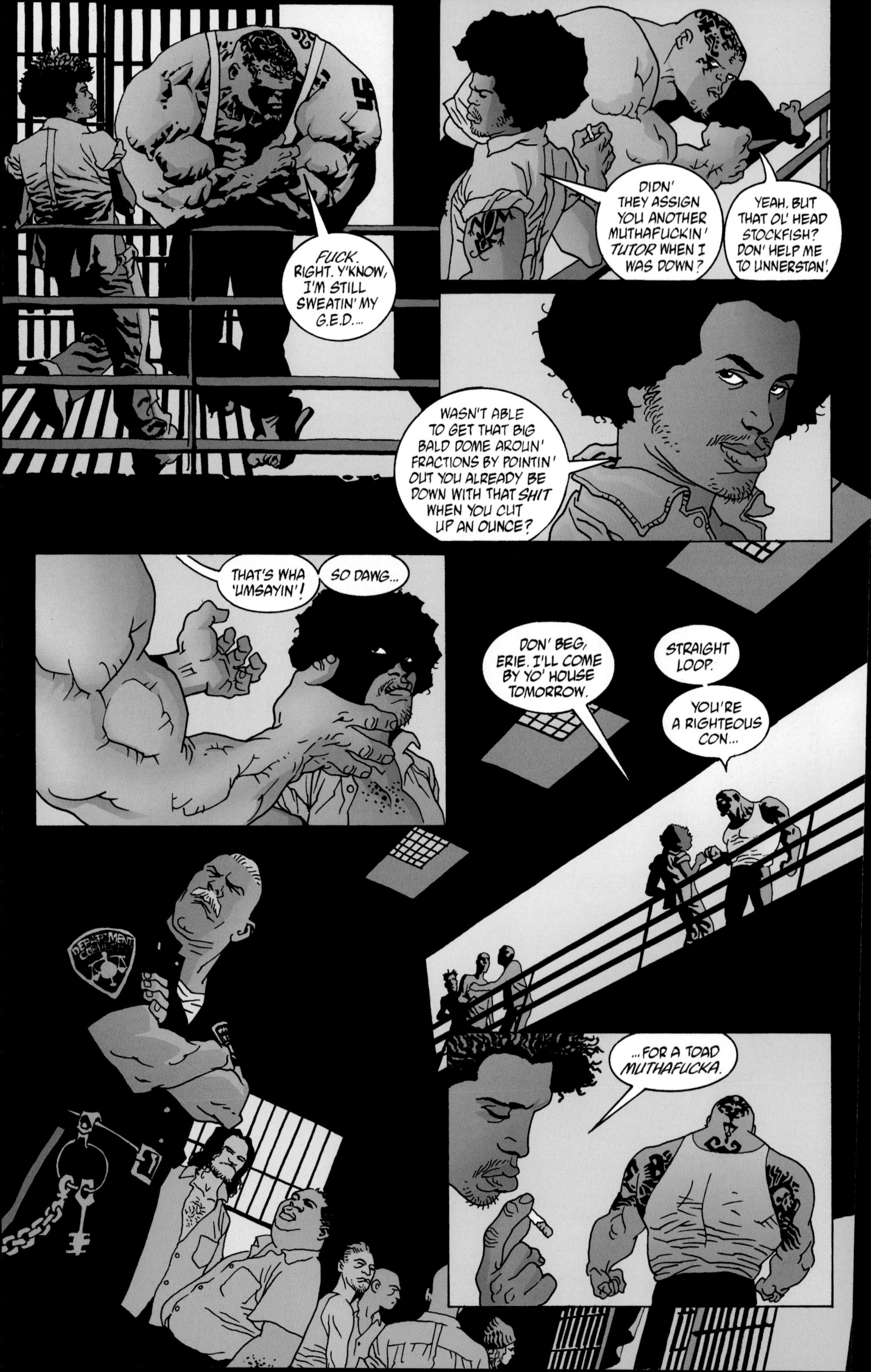
FUCK. RIGHT. Y'KNOW, I'M STILL SWEATIN' MY G.E.D....
DIDN' THEY ASSIGN YOU ANOTHER MUTHAFUCKIN' TUTOR WHEN I WAS DOWN?
YEAH, BUT THAT OL' HEAD STOCKFISH? DON' HELP ME TO UNNERSTAN'.
WASN'T ABLE TO GET THAT BIG BALD DOME AROUN' FRACTIONS BY POINTIN' OUT YOU ALREADY BE DOWN WITH THAT SHIT WHEN YOU CUT UP AN OUNCE?
THAT'S WHA 'UMSAYIN'!
SO DAWG...
DON' BEG, ERIE. I'LL COME BY YO' HOUSE TOMORROW.
STRAIGHT LOOP.
YOU'RE A RIGHTEOUS CON...
...FOR A TOAD MUTHAFUCKA.

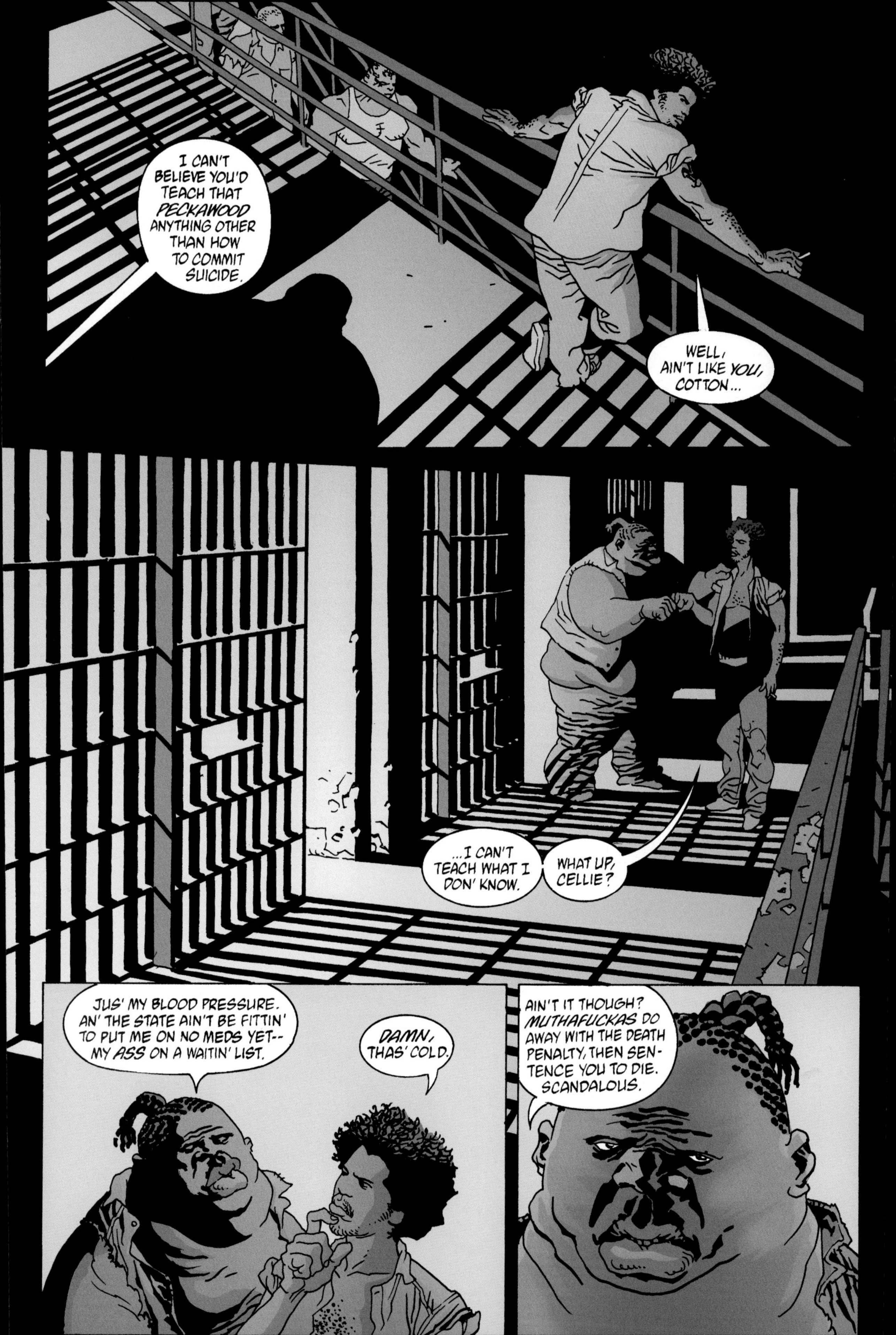
I CAN'T BELIEVE YOU'D TEACH THAT *PECKAWOOD* ANYTHING OTHER THAN HOW TO COMMIT SUICIDE.
WELL, AIN'T LIKE *YOU*, COTTON...
...I CAN'T TEACH WHAT I DON' KNOW.
WHAT UP, CELLIE?
JUS' MY BLOOD PRESSURE. AN' THE STATE AIN'T BE FITTIN' TO PUT ME ON NO MEDS YET-- MY *ASS* ON A WAITIN' LIST.
DAMN, THAS' COLD.
AIN'T IT THOUGH? *MUTHAFUCKAS* DO AWAY WITH THE DEATH PENALTY, THEN SEN-TENCE YOU TO DIE. SCANDALOUS.

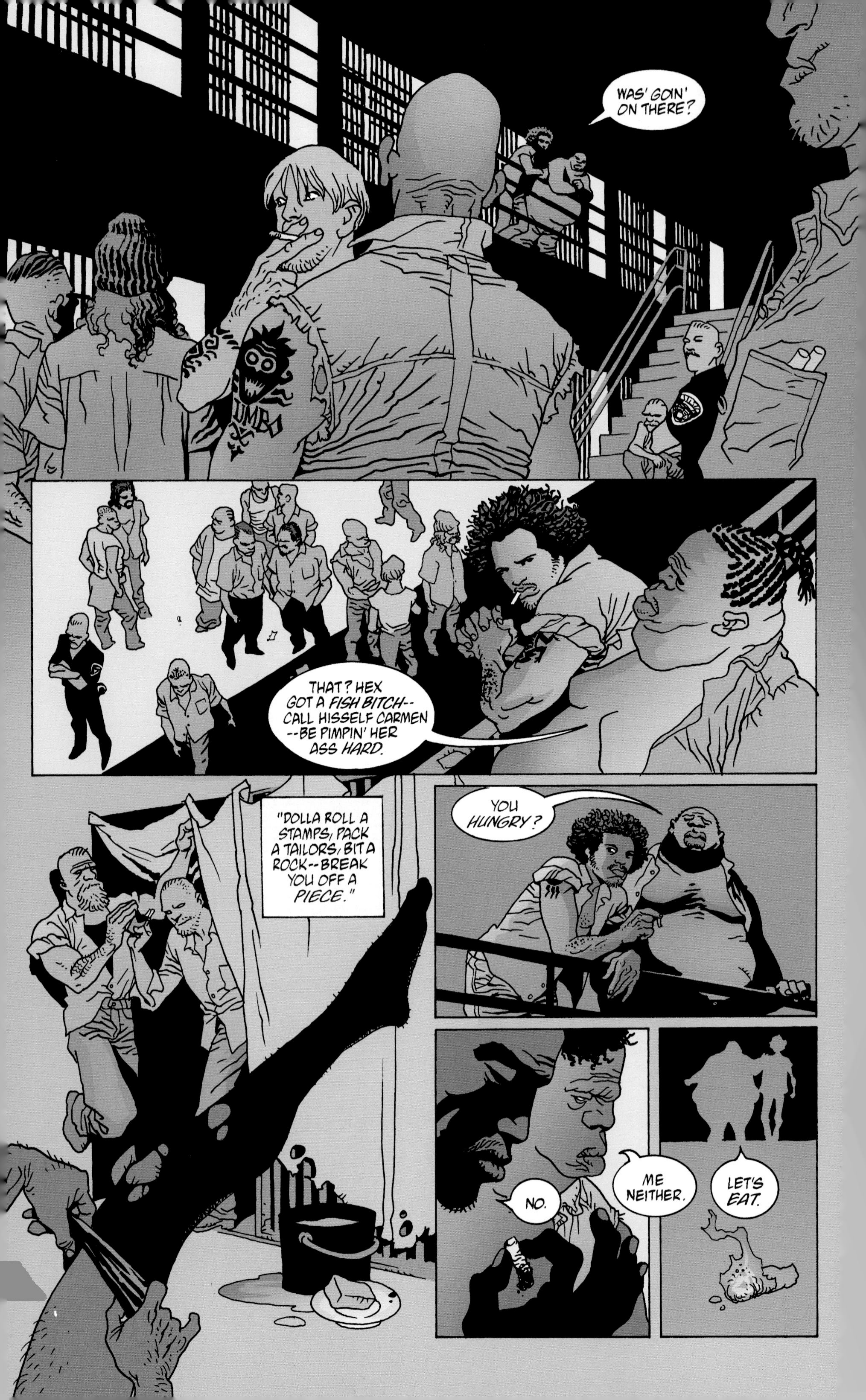
WAS' GOIN' ON THERE?
THAT? HEX GOT A FISH BITCH-- CALL HISSELF CARMEN --BE PIMPIN' HER ASS HARD.
"DOLLA ROLL A STAMPS, PACK A TAILORS, BIT A ROCK--BREAK YOU OFF A PIECE."
YOU HUNGRY?
NO.
ME NEITHER.
LET'S EAT.

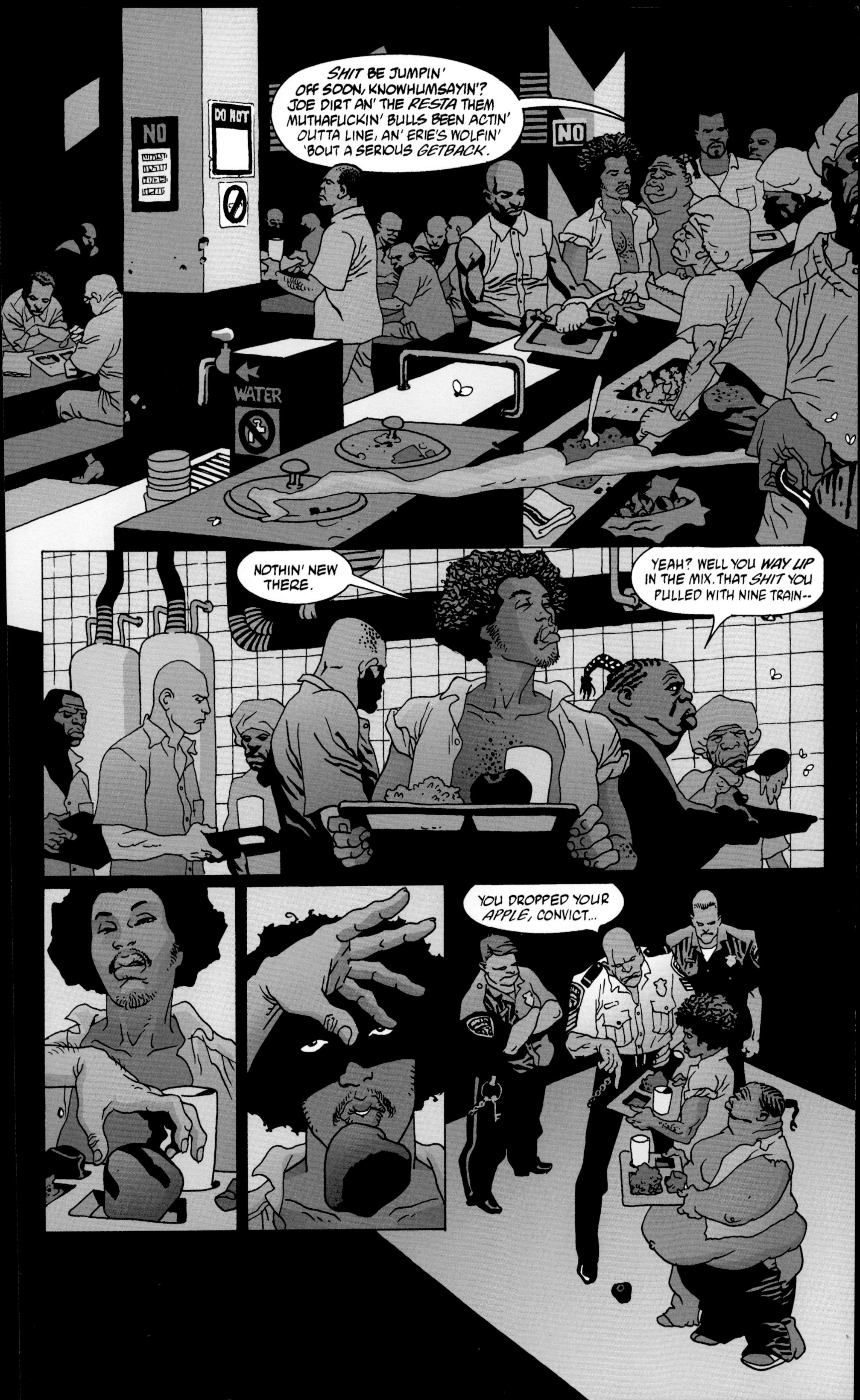
SHIT BE JUMPIN' OFF SOON, KNOWHUMSAYIN'? JOE DIRT AN' THE RESTA THEM MUTHAFUCKIN' BULLS BEEN ACTIN' OUTTA LINE, AN' ERIE'S WOLFIN' 'BOUT A SERIOUS GETBACK.
NO
DO NOT
NO
WATER
NOTHIN' NEW THERE.
YEAH? WELL YOU WAY UP IN THE MIX. THAT SHIT YOU PULLED WITH NINE TRAIN--
YOU DROPPED YOUR APPLE, CONVICT...

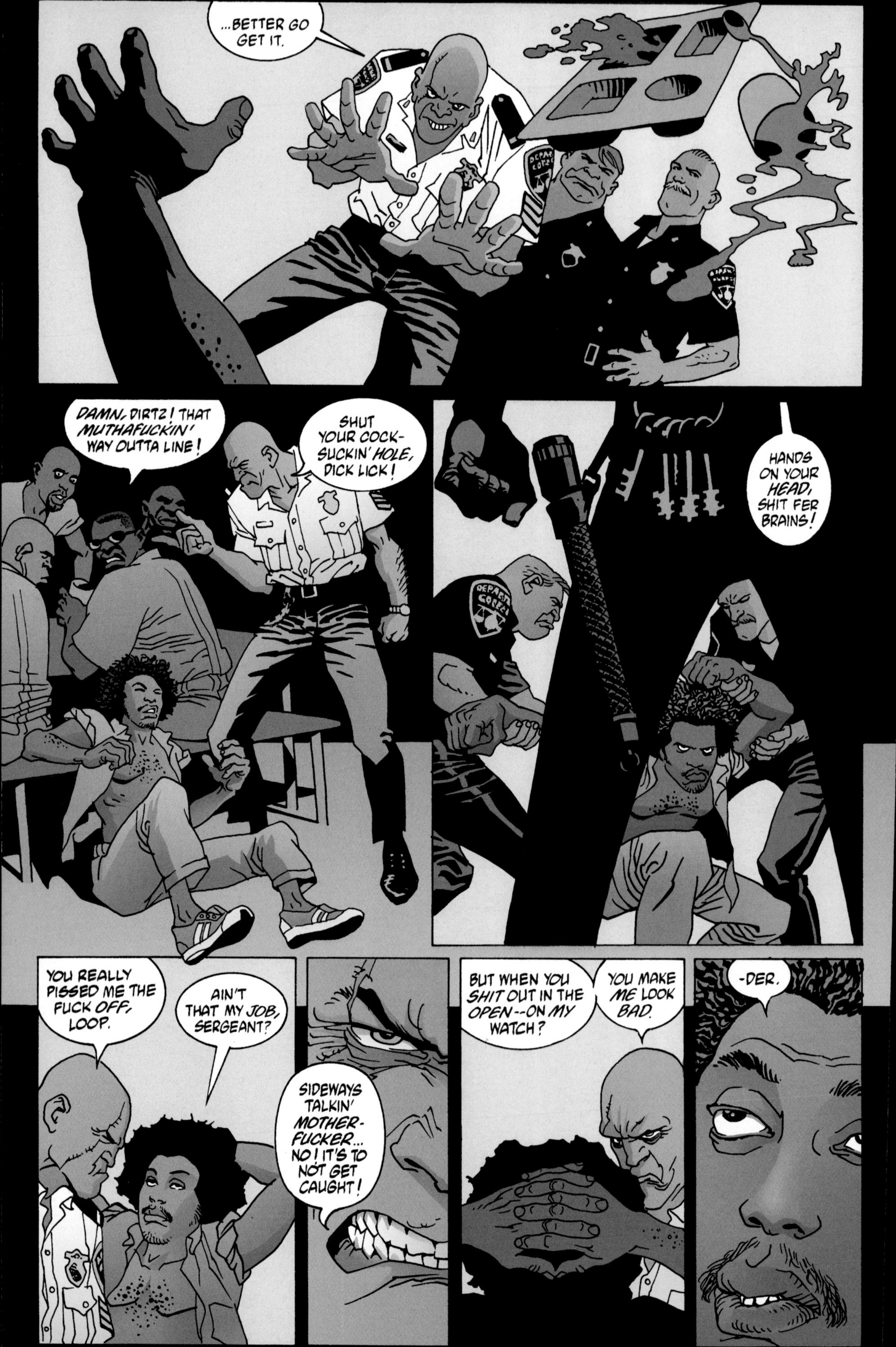
...BETTER GO GET IT.
DAMN, DIRTZ! THAT MUTHAFUCKIN' WAY OUTTA LINE!
SHUT YOUR COCK-SUCKIN' HOLE, DICK LICK!
HANDS ON YOUR HEAD, SHIT FER BRAINS!
YOU REALLY PISSED ME THE FUCK OFF, LOOP.
AIN'T THAT MY JOB, SERGEANT?
SIDEWAYS TALKIN' MOTHER-FUCKER... NO! IT'S TO NOT GET CAUGHT!
BUT WHEN YOU SHIT OUT IN THE OPEN--ON MY WATCH?
YOU MAKE ME LOOK BAD.
-DER.

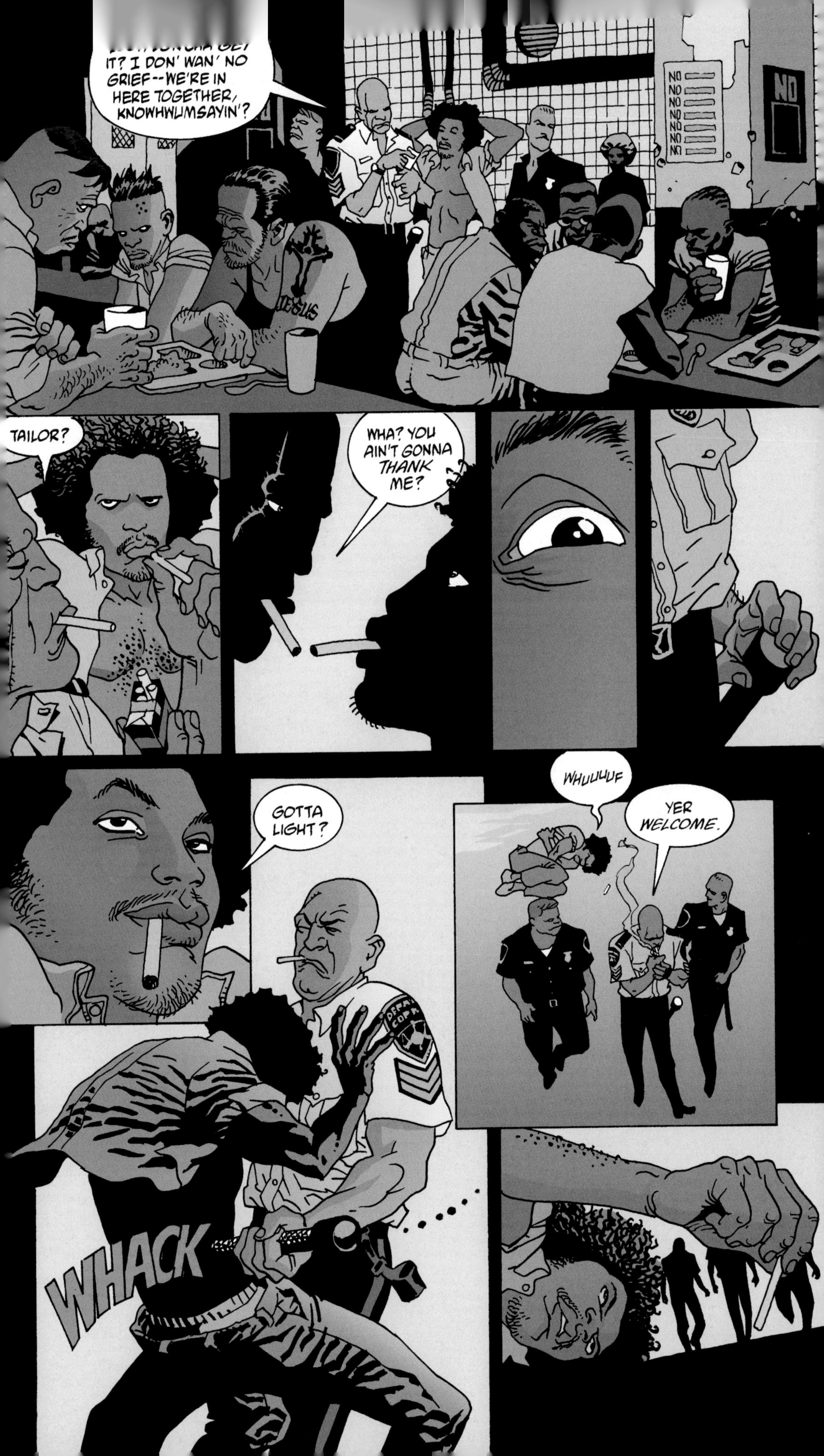
IT? I DON' WAN' NO GRIEF--WE'RE IN HERE TOGETHER, KNOWHWUMSAYIN'?
NO
TAILOR?
WHA? YOU AIN'T GONNA THANK ME?
GOTTA LIGHT?
WHACK
WHUUUUF
YER WELCOME.

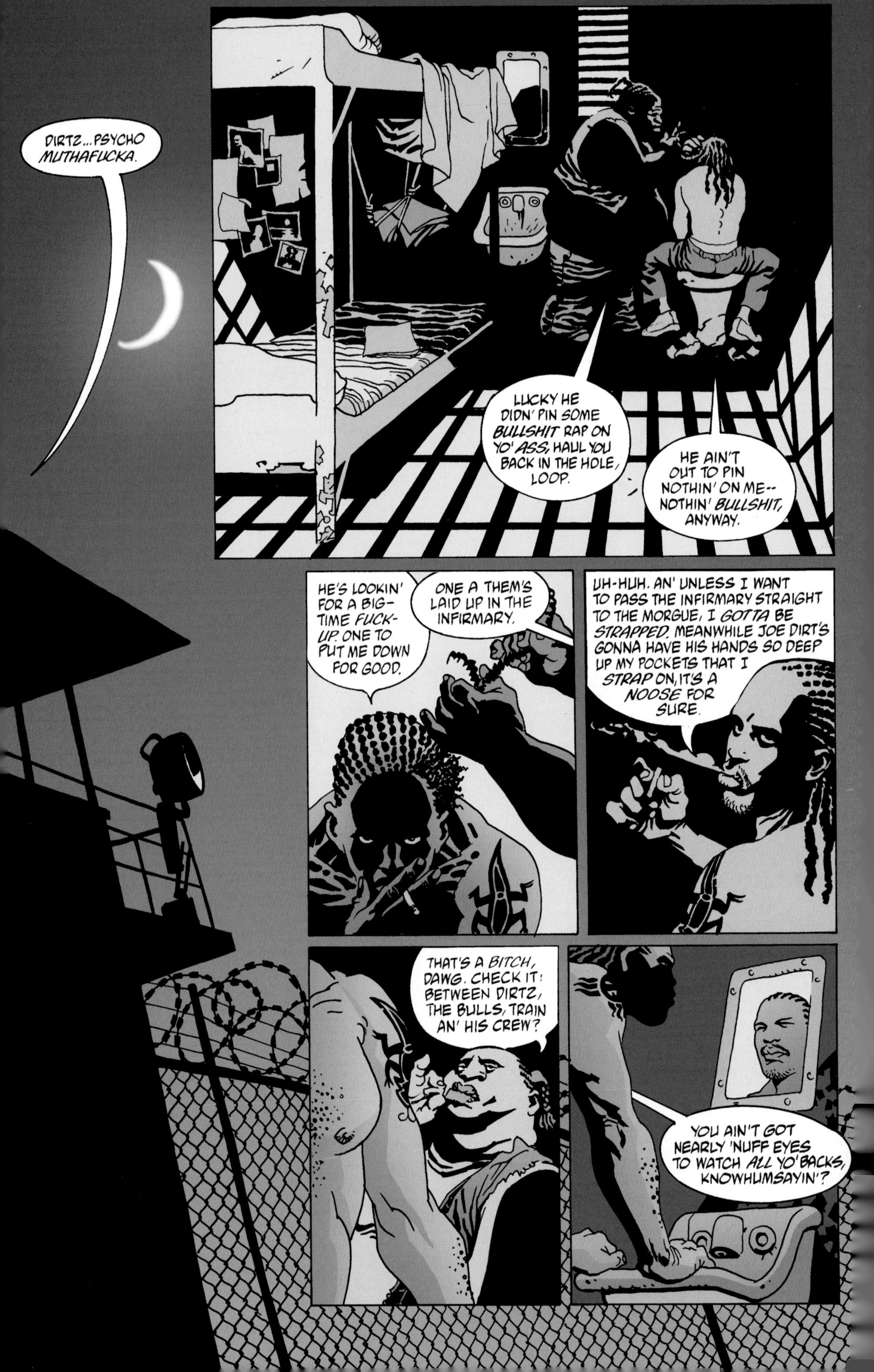
DIRTZ...PSYCHO MUTHAFUCKA.
LUCKY HE DIDN' PIN SOME BULLSHIT RAP ON YO' ASS, HAUL YOU BACK IN THE HOLE, LOOP.
HE AIN'T OUT TO PIN NOTHIN' ON ME-- NOTHIN' BULLSHIT, ANYWAY.
HE'S LOOKIN' FOR A BIG-TIME FUCK-UP. ONE TO PUT ME DOWN FOR GOOD.
ONE A THEM'S LAID UP IN THE INFIRMARY.
UH-HUH. AN' UNLESS I WANT TO PASS THE INFIRMARY STRAIGHT TO THE MORGUE, I GOTTA BE STRAPPED. MEANWHILE JOE DIRT'S GONNA HAVE HIS HANDS SO DEEP UP MY POCKETS THAT I STRAP ON, IT'S A NOOSE FOR SURE.
THAT'S A BITCH, DAWG. CHECK IT: BETWEEN DIRTZ, THE BULLS, TRAIN AN' HIS CREW?
YOU AIN'T GOT NEARLY 'NUFF EYES TO WATCH ALL YO' BACKS, KNOWHUMSAYIN'?

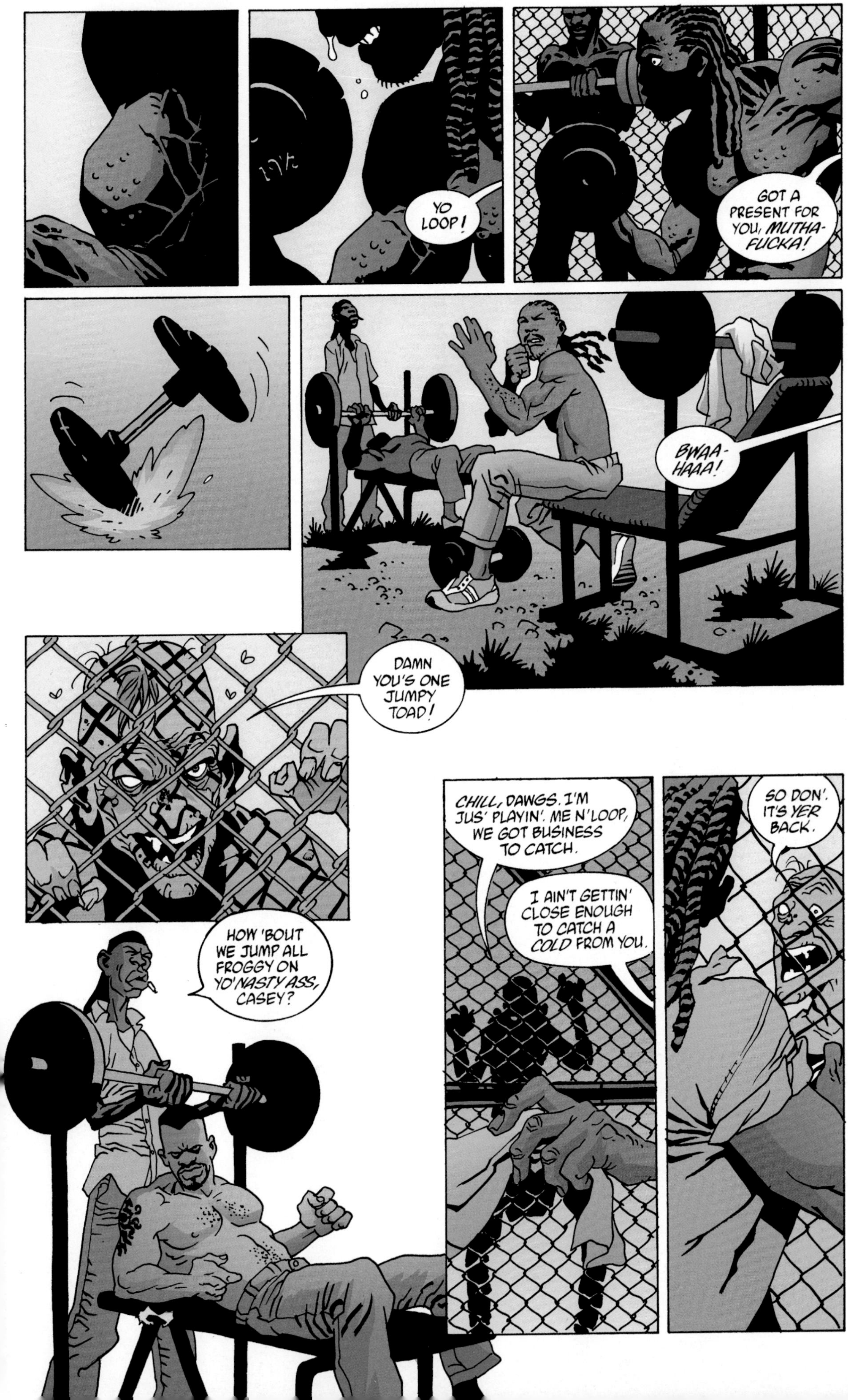
YO LOOP!
GOT A PRESENT FOR YOU, MUTHA-FUCKA!
BWAA-HAAA!
DAMN YOU'S ONE JUMPY TOAD!
HOW 'BOUT WE JUMP ALL FROGGY ON YO' NASTY ASS, CASEY?
CHILL, DAWGS. I'M JUS' PLAYIN'. ME N' LOOP, WE GOT BUSINESS TO CATCH.
I AIN'T GETTIN' CLOSE ENOUGH TO CATCH A COLD FROM YOU.
SO DON'. IT'S YER BACK.

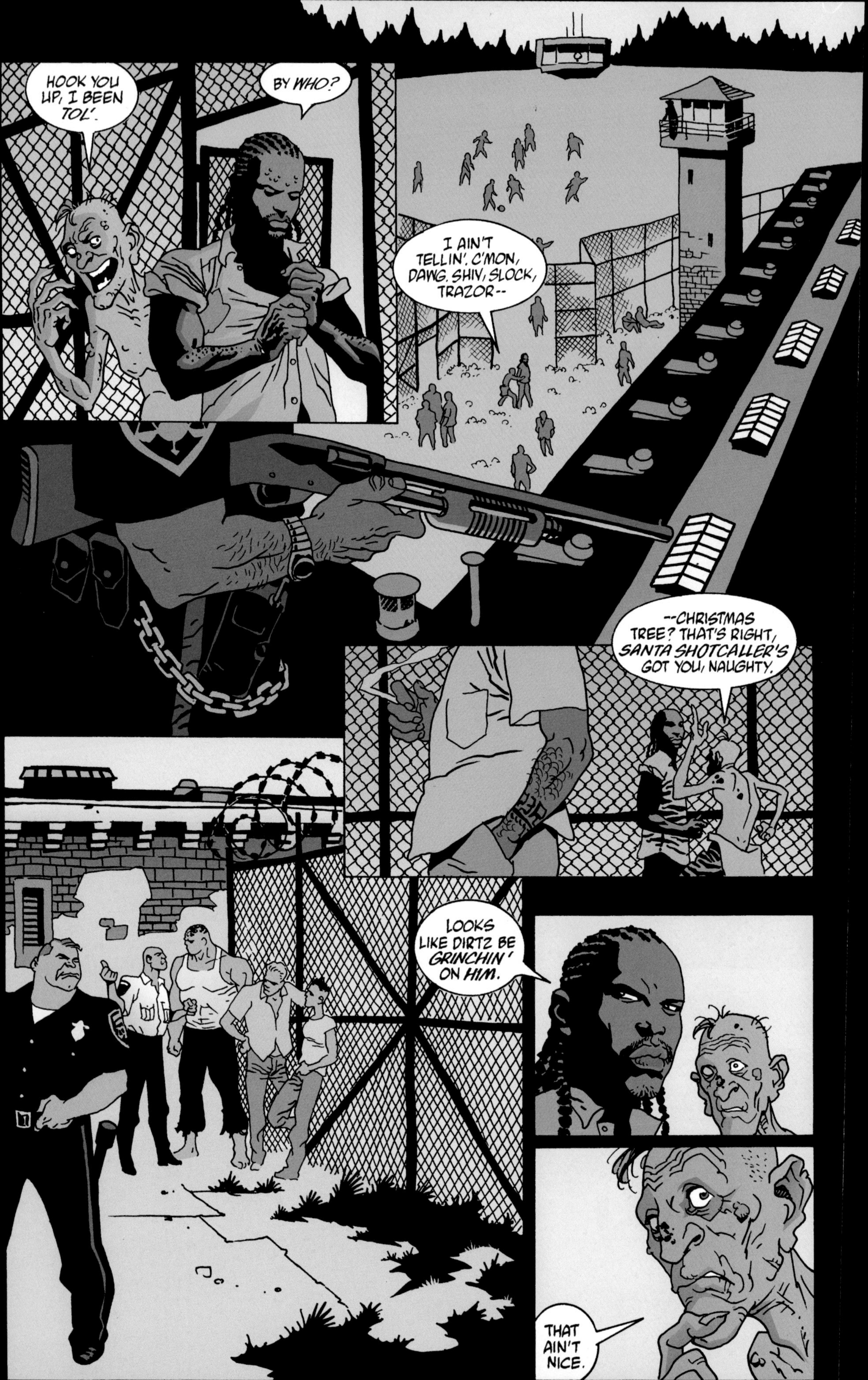
HOOK YOU UP, I BEEN TOL'.
BY WHO?
I AIN'T TELLIN'. C'MON, DAWG. SHIV, SLOCK, TRAZOR--
--CHRISTMAS TREE? THAT'S RIGHT, SANTA SHOTCALLER'S GOT YOU, NAUGHTY.
LOOKS LIKE DIRTZ BE GRINCHIN' ON HIM.
THAT AIN'T NICE.

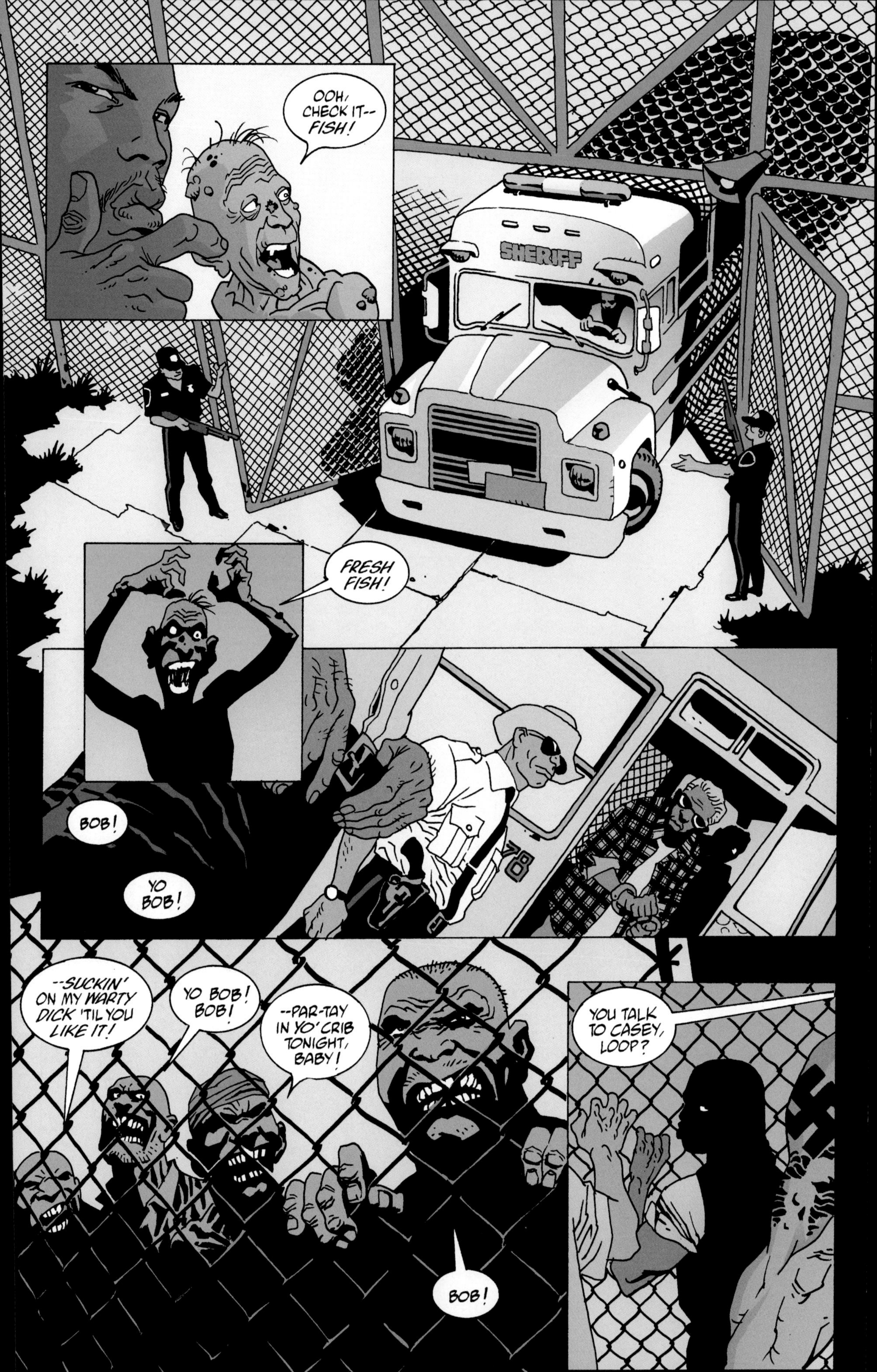
OOH, CHECK IT-- FISH!
FRESH FISH!
BOB!
YO BOB!
--SUCKIN' ON MY WARTY DICK 'TIL YOU LIKE IT!
YO BOB! BOB!
--PAR-TAY IN YO' CRIB TONIGHT, BABY!
BOB!
YOU TALK TO CASEY, LOOP?

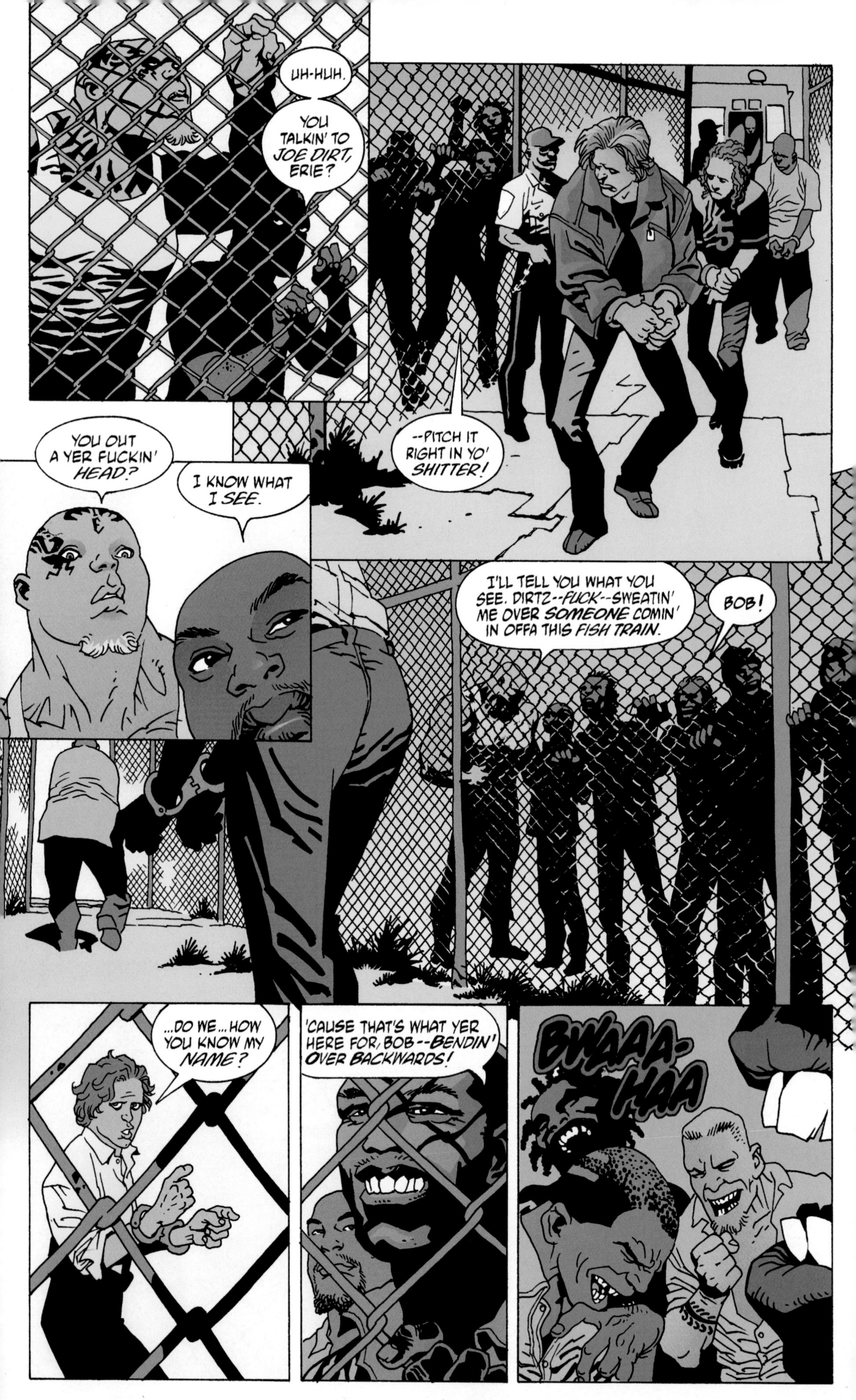

UH-HUH.
YOU TALKIN' TO JOE DIRT, ERIE?
--PITCH IT RIGHT IN YO' SHITTER!
YOU OUT A YER FUCKIN' HEAD?
I KNOW WHAT I SEE.
I'LL TELL YOU WHAT YOU SEE. DIRTZ--FUCK--SWEATIN' ME OVER SOMEONE COMIN' IN OFFA THIS FISH TRAIN.
BOB!
...DO WE... HOW YOU KNOW MY NAME?
'CAUSE THAT'S WHAT YER HERE FOR, BOB--BENDIN' OVER BACKWARDS!
BWAAA-HAA

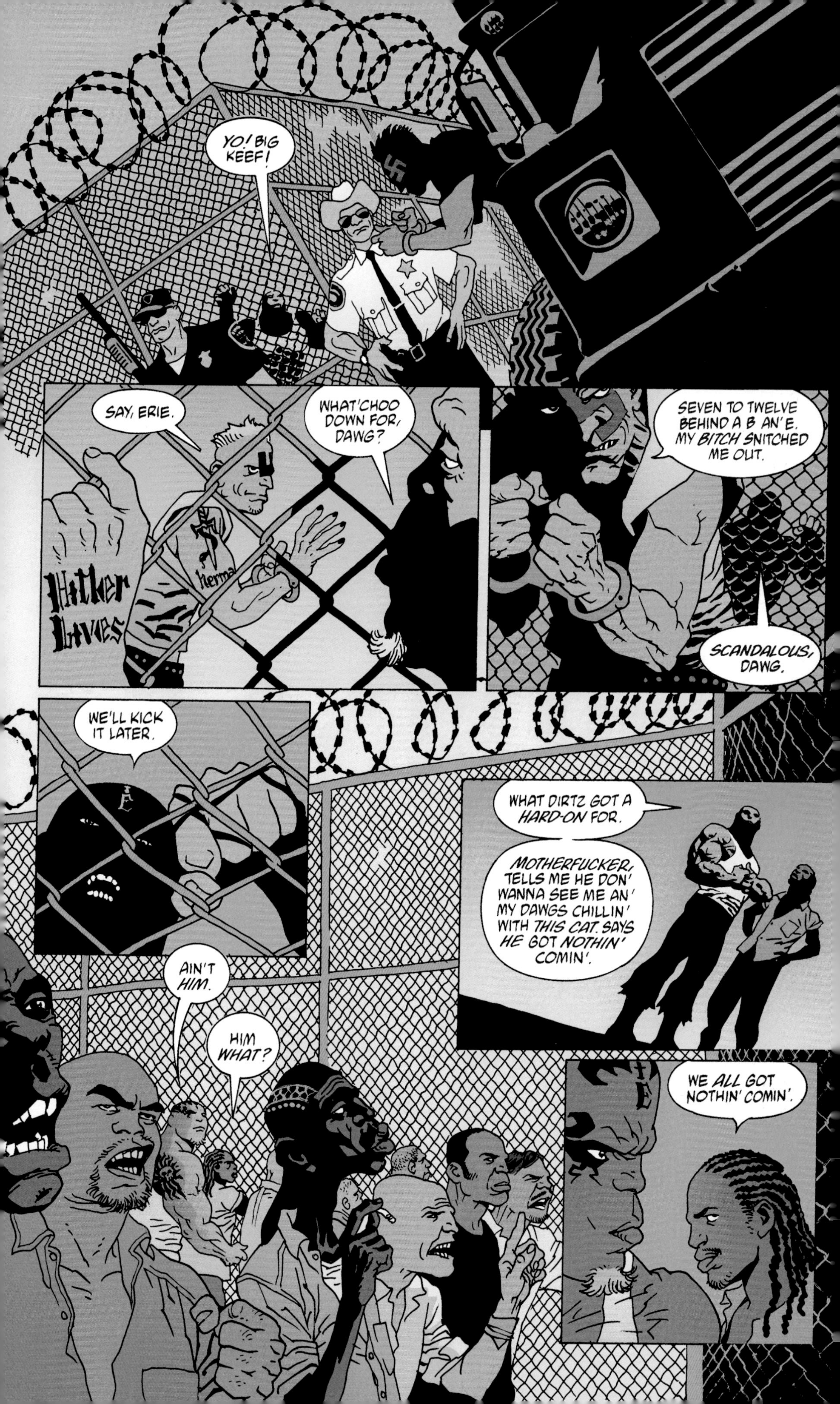

YO! BIG KEEF!
SAY, ERIE.
WHAT'CHOO DOWN FOR, DAWG?
SEVEN TO TWELVE BEHIND A B AN' E. MY BITCH SNITCHED ME OUT.
SCANDALOUS, DAWG.
Hitler Lives
WE'LL KICK IT LATER.
WHAT DIRTZ GOT A HARD-ON FOR.
MOTHERFUCKER, TELLS ME HE DON' WANNA SEE ME AN' MY DAWGS CHILLIN' WITH THIS CAT. SAYS HE GOT NOTHIN' COMIN'.
AIN'T HIM.
HIM WHAT?
WE ALL GOT NOTHIN' COMIN'.

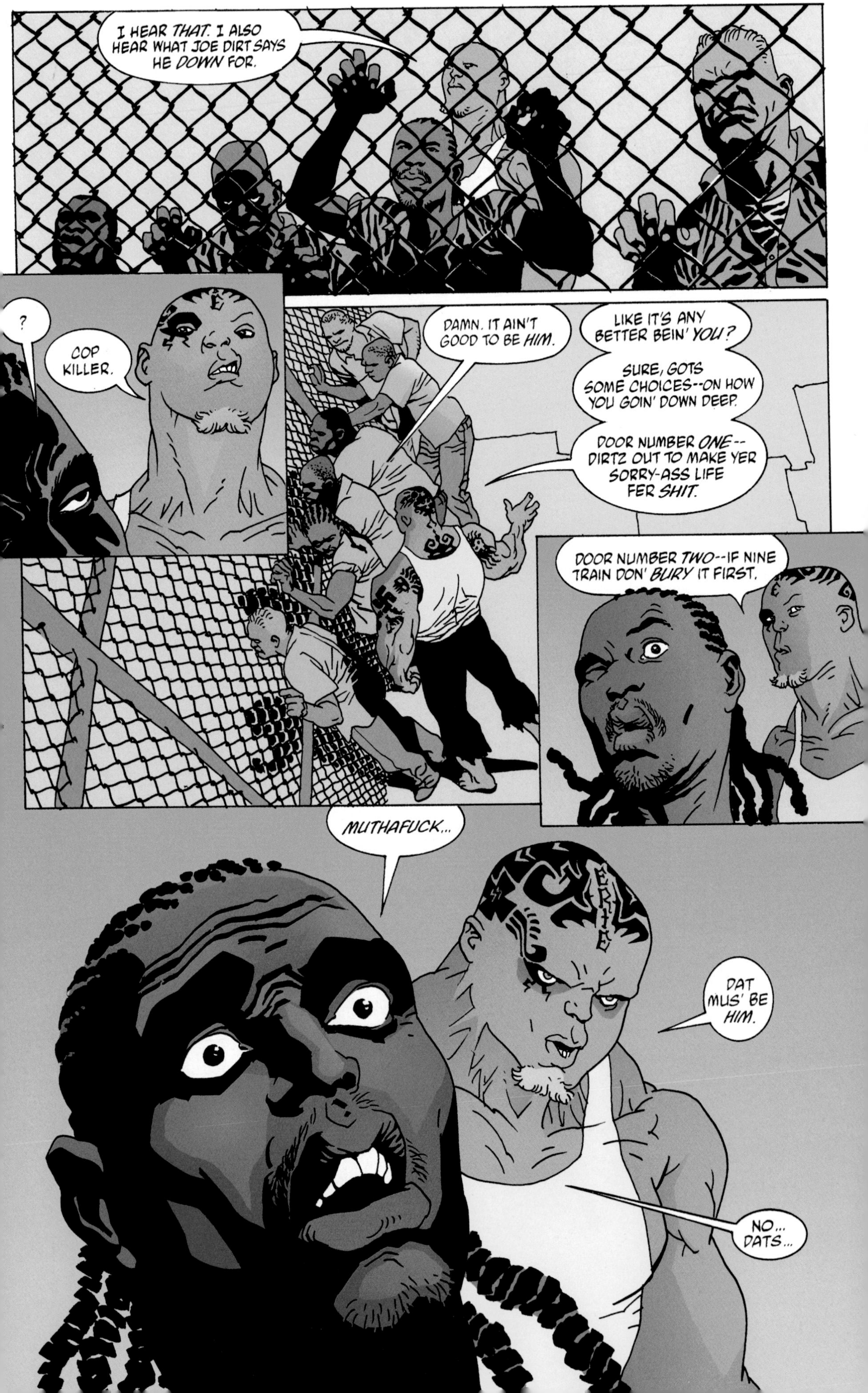
I HEAR *THAT.* I ALSO HEAR WHAT JOE DIRT SAYS HE *DOWN* FOR.
?
COP KILLER.
DAMN. IT AIN'T GOOD TO BE *HIM.*
LIKE IT'S ANY BETTER BEIN' *YOU?*
SURE, GOTS SOME CHOICES--ON HOW YOU GOIN' DOWN DEEP.
DOOR NUMBER *ONE*--DIRTZ OUT TO MAKE YER SORRY-ASS LIFE FER *SHIT.*
DOOR NUMBER *TWO*--IF NINE TRAIN DON' *BURY* IT FIRST.
MUTHAFUCK...
DAT MUS' BE *HIM.*
NO... DATS...

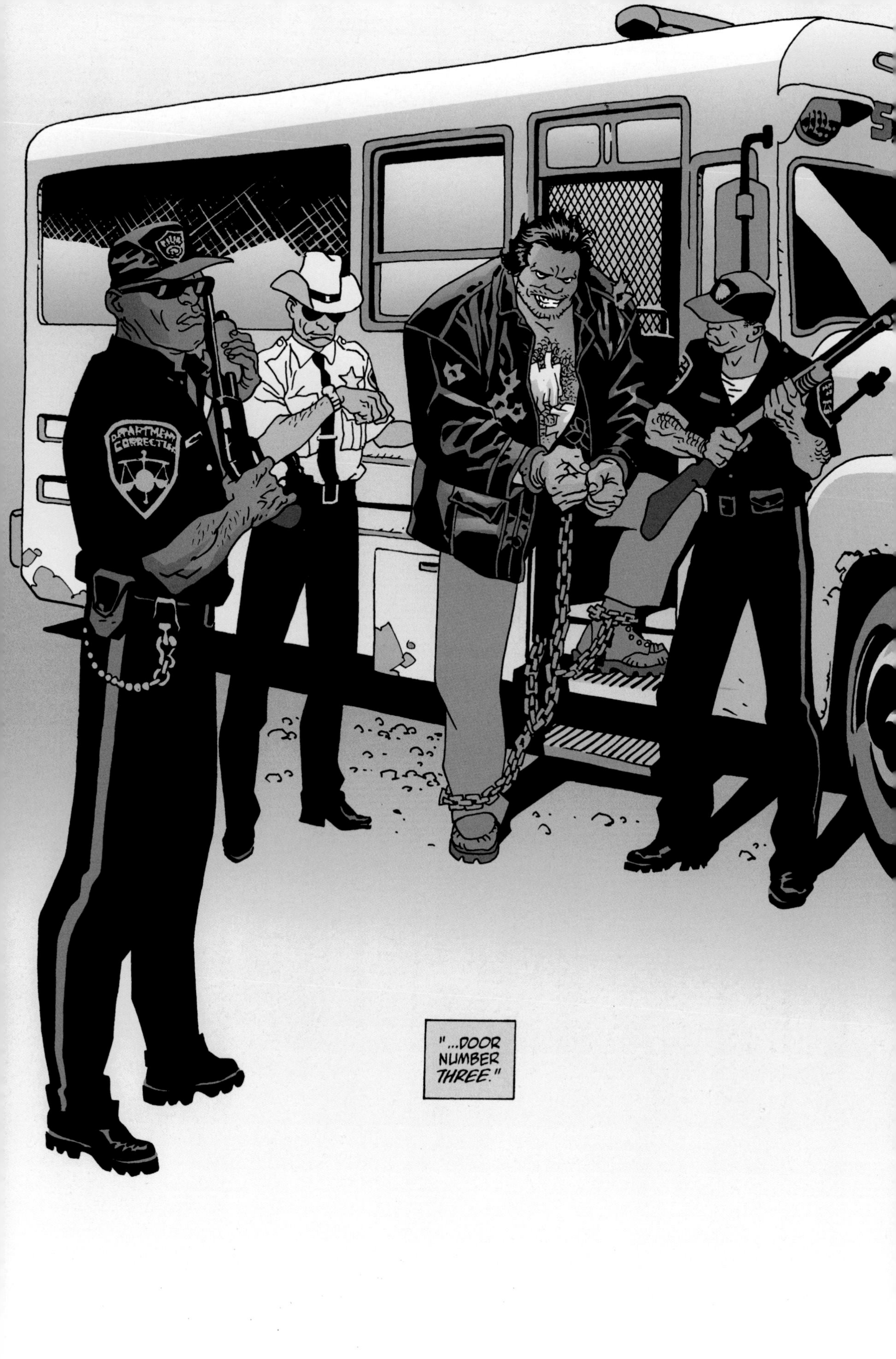
"...DOOR NUMBER THREE."

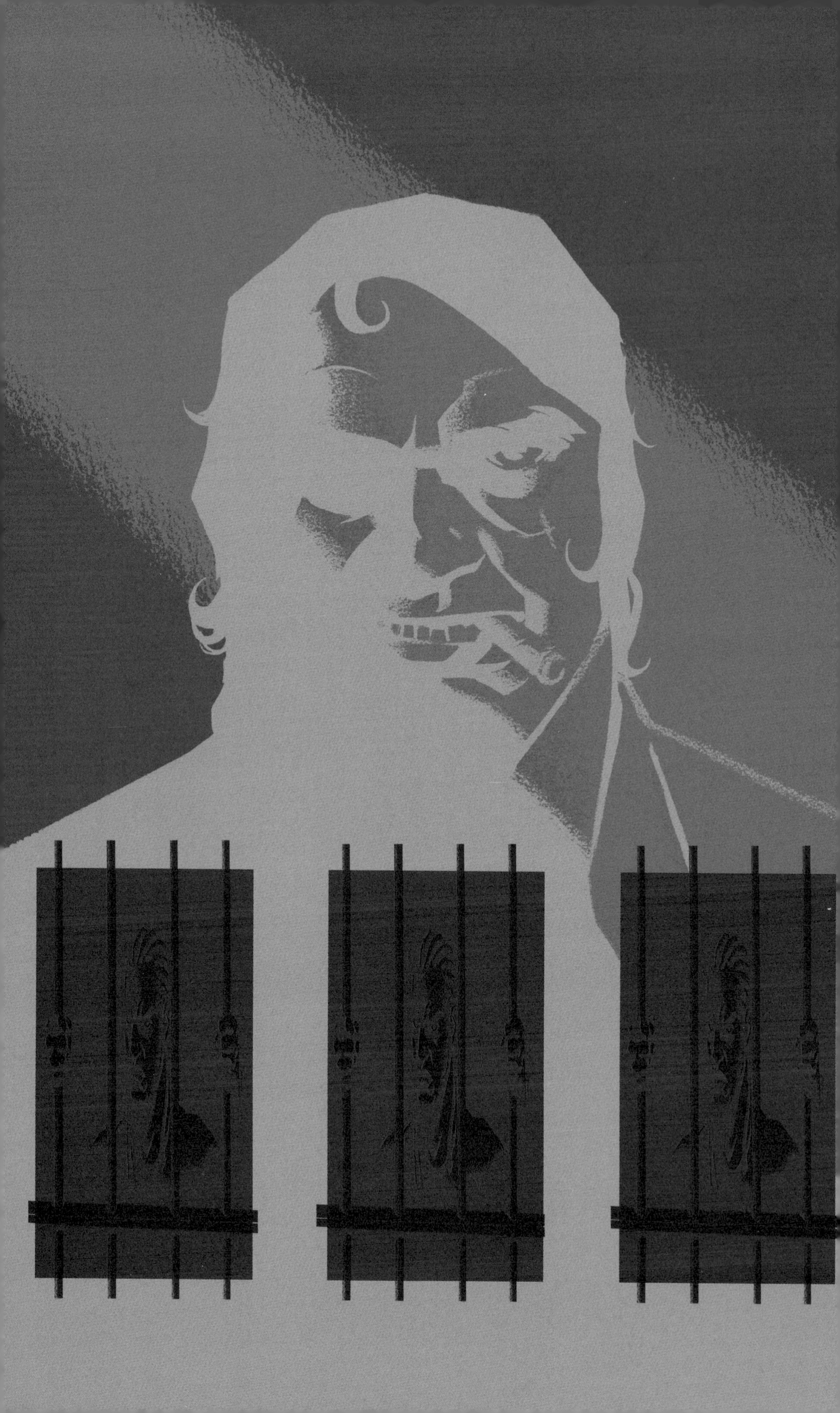

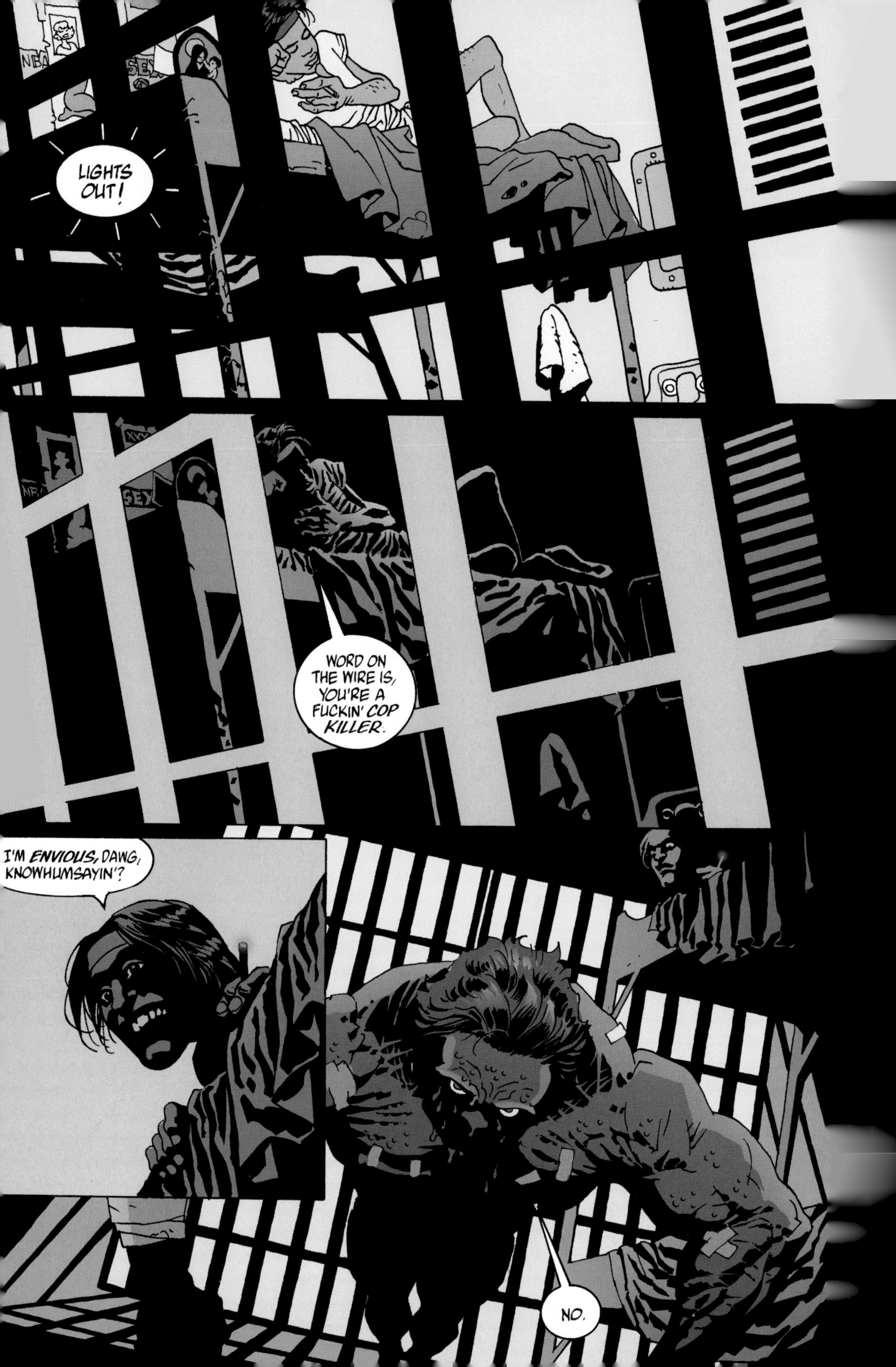
LIGHTS OUT!
WORD ON THE WIRE IS, YOU'RE A FUCKIN' COP KILLER.
I'M ENVIOUS, DAWG, KNOWHUMSAYIN'?
NO.

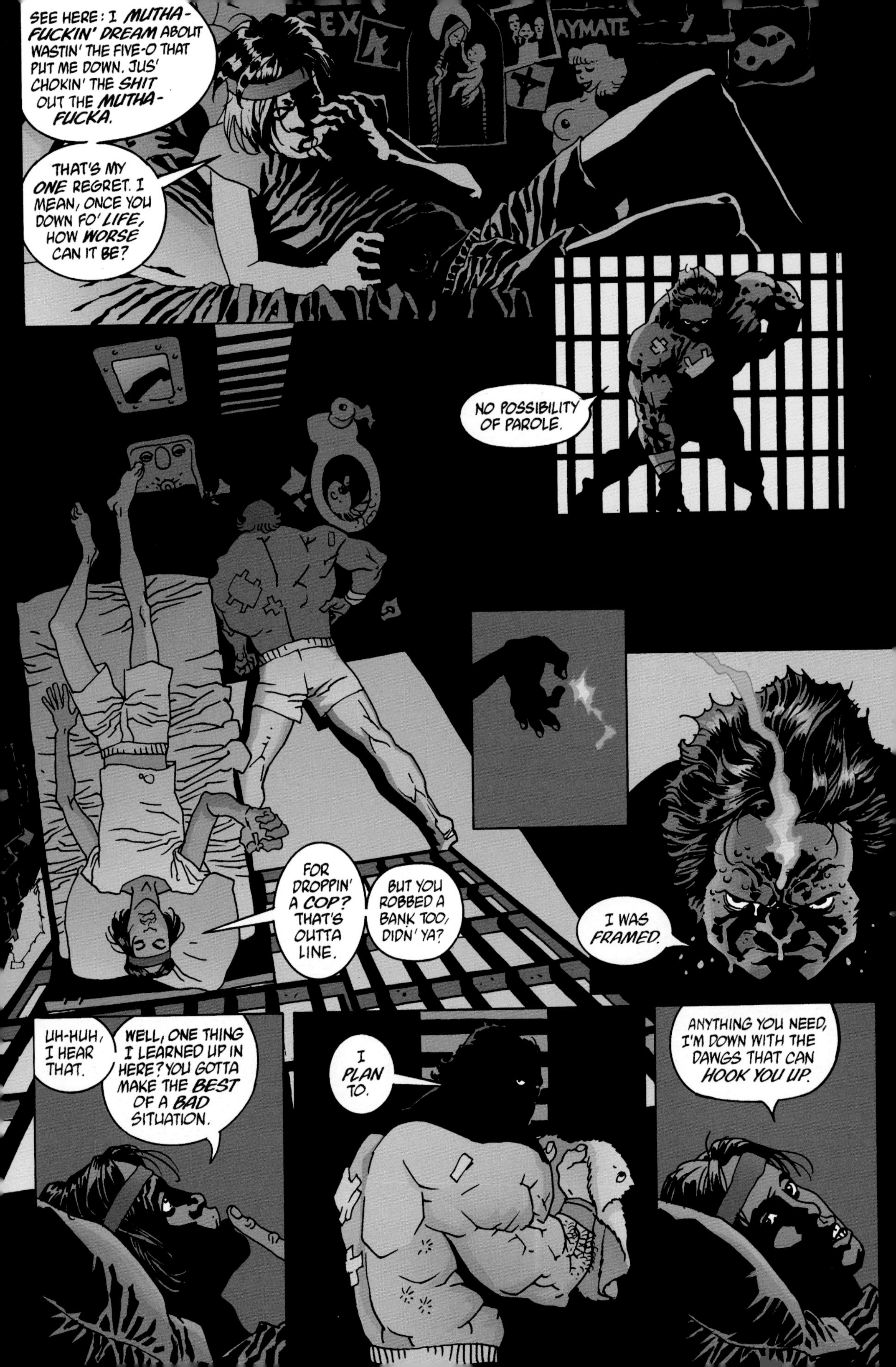

SEE HERE: I MUTHA-FUCKIN' DREAM ABOUT WASTIN' THE FIVE-O THAT PUT ME DOWN. JUS' CHOKIN' THE SHIT OUT THE MUTHA-FUCKA.
THAT'S MY ONE REGRET. I MEAN, ONCE YOU DOWN FO' LIFE, HOW WORSE CAN IT BE?
NO POSSIBILITY OF PAROLE.
FOR DROPPIN' A COP? THAT'S OUTTA LINE.
BUT YOU ROBBED A BANK TOO, DIDN' YA?
I WAS FRAMED.
UH-HUH, I HEAR THAT.
WELL, ONE THING I LEARNED UP IN HERE? YOU GOTTA MAKE THE BEST OF A BAD SITUATION.
I PLAN TO.
ANYTHING YOU NEED, I'M DOWN WITH THE DAWGS THAT CAN HOOK YOU UP.

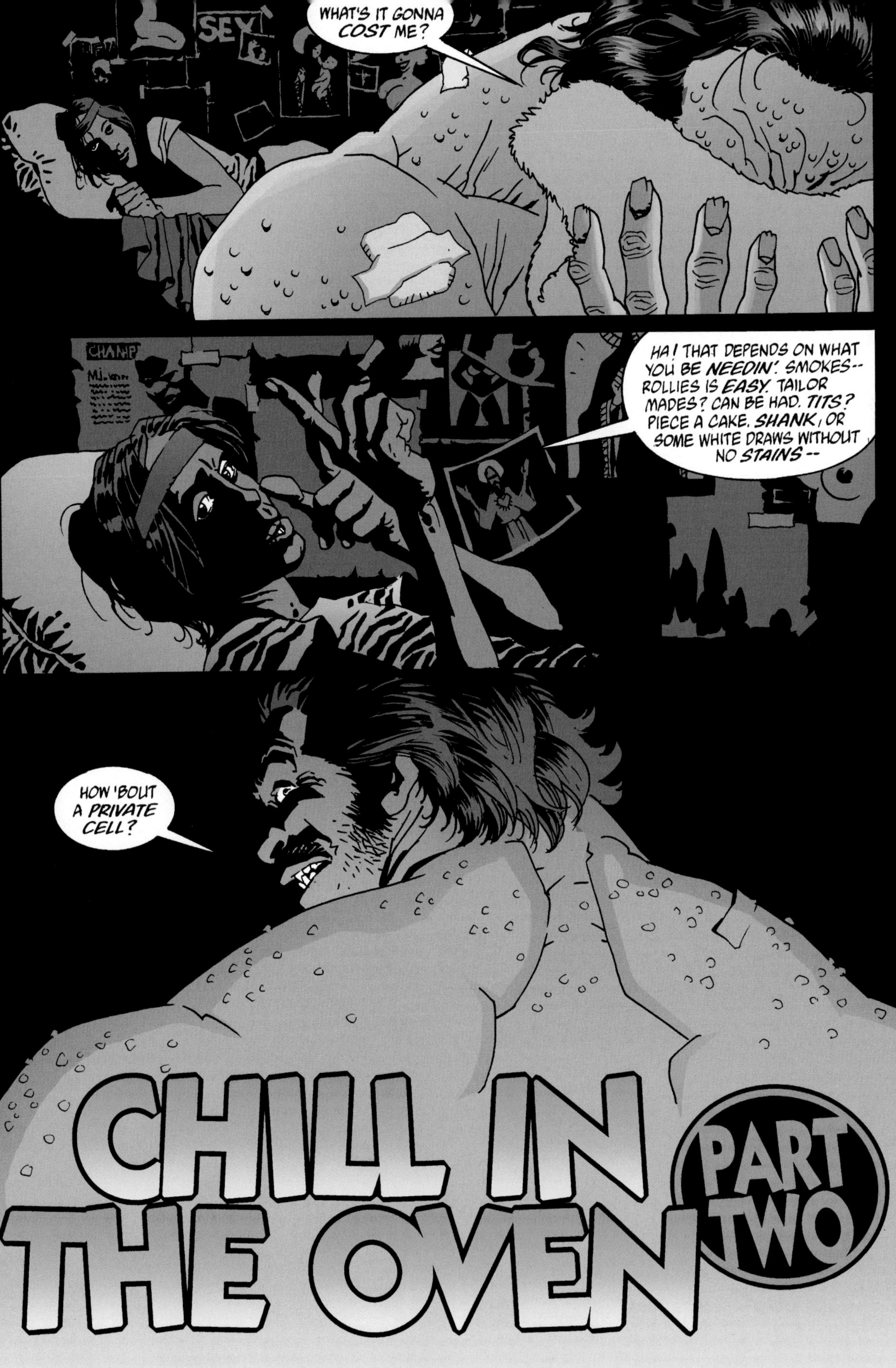

WHAT'S IT GONNA COST ME?
HA! THAT DEPENDS ON WHAT YOU BE NEEDIN'. SMOKES-- ROLLIES IS EASY. TAILOR MADES? CAN BE HAD. TITS? PIECE A CAKE. SHANK, OR SOME WHITE DRAWS WITHOUT NO STAINS--
HOW 'BOUT A PRIVATE CELL?
CHILL IN THE OVEN
PART TWO

BRIAN AZZARELLO writer | EDUARDO RISSO artist | PATRICIA MULVIHILL colorist | CLEM ROBINS letterer | ZYLONOL separations | DAVE JOHNSON cover | ZACHARY RAU ass't ed | WILL DENNIS editor

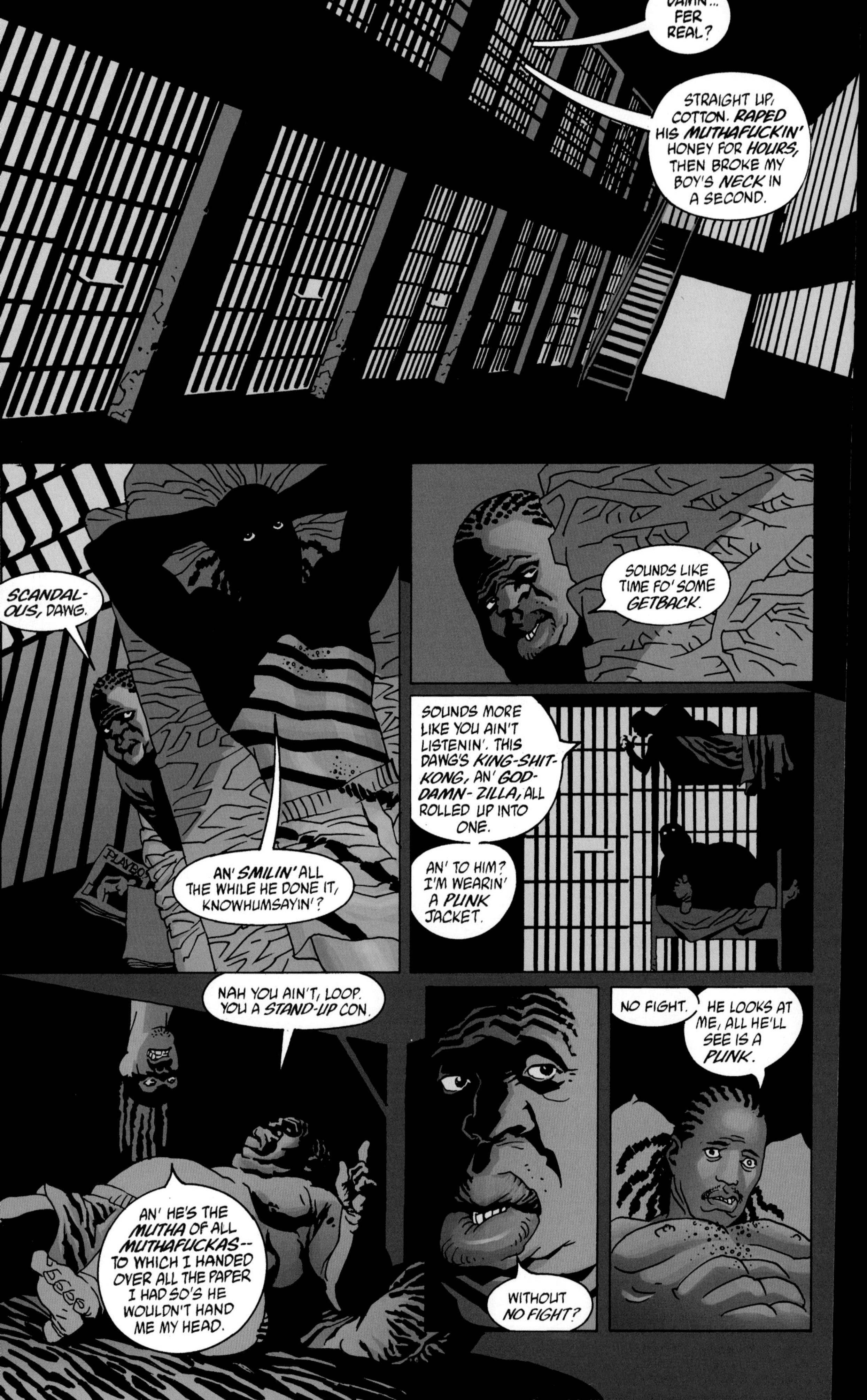
DAMN... FER REAL?
STRAIGHT UP, COTTON. RAPED HIS MUTHAFUCKIN' HONEY FOR HOURS, THEN BROKE MY BOY'S NECK IN A SECOND.
SCANDAL-OUS, DAWG.
AN' SMILIN' ALL THE WHILE HE DONE IT, KNOWHUMSAYIN'?
SOUNDS LIKE TIME FO' SOME GETBACK.
SOUNDS MORE LIKE YOU AIN'T LISTENIN'. THIS DAWG'S KING-SHIT-KONG, AN' GOD-DAMN-ZILLA, ALL ROLLED UP INTO ONE.
AN' TO HIM? I'M WEARIN' A PUNK JACKET.
NAH YOU AIN'T, LOOP. YOU A STAND-UP CON.
AN' HE'S THE MUTHA OF ALL MUTHAFUCKAS-- TO WHICH I HANDED OVER ALL THE PAPER I HAD SO'S HE WOULDN'T HAND ME MY HEAD.
WITHOUT NO FIGHT?
NO FIGHT.
HE LOOKS AT ME, ALL HE'LL SEE IS A PUNK.

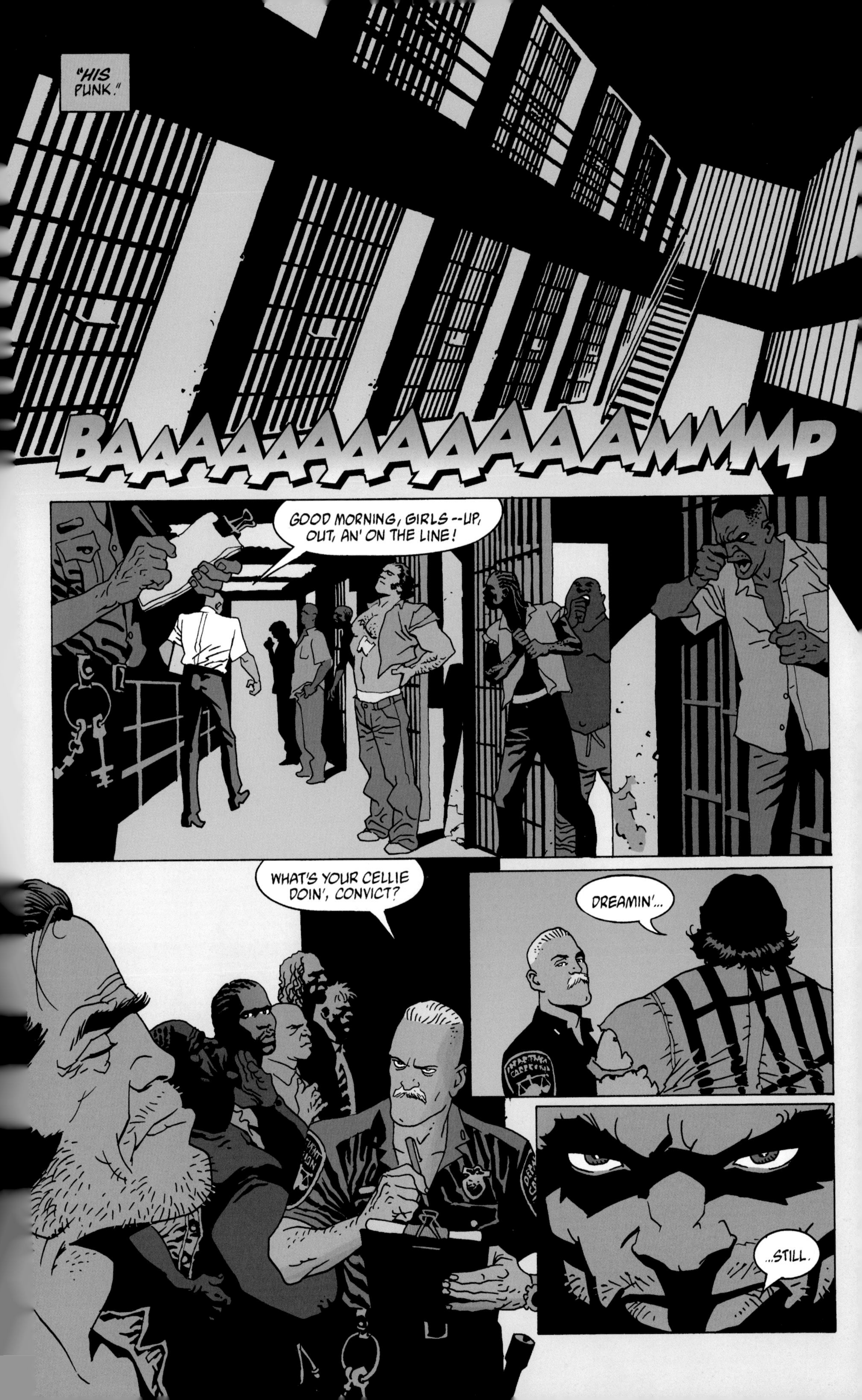
"HIS PUNK."
BAAAAAAAAAAAAMMMP
GOOD MORNING, GIRLS --UP, OUT, AN' ON THE LINE!
WHAT'S YOUR CELLIE DOIN', CONVICT?
DREAMIN'...
...STILL.

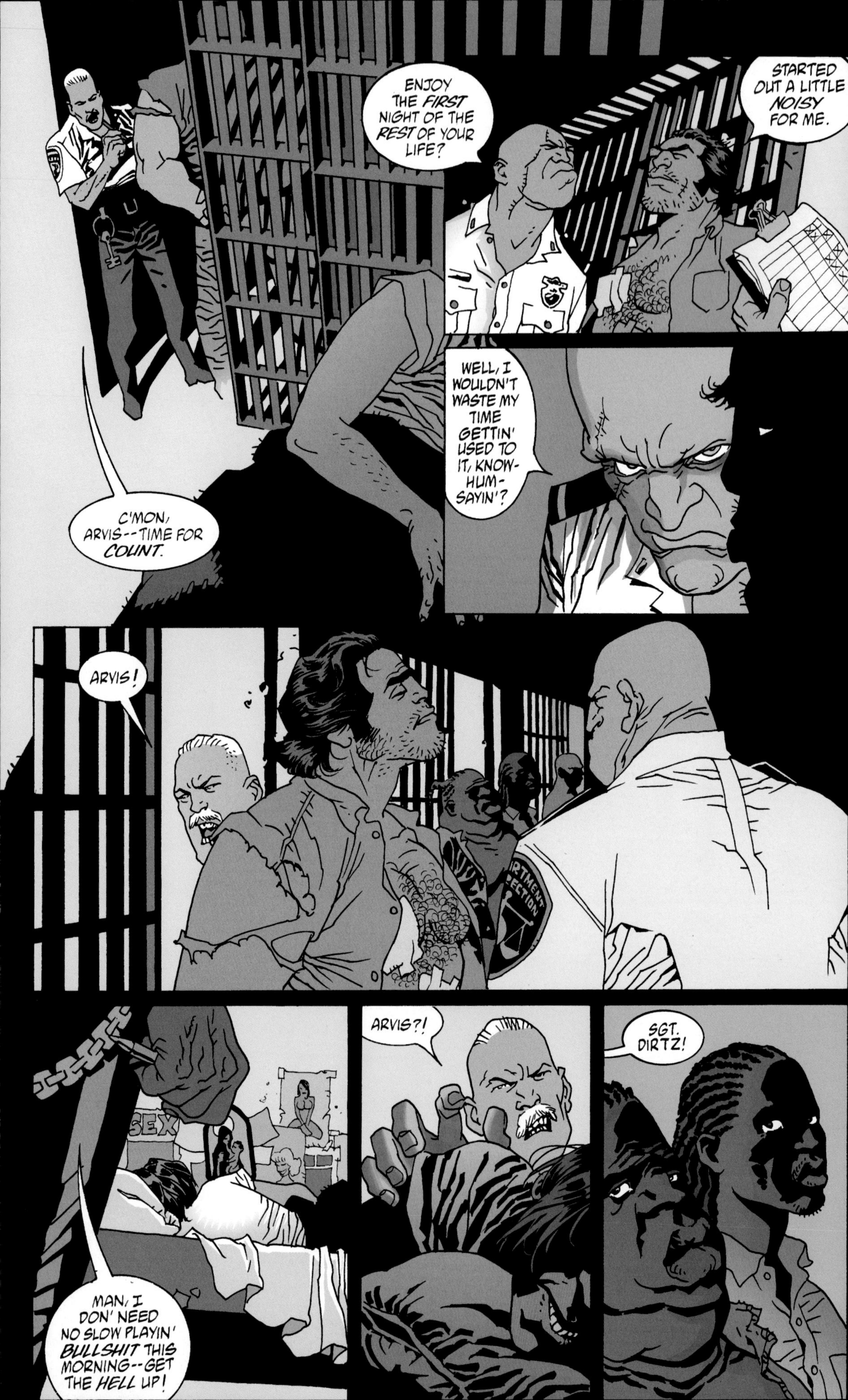
ENJOY THE FIRST NIGHT OF THE REST OF YOUR LIFE?
STARTED OUT A LITTLE NOISY FOR ME.
WELL, I WOULDN'T WASTE MY TIME GETTIN' USED TO IT, KNOW-HUM-SAYIN'?
C'MON, ARVIS--TIME FOR COUNT.
ARVIS!
ARVIS?!
SGT. DIRTZ!
SEX
MAN, I DON' NEED NO SLOW PLAYIN' BULLSHIT THIS MORNING--GET THE HELL UP!

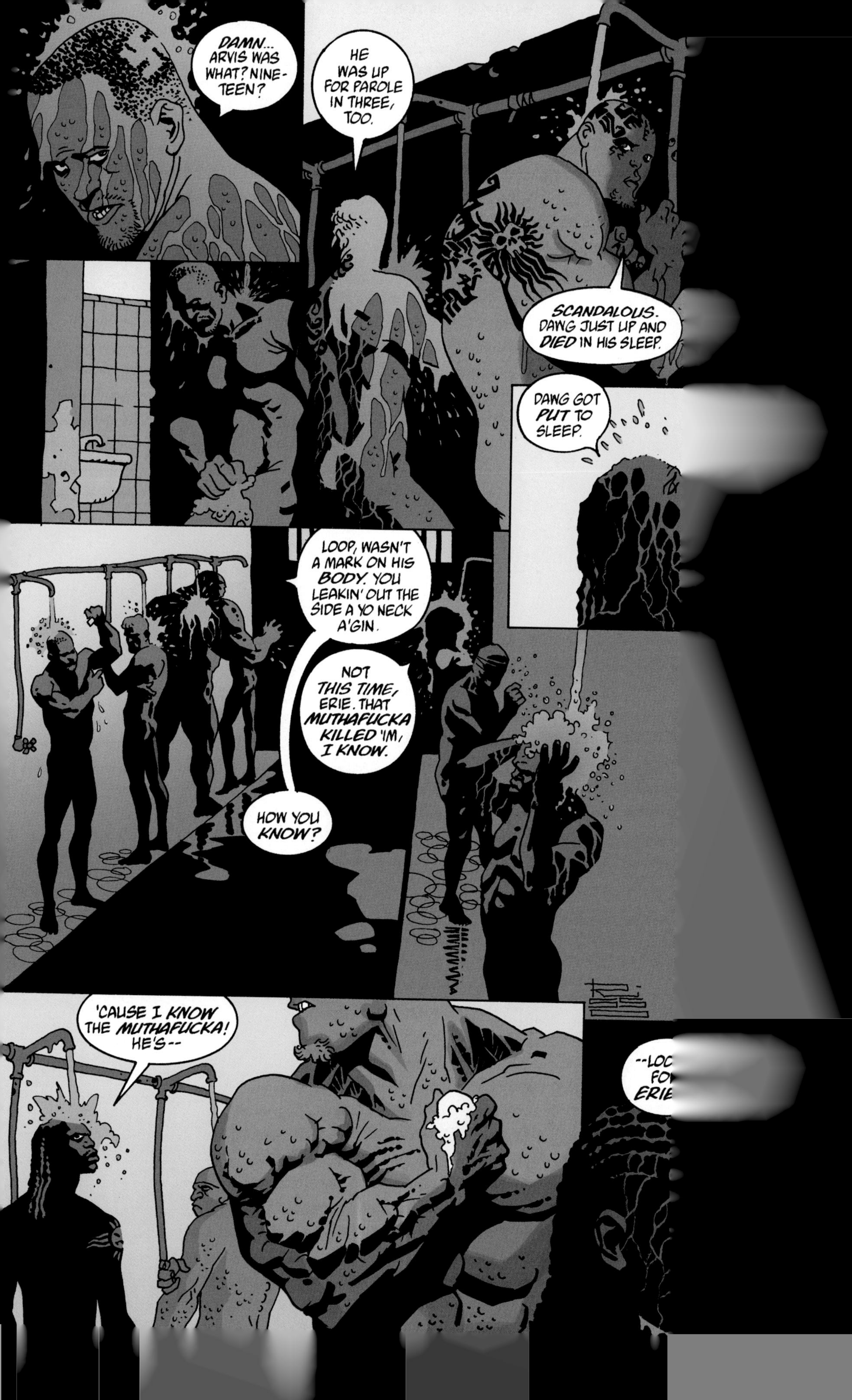
DAMN... ARVIS WAS WHAT? NINE-TEEN?
HE WAS UP FOR PAROLE IN THREE, TOO.
SCANDALOUS. DAWG JUST UP AND DIED IN HIS SLEEP.
DAWG GOT PUT TO SLEEP.
LOOP, WASN'T A MARK ON HIS BODY. YOU LEAKIN' OUT THE SIDE A YO NECK A'GIN.
NOT THIS TIME, ERIE. THAT MUTHAFUCKA KILLED 'IM, I KNOW.
HOW YOU KNOW?
'CAUSE I KNOW THE MUTHAFUCKA! HE'S--

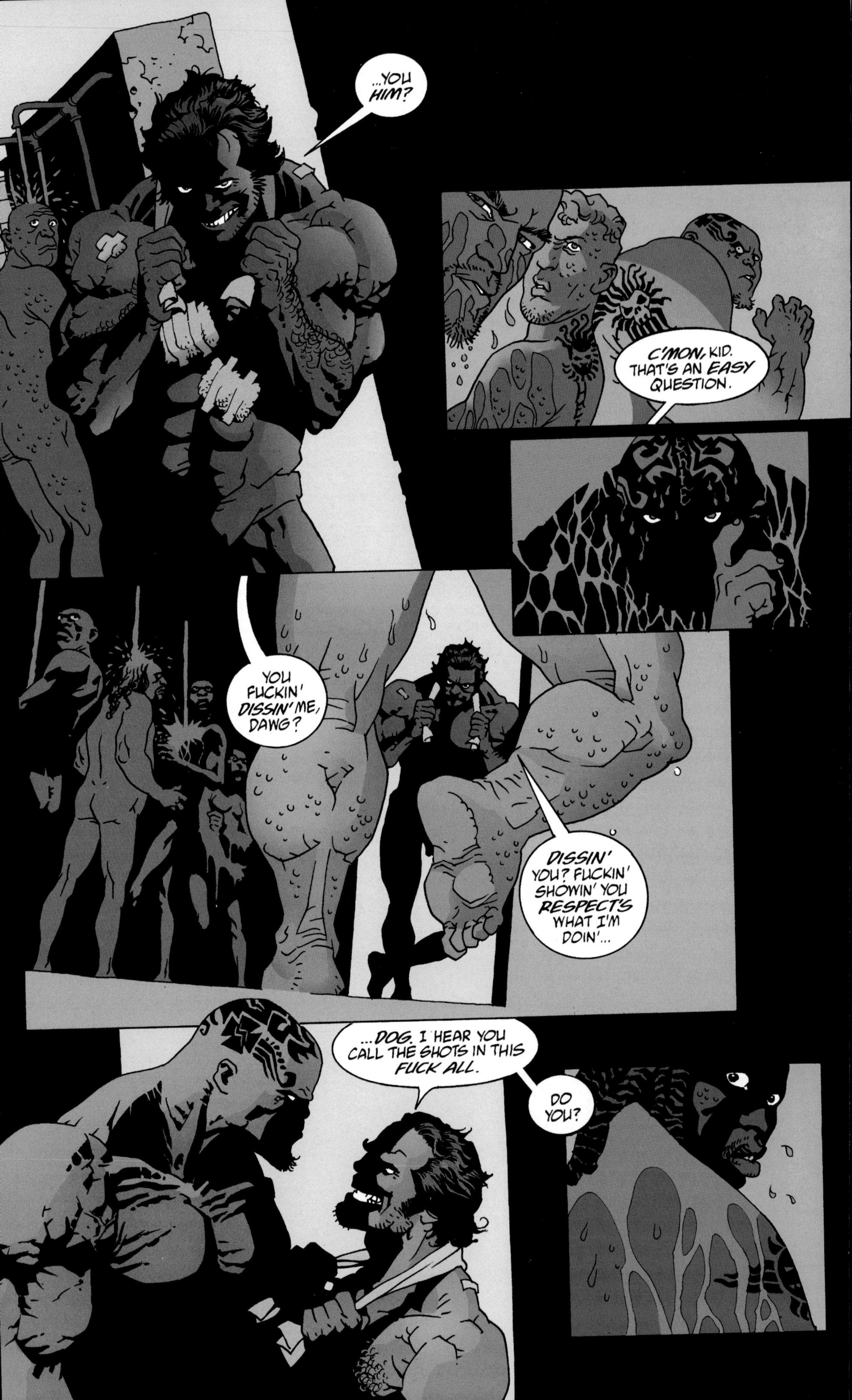
...YOU HIM?
C'MON, KID. THAT'S AN EASY QUESTION.
YOU FUCKIN' DISSIN' ME, DAWG?
DISSIN' YOU? FUCKIN' SHOWIN' YOU RESPECT'S WHAT I'M DOIN'...
...DOG. I HEAR YOU CALL THE SHOTS IN THIS FUCK ALL.
DO YOU?

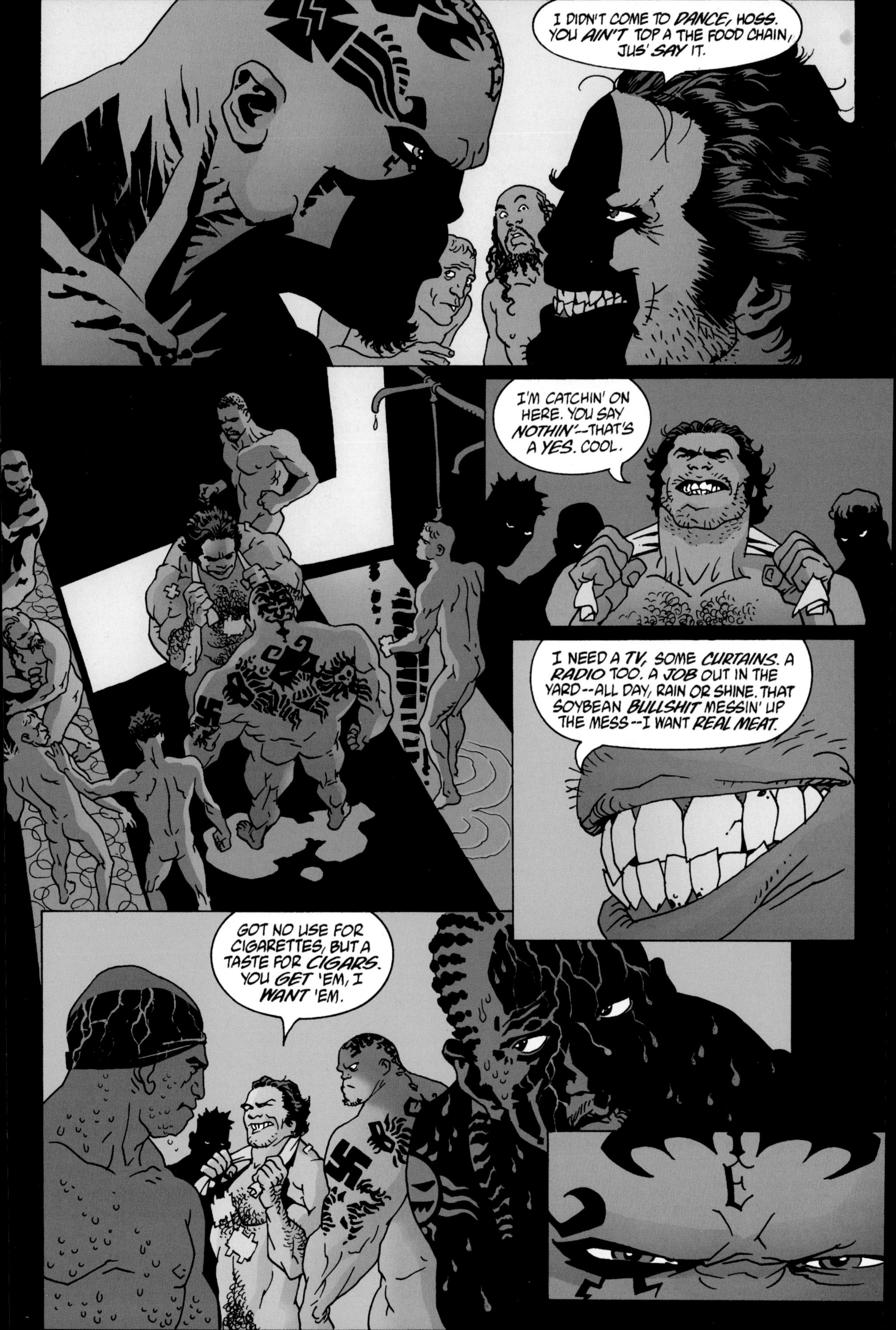
I DIDN'T COME TO DANCE, HOSS. YOU AIN'T TOP A THE FOOD CHAIN, JUS' SAY IT.
I'M CATCHIN' ON HERE. YOU SAY NOTHIN'--THAT'S A YES. COOL.
I NEED A TV, SOME CURTAINS. A RADIO TOO. A JOB OUT IN THE YARD--ALL DAY, RAIN OR SHINE. THAT SOYBEAN BULLSHIT MESSIN' UP THE MESS--I WANT REAL MEAT.
GOT NO USE FOR CIGARETTES, BUT A TASTE FOR CIGARS. YOU GET 'EM, I WANT 'EM.

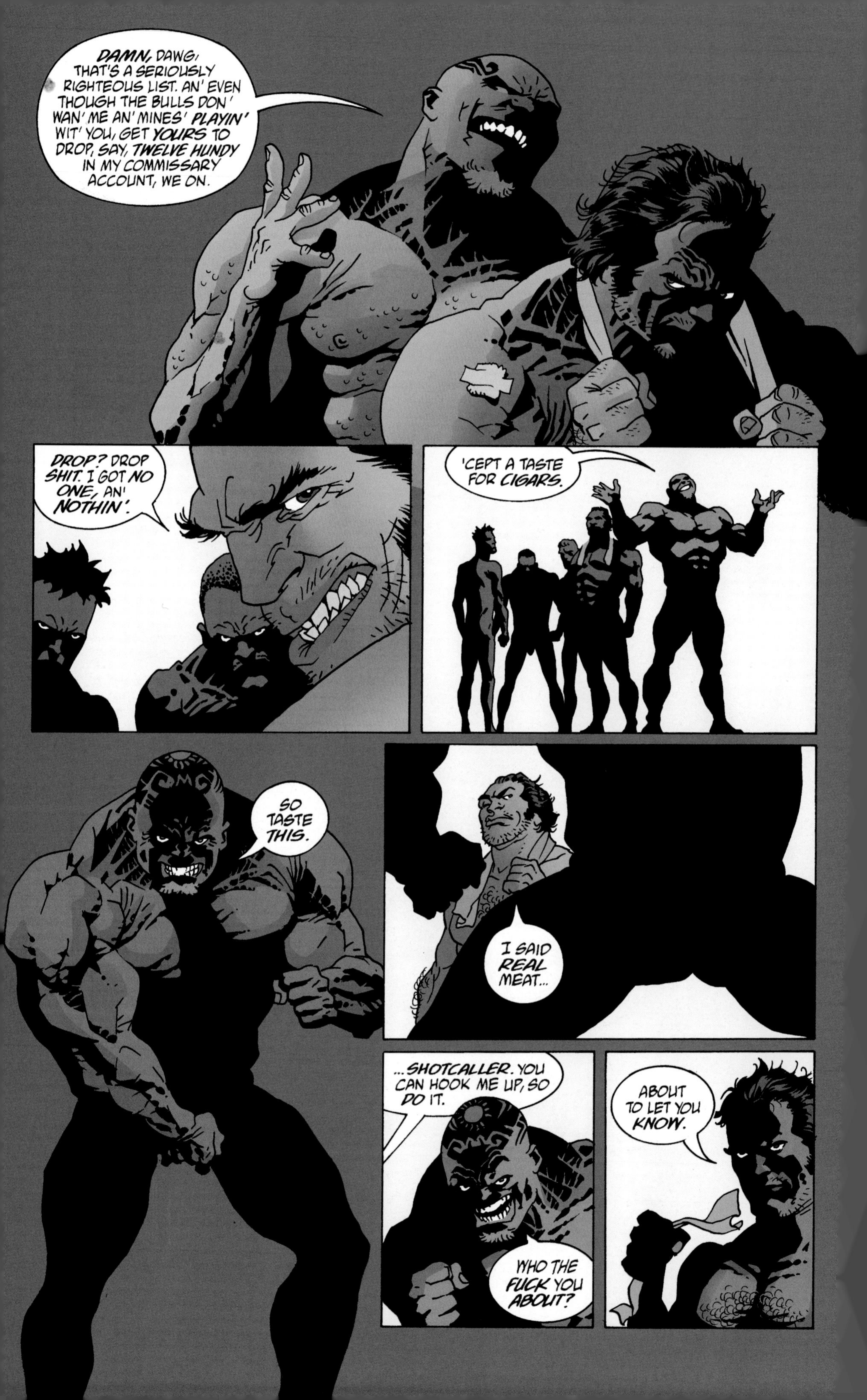
DAMN, DAWG, THAT'S A SERIOUSLY RIGHTEOUS LIST. AN' EVEN THOUGH THE BULLS DON' WAN' ME AN' MINES' PLAYIN' WIT' YOU, GET YOURS TO DROP, SAY, TWELVE HUNDY IN MY COMMISSARY ACCOUNT, WE ON.
DROP? DROP SHIT. I GOT NO ONE, AN' NOTHIN'.
'CEPT A TASTE FOR CIGARS.
SO TASTE THIS.
I SAID REAL MEAT...
...SHOTCALLER. YOU CAN HOOK ME UP, SO DO IT.
WHO THE FUCK YOU ABOUT?
ABOUT TO LET YOU KNOW.

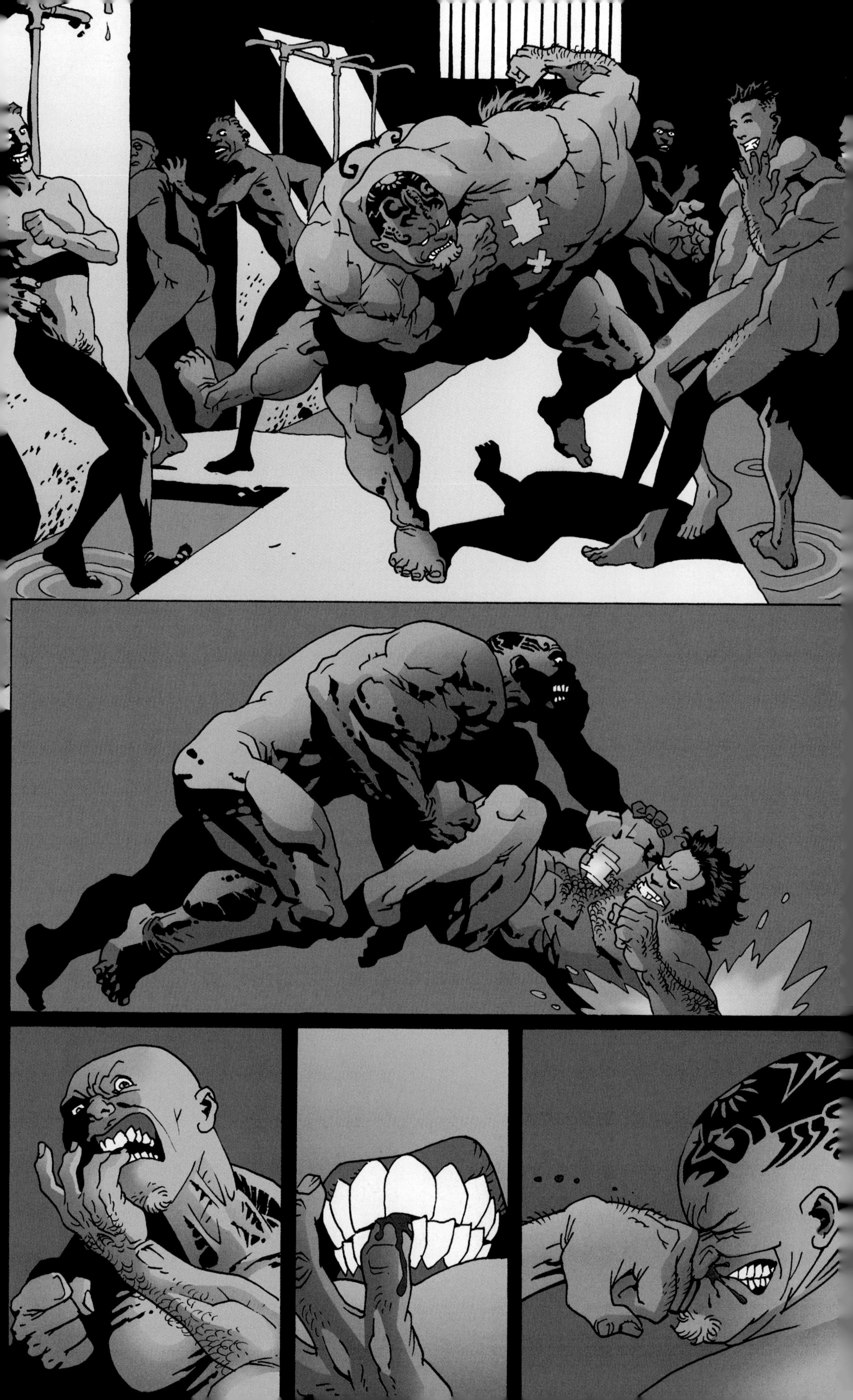

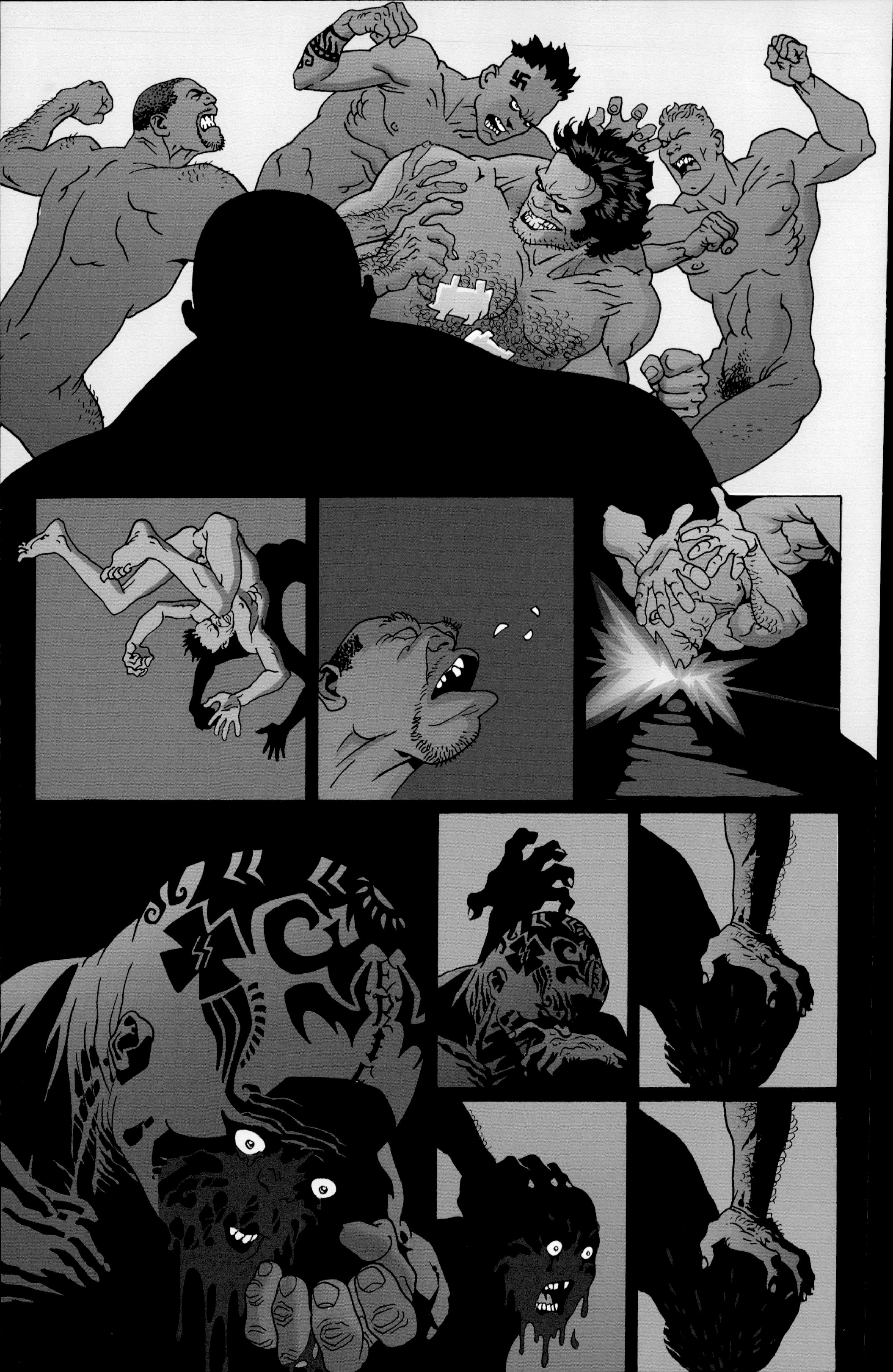

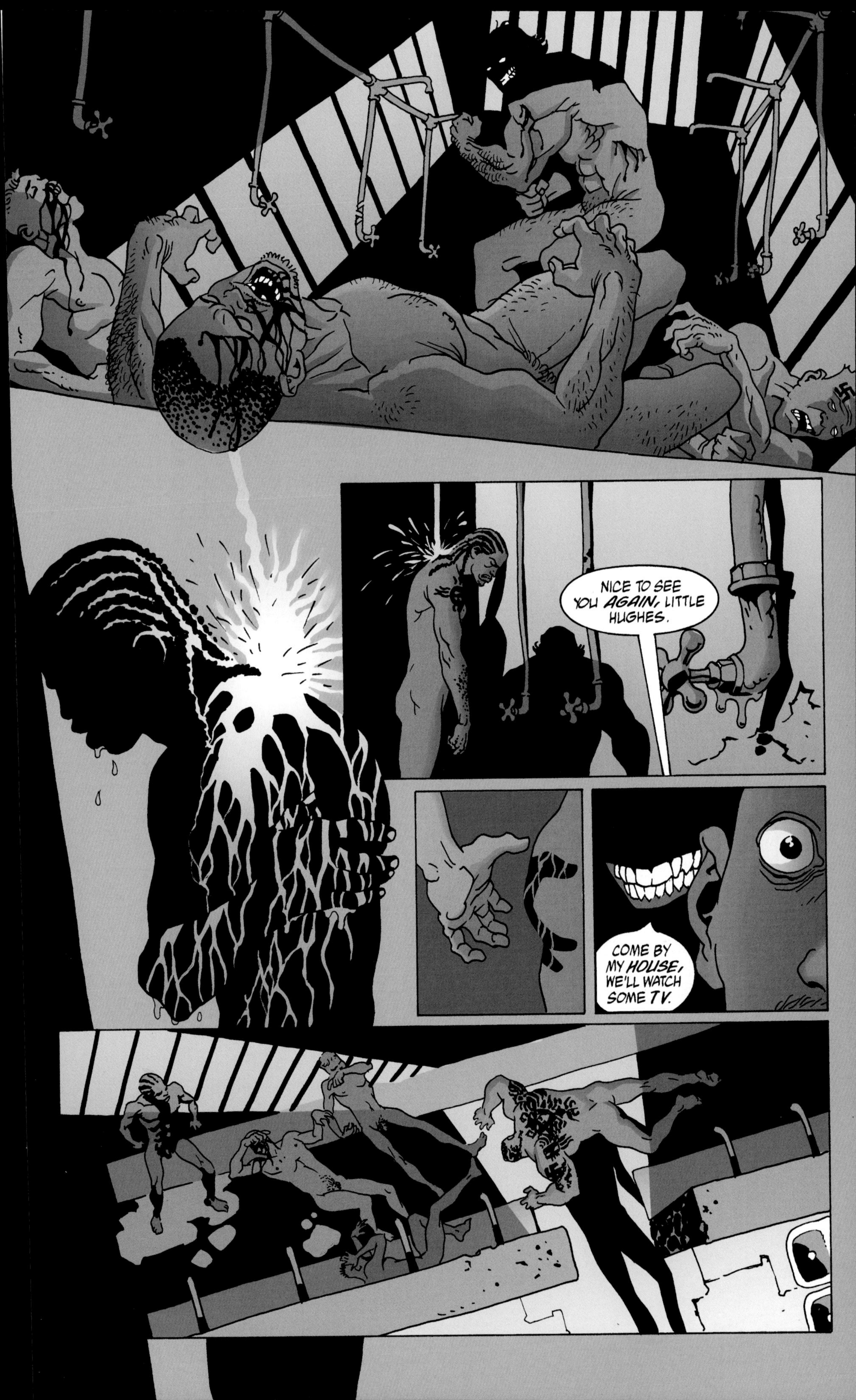
NICE TO SEE YOU AGAIN, LITTLE HUGHES.
COME BY MY HOUSE, WE'LL WATCH SOME TV.

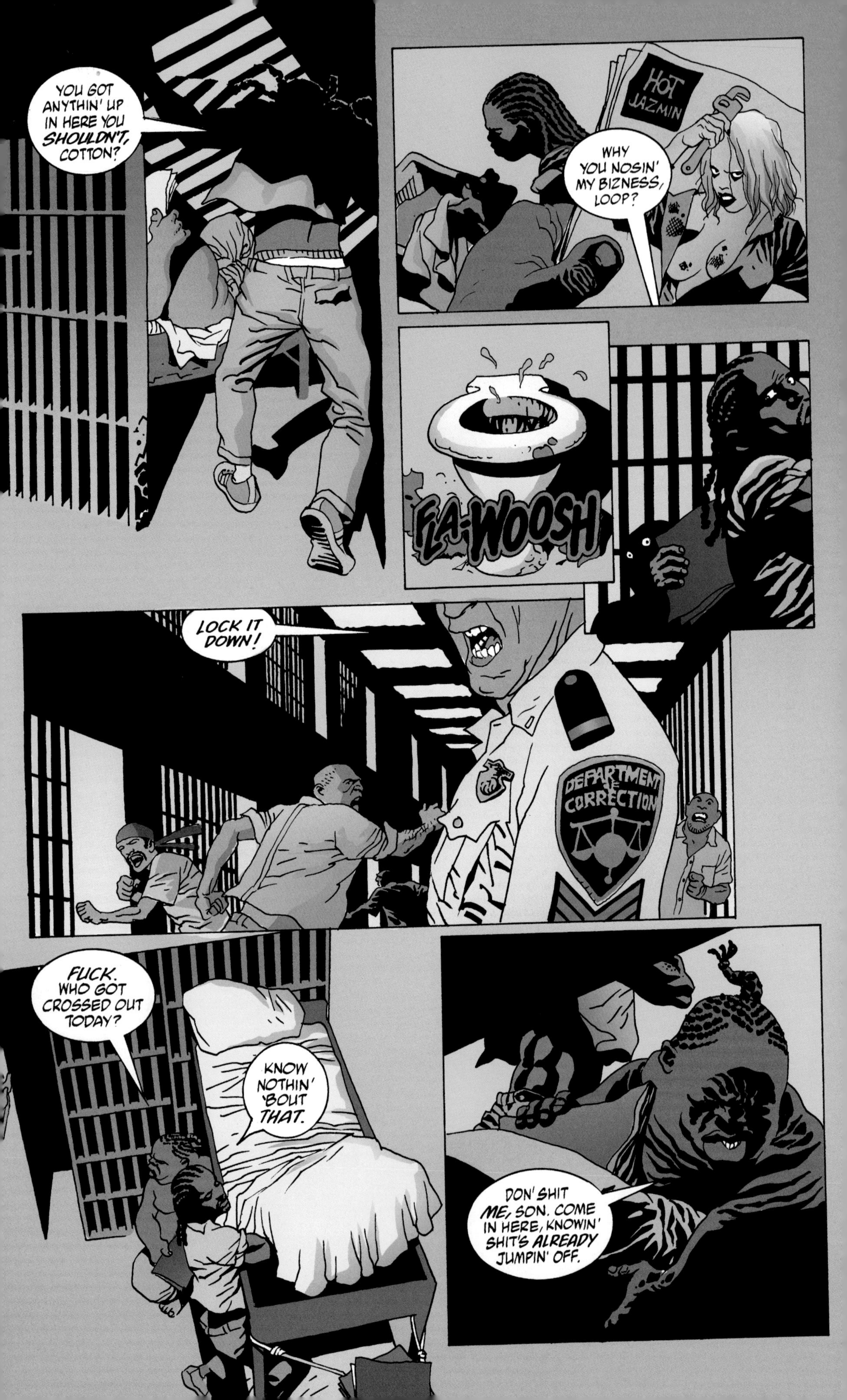
YOU GOT ANYTHIN' UP IN HERE YOU SHOULDN'T, COTTON?
HOT JAZMIN
WHY YOU NOSIN' MY BIZNESS, LOOP?
FLA-WOOSH
LOCK IT DOWN!
DEPARTMENT OF CORRECTION
FUCK. WHO GOT CROSSED OUT TODAY?
KNOW NOTHIN' 'BOUT THAT.
DON' SHIT ME, SON. COME IN HERE, KNOWIN' SHIT'S ALREADY JUMPIN' OFF.

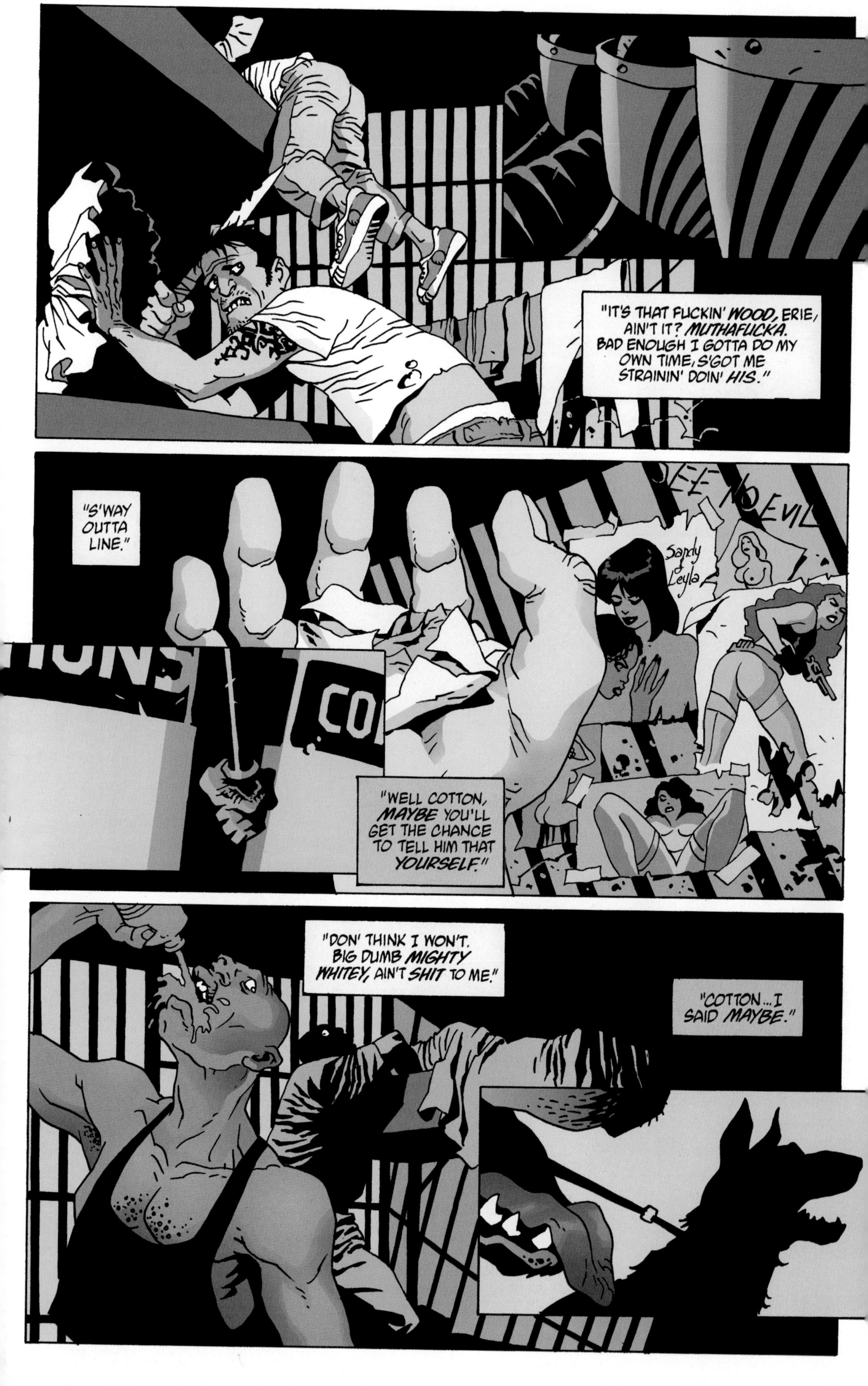
"IT'S THAT FUCKIN' WOOD, ERIE, AIN'T IT? MUTHAFUCKA. BAD ENOUGH I GOTTA DO MY OWN TIME, S'GOT ME STRAININ' DOIN' HIS."
"S'WAY OUTTA LINE."
SEE NO EVIL
Sandy
Leyla
CO
"WELL COTTON, MAYBE YOU'LL GET THE CHANCE TO TELL HIM THAT YOURSELF."
"DON' THINK I WON'T. BIG DUMB MIGHTY WHITEY, AIN'T SHIT TO ME."
"COTTON...I SAID MAYBE."

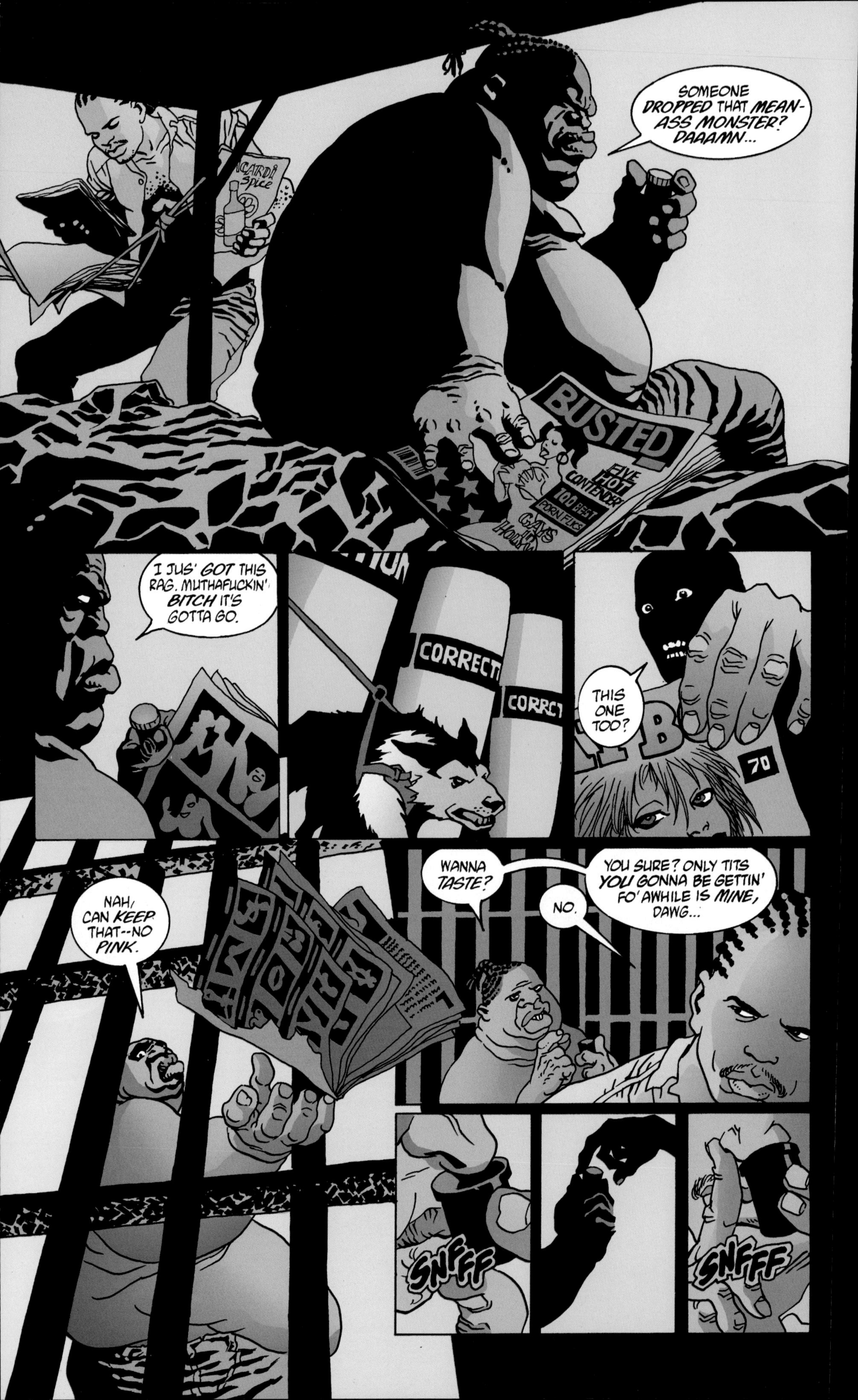
SOMEONE DROPPED THAT MEAN-ASS MONSTER? DAAAMN...
BACARDI Spice
BUSTED
FIVE HOT CONTENDER
100 BEST PORN FLICS
I JUS' GOT THIS RAG. MUTHAFUCKIN' BITCH IT'S GOTTA GO.
CORRECT
CORRCT
THIS ONE TOO?
70
NAH, CAN KEEP THAT--NO PINK.
WANNA TASTE?
NO.
YOU SURE? ONLY TITS YOU GONNA BE GETTIN' FO'AWHILE IS MINE, DAWG...
SNFFF
SNFFFF

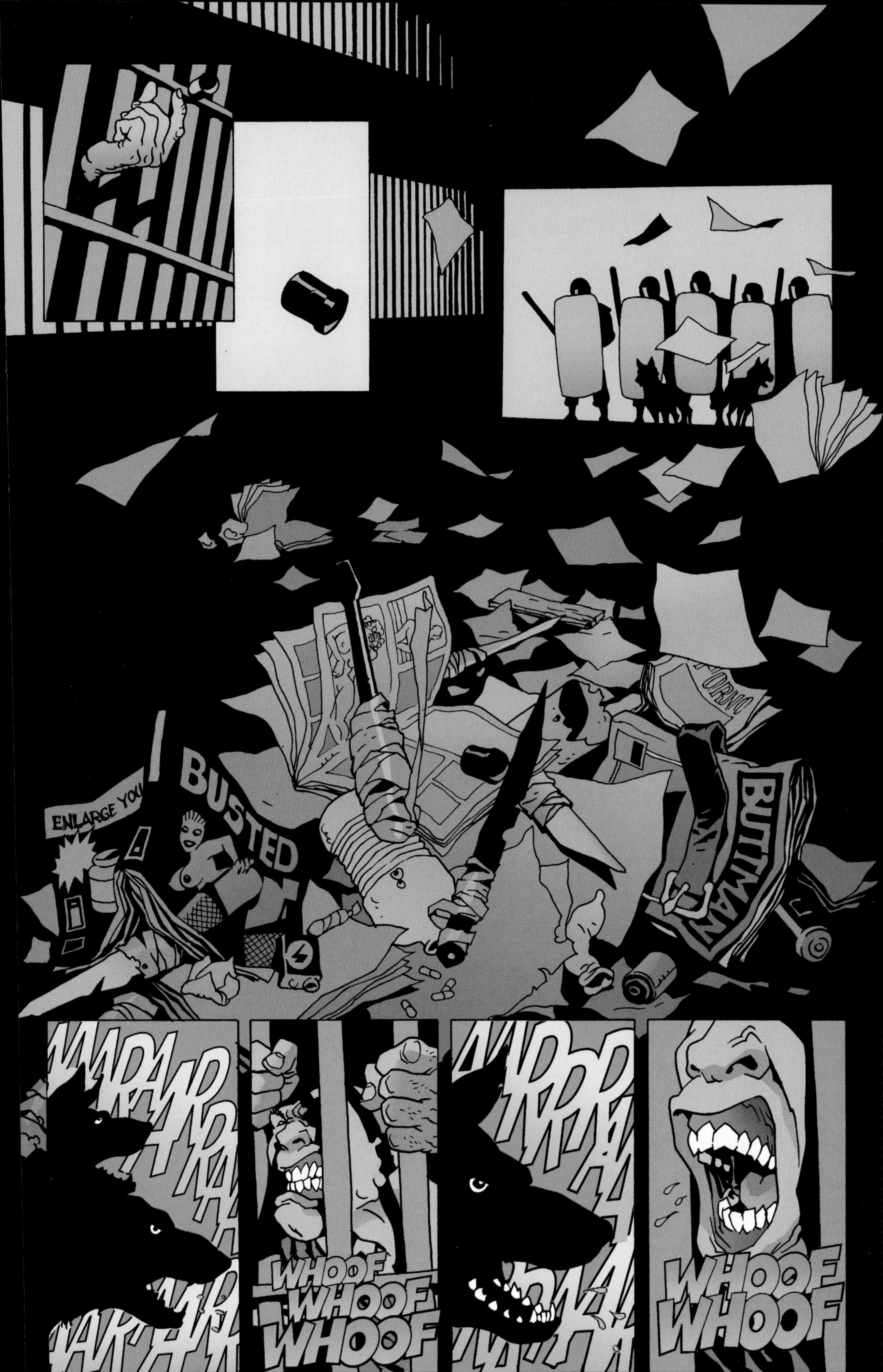
ENLARGE YOU
BUSTED
BUTTMAN
WHOOF
WHOOF
WHOOF
WHOOF
WHOOF

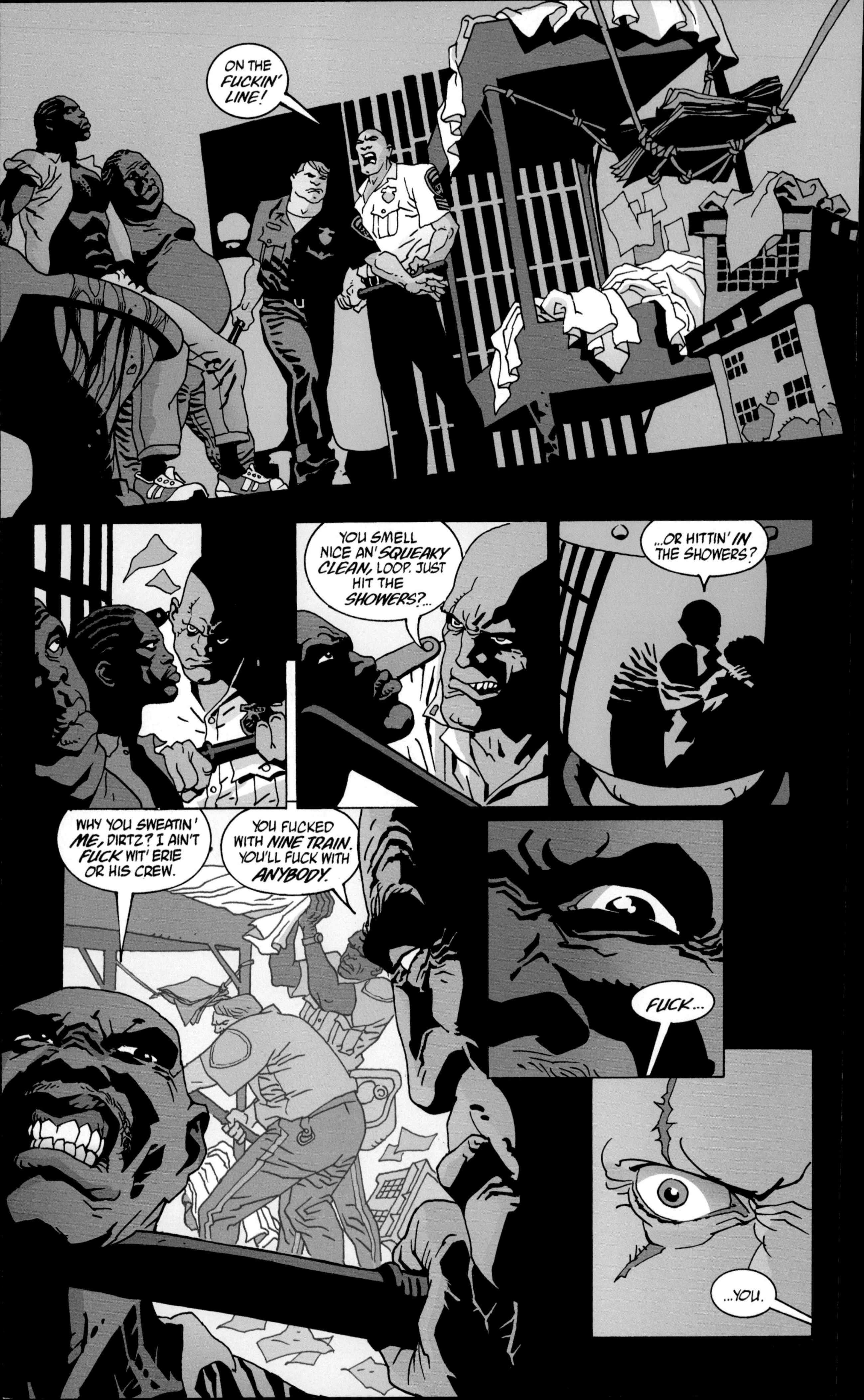
ON THE FUCKIN' LINE!
YOU SMELL NICE AN' SQUEAKY CLEAN, LOOP. JUST HIT THE SHOWERS?...
...OR HITTIN' IN THE SHOWERS?
WHY YOU SWEATIN' ME, DIRTZ? I AIN'T FUCK WIT' ERIE OR HIS CREW.
YOU FUCKED WITH NINE TRAIN. YOU'LL FUCK WITH ANYBODY.
FUCK...
...YOU.

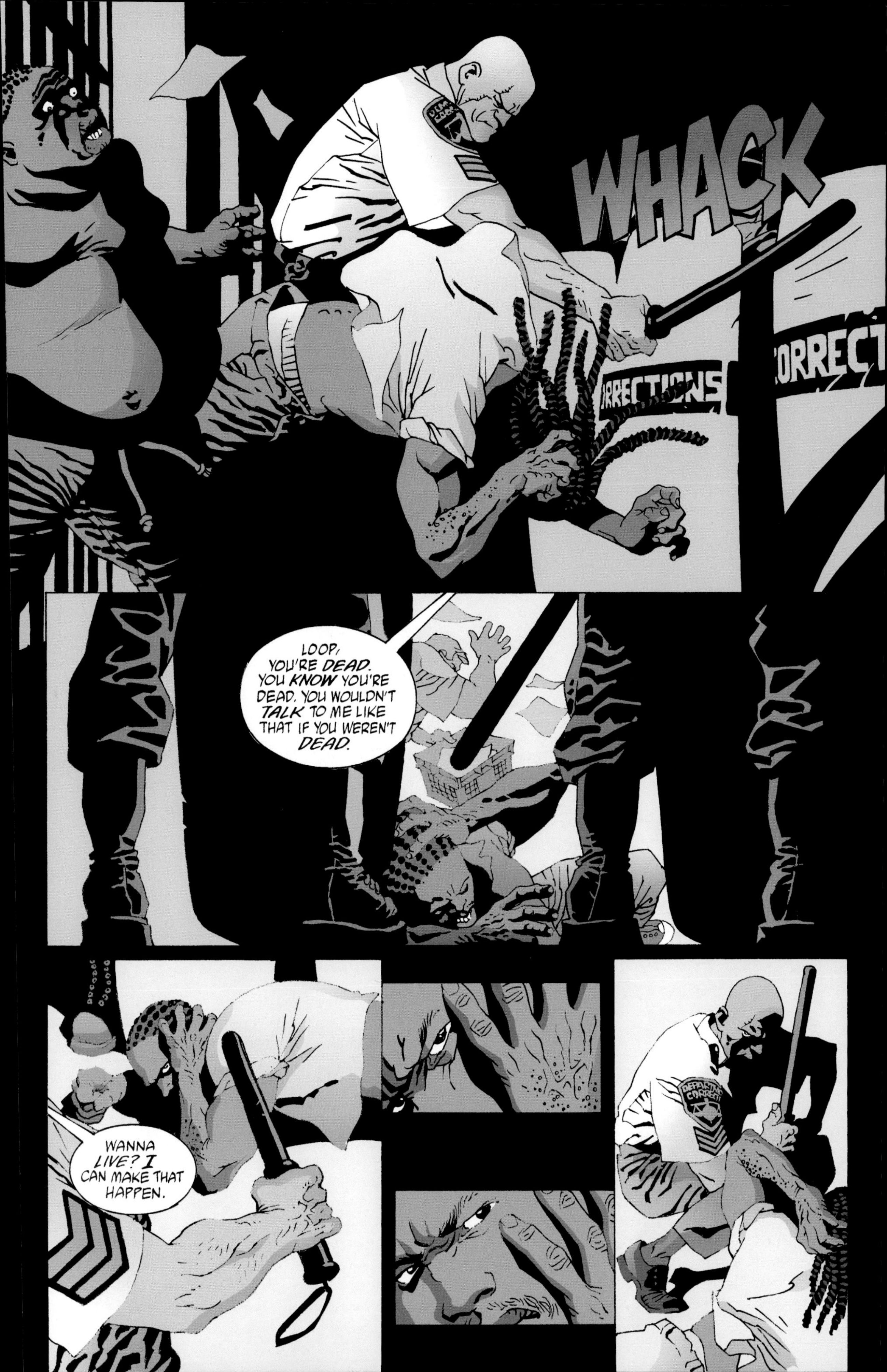
WHACK
RRECTIONS
CORRECT
LOOP, YOU'RE DEAD. YOU KNOW YOU'RE DEAD. YOU WOULDN'T TALK TO ME LIKE THAT IF YOU WEREN'T DEAD.
WANNA LIVE? I CAN MAKE THAT HAPPEN.

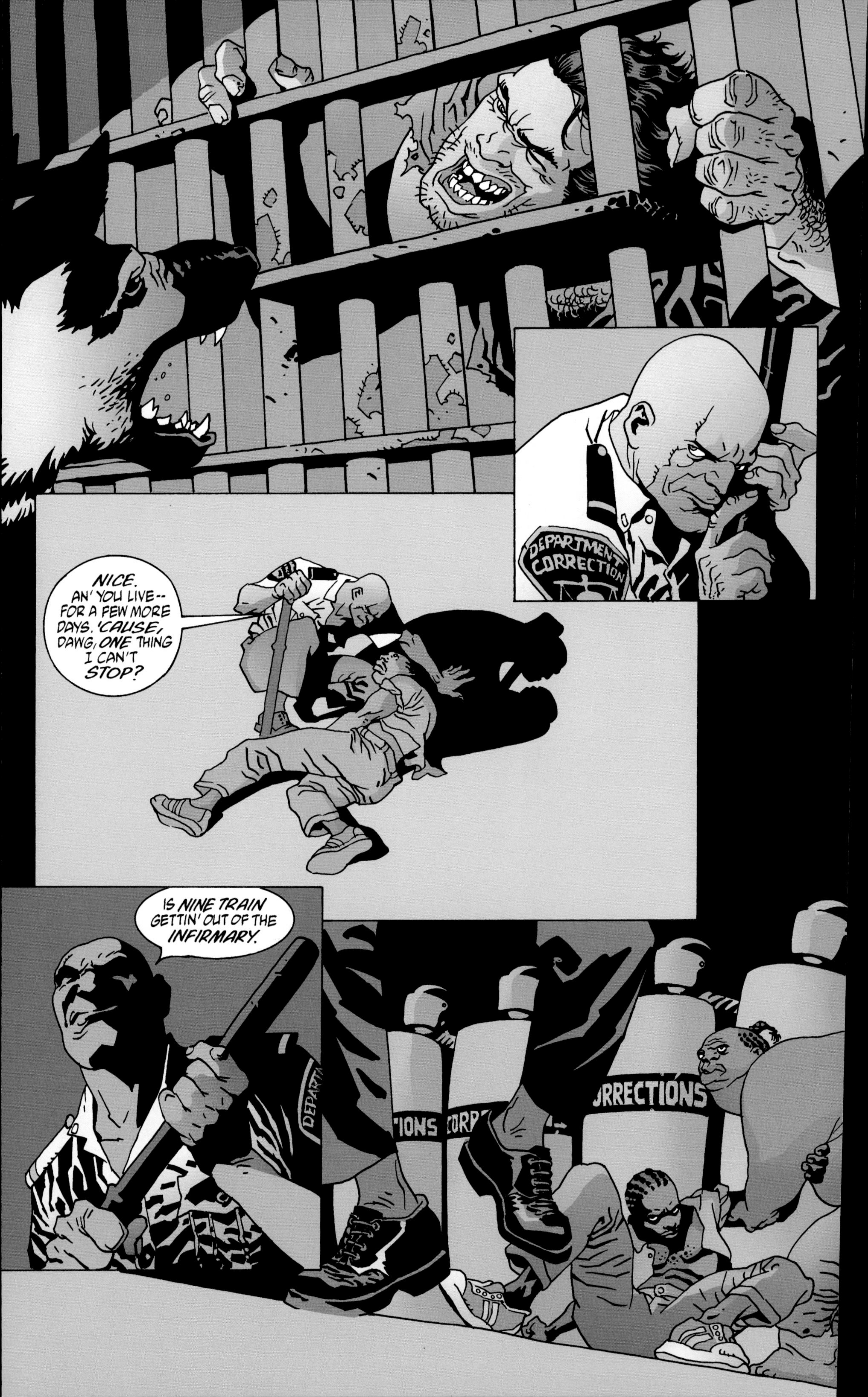
DEPARTMENT CORRECTION
NICE. AN' YOU LIVE-- FOR A FEW MORE DAYS. 'CAUSE, DAWG, ONE THING I CAN'T STOP?
IS NINE TRAIN GETTIN' OUT OF THE INFIRMARY.
CORRECTIONS

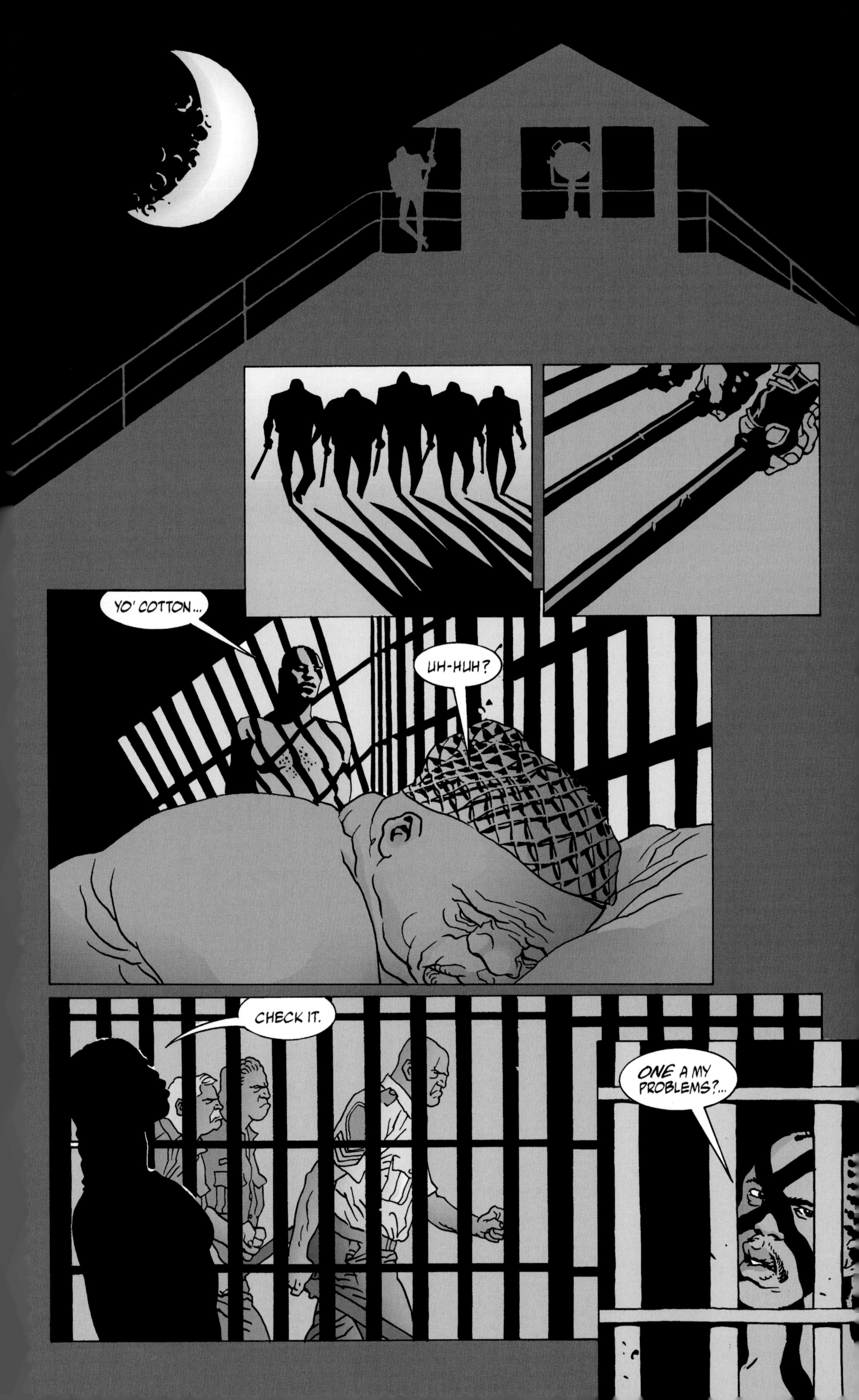

YO' COTTON...
UH-HUH?
CHECK IT.
ONE A MY PROBLEMS?...

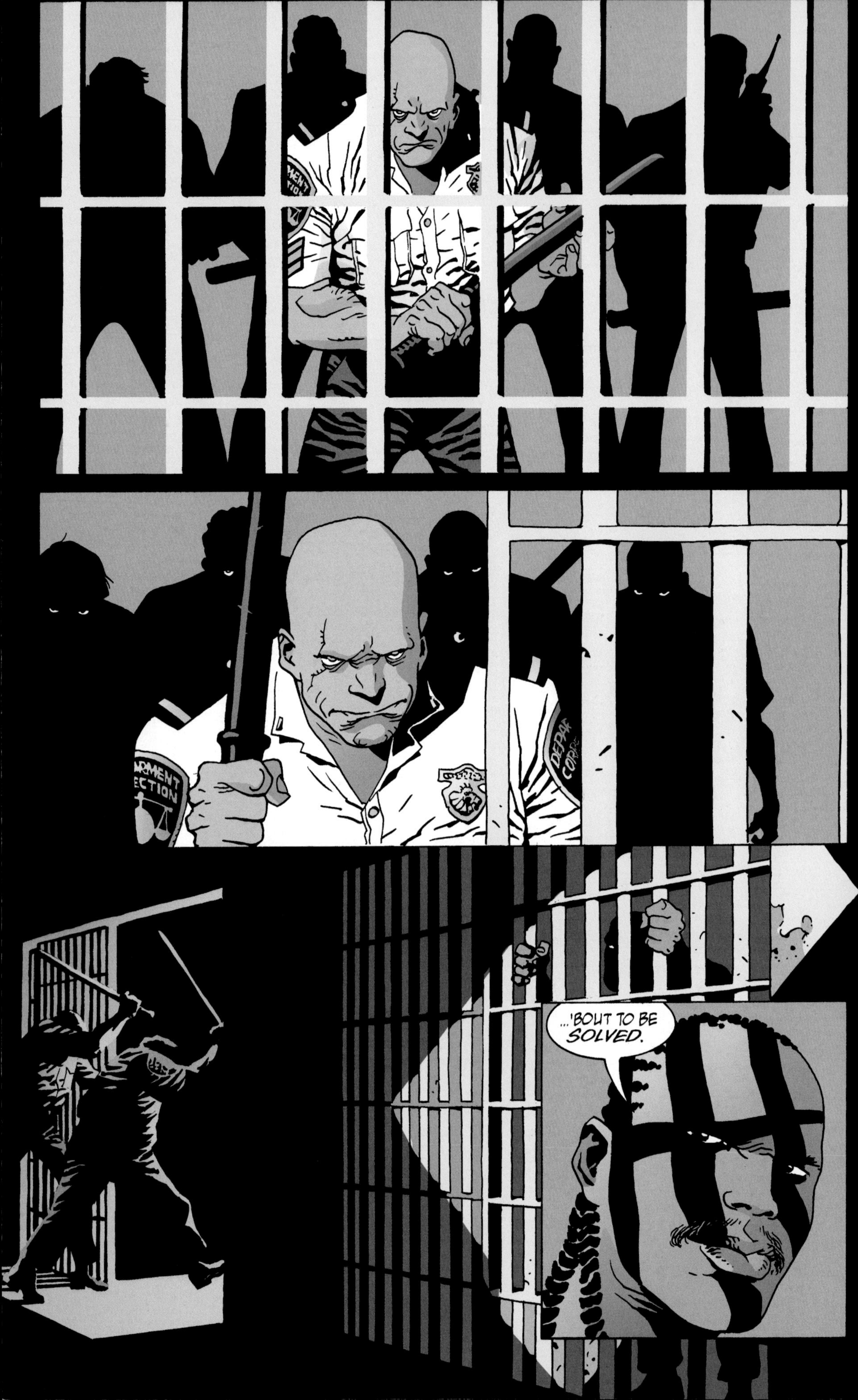
...'BOUT TO BE SOLVED.

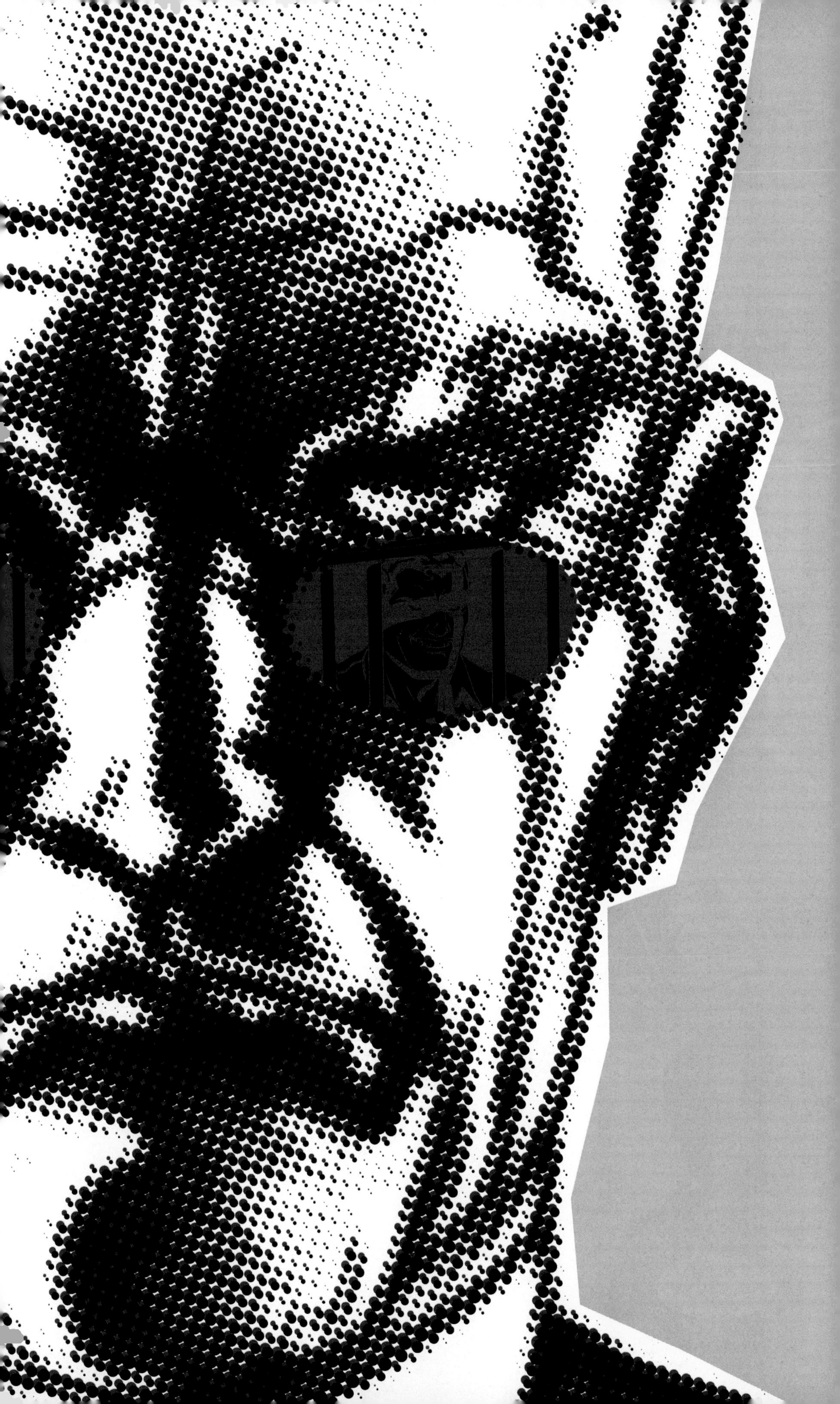

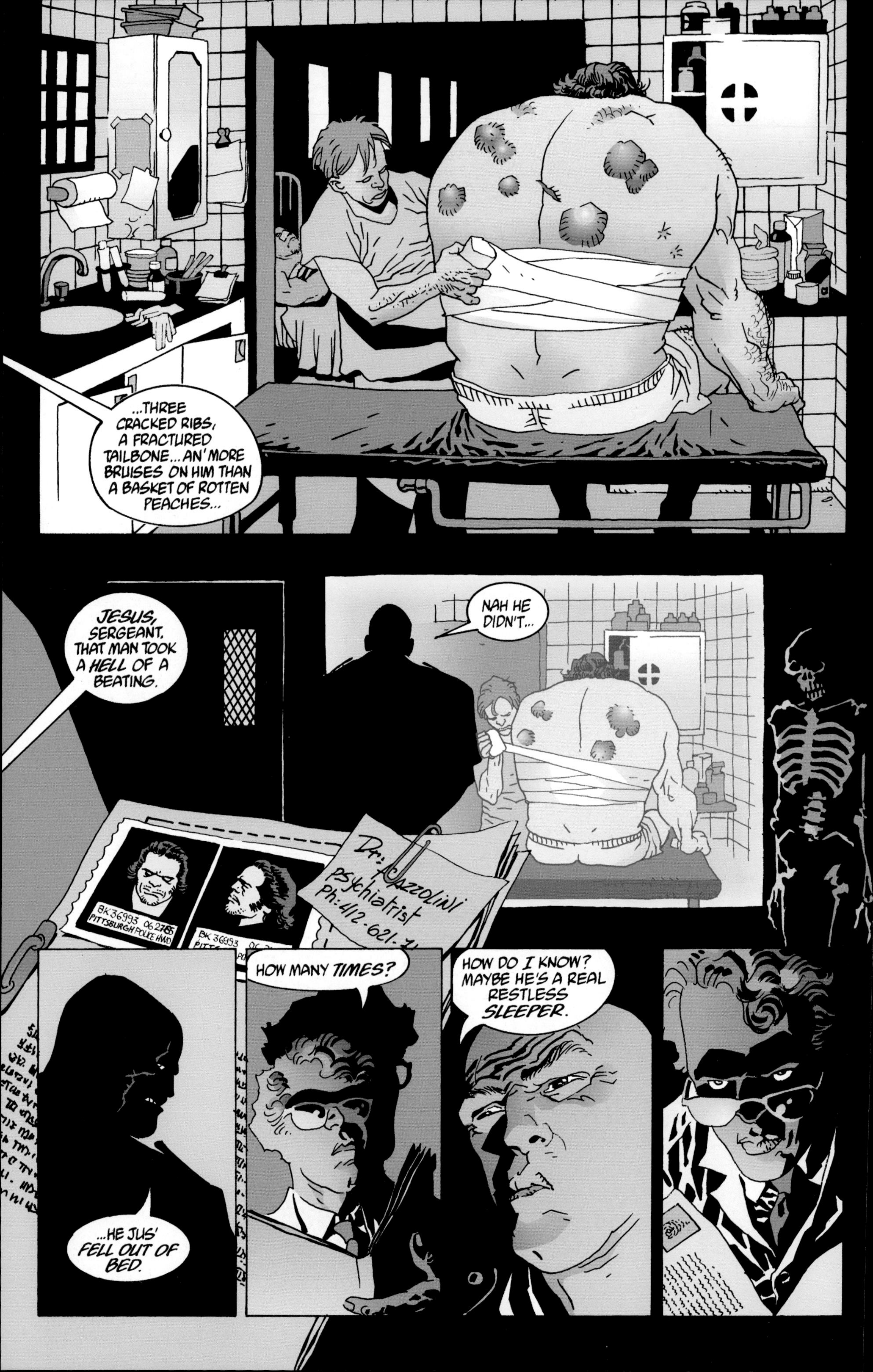

...THREE CRACKED RIBS, A FRACTURED TAILBONE... AN' MORE BRUISES ON HIM THAN A BASKET OF ROTTEN PEACHES...
JESUS, SERGEANT. THAT MAN TOOK A HELL OF A BEATING.
NAH HE DIDN'T...
...HE JUS' FELL OUT OF BED.
HOW MANY TIMES?
HOW DO I KNOW? MAYBE HE'S A REAL RESTLESS SLEEPER.
BK 36993
PITTSBURGH POLICE HWD
psychiatrist

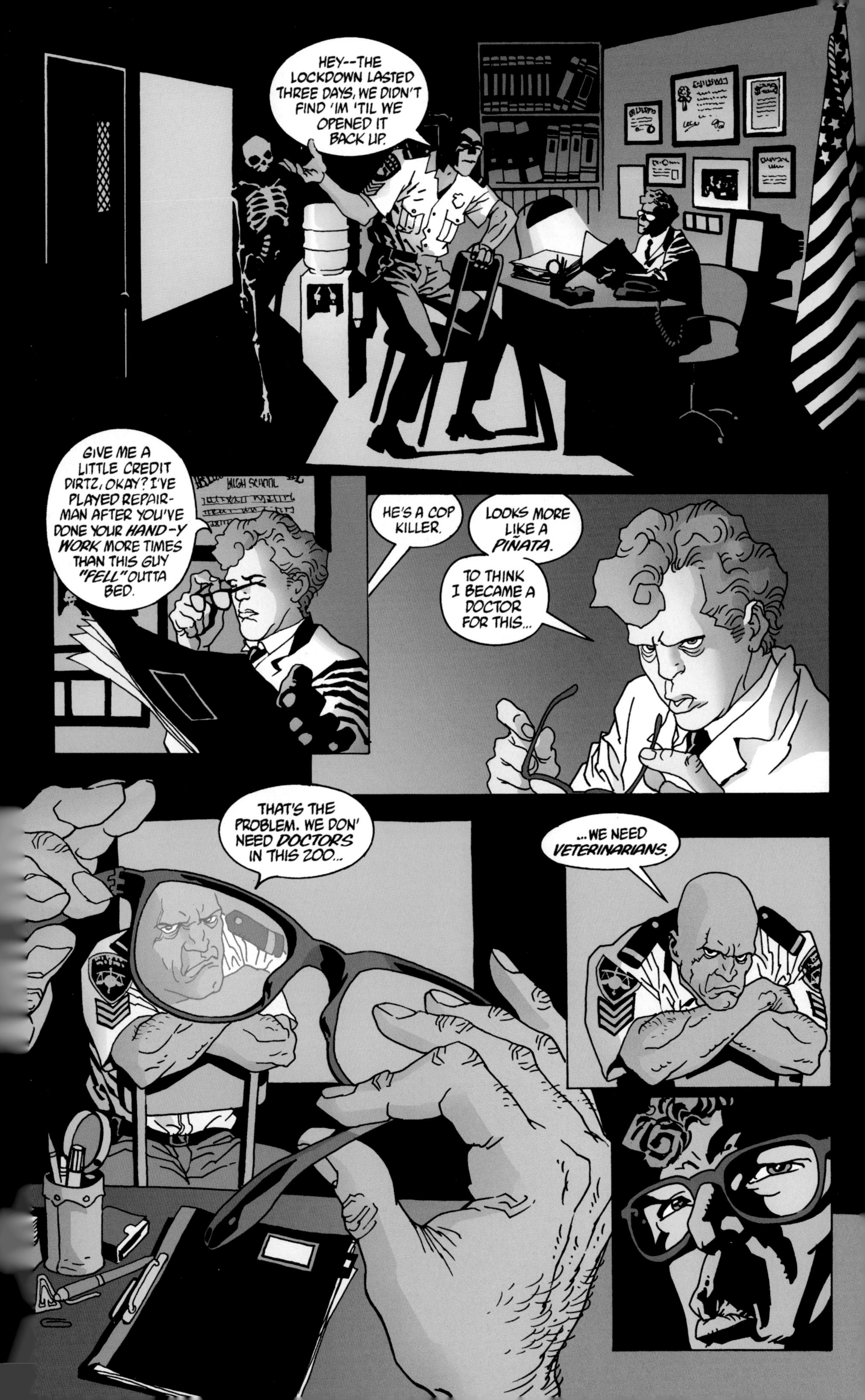
HEY--THE LOCKDOWN LASTED THREE DAYS, WE DIDN'T FIND 'IM 'TIL WE OPENED IT BACK UP.
GIVE ME A LITTLE CREDIT DIRTZ, OKAY? I'VE PLAYED REPAIR-MAN AFTER YOU'VE DONE YOUR HAND-Y WORK MORE TIMES THAN THIS GUY "FELL" OUTTA BED.
HIGH SCHOOL
HE'S A COP KILLER.
LOOKS MORE LIKE A PIÑATA.
TO THINK I BECAME A DOCTOR FOR THIS...
THAT'S THE PROBLEM. WE DON' NEED DOCTORS IN THIS ZOO...
...WE NEED VETERINARIANS.

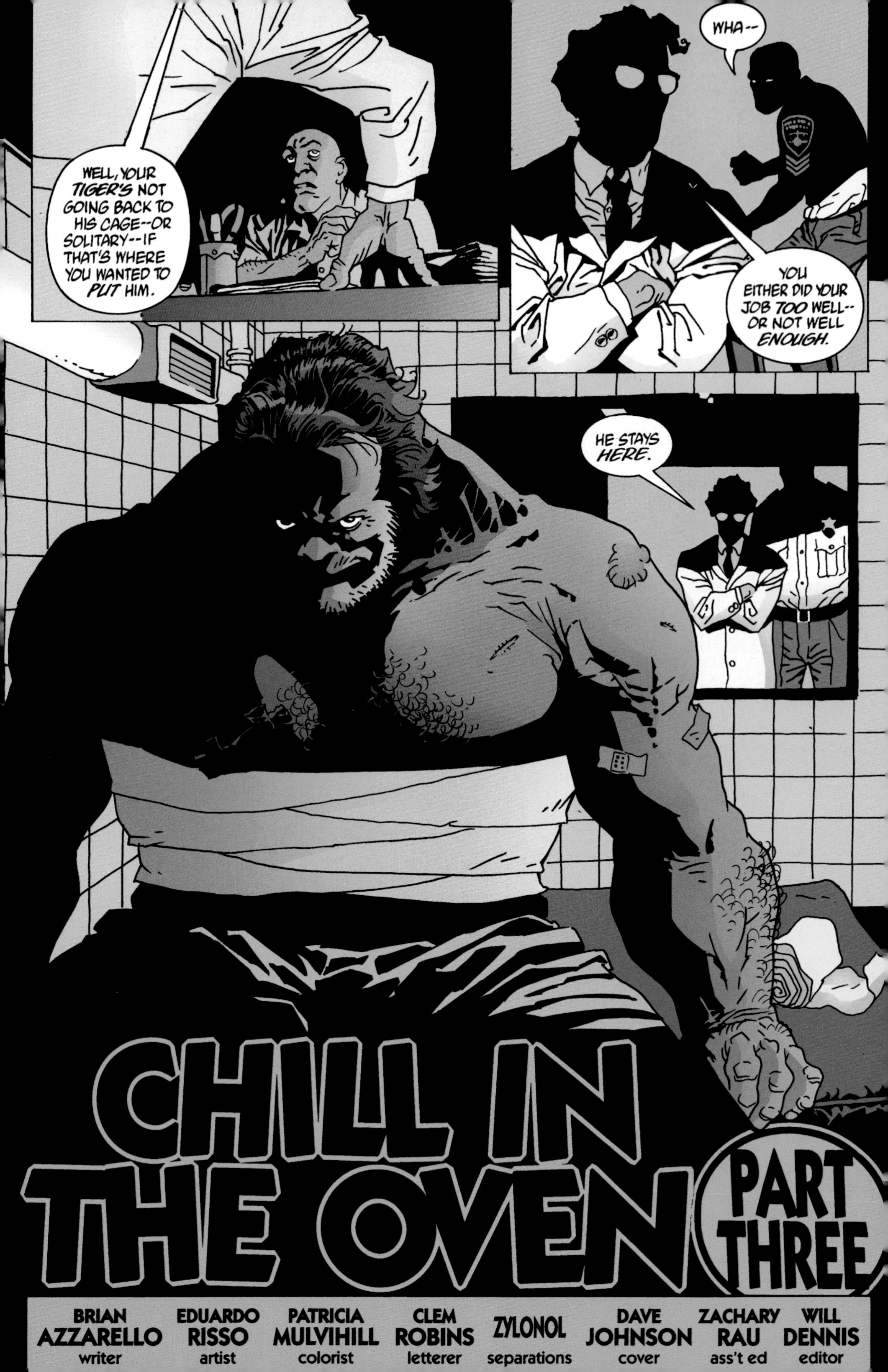
WELL, YOUR TIGER'S NOT GOING BACK TO HIS CAGE--OR SOLITARY--IF THAT'S WHERE YOU WANTED TO PUT HIM.
WHA--
YOU EITHER DID YOUR JOB TOO WELL--OR NOT WELL ENOUGH.
HE STAYS HERE.
CHILL IN THE OVEN
PART THREE
BRIAN AZZARELLO writer
EDUARDO RISSO artist
PATRICIA MULVIHILL colorist
CLEM ROBINS letterer
ZYLONOL separations
DAVE JOHNSON cover
ZACHARY RAU ass't ed
WILL DENNIS editor

NICE MOVE, YOUNG BLOOD. YOU BEEN LEARNIN' SOMETHIN' *FINALLY.*

UH-HUH. I BEEN STUDYIN' YO' *ASS,* OLD HEAD. HOW MANY GAMES WE PLAY?

HUN'RED.

AN' HOW MANY I *WON?*

YOU *AIN'T.*

SO MAYBE IT'S TIME I GOT *LUCKY.*

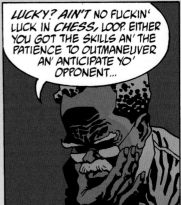

LUCKY? AIN'T NO FUCKIN' LUCK IN *CHESS,* LOOP. EITHER YOU GOT THE SKILLS AN' THE PATIENCE TO OUTMANEUVER AN' ANTICIPATE YO' OPPONENT...

...OR YOU *AIN'T.* CHECK-MATE.

ONE-OH-ONE TO NONE.

YO' LOOPY LOOP...

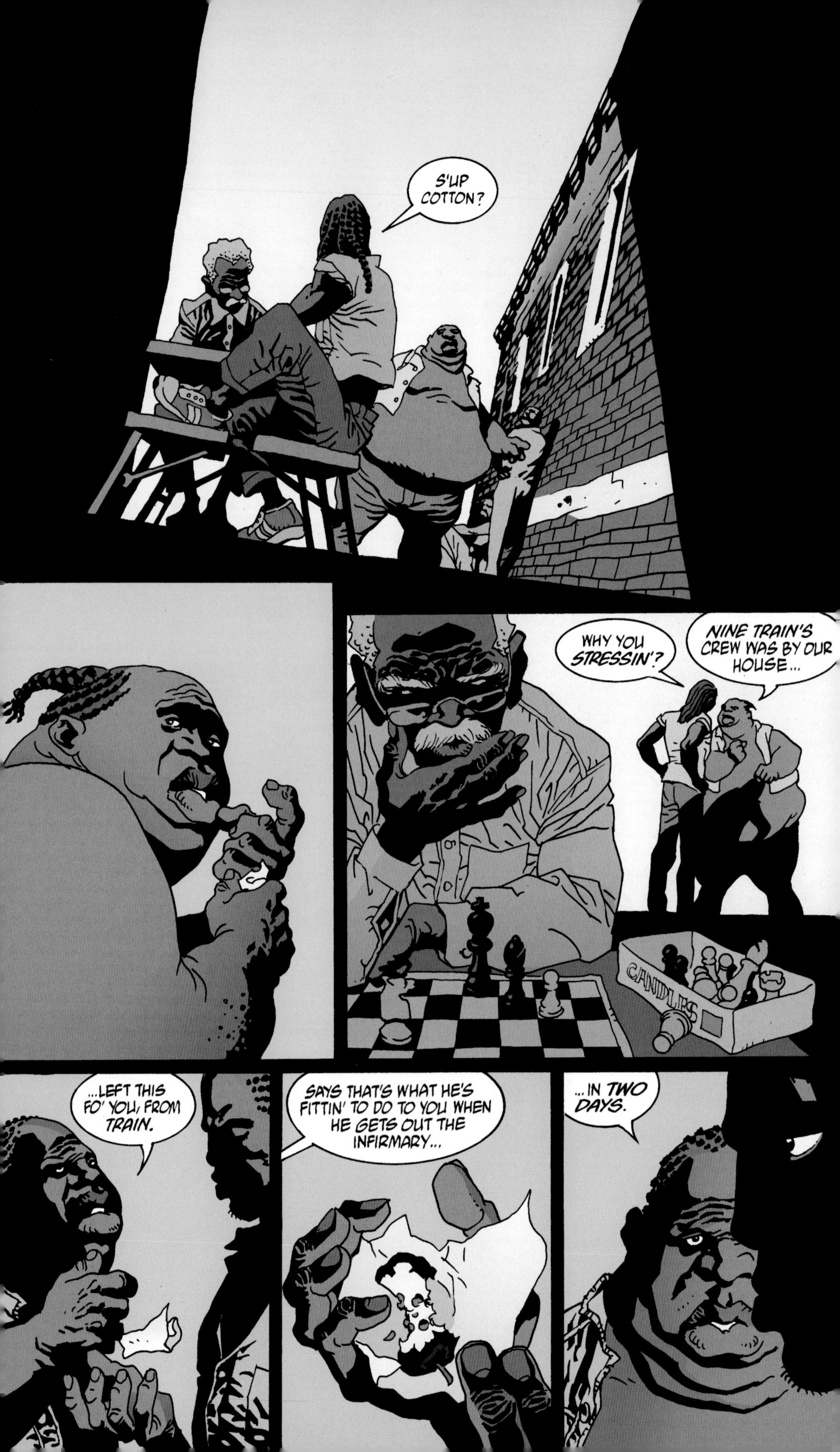
S'UP COTTON?
WHY YOU STRESSIN'?
NINE TRAIN'S CREW WAS BY OUR HOUSE...
...LEFT THIS FO' YOU, FROM TRAIN.
SAYS THAT'S WHAT HE'S FITTIN' TO DO TO YOU WHEN HE GETS OUT THE INFIRMARY...
...IN TWO DAYS.
CANDLES

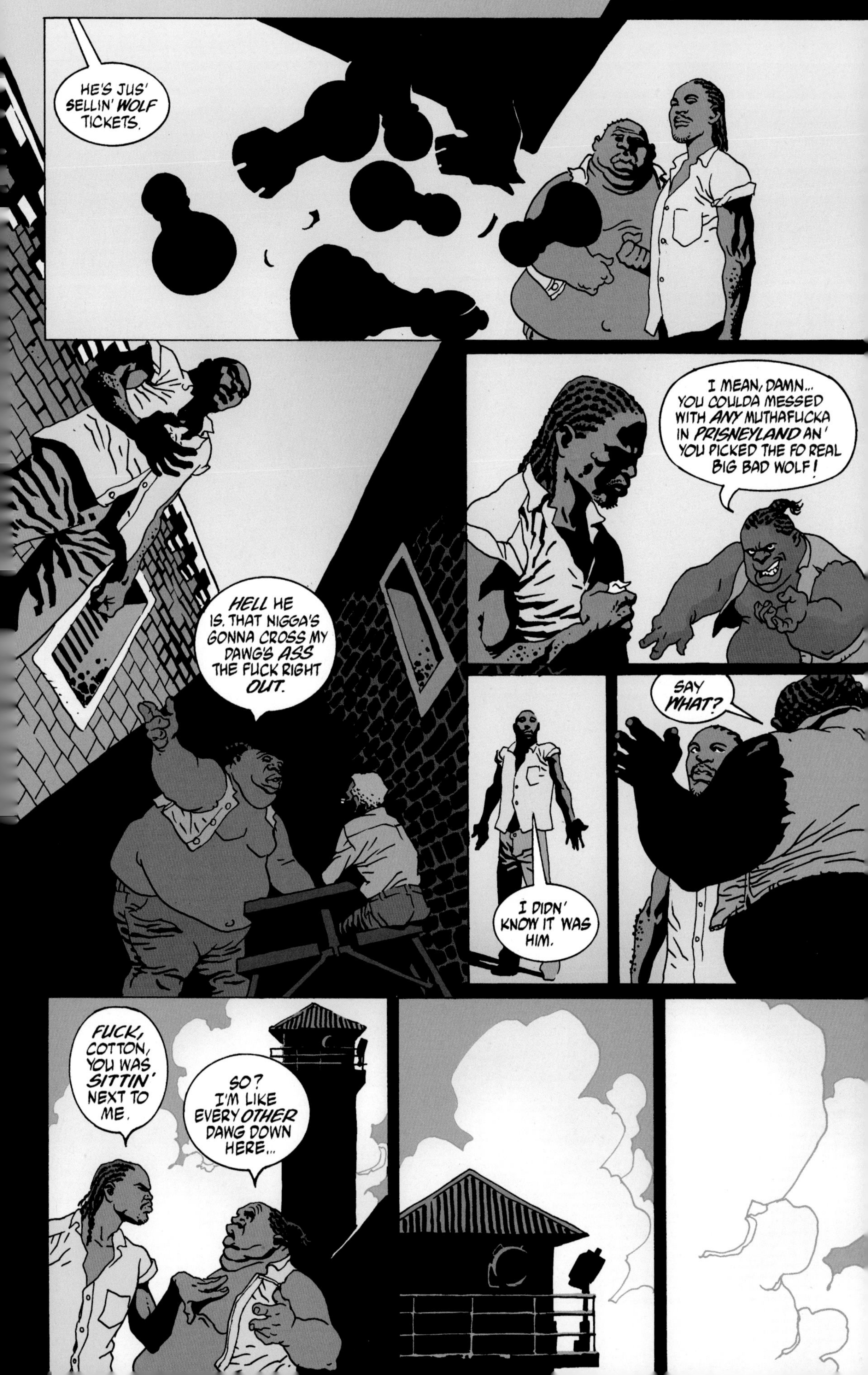
HE'S JUS' SELLIN' WOLF TICKETS.
HELL HE IS. THAT NIGGA'S GONNA CROSS MY DAWG'S ASS THE FUCK RIGHT OUT.
I MEAN, DAMN... YOU COULDA MESSED WITH ANY MUTHAFUCKA IN PRISNEYLAND AN' YOU PICKED THE FO REAL BIG BAD WOLF!
I DIDN' KNOW IT WAS HIM.
SAY WHAT?
FUCK, COTTON, YOU WAS SITTIN' NEXT TO ME.
SO? I'M LIKE EVERY OTHER DAWG DOWN HERE...

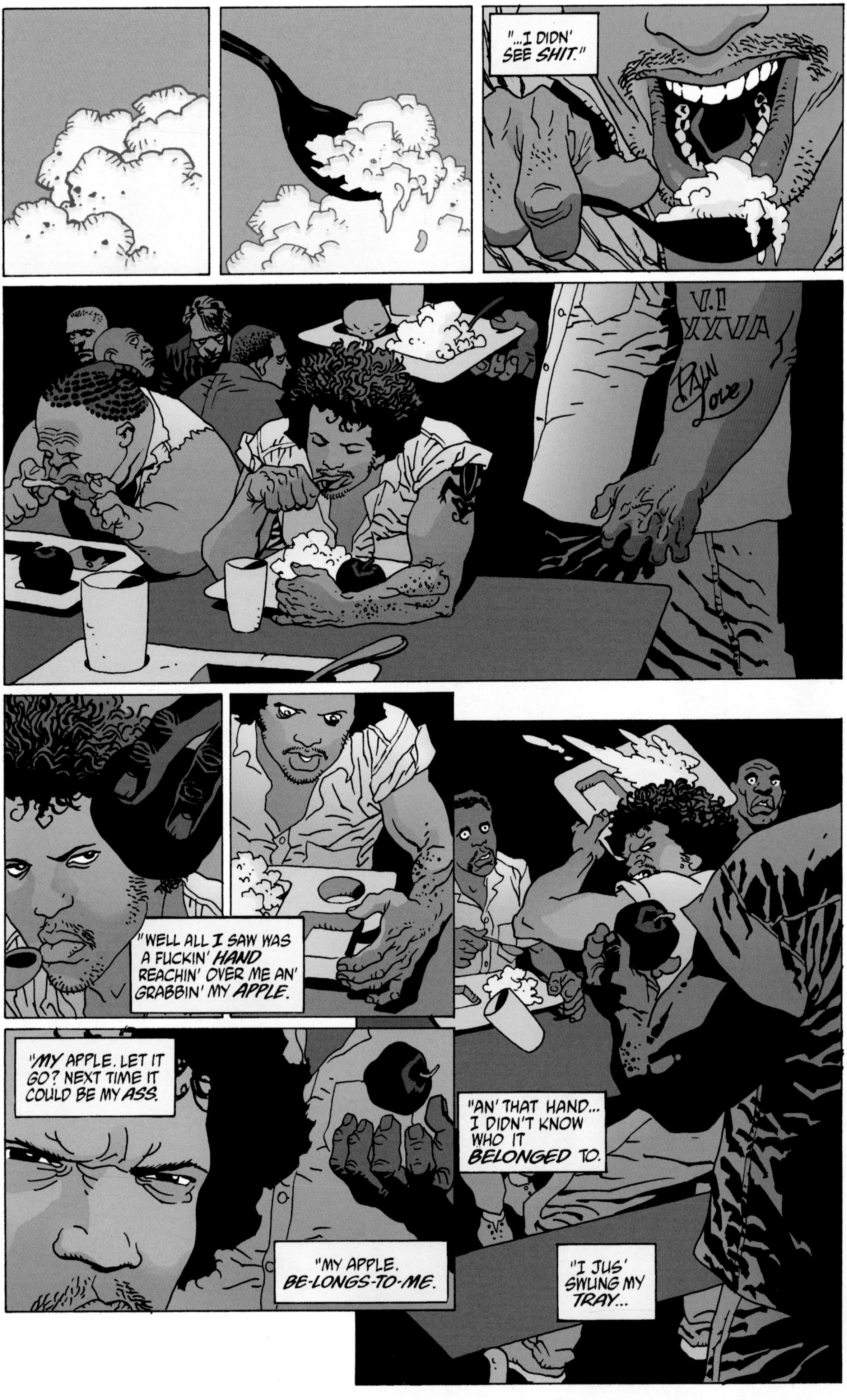
"...I DIDN' SEE SHIT."
V.I XXVIA
PAIN LOVE
"WELL ALL I SAW WAS A FUCKIN' HAND REACHIN' OVER ME AN' GRABBIN' MY APPLE.
"MY APPLE. LET IT GO? NEXT TIME IT COULD BE MY ASS.
"MY APPLE. BE-LONGS-TO-ME.
"AN' THAT HAND... I DIDN'T KNOW WHO IT BELONGED TO.
"I JUS' SWUNG MY TRAY...

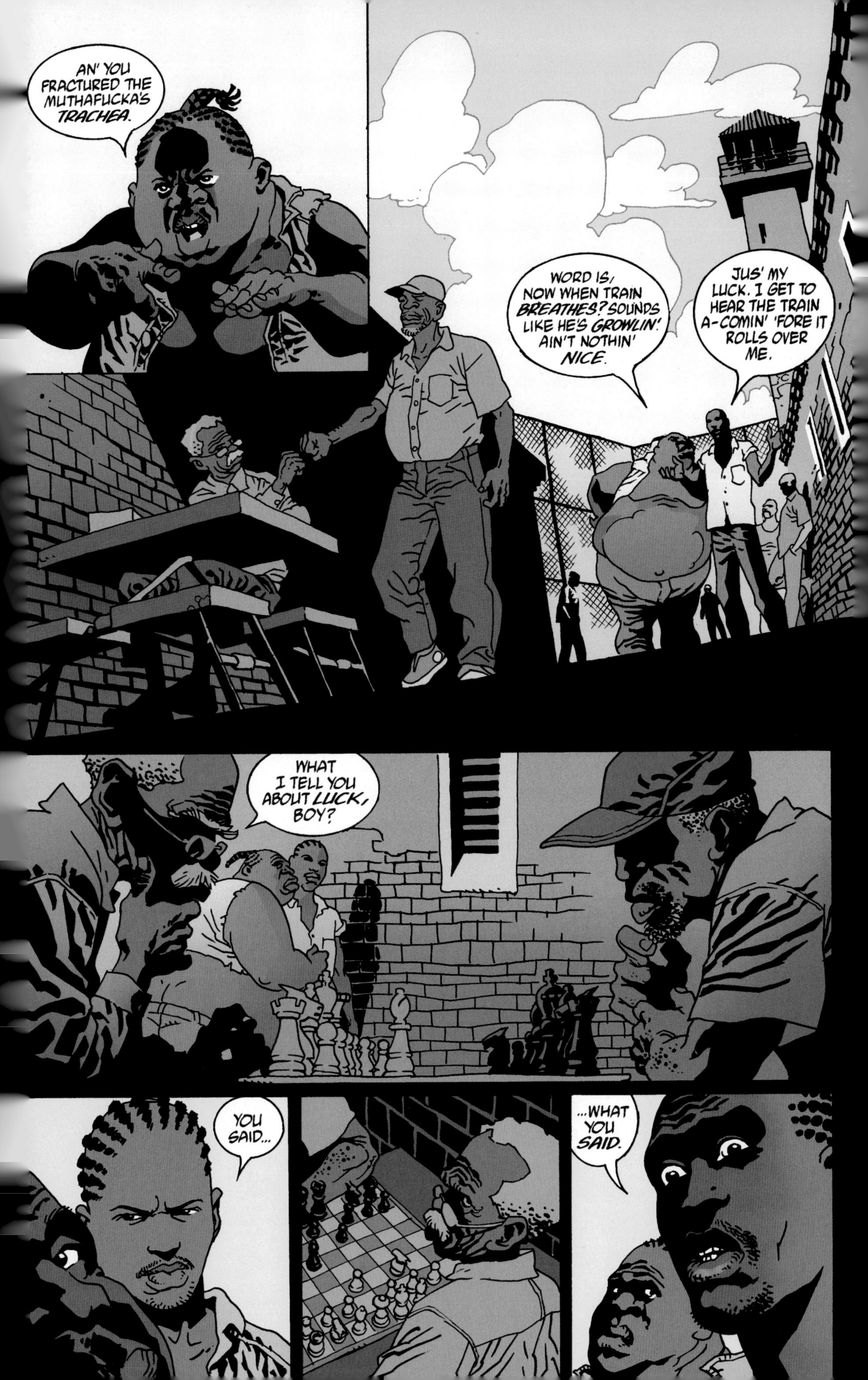
AN' YOU FRACTURED THE MUTHAFUCKA'S *TRACHEA*.
WORD IS, NOW WHEN TRAIN *BREATHES?* SOUNDS LIKE HE'S *GROWLIN'* AIN'T NOTHIN' *NICE*.
JUS' MY LUCK. I GET TO HEAR THE TRAIN A-COMIN' 'FORE IT ROLLS OVER ME.
WHAT I TELL YOU ABOUT *LUCK*, BOY?
YOU SAID...
...WHAT YOU *SAID*.

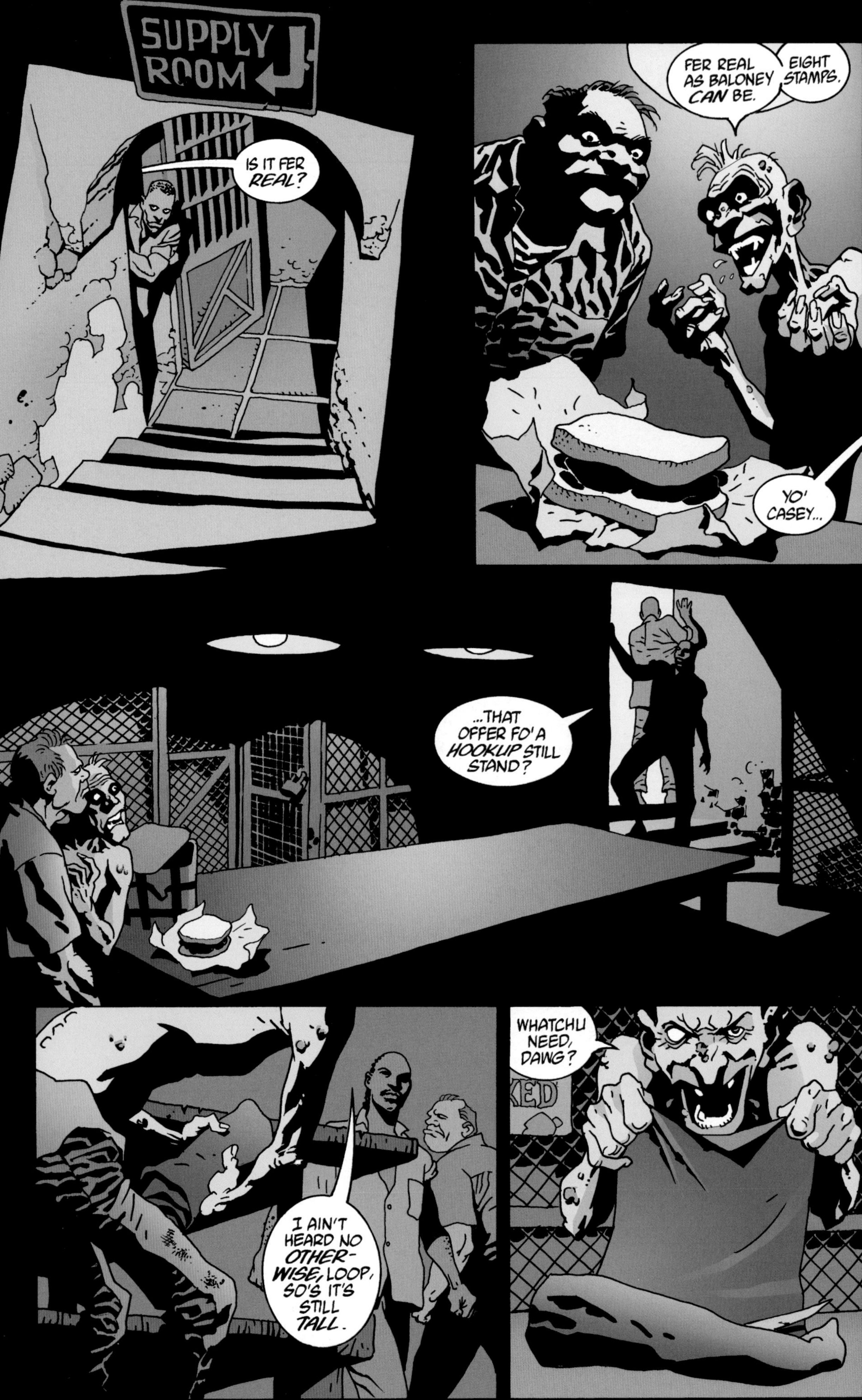
SUPPLY ROOM
IS IT FER REAL?
FER REAL AS BALONEY CAN BE.
EIGHT STAMPS.
YO' CASEY...
...THAT OFFER FO'A HOOKUP STILL STAND?
I AIN'T HEARD NO OTHER-WISE, LOOP, SO'S IT'S STILL TALL.
WHATCHU NEED, DAWG?

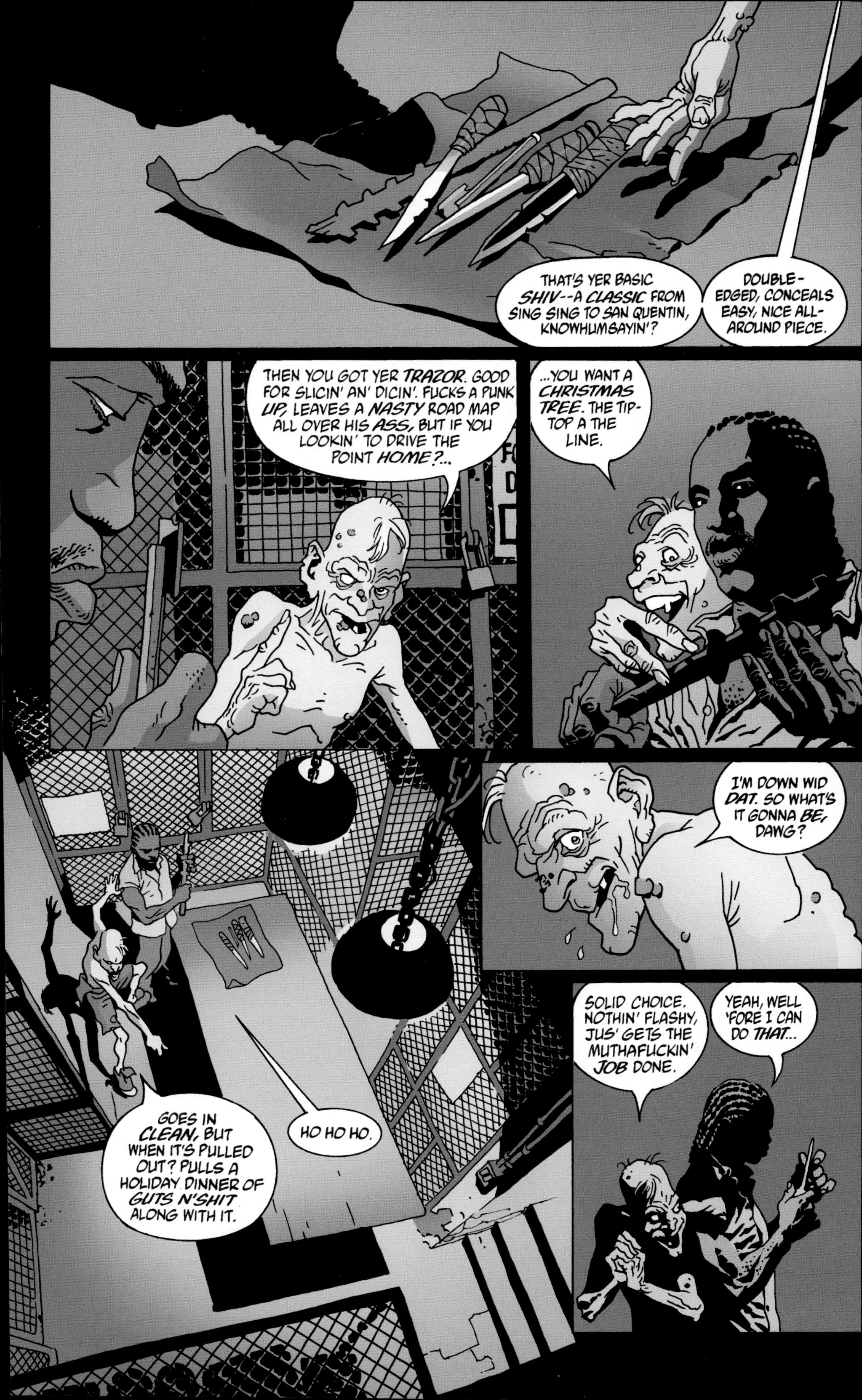
THAT'S YER BASIC SHIV--A CLASSIC FROM SING SING TO SAN QUENTIN, KNOWHUMSAYIN'?
DOUBLE-EDGED, CONCEALS EASY, NICE ALL-AROUND PIECE.
THEN YOU GOT YER TRAZOR. GOOD FOR SLICIN' AN' DICIN'. FUCKS A PUNK UP, LEAVES A NASTY ROAD MAP ALL OVER HIS ASS, BUT IF YOU LOOKIN' TO DRIVE THE POINT HOME?...
...YOU WANT A CHRISTMAS TREE. THE TIP-TOP A THE LINE.
GOES IN CLEAN, BUT WHEN IT'S PULLED OUT? PULLS A HOLIDAY DINNER OF GUTS N'SHIT ALONG WITH IT.
HO HO HO.
I'M DOWN WID DAT. SO WHAT'S IT GONNA BE, DAWG?
SOLID CHOICE. NOTHIN' FLASHY, JUS' GETS THE MUTHAFUCKIN' JOB DONE.
YEAH, WELL 'FORE I CAN DO THAT...

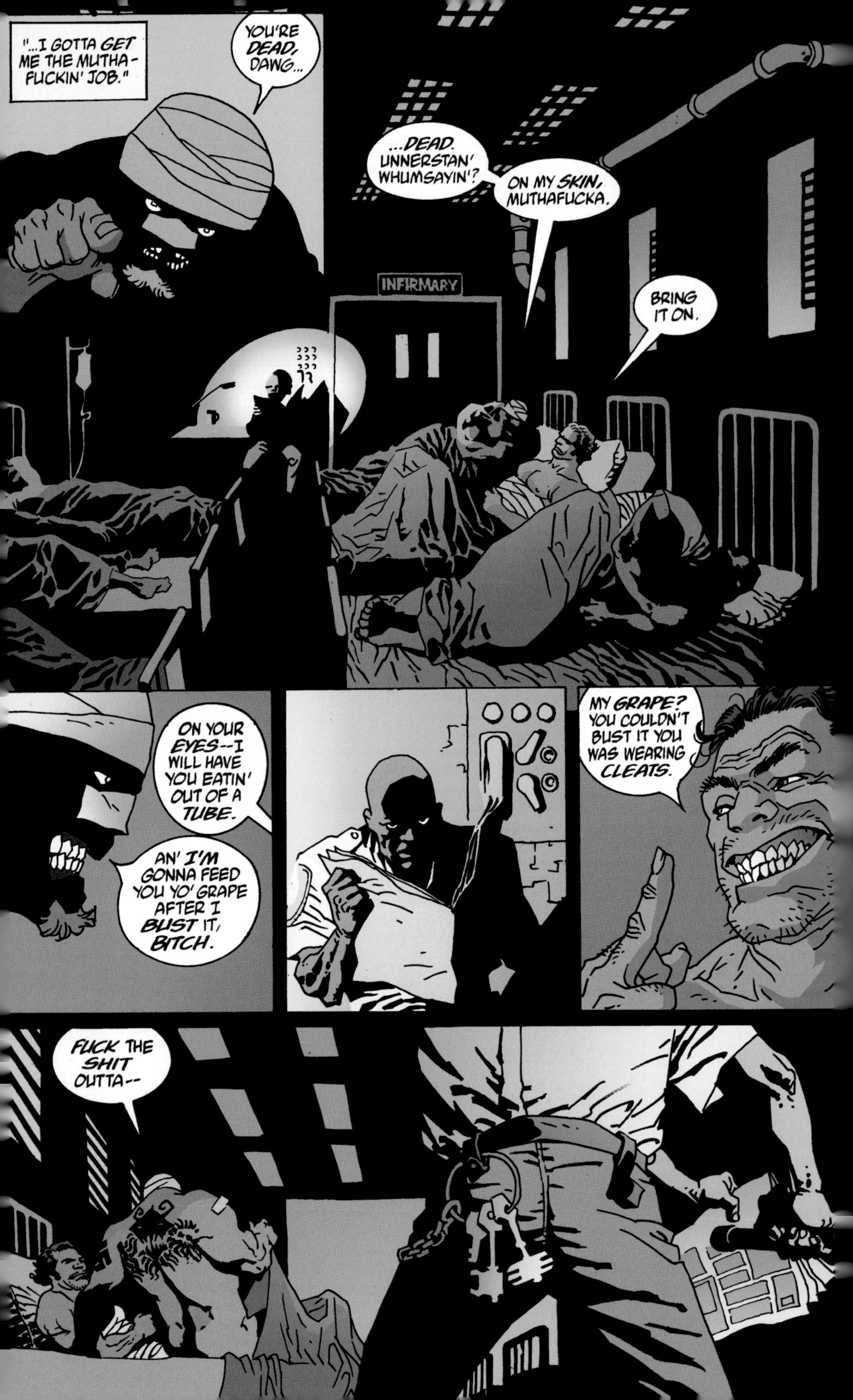
"...I GOTTA GET ME THE MUTHA-FUCKIN' JOB."
YOU'RE DEAD, DAWG...
...DEAD. UNNERSTAN' WHUMSAYIN'?
ON MY SKIN, MUTHAFUCKA.
INFIRMARY
BRING IT ON.
ON YOUR EYES--I WILL HAVE YOU EATIN' OUT OF A TUBE.
AN' I'M GONNA FEED YOU YO' GRAPE AFTER I BUST IT, BITCH.
MY GRAPE? YOU COULDN'T BUST IT YOU WAS WEARING CLEATS.
FUCK THE SHIT OUTTA--

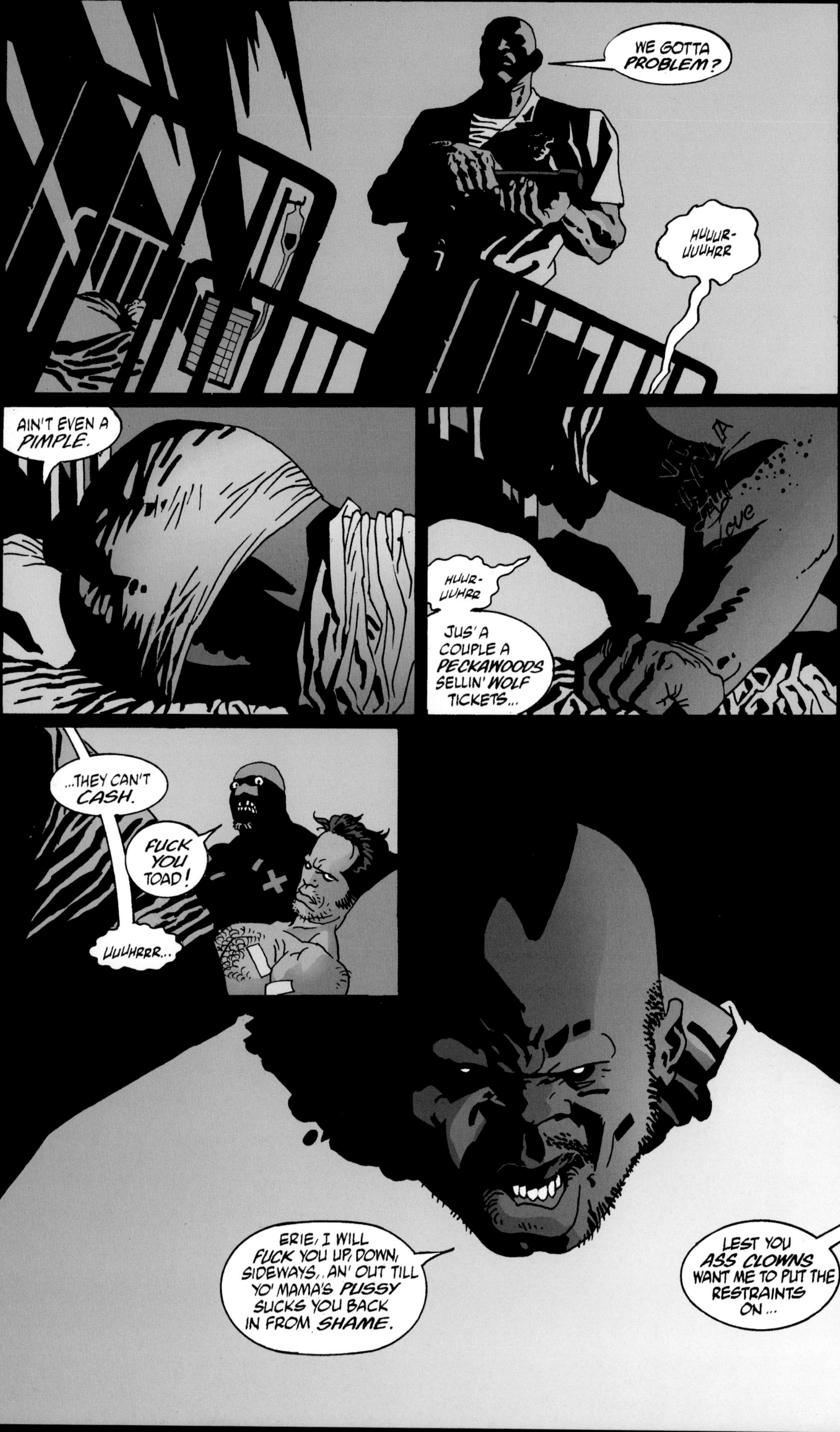
WE GOTTA PROBLEM?
HUUUR-UUUHRR
AIN'T EVEN A PIMPLE.
HUUR-UUHRR
JUS' A COUPLE A PECKAWOODS SELLIN' WOLF TICKETS...
...THEY CAN'T CASH.
FUCK YOU TOAD!
UUUHRRR...
ERIE, I WILL FUCK YOU UP, DOWN, SIDEWAYS, AN' OUT TILL YO' MAMA'S PUSSY SUCKS YOU BACK IN FROM SHAME.
LEST YOU ASS CLOWNS WANT ME TO PUT THE RESTRAINTS ON...

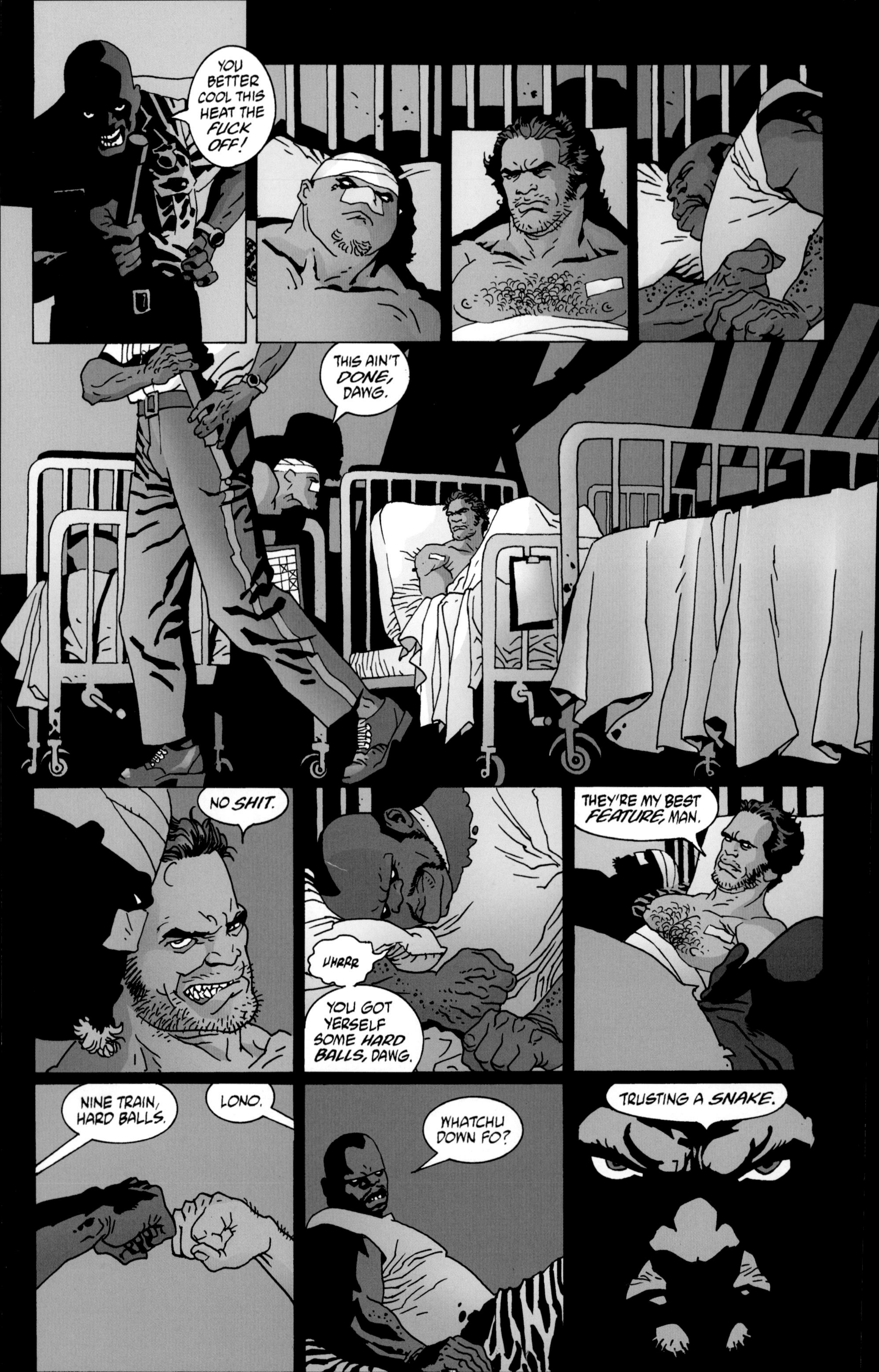
YOU BETTER COOL THIS HEAT THE FUCK OFF!
THIS AIN'T DONE, DAWG.
NO SHIT.
UHRRR
YOU GOT YERSELF SOME HARD BALLS, DAWG.
THEY'RE MY BEST FEATURE, MAN.
NINE TRAIN, HARD BALLS.
LONO.
WHATCHU DOWN FO?
TRUSTING A SNAKE.

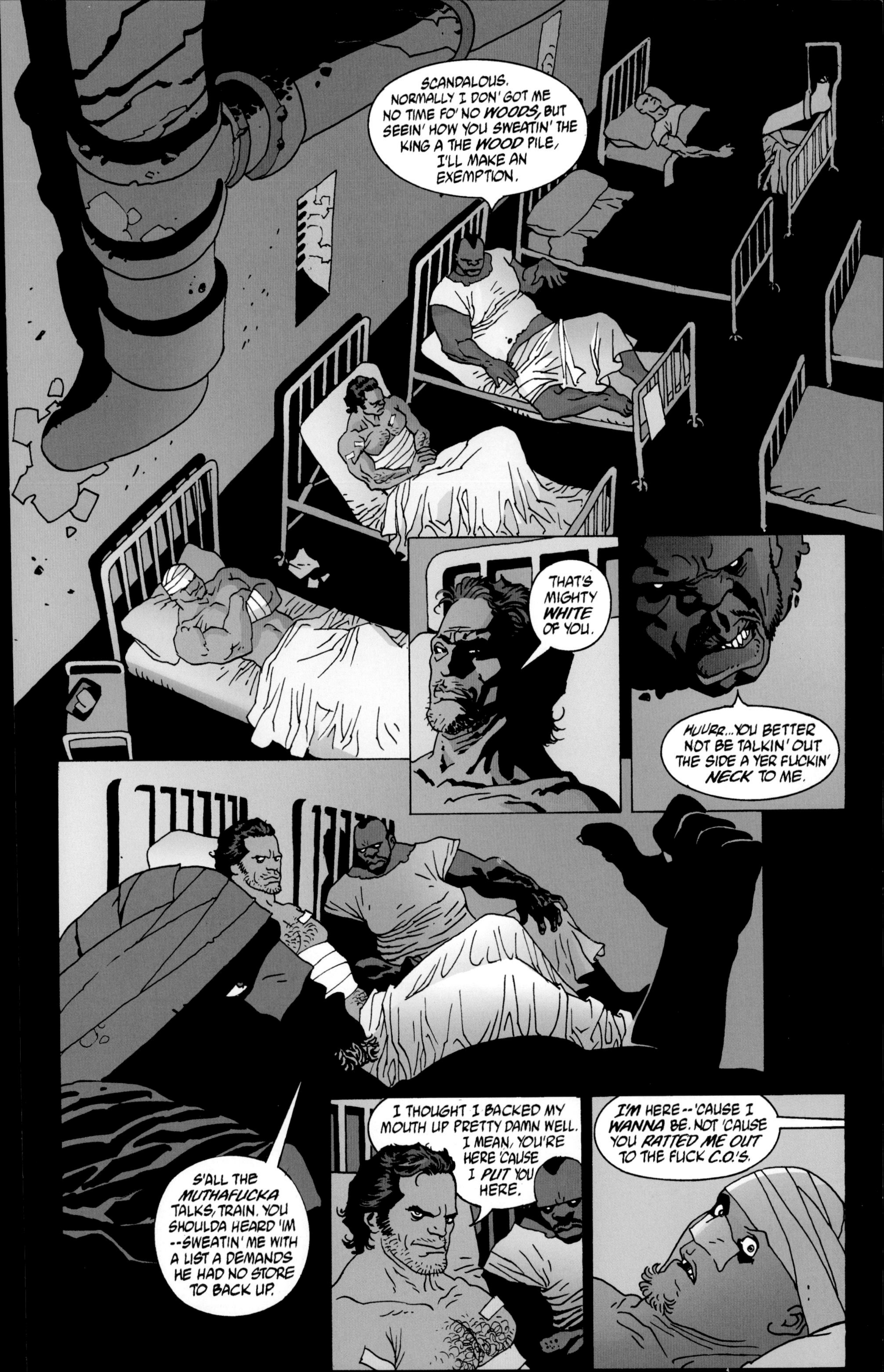
SCANDALOUS. NORMALLY I DON' GOT ME NO TIME FO' NO WOODS, BUT SEEIN' HOW YOU SWEATIN' THE KING A THE WOOD PILE, I'LL MAKE AN EXEMPTION.
THAT'S MIGHTY WHITE OF YOU.
HUURR... YOU BETTER NOT BE TALKIN' OUT THE SIDE A YER FUCKIN' NECK TO ME.
S'ALL THE MUTHAFUCKA TALKS, TRAIN. YOU SHOULDA HEARD 'IM --SWEATIN' ME WITH A LIST A DEMANDS HE HAD NO STORE TO BACK UP.
I THOUGHT I BACKED MY MOUTH UP PRETTY DAMN WELL.
I MEAN, YOU'RE HERE 'CAUSE I PUT YOU HERE.
I'M HERE-- 'CAUSE I WANNA BE. NOT 'CAUSE YOU RATTED ME OUT TO THE FUCK C.O.'S.

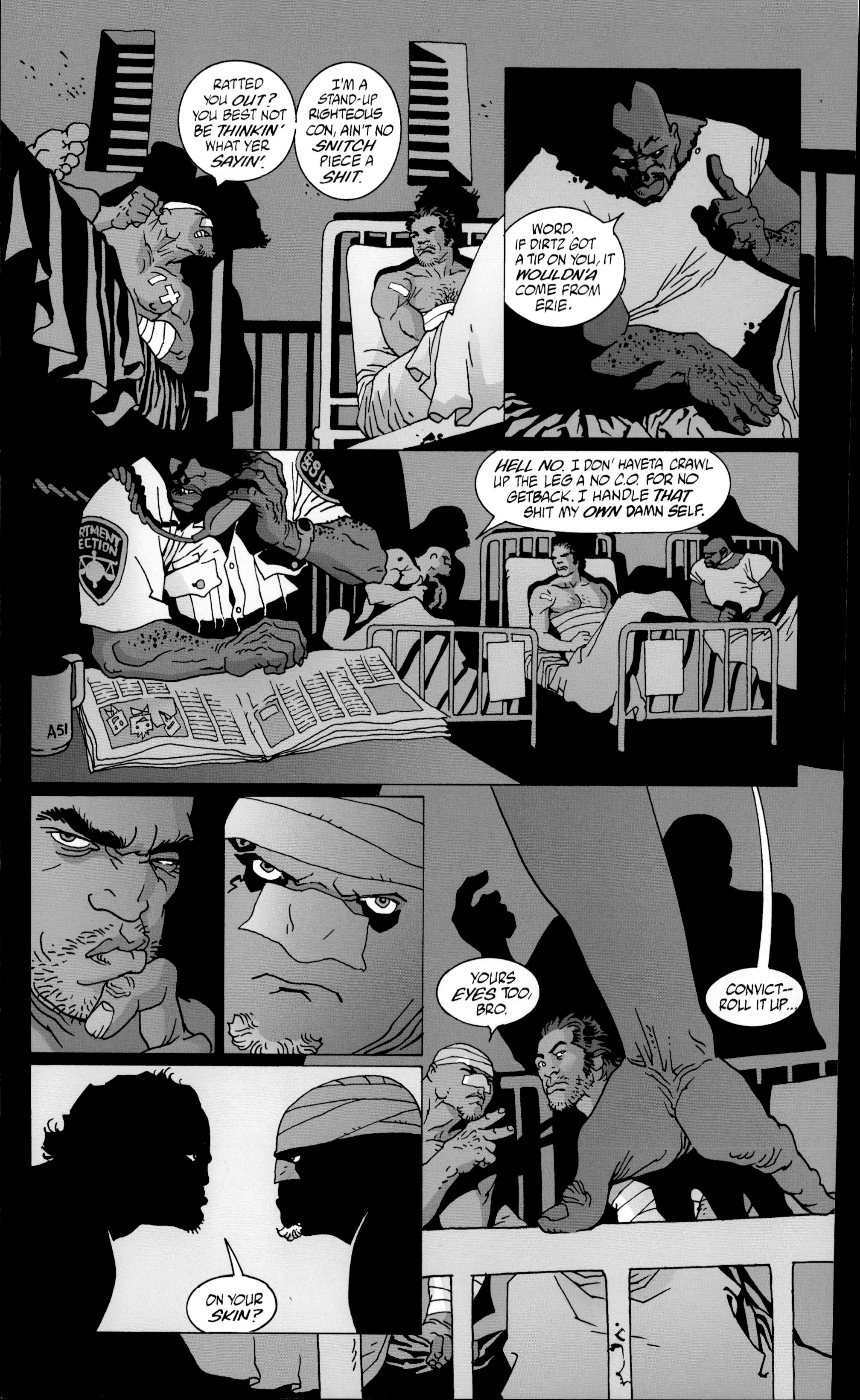
RATTED YOU OUT? YOU BEST NOT BE THINKIN' WHAT YER SAYIN'.
I'M A STAND-UP RIGHTEOUS CON, AIN'T NO SNITCH PIECE A SHIT.
WORD. IF DIRTZ GOT A TIP ON YOU, IT WOULDN'A COME FROM ERIE.
HELL NO. I DON' HAVETA CRAWL UP THE LEG A NO C.O. FOR NO GETBACK. I HANDLE THAT SHIT MY OWN DAMN SELF.
YOURS EYES TOO, BRO.
CONVICT-- ROLL IT UP...
ON YOUR SKIN?

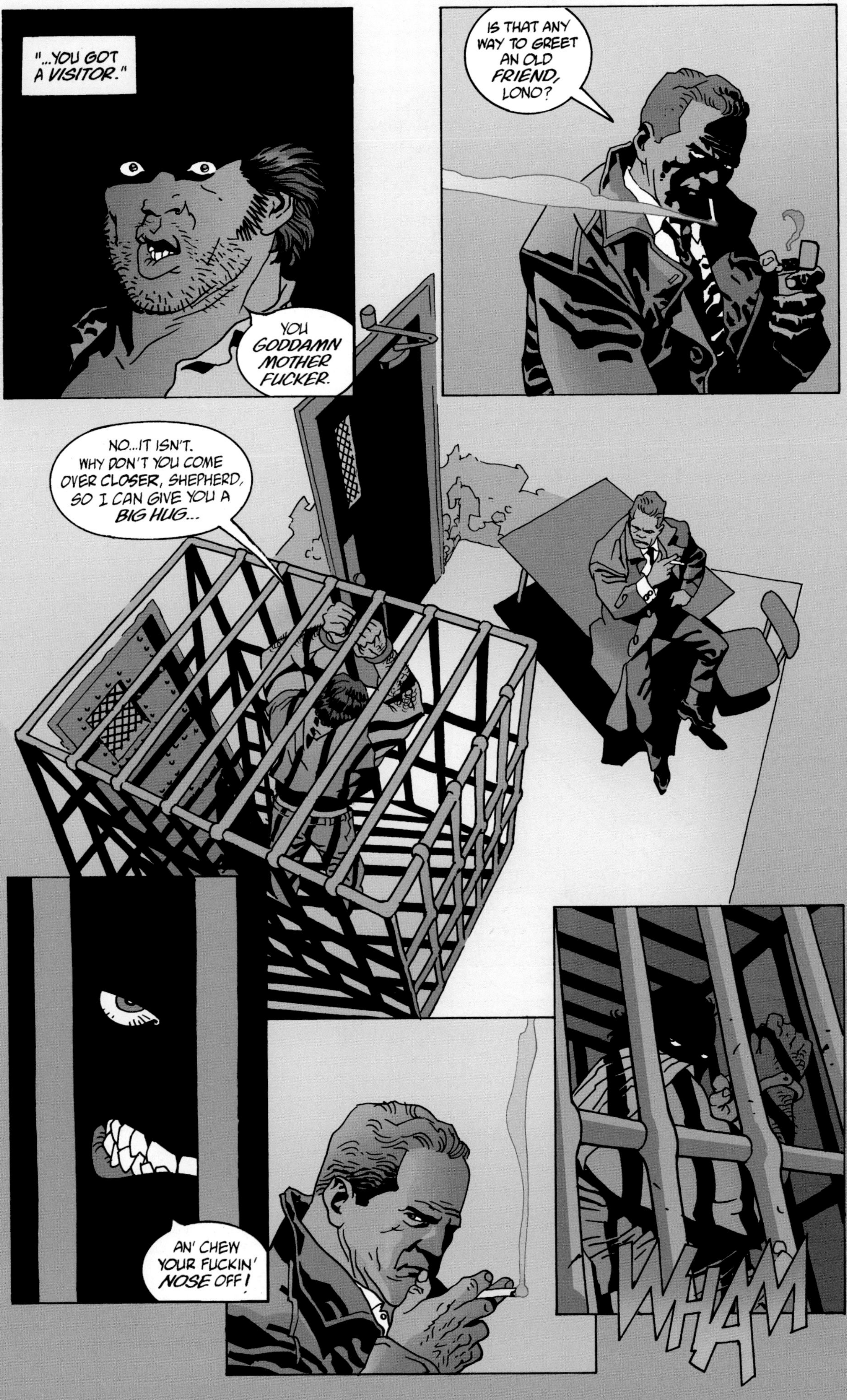
"...YOU GOT A VISITOR."
YOU GODDAMN MOTHER FUCKER.
IS THAT ANY WAY TO GREET AN OLD FRIEND, LONO?
NO...IT ISN'T. WHY DON'T YOU COME OVER CLOSER, SHEPHERD, SO I CAN GIVE YOU A BIG HUG...
AN' CHEW YOUR FUCKIN' NOSE OFF!
WHAM

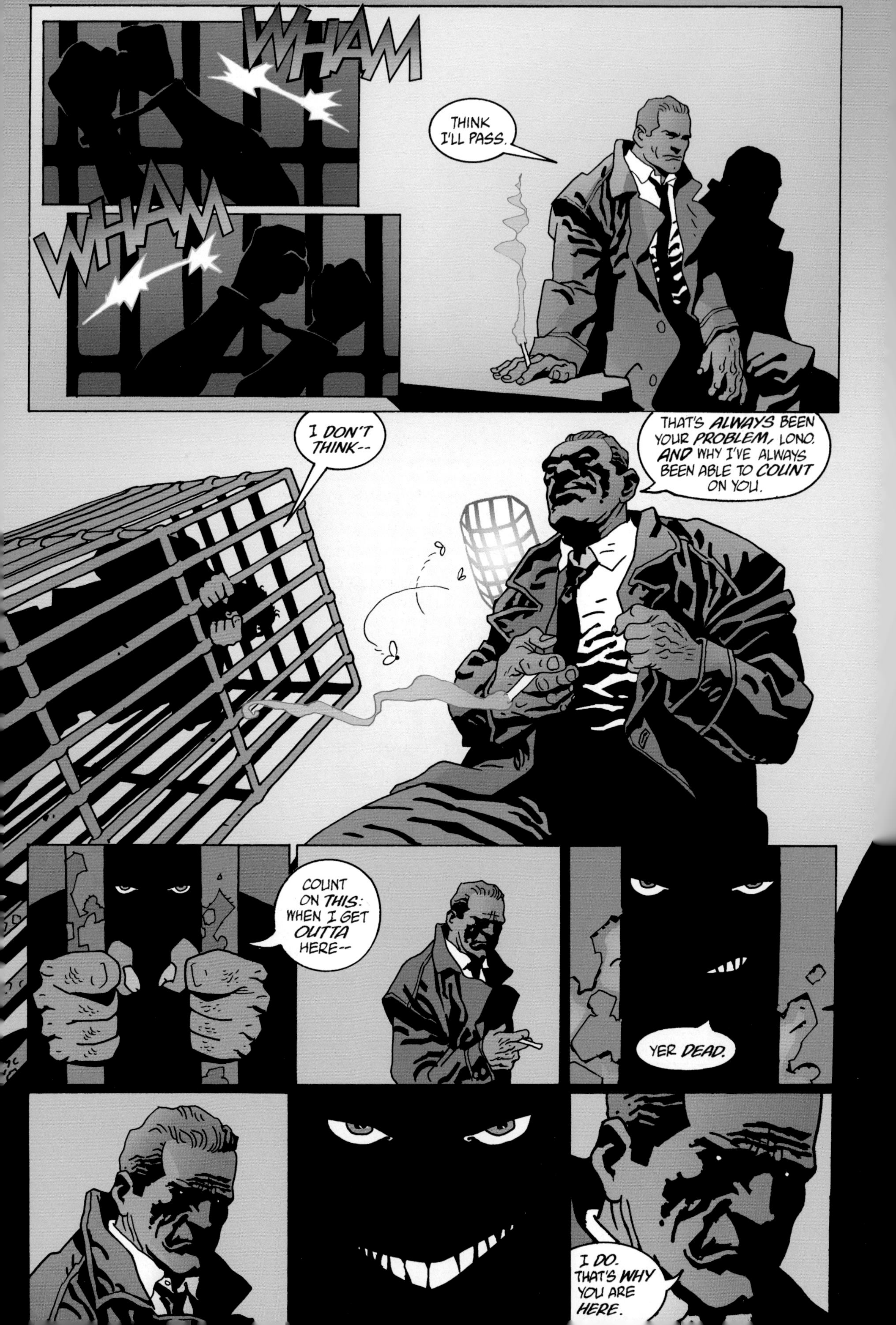
WHAM
WHAM
THINK I'LL PASS.
I DON'T THINK--
THAT'S ALWAYS BEEN YOUR PROBLEM, LONO. AND WHY I'VE ALWAYS BEEN ABLE TO COUNT ON YOU.
COUNT ON THIS: WHEN I GET OUTTA HERE--
YER DEAD.
I DO. THAT'S WHY YOU ARE HERE.

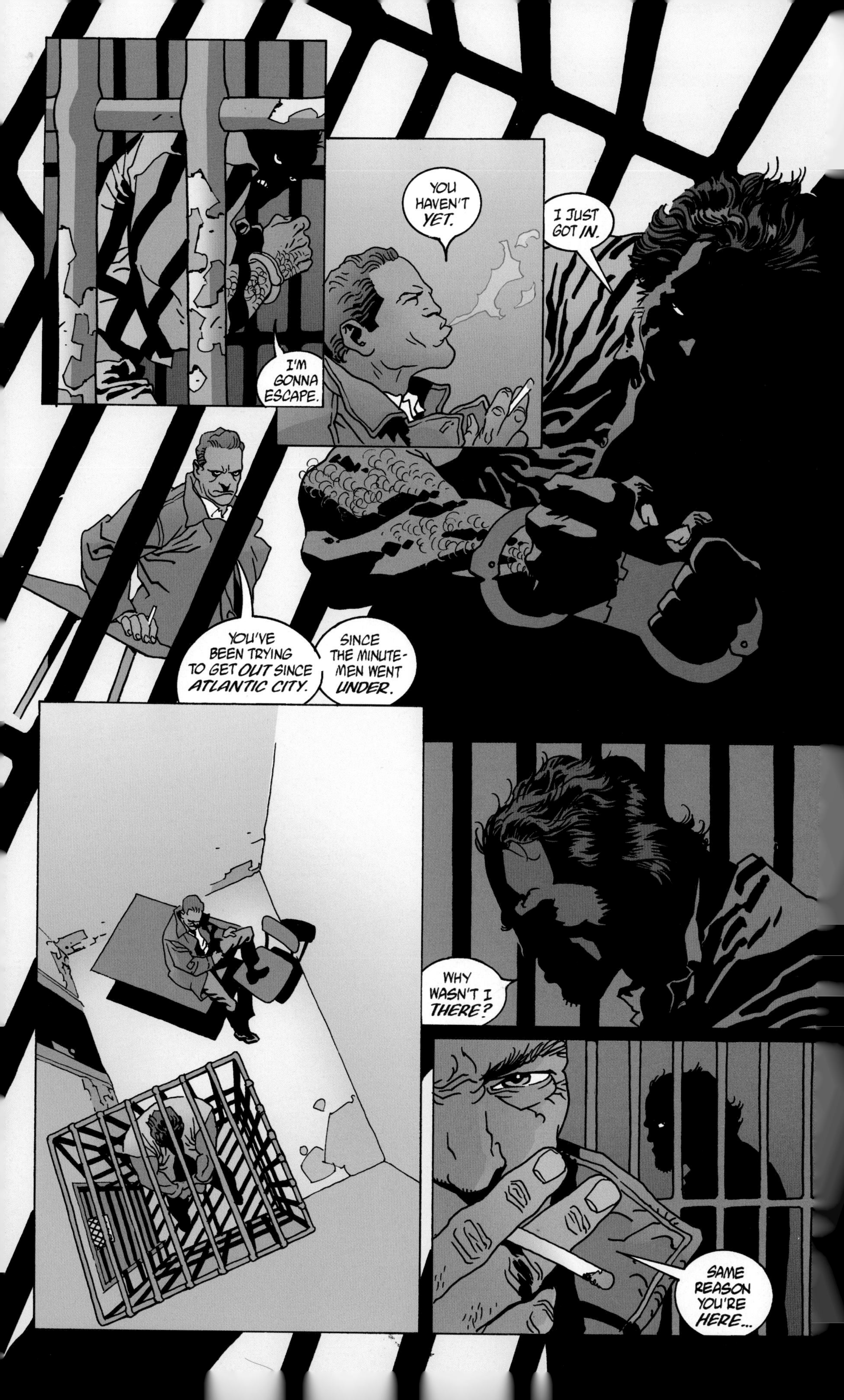
I'M GONNA ESCAPE.
YOU HAVEN'T YET.
I JUST GOT IN.
YOU'VE BEEN TRYING TO GET OUT SINCE ATLANTIC CITY.
SINCE THE MINUTEMEN WENT UNDER.
WHY WASN'T I THERE?
SAME REASON YOU'RE HERE...

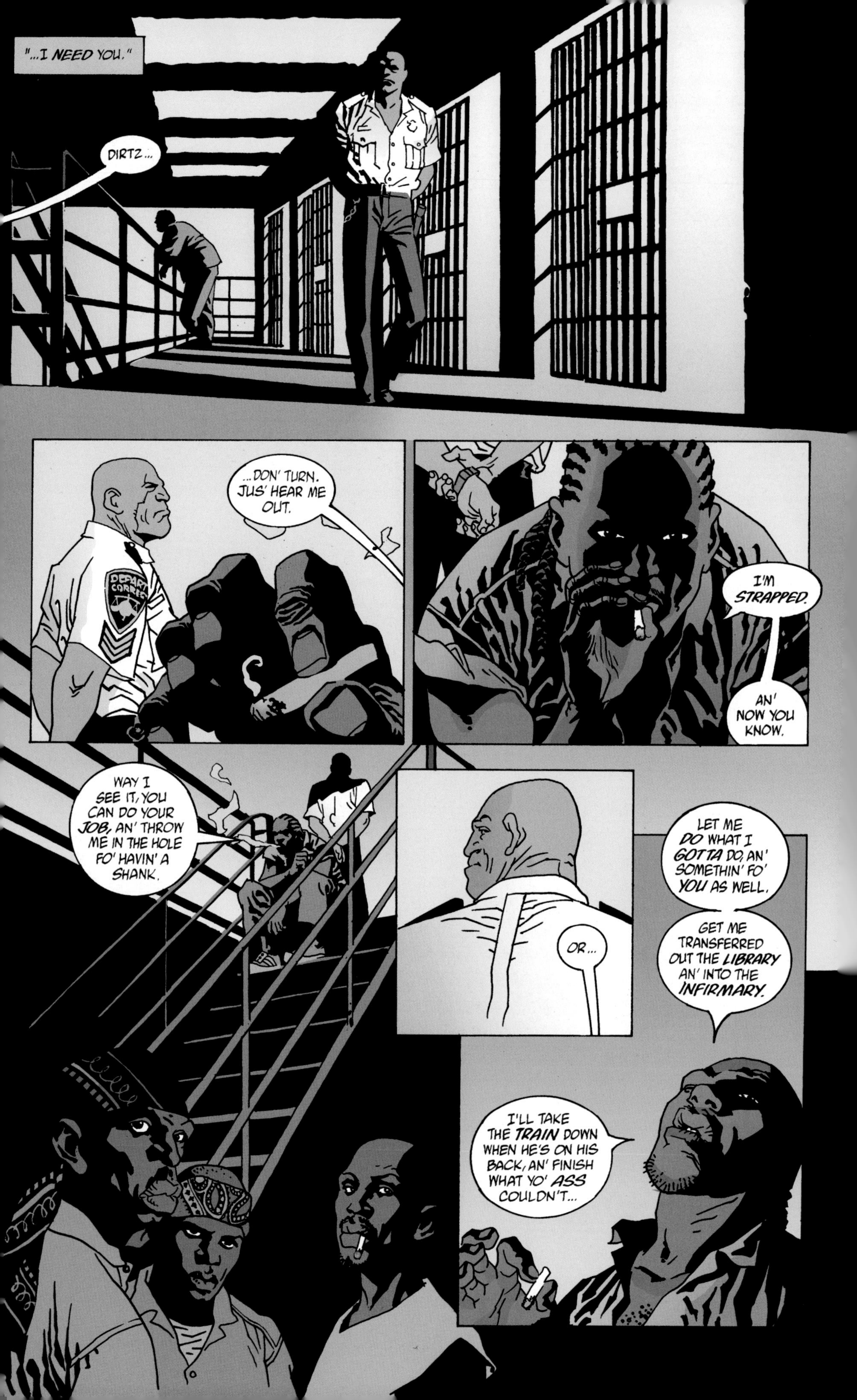
"...I NEED YOU."
DIRTZ...
...DON' TURN. JUS' HEAR ME OUT.
I'M STRAPPED.
AN' NOW YOU KNOW.
WAY I SEE IT, YOU CAN DO YOUR JOB, AN' THROW ME IN THE HOLE FO' HAVIN' A SHANK.
OR...
LET ME DO WHAT I GOTTA DO, AN' SOMETHIN' FO' YOU AS WELL.
GET ME TRANSFERRED OUT THE LIBRARY AN' INTO THE INFIRMARY.
I'LL TAKE THE TRAIN DOWN WHEN HE'S ON HIS BACK, AN' FINISH WHAT YO' ASS COULDN'T...

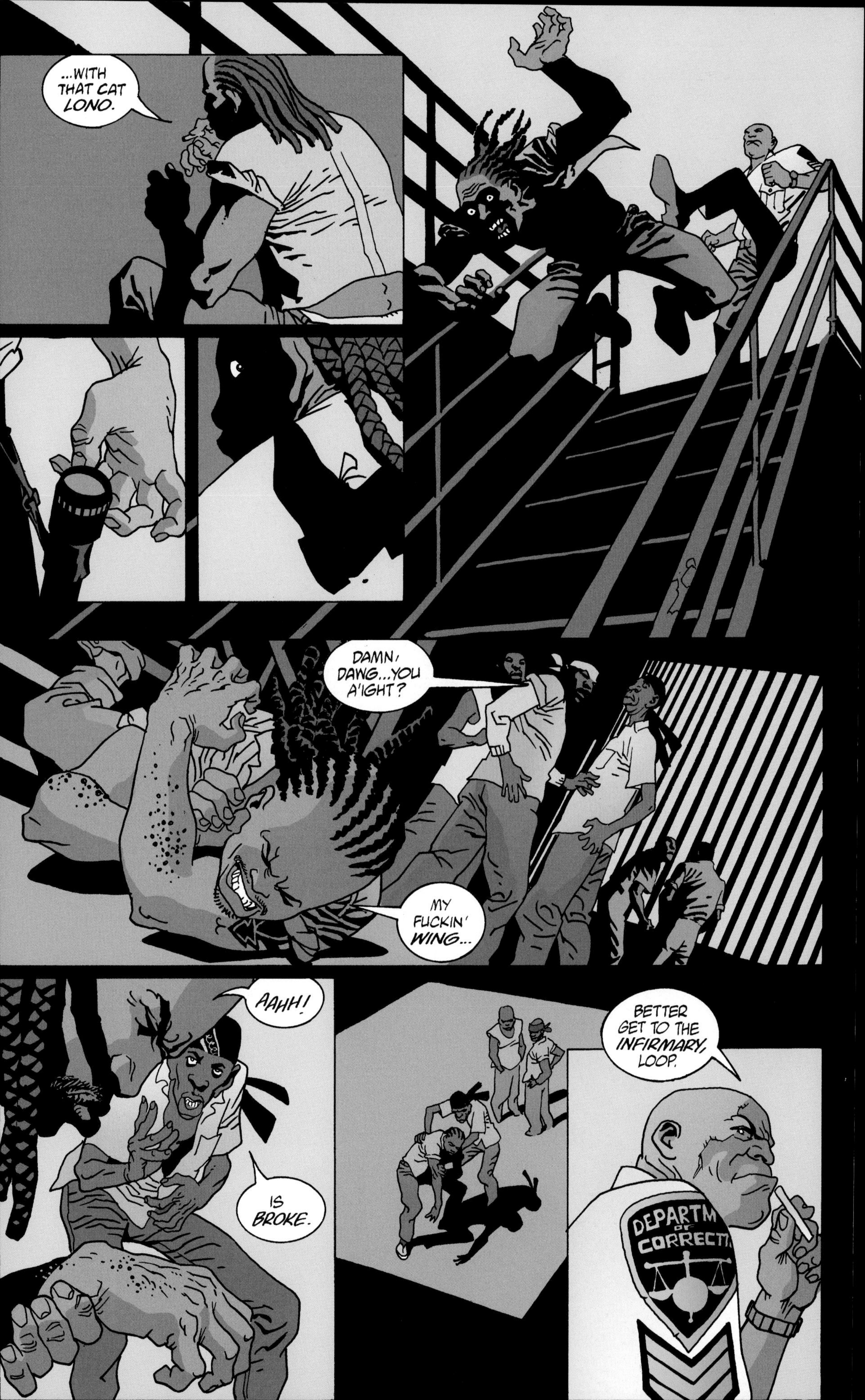
...WITH THAT CAT LONO.
DAMN, DAWG...YOU A'IGHT?
MY FUCKIN' WING...
AAHH!
IS BROKE.
BETTER GET TO THE INFIRMARY, LOOP.
DEPARTM
CORRECTI

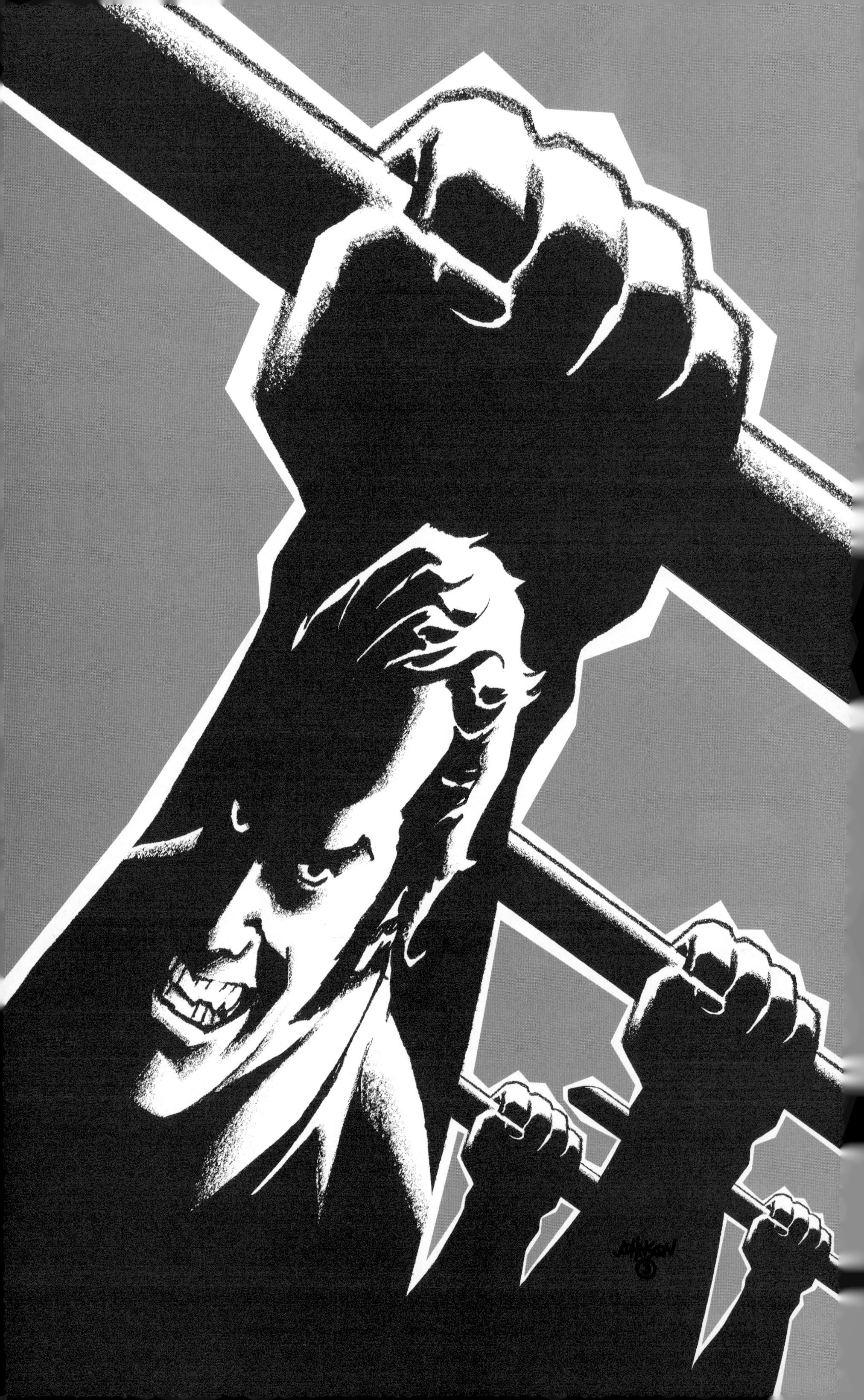

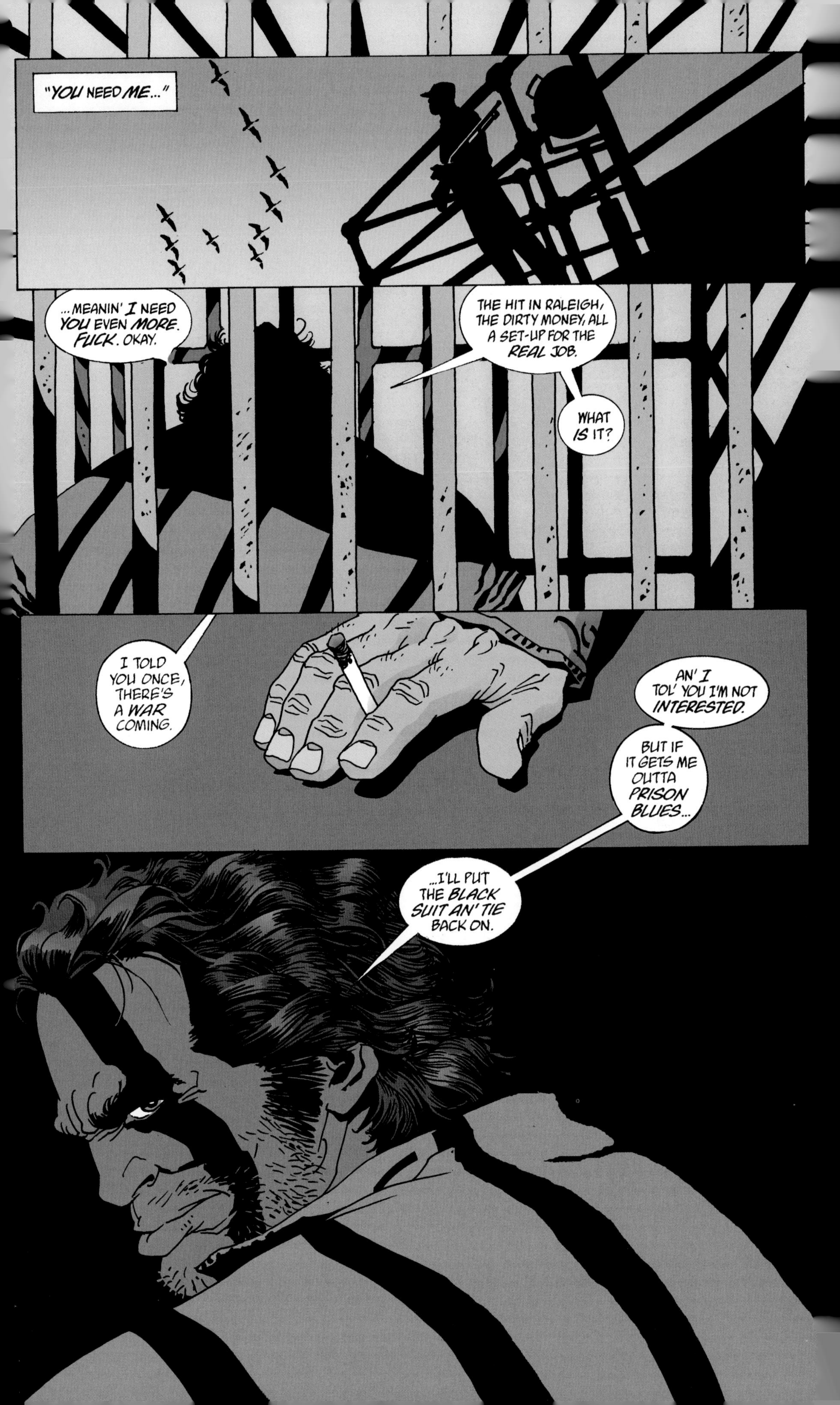
"YOU NEED ME..."
...MEANIN' I NEED YOU EVEN MORE. FUCK. OKAY.
THE HIT IN RALEIGH, THE DIRTY MONEY, ALL A SET-UP FOR THE REAL JOB.
WHAT IS IT?
I TOLD YOU ONCE, THERE'S A WAR COMING.
AN' I TOL' YOU I'M NOT INTERESTED.
BUT IF IT GETS ME OUTTA PRISON BLUES...
...I'LL PUT THE BLACK SUIT AN' TIE BACK ON.

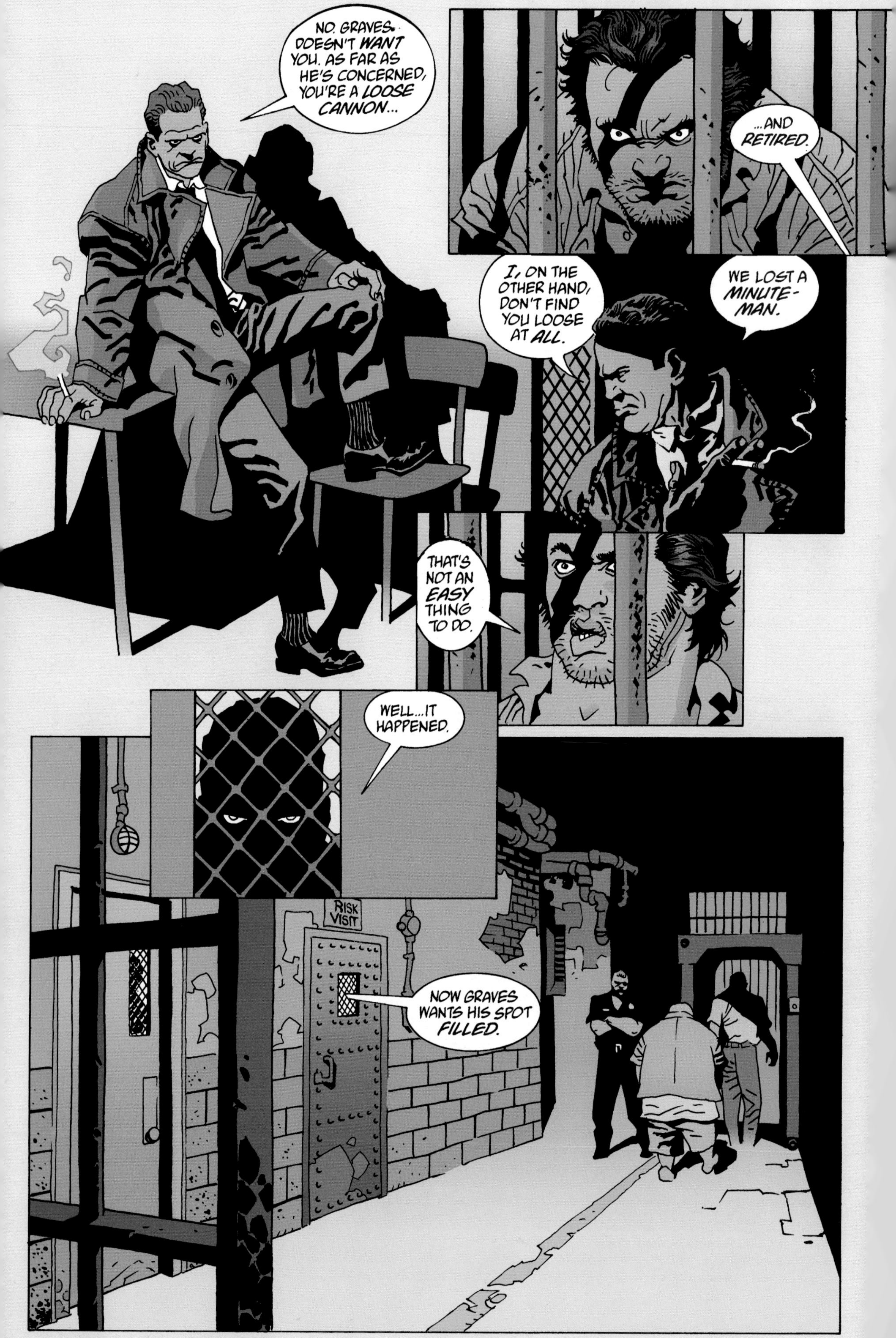
NO. GRAVES DOESN'T WANT YOU. AS FAR AS HE'S CONCERNED, YOU'RE A LOOSE CANNON...
...AND RETIRED.
I, ON THE OTHER HAND, DON'T FIND YOU LOOSE AT ALL.
WE LOST A MINUTE-MAN.
THAT'S NOT AN EASY THING TO DO.
WELL...IT HAPPENED.
RISK VISIT
NOW GRAVES WANTS HIS SPOT FILLED.

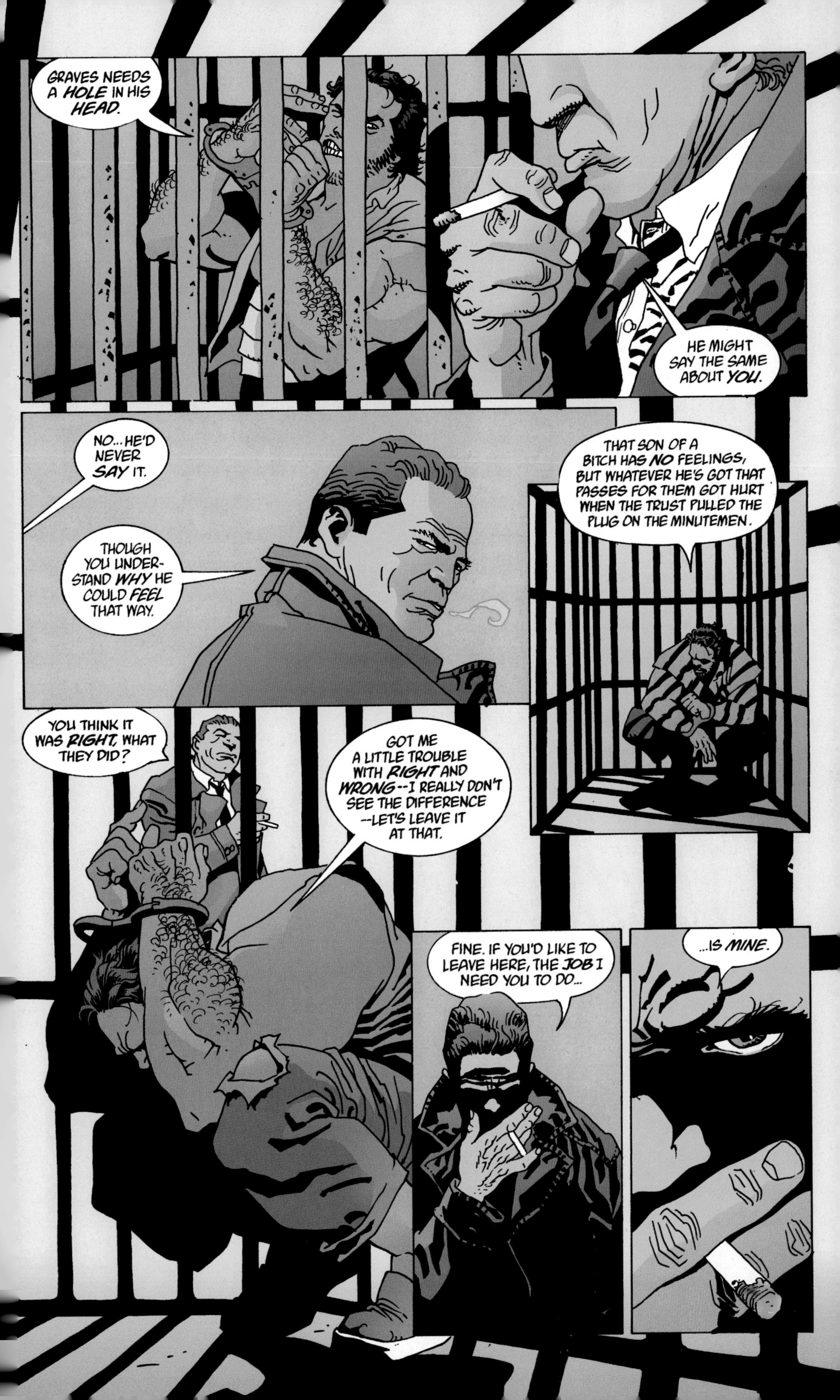
GRAVES NEEDS A HOLE IN HIS HEAD.
HE MIGHT SAY THE SAME ABOUT YOU.
NO... HE'D NEVER SAY IT.
THOUGH YOU UNDER-STAND WHY HE COULD FEEL THAT WAY.
THAT SON OF A BITCH HAS NO FEELINGS, BUT WHATEVER HE'S GOT THAT PASSES FOR THEM GOT HURT WHEN THE TRUST PULLED THE PLUG ON THE MINUTEMEN.
YOU THINK IT WAS RIGHT, WHAT THEY DID?
GOT ME A LITTLE TROUBLE WITH RIGHT AND WRONG--I REALLY DON'T SEE THE DIFFERENCE --LET'S LEAVE IT AT THAT.
FINE. IF YOU'D LIKE TO LEAVE HERE, THE JOB I NEED YOU TO DO...
...IS MINE.

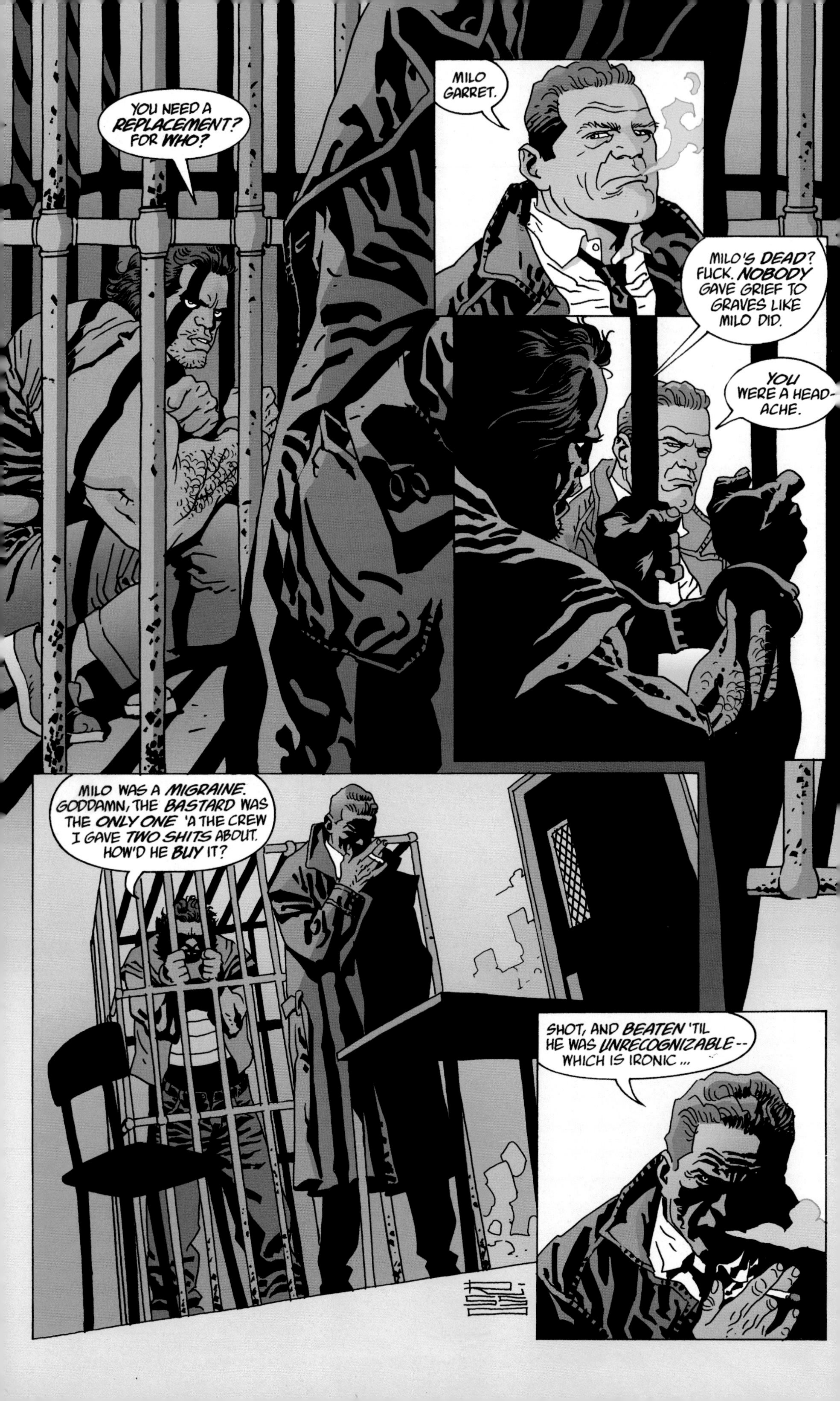
YOU NEED A REPLACEMENT? FOR WHO?
MILO GARRET.
MILO'S DEAD? FUCK. NOBODY GAVE GRIEF TO GRAVES LIKE MILO DID.
YOU WERE A HEAD-ACHE.
MILO WAS A MIGRAINE. GODDAMN, THE BASTARD WAS THE ONLY ONE 'A THE CREW I GAVE TWO SHITS ABOUT. HOW'D HE BUY IT?
SHOT, AND BEATEN 'TIL HE WAS UNRECOGNIZABLE-- WHICH IS IRONIC ...

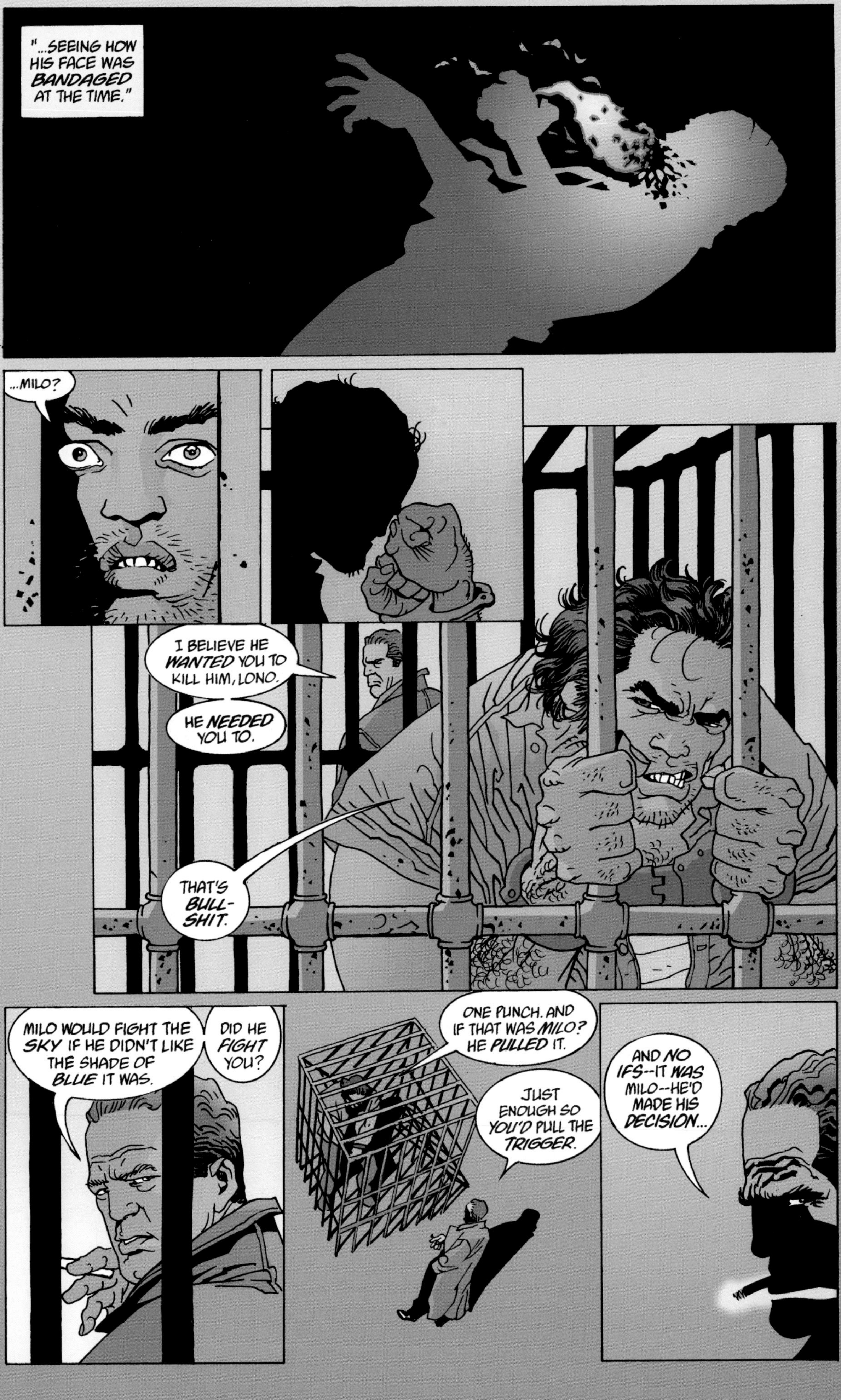

"...SEEING HOW HIS FACE WAS BANDAGED AT THE TIME."
...MILO?
I BELIEVE HE WANTED YOU TO KILL HIM, LONO.
HE NEEDED YOU TO.
THAT'S BULL-SHIT.
MILO WOULD FIGHT THE SKY IF HE DIDN'T LIKE THE SHADE OF BLUE IT WAS.
DID HE FIGHT YOU?
ONE PUNCH. AND IF THAT WAS MILO? HE PULLED IT.
JUST ENOUGH SO YOU'D PULL THE TRIGGER.
AND NO IFS--IT WAS MILO--HE'D MADE HIS DECISION...

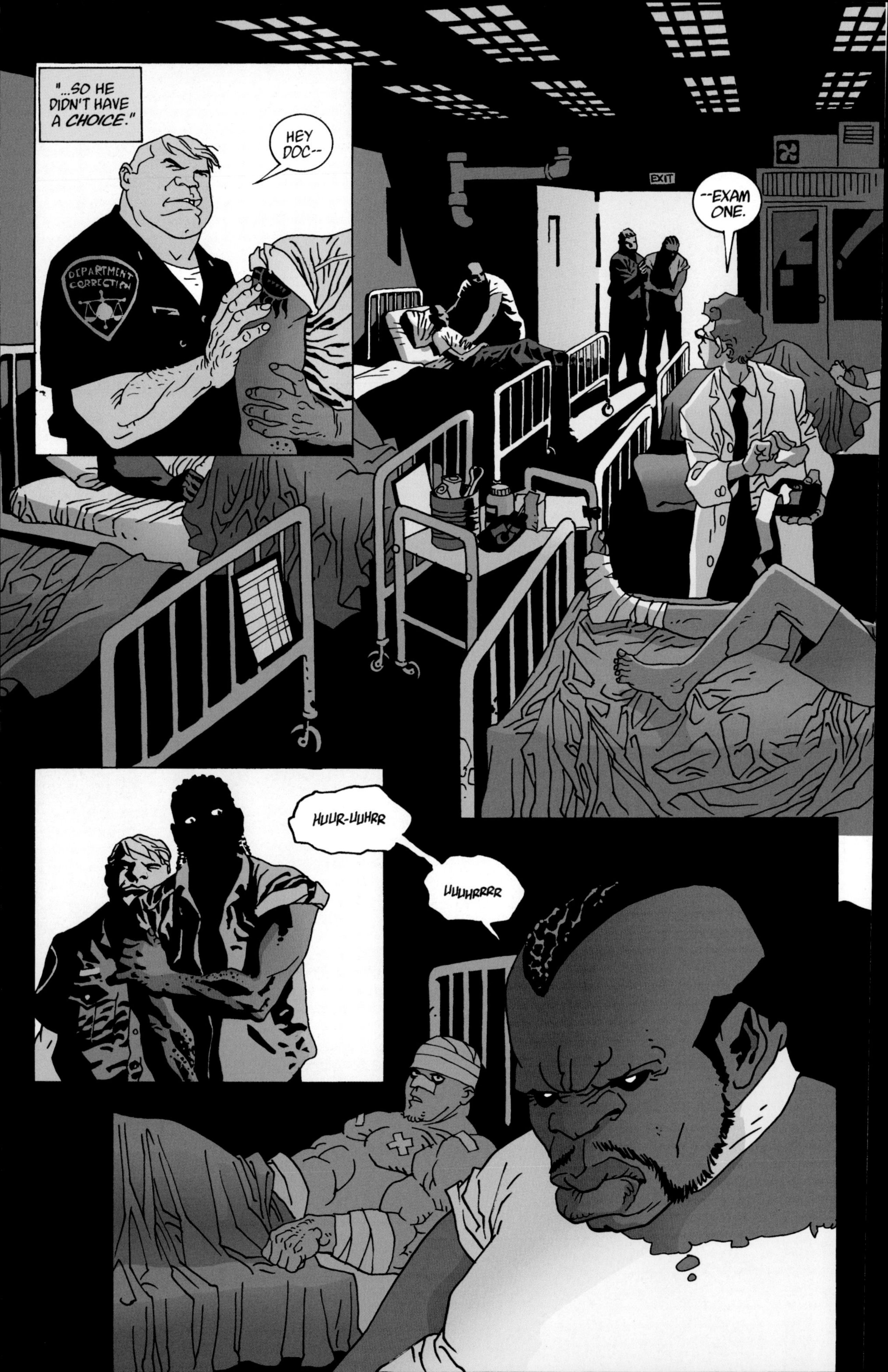
"...SO HE DIDN'T HAVE A *CHOICE*."
HEY DOC--
EXIT
--EXAM ONE.
DEPARTMENT CORRECTION
HUUR-UUHRR
UUUHRRRR

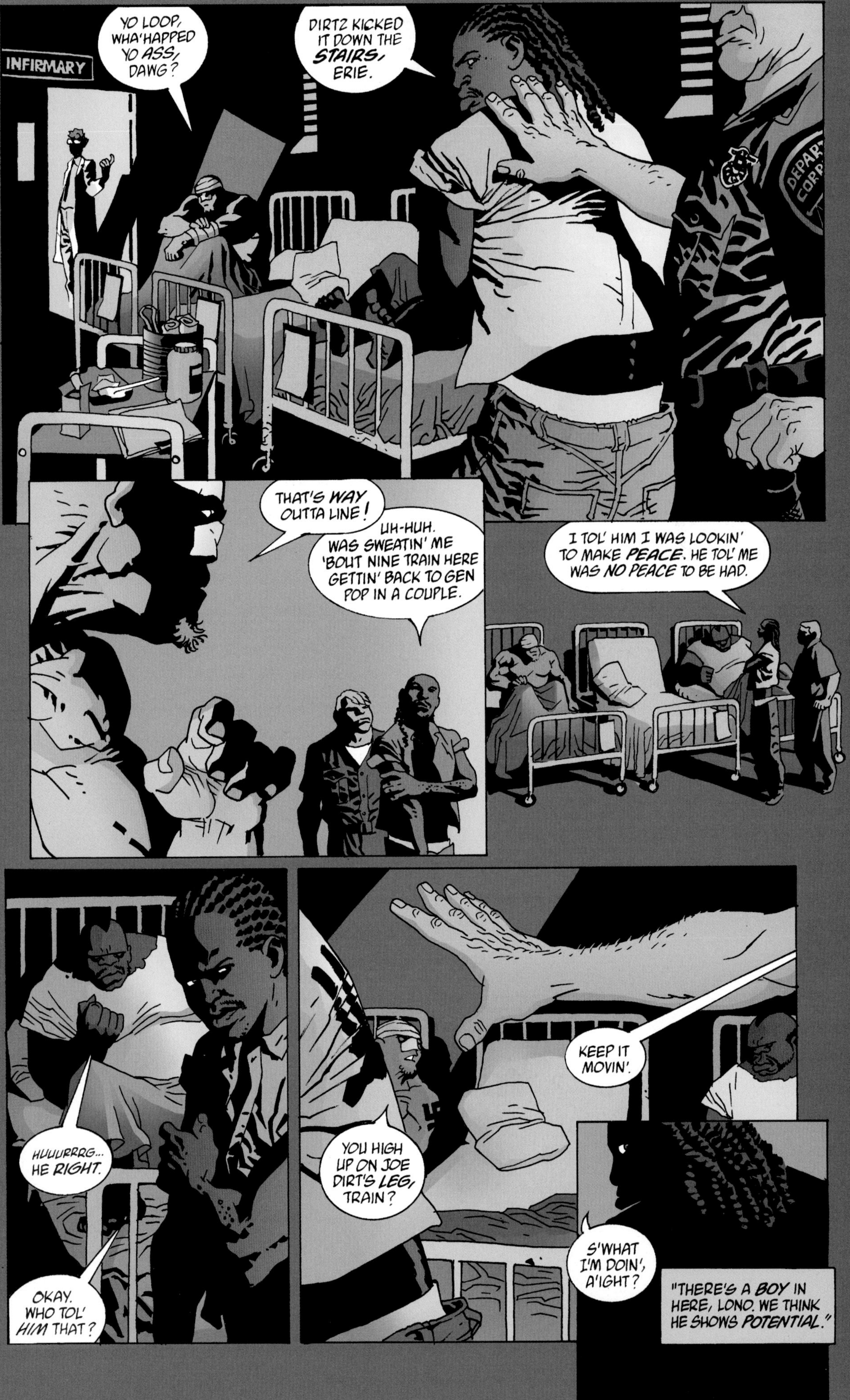
INFIRMARY
YO LOOP, WHA'HAPPED YO ASS, DAWG?
DIRTZ KICKED IT DOWN THE STAIRS, ERIE.
THAT'S WAY OUTTA LINE!
UH-HUH. WAS SWEATIN' ME 'BOUT NINE TRAIN HERE GETTIN' BACK TO GEN POP IN A COUPLE.
I TOL' HIM I WAS LOOKIN' TO MAKE PEACE. HE TOL' ME WAS NO PEACE TO BE HAD.
HUUURRRG... HE RIGHT.
OKAY. WHO TOL' HIM THAT?
YOU HIGH UP ON JOE DIRT'S LEG, TRAIN?
KEEP IT MOVIN'.
S'WHAT I'M DOIN', A'IGHT?
"THERE'S A BOY IN HERE, LONO. WE THINK HE SHOWS POTENTIAL."

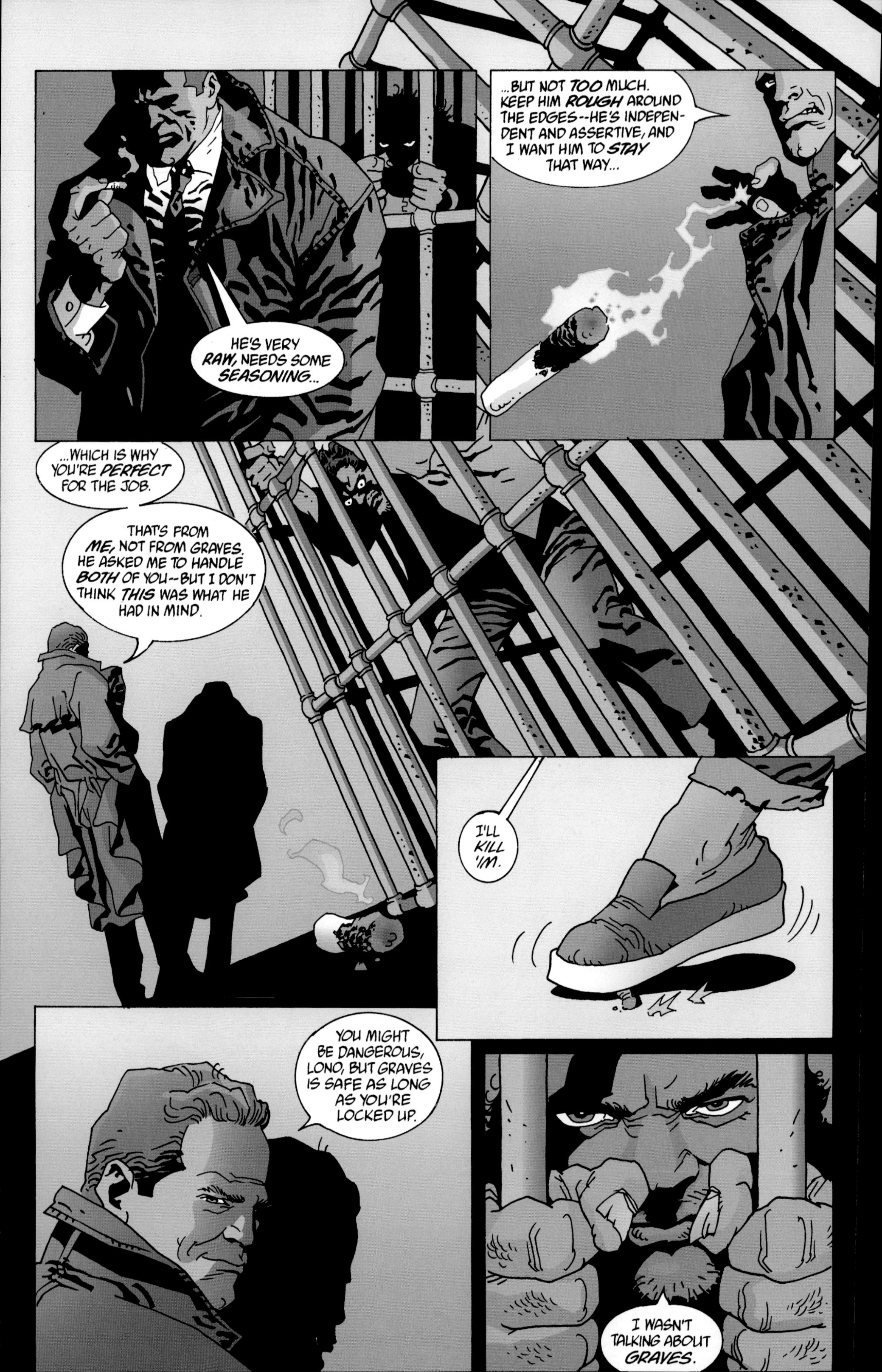
HE'S VERY RAW, NEEDS SOME SEASONING...
...BUT NOT TOO MUCH. KEEP HIM ROUGH AROUND THE EDGES--HE'S INDEPENDENT AND ASSERTIVE, AND I WANT HIM TO STAY THAT WAY...
...WHICH IS WHY YOU'RE PERFECT FOR THE JOB.
THAT'S FROM ME, NOT FROM GRAVES. HE ASKED ME TO HANDLE BOTH OF YOU--BUT I DON'T THINK THIS WAS WHAT HE HAD IN MIND.
I'LL KILL 'IM.
YOU MIGHT BE DANGEROUS, LONO, BUT GRAVES IS SAFE AS LONG AS YOU'RE LOCKED UP.
I WASN'T TALKING ABOUT GRAVES.

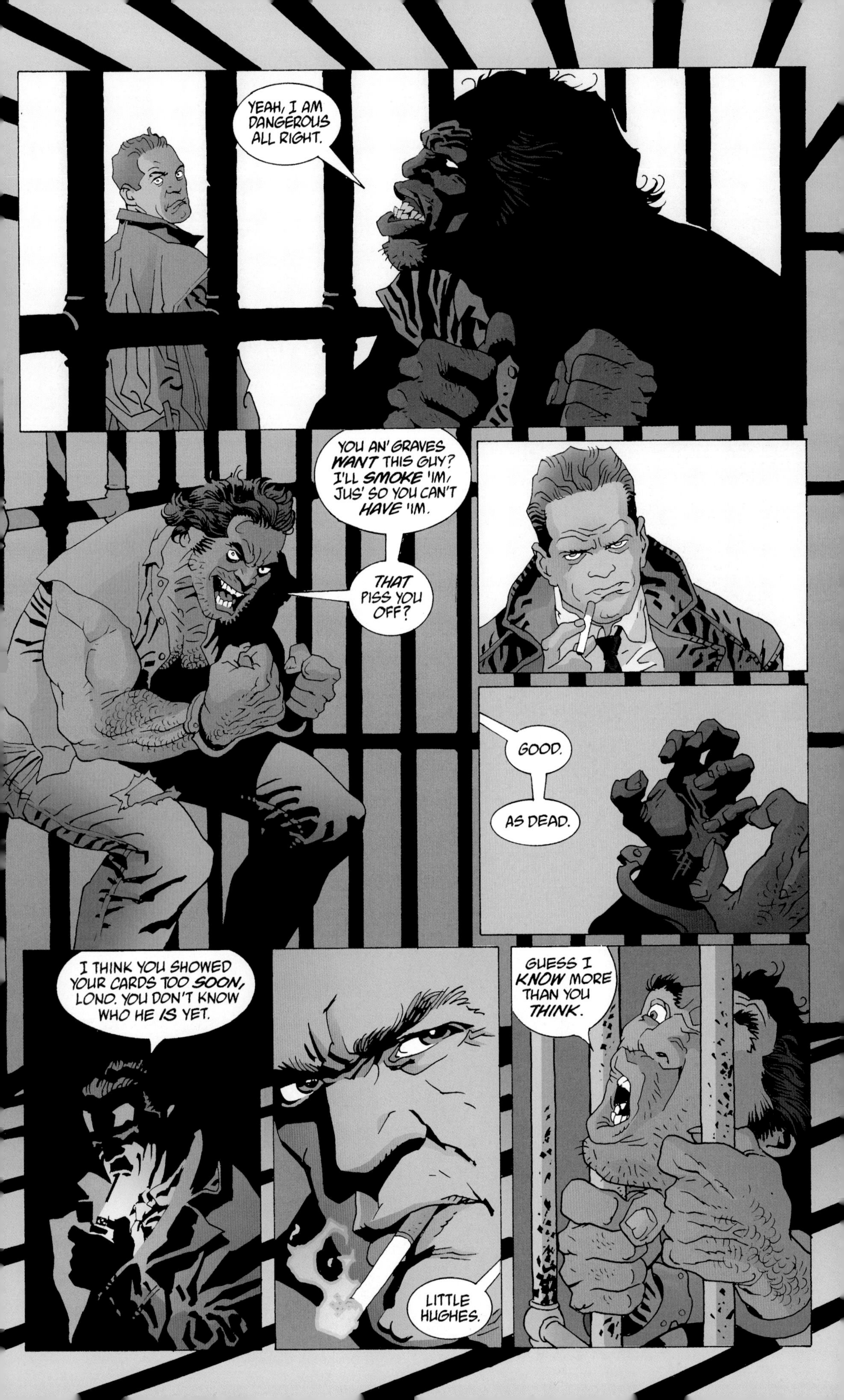
YEAH, I AM DANGEROUS ALL RIGHT.
YOU AN' GRAVES WANT THIS GUY? I'LL SMOKE 'IM, JUS' SO YOU CAN'T HAVE 'IM.
THAT PISS YOU OFF?
GOOD.
AS DEAD.
I THINK YOU SHOWED YOUR CARDS TOO SOON, LONO. YOU DON'T KNOW WHO HE IS YET.
LITTLE HUGHES.
GUESS I KNOW MORE THAN YOU THINK.

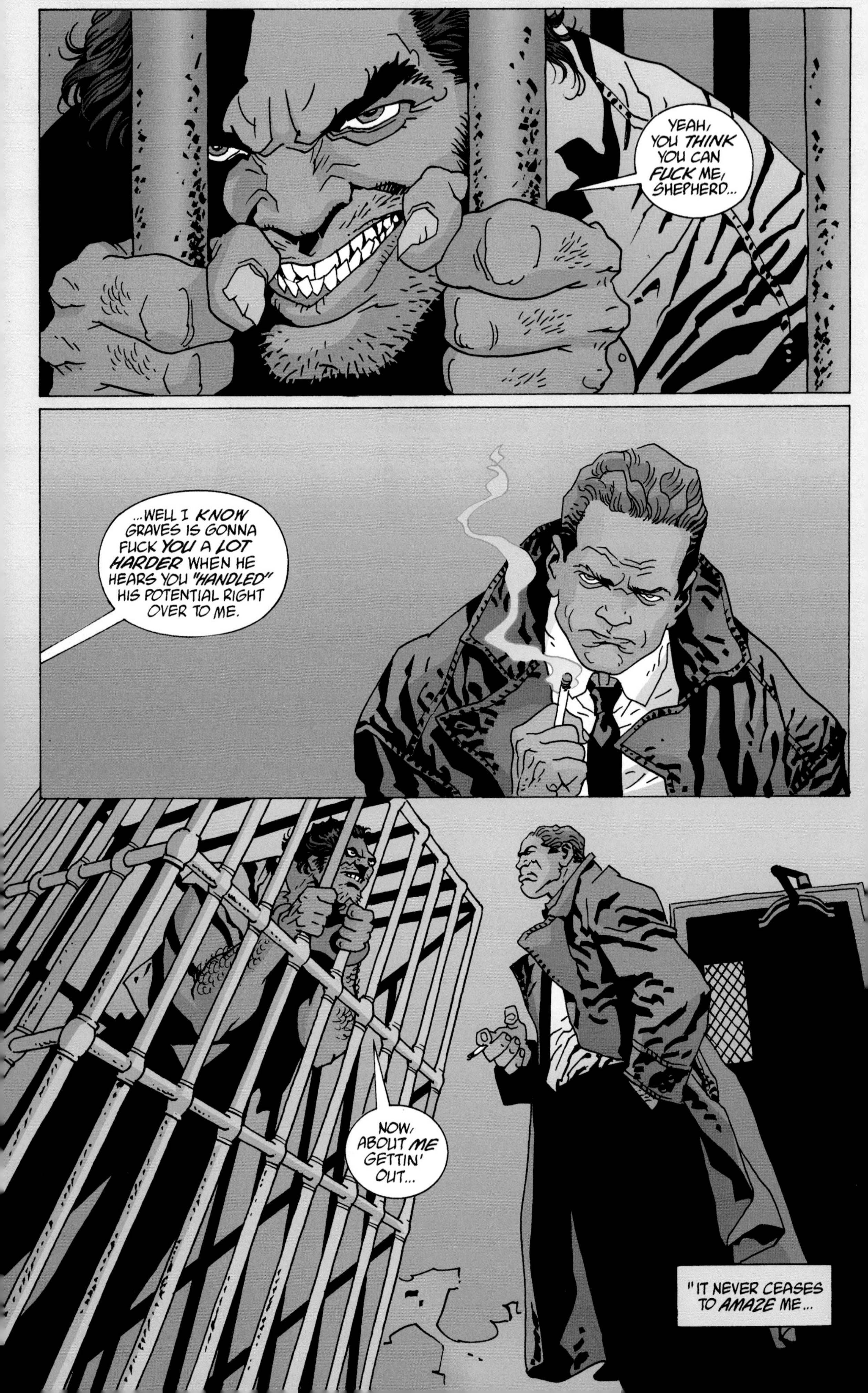
YEAH, YOU *THINK* YOU CAN *FUCK* ME, SHEPHERD...
...WELL I *KNOW* GRAVES IS GONNA FUCK *YOU* A *LOT HARDER* WHEN HE HEARS YOU *"HANDLED"* HIS POTENTIAL RIGHT OVER TO ME.
NOW, ABOUT *ME* GETTIN' OUT...
"IT NEVER CEASES TO *AMAZE* ME...

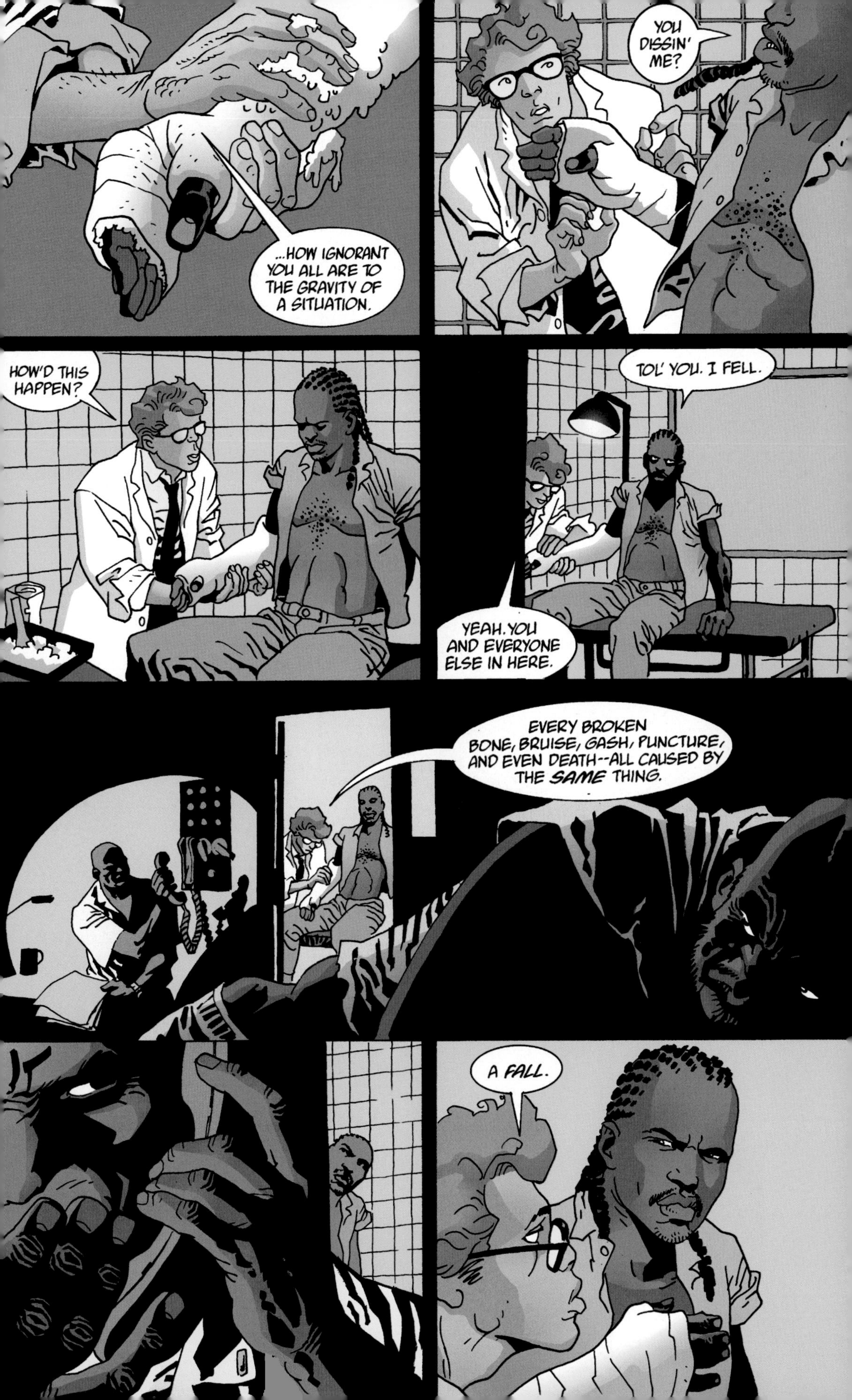
...HOW IGNORANT YOU ALL ARE TO THE GRAVITY OF A SITUATION.
YOU DISSIN' ME?
HOW'D THIS HAPPEN?
TOL' YOU. I FELL.
YEAH. YOU AND EVERYONE ELSE IN HERE.
EVERY BROKEN BONE, BRUISE, GASH, PUNCTURE, AND EVEN DEATH--ALL CAUSED BY THE SAME THING.
A FALL.

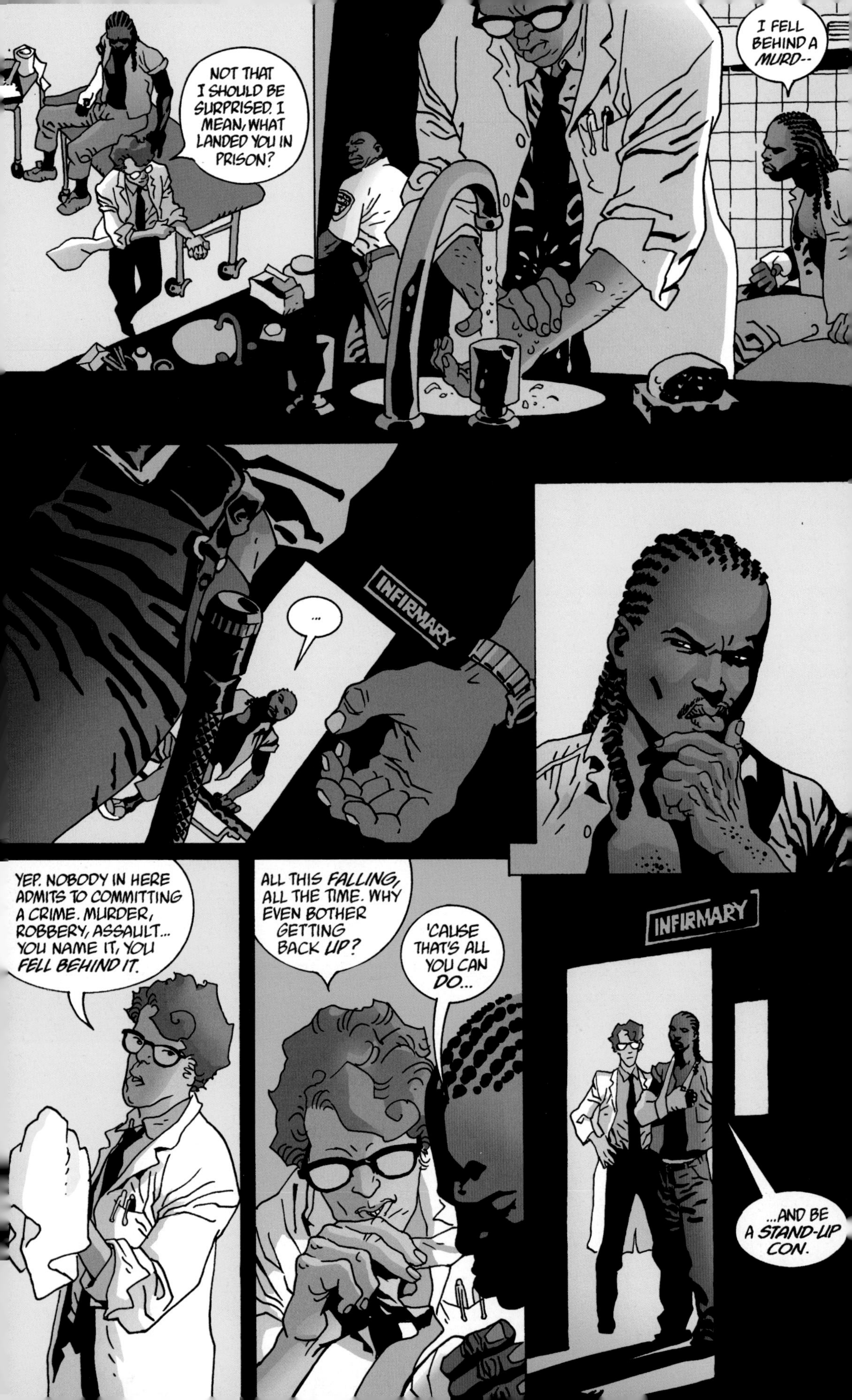
NOT THAT I SHOULD BE SURPRISED. I MEAN, WHAT LANDED YOU IN PRISON?
I FELL BEHIND A MURD--
INFIRMARY
...
YEP. NOBODY IN HERE ADMITS TO COMMITTING A CRIME. MURDER, ROBBERY, ASSAULT... YOU NAME IT, YOU FELL BEHIND IT.
ALL THIS FALLING, ALL THE TIME. WHY EVEN BOTHER GETTING BACK UP?
'CAUSE THAT'S ALL YOU CAN DO...
INFIRMARY
...AND BE A STAND-UP CON.

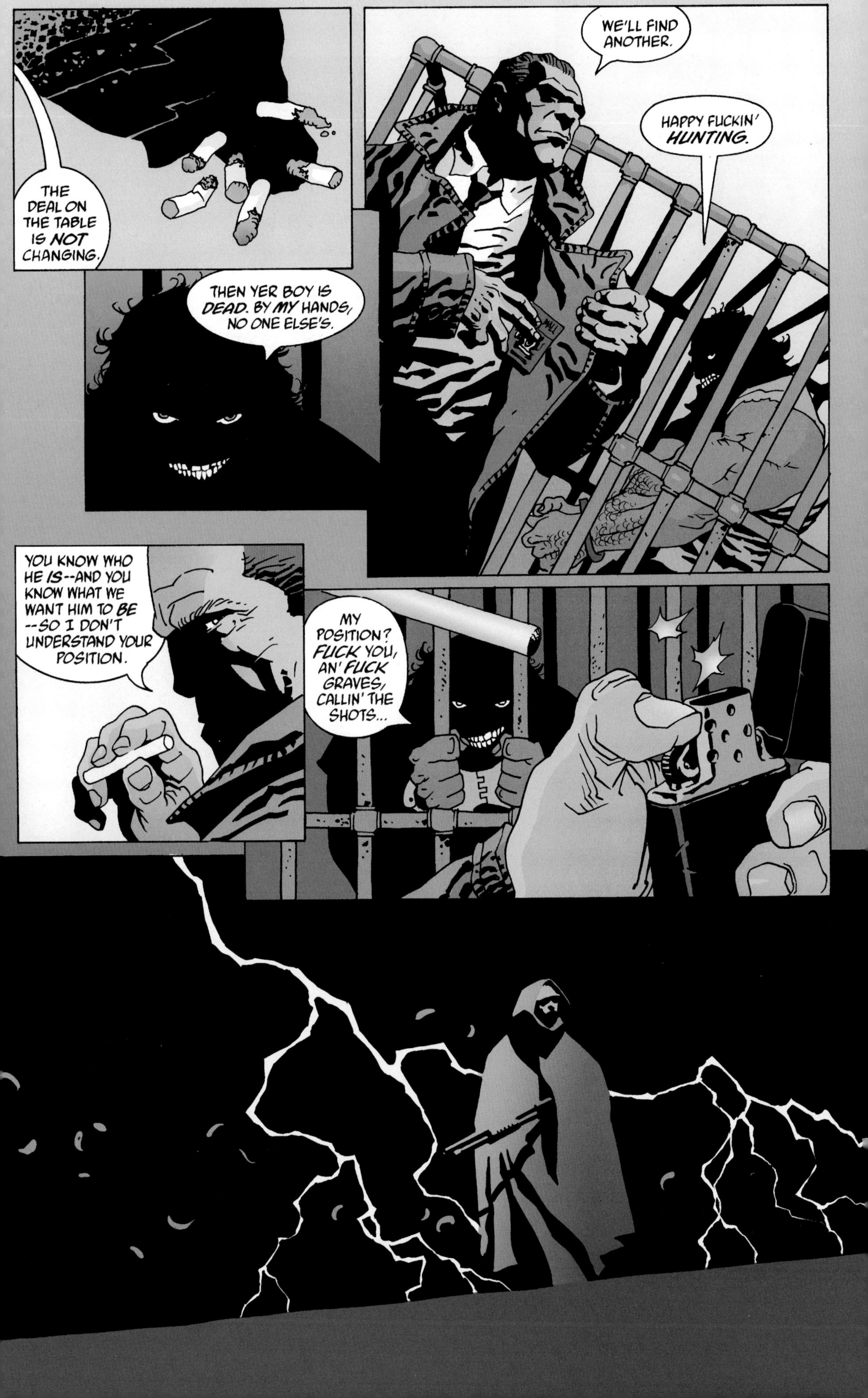
THE DEAL ON THE TABLE IS NOT CHANGING.
WE'LL FIND ANOTHER.
HAPPY FUCKIN' HUNTING.
THEN YER BOY IS DEAD. BY MY HANDS, NO ONE ELSE'S.
YOU KNOW WHO HE IS--AND YOU KNOW WHAT WE WANT HIM TO BE --SO I DON'T UNDERSTAND YOUR POSITION.
MY POSITION? FUCK YOU, AN' FUCK GRAVES, CALLIN' THE SHOTS...

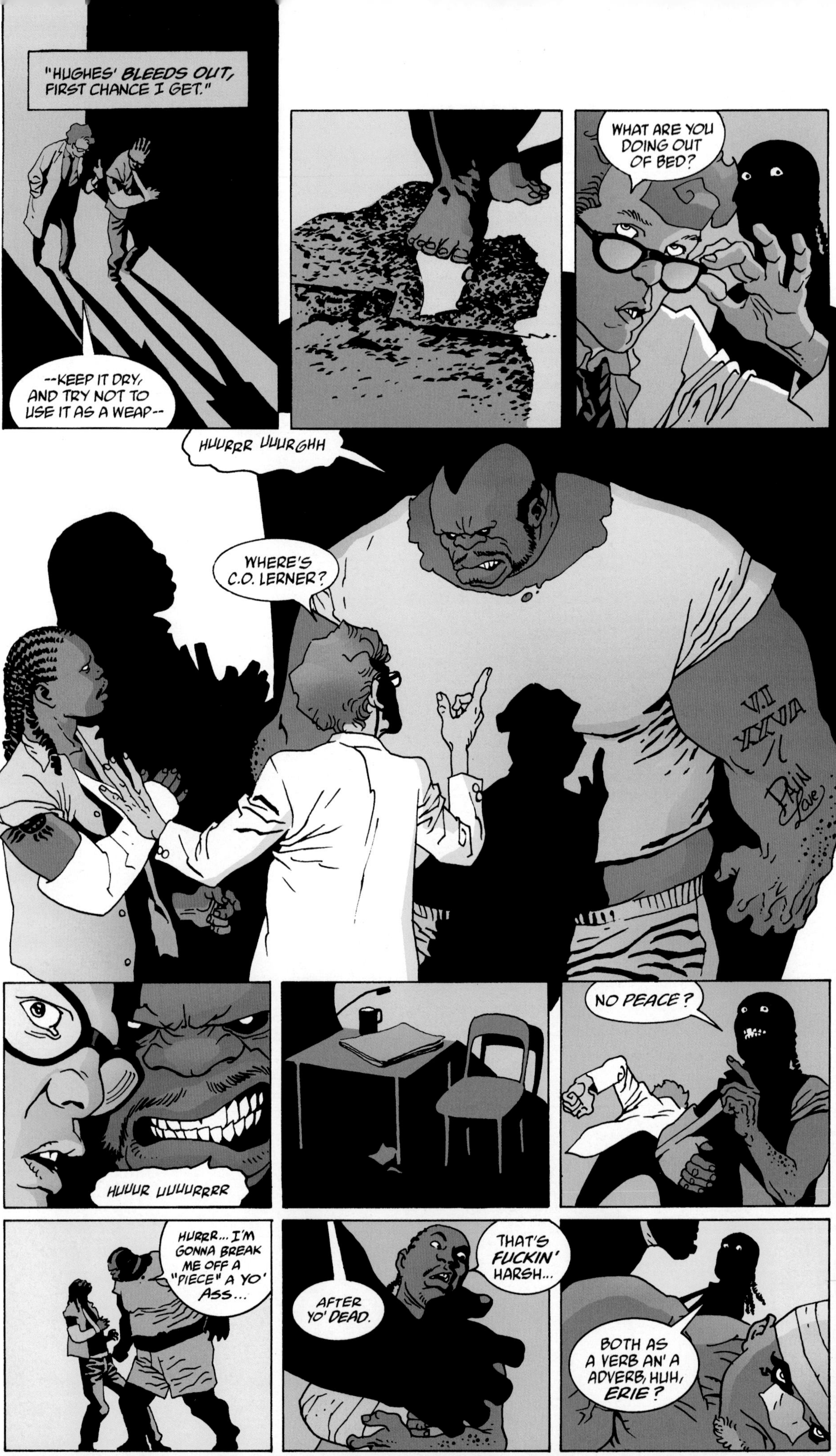

"HUGHES' BLEEDS OUT, FIRST CHANCE I GET."
--KEEP IT DRY, AND TRY NOT TO USE IT AS A WEAP--
WHAT ARE YOU DOING OUT OF BED?
HUURRR UUURGHH
WHERE'S C.O. LERNER?
VI XXVI
PAIN Love
HUUUR UUUURRRR
NO PEACE?
HURRR... I'M GONNA BREAK ME OFF A "PIECE" A YO' ASS...
AFTER YO' DEAD.
THAT'S FUCKIN' HARSH...
BOTH AS A VERB AN' A ADVERB, HUH, ERIE?

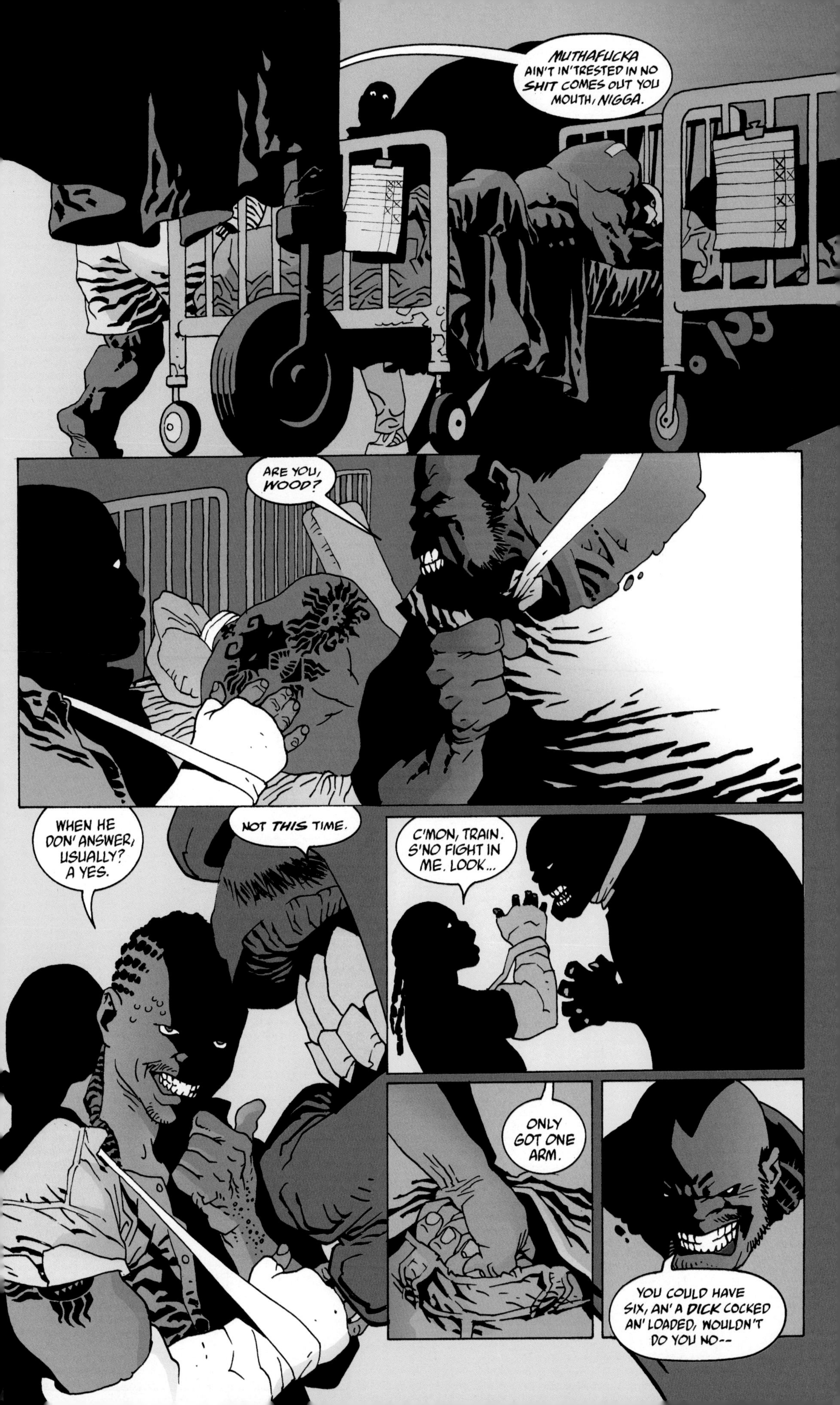
MUTHAFUCKA AIN'T IN'TRESTED IN NO SHIT COMES OUT YOU MOUTH, NIGGA.
ARE YOU, WOOD?
WHEN HE DON' ANSWER, USUALLY? A YES.
NOT THIS TIME.
C'MON, TRAIN. S'NO FIGHT IN ME. LOOK...
ONLY GOT ONE ARM.
YOU COULD HAVE SIX, AN' A DICK COCKED AN' LOADED, WOULDN'T DO YOU NO--

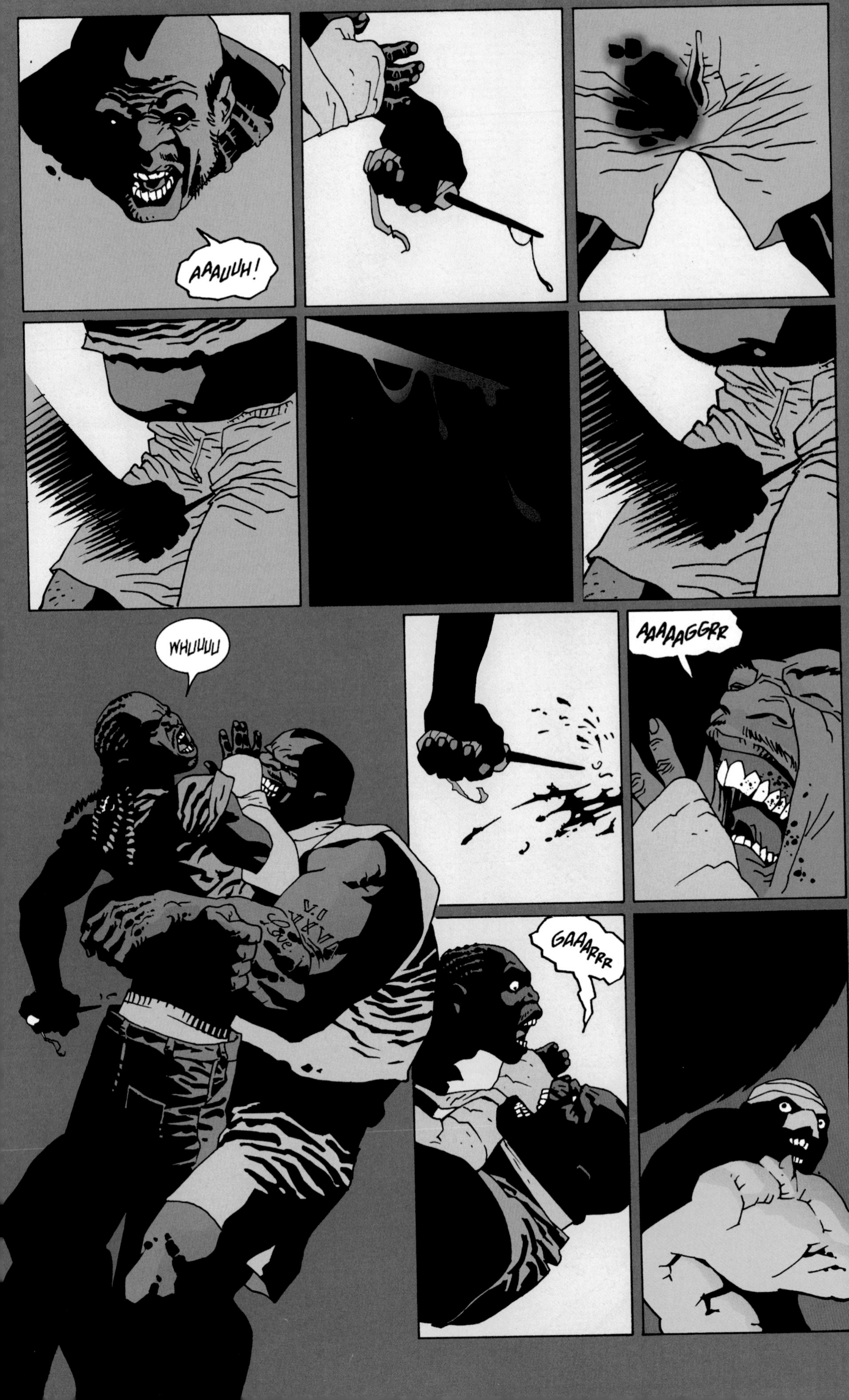
AAAUUH!
WHUUUU
AAAAAGGRR
GAAARRR

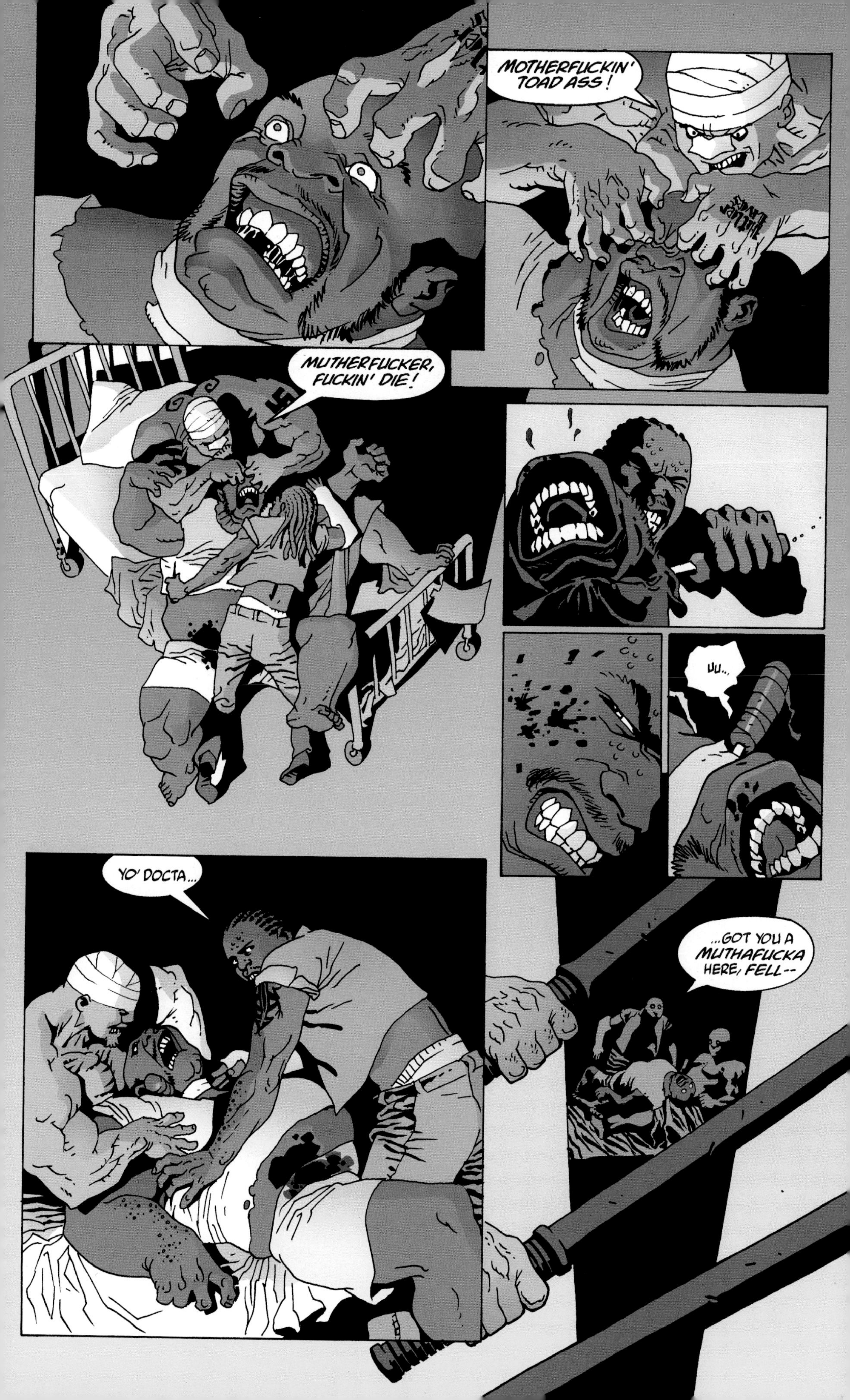
MOTHERFUCKIN' TOAD ASS!
MUTHERFUCKER, FUCKIN' DIE!
UU...
YO' DOCTA...
...GOT YOU A MUTHAFUCKA HERE, FELL--

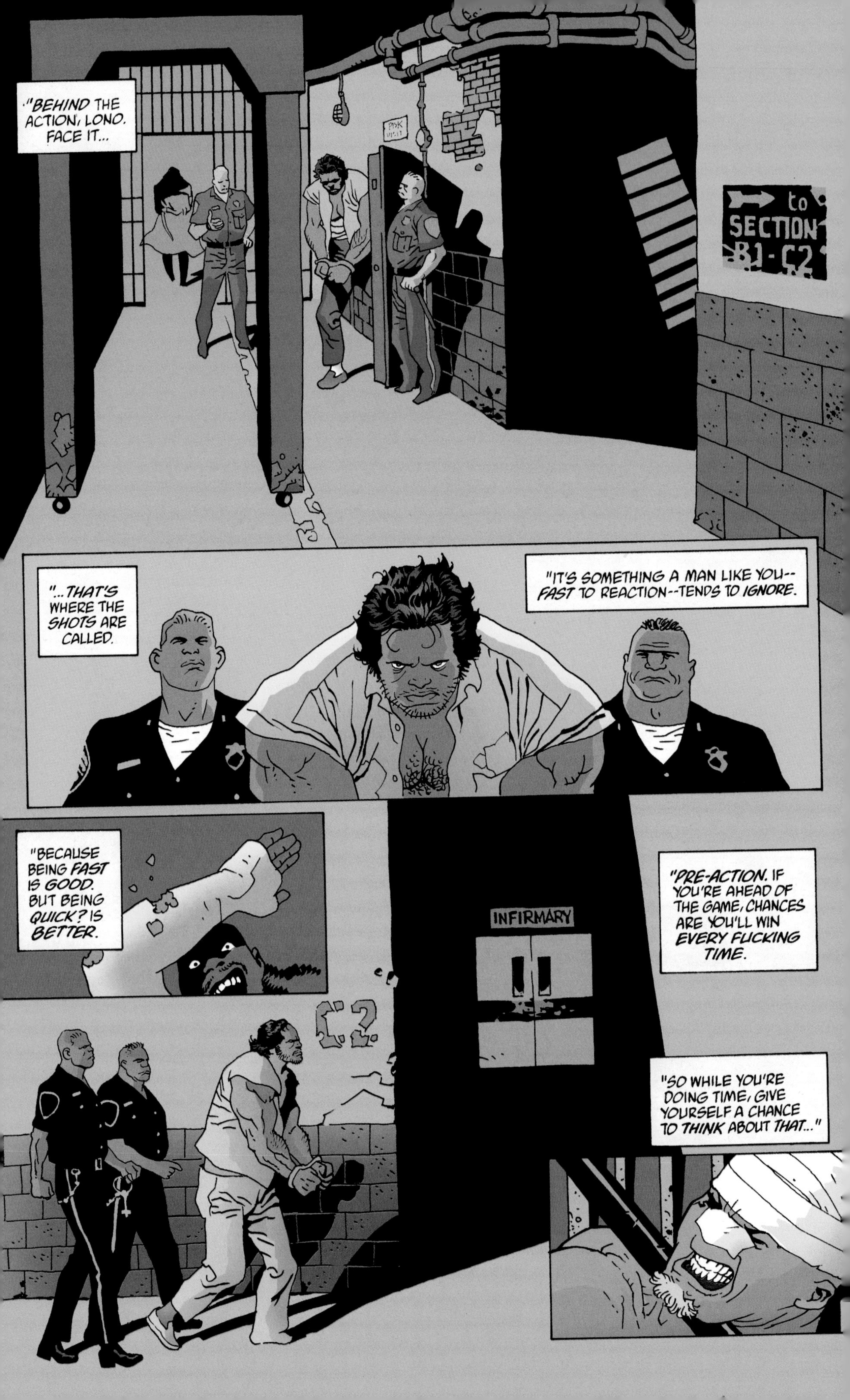

"BEHIND THE ACTION, LONO. FACE IT...
to SECTION B1-C2
"...THAT'S WHERE THE SHOTS ARE CALLED.
"IT'S SOMETHING A MAN LIKE YOU--FAST TO REACTION--TENDS TO IGNORE.
"BECAUSE BEING FAST IS GOOD. BUT BEING QUICK? IS BETTER.
INFIRMARY
"PRE-ACTION. IF YOU'RE AHEAD OF THE GAME, CHANCES ARE YOU'LL WIN EVERY FUCKING TIME.
C2
"SO WHILE YOU'RE DOING TIME, GIVE YOURSELF A CHANCE TO THINK ABOUT THAT..."

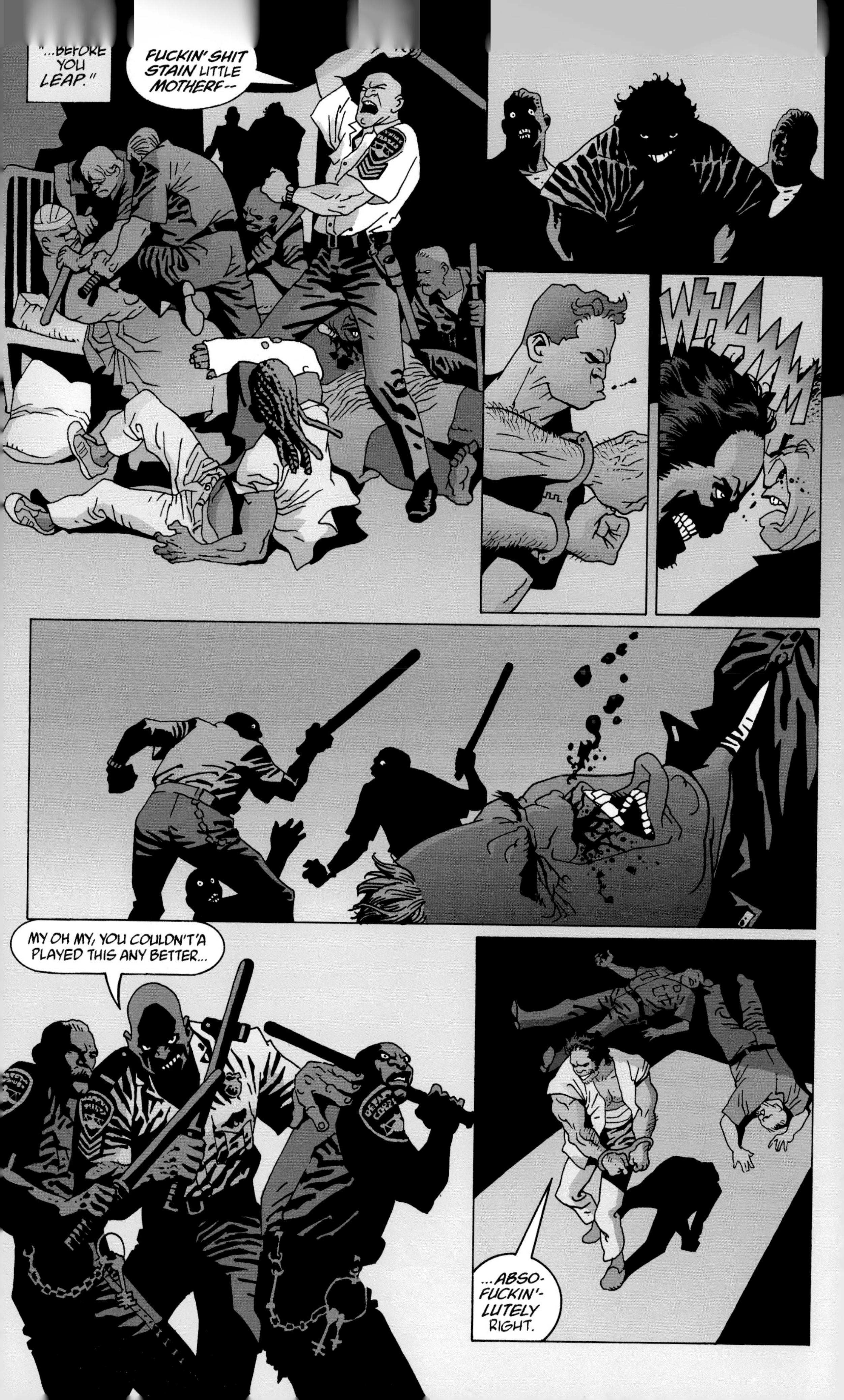
"...BEFORE YOU LEAP."
FUCKIN' SHIT STAIN LITTLE MOTHERF--
WHAM
MY OH MY, YOU COULDN'T'A PLAYED THIS ANY BETTER...
...ABSO-FUCKIN'-LUTELY RIGHT.

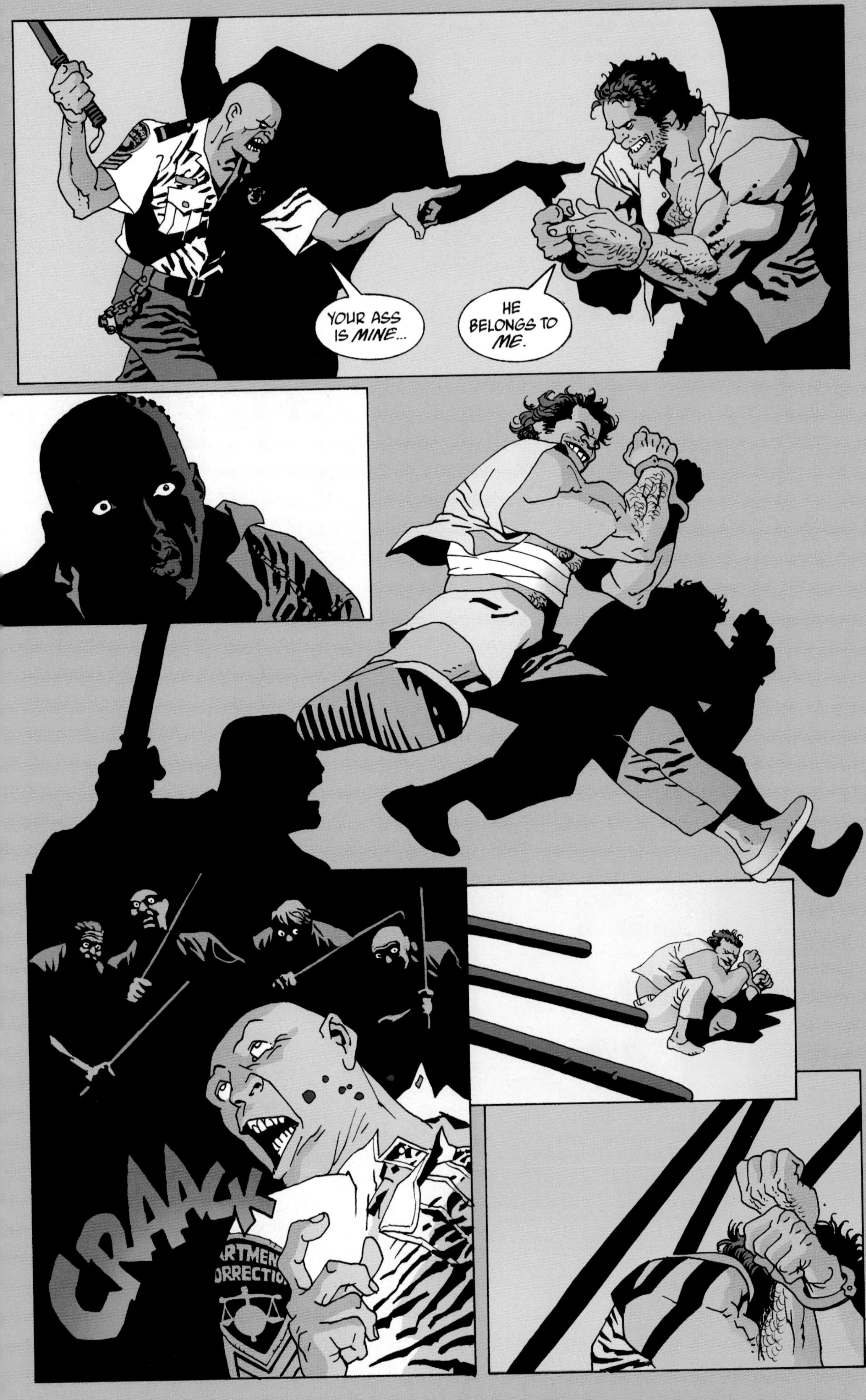
YOUR ASS IS MINE...
HE BELONGS TO ME.
CRAACK

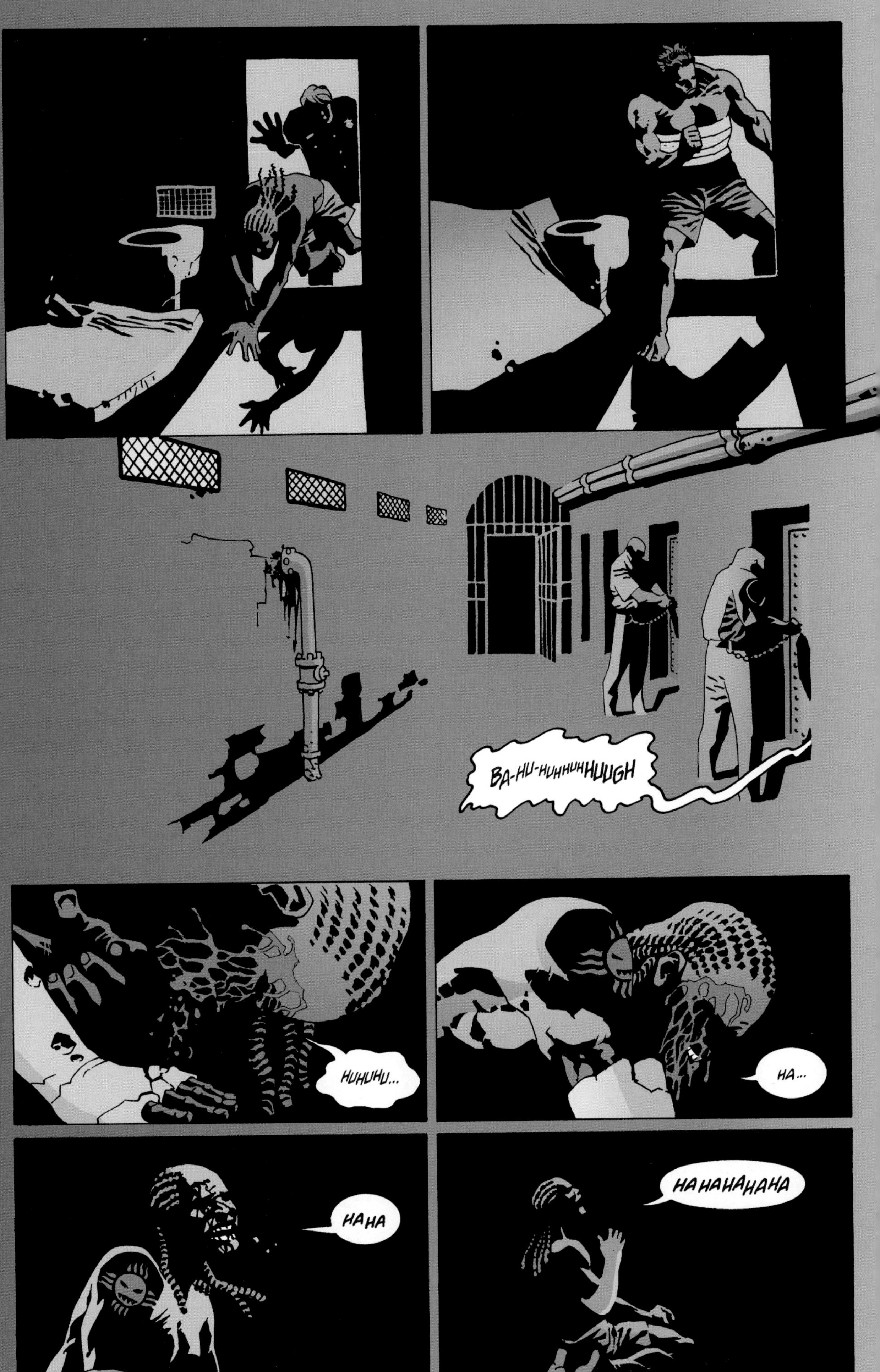
BA-HU-HUHHUHHUUGH
HUHUHU...
HA...
HAHA
HAHAHAHAHA

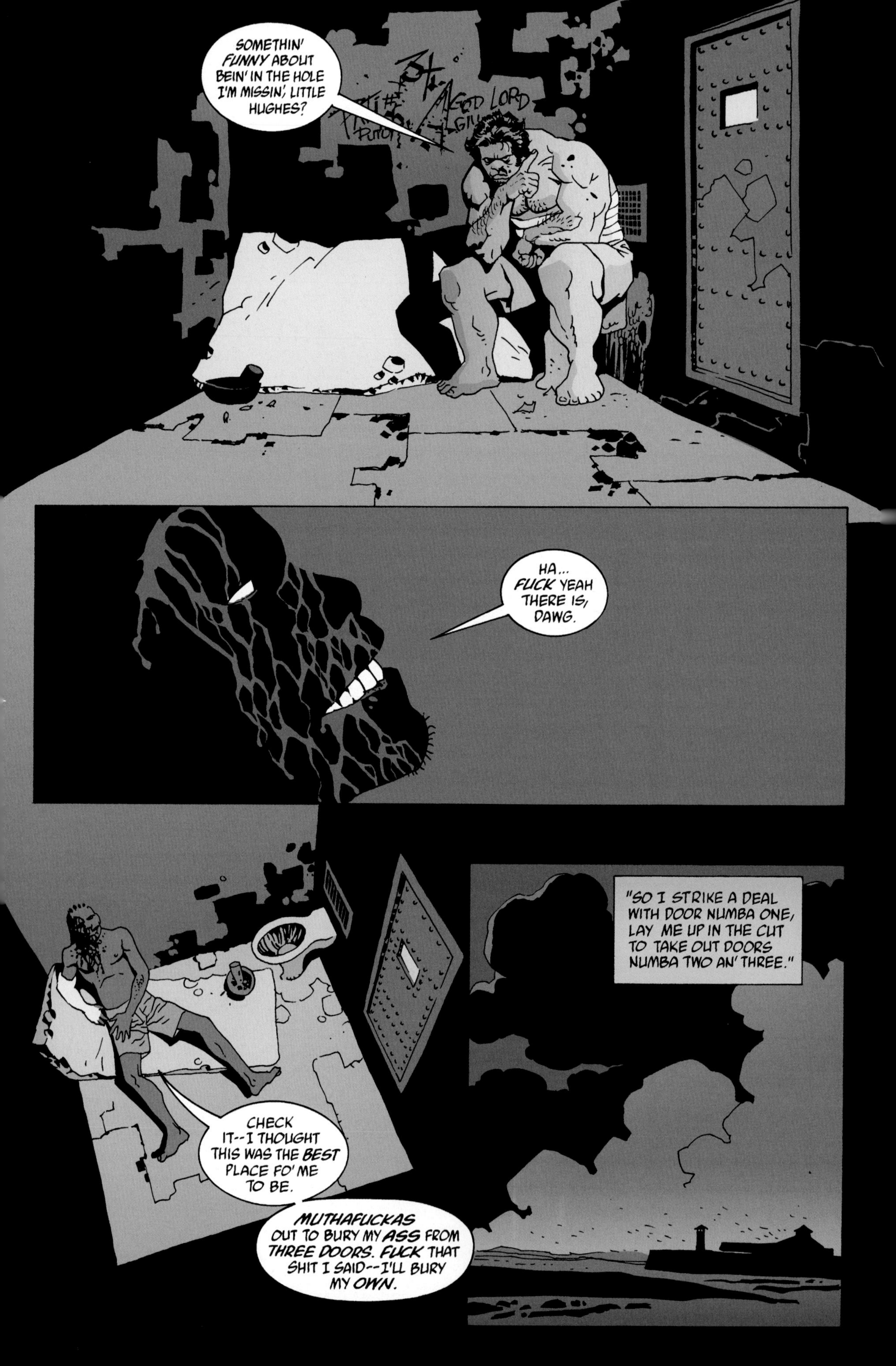
SOMETHIN' FUNNY ABOUT BEIN' IN THE HOLE I'M MISSIN', LITTLE HUGHES?
HA... FUCK YEAH THERE IS, DAWG.
CHECK IT--I THOUGHT THIS WAS THE BEST PLACE FO' ME TO BE.
MUTHAFUCKAS OUT TO BURY MY ASS FROM THREE DOORS. FUCK THAT SHIT I SAID--I'LL BURY MY OWN.
"SO I STRIKE A DEAL WITH DOOR NUMBA ONE, LAY ME UP IN THE CUT TO TAKE OUT DOORS NUMBA TWO AN' THREE."

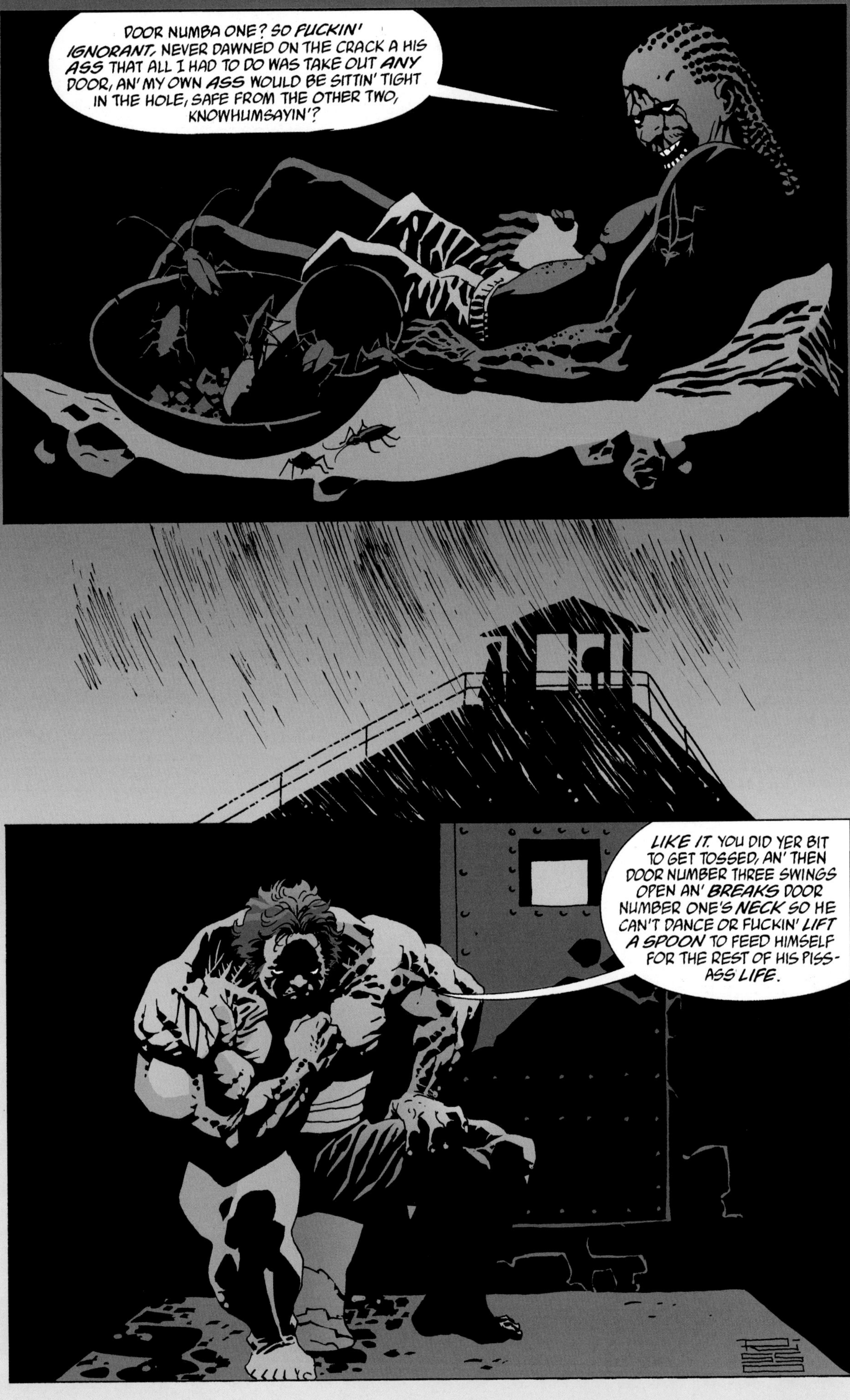
DOOR NUMBA ONE? SO FUCKIN' IGNORANT, NEVER DAWNED ON THE CRACK A HIS ASS THAT ALL I HAD TO DO WAS TAKE OUT ANY DOOR, AN' MY OWN ASS WOULD BE SITTIN' TIGHT IN THE HOLE, SAFE FROM THE OTHER TWO, KNOWHUMSAYIN'?
LIKE IT. YOU DID YER BIT TO GET TOSSED, AN' THEN DOOR NUMBER THREE SWINGS OPEN AN' BREAKS DOOR NUMBER ONE'S NECK SO HE CAN'T DANCE OR FUCKIN' LIFT A SPOON TO FEED HIMSELF FOR THE REST OF HIS PISS-ASS LIFE.

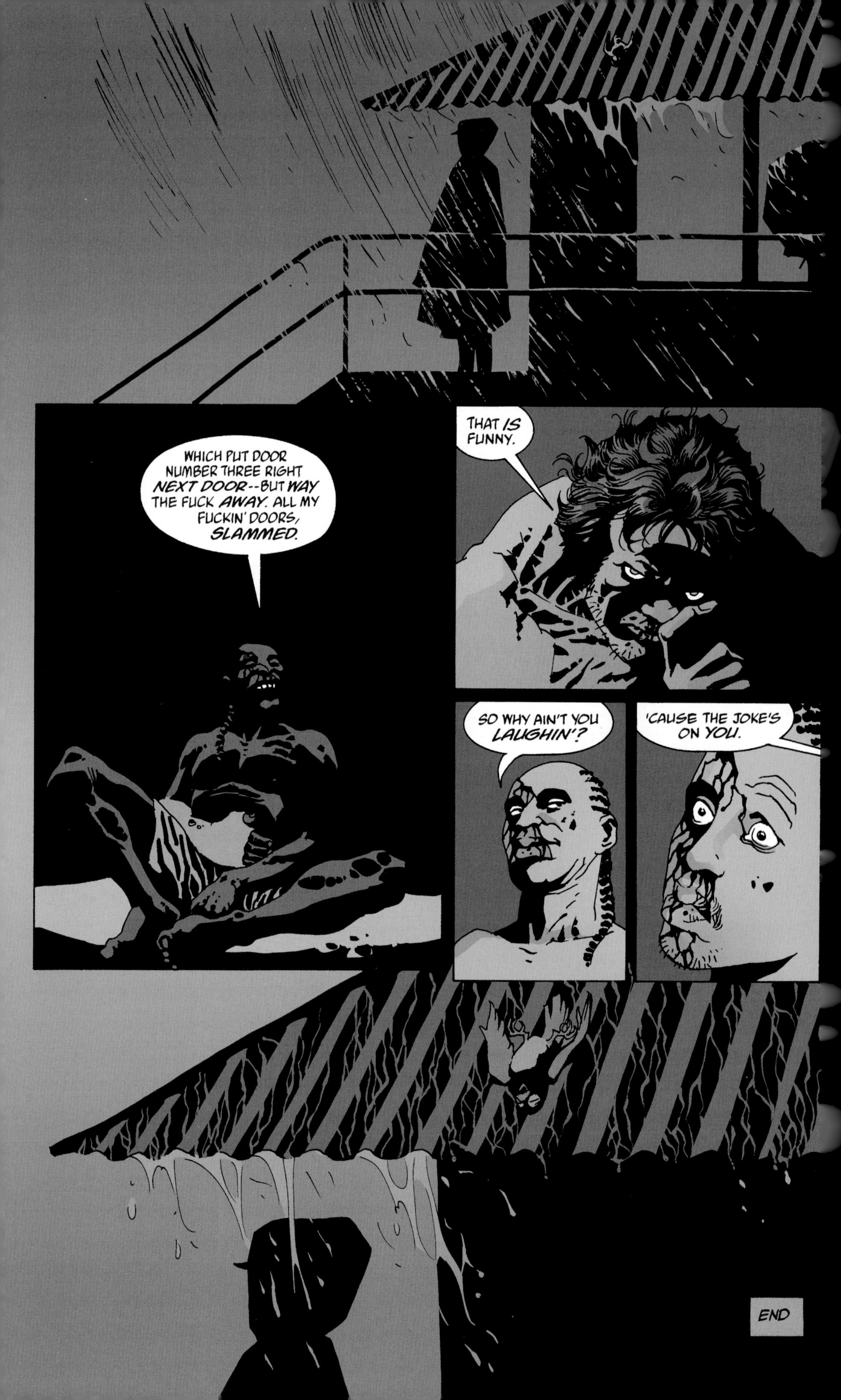
WHICH PUT DOOR NUMBER THREE RIGHT *NEXT DOOR*--BUT *WAY* THE FUCK *AWAY*. ALL MY FUCKIN' DOORS, *SLAMMED*.
THAT *IS* FUNNY.
SO WHY AIN'T YOU *LAUGHIN'*?
'CAUSE THE JOKE'S ON *YOU*.
END

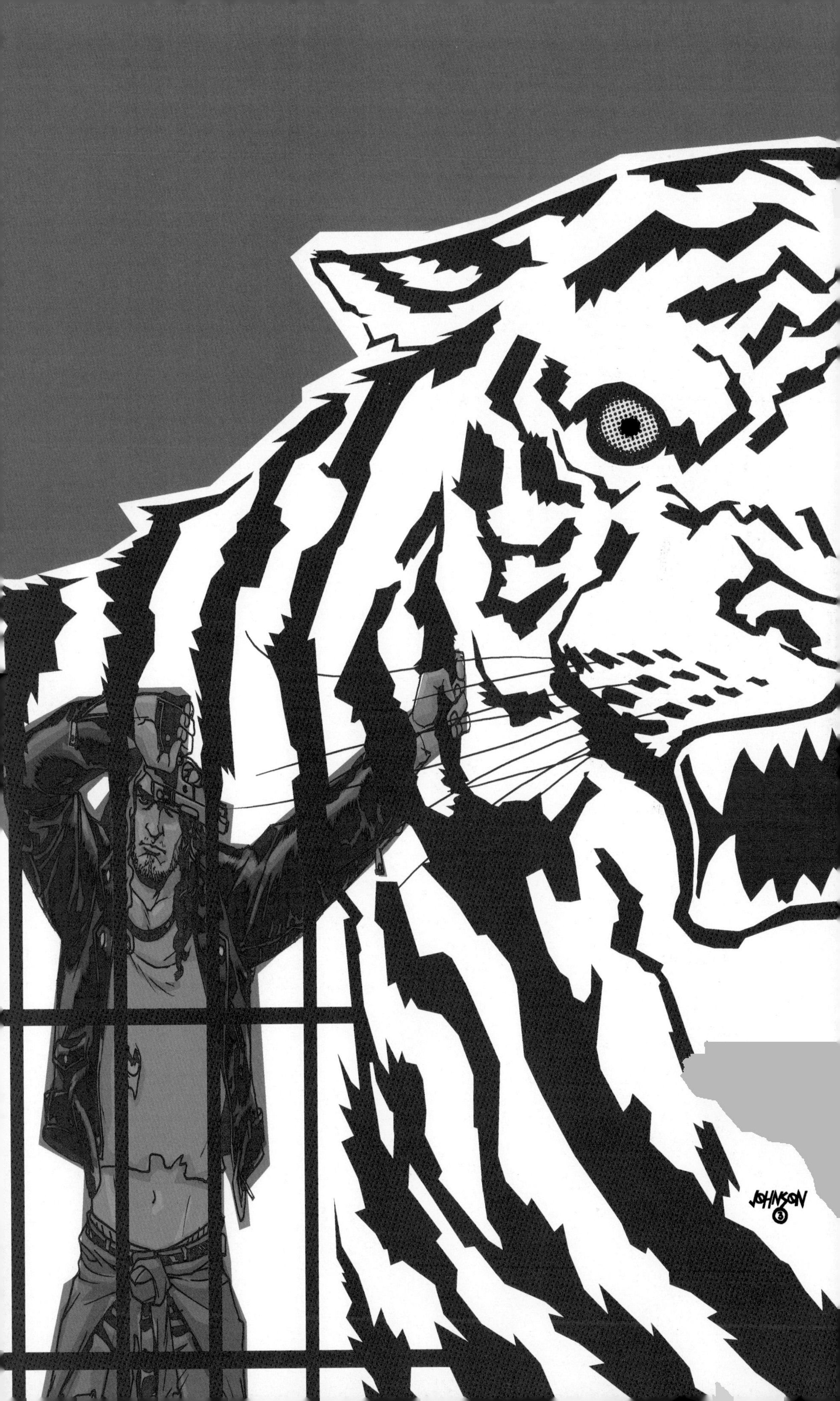
JOHNSON

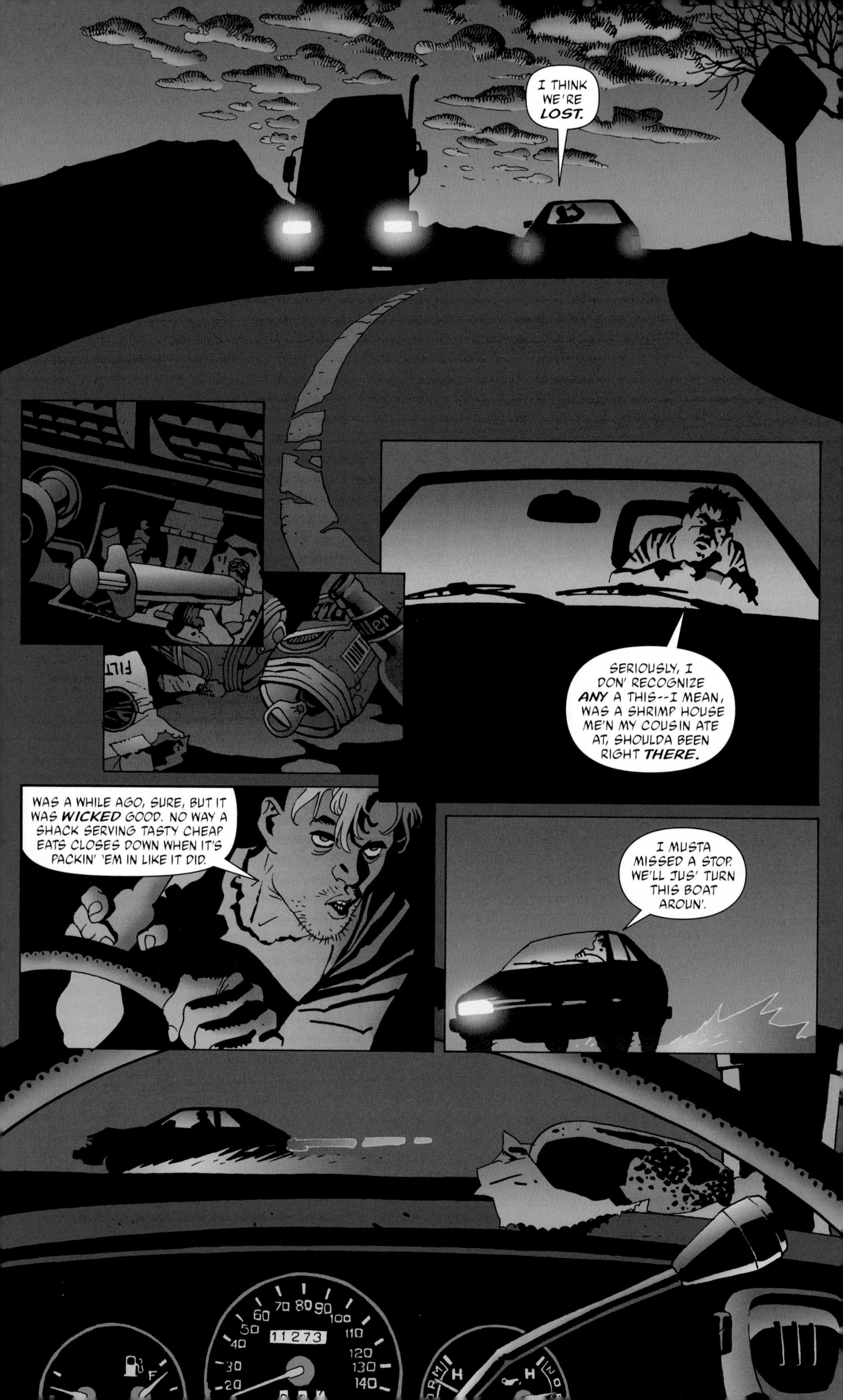
I THINK WE'RE LOST.
SERIOUSLY, I DON' RECOGNIZE ANY A THIS--I MEAN, WAS A SHRIMP HOUSE ME'N MY COUSIN ATE AT, SHOULDA BEEN RIGHT THERE.
WAS A WHILE AGO, SURE, BUT IT WAS WICKED GOOD. NO WAY A SHACK SERVING TASTY CHEAP EATS CLOSES DOWN WHEN IT'S PACKIN' 'EM IN LIKE IT DID.
I MUSTA MISSED A STOP. WE'LL JUS' TURN THIS BOAT AROUN'.

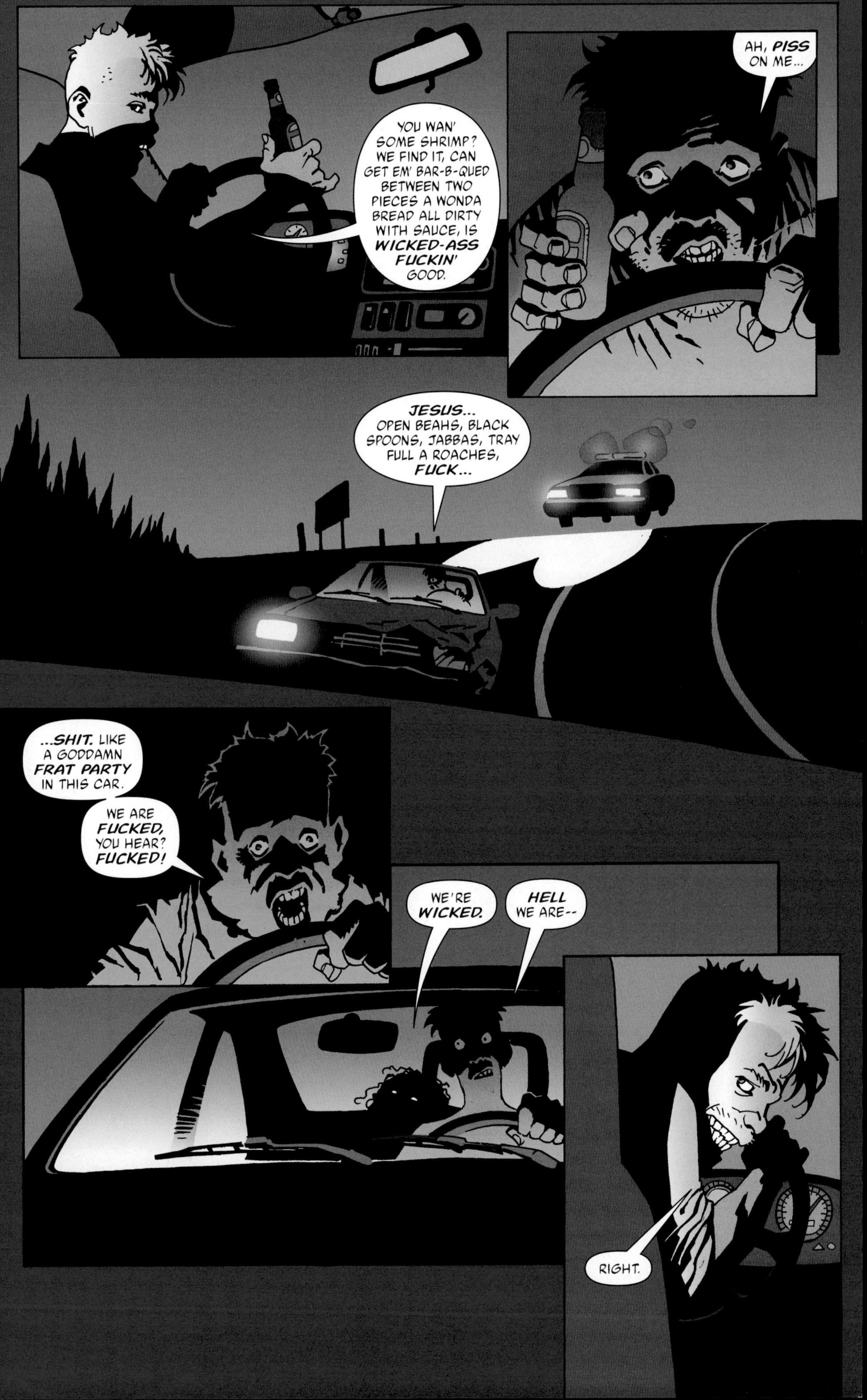
YOU WAN' SOME SHRIMP? WE FIND IT, CAN GET EM' BAR-B-QUED BETWEEN TWO PIECES A WONDA BREAD ALL DIRTY WITH SAUCE, IS WICKED-ASS FUCKIN' GOOD.
AH, PISS ON ME...
JESUS... OPEN BEAHS, BLACK SPOONS, JABBAS, TRAY FULL A ROACHES, FUCK...
...SHIT. LIKE A GODDAMN FRAT PARTY IN THIS CAR.
WE ARE FUCKED, YOU HEAR? FUCKED!
WE'RE WICKED.
HELL WE ARE--
RIGHT.

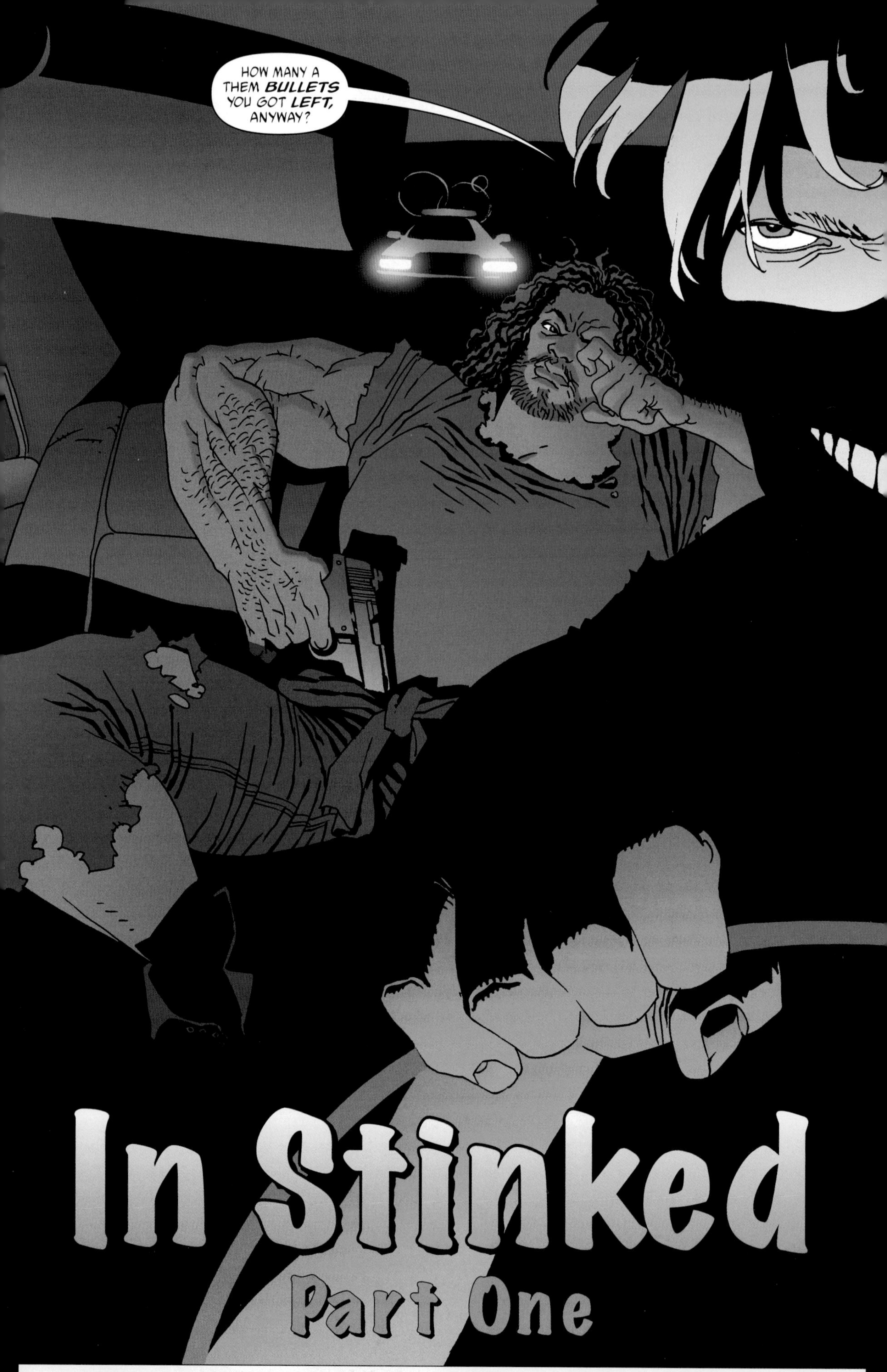
HOW MANY A THEM BULLETS YOU GOT LEFT, ANYWAY?
In Stinked
Part One

Brian Azzarello	Eduardo Risso	Patricia Mulvihill	Clem Robins	Dave Johnson	Zachary Rau	Will Dennis
WRITER	ARTIST	COLORIST	LETTERER	COVER	ASS'T ED	EDITOR

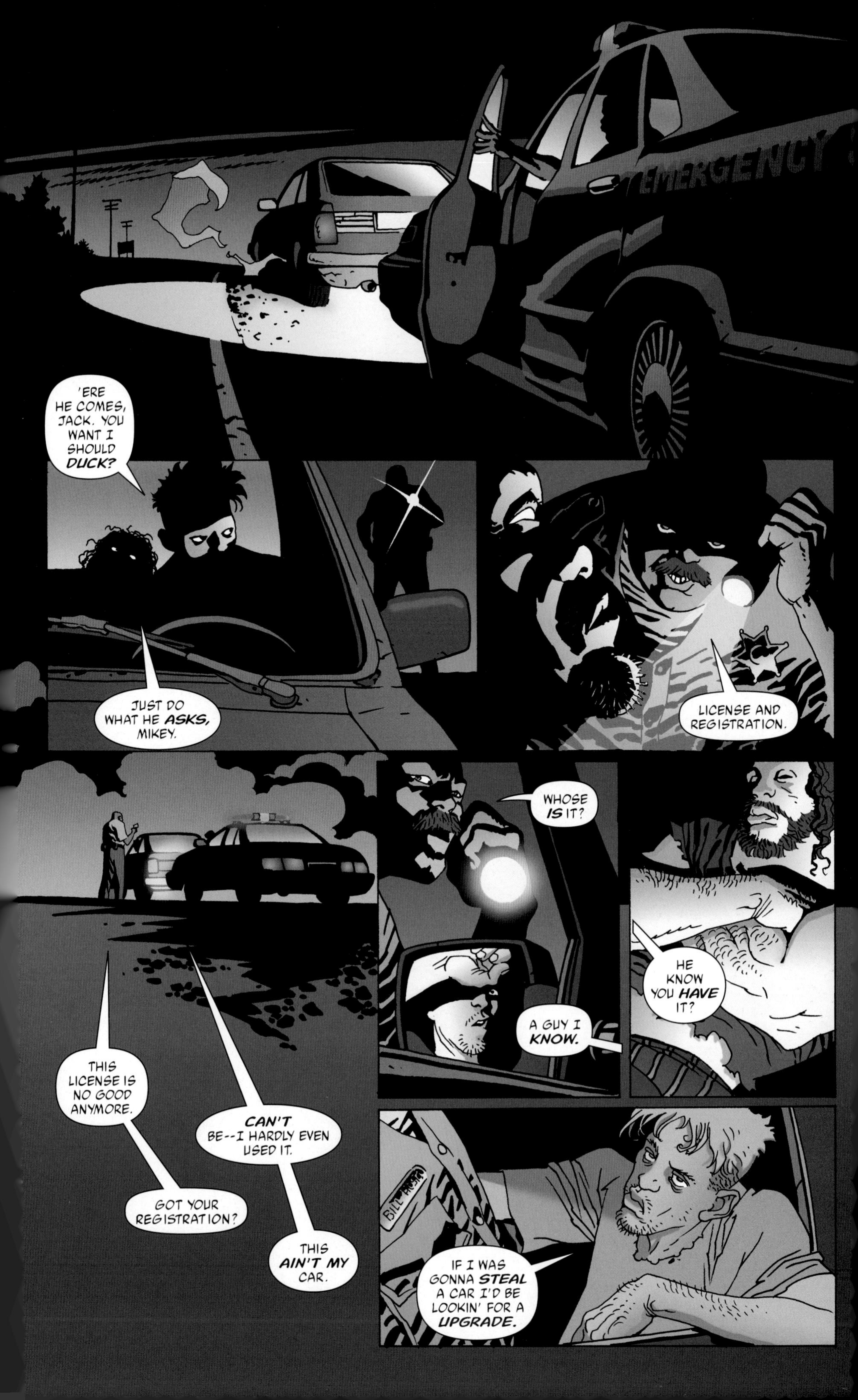
EMERGENCY
'ERE HE COMES, JACK. YOU WANT I SHOULD DUCK?
JUST DO WHAT HE ASKS, MIKEY.
LICENSE AND REGISTRATION.
THIS LICENSE IS NO GOOD ANYMORE.
CAN'T BE--I HARDLY EVEN USED IT.
GOT YOUR REGISTRATION?
THIS AIN'T MY CAR.
WHOSE IS IT?
A GUY I KNOW.
HE KNOW YOU HAVE IT?
IF I WAS GONNA STEAL A CAR I'D BE LOOKIN' FOR A UPGRADE.

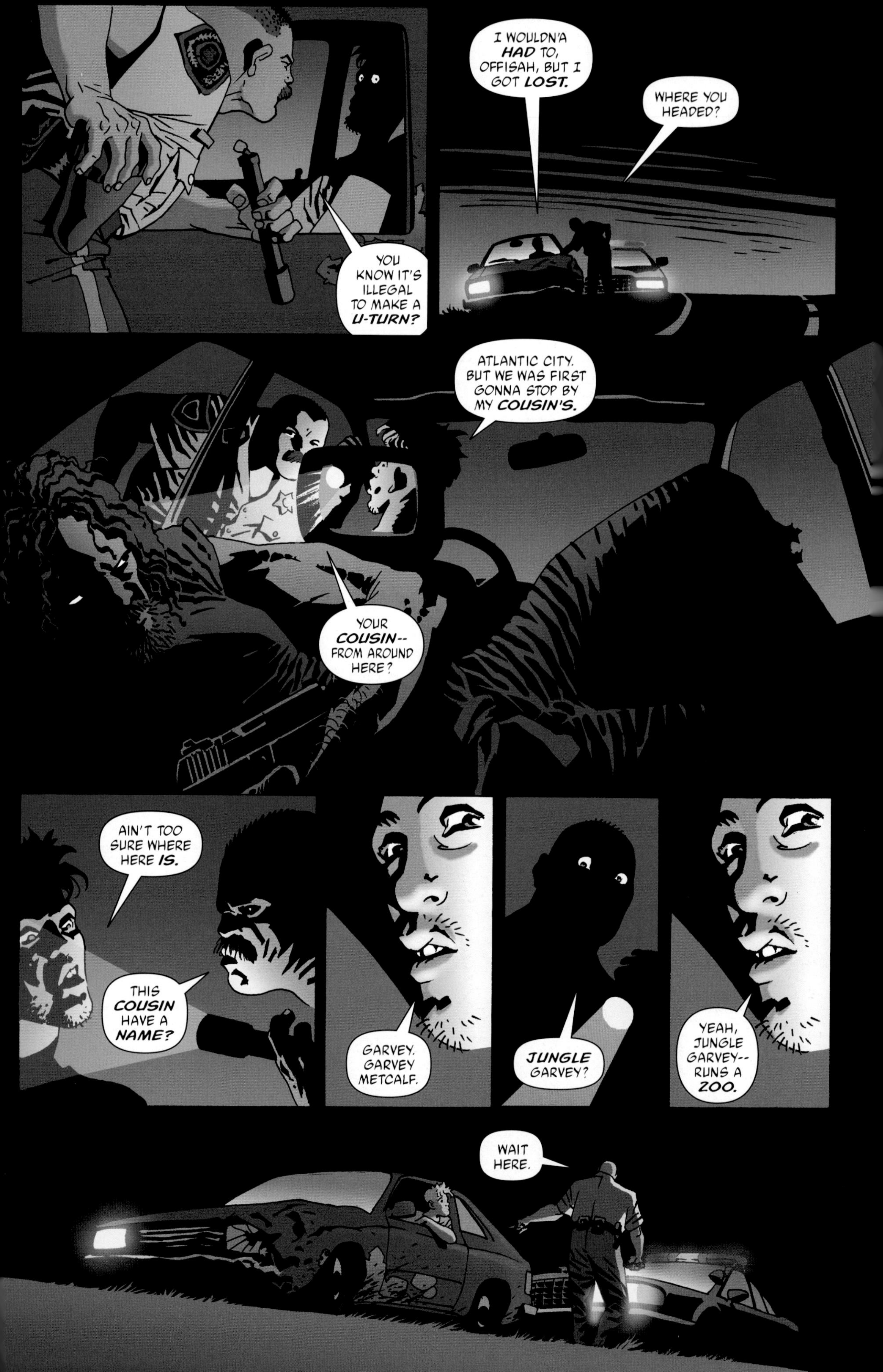
YOU KNOW IT'S ILLEGAL TO MAKE A U-TURN?
I WOULDN'A HAD TO, OFFISAH, BUT I GOT LOST.
WHERE YOU HEADED?
ATLANTIC CITY. BUT WE WAS FIRST GONNA STOP BY MY COUSIN'S.
YOUR COUSIN-- FROM AROUND HERE?
AIN'T TOO SURE WHERE HERE IS.
THIS COUSIN HAVE A NAME?
GARVEY. GARVEY METCALF.
JUNGLE GARVEY?
YEAH, JUNGLE GARVEY-- RUNS A ZOO.
WAIT HERE.

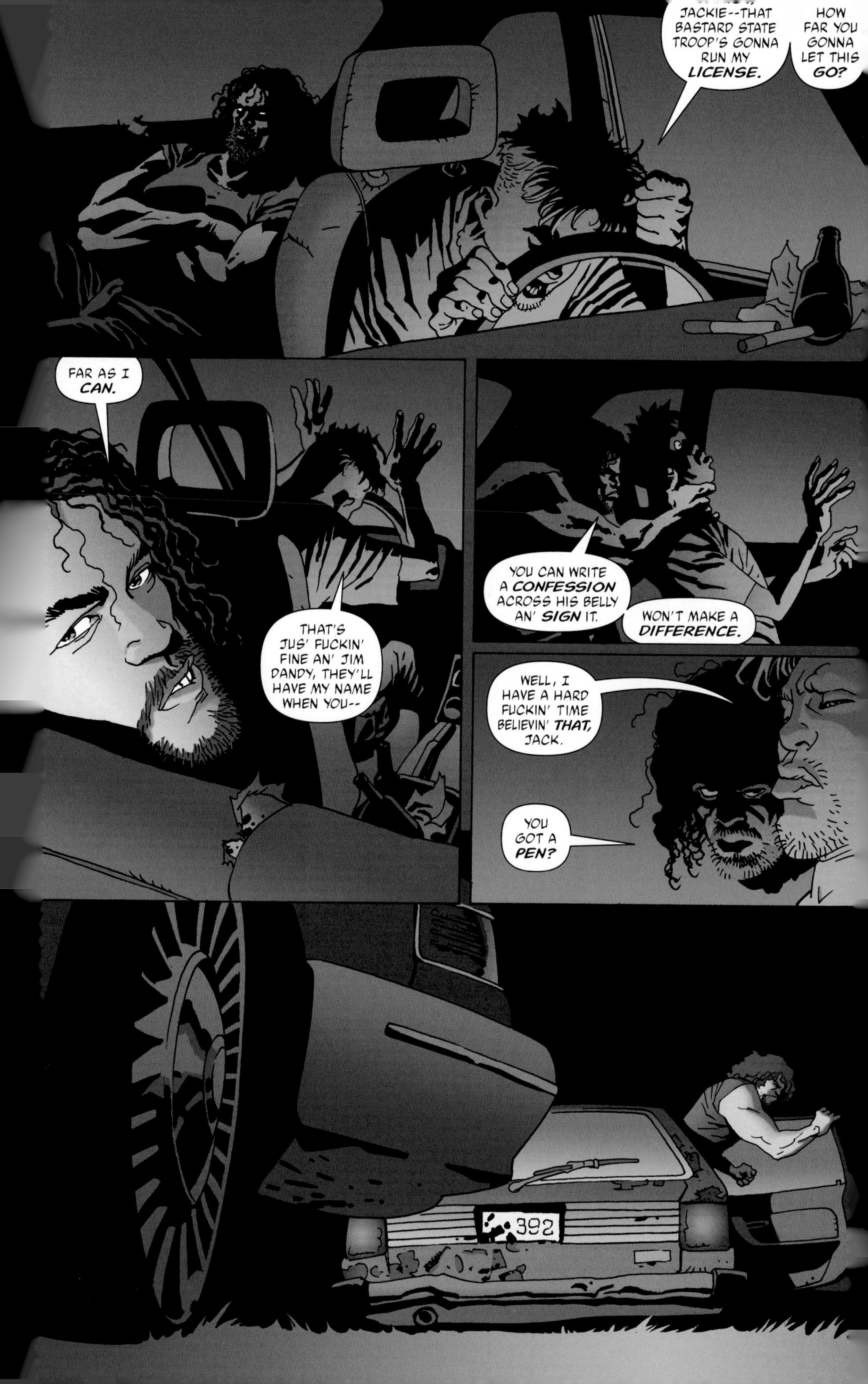
JACKIE--THAT BASTARD STATE TROOP'S GONNA RUN MY LICENSE.
HOW FAR YOU GONNA LET THIS GO?
FAR AS I CAN.
THAT'S JUS' FUCKIN' FINE AN' JIM DANDY, THEY'LL HAVE MY NAME WHEN YOU--
YOU CAN WRITE A CONFESSION ACROSS HIS BELLY AN' SIGN IT.
WON'T MAKE A DIFFERENCE.
WELL, I HAVE A HARD FUCKIN' TIME BELIEVIN' THAT, JACK.
YOU GOT A PEN?
392

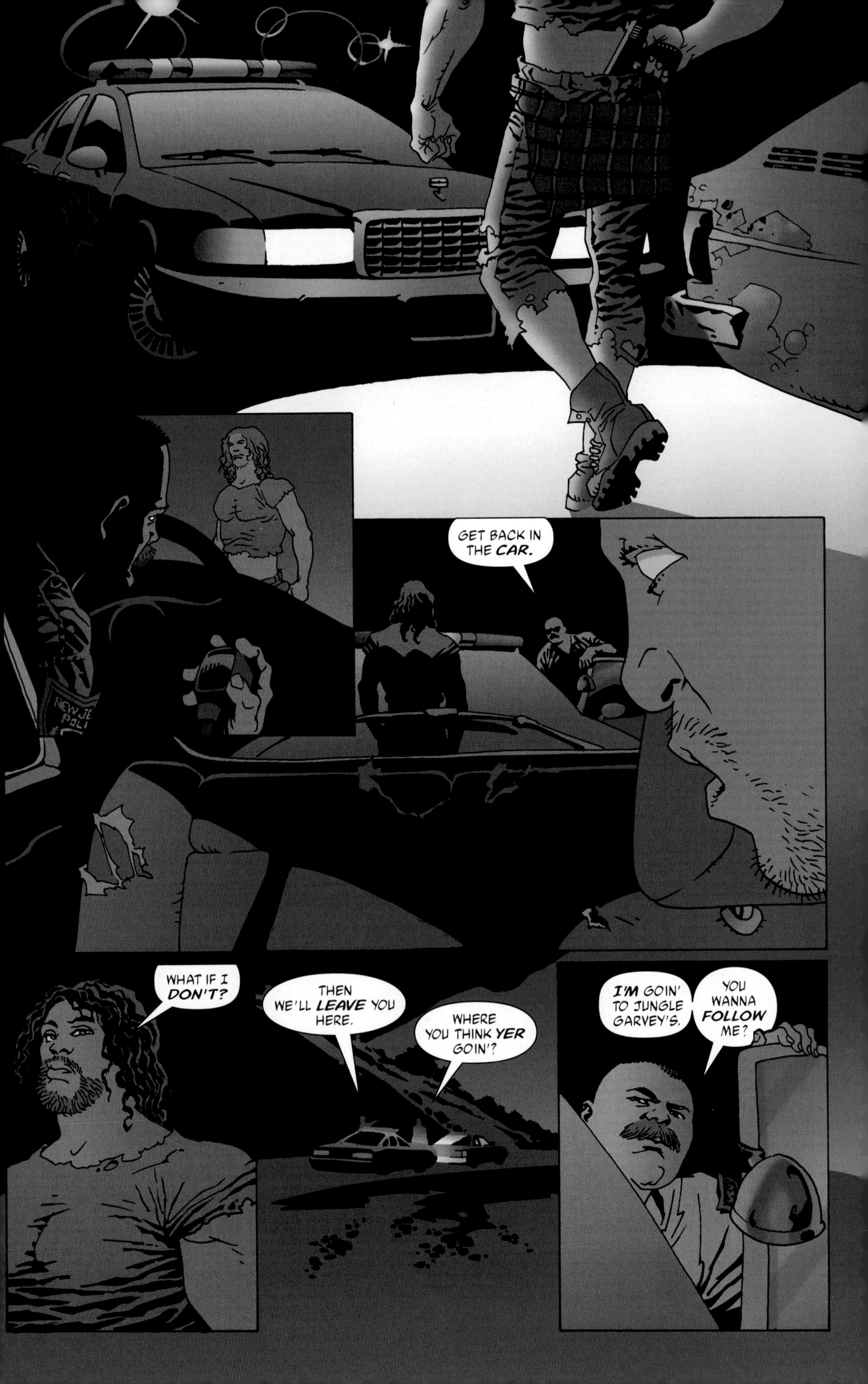
GET BACK IN THE **CAR.**
WHAT IF I **DON'T?**
THEN WE'LL **LEAVE** YOU HERE.
WHERE YOU THINK **YER** GOIN'?
I'M GOIN' TO JUNGLE GARVEY'S.
YOU WANNA **FOLLOW** ME?

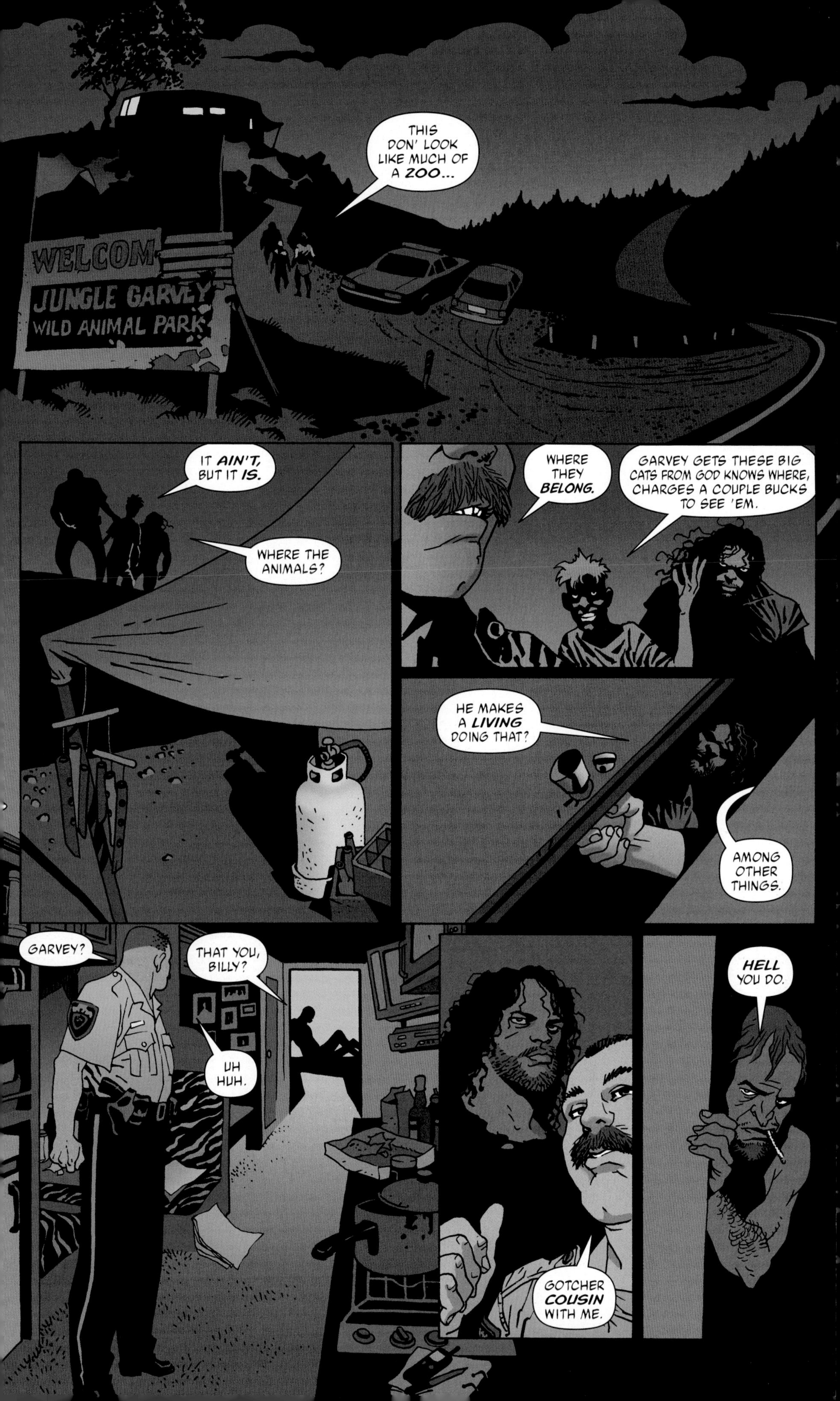
THIS DON' LOOK LIKE MUCH OF A ZOO...
WELCOM
JUNGLE GARVEY WILD ANIMAL PARK
IT AIN'T, BUT IT IS.
WHERE THE ANIMALS?
WHERE THEY BELONG.
GARVEY GETS THESE BIG CATS FROM GOD KNOWS WHERE, CHARGES A COUPLE BUCKS TO SEE 'EM.
HE MAKES A LIVING DOING THAT?
AMONG OTHER THINGS.
GARVEY?
THAT YOU, BILLY?
UH HUH.
GOTCHER COUSIN WITH ME.
HELL YOU DO.

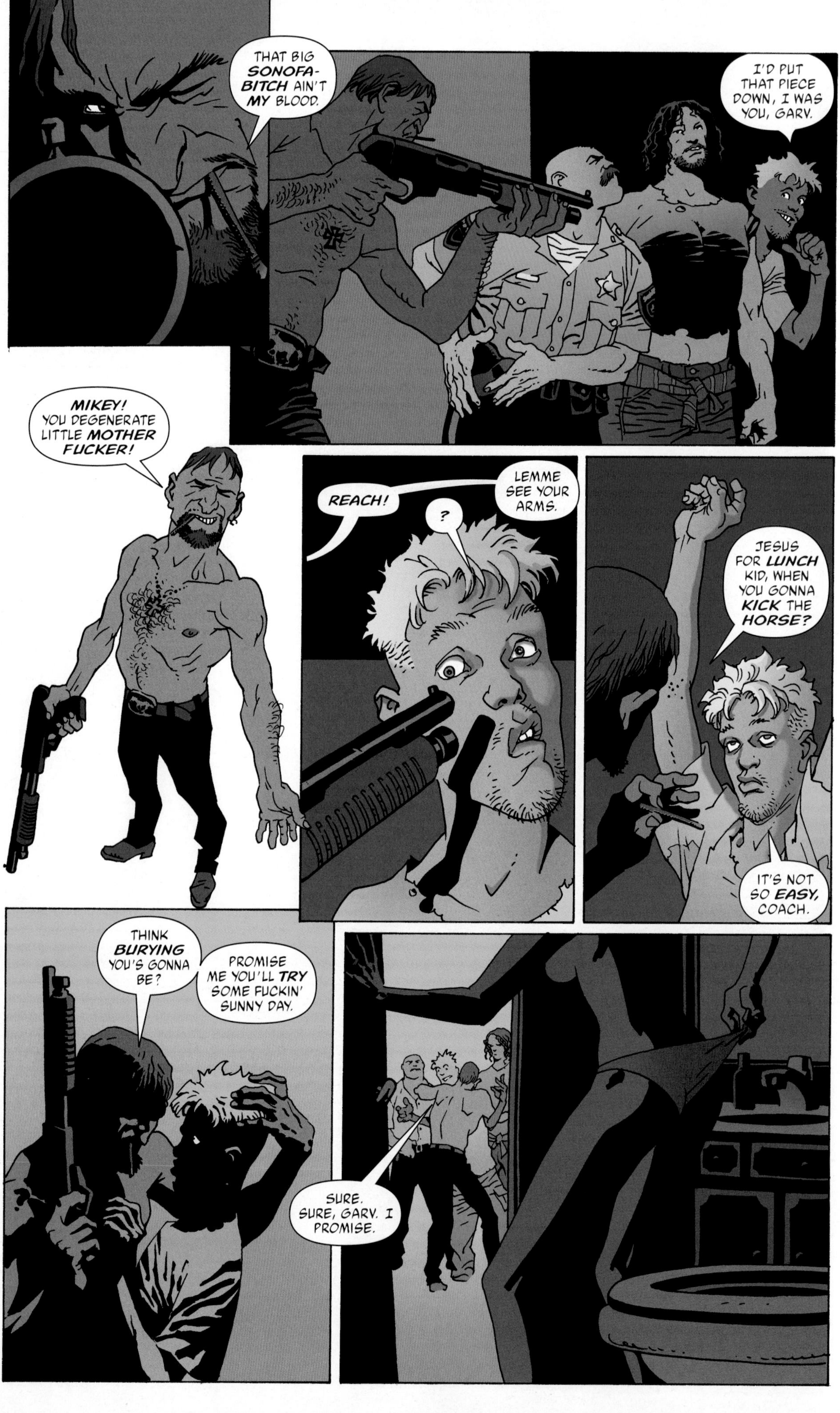
THAT BIG SONOFA-BITCH AIN'T MY BLOOD.
I'D PUT THAT PIECE DOWN, I WAS YOU, GARV.
MIKEY! YOU DEGENERATE LITTLE MOTHER FUCKER!
REACH!
LEMME SEE YOUR ARMS.
?
JESUS FOR LUNCH KID, WHEN YOU GONNA KICK THE HORSE?
IT'S NOT SO EASY, COACH.
THINK BURYING YOU'S GONNA BE?
PROMISE ME YOU'LL TRY SOME FUCKIN' SUNNY DAY.
SURE. SURE, GARV. I PROMISE.

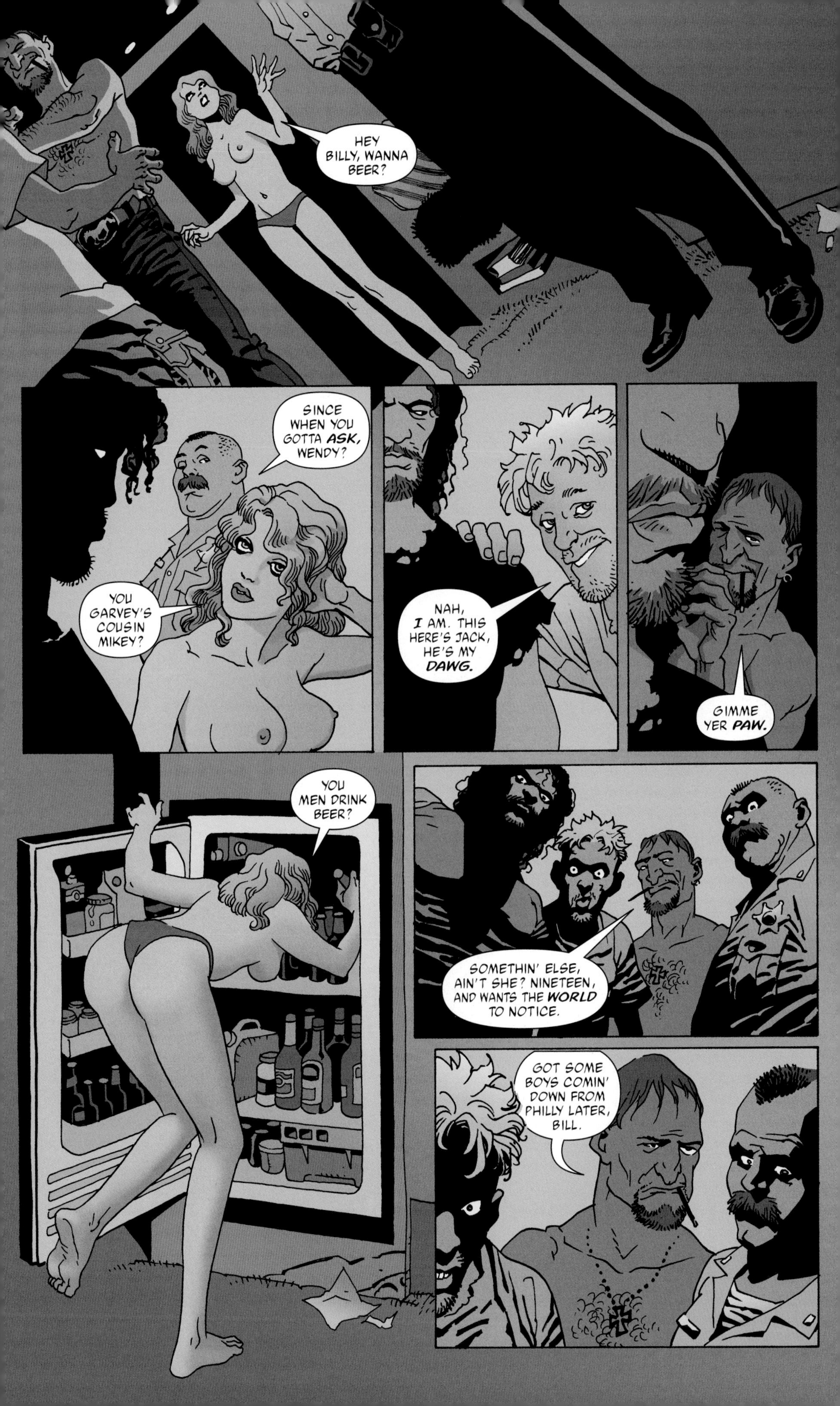
HEY BILLY, WANNA BEER?
SINCE WHEN YOU GOTTA ASK, WENDY?
YOU GARVEY'S COUSIN MIKEY?
NAH, I AM. THIS HERE'S JACK, HE'S MY DAWG.
GIMME YER PAW.
YOU MEN DRINK BEER?
SOMETHIN' ELSE, AIN'T SHE? NINETEEN, AND WANTS THE WORLD TO NOTICE.
GOT SOME BOYS COMIN' DOWN FROM PHILLY LATER, BILL.

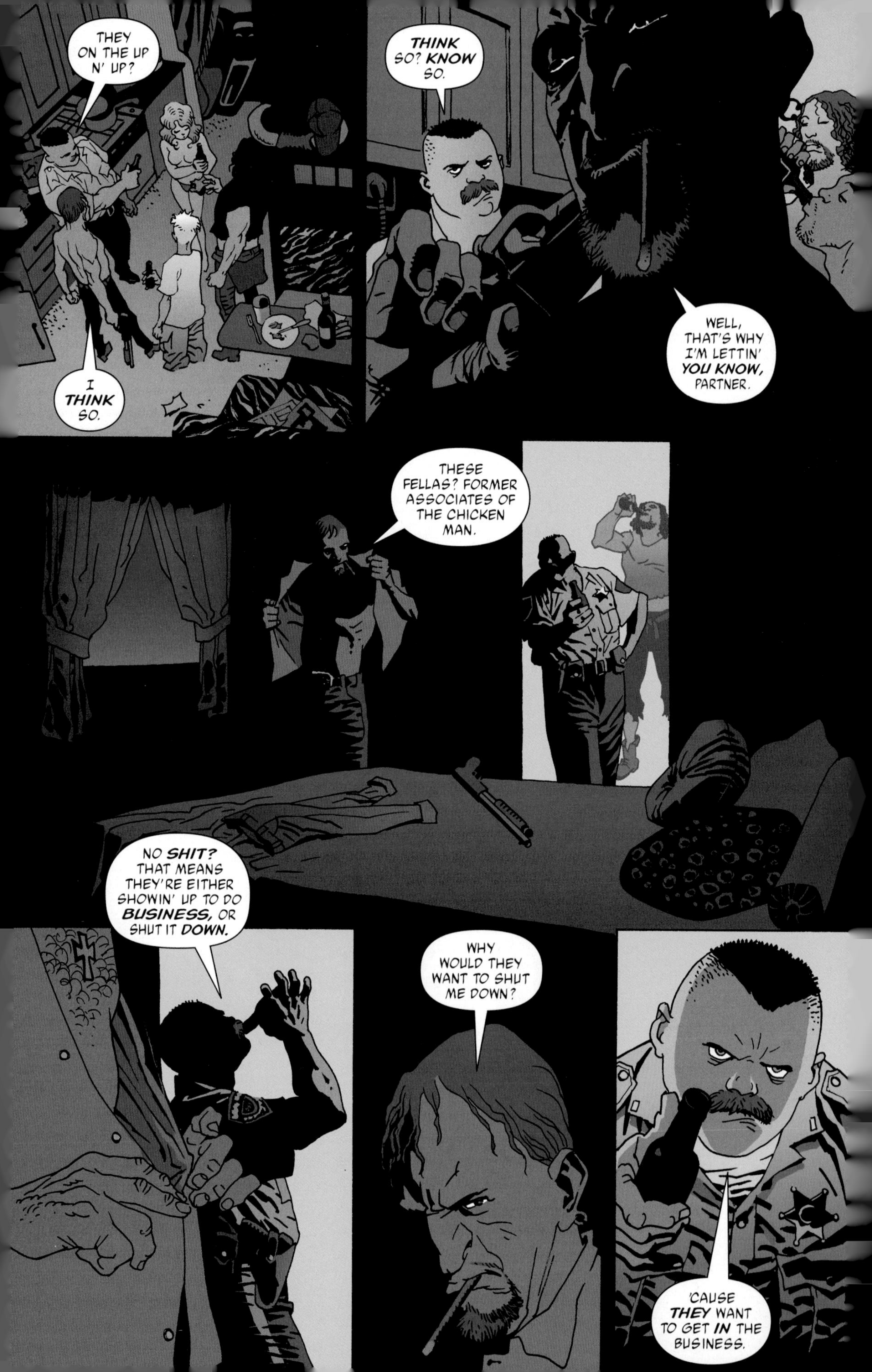
THEY ON THE UP N' UP?
I THINK SO.
THINK SO? KNOW SO.
WELL, THAT'S WHY I'M LETTIN' YOU KNOW, PARTNER.
THESE FELLAS? FORMER ASSOCIATES OF THE CHICKEN MAN.
NO SHIT? THAT MEANS THEY'RE EITHER SHOWIN' UP TO DO BUSINESS, OR SHUT IT DOWN.
WHY WOULD THEY WANT TO SHUT ME DOWN?
'CAUSE THEY WANT TO GET IN THE BUSINESS.

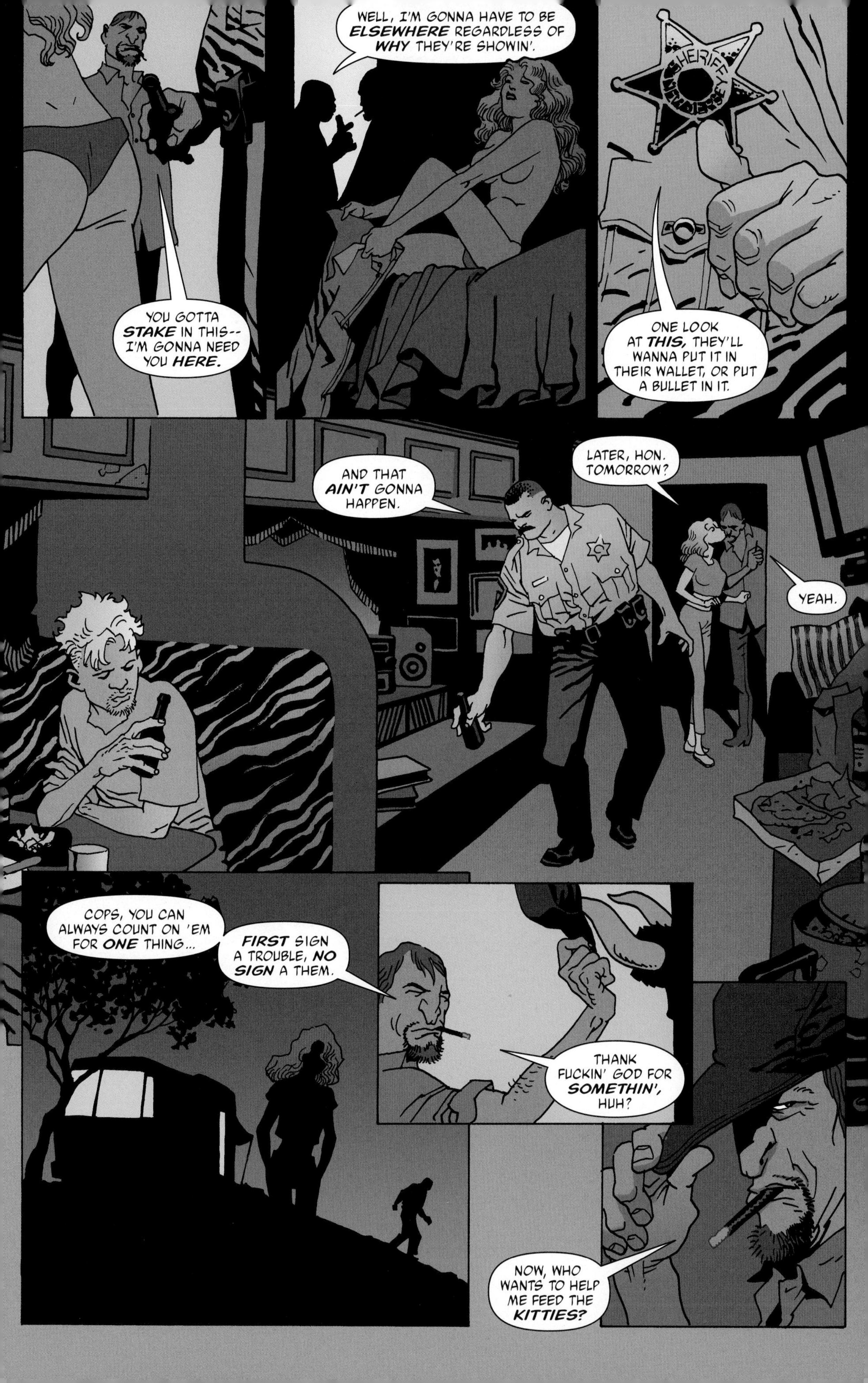
YOU GOTTA STAKE IN THIS-- I'M GONNA NEED YOU HERE.
WELL, I'M GONNA HAVE TO BE ELSEWHERE REGARDLESS OF WHY THEY'RE SHOWIN'.
SHERIFF
ONE LOOK AT THIS, THEY'LL WANNA PUT IT IN THEIR WALLET, OR PUT A BULLET IN IT.
AND THAT AIN'T GONNA HAPPEN.
LATER, HON. TOMORROW?
YEAH.
COPS, YOU CAN ALWAYS COUNT ON 'EM FOR ONE THING...
FIRST SIGN A TROUBLE, NO SIGN A THEM.
THANK FUCKIN' GOD FOR SOMETHIN', HUH?
NOW, WHO WANTS TO HELP ME FEED THE KITTIES?

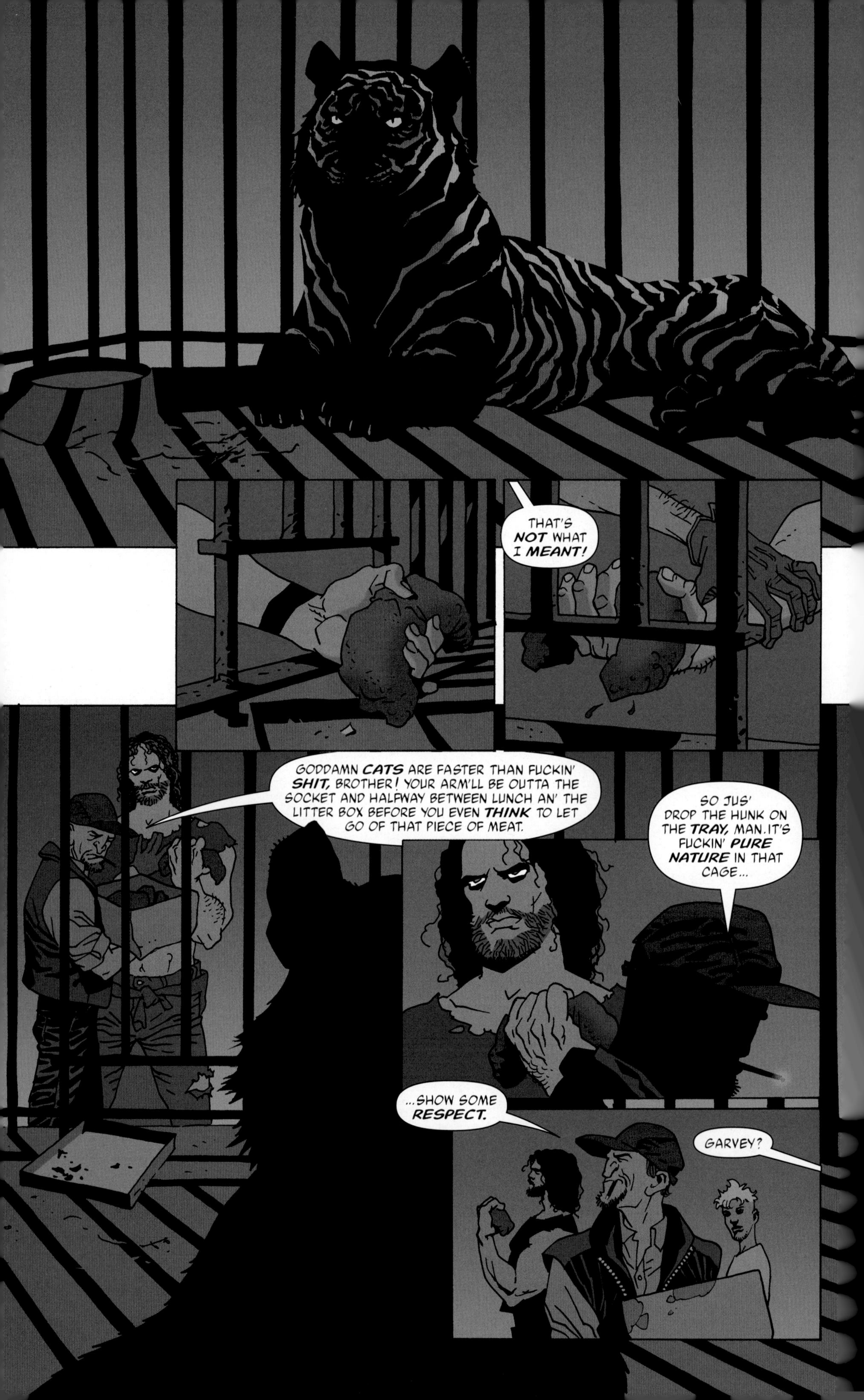
THAT'S **NOT** WHAT I **MEANT!**
GODDAMN **CATS** ARE FASTER THAN FUCKIN' **SHIT,** BROTHER! YOUR ARM'LL BE OUTTA THE SOCKET AND HALFWAY BETWEEN LUNCH AN' THE LITTER BOX BEFORE YOU EVEN **THINK** TO LET GO OF THAT PIECE OF MEAT.
SO JUS' DROP THE HUNK ON THE **TRAY,** MAN. IT'S FUCKIN' **PURE NATURE** IN THAT CAGE...
...SHOW SOME **RESPECT.**
GARVEY?

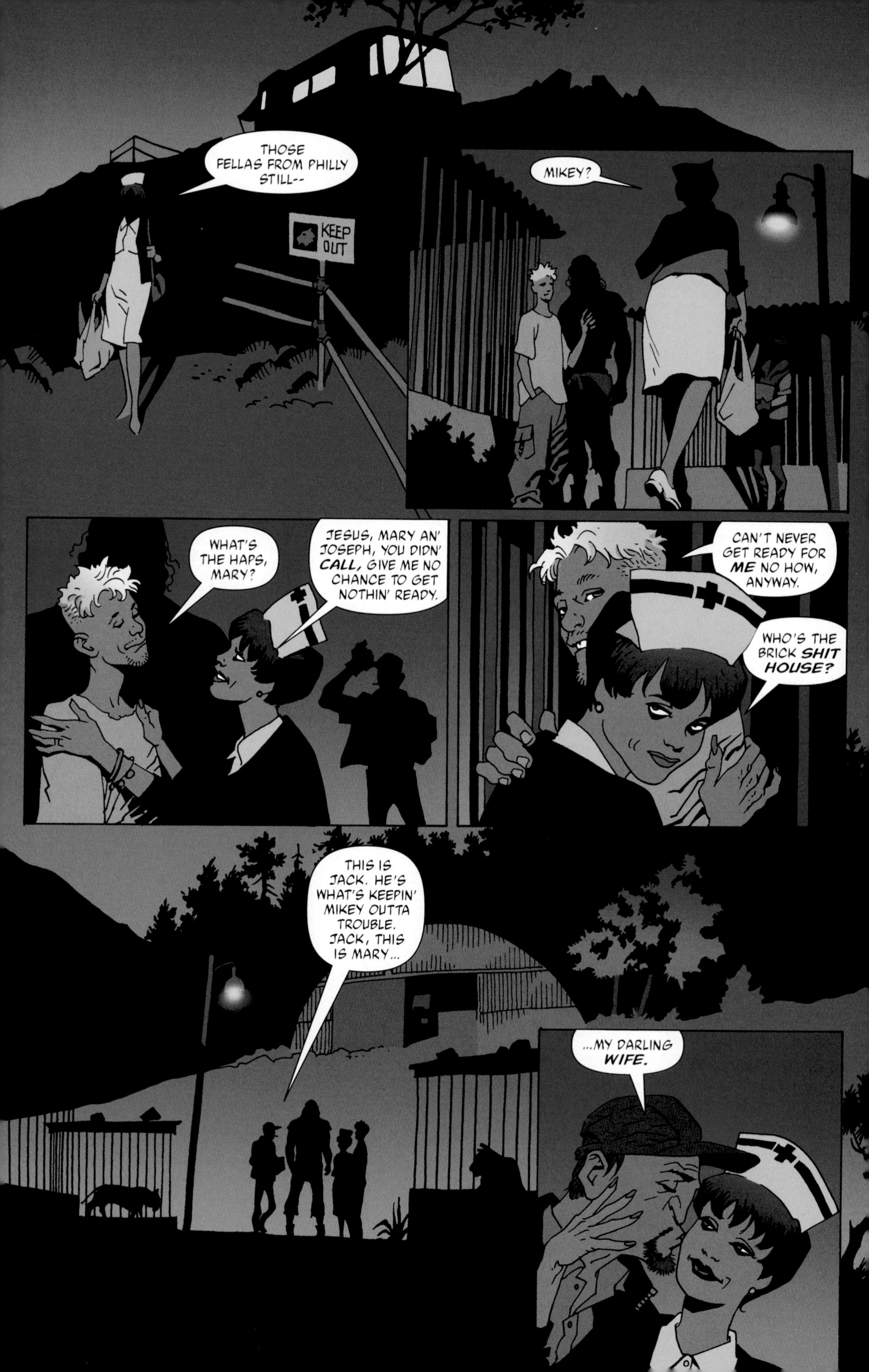
THOSE FELLAS FROM PHILLY STILL--
KEEP OUT
MIKEY?
WHAT'S THE HAPS, MARY?
JESUS, MARY AN' JOSEPH, YOU DIDN' **CALL**, GIVE ME NO CHANCE TO GET NOTHIN' READY.
CAN'T NEVER GET READY FOR **ME** NO HOW, ANYWAY.
WHO'S THE BRICK **SHIT HOUSE?**
THIS IS JACK. HE'S WHAT'S KEEPIN' MIKEY OUTTA TROUBLE. JACK, THIS IS MARY...
...MY DARLING **WIFE.**

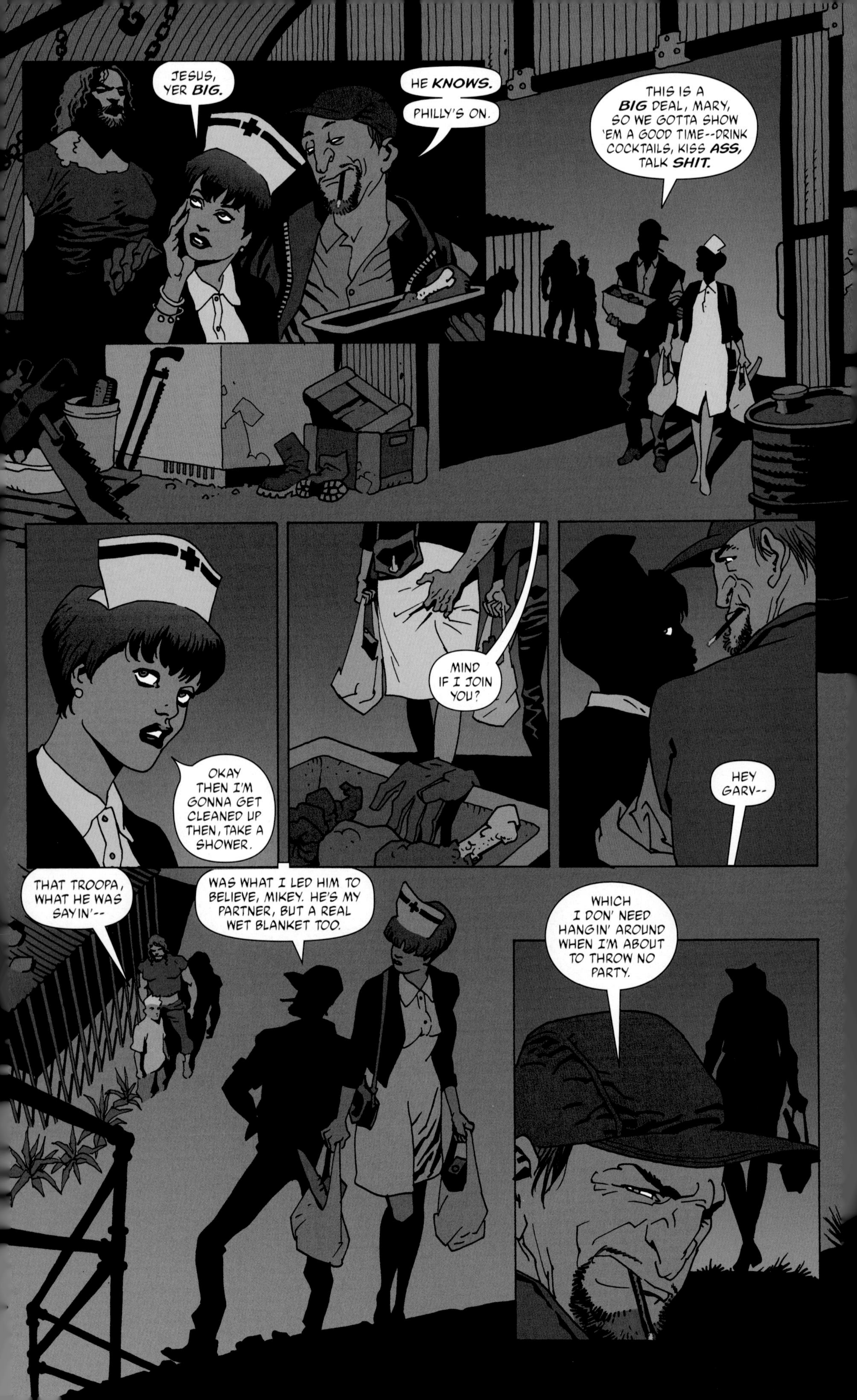

JESUS, YER *BIG.*
HE *KNOWS.*
PHILLY'S ON.
THIS IS A *BIG* DEAL, MARY, SO WE GOTTA SHOW 'EM A GOOD TIME--DRINK COCKTAILS, KISS *ASS,* TALK *SHIT.*
OKAY THEN I'M GONNA GET CLEANED UP THEN, TAKE A SHOWER.
MIND IF I JOIN YOU?
HEY GARV--
THAT TROOPA, WHAT HE WAS SAYIN'--
WAS WHAT I LED HIM TO BELIEVE, MIKEY. HE'S MY PARTNER, BUT A REAL WET BLANKET TOO.
WHICH I DON' NEED HANGIN' AROUND WHEN I'M ABOUT TO THROW NO PARTY.

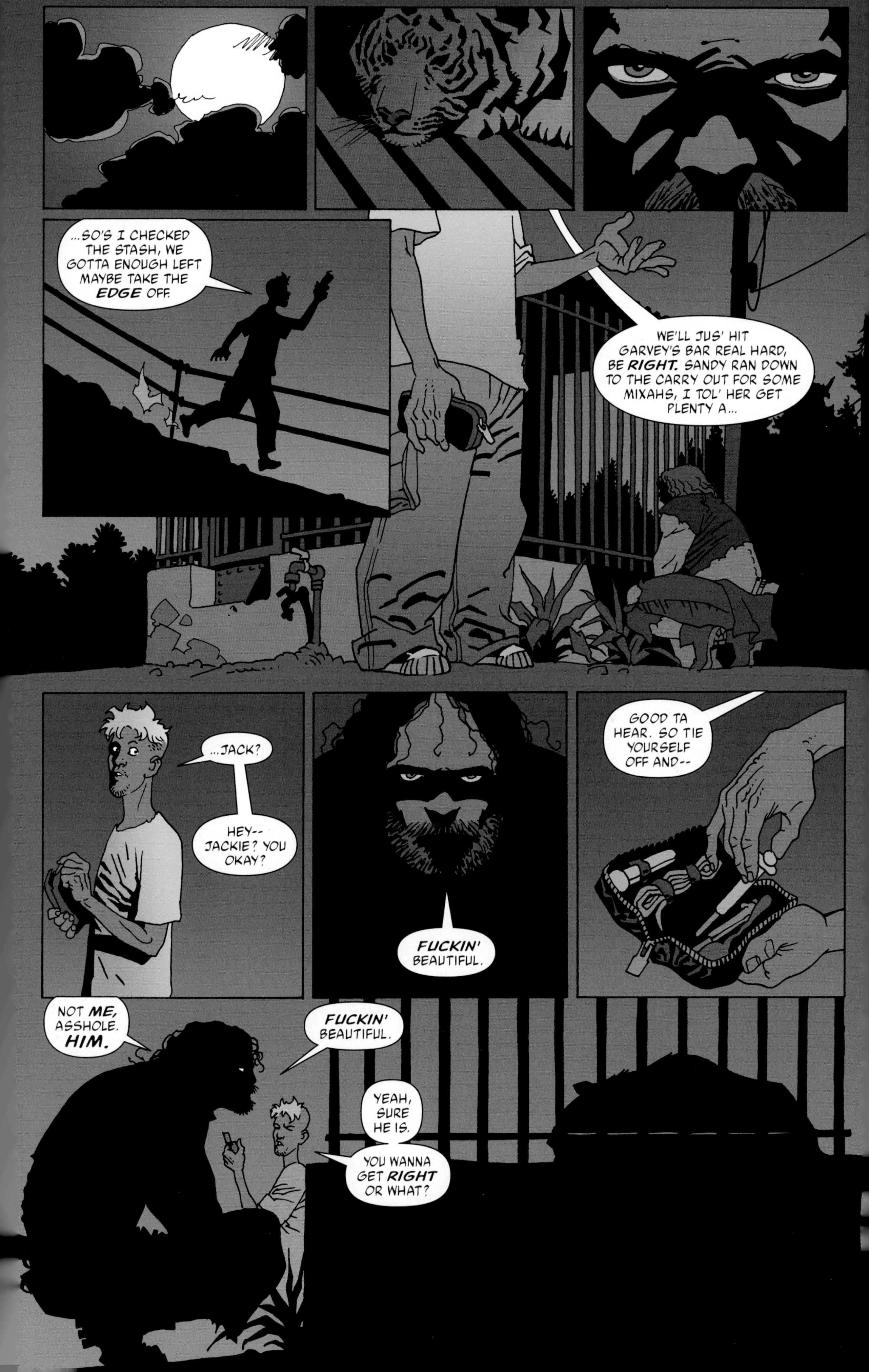
...SO'S I CHECKED THE STASH, WE GOTTA ENOUGH LEFT MAYBE TAKE THE EDGE OFF.
WE'LL JUS' HIT GARVEY'S BAR REAL HARD, BE RIGHT. SANDY RAN DOWN TO THE CARRY OUT FOR SOME MIXAHS, I TOL' HER GET PLENTY A...
...JACK?
HEY-- JACKIE? YOU OKAY?
FUCKIN' BEAUTIFUL.
GOOD TA HEAR. SO TIE YOURSELF OFF AND--
NOT ME, ASSHOLE. HIM.
FUCKIN' BEAUTIFUL.
YEAH, SURE HE IS.
YOU WANNA GET RIGHT OR WHAT?

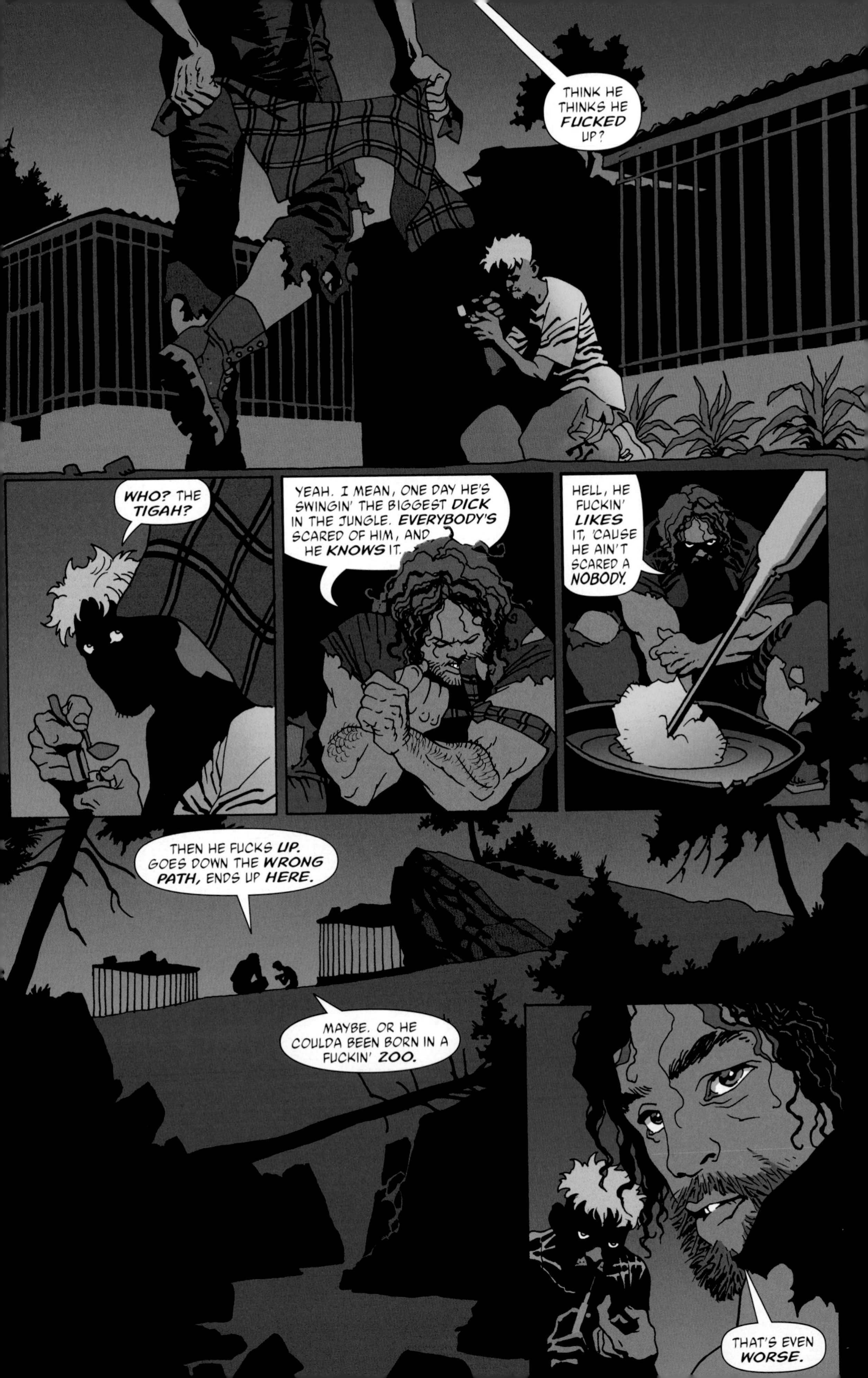
THINK HE THINKS HE FUCKED UP?
WHO? THE TIGAH?
YEAH. I MEAN, ONE DAY HE'S SWINGIN' THE BIGGEST DICK IN THE JUNGLE. EVERYBODY'S SCARED OF HIM, AND HE KNOWS IT.
HELL, HE FUCKIN' LIKES IT, 'CAUSE HE AIN'T SCARED A NOBODY.
THEN HE FUCKS UP. GOES DOWN THE WRONG PATH, ENDS UP HERE.
MAYBE. OR HE COULDA BEEN BORN IN A FUCKIN' ZOO.
THAT'S EVEN WORSE.

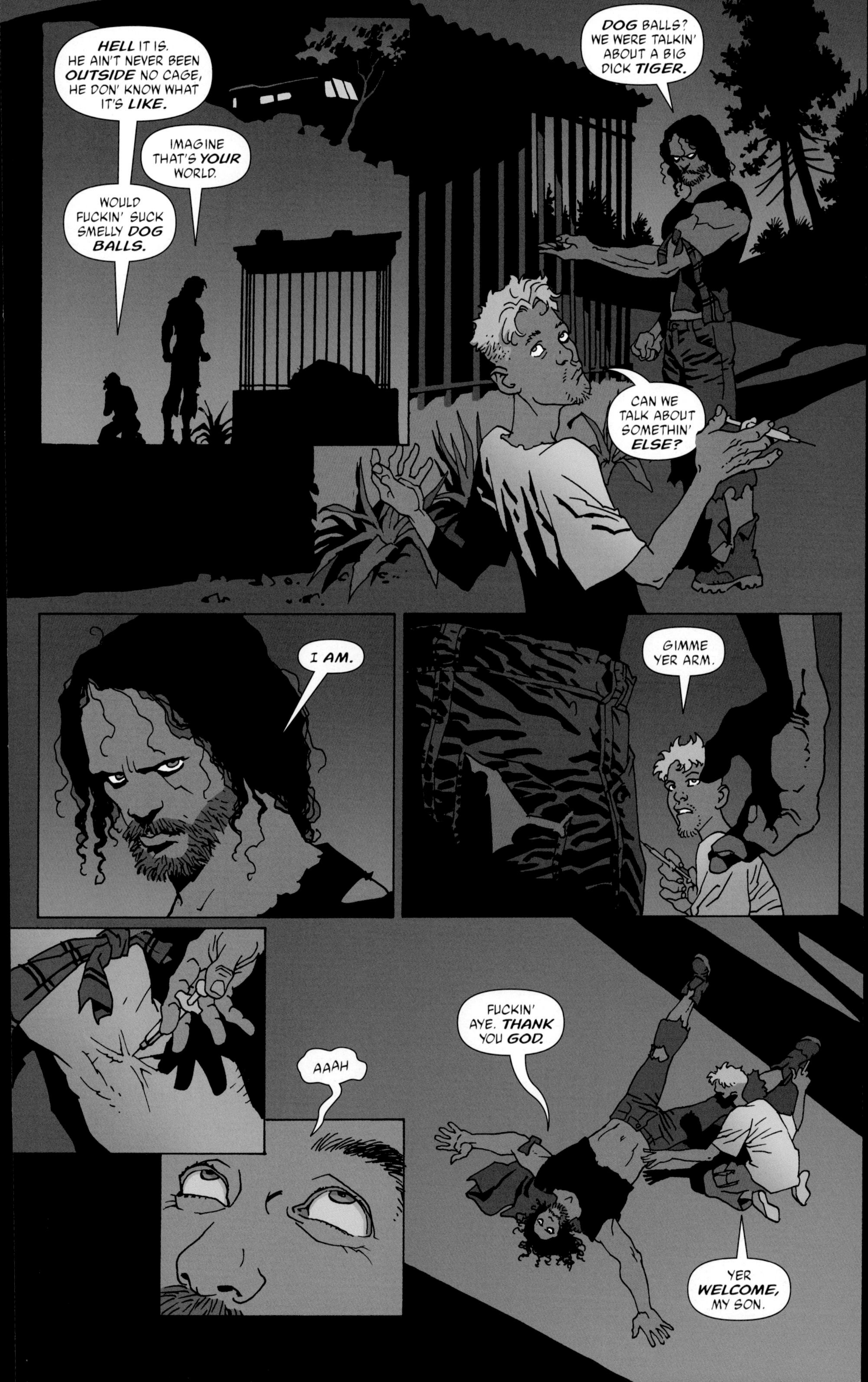
HELL IT IS. HE AIN'T NEVER BEEN OUTSIDE NO CAGE, HE DON' KNOW WHAT IT'S LIKE.
IMAGINE THAT'S YOUR WORLD.
WOULD FUCKIN' SUCK SMELLY DOG BALLS.
DOG BALLS? WE WERE TALKIN' ABOUT A BIG DICK TIGER.
CAN WE TALK ABOUT SOMETHIN' ELSE?
I AM.
GIMME YER ARM.
AAAH
FUCKIN' AYE. THANK YOU GOD.
YER WELCOME, MY SON.

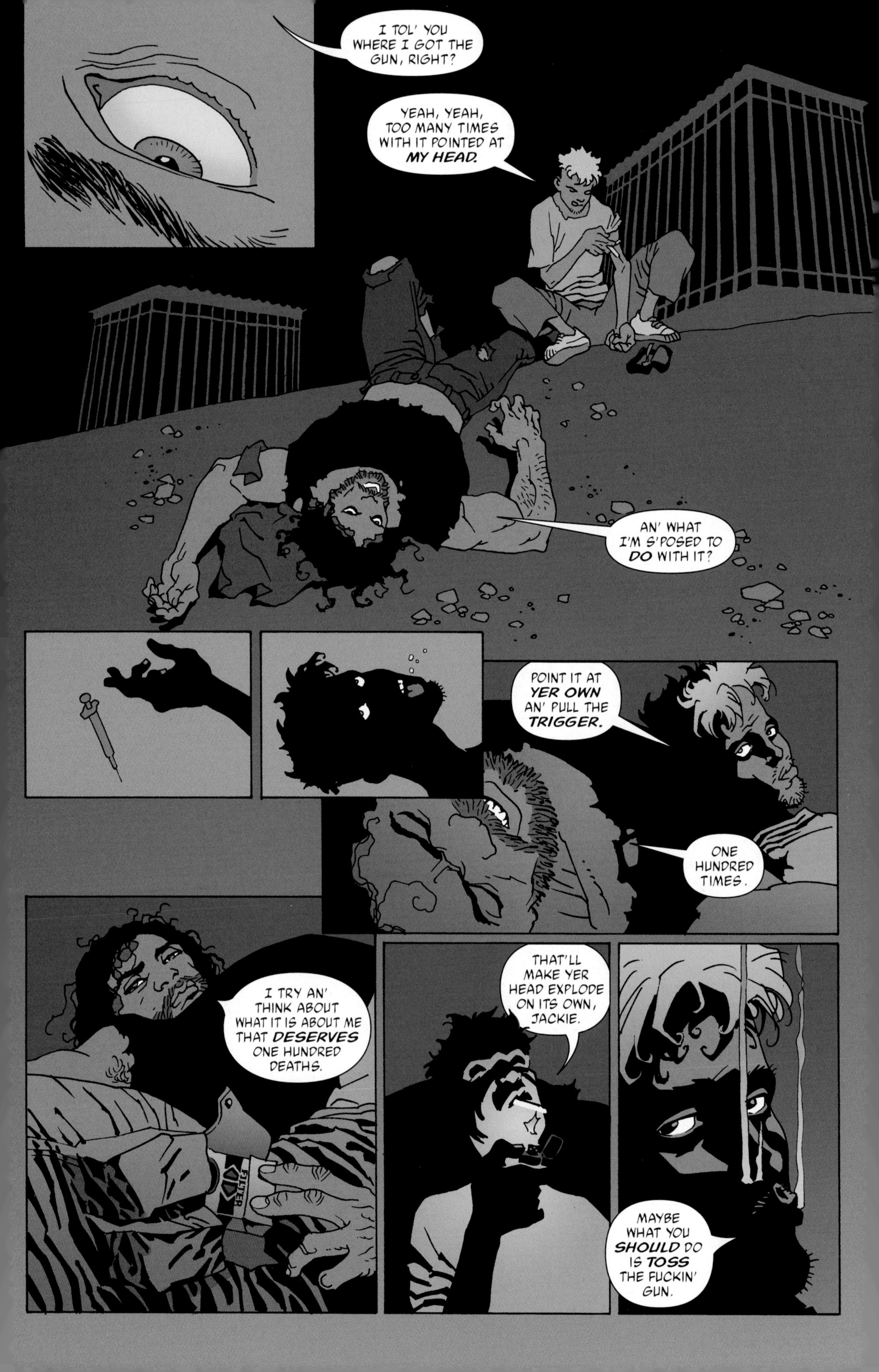

I TOL' YOU WHERE I GOT THE GUN, RIGHT?
YEAH, YEAH, TOO MANY TIMES WITH IT POINTED AT MY HEAD.
AN' WHAT I'M S'POSED TO DO WITH IT?
POINT IT AT YER OWN AN' PULL THE TRIGGER.
ONE HUNDRED TIMES.
I TRY AN' THINK ABOUT WHAT IT IS ABOUT ME THAT DESERVES ONE HUNDRED DEATHS.
THAT'LL MAKE YER HEAD EXPLODE ON ITS OWN, JACKIE.
MAYBE WHAT YOU SHOULD DO IS TOSS THE FUCKIN' GUN.

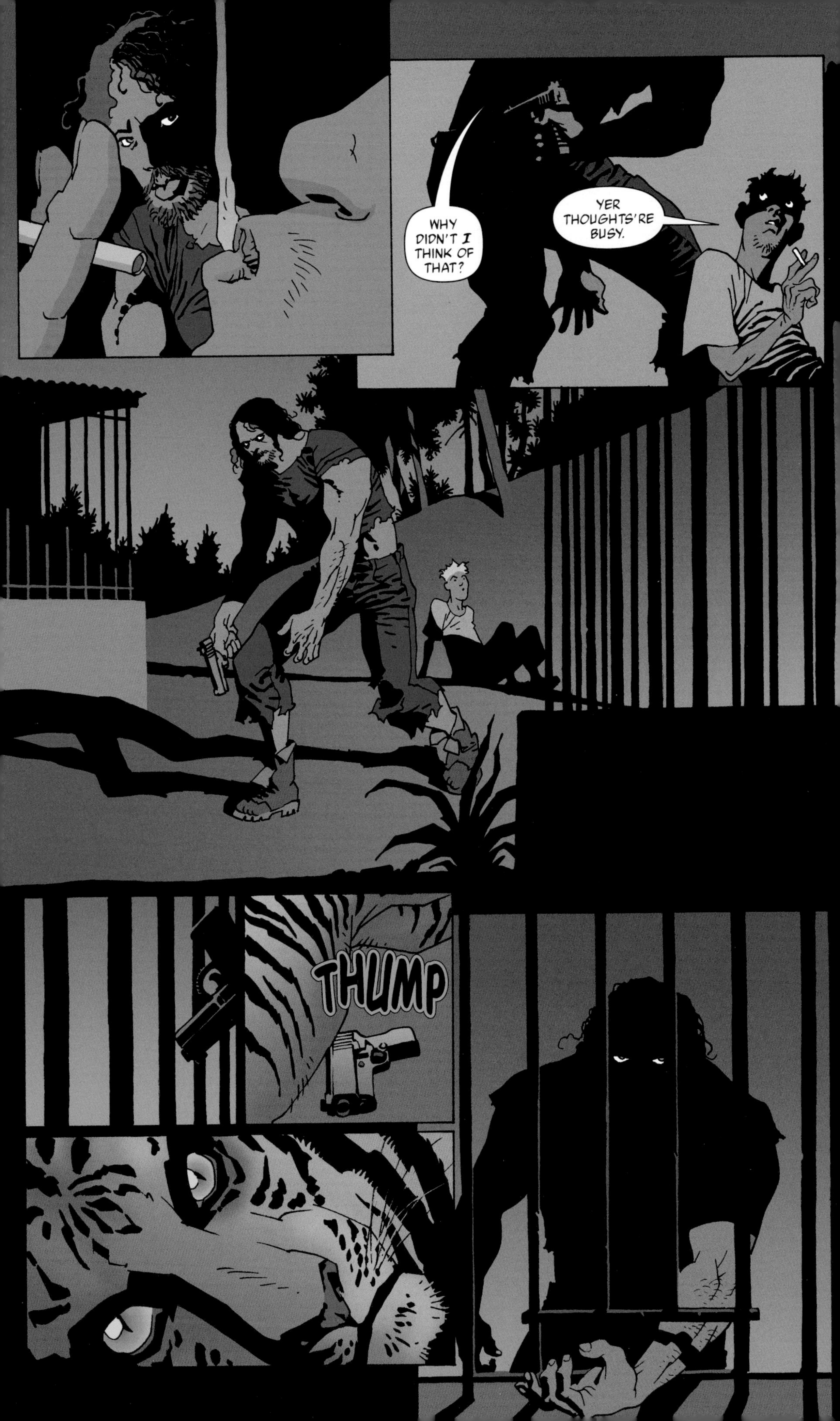
WHY DIDN'T I THINK OF THAT?
YER THOUGHTS'RE BUSY.
THUMP

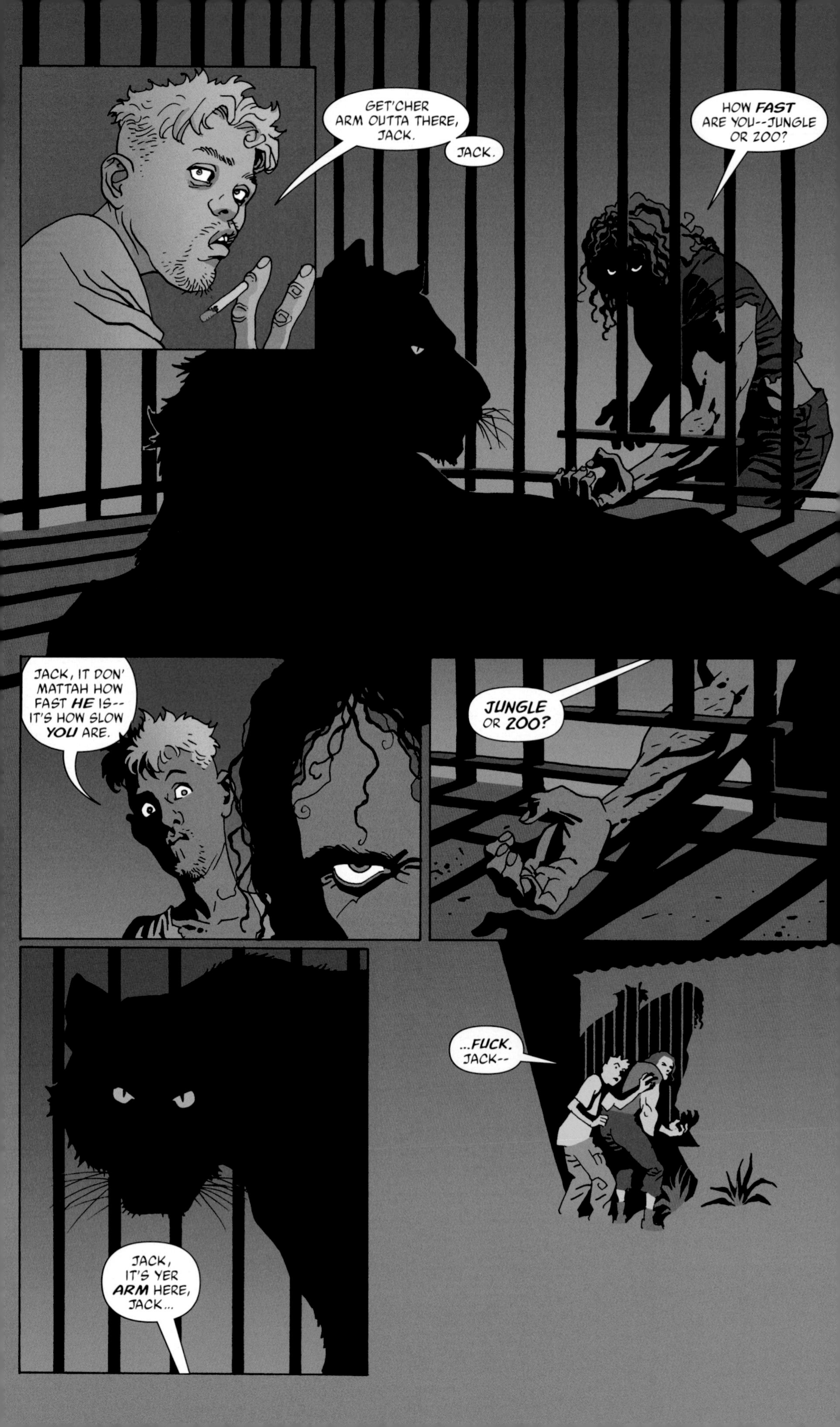
GET'CHER ARM OUTTA THERE, JACK.
JACK.
HOW FAST ARE YOU--JUNGLE OR ZOO?
JACK, IT DON' MATTAH HOW FAST HE IS-- IT'S HOW SLOW YOU ARE.
JUNGLE OR ZOO?
JACK, IT'S YER ARM HERE, JACK...
...FUCK. JACK--

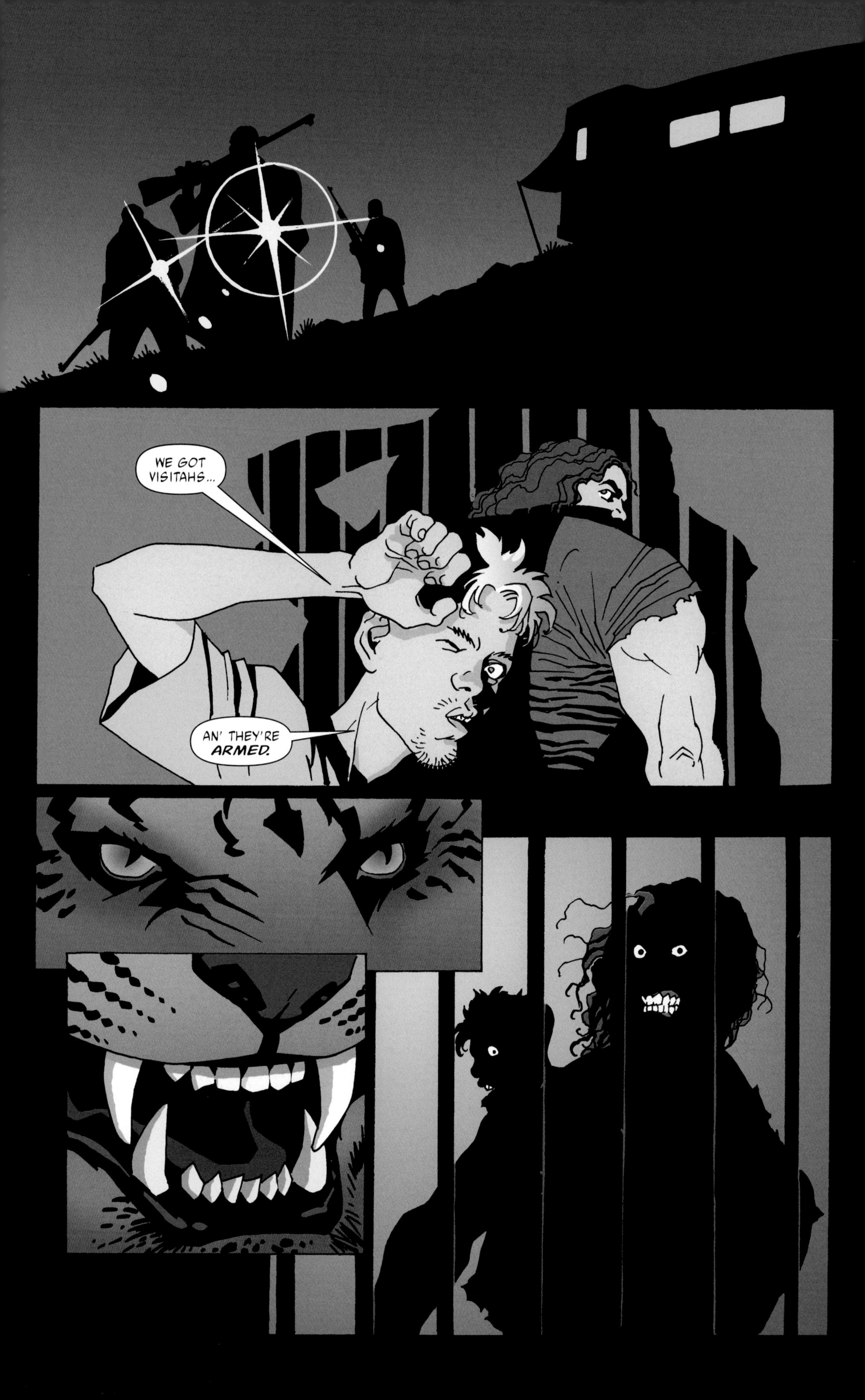
WE GOT VISITAHS...
AN' THEY'RE ARMED.

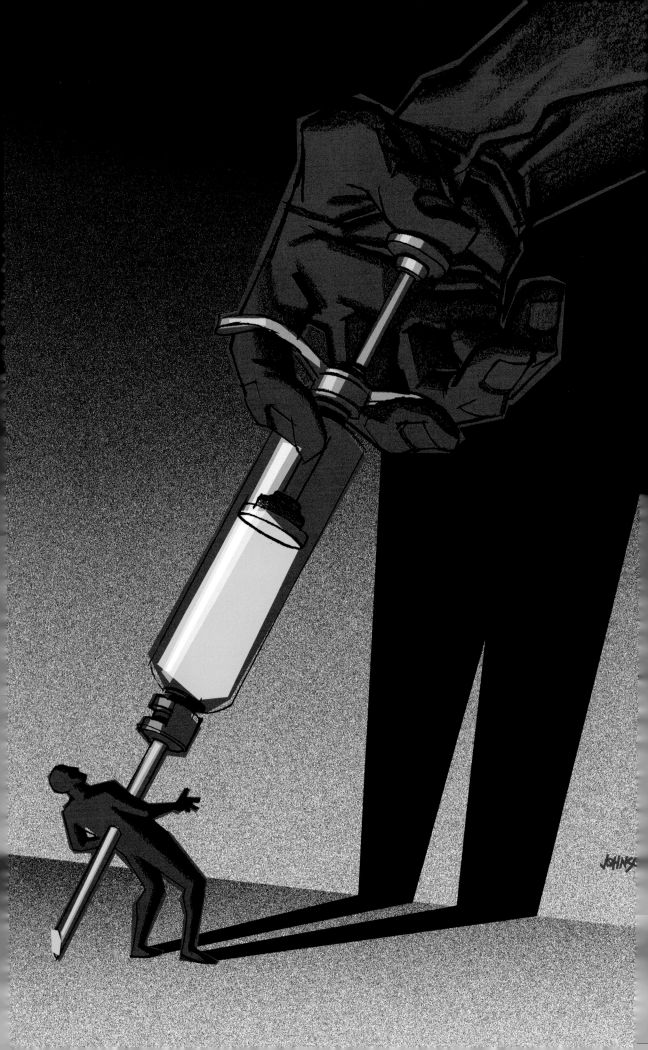

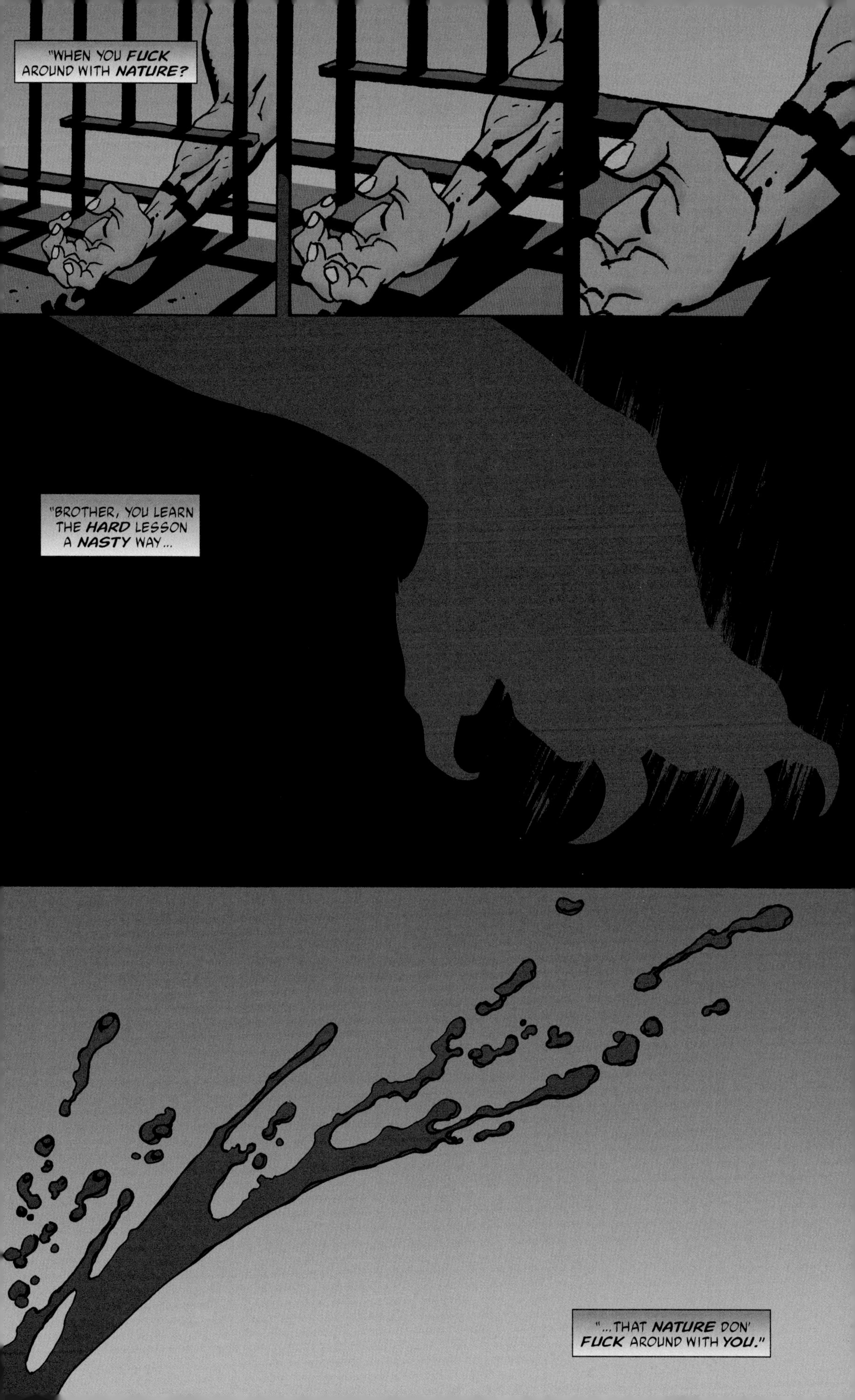
"WHEN YOU FUCK AROUND WITH NATURE?
"BROTHER, YOU LEARN THE HARD LESSON A NASTY WAY...
"...THAT NATURE DON' FUCK AROUND WITH YOU."

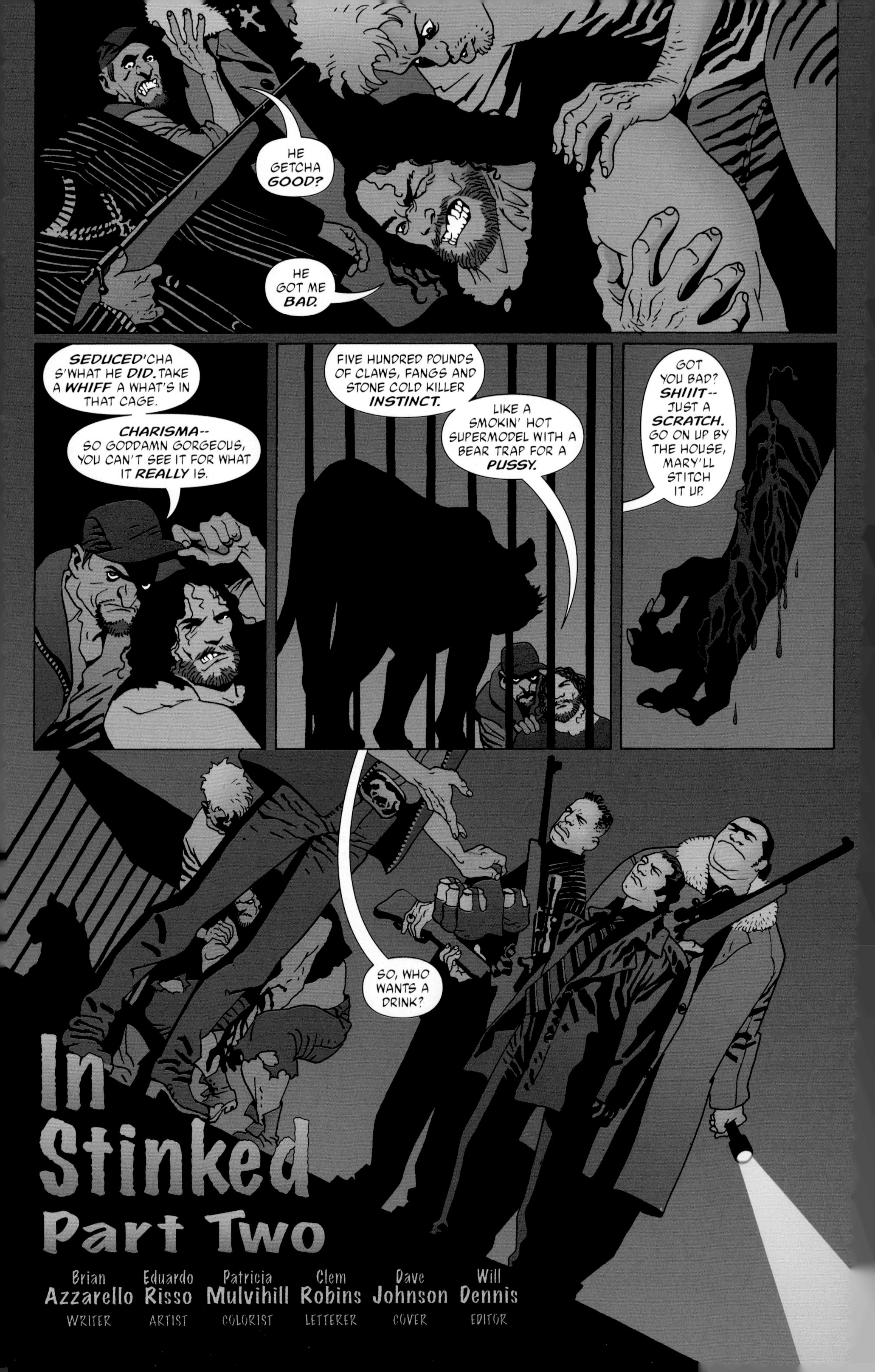
HE GETCHA GOOD?
HE GOT ME BAD.
SEDUCED'CHA S'WHAT HE DID. TAKE A WHIFF A WHAT'S IN THAT CAGE.
CHARISMA-- SO GODDAMN GORGEOUS, YOU CAN'T SEE IT FOR WHAT IT REALLY IS.
FIVE HUNDRED POUNDS OF CLAWS, FANGS AND STONE COLD KILLER INSTINCT.
LIKE A SMOKIN' HOT SUPERMODEL WITH A BEAR TRAP FOR A PUSSY.
GOT YOU BAD? SHIIIT-- JUST A SCRATCH. GO ON UP BY THE HOUSE, MARY'LL STITCH IT UP.
SO, WHO WANTS A DRINK?
In Stinked
Part Two
Brian Azzarello WRITER
Eduardo Risso ARTIST
Patricia Mulvihill COLORIST
Clem Robins LETTERER
Dave Johnson COVER
Will Dennis EDITOR

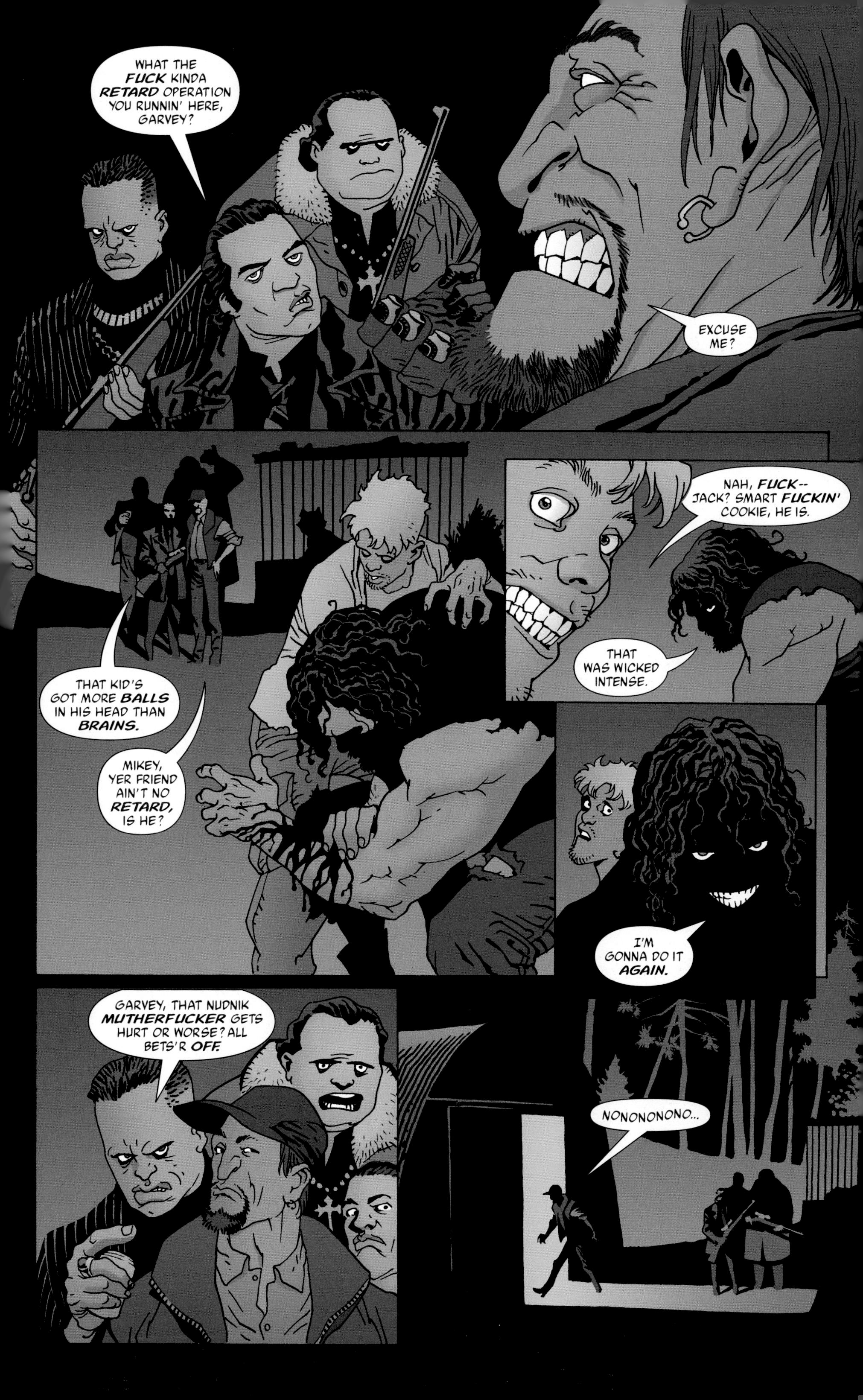
WHAT THE FUCK KINDA RETARD OPERATION YOU RUNNIN' HERE, GARVEY?
EXCUSE ME?
THAT KID'S GOT MORE BALLS IN HIS HEAD THAN BRAINS.
MIKEY, YER FRIEND AIN'T NO RETARD, IS HE?
NAH, FUCK-- JACK? SMART FUCKIN' COOKIE, HE IS.
THAT WAS WICKED INTENSE.
I'M GONNA DO IT AGAIN.
GARVEY, THAT NUDNIK MUTHERFUCKER GETS HURT OR WORSE? ALL BETS'R OFF.
NONONONONO...

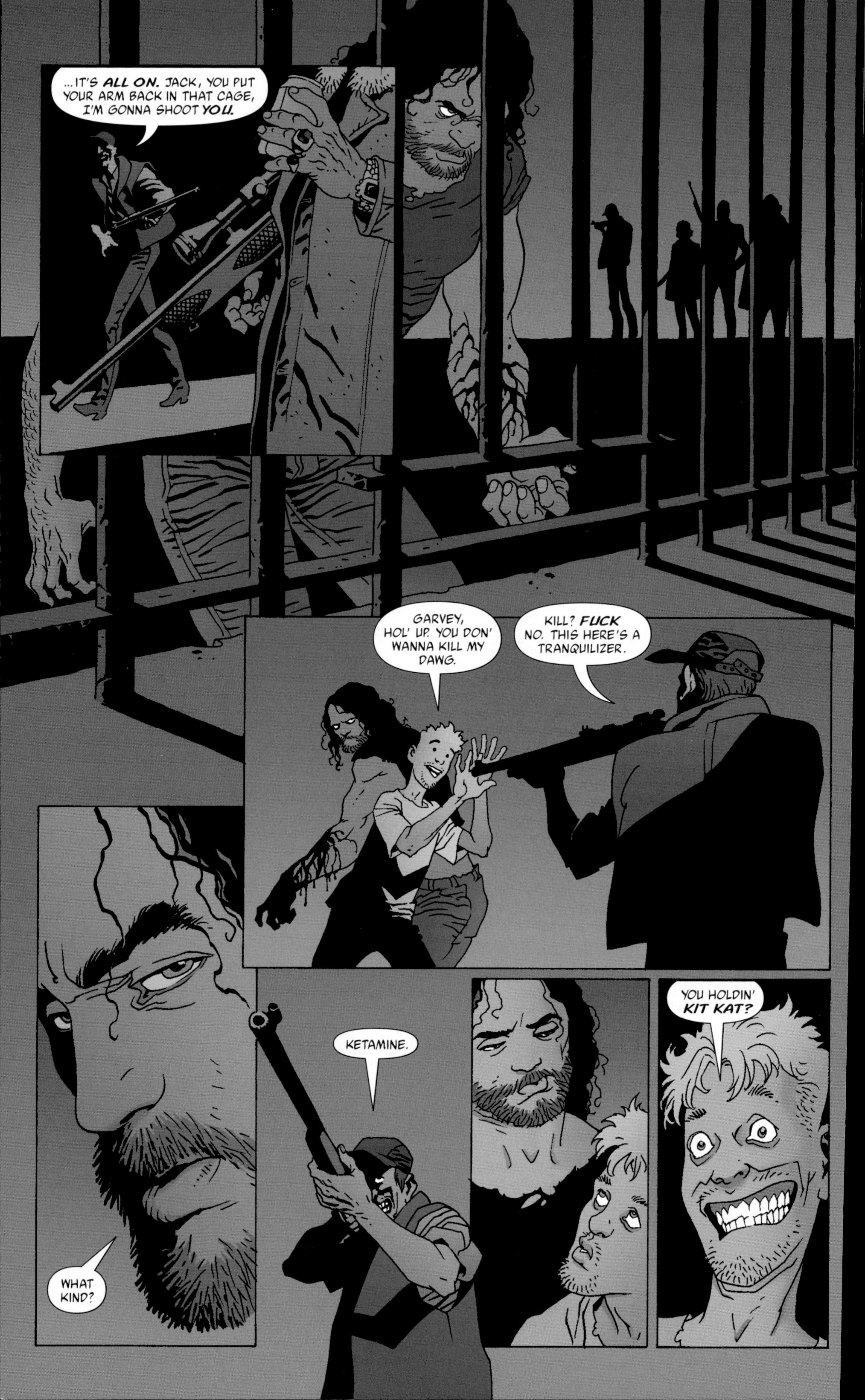
...IT'S ALL ON. JACK, YOU PUT YOUR ARM BACK IN THAT CAGE, I'M GONNA SHOOT YOU.
GARVEY, HOL' UP. YOU DON' WANNA KILL MY DAWG.
KILL? FUCK NO. THIS HERE'S A TRANQUILIZER.
WHAT KIND?
KETAMINE.
YOU HOLDIN' KIT KAT?

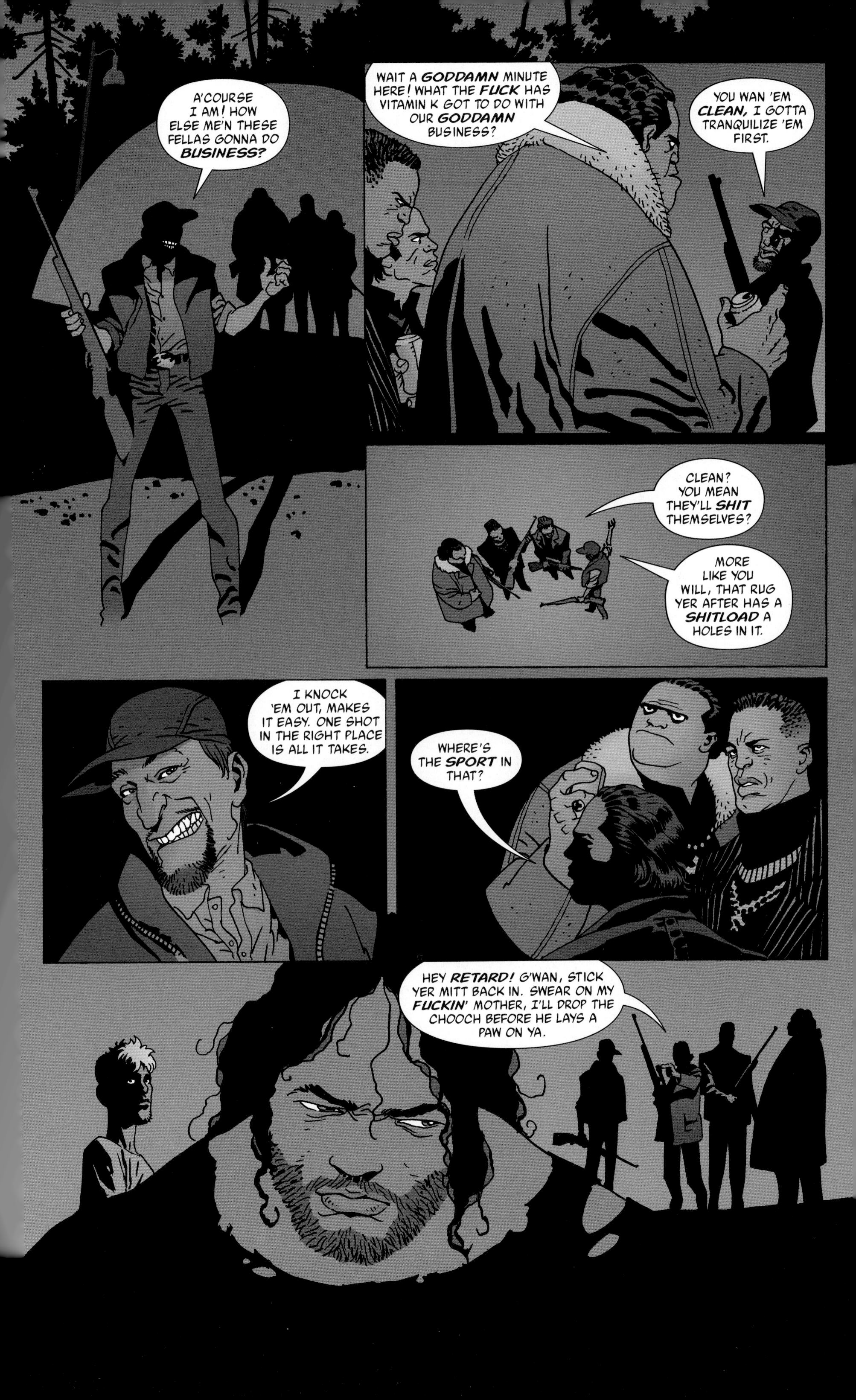
A'COURSE I AM! HOW ELSE ME'N THESE FELLAS GONNA DO BUSINESS?
WAIT A GODDAMN MINUTE HERE! WHAT THE FUCK HAS VITAMIN K GOT TO DO WITH OUR GODDAMN BUSINESS?
YOU WAN 'EM CLEAN, I GOTTA TRANQUILIZE 'EM FIRST.
CLEAN? YOU MEAN THEY'LL SHIT THEMSELVES?
MORE LIKE YOU WILL, THAT RUG YER AFTER HAS A SHITLOAD A HOLES IN IT.
I KNOCK 'EM OUT, MAKES IT EASY. ONE SHOT IN THE RIGHT PLACE IS ALL IT TAKES.
WHERE'S THE SPORT IN THAT?
HEY RETARD! G'WAN, STICK YER MITT BACK IN. SWEAR ON MY FUCKIN' MOTHER, I'LL DROP THE CHOOCH BEFORE HE LAYS A PAW ON YA.

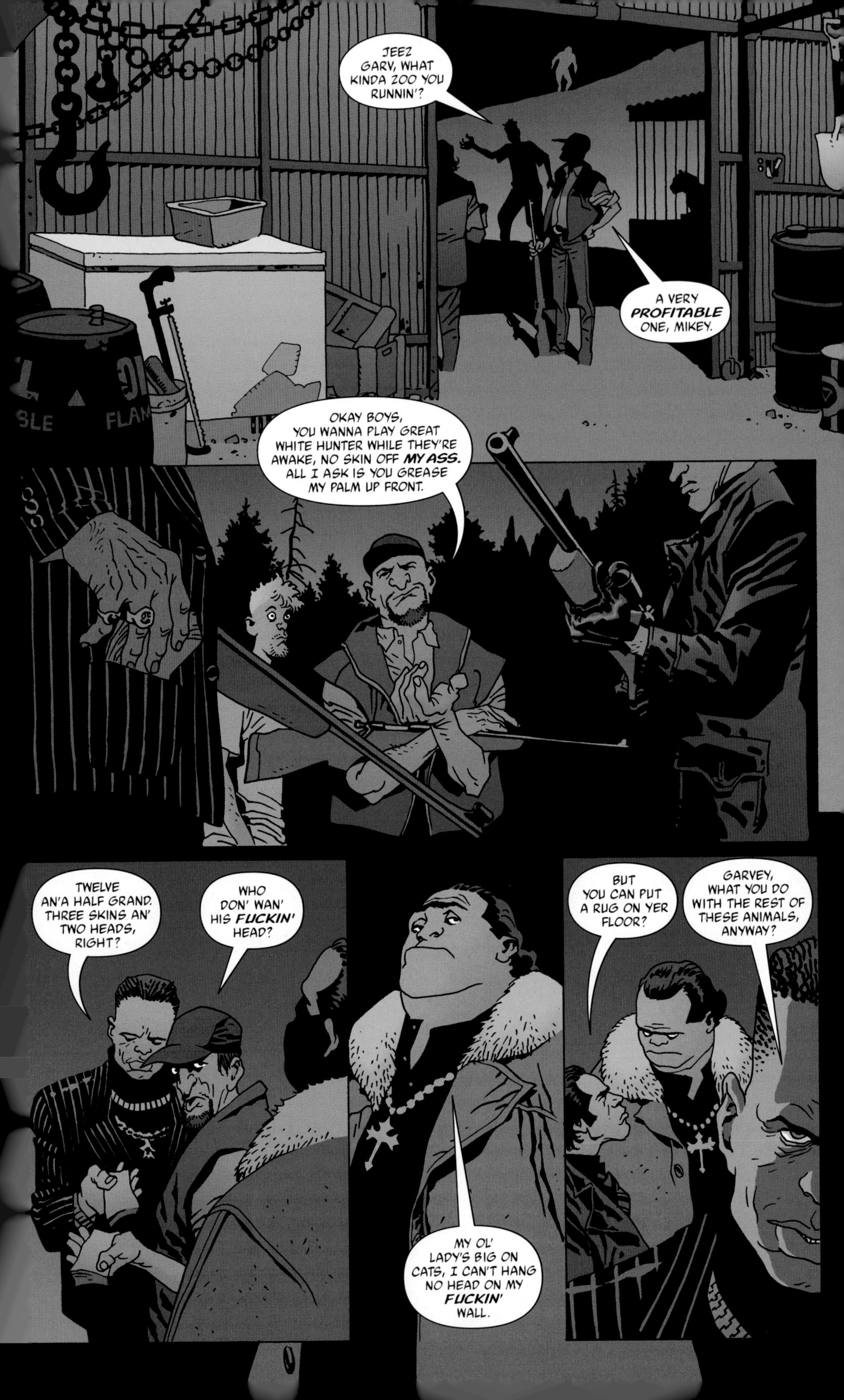
JEEZ GARV, WHAT KINDA ZOO YOU RUNNIN'?
A VERY PROFITABLE ONE, MIKEY.
OKAY BOYS, YOU WANNA PLAY GREAT WHITE HUNTER WHILE THEY'RE AWAKE, NO SKIN OFF MY ASS. ALL I ASK IS YOU GREASE MY PALM UP FRONT.
TWELVE AN'A HALF GRAND. THREE SKINS AN' TWO HEADS, RIGHT?
WHO DON' WAN' HIS FUCKIN' HEAD?
MY OL' LADY'S BIG ON CATS, I CAN'T HANG NO HEAD ON MY FUCKIN' WALL.
BUT YOU CAN PUT A RUG ON YER FLOOR?
GARVEY, WHAT YOU DO WITH THE REST OF THESE ANIMALS, ANYWAY?

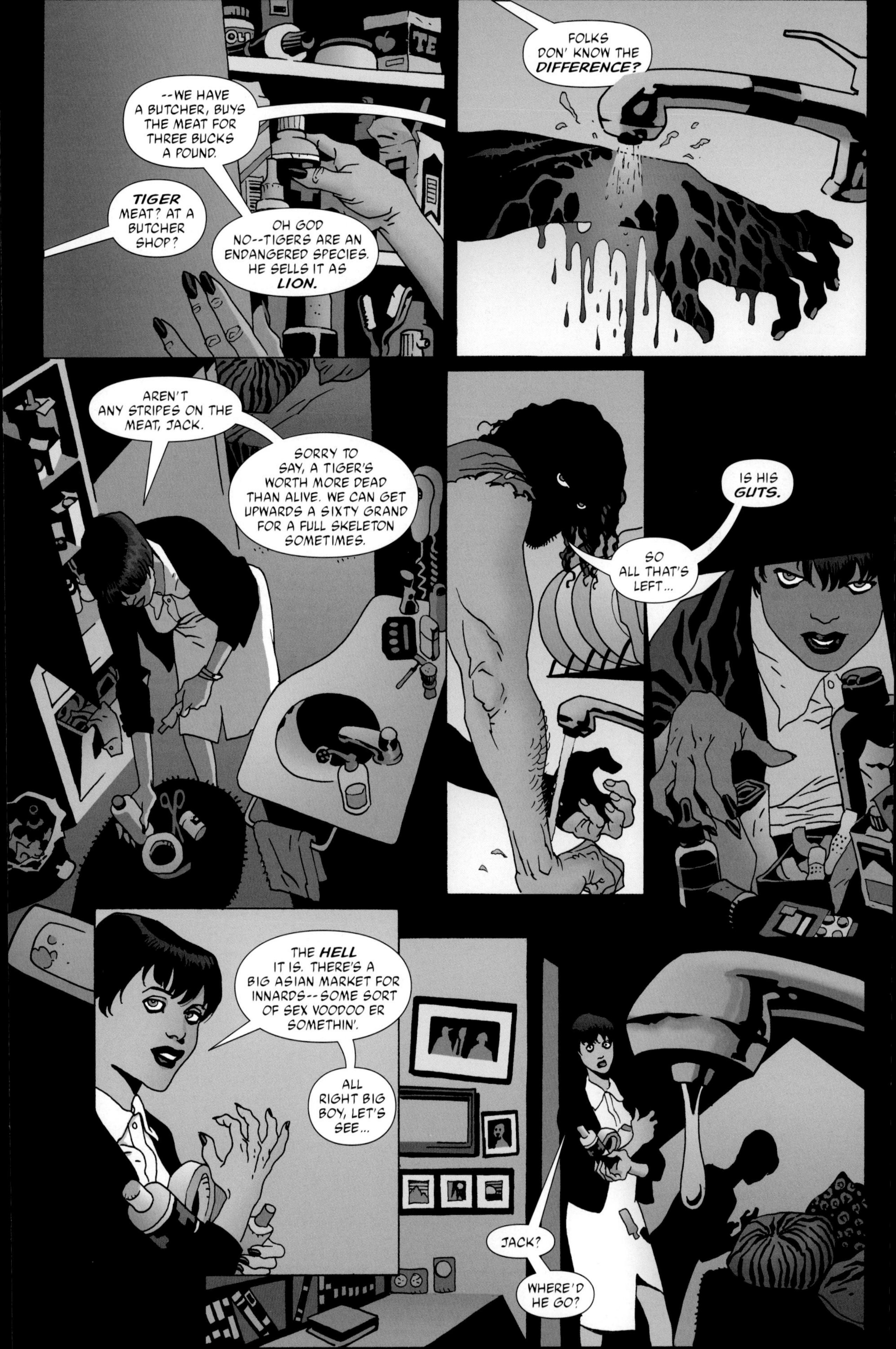
--WE HAVE A BUTCHER, BUYS THE MEAT FOR THREE BUCKS A POUND.
TIGER MEAT? AT A BUTCHER SHOP?
OH GOD NO--TIGERS ARE AN ENDANGERED SPECIES. HE SELLS IT AS LION.
FOLKS DON' KNOW THE DIFFERENCE?
AREN'T ANY STRIPES ON THE MEAT, JACK.
SORRY TO SAY, A TIGER'S WORTH MORE DEAD THAN ALIVE. WE CAN GET UPWARDS A SIXTY GRAND FOR A FULL SKELETON SOMETIMES.
SO ALL THAT'S LEFT...
IS HIS GUTS.
THE HELL IT IS. THERE'S A BIG ASIAN MARKET FOR INNARDS--SOME SORT OF SEX VOODOO ER SOMETHIN'.
ALL RIGHT BIG BOY, LET'S SEE...
JACK?
WHERE'D HE GO?

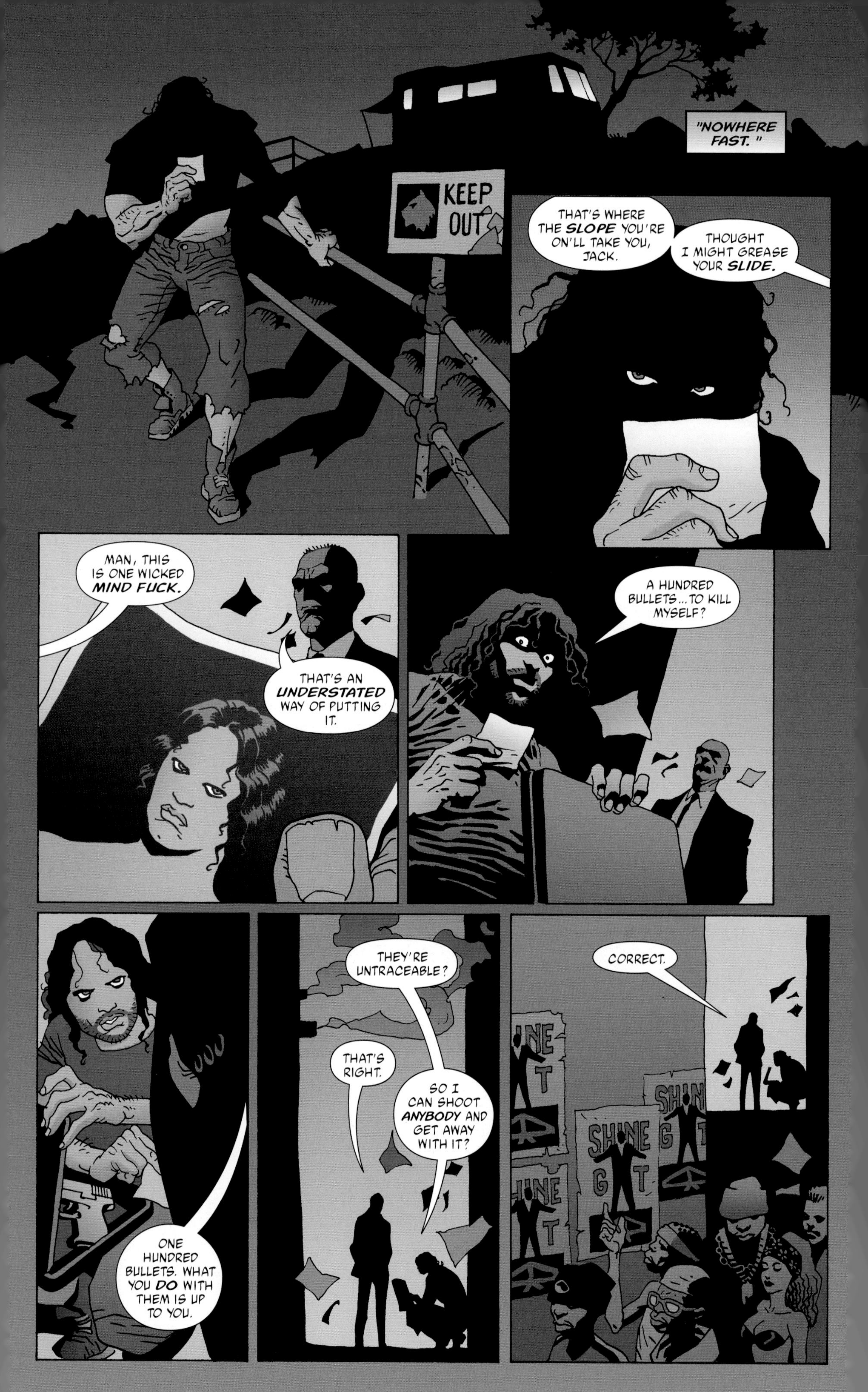
"NOWHERE FAST."
KEEP OUT
THAT'S WHERE THE SLOPE YOU'RE ON'LL TAKE YOU, JACK.
THOUGHT I MIGHT GREASE YOUR SLIDE.
MAN, THIS IS ONE WICKED MIND FUCK.
THAT'S AN UNDERSTATED WAY OF PUTTING IT.
A HUNDRED BULLETS...TO KILL MYSELF?
ONE HUNDRED BULLETS. WHAT YOU DO WITH THEM IS UP TO YOU.
THEY'RE UNTRACEABLE?
THAT'S RIGHT.
SO I CAN SHOOT ANYBODY AND GET AWAY WITH IT?
CORRECT.

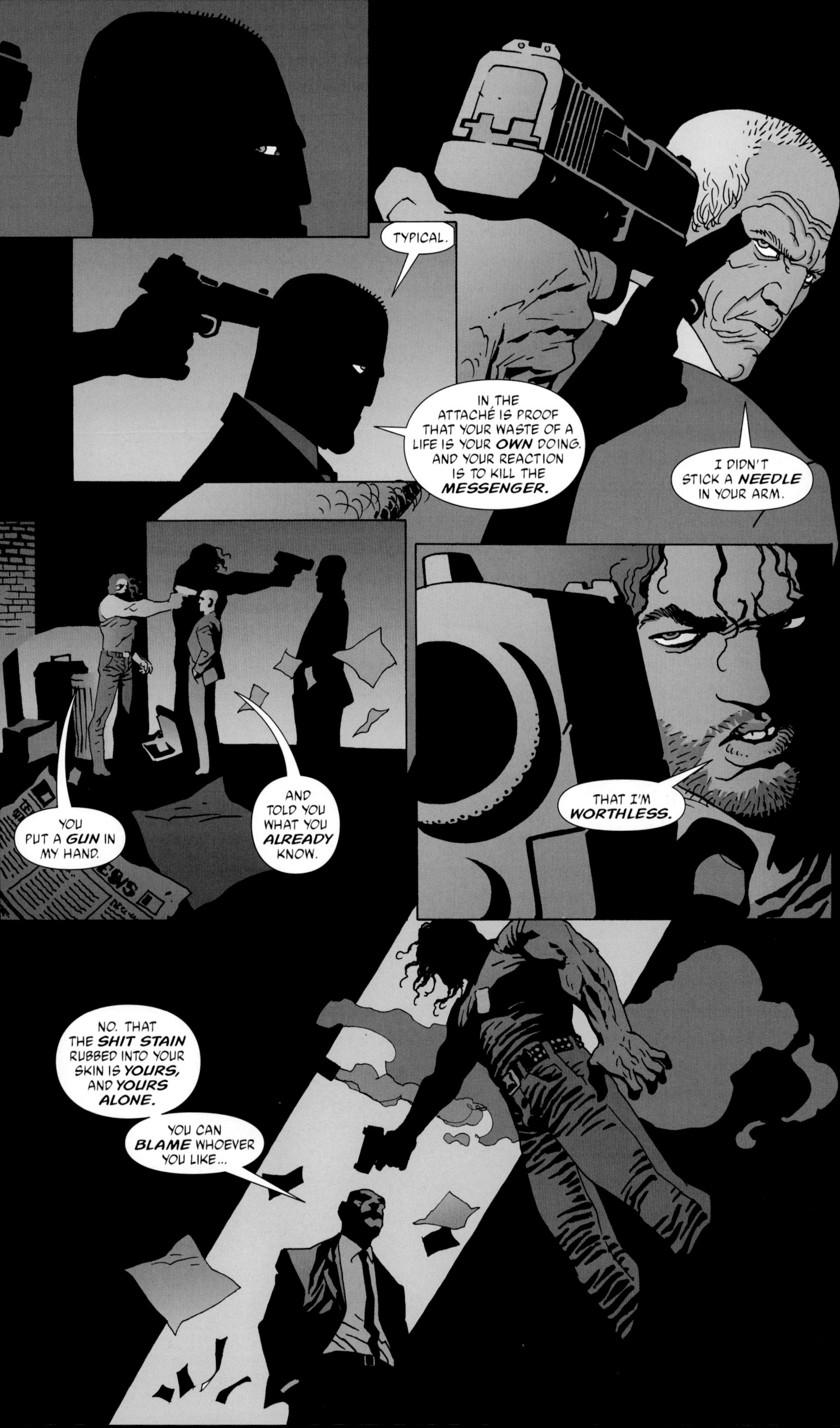
TYPICAL.
IN THE ATTACHÉ IS PROOF THAT YOUR WASTE OF A LIFE IS YOUR **OWN** DOING. AND YOUR REACTION IS TO KILL THE **MESSENGER.**
I DIDN'T STICK A **NEEDLE** IN YOUR ARM.
YOU PUT A **GUN** IN MY HAND.
AND TOLD YOU WHAT YOU **ALREADY** KNOW.
THAT I'M **WORTHLESS.**
NO. THAT THE **SHIT STAIN** RUBBED INTO YOUR SKIN IS **YOURS,** AND **YOURS ALONE.**
YOU CAN **BLAME** WHOEVER YOU LIKE...

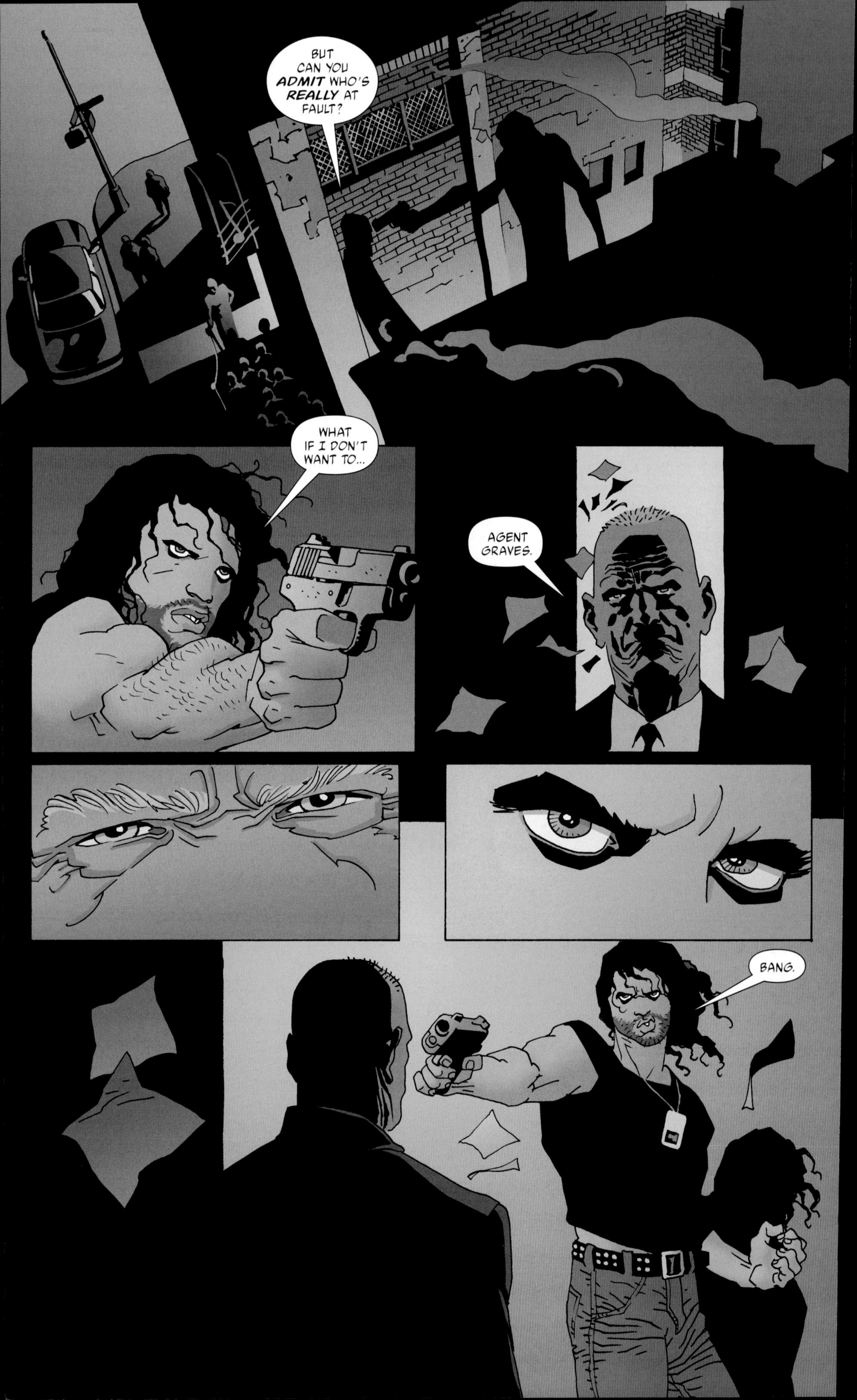
BUT CAN YOU ADMIT WHO'S REALLY AT FAULT?
WHAT IF I DON'T WANT TO...
AGENT GRAVES.
BANG.

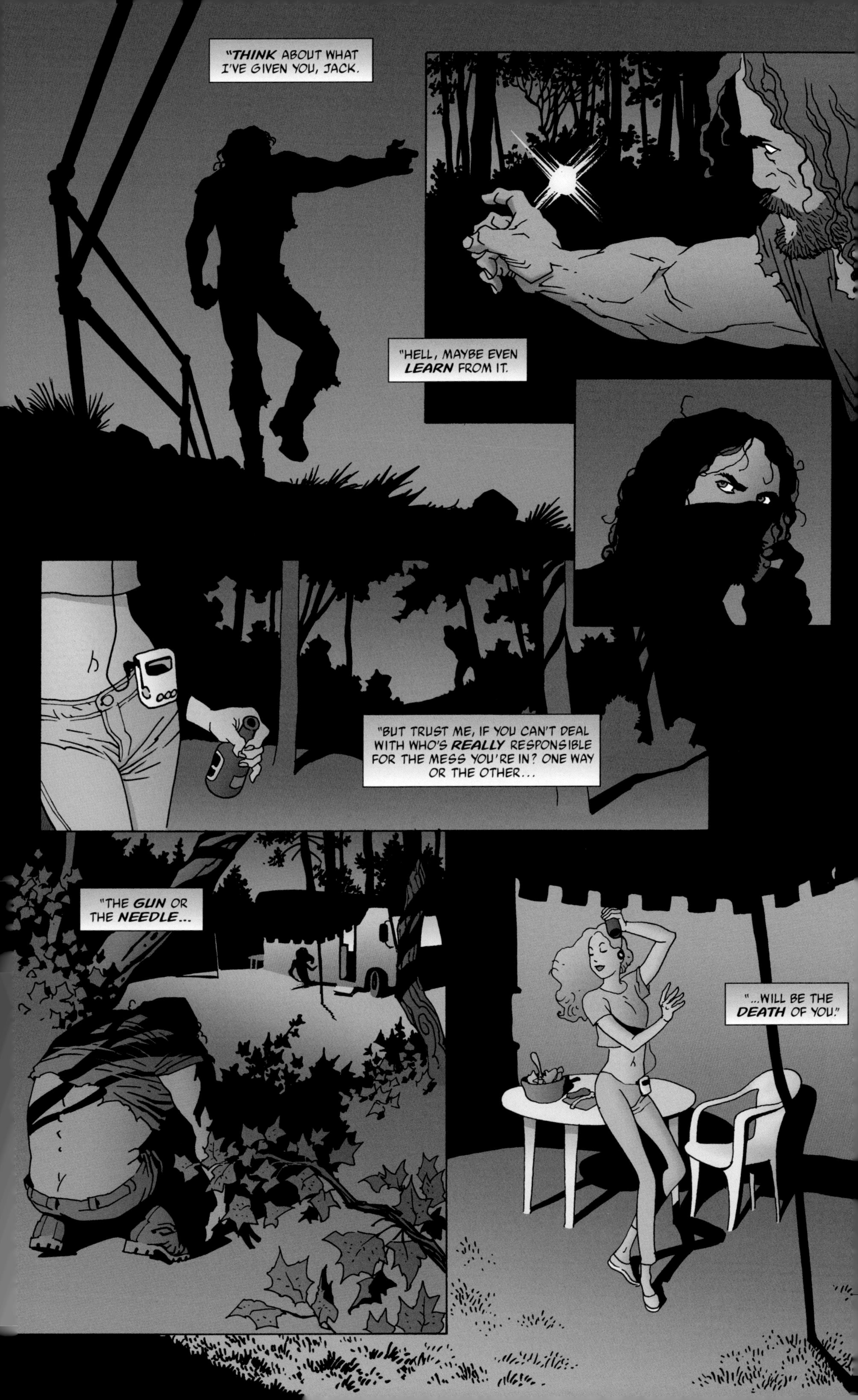
"THINK ABOUT WHAT I'VE GIVEN YOU, JACK.
"HELL, MAYBE EVEN LEARN FROM IT.
"BUT TRUST ME, IF YOU CAN'T DEAL WITH WHO'S REALLY RESPONSIBLE FOR THE MESS YOU'RE IN? ONE WAY OR THE OTHER...
"THE GUN OR THE NEEDLE...
"...WILL BE THE DEATH OF YOU."

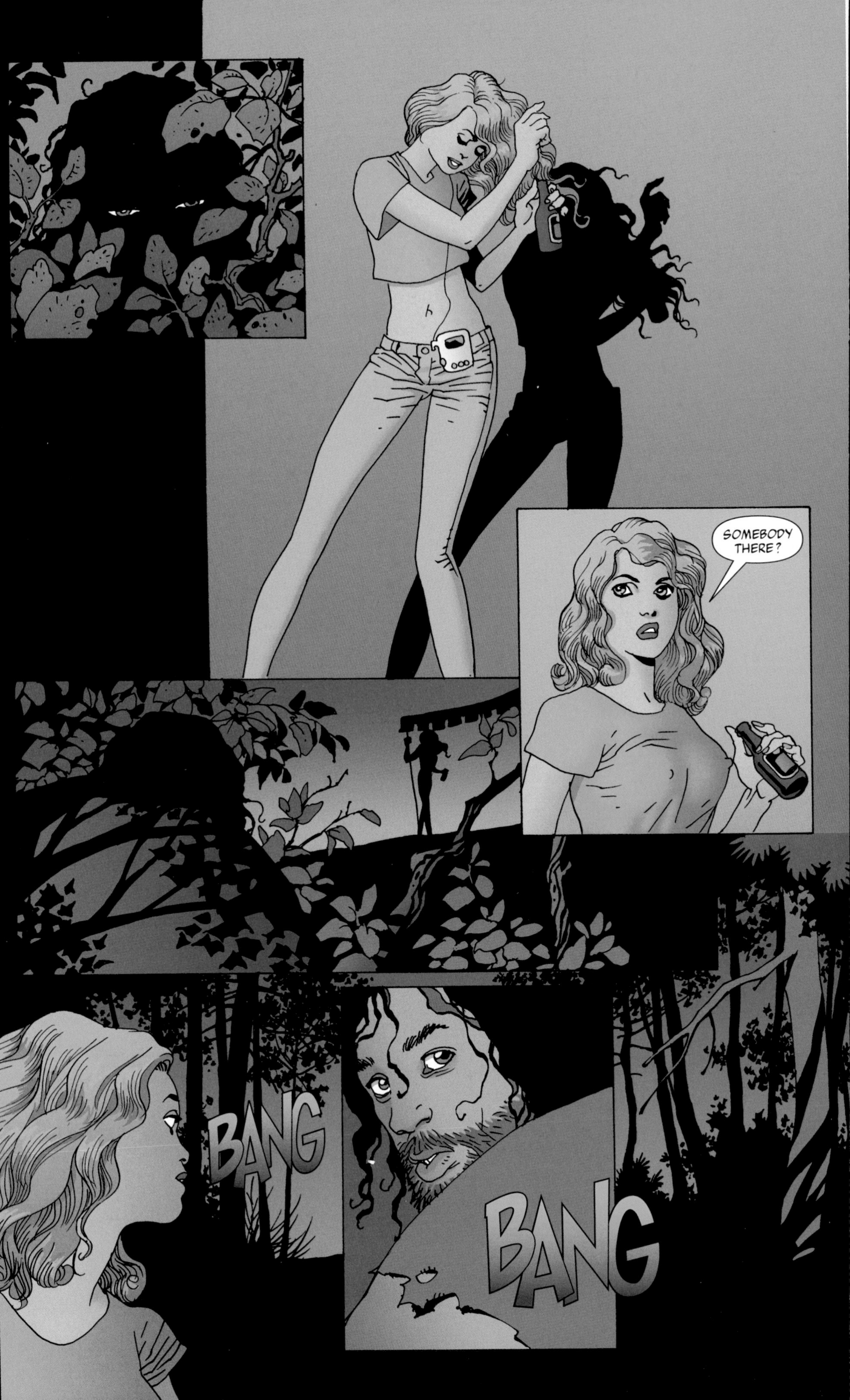
SOMEBODY THERE?
BANG
BANG

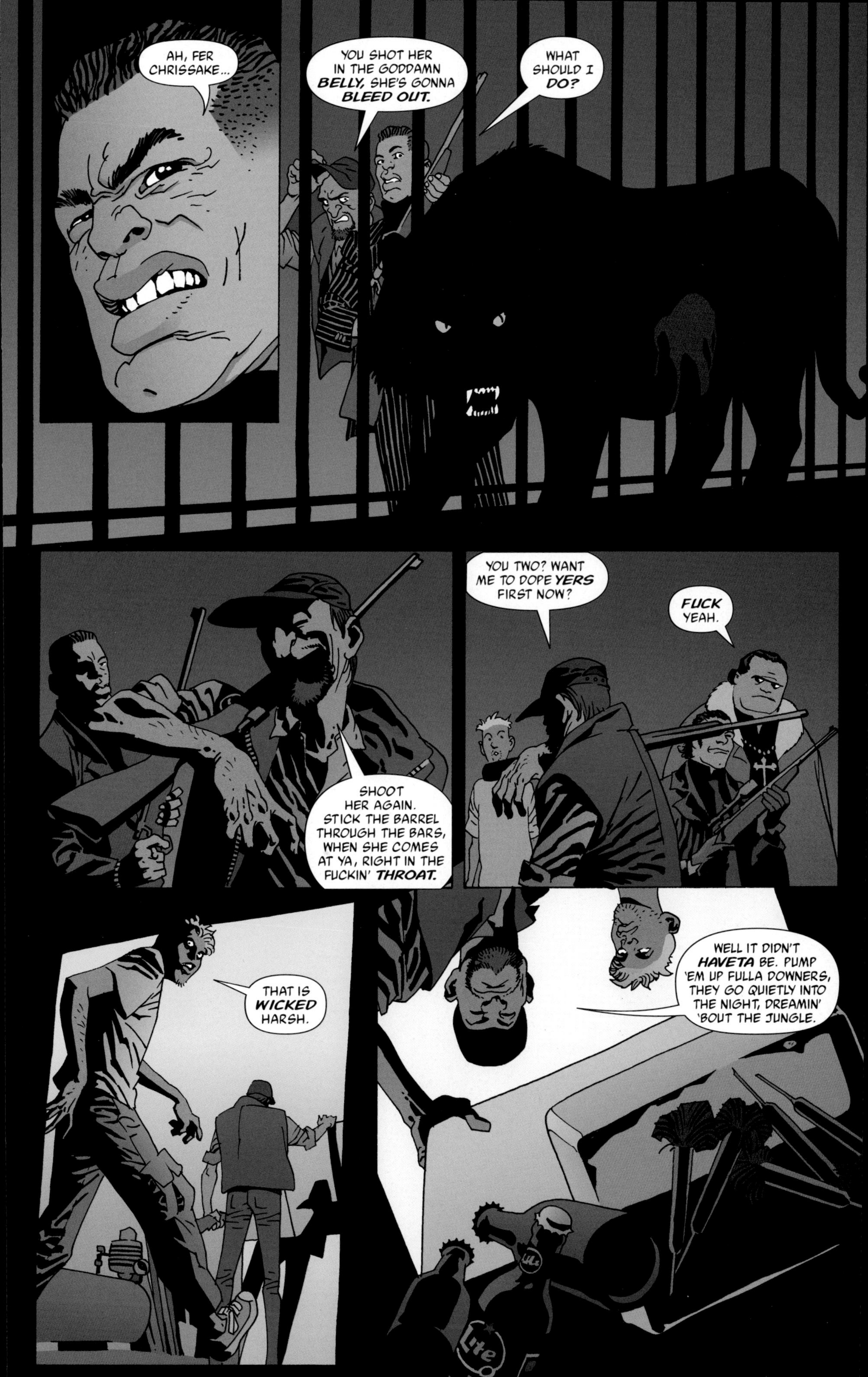
AH, FER CHRISSAKE...
YOU SHOT HER IN THE GODDAMN BELLY, SHE'S GONNA BLEED OUT.
WHAT SHOULD I DO?
SHOOT HER AGAIN. STICK THE BARREL THROUGH THE BARS, WHEN SHE COMES AT YA, RIGHT IN THE FUCKIN' THROAT.
YOU TWO? WANT ME TO DOPE YERS FIRST NOW?
FUCK YEAH.
THAT IS WICKED HARSH.
WELL IT DIDN'T HAVETA BE. PUMP 'EM UP FULLA DOWNERS, THEY GO QUIETLY INTO THE NIGHT, DREAMIN' 'BOUT THE JUNGLE.

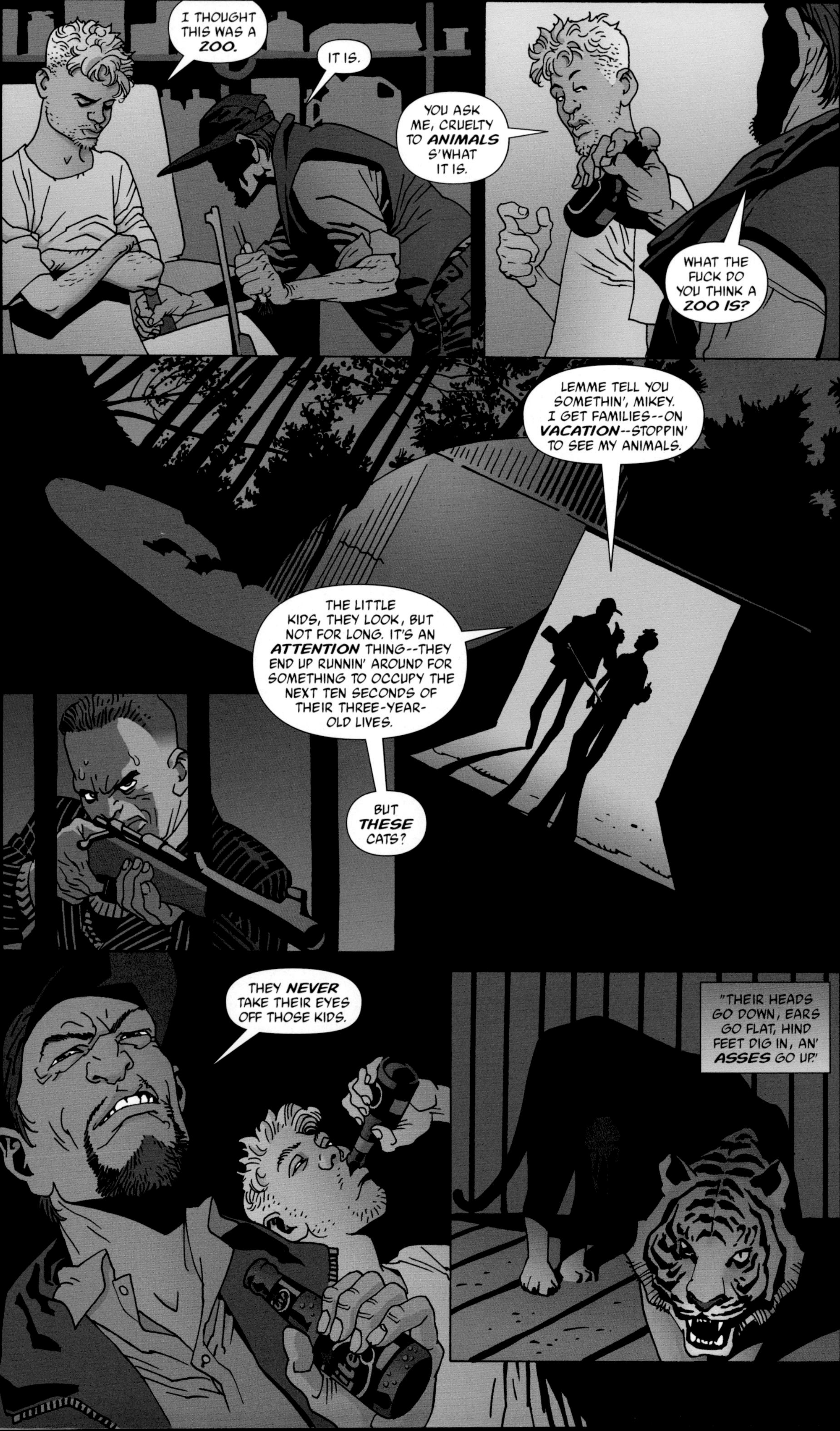

I THOUGHT THIS WAS A ZOO.
IT IS.
YOU ASK ME, CRUELTY TO ANIMALS S'WHAT IT IS.
WHAT THE FUCK DO YOU THINK A ZOO IS?
LEMME TELL YOU SOMETHIN', MIKEY. I GET FAMILIES--ON VACATION--STOPPIN' TO SEE MY ANIMALS.
THE LITTLE KIDS, THEY LOOK, BUT NOT FOR LONG. IT'S AN ATTENTION THING--THEY END UP RUNNIN' AROUND FOR SOMETHING TO OCCUPY THE NEXT TEN SECONDS OF THEIR THREE-YEAR-OLD LIVES.
BUT THESE CATS?
THEY NEVER TAKE THEIR EYES OFF THOSE KIDS.
"THEIR HEADS GO DOWN, EARS GO FLAT, HIND FEET DIG IN, AN' ASSES GO UP."

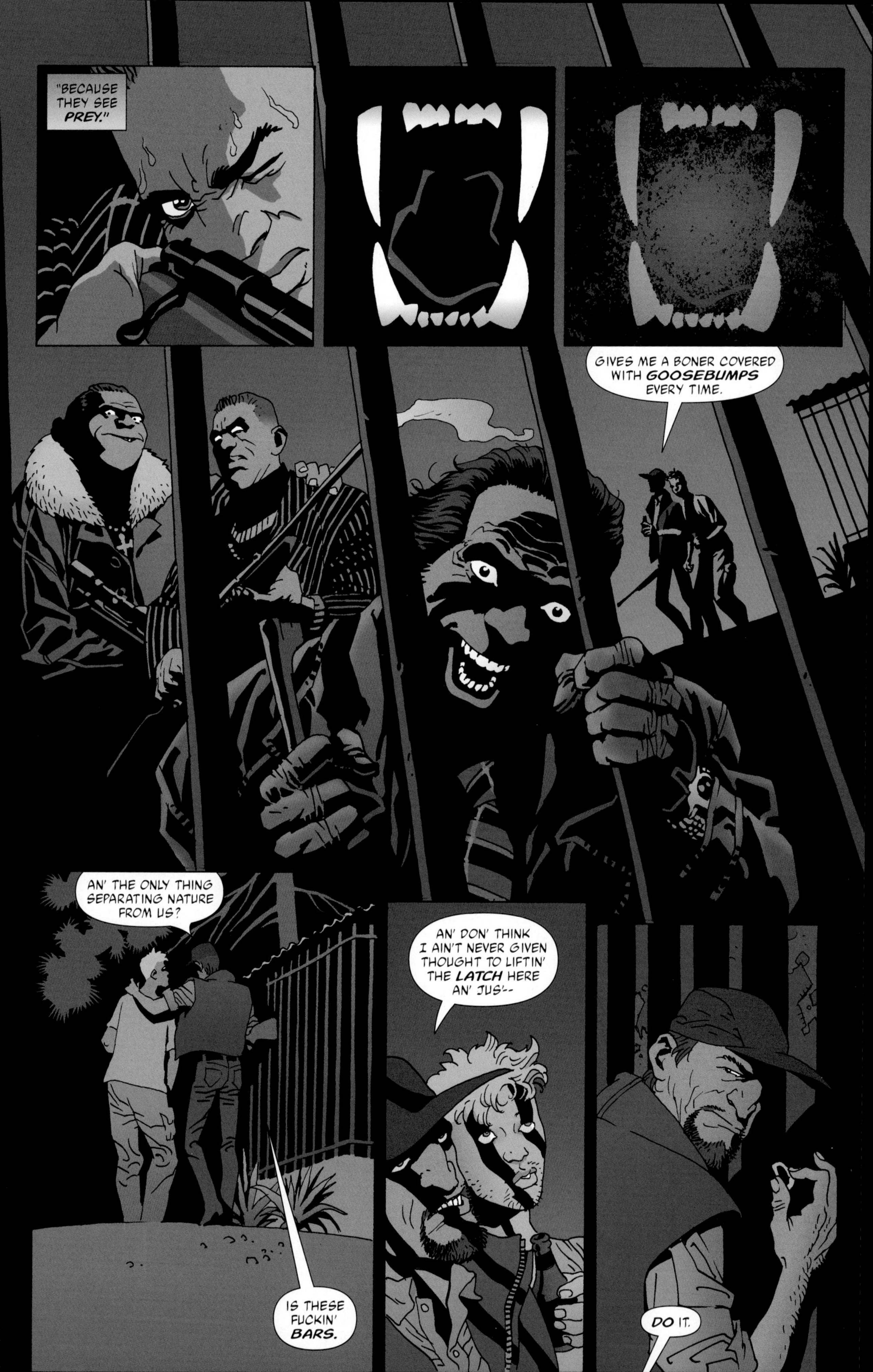
"BECAUSE THEY SEE PREY."
GIVES ME A BONER COVERED WITH GOOSEBUMPS EVERY TIME.
AN' THE ONLY THING SEPARATING NATURE FROM US?
IS THESE FUCKIN' BARS.
AN' DON' THINK I AIN'T NEVER GIVEN THOUGHT TO LIFTIN' THE LATCH HERE AN' JUS'--
DO IT.

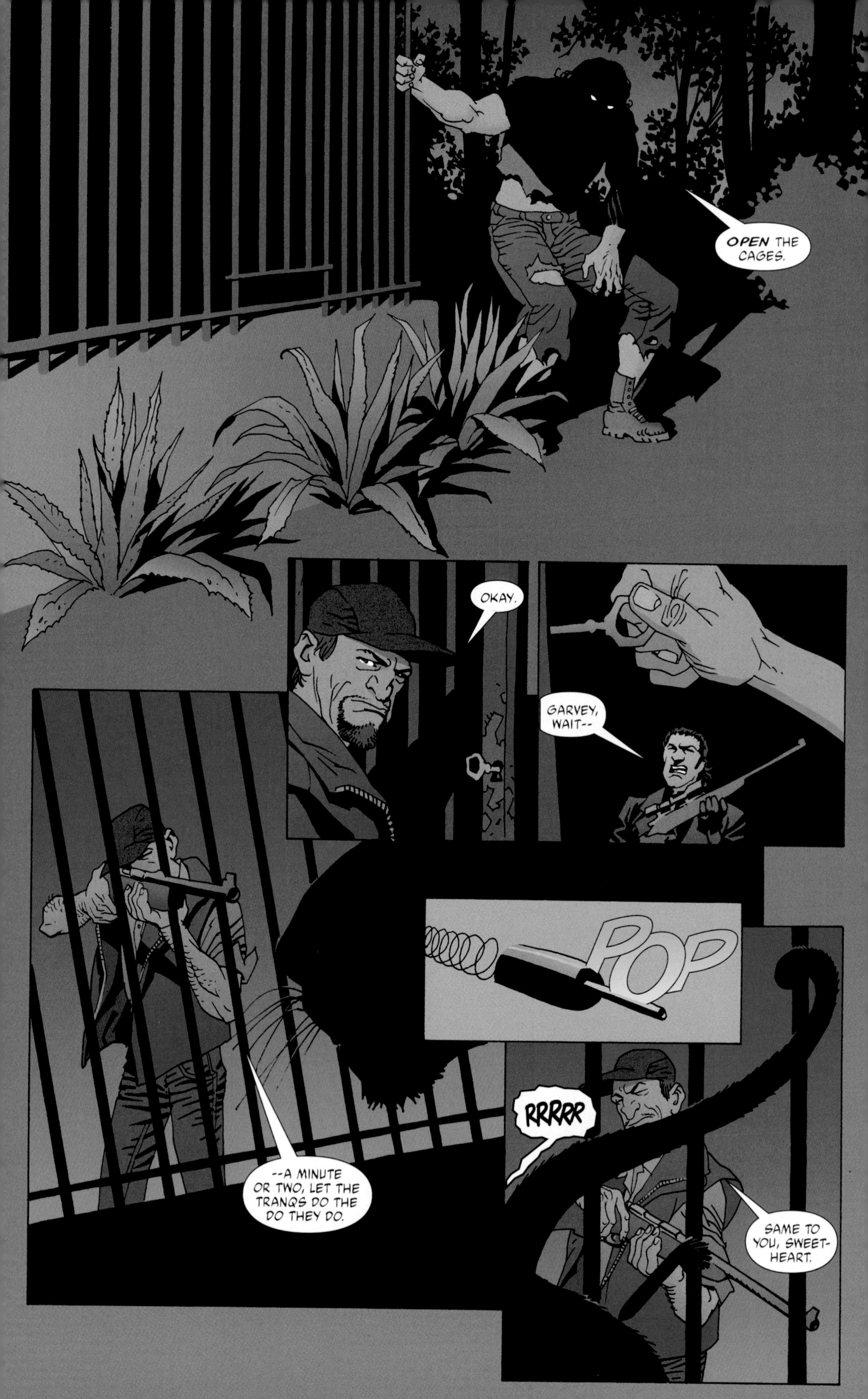
OPEN THE CAGES.
OKAY.
GARVEY, WAIT--
--A MINUTE OR TWO, LET THE TRANQS DO THE DO THEY DO.
POP
RRRRR
SAME TO YOU, SWEET-HEART.

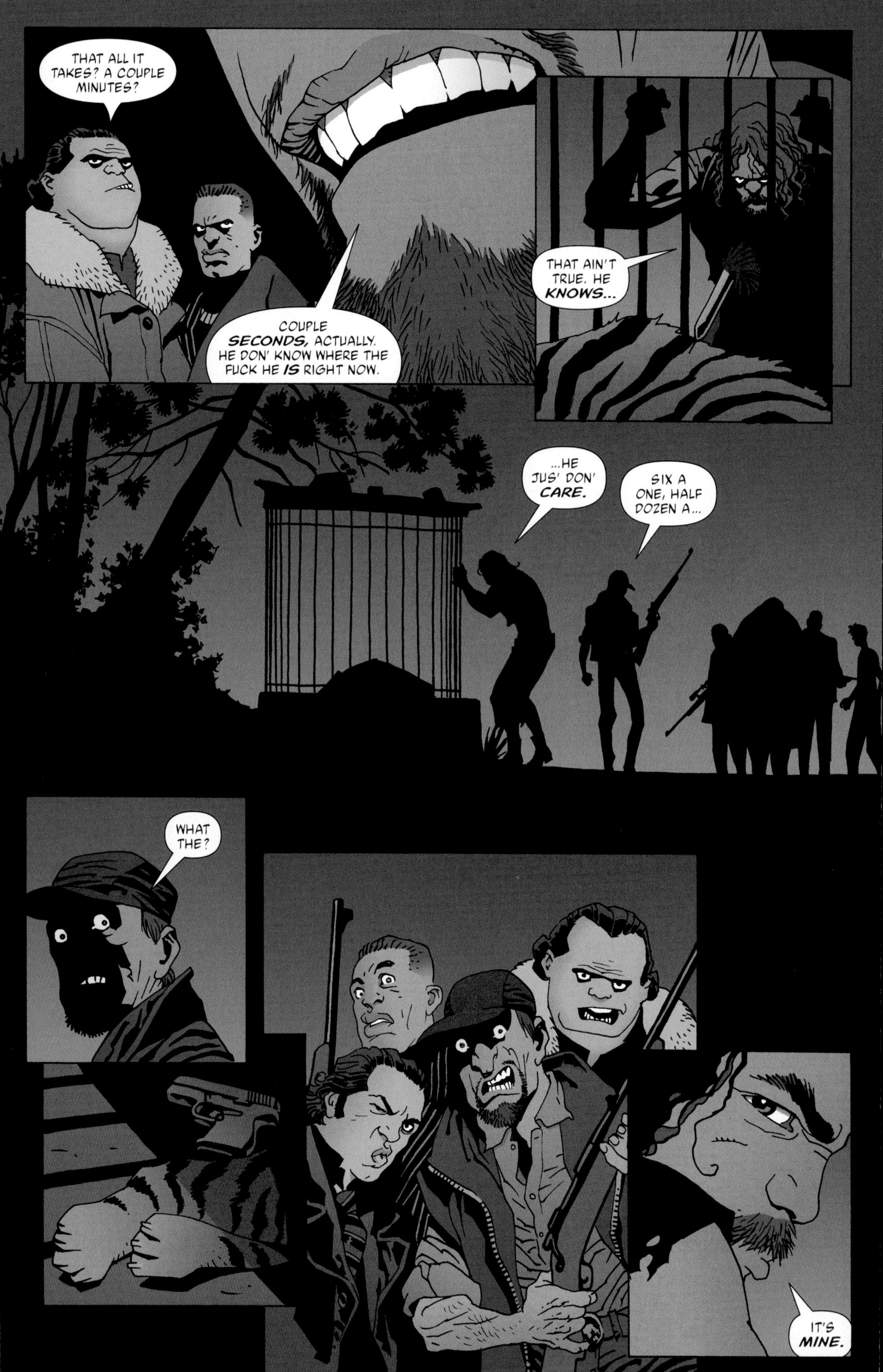

THAT ALL IT TAKES? A COUPLE MINUTES?
COUPLE **SECONDS,** ACTUALLY. HE DON' KNOW WHERE THE FUCK HE ***IS*** RIGHT NOW.
THAT AIN'T TRUE. HE ***KNOWS...***
...HE JUS' DON' ***CARE.***
SIX A ONE, HALF DOZEN A...
WHAT THE?
IT'S ***MINE.***

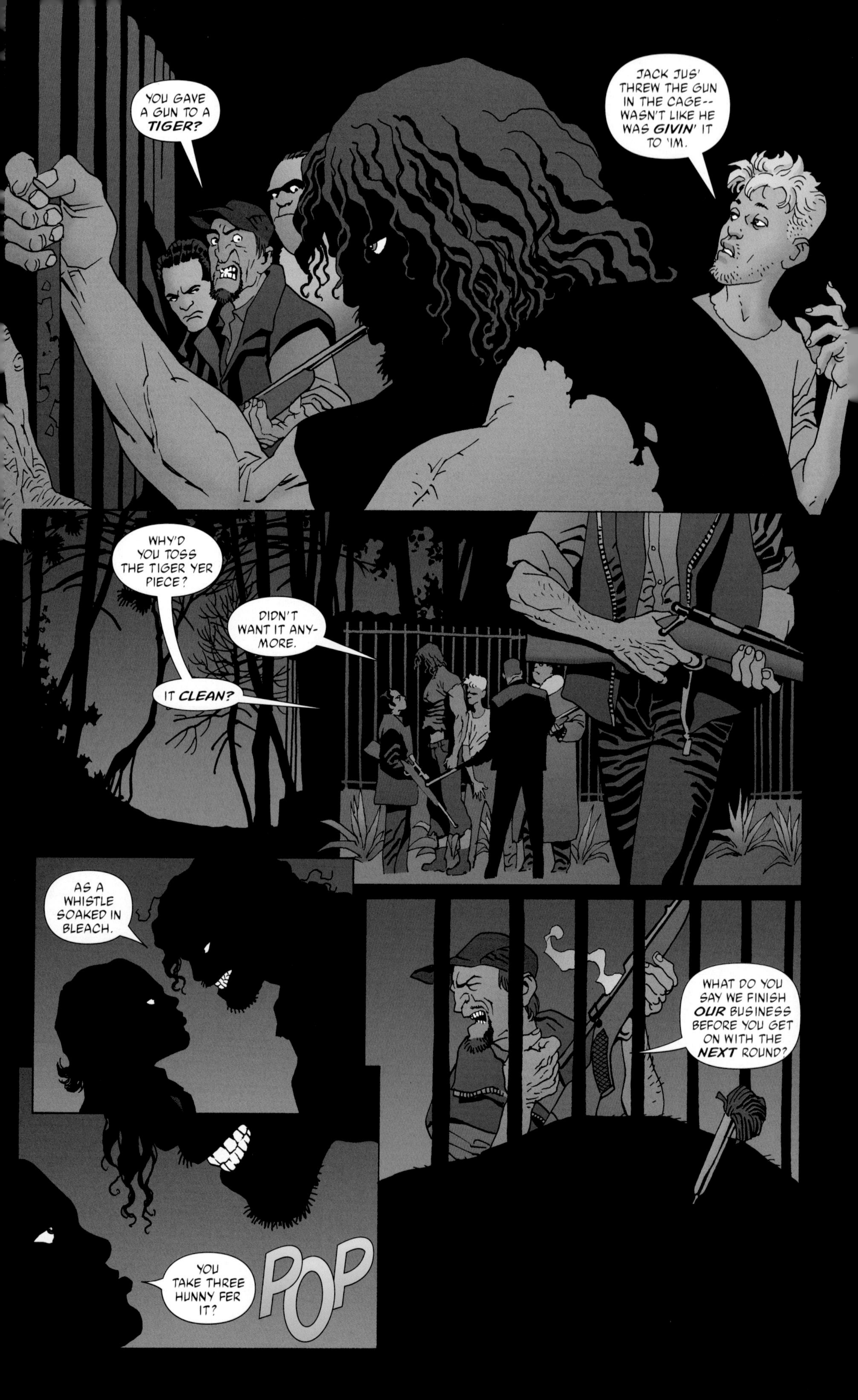
YOU GAVE A GUN TO A TIGER?
JACK JUS' THREW THE GUN IN THE CAGE-- WASN'T LIKE HE WAS GIVIN' IT TO 'IM.
WHY'D YOU TOSS THE TIGER YER PIECE?
DIDN'T WANT IT ANY-MORE.
IT CLEAN?
AS A WHISTLE SOAKED IN BLEACH.
WHAT DO YOU SAY WE FINISH OUR BUSINESS BEFORE YOU GET ON WITH THE NEXT ROUND?
YOU TAKE THREE HUNNY FER IT?
POP

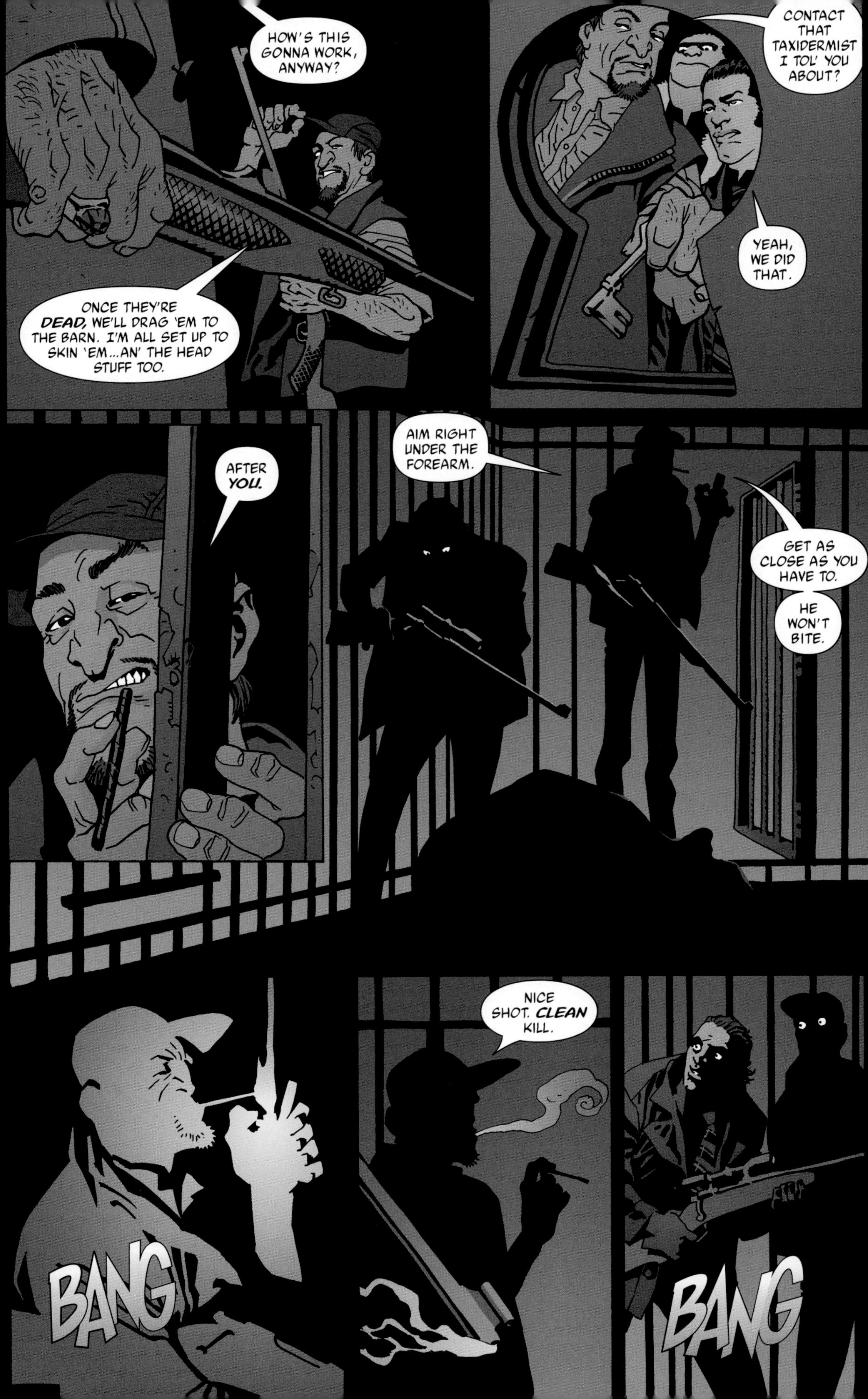
HOW'S THIS GONNA WORK, ANYWAY?
ONCE THEY'RE DEAD, WE'LL DRAG 'EM TO THE BARN. I'M ALL SET UP TO SKIN 'EM...AN' THE HEAD STUFF TOO.
CONTACT THAT TAXIDERMIST I TOL' YOU ABOUT?
YEAH, WE DID THAT.
AFTER YOU.
AIM RIGHT UNDER THE FOREARM.
GET AS CLOSE AS YOU HAVE TO.
HE WON'T BITE.
BANG
NICE SHOT. CLEAN KILL.
BANG

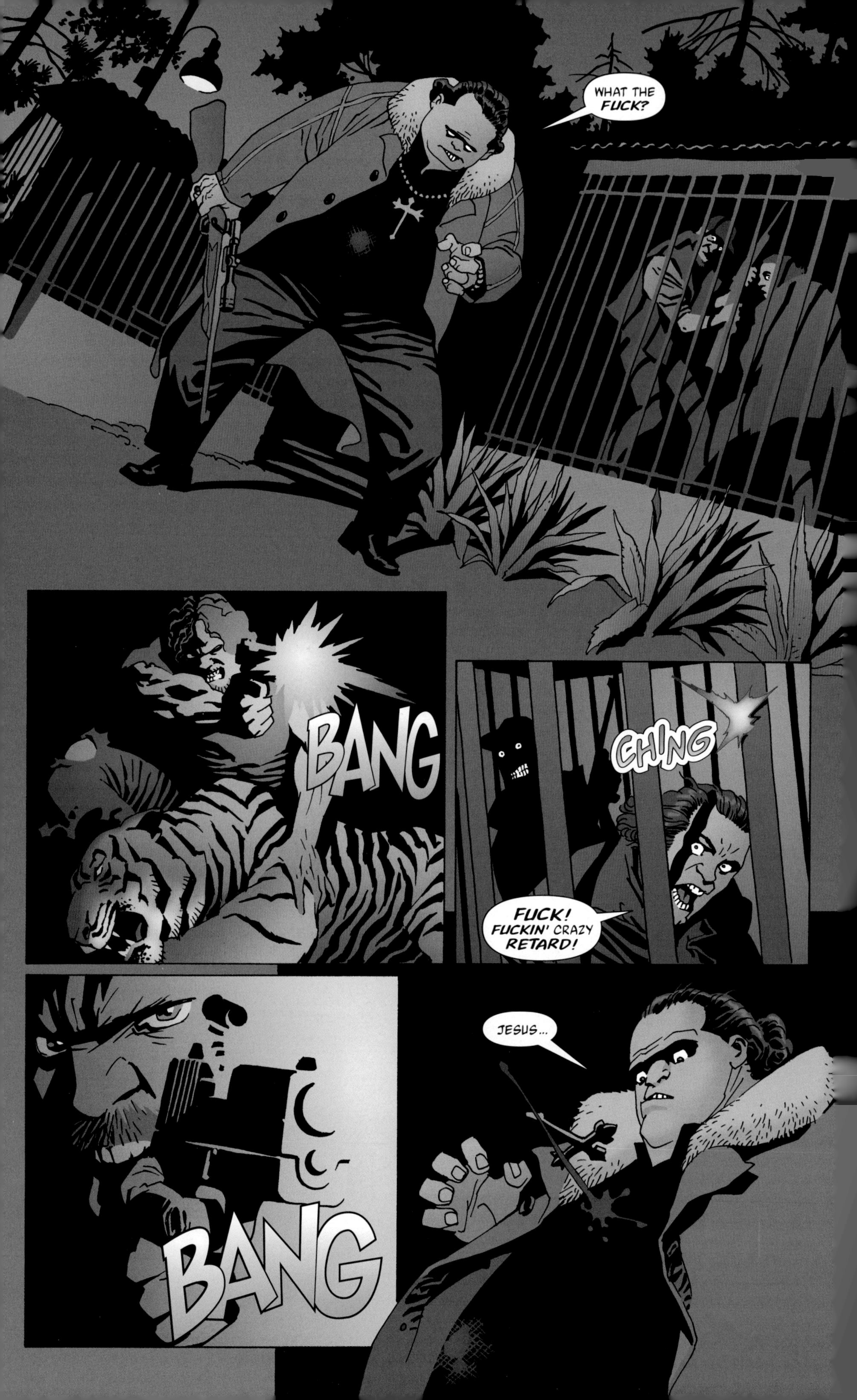
WHAT THE FUCK?
BANG
CHING
FUCK! FUCKIN' CRAZY RETARD!
BANG
JESUS...

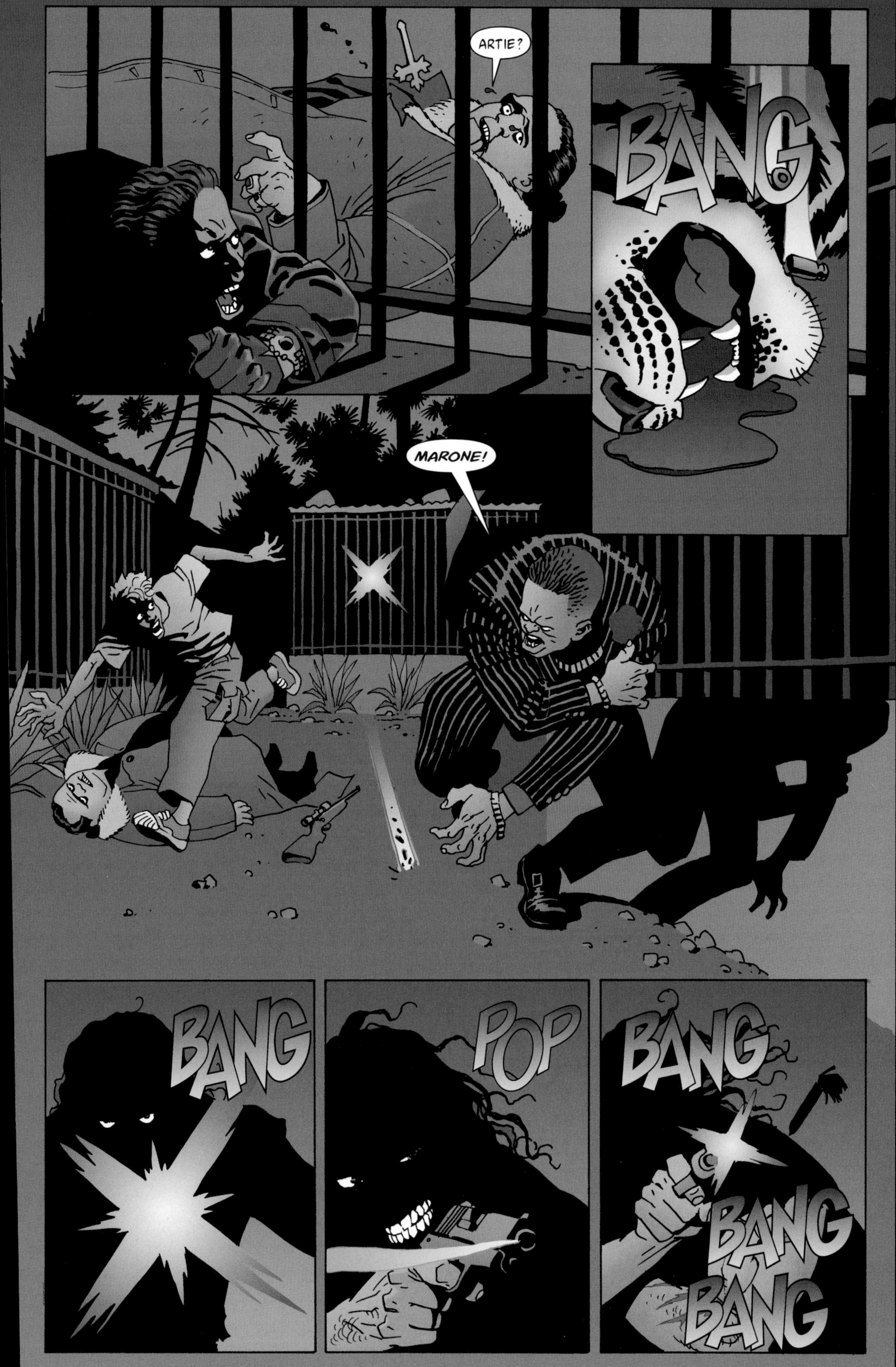
ARTIE?
BANG
MARONE!
BANG
POP
BANG
BANG
BANG

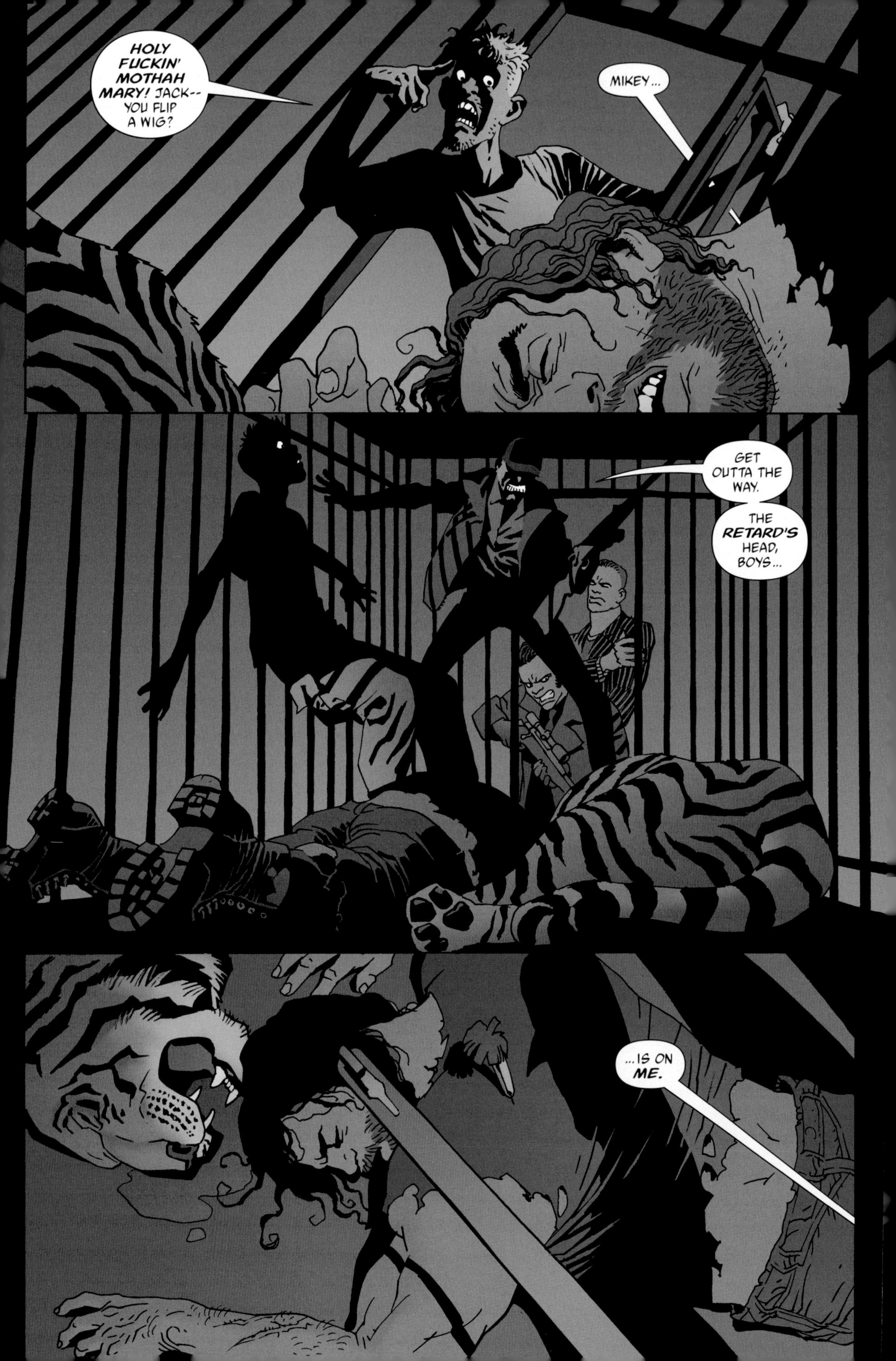
HOLY FUCKIN' MOTHAH MARY! JACK-- YOU FLIP A WIG?
MIKEY...
GET OUTTA THE WAY.
THE RETARD'S HEAD, BOYS...
...IS ON ME.

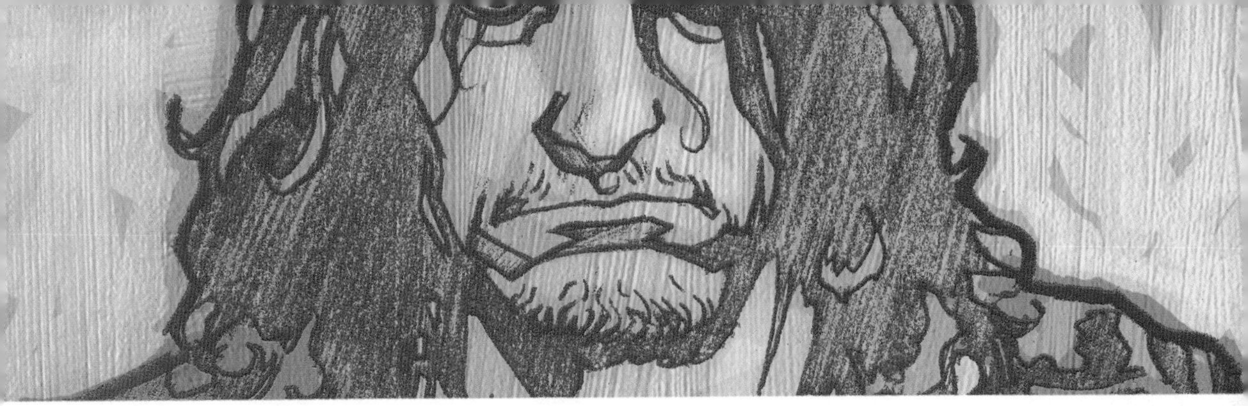

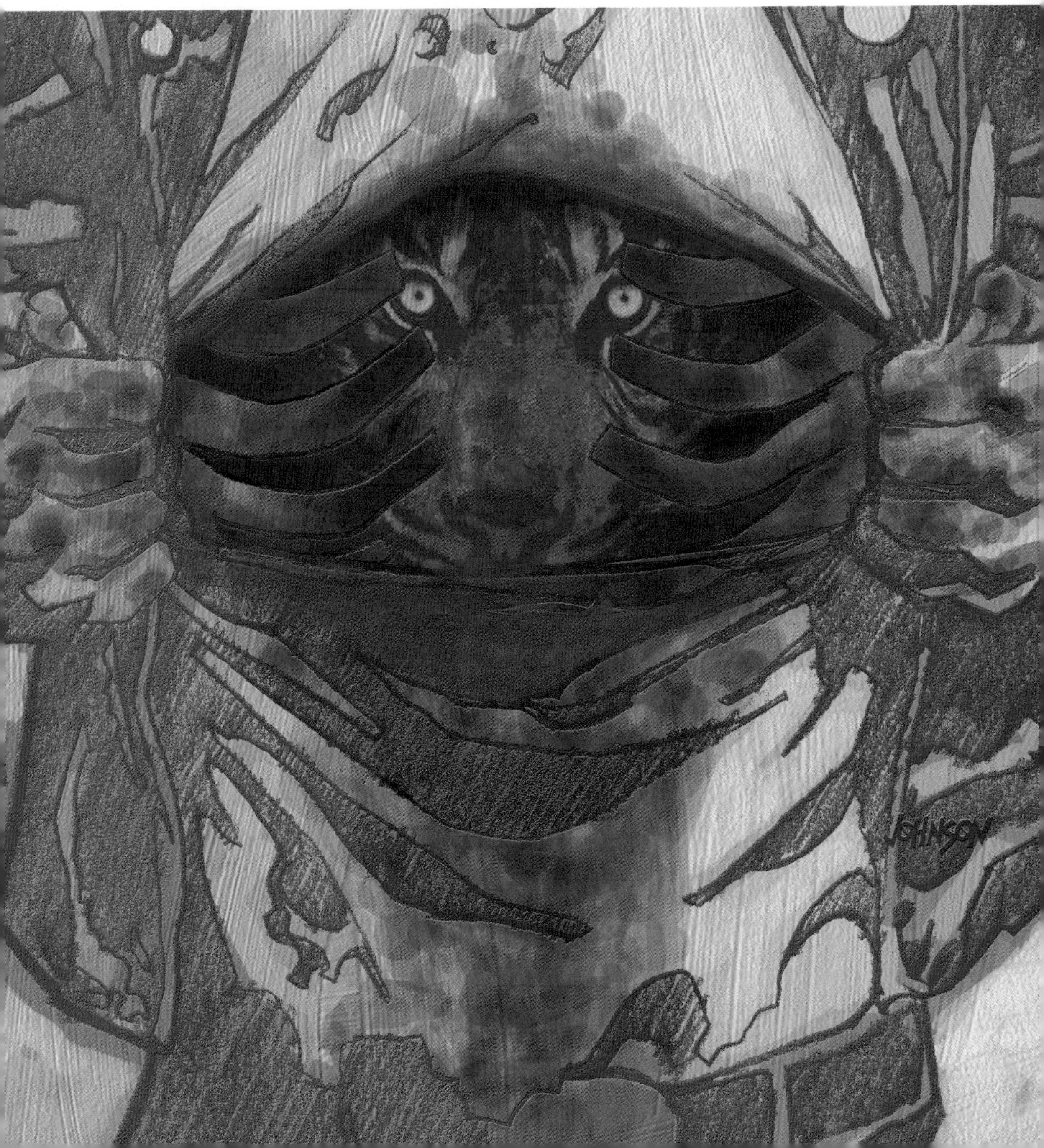
JOHNSON

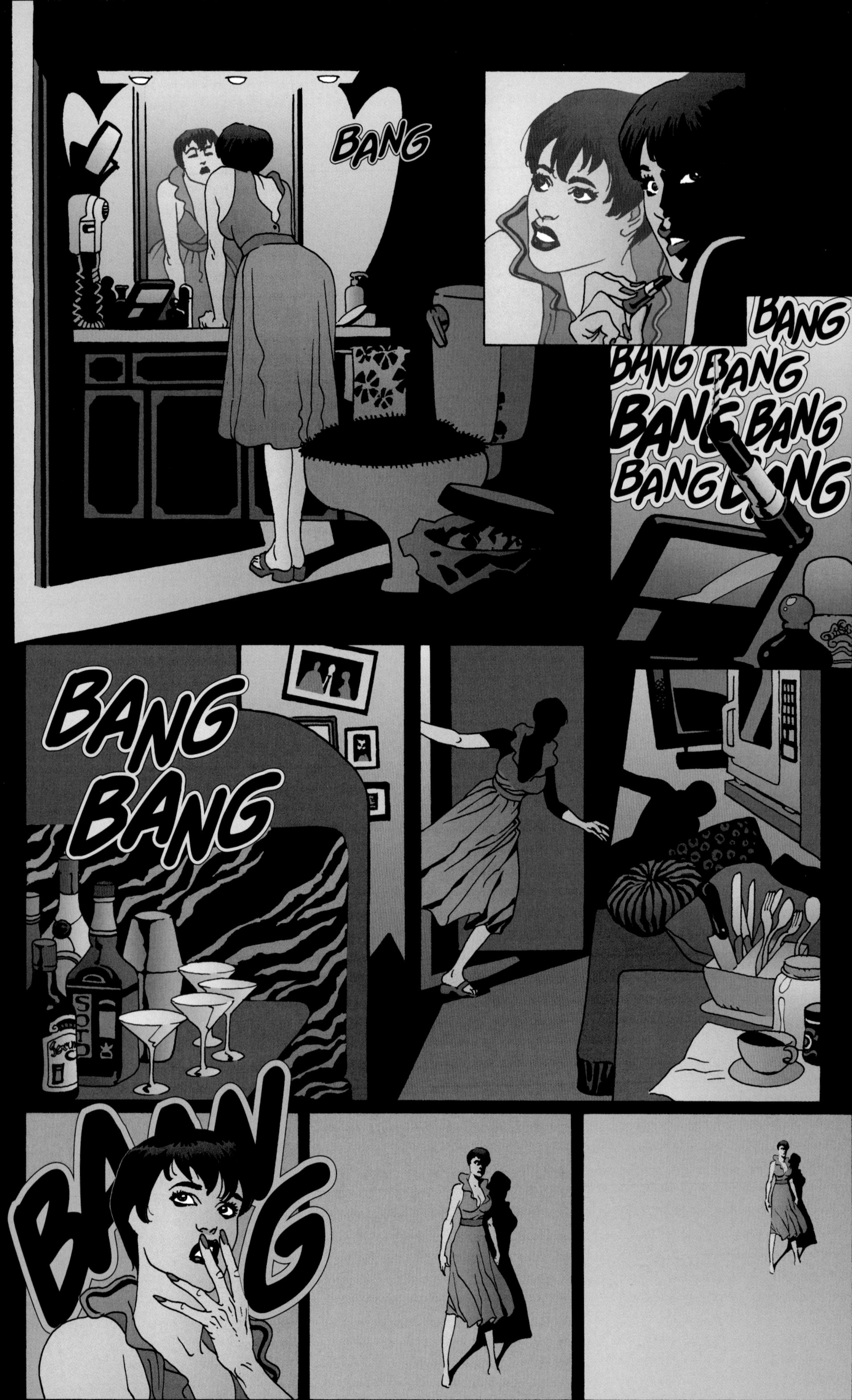
BANG
BANG
BANG BANG
BANG BANG
BANG BANG
BANG
BANG

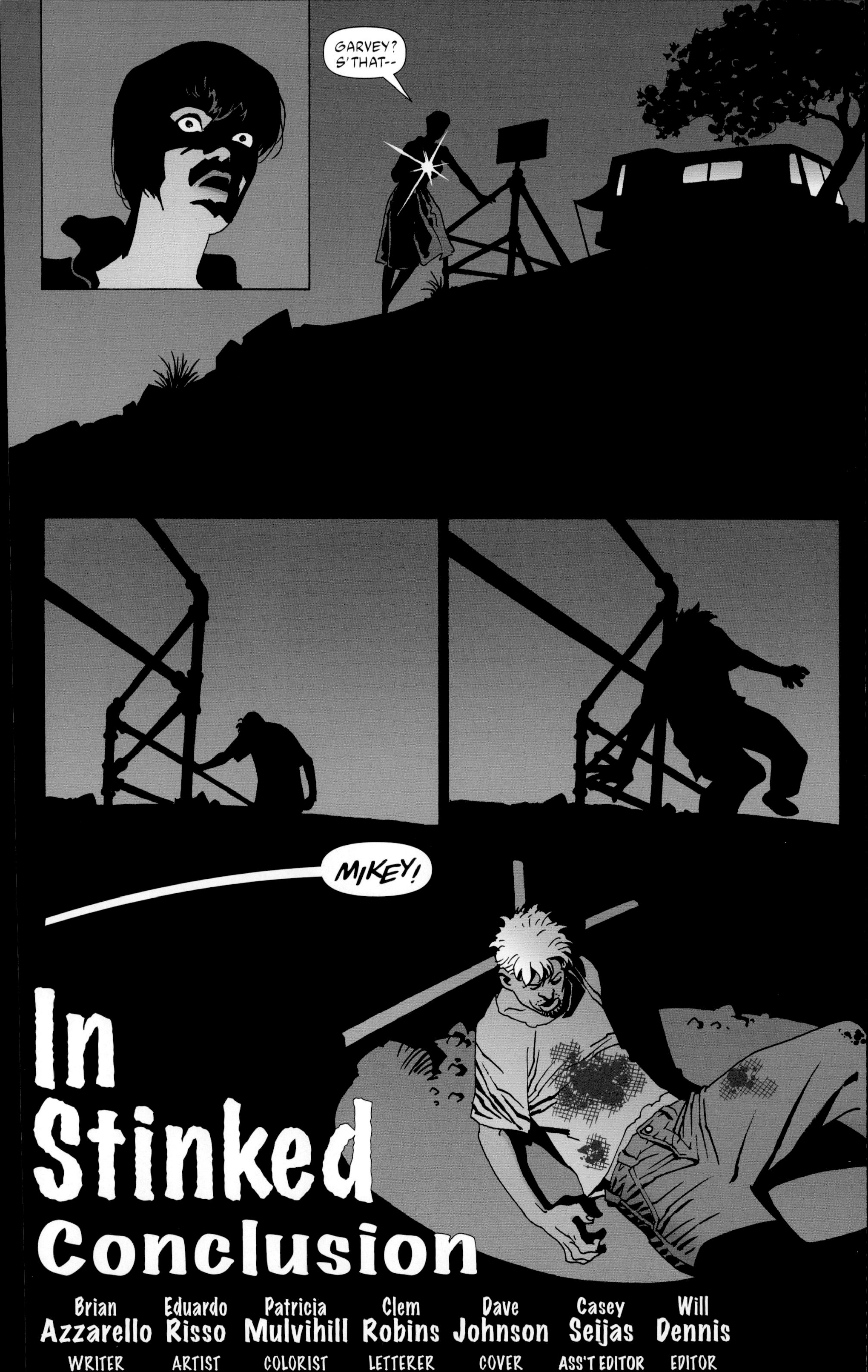

GARVEY? S'THAT--
MIKEY!
In Stinked
Conclusion
Brian Azzarello WRITER
Eduardo Risso ARTIST
Patricia Mulvihill COLORIST
Clem Robins LETTERER
Dave Johnson COVER
Casey Seijas ASS'T EDITOR
Will Dennis EDITOR

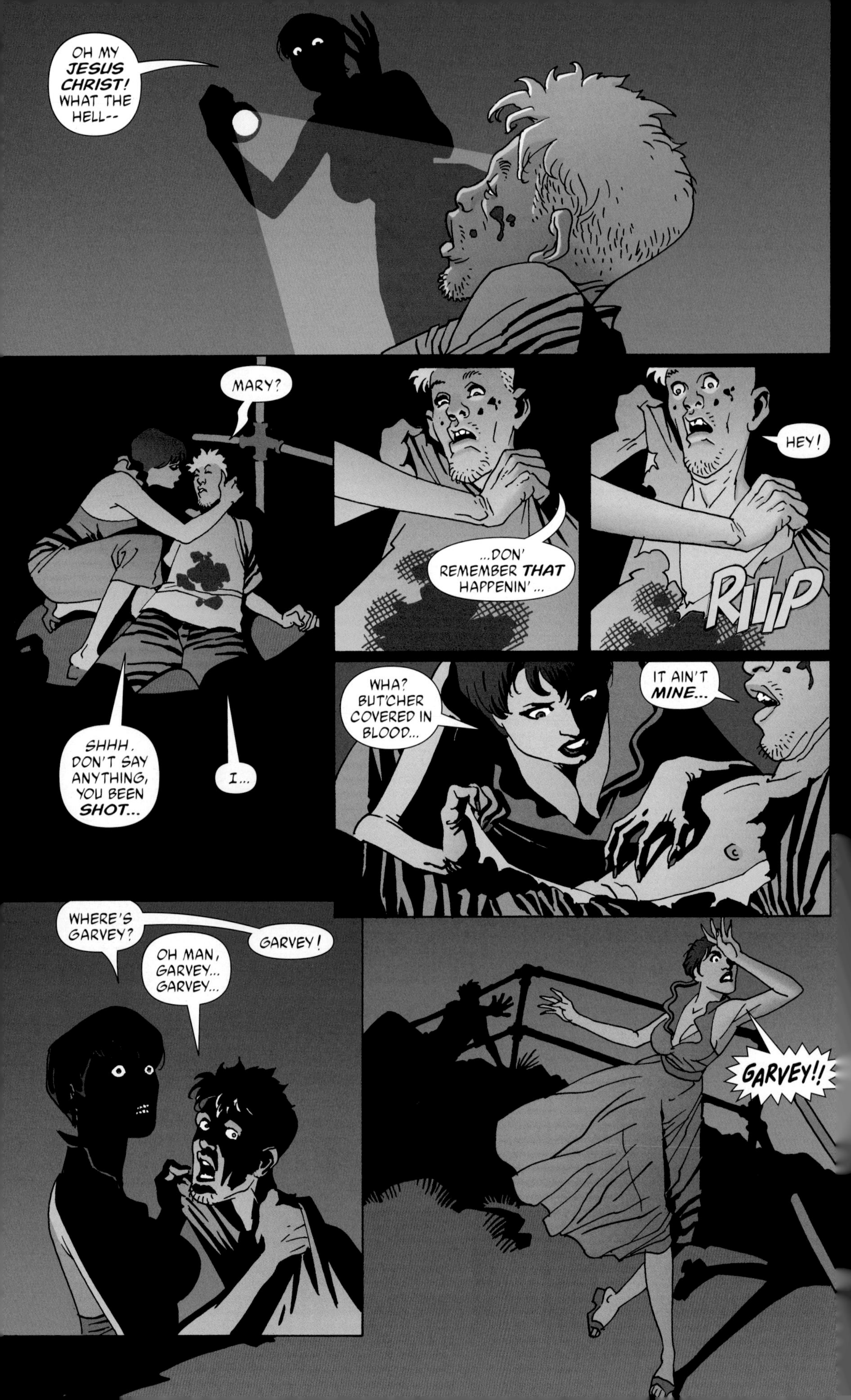
OH MY JESUS CHRIST! WHAT THE HELL--
MARY?
SHHH. DON'T SAY ANYTHING, YOU BEEN SHOT...
I...
...DON' REMEMBER THAT HAPPENIN'...
HEY!
RIIIP
WHA? BUT'CHER COVERED IN BLOOD...
IT AIN'T MINE...
WHERE'S GARVEY?
GARVEY!
OH MAN, GARVEY... GARVEY...
GARVEY!!

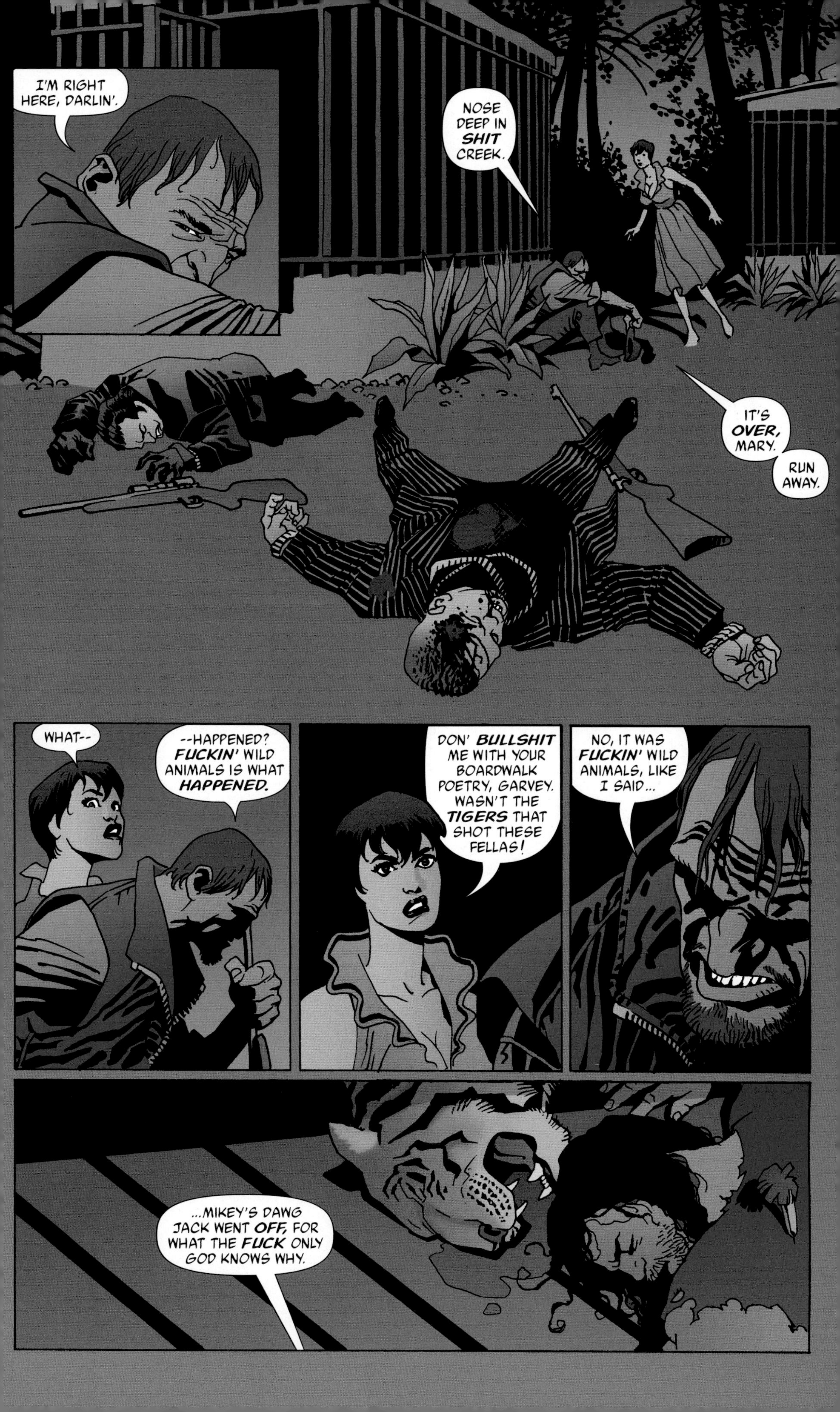
I'M RIGHT HERE, DARLIN'.
NOSE DEEP IN SHIT CREEK.
IT'S OVER, MARY.
RUN AWAY.
WHAT--
--HAPPENED? FUCKIN' WILD ANIMALS IS WHAT HAPPENED.
DON' BULLSHIT ME WITH YOUR BOARDWALK POETRY, GARVEY. WASN'T THE TIGERS THAT SHOT THESE FELLAS!
NO, IT WAS FUCKIN' WILD ANIMALS, LIKE I SAID...
...MIKEY'S DAWG JACK WENT OFF, FOR WHAT THE FUCK ONLY GOD KNOWS WHY.

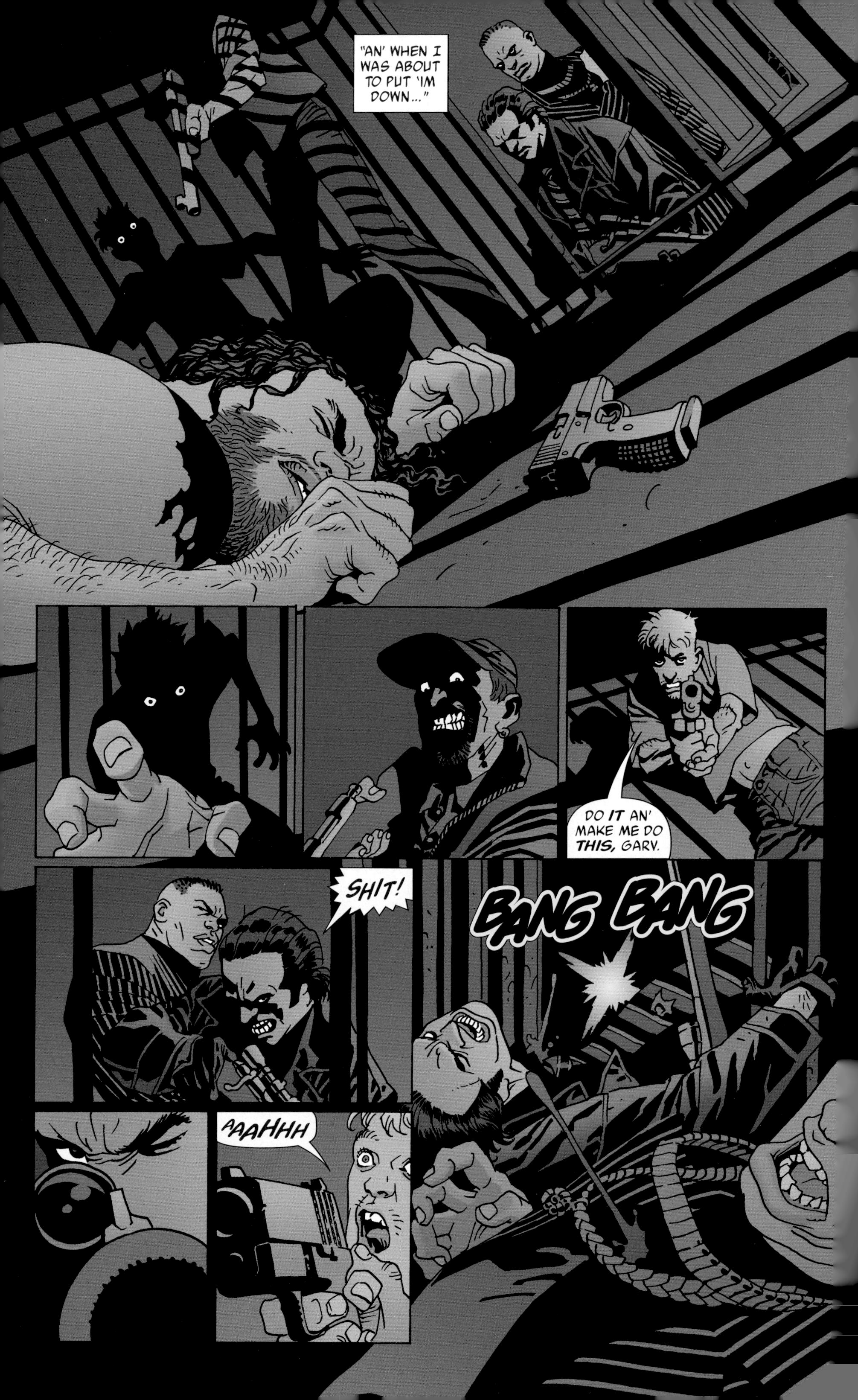
"AN' WHEN I WAS ABOUT TO PUT 'IM DOWN..."
DO IT AN' MAKE ME DO THIS, GARV.
SHIT!
BANG BANG
AAAHHH

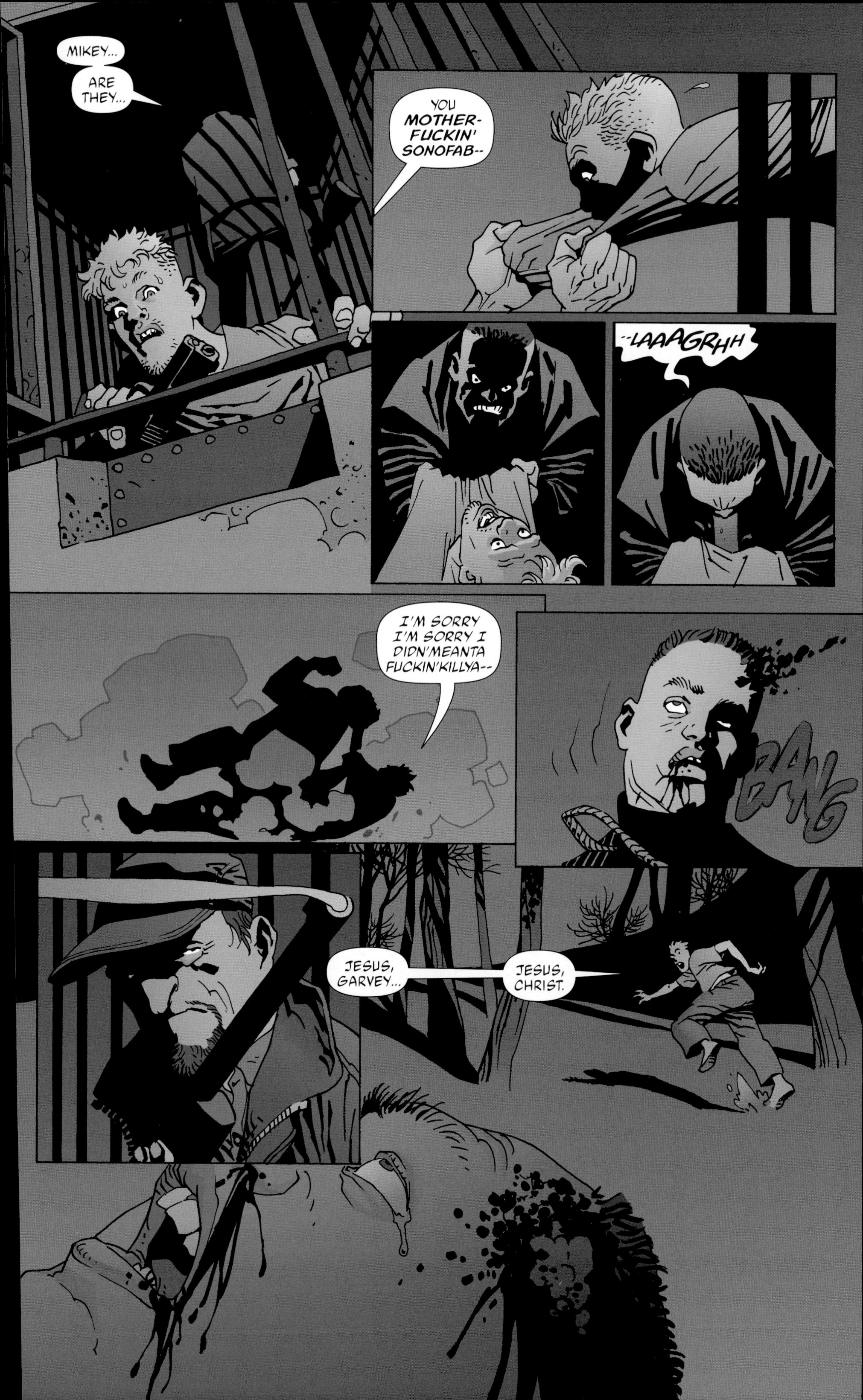
MIKEY...
ARE THEY...
YOU MOTHER-FUCKIN' SONOFAB--
--LAAAGRHH
I'M SORRY I'M SORRY I DIDN'MEANTA FUCKIN'KILLYA--
BANG
JESUS, GARVEY...
JESUS, CHRIST.

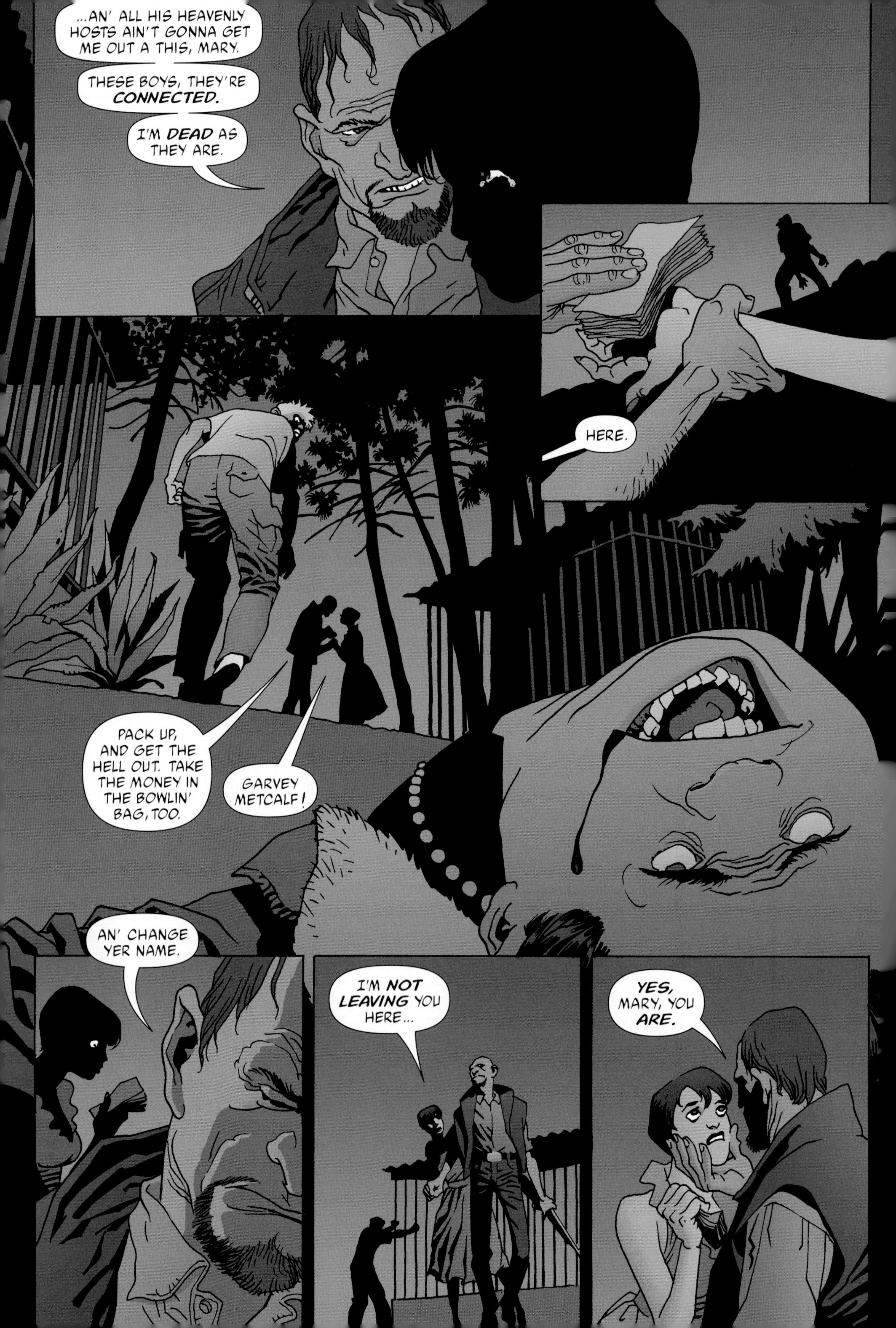
...AN' ALL HIS HEAVENLY HOSTS AIN'T GONNA GET ME OUT A THIS, MARY.
THESE BOYS, THEY'RE CONNECTED.
I'M DEAD AS THEY ARE.
HERE.
PACK UP, AND GET THE HELL OUT. TAKE THE MONEY IN THE BOWLIN' BAG, TOO.
GARVEY METCALF!
AN' CHANGE YER NAME.
I'M NOT LEAVING YOU HERE...
YES, MARY, YOU ARE.

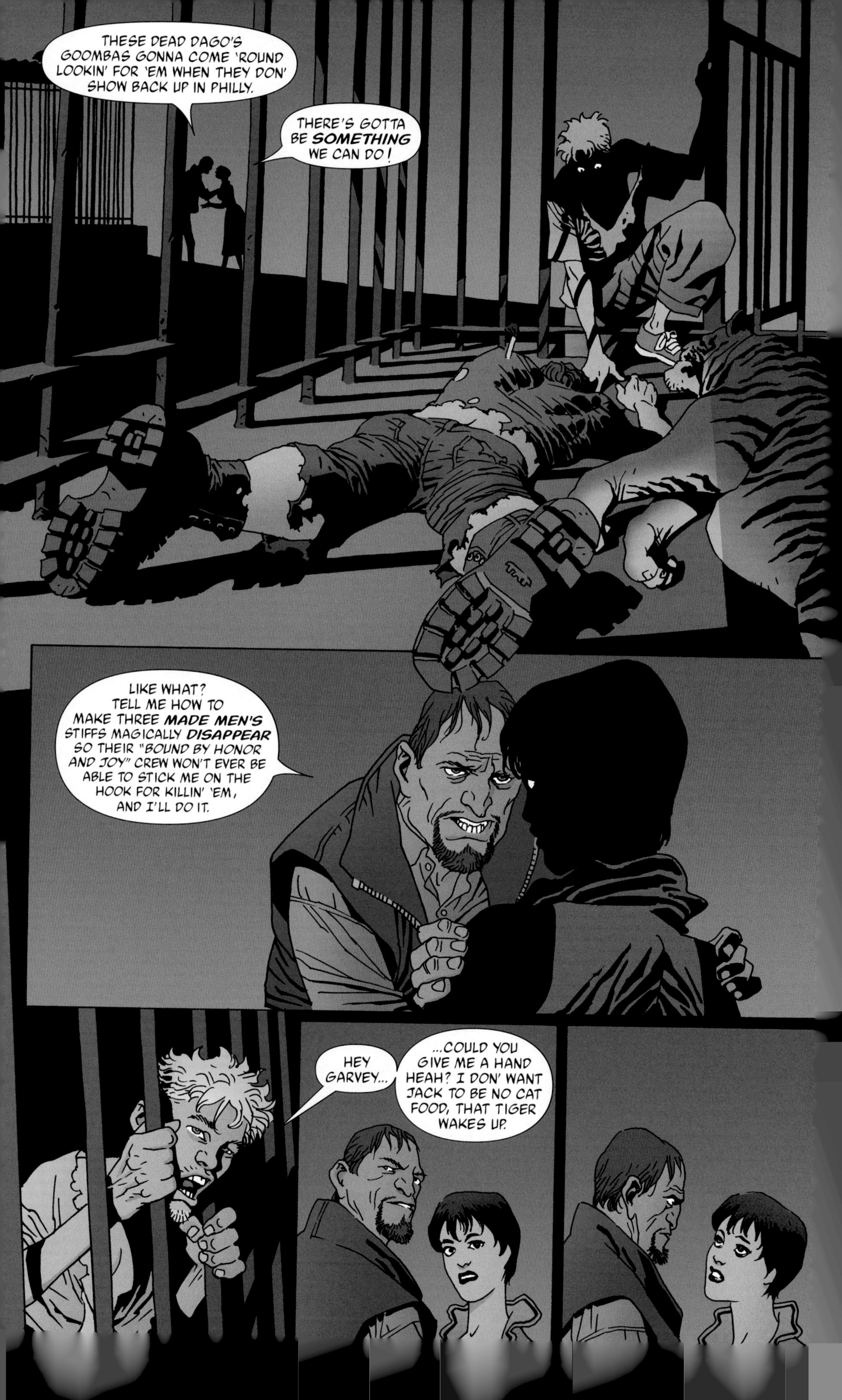
THESE DEAD DAGO'S GOOMBAS GONNA COME 'ROUND LOOKIN' FOR 'EM WHEN THEY DON' SHOW BACK UP IN PHILLY.
THERE'S GOTTA BE SOMETHING WE CAN DO!
LIKE WHAT? TELL ME HOW TO MAKE THREE MADE MEN'S STIFFS MAGICALLY DISAPPEAR SO THEIR "BOUND BY HONOR AND JOY" CREW WON'T EVER BE ABLE TO STICK ME ON THE HOOK FOR KILLIN' 'EM, AND I'LL DO IT.
HEY GARVEY...
...COULD YOU GIVE ME A HAND HEAH? I DON' WANT JACK TO BE NO CAT FOOD, THAT TIGER WAKES UP.

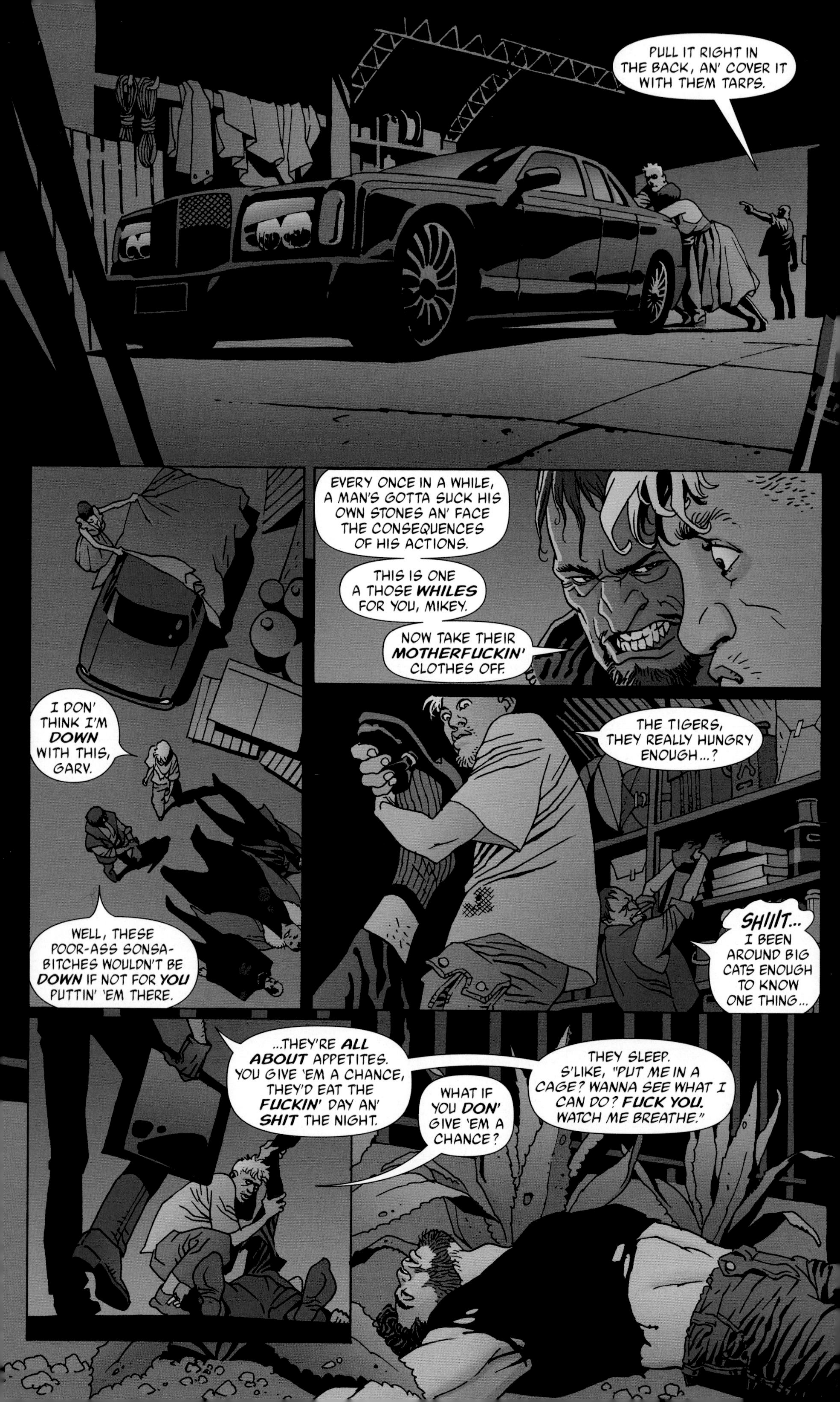
PULL IT RIGHT IN THE BACK, AN' COVER IT WITH THEM TARPS.
EVERY ONCE IN A WHILE, A MAN'S GOTTA SUCK HIS OWN STONES AN' FACE THE CONSEQUENCES OF HIS ACTIONS.
THIS IS ONE A THOSE WHILES FOR YOU, MIKEY.
NOW TAKE THEIR MOTHERFUCKIN' CLOTHES OFF.
I DON' THINK I'M DOWN WITH THIS, GARV.
WELL, THESE POOR-ASS SONSA-BITCHES WOULDN'T BE DOWN IF NOT FOR YOU PUTTIN' 'EM THERE.
THE TIGERS, THEY REALLY HUNGRY ENOUGH...?
SHIIIT... I BEEN AROUND BIG CATS ENOUGH TO KNOW ONE THING...
...THEY'RE ALL ABOUT APPETITES. YOU GIVE 'EM A CHANCE, THEY'D EAT THE FUCKIN' DAY AN' SHIT THE NIGHT.
WHAT IF YOU DON' GIVE 'EM A CHANCE?
THEY SLEEP. S'LIKE, "PUT ME IN A CAGE? WANNA SEE WHAT I CAN DO? FUCK YOU. WATCH ME BREATHE."

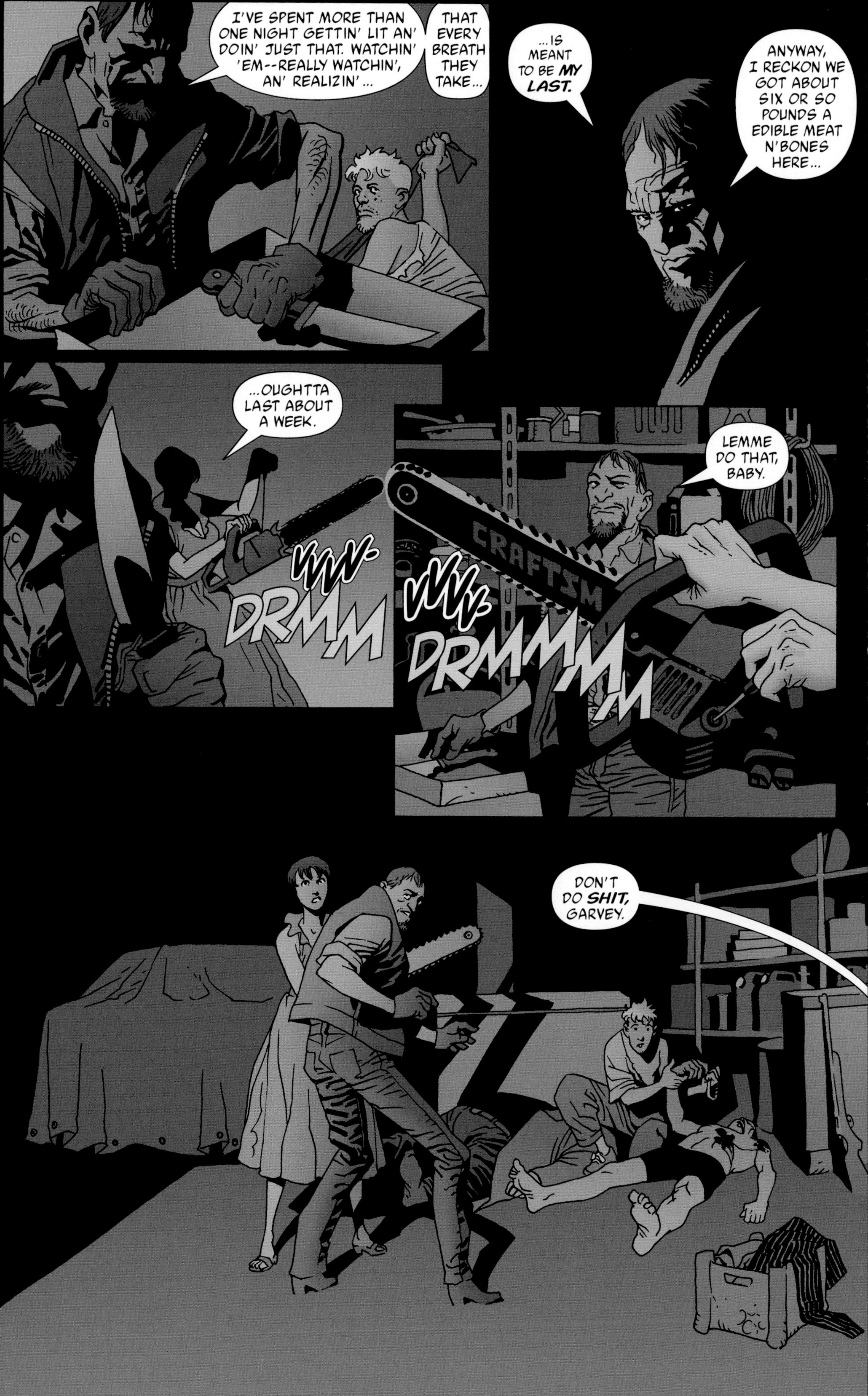
I'VE SPENT MORE THAN ONE NIGHT GETTIN' LIT AN' DOIN' JUST THAT. WATCHIN' 'EM--REALLY WATCHIN', AN' REALIZIN'...
THAT EVERY BREATH THEY TAKE...
...IS MEANT TO BE MY LAST.
ANYWAY, I RECKON WE GOT ABOUT SIX OR SO POUNDS A EDIBLE MEAT N'BONES HERE...
...OUGHTTA LAST ABOUT A WEEK.
VVVV-
DRMM
LEMME DO THAT, BABY.
CRAFTSM
VVVV-
DRMMMMM
DON'T DO SHIT, GARVEY.

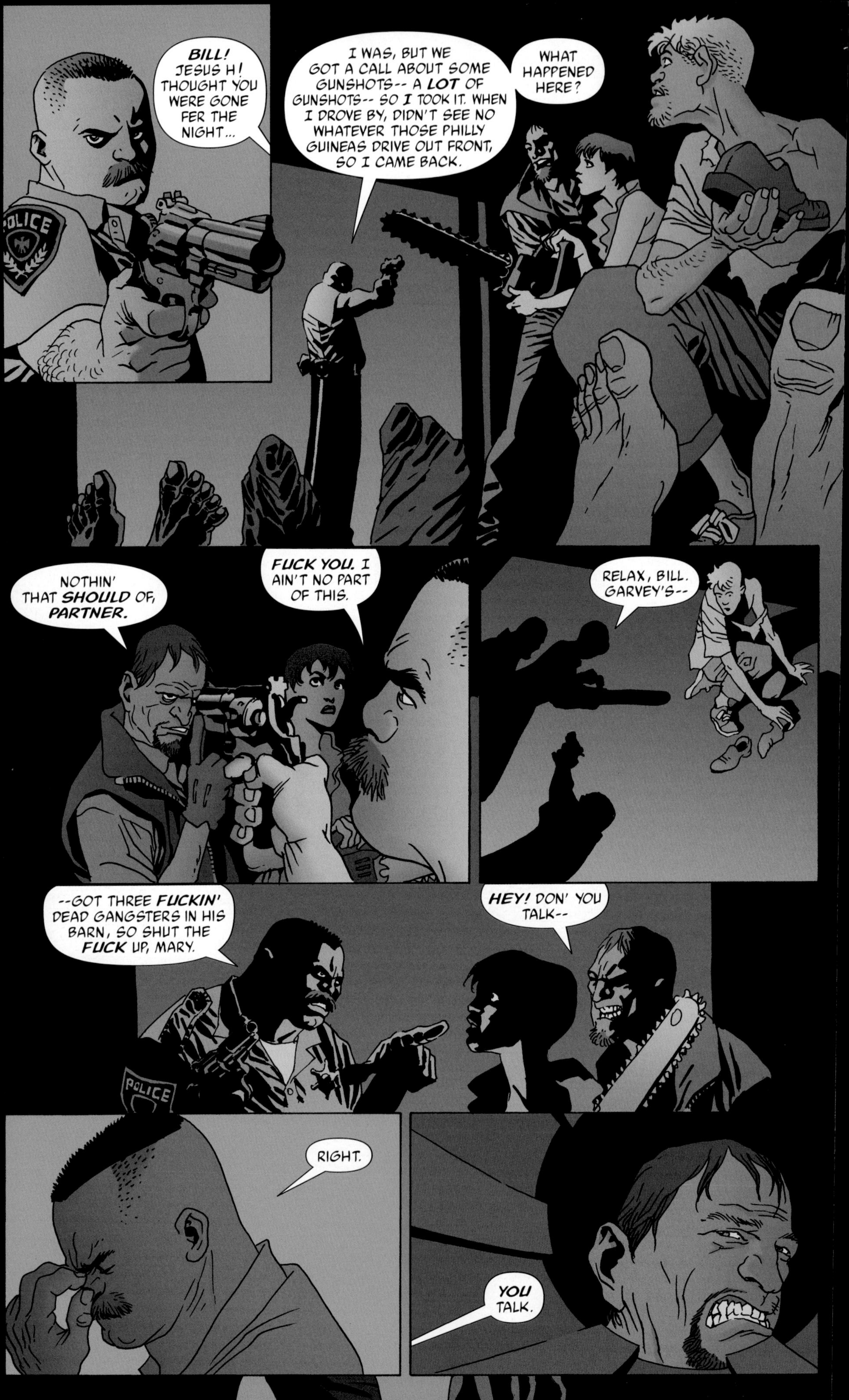
BILL! JESUS H! THOUGHT YOU WERE GONE FER THE NIGHT...
I WAS, BUT WE GOT A CALL ABOUT SOME GUNSHOTS-- A LOT OF GUNSHOTS-- SO I TOOK IT. WHEN I DROVE BY, DIDN'T SEE NO WHATEVER THOSE PHILLY GUINEAS DRIVE OUT FRONT, SO I CAME BACK.
WHAT HAPPENED HERE?
NOTHIN' THAT SHOULD OF, PARTNER.
FUCK YOU. I AIN'T NO PART OF THIS.
RELAX, BILL. GARVEY'S--
--GOT THREE FUCKIN' DEAD GANGSTERS IN HIS BARN, SO SHUT THE FUCK UP, MARY.
HEY! DON' YOU TALK--
RIGHT.
YOU TALK.

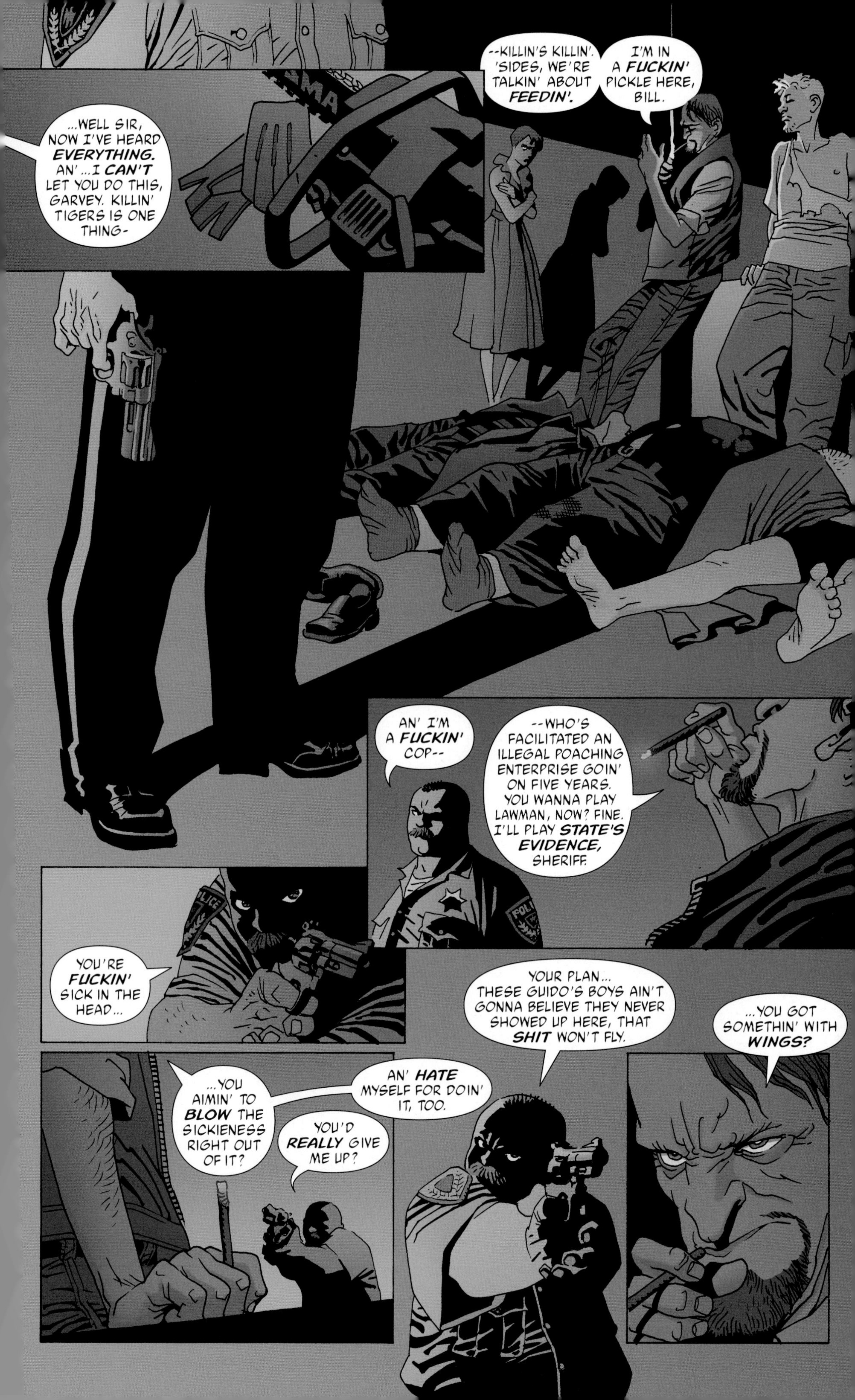
...WELL SIR, NOW I'VE HEARD EVERYTHING. AN'...I CAN'T LET YOU DO THIS, GARVEY. KILLIN' TIGERS IS ONE THING-
--KILLIN'S KILLIN'. 'SIDES, WE'RE TALKIN' ABOUT FEEDIN'.
I'M IN A FUCKIN' PICKLE HERE, BILL.
AN' I'M A FUCKIN' COP--
--WHO'S FACILITATED AN ILLEGAL POACHING ENTERPRISE GOIN' ON FIVE YEARS. YOU WANNA PLAY LAWMAN, NOW? FINE. I'LL PLAY STATE'S EVIDENCE, SHERIFF.
YOU'RE FUCKIN' SICK IN THE HEAD...
...YOU AIMIN' TO BLOW THE SICKIENESS RIGHT OUT OF IT?
AN' HATE MYSELF FOR DOIN' IT, TOO.
YOU'D REALLY GIVE ME UP?
YOUR PLAN... THESE GUIDO'S BOYS AIN'T GONNA BELIEVE THEY NEVER SHOWED UP HERE, THAT SHIT WON'T FLY.
...YOU GOT SOMETHIN' WITH WINGS?

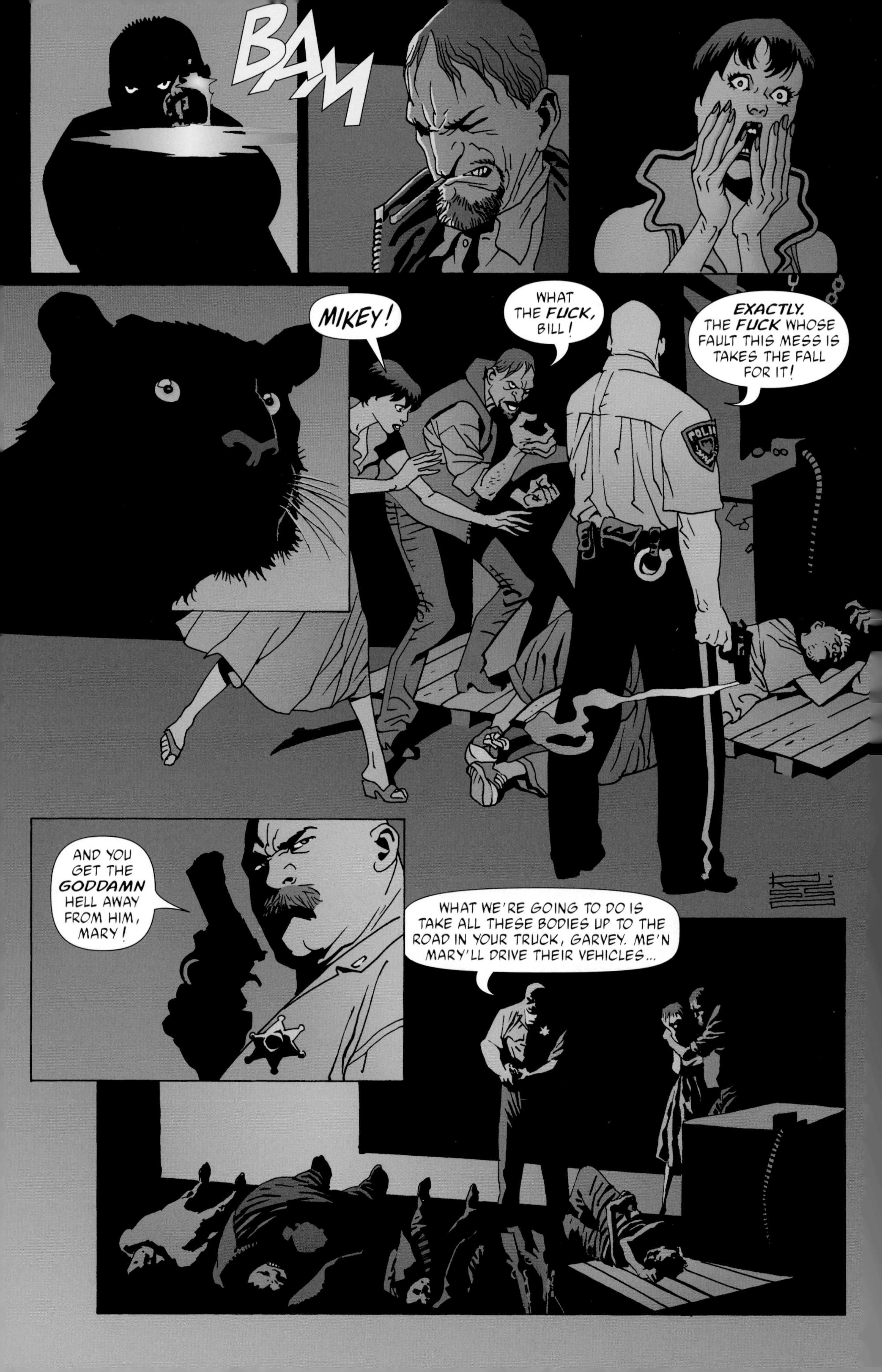
BAM
MIKEY!
WHAT THE FUCK, BILL!
EXACTLY. THE FUCK WHOSE FAULT THIS MESS IS TAKES THE FALL FOR IT!
AND YOU GET THE GODDAMN HELL AWAY FROM HIM, MARY!
WHAT WE'RE GOING TO DO IS TAKE ALL THESE BODIES UP TO THE ROAD IN YOUR TRUCK, GARVEY. ME'N MARY'LL DRIVE THEIR VEHICLES...

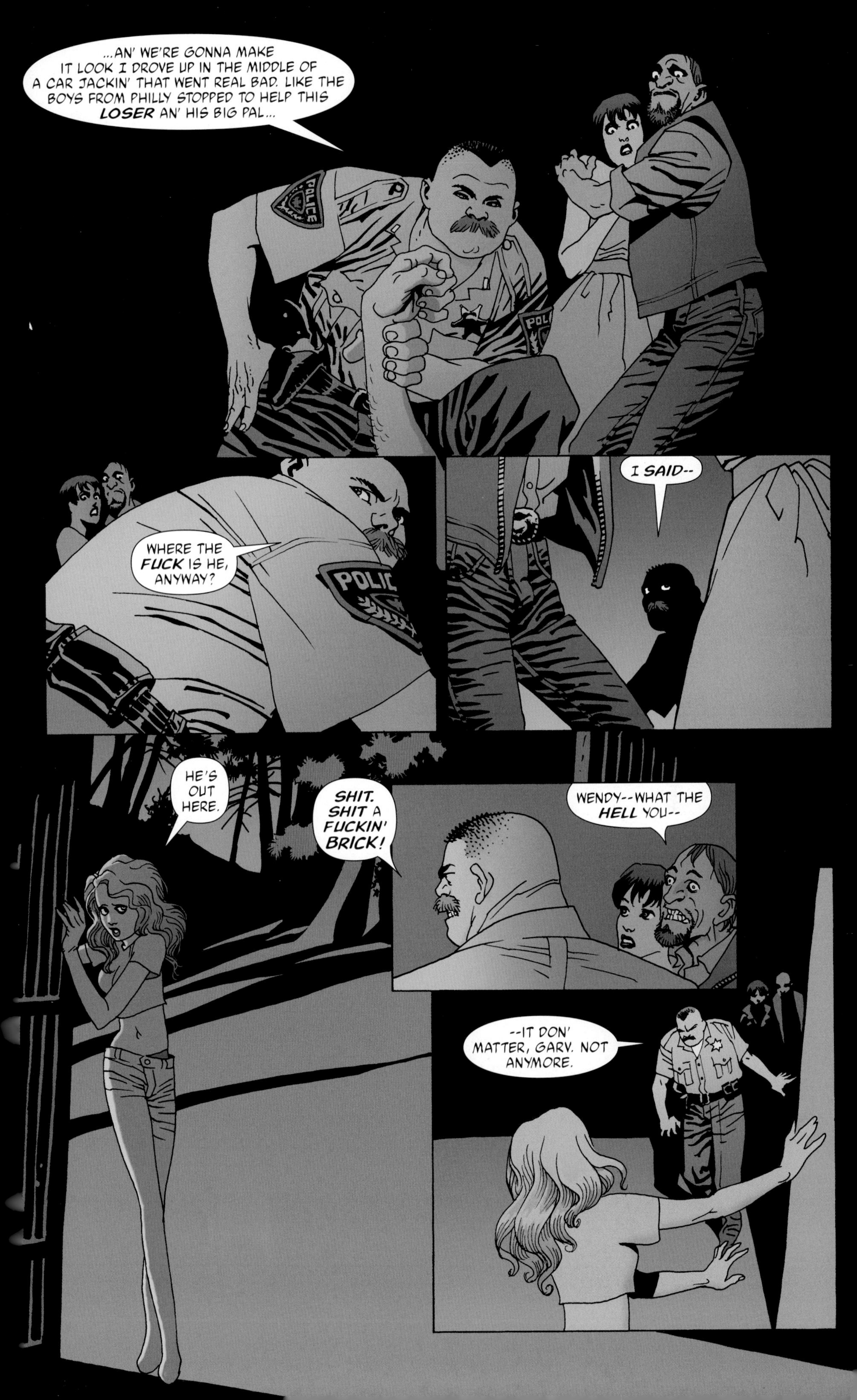
...AN' WE'RE GONNA MAKE IT LOOK I DROVE UP IN THE MIDDLE OF A CAR JACKIN' THAT WENT REAL BAD. LIKE THE BOYS FROM PHILLY STOPPED TO HELP THIS LOSER AN' HIS BIG PAL...
POLICE
WHERE THE FUCK IS HE, ANYWAY?
POLICE
I SAID--
HE'S OUT HERE.
SHIT. SHIT A FUCKIN' BRICK!
WENDY--WHAT THE HELL YOU--
--IT DON' MATTER, GARV. NOT ANYMORE.

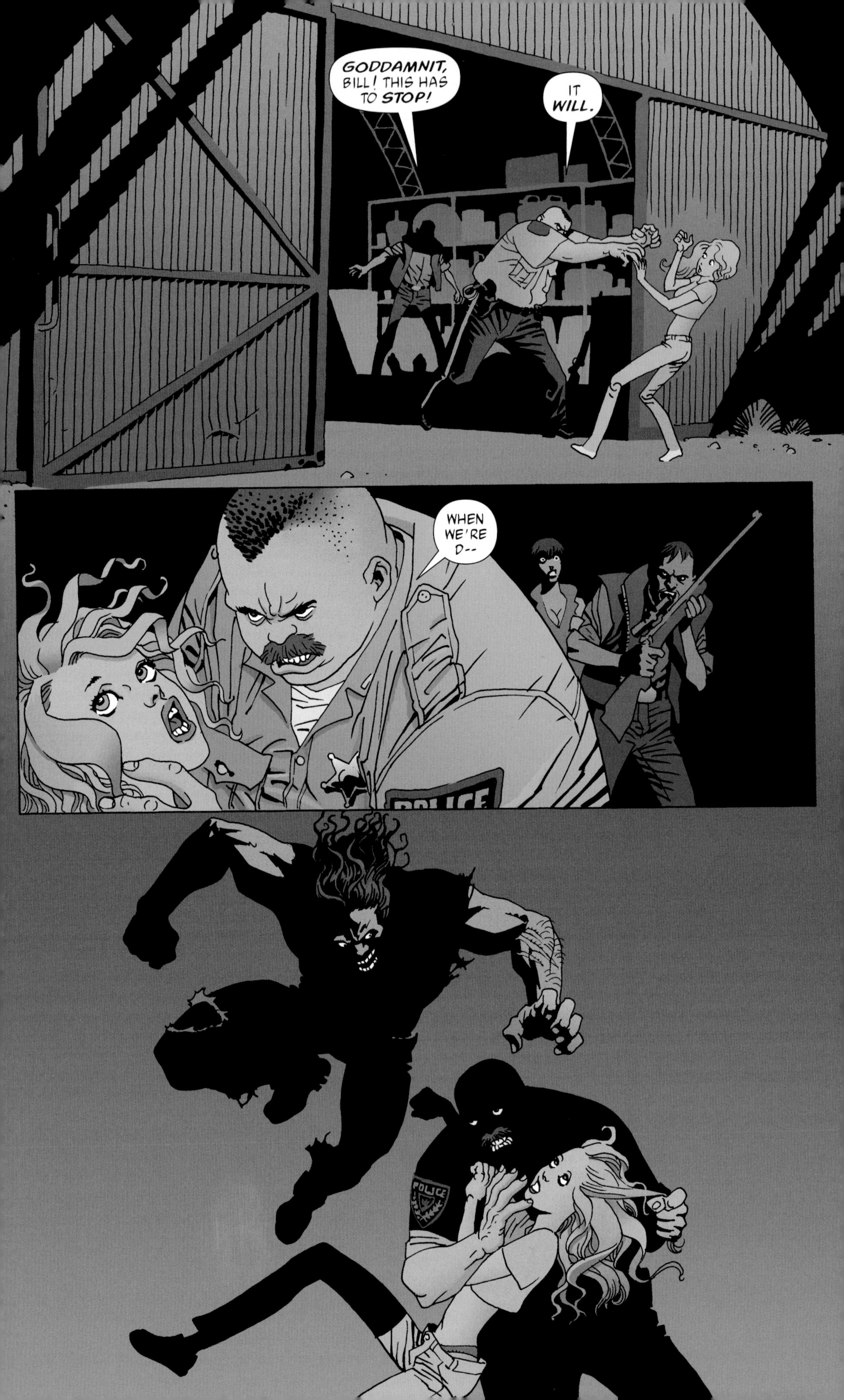
GODDAMNIT, BILL! THIS HAS TO STOP!
IT WILL.
WHEN WE'RE D--
POLICE
POLICE

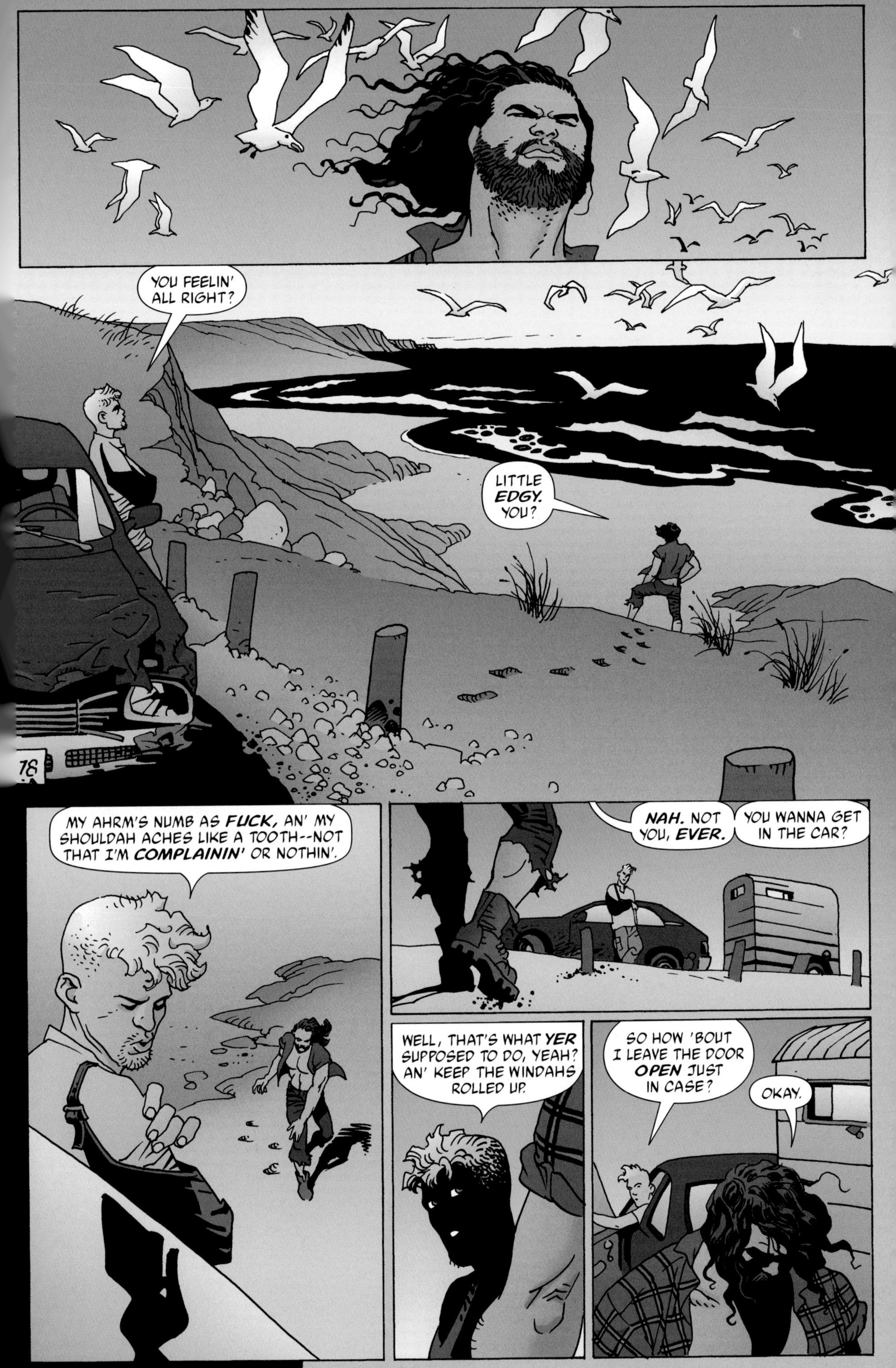

YOU FEELIN' ALL RIGHT?
LITTLE EDGY. YOU?
MY AHRM'S NUMB AS FUCK, AN' MY SHOULDAH ACHES LIKE A TOOTH--NOT THAT I'M COMPLAININ' OR NOTHIN'.
NAH. NOT YOU, EVER.
YOU WANNA GET IN THE CAR?
WELL, THAT'S WHAT YER SUPPOSED TO DO, YEAH? AN' KEEP THE WINDAHS ROLLED UP.
SO HOW 'BOUT I LEAVE THE DOOR OPEN JUST IN CASE?
OKAY.

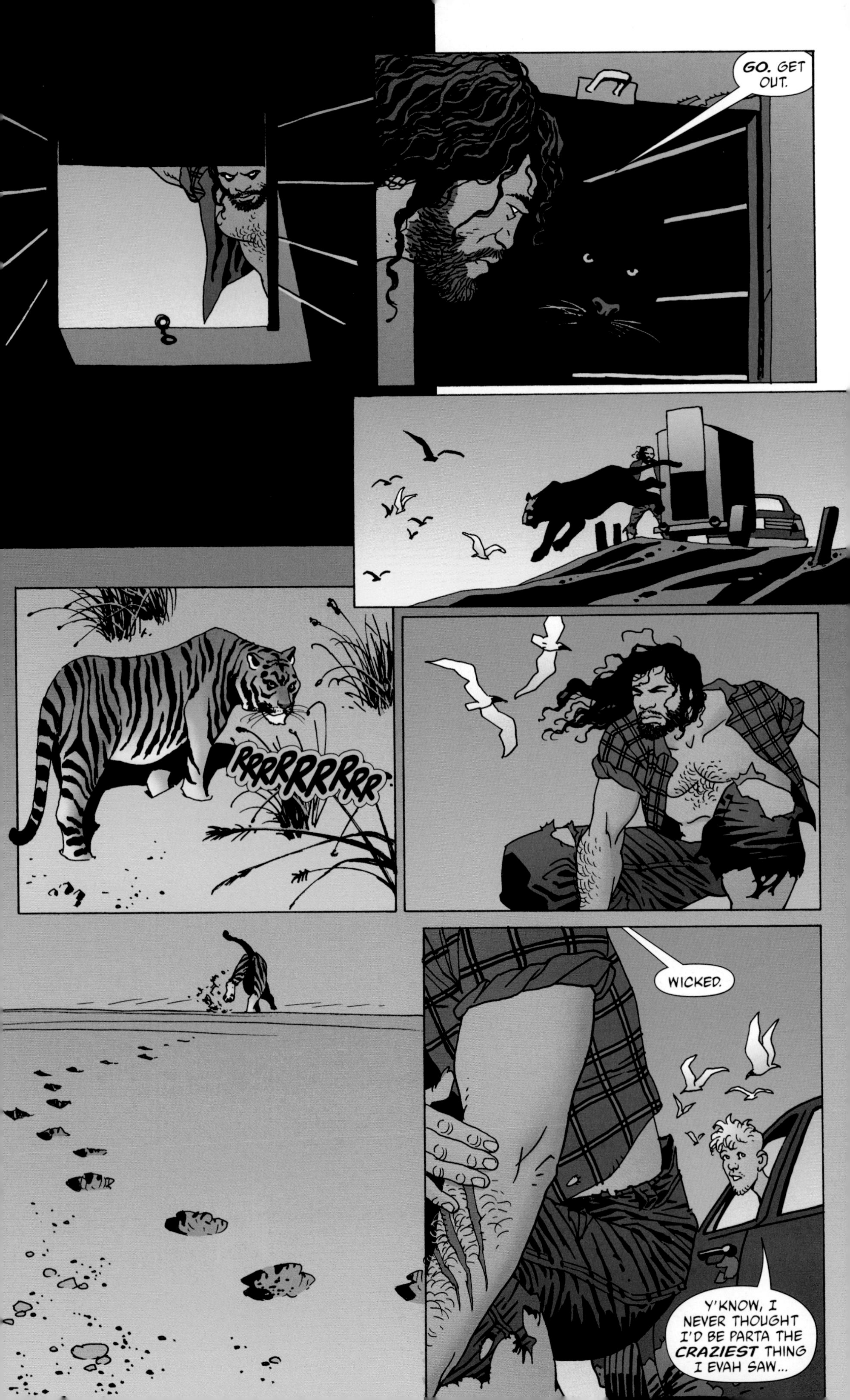
GO. GET OUT.
RRRRRRRRRR
WICKED.
Y'KNOW, I NEVER THOUGHT I'D BE PARTA THE CRAZIEST THING I EVAH SAW...

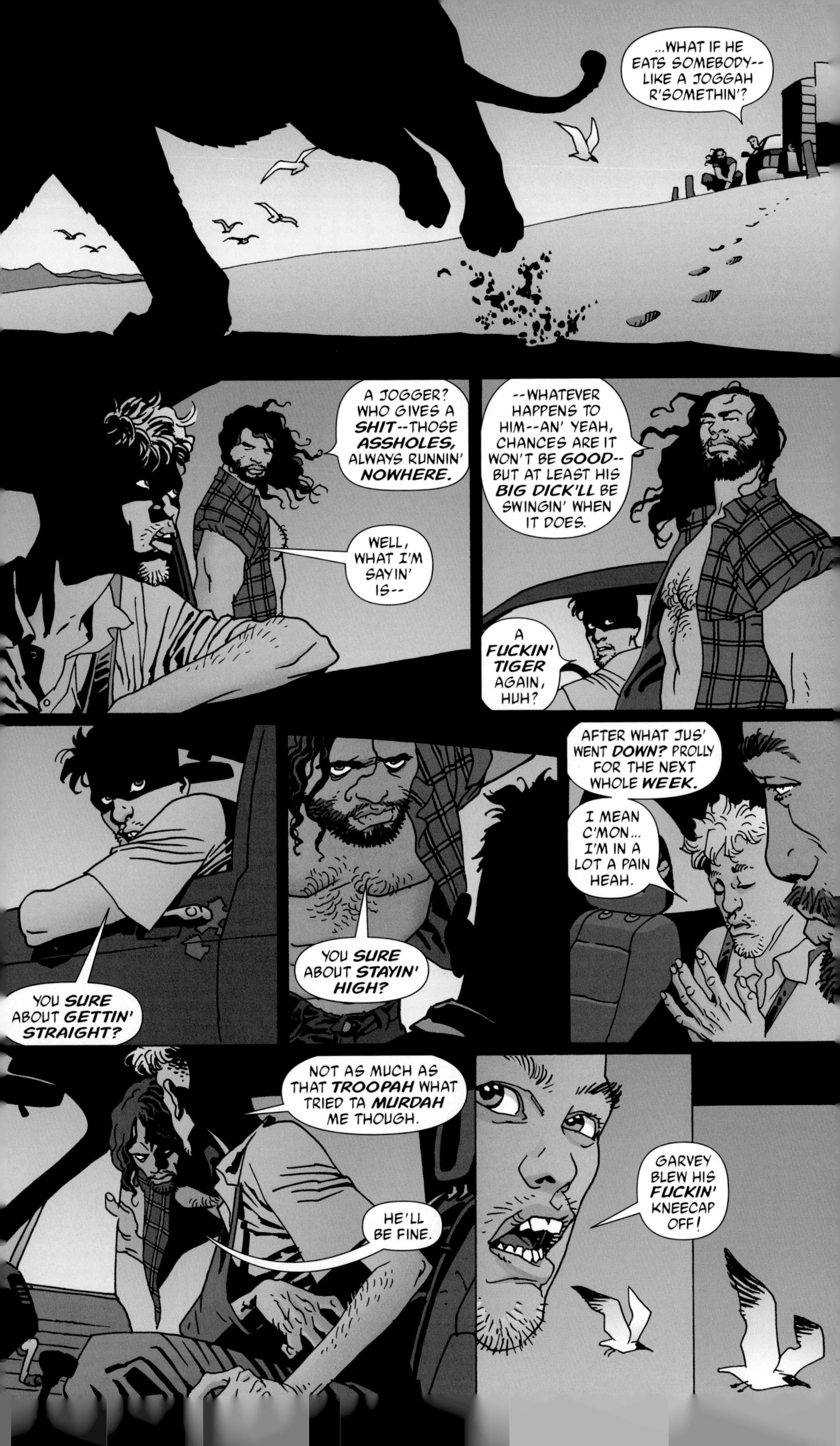
...WHAT IF HE EATS SOMEBODY-- LIKE A JOGGAH R'SOMETHIN'?
A JOGGER? WHO GIVES A SHIT--THOSE ASSHOLES, ALWAYS RUNNIN' NOWHERE.
WELL, WHAT I'M SAYIN' IS--
--WHATEVER HAPPENS TO HIM--AN' YEAH, CHANCES ARE IT WON'T BE GOOD-- BUT AT LEAST HIS BIG DICK'LL BE SWINGIN' WHEN IT DOES.
A FUCKIN' TIGER AGAIN, HUH?
YOU SURE ABOUT GETTIN' STRAIGHT?
YOU SURE ABOUT STAYIN' HIGH?
AFTER WHAT JUS' WENT DOWN? PROLLY FOR THE NEXT WHOLE WEEK.
I MEAN C'MON... I'M IN A LOT A PAIN HEAH.
NOT AS MUCH AS THAT TROOPAH WHAT TRIED TA MURDAH ME THOUGH.
HE'LL BE FINE.
GARVEY BLEW HIS FUCKIN' KNEECAP OFF!

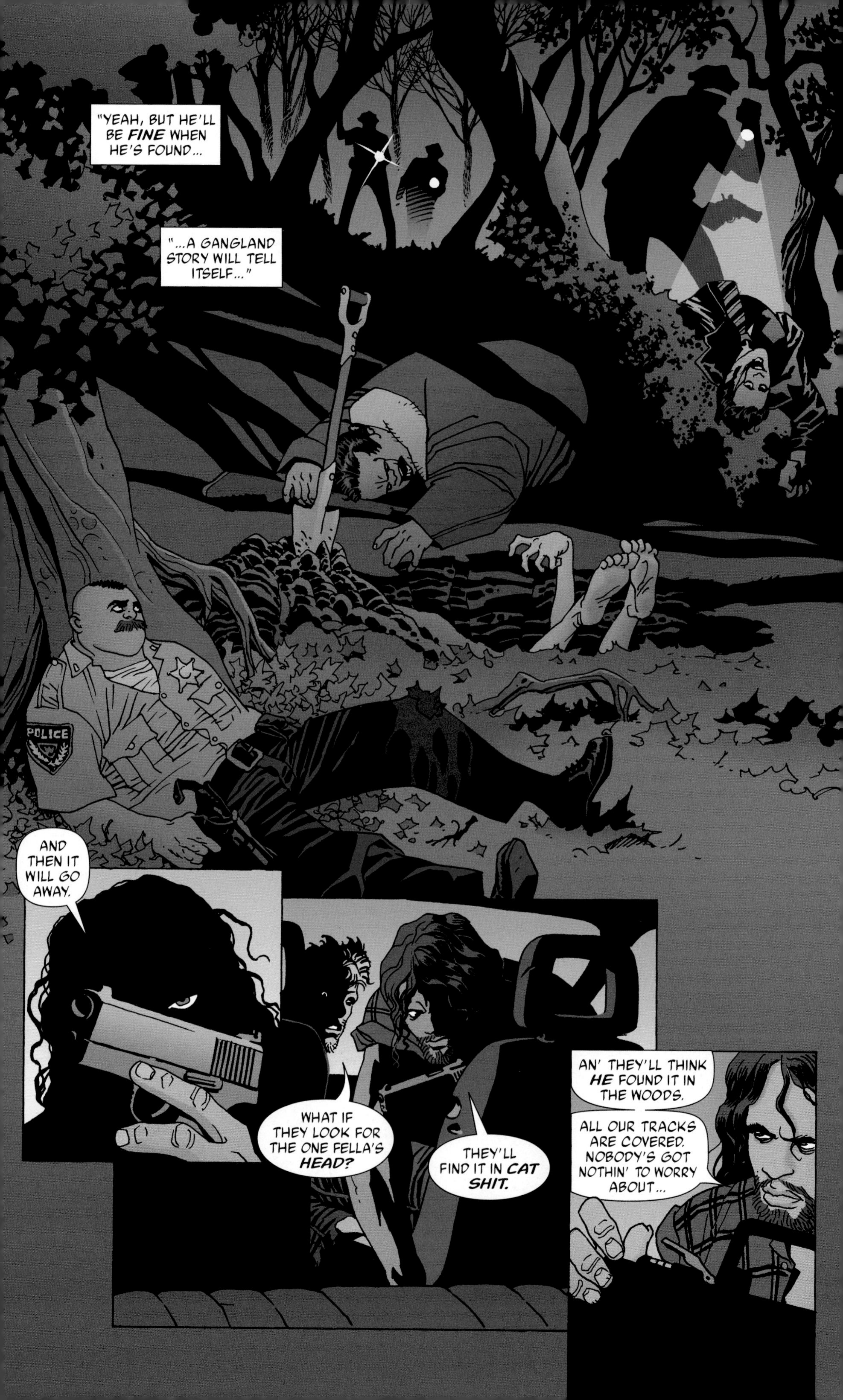

"YEAH, BUT HE'LL BE FINE WHEN HE'S FOUND...
"...A GANGLAND STORY WILL TELL ITSELF..."
AND THEN IT WILL GO AWAY.
WHAT IF THEY LOOK FOR THE ONE FELLA'S HEAD?
THEY'LL FIND IT IN CAT SHIT.
AN' THEY'LL THINK HE FOUND IT IN THE WOODS.
ALL OUR TRACKS ARE COVERED. NOBODY'S GOT NOTHIN' TO WORRY ABOUT...

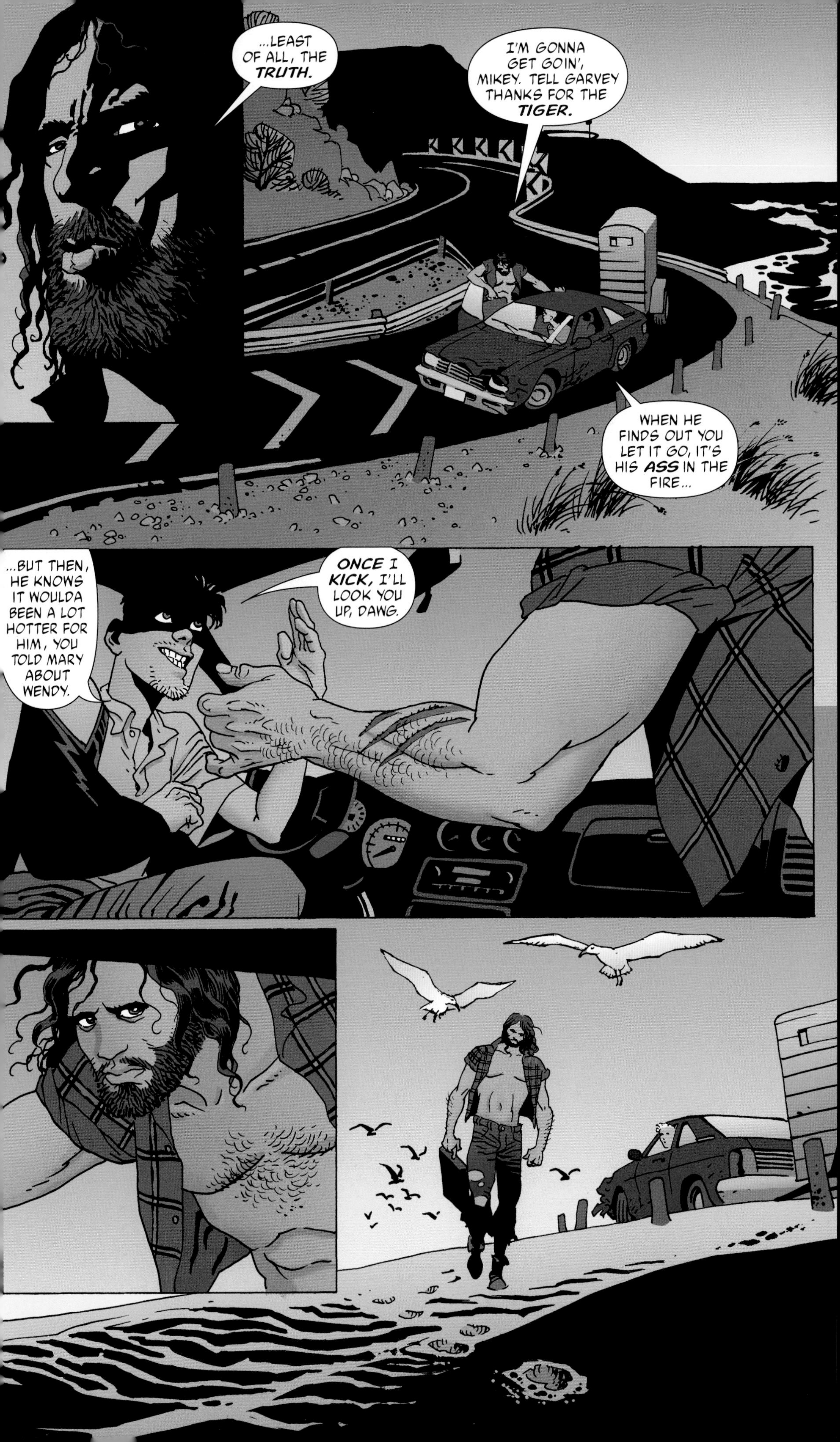
...LEAST OF ALL, THE TRUTH.
I'M GONNA GET GOIN', MIKEY. TELL GARVEY THANKS FOR THE TIGER.
WHEN HE FINDS OUT YOU LET IT GO, IT'S HIS ASS IN THE FIRE...
...BUT THEN, HE KNOWS IT WOULDA BEEN A LOT HOTTER FOR HIM, YOU TOLD MARY ABOUT WENDY.
ONCE I KICK, I'LL LOOK YOU UP, DAWG.

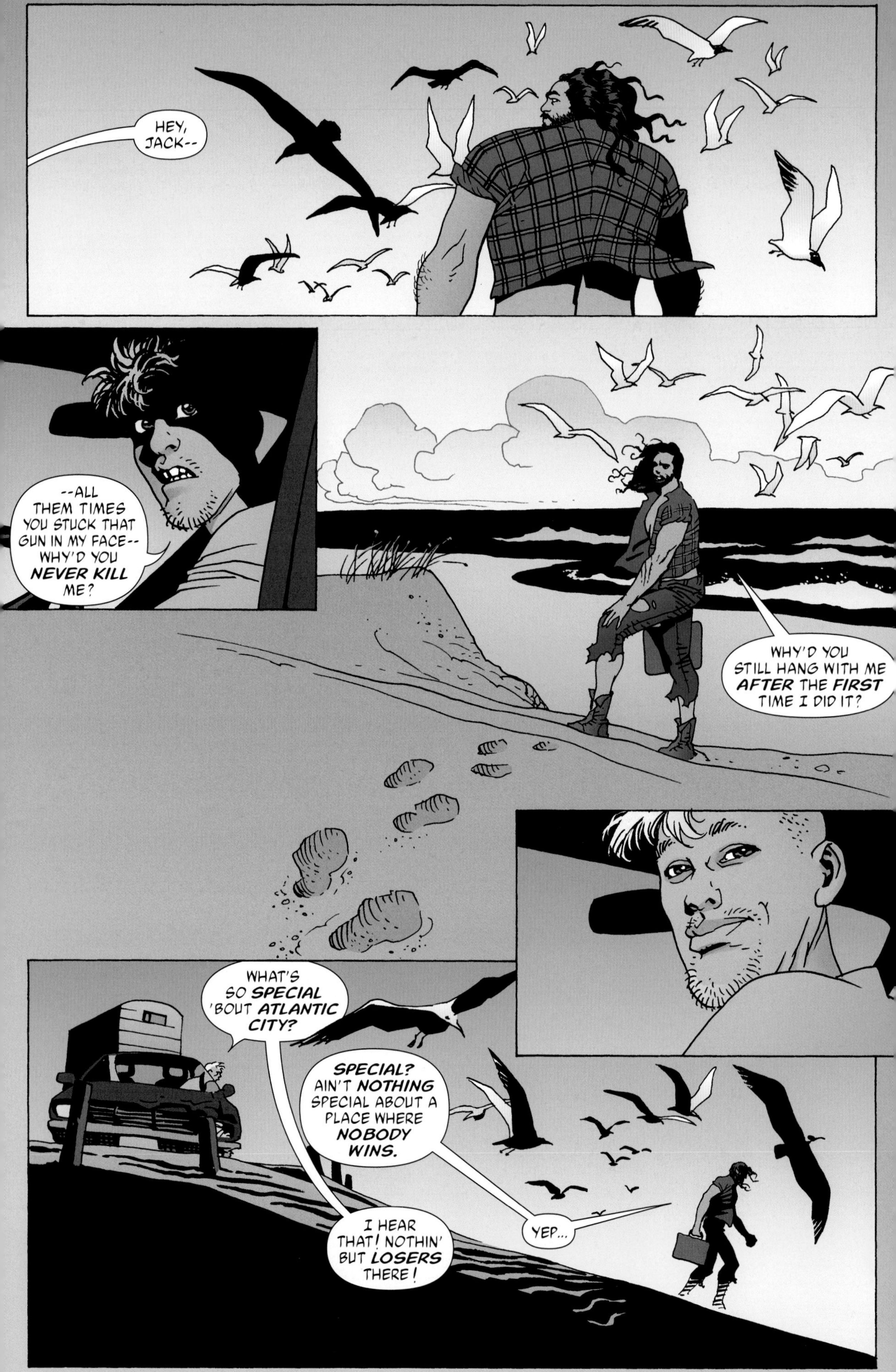

HEY, JACK--
--ALL THEM TIMES YOU STUCK THAT GUN IN MY FACE-- WHY'D YOU NEVER KILL ME?
WHY'D YOU STILL HANG WITH ME AFTER THE FIRST TIME I DID IT?
WHAT'S SO SPECIAL 'BOUT ATLANTIC CITY?
SPECIAL? AIN'T NOTHING SPECIAL ABOUT A PLACE WHERE NOBODY WINS.
I HEAR THAT! NOTHIN' BUT LOSERS THERE!
YEP...

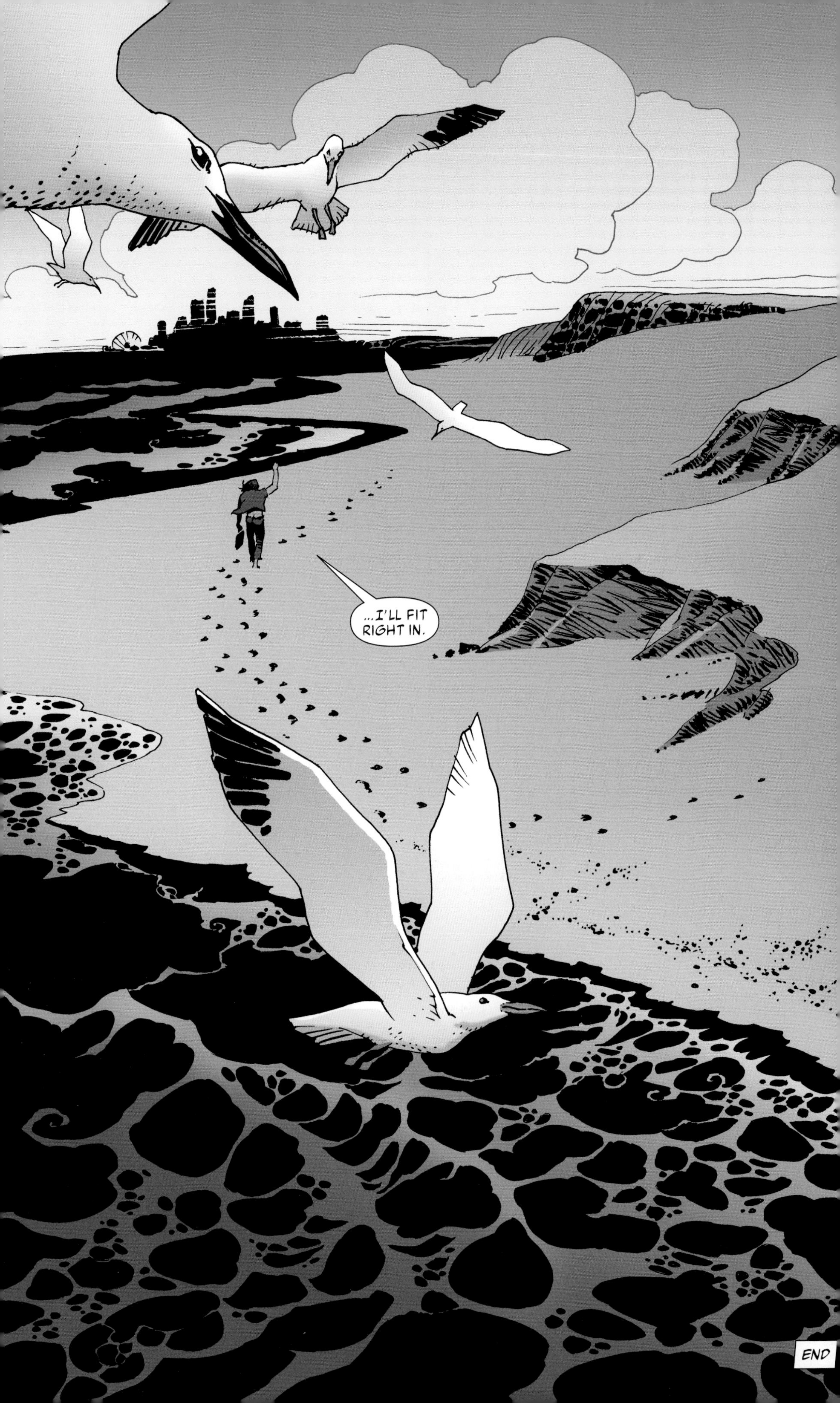
...I'LL FIT RIGHT IN.
END

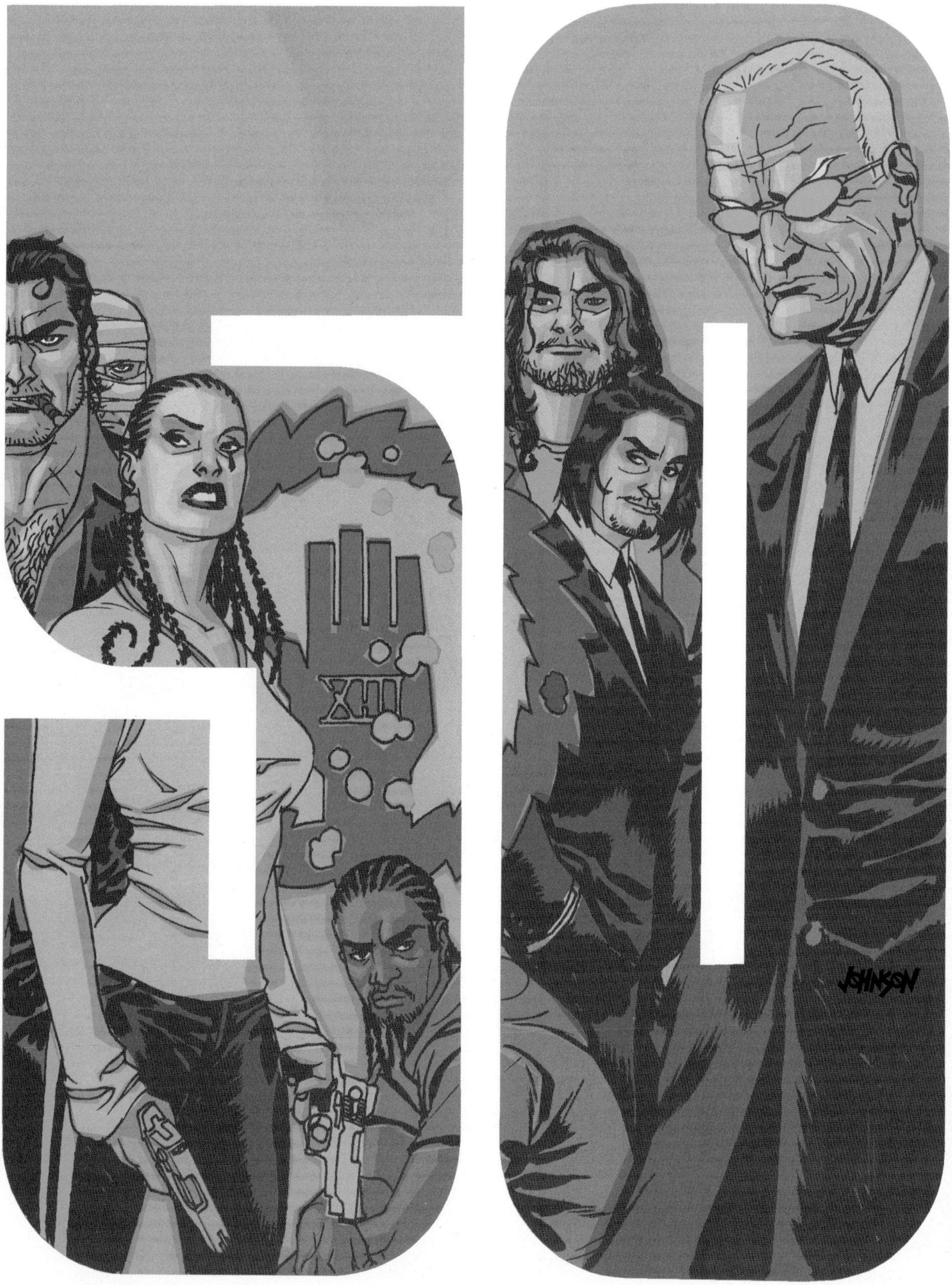
XIII
JOHNSON

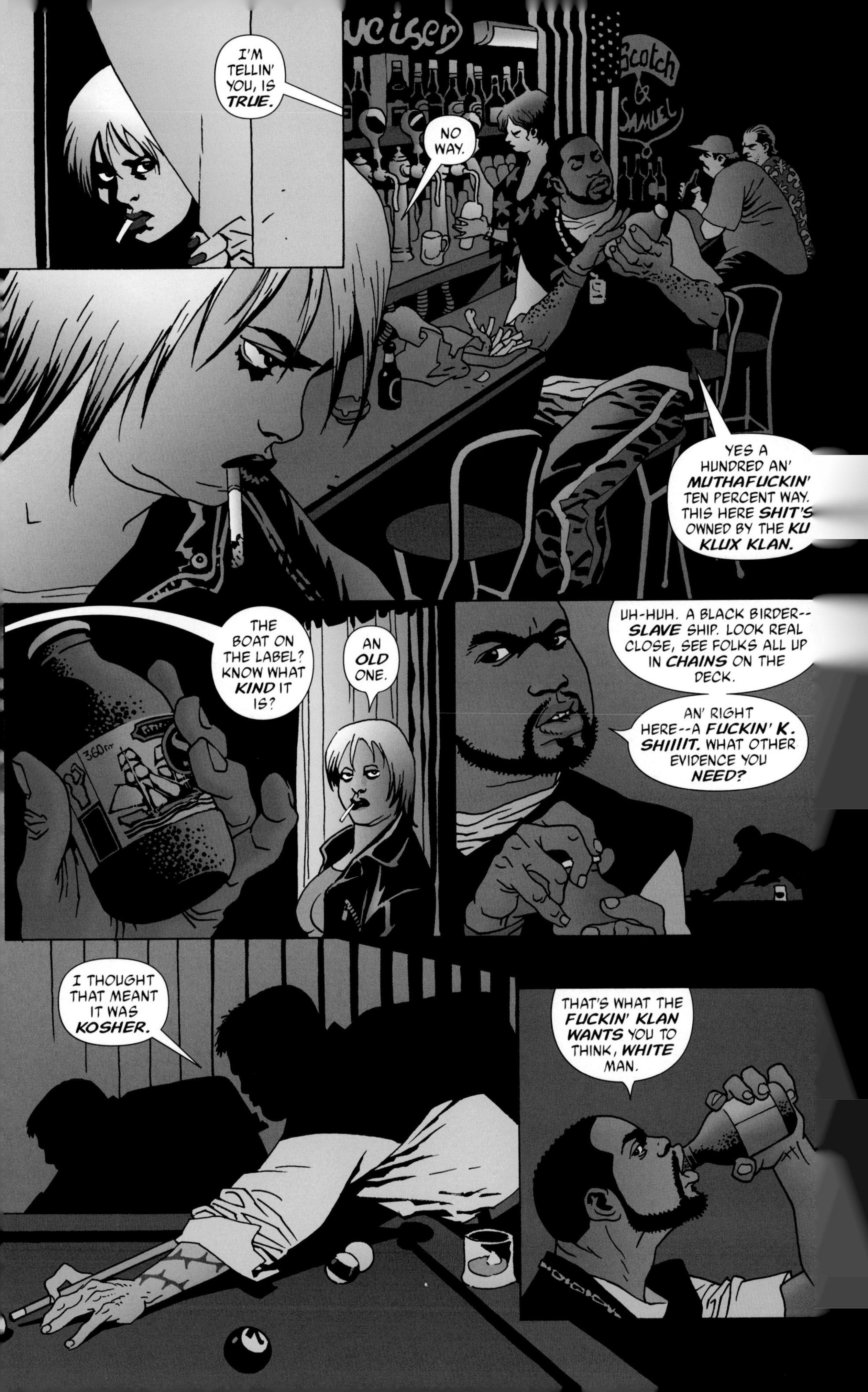
I'M TELLIN' YOU, IS TRUE.
NO WAY.
YES A HUNDRED AN' MUTHAFUCKIN' TEN PERCENT WAY. THIS HERE SHIT'S OWNED BY THE KU KLUX KLAN.
THE BOAT ON THE LABEL? KNOW WHAT KIND IT IS?
AN OLD ONE.
UH-HUH. A BLACK BIRDER--SLAVE SHIP. LOOK REAL CLOSE, SEE FOLKS ALL UP IN CHAINS ON THE DECK.
AN' RIGHT HERE--A FUCKIN' K. SHIIIIT. WHAT OTHER EVIDENCE YOU NEED?
I THOUGHT THAT MEANT IT WAS KOSHER.
THAT'S WHAT THE FUCKIN' KLAN WANTS YOU TO THINK, WHITE MAN.

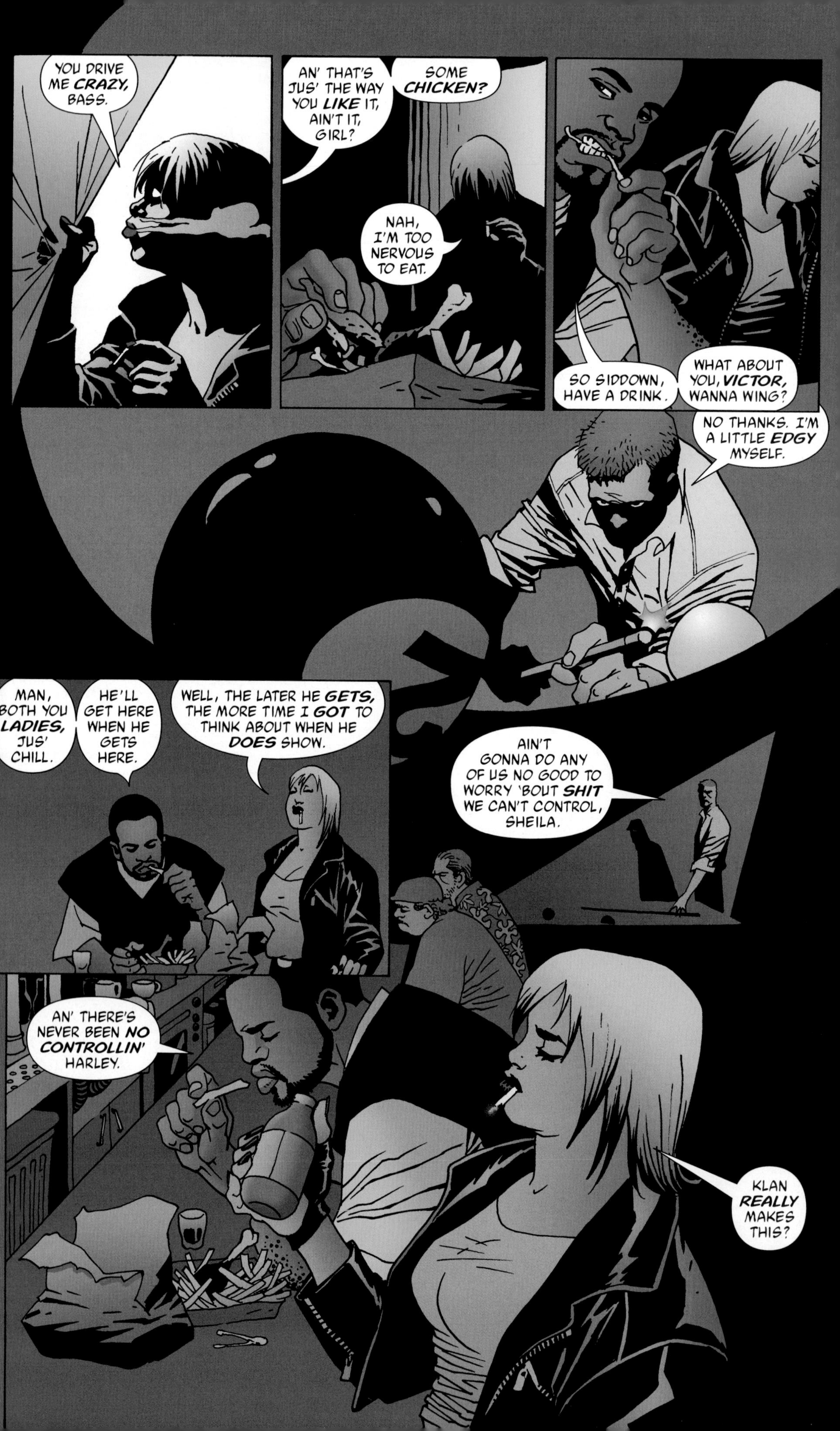

YOU DRIVE ME CRAZY, BASS.
AN' THAT'S JUS' THE WAY YOU LIKE IT, AIN'T IT, GIRL?
SOME CHICKEN?
NAH, I'M TOO NERVOUS TO EAT.
SO SIDDOWN, HAVE A DRINK.
WHAT ABOUT YOU, VICTOR, WANNA WING?
NO THANKS. I'M A LITTLE EDGY MYSELF.
MAN, BOTH YOU LADIES, JUS' CHILL.
HE'LL GET HERE WHEN HE GETS HERE.
WELL, THE LATER HE GETS, THE MORE TIME I GOT TO THINK ABOUT WHEN HE DOES SHOW.
AIN'T GONNA DO ANY OF US NO GOOD TO WORRY 'BOUT SHIT WE CAN'T CONTROL, SHEILA.
AN' THERE'S NEVER BEEN NO CONTROLLIN' HARLEY.
KLAN REALLY MAKES THIS?

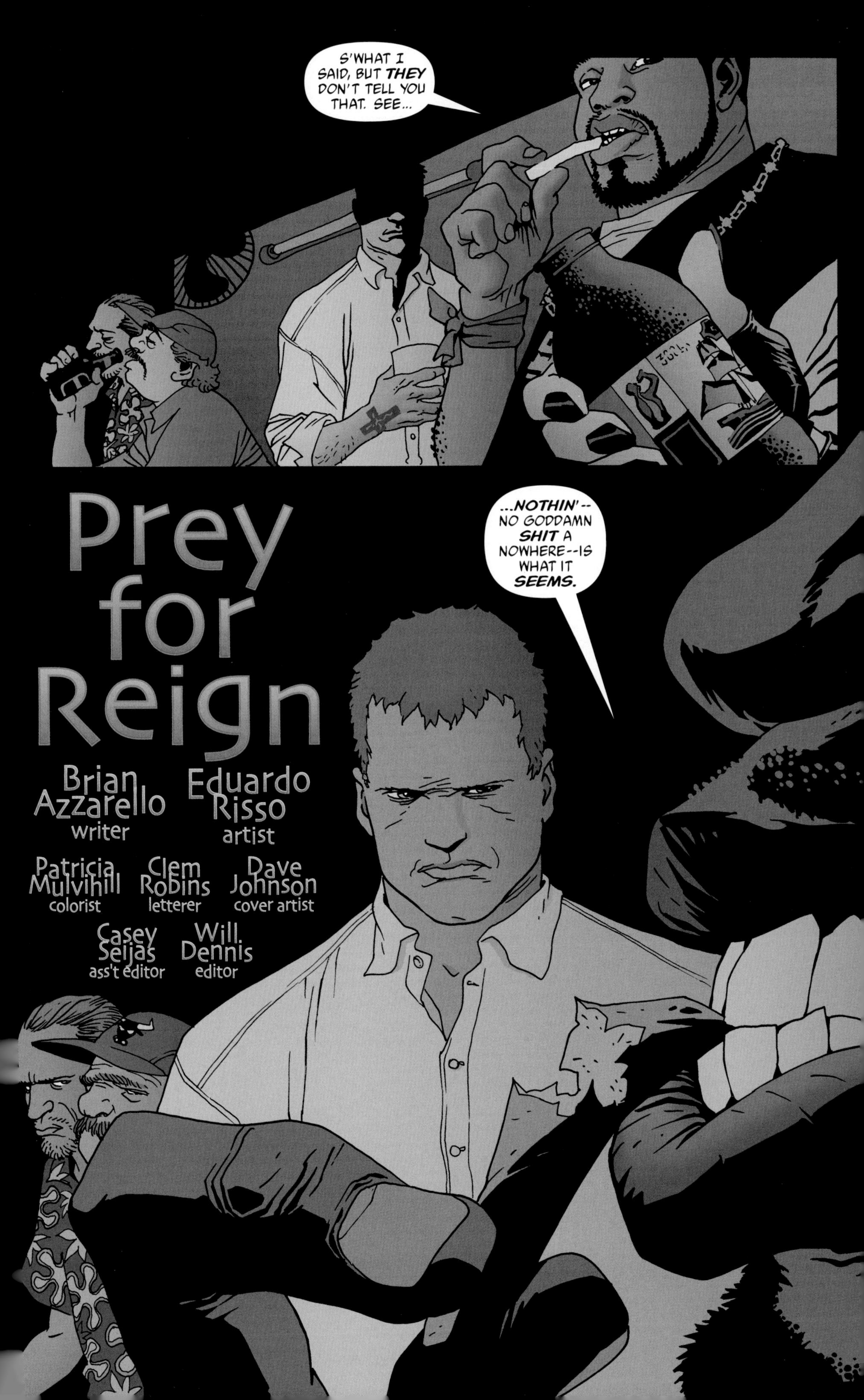
S'WHAT I SAID, BUT THEY DON'T TELL YOU THAT. SEE...
...NOTHIN' -- NO GODDAMN SHIT A NOWHERE--IS WHAT IT SEEMS.
Prey for Reign
Brian Azzarello writer
Eduardo Risso artist
Patricia Mulvihill colorist
Clem Robins letterer
Dave Johnson cover artist
Casey Seijas ass't editor
Will Dennis editor

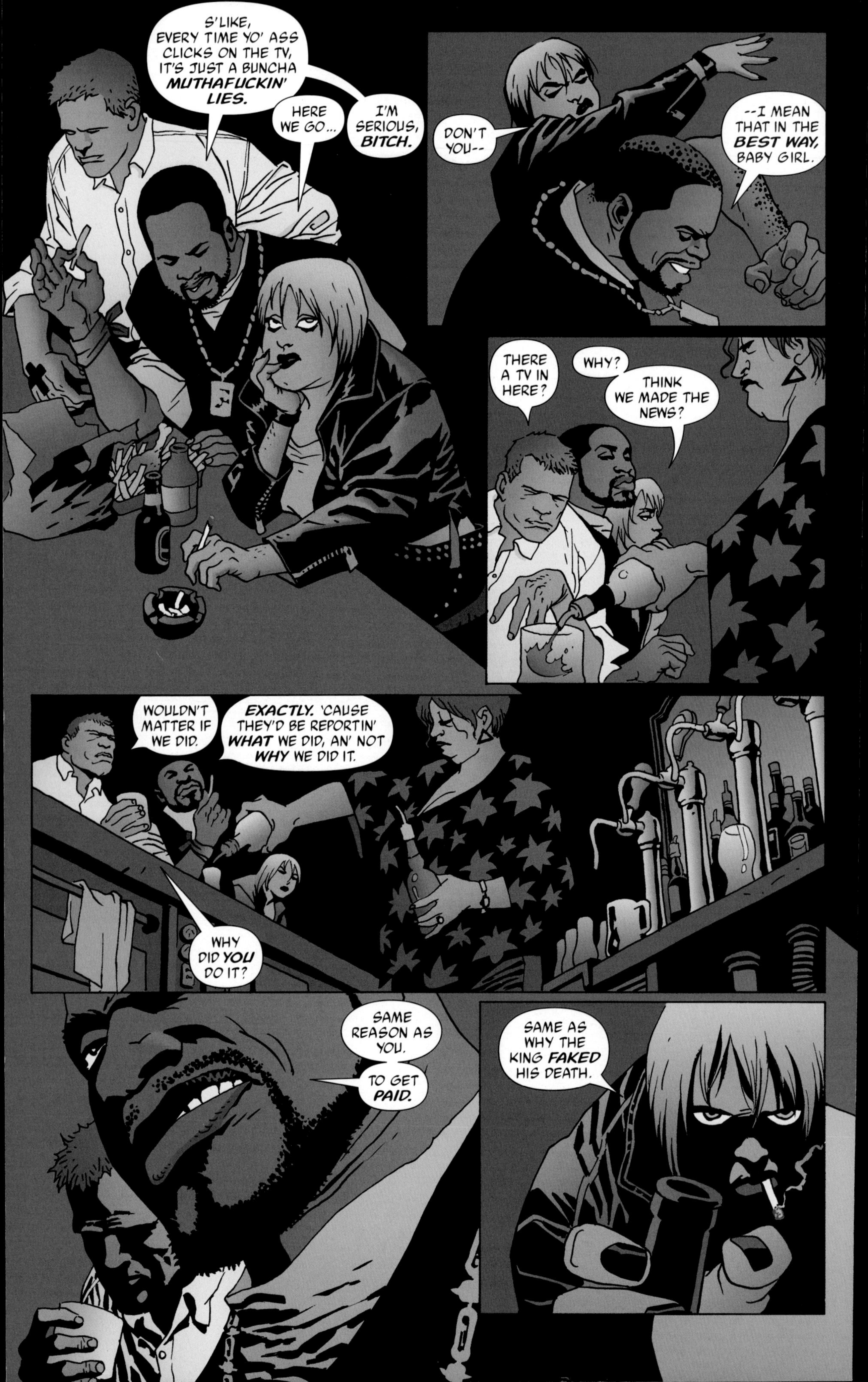

S'LIKE, EVERY TIME YO' ASS CLICKS ON THE TV, IT'S JUST A BUNCHA **MUTHAFUCKIN' LIES.**
HERE WE GO...
I'M SERIOUS, **BITCH.**
DON'T YOU--
--I MEAN THAT IN THE **BEST WAY,** BABY GIRL.
THERE A TV IN HERE?
WHY?
THINK WE MADE THE NEWS?
WOULDN'T MATTER IF WE DID.
EXACTLY. 'CAUSE THEY'D BE REPORTIN' **WHAT** WE DID, AN' NOT **WHY** WE DID IT.
WHY DID **YOU** DO IT?
SAME REASON AS YOU.
TO GET **PAID.**
SAME AS WHY THE KING **FAKED** HIS DEATH.

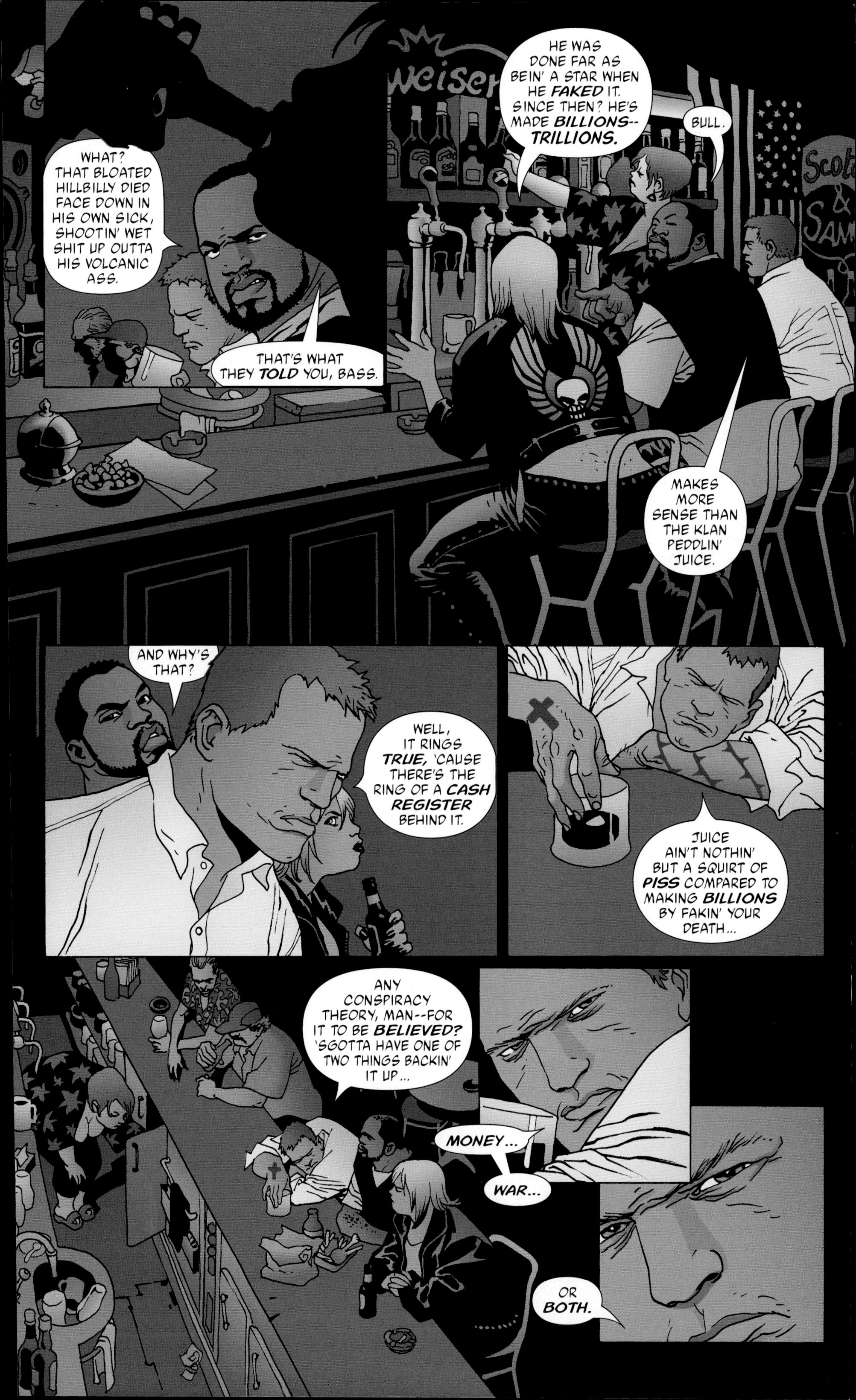
WHAT? THAT BLOATED HILLBILLY DIED FACE DOWN IN HIS OWN SICK, SHOOTIN' WET SHIT UP OUTTA HIS VOLCANIC ASS.
THAT'S WHAT THEY TOLD YOU, BASS.
HE WAS DONE FAR AS BEIN' A STAR WHEN HE FAKED IT. SINCE THEN? HE'S MADE BILLIONS--TRILLIONS.
BULL.
MAKES MORE SENSE THAN THE KLAN PEDDLIN' JUICE.
AND WHY'S THAT?
WELL, IT RINGS TRUE, 'CAUSE THERE'S THE RING OF A CASH REGISTER BEHIND IT.
JUICE AIN'T NOTHIN' BUT A SQUIRT OF PISS COMPARED TO MAKING BILLIONS BY FAKIN' YOUR DEATH...
ANY CONSPIRACY THEORY, MAN--FOR IT TO BE BELIEVED? 'SGOTTA HAVE ONE OF TWO THINGS BACKIN' IT UP...
MONEY...
WAR...
OR BOTH.

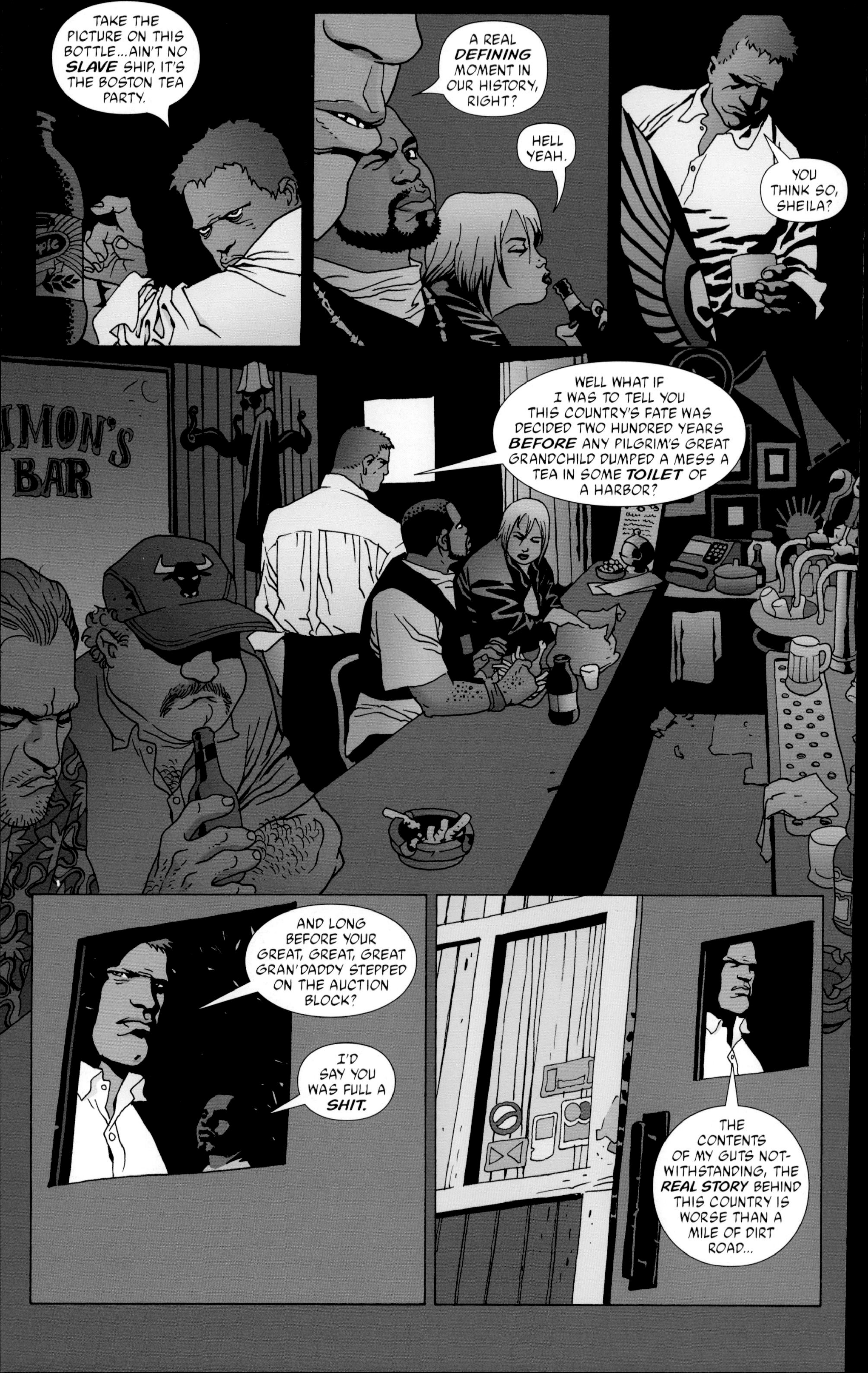
TAKE THE PICTURE ON THIS BOTTLE...AIN'T NO **SLAVE** SHIP, IT'S THE BOSTON TEA PARTY.
A REAL **DEFINING** MOMENT IN OUR HISTORY, RIGHT?
HELL YEAH.
YOU THINK SO, SHEILA?
SIMON'S BAR
WELL WHAT IF I WAS TO TELL YOU THIS COUNTRY'S FATE WAS DECIDED TWO HUNDRED YEARS **BEFORE** ANY PILGRIM'S GREAT GRANDCHILD DUMPED A MESS A TEA IN SOME **TOILET** OF A HARBOR?
AND LONG BEFORE YOUR GREAT, GREAT, GREAT GRAN'DADDY STEPPED ON THE AUCTION BLOCK?
I'D SAY YOU WAS FULL A **SHIT.**
THE CONTENTS OF MY GUTS NOT-WITHSTANDING, THE **REAL STORY** BEHIND THIS COUNTRY IS WORSE THAN A MILE OF DIRT ROAD...

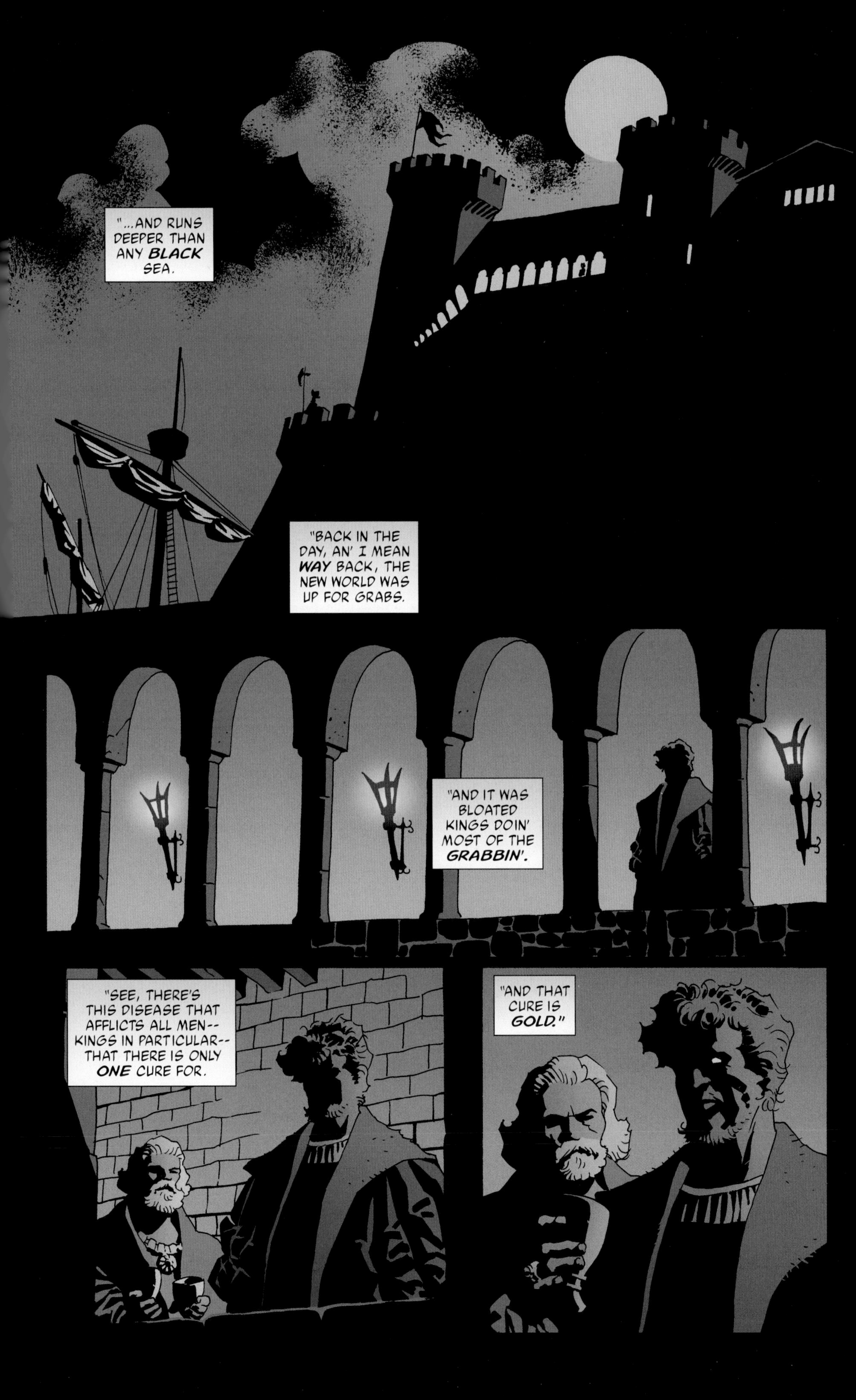
"...AND RUNS DEEPER THAN ANY BLACK SEA.
"BACK IN THE DAY, AN' I MEAN WAY BACK, THE NEW WORLD WAS UP FOR GRABS.
"AND IT WAS BLOATED KINGS DOIN' MOST OF THE GRABBIN'.
"SEE, THERE'S THIS DISEASE THAT AFFLICTS ALL MEN-- KINGS IN PARTICULAR-- THAT THERE IS ONLY ONE CURE FOR.
"AND THAT CURE IS GOLD."

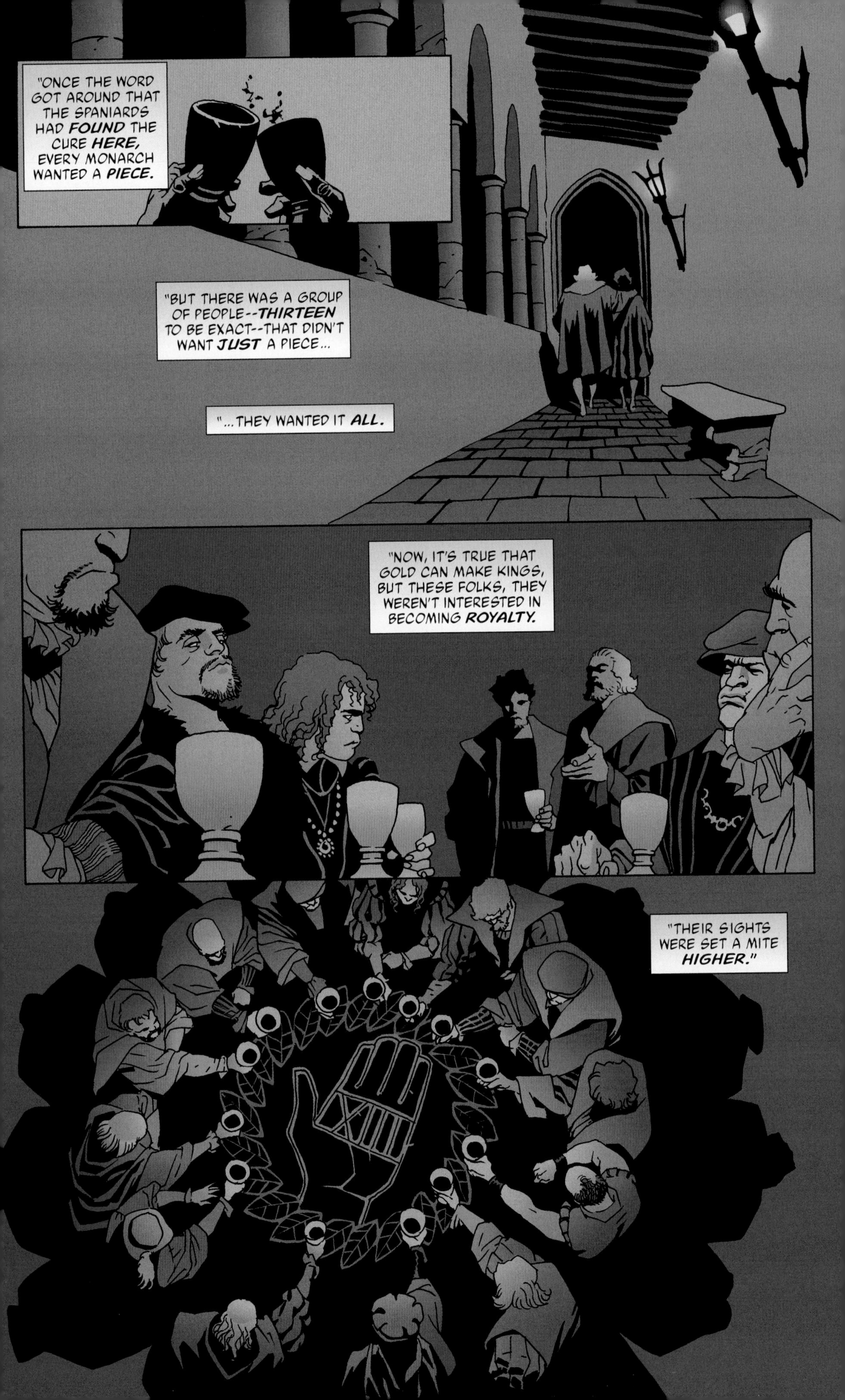
"ONCE THE WORD GOT AROUND THAT THE SPANIARDS HAD **FOUND** THE CURE **HERE**, EVERY MONARCH WANTED A **PIECE**.
"BUT THERE WAS A GROUP OF PEOPLE--**THIRTEEN** TO BE EXACT--THAT DIDN'T WANT **JUST** A PIECE...
"...THEY WANTED IT **ALL**.
"NOW, IT'S TRUE THAT GOLD CAN MAKE KINGS, BUT THESE FOLKS, THEY WEREN'T INTERESTED IN BECOMING **ROYALTY**.
"THEIR SIGHTS WERE SET A MITE **HIGHER**."

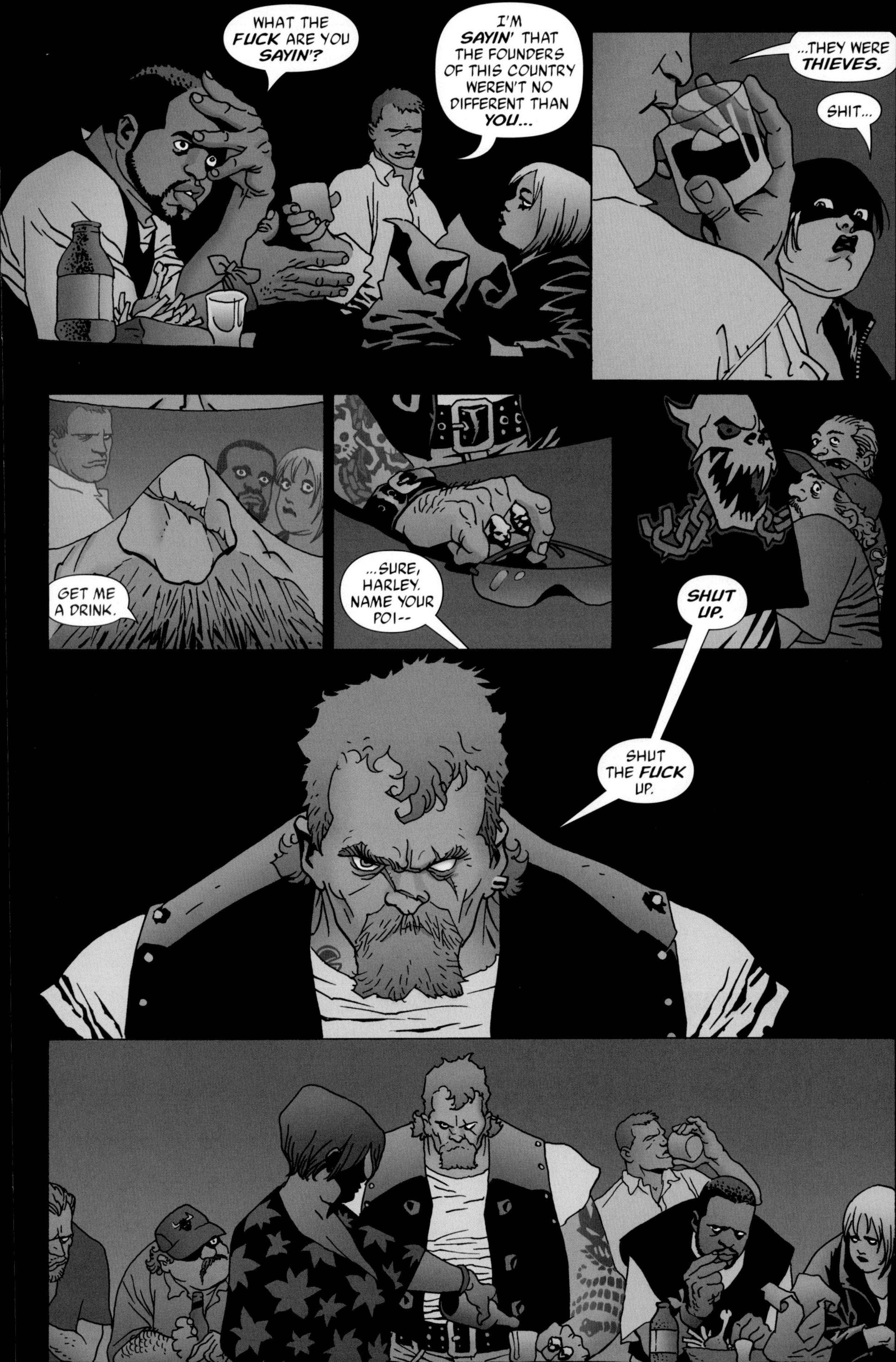
WHAT THE FUCK ARE YOU SAYIN'?
I'M SAYIN' THAT THE FOUNDERS OF THIS COUNTRY WEREN'T NO DIFFERENT THAN YOU...
...THEY WERE THIEVES.
SHIT...
GET ME A DRINK.
...SURE, HARLEY. NAME YOUR POI--
SHUT UP.
SHUT THE FUCK UP.

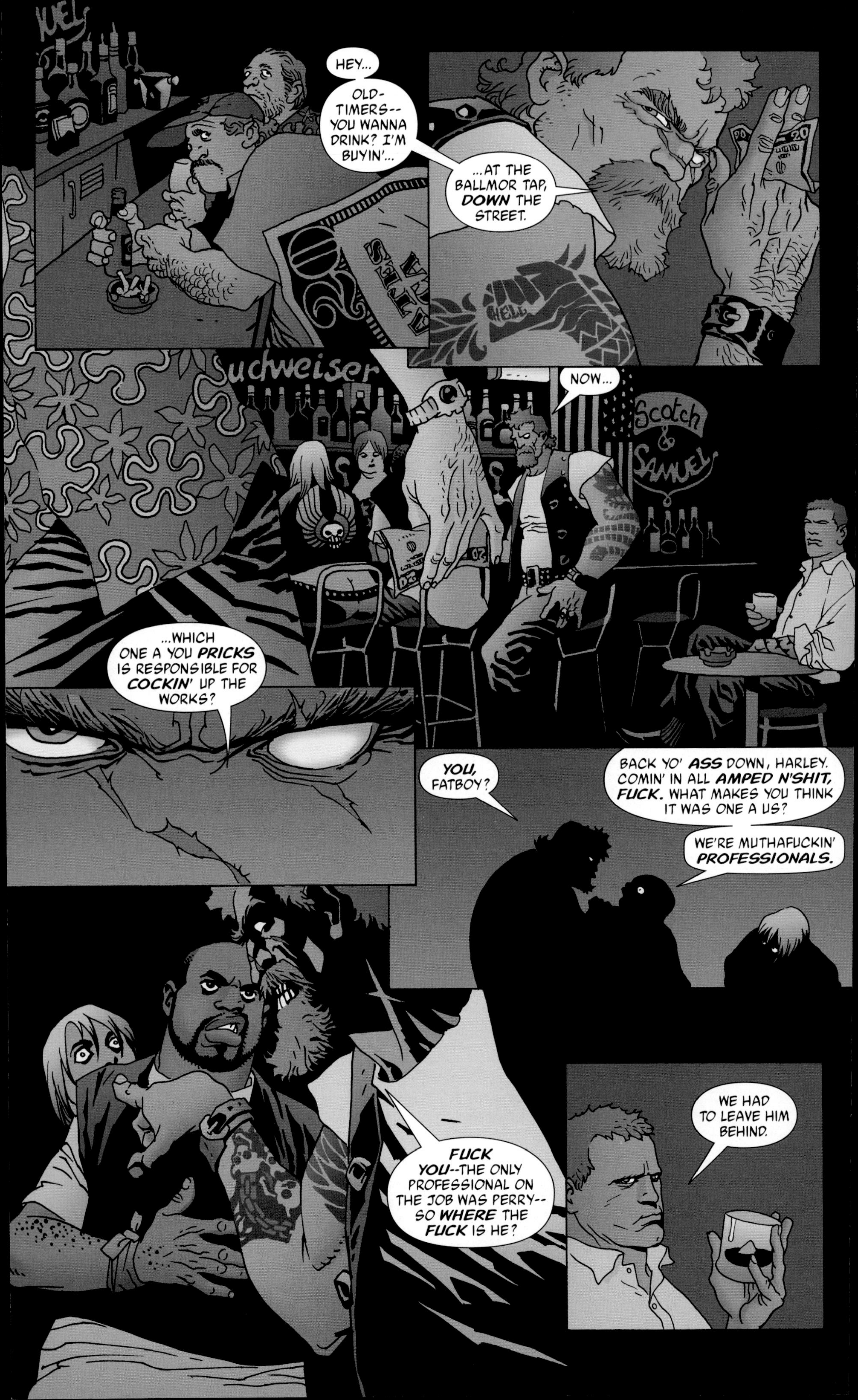
HEY...
OLD-TIMERS--YOU WANNA DRINK? I'M BUYIN'...
...AT THE BALLMOR TAP, DOWN THE STREET.
NOW...
...WHICH ONE A YOU PRICKS IS RESPONSIBLE FOR COCKIN' UP THE WORKS?
YOU, FATBOY?
BACK YO' ASS DOWN, HARLEY. COMIN' IN ALL AMPED N'SHIT, FUCK. WHAT MAKES YOU THINK IT WAS ONE A US?
WE'RE MUTHAFUCKIN' PROFESSIONALS.
FUCK YOU--THE ONLY PROFESSIONAL ON THE JOB WAS PERRY--SO WHERE THE FUCK IS HE?
WE HAD TO LEAVE HIM BEHIND.

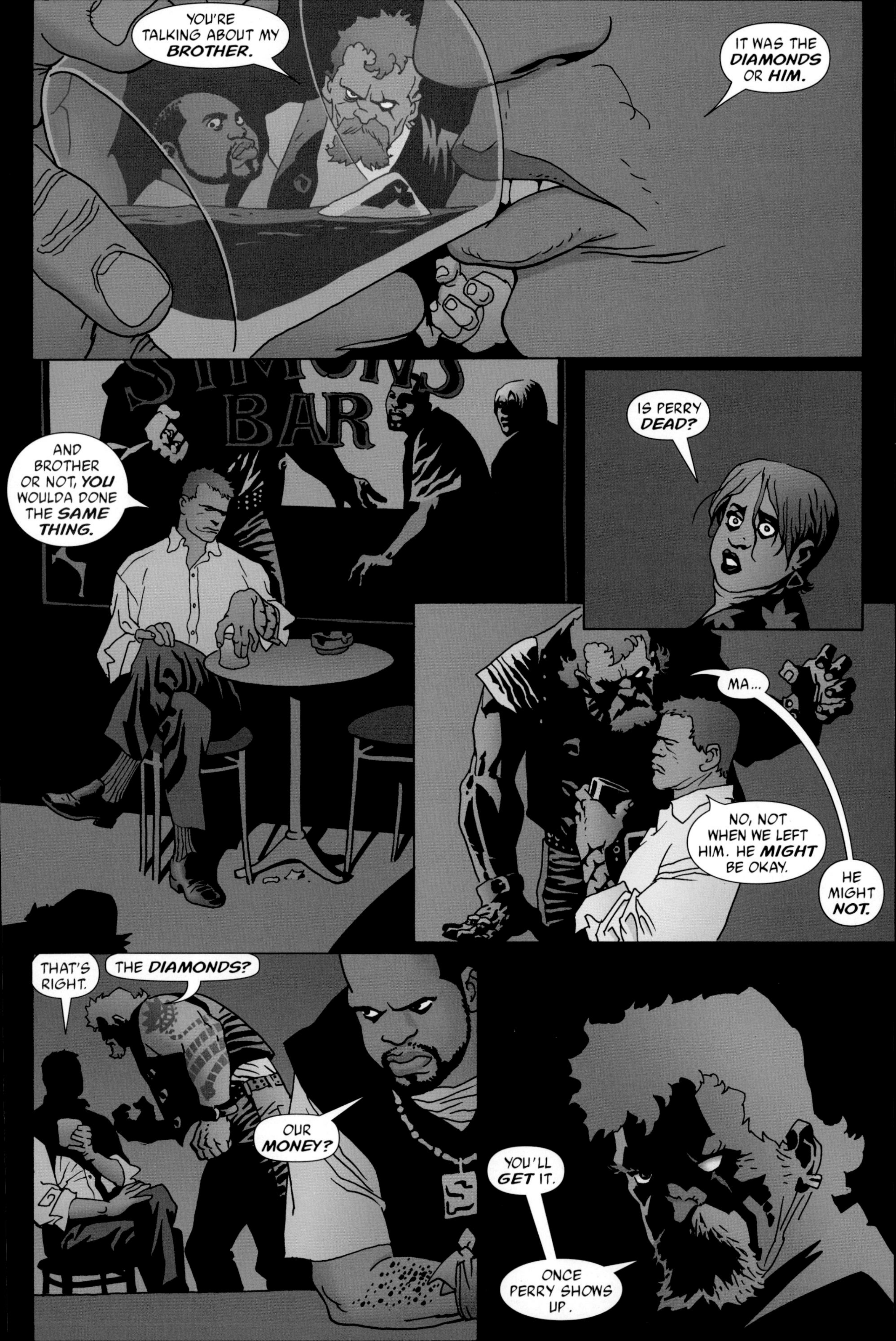
YOU'RE TALKING ABOUT MY BROTHER.
IT WAS THE DIAMONDS OR HIM.
AND BROTHER OR NOT, YOU WOULDA DONE THE SAME THING.
IS PERRY DEAD?
MA...
NO, NOT WHEN WE LEFT HIM. HE MIGHT BE OKAY.
HE MIGHT NOT.
THAT'S RIGHT.
THE DIAMONDS?
OUR MONEY?
YOU'LL GET IT.
ONCE PERRY SHOWS UP.

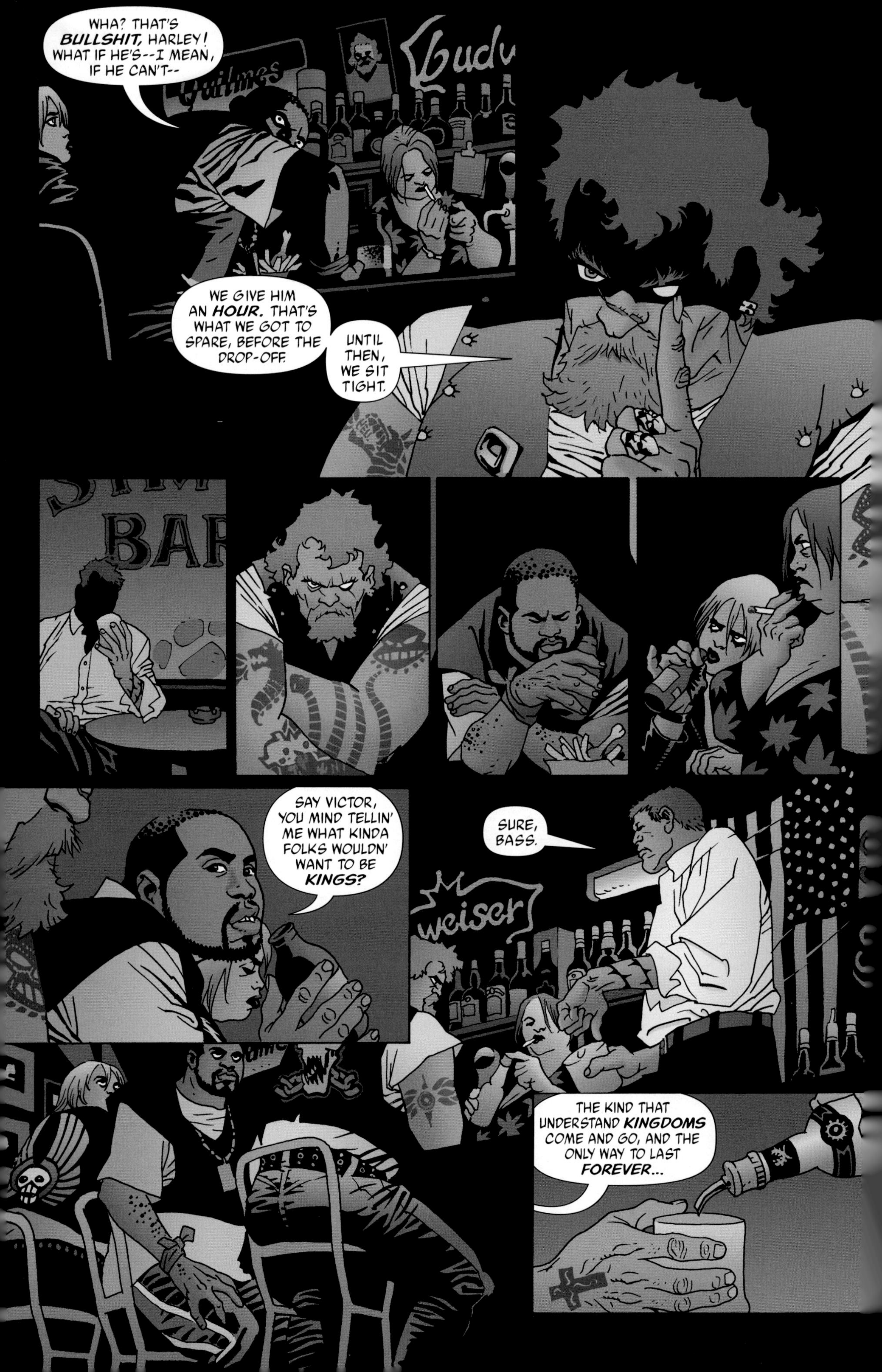
WHA? THAT'S **BULLSHIT,** HARLEY! WHAT IF HE'S--I MEAN, IF HE CAN'T--
WE GIVE HIM AN **HOUR.** THAT'S WHAT WE GOT TO SPARE, BEFORE THE DROP-OFF.
UNTIL THEN, WE SIT TIGHT.
SAY VICTOR, YOU MIND TELLIN' ME WHAT KINDA FOLKS WOULDN' WANT TO BE **KINGS?**
SURE, BASS.
THE KIND THAT UNDERSTAND **KINGDOMS** COME AND GO, AND THE ONLY WAY TO LAST **FOREVER...**

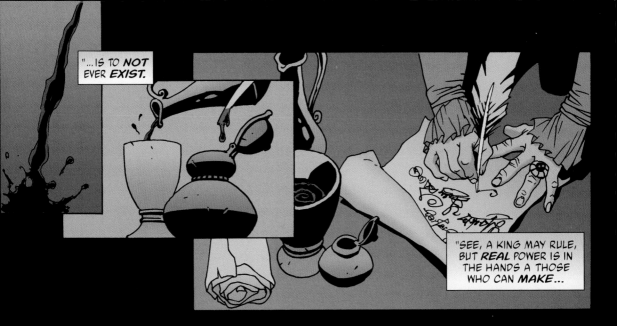

"...IS TO **NOT** EVER **EXIST.**"

"SEE, A KING MAY RULE, BUT **REAL** POWER IS IN THE HANDS A THOSE WHO CAN **MAKE...**"

"...OR **BREAK** 'EM. THAT'S BEEN THE WAY IT IS..."

"...**FOREVER.**"

"AND WHILE THESE FOLKS HAD BEEN AROUND JUST ABOUT AS LONG..."

"...THE IDEA OF CREATING A BINDING **TRUST** WAS NEW."

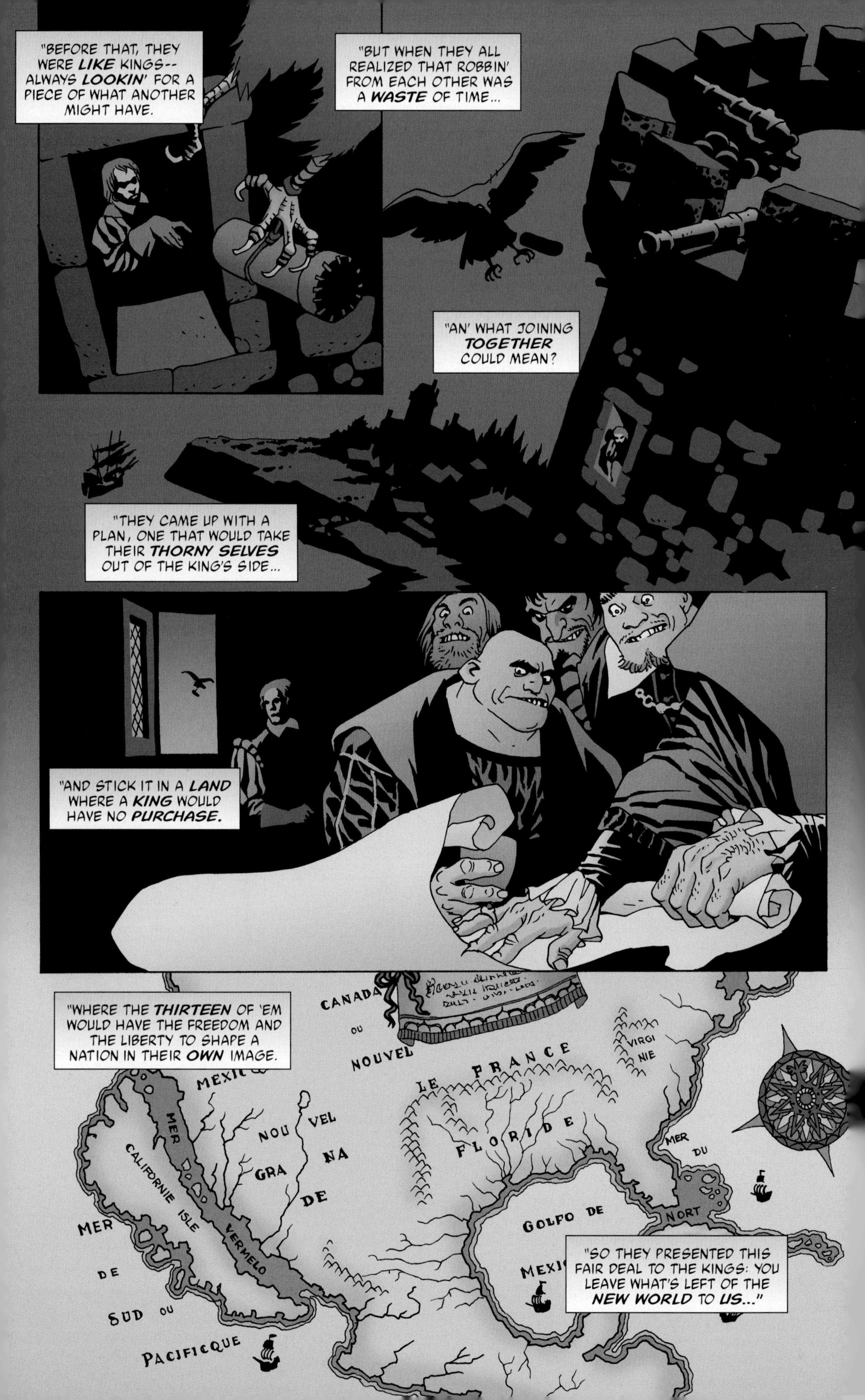
"BEFORE THAT, THEY WERE LIKE KINGS-- ALWAYS LOOKIN' FOR A PIECE OF WHAT ANOTHER MIGHT HAVE.
"BUT WHEN THEY ALL REALIZED THAT ROBBIN' FROM EACH OTHER WAS A WASTE OF TIME...
"AN' WHAT JOINING TOGETHER COULD MEAN?
"THEY CAME UP WITH A PLAN, ONE THAT WOULD TAKE THEIR THORNY SELVES OUT OF THE KING'S SIDE...
"AND STICK IT IN A LAND WHERE A KING WOULD HAVE NO PURCHASE.
"WHERE THE THIRTEEN OF 'EM WOULD HAVE THE FREEDOM AND THE LIBERTY TO SHAPE A NATION IN THEIR OWN IMAGE.
CANADA
OU
NOUVEL
LE FRANCE
VIRGI NIE
MEXIC
MER
CALIFORNIE ISLE
VERMELO
NOU VEL GRA NA DE
FLORIDE
MER DU NORT
GOLFO DE MEXIC
MER DE SUD OU PACIFICQUE
"SO THEY PRESENTED THIS FAIR DEAL TO THE KINGS: YOU LEAVE WHAT'S LEFT OF THE NEW WORLD TO US..."

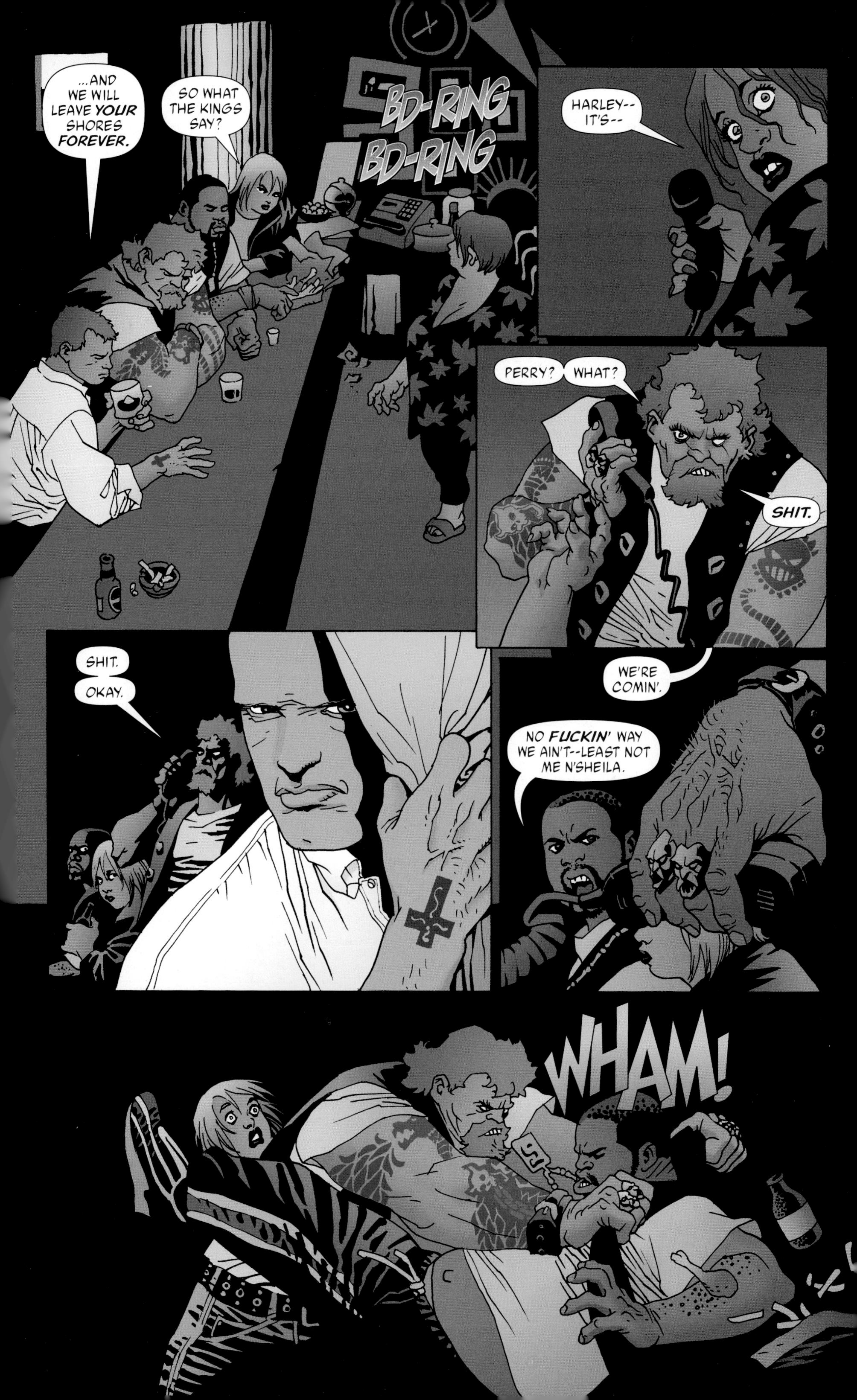
...AND WE WILL LEAVE YOUR SHORES FOREVER.
SO WHAT THE KINGS SAY?
BD-RING BD-RING
HARLEY-- IT'S--
PERRY?
WHAT?
SHIT.
SHIT.
OKAY.
WE'RE COMIN'.
NO FUCKIN' WAY WE AIN'T--LEAST NOT ME N'SHEILA.
WHAM!

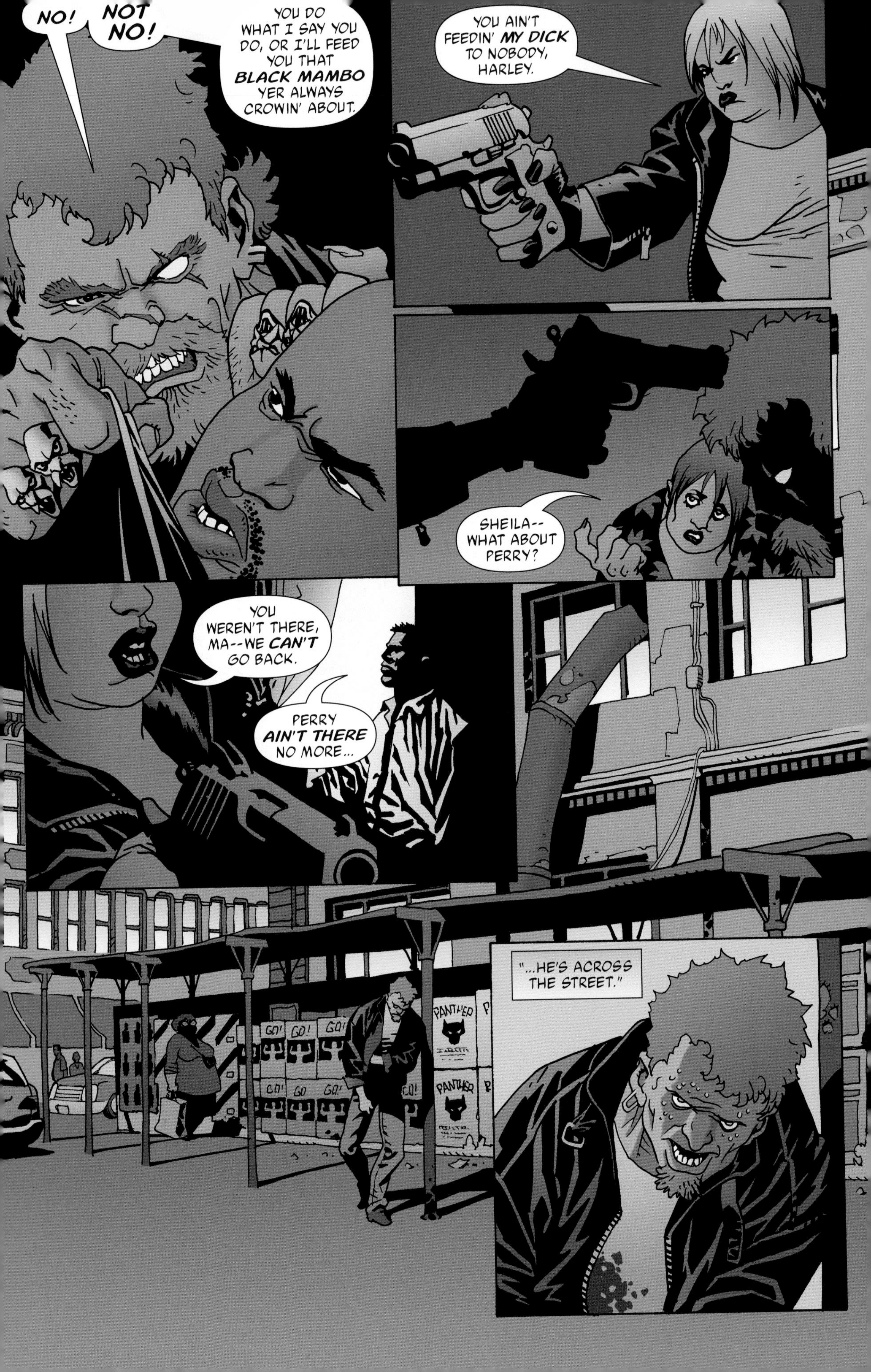
NO!
NOT NO!
YOU DO WHAT I SAY YOU DO, OR I'LL FEED YOU THAT BLACK MAMBO YER ALWAYS CROWIN' ABOUT.
YOU AIN'T FEEDIN' MY DICK TO NOBODY, HARLEY.
SHEILA-- WHAT ABOUT PERRY?
YOU WEREN'T THERE, MA--WE CAN'T GO BACK.
PERRY AIN'T THERE NO MORE...
"...HE'S ACROSS THE STREET."
GO!
GO!
GO!
PANTHER
PANTHER

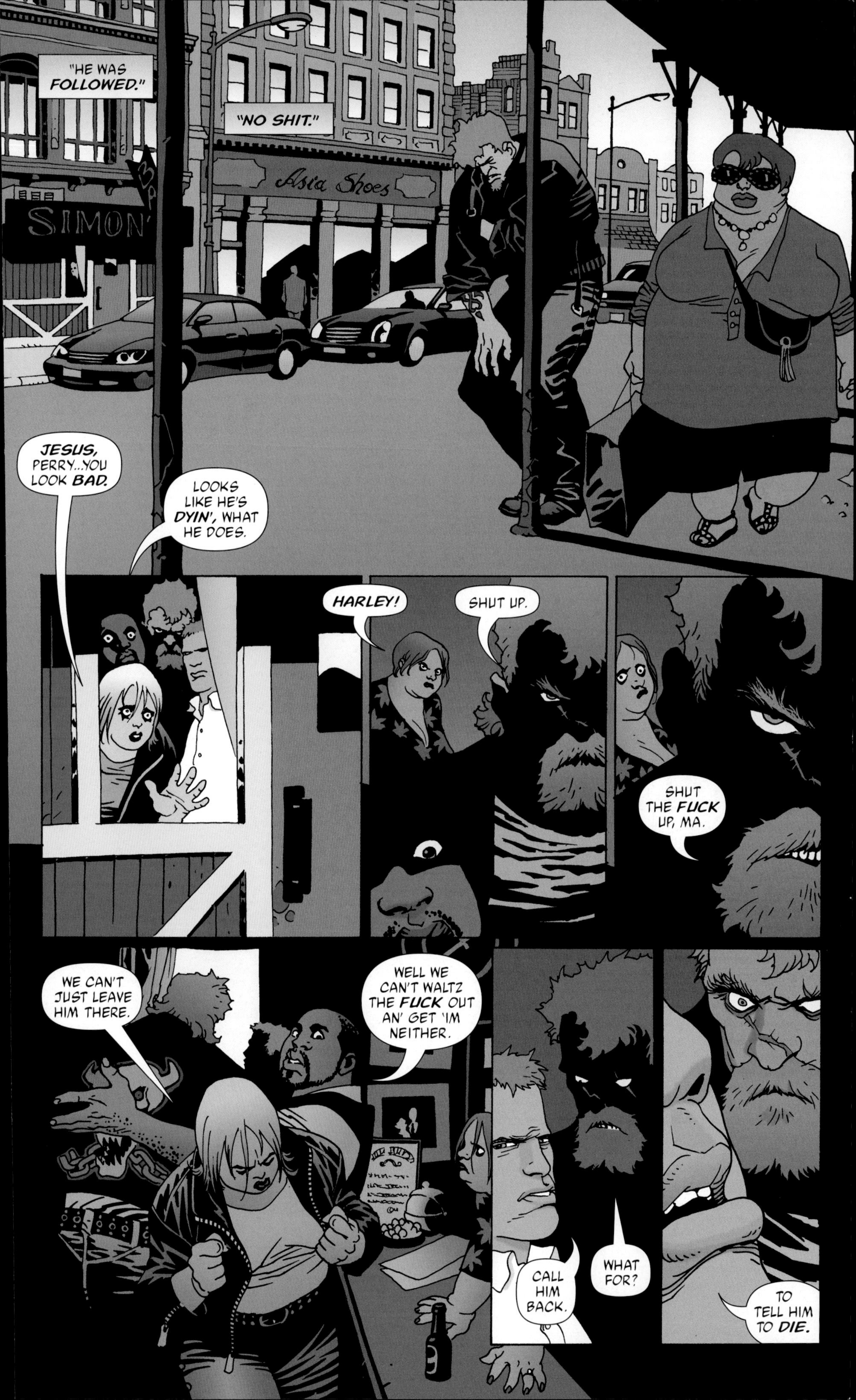
"HE WAS FOLLOWED."
"NO SHIT."
Asia Shoes
SIMON
JESUS, PERRY...YOU LOOK BAD.
LOOKS LIKE HE'S DYIN', WHAT HE DOES.
HARLEY!
SHUT UP.
SHUT THE FUCK UP, MA.
WE CAN'T JUST LEAVE HIM THERE.
WELL WE CAN'T WALTZ THE FUCK OUT AN' GET 'IM NEITHER.
CALL HIM BACK.
WHAT FOR?
TO TELL HIM TO DIE.

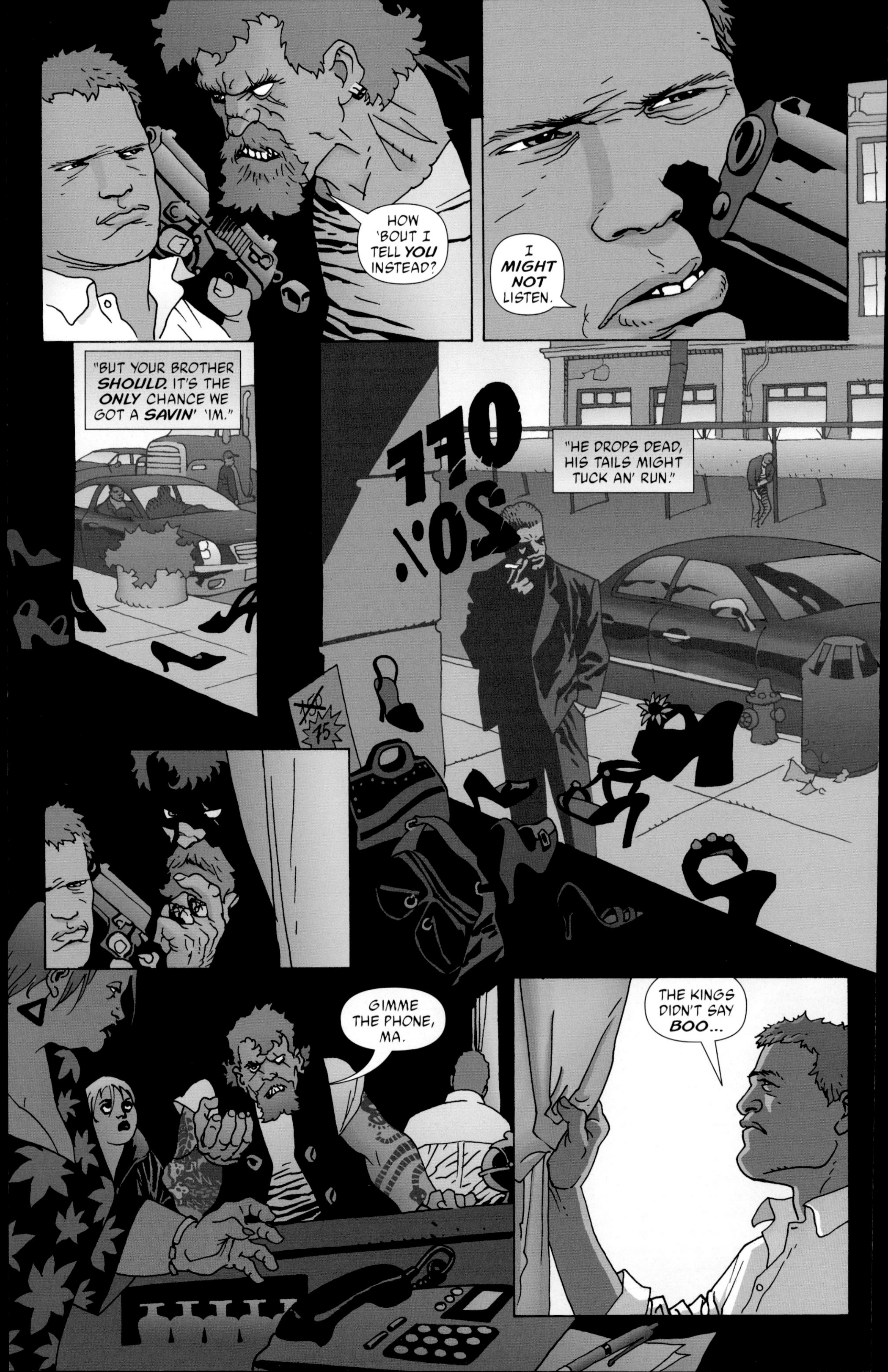
HOW 'BOUT I TELL YOU INSTEAD?
I MIGHT NOT LISTEN.
"BUT YOUR BROTHER SHOULD. IT'S THE ONLY CHANCE WE GOT A SAVIN' 'IM."
20% OFF
"HE DROPS DEAD, HIS TAILS MIGHT TUCK AN' RUN."
GIMME THE PHONE, MA.
THE KINGS DIDN'T SAY BOO...

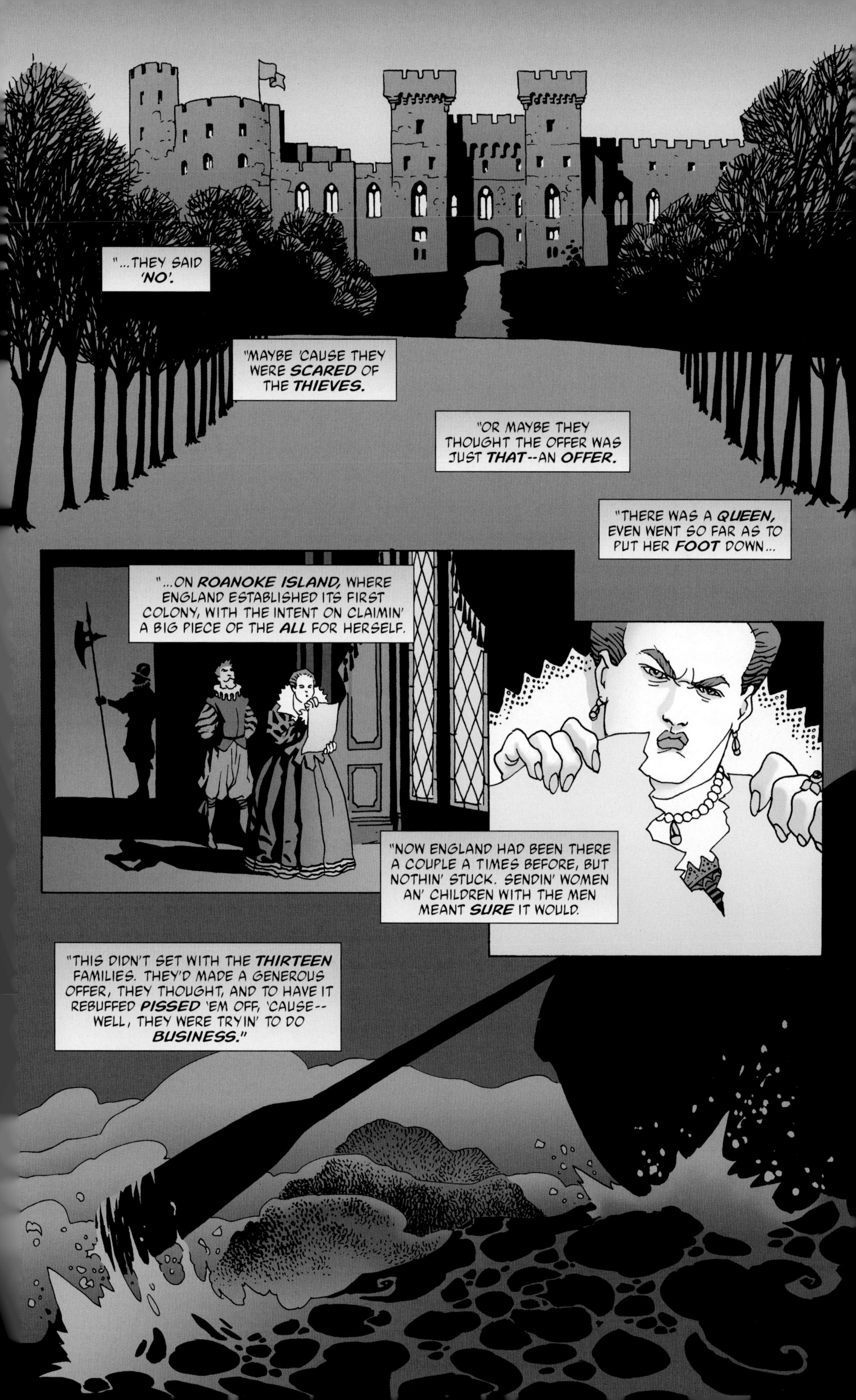
"...THEY SAID 'NO'.
"MAYBE 'CAUSE THEY WERE SCARED OF THE THIEVES.
"OR MAYBE THEY THOUGHT THE OFFER WAS JUST THAT--AN OFFER.
"THERE WAS A QUEEN, EVEN WENT SO FAR AS TO PUT HER FOOT DOWN...
"...ON ROANOKE ISLAND, WHERE ENGLAND ESTABLISHED ITS FIRST COLONY, WITH THE INTENT ON CLAIMIN' A BIG PIECE OF THE ALL FOR HERSELF.
"NOW ENGLAND HAD BEEN THERE A COUPLE A TIMES BEFORE, BUT NOTHIN' STUCK. SENDIN' WOMEN AN' CHILDREN WITH THE MEN MEANT SURE IT WOULD.
"THIS DIDN'T SET WITH THE THIRTEEN FAMILIES. THEY'D MADE A GENEROUS OFFER, THEY THOUGHT, AND TO HAVE IT REBUFFED PISSED 'EM OFF, 'CAUSE--WELL, THEY WERE TRYIN' TO DO BUSINESS."

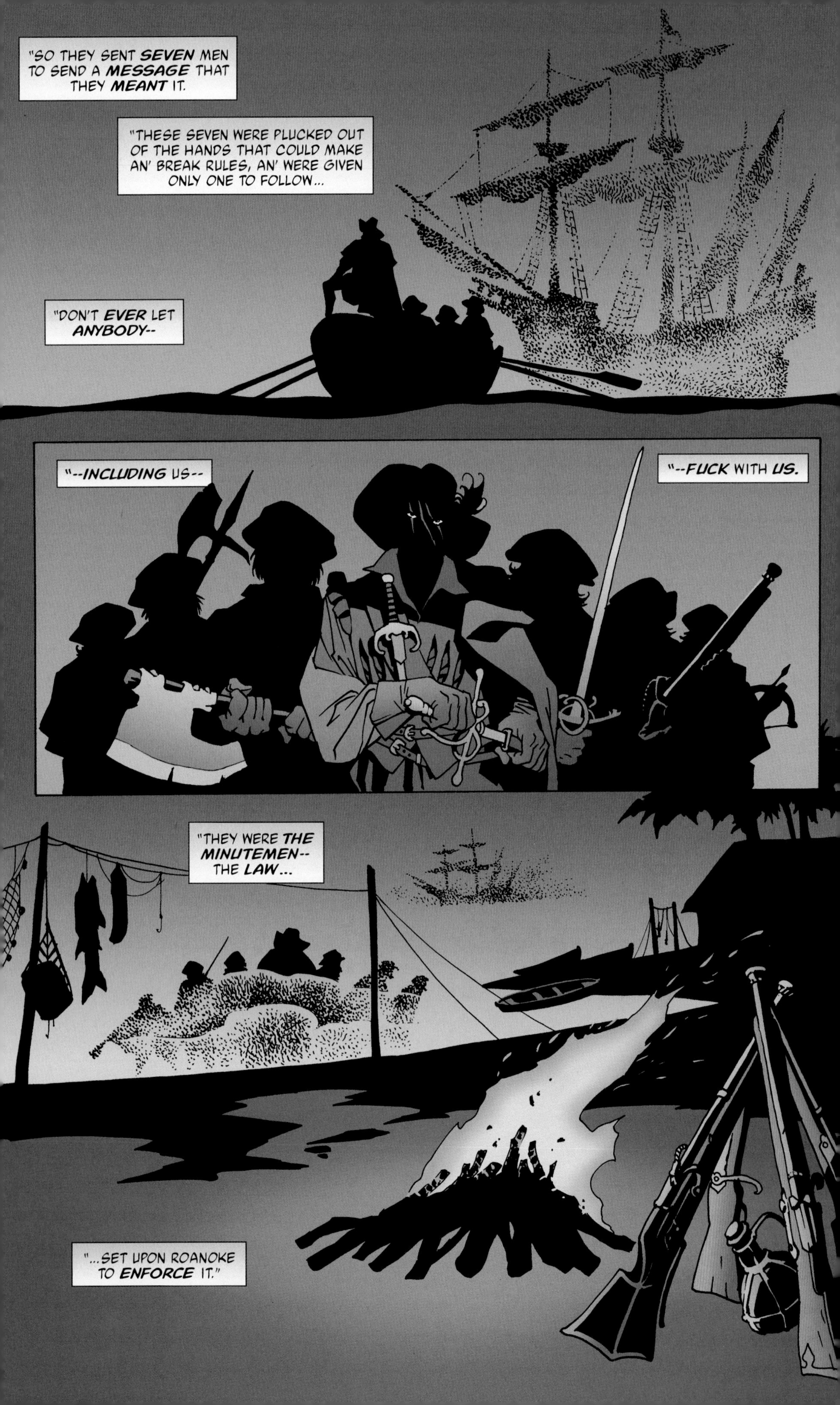

"SO THEY SENT SEVEN MEN TO SEND A MESSAGE THAT THEY MEANT IT.
"THESE SEVEN WERE PLUCKED OUT OF THE HANDS THAT COULD MAKE AN' BREAK RULES, AN' WERE GIVEN ONLY ONE TO FOLLOW...
"DON'T EVER LET ANYBODY--
"--INCLUDING US--
"--FUCK WITH US.
"THEY WERE THE MINUTEMEN-- THE LAW...
"...SET UPON ROANOKE TO ENFORCE IT."

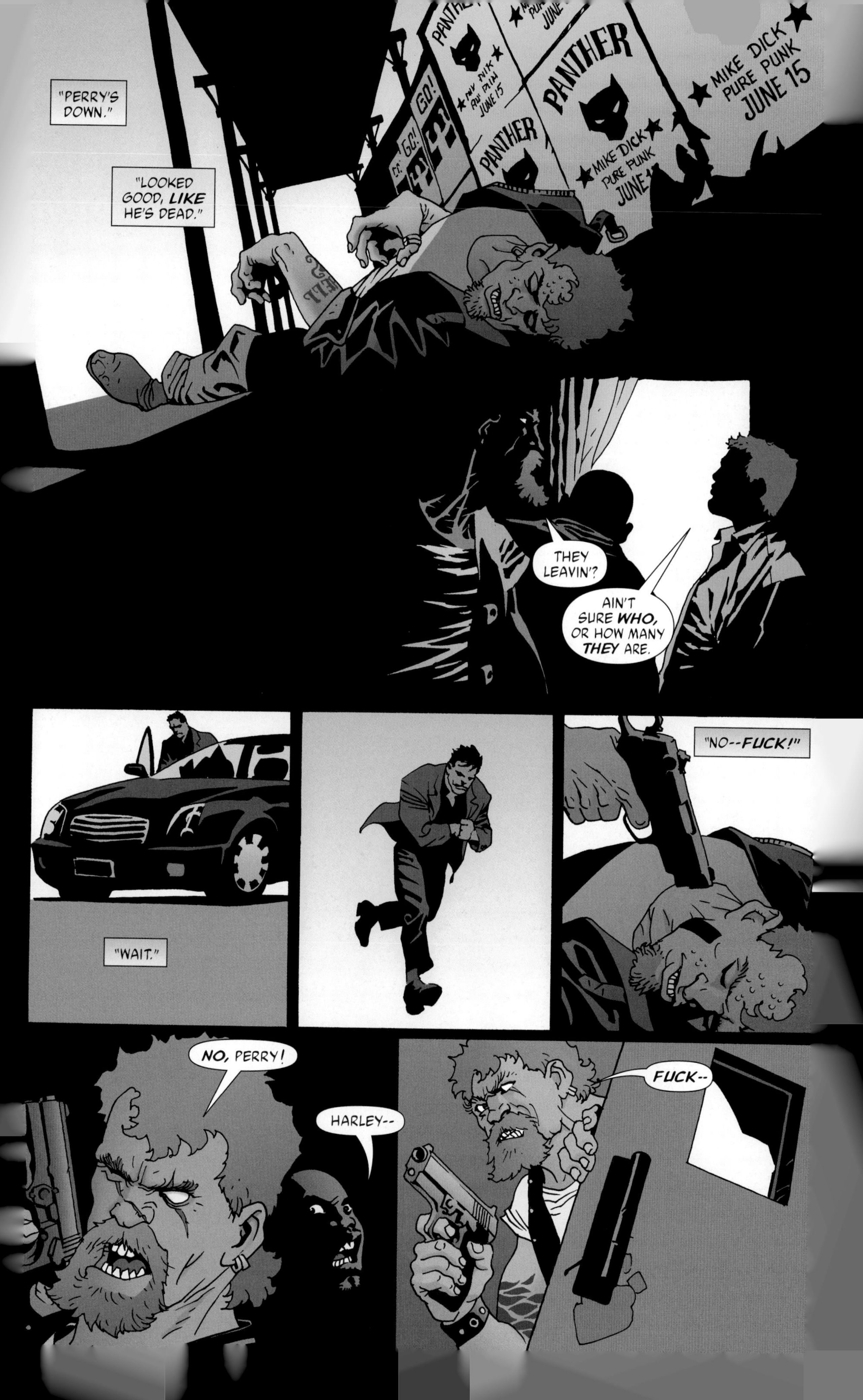
PANTHER
MIKE DICK
PURE PUNK
JUNE 15
"PERRY'S DOWN."
"LOOKED GOOD, LIKE HE'S DEAD."
THEY LEAVIN'?
AIN'T SURE WHO, OR HOW MANY THEY ARE.
"WAIT."
"NO--FUCK!"
NO, PERRY!
HARLEY--
FUCK--

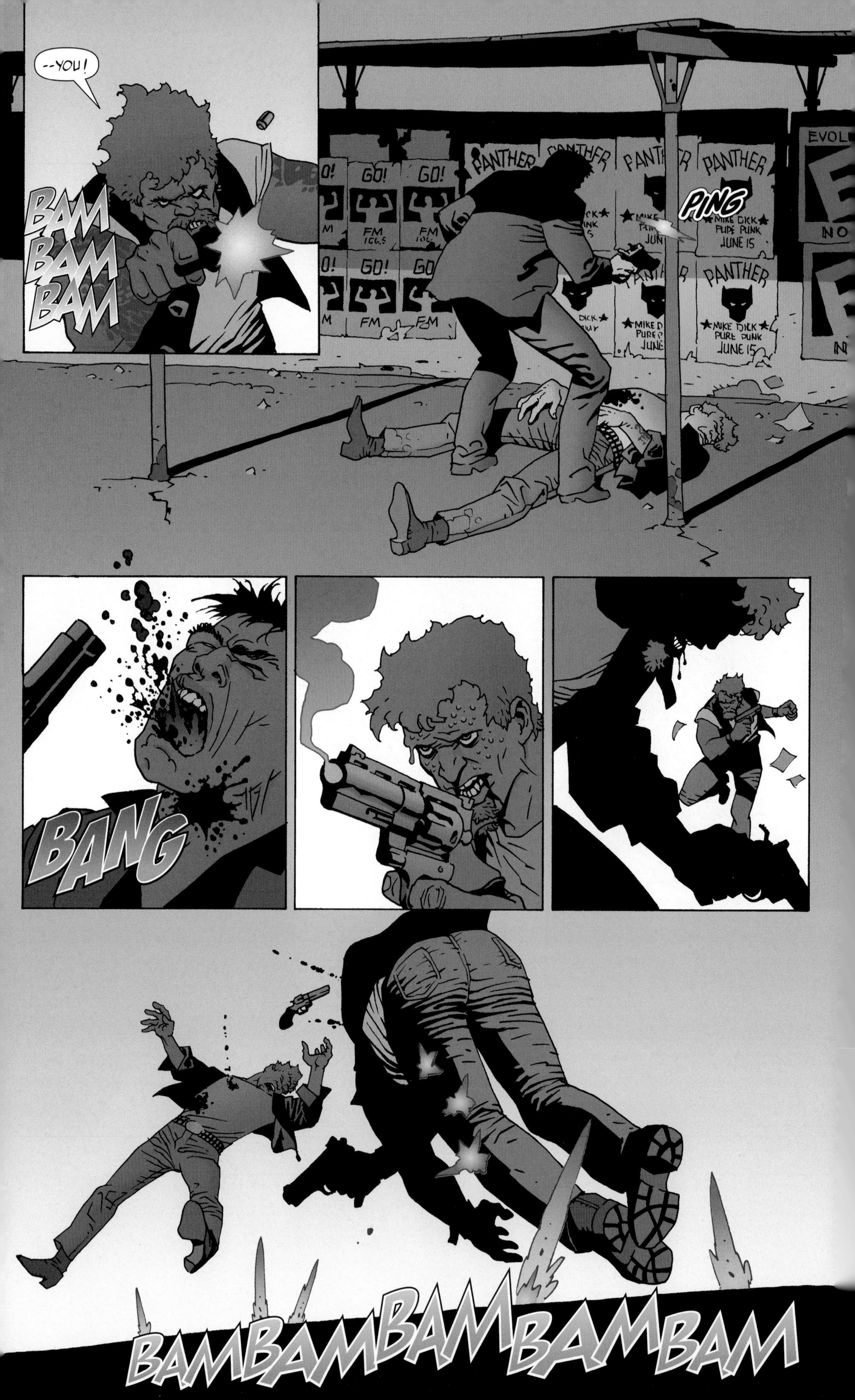
--YOU!
BAM BAM BAM
PANTHER
GO!
FM
MIKE DICK
PURE PUNK
JUNE 15
PING
BANG
BAMBAMBAMBAMBAM

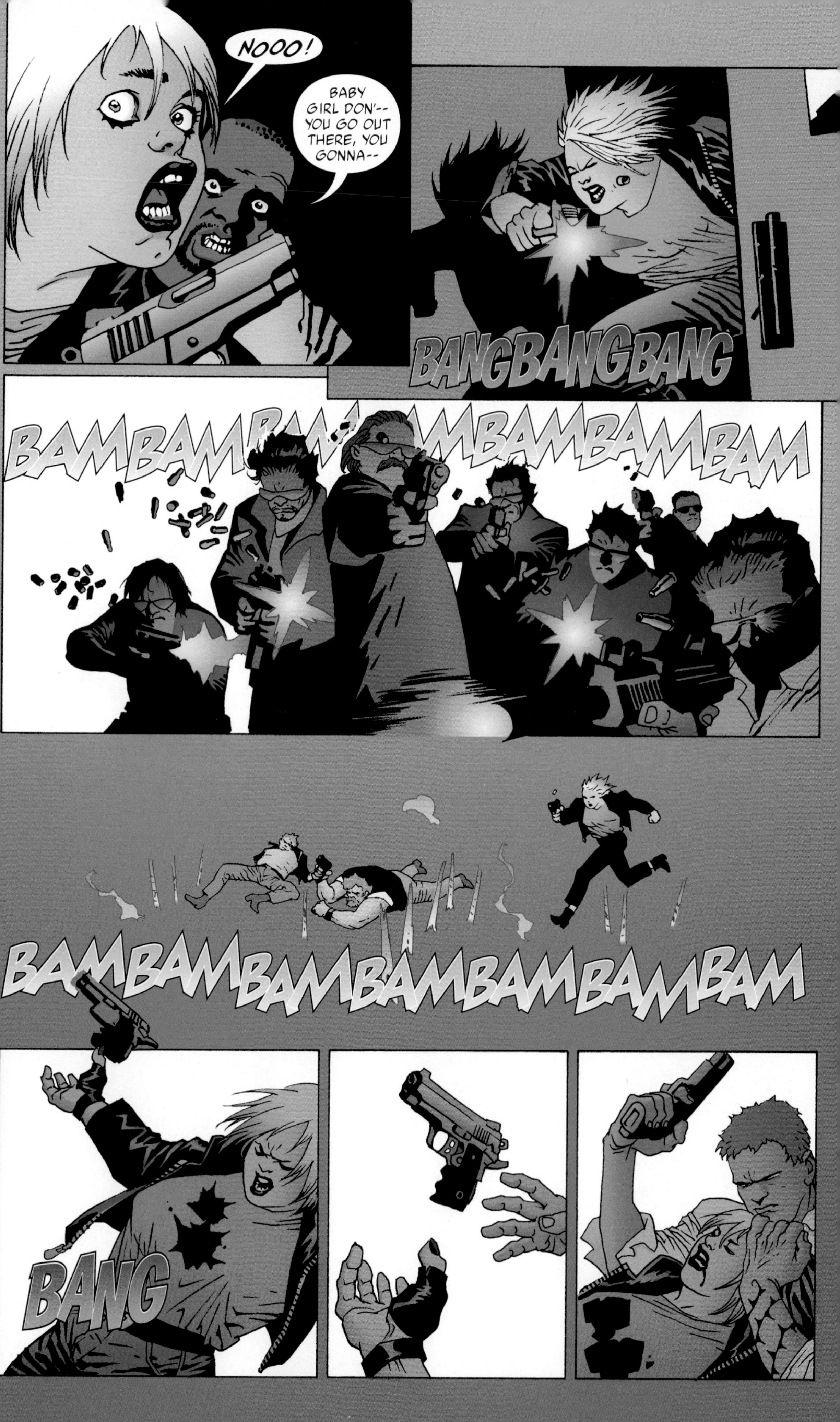
NOOO!
BABY GIRL DON'-- YOU GO OUT THERE, YOU GONNA--
BANGBANGBANG
BAMBAMBAMBAMBAMBAMBAMBAM
BAMBAMBAMBAMBAMBAMBAMBAM
BANG

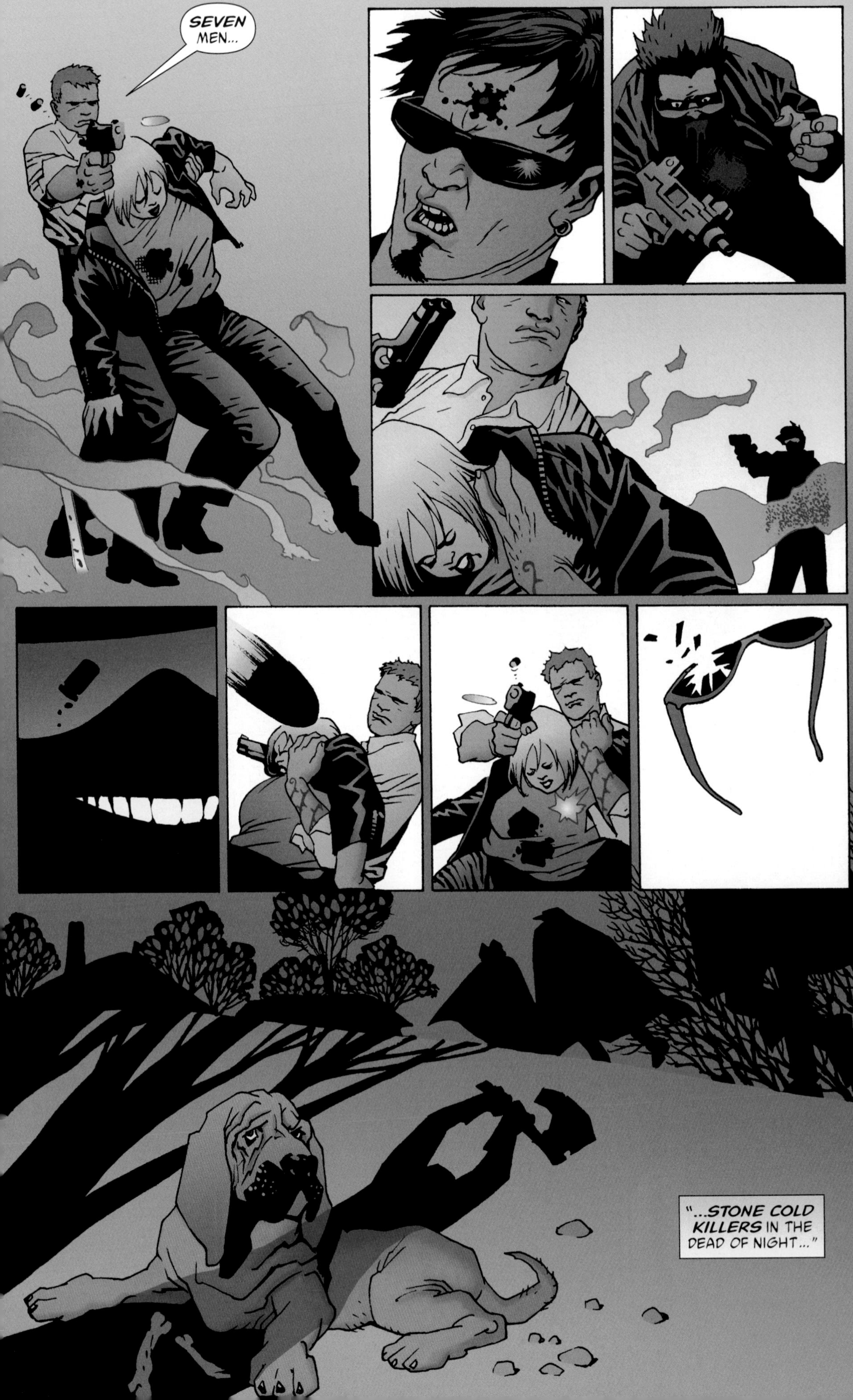
SEVEN MEN...
"...STONE COLD KILLERS IN THE DEAD OF NIGHT..."

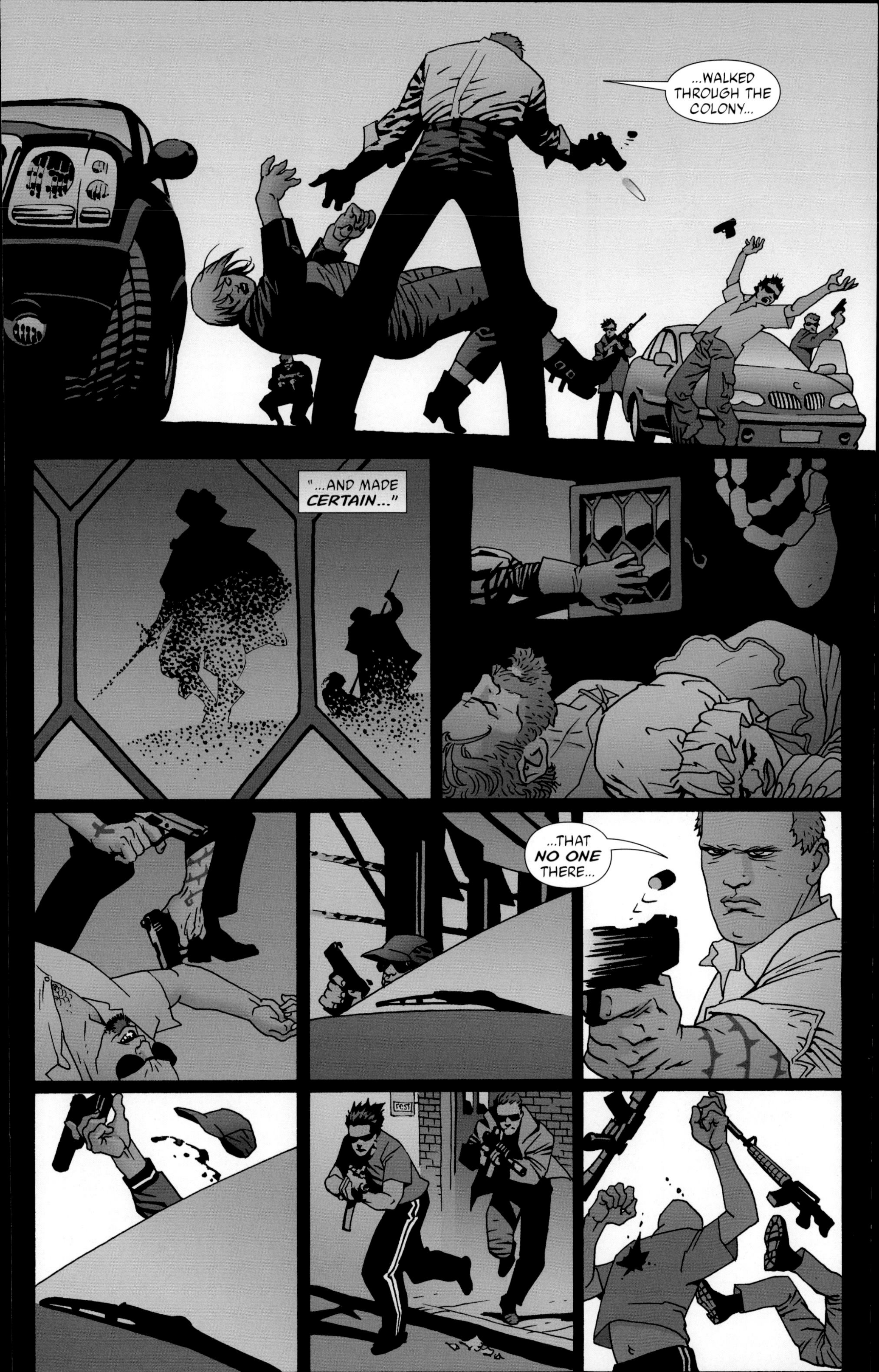
...WALKED THROUGH THE COLONY...
"...AND MADE CERTAIN..."
...THAT NO ONE THERE...

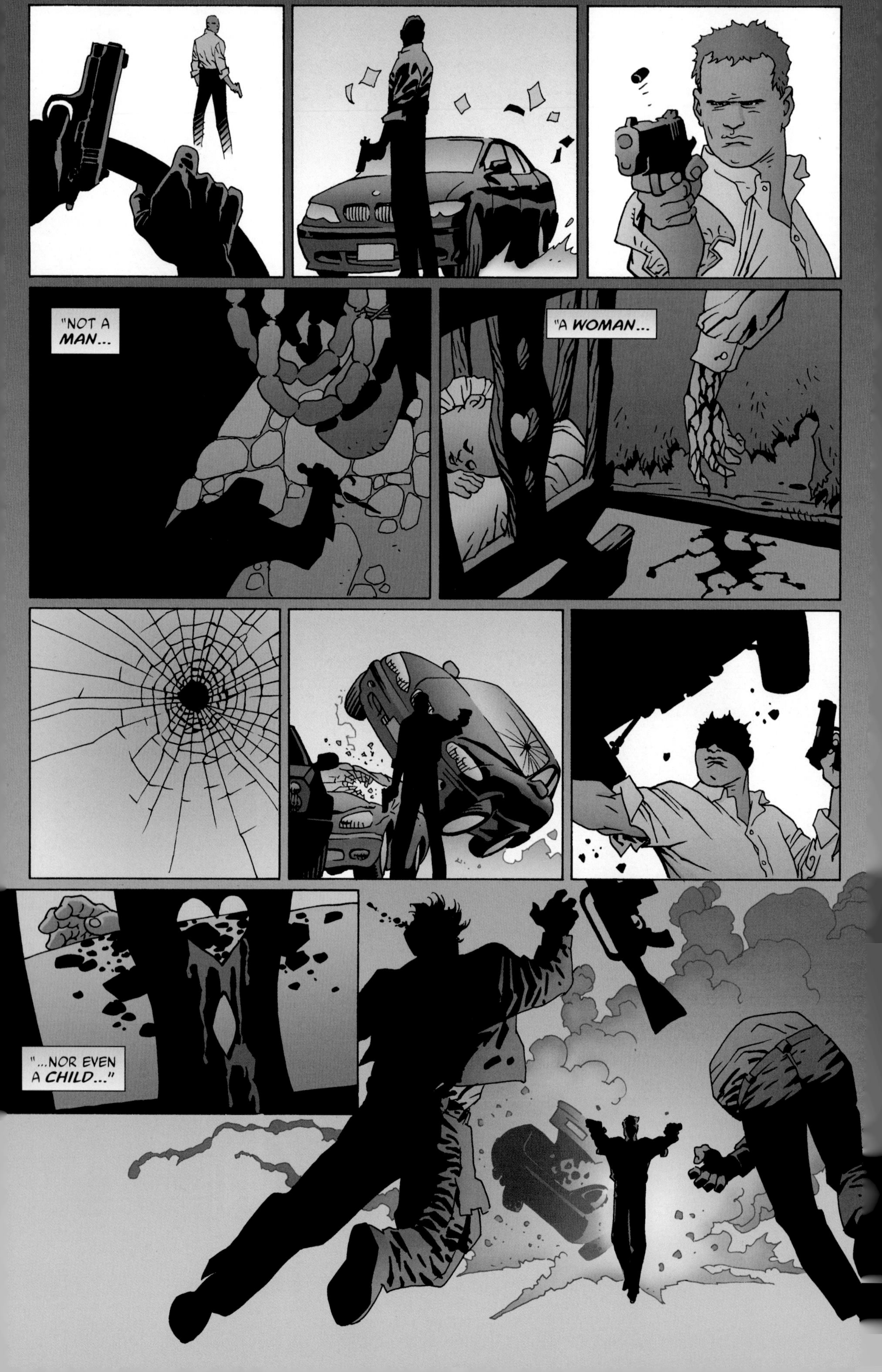
"NOT A MAN...
"A WOMAN...
"...NOR EVEN A CHILD..."

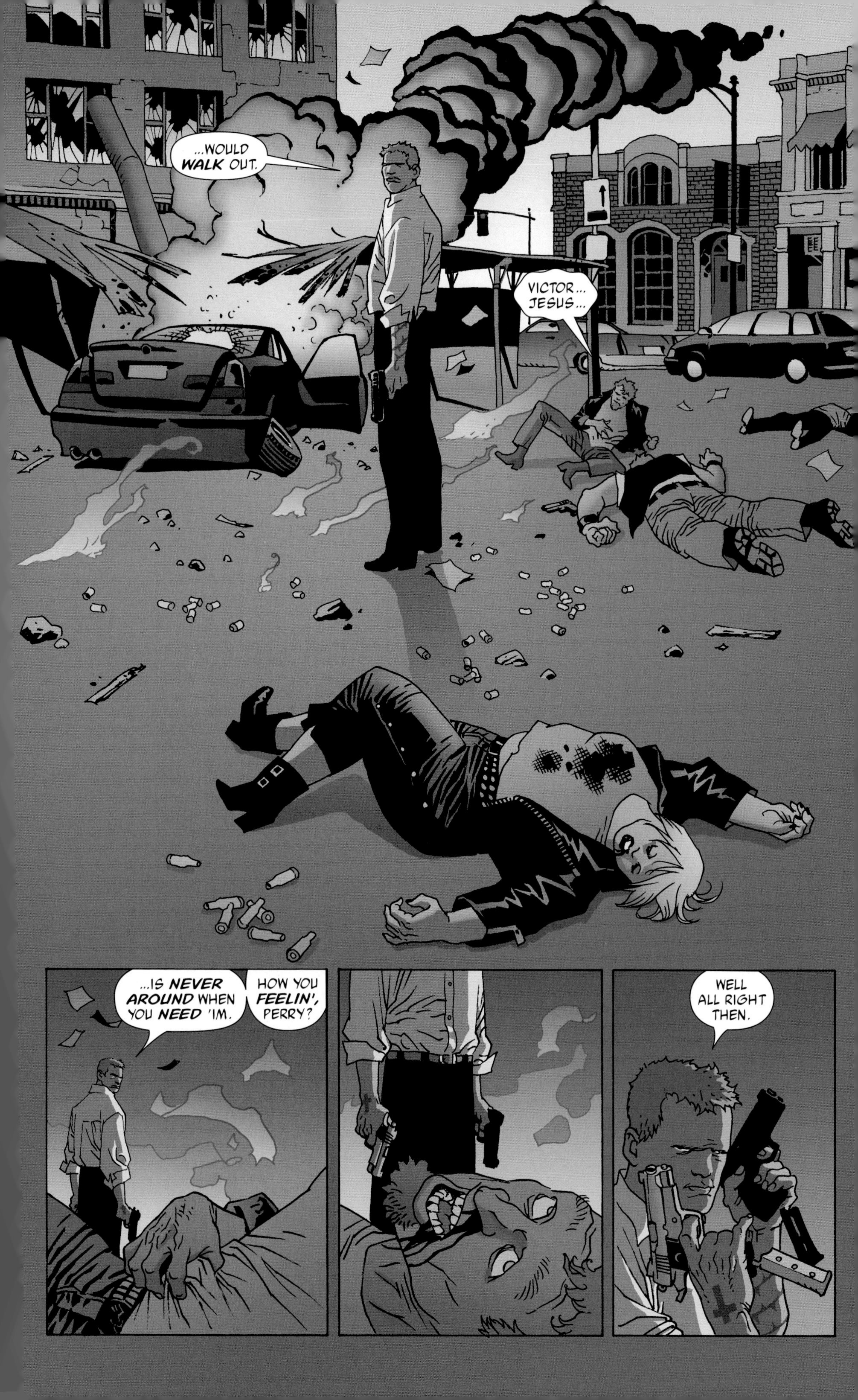
...WOULD WALK OUT.
VICTOR... JESUS...
...IS NEVER AROUND WHEN YOU NEED 'IM.
HOW YOU FEELIN', PERRY?
WELL ALL RIGHT THEN.

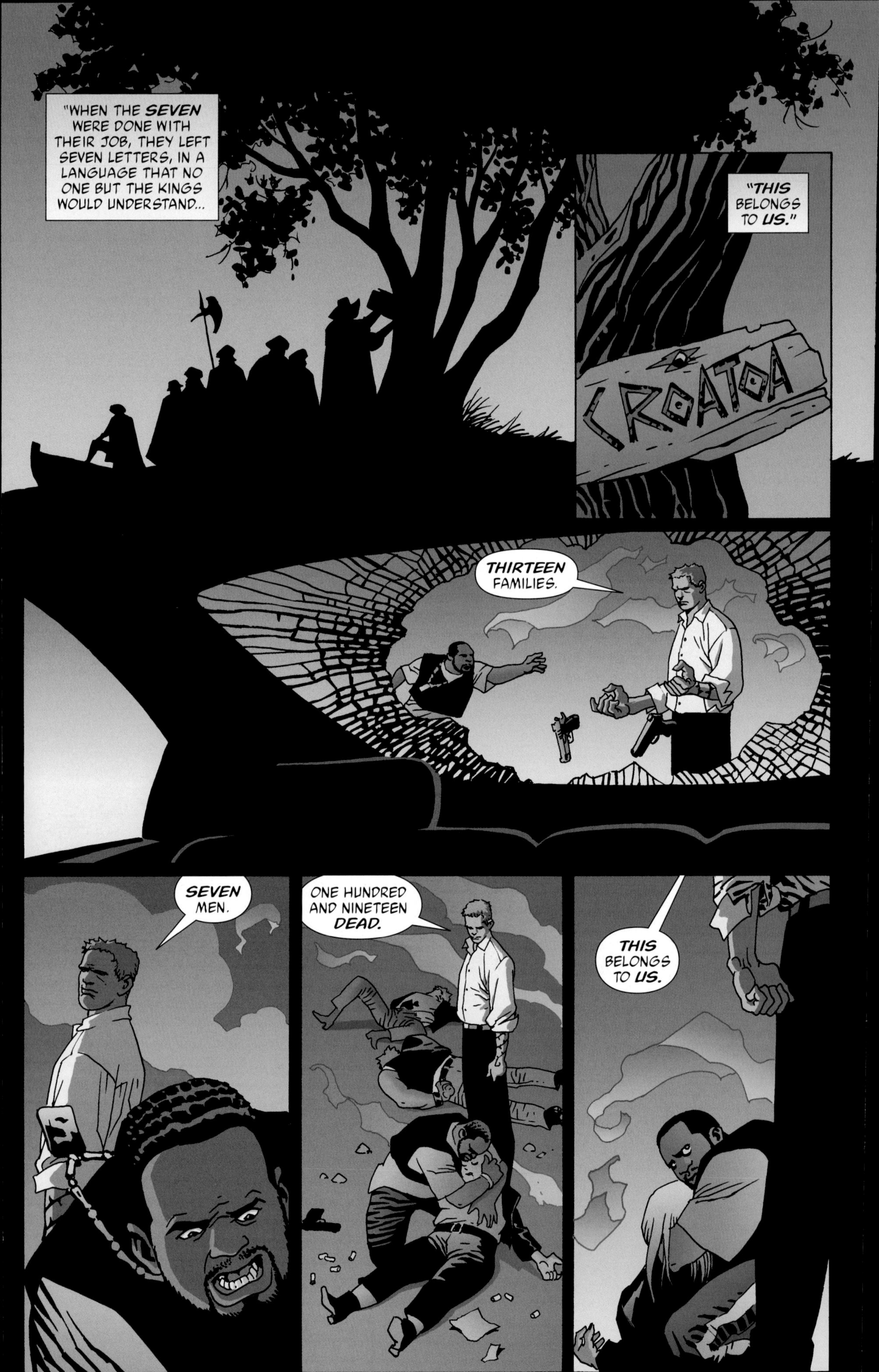
"WHEN THE SEVEN WERE DONE WITH THEIR JOB, THEY LEFT SEVEN LETTERS, IN A LANGUAGE THAT NO ONE BUT THE KINGS WOULD UNDERSTAND...
"THIS BELONGS TO US."
CROATOA
THIRTEEN FAMILIES.
SEVEN MEN.
ONE HUNDRED AND NINETEEN DEAD.
THIS BELONGS TO US.

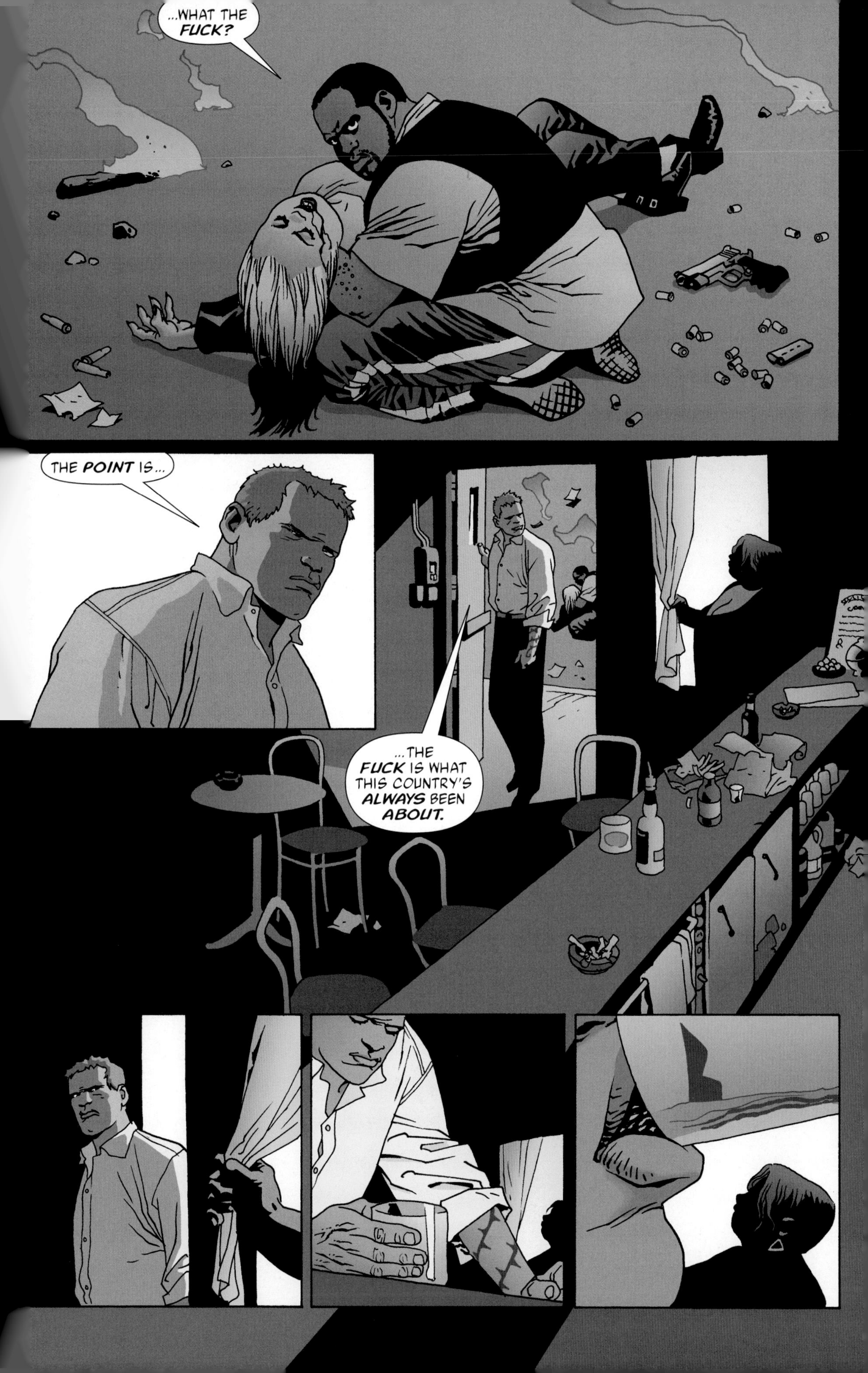
...WHAT THE FUCK?
THE POINT IS...
...THE FUCK IS WHAT THIS COUNTRY'S ALWAYS BEEN ABOUT.

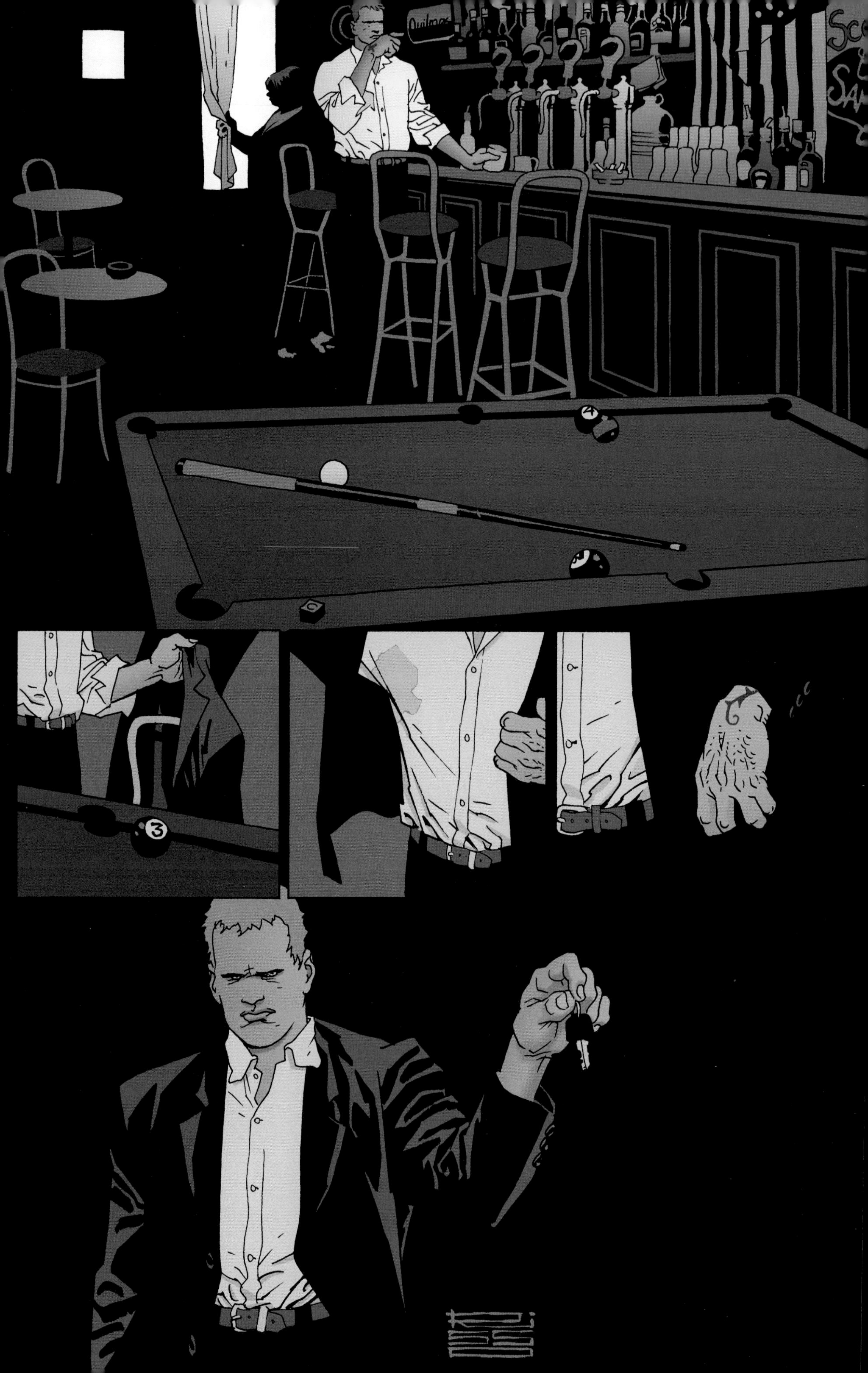

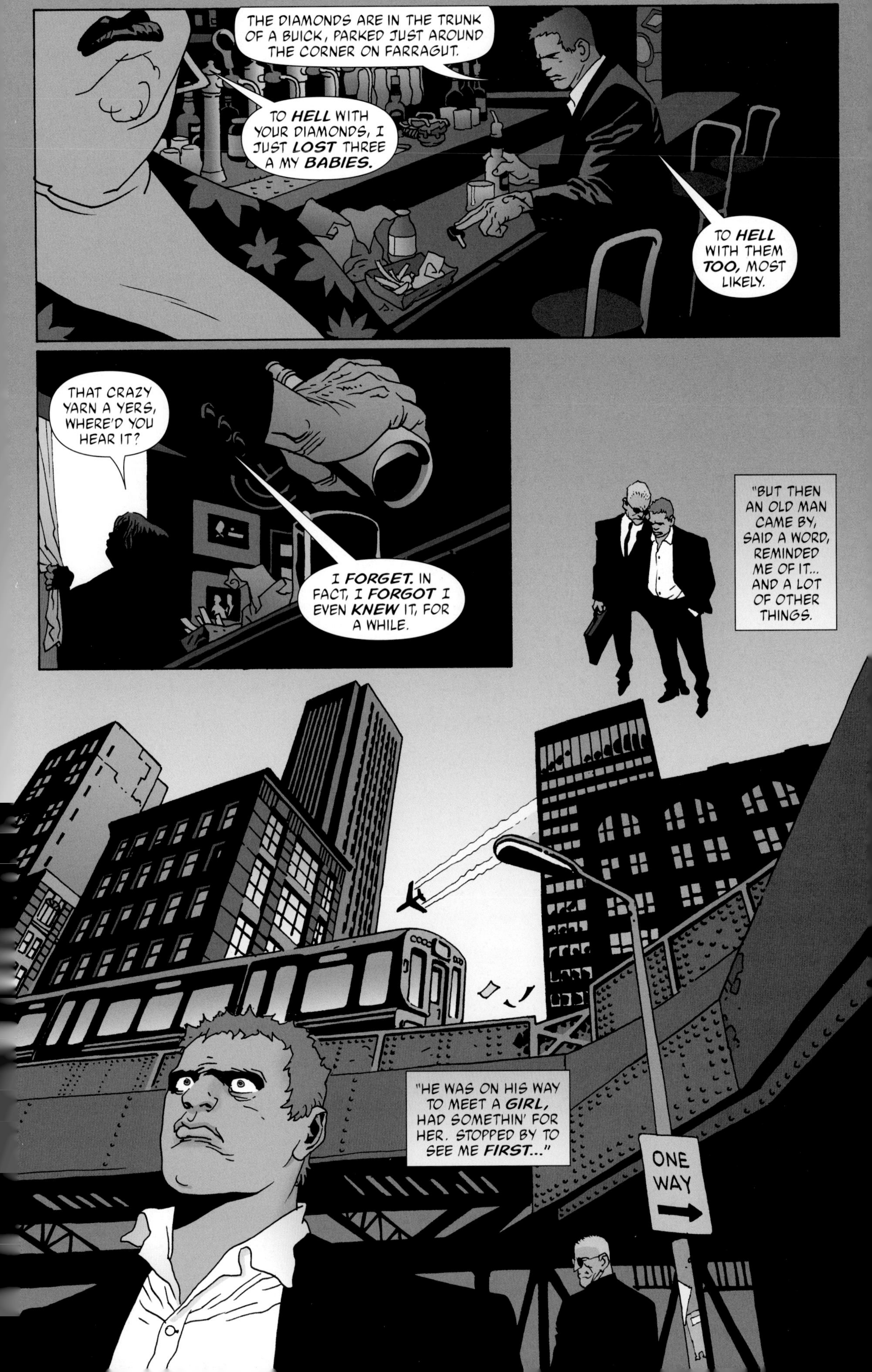
THE DIAMONDS ARE IN THE TRUNK OF A BUICK, PARKED JUST AROUND THE CORNER ON FARRAGUT.
TO HELL WITH YOUR DIAMONDS, I JUST LOST THREE A MY BABIES.
TO HELL WITH THEM TOO, MOST LIKELY.
THAT CRAZY YARN A YERS, WHERE'D YOU HEAR IT?
I FORGET. IN FACT, I FORGOT I EVEN KNEW IT, FOR A WHILE.
"BUT THEN AN OLD MAN CAME BY, SAID A WORD, REMINDED ME OF IT... AND A LOT OF OTHER THINGS.
"HE WAS ON HIS WAY TO MEET A GIRL, HAD SOMETHIN' FOR HER. STOPPED BY TO SEE ME FIRST..."
ONE WAY

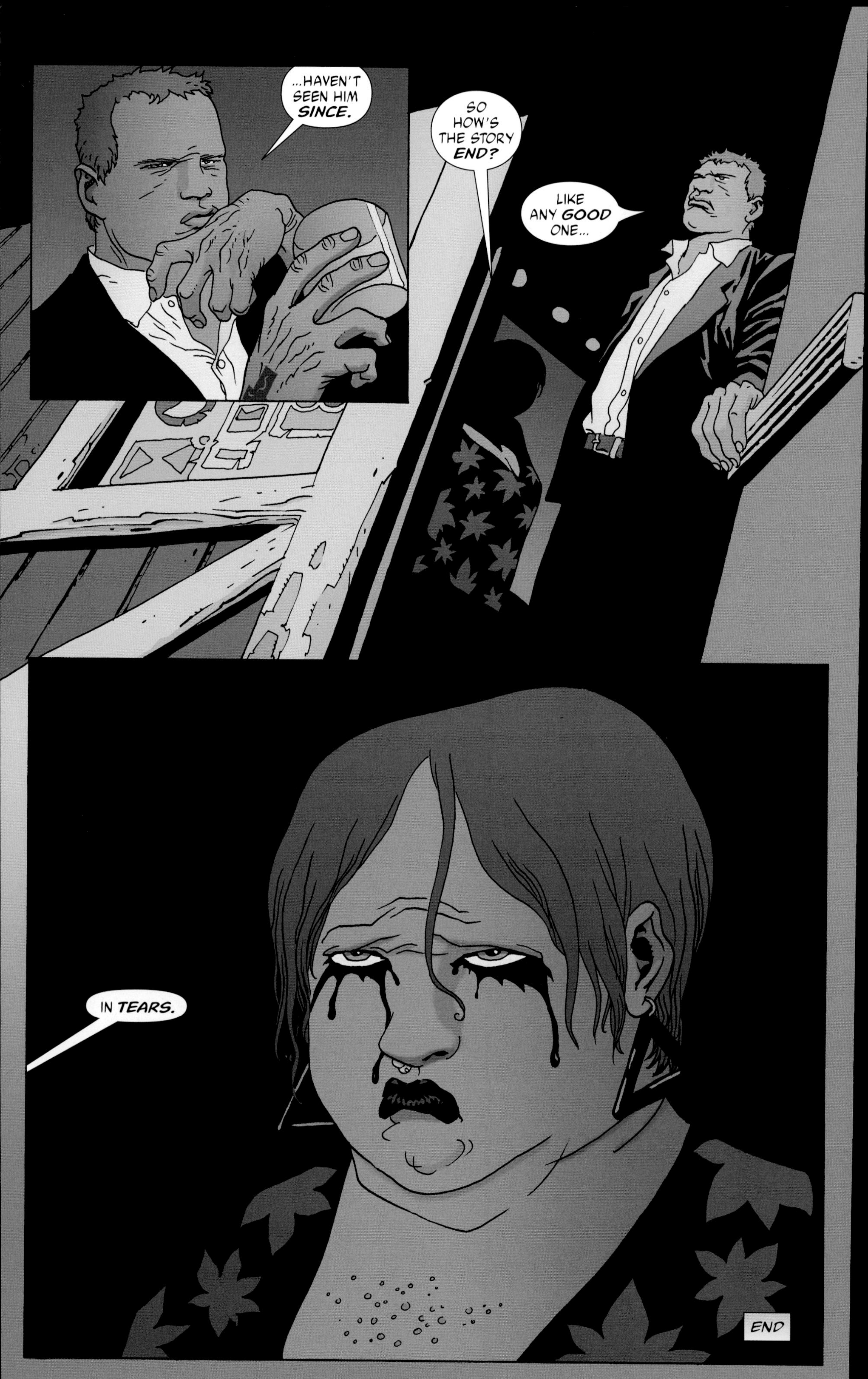
...HAVEN'T SEEN HIM SINCE.
SO HOW'S THE STORY END?
LIKE ANY GOOD ONE...
IN TEARS.
END

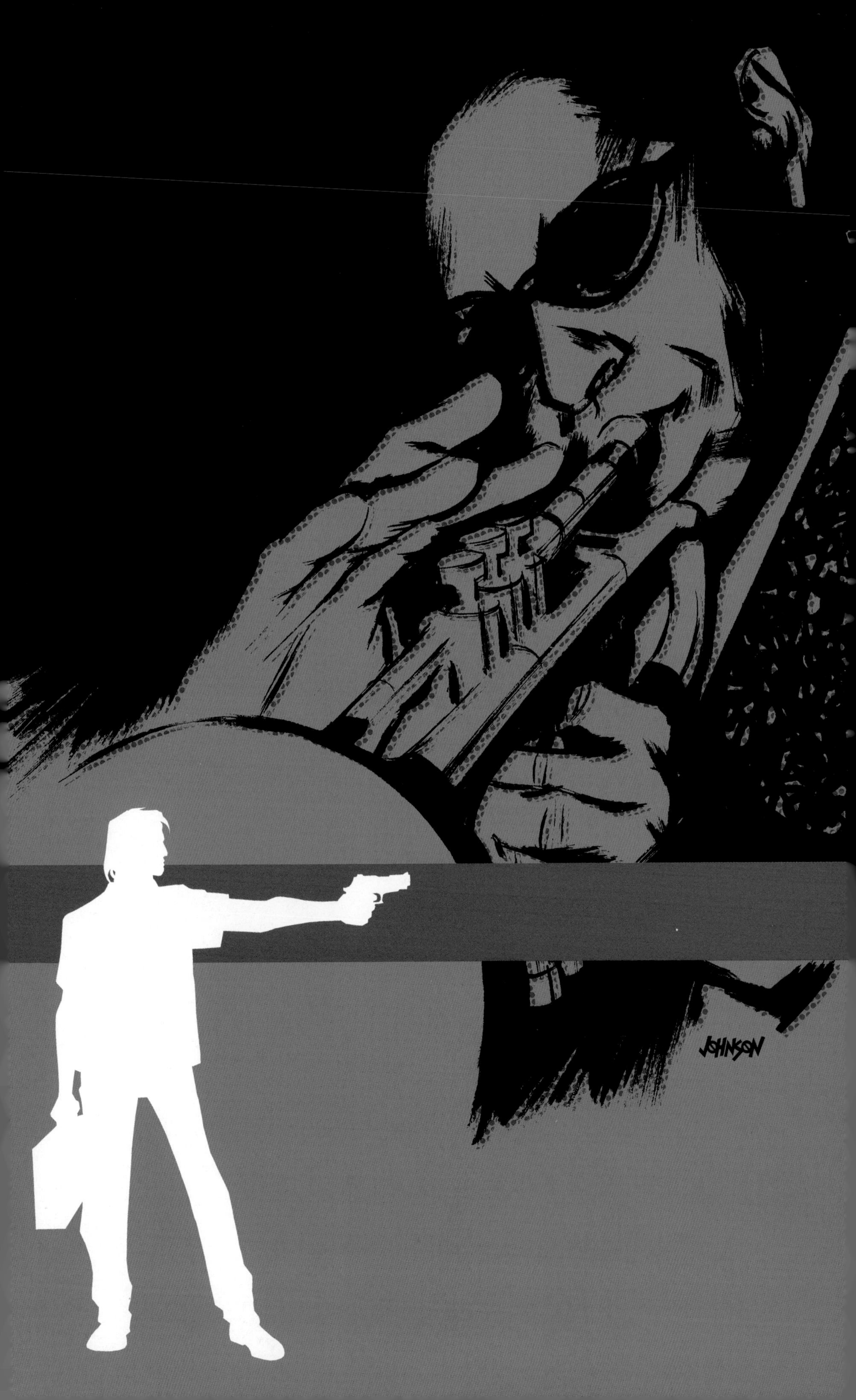
JOHNSON

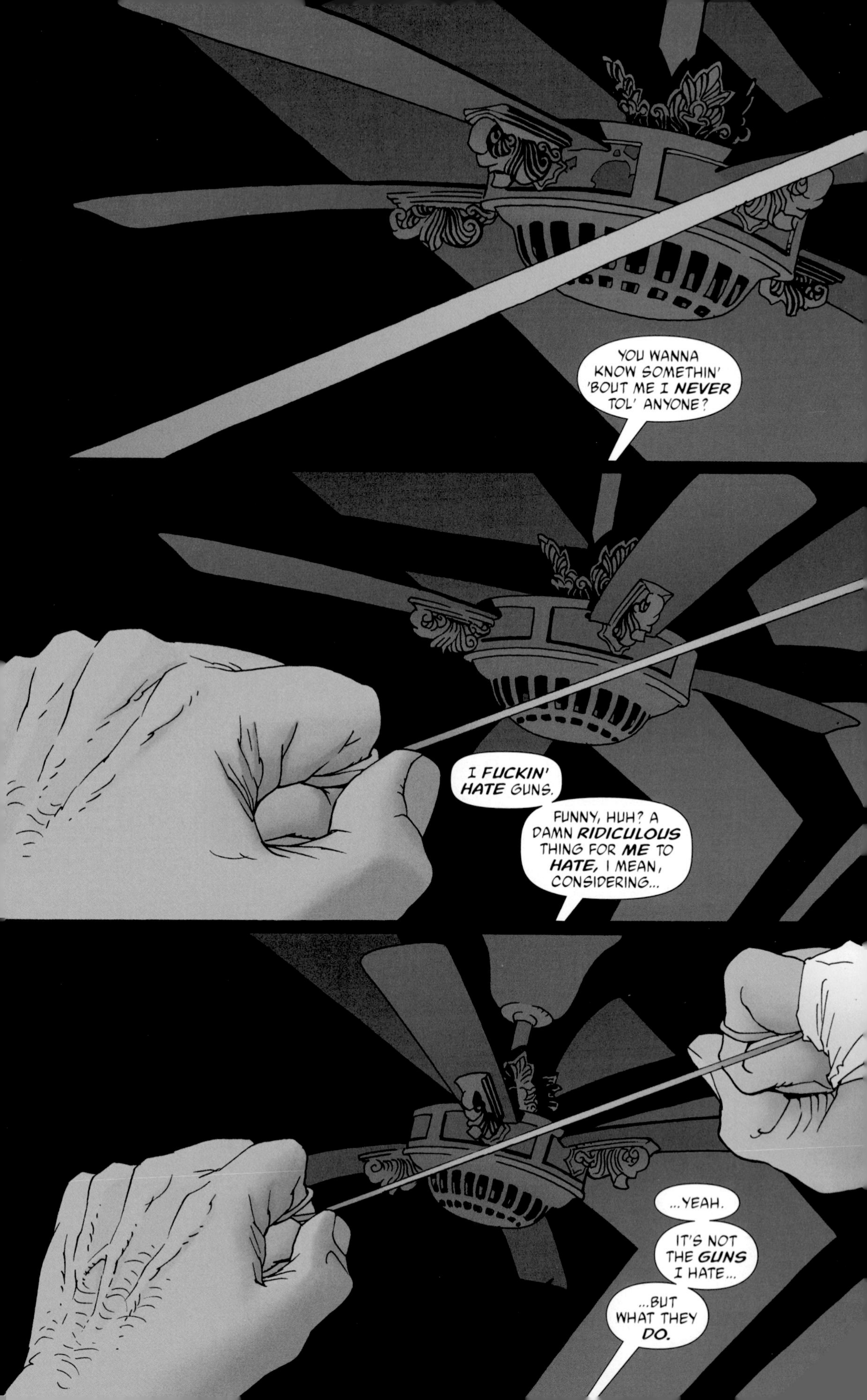
YOU WANNA KNOW SOMETHIN' 'BOUT ME I NEVER TOL' ANYONE?
I FUCKIN' HATE GUNS.
FUNNY, HUH? A DAMN RIDICULOUS THING FOR ME TO HATE, I MEAN, CONSIDERING...
...YEAH.
IT'S NOT THE GUNS I HATE...
...BUT WHAT THEY DO.

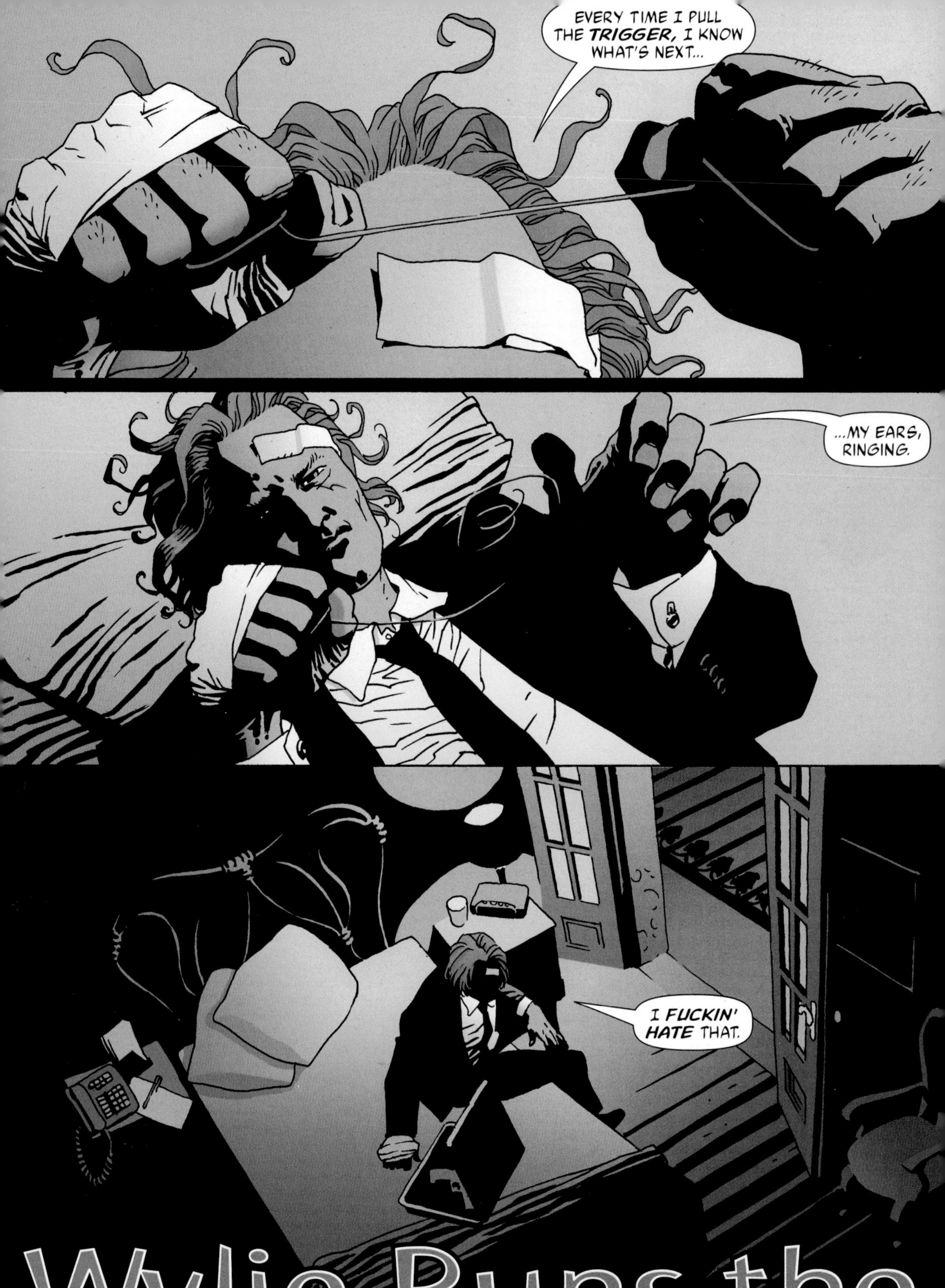
EVERY TIME I PULL THE TRIGGER, I KNOW WHAT'S NEXT...
...MY EARS, RINGING.
I FUCKIN' HATE THAT.

Wylie Runs the Voodoo Down Part One

Brian Azzarello writer · Eduardo Risso artist · Patricia Mulvihill colorist · Clem Robins letterer · Dave Johnson cover · Casey Seijas asst ed · Will Dennis editor

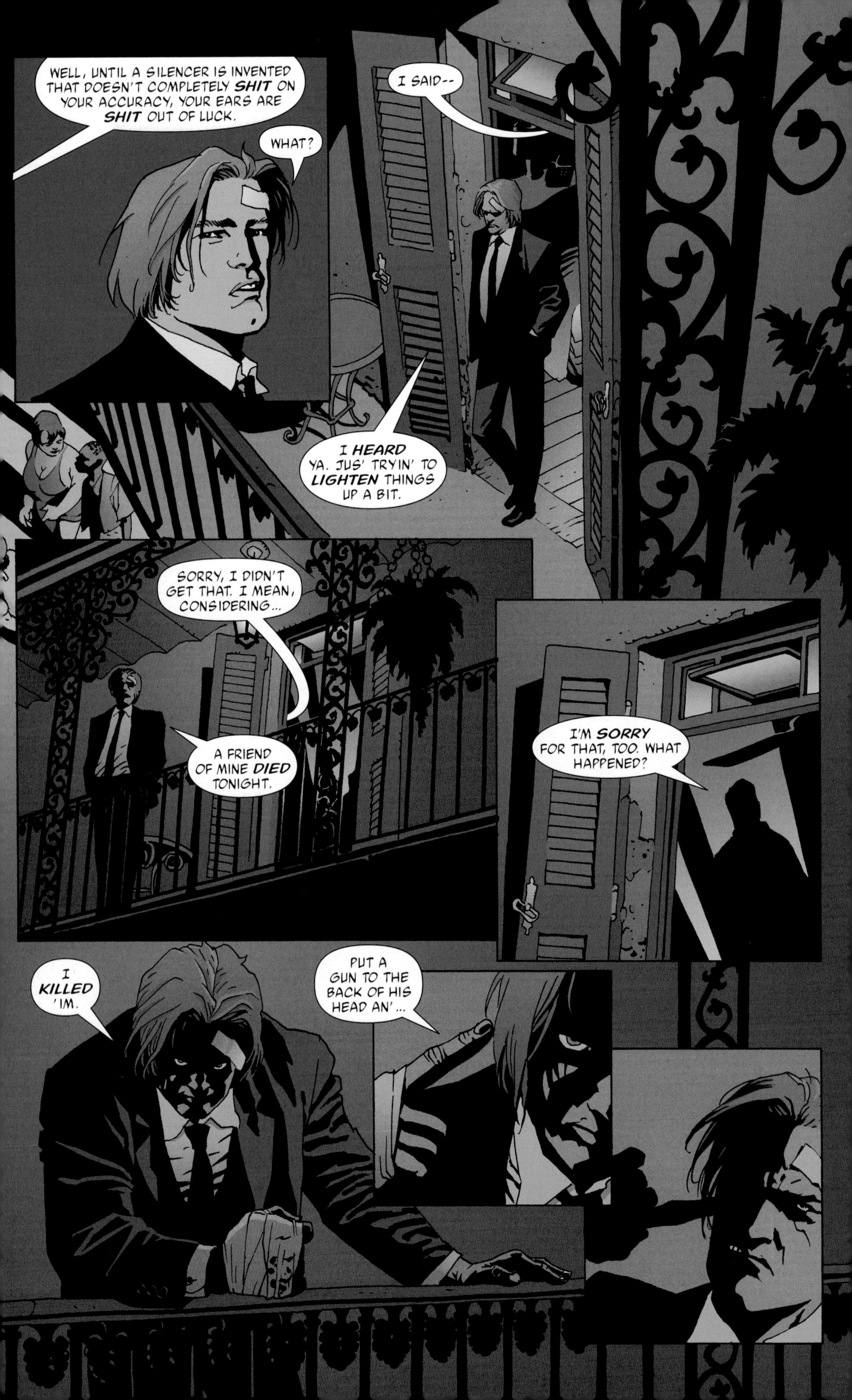
WELL, UNTIL A SILENCER IS INVENTED THAT DOESN'T COMPLETELY SHIT ON YOUR ACCURACY, YOUR EARS ARE SHIT OUT OF LUCK.
WHAT?
I SAID--
I HEARD YA. JUS' TRYIN' TO LIGHTEN THINGS UP A BIT.
SORRY, I DIDN'T GET THAT. I MEAN, CONSIDERING...
A FRIEND OF MINE DIED TONIGHT.
I'M SORRY FOR THAT, TOO. WHAT HAPPENED?
I KILLED 'IM.
PUT A GUN TO THE BACK OF HIS HEAD AN'...

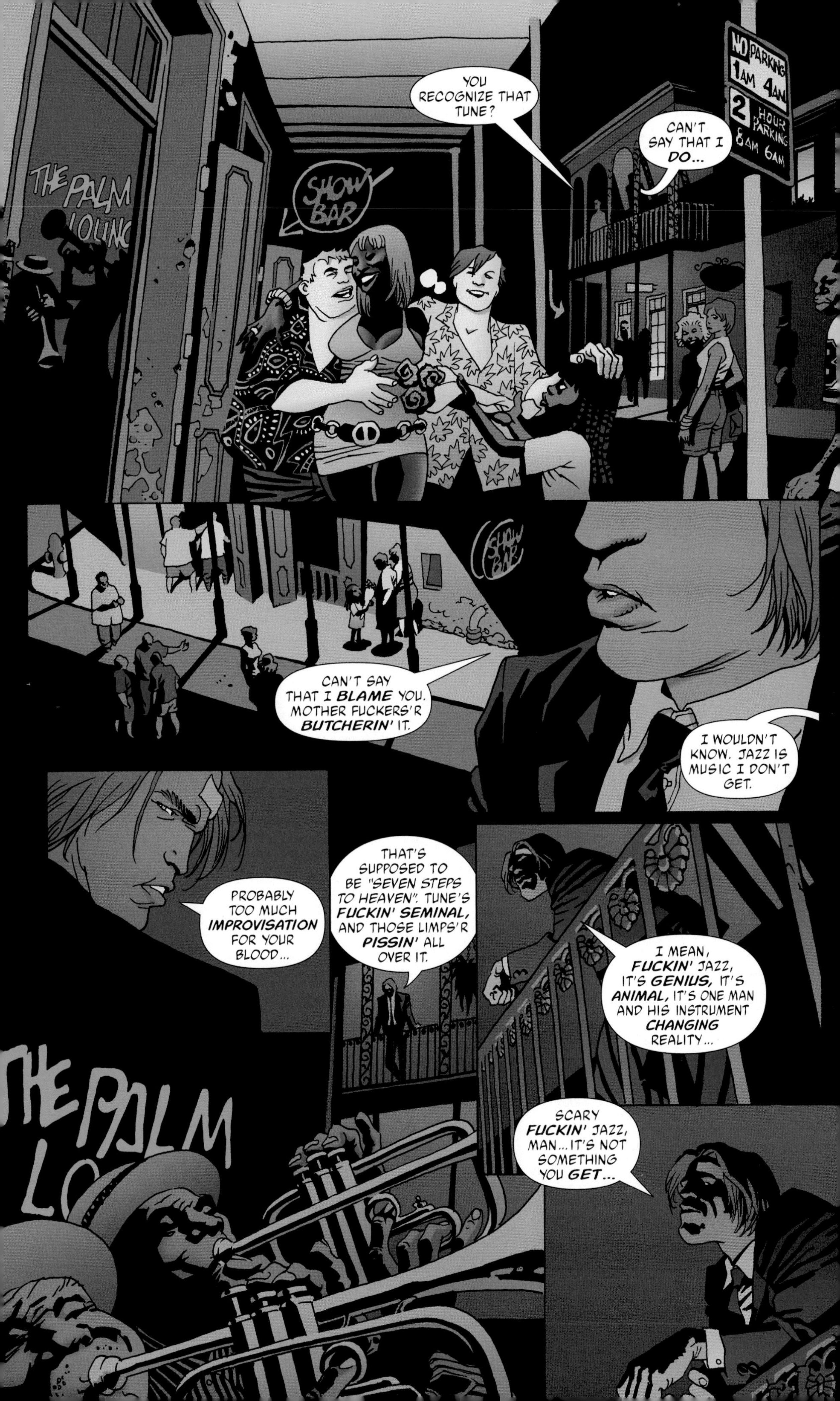
THE PALM LOUNG
SHOW BAR
NO PARKING 1AM 4AM
2 HOUR PARKING 8AM 6AM
YOU RECOGNIZE THAT TUNE?
CAN'T SAY THAT I DO...
CAN'T SAY THAT I BLAME YOU. MOTHER FUCKERS'R BUTCHERIN' IT.
I WOULDN'T KNOW. JAZZ IS MUSIC I DON'T GET.
PROBABLY TOO MUCH IMPROVISATION FOR YOUR BLOOD...
THAT'S SUPPOSED TO BE "SEVEN STEPS TO HEAVEN". TUNE'S FUCKIN' SEMINAL, AND THOSE LIMPS'R PISSIN' ALL OVER IT.
I MEAN, FUCKIN' JAZZ, IT'S GENIUS, IT'S ANIMAL, IT'S ONE MAN AND HIS INSTRUMENT CHANGING REALITY...
SCARY FUCKIN' JAZZ, MAN... IT'S NOT SOMETHING YOU GET...
THE PALM

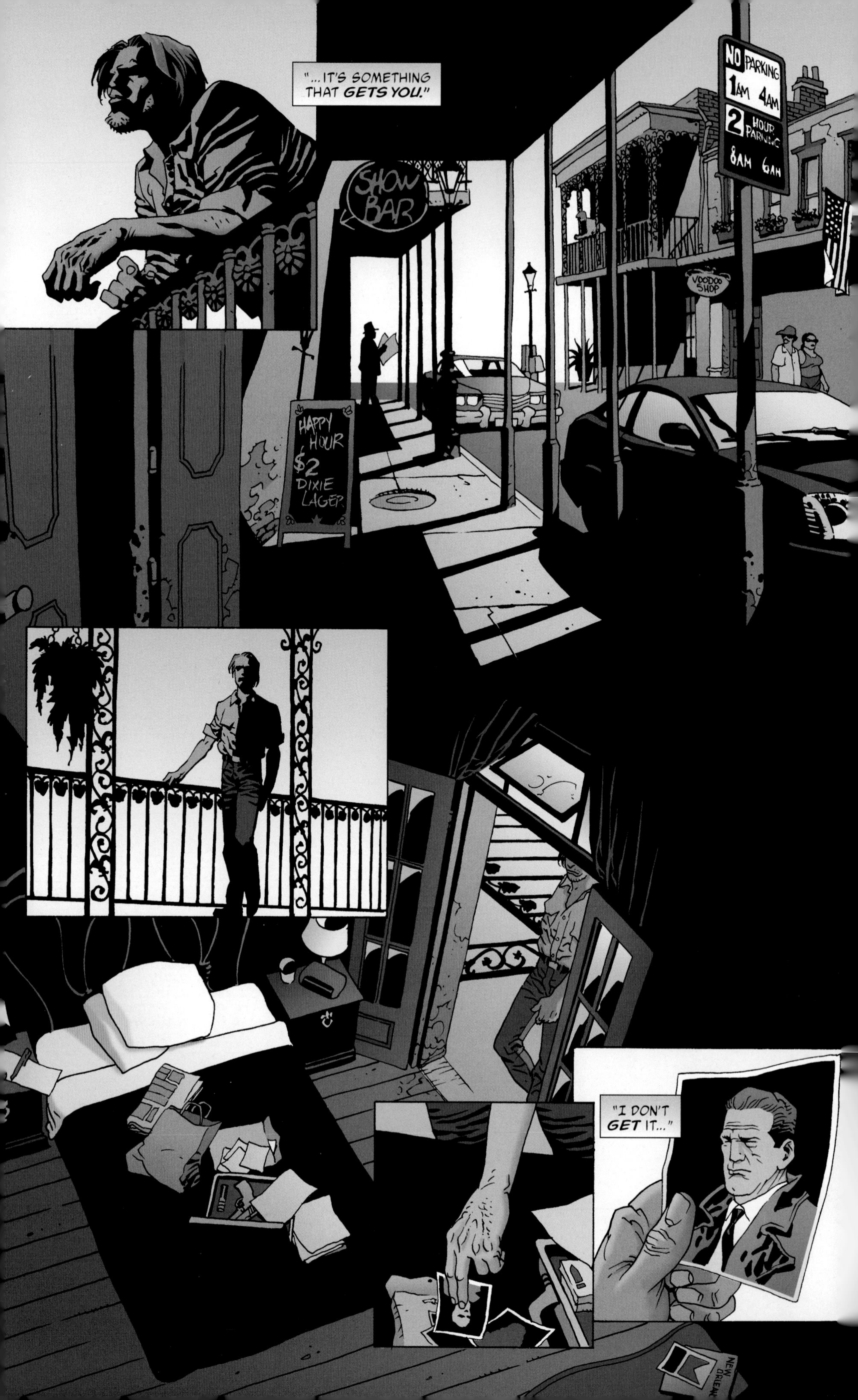
"...IT'S SOMETHING THAT GETS YOU."
NO PARKING
1AM 4AM
2 HOUR PARKING
8AM 6AM
SHOW BAR
VOODOO SHOP
HAPPY HOUR $2 DIXIE LAGER
"I DON'T GET IT..."

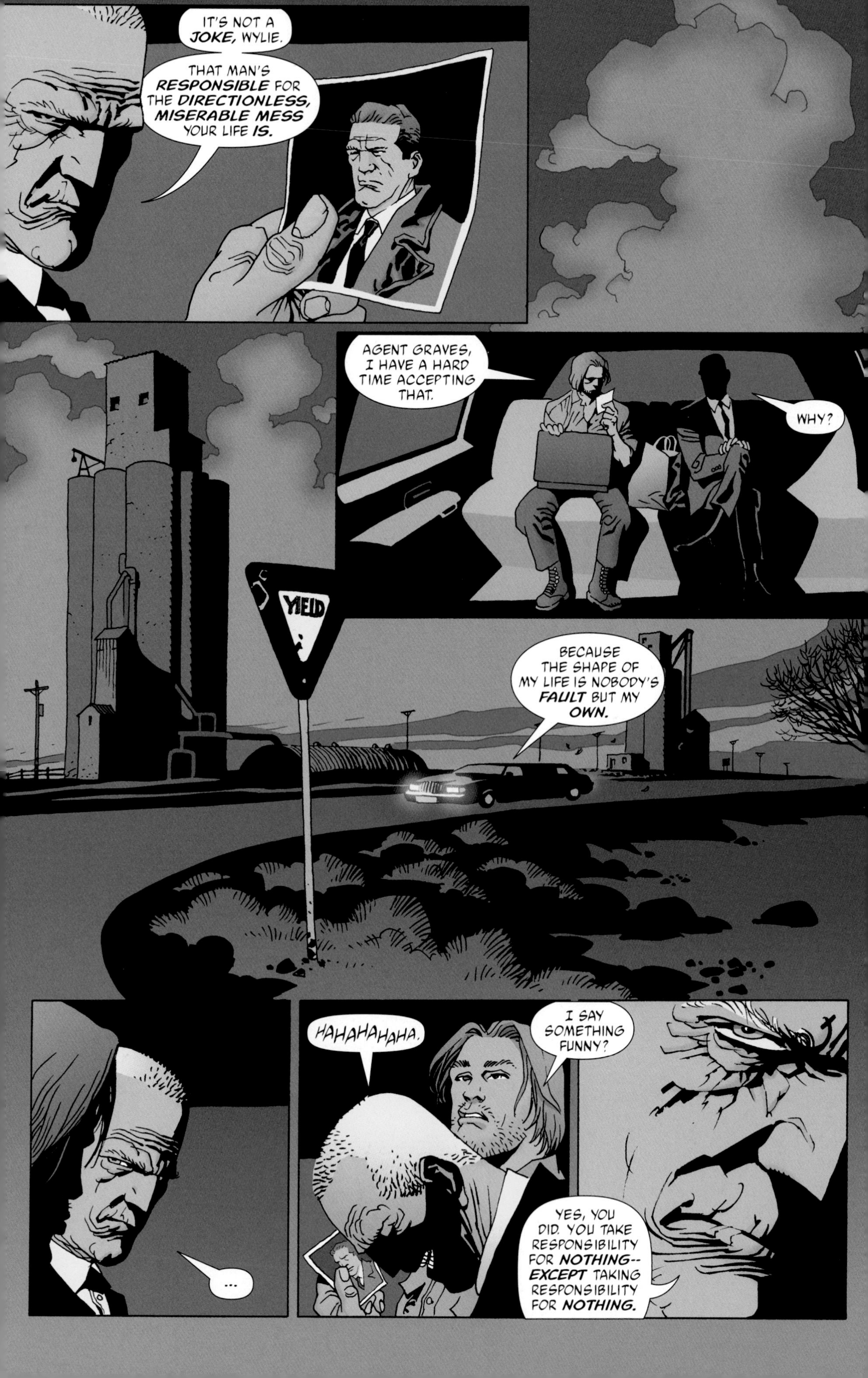
IT'S NOT A JOKE, WYLIE.
THAT MAN'S RESPONSIBLE FOR THE DIRECTIONLESS, MISERABLE MESS YOUR LIFE IS.
AGENT GRAVES, I HAVE A HARD TIME ACCEPTING THAT.
WHY?
YIELD
BECAUSE THE SHAPE OF MY LIFE IS NOBODY'S FAULT BUT MY OWN.
...
HAHAHAHAHAHA.
I SAY SOMETHING FUNNY?
YES, YOU DID. YOU TAKE RESPONSIBILITY FOR NOTHING-- EXCEPT TAKING RESPONSIBILITY FOR NOTHING.

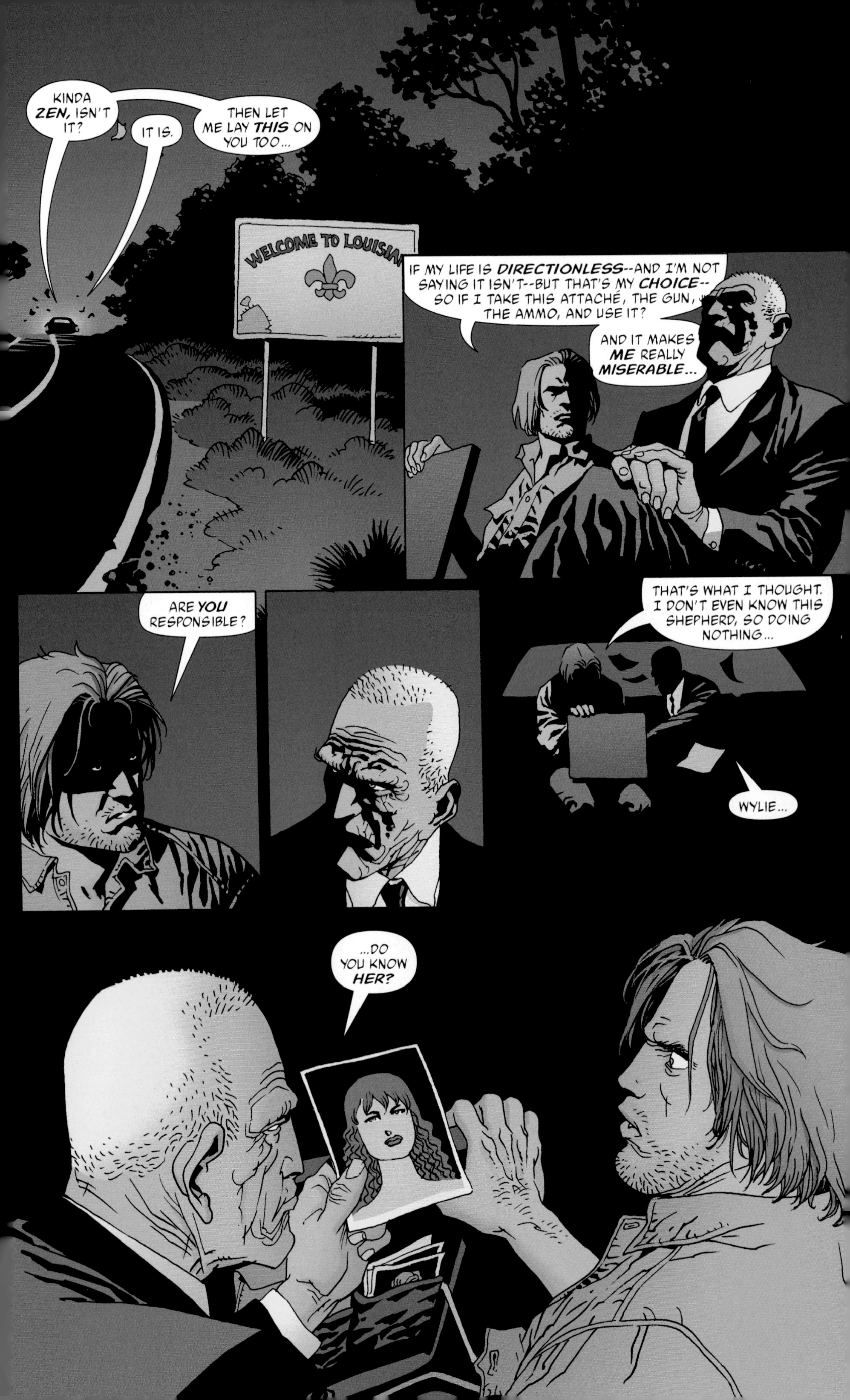
KINDA ZEN, ISN'T IT?
IT IS.
THEN LET ME LAY THIS ON YOU TOO...
WELCOME TO LOUISIAN
IF MY LIFE IS DIRECTIONLESS--AND I'M NOT SAYING IT ISN'T--BUT THAT'S MY CHOICE--SO IF I TAKE THIS ATTACHÉ, THE GUN, THE AMMO, AND USE IT?
AND IT MAKES ME REALLY MISERABLE...
ARE YOU RESPONSIBLE?
THAT'S WHAT I THOUGHT. I DON'T EVEN KNOW THIS SHEPHERD, SO DOING NOTHING...
WYLIE...
...DO YOU KNOW HER?

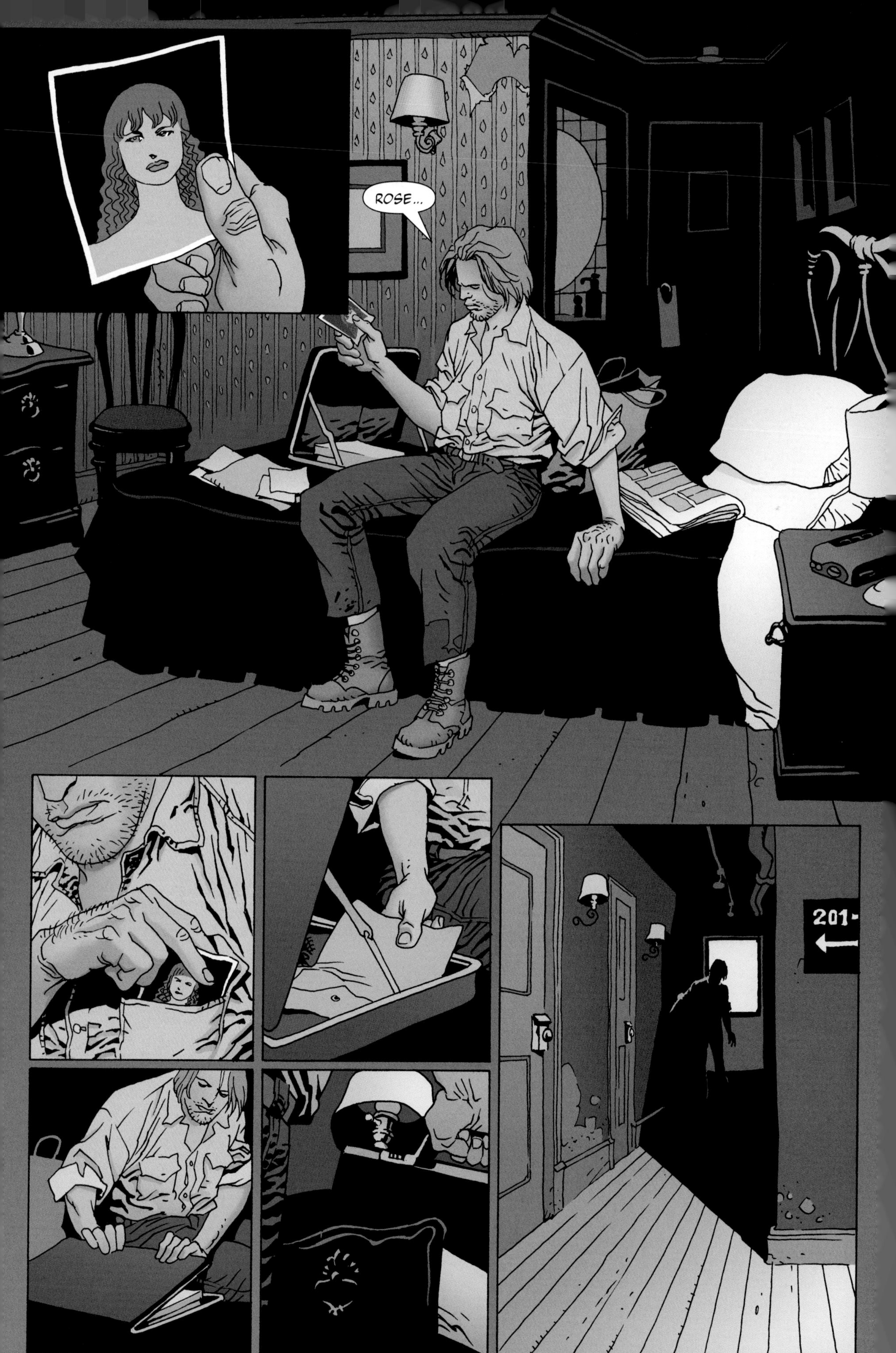
ROSE...
201-

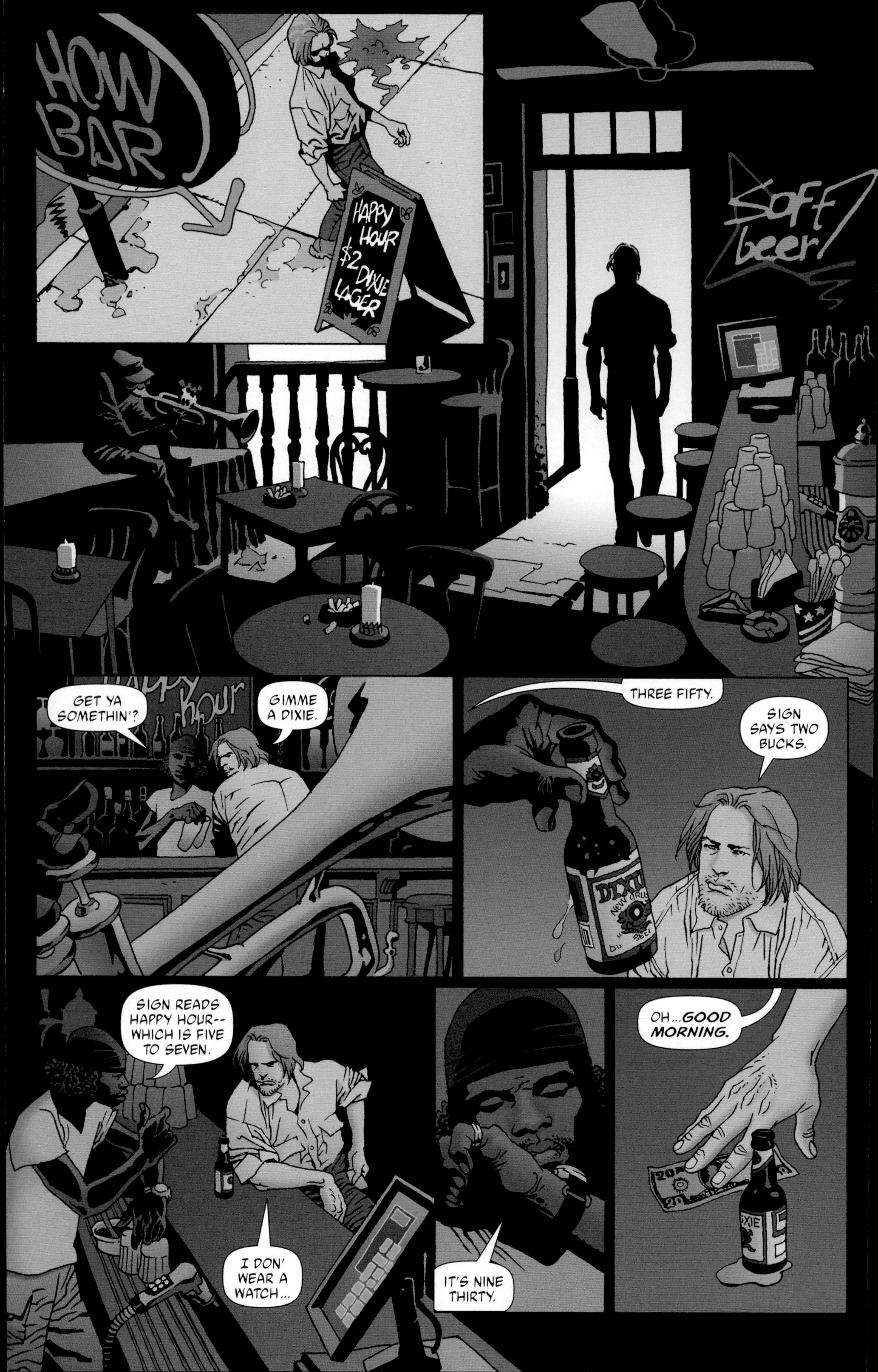
HOW BAR
HAPPY HOUR $2 DIXIE LAGER
Soft beer
GET YA SOMETHIN'?
GIMME A DIXIE.
THREE FIFTY.
SIGN SAYS TWO BUCKS.
SIGN READS HAPPY HOUR-- WHICH IS FIVE TO SEVEN.
I DON' WEAR A WATCH...
IT'S NINE THIRTY.
OH...**GOOD MORNING.**

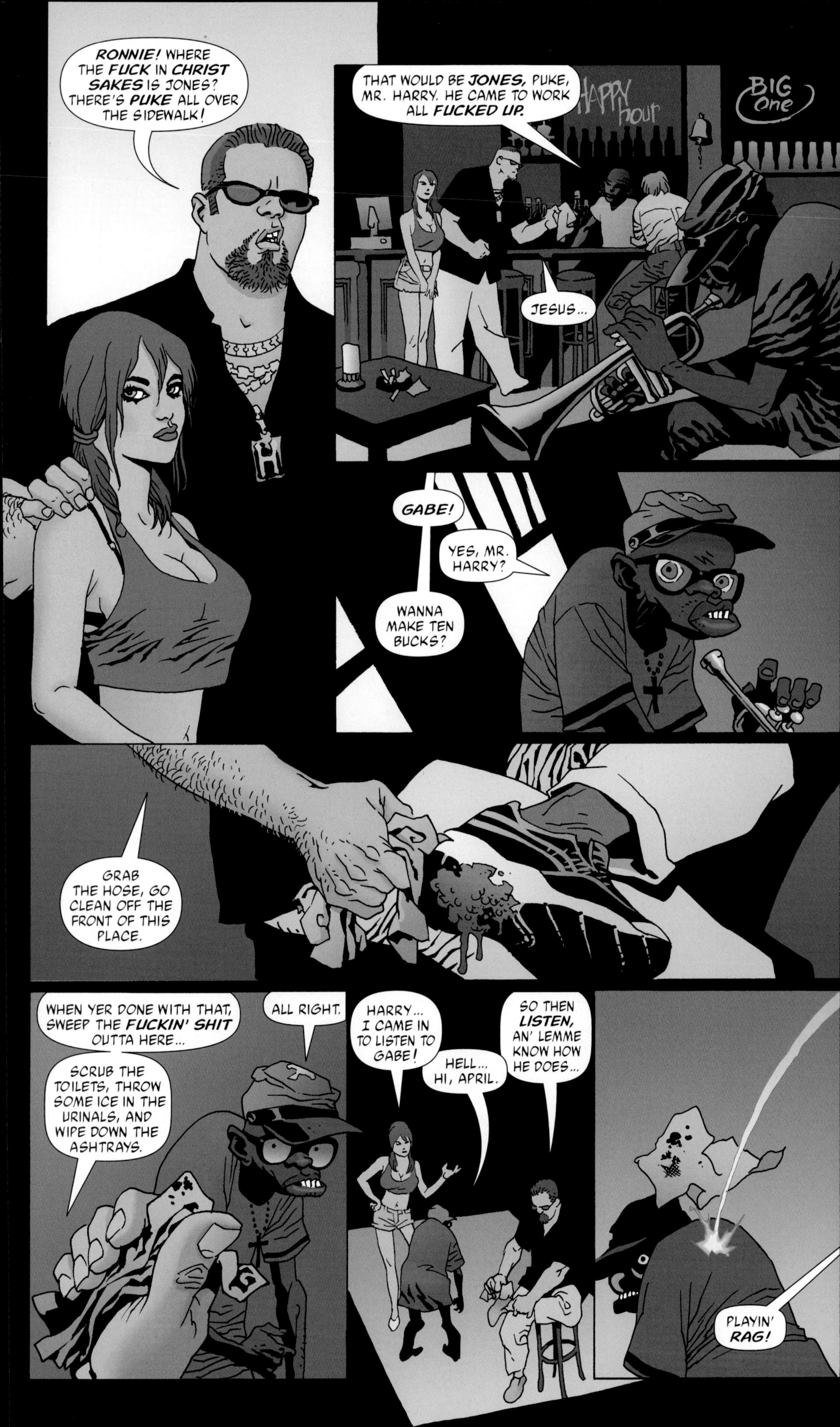
RONNIE! WHERE THE FUCK IN CHRIST SAKES IS JONES? THERE'S PUKE ALL OVER THE SIDEWALK!
THAT WOULD BE JONES, PUKE, MR. HARRY. HE CAME TO WORK ALL FUCKED UP.
HAPPY hour
BIG One
JESUS...
GABE!
YES, MR. HARRY?
WANNA MAKE TEN BUCKS?
GRAB THE HOSE, GO CLEAN OFF THE FRONT OF THIS PLACE.
WHEN YER DONE WITH THAT, SWEEP THE FUCKIN' SHIT OUTTA HERE...
SCRUB THE TOILETS, THROW SOME ICE IN THE URINALS, AND WIPE DOWN THE ASHTRAYS.
ALL RIGHT.
HARRY... I CAME IN TO LISTEN TO GABE!
HELL... HI, APRIL.
SO THEN LISTEN, AN' LEMME KNOW HOW HE DOES...
PLAYIN' RAG!

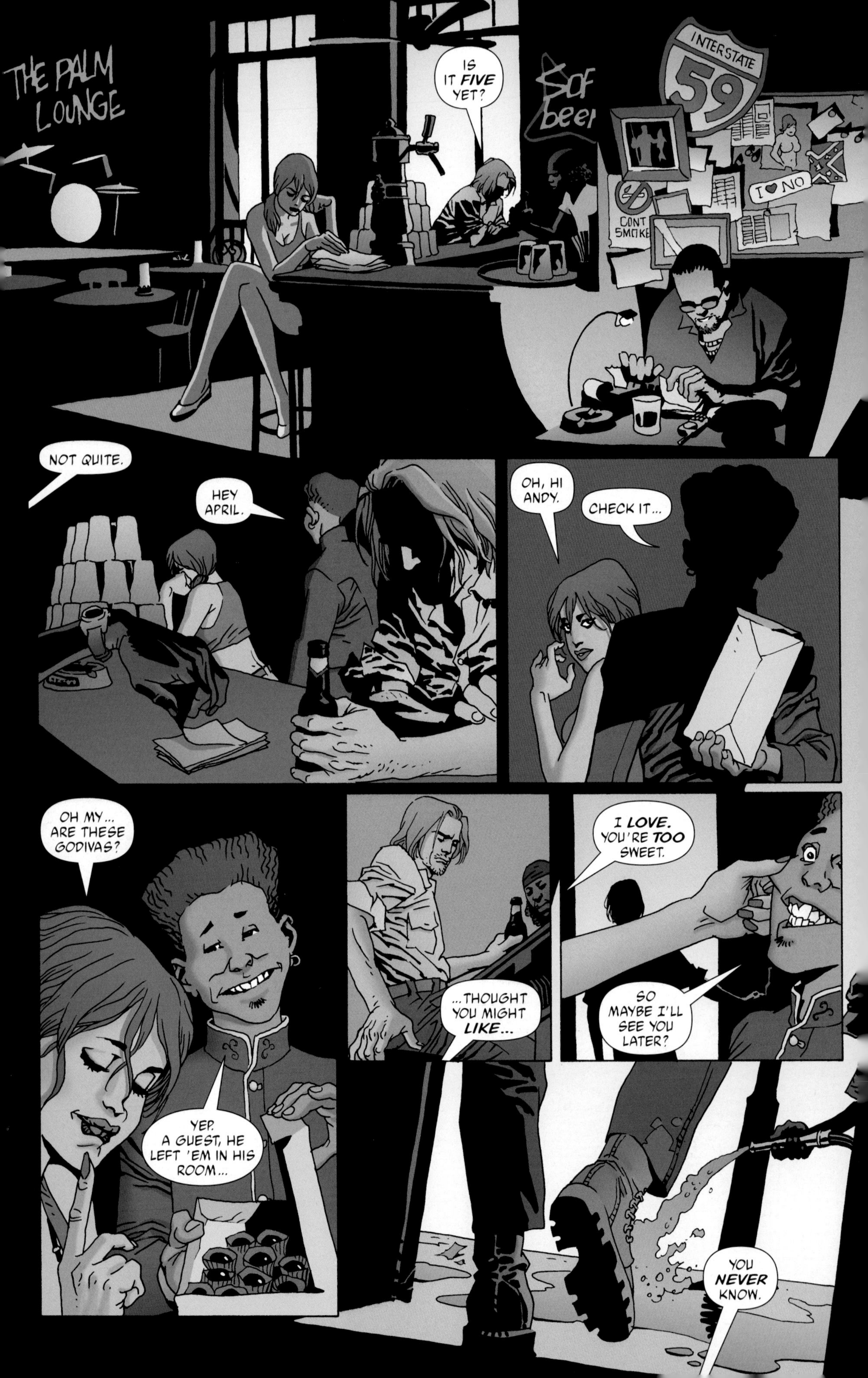
THE PALM LOUNGE
INTERSTATE 59
IS IT FIVE YET?
I ♥ NO
NOT QUITE.
HEY APRIL.
OH, HI ANDY.
CHECK IT...
OH MY... ARE THESE GODIVAS?
YEP. A GUEST, HE LEFT 'EM IN HIS ROOM...
...THOUGHT YOU MIGHT LIKE...
I LOVE. YOU'RE TOO SWEET.
SO MAYBE I'LL SEE YOU LATER?
YOU NEVER KNOW.

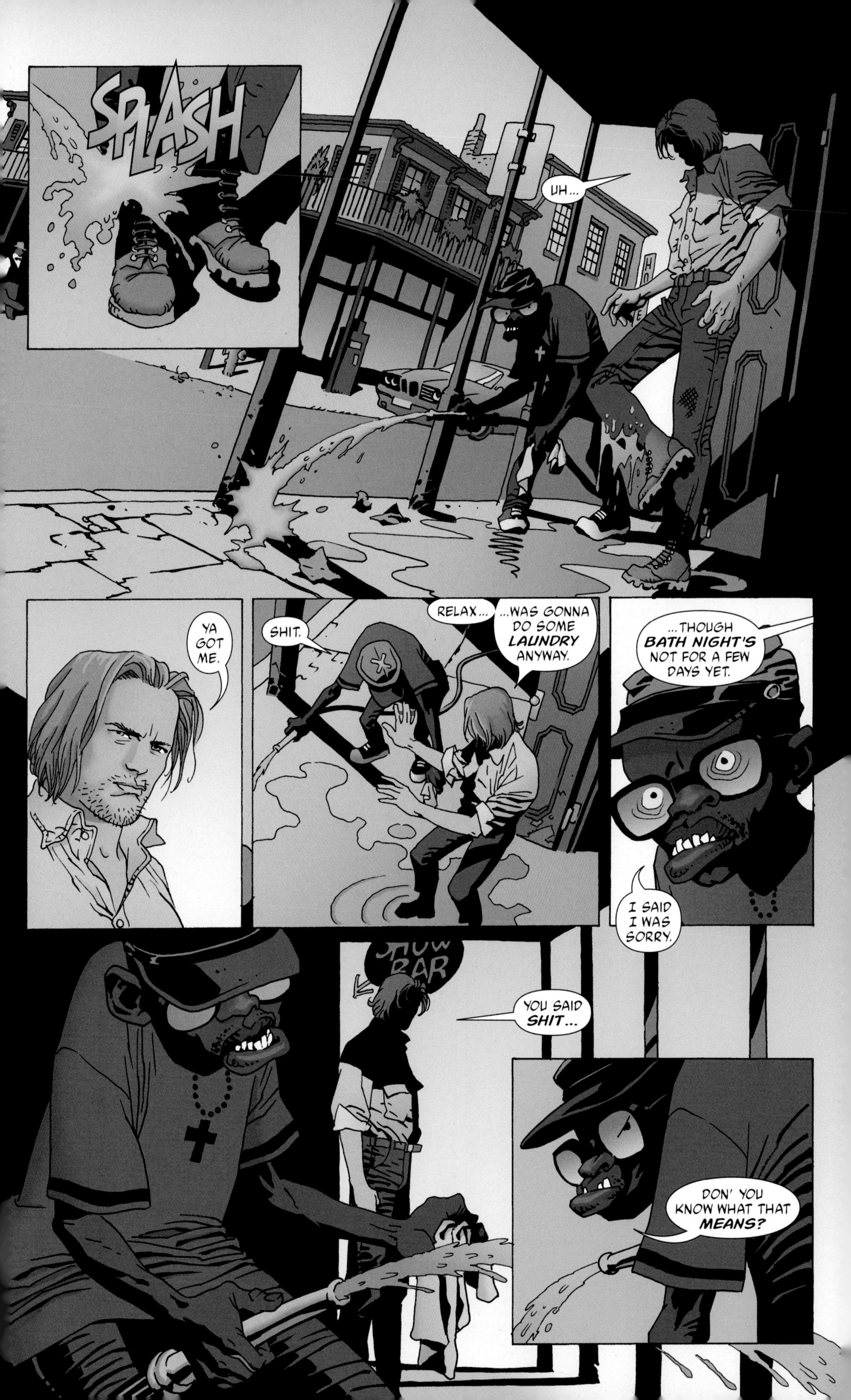
SPLASH
UH...
YA GOT ME.
SHIT.
RELAX...
...WAS GONNA DO SOME LAUNDRY ANYWAY.
...THOUGH BATH NIGHT'S NOT FOR A FEW DAYS YET.
I SAID I WAS SORRY.
YOU SAID SHIT...
DON' YOU KNOW WHAT THAT MEANS?

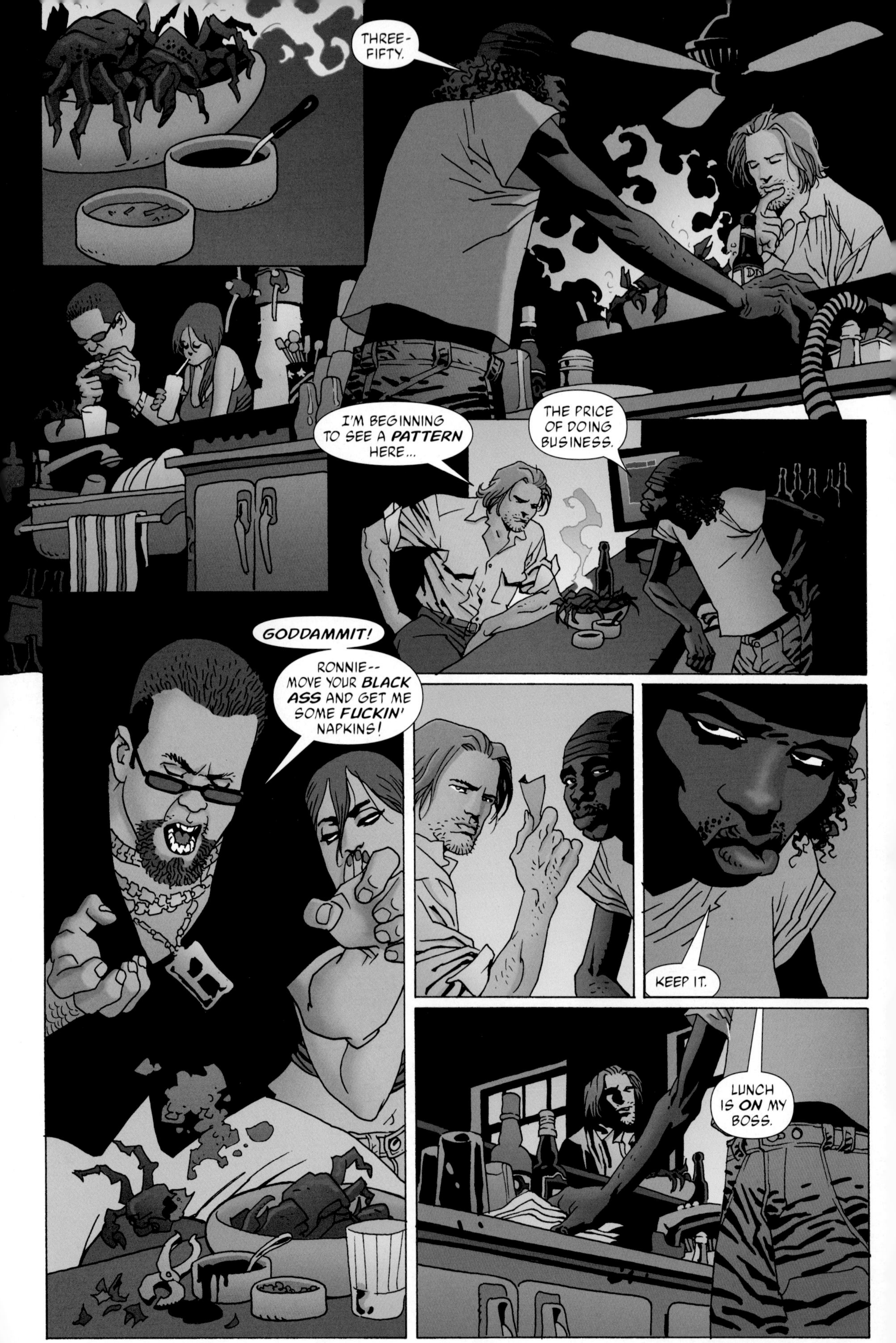
THREE-FIFTY.
I'M BEGINNING TO SEE A PATTERN HERE...
THE PRICE OF DOING BUSINESS.
GODDAMMIT!
RONNIE-- MOVE YOUR BLACK ASS AND GET ME SOME FUCKIN' NAPKINS!
KEEP IT.
LUNCH IS ON MY BOSS.

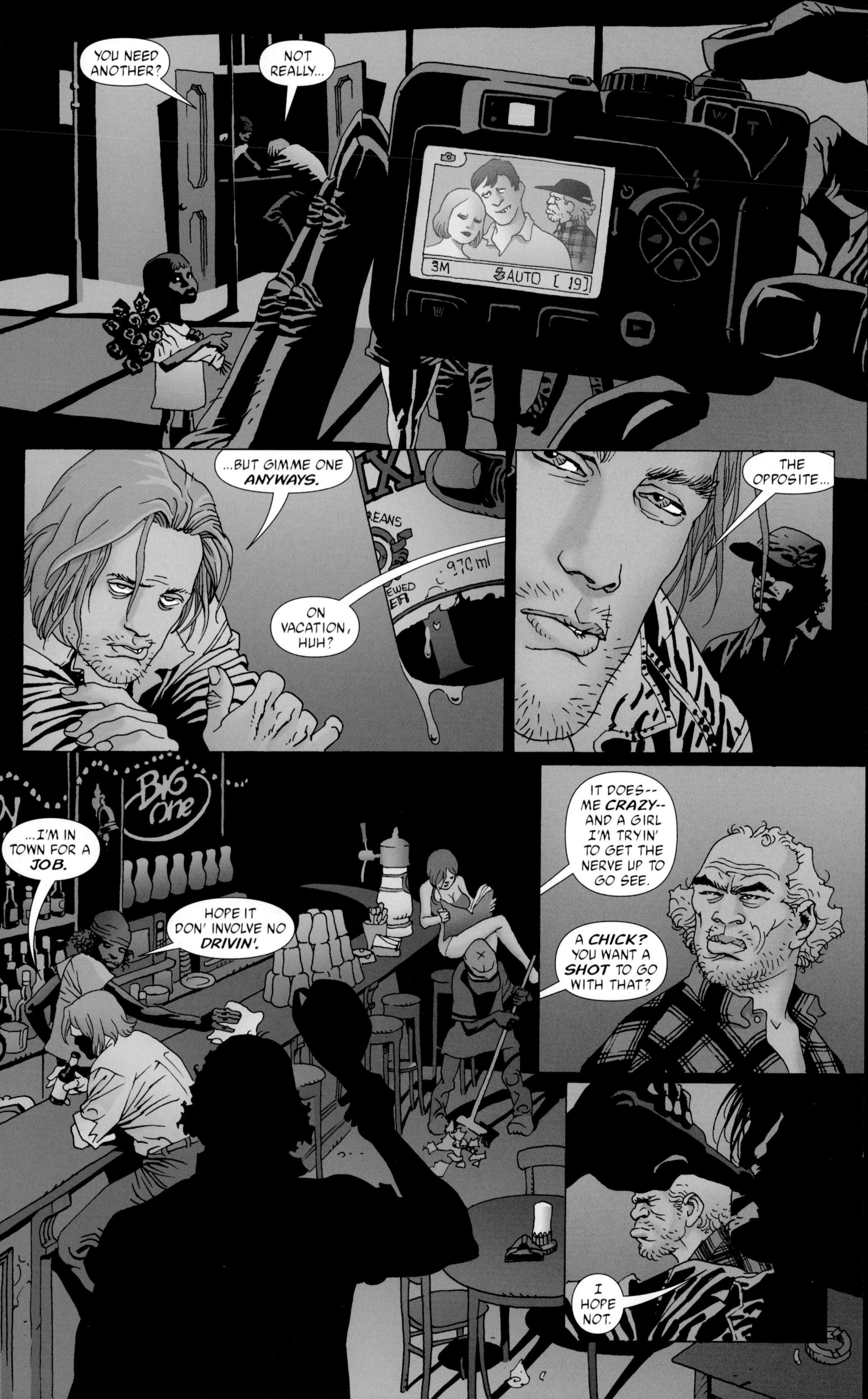
YOU NEED ANOTHER?
NOT REALLY...
3M
AUTO [19]
...BUT GIMME ONE ANYWAYS.
ON VACATION, HUH?
970 ml
THE OPPOSITE...
...I'M IN TOWN FOR A JOB.
HOPE IT DON' INVOLVE NO DRIVIN'.
Big One
IT DOES-- ME CRAZY-- AND A GIRL I'M TRYIN' TO GET THE NERVE UP TO GO SEE.
A CHICK? YOU WANT A SHOT TO GO WITH THAT?
I HOPE NOT.

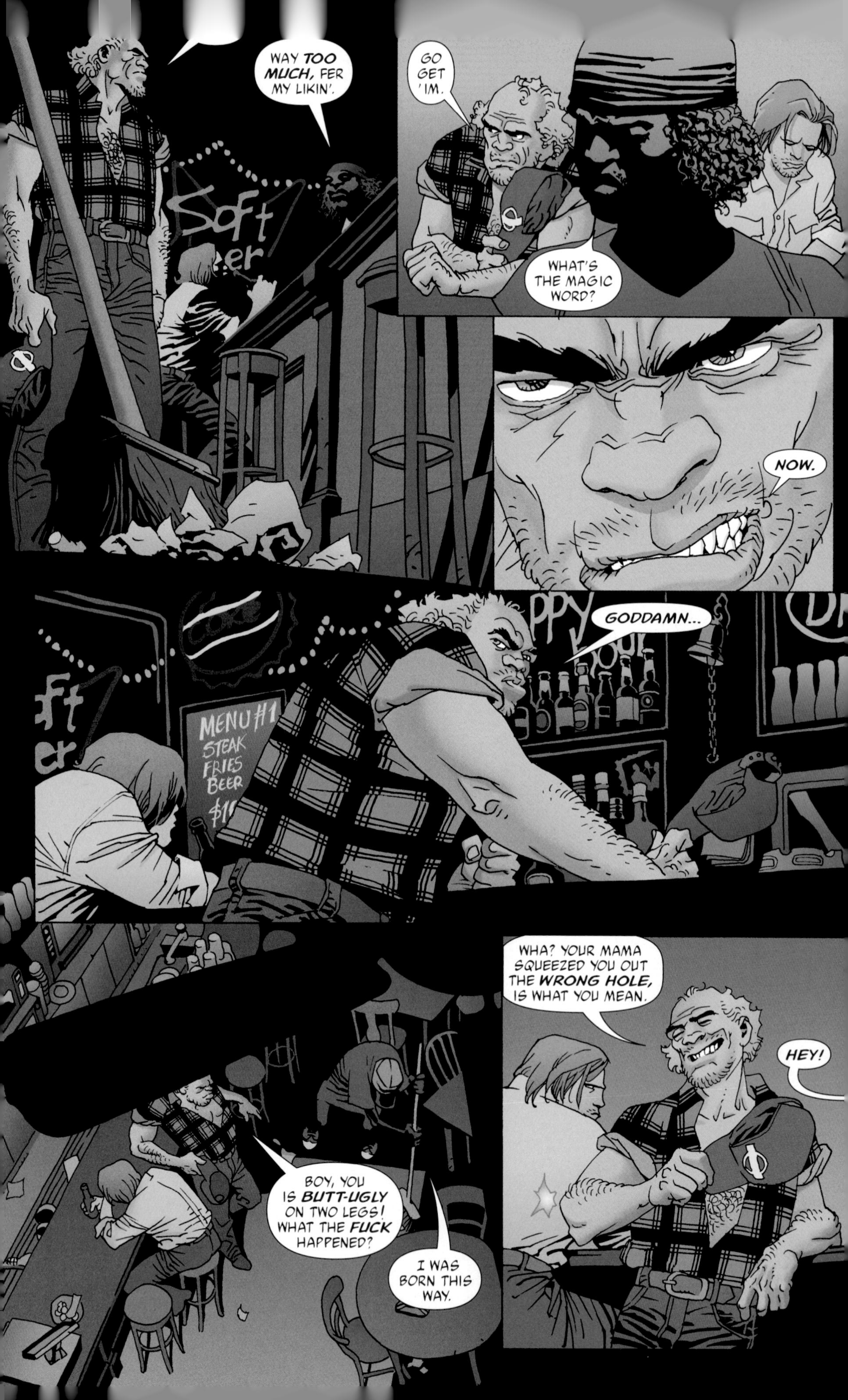
WAY TOO MUCH, FER MY LIKIN'.
Soft
GO GET 'IM.
WHAT'S THE MAGIC WORD?
NOW.
GODDAMN...
MENU #1 STEAK FRIES BEER
WHA? YOUR MAMA SQUEEZED YOU OUT THE WRONG HOLE, IS WHAT YOU MEAN.
HEY!
BOY, YOU IS BUTT-UGLY ON TWO LEGS! WHAT THE FUCK HAPPENED?
I WAS BORN THIS WAY.

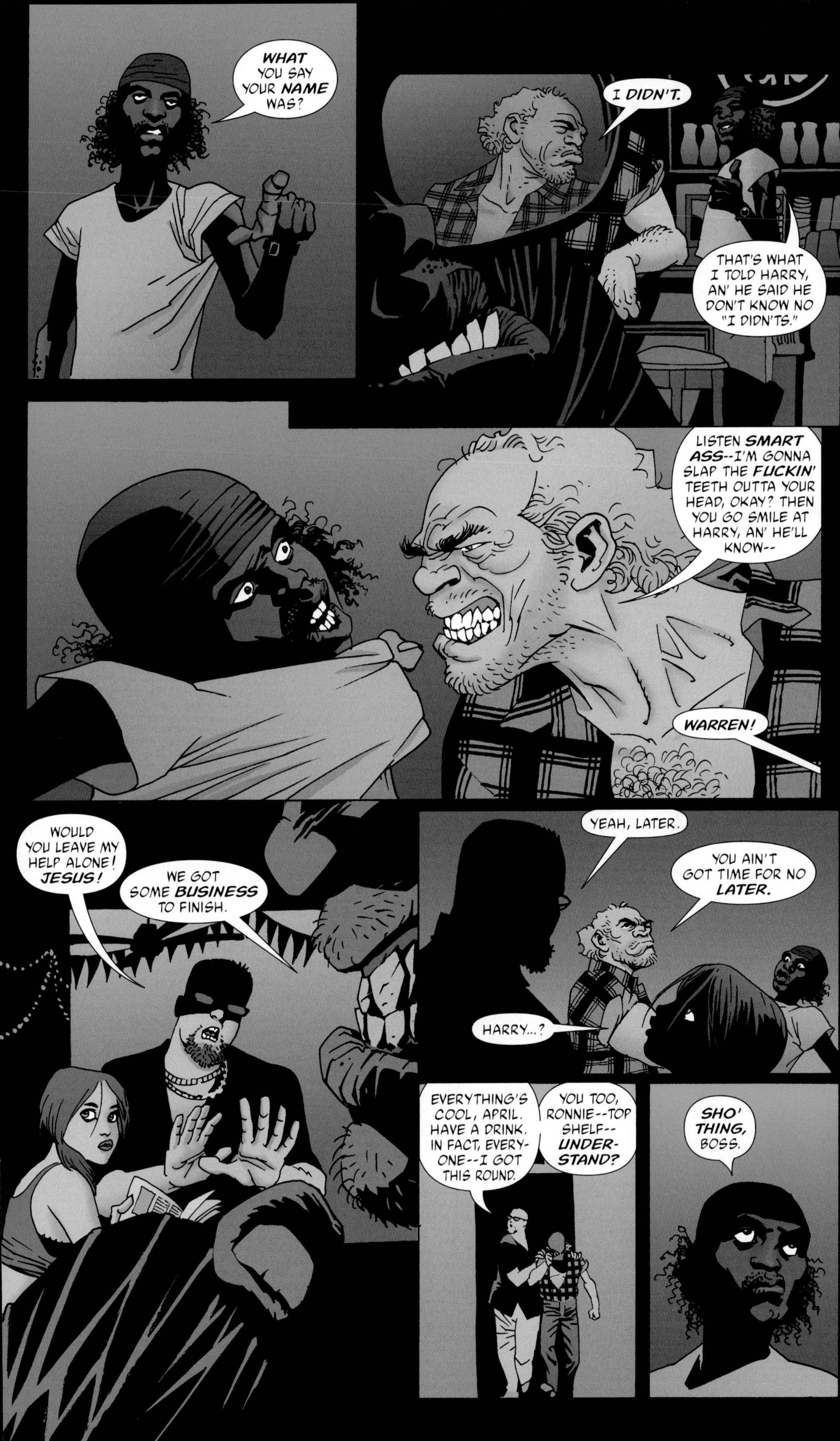
WHAT YOU SAY YOUR NAME WAS?
I DIDN'T.
THAT'S WHAT I TOLD HARRY, AN' HE SAID HE DON'T KNOW NO "I DIDN'TS."
LISTEN SMART ASS--I'M GONNA SLAP THE FUCKIN' TEETH OUTTA YOUR HEAD, OKAY? THEN YOU GO SMILE AT HARRY, AN' HE'LL KNOW--
WARREN!
WOULD YOU LEAVE MY HELP ALONE! JESUS!
WE GOT SOME BUSINESS TO FINISH.
YEAH, LATER.
YOU AIN'T GOT TIME FOR NO LATER.
HARRY...?
EVERYTHING'S COOL, APRIL. HAVE A DRINK. IN FACT, EVERY-ONE--I GOT THIS ROUND.
YOU TOO, RONNIE--TOP SHELF--UNDER-STAND?
SHO' THING, BOSS.

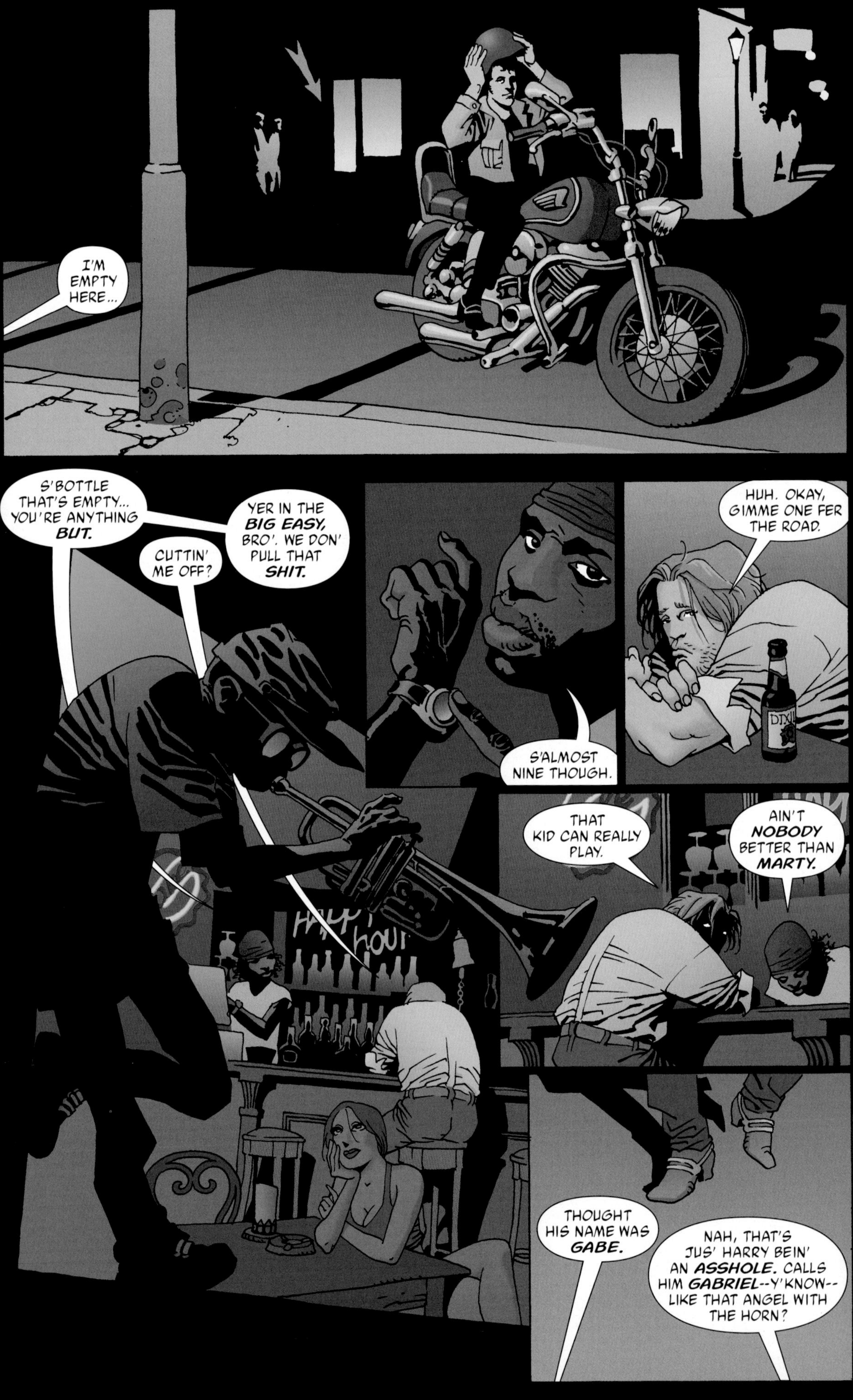
I'M EMPTY HERE...
S'BOTTLE THAT'S EMPTY... YOU'RE ANYTHING BUT.
CUTTIN' ME OFF?
YER IN THE BIG EASY, BRO'. WE DON' PULL THAT SHIT.
S'ALMOST NINE THOUGH.
HUH. OKAY, GIMME ONE FER THE ROAD.
THAT KID CAN REALLY PLAY.
AIN'T NOBODY BETTER THAN MARTY.
THOUGHT HIS NAME WAS GABE.
NAH, THAT'S JUS' HARRY BEIN' AN ASSHOLE. CALLS HIM GABRIEL--Y'KNOW--LIKE THAT ANGEL WITH THE HORN?

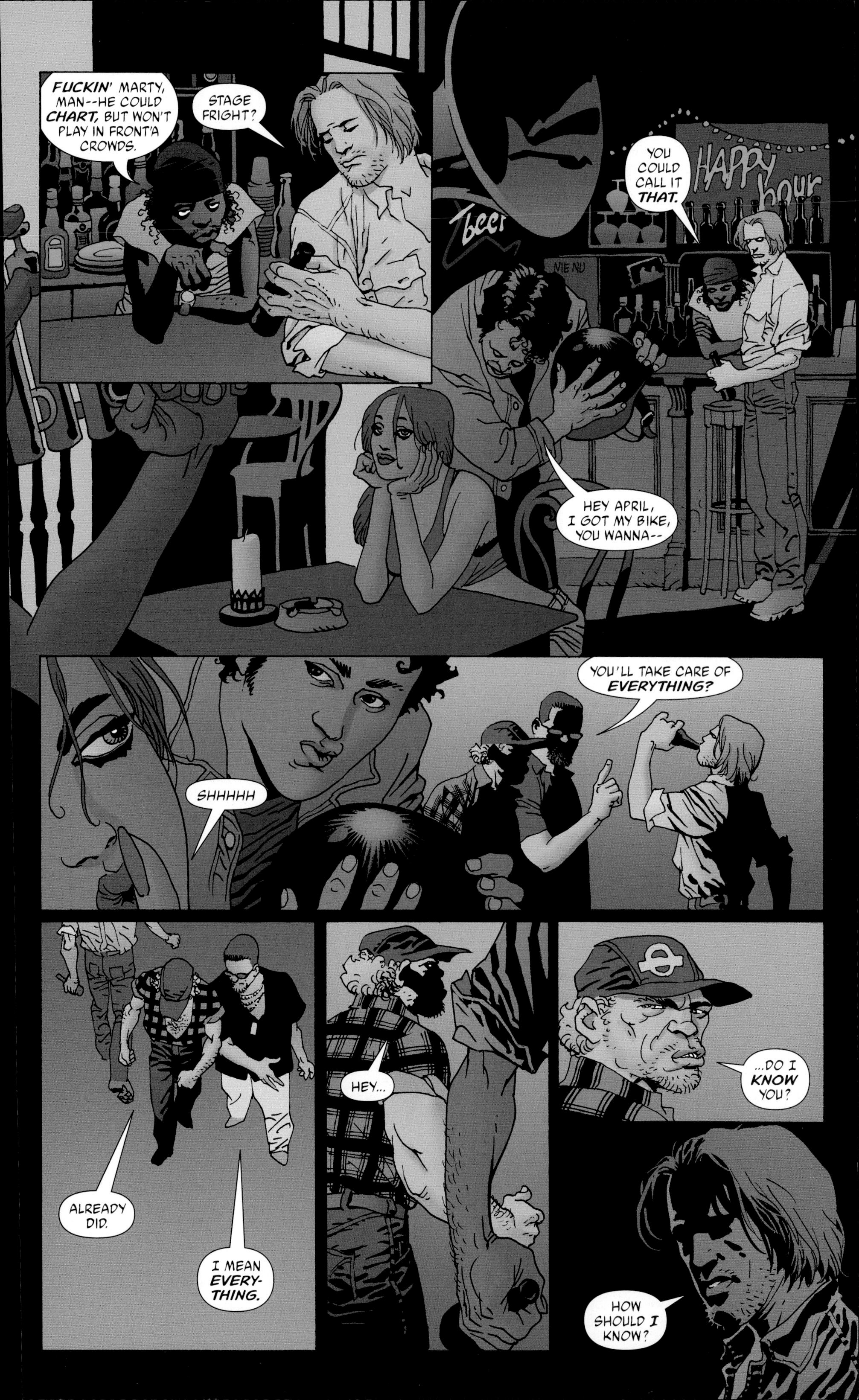
FUCKIN' MARTY, MAN--HE COULD CHART, BUT WON'T PLAY IN FRONT'A CROWDS.
STAGE FRIGHT?
YOU COULD CALL IT THAT.
HAPPY hour
beer
HEY APRIL, I GOT MY BIKE, YOU WANNA--
YOU'LL TAKE CARE OF EVERYTHING?
SHHHHH
ALREADY DID.
I MEAN EVERY-THING.
HEY...
...DO I KNOW YOU?
HOW SHOULD I KNOW?

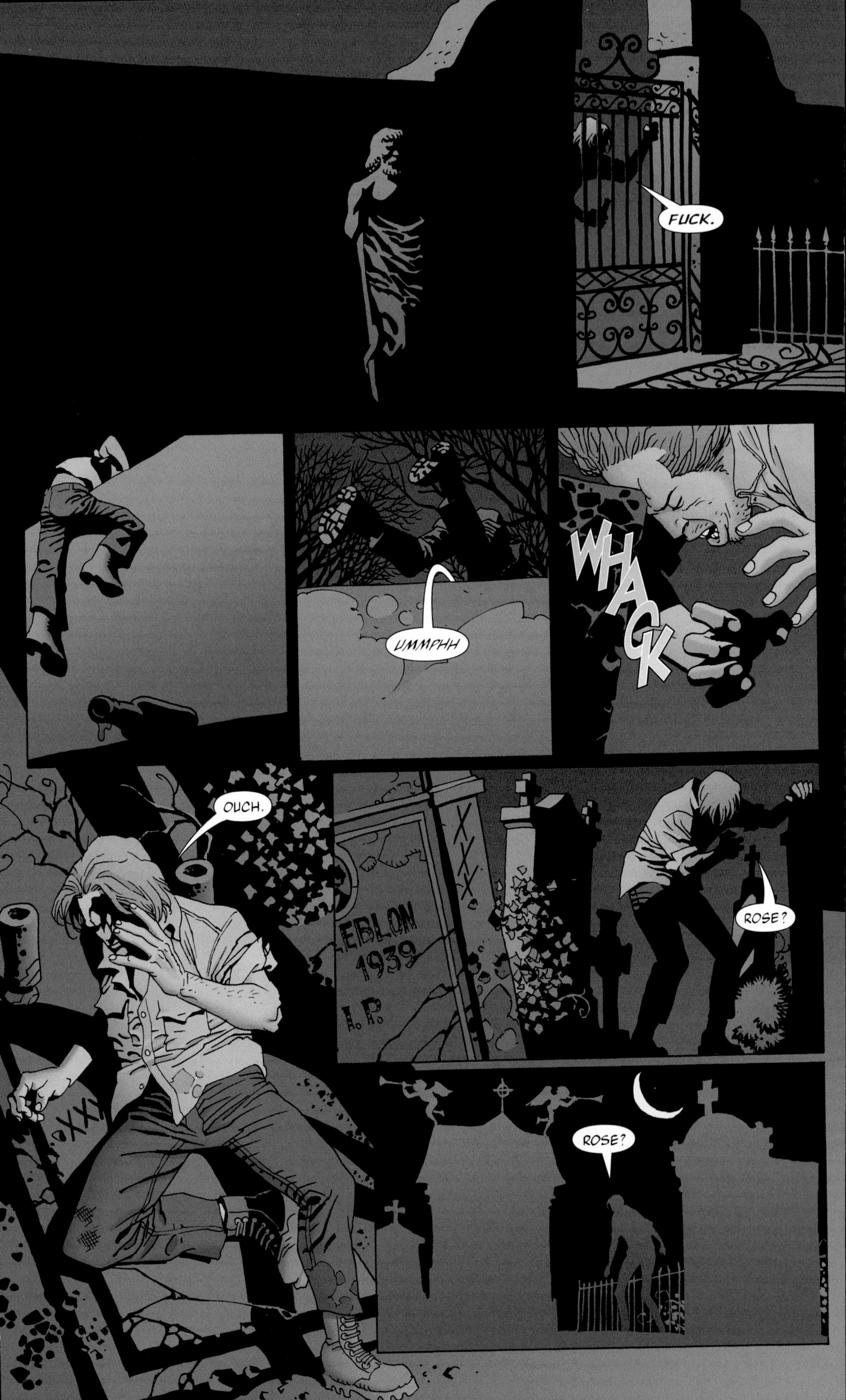
FUCK.
UMMPHH
WHACK
OUCH.
EBLON
1939
I. P.
ROSE?
ROSE?

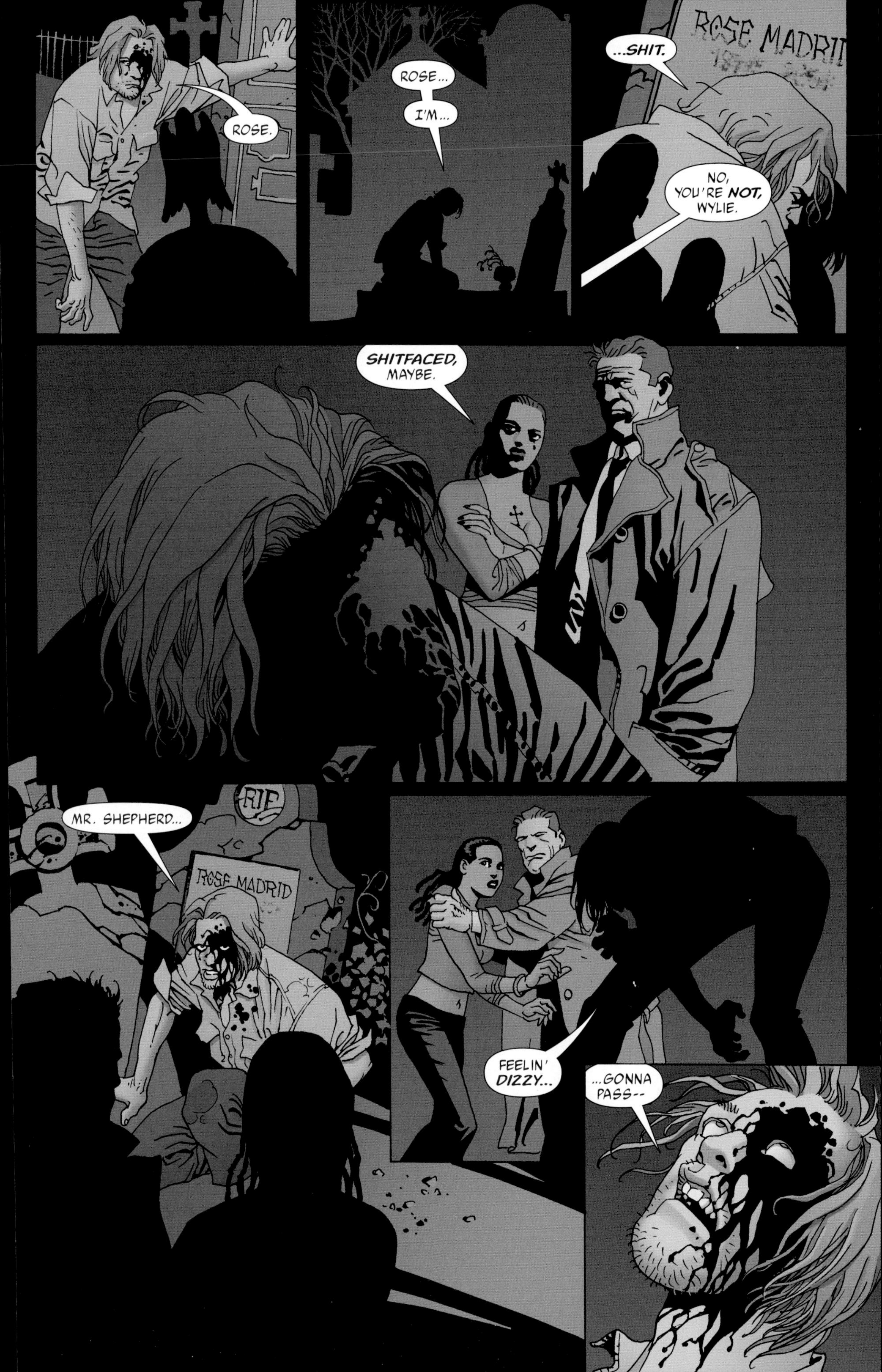
ROSE.
ROSE...
I'M...
...SHIT.
ROSE MADRID
NO, YOU'RE NOT, WYLIE.
SHITFACED, MAYBE.
MR. SHEPHERD...
RIP
ROSE MADRID
FEELIN' DIZZY...
...GONNA PASS--

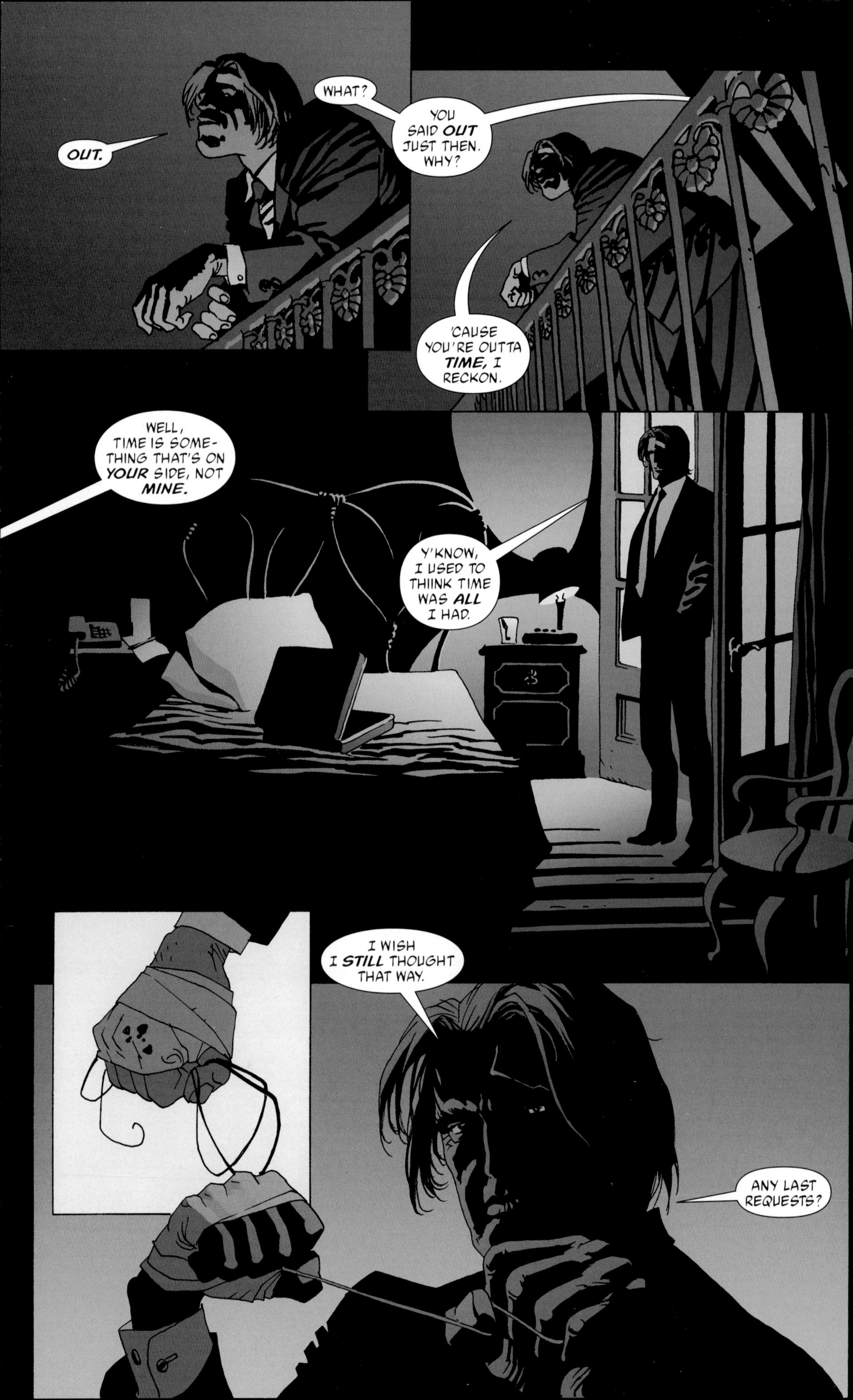
OUT.
WHAT?
YOU SAID OUT JUST THEN. WHY?
'CAUSE YOU'RE OUTTA TIME, I RECKON.
WELL, TIME IS SOMETHING THAT'S ON YOUR SIDE, NOT MINE.
Y'KNOW, I USED TO THIINK TIME WAS ALL I HAD.
I WISH I STILL THOUGHT THAT WAY.
ANY LAST REQUESTS?

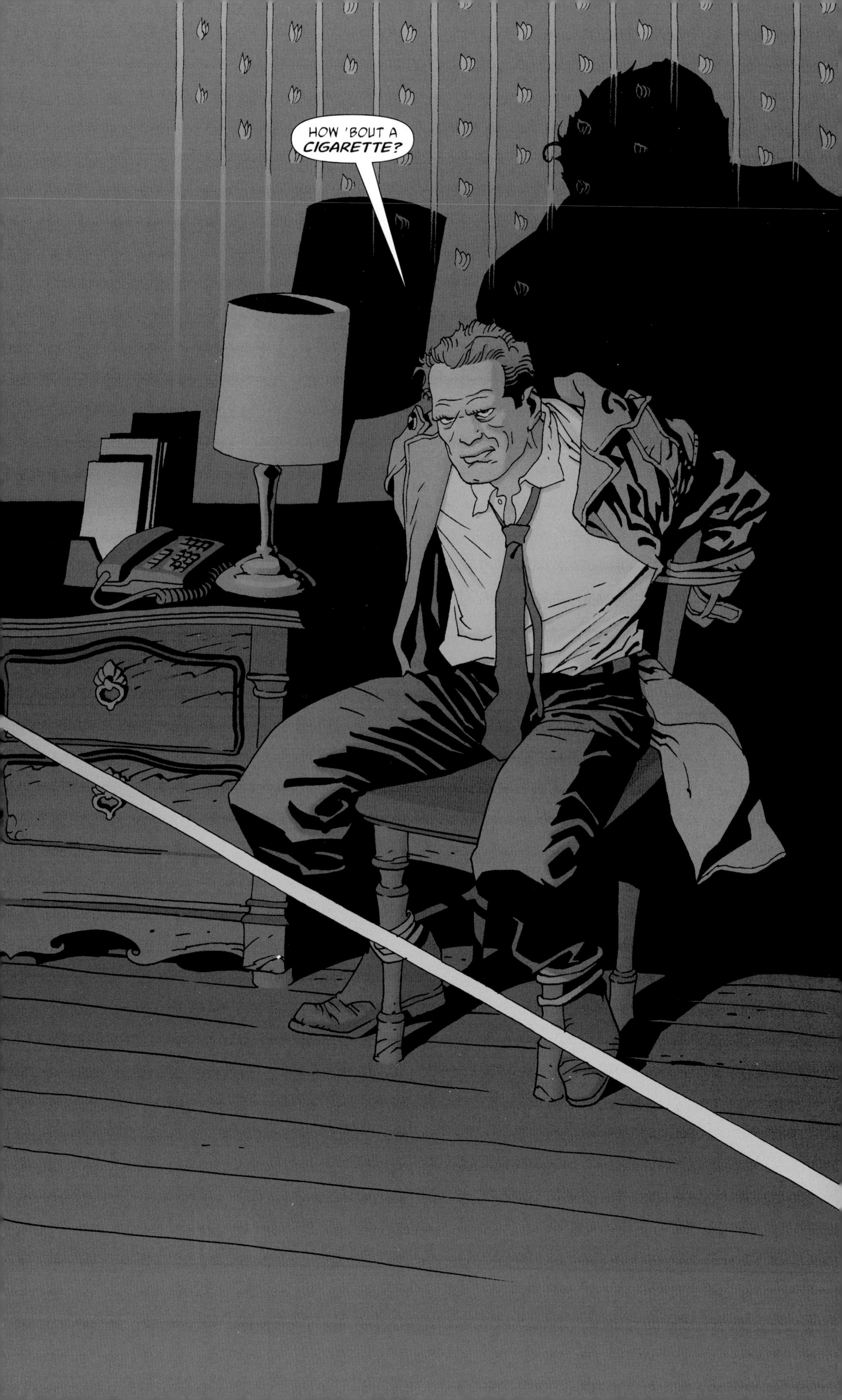
HOW 'BOUT A
CIGARETTE?

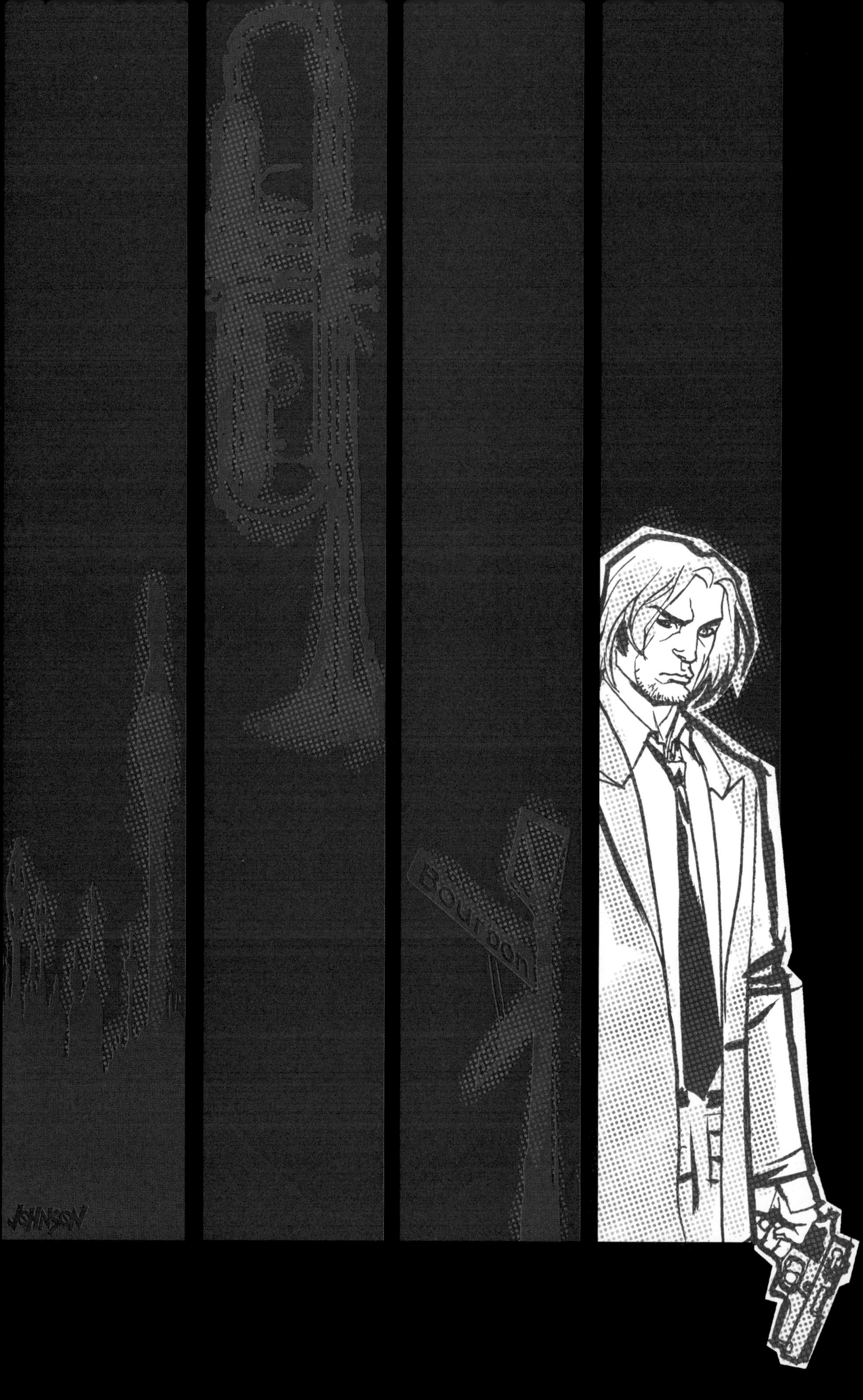
Bourbon
JOHNSON

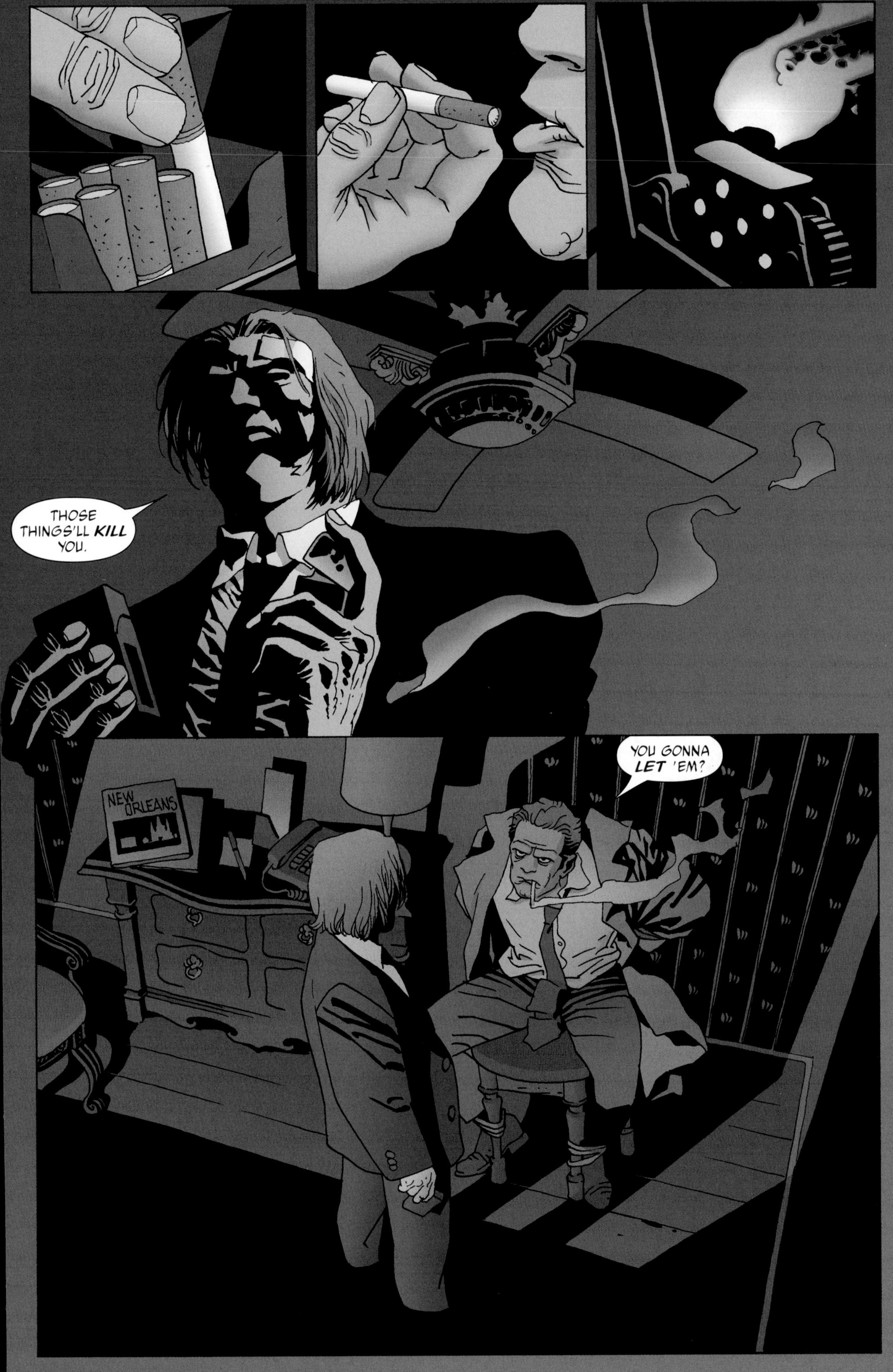
THOSE THINGS'LL KILL YOU.
NEW ORLEANS
YOU GONNA LET 'EM?

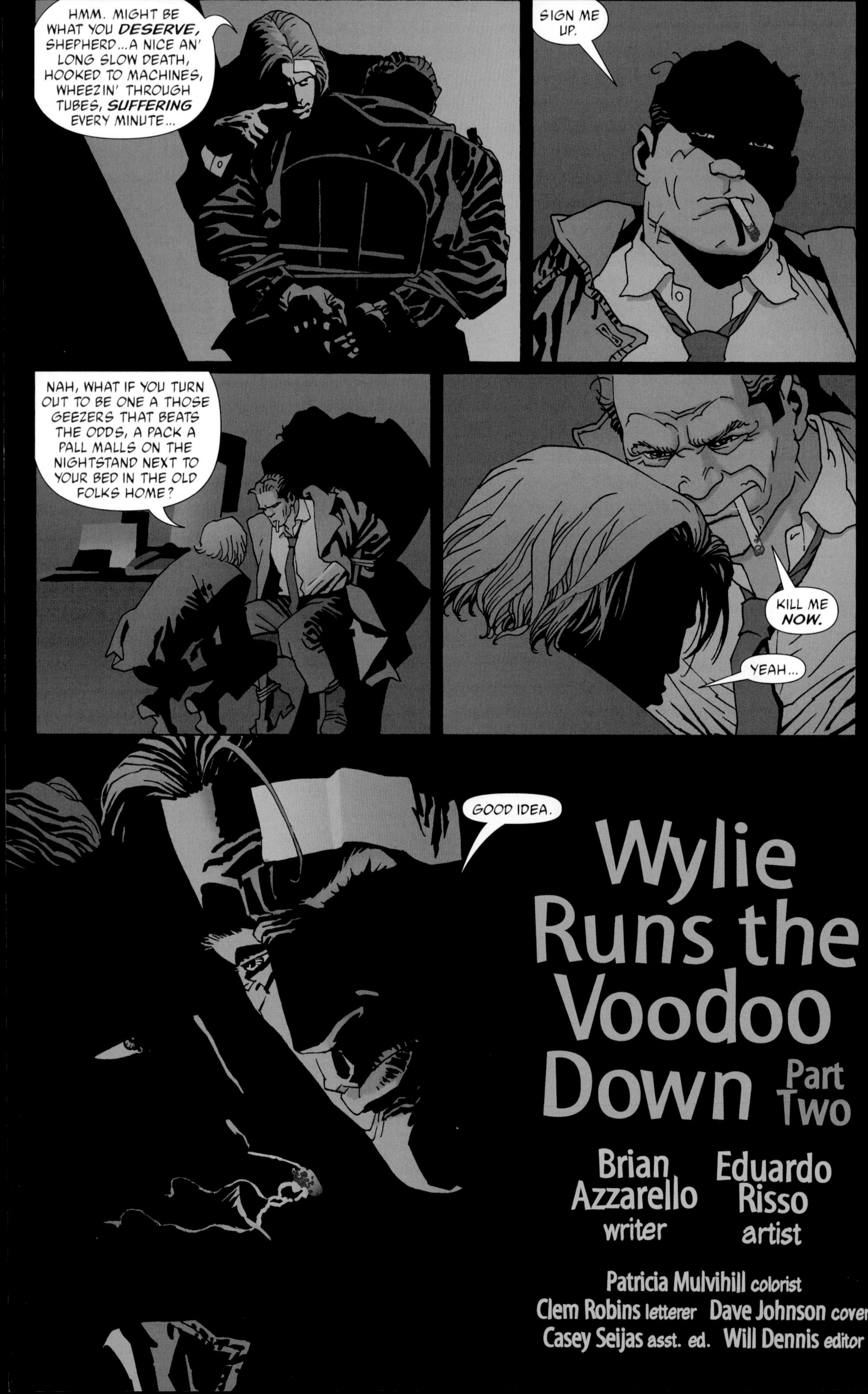
HMM. MIGHT BE WHAT YOU DESERVE, SHEPHERD...A NICE AN' LONG SLOW DEATH, HOOKED TO MACHINES, WHEEZIN' THROUGH TUBES, SUFFERING EVERY MINUTE...
SIGN ME UP.
NAH, WHAT IF YOU TURN OUT TO BE ONE A THOSE GEEZERS THAT BEATS THE ODDS, A PACK A PALL MALLS ON THE NIGHTSTAND NEXT TO YOUR BED IN THE OLD FOLKS HOME?
KILL ME NOW.
YEAH...
GOOD IDEA.
Wylie Runs the Voodoo Down Part Two
Brian Azzarello writer
Eduardo Risso artist
Patricia Mulvihill colorist
Clem Robins letterer
Dave Johnson cover
Casey Seijas asst. ed.
Will Dennis editor

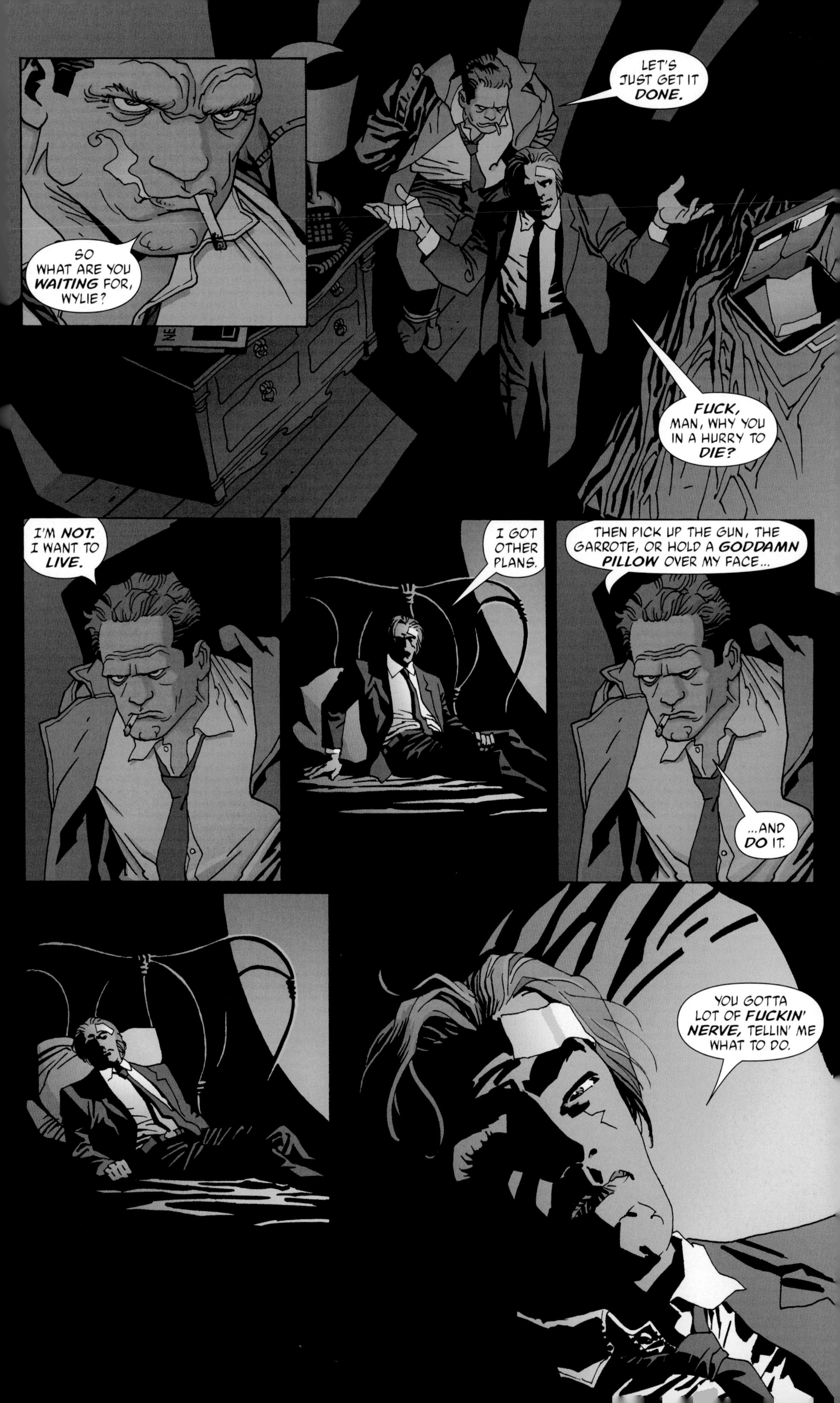
SO WHAT ARE YOU **WAITING** FOR, WYLIE?
LET'S JUST GET IT **DONE.**
FUCK, MAN, WHY YOU IN A HURRY TO **DIE?**
I'M **NOT.** I WANT TO **LIVE.**
I GOT OTHER PLANS.
THEN PICK UP THE GUN, THE GARROTE, OR HOLD A **GODDAMN PILLOW** OVER MY FACE...
...AND **DO** IT.
YOU GOTTA LOT OF **FUCKIN' NERVE,** TELLIN' ME WHAT TO DO.

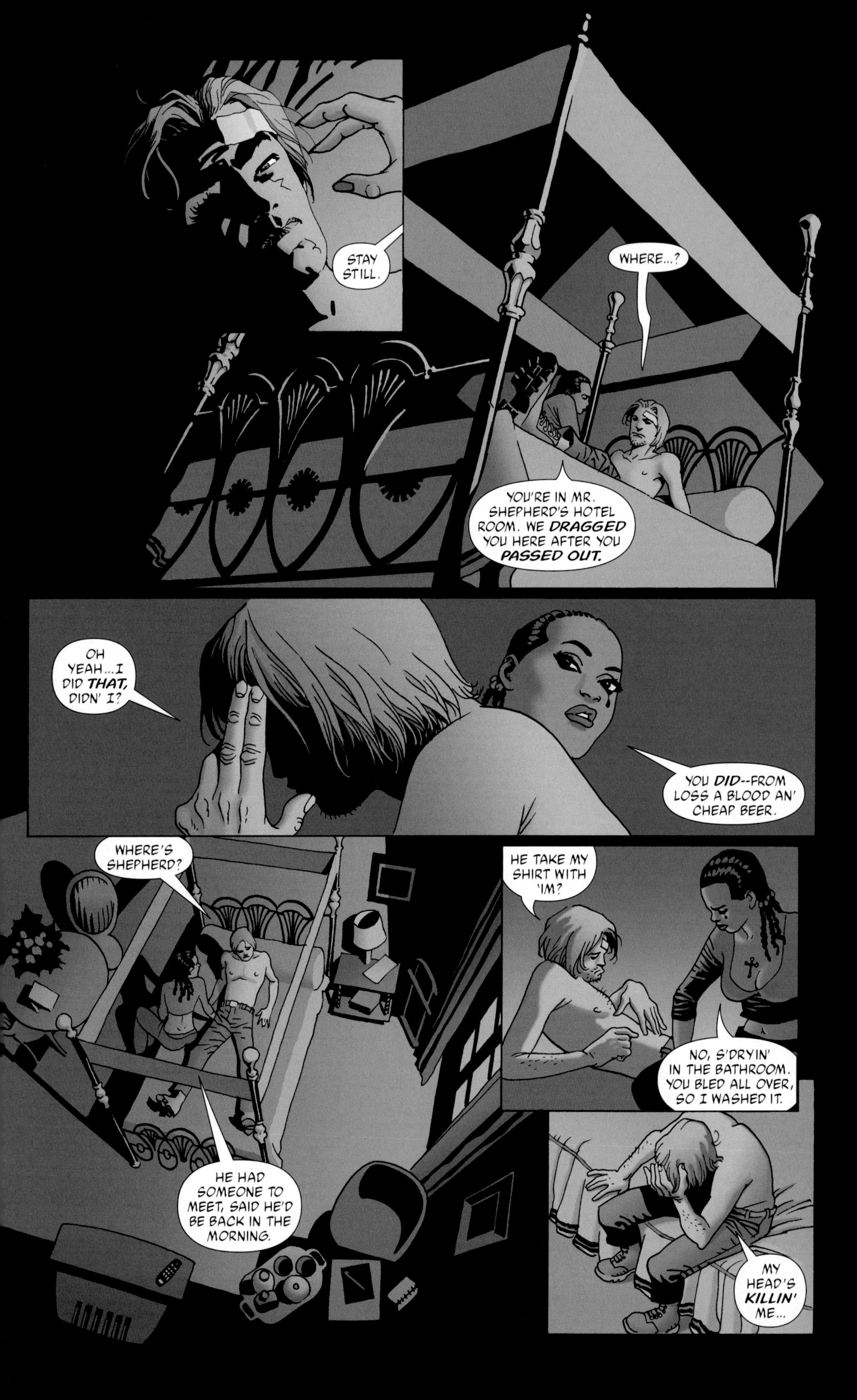
STAY STILL.
WHERE...?
YOU'RE IN MR. SHEPHERD'S HOTEL ROOM. WE **DRAGGED** YOU HERE AFTER YOU **PASSED OUT.**
OH YEAH...I DID **THAT,** DIDN' I?
YOU **DID**--FROM LOSS A BLOOD AN' CHEAP BEER.
WHERE'S SHEPHERD?
HE HAD SOMEONE TO MEET, SAID HE'D BE BACK IN THE MORNING.
HE TAKE MY SHIRT WITH 'IM?
NO, S'DRYIN' IN THE BATHROOM. YOU BLED ALL OVER, SO I WASHED IT.
MY HEAD'S **KILLIN'** ME...

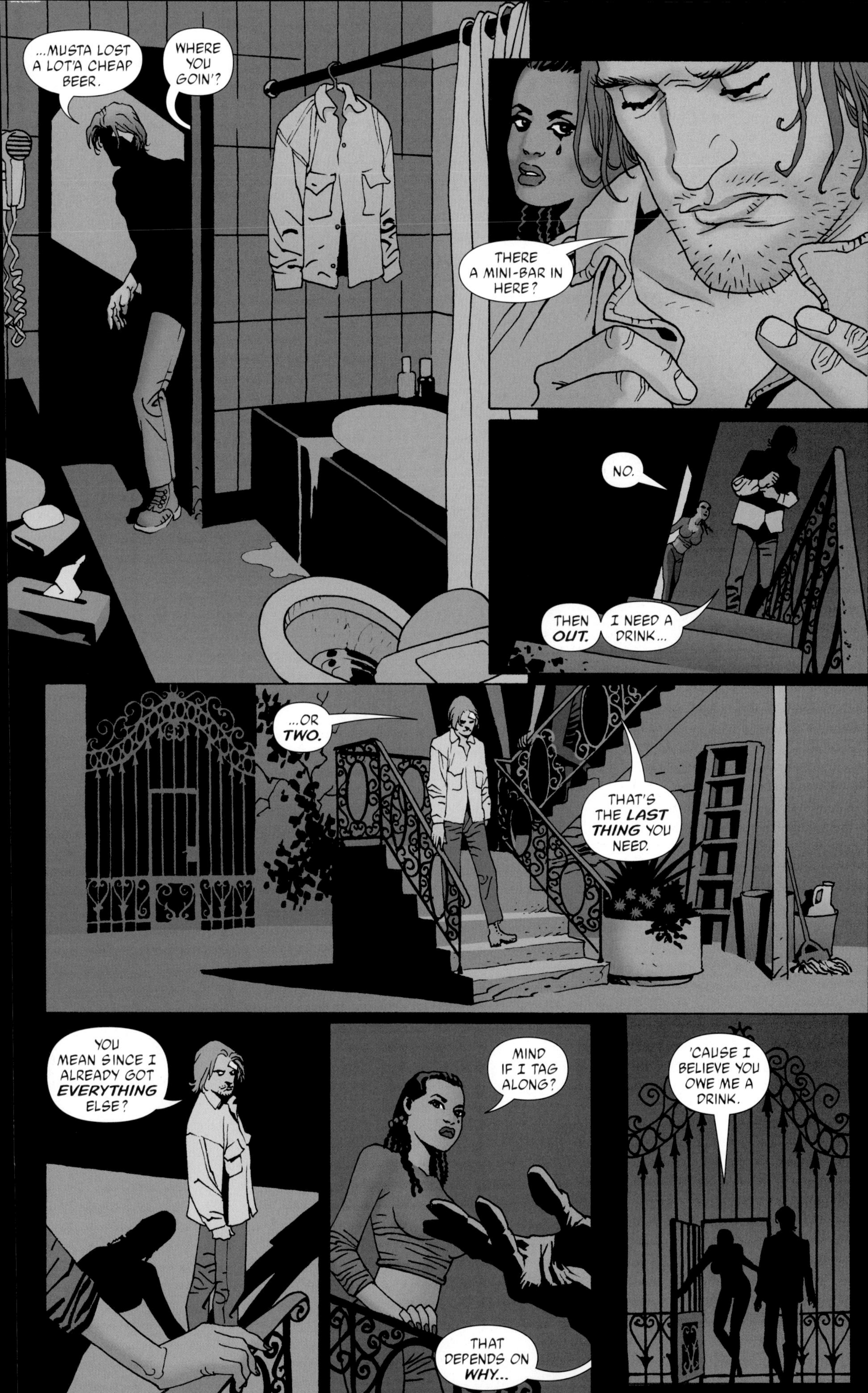
...MUSTA LOST A LOT'A CHEAP BEER.
WHERE YOU GOIN'?
THERE A MINI-BAR IN HERE?
NO.
THEN **OUT.**
I NEED A DRINK...
...OR **TWO.**
THAT'S THE **LAST THING** YOU NEED.
YOU MEAN SINCE I ALREADY GOT **EVERYTHING** ELSE?
MIND IF I TAG ALONG?
THAT DEPENDS ON **WHY...**
'CAUSE I BELIEVE YOU OWE ME A DRINK.

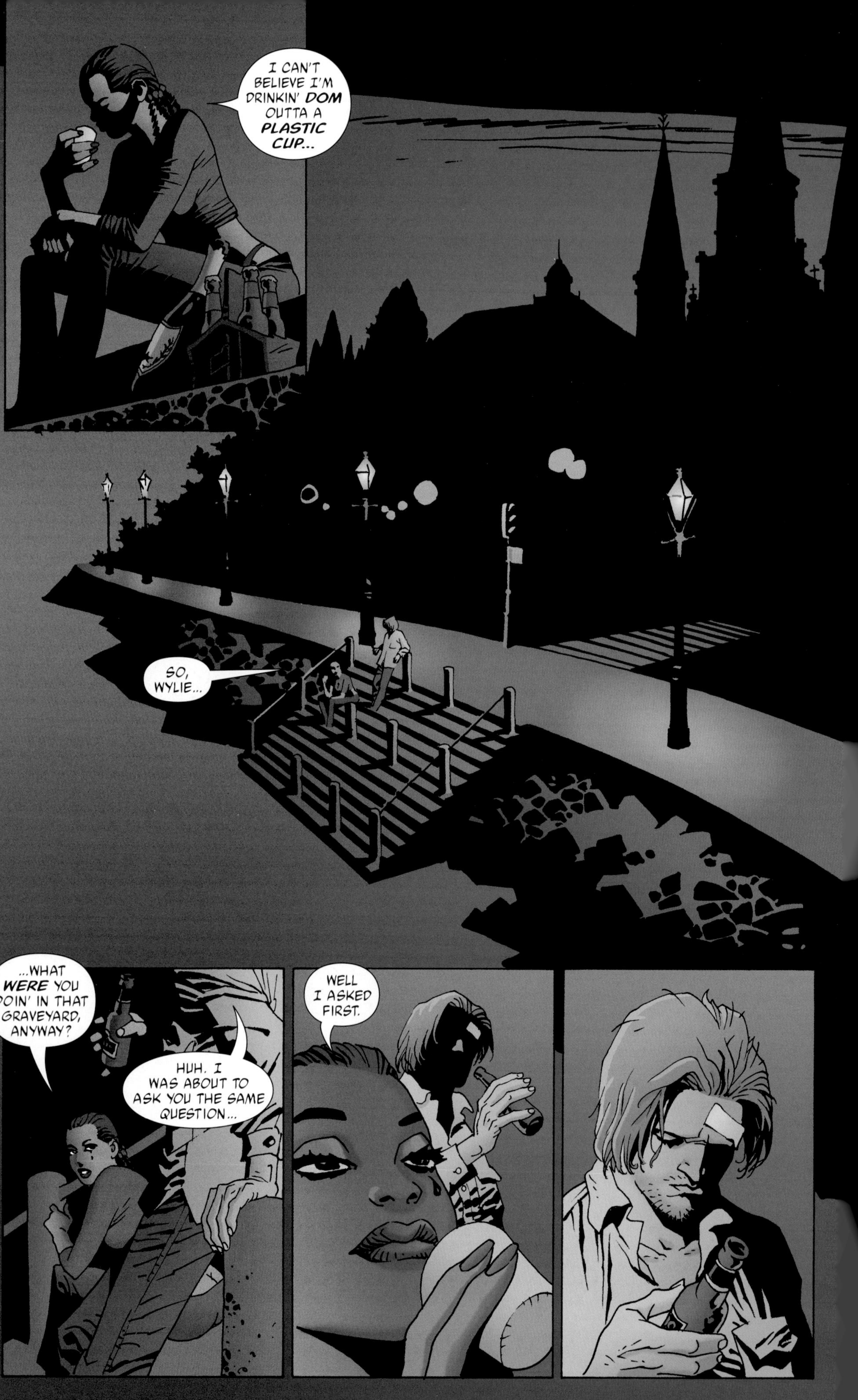
I CAN'T BELIEVE I'M DRINKIN' DOM OUTTA A PLASTIC CUP...
SO, WYLIE...
...WHAT WERE YOU DOIN' IN THAT GRAVEYARD, ANYWAY?
HUH. I WAS ABOUT TO ASK YOU THE SAME QUESTION...
WELL I ASKED FIRST.

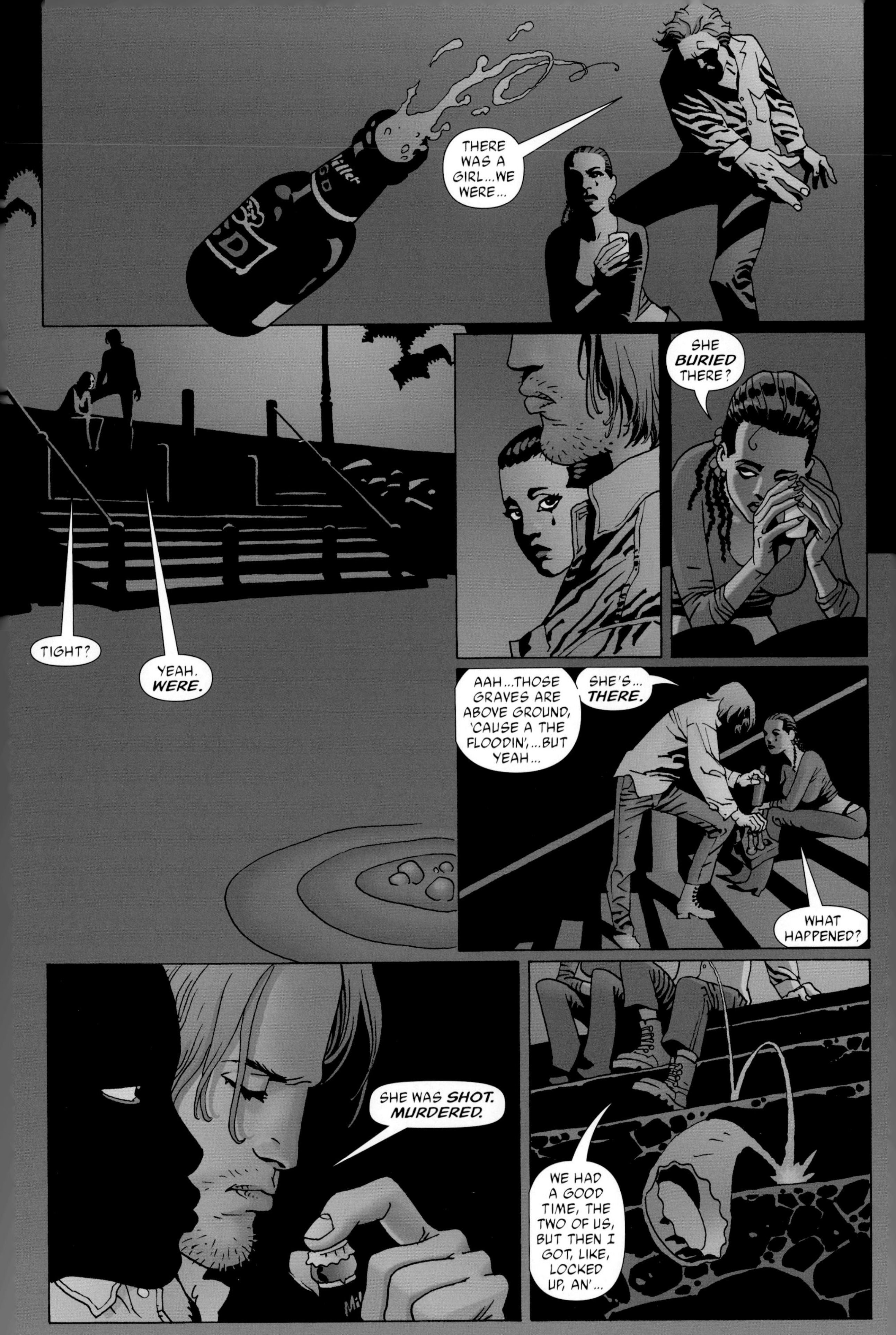
THERE WAS A GIRL...WE WERE...
TIGHT?
YEAH. WERE.
SHE BURIED THERE?
SHE'S... THERE.
AAH...THOSE GRAVES ARE ABOVE GROUND, 'CAUSE A THE FLOODIN',...BUT YEAH...
WHAT HAPPENED?
SHE WAS SHOT. MURDERED.
WE HAD A GOOD TIME, THE TWO OF US, BUT THEN I GOT, LIKE, LOCKED UP, AN'...

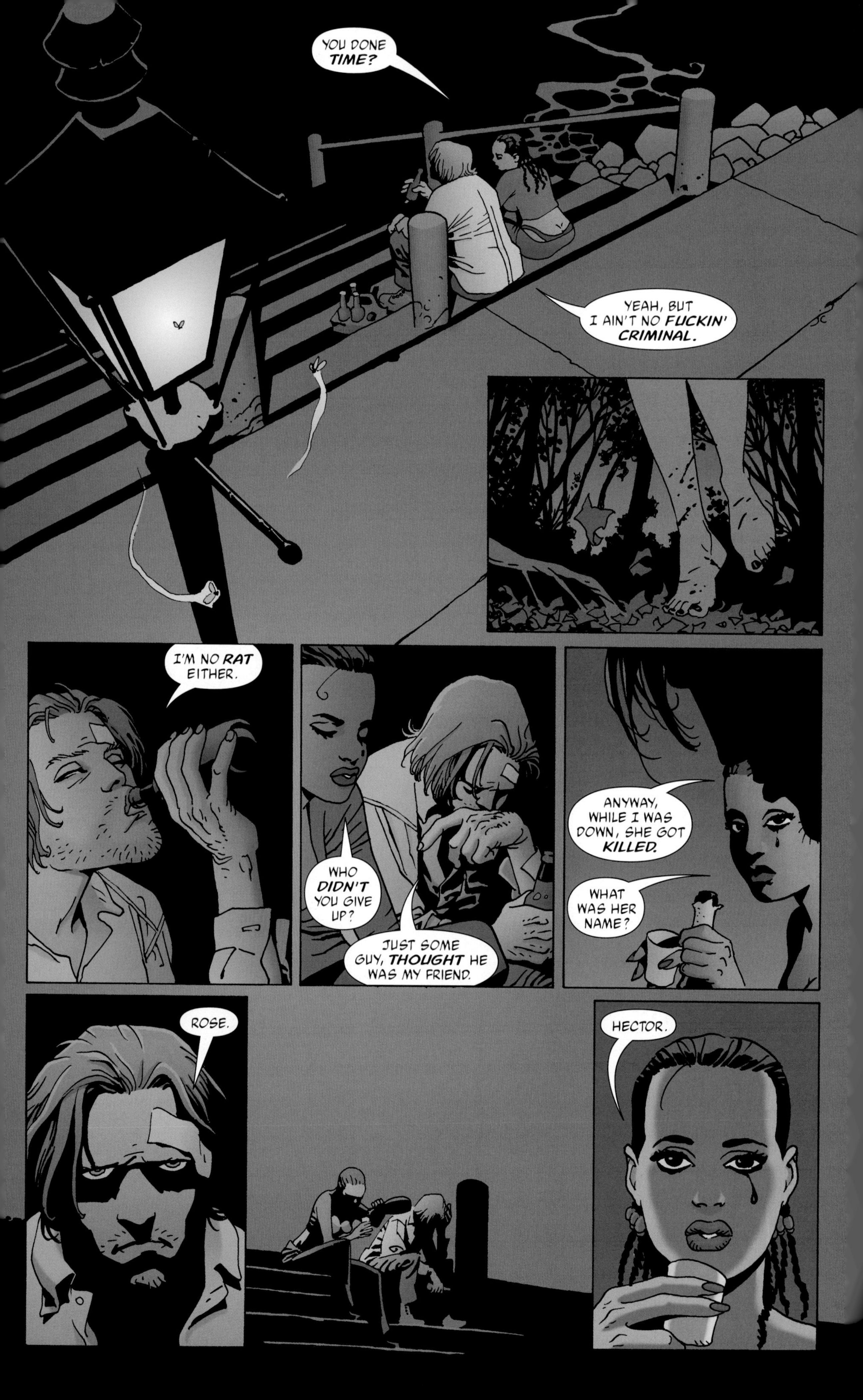
YOU DONE TIME?
YEAH, BUT I AIN'T NO FUCKIN' CRIMINAL.
I'M NO RAT EITHER.
WHO DIDN'T YOU GIVE UP?
JUST SOME GUY, THOUGHT HE WAS MY FRIEND.
ANYWAY, WHILE I WAS DOWN, SHE GOT KILLED.
WHAT WAS HER NAME?
ROSE.
HECTOR.

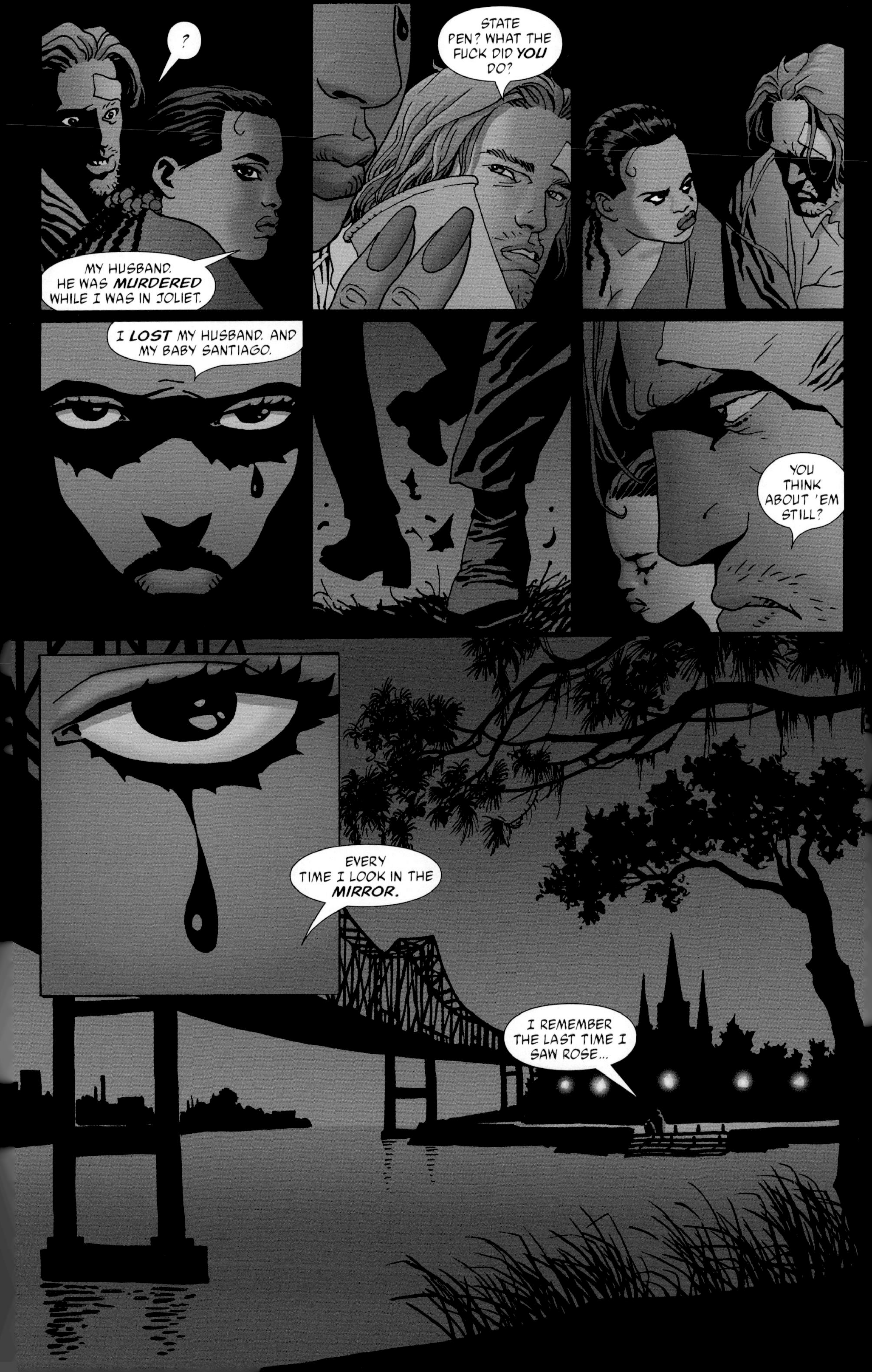
?
MY HUSBAND. HE WAS MURDERED WHILE I WAS IN JOLIET.
STATE PEN? WHAT THE FUCK DID YOU DO?
I LOST MY HUSBAND. AND MY BABY SANTIAGO.
YOU THINK ABOUT 'EM STILL?
EVERY TIME I LOOK IN THE MIRROR.
I REMEMBER THE LAST TIME I SAW ROSE...

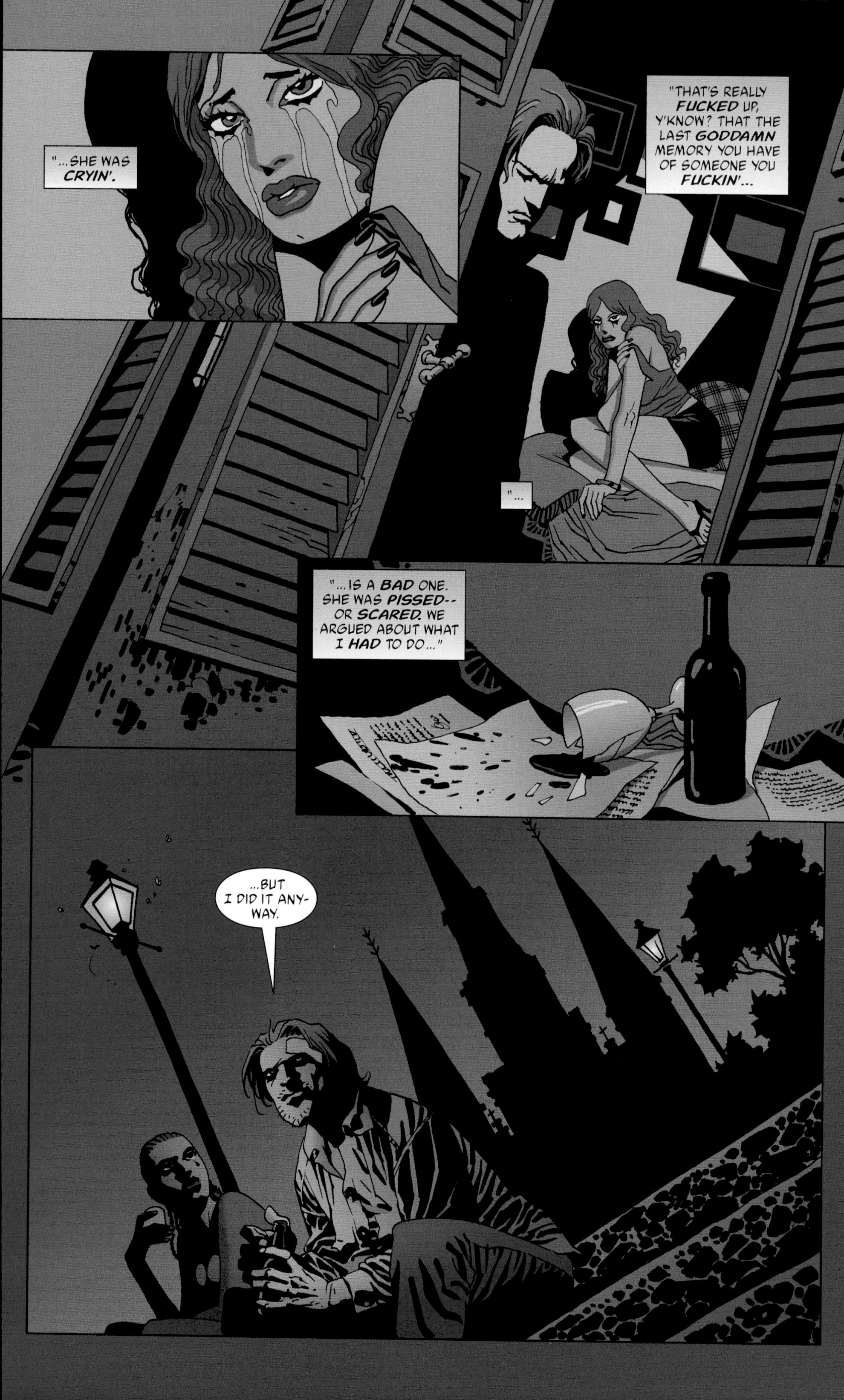
"...SHE WAS CRYIN'.
"THAT'S REALLY FUCKED UP, Y'KNOW? THAT THE LAST GODDAMN MEMORY YOU HAVE OF SOMEONE YOU FUCKIN'...
"...
"...IS A BAD ONE. SHE WAS PISSED-- OR SCARED. WE ARGUED ABOUT WHAT I HAD TO DO..."
...BUT I DID IT ANY-WAY.

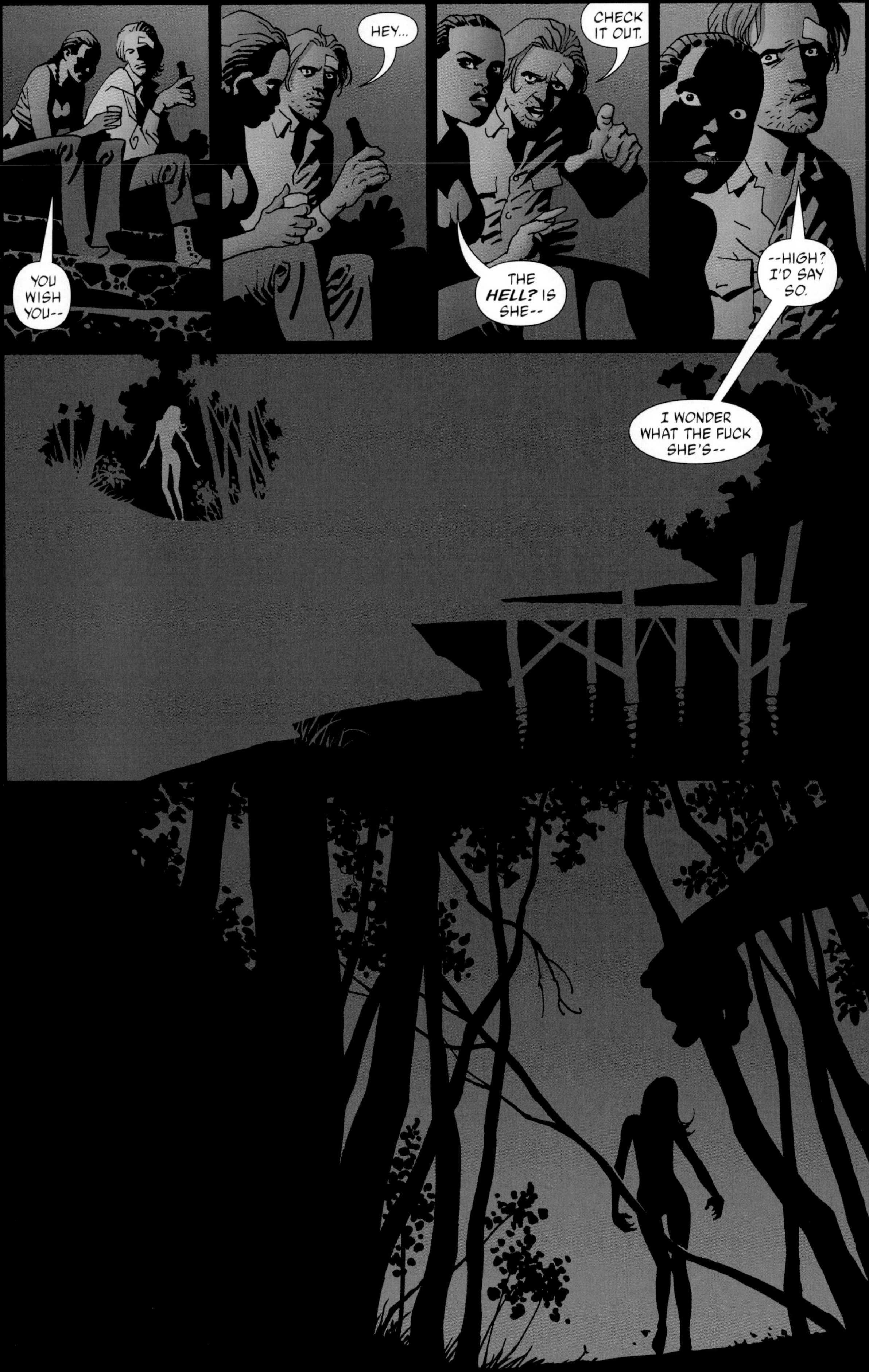
YOU WISH YOU--
HEY...
CHECK IT OUT.
THE **HELL?** IS SHE--
--HIGH? I'D SAY SO.
I WONDER WHAT THE FUCK SHE'S--

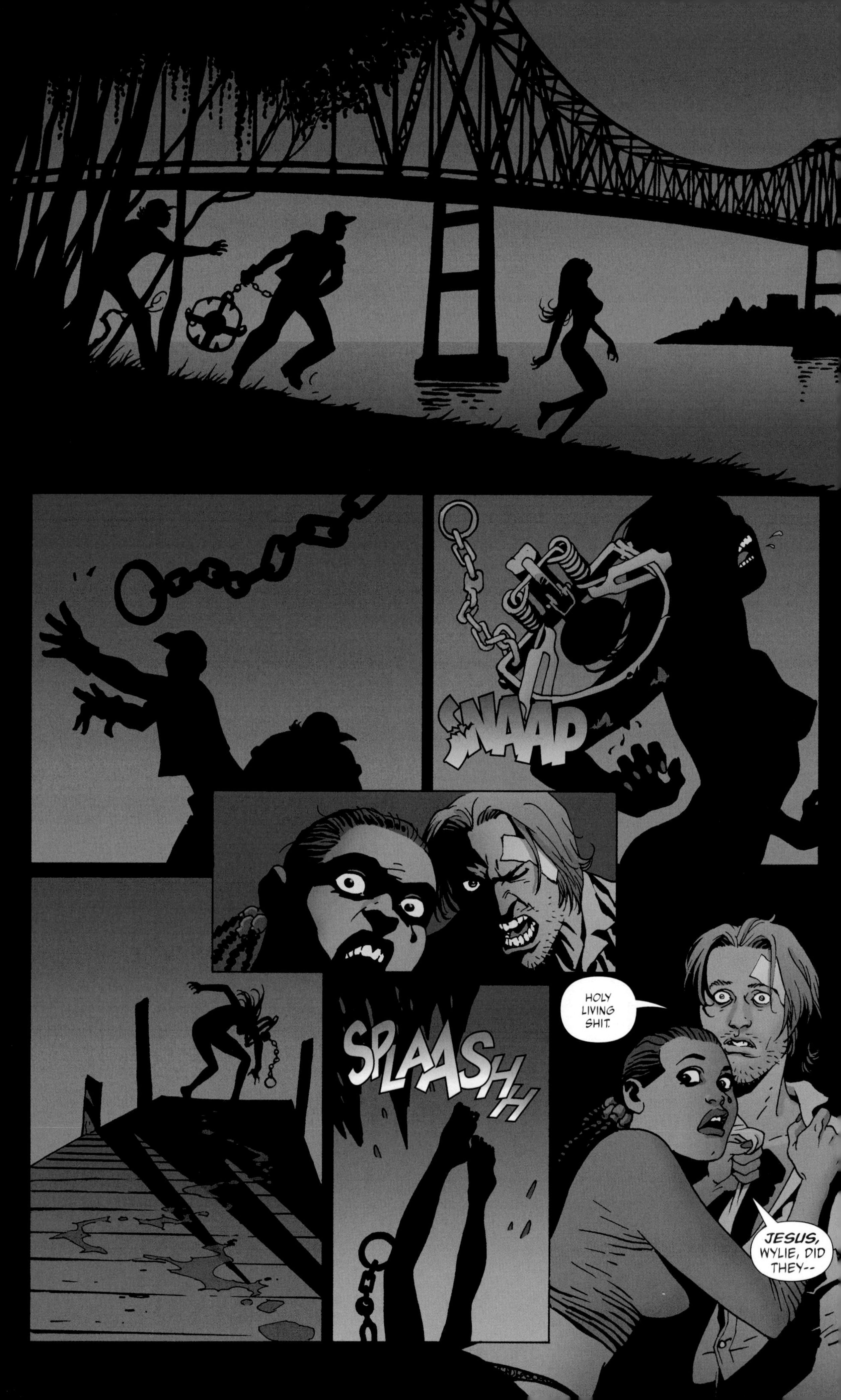
SNAAP
SPLAASHH
HOLY LIVING SHIT.
JESUS, WYLIE, DID THEY--

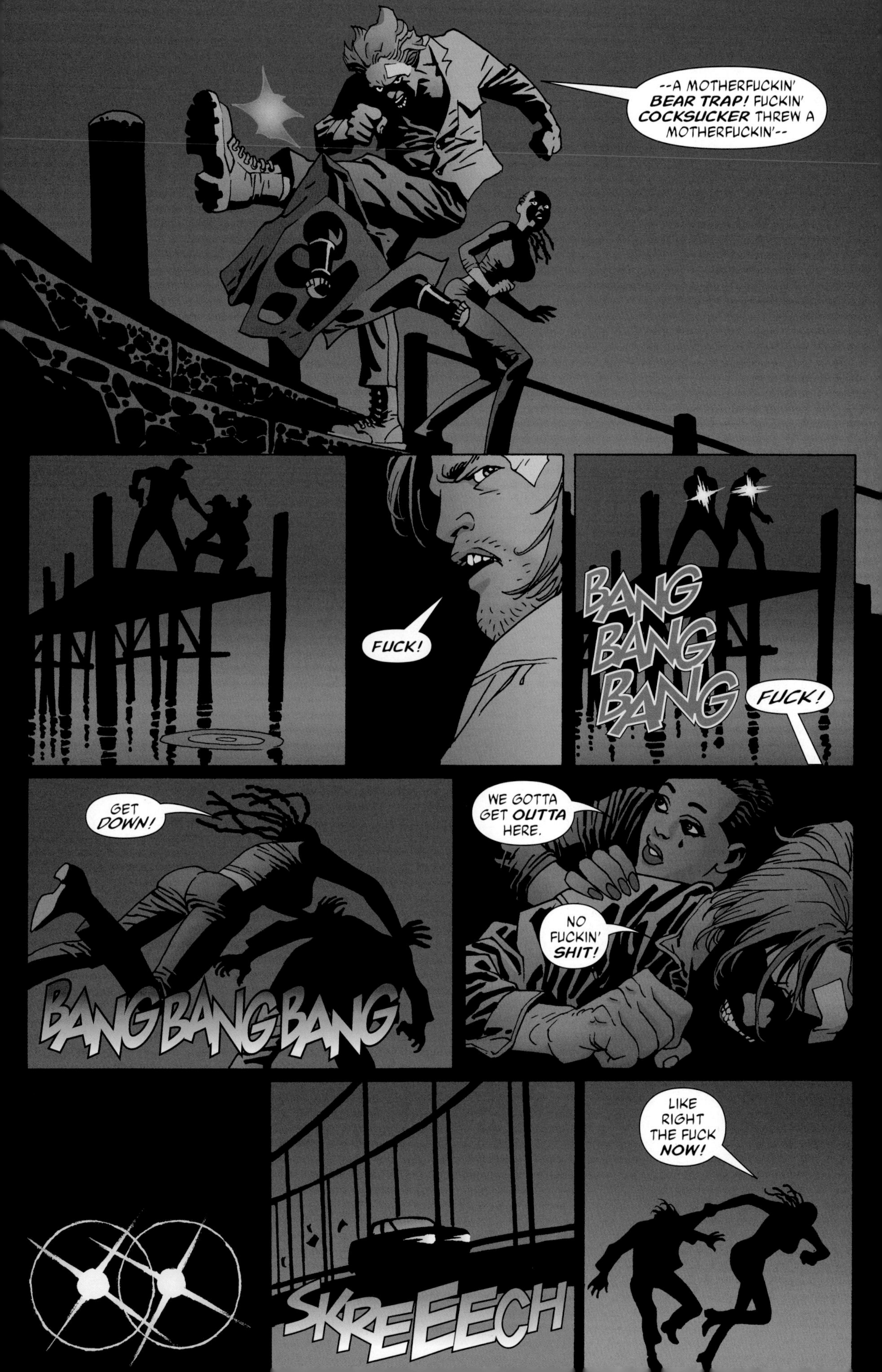
--A MOTHERFUCKIN' BEAR TRAP! FUCKIN' COCKSUCKER THREW A MOTHERFUCKIN'--
FUCK!
BANG BANG BANG
FUCK!
GET DOWN!
BANG BANG BANG
WE GOTTA GET OUTTA HERE.
NO FUCKIN' SHIT!
SKREEEECH
LIKE RIGHT THE FUCK NOW!

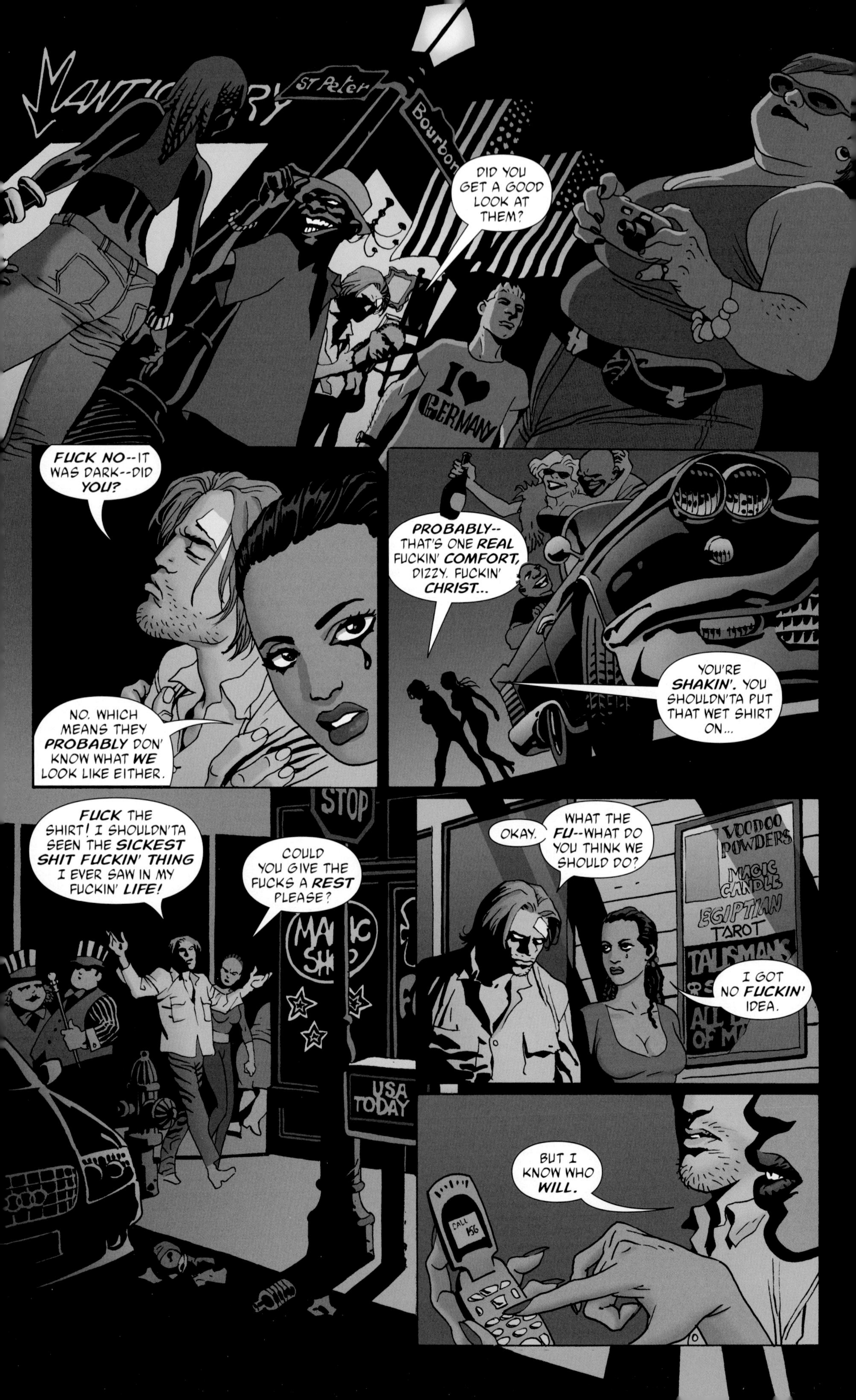
St Peter
Bourbon
DID YOU GET A GOOD LOOK AT THEM?
FUCK NO--IT WAS DARK--DID YOU?
NO. WHICH MEANS THEY PROBABLY DON' KNOW WHAT WE LOOK LIKE EITHER.
PROBABLY--THAT'S ONE REAL FUCKIN' COMFORT, DIZZY. FUCKIN' CHRIST...
YOU'RE SHAKIN'. YOU SHOULDN'TA PUT THAT WET SHIRT ON...
STOP
FUCK THE SHIRT! I SHOULDN'TA SEEN THE SICKEST SHIT FUCKIN' THING I EVER SAW IN MY FUCKIN' LIFE!
COULD YOU GIVE THE FUCKS A REST PLEASE?
USA TODAY
OKAY.
WHAT THE FU--WHAT DO YOU THINK WE SHOULD DO?
VOODOO POWDERS
MAGIC CANDLE
EGIPTIAN TAROT
TALISMANS
I GOT NO FUCKIN' IDEA.
BUT I KNOW WHO WILL.

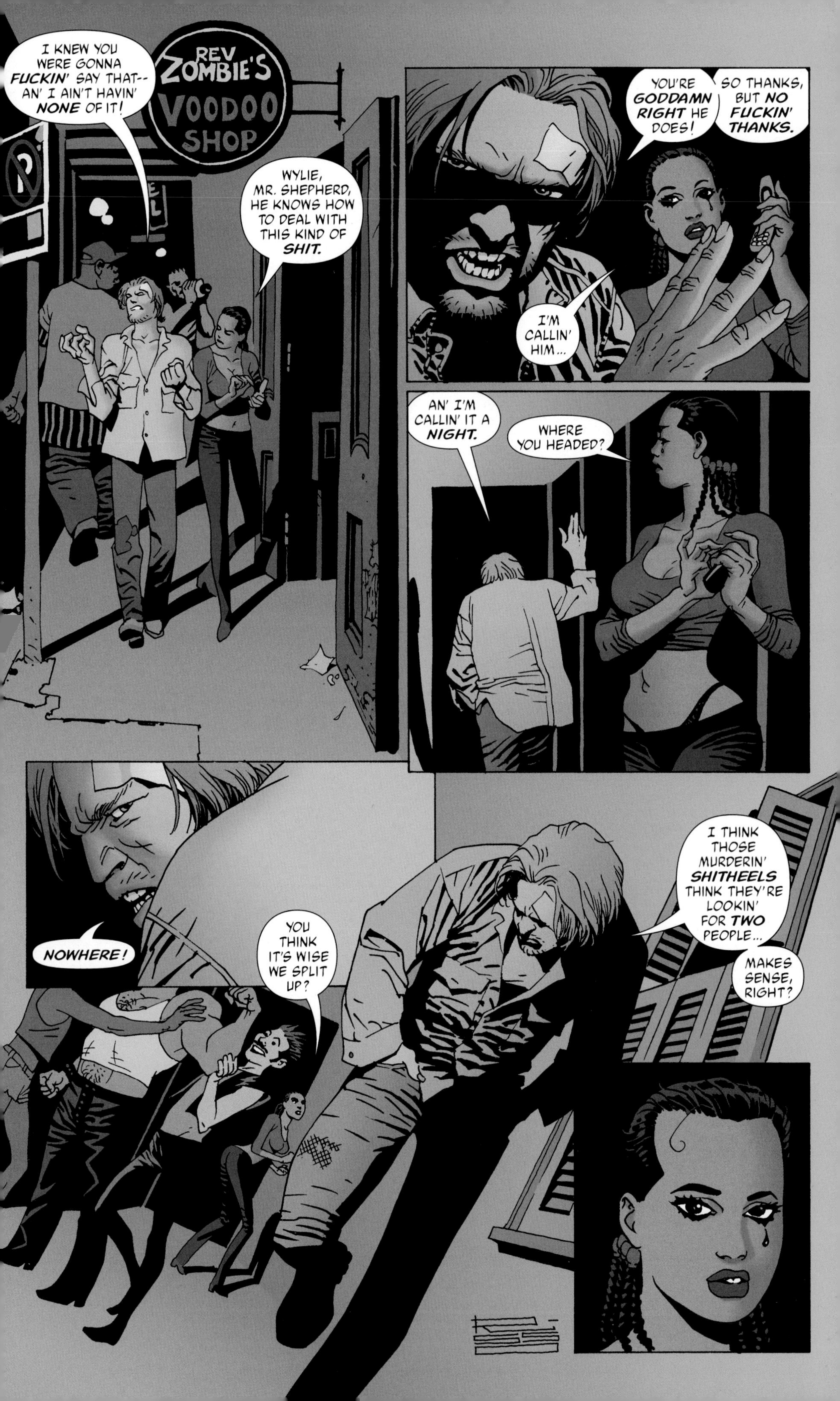
I KNEW YOU WERE GONNA FUCKIN' SAY THAT-- AN' I AIN'T HAVIN' NONE OF IT!
REV ZOMBIE'S VOODOO SHOP
WYLIE, MR. SHEPHERD, HE KNOWS HOW TO DEAL WITH THIS KIND OF SHIT.
YOU'RE GODDAMN RIGHT HE DOES!
SO THANKS, BUT NO FUCKIN' THANKS.
I'M CALLIN' HIM...
AN' I'M CALLIN' IT A NIGHT.
WHERE YOU HEADED?
NOWHERE!
YOU THINK IT'S WISE WE SPLIT UP?
I THINK THOSE MURDERIN' SHITHEELS THINK THEY'RE LOOKIN' FOR TWO PEOPLE...
MAKES SENSE, RIGHT?

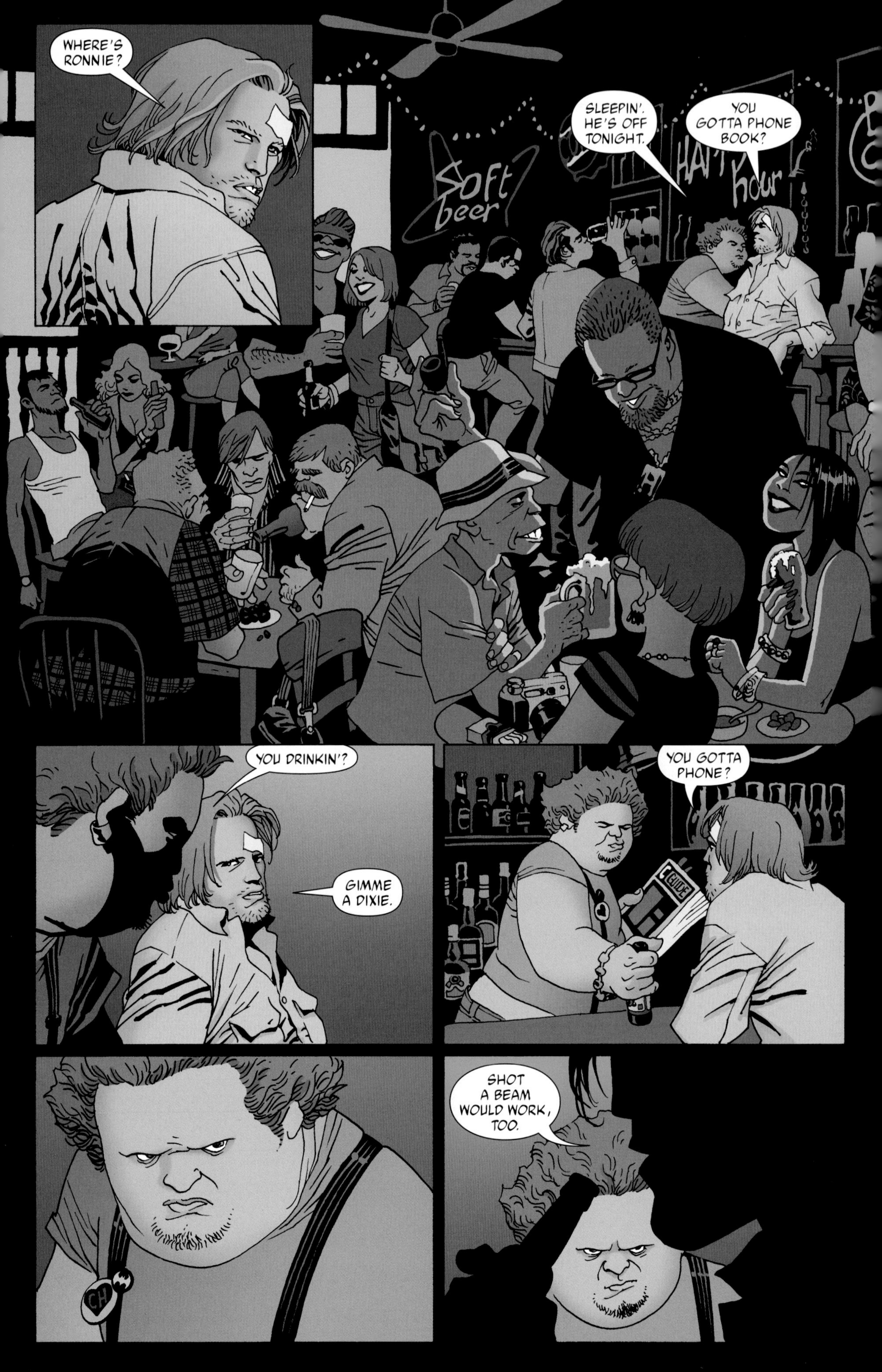
WHERE'S RONNIE?
SLEEPIN'. HE'S OFF TONIGHT.
YOU GOTTA PHONE BOOK?
Soft beer
YOU DRINKIN'?
GIMME A DIXIE.
YOU GOTTA PHONE?
SHOT A BEAM WOULD WORK, TOO.

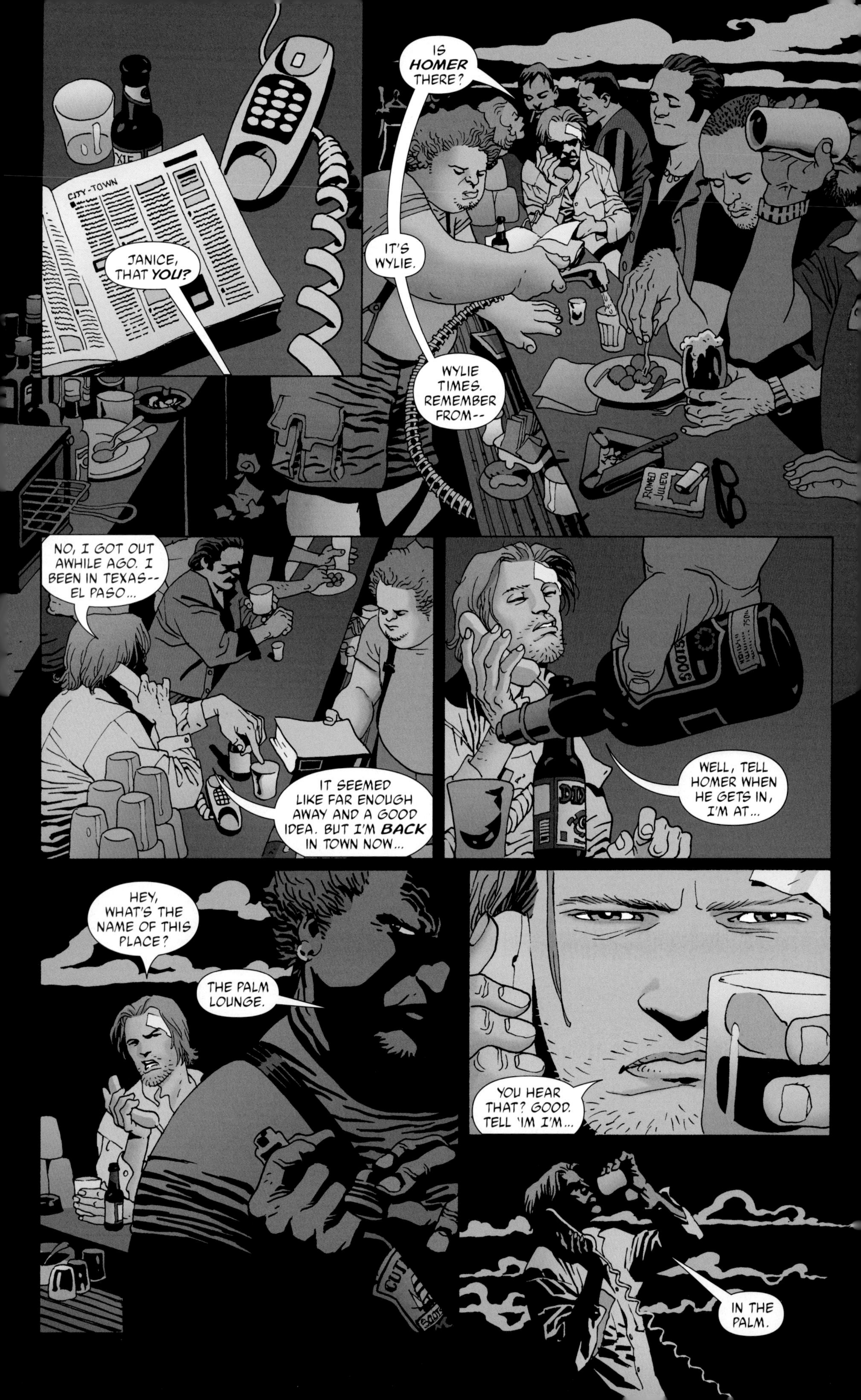
JANICE, THAT YOU?
IS HOMER THERE?
IT'S WYLIE.
WYLIE TIMES. REMEMBER FROM--
NO, I GOT OUT AWHILE AGO. I BEEN IN TEXAS-- EL PASO...
IT SEEMED LIKE FAR ENOUGH AWAY AND A GOOD IDEA. BUT I'M BACK IN TOWN NOW...
WELL, TELL HOMER WHEN HE GETS IN, I'M AT...
HEY, WHAT'S THE NAME OF THIS PLACE?
THE PALM LOUNGE.
YOU HEAR THAT? GOOD. TELL 'IM I'M...
IN THE PALM.

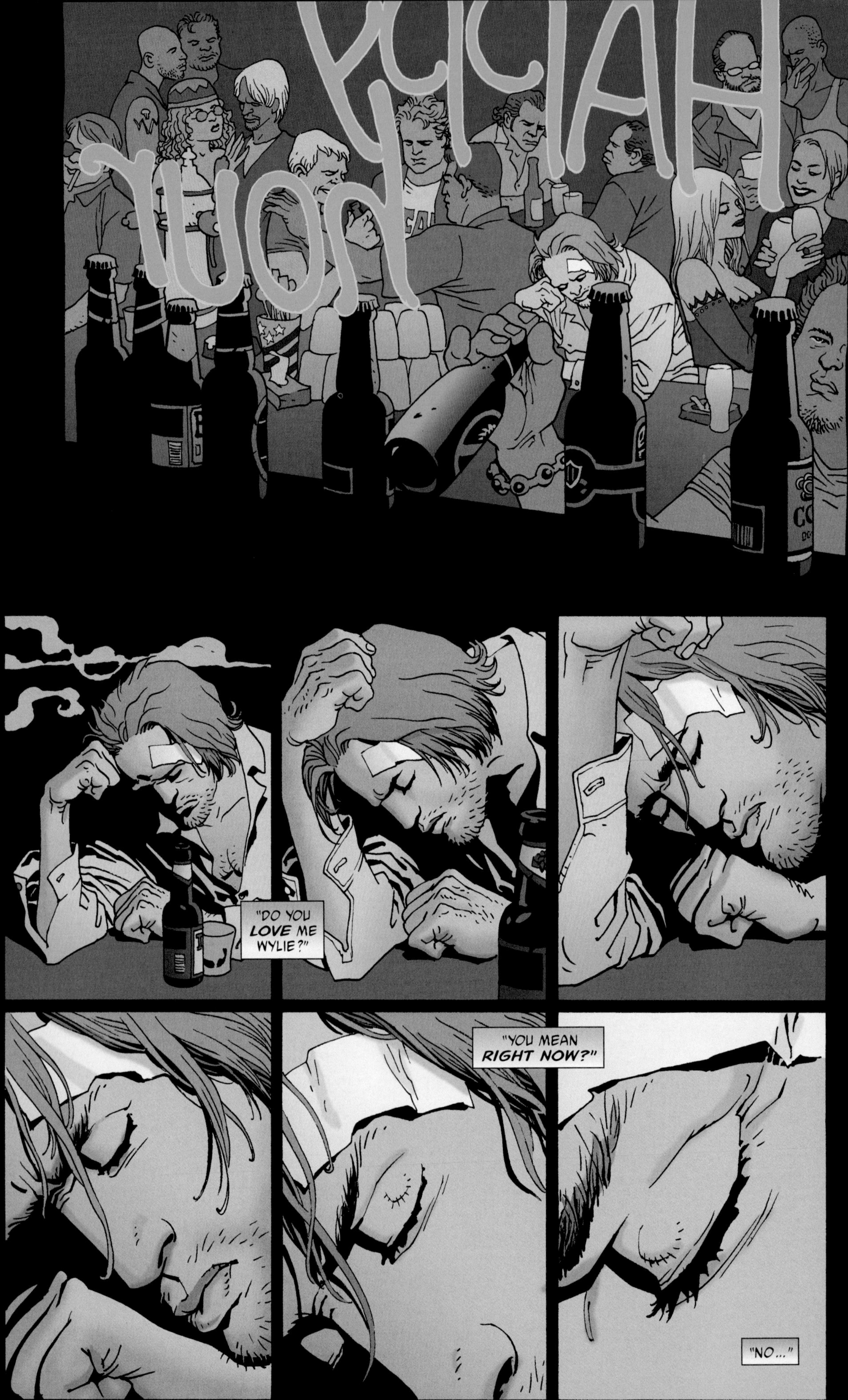
HAPPY HOUR
"DO YOU LOVE ME WYLIE?"
"YOU MEAN RIGHT NOW?"
"NO..."

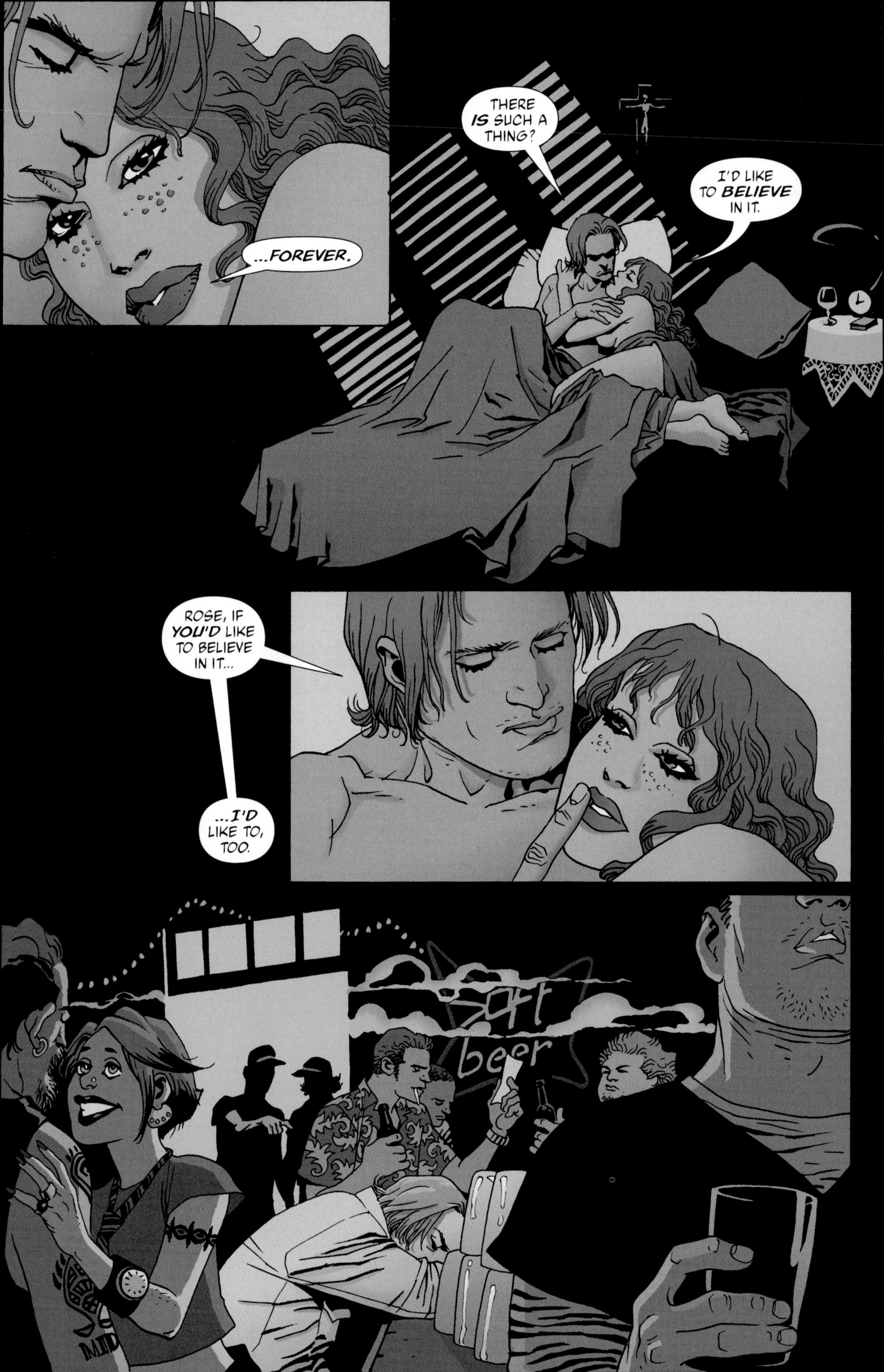
...FOREVER.
THERE IS SUCH A THING?
I'D LIKE TO BELIEVE IN IT.
ROSE, IF YOU'D LIKE TO BELIEVE IN IT...
...I'D LIKE TO, TOO.
Soft beer

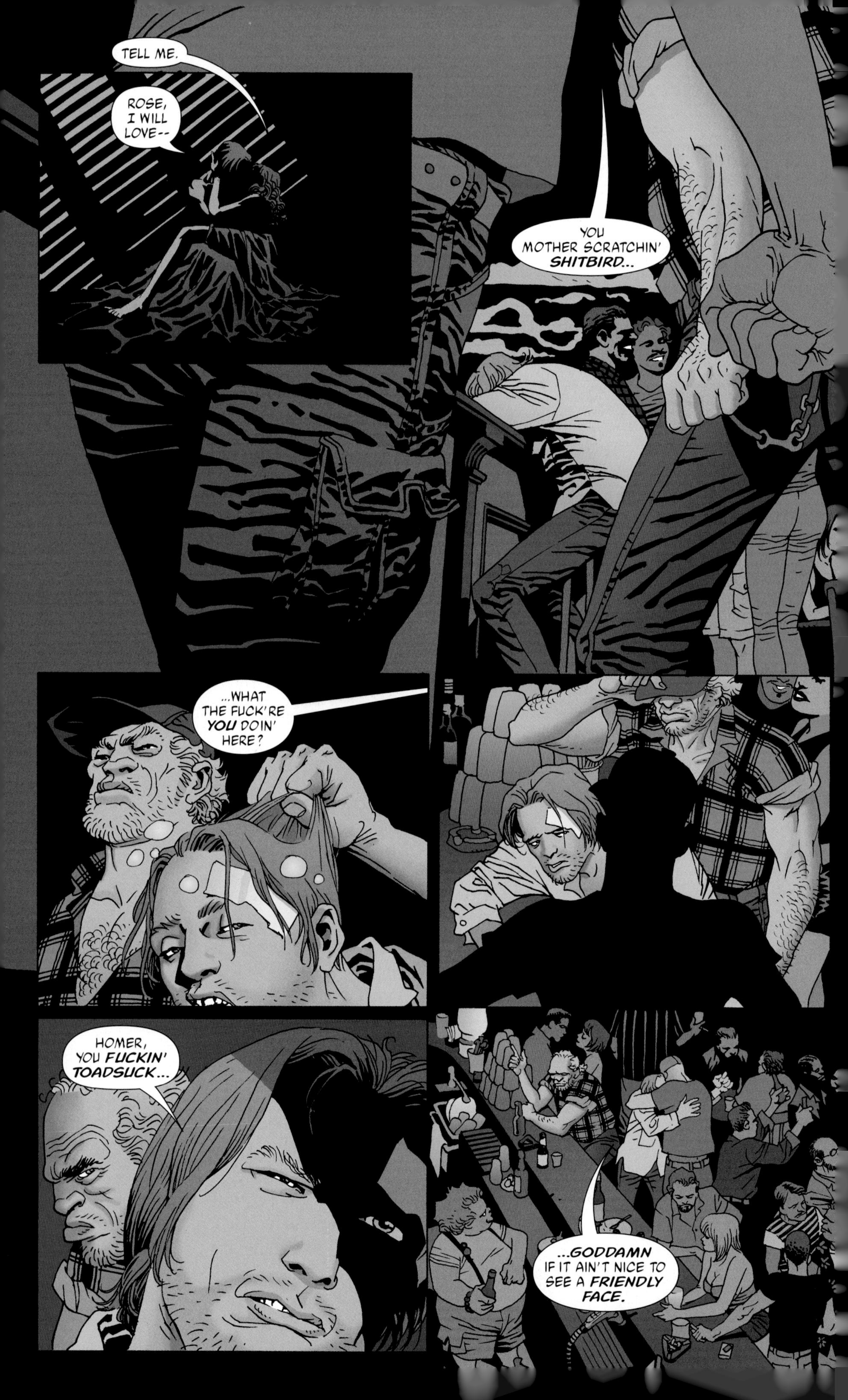
TELL ME.
ROSE, I WILL LOVE--
YOU MOTHER SCRATCHIN' SHITBIRD...
...WHAT THE FUCK'RE YOU DOIN' HERE?
HOMER, YOU FUCKIN' TOADSUCK...
...GODDAMN IF IT AIN'T NICE TO SEE A FRIENDLY FACE.

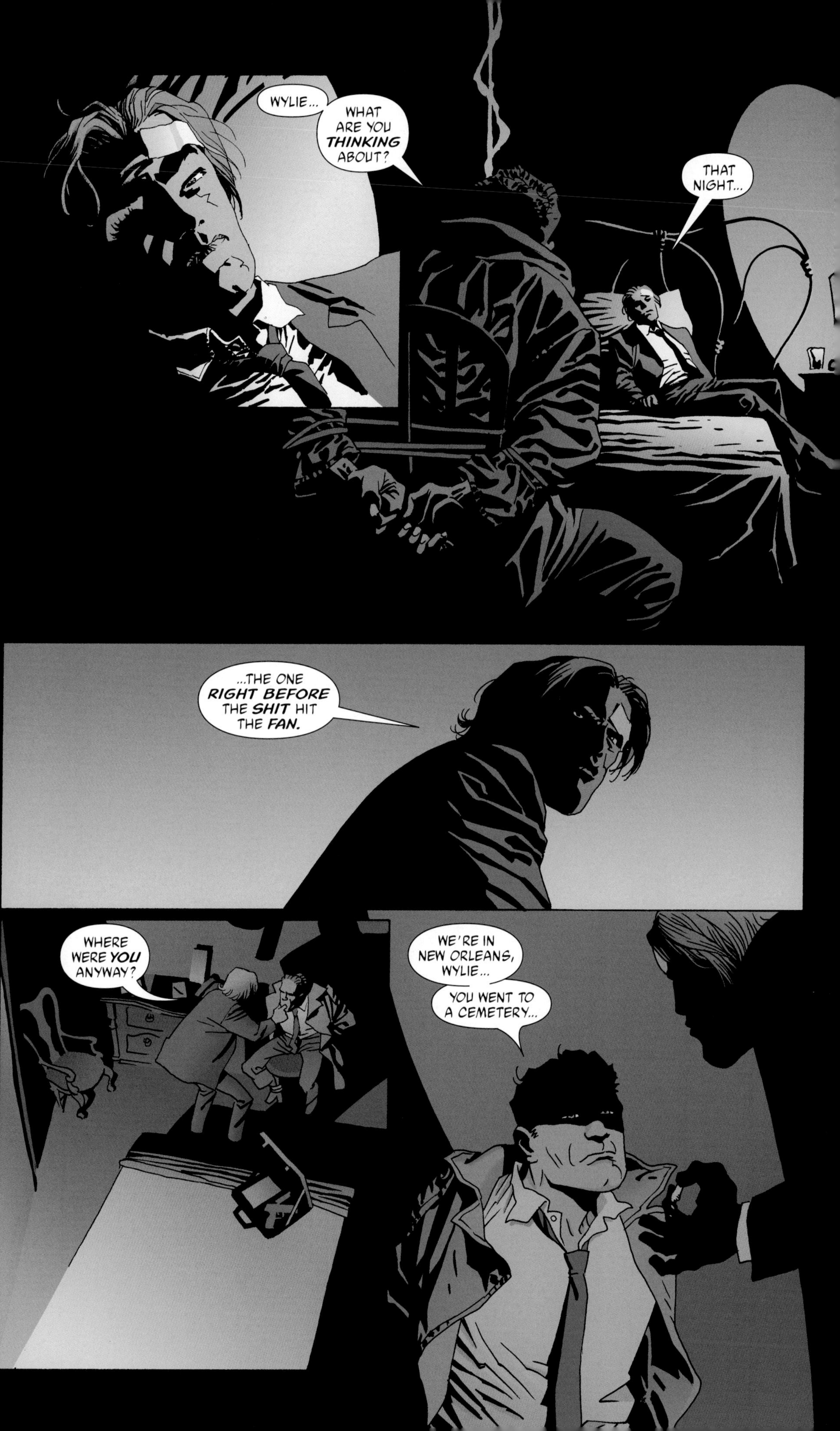
WYLIE...
WHAT ARE YOU THINKING ABOUT?
THAT NIGHT...
...THE ONE RIGHT BEFORE THE SHIT HIT THE FAN.
WHERE WERE YOU ANYWAY?
WE'RE IN NEW ORLEANS, WYLIE...
YOU WENT TO A CEMETERY...

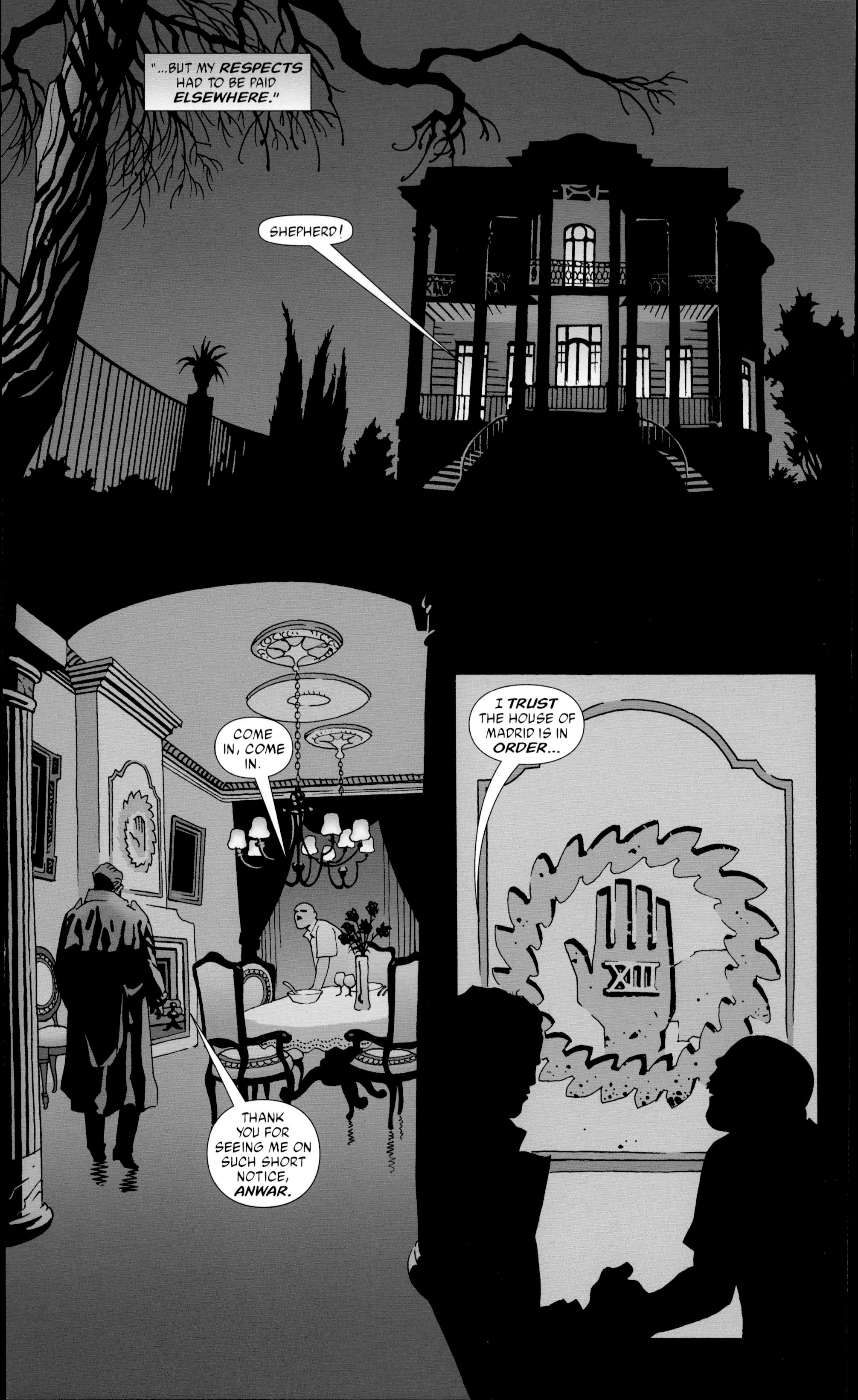
"...BUT MY RESPECTS HAD TO BE PAID ELSEWHERE."
SHEPHERD!
COME IN, COME IN.
THANK YOU FOR SEEING ME ON SUCH SHORT NOTICE, ANWAR.
I TRUST THE HOUSE OF MADRID IS IN ORDER...
XIII

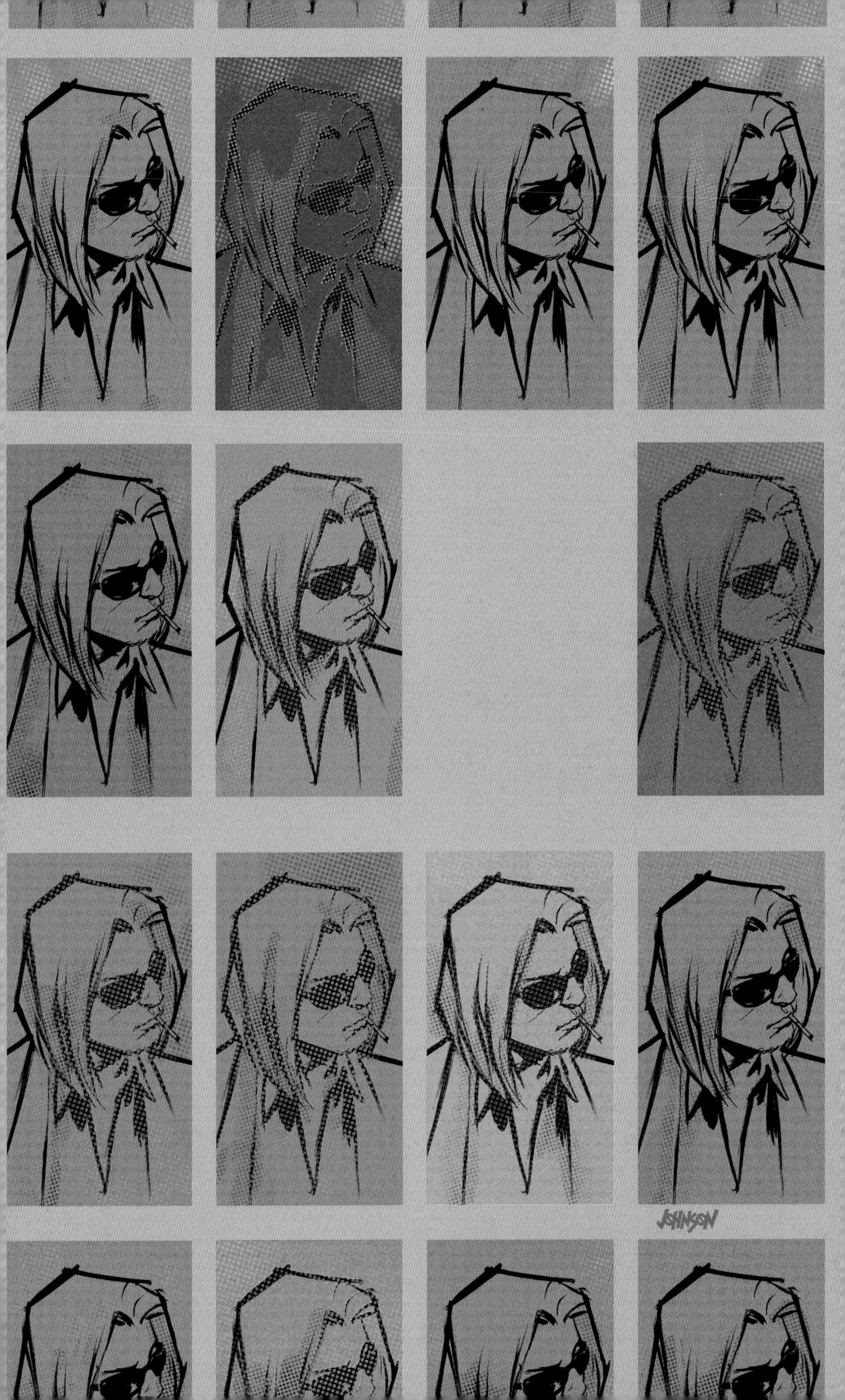
JOHNSON

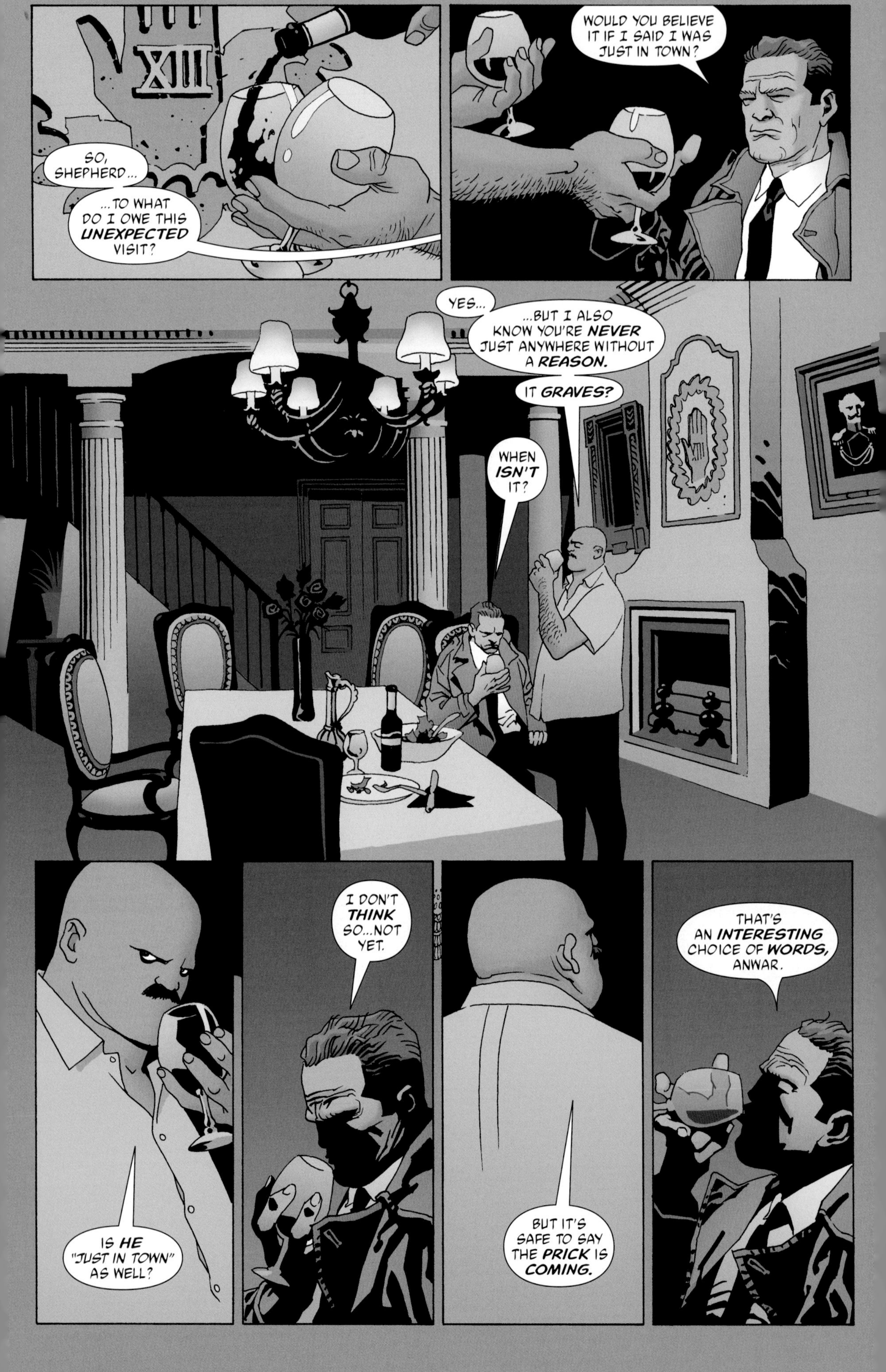
SO, SHEPHERD...
...TO WHAT DO I OWE THIS UNEXPECTED VISIT?
WOULD YOU BELIEVE IT IF I SAID I WAS JUST IN TOWN?
YES...
...BUT I ALSO KNOW YOU'RE NEVER JUST ANYWHERE WITHOUT A REASON.
IT GRAVES?
WHEN ISN'T IT?
IS HE "JUST IN TOWN" AS WELL?
I DON'T THINK SO...NOT YET.
BUT IT'S SAFE TO SAY THE PRICK IS COMING.
THAT'S AN INTERESTING CHOICE OF WORDS, ANWAR.

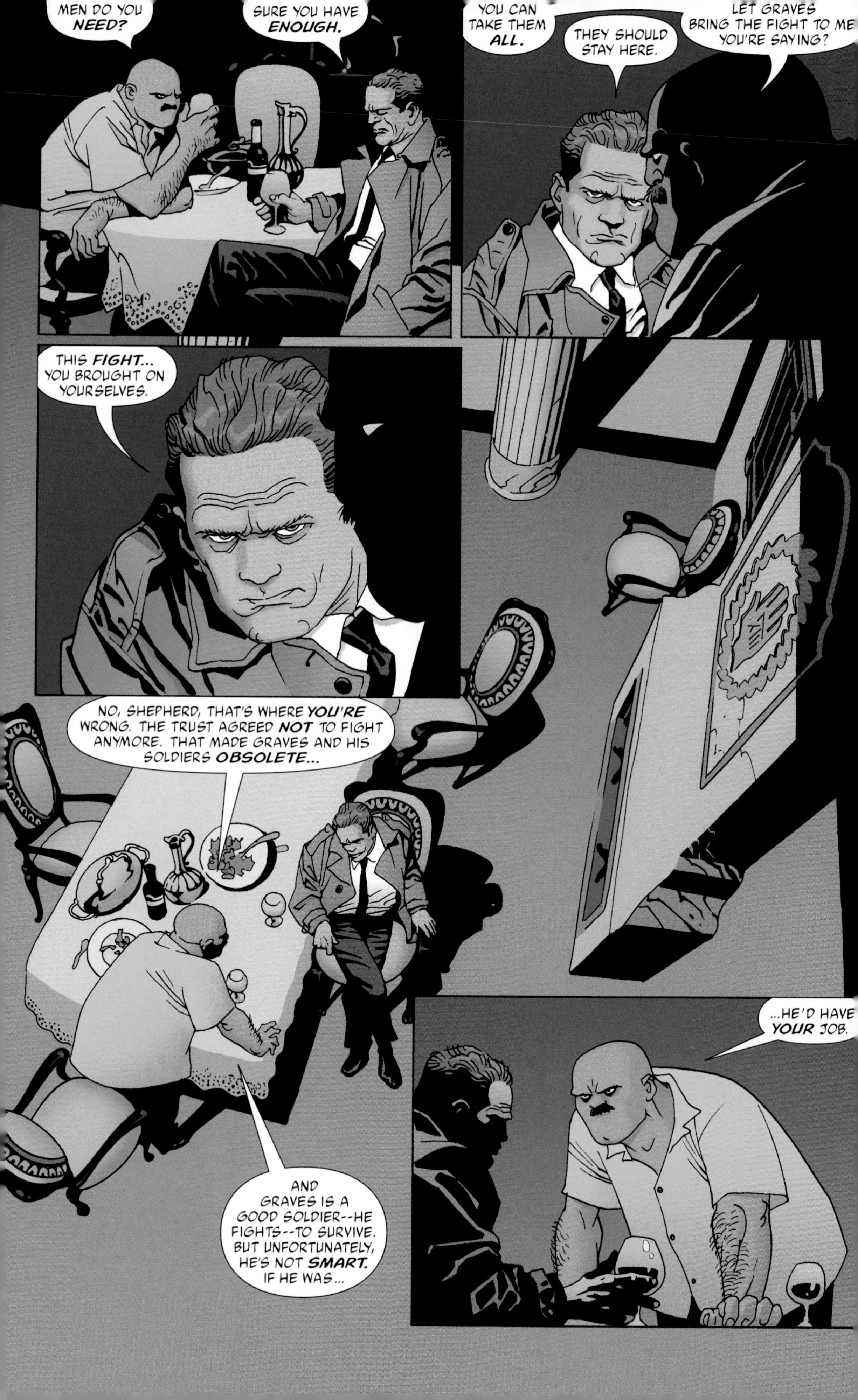
MEN DO YOU NEED?
SURE YOU HAVE ENOUGH.
YOU CAN TAKE THEM ALL.
THEY SHOULD STAY HERE.
LET GRAVES BRING THE FIGHT TO ME YOU'RE SAYING?
THIS FIGHT... YOU BROUGHT ON YOURSELVES.
NO, SHEPHERD, THAT'S WHERE YOU'RE WRONG. THE TRUST AGREED NOT TO FIGHT ANYMORE. THAT MADE GRAVES AND HIS SOLDIERS OBSOLETE...
AND GRAVES IS A GOOD SOLDIER--HE FIGHTS--TO SURVIVE. BUT UNFORTUNATELY, HE'S NOT SMART. IF HE WAS...
...HE'D HAVE YOUR JOB.

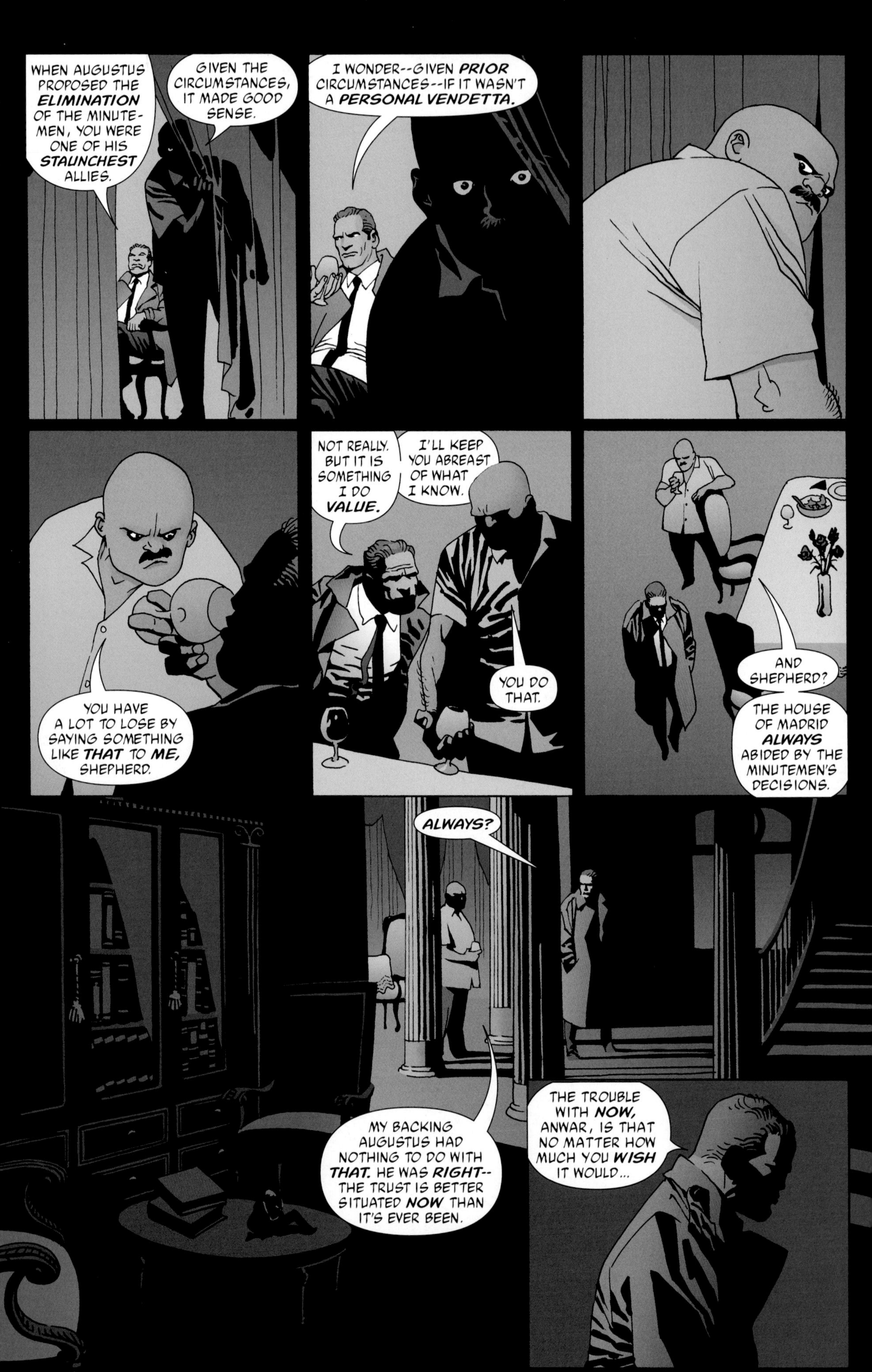

WHEN AUGUSTUS PROPOSED THE ELIMINATION OF THE MINUTE-MEN, YOU WERE ONE OF HIS STAUNCHEST ALLIES.
GIVEN THE CIRCUMSTANCES, IT MADE GOOD SENSE.
I WONDER--GIVEN PRIOR CIRCUMSTANCES--IF IT WASN'T A PERSONAL VENDETTA.
YOU HAVE A LOT TO LOSE BY SAYING SOMETHING LIKE THAT TO ME, SHEPHERD.
NOT REALLY. BUT IT IS SOMETHING I DO VALUE.
I'LL KEEP YOU ABREAST OF WHAT I KNOW.
YOU DO THAT.
AND SHEPHERD?
THE HOUSE OF MADRID ALWAYS ABIDED BY THE MINUTEMEN'S DECISIONS.
ALWAYS?
MY BACKING AUGUSTUS HAD NOTHING TO DO WITH THAT. HE WAS RIGHT-- THE TRUST IS BETTER SITUATED NOW THAN IT'S EVER BEEN.
THE TROUBLE WITH NOW, ANWAR, IS THAT NO MATTER HOW MUCH YOU WISH IT WOULD...

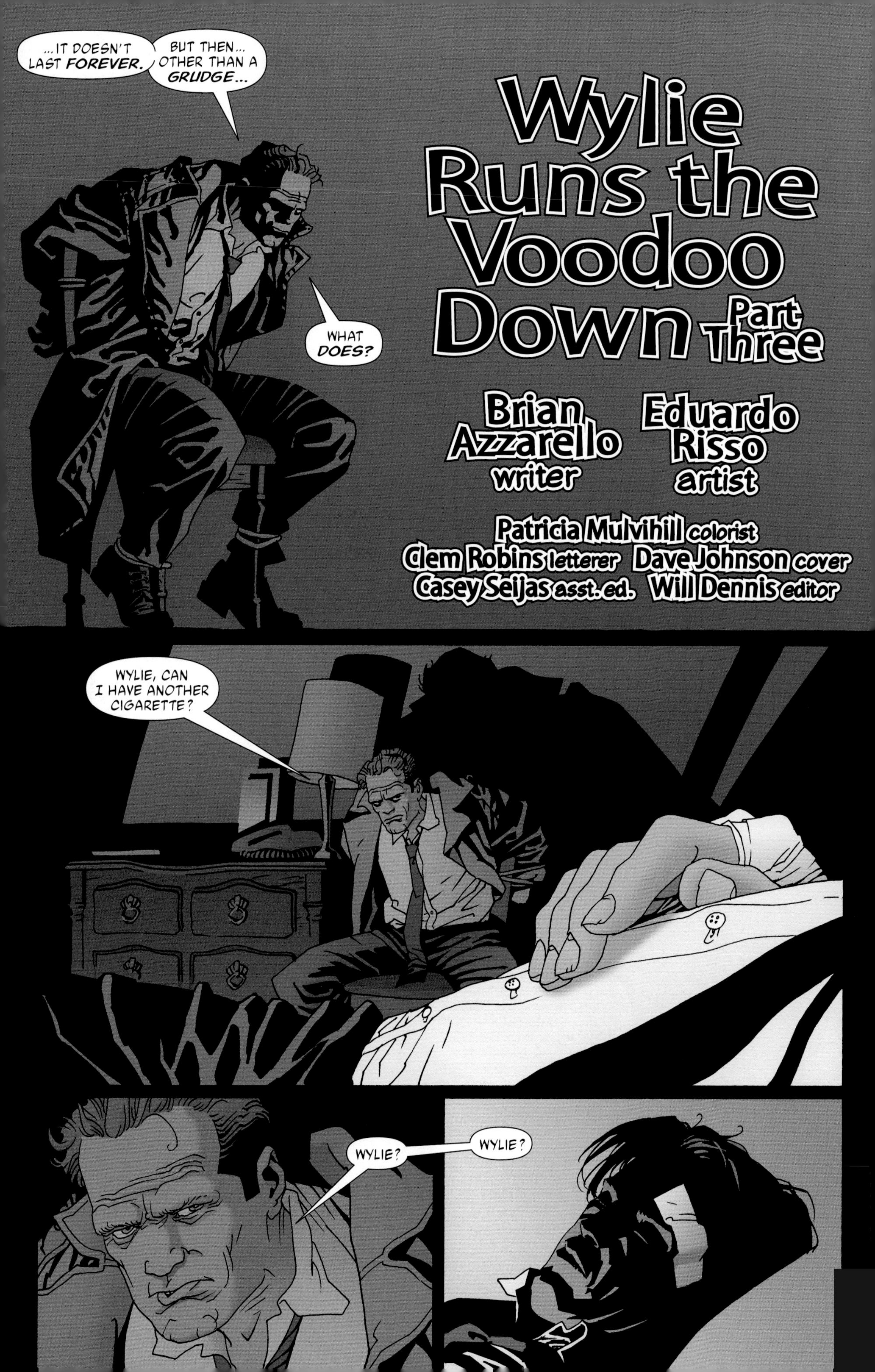
...IT DOESN'T LAST FOREVER.
BUT THEN... OTHER THAN A GRUDGE...
WHAT DOES?
Wylie Runs the Voodoo Down Part Three
Brian Azzarello writer
Eduardo Risso artist
Patricia Mulvihill colorist
Clem Robins letterer
Dave Johnson cover
Casey Seijas asst. ed.
Will Dennis editor
WYLIE, CAN I HAVE ANOTHER CIGARETTE?
WYLIE?
WYLIE?

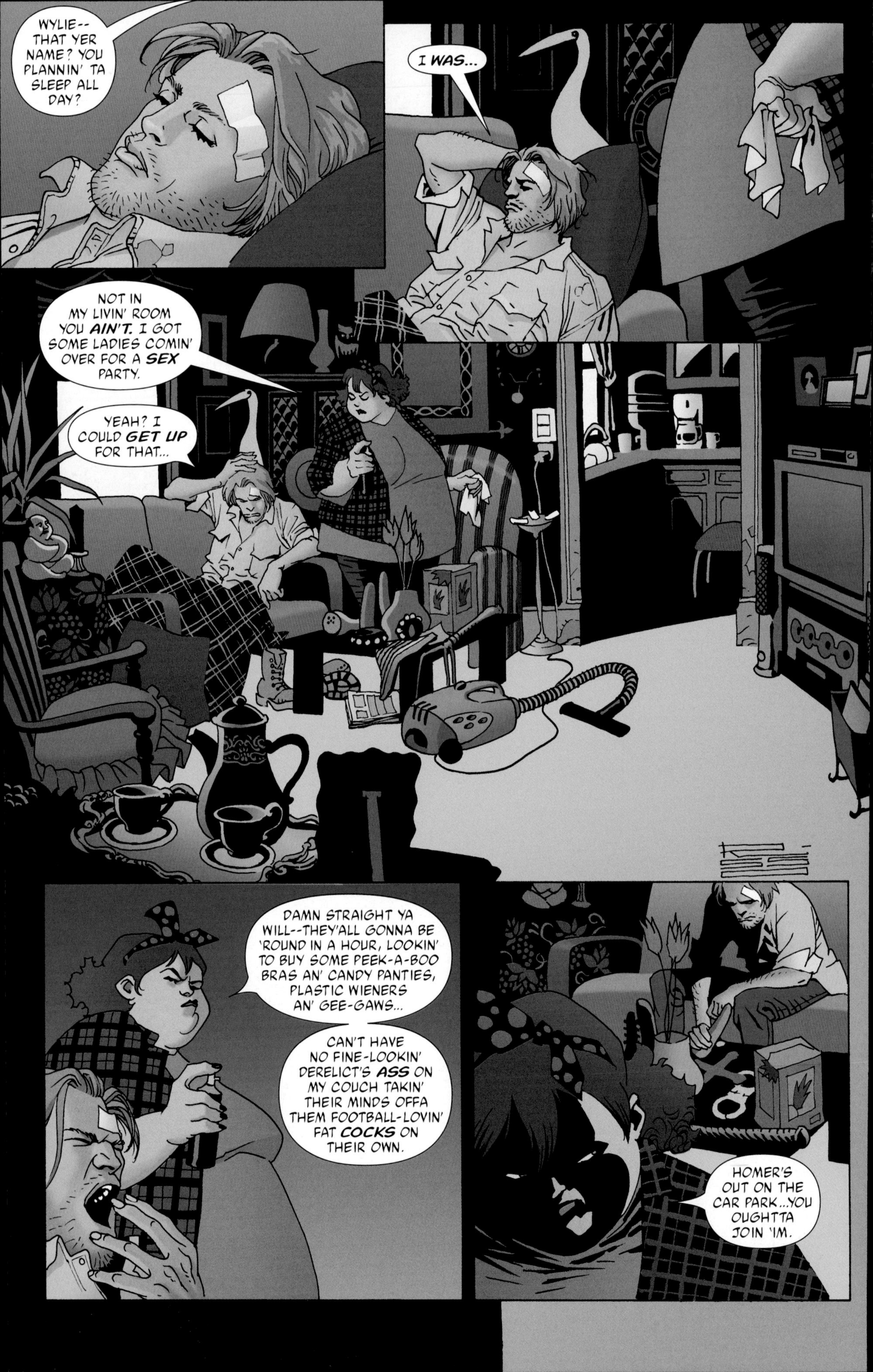
WYLIE--THAT YER NAME? YOU PLANNIN' TA SLEEP ALL DAY?
I WAS...
NOT IN MY LIVIN' ROOM YOU AIN'T. I GOT SOME LADIES COMIN' OVER FOR A SEX PARTY.
YEAH? I COULD GET UP FOR THAT...
DAMN STRAIGHT YA WILL--THEY'ALL GONNA BE 'ROUND IN A HOUR, LOOKIN' TO BUY SOME PEEK-A-BOO BRAS AN' CANDY PANTIES, PLASTIC WIENERS AN' GEE-GAWS...
CAN'T HAVE NO FINE-LOOKIN' DERELICT'S ASS ON MY COUCH TAKIN' THEIR MINDS OFFA THEM FOOTBALL-LOVIN' FAT COCKS ON THEIR OWN.
HOMER'S OUT ON THE CAR PARK...YOU OUGHTTA JOIN 'IM.

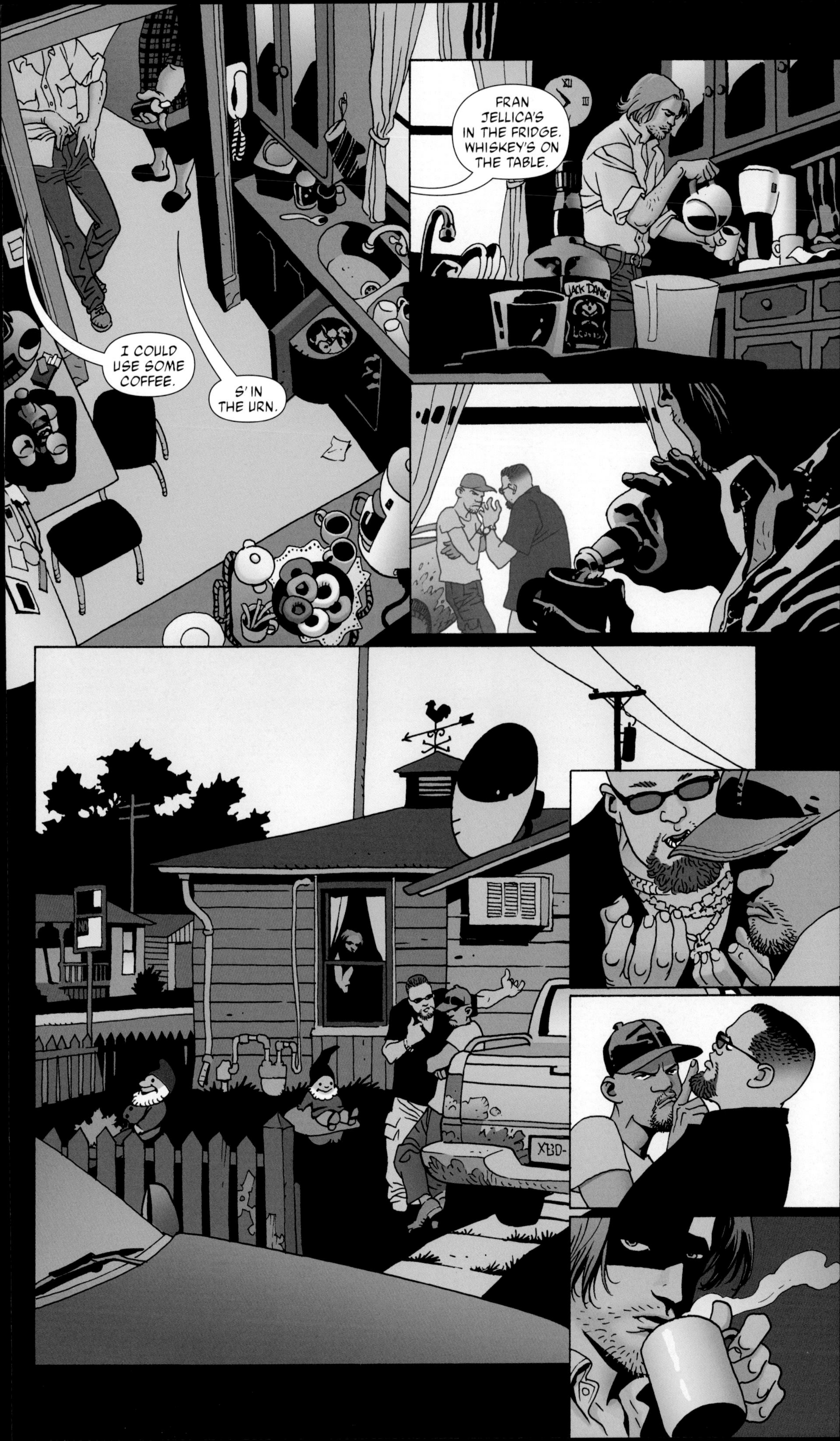

I COULD USE SOME COFFEE.
S' IN THE URN.
FRAN JELLICA'S IN THE FRIDGE. WHISKEY'S ON THE TABLE.

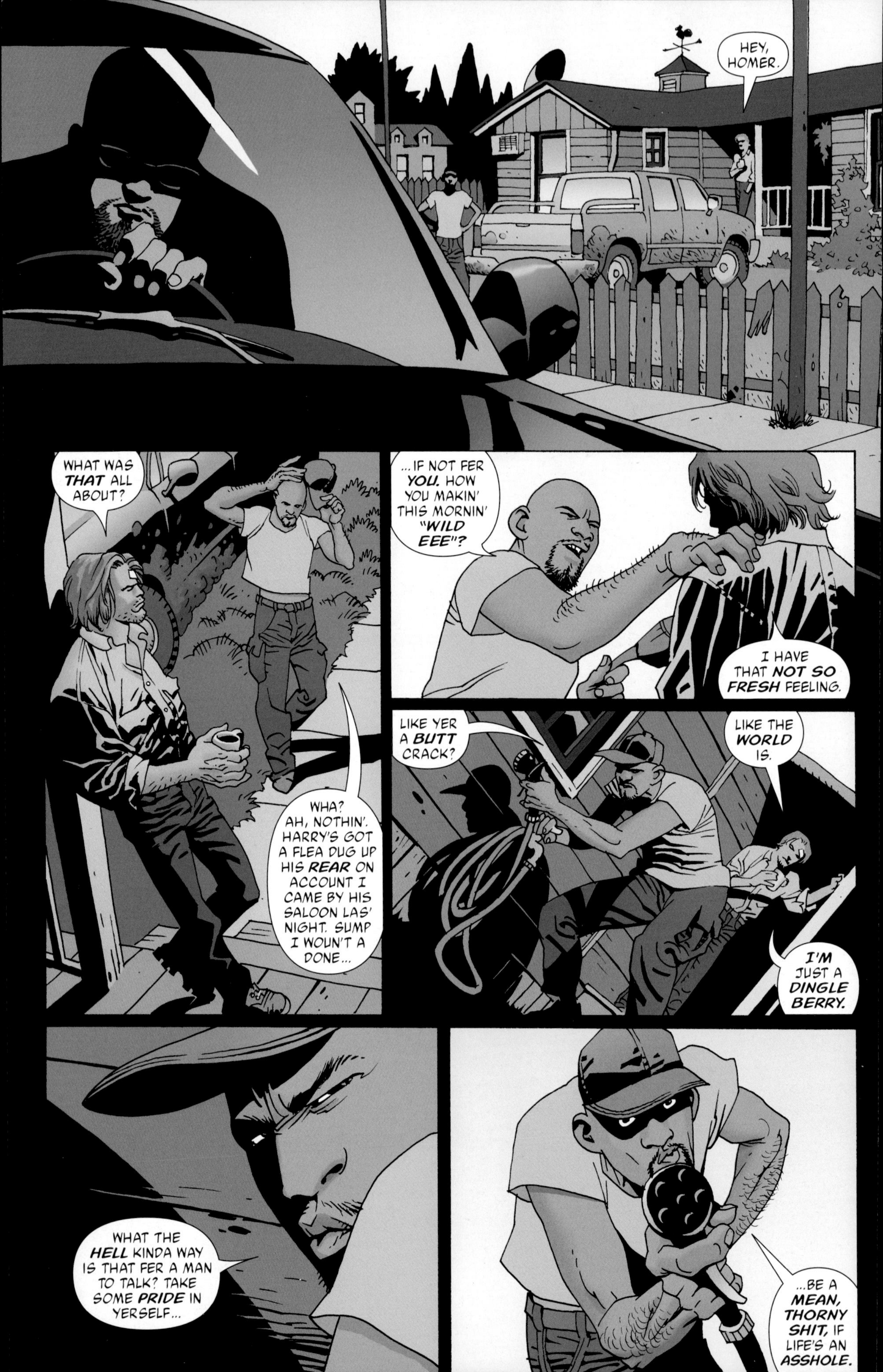
HEY, HOMER.
WHAT WAS **THAT** ALL ABOUT?
WHA? AH, NOTHIN'. HARRY'S GOT A FLEA DUG UP HIS **REAR** ON ACCOUNT I CAME BY HIS SALOON LAS' NIGHT. SUMP I WOUN'T A DONE...
...IF NOT FER **YOU.** HOW YOU MAKIN' THIS MORNIN' **"WILD EEE"**?
I HAVE THAT **NOT SO FRESH** FEELING.
LIKE YER A **BUTT** CRACK?
LIKE THE **WORLD** IS.
I'M JUST A **DINGLE BERRY.**
WHAT THE **HELL** KINDA WAY IS THAT FER A MAN TO TALK? TAKE SOME **PRIDE** IN YERSELF...
...BE A **MEAN, THORNY SHIT,** IF LIFE'S AN **ASSHOLE.**

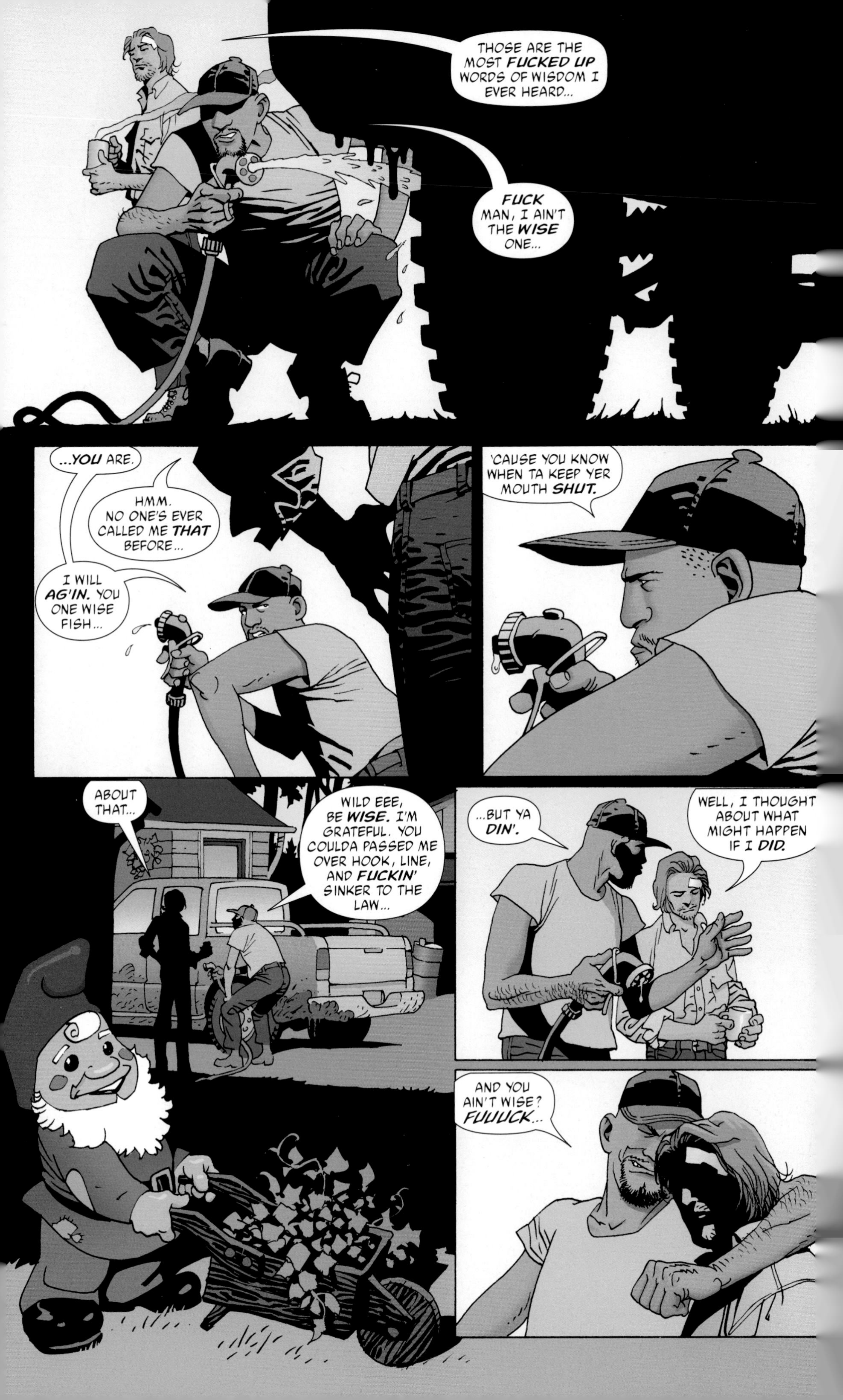
THOSE ARE THE MOST FUCKED UP WORDS OF WISDOM I EVER HEARD...
FUCK MAN, I AIN'T THE WISE ONE...
...YOU ARE.
HMM. NO ONE'S EVER CALLED ME THAT BEFORE...
I WILL AG'IN. YOU ONE WISE FISH...
'CAUSE YOU KNOW WHEN TA KEEP YER MOUTH SHUT.
ABOUT THAT...
WILD EEE, BE WISE. I'M GRATEFUL. YOU COULDA PASSED ME OVER HOOK, LINE, AND FUCKIN' SINKER TO THE LAW...
...BUT YA DIN'.
WELL, I THOUGHT ABOUT WHAT MIGHT HAPPEN IF I DID.
AND YOU AIN'T WISE? FUUUCK...

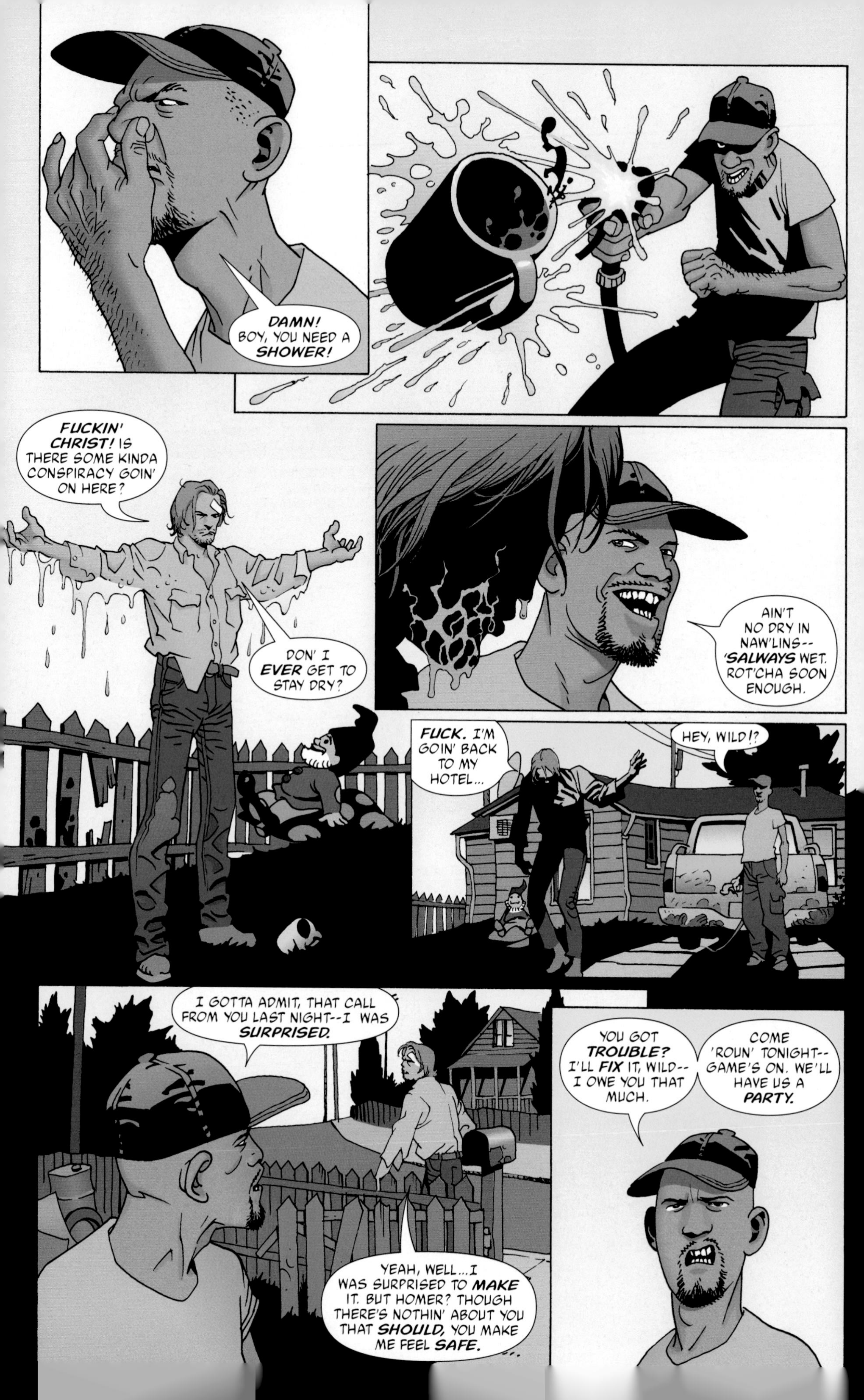
DAMN! BOY, YOU NEED A SHOWER!
FUCKIN' CHRIST! IS THERE SOME KINDA CONSPIRACY GOIN' ON HERE?
DON' I EVER GET TO STAY DRY?
AIN'T NO DRY IN NAW'LINS-- 'SALWAYS WET. ROT'CHA SOON ENOUGH.
FUCK. I'M GOIN' BACK TO MY HOTEL...
HEY, WILD!?
I GOTTA ADMIT, THAT CALL FROM YOU LAST NIGHT--I WAS SURPRISED.
YEAH, WELL...I WAS SURPRISED TO MAKE IT. BUT HOMER? THOUGH THERE'S NOTHIN' ABOUT YOU THAT SHOULD, YOU MAKE ME FEEL SAFE.
YOU GOT TROUBLE? I'LL FIX IT, WILD-- I OWE YOU THAT MUCH.
COME 'ROUN' TONIGHT-- GAME'S ON. WE'LL HAVE US A PARTY.

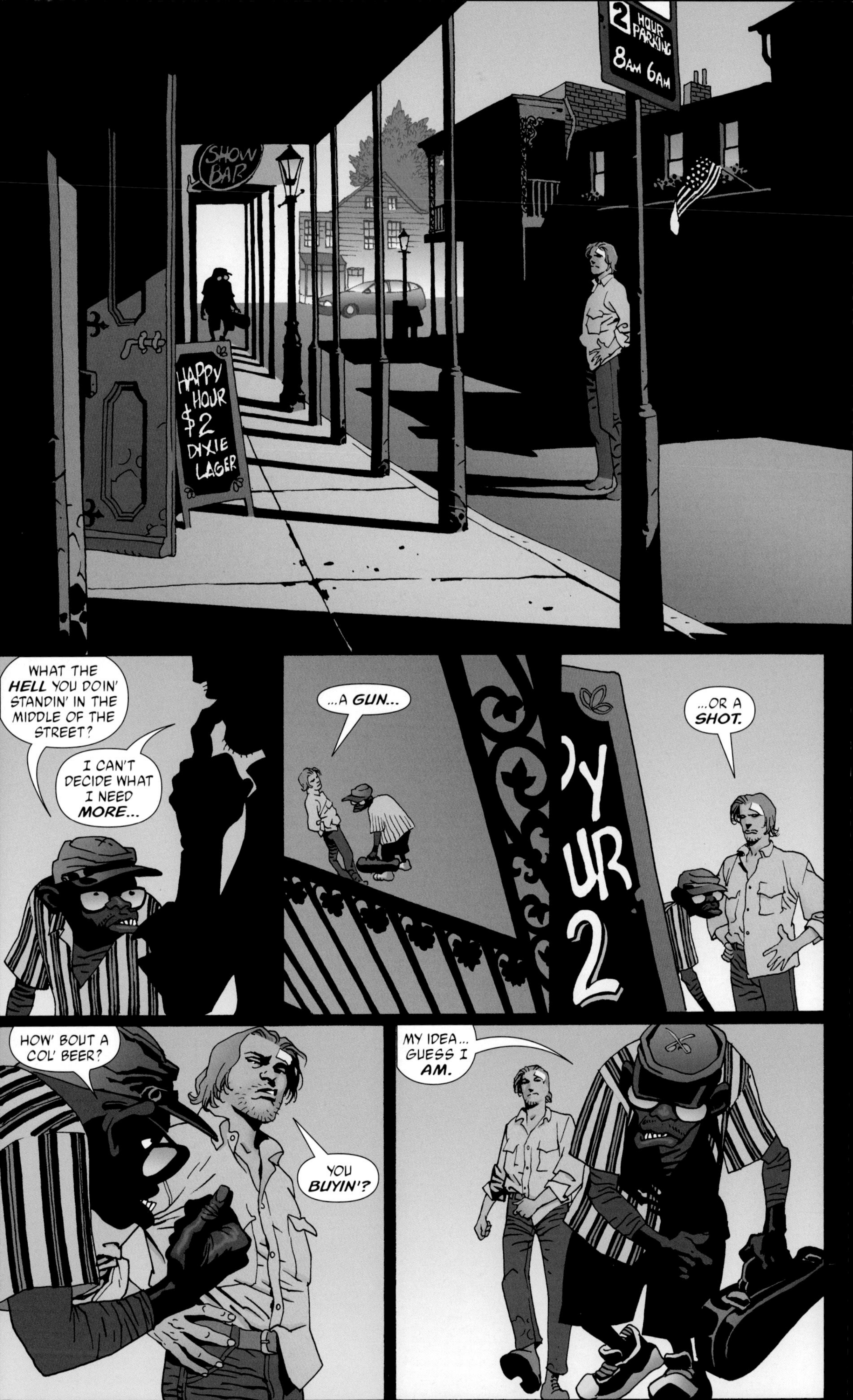
2 HOUR PARKING
8AM 6AM
SHOW BAR
HAPPY HOUR $2 DIXIE LAGER
WHAT THE HELL YOU DOIN' STANDIN' IN THE MIDDLE OF THE STREET?
I CAN'T DECIDE WHAT I NEED MORE...
...A GUN...
...OR A SHOT.
HOW' BOUT A COL' BEER?
YOU BUYIN'?
MY IDEA... GUESS I AM.

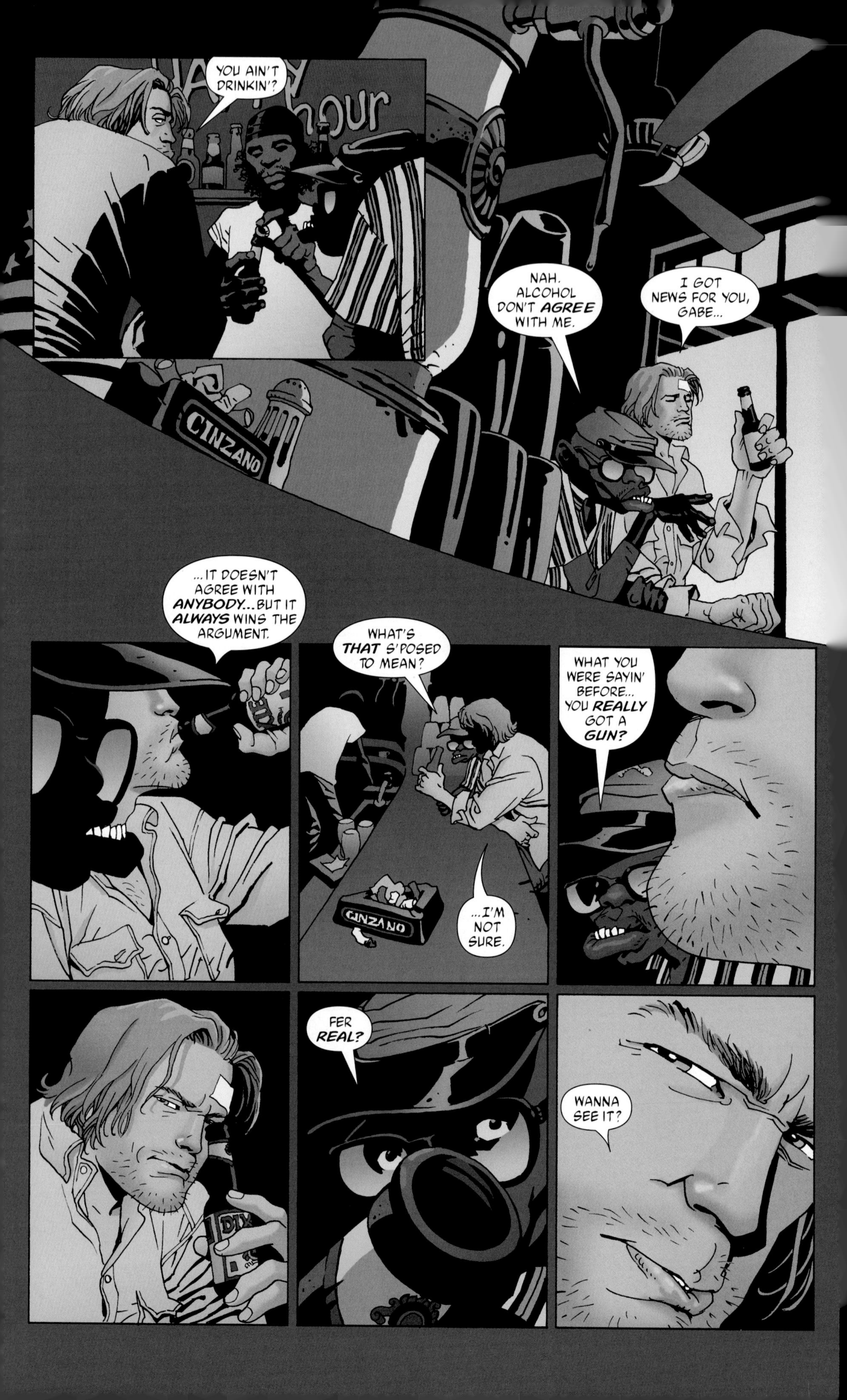

YOU AIN'T DRINKIN'?
happy hour
NAH. ALCOHOL DON'T AGREE WITH ME.
I GOT NEWS FOR YOU, GABE...
CINZANO
...IT DOESN'T AGREE WITH ANYBODY...BUT IT ALWAYS WINS THE ARGUMENT.
WHAT'S THAT S'POSED TO MEAN?
...I'M NOT SURE.
CINZANO
WHAT YOU WERE SAYIN' BEFORE... YOU REALLY GOT A GUN?
FER REAL?
WANNA SEE IT?

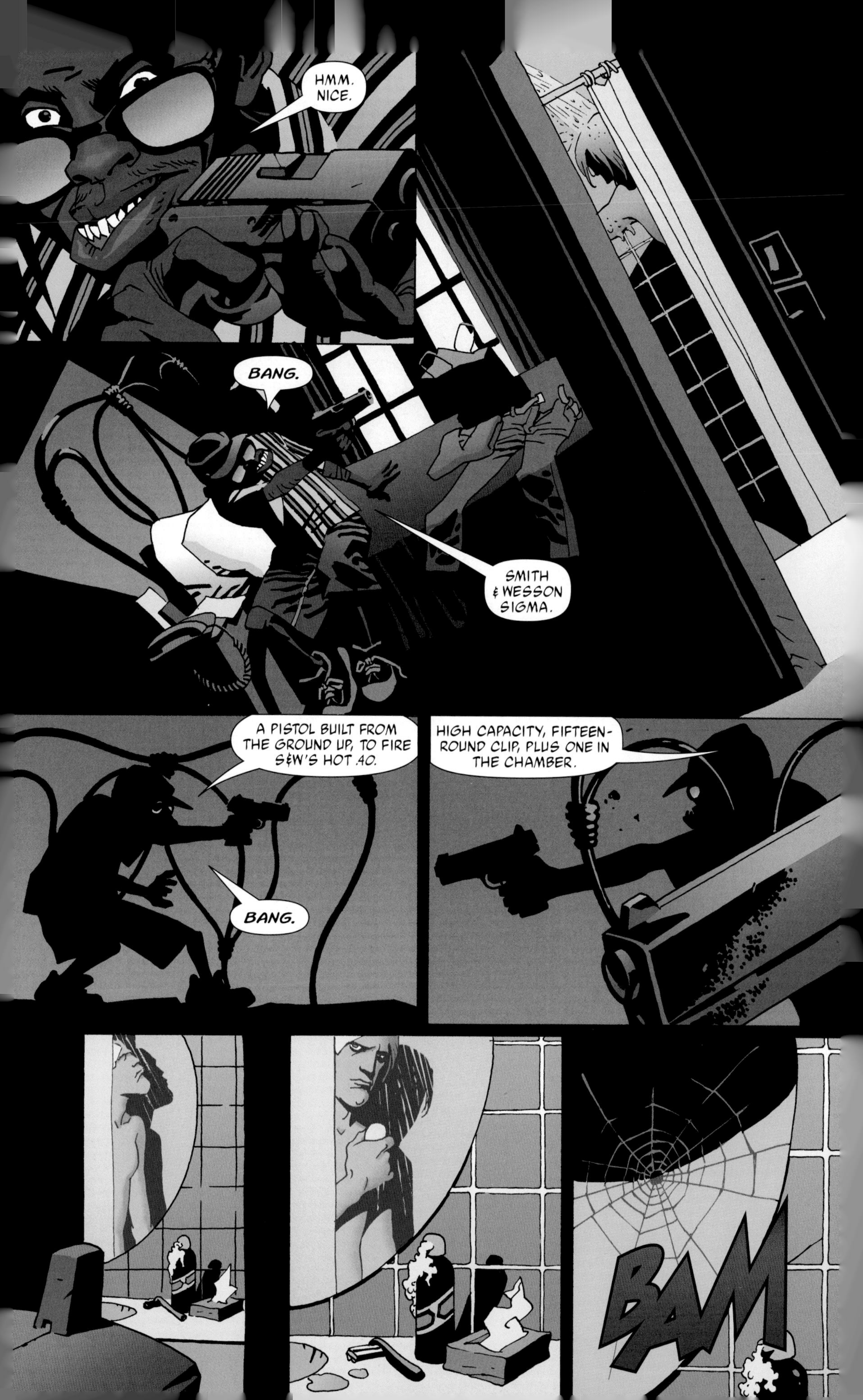
HMM. NICE.
BANG.
SMITH & WESSON SIGMA.
A PISTOL BUILT FROM THE GROUND UP, TO FIRE S&W'S HOT .40.
BANG.
HIGH CAPACITY, FIFTEEN-ROUND CLIP, PLUS ONE IN THE CHAMBER.
BAM

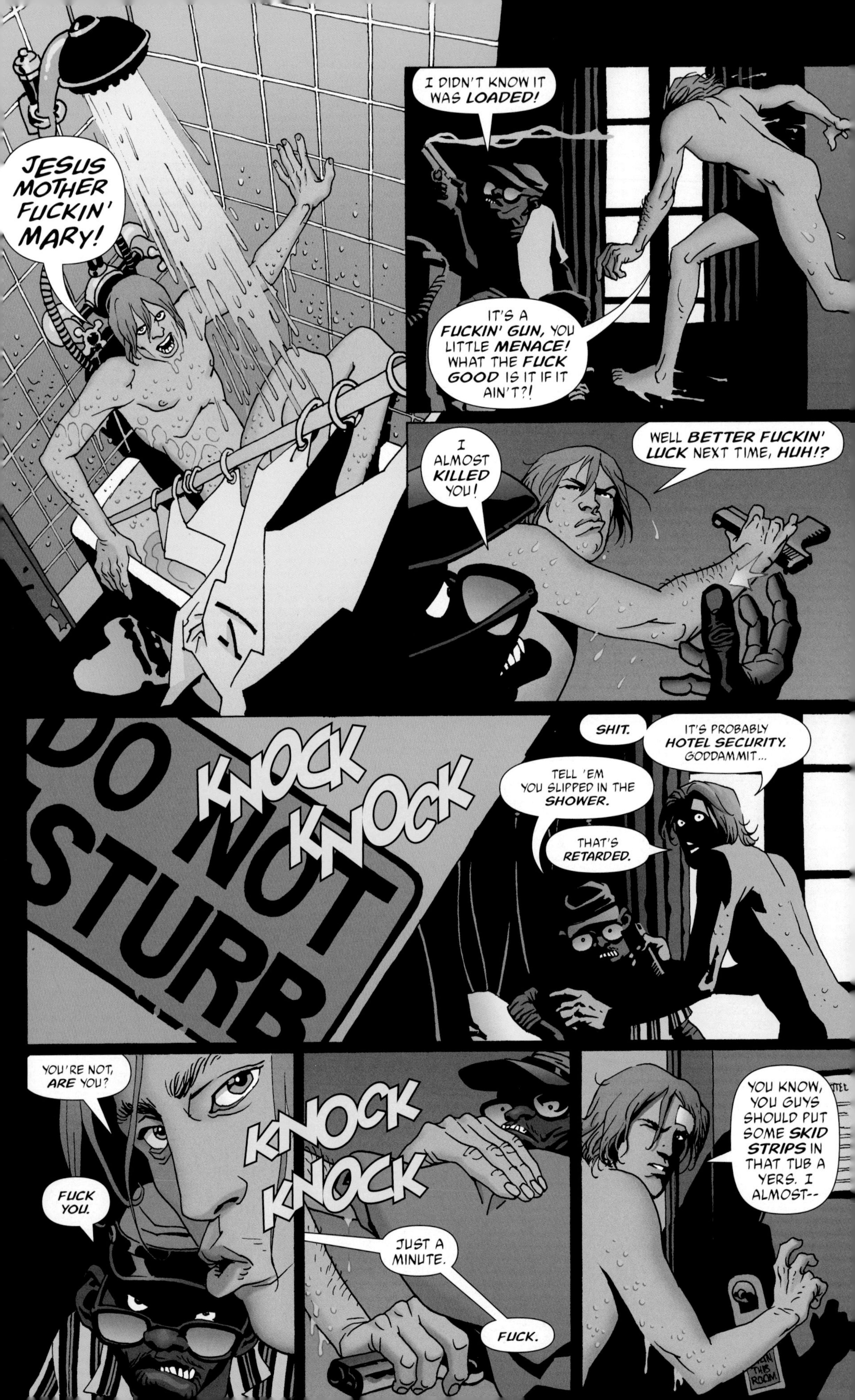
JESUS MOTHER FUCKIN' MARY!
I DIDN'T KNOW IT WAS LOADED!
IT'S A FUCKIN' GUN, YOU LITTLE MENACE! WHAT THE FUCK GOOD IS IT IF IT AIN'T?!
I ALMOST KILLED YOU!
WELL BETTER FUCKIN' LUCK NEXT TIME, HUH!?
DO NOT
STURB
KNOCK KNOCK
SHIT.
IT'S PROBABLY HOTEL SECURITY. GODDAMMIT...
TELL 'EM YOU SLIPPED IN THE SHOWER.
THAT'S RETARDED.
YOU'RE NOT, ARE YOU?
FUCK YOU.
KNOCK KNOCK
JUST A MINUTE.
FUCK.
YOU KNOW, YOU GUYS SHOULD PUT SOME SKID STRIPS IN THAT TUB A YERS. I ALMOST--

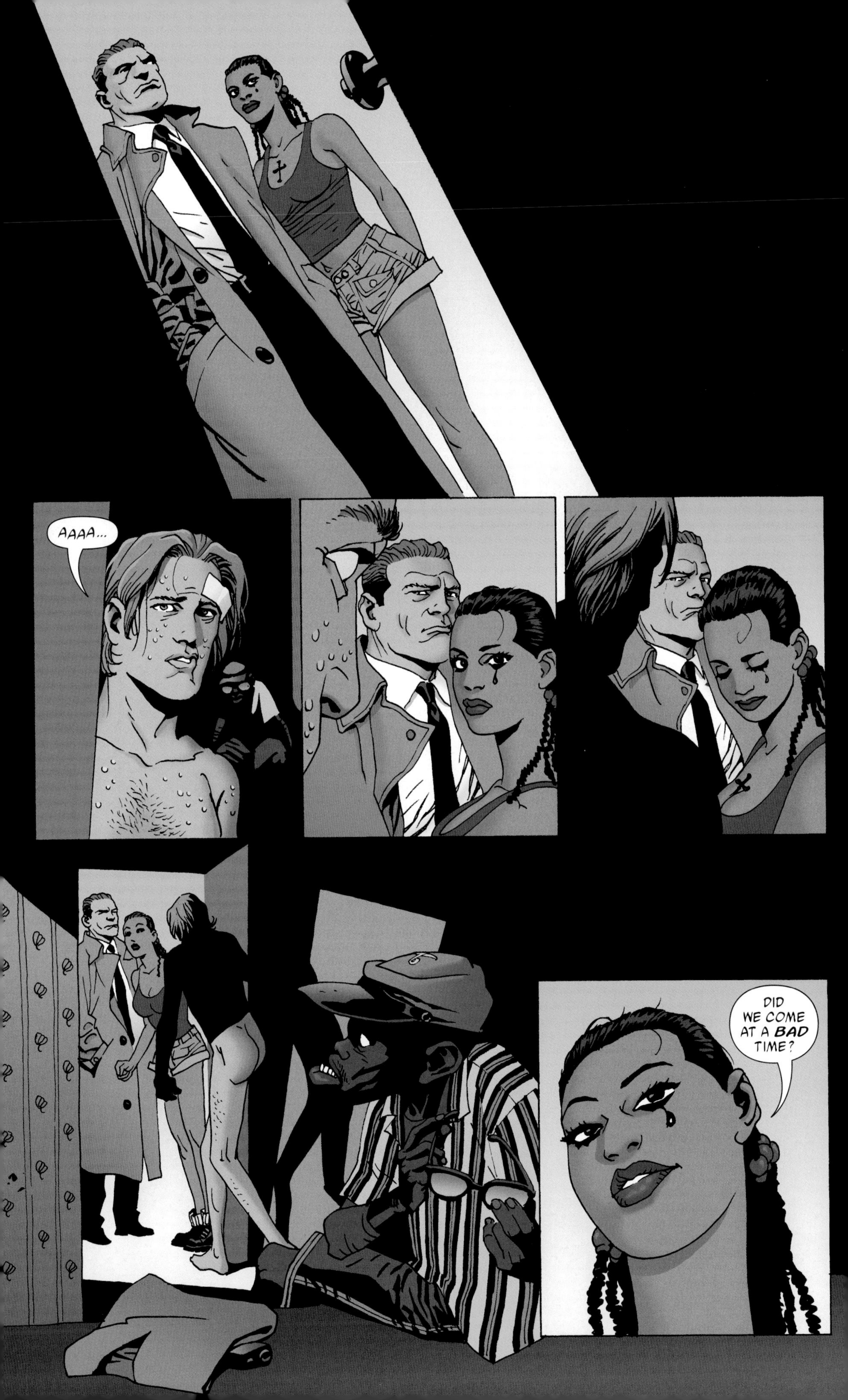
AAAA...
DID WE COME AT A *BAD* TIME?

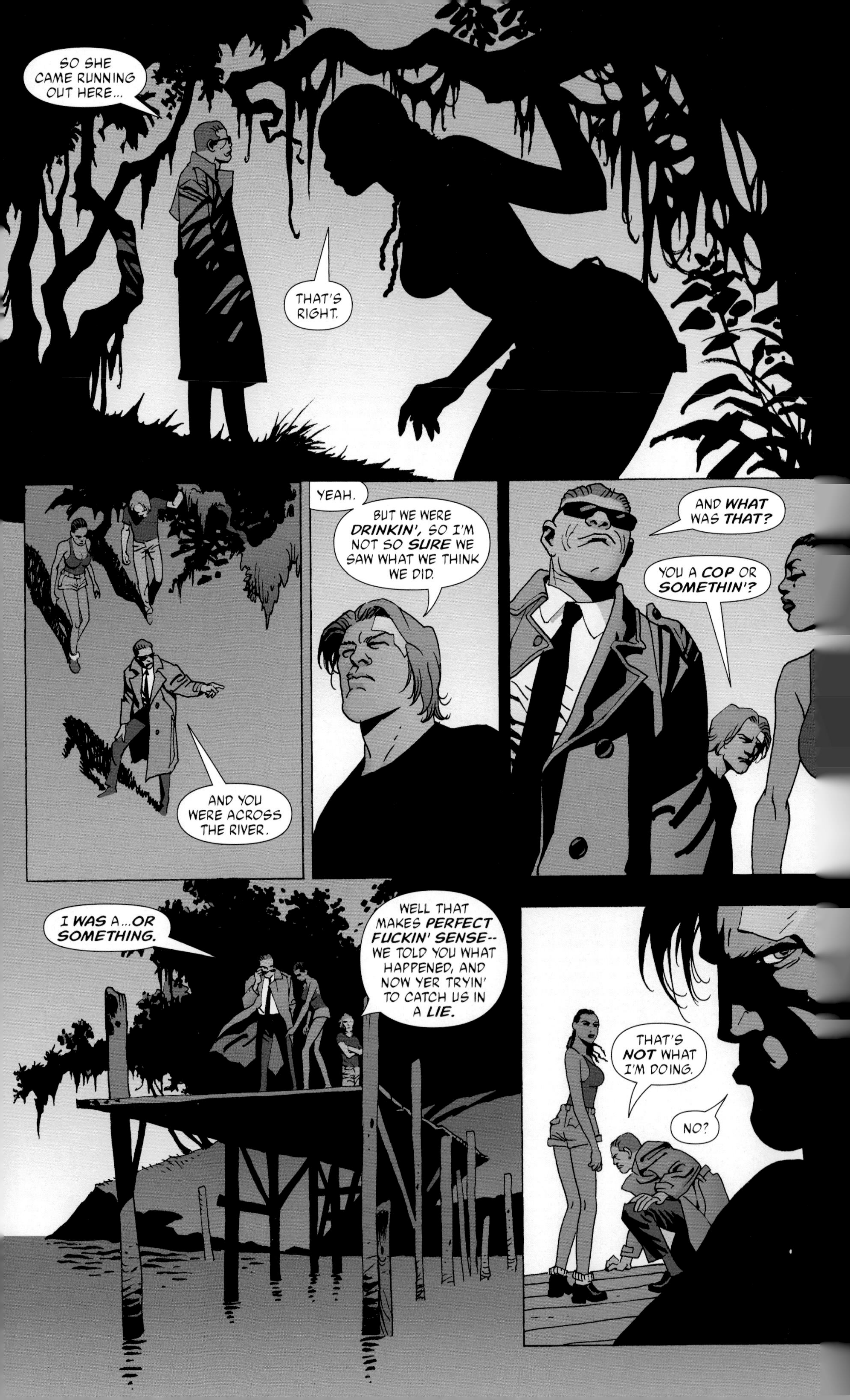
SO SHE CAME RUNNING OUT HERE...
THAT'S RIGHT.
YEAH.
BUT WE WERE DRINKIN', SO I'M NOT SO SURE WE SAW WHAT WE THINK WE DID.
AND YOU WERE ACROSS THE RIVER.
AND WHAT WAS THAT?
YOU A COP OR SOMETHIN'?
I WAS A...OR SOMETHING.
WELL THAT MAKES PERFECT FUCKIN' SENSE-- WE TOLD YOU WHAT HAPPENED, AND NOW YER TRYIN' TO CATCH US IN A LIE.
THAT'S NOT WHAT I'M DOING.
NO?

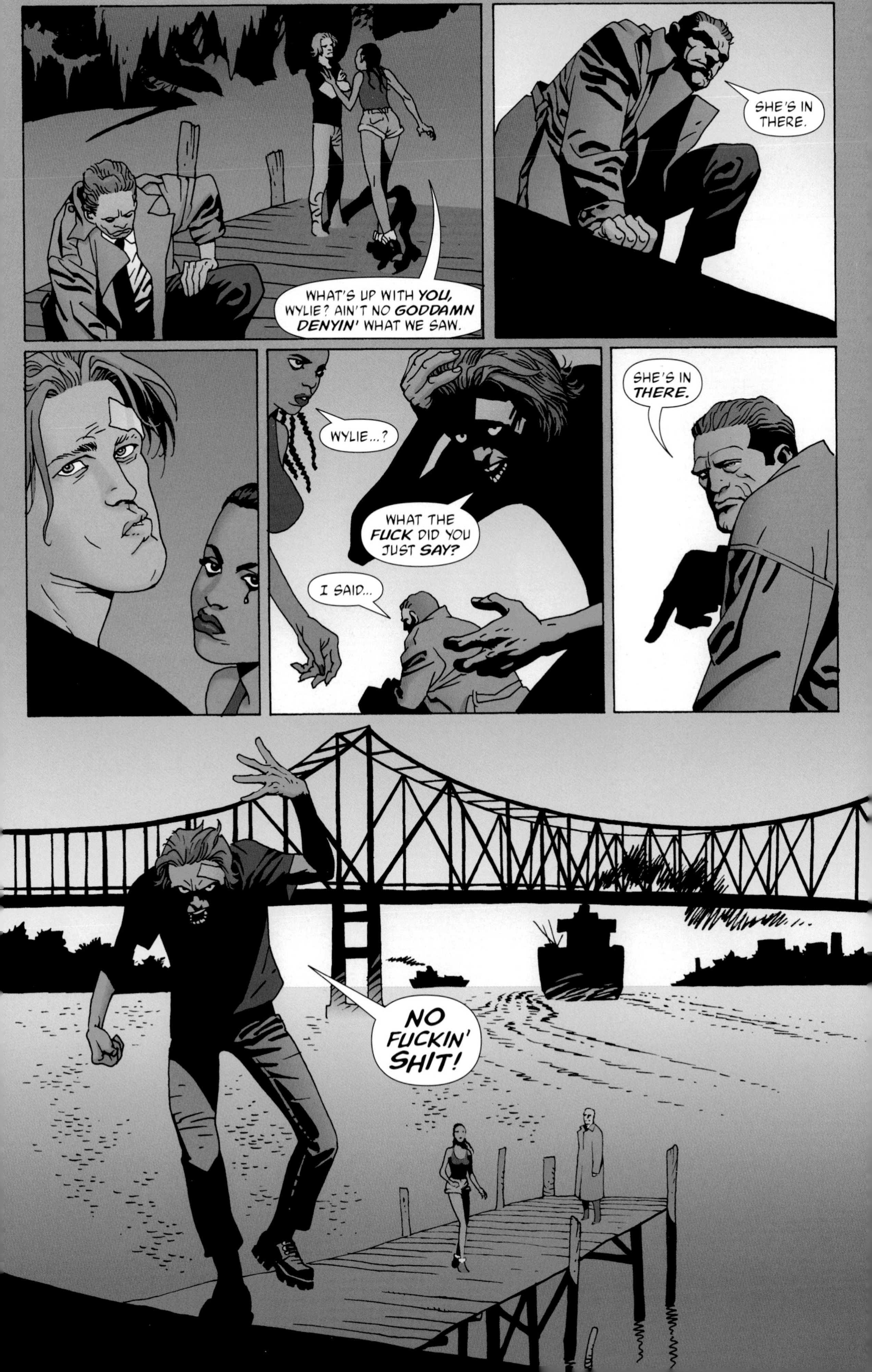
WHAT'S UP WITH YOU, WYLIE? AIN'T NO GODDAMN DENYIN' WHAT WE SAW.
SHE'S IN THERE.
WYLIE...?
WHAT THE FUCK DID YOU JUST SAY?
I SAID...
SHE'S IN THERE.
NO FUCKIN' SHIT!

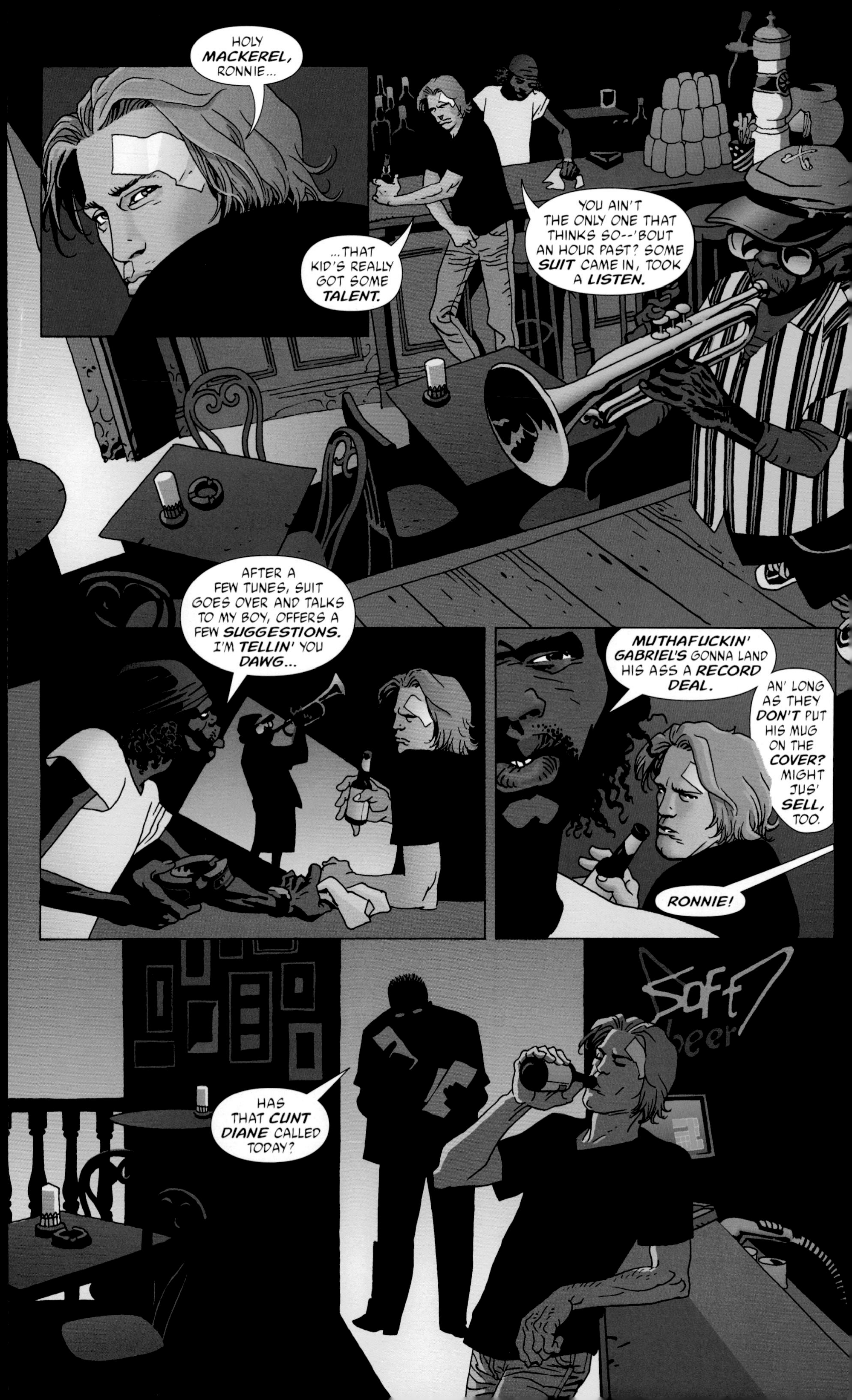
HOLY MACKEREL, RONNIE...
...THAT KID'S REALLY GOT SOME TALENT.
YOU AIN'T THE ONLY ONE THAT THINKS SO--'BOUT AN HOUR PAST? SOME SUIT CAME IN, TOOK A LISTEN.
AFTER A FEW TUNES, SUIT GOES OVER AND TALKS TO MY BOY, OFFERS A FEW SUGGESTIONS. I'M TELLIN' YOU DAWG...
MUTHAFUCKIN' GABRIEL'S GONNA LAND HIS ASS A RECORD DEAL.
AN' LONG AS THEY DON'T PUT HIS MUG ON THE COVER? MIGHT JUS' SELL, TOO.
RONNIE!
Soft beer
HAS THAT CUNT DIANE CALLED TODAY?

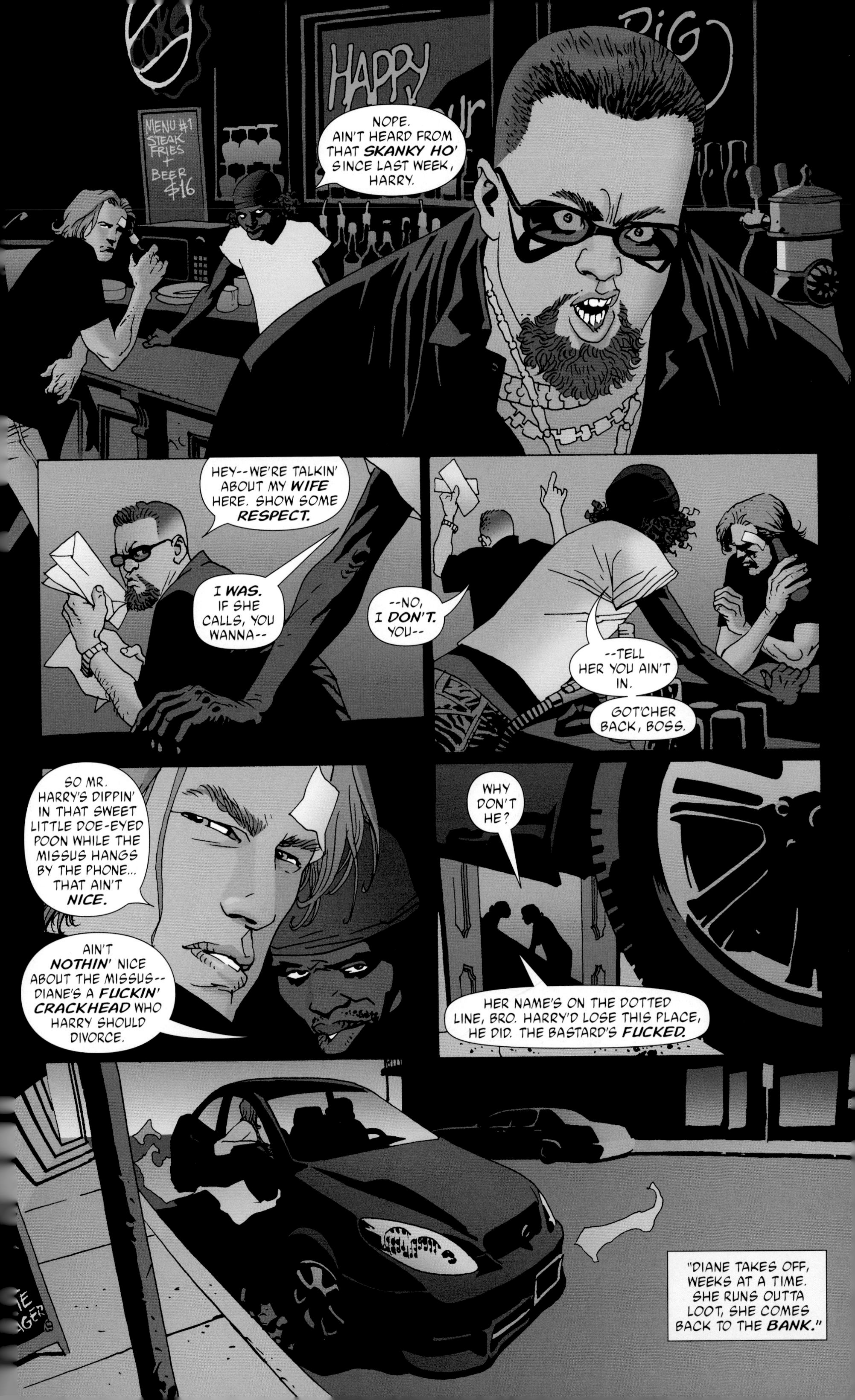
HAPPY
MENU #1 STEAK FRIES + BEER $16
NOPE. AIN'T HEARD FROM THAT SKANKY HO' SINCE LAST WEEK, HARRY.
HEY--WE'RE TALKIN' ABOUT MY WIFE HERE. SHOW SOME RESPECT.
I WAS. IF SHE CALLS, YOU WANNA--
--NO, I DON'T. YOU--
--TELL HER YOU AIN'T IN.
GOT'CHER BACK, BOSS.
SO MR. HARRY'S DIPPIN' IN THAT SWEET LITTLE DOE-EYED POON WHILE THE MISSUS HANGS BY THE PHONE... THAT AIN'T NICE.
AIN'T NOTHIN' NICE ABOUT THE MISSUS--DIANE'S A FUCKIN' CRACKHEAD WHO HARRY SHOULD DIVORCE.
WHY DON'T HE?
HER NAME'S ON THE DOTTED LINE, BRO. HARRY'D LOSE THIS PLACE, HE DID. THE BASTARD'S FUCKED.
"DIANE TAKES OFF, WEEKS AT A TIME. SHE RUNS OUTTA LOOT, SHE COMES BACK TO THE BANK."

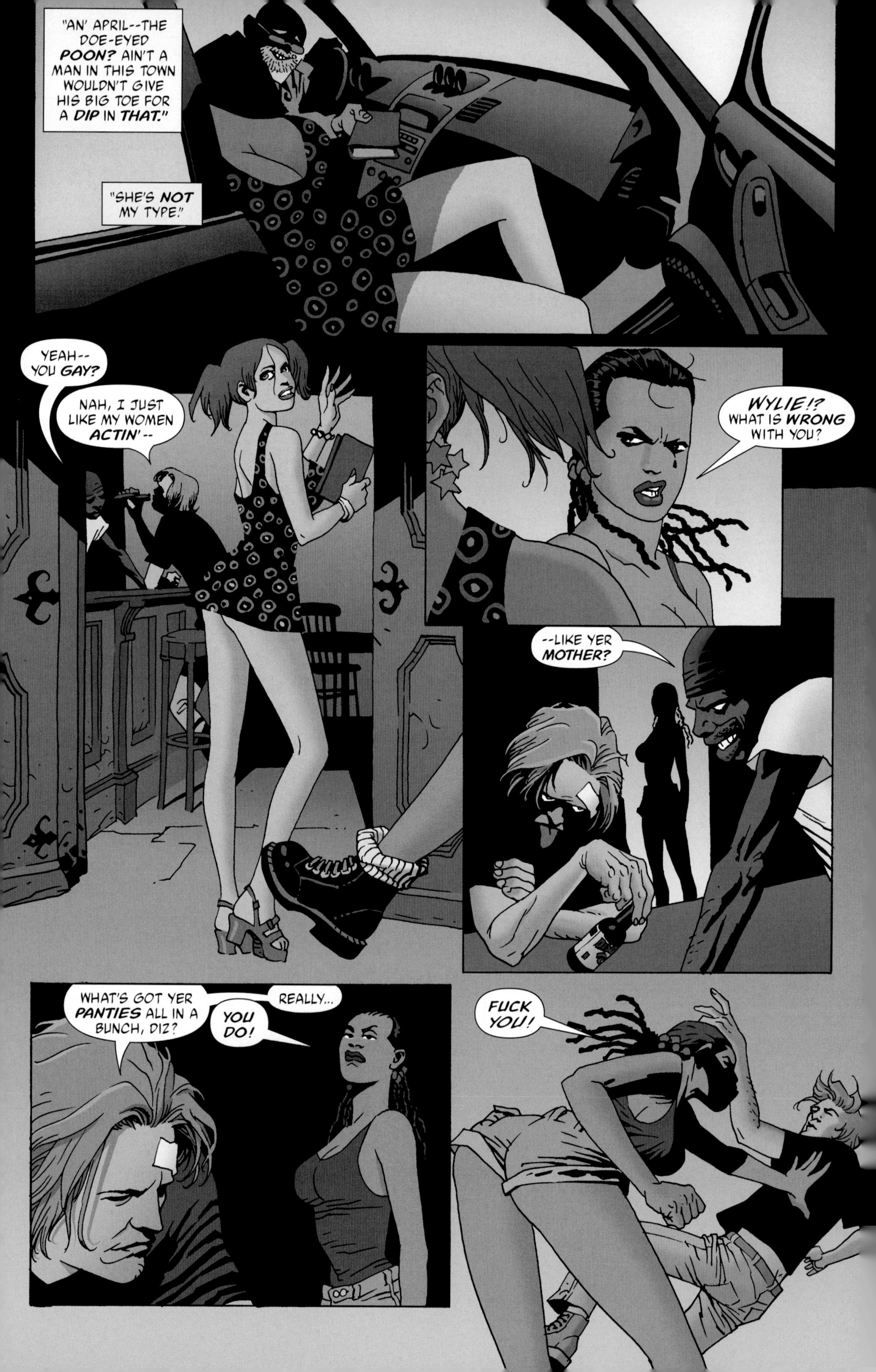
"AN' APRIL--THE DOE-EYED POON? AIN'T A MAN IN THIS TOWN WOULDN'T GIVE HIS BIG TOE FOR A DIP IN THAT."
"SHE'S NOT MY TYPE."
YEAH-- YOU GAY?
NAH, I JUST LIKE MY WOMEN ACTIN'--
WYLIE!? WHAT IS WRONG WITH YOU?
--LIKE YER MOTHER?
WHAT'S GOT YER PANTIES ALL IN A BUNCH, DIZ?
REALLY...
YOU DO!
FUCK YOU!

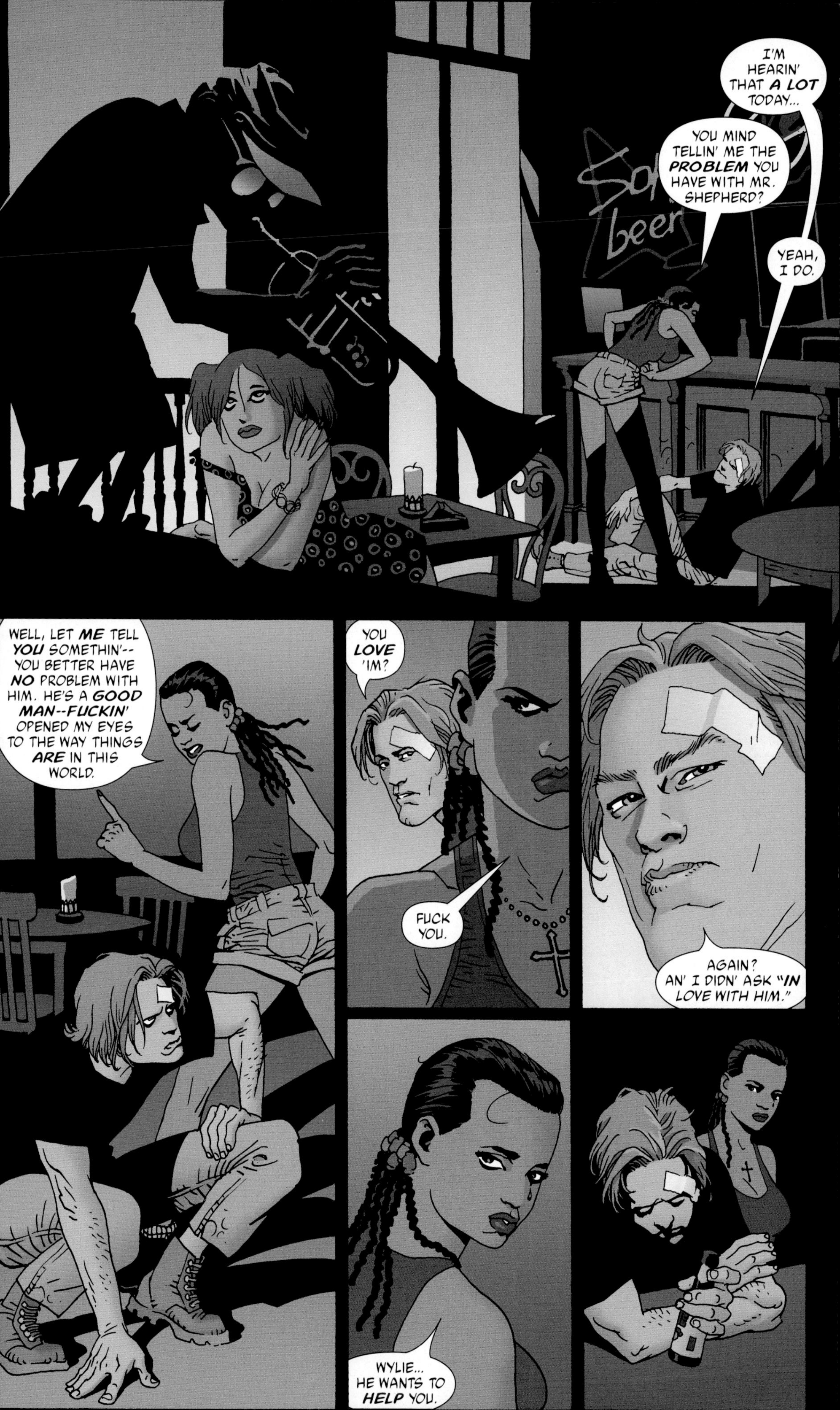
I'M HEARIN' THAT A LOT TODAY...
YOU MIND TELLIN' ME THE PROBLEM YOU HAVE WITH MR. SHEPHERD?
YEAH, I DO.
WELL, LET ME TELL YOU SOMETHIN'-- YOU BETTER HAVE NO PROBLEM WITH HIM. HE'S A GOOD MAN--FUCKIN' OPENED MY EYES TO THE WAY THINGS ARE IN THIS WORLD.
YOU LOVE 'IM?
FUCK YOU.
AGAIN? AN' I DIDN' ASK "IN LOVE WITH HIM."
WYLIE... HE WANTS TO HELP YOU.

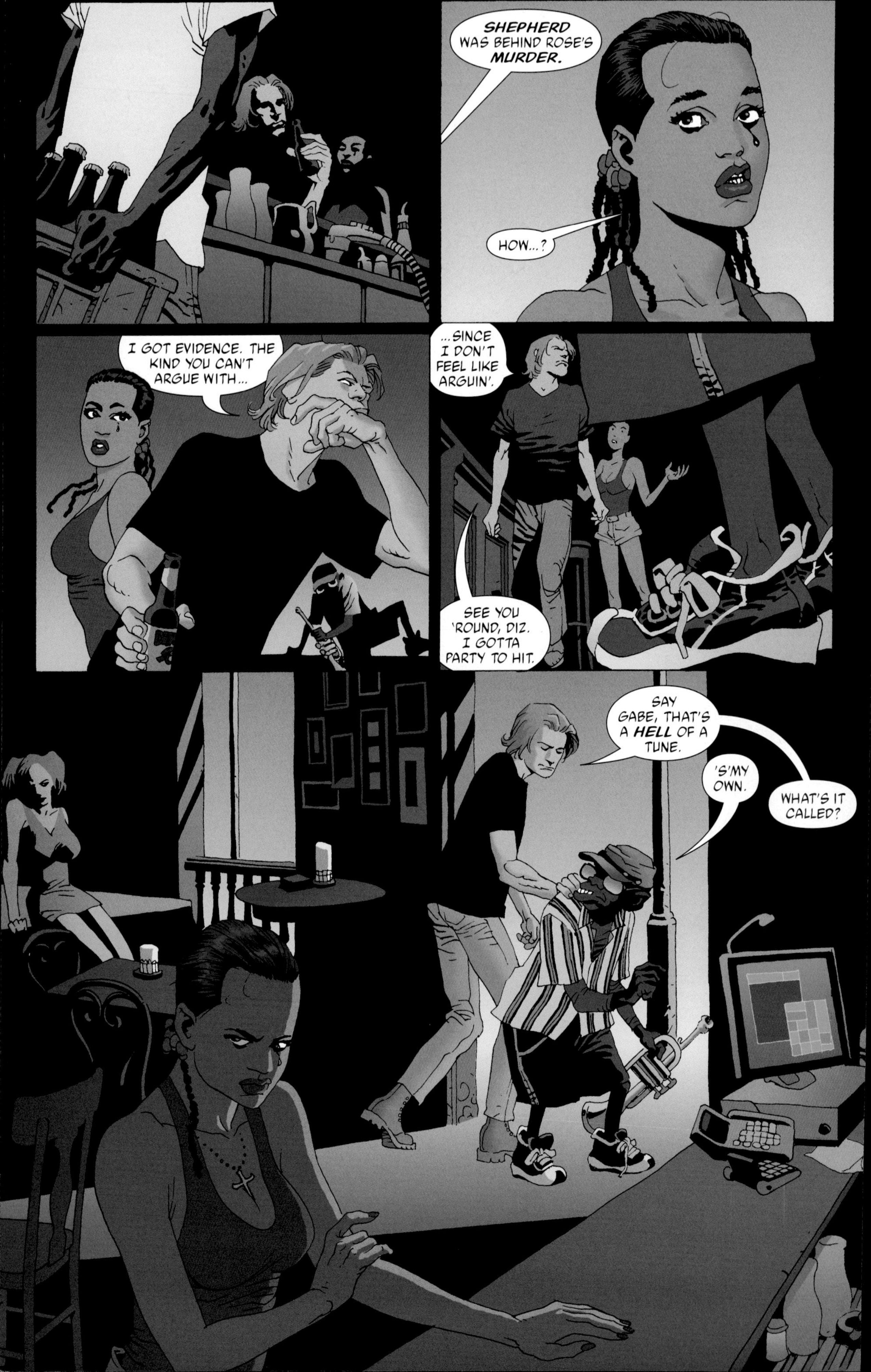
SHEPHERD WAS BEHIND ROSE'S MURDER.
HOW...?
I GOT EVIDENCE. THE KIND YOU CAN'T ARGUE WITH...
...SINCE I DON'T FEEL LIKE ARGUIN'.
SEE YOU 'ROUND, DIZ. I GOTTA PARTY TO HIT.
SAY GABE, THAT'S A HELL OF A TUNE.
'S'MY OWN.
WHAT'S IT CALLED?

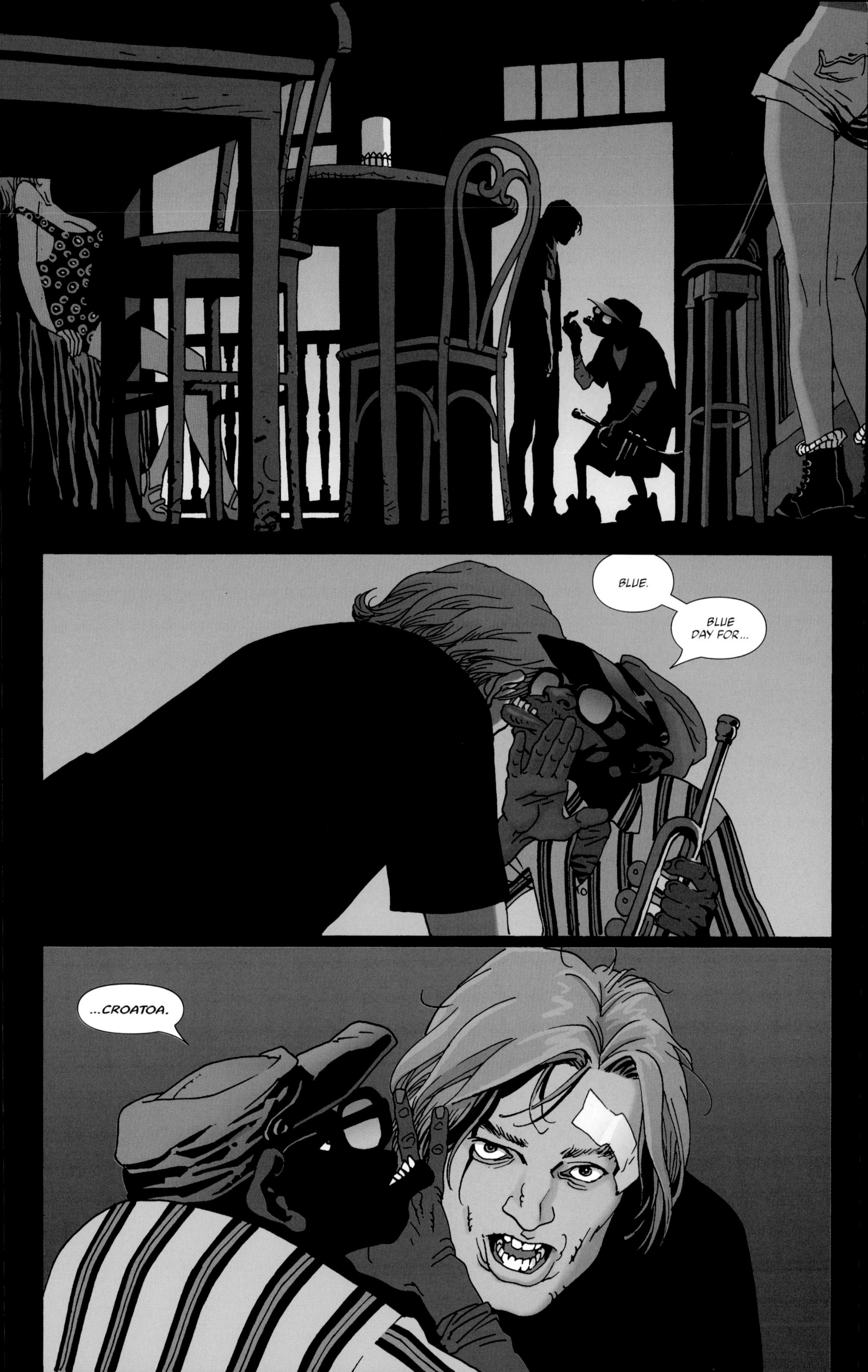
BLUE.
BLUE DAY FOR...
...CROATOA.

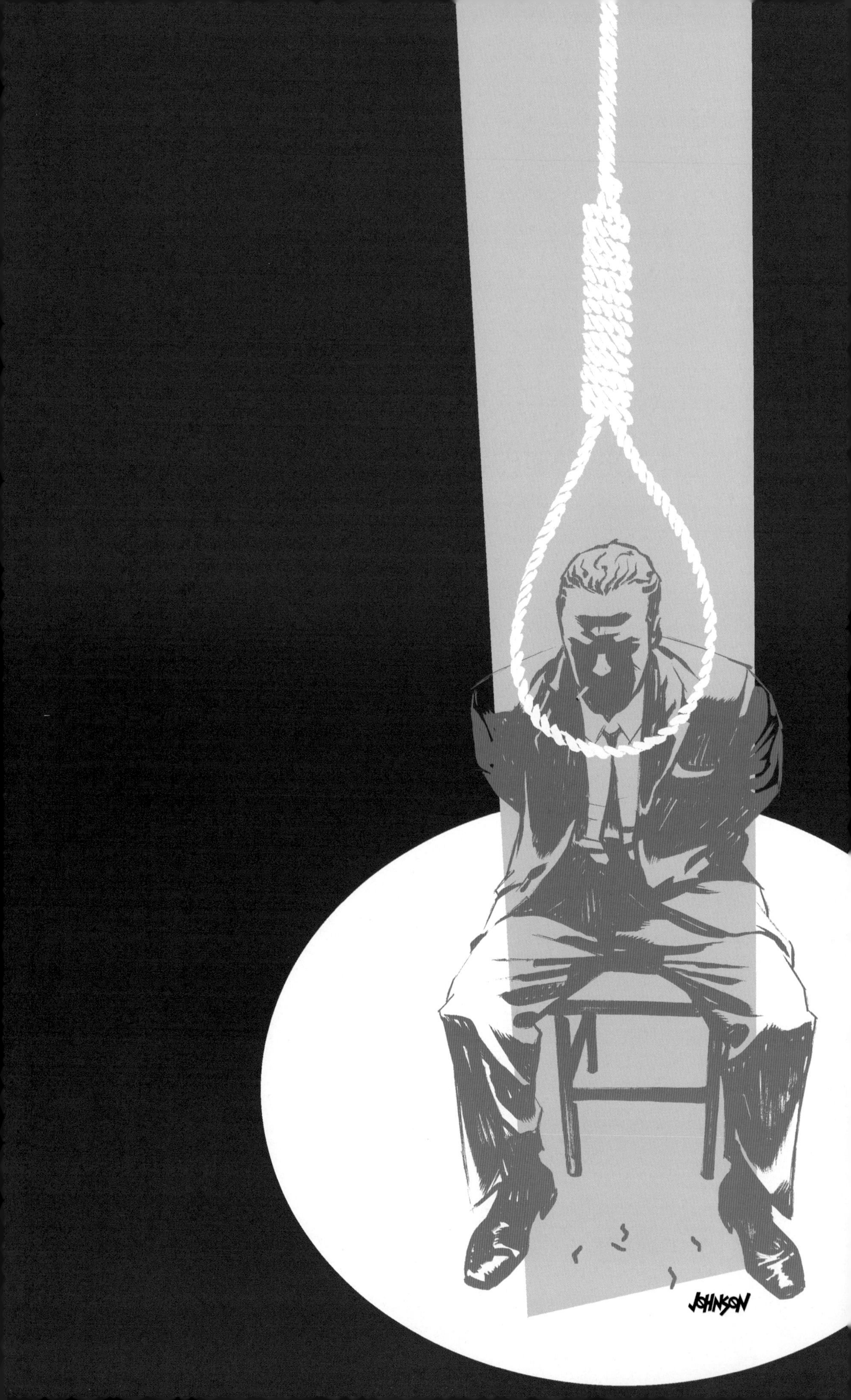
JOHNSON

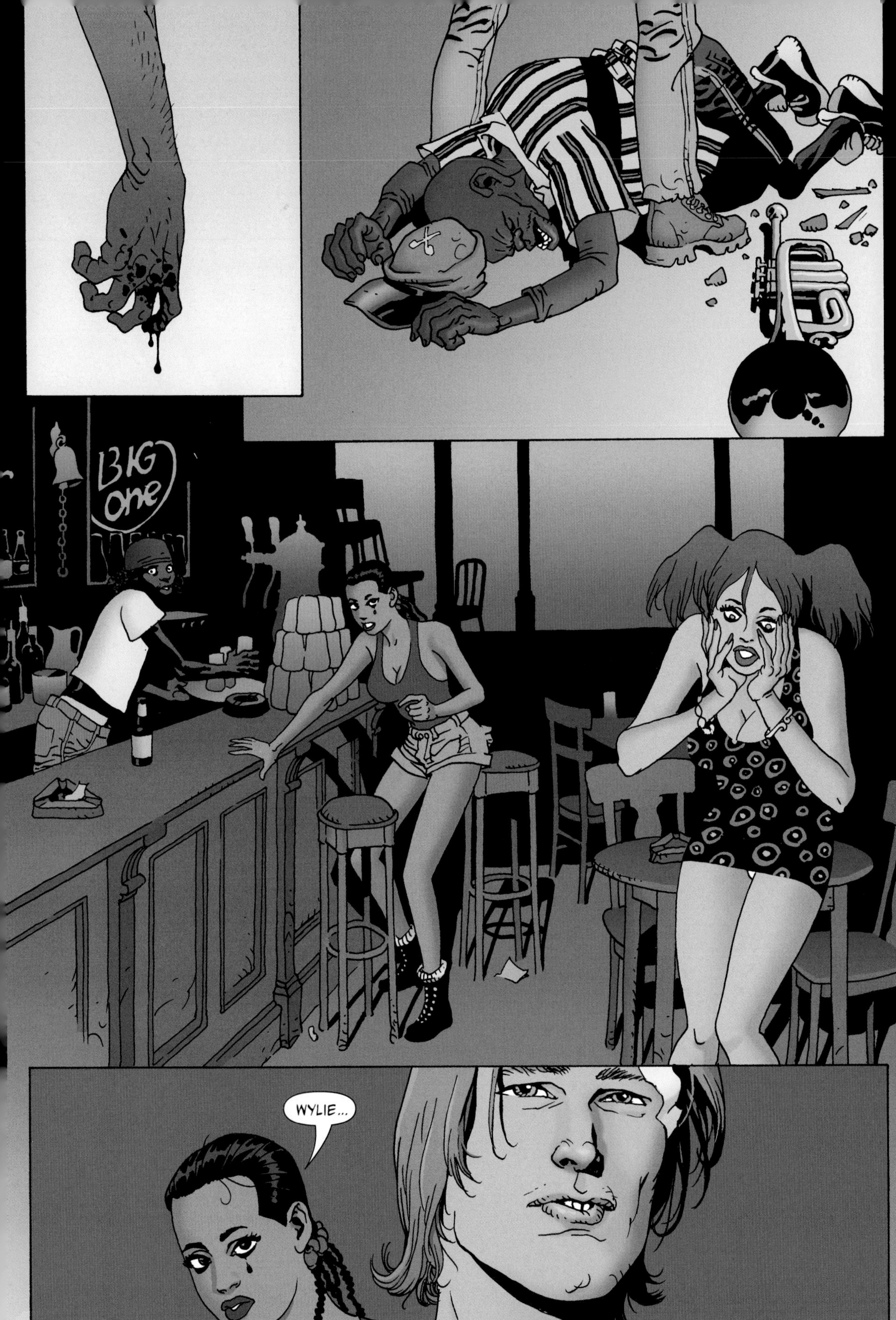

BIG one
WYLIE...

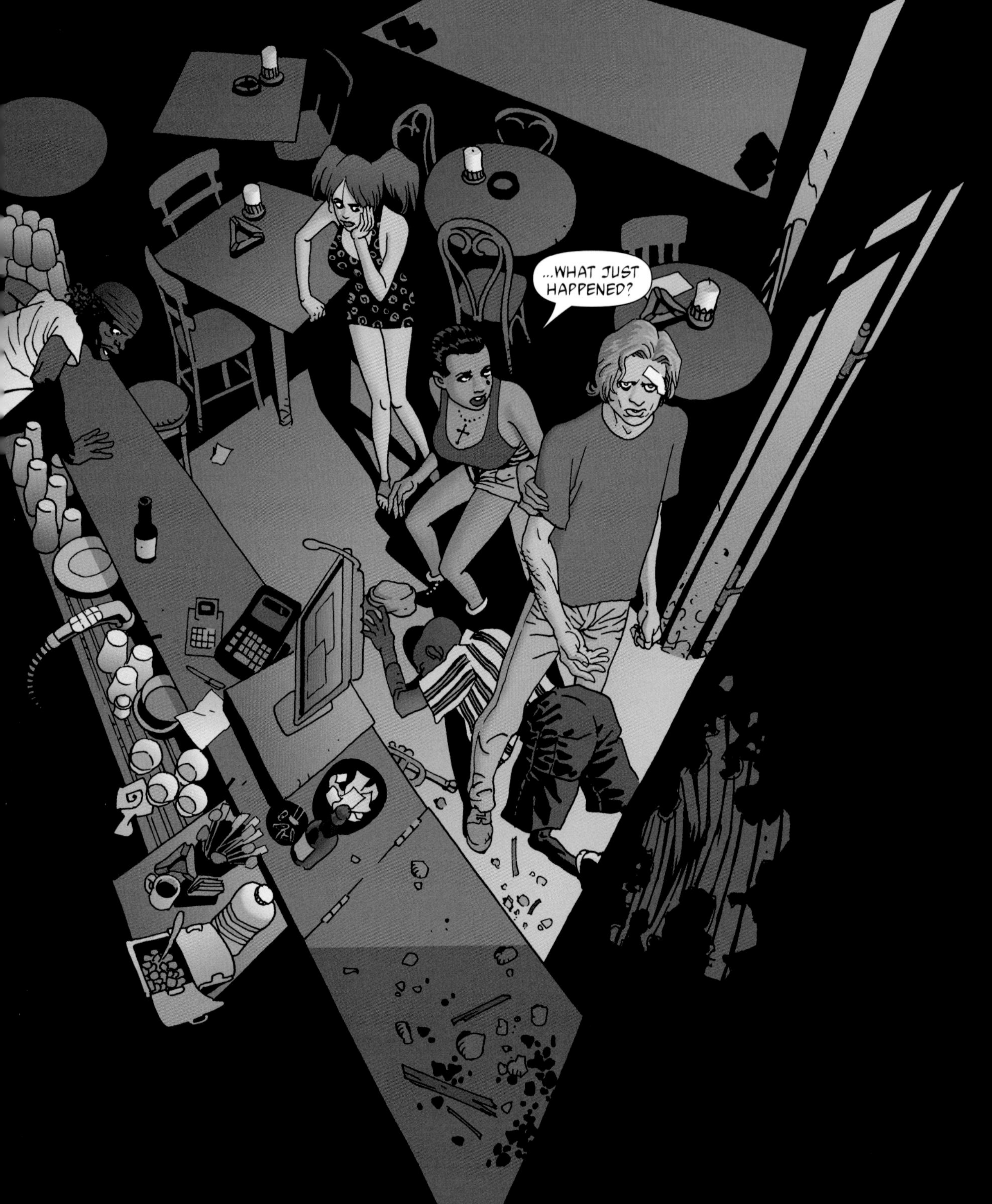
...WHAT JUST HAPPENED?

Wylie Runs the Voodoo Down Part Four

Brian Azzarello writer **Eduardo Risso** artist
Patricia Mulvihill colorist
Clem Robins letterer **Dave Johnson** cover
Casey Seijas asst. ed. **Will Dennis** editor

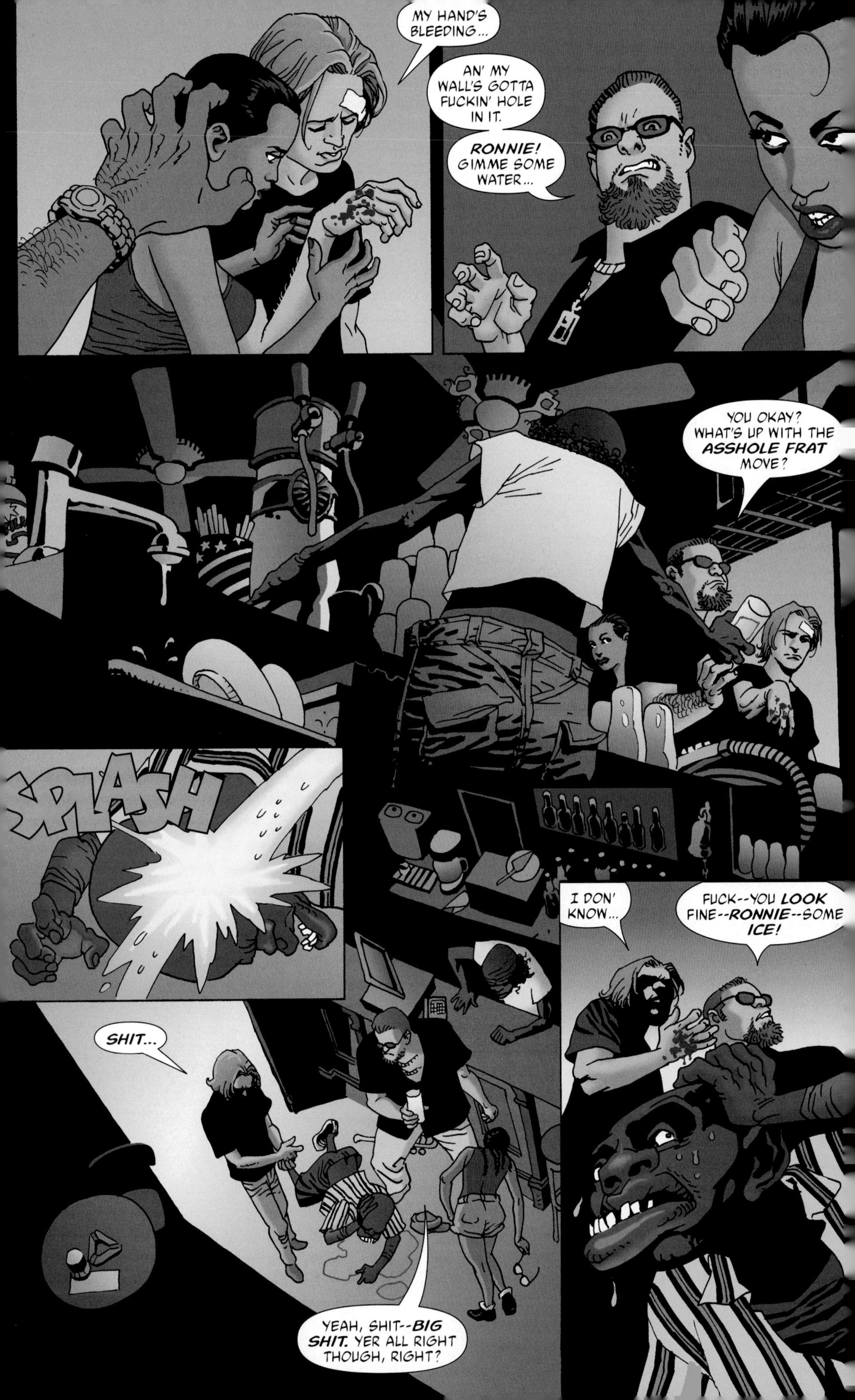
MY HAND'S BLEEDING...
AN' MY WALL'S GOTTA FUCKIN' HOLE IN IT.
RONNIE! GIMME SOME WATER...
YOU OKAY? WHAT'S UP WITH THE ASSHOLE FRAT MOVE?
SPLASH
I DON' KNOW...
FUCK--YOU LOOK FINE--RONNIE--SOME ICE!
SHIT...
YEAH, SHIT--BIG SHIT. YER ALL RIGHT THOUGH, RIGHT?

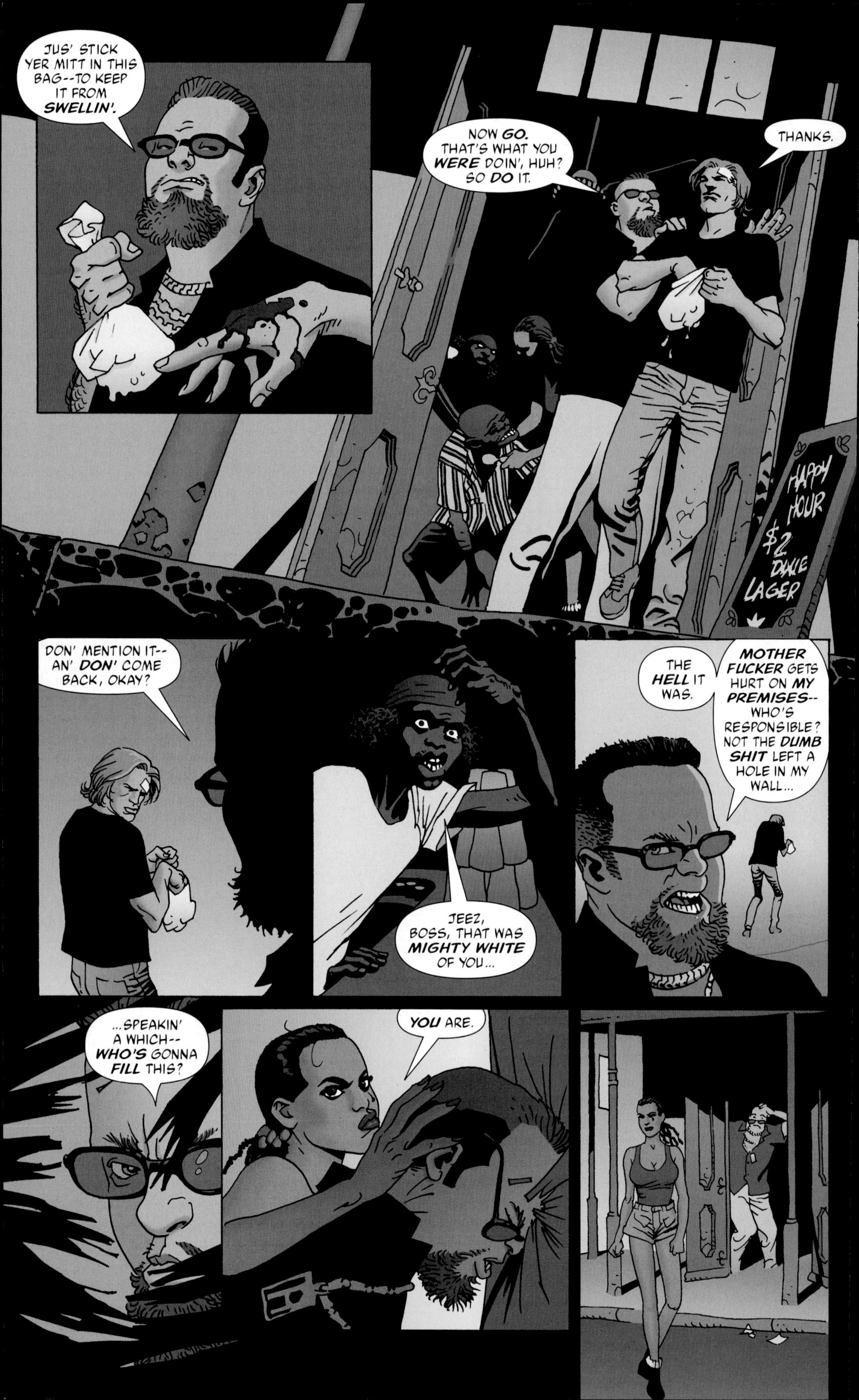
JUS' STICK YER MITT IN THIS BAG--TO KEEP IT FROM SWELLIN'.
NOW GO. THAT'S WHAT YOU WERE DOIN', HUH? SO DO IT.
THANKS.
HAPPY HOUR $2 DIXIE LAGER
DON' MENTION IT--AN' DON' COME BACK, OKAY?
JEEZ, BOSS, THAT WAS MIGHTY WHITE OF YOU...
THE HELL IT WAS.
MOTHER FUCKER GETS HURT ON MY PREMISES--WHO'S RESPONSIBLE? NOT THE DUMB SHIT LEFT A HOLE IN MY WALL...
...SPEAKIN' A WHICH--WHO'S GONNA FILL THIS?
YOU ARE.

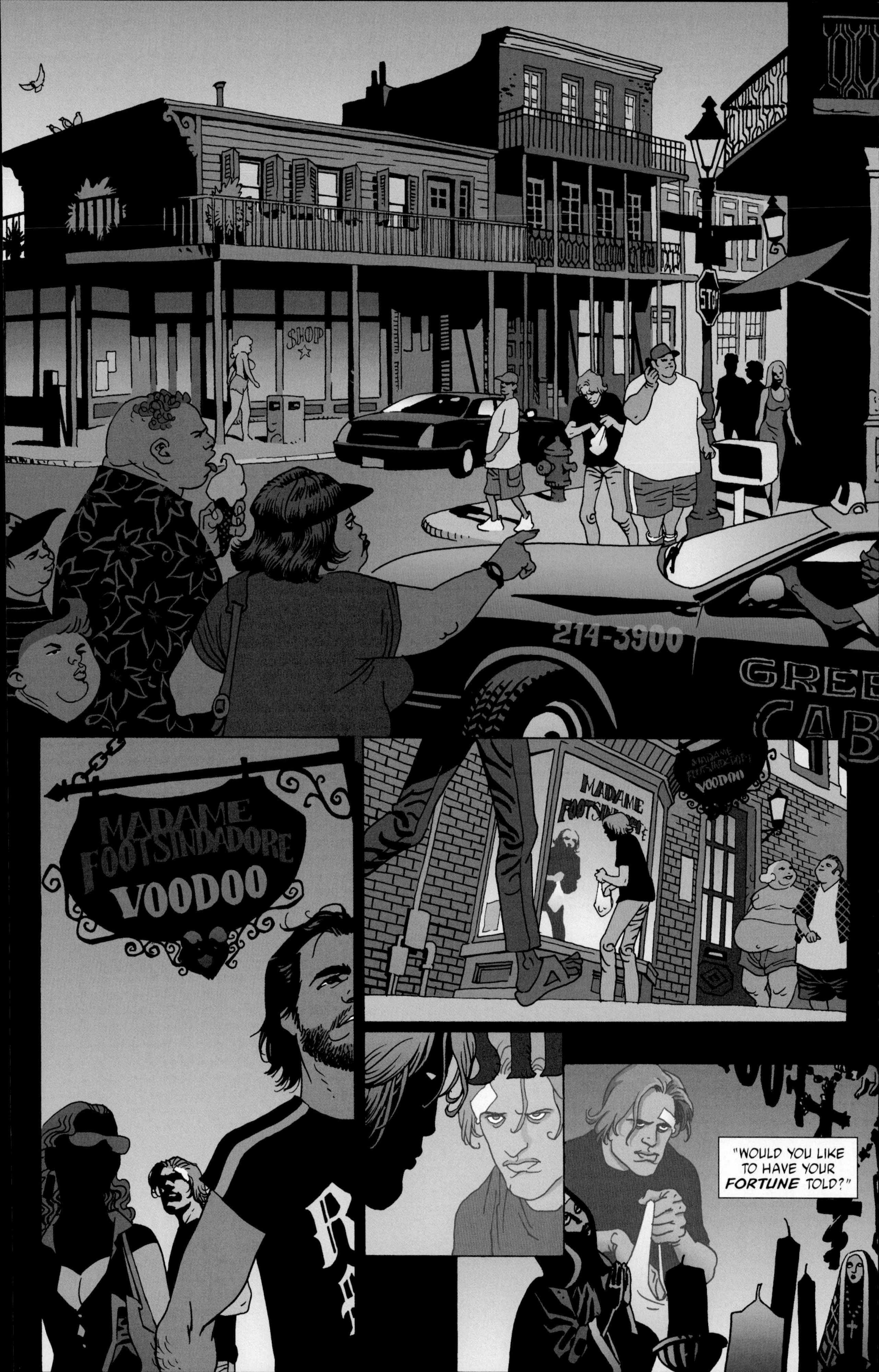

SHOP
STOP
214-3900
MADAME FOOTSINDADORE VOODOO
MADAME FOOTSINDADORE
"WOULD YOU LIKE TO HAVE YOUR FORTUNE TOLD?"

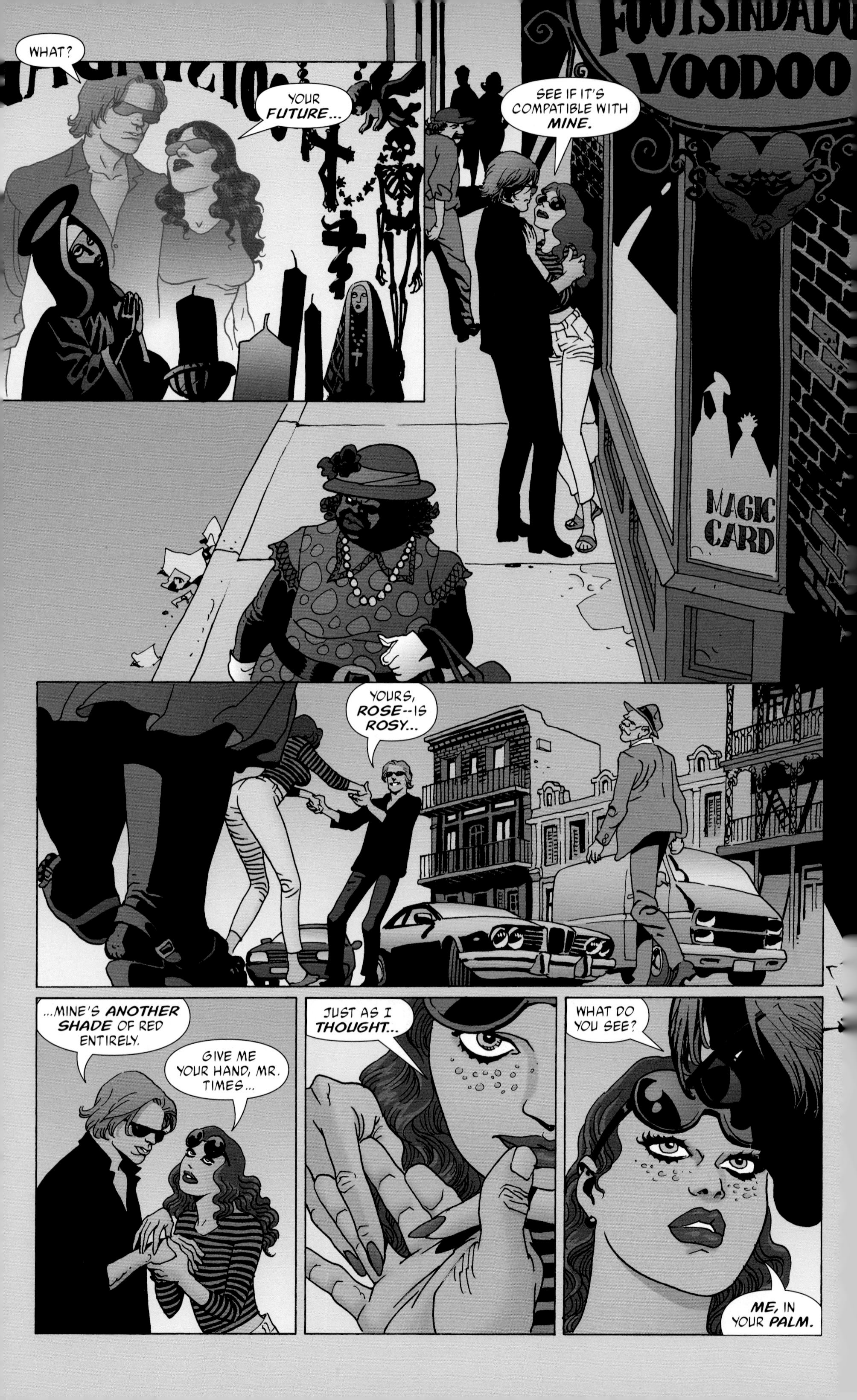
WHAT?
YOUR FUTURE...
SEE IF IT'S COMPATIBLE WITH MINE.
VOODOO
MAGIC CARD
YOURS, ROSE--IS ROSY...
...MINE'S ANOTHER SHADE OF RED ENTIRELY.
GIVE ME YOUR HAND, MR. TIMES...
JUST AS I THOUGHT...
WHAT DO YOU SEE?
ME, IN YOUR PALM.

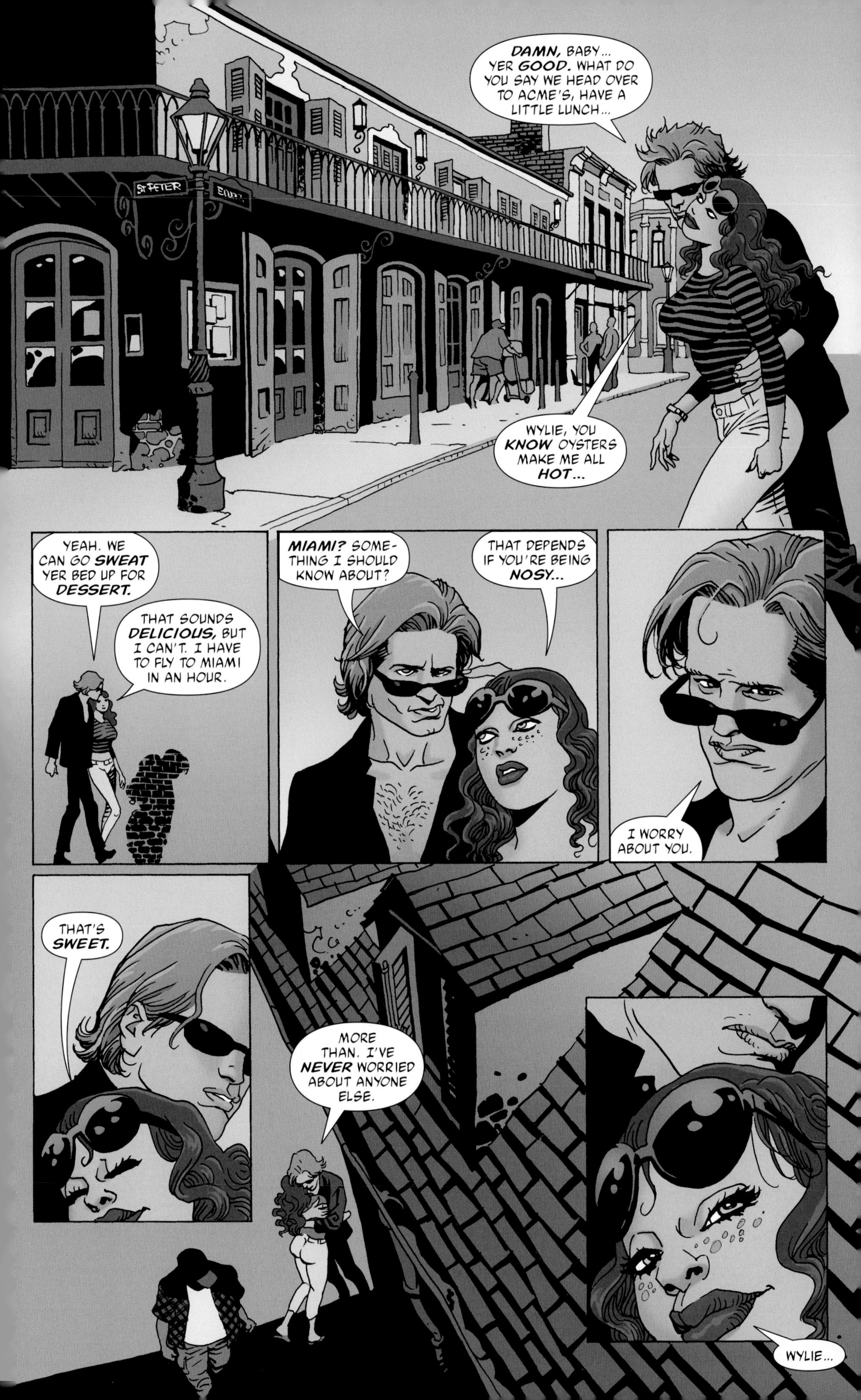
DAMN, BABY... YER GOOD. WHAT DO YOU SAY WE HEAD OVER TO ACME'S, HAVE A LITTLE LUNCH...
ST PETER
WYLIE, YOU KNOW OYSTERS MAKE ME ALL HOT...
YEAH. WE CAN GO SWEAT YER BED UP FOR DESSERT.
THAT SOUNDS DELICIOUS, BUT I CAN'T. I HAVE TO FLY TO MIAMI IN AN HOUR.
MIAMI? SOMETHING I SHOULD KNOW ABOUT?
THAT DEPENDS IF YOU'RE BEING NOSY...
I WORRY ABOUT YOU.
THAT'S SWEET.
MORE THAN. I'VE NEVER WORRIED ABOUT ANYONE ELSE.
WYLIE...

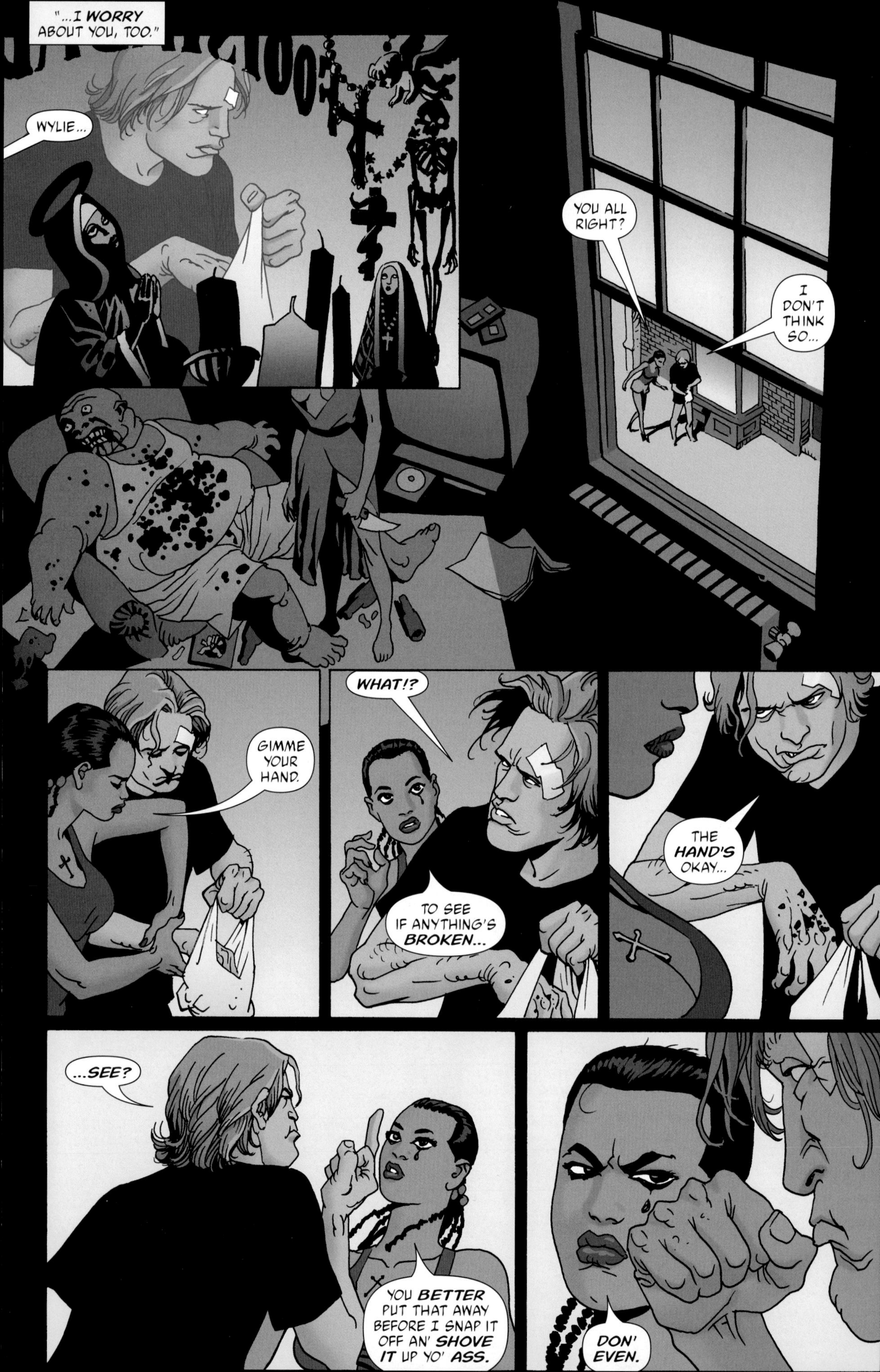
"...I WORRY ABOUT YOU, TOO."
WYLIE...
YOU ALL RIGHT?
I DON'T THINK SO...
GIMME YOUR HAND.
WHAT!?
TO SEE IF ANYTHING'S BROKEN...
THE HAND'S OKAY...
...SEE?
YOU BETTER PUT THAT AWAY BEFORE I SNAP IT OFF AN' SHOVE IT UP YO' ASS.
DON' EVEN.

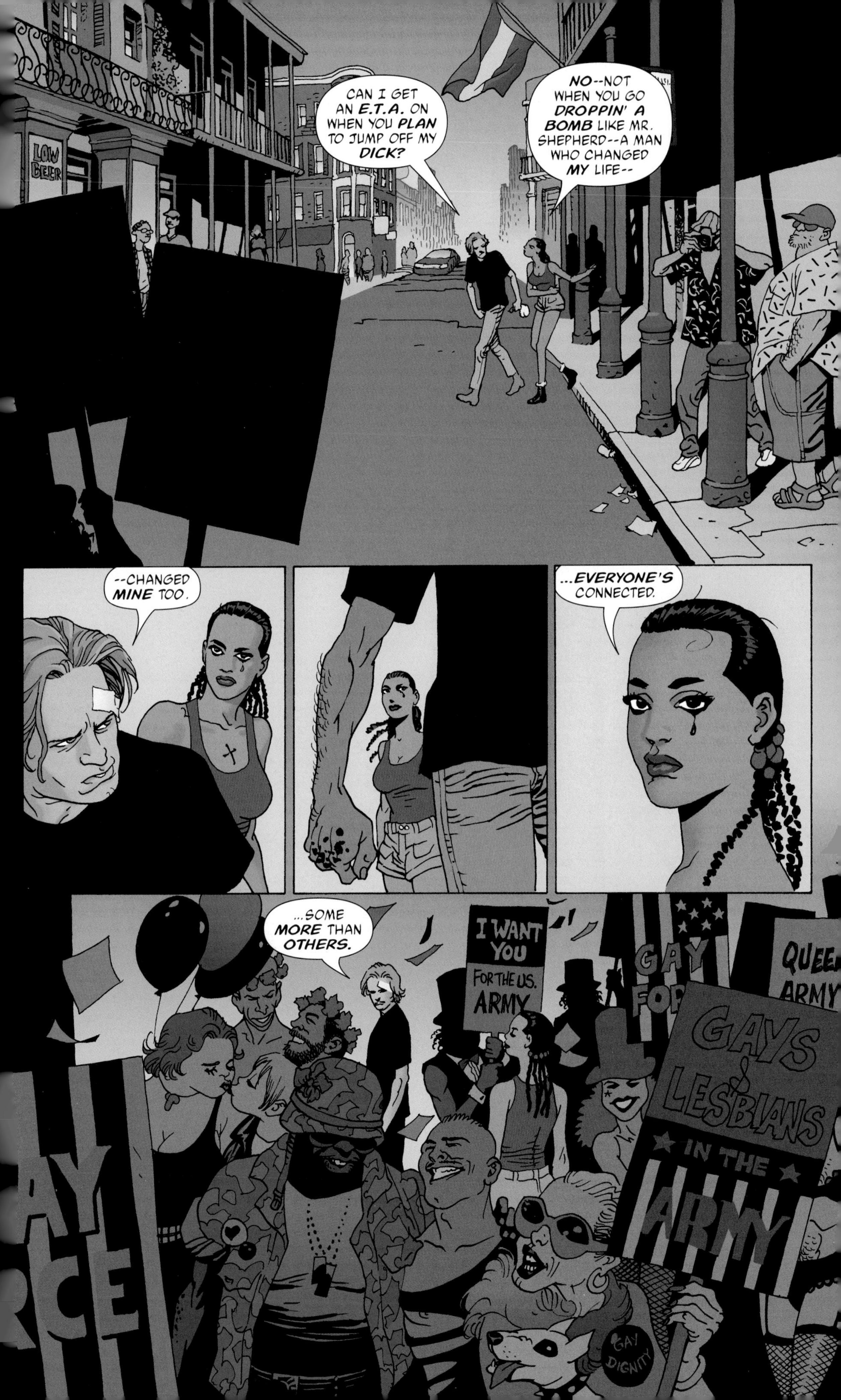

LOW BEER
CAN I GET AN E.T.A. ON WHEN YOU PLAN TO JUMP OFF MY DICK?
NO--NOT WHEN YOU GO DROPPIN' A BOMB LIKE MR. SHEPHERD--A MAN WHO CHANGED MY LIFE--
--CHANGED MINE TOO.
...EVERYONE'S CONNECTED.
...SOME MORE THAN OTHERS.
I WANT YOU FOR THE U.S. ARMY
GAYS & LESBIANS IN THE ARMY
GAY DIGNITY

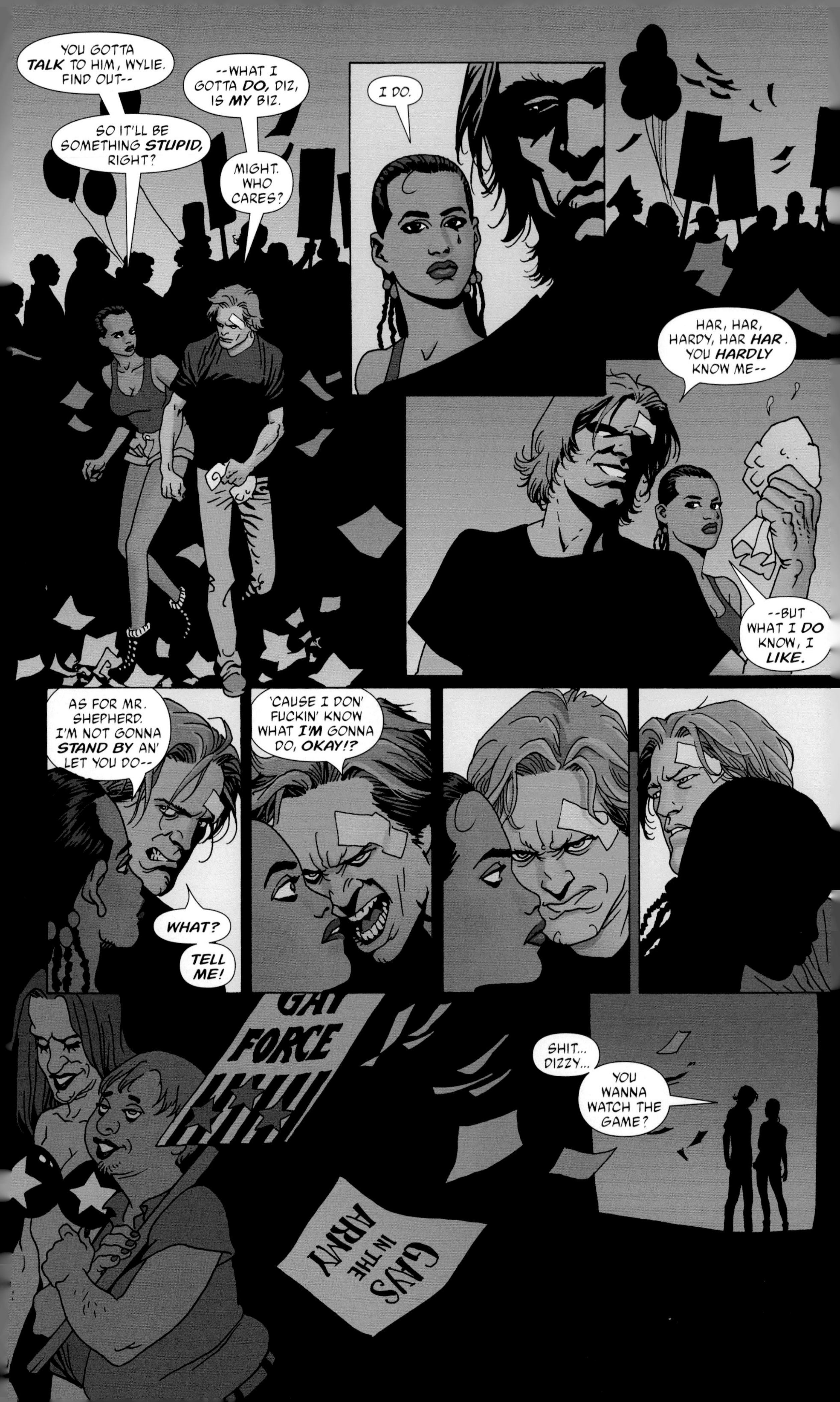
YOU GOTTA TALK TO HIM, WYLIE. FIND OUT--
--WHAT I GOTTA DO, DIZ, IS MY BIZ.
SO IT'LL BE SOMETHING STUPID, RIGHT?
MIGHT. WHO CARES?
I DO.
HAR, HAR, HARDY, HAR HAR. YOU HARDLY KNOW ME--
--BUT WHAT I DO KNOW, I LIKE.
AS FOR MR. SHEPHERD. I'M NOT GONNA STAND BY AN' LET YOU DO--
WHAT?
TELL ME!
'CAUSE I DON' FUCKIN' KNOW WHAT I'M GONNA DO, OKAY!?
GAY FORCE
GAYS IN THE ARMY
SHIT... DIZZY...
YOU WANNA WATCH THE GAME?

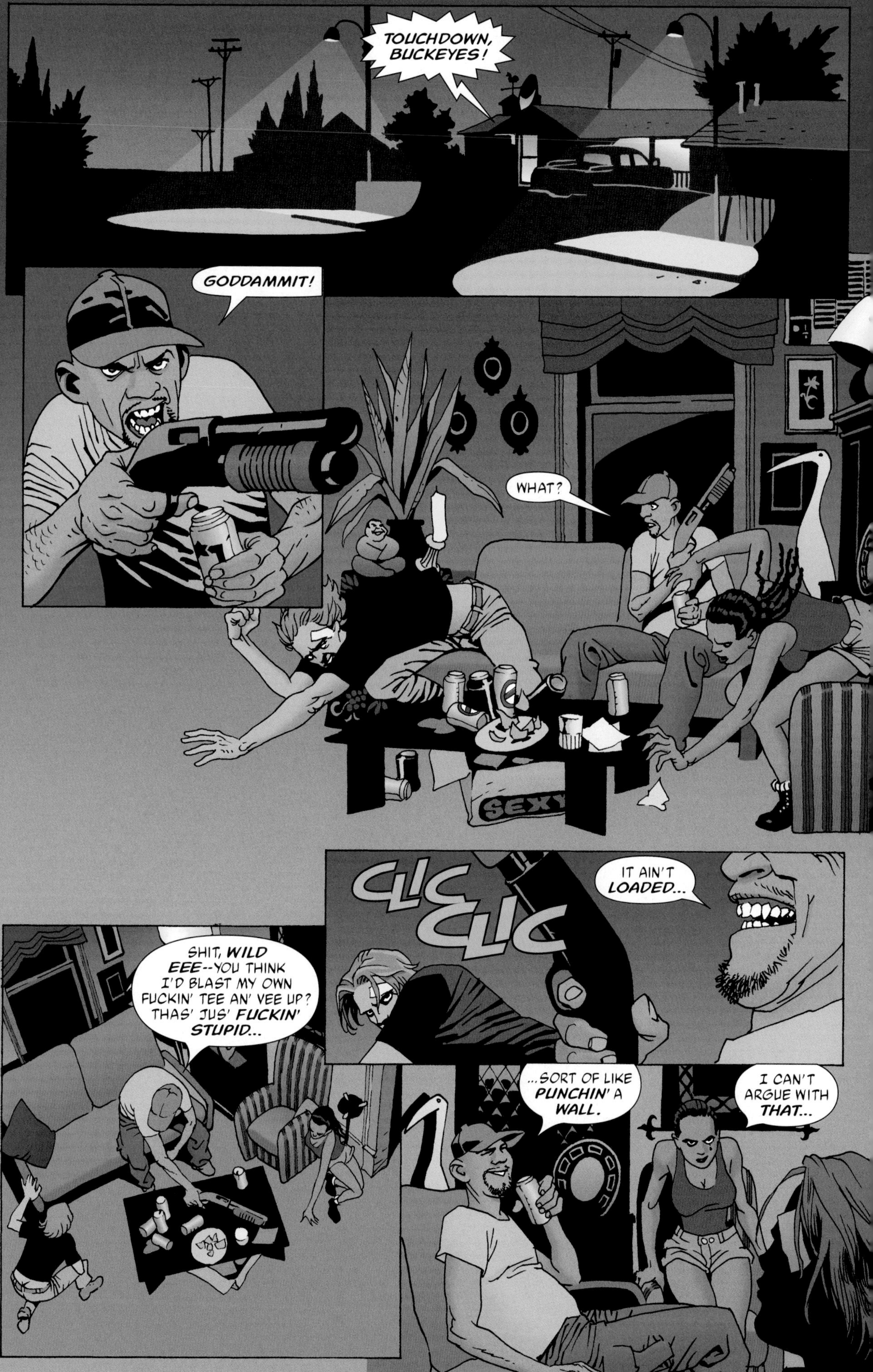
TOUCHDOWN, BUCKEYES!
GODDAMMIT!
WHAT?
SEXY
CLIC
CLIC
IT AIN'T LOADED...
SHIT, WILD EEE--YOU THINK I'D BLAST MY OWN FUCKIN' TEE AN' VEE UP? THAS' JUS' FUCKIN' STUPID...
...SORT OF LIKE PUNCHIN' A WALL.
I CAN'T ARGUE WITH THAT...

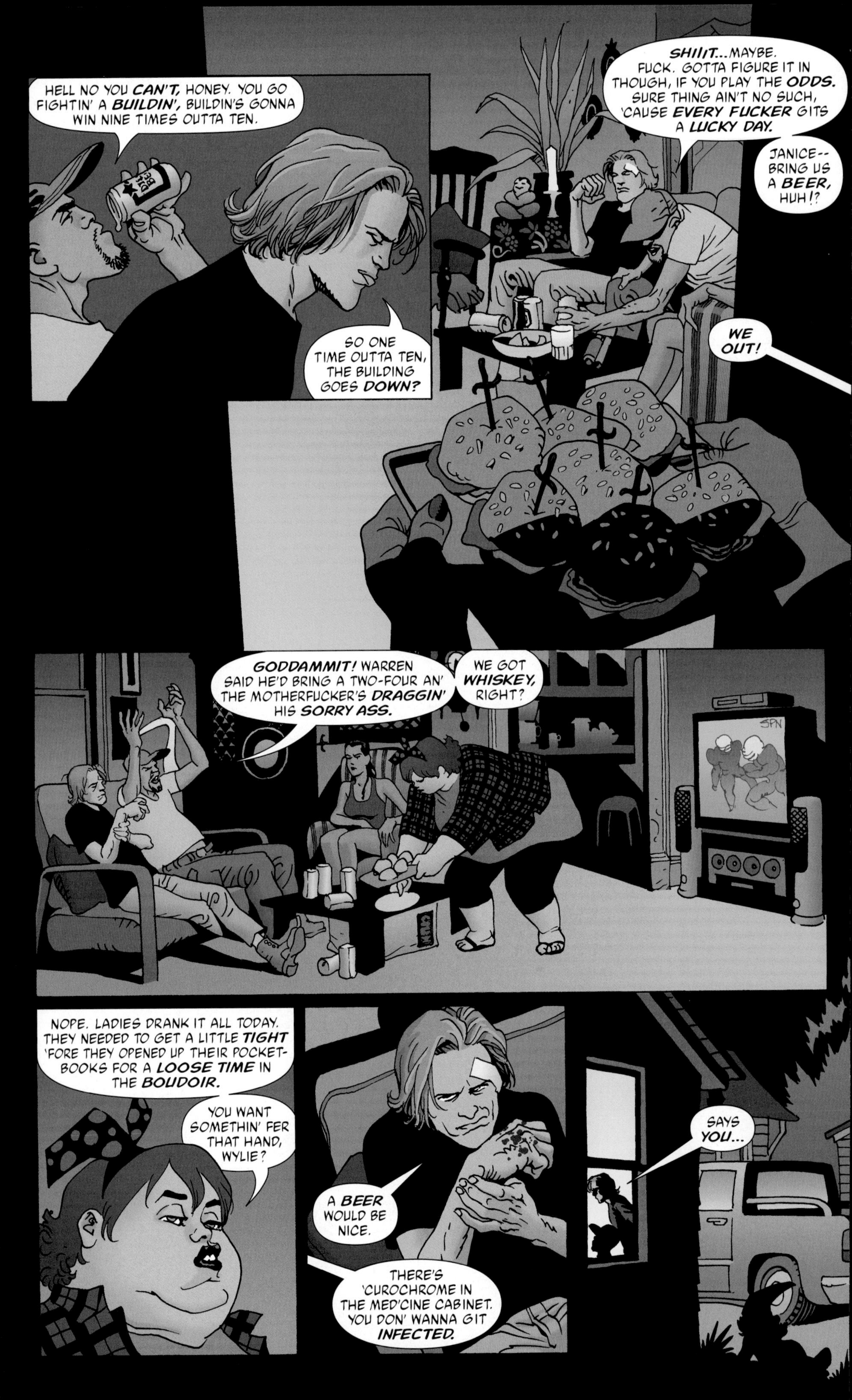
HELL NO YOU CAN'T, HONEY. YOU GO FIGHTIN' A BUILDIN', BUILDIN'S GONNA WIN NINE TIMES OUTTA TEN.
SO ONE TIME OUTTA TEN, THE BUILDING GOES DOWN?
SHIIIT... MAYBE. FUCK. GOTTA FIGURE IT IN THOUGH, IF YOU PLAY THE ODDS. SURE THING AIN'T NO SUCH, 'CAUSE EVERY FUCKER GITS A LUCKY DAY.
JANICE-- BRING US A BEER, HUH!?
WE OUT!
GODDAMMIT! WARREN SAID HE'D BRING A TWO-FOUR AN' THE MOTHERFUCKER'S DRAGGIN' HIS SORRY ASS.
WE GOT WHISKEY, RIGHT?
NOPE. LADIES DRANK IT ALL TODAY. THEY NEEDED TO GET A LITTLE TIGHT 'FORE THEY OPENED UP THEIR POCKETBOOKS FOR A LOOSE TIME IN THE BOUDOIR.
YOU WANT SOMETHIN' FER THAT HAND, WYLIE?
A BEER WOULD BE NICE.
THERE'S 'CUROCHROME IN THE MED'CINE CABINET. YOU DON' WANNA GIT INFECTED.
SAYS YOU...

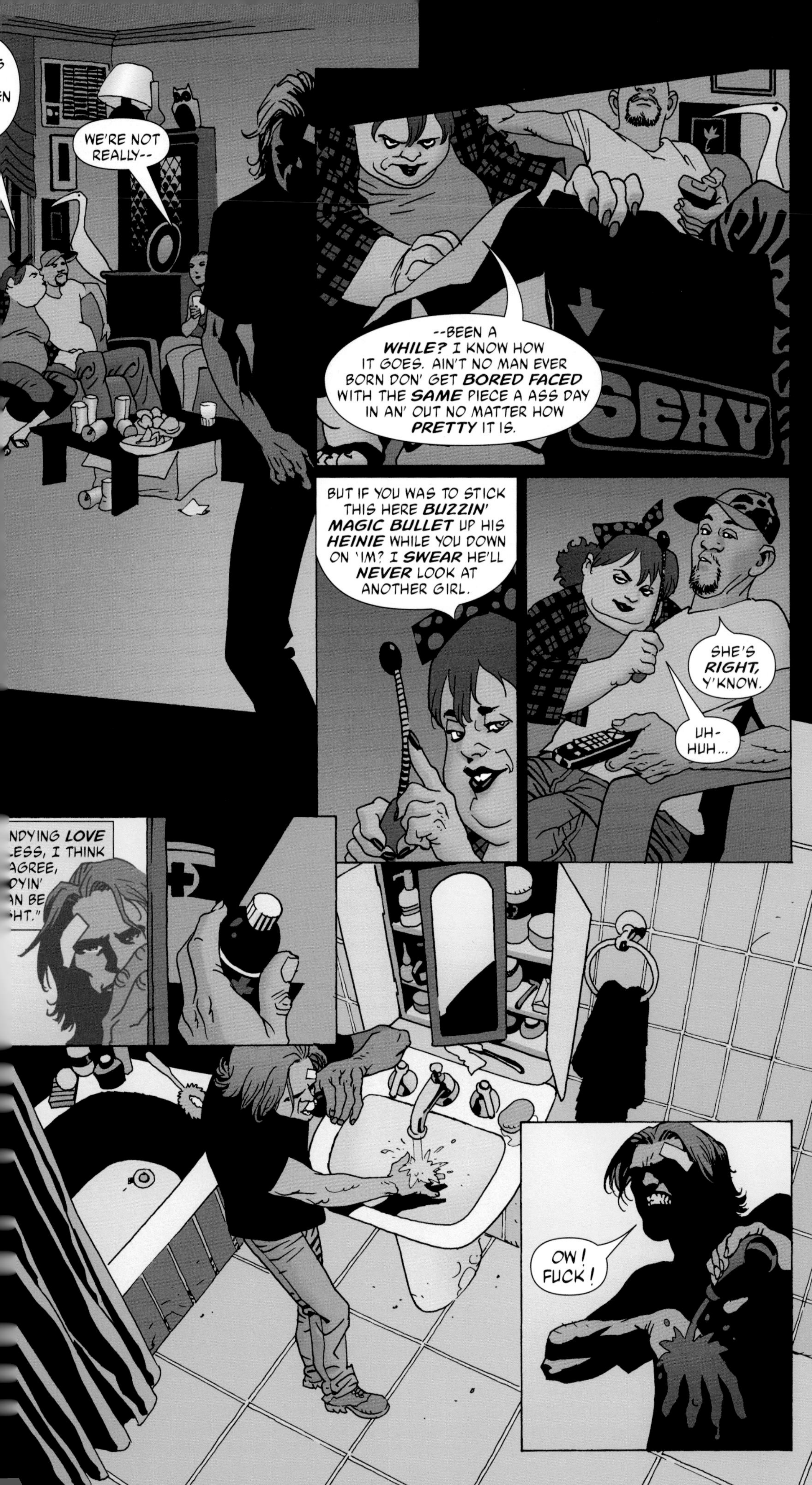
WE'RE NOT REALLY--
--BEEN A WHILE? I KNOW HOW IT GOES. AIN'T NO MAN EVER BORN DON' GET BORED FACED WITH THE SAME PIECE A ASS DAY IN AN' OUT NO MATTER HOW PRETTY IT IS.
SEXY
BUT IF YOU WAS TO STICK THIS HERE BUZZIN' MAGIC BULLET UP HIS HEINIE WHILE YOU DOWN ON 'IM? I SWEAR HE'LL NEVER LOOK AT ANOTHER GIRL.
SHE'S RIGHT, Y'KNOW.
UH-HUH...
NDYING LOVE
LESS, I THINK
AGREE,
DYIN'
AN BE
GHT."
OW! FUCK!

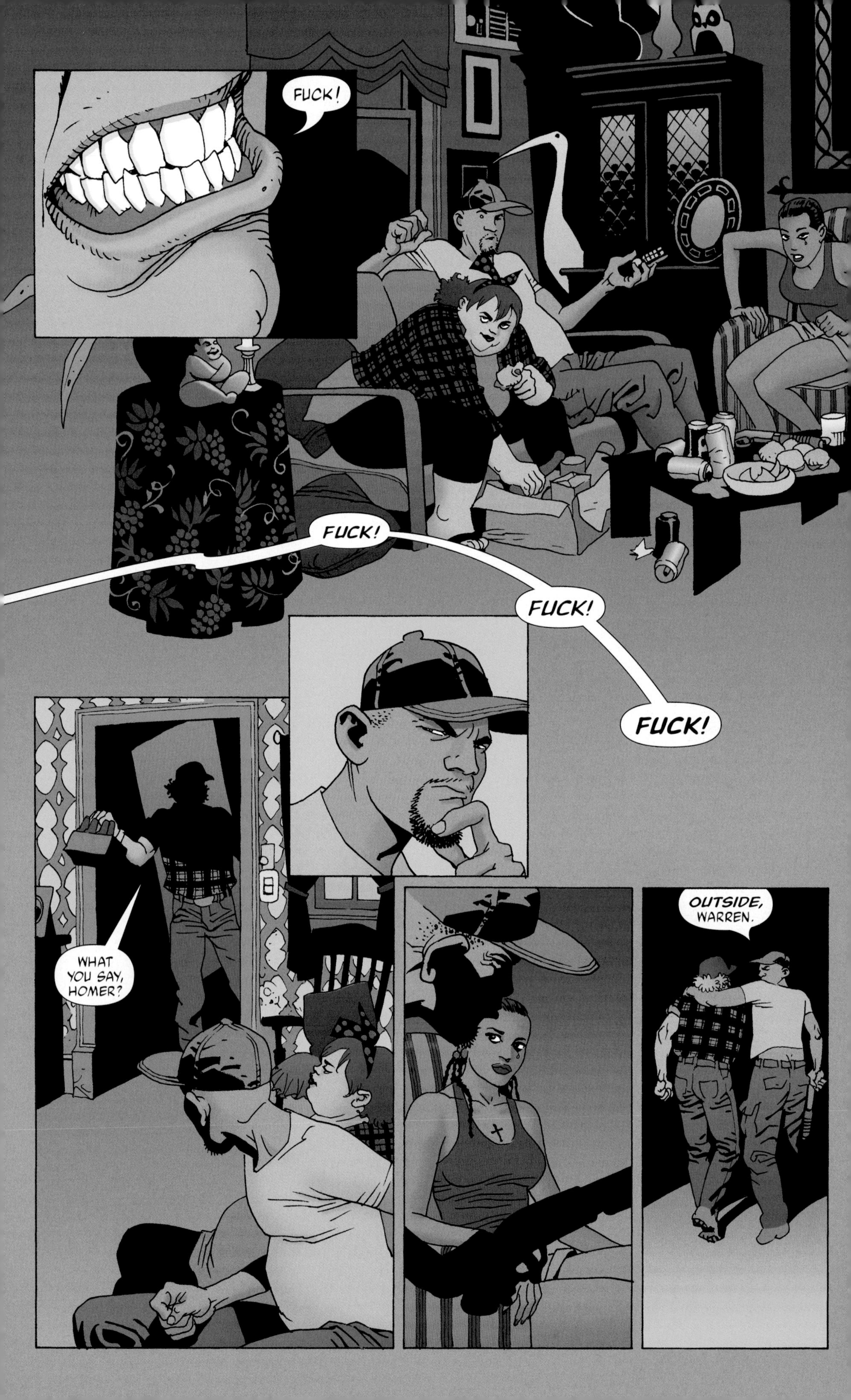

FUCK!
FUCK!
FUCK!
FUCK!
WHAT YOU SAY, HOMER?
OUTSIDE, WARREN.

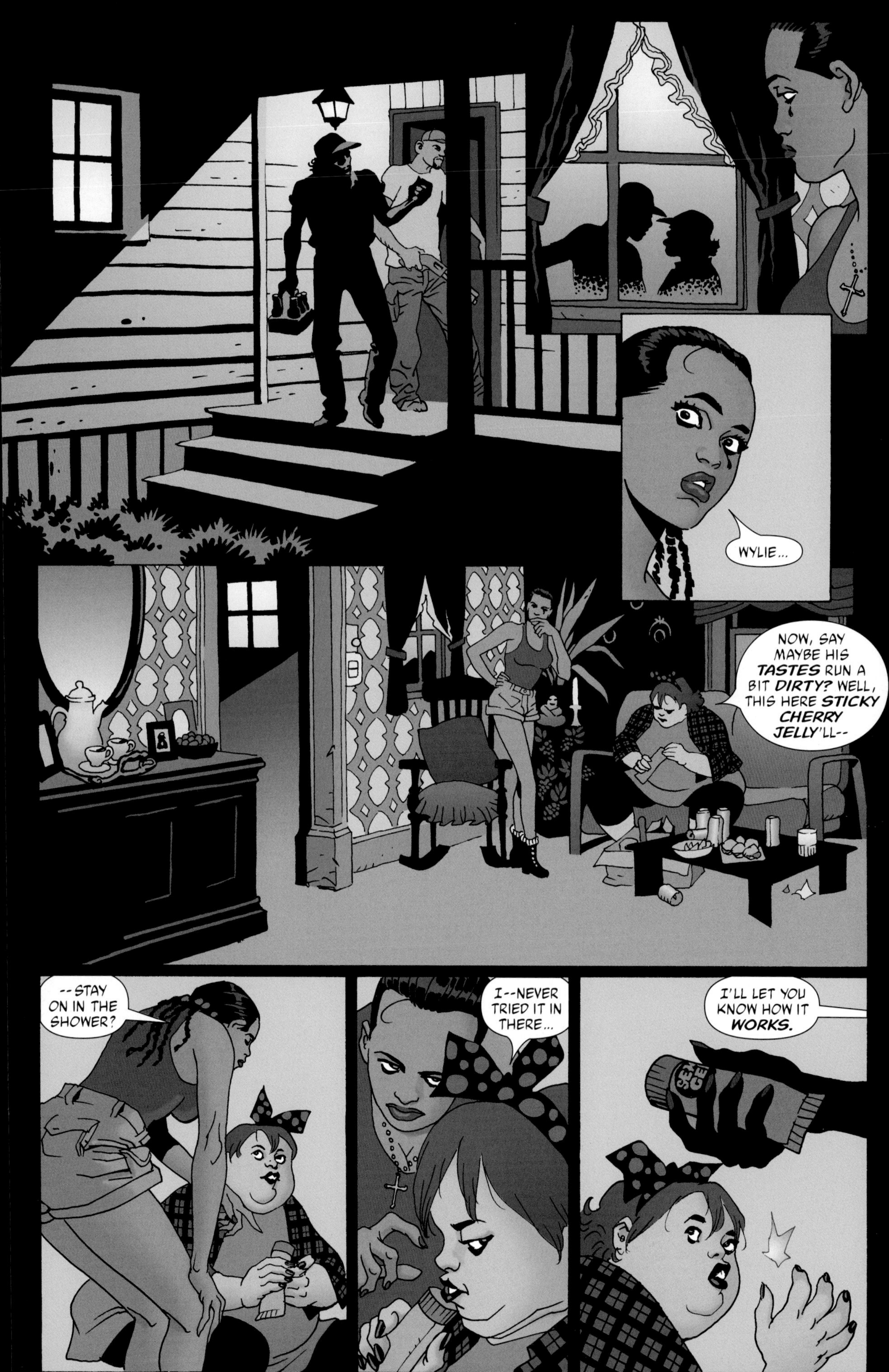
WYLIE...
NOW, SAY MAYBE HIS ***TASTES*** RUN A BIT ***DIRTY?*** WELL, THIS HERE ***STICKY CHERRY JELLY***'LL--
--STAY ON IN THE SHOWER?
I--NEVER TRIED IT IN THERE...
I'LL LET YOU KNOW HOW IT ***WORKS.***

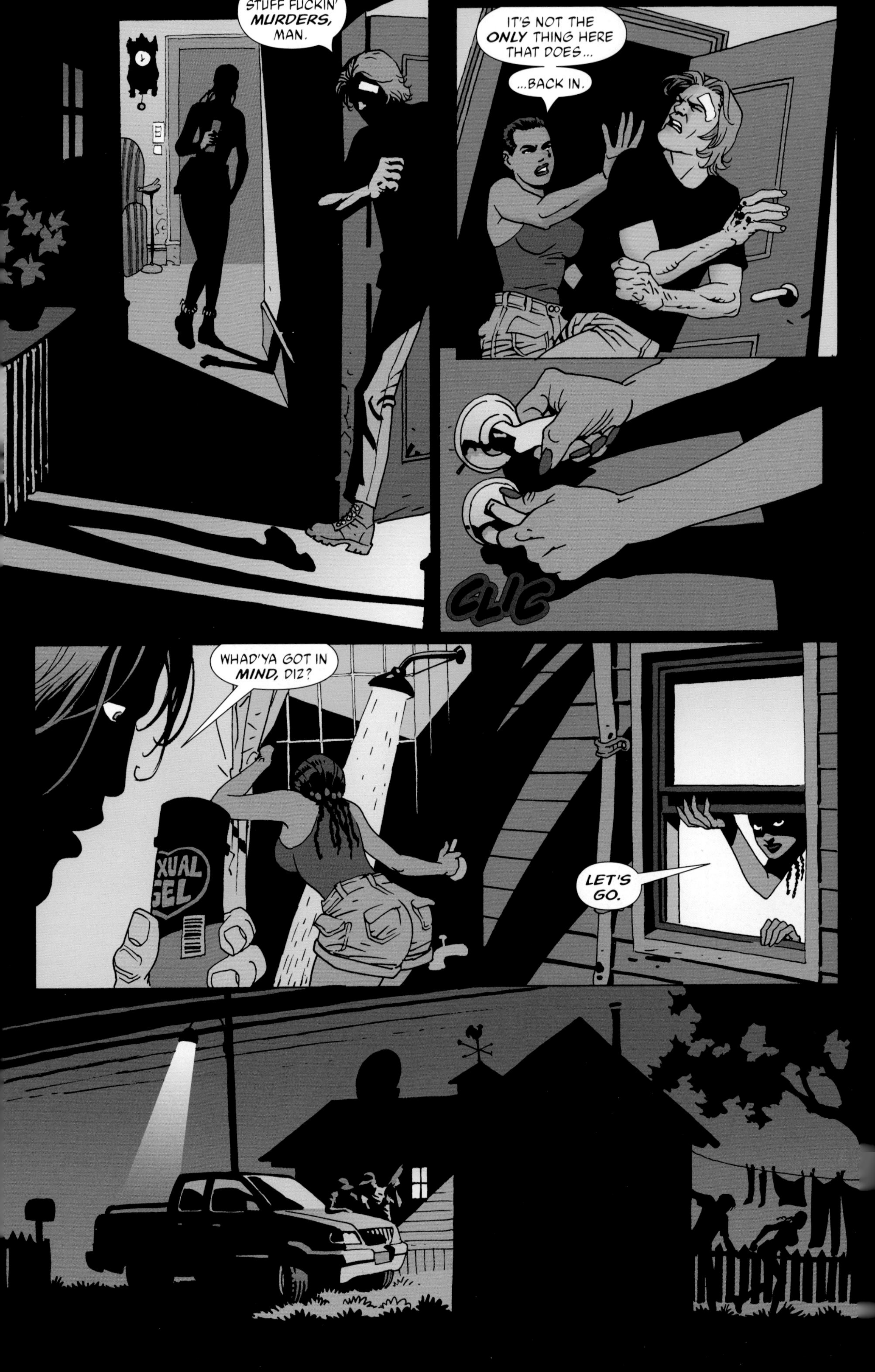
THAT STUFF FUCKIN' MURDERS, MAN.
IT'S NOT THE ONLY THING HERE THAT DOES...
...BACK IN.
CLIC
WHAD'YA GOT IN MIND, DIZ?
XUAL GEL
LET'S GO.

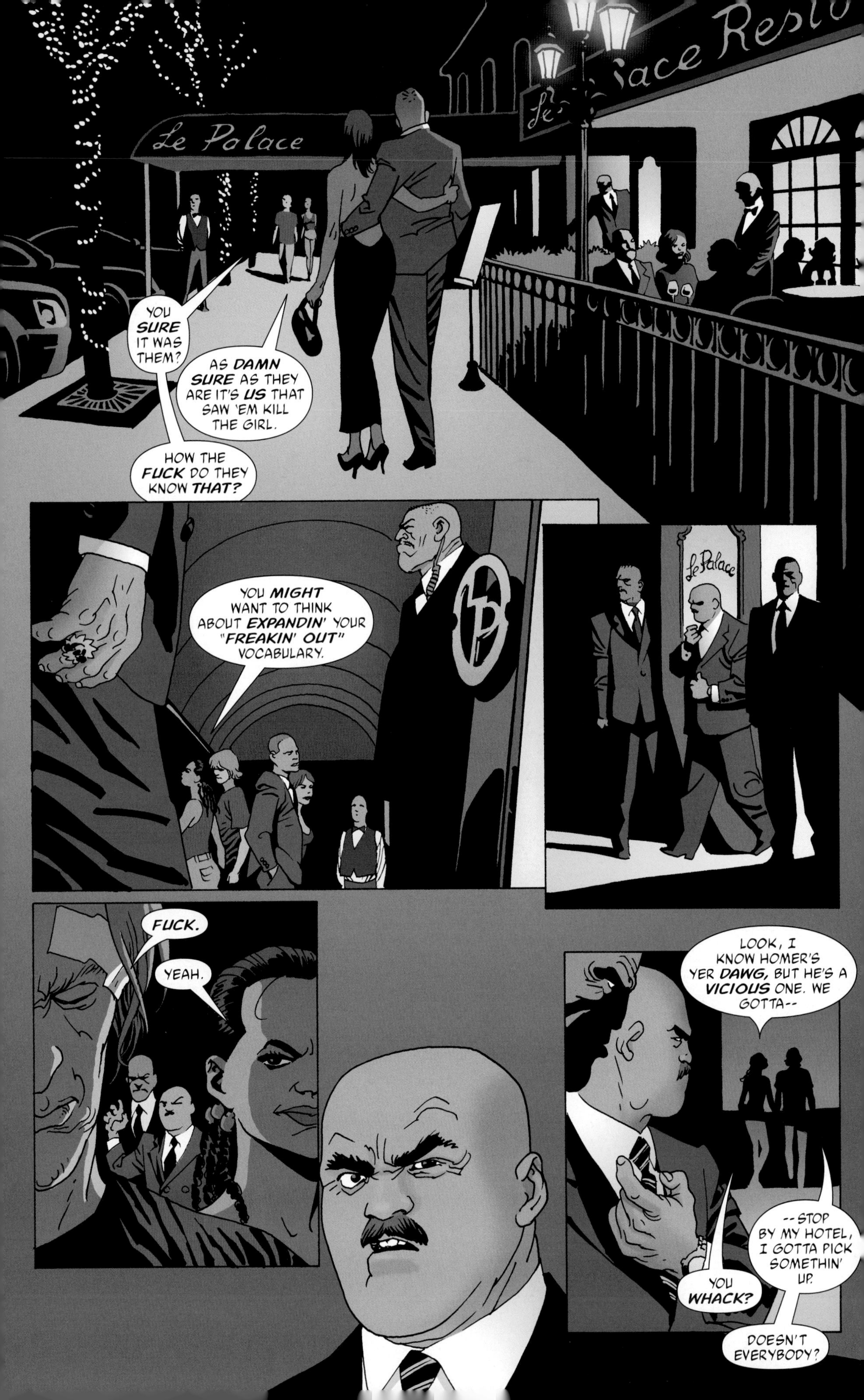

Le Palace
Le Palace Resto
YOU SURE IT WAS THEM?
AS DAMN SURE AS THEY ARE IT'S US THAT SAW 'EM KILL THE GIRL.
HOW THE FUCK DO THEY KNOW THAT?
YOU MIGHT WANT TO THINK ABOUT EXPANDIN' YOUR "FREAKIN' OUT" VOCABULARY.
Le Palace
FUCK.
YEAH.
LOOK, I KNOW HOMER'S YER DAWG, BUT HE'S A VICIOUS ONE. WE GOTTA--
--STOP BY MY HOTEL, I GOTTA PICK SOMETHIN' UP.
YOU WHACK?
DOESN'T EVERYBODY?

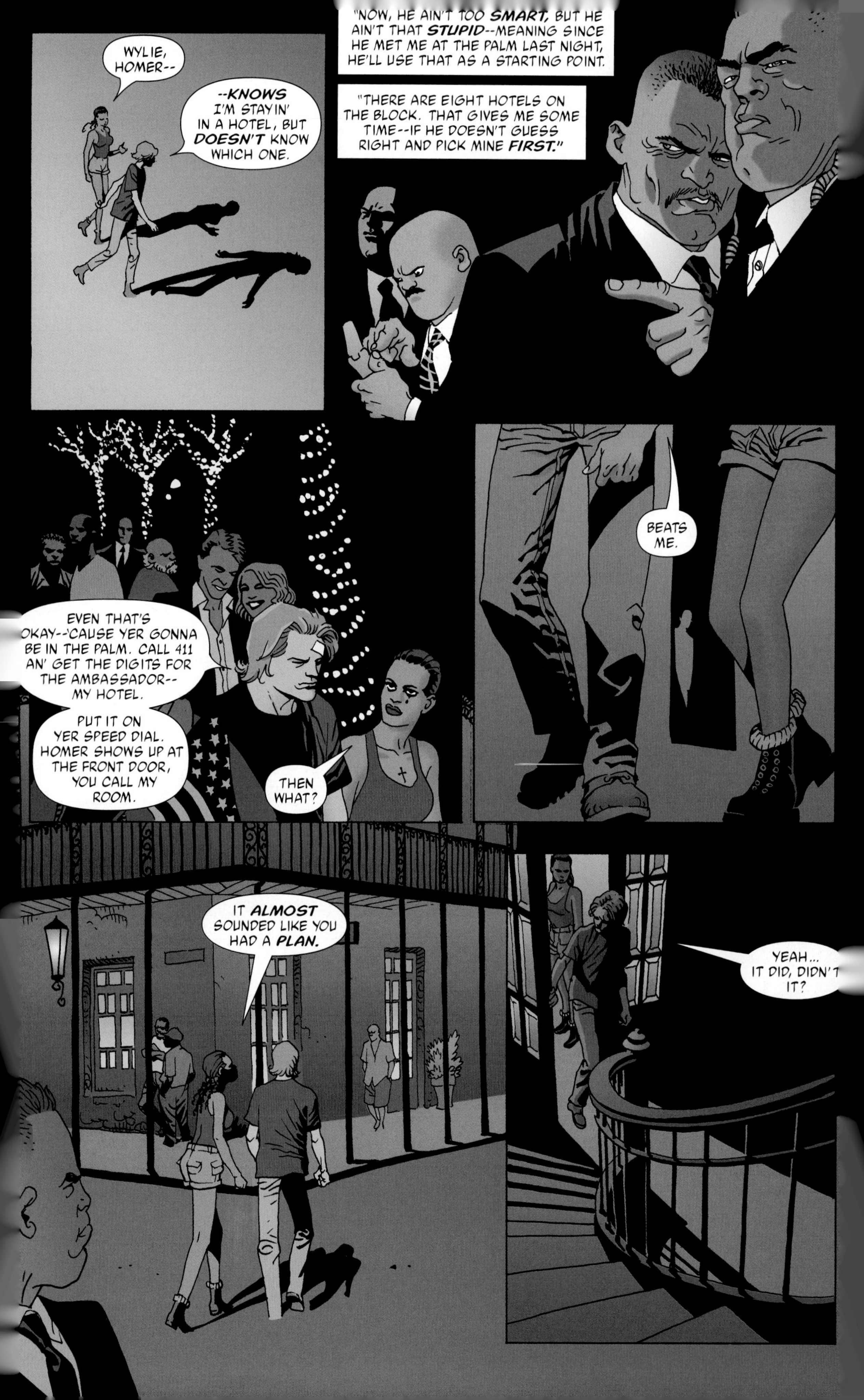
WYLIE, HOMER--
--KNOWS I'M STAYIN' IN A HOTEL, BUT DOESN'T KNOW WHICH ONE.
"NOW, HE AIN'T TOO SMART, BUT HE AIN'T THAT STUPID--MEANING SINCE HE MET ME AT THE PALM LAST NIGHT, HE'LL USE THAT AS A STARTING POINT.
"THERE ARE EIGHT HOTELS ON THE BLOCK. THAT GIVES ME SOME TIME--IF HE DOESN'T GUESS RIGHT AND PICK MINE FIRST."
EVEN THAT'S OKAY--'CAUSE YER GONNA BE IN THE PALM. CALL 411 AN' GET THE DIGITS FOR THE AMBASSADOR--MY HOTEL.
PUT IT ON YER SPEED DIAL. HOMER SHOWS UP AT THE FRONT DOOR, YOU CALL MY ROOM.
THEN WHAT?
BEATS ME.
IT ALMOST SOUNDED LIKE YOU HAD A PLAN.
YEAH... IT DID, DIDN'T IT?

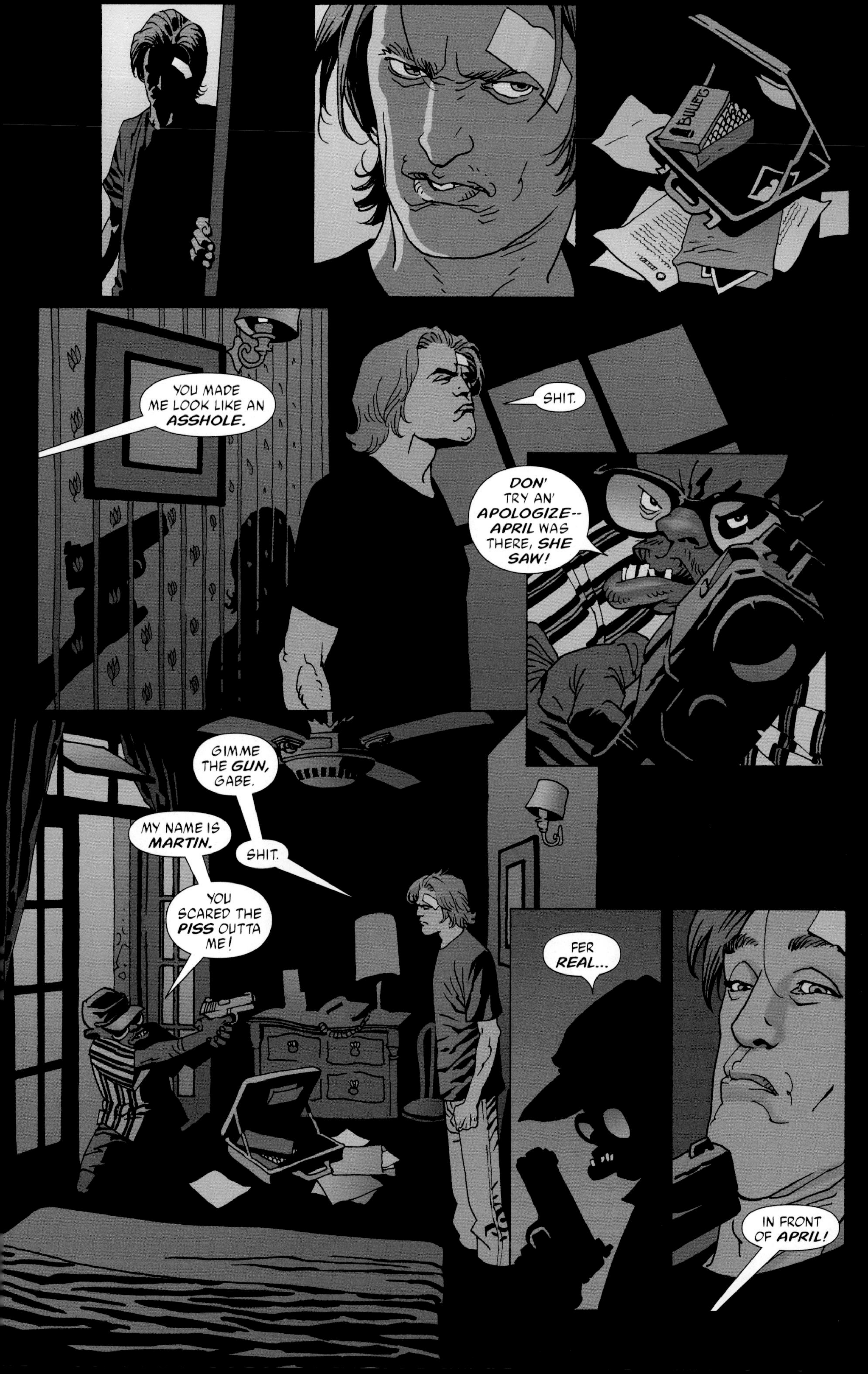
YOU MADE ME LOOK LIKE AN ASSHOLE.
SHIT.
DON' TRY AN' APOLOGIZE-- APRIL WAS THERE, SHE SAW!
GIMME THE GUN, GABE.
MY NAME IS MARTIN.
SHIT.
YOU SCARED THE PISS OUTTA ME!
FER REAL...
IN FRONT OF APRIL!

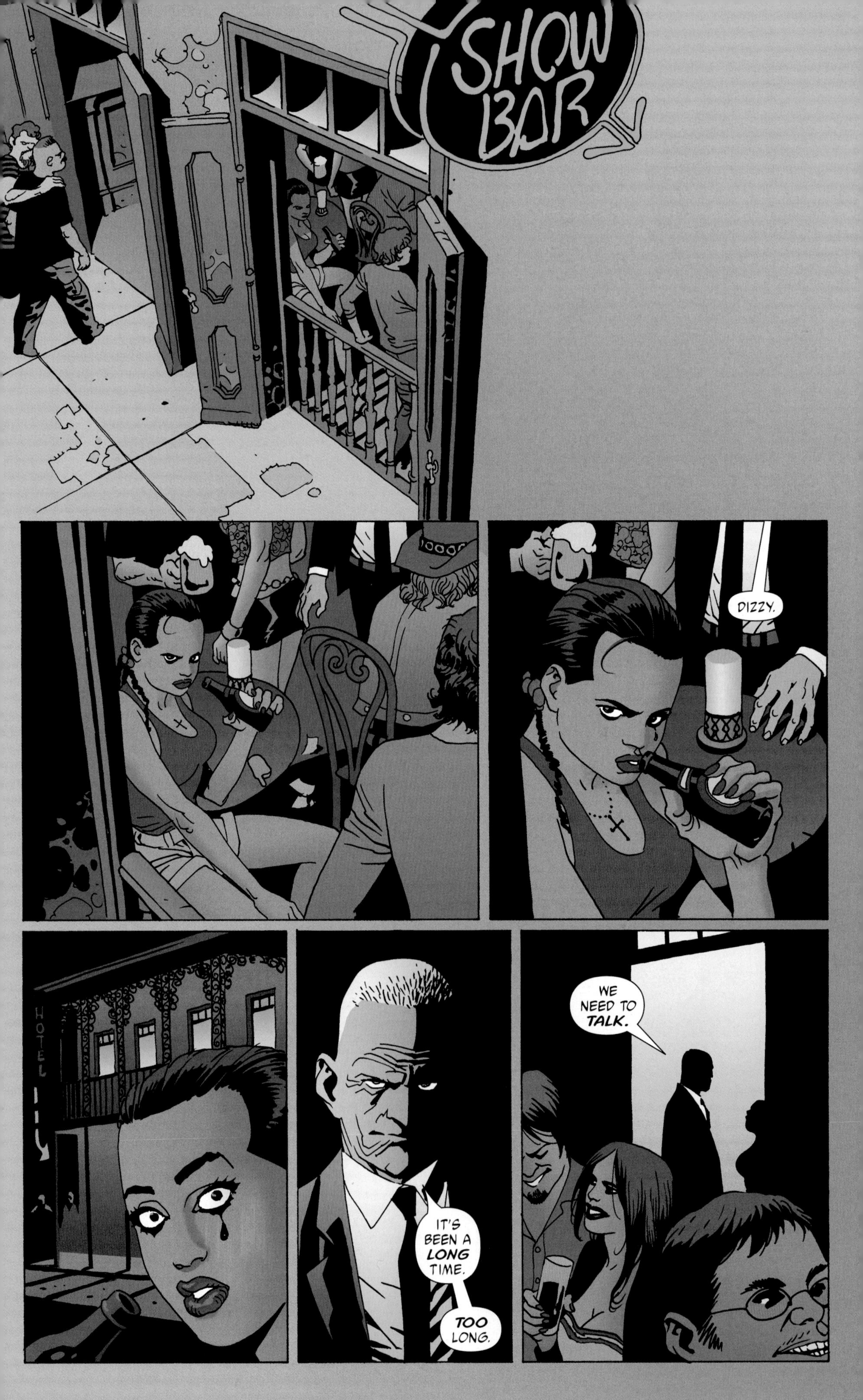
SHOW BAR
DIZZY.
HOTEL
IT'S BEEN A LONG TIME.
TOO LONG.
WE NEED TO TALK.

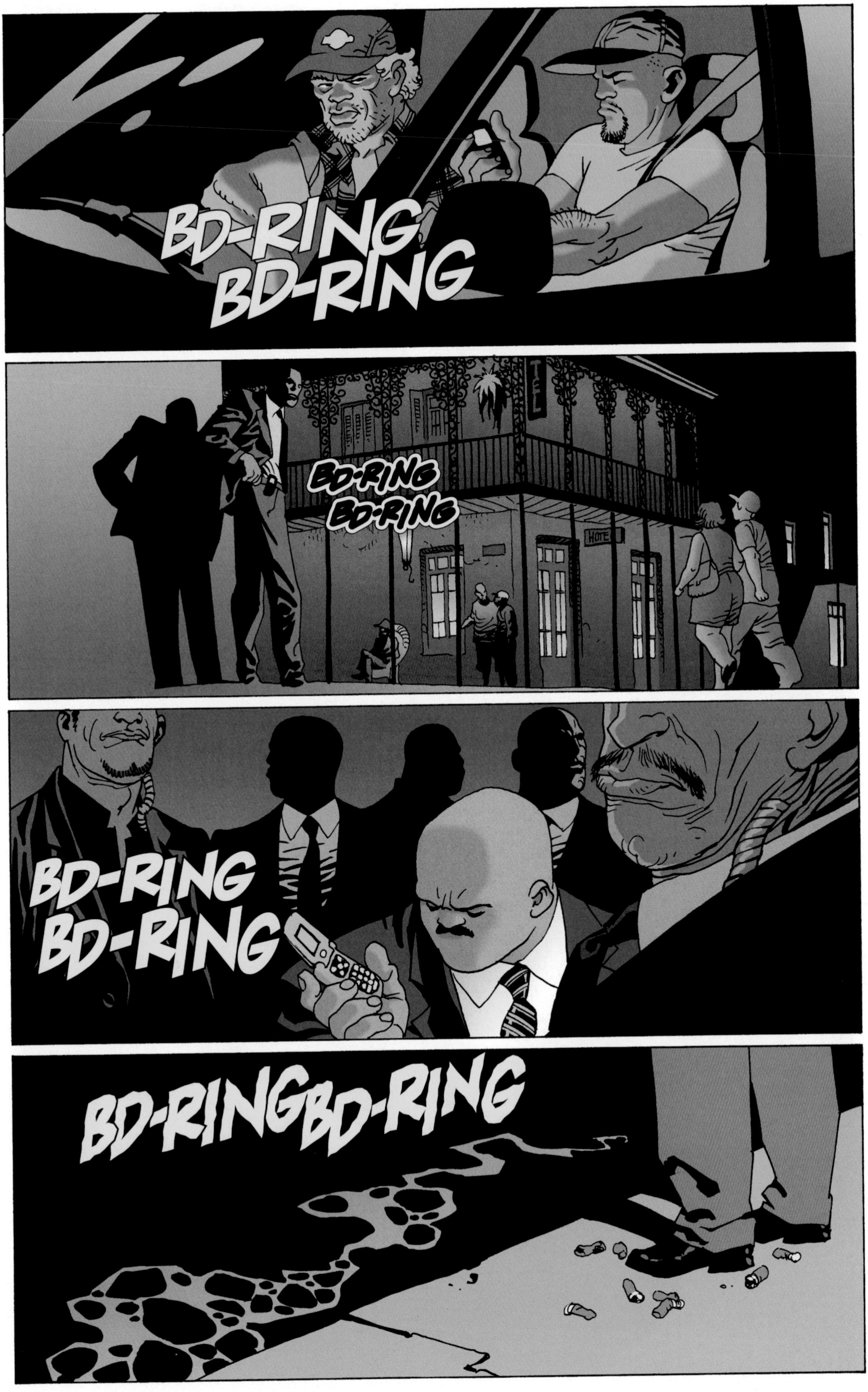
BD-RING
BD-RING
BD-RING
BD-RING
BD-RING
BD-RING
BD-RINGBD-RING

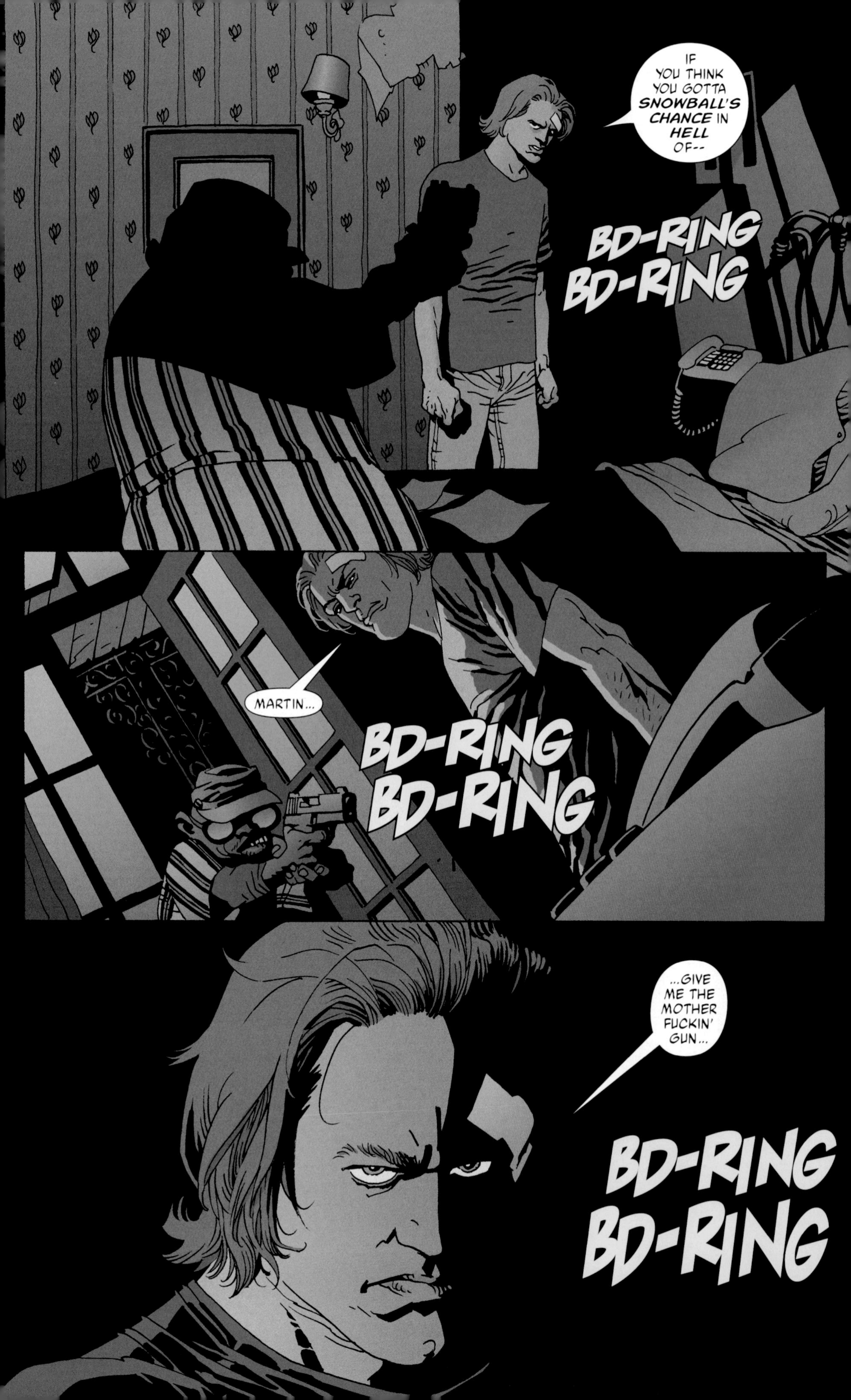
IF YOU THINK YOU GOTTA SNOWBALL'S CHANCE IN HELL OF--
BD-RING BD-RING
MARTIN...
BD-RING BD-RING
...GIVE ME THE MOTHER FUCKIN' GUN...
BD-RING BD-RING

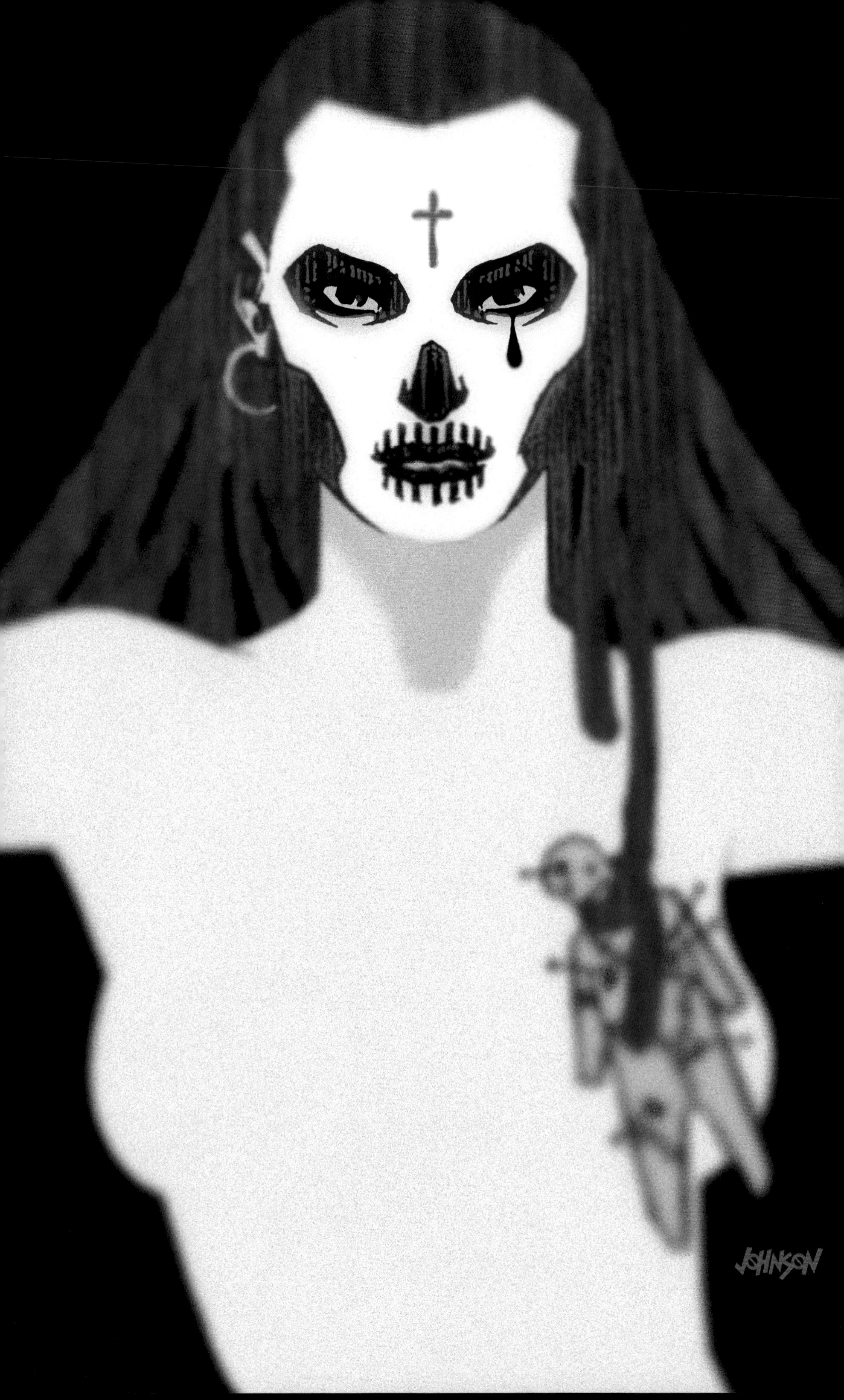
JOHNSON

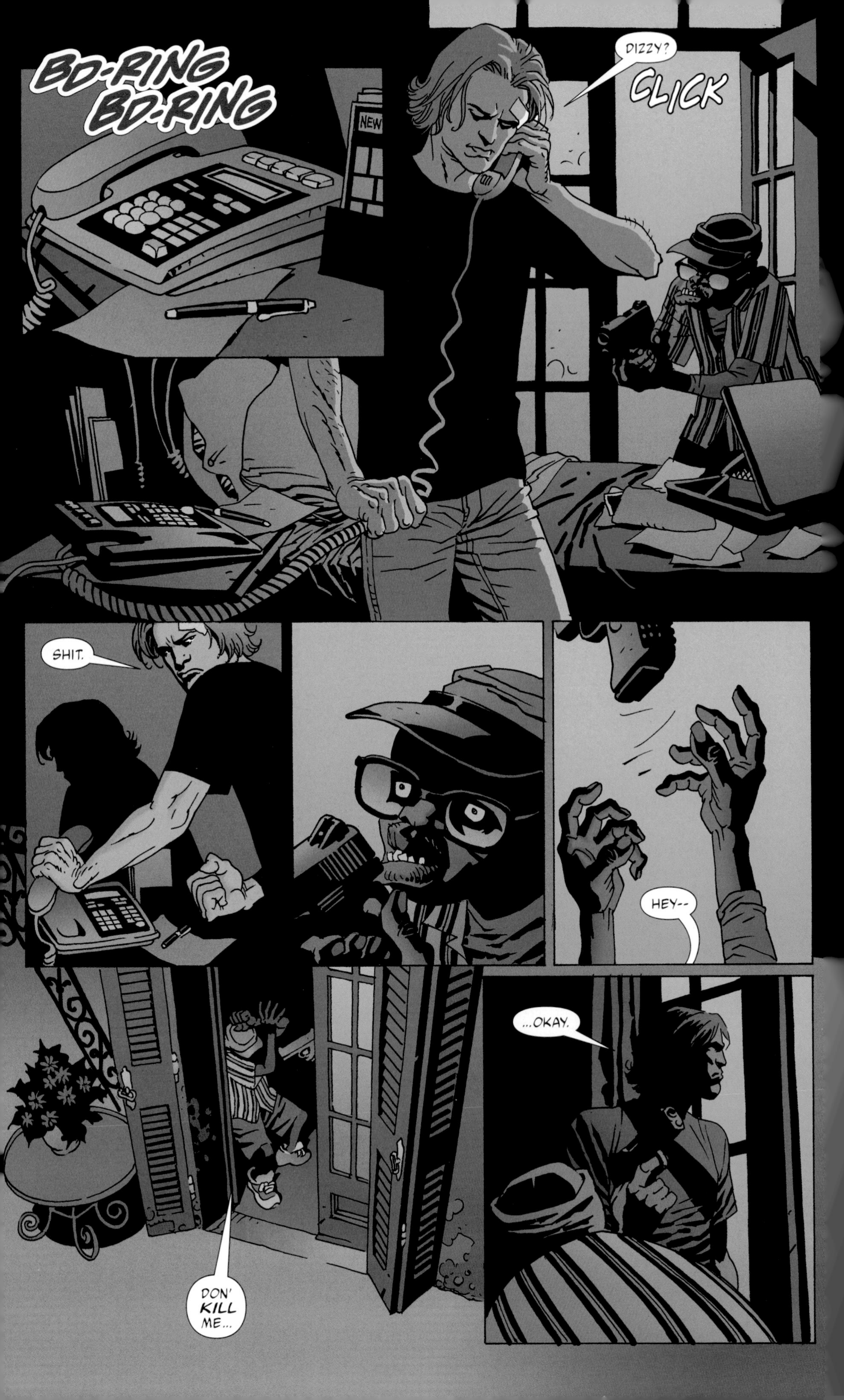
BD-RING
BD-RING
DIZZY?
CLICK
SHIT.
HEY--
DON' KILL ME...
...OKAY.

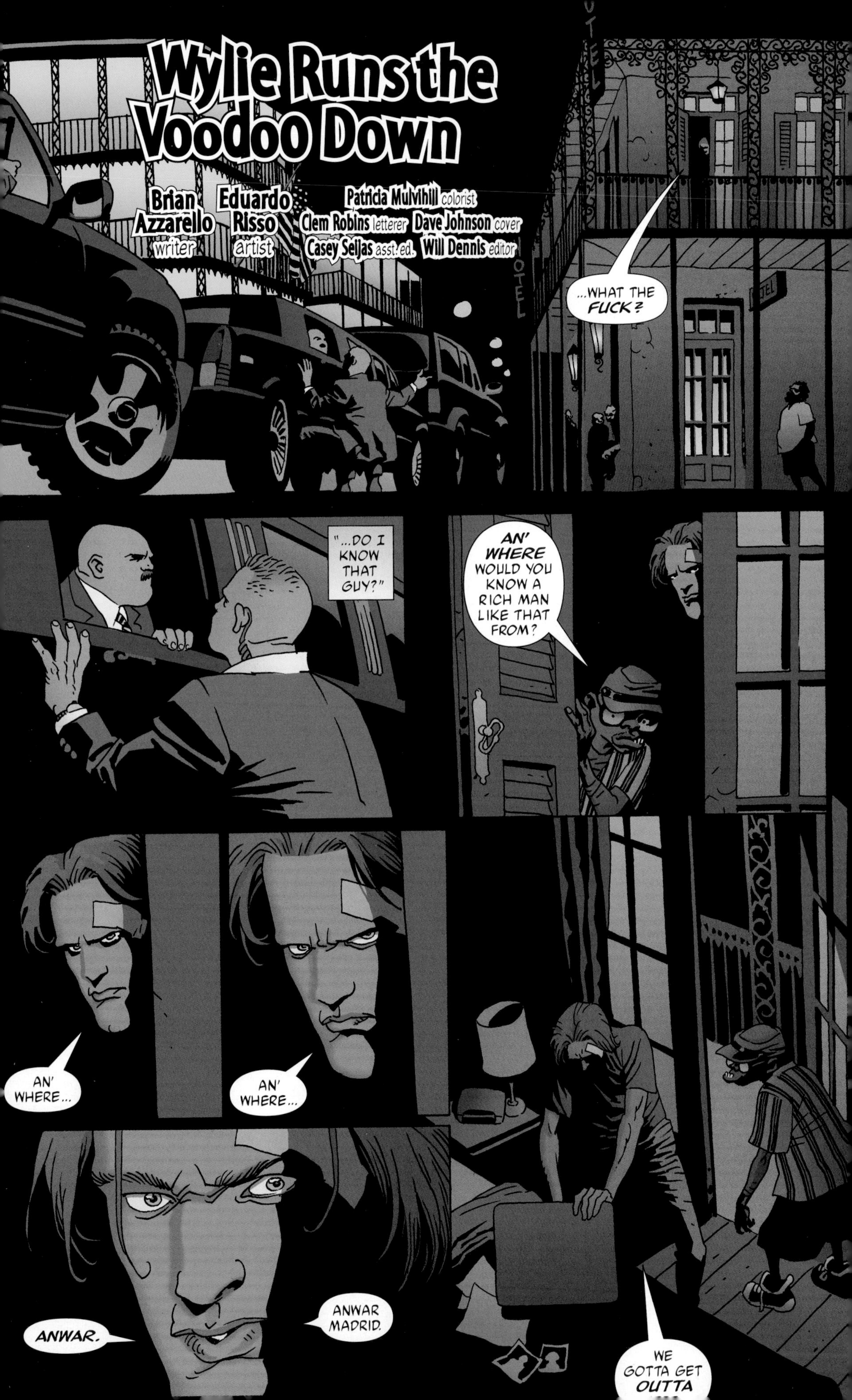
Wylie Runs the Voodoo Down
Brian Azzarello writer
Eduardo Risso artist
Patricia Mulvihill colorist
Clem Robins letterer
Dave Johnson cover
Casey Seijas asst. ed.
Will Dennis editor
...WHAT THE FUCK?
"...DO I KNOW THAT GUY?"
AN' WHERE WOULD YOU KNOW A RICH MAN LIKE THAT FROM?
AN' WHERE...
AN' WHERE...
ANWAR.
ANWAR MADRID.
WE GOTTA GET OUTTA

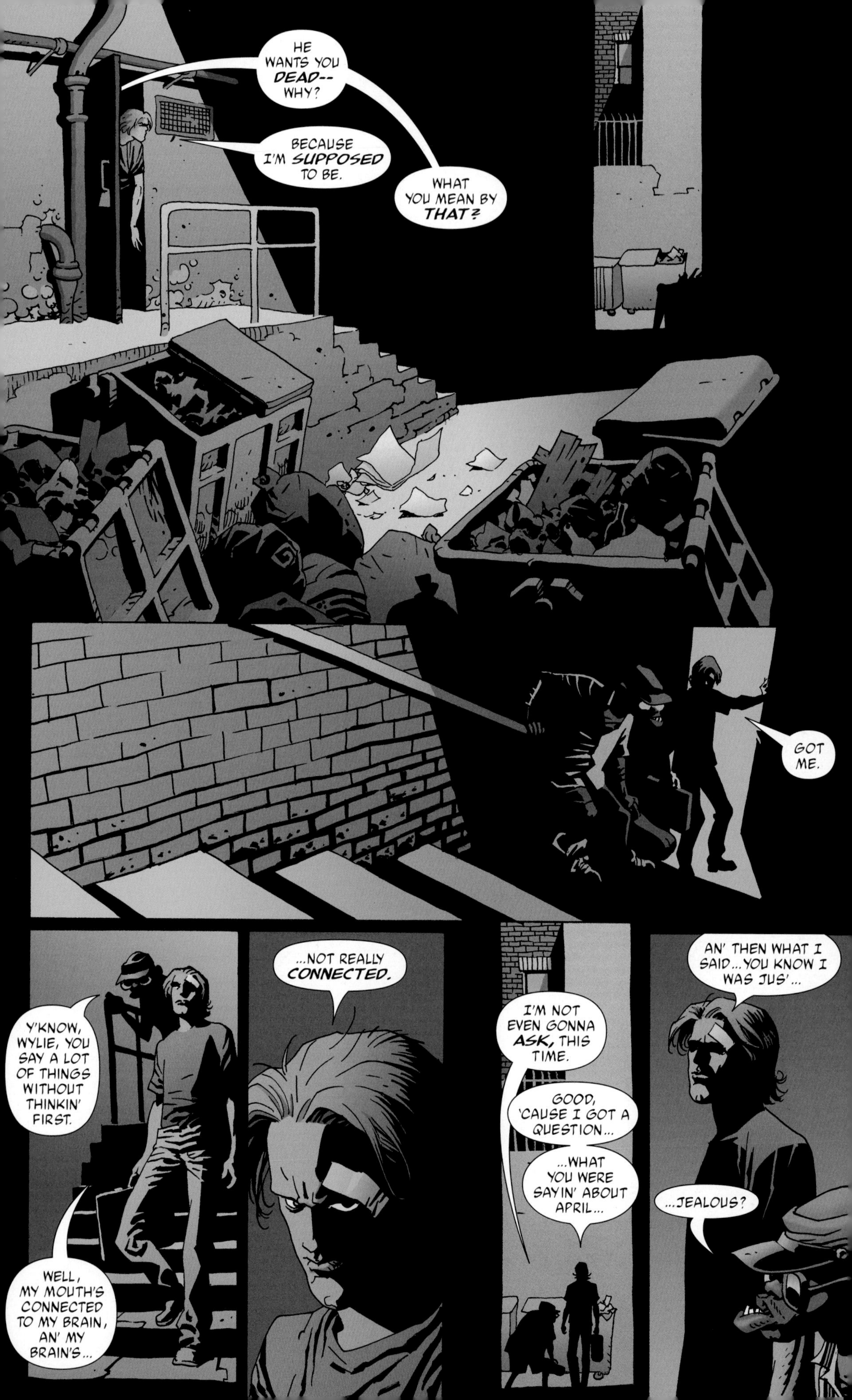
HE WANTS YOU DEAD-- WHY?
BECAUSE I'M SUPPOSED TO BE.
WHAT YOU MEAN BY THAT?
GOT ME.
Y'KNOW, WYLIE, YOU SAY A LOT OF THINGS WITHOUT THINKIN' FIRST.
WELL, MY MOUTH'S CONNECTED TO MY BRAIN, AN' MY BRAIN'S...
...NOT REALLY CONNECTED.
I'M NOT EVEN GONNA ASK, THIS TIME.
GOOD, 'CAUSE I GOT A QUESTION...
...WHAT YOU WERE SAYIN' ABOUT APRIL...
AN' THEN WHAT I SAID... YOU KNOW I WAS JUS'...
...JEALOUS?

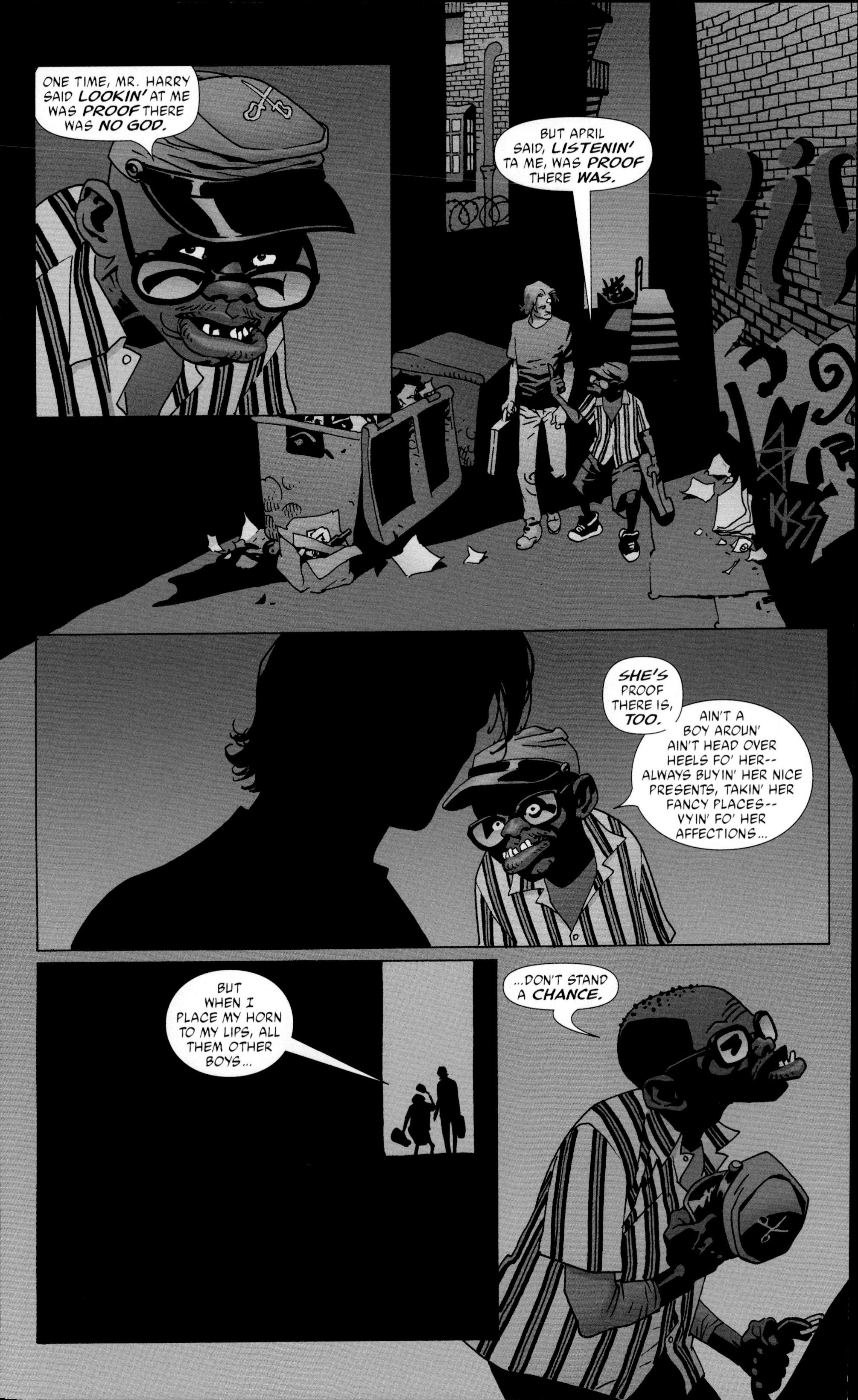
ONE TIME, MR. HARRY SAID LOOKIN' AT ME WAS PROOF THERE WAS NO GOD.
BUT APRIL SAID, LISTENIN' TA ME, WAS PROOF THERE WAS.
SHE'S PROOF THERE IS, TOO.
AIN'T A BOY AROUN' AIN'T HEAD OVER HEELS FO' HER-- ALWAYS BUYIN' HER NICE PRESENTS, TAKIN' HER FANCY PLACES-- VYIN' FO' HER AFFECTIONS...
BUT WHEN I PLACE MY HORN TO MY LIPS, ALL THEM OTHER BOYS...
...DON'T STAND A CHANCE.

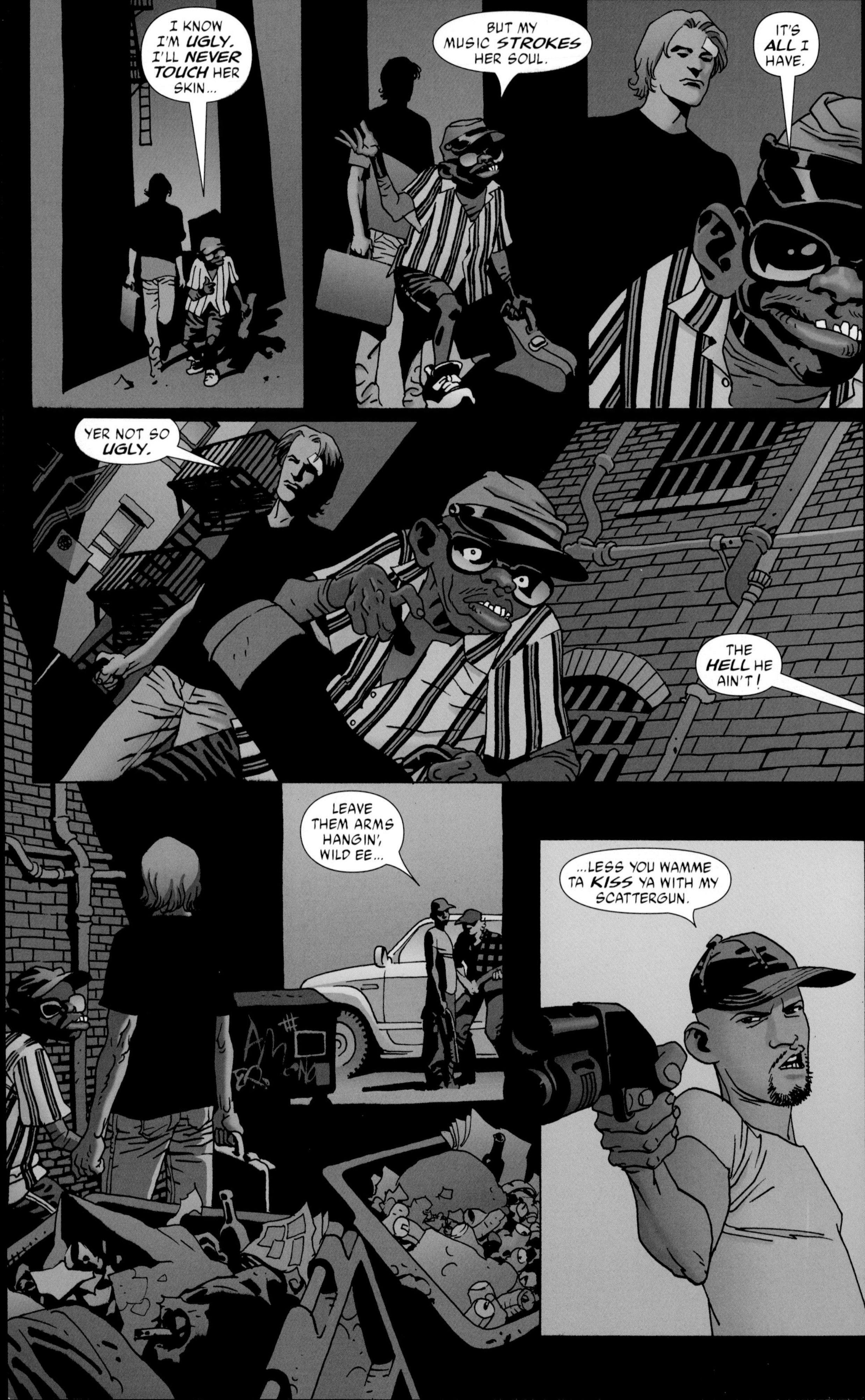

I KNOW I'M UGLY. I'LL NEVER TOUCH HER SKIN...
BUT MY MUSIC STROKES HER SOUL.
IT'S ALL I HAVE.
YER NOT SO UGLY.
THE HELL HE AIN'T!
LEAVE THEM ARMS HANGIN', WILD EE...
...LESS YOU WAMME TA KISS YA WITH MY SCATTERGUN.

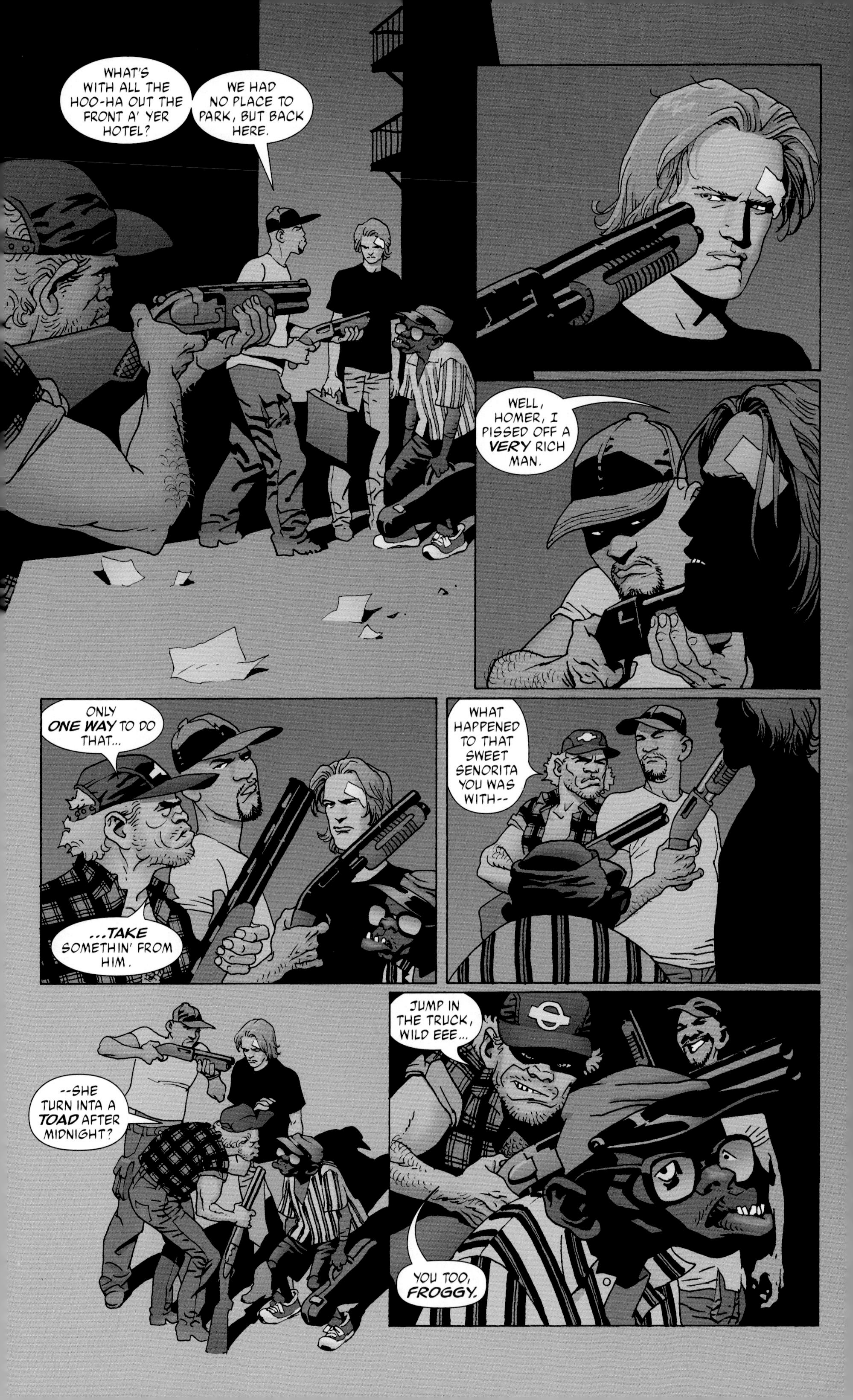
WHAT'S WITH ALL THE HOO-HA OUT THE FRONT A' YER HOTEL?
WE HAD NO PLACE TO PARK, BUT BACK HERE.
WELL, HOMER, I PISSED OFF A VERY RICH MAN.
ONLY ONE WAY TO DO THAT...
...TAKE SOMETHIN' FROM HIM.
WHAT HAPPENED TO THAT SWEET SENORITA YOU WAS WITH--
--SHE TURN INTA A TOAD AFTER MIDNIGHT?
JUMP IN THE TRUCK, WILD EEE...
YOU TOO, FROGGY.

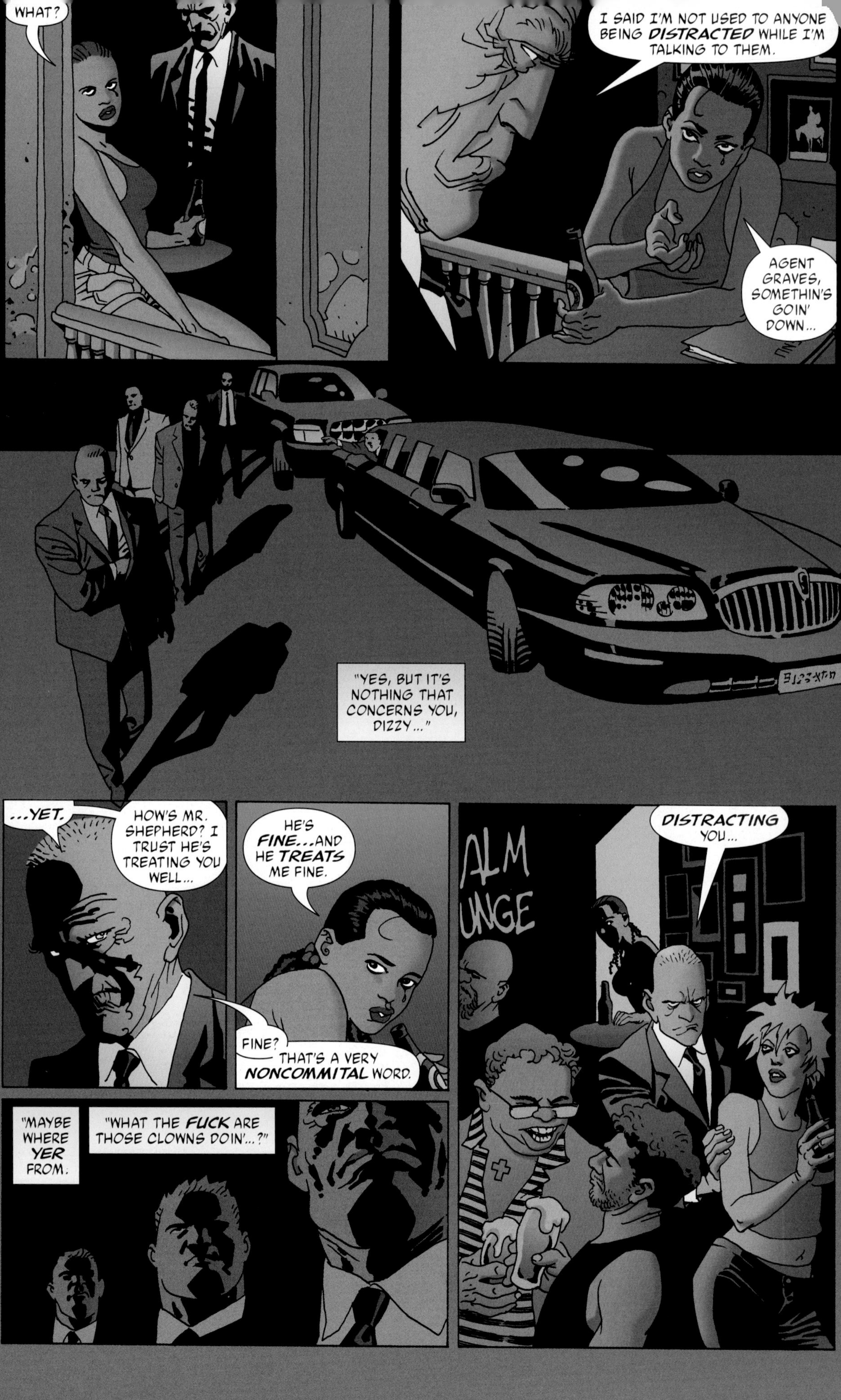
WHAT?
I SAID I'M NOT USED TO ANYONE BEING DISTRACTED WHILE I'M TALKING TO THEM.
AGENT GRAVES, SOMETHIN'S GOIN' DOWN...
"YES, BUT IT'S NOTHING THAT CONCERNS YOU, DIZZY..."
...YET.
HOW'S MR. SHEPHERD? I TRUST HE'S TREATING YOU WELL...
HE'S FINE...AND HE TREATS ME FINE.
FINE? THAT'S A VERY NONCOMMITAL WORD.
DISTRACTING YOU...
ALM
UNGE
"MAYBE WHERE YER FROM.
"WHAT THE FUCK ARE THOSE CLOWNS DOIN'...?"

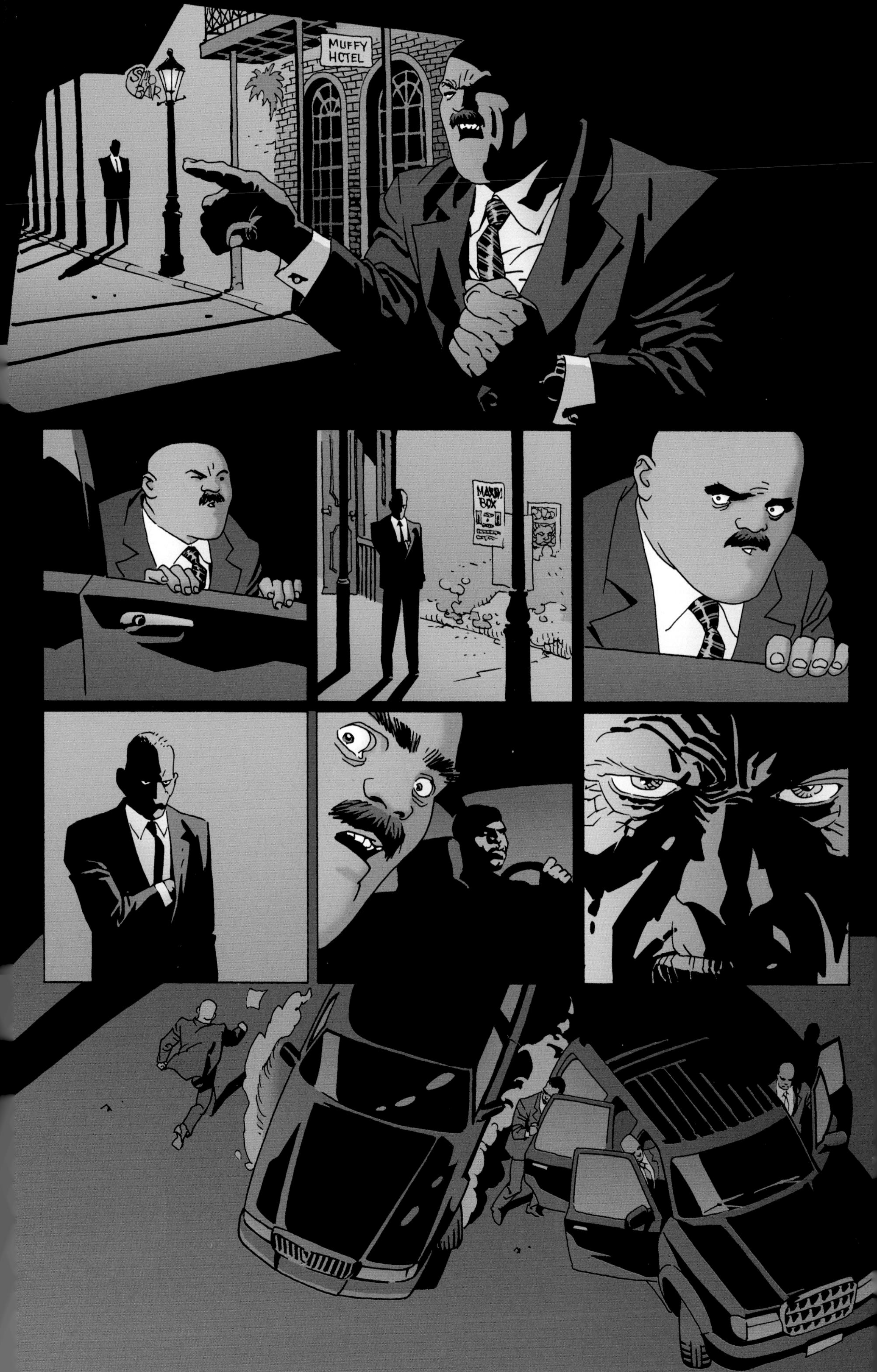
MUFFY
HOTEL
SHO
BAR

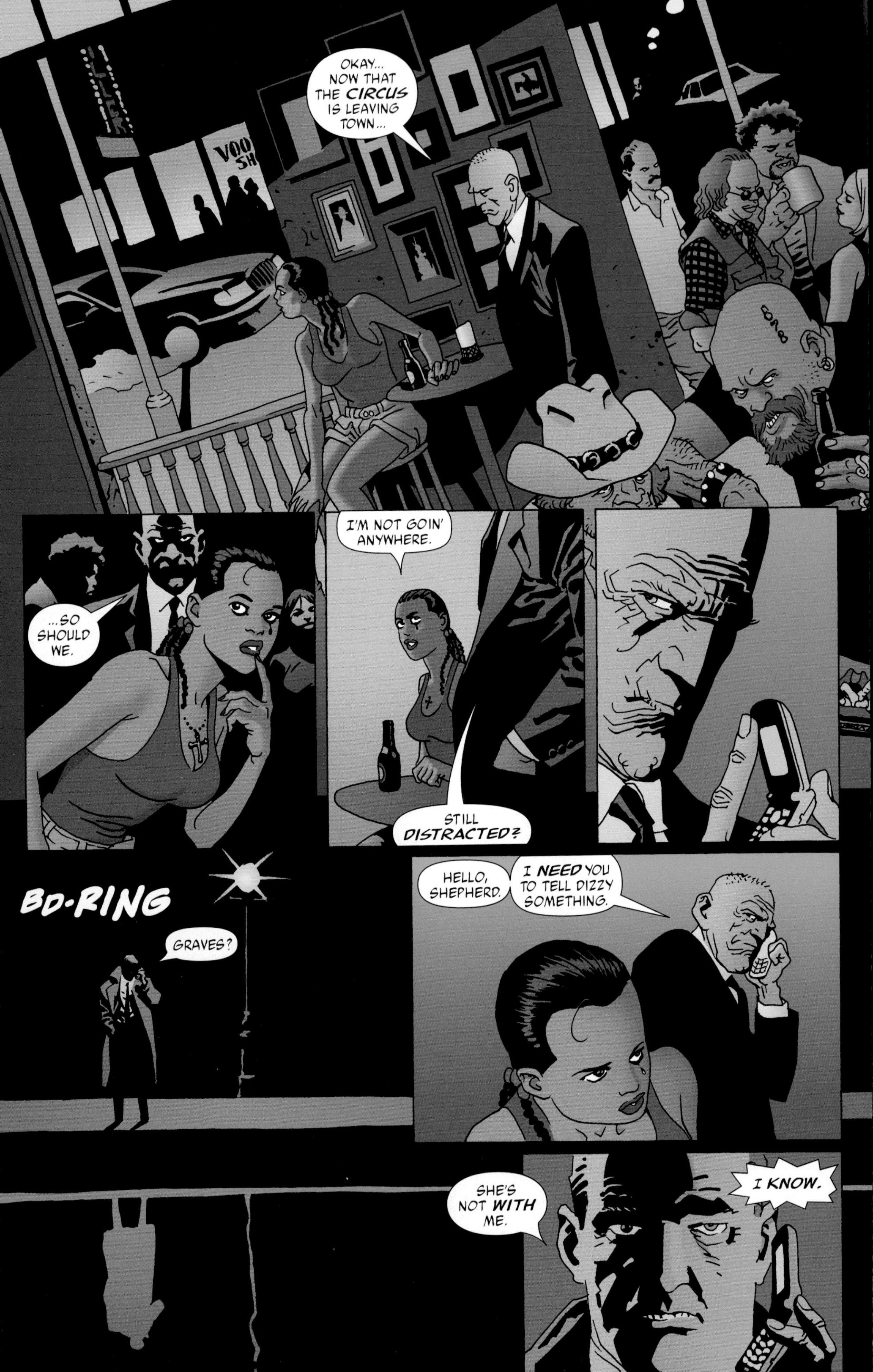

OKAY... NOW THAT THE CIRCUS IS LEAVING TOWN...
...SO SHOULD WE.
I'M NOT GOIN' ANYWHERE.
STILL DISTRACTED?
BD-RING
GRAVES?
HELLO, SHEPHERD.
I NEED YOU TO TELL DIZZY SOMETHING.
SHE'S NOT WITH ME.
I KNOW.

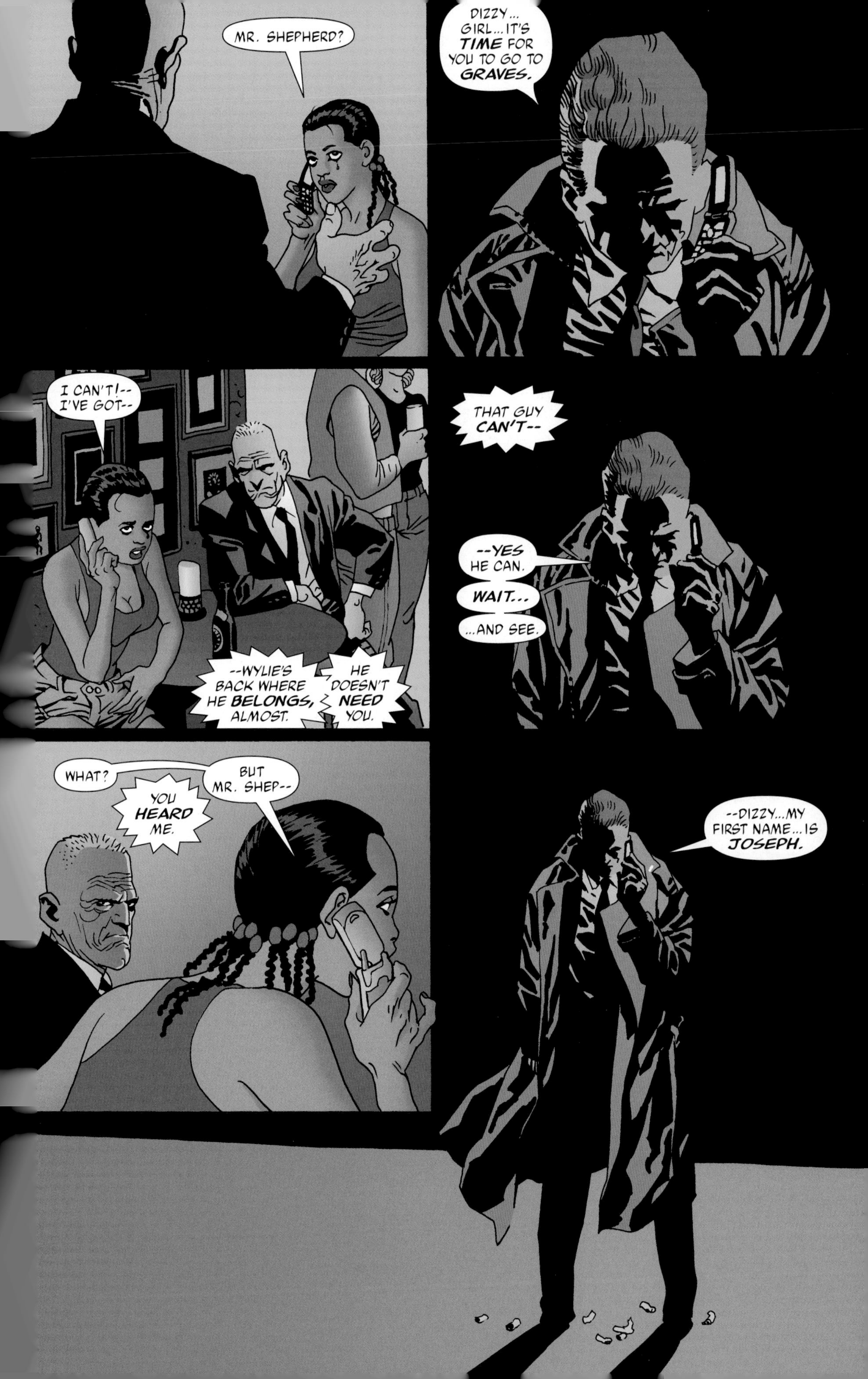
MR. SHEPHERD?
DIZZY... GIRL... IT'S TIME FOR YOU TO GO TO GRAVES.
I CAN'T!-- I'VE GOT--
--WYLIE'S BACK WHERE HE BELONGS, ALMOST.
HE DOESN'T NEED YOU.
THAT GUY CAN'T--
--YES HE CAN.
WAIT...
...AND SEE.
WHAT?
BUT MR. SHEP--
YOU HEARD ME.
--DIZZY...MY FIRST NAME...IS JOSEPH.

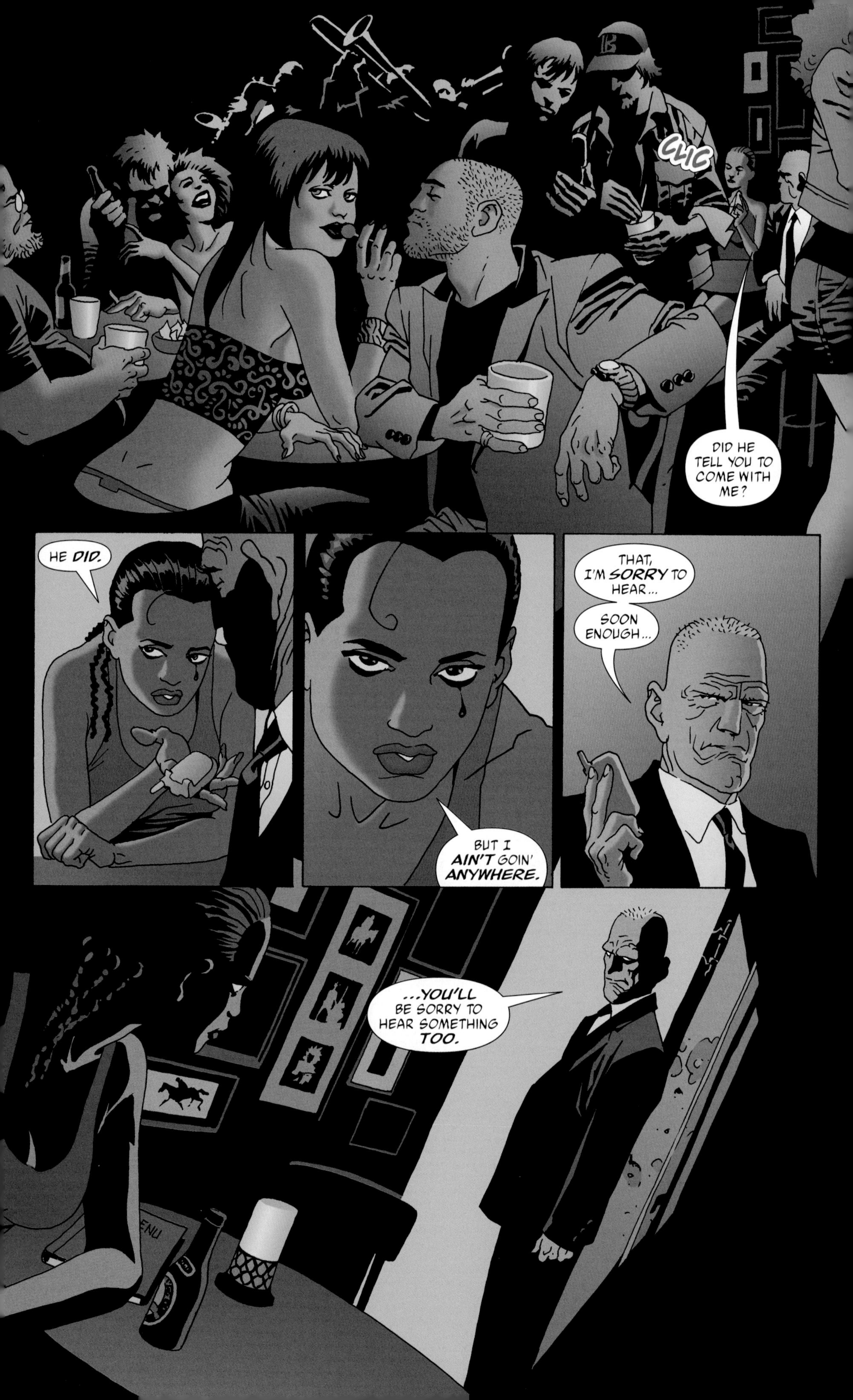
CLIC
DID HE TELL YOU TO COME WITH ME?
HE DID.
BUT I AIN'T GOIN' ANYWHERE.
THAT, I'M SORRY TO HEAR...
SOON ENOUGH...
...YOU'LL BE SORRY TO HEAR SOMETHING TOO.

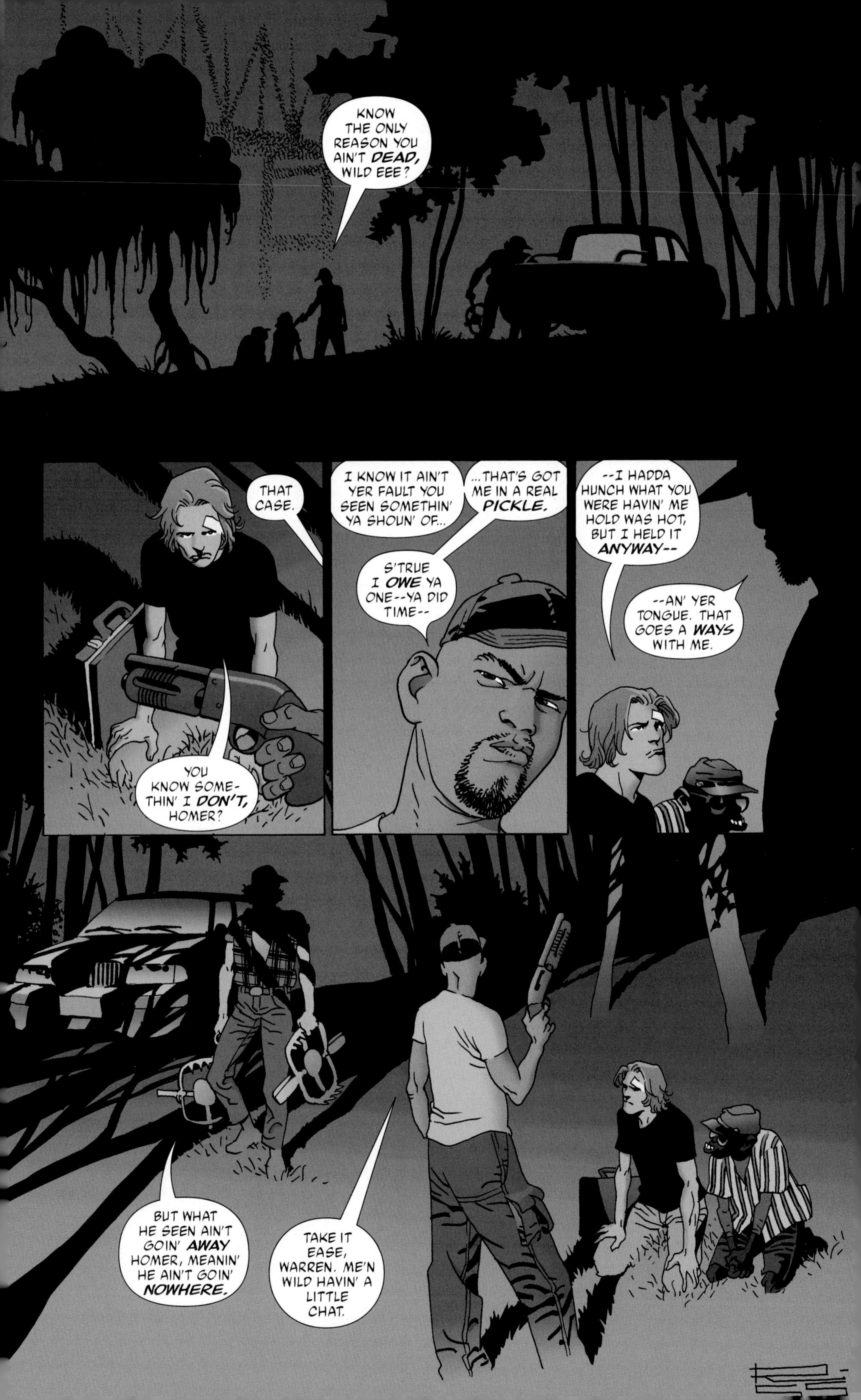
KNOW THE ONLY REASON YOU AIN'T DEAD, WILD EEE?
THAT CASE.
YOU KNOW SOME-THIN' I DON'T, HOMER?
I KNOW IT AIN'T YER FAULT YOU SEEN SOMETHIN' YA SHOUN' OF...
...THAT'S GOT ME IN A REAL PICKLE.
S'TRUE I OWE YA ONE--YA DID TIME--
--I HADDA HUNCH WHAT YOU WERE HAVIN' ME HOLD WAS HOT, BUT I HELD IT ANYWAY--
--AN' YER TONGUE. THAT GOES A WAYS WITH ME.
BUT WHAT HE SEEN AIN'T GOIN' AWAY HOMER, MEANIN' HE AIN'T GOIN' NOWHERE.
TAKE IT EASE, WARREN. ME'N WILD HAVIN' A LITTLE CHAT.

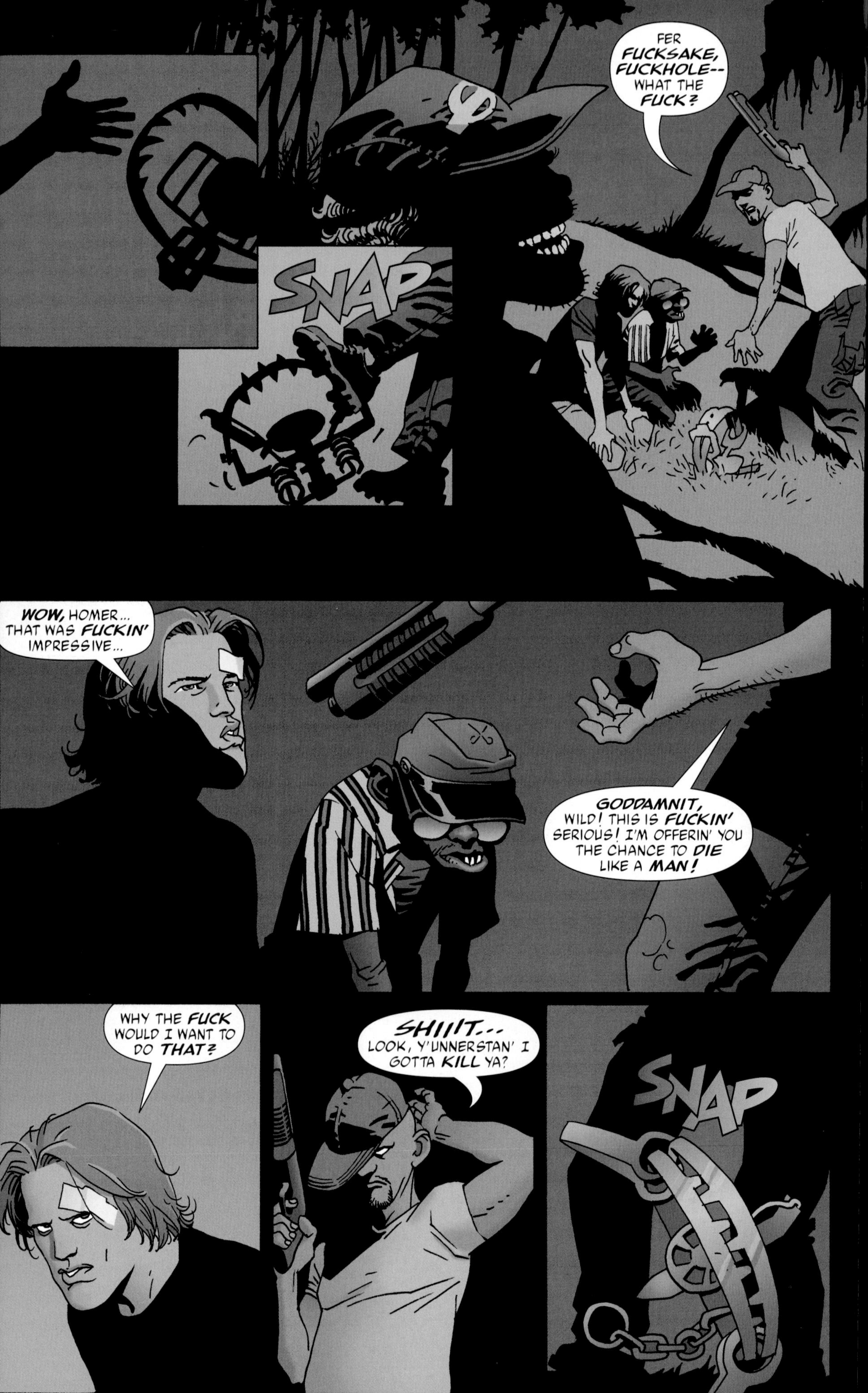
FER FUCKSAKE, FUCKHOLE-- WHAT THE FUCK?
SNAP
WOW, HOMER... THAT WAS FUCKIN' IMPRESSIVE...
GODDAMNIT, WILD! THIS IS FUCKIN' SERIOUS! I'M OFFERIN' YOU THE CHANCE TO DIE LIKE A MAN!
WHY THE FUCK WOULD I WANT TO DO THAT?
SHIIIT... LOOK, Y'UNNERSTAN' I GOTTA KILL YA?
SNAP

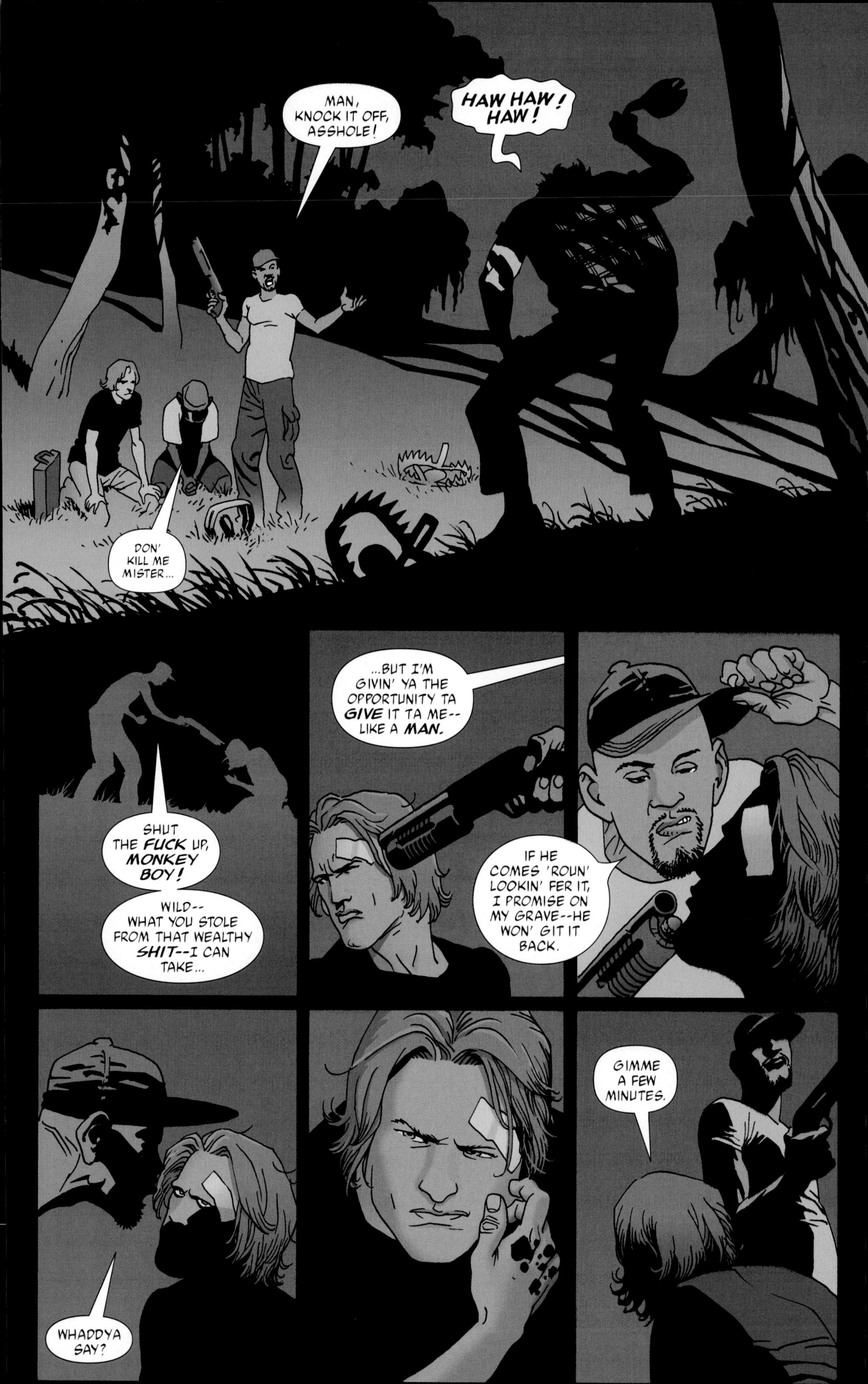
MAN, KNOCK IT OFF, ASSHOLE!
HAW HAW! HAW!
DON' KILL ME MISTER...
SHUT THE FUCK UP, MONKEY BOY!
WILD-- WHAT YOU STOLE FROM THAT WEALTHY SHIT--I CAN TAKE...
...BUT I'M GIVIN' YA THE OPPORTUNITY TA GIVE IT TA ME-- LIKE A MAN.
IF HE COMES 'ROUN' LOOKIN' FER IT, I PROMISE ON MY GRAVE--HE WON' GIT IT BACK.
WHADDYA SAY?
GIMME A FEW MINUTES.

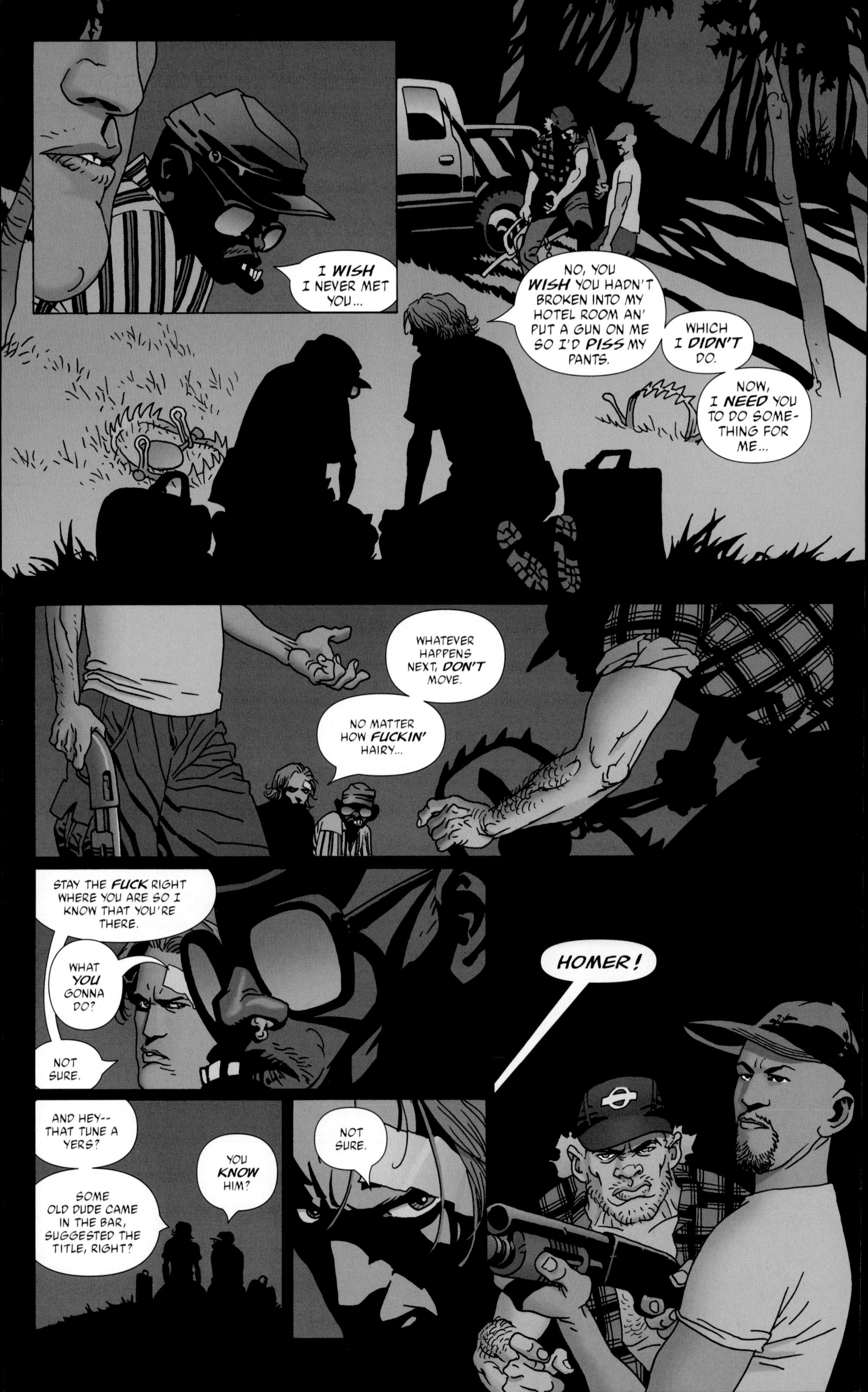

I WISH I NEVER MET YOU...
NO, YOU WISH YOU HADN'T BROKEN INTO MY HOTEL ROOM AN' PUT A GUN ON ME SO I'D PISS MY PANTS.
WHICH I DIDN'T DO.
NOW, I NEED YOU TO DO SOMETHING FOR ME...
WHATEVER HAPPENS NEXT, DON'T MOVE.
NO MATTER HOW FUCKIN' HAIRY...
STAY THE FUCK RIGHT WHERE YOU ARE SO I KNOW THAT YOU'RE THERE.
WHAT YOU GONNA DO?
NOT SURE.
HOMER!
AND HEY-- THAT TUNE A YERS?
SOME OLD DUDE CAME IN THE BAR, SUGGESTED THE TITLE, RIGHT?
YOU KNOW HIM?
NOT SURE.

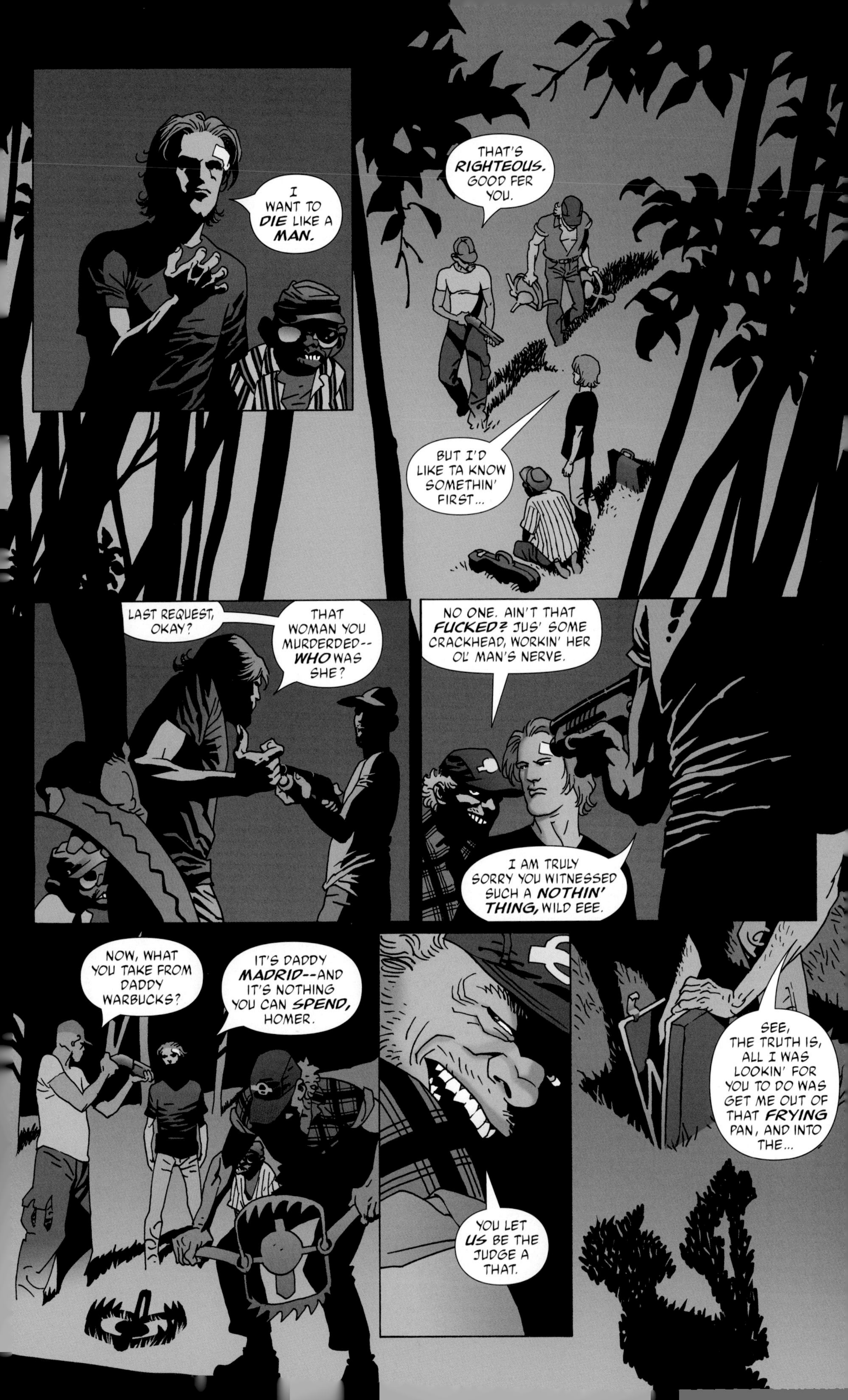
I WANT TO DIE LIKE A MAN.
THAT'S RIGHTEOUS. GOOD FER YOU.
BUT I'D LIKE TA KNOW SOMETHIN' FIRST...
LAST REQUEST, OKAY?
THAT WOMAN YOU MURDERDED-- WHO WAS SHE?
NO ONE. AIN'T THAT FUCKED? JUS' SOME CRACKHEAD, WORKIN' HER OL' MAN'S NERVE.
I AM TRULY SORRY YOU WITNESSED SUCH A NOTHIN' THING, WILD EEE.
NOW, WHAT YOU TAKE FROM DADDY WARBUCKS?
IT'S DADDY MADRID--AND IT'S NOTHING YOU CAN SPEND, HOMER.
YOU LET US BE THE JUDGE A THAT.
SEE, THE TRUTH IS, ALL I WAS LOOKIN' FOR YOU TO DO WAS GET ME OUT OF THAT FRYING PAN, AND INTO THE...

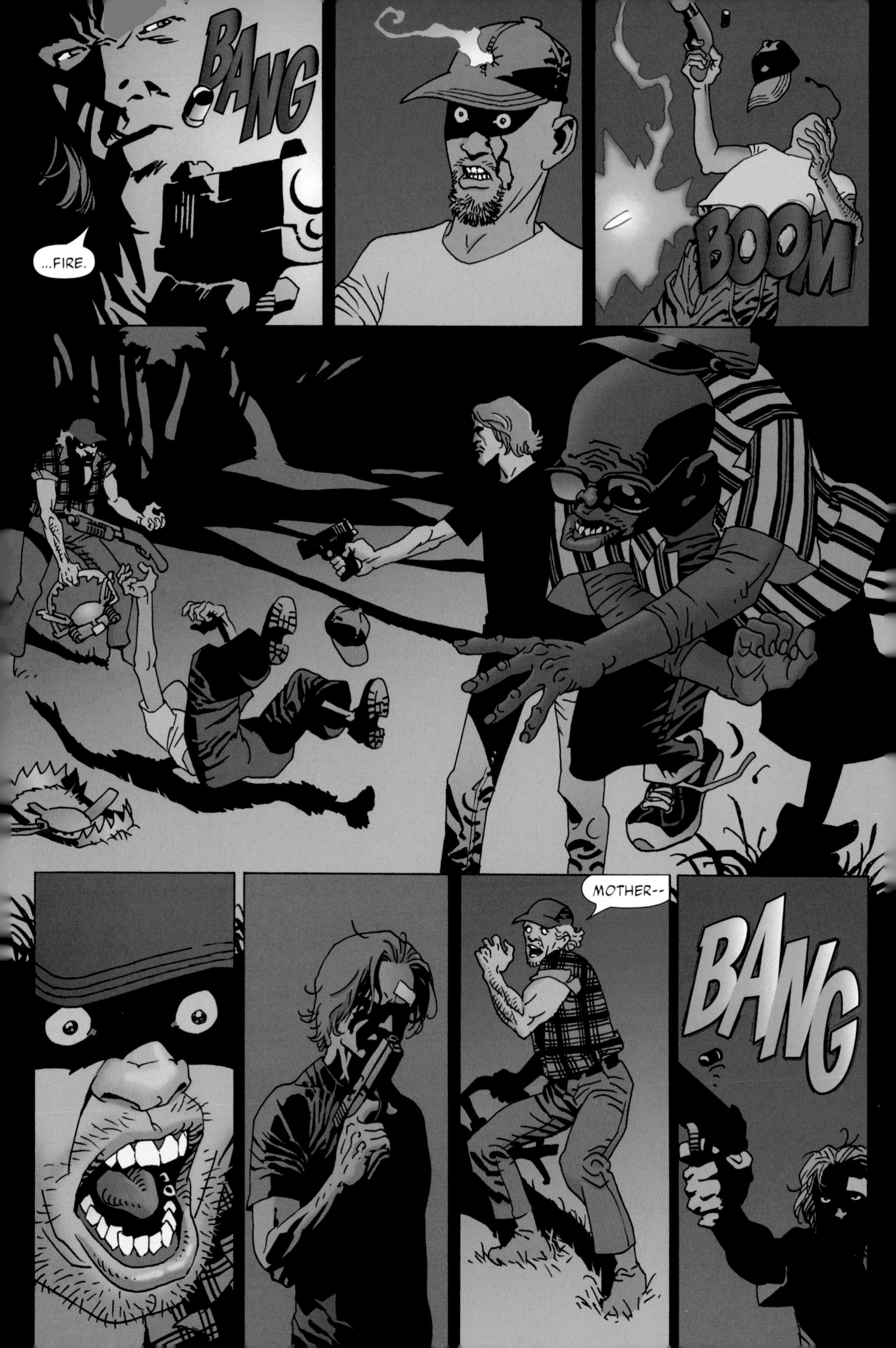
BANG
...FIRE.
BOOM
MOTHER--
BANG

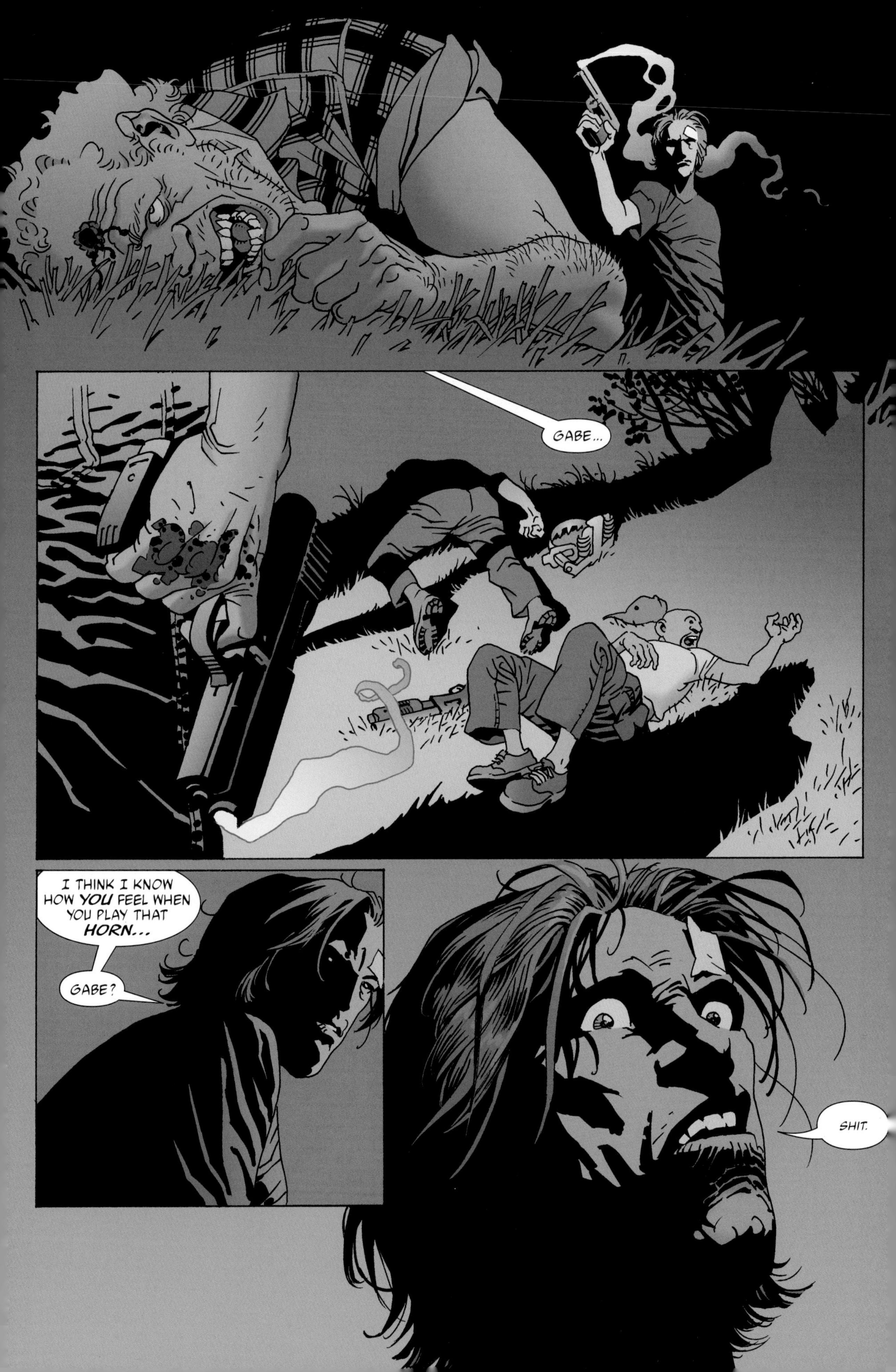
GABE...
I THINK I KNOW HOW YOU FEEL WHEN YOU PLAY THAT HORN...
GABE?
SHIT.

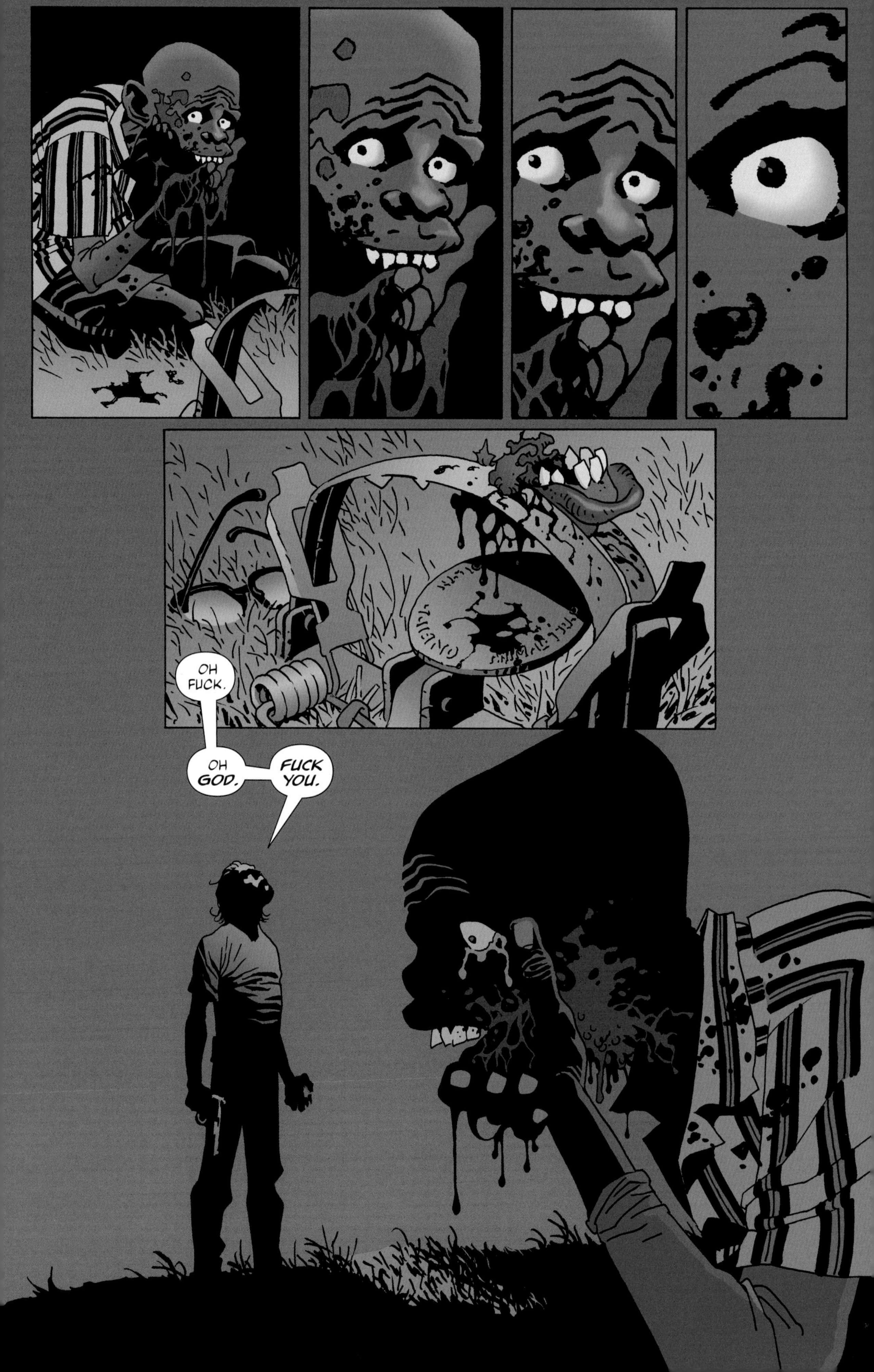
OH FUCK.
OH GOD.
FUCK YOU.

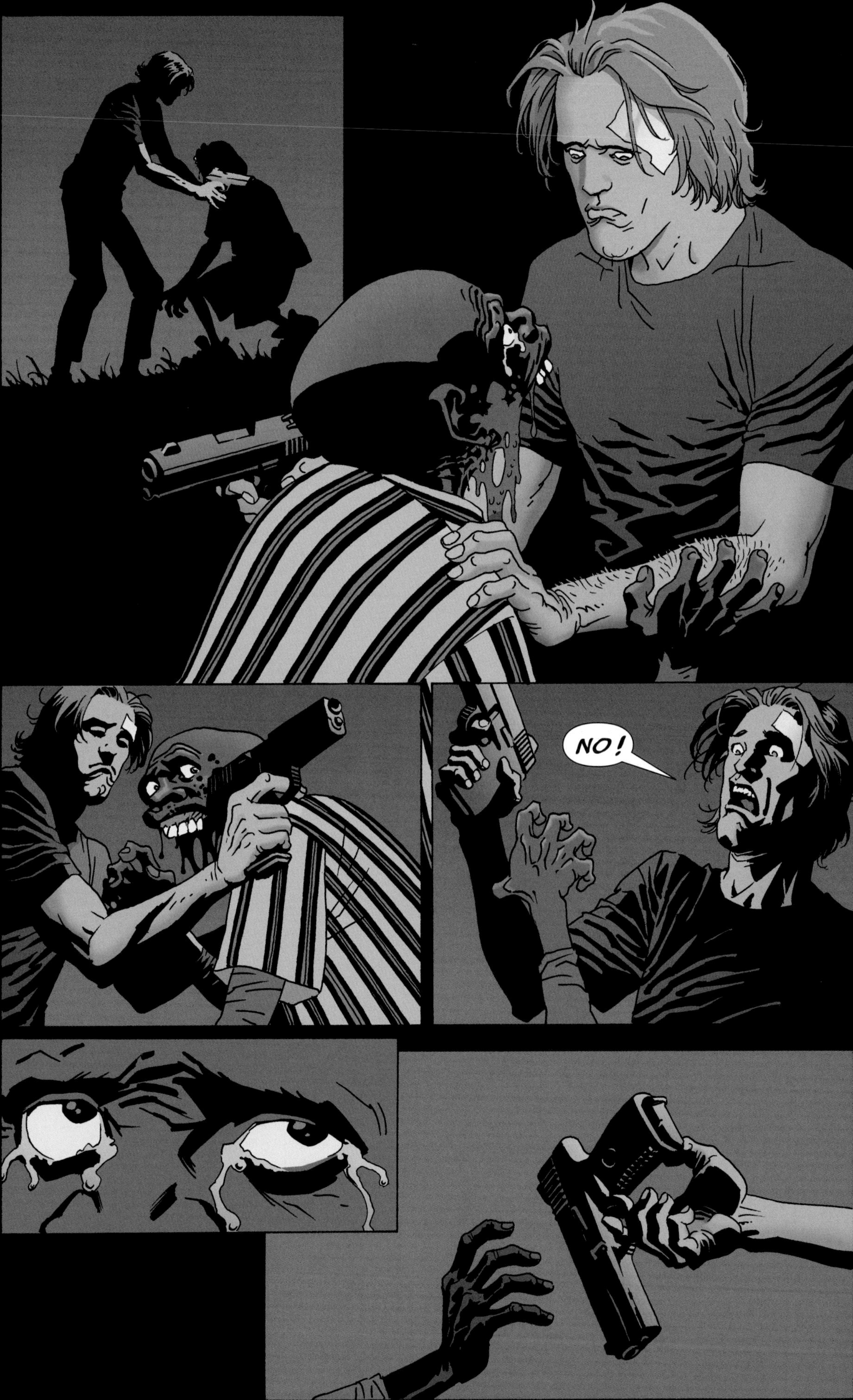
NO!

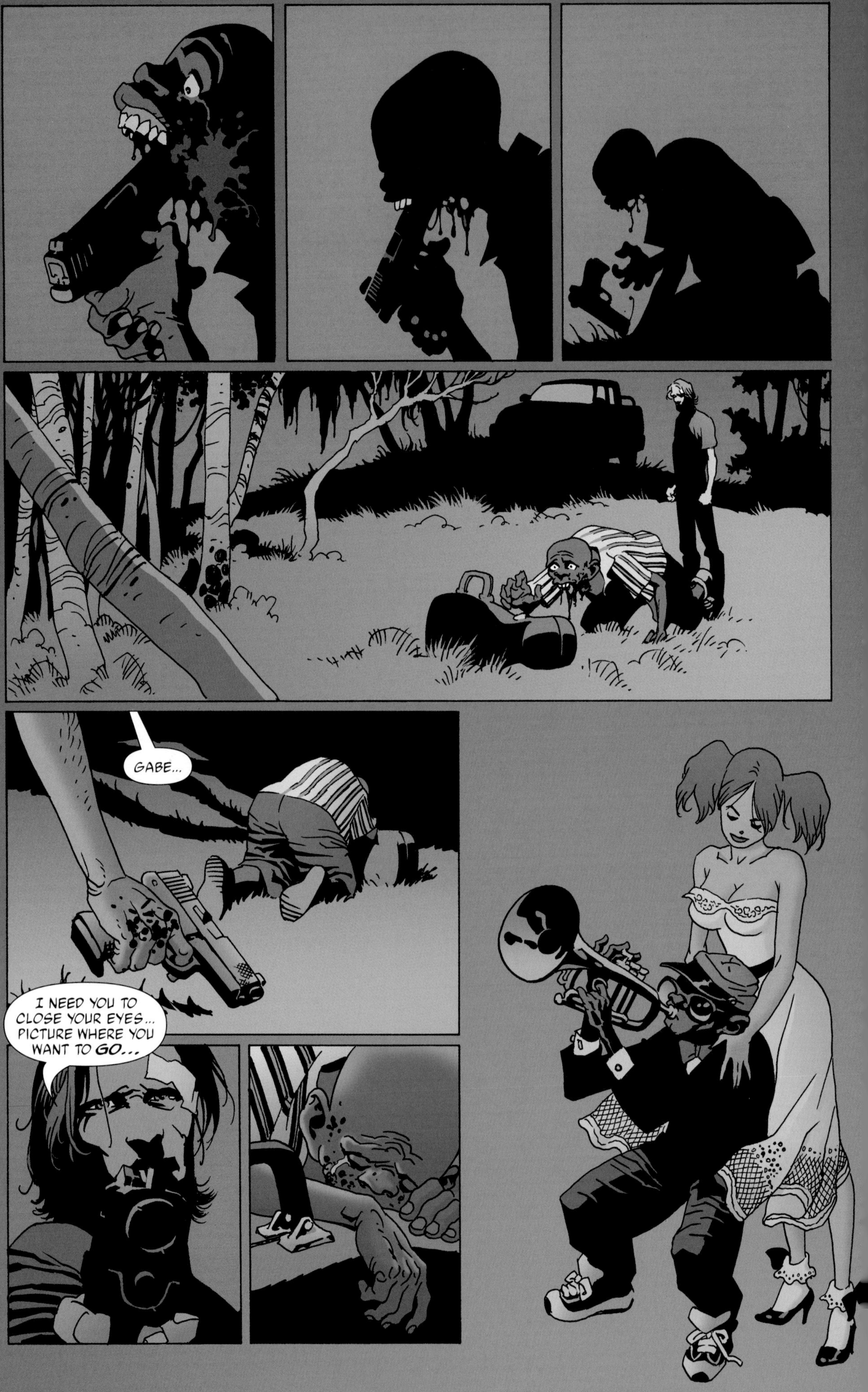
GABE...
I NEED YOU TO CLOSE YOUR EYES... PICTURE WHERE YOU WANT TO GO...

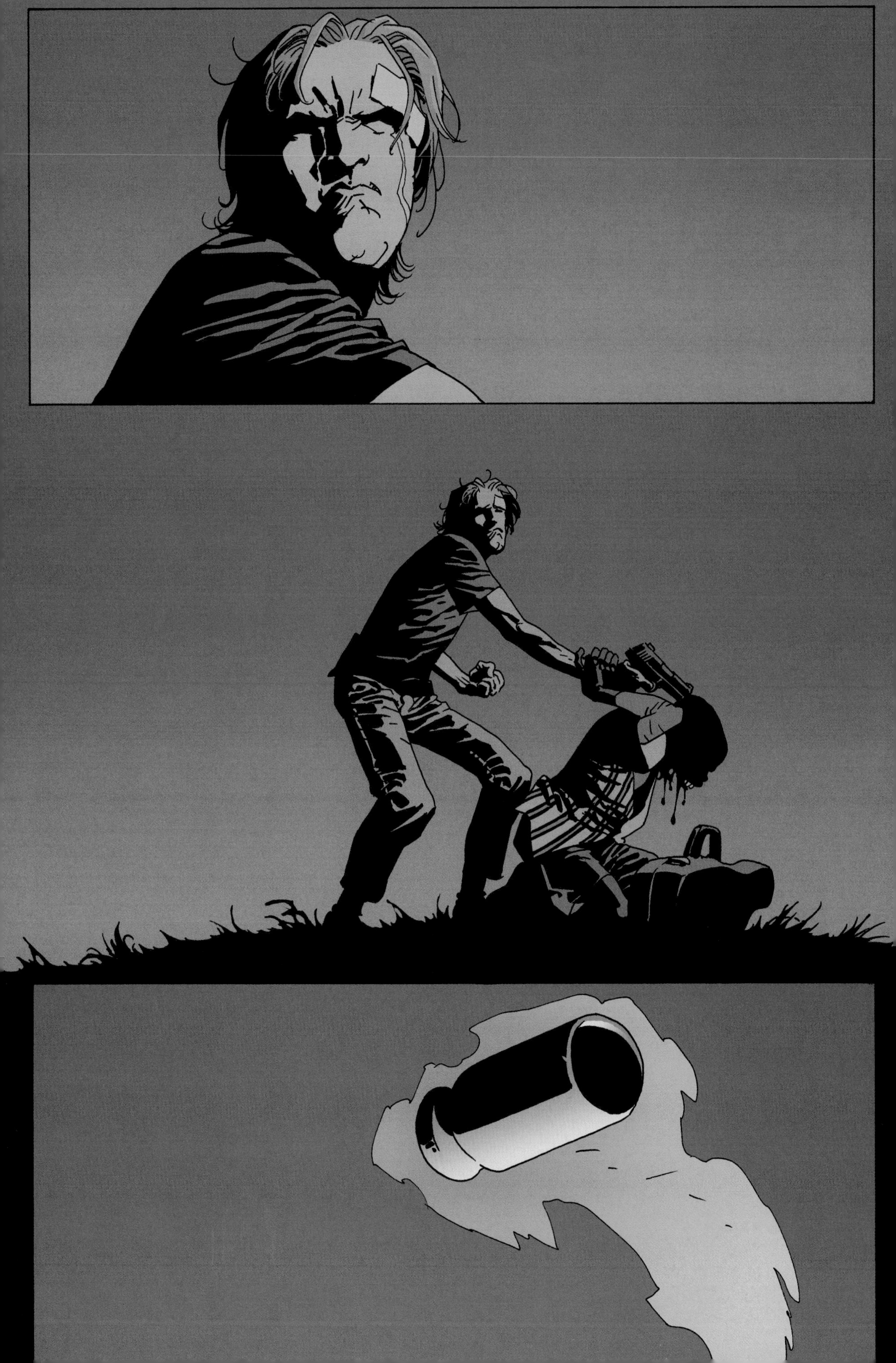

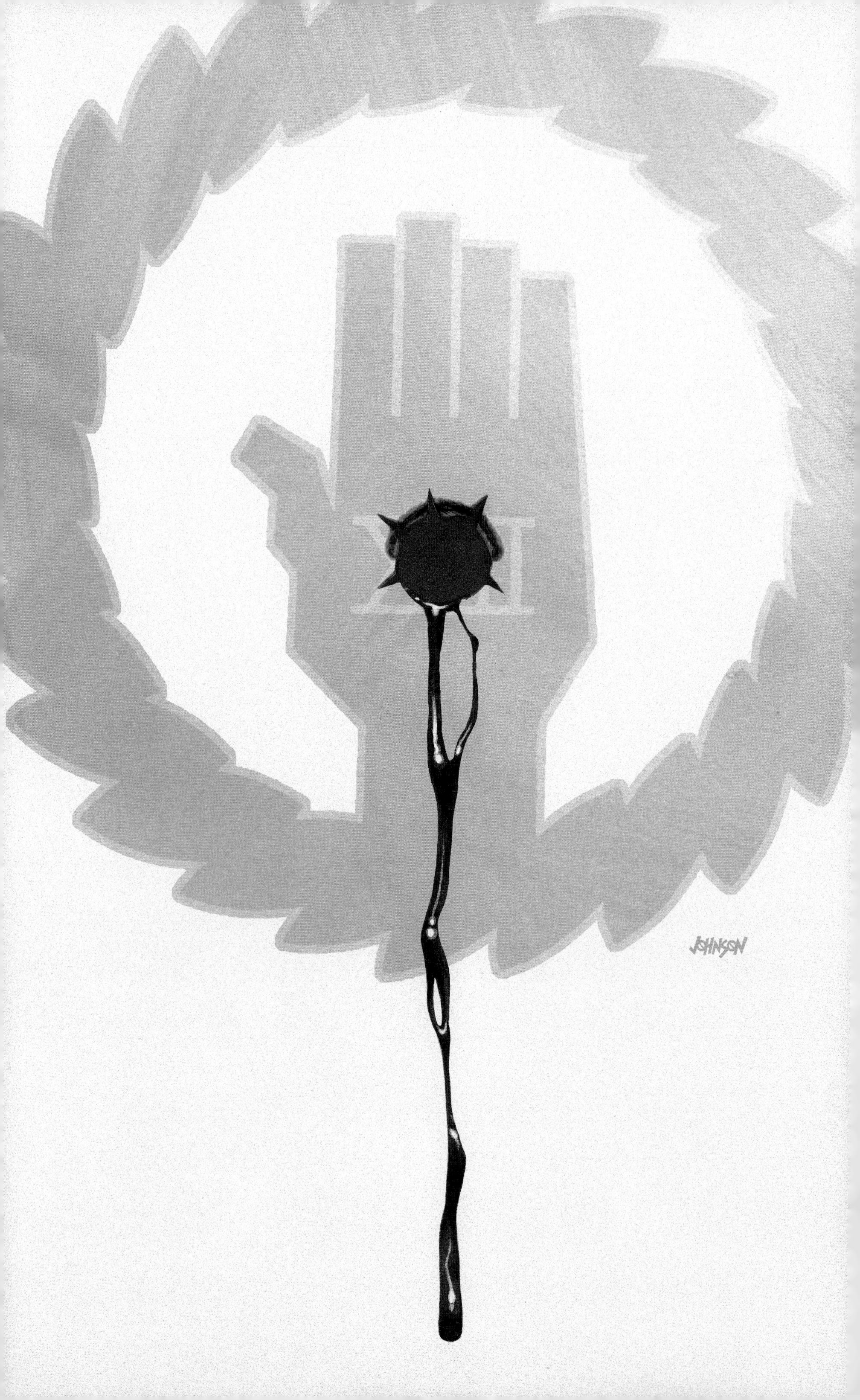
JOHNSON

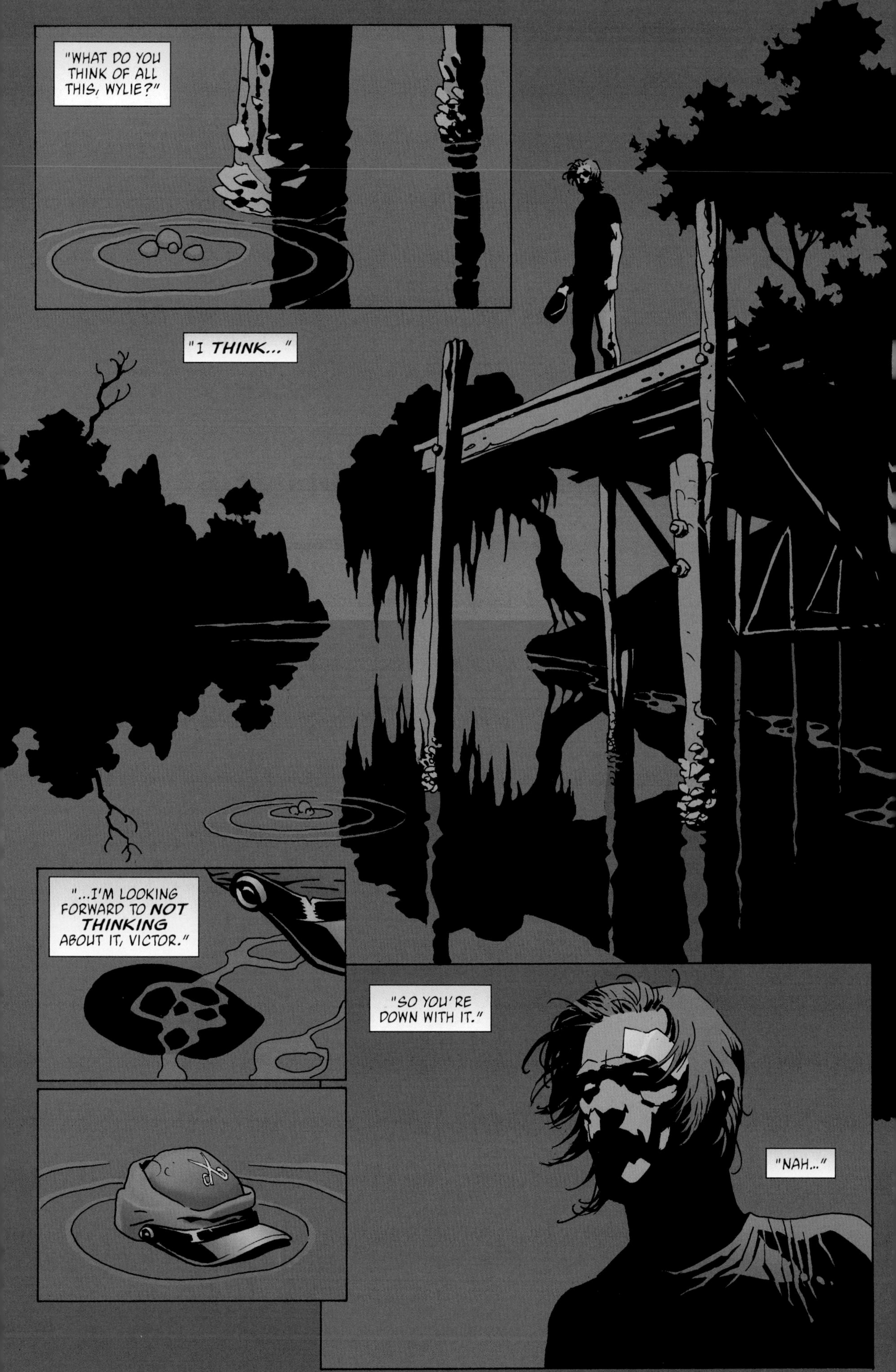
"WHAT DO YOU THINK OF ALL THIS, WYLIE?"
"I THINK..."
"...I'M LOOKING FORWARD TO NOT THINKING ABOUT IT, VICTOR."
"SO YOU'RE DOWN WITH IT."
"NAH..."

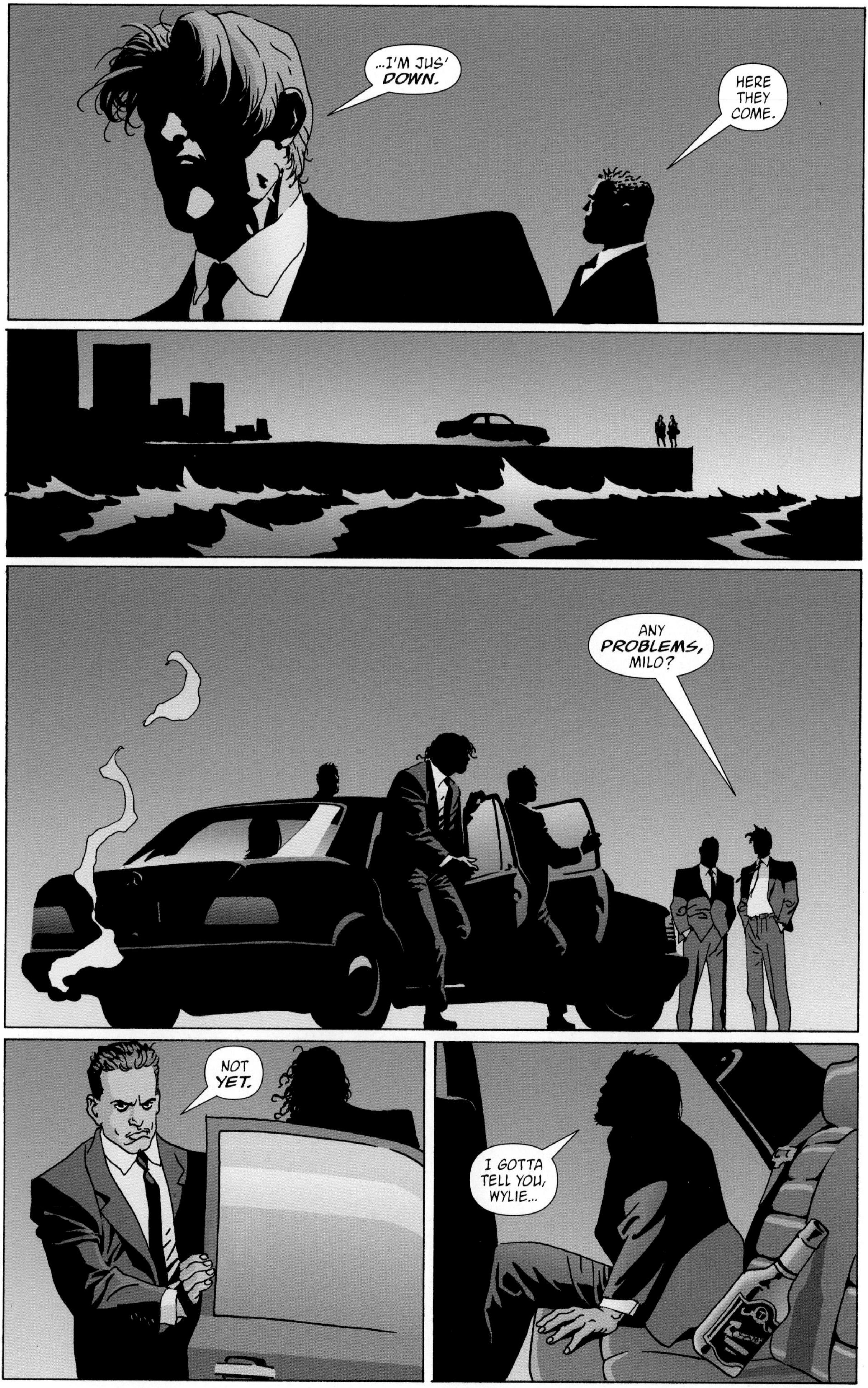
...I'M JUS' DOWN.
HERE THEY COME.
ANY PROBLEMS, MILO?
NOT YET.
I GOTTA TELL YOU, WYLIE...

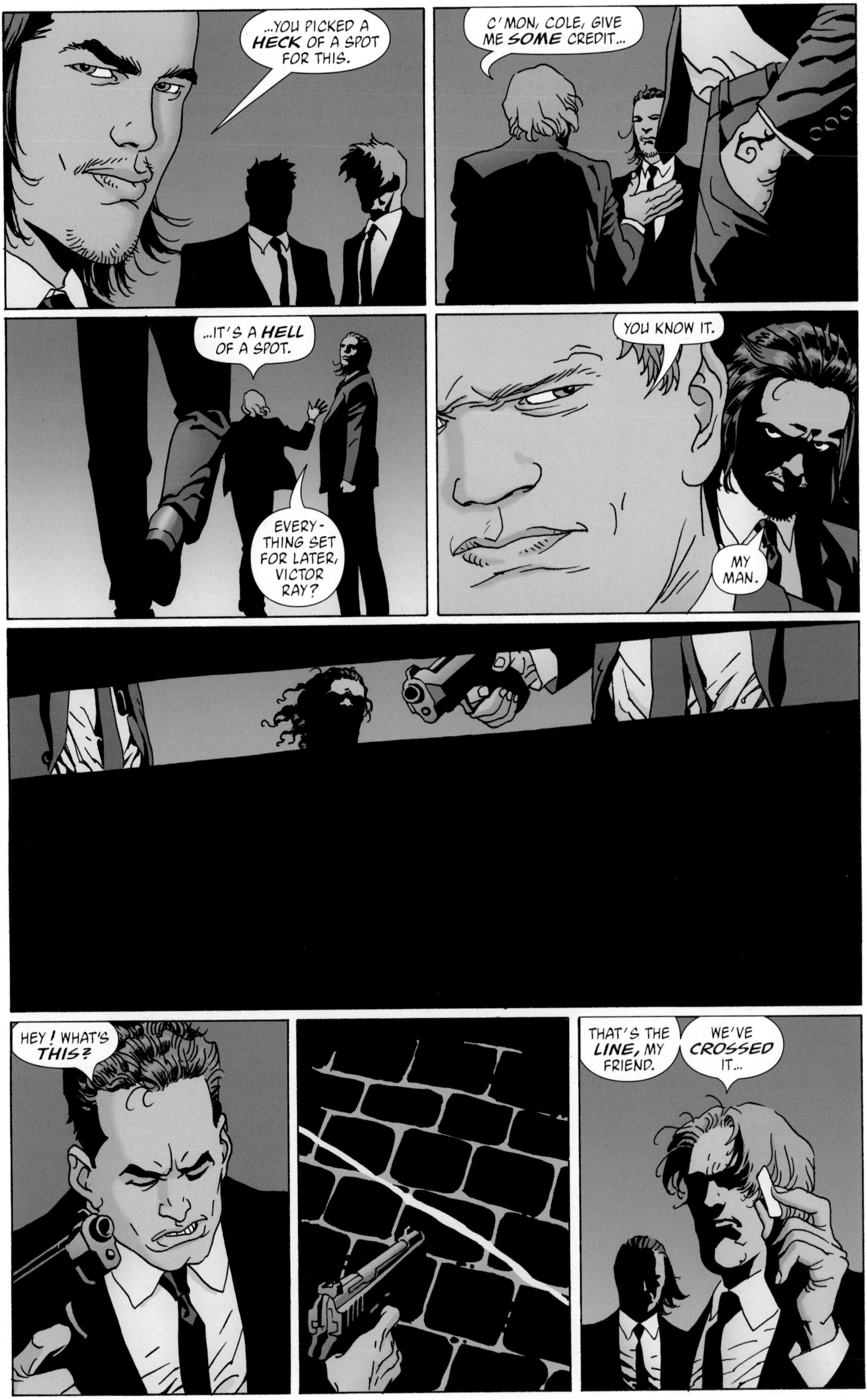
...YOU PICKED A HECK OF A SPOT FOR THIS.
C'MON, COLE, GIVE ME SOME CREDIT...
...IT'S A HELL OF A SPOT.
EVERY-THING SET FOR LATER, VICTOR RAY?
YOU KNOW IT.
MY MAN.
HEY! WHAT'S THIS?
THAT'S THE LINE, MY FRIEND.
WE'VE CROSSED IT...

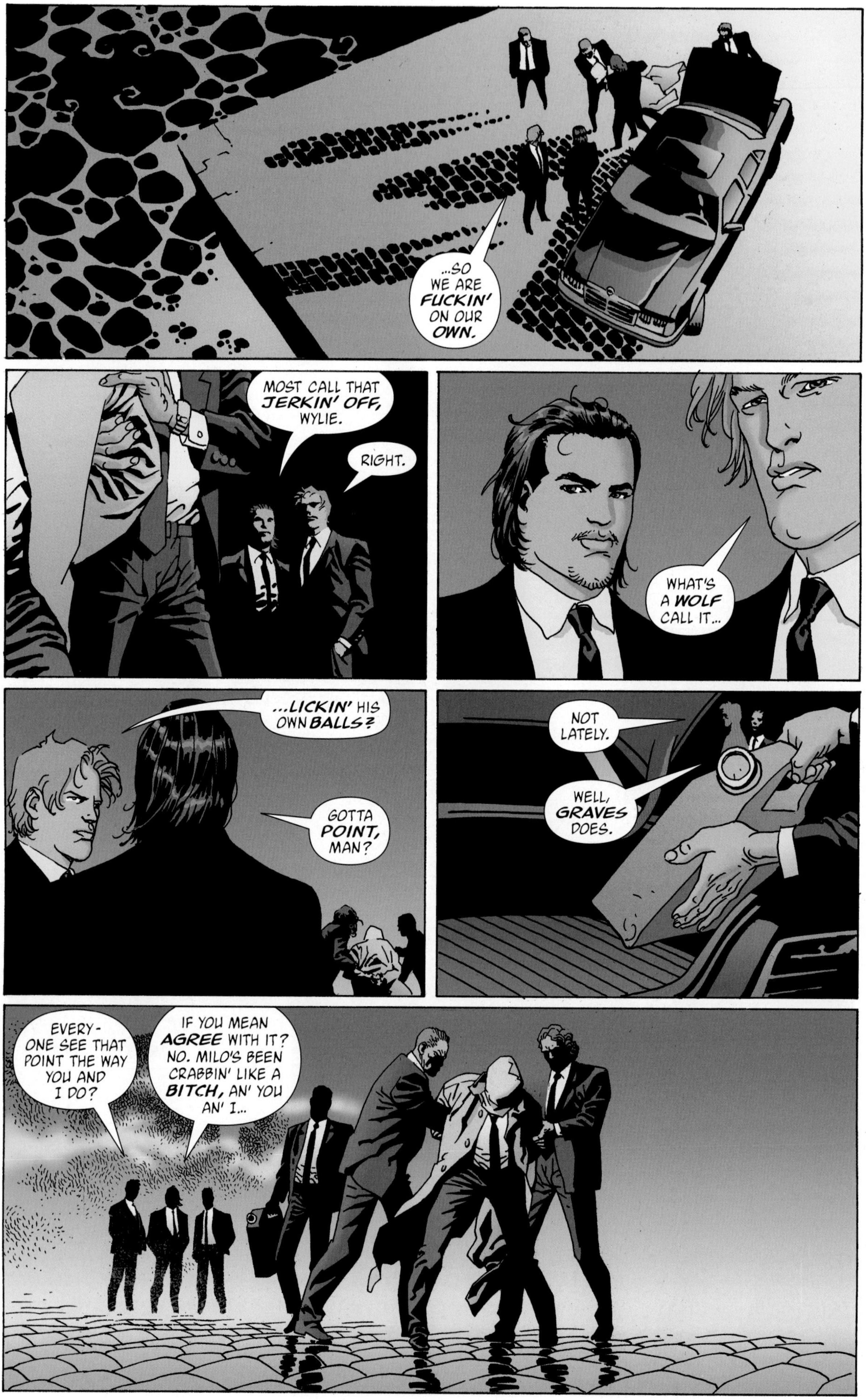
...SO WE ARE FUCKIN' ON OUR OWN.
MOST CALL THAT JERKIN' OFF, WYLIE.
RIGHT.
WHAT'S A WOLF CALL IT...
...LICKIN' HIS OWN BALLS?
GOTTA POINT, MAN?
NOT LATELY.
WELL, GRAVES DOES.
EVERY-ONE SEE THAT POINT THE WAY YOU AND I DO?
IF YOU MEAN AGREE WITH IT? NO. MILO'S BEEN CRABBIN' LIKE A BITCH, AN' YOU AN' I...

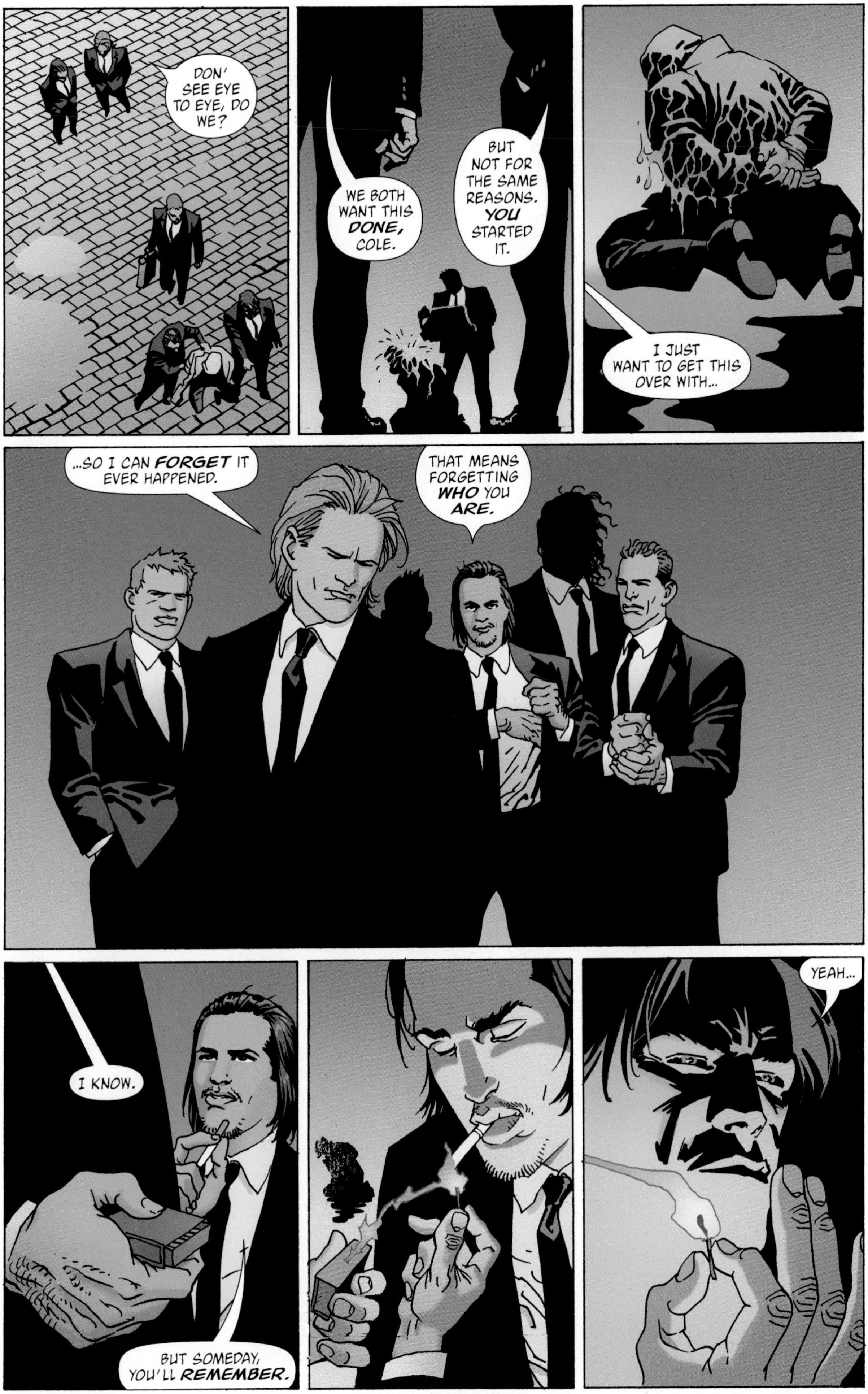
DON' SEE EYE TO EYE, DO WE?
WE BOTH WANT THIS DONE, COLE.
BUT NOT FOR THE SAME REASONS. YOU STARTED IT.
I JUST WANT TO GET THIS OVER WITH...
...SO I CAN FORGET IT EVER HAPPENED.
THAT MEANS FORGETTING WHO YOU ARE.
I KNOW.
BUT SOMEDAY, YOU'LL REMEMBER.
YEAH...

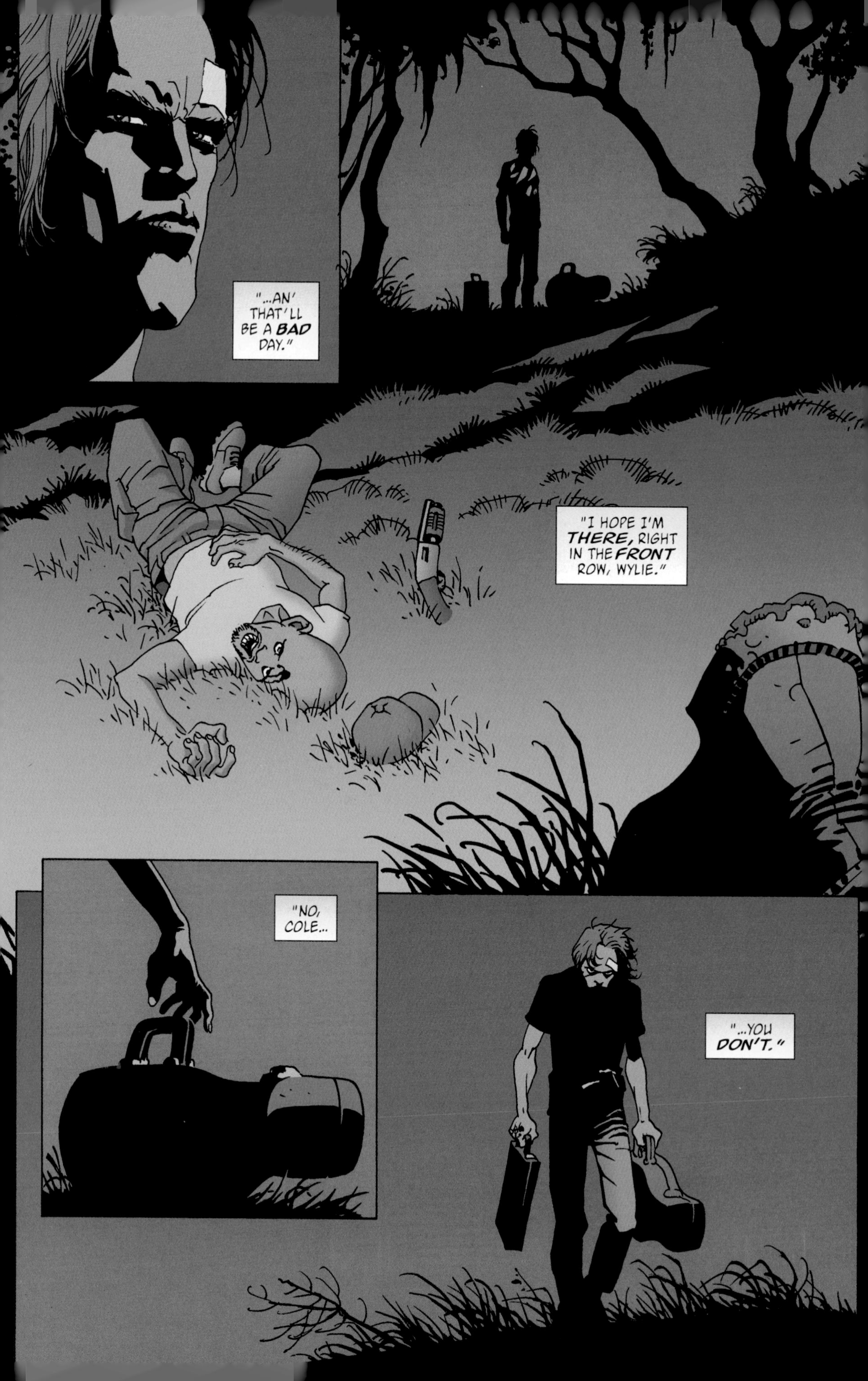
"...AN' THAT'LL BE A BAD DAY."
"I HOPE I'M THERE, RIGHT IN THE FRONT ROW, WYLIE."
"NO, COLE...
"...YOU DON'T."

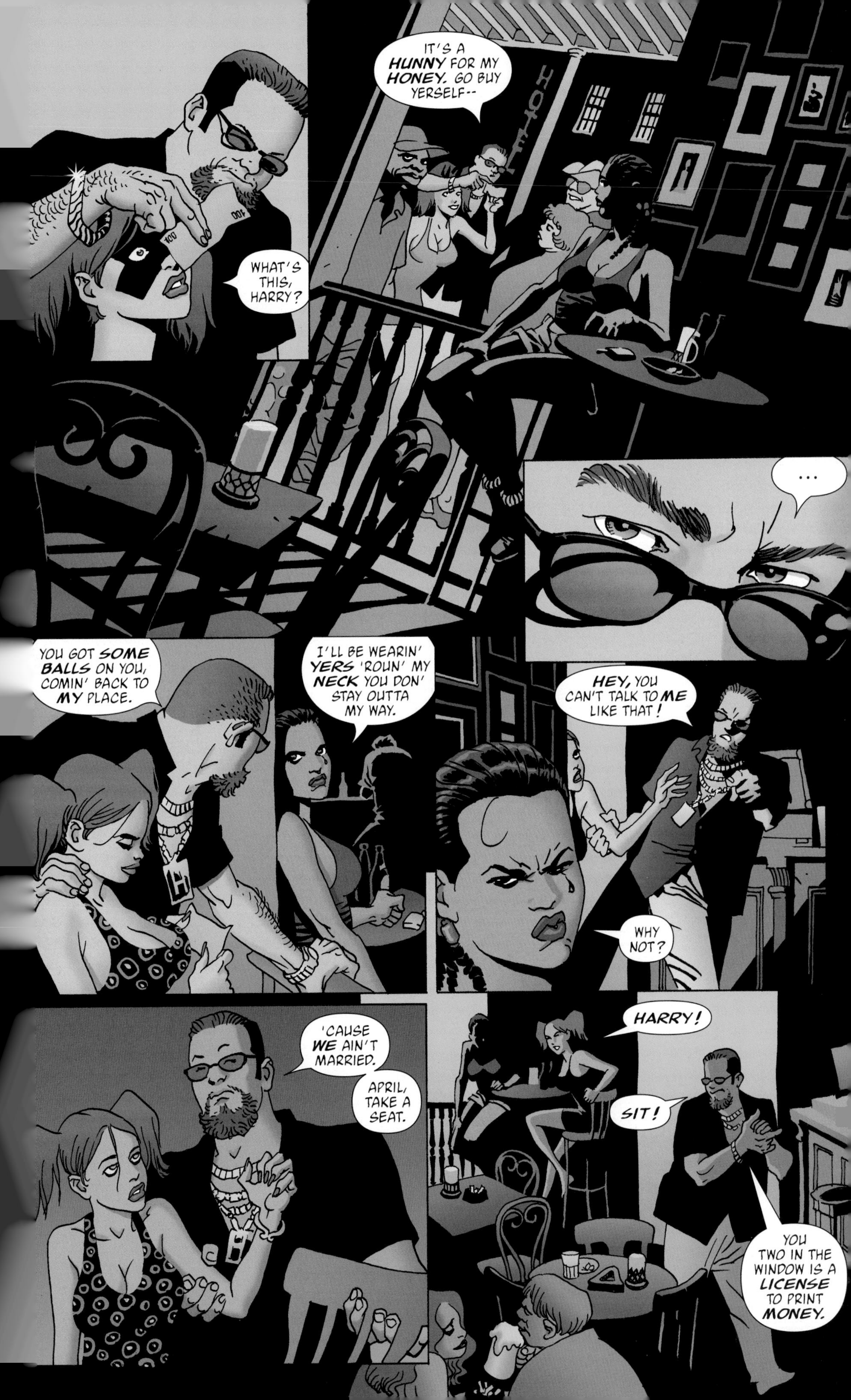
IT'S A HUNNY FOR MY HONEY. GO BUY YERSELF--
WHAT'S THIS, HARRY?
...
YOU GOT SOME BALLS ON YOU, COMIN' BACK TO MY PLACE.
I'LL BE WEARIN' YERS 'ROUN' MY NECK YOU DON' STAY OUTTA MY WAY.
HEY, YOU CAN'T TALK TO ME LIKE THAT!
WHY NOT?
'CAUSE WE AIN'T MARRIED.
APRIL, TAKE A SEAT.
HARRY!
SIT!
YOU TWO IN THE WINDOW IS A LICENSE TO PRINT MONEY.

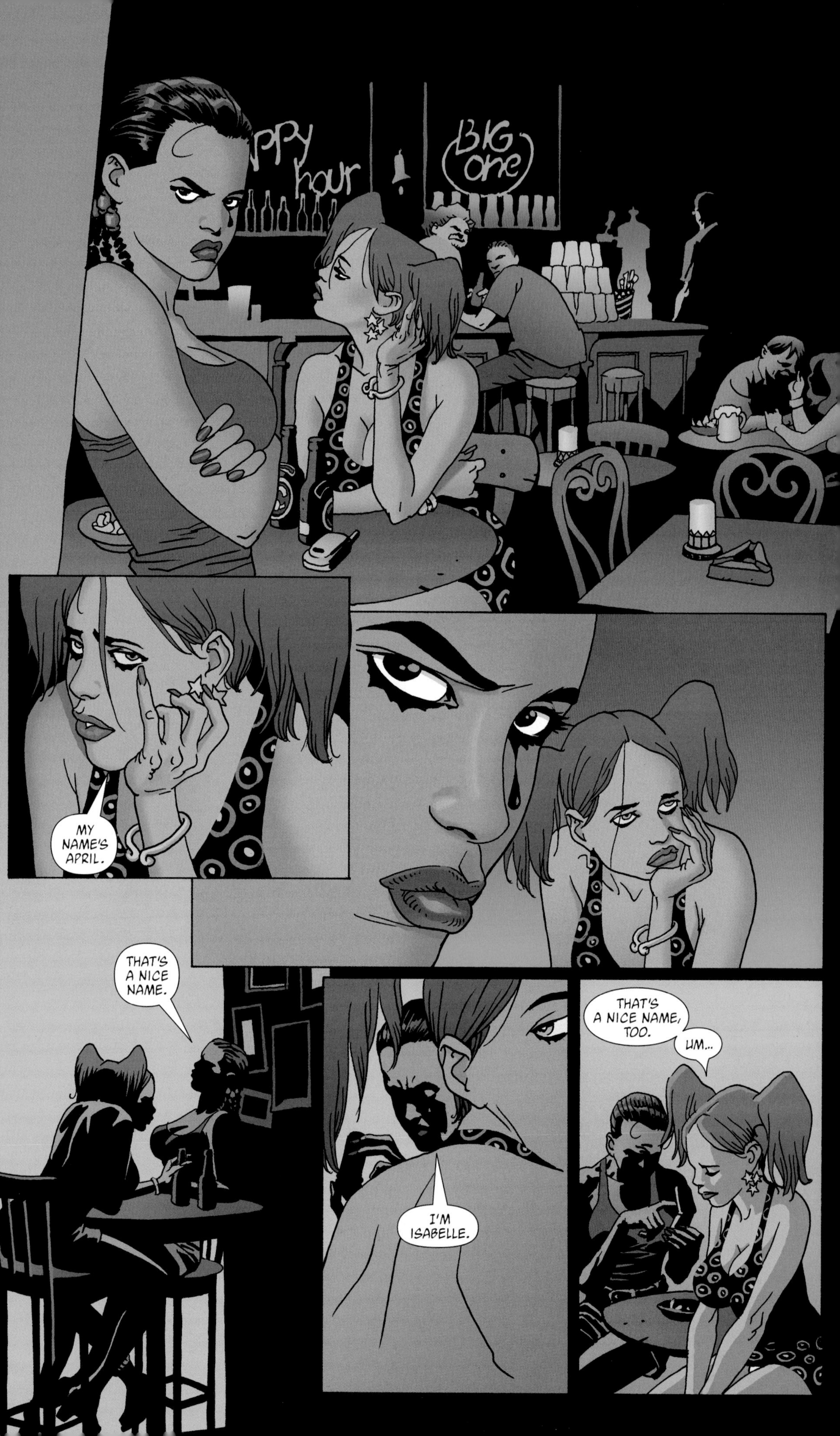
PPY
hour
BIG
one
MY NAME'S APRIL.
THAT'S A NICE NAME.
I'M ISABELLE.
THAT'S A NICE NAME, TOO.
UM...

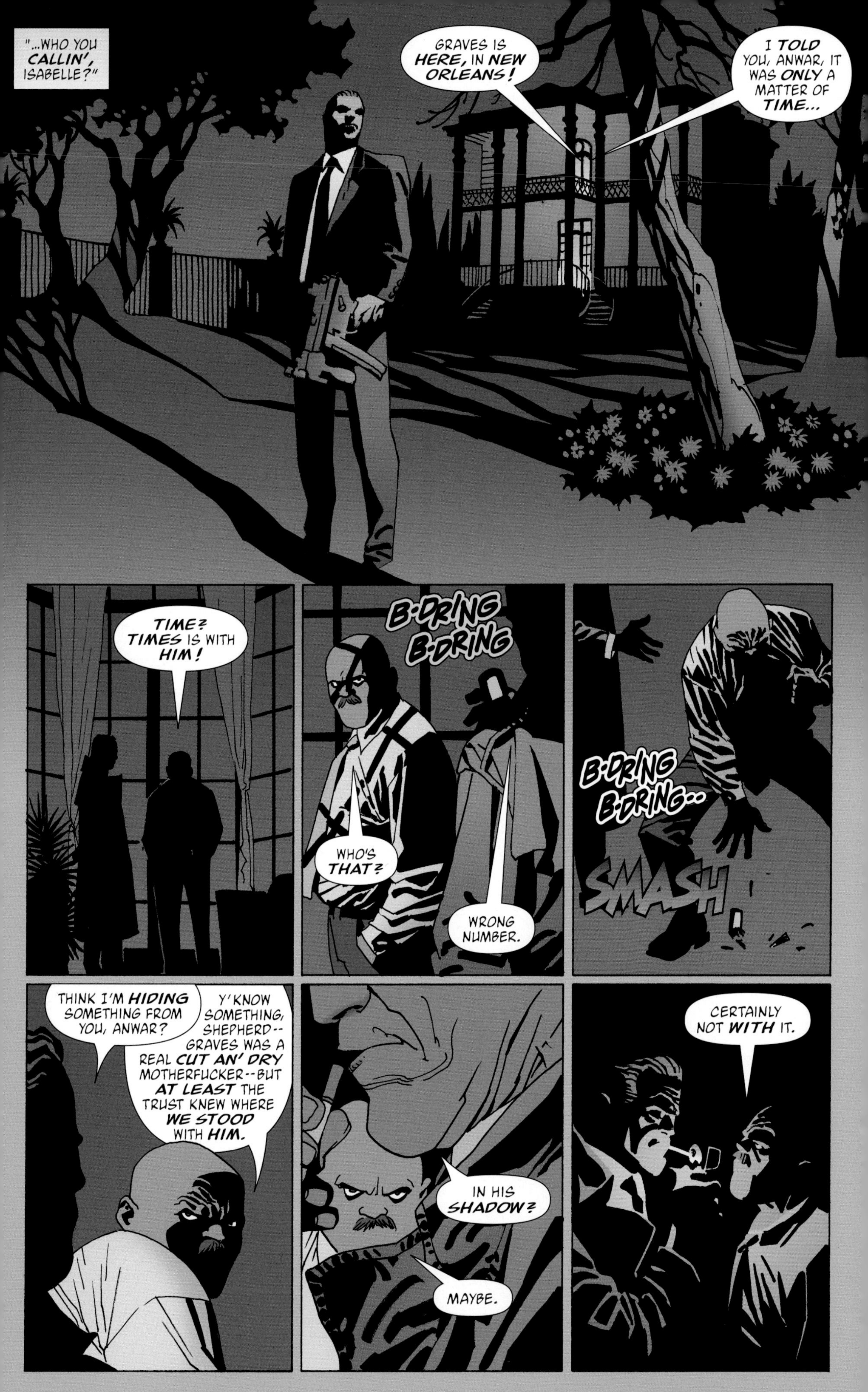
"...WHO YOU CALLIN', ISABELLE?"
GRAVES IS HERE, IN NEW ORLEANS!
I TOLD YOU, ANWAR, IT WAS ONLY A MATTER OF TIME...
TIME? TIMES IS WITH HIM!
B-DRING B-DRING
WHO'S THAT?
WRONG NUMBER.
B-DRING B-DRING..
SMASH
THINK I'M HIDING SOMETHING FROM YOU, ANWAR?
Y'KNOW SOMETHING, SHEPHERD-- GRAVES WAS A REAL CUT AN' DRY MOTHERFUCKER--BUT AT LEAST THE TRUST KNEW WHERE WE STOOD WITH HIM.
IN HIS SHADOW?
MAYBE.
CERTAINLY NOT WITH IT.

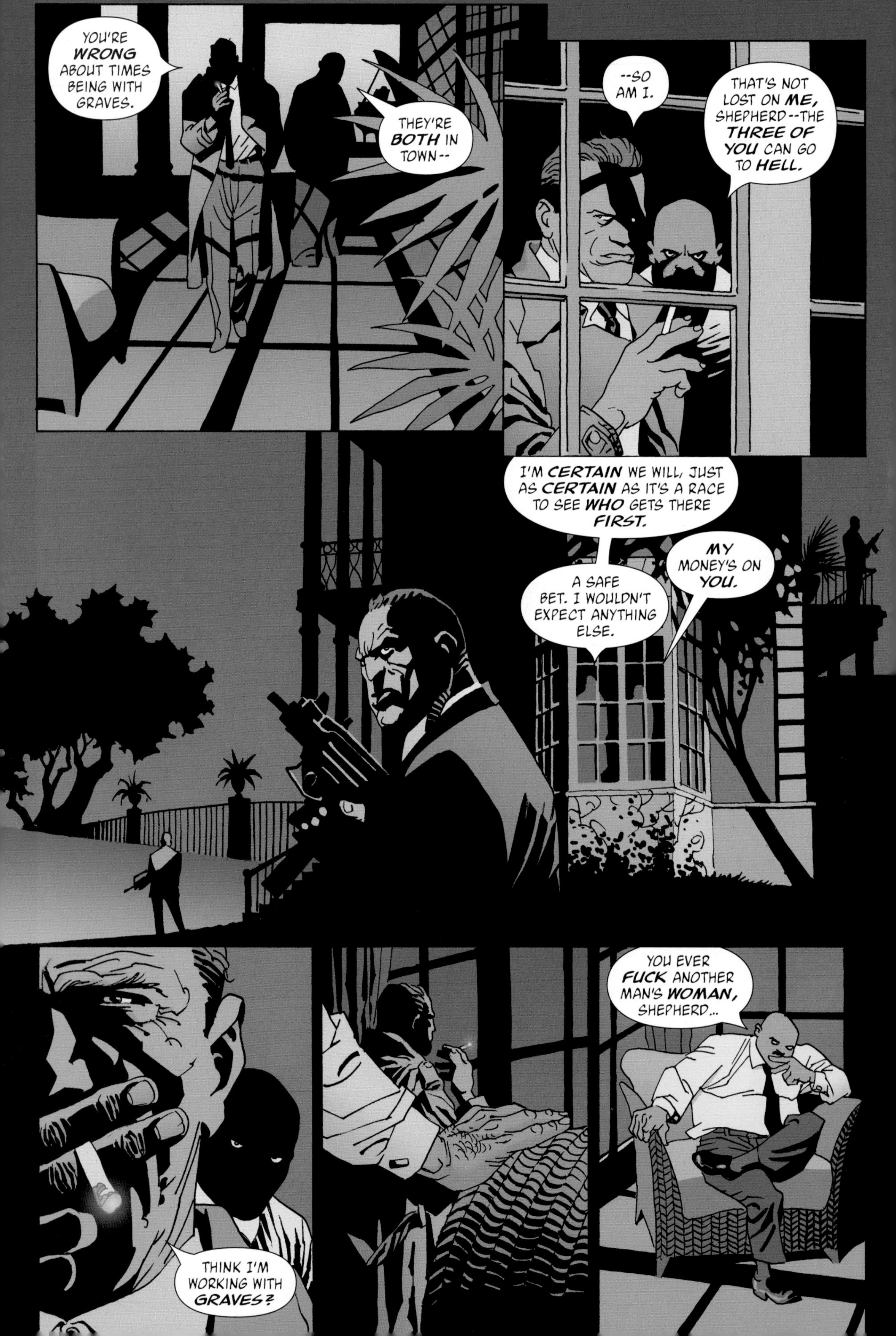

YOU'RE WRONG ABOUT TIMES BEING WITH GRAVES.
THEY'RE BOTH IN TOWN--
--SO AM I.
THAT'S NOT LOST ON ME, SHEPHERD--THE THREE OF YOU CAN GO TO HELL.
I'M CERTAIN WE WILL, JUST AS CERTAIN AS IT'S A RACE TO SEE WHO GETS THERE FIRST.
A SAFE BET. I WOULDN'T EXPECT ANYTHING ELSE.
MY MONEY'S ON YOU.
THINK I'M WORKING WITH GRAVES?
YOU EVER FUCK ANOTHER MAN'S WOMAN, SHEPHERD...

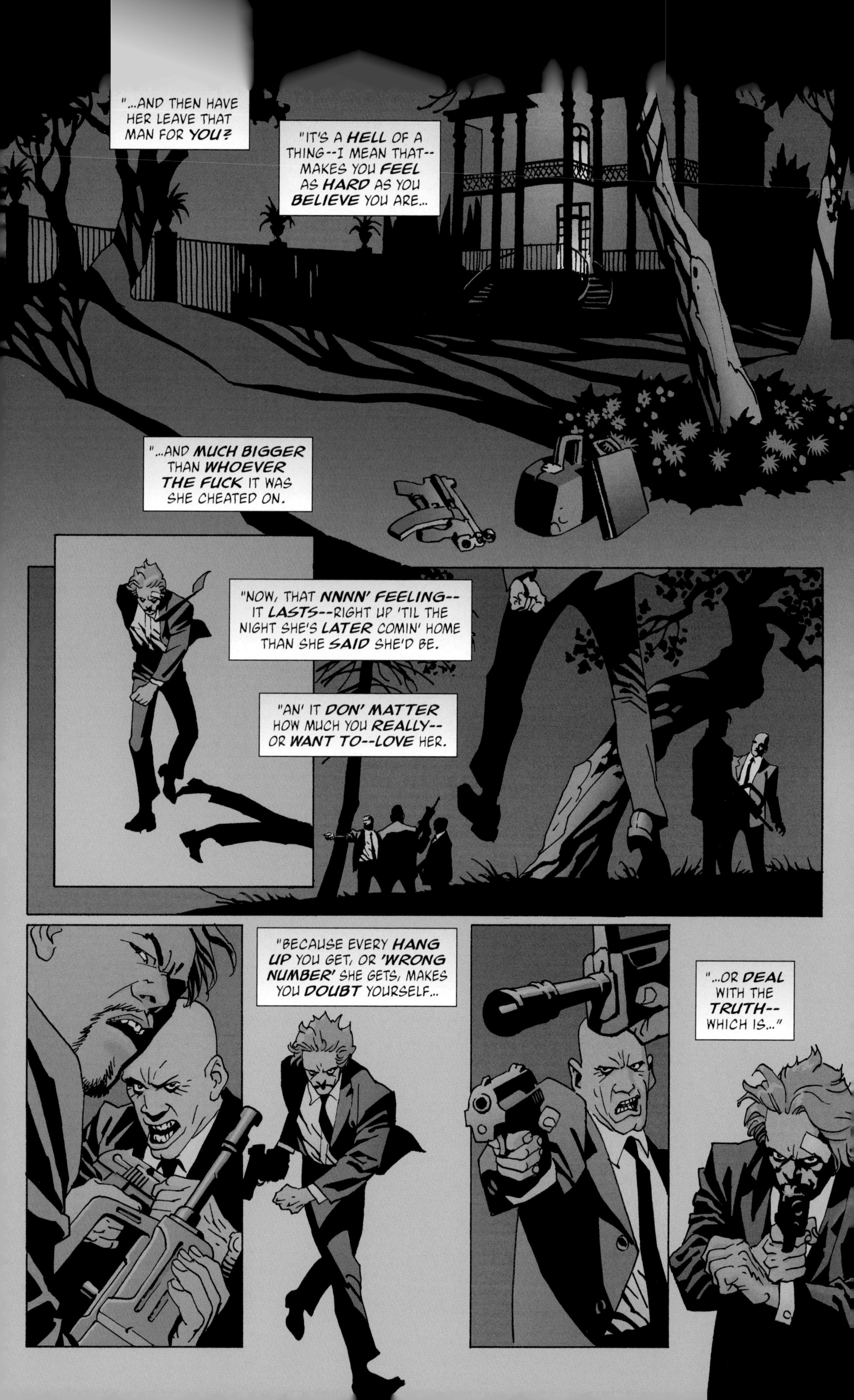
"...AND THEN HAVE HER LEAVE THAT MAN FOR YOU?
"IT'S A HELL OF A THING--I MEAN THAT--MAKES YOU FEEL AS HARD AS YOU BELIEVE YOU ARE...
"...AND MUCH BIGGER THAN WHOEVER THE FUCK IT WAS SHE CHEATED ON.
"NOW, THAT NNNN' FEELING--IT LASTS--RIGHT UP 'TIL THE NIGHT SHE'S LATER COMIN' HOME THAN SHE SAID SHE'D BE.
"AN' IT DON' MATTER HOW MUCH YOU REALLY--OR WANT TO--LOVE HER.
"BECAUSE EVERY HANG UP YOU GET, OR 'WRONG NUMBER' SHE GETS, MAKES YOU DOUBT YOURSELF...
"...OR DEAL WITH THE TRUTH--WHICH IS..."

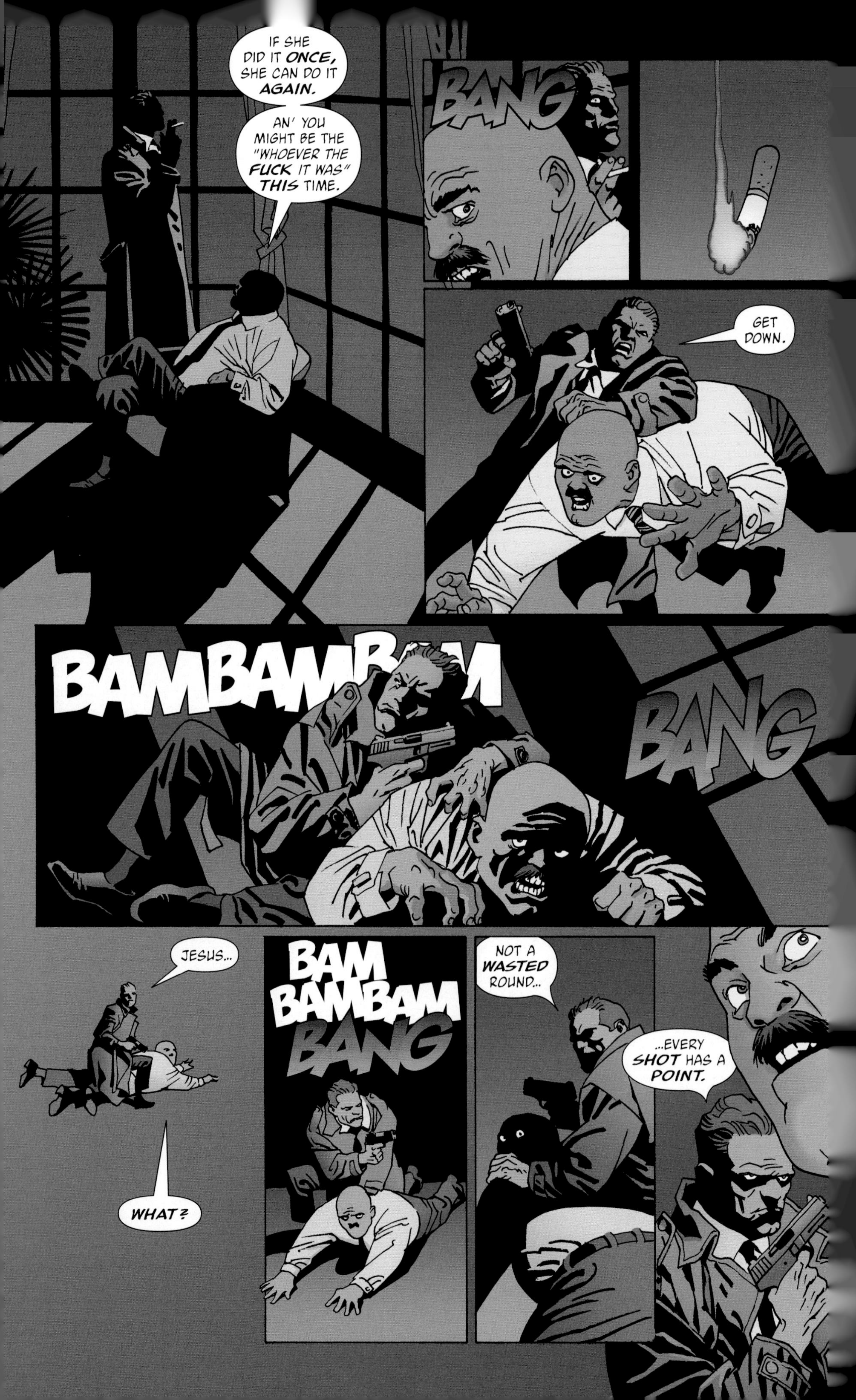
IF SHE DID IT ONCE, SHE CAN DO IT AGAIN.
AN' YOU MIGHT BE THE "WHOEVER THE FUCK IT WAS" THIS TIME.
BANG
GET DOWN.
BAMBAMBAM
BANG
JESUS...
WHAT?
BAM BAMBAMBAM BANG
NOT A WASTED ROUND...
...EVERY SHOT HAS A POINT.

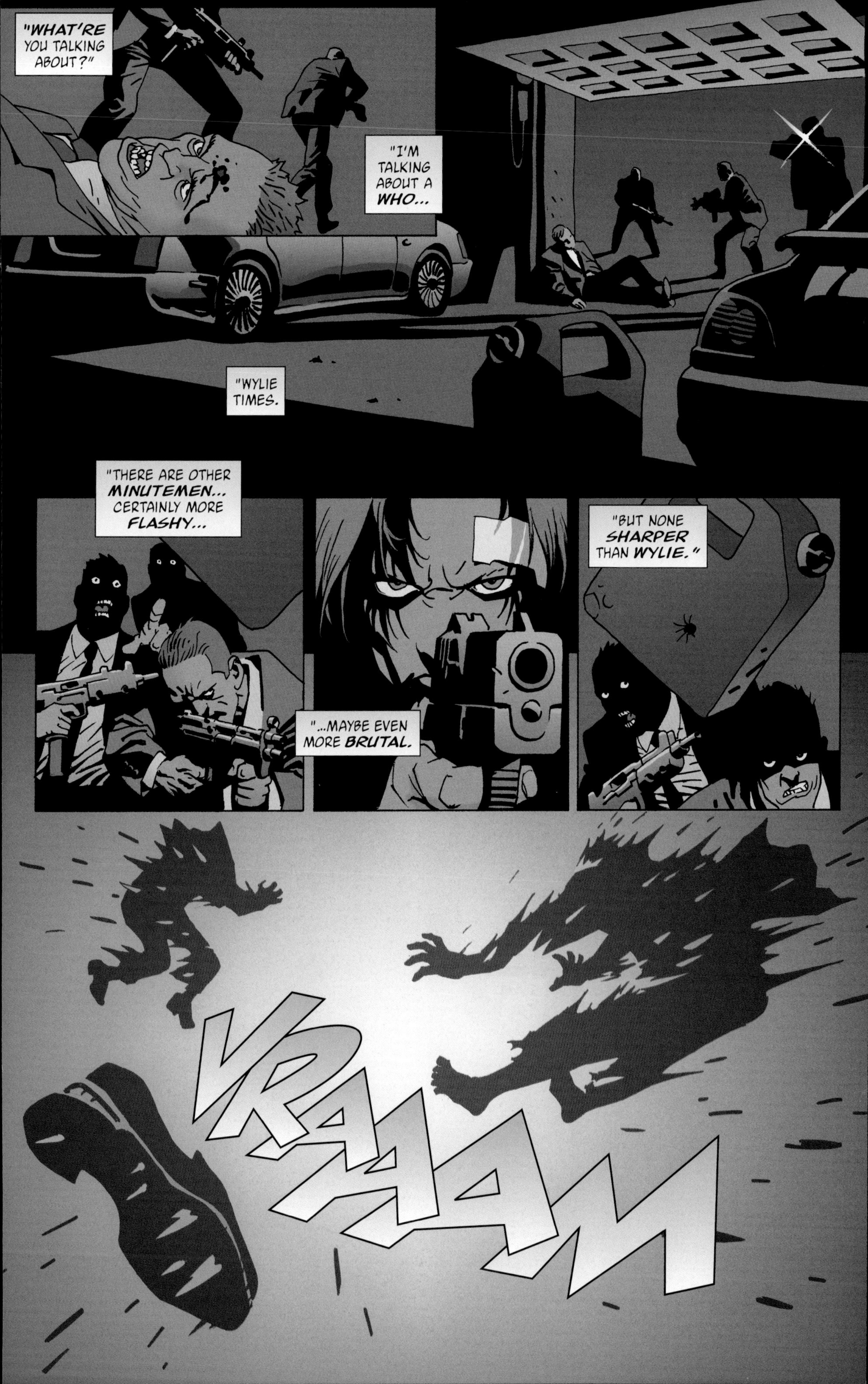
"WHAT'RE YOU TALKING ABOUT?"
"I'M TALKING ABOUT A WHO...
"WYLIE TIMES.
"THERE ARE OTHER MINUTEMEN... CERTAINLY MORE FLASHY...
"...MAYBE EVEN MORE BRUTAL.
"BUT NONE SHARPER THAN WYLIE."
VRAAAM

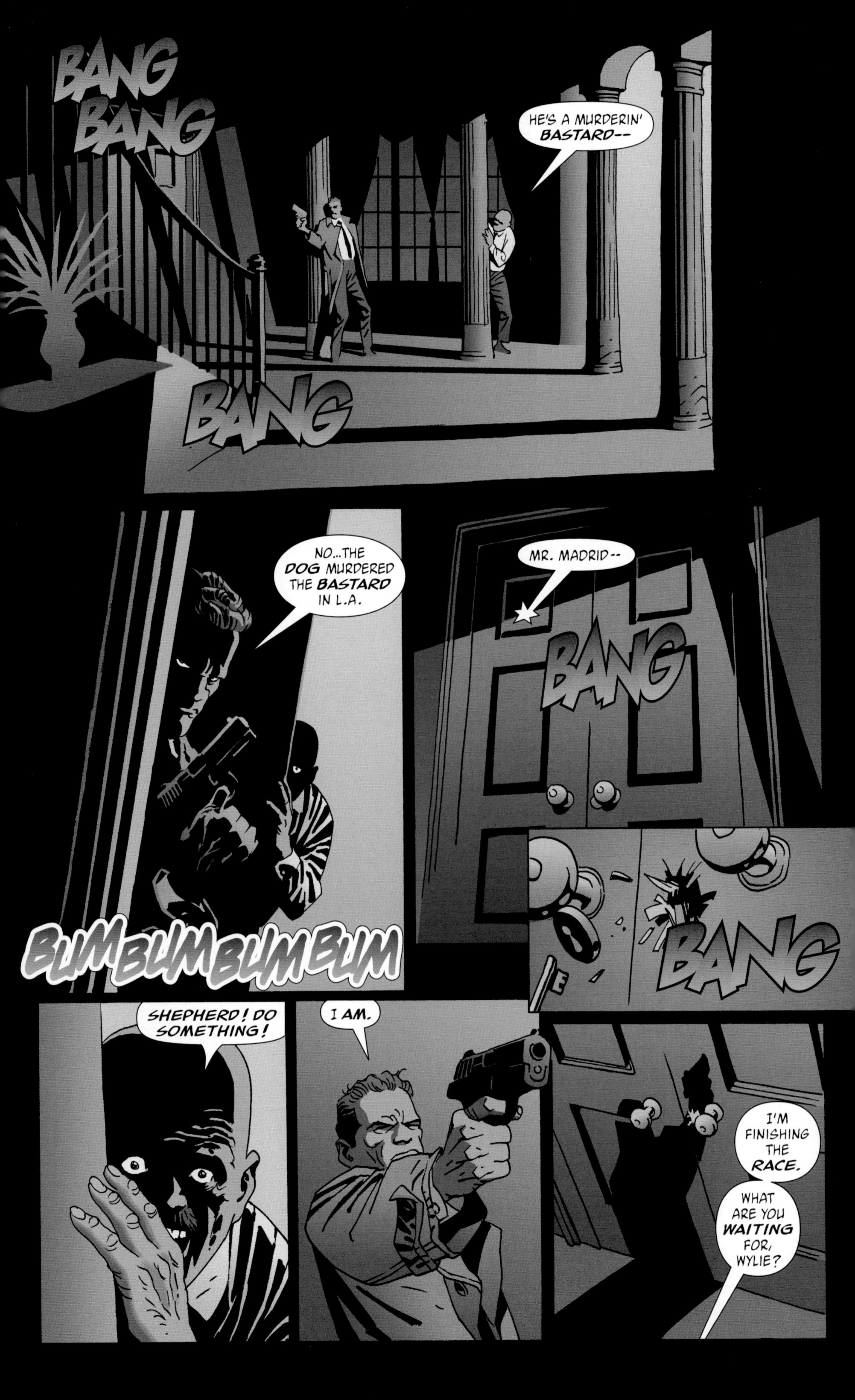
BANG
BANG
HE'S A MURDERIN' BASTARD--
BANG
NO...THE DOG MURDERED THE BASTARD IN L.A.
BLUM BLUM BLUM BLUM
MR. MADRID--
BANG
BANG
SHEPHERD! DO SOMETHING!
I AM.
I'M FINISHING THE RACE.
WHAT ARE YOU WAITING FOR, WYLIE?

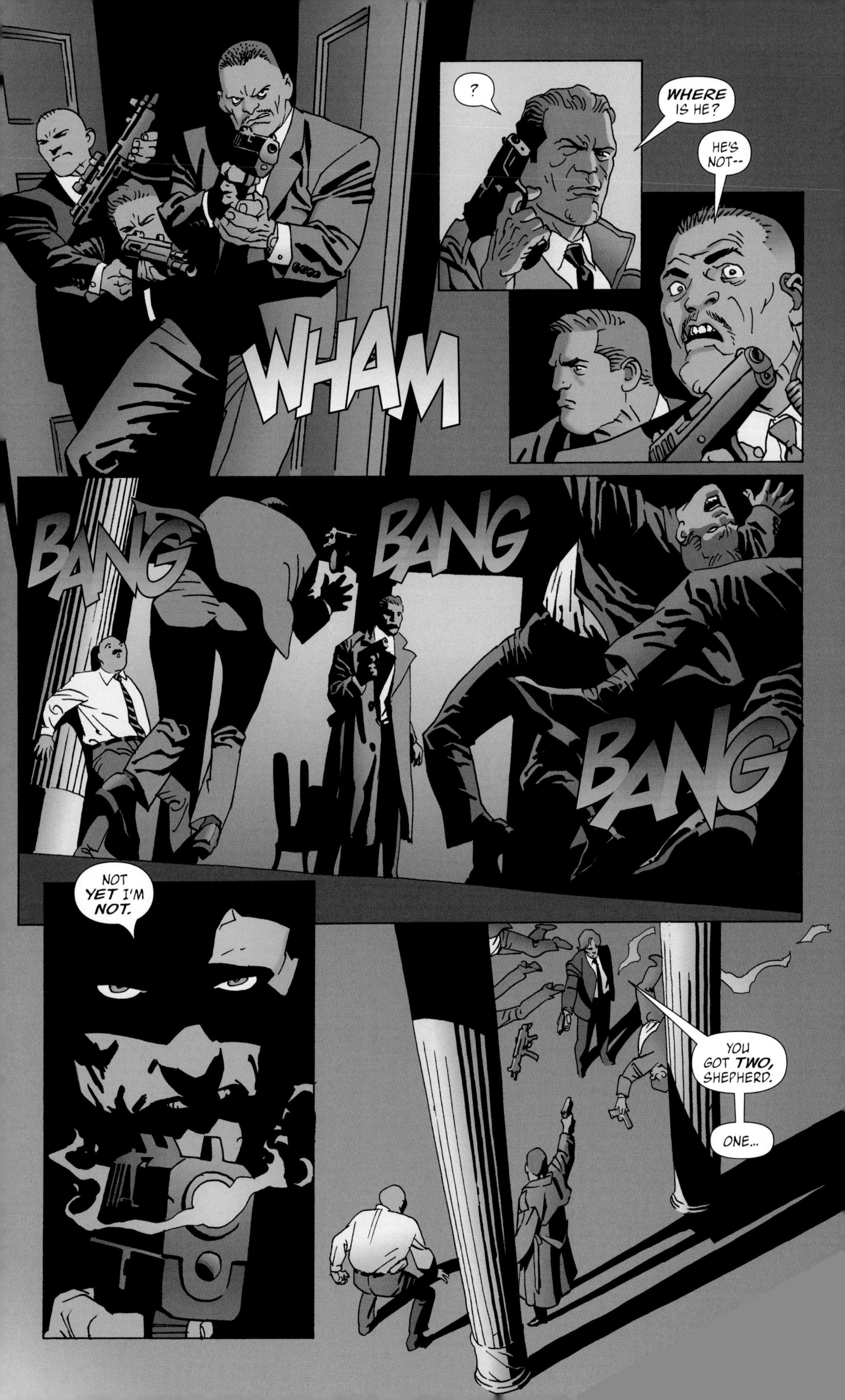
WHAM
?
WHERE IS HE?
HE'S NOT--
BANG
BANG
BANG
NOT YET I'M NOT.
YOU GOT TWO, SHEPHERD.
ONE...

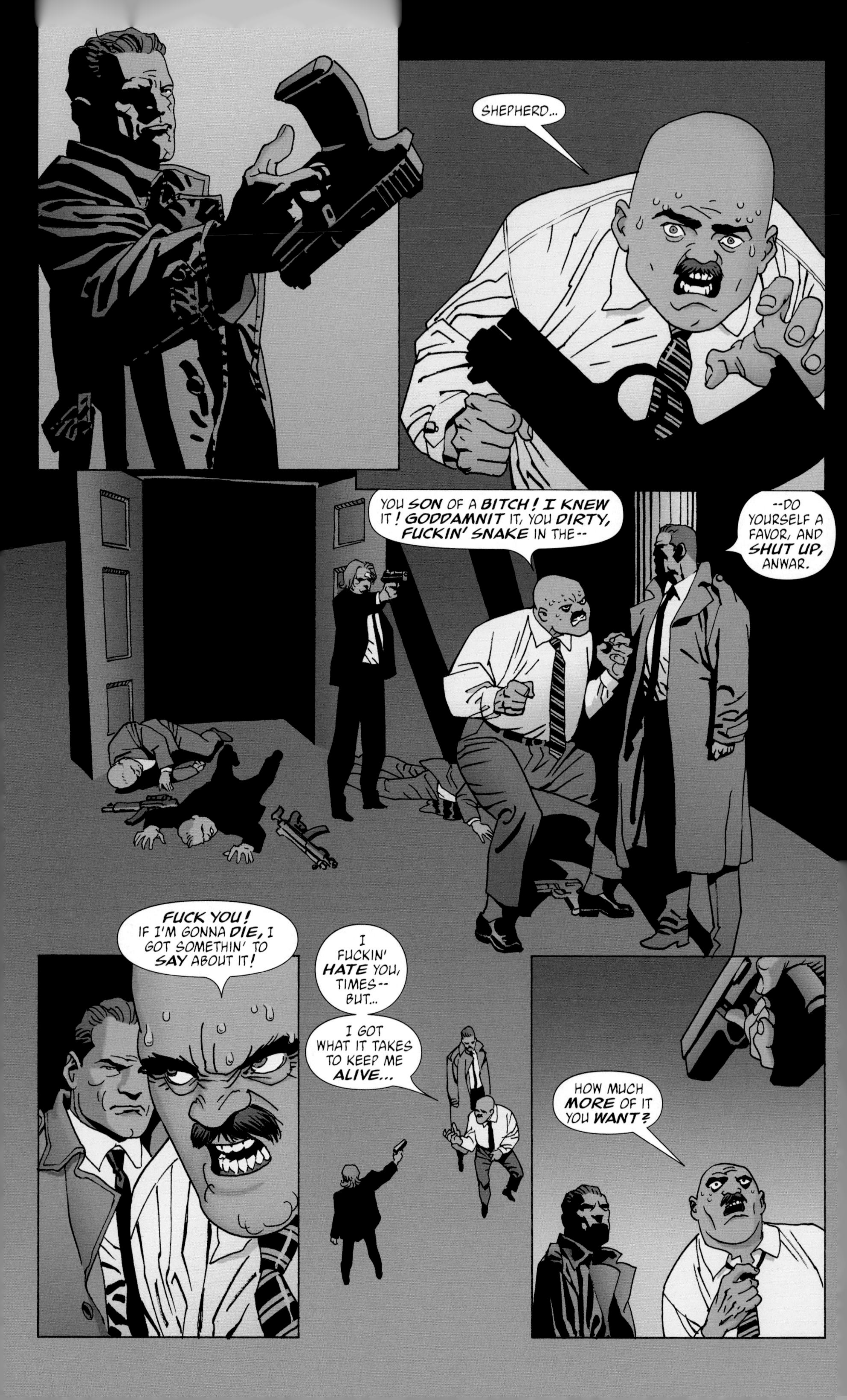
SHEPHERD...
YOU SON OF A BITCH! I KNEW IT! GODDAMNIT IT, YOU DIRTY, FUCKIN' SNAKE IN THE--
--DO YOURSELF A FAVOR, AND SHUT UP, ANWAR.
FUCK YOU! IF I'M GONNA DIE, I GOT SOMETHIN' TO SAY ABOUT IT!
I FUCKIN' HATE YOU, TIMES-- BUT...
I GOT WHAT IT TAKES TO KEEP ME ALIVE...
HOW MUCH MORE OF IT YOU WANT?

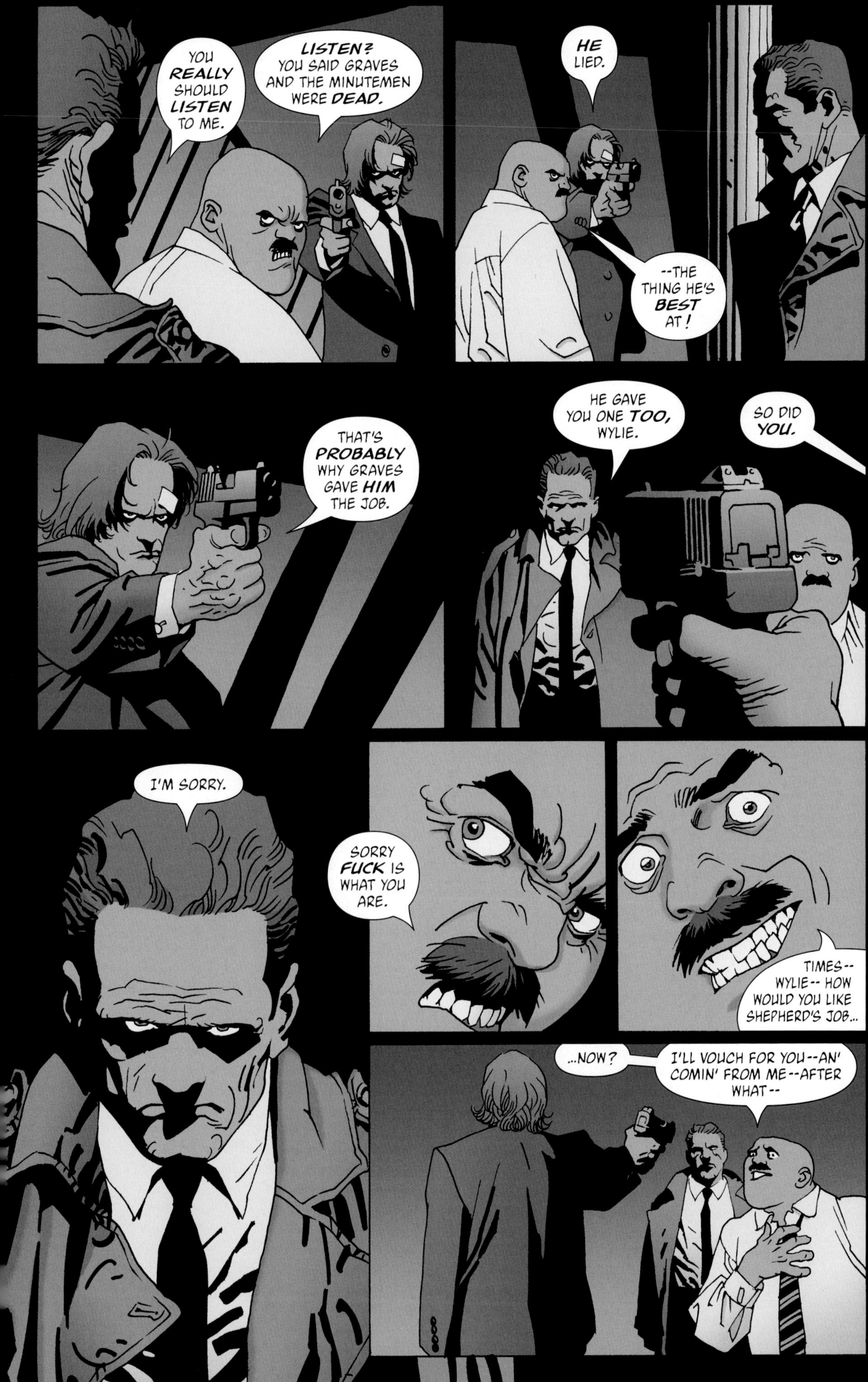
YOU REALLY SHOULD LISTEN TO ME.
LISTEN? YOU SAID GRAVES AND THE MINUTEMEN WERE DEAD.
HE LIED.
--THE THING HE'S BEST AT!
THAT'S PROBABLY WHY GRAVES GAVE HIM THE JOB.
HE GAVE YOU ONE TOO, WYLIE.
SO DID YOU.
I'M SORRY.
SORRY FUCK IS WHAT YOU ARE.
TIMES-- WYLIE-- HOW WOULD YOU LIKE SHEPHERD'S JOB...
...NOW?
I'LL VOUCH FOR YOU--AN' COMIN' FROM ME--AFTER WHAT--

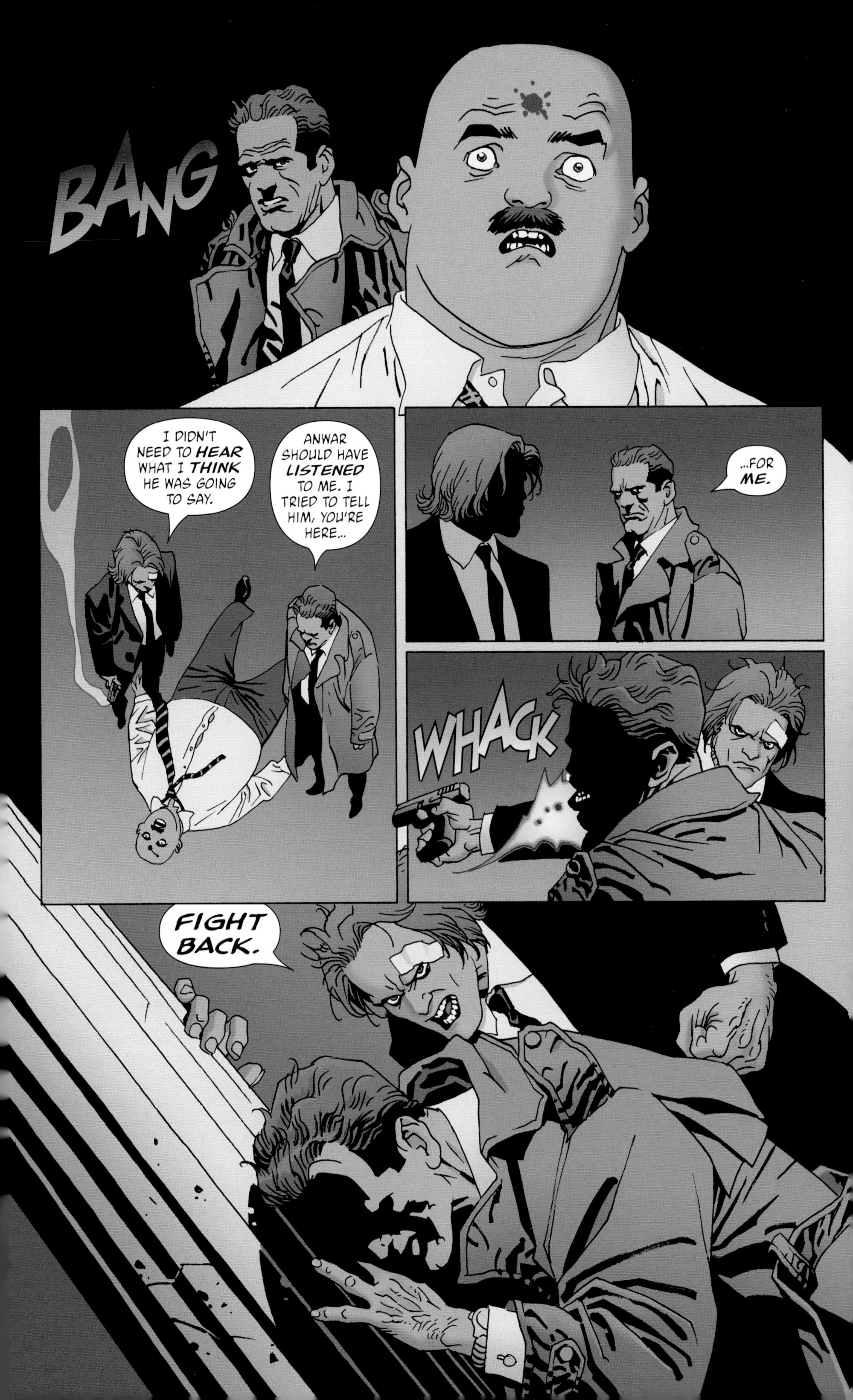
BANG
I DIDN'T NEED TO HEAR WHAT I THINK HE WAS GOING TO SAY.
ANWAR SHOULD HAVE LISTENED TO ME. I TRIED TO TELL HIM, YOU'RE HERE...
...FOR ME.
WHACK
FIGHT BACK.

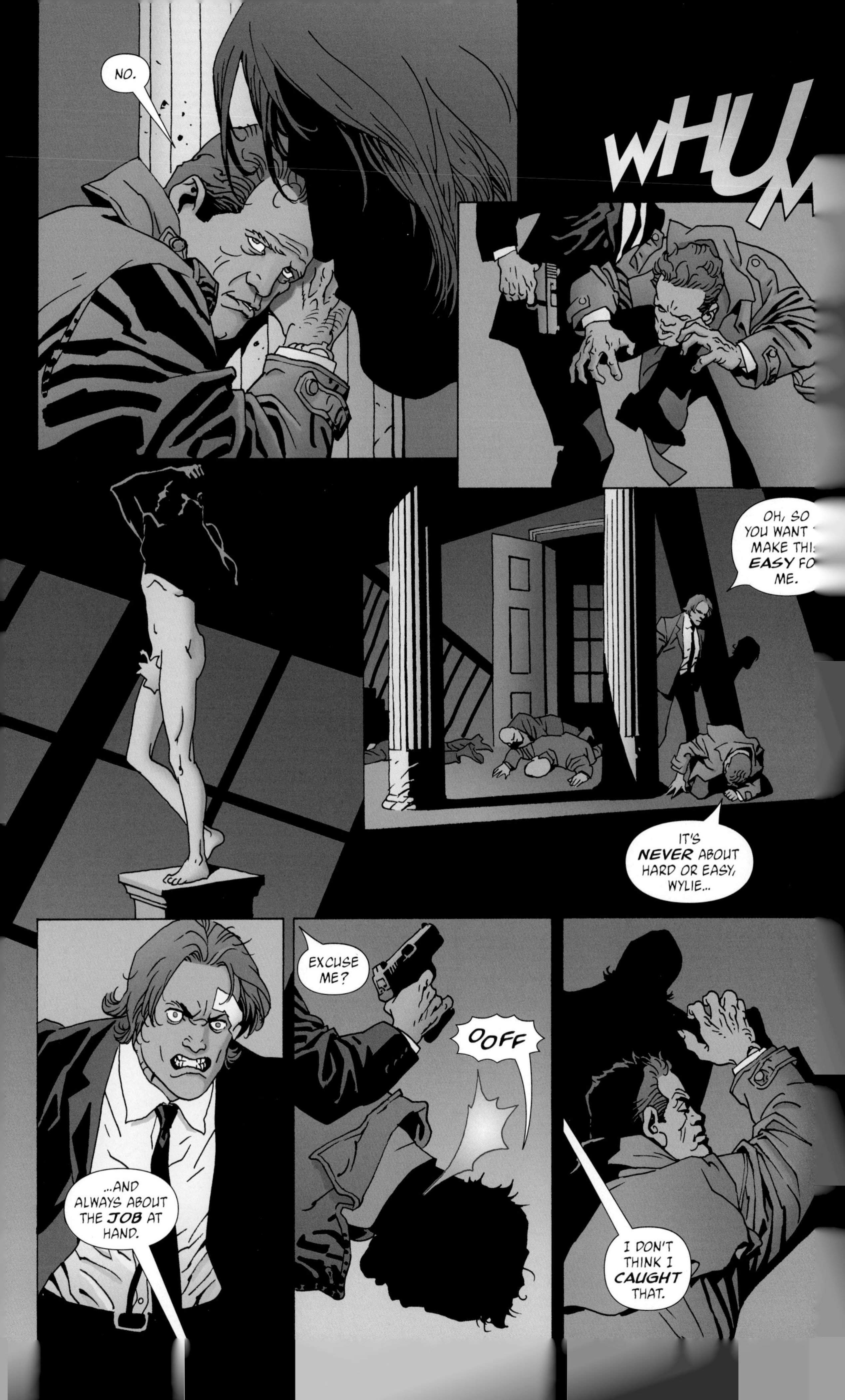
NO.
WHUM
OH, SO YOU WANT T MAKE THIS EASY FO ME.
IT'S NEVER ABOUT HARD OR EASY, WYLIE...
...AND ALWAYS ABOUT THE JOB AT HAND.
EXCUSE ME?
OOFF
I DON'T THINK I CAUGHT THAT.

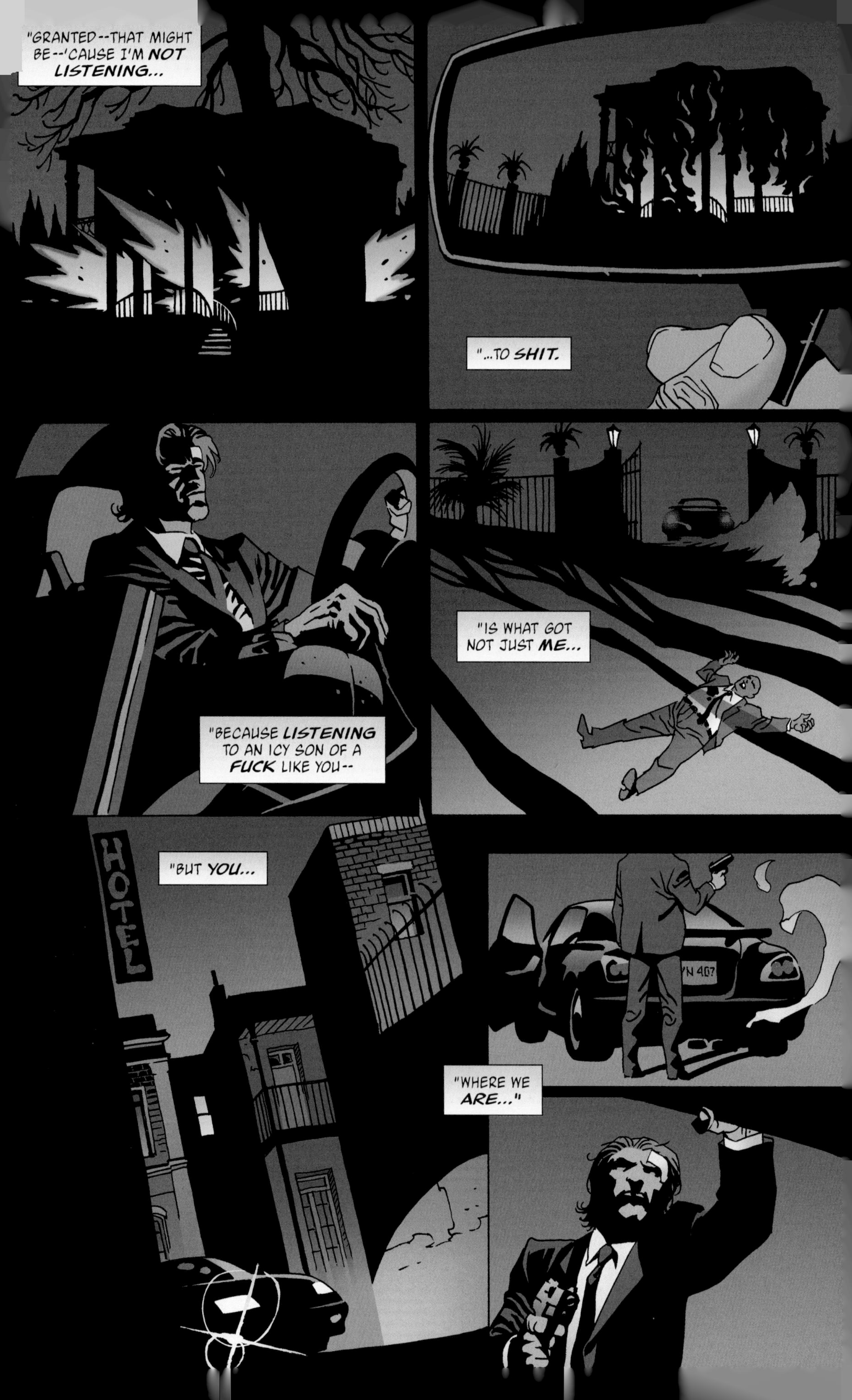
"GRANTED--THAT MIGHT BE--'CAUSE I'M NOT LISTENING...
"...TO SHIT.
"BECAUSE LISTENING TO AN ICY SON OF A FUCK LIKE YOU--
"IS WHAT GOT NOT JUST ME...
"BUT YOU...
"WHERE WE ARE..."
HOTEL

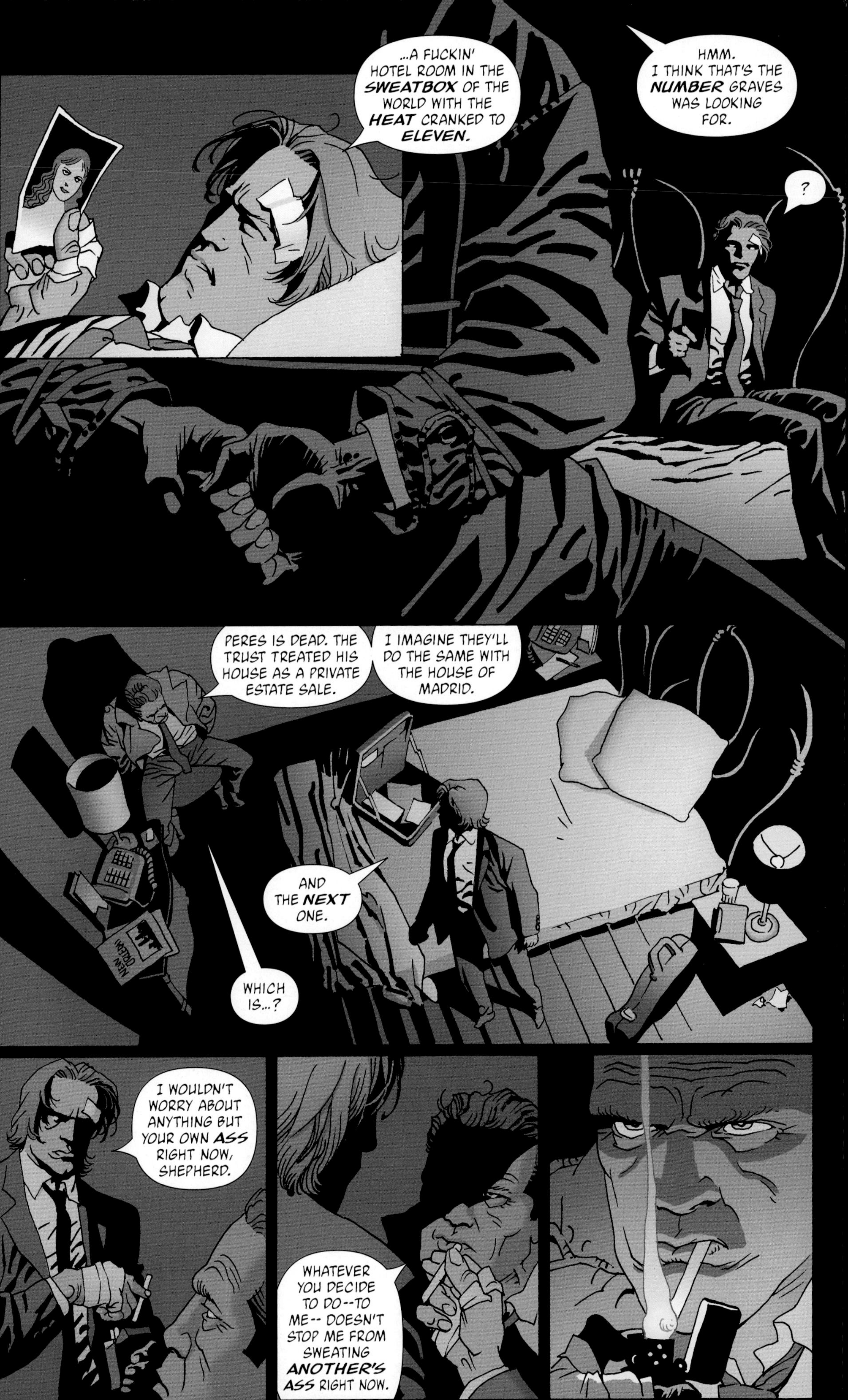
...A FUCKIN' HOTEL ROOM IN THE SWEATBOX OF THE WORLD WITH THE HEAT CRANKED TO ELEVEN.
HMM. I THINK THAT'S THE NUMBER GRAVES WAS LOOKING FOR.
?
PERES IS DEAD. THE TRUST TREATED HIS HOUSE AS A PRIVATE ESTATE SALE.
I IMAGINE THEY'LL DO THE SAME WITH THE HOUSE OF MADRID.
AND THE NEXT ONE.
WHICH IS...?
I WOULDN'T WORRY ABOUT ANYTHING BUT YOUR OWN ASS RIGHT NOW, SHEPHERD.
WHATEVER YOU DECIDE TO DO--TO ME-- DOESN'T STOP ME FROM SWEATING ANOTHER'S ASS RIGHT NOW.

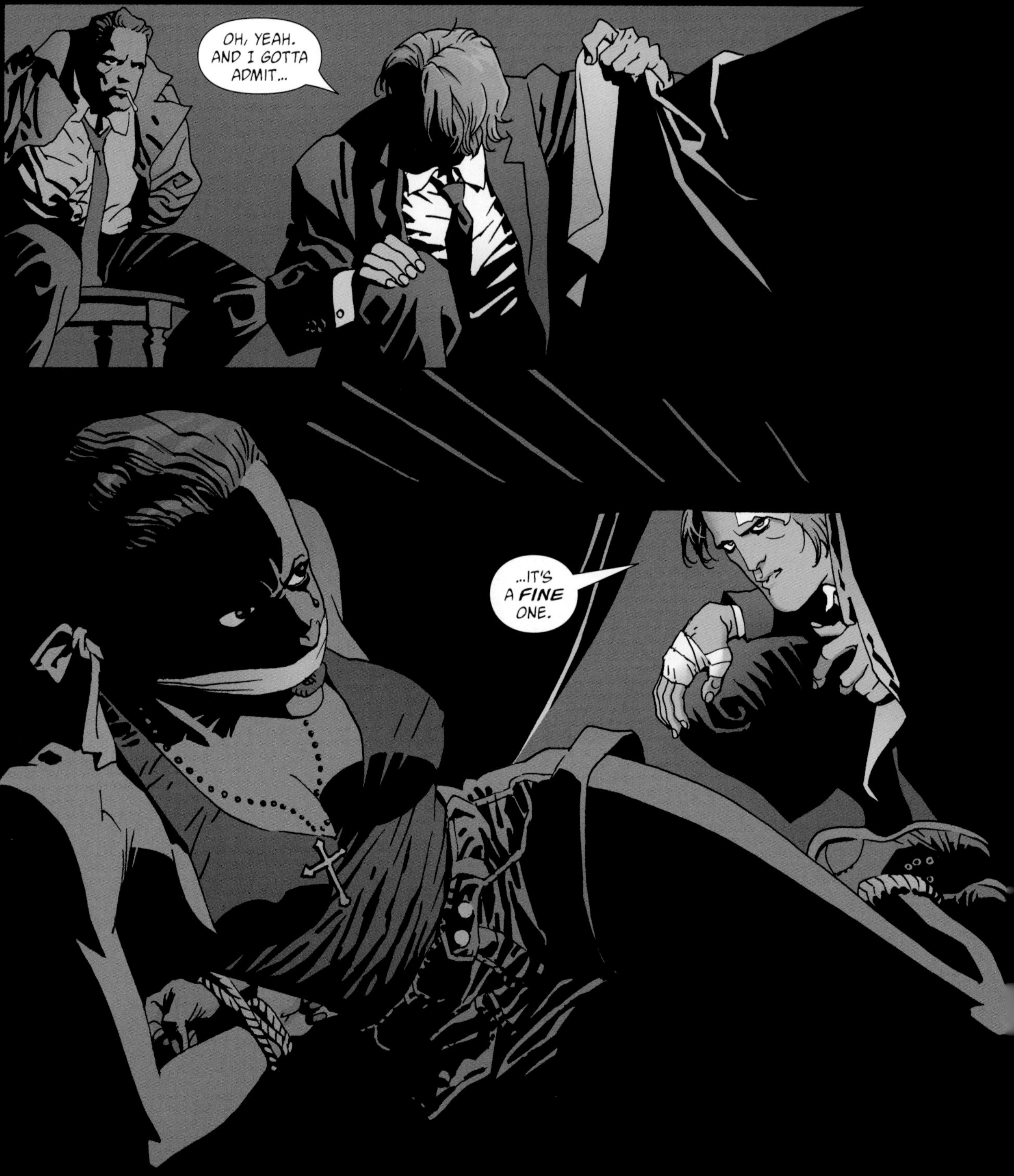
OH, YEAH. AND I GOTTA ADMIT...
...IT'S A FINE ONE.

Wylie Runs the Voodoo Down Part Six

Brian Azzarello writer
Eduardo Risso artist
Patricia Mulvihill colorist
Clem Robins letterer **Dave Johnson** cover
Casey Seijas asst. ed. **Will Dennis** editor

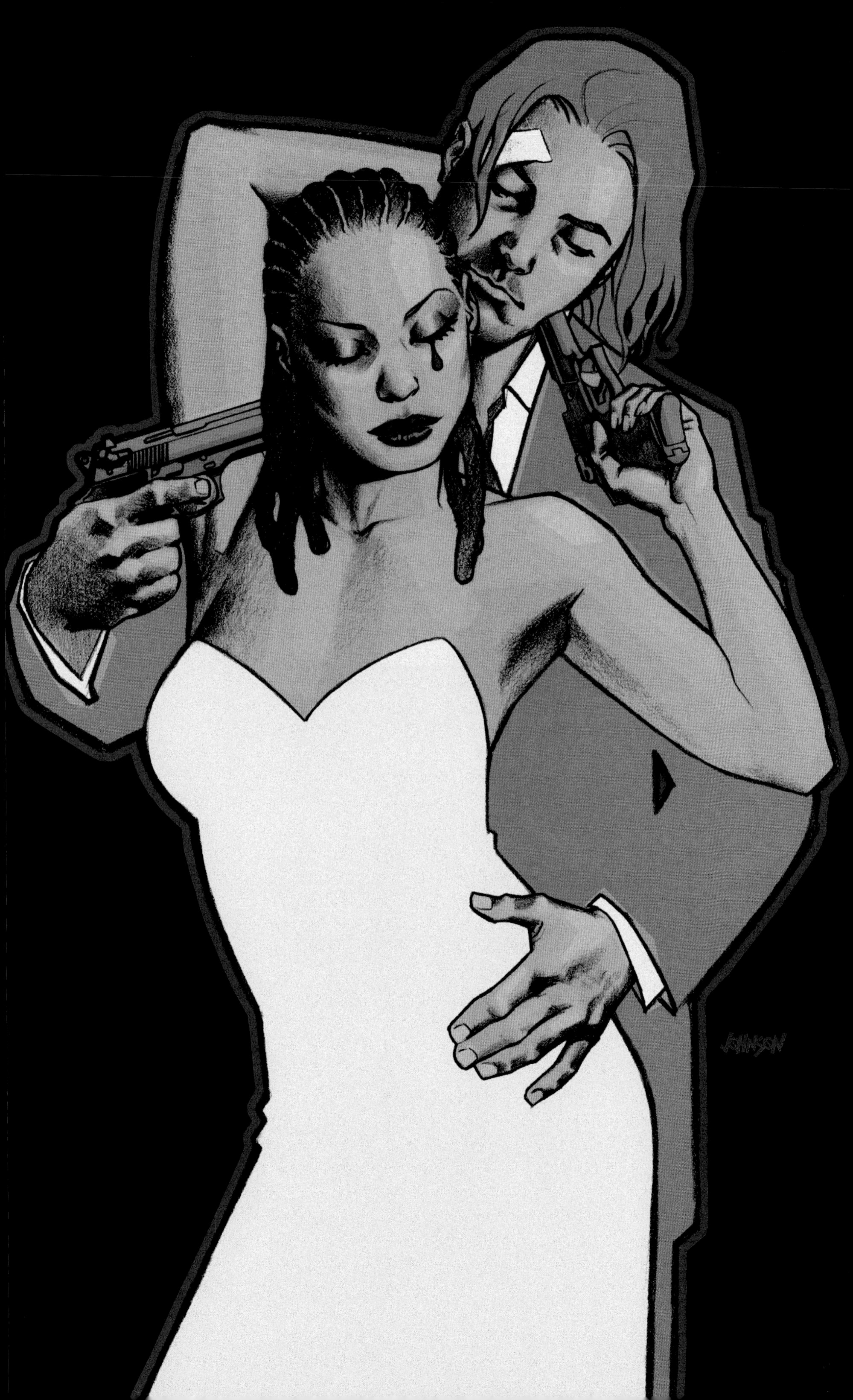
JOHNSON

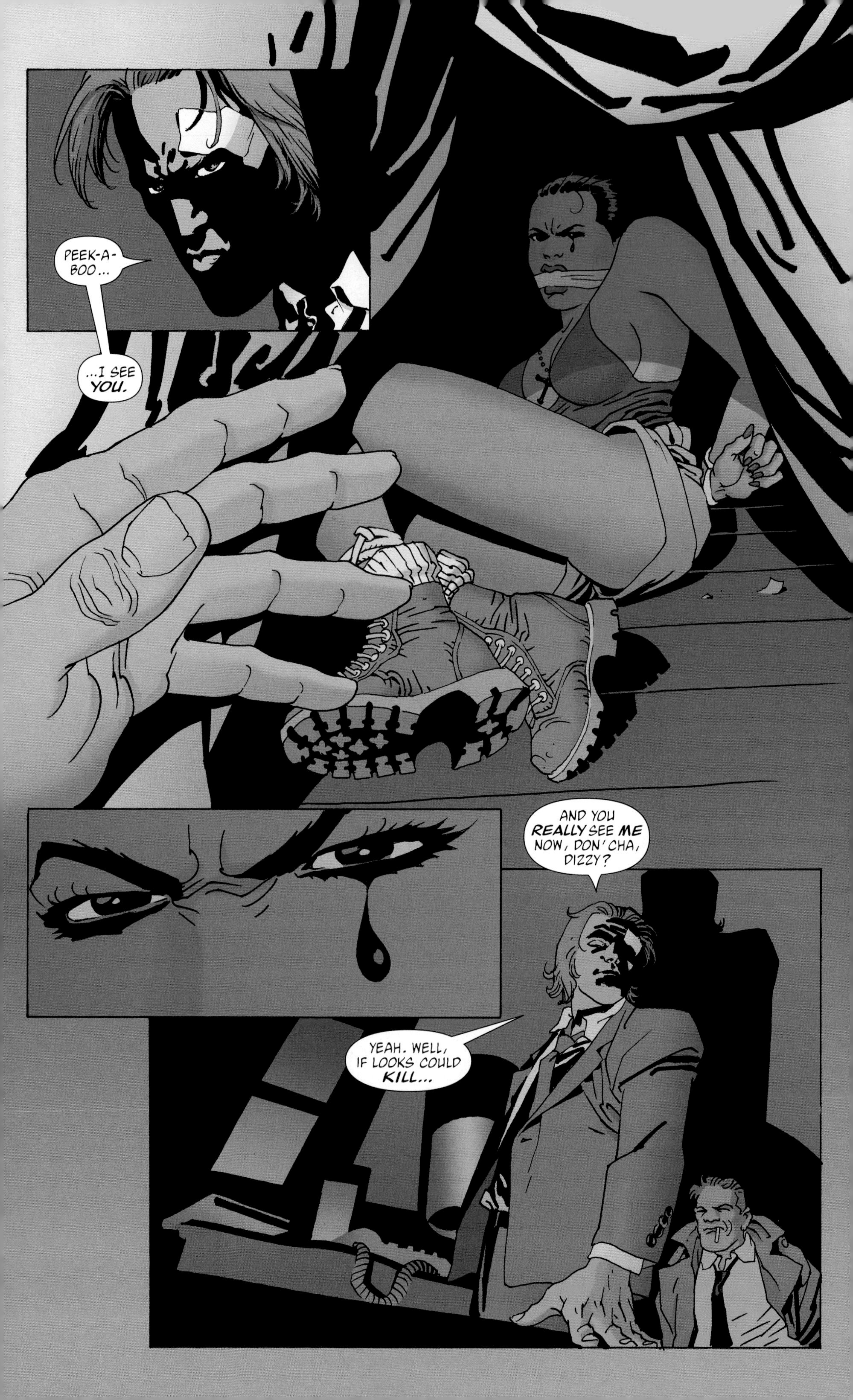
PEEK-A-BOO...
...I SEE YOU.
AND YOU REALLY SEE ME NOW, DON'CHA, DIZZY?
YEAH. WELL, IF LOOKS COULD KILL...

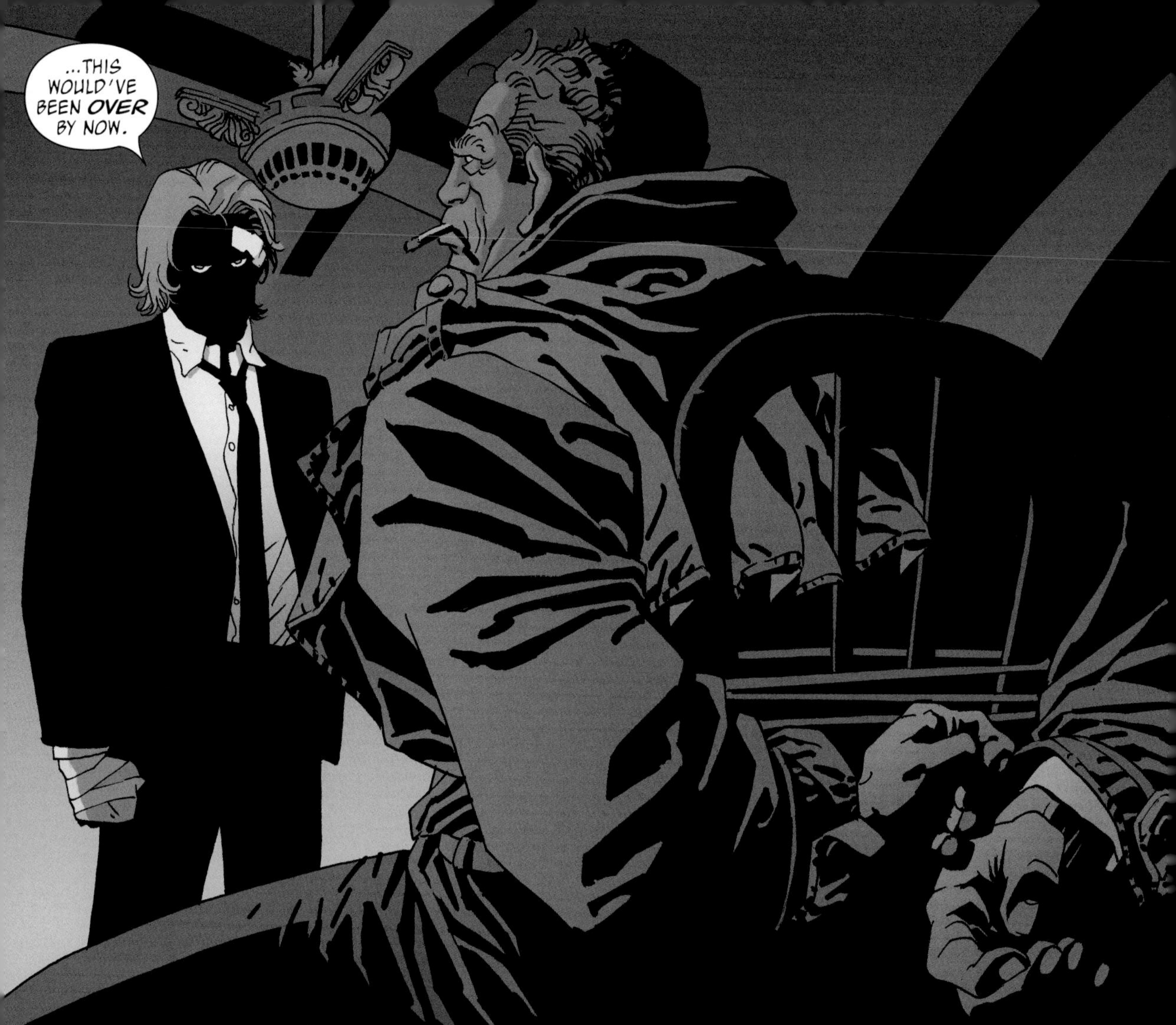
...THIS WOULD'VE BEEN OVER BY NOW.

Wylie Runs the Voodoo Down

Conclusion

Brian Azzarello writer

Eduardo Risso artist

Patricia Mulvihill colorist

Clem Robins letterer **Dave Johnson** cover

Casey Seijas asst. ed. **Will Dennis** editor

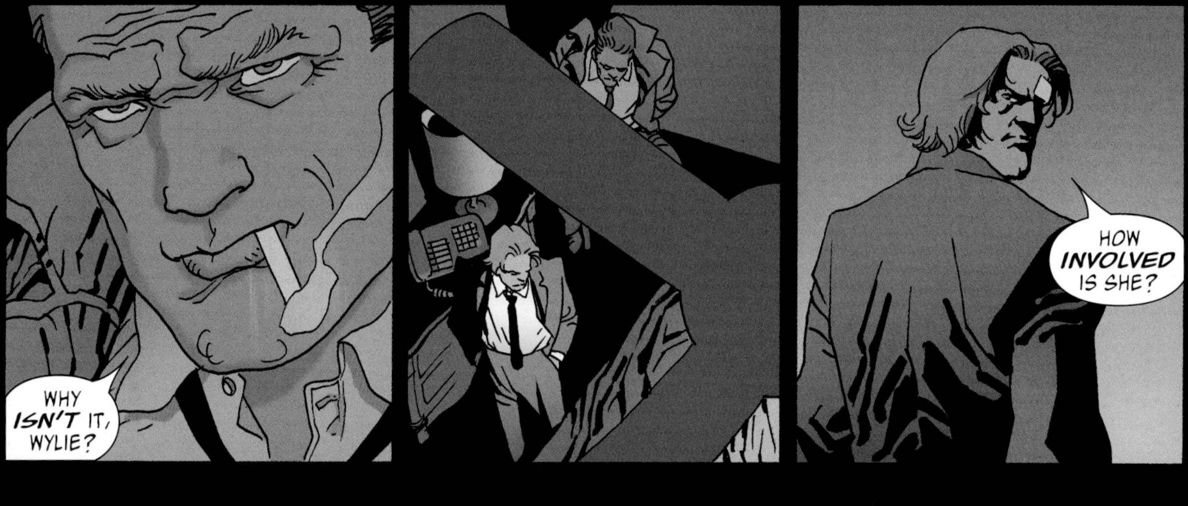
WHY ISN'T IT, WYLIE?
HOW INVOLVED IS SHE?

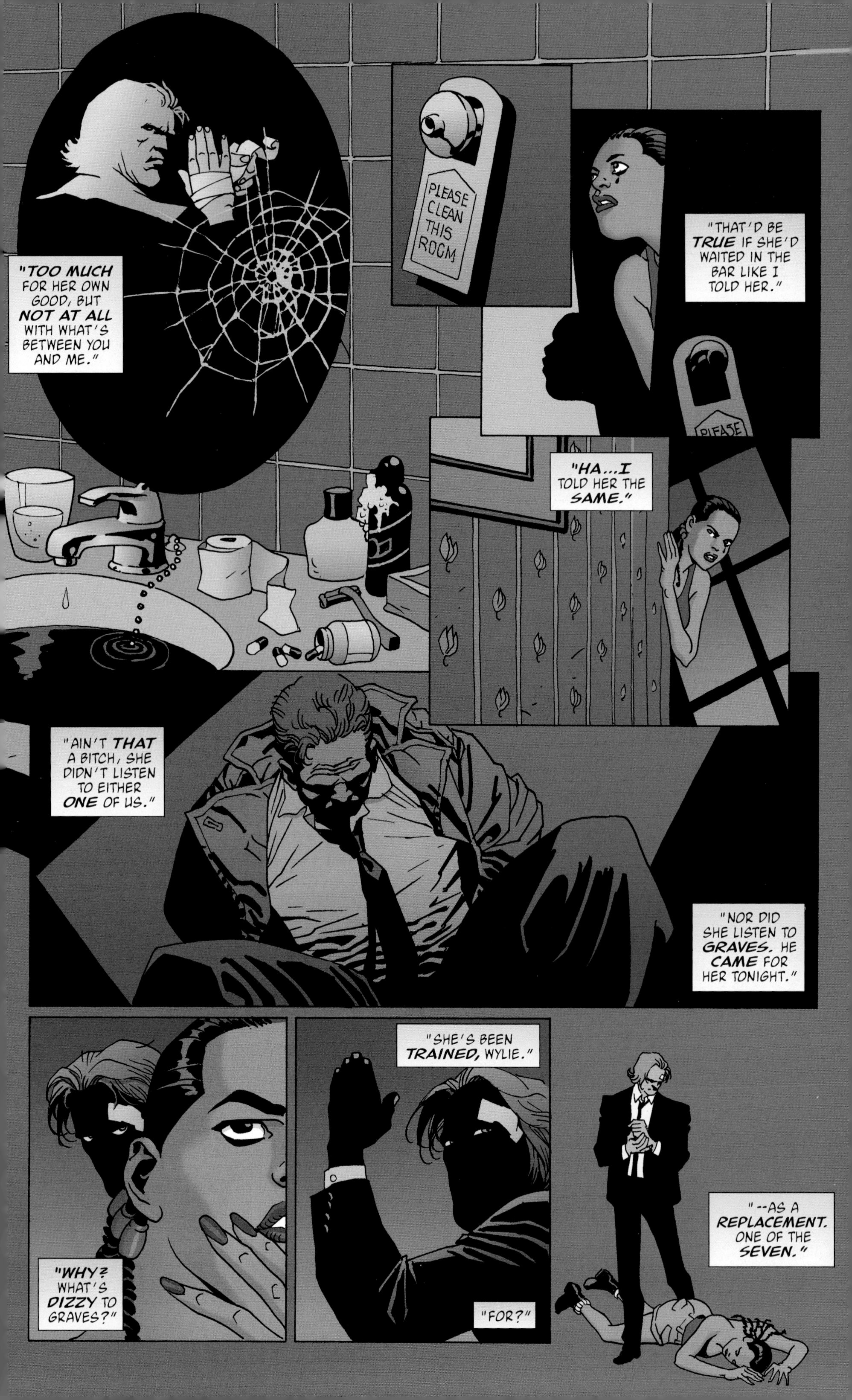
"TOO MUCH FOR HER OWN GOOD, BUT NOT AT ALL WITH WHAT'S BETWEEN YOU AND ME."
PLEASE CLEAN THIS ROOM
"THAT'D BE TRUE IF SHE'D WAITED IN THE BAR LIKE I TOLD HER."
"HA...I TOLD HER THE SAME."
"AIN'T THAT A BITCH, SHE DIDN'T LISTEN TO EITHER ONE OF US."
"NOR DID SHE LISTEN TO GRAVES. HE CAME FOR HER TONIGHT."
"WHY? WHAT'S DIZZY TO GRAVES?"
"SHE'S BEEN TRAINED, WYLIE."
"FOR?"
"--AS A REPLACEMENT. ONE OF THE SEVEN."

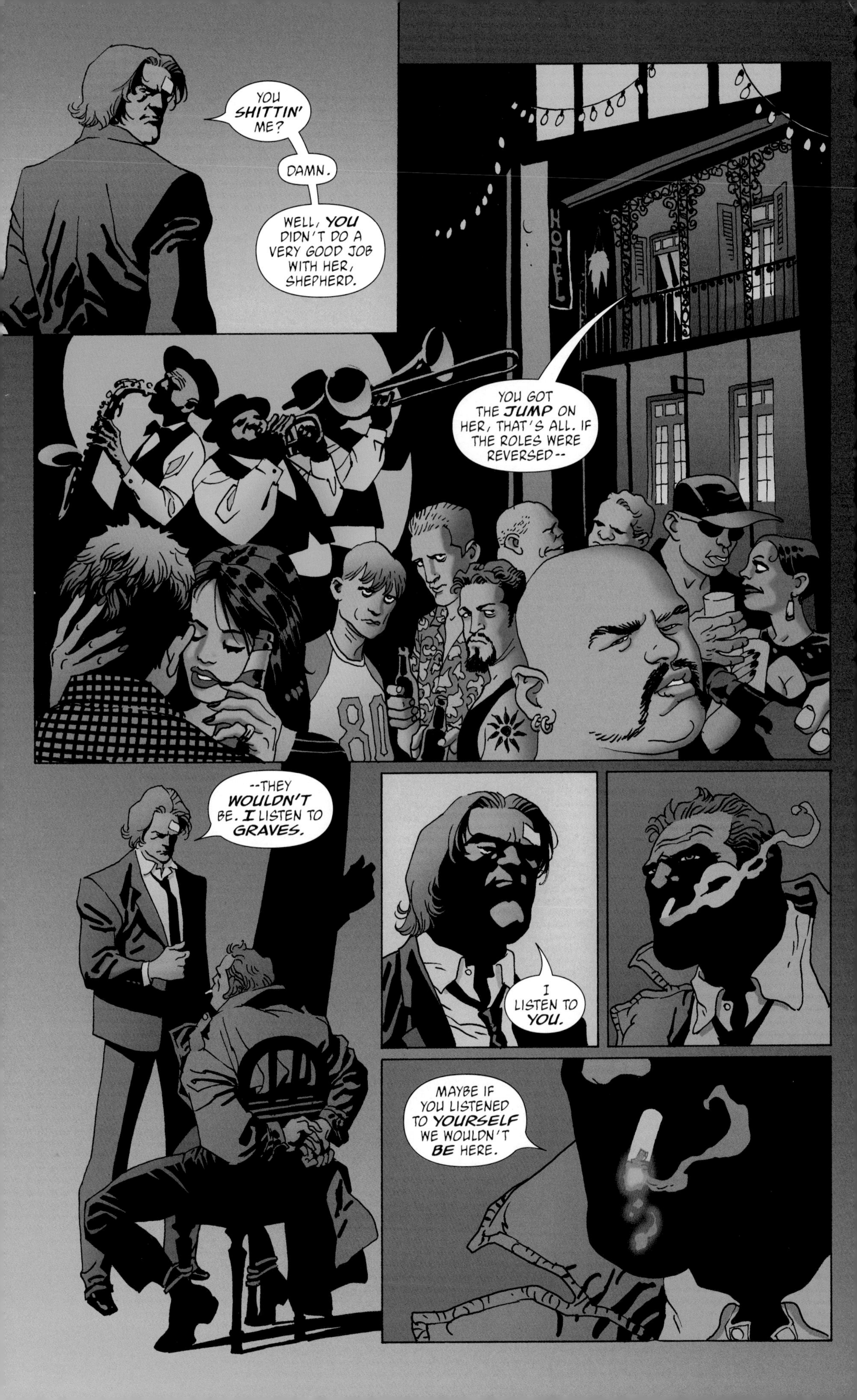

YOU SHITTIN' ME?
DAMN.
WELL, YOU DIDN'T DO A VERY GOOD JOB WITH HER, SHEPHERD.
YOU GOT THE JUMP ON HER, THAT'S ALL. IF THE ROLES WERE REVERSED--
--THEY WOULDN'T BE. I LISTEN TO GRAVES.
I LISTEN TO YOU.
MAYBE IF YOU LISTENED TO YOURSELF WE WOULDN'T BE HERE.

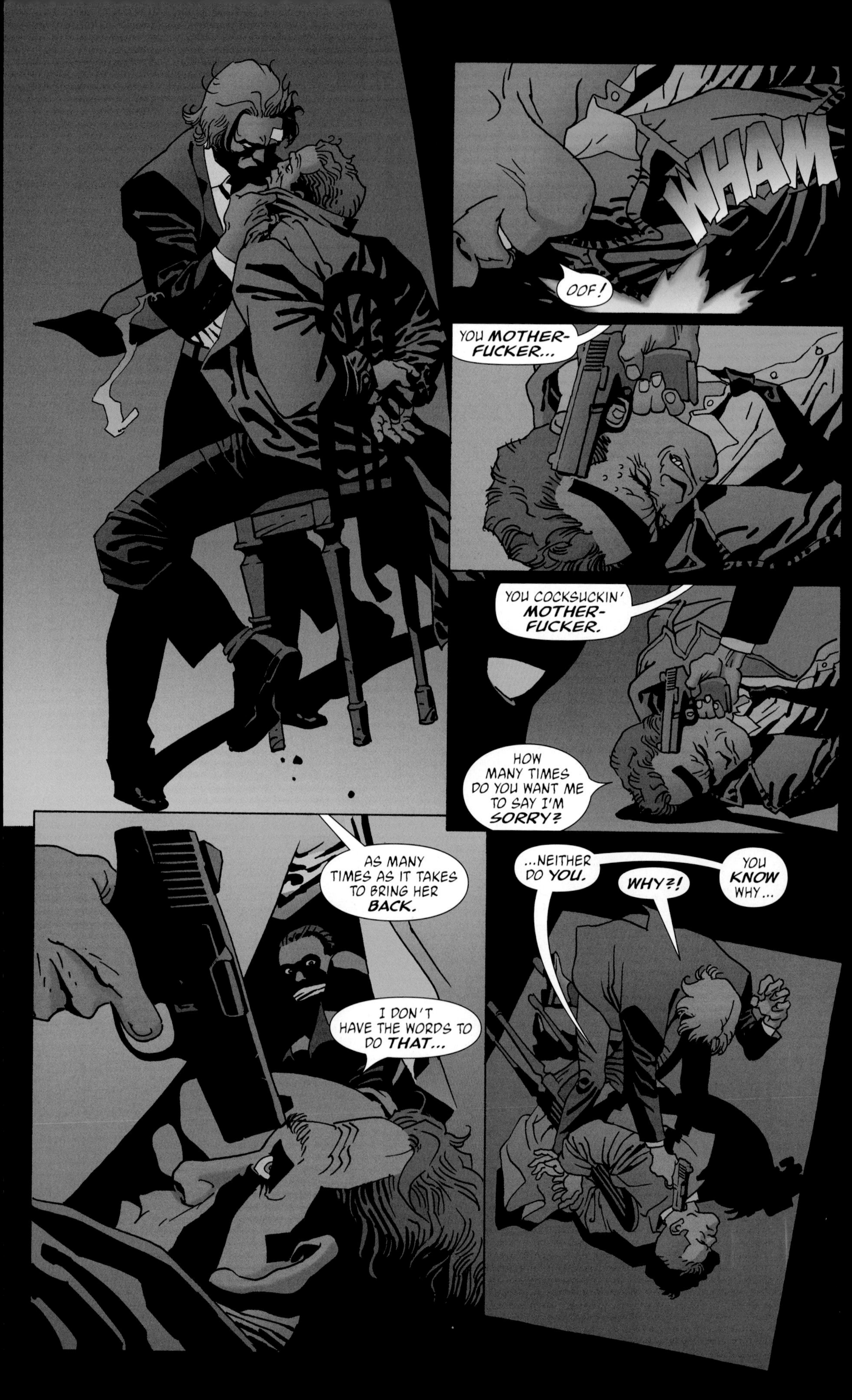
WHAM
OOF!
YOU MOTHER-FUCKER...
YOU COCKSUCKIN' MOTHER-FUCKER.
HOW MANY TIMES DO YOU WANT ME TO SAY I'M SORRY?
AS MANY TIMES AS IT TAKES TO BRING HER BACK.
I DON'T HAVE THE WORDS TO DO THAT...
...NEITHER DO YOU.
WHY?!
YOU KNOW WHY...

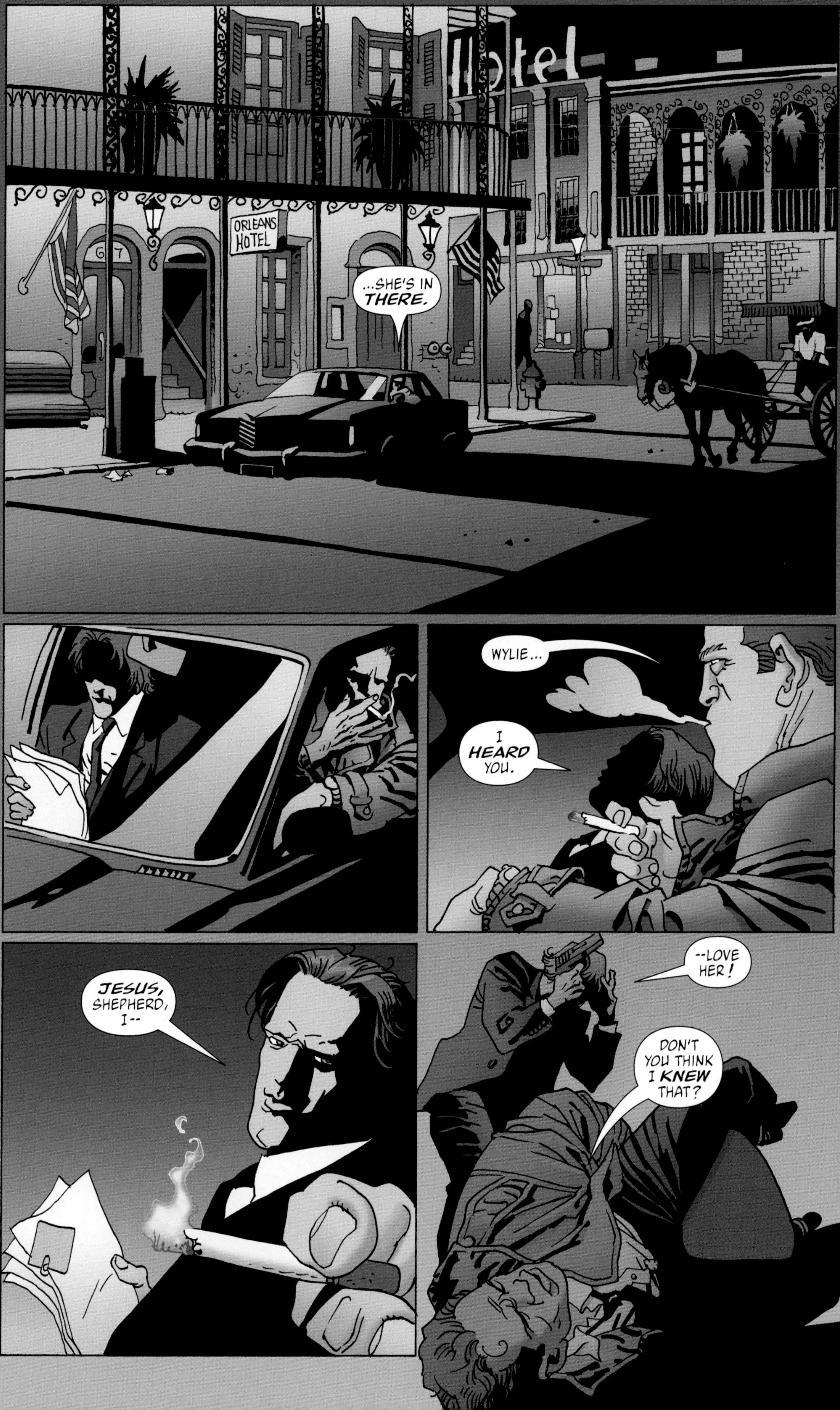
Hotel
ORLEANS HOTEL
...SHE'S IN THERE.
WYLIE...
I HEARD YOU.
JESUS, SHEPHERD, I--
--LOVE HER!
DON'T YOU THINK I KNEW THAT?

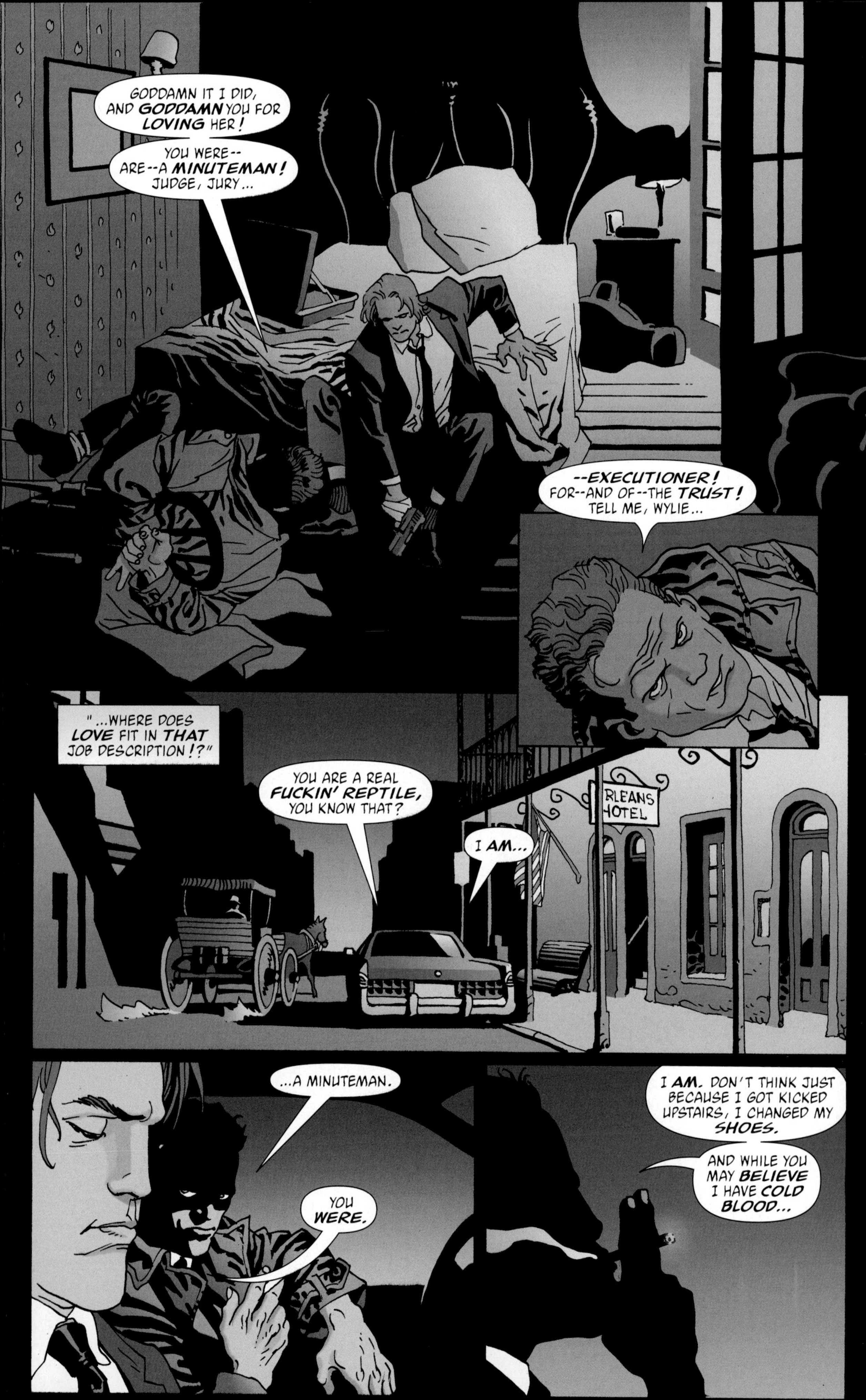

GODDAMN IT I DID, AND GODDAMN YOU FOR LOVING HER!
YOU WERE-- ARE--A MINUTEMAN! JUDGE, JURY...
--EXECUTIONER! FOR--AND OF--THE TRUST! TELL ME, WYLIE...
"...WHERE DOES LOVE FIT IN THAT JOB DESCRIPTION!?"
YOU ARE A REAL FUCKIN' REPTILE, YOU KNOW THAT?
I AM...
RLEANS HOTEL
...A MINUTEMAN.
YOU WERE.
I AM. DON'T THINK JUST BECAUSE I GOT KICKED UPSTAIRS, I CHANGED MY SHOES.
AND WHILE YOU MAY BELIEVE I HAVE COLD BLOOD...

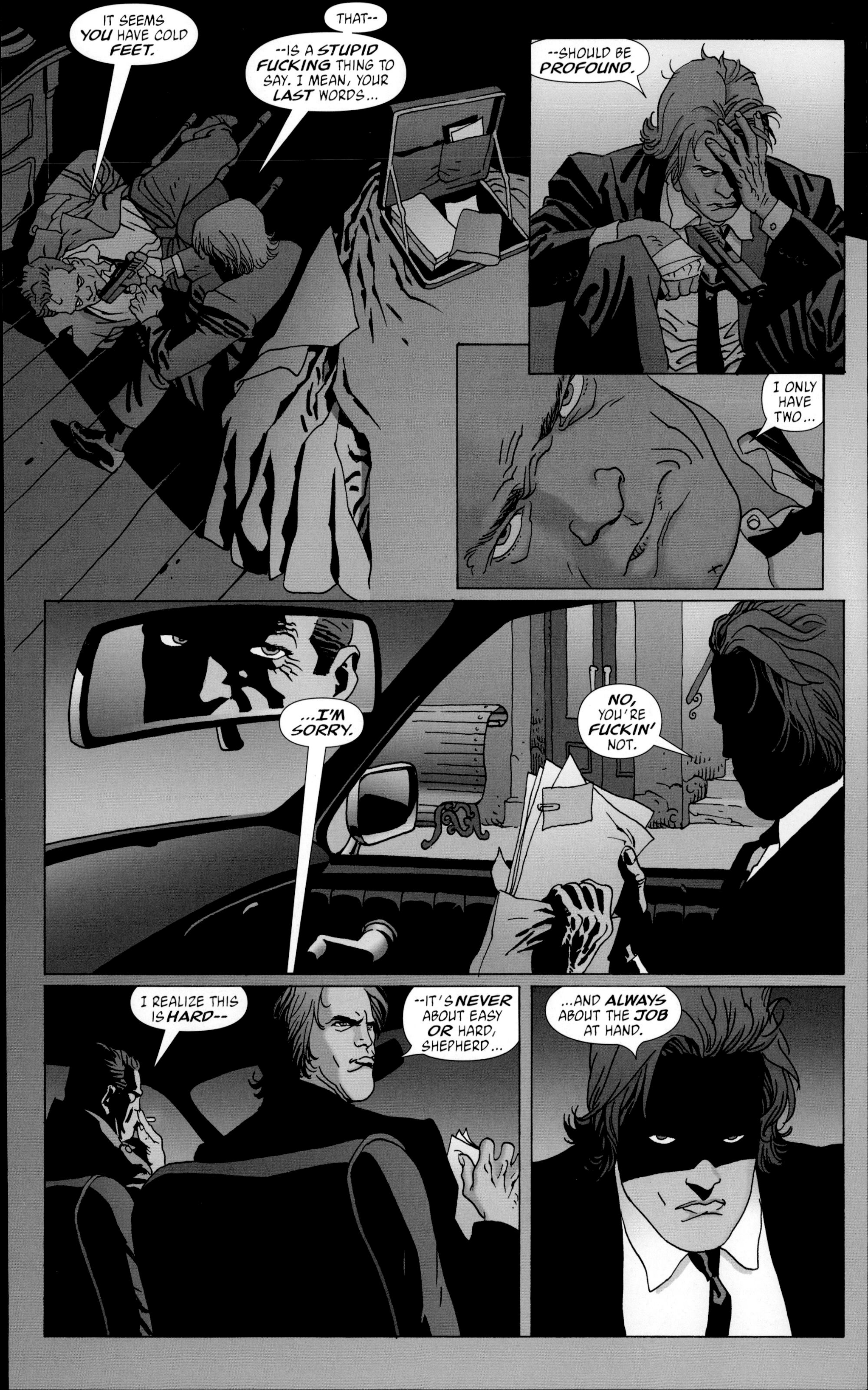
IT SEEMS YOU HAVE COLD FEET.
THAT--
--IS A STUPID FUCKING THING TO SAY. I MEAN, YOUR LAST WORDS...
--SHOULD BE PROFOUND.
I ONLY HAVE TWO...
...I'M SORRY.
NO, YOU'RE FUCKIN' NOT.
I REALIZE THIS IS HARD--
--IT'S NEVER ABOUT EASY OR HARD, SHEPHERD...
...AND ALWAYS ABOUT THE JOB AT HAND.

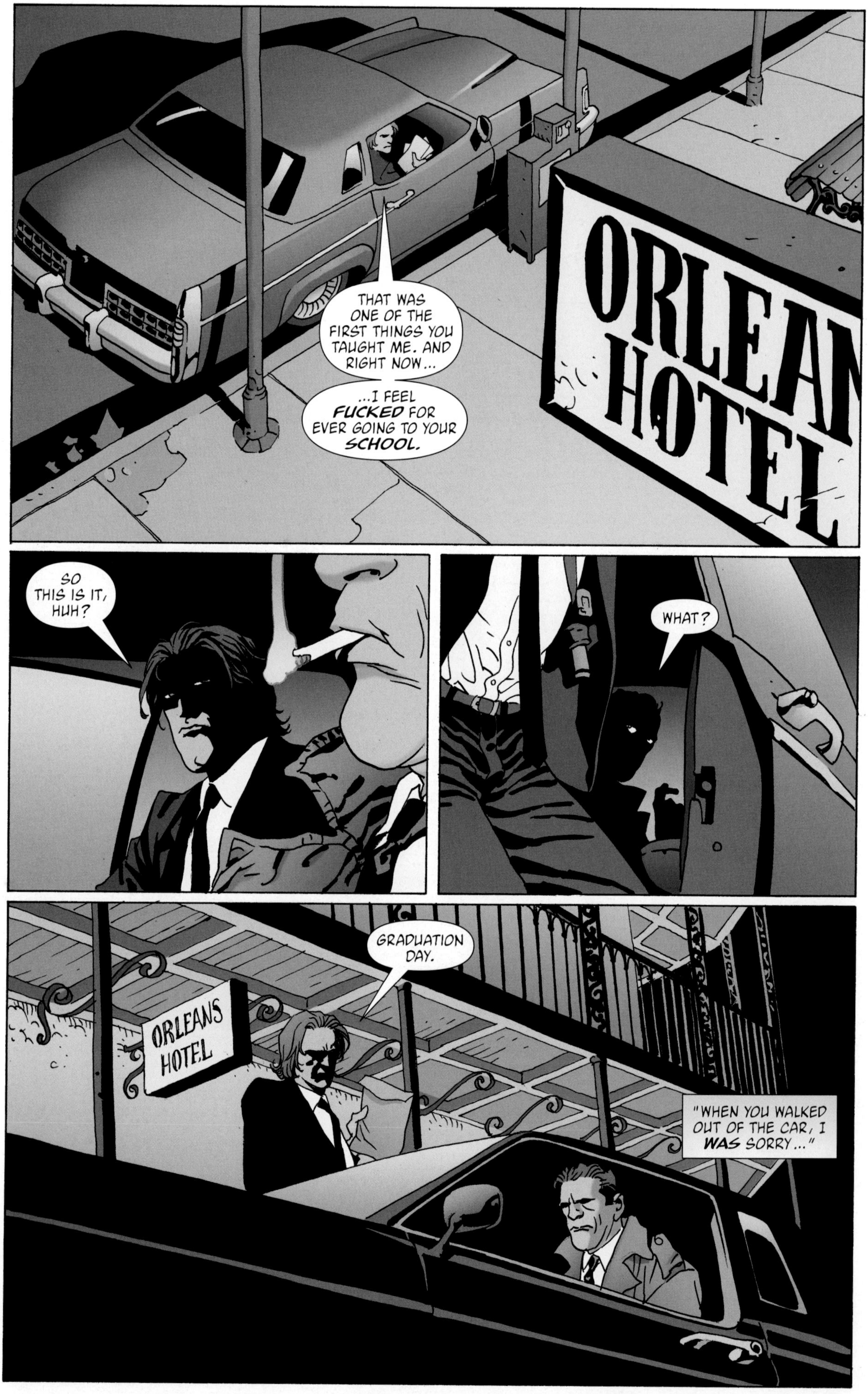
ORLEANS HOTEL
THAT WAS ONE OF THE FIRST THINGS YOU TAUGHT ME. AND RIGHT NOW...
...I FEEL FUCKED FOR EVER GOING TO YOUR SCHOOL.
SO THIS IS IT, HUH?
WHAT?
GRADUATION DAY.
ORLEANS HOTEL
"WHEN YOU WALKED OUT OF THE CAR, I WAS SORRY..."

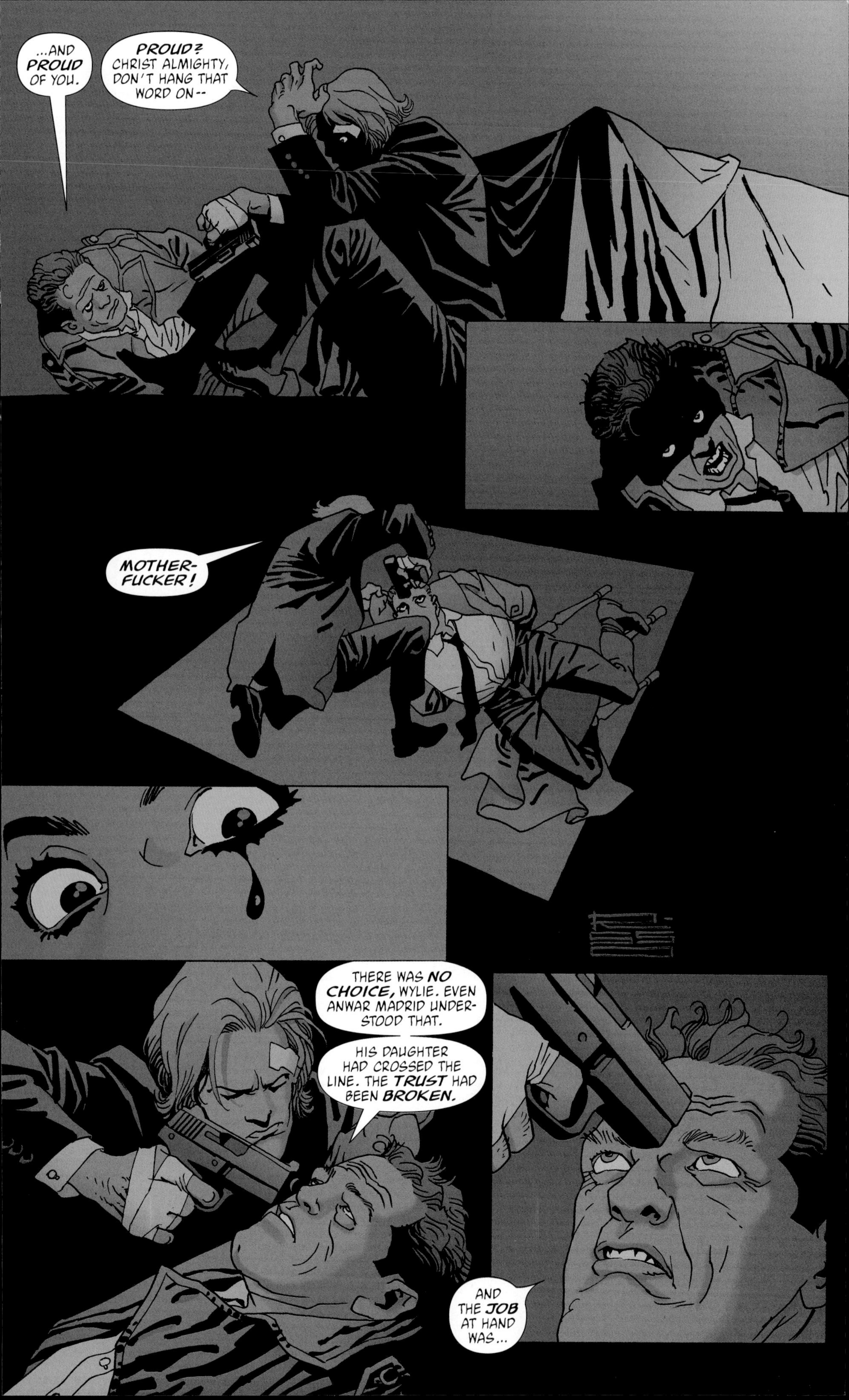
...AND PROUD OF YOU.
PROUD? CHRIST ALMIGHTY, DON'T HANG THAT WORD ON--
MOTHER-FUCKER!
THERE WAS NO CHOICE, WYLIE. EVEN ANWAR MADRID UNDER-STOOD THAT.
HIS DAUGHTER HAD CROSSED THE LINE. THE TRUST HAD BEEN BROKEN.
AND THE JOB AT HAND WAS...

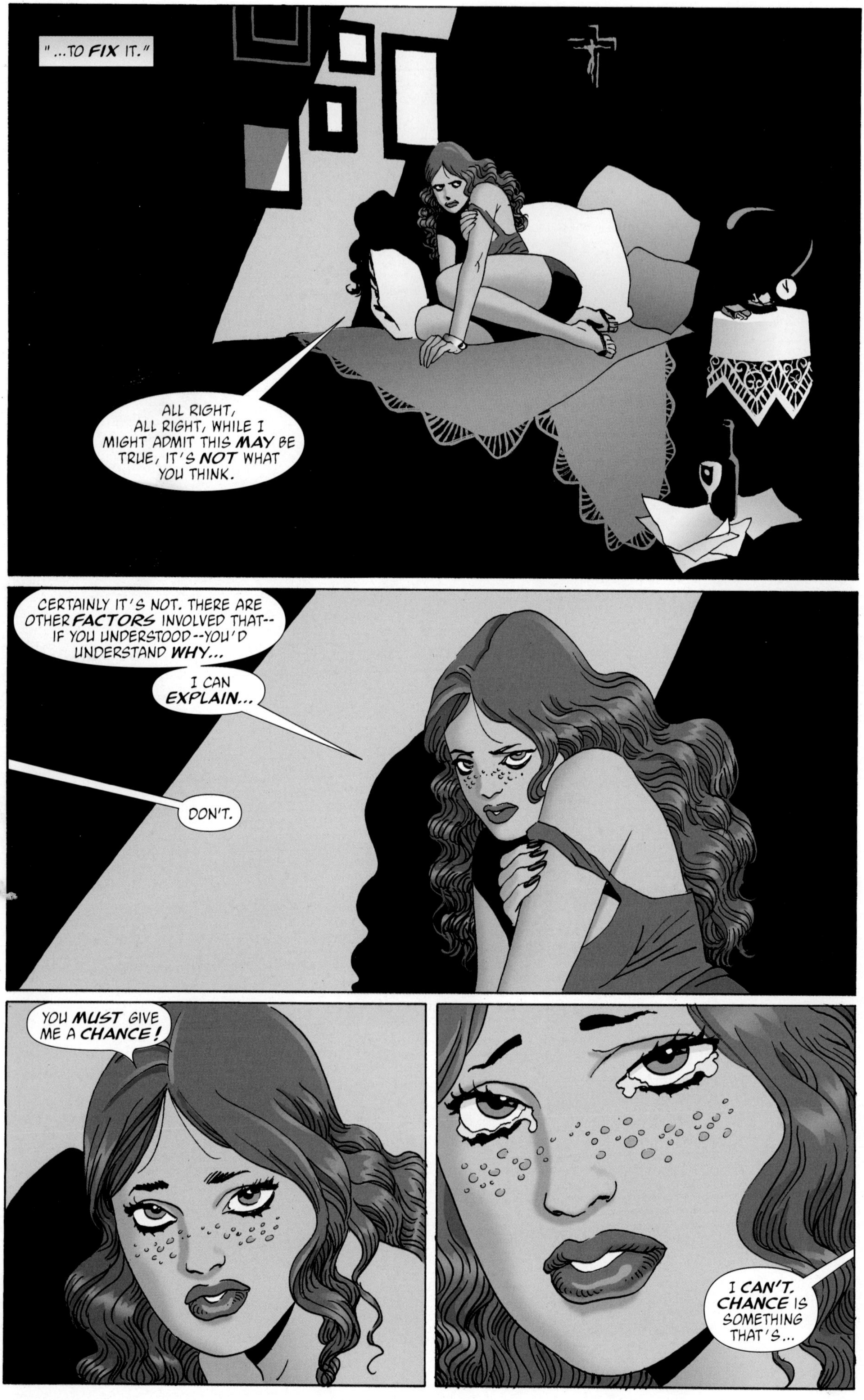
"...TO FIX IT."
ALL RIGHT, ALL RIGHT, WHILE I MIGHT ADMIT THIS MAY BE TRUE, IT'S NOT WHAT YOU THINK.
CERTAINLY IT'S NOT. THERE ARE OTHER FACTORS INVOLVED THAT-- IF YOU UNDERSTOOD--YOU'D UNDERSTAND WHY...
I CAN EXPLAIN...
DON'T.
YOU MUST GIVE ME A CHANCE!
I CAN'T. CHANCE IS SOMETHING THAT'S...

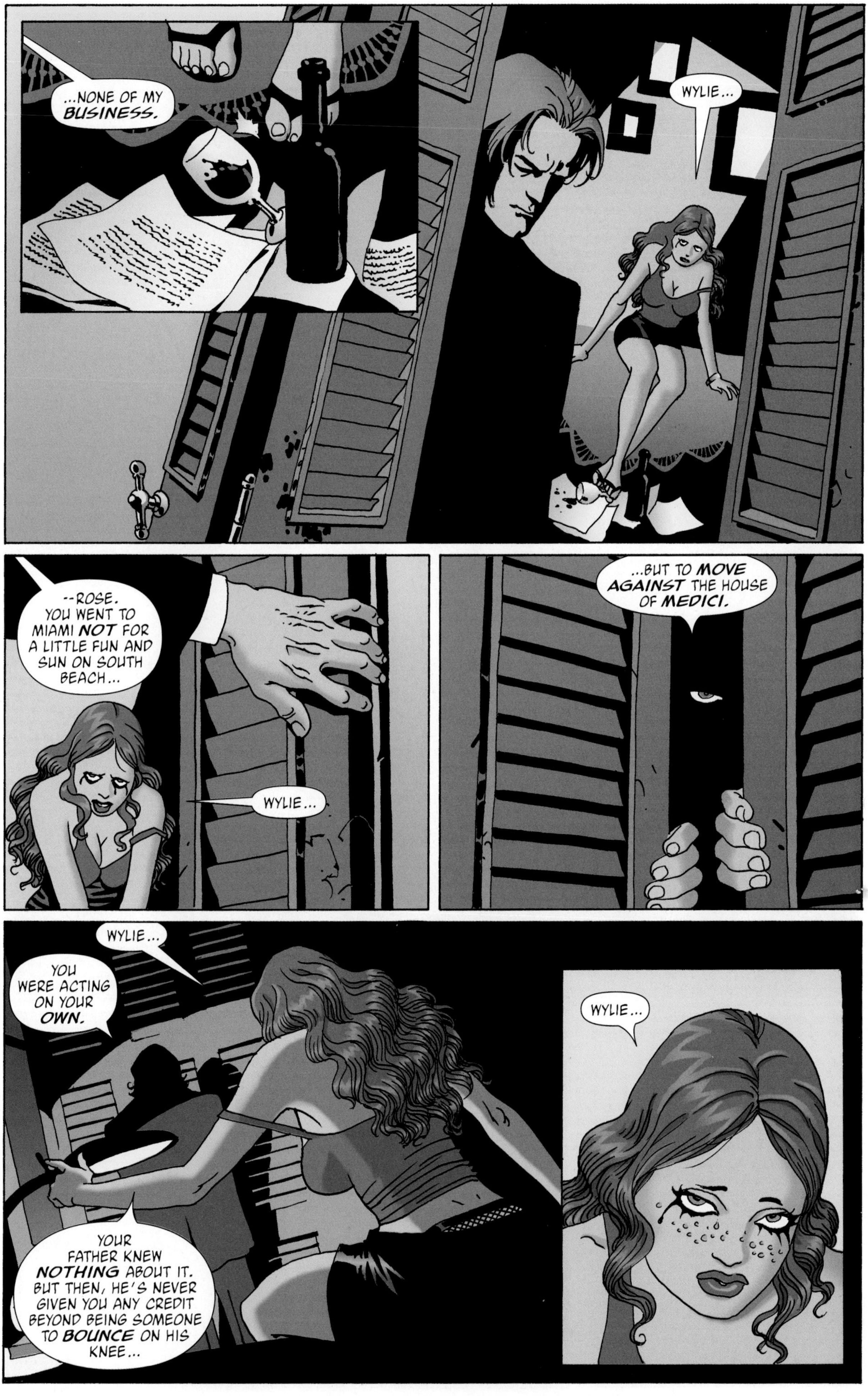
...NONE OF MY BUSINESS.
WYLIE...
--ROSE. YOU WENT TO MIAMI NOT FOR A LITTLE FUN AND SUN ON SOUTH BEACH...
WYLIE...
...BUT TO MOVE AGAINST THE HOUSE OF MEDICI.
WYLIE...
YOU WERE ACTING ON YOUR OWN.
YOUR FATHER KNEW NOTHING ABOUT IT. BUT THEN, HE'S NEVER GIVEN YOU ANY CREDIT BEYOND BEING SOMEONE TO BOUNCE ON HIS KNEE...
WYLIE...

...I BOUNCE IN YOUR LAP.

YEAH YOU DO, BABY.

C'MERE.

WHAT ARE WE GOING TO DO?

WE'RE GONNA FUCK--THE TRUST, GRAVES, AND SHEPHERD.

WE'RE GONNA RUN, WE'RE GONNA CHANGE OUR NAMES, AND WE'RE GONNA LIVE HAPPILY EVER AFTER.

WE'RE GONNA HAVE KIDS. I'M GONNA LOSE MY HAIR, YER BEAUTIFUL TITS ARE GONNA SAG, BUT I'LL STILL LAY MY BALD DOME ON THEM AND LICK YOUR NIPPLES CRAZY.

WE'RE GONNA FORGET YER A FILTHY RICH GIRL, AND THAT I'M A STINKIN' ASSASSIN. BUT WE'LL NEVER--EVER--FORGET HOW MUCH WE LOVE EACH OTHER.

HOW'S THAT SOUND?

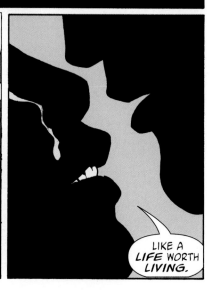

LIKE A LIFE WORTH LIVING.

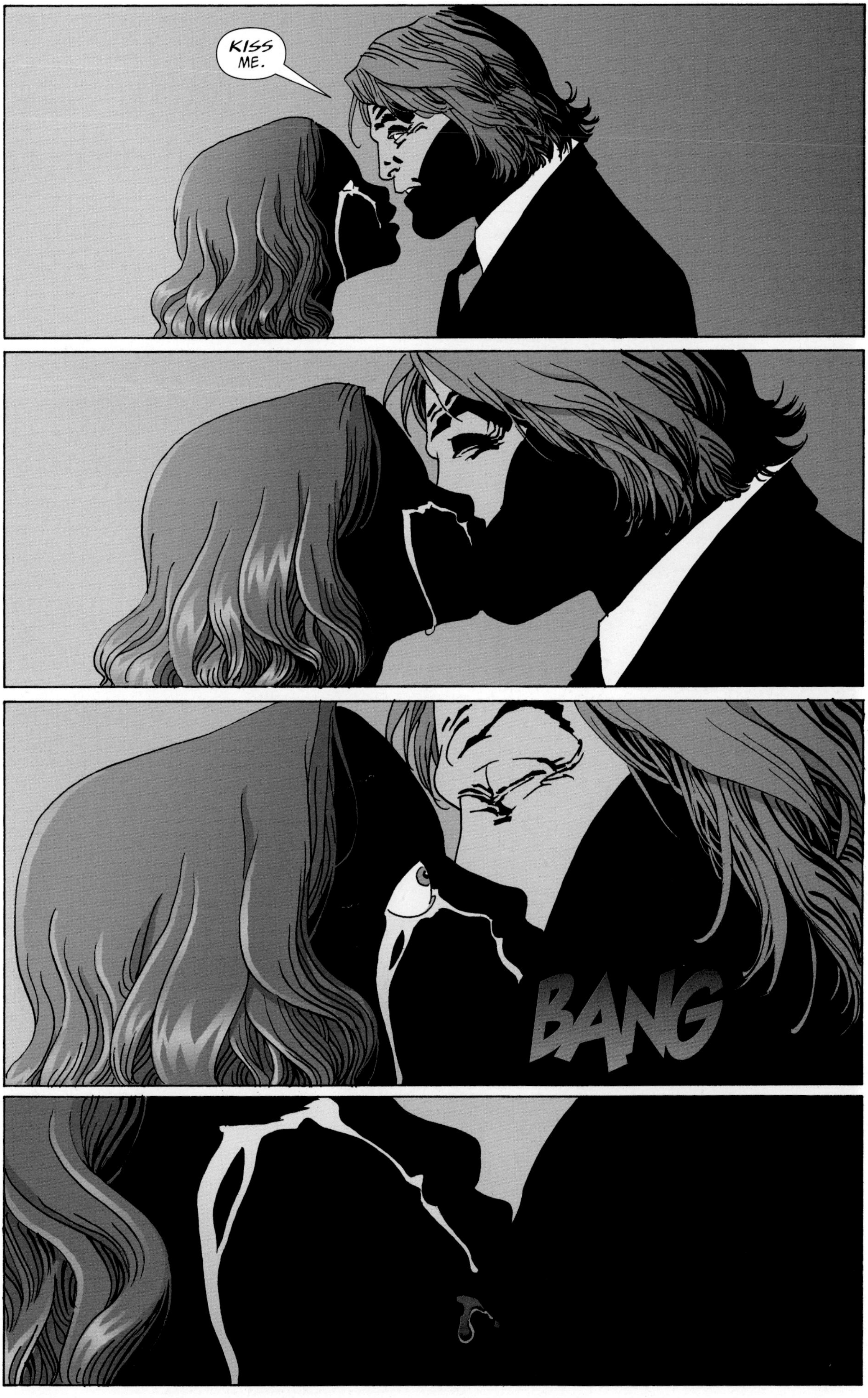
KISS ME.
BANG

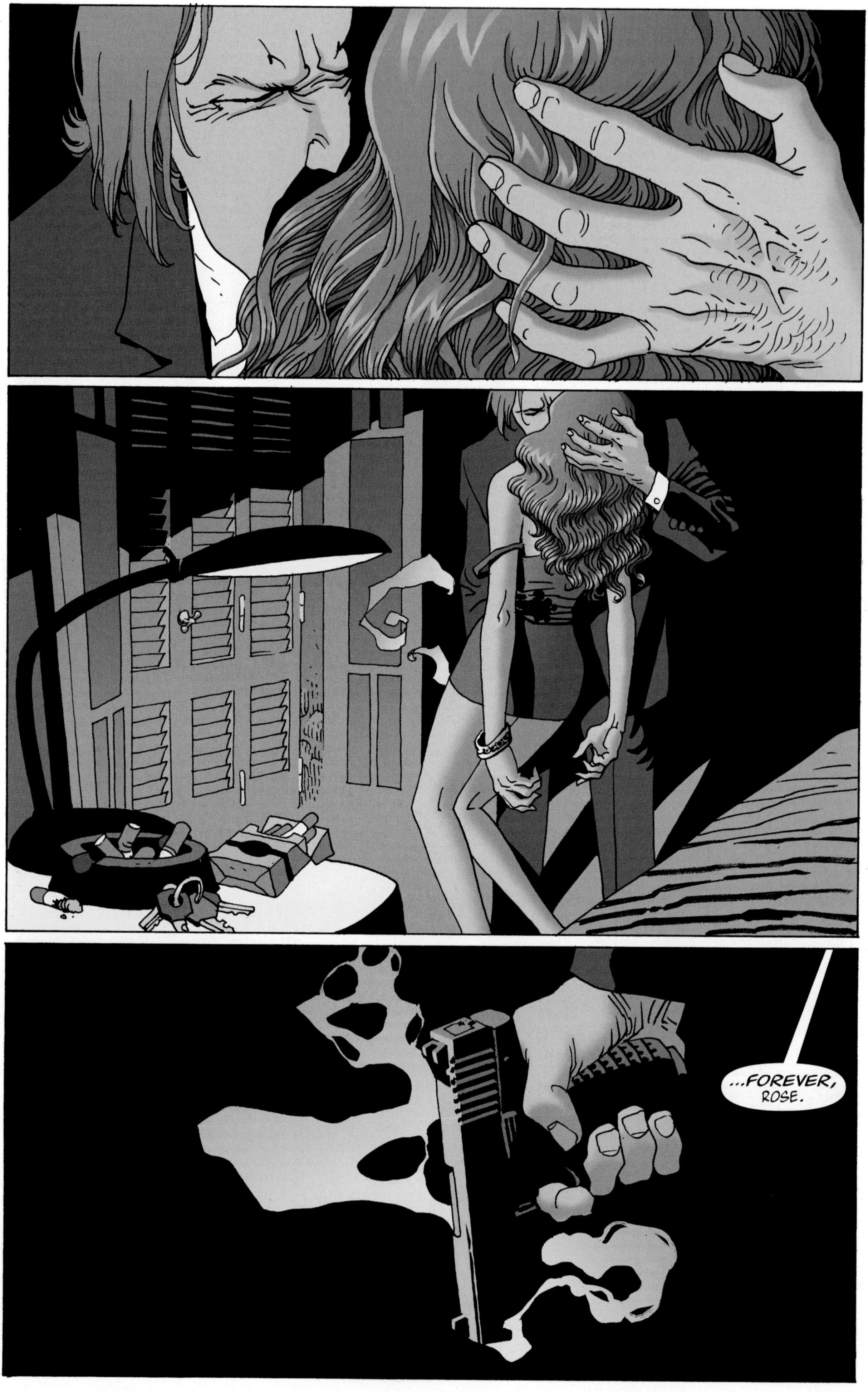
...FOREVER, ROSE.

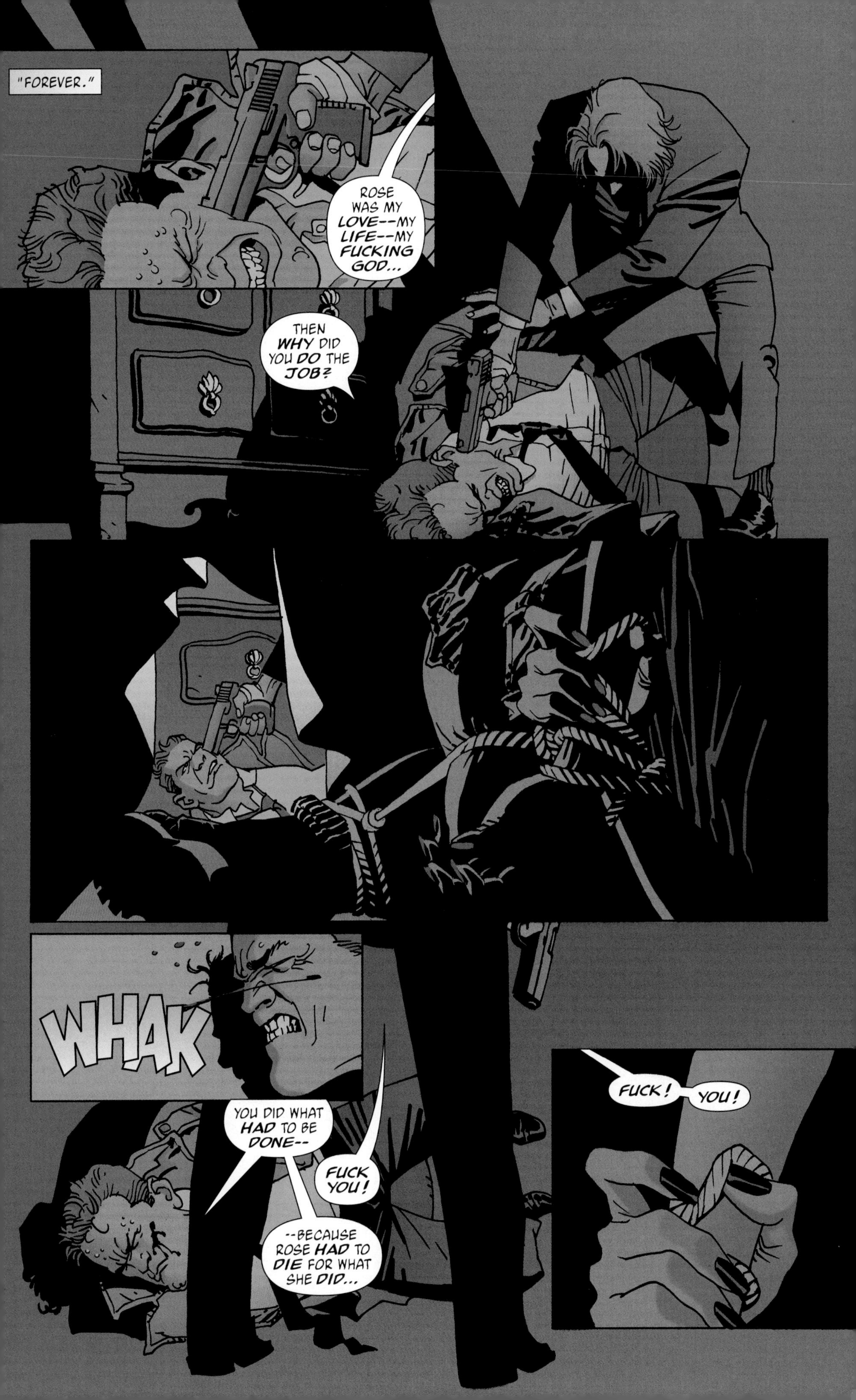
"FOREVER."
ROSE WAS MY LOVE--MY LIFE--MY FUCKING GOD...
THEN WHY DID YOU DO THE JOB?
WHAK
YOU DID WHAT HAD TO BE DONE--
FUCK YOU!
--BECAUSE ROSE HAD TO DIE FOR WHAT SHE DID...
FUCK!
YOU!

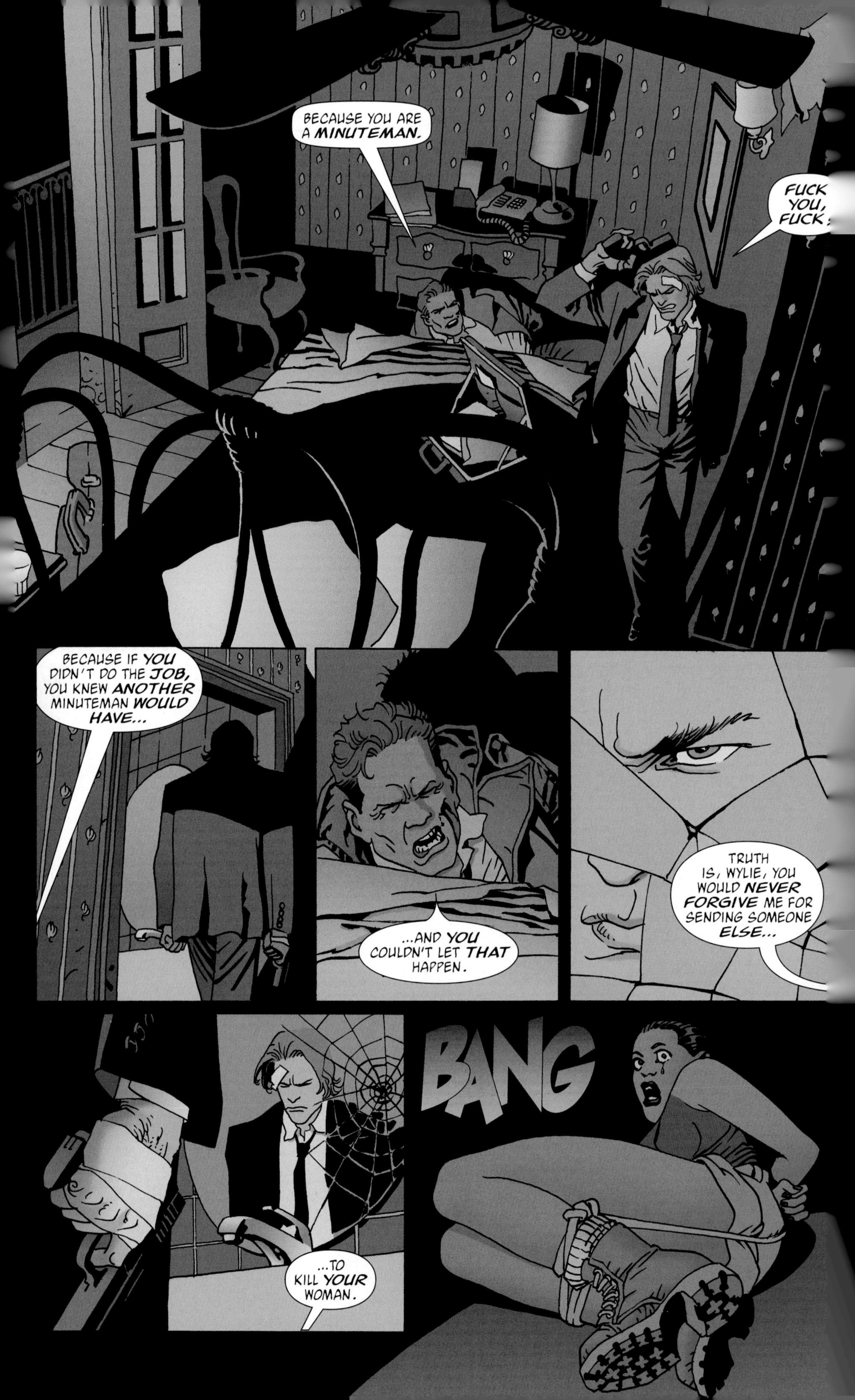
BECAUSE YOU ARE A MINUTEMAN.
FUCK YOU, FUCK!
BECAUSE IF YOU DIDN'T DO THE JOB, YOU KNEW ANOTHER MINUTEMAN WOULD HAVE...
...AND YOU COULDN'T LET THAT HAPPEN.
TRUTH IS, WYLIE, YOU WOULD NEVER FORGIVE ME FOR SENDING SOMEONE ELSE...
...TO KILL YOUR WOMAN.
BANG

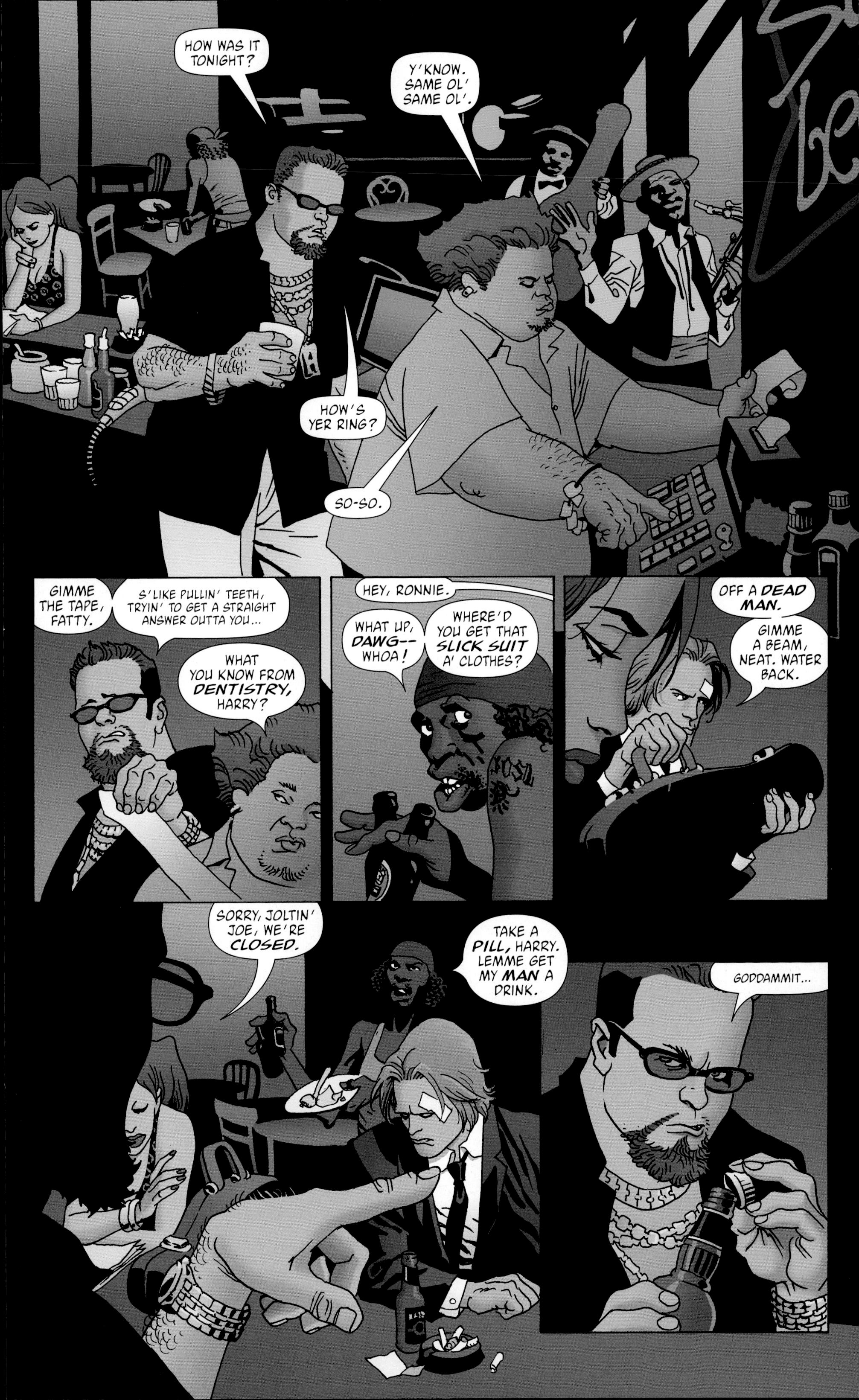
HOW WAS IT TONIGHT?
Y'KNOW. SAME OL' SAME OL'.
HOW'S YER RING?
SO-SO.
GIMME THE TAPE, FATTY.
S'LIKE PULLIN' TEETH, TRYIN' TO GET A STRAIGHT ANSWER OUTTA YOU...
WHAT YOU KNOW FROM DENTISTRY, HARRY?
HEY, RONNIE.
WHAT UP, DAWG-- WHOA!
WHERE'D YOU GET THAT SLICK SUIT A' CLOTHES?
OFF A DEAD MAN.
GIMME A BEAM, NEAT. WATER BACK.
SORRY, JOLTIN' JOE, WE'RE CLOSED.
TAKE A PILL, HARRY. LEMME GET MY MAN A DRINK.
GODDAMMIT...

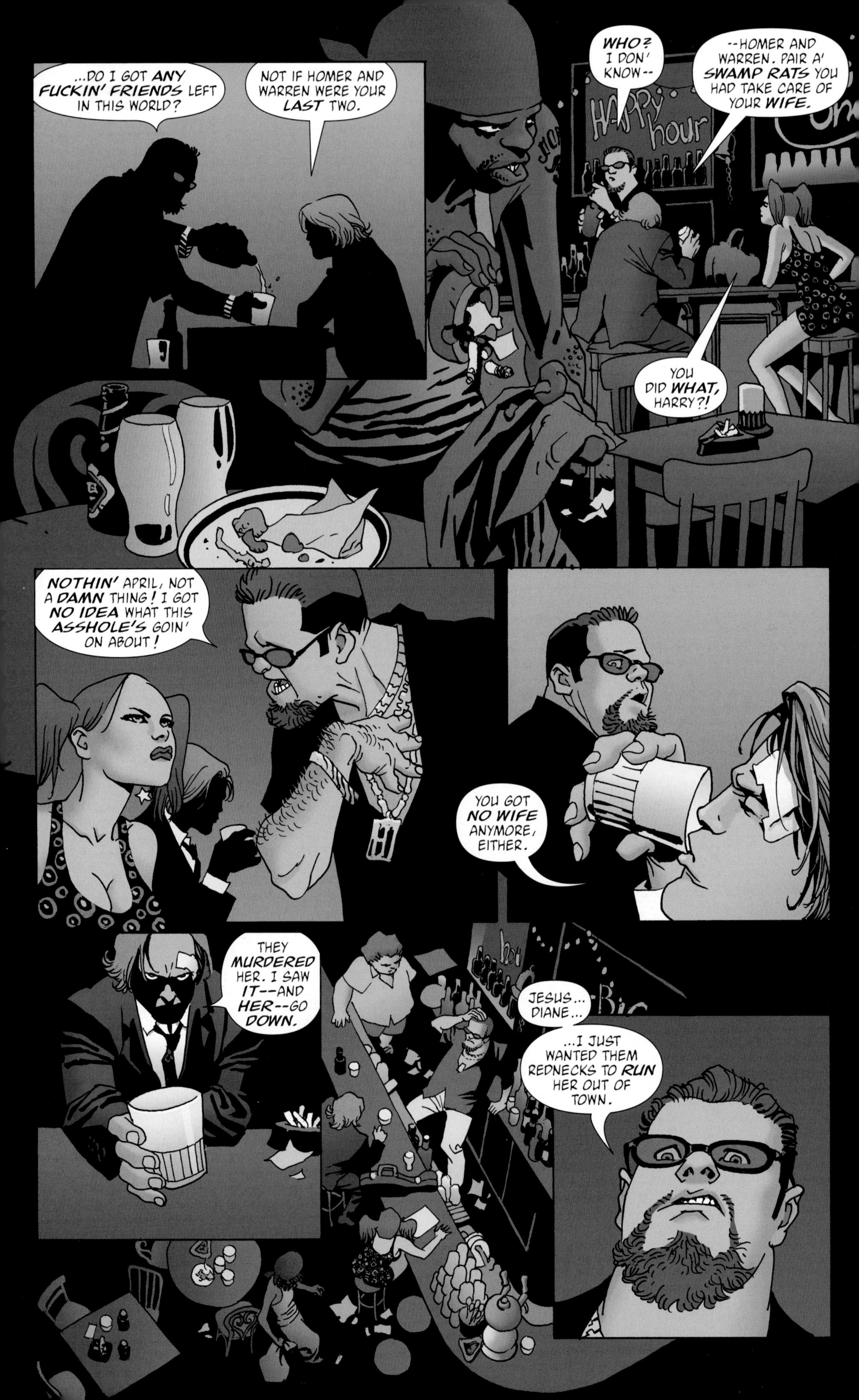
...DO I GOT ANY FUCKIN' FRIENDS LEFT IN THIS WORLD?
NOT IF HOMER AND WARREN WERE YOUR LAST TWO.
WHO? I DON' KNOW--
--HOMER AND WARREN. PAIR A' SWAMP RATS YOU HAD TAKE CARE OF YOUR WIFE.
HAPPY hour
YOU DID WHAT, HARRY?!
NOTHIN' APRIL, NOT A DAMN THING! I GOT NO IDEA WHAT THIS ASSHOLE'S GOIN' ON ABOUT!
YOU GOT NO WIFE ANYMORE, EITHER.
THEY MURDERED HER. I SAW IT--AND HER--GO DOWN.
JESUS... DIANE...
...I JUST WANTED THEM REDNECKS TO RUN HER OUT OF TOWN.

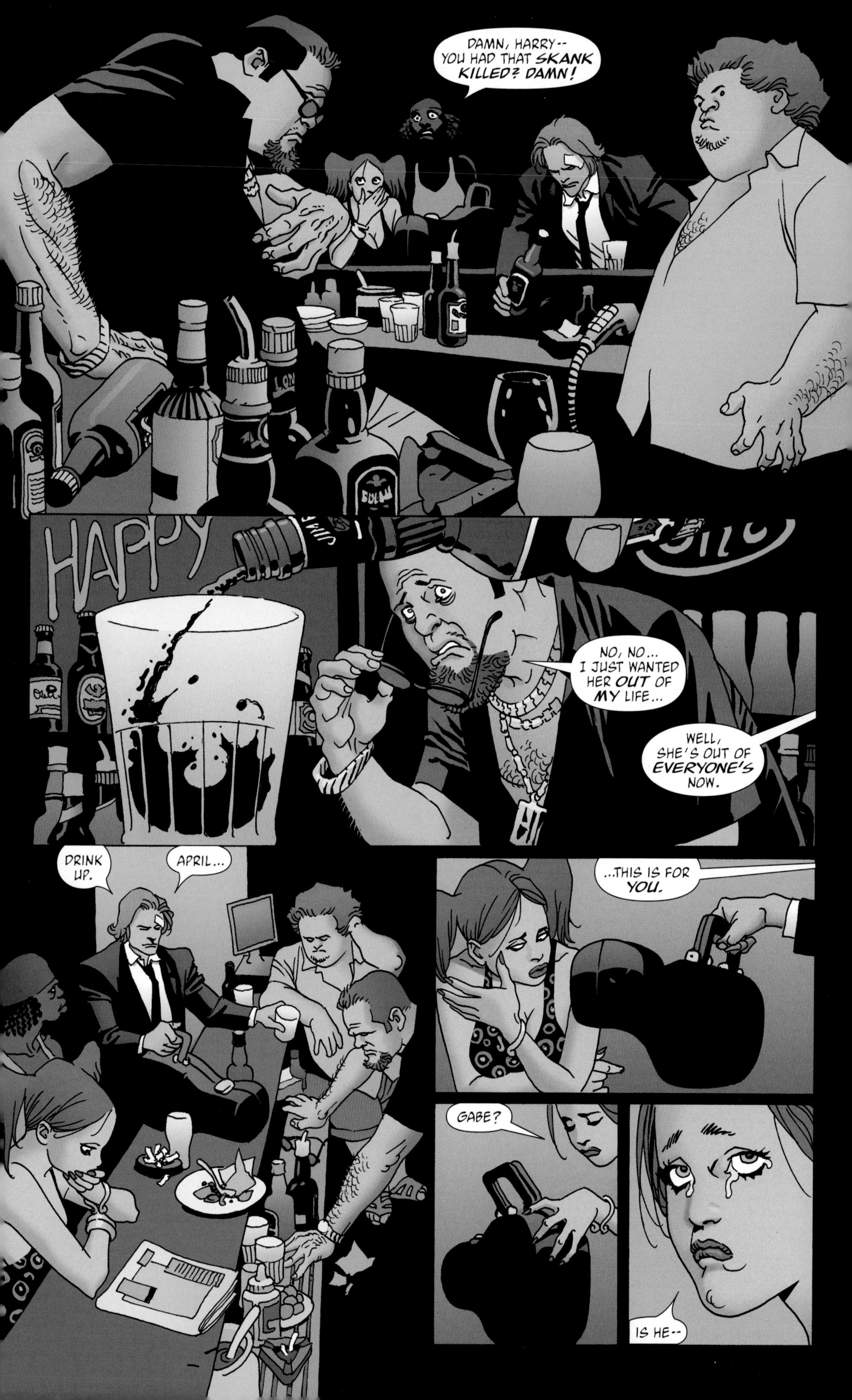
DAMN, HARRY--
YOU HAD THAT SKANK KILLED? DAMN!
NO, NO... I JUST WANTED HER OUT OF MY LIFE...
WELL, SHE'S OUT OF EVERYONE'S NOW.
DRINK UP.
APRIL...
...THIS IS FOR YOU.
GABE?
IS HE--

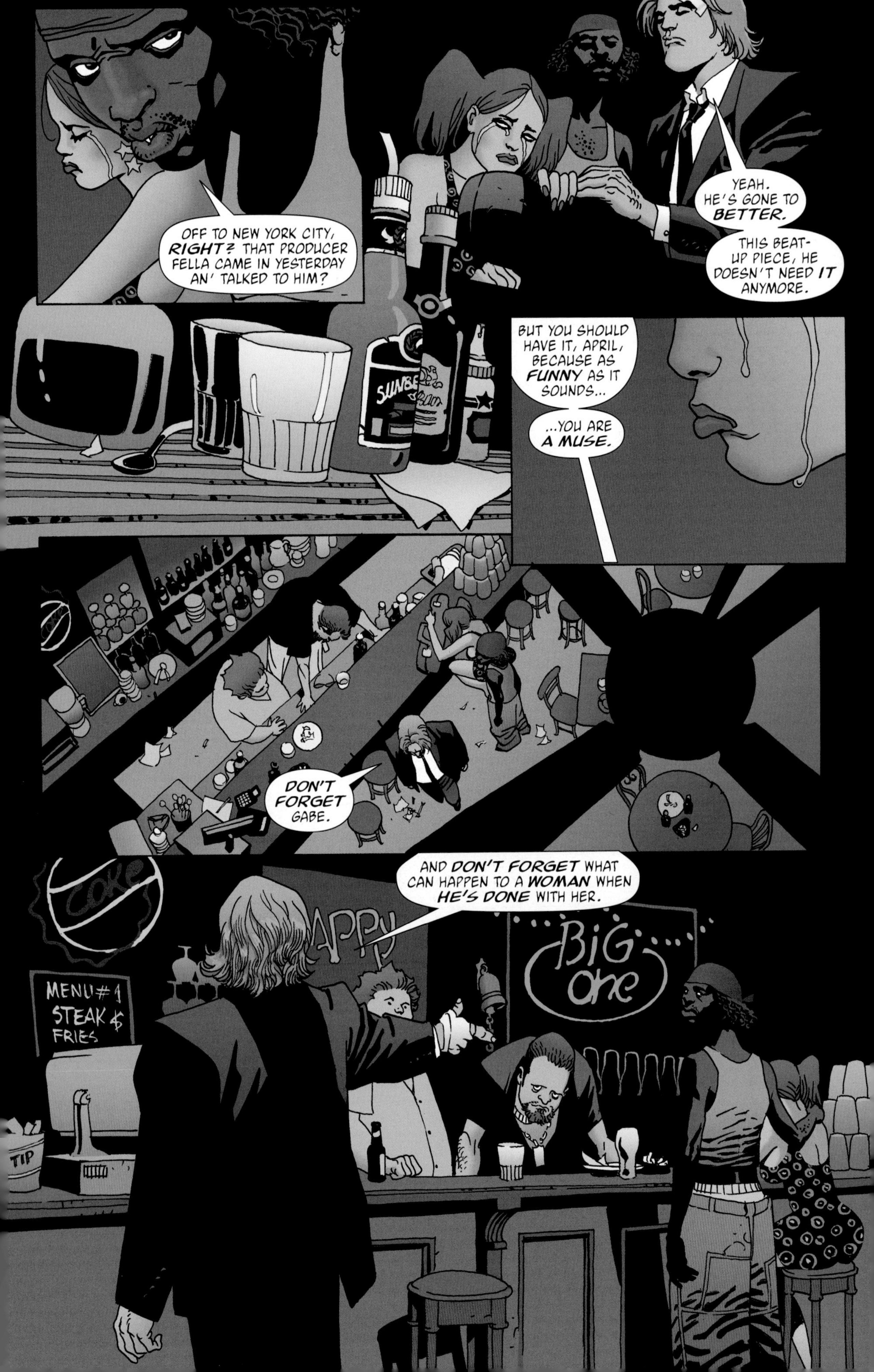
OFF TO NEW YORK CITY, RIGHT? THAT PRODUCER FELLA CAME IN YESTERDAY AN' TALKED TO HIM?
YEAH. HE'S GONE TO BETTER.
THIS BEAT-UP PIECE, HE DOESN'T NEED IT ANYMORE.
BUT YOU SHOULD HAVE IT, APRIL, BECAUSE AS FUNNY AS IT SOUNDS...
...YOU ARE A MUSE.
DON'T FORGET GABE.
AND DON'T FORGET WHAT CAN HAPPEN TO A WOMAN WHEN HE'S DONE WITH HER.
COKE
BIG ONE
MENU #1 STEAK $ FRIES
TIP

YOU READY TO GO?

I GOT *SHOTGUN*.

YOU DRIVE.

BUCKLE UP, BAY--

--KID.

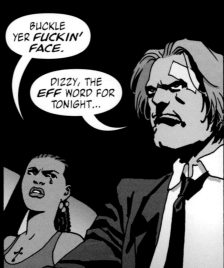

BUCKLE YER *FUCKIN'* FACE.

DIZZY, THE *EFF* WORD FOR TONIGHT...

...IS *FORGIVE*.

SINCE *FORGET* IS OFF THE TABLE.

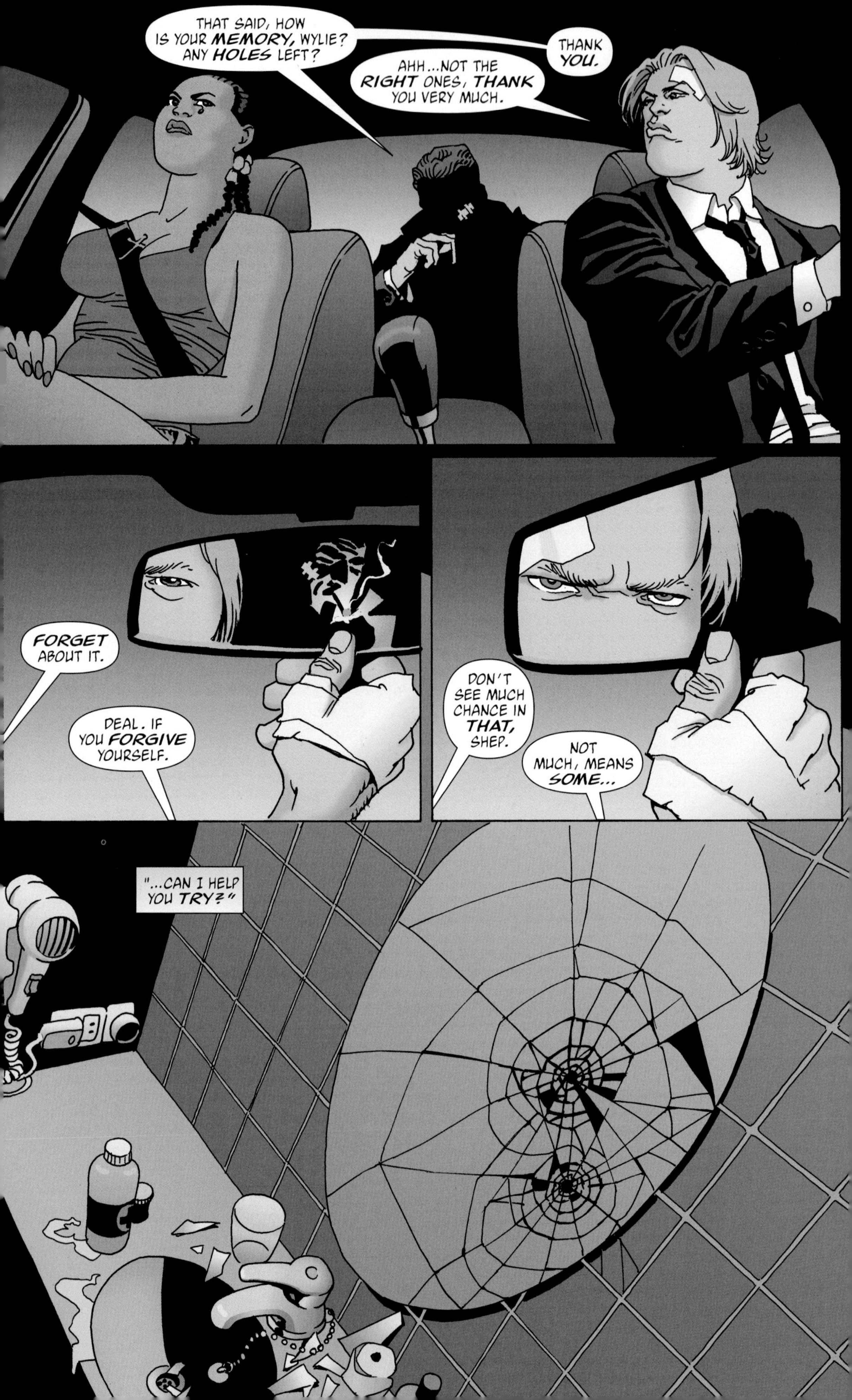
THAT SAID, HOW IS YOUR MEMORY, WYLIE? ANY HOLES LEFT?
AHH...NOT THE RIGHT ONES, THANK YOU VERY MUCH.
THANK YOU.
FORGET ABOUT IT.
DEAL. IF YOU FORGIVE YOURSELF.
DON'T SEE MUCH CHANCE IN THAT, SHEP.
NOT MUCH, MEANS SOME...
"...CAN I HELP YOU TRY?"

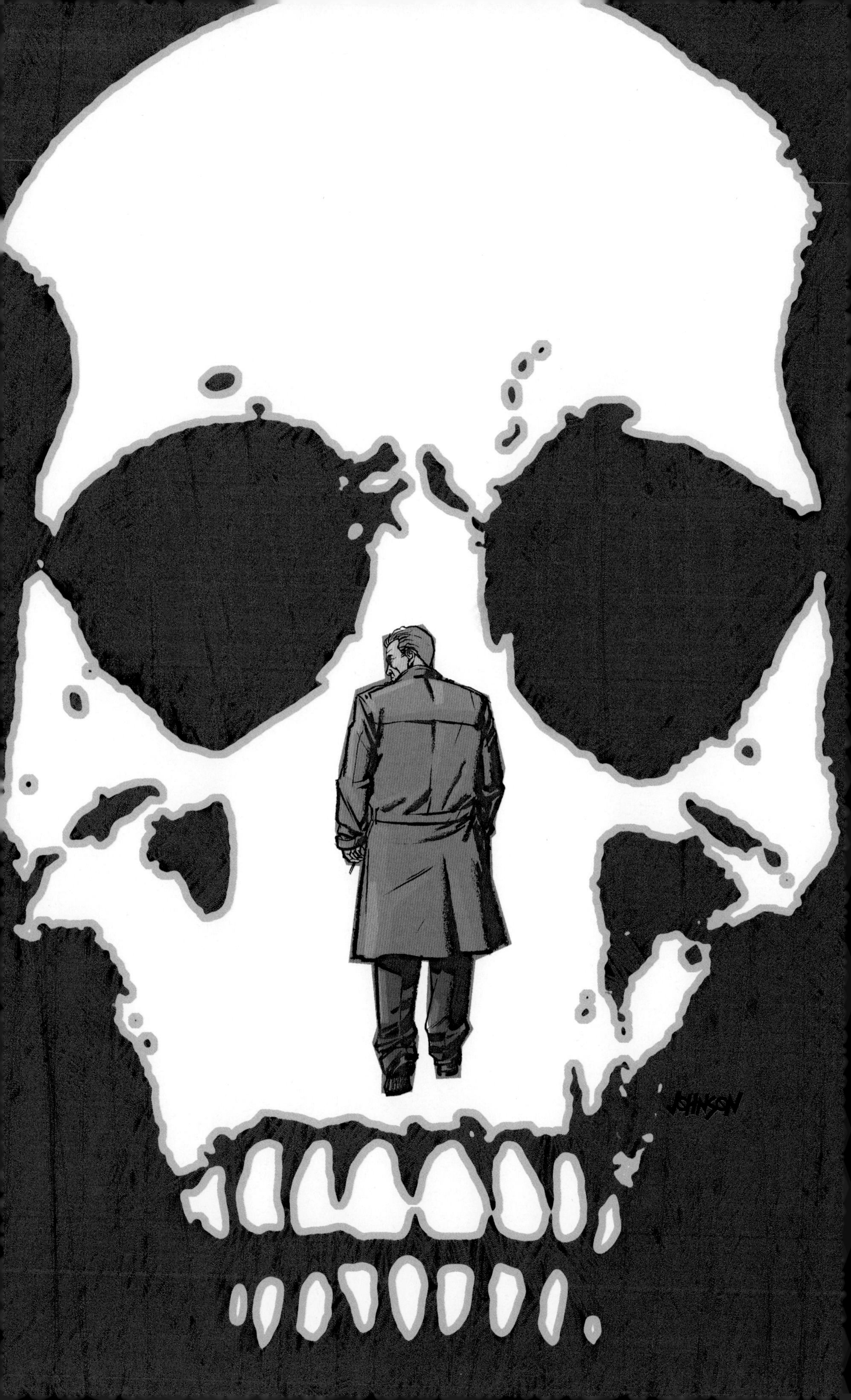
JOHNSON

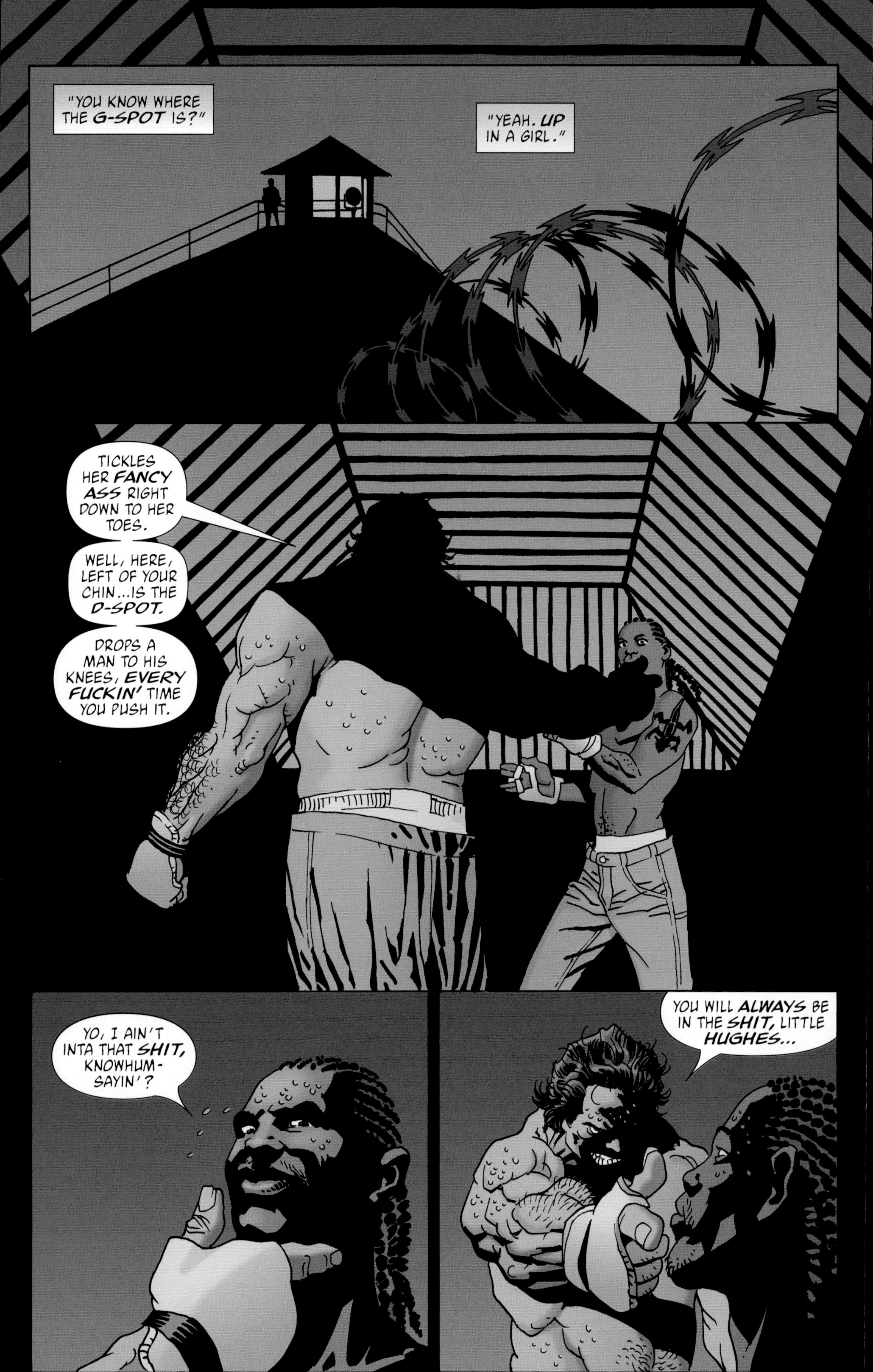
"YOU KNOW WHERE THE G-SPOT IS?"
"YEAH. UP IN A GIRL."
TICKLES HER FANCY ASS RIGHT DOWN TO HER TOES.
WELL, HERE, LEFT OF YOUR CHIN...IS THE D-SPOT.
DROPS A MAN TO HIS KNEES, EVERY FUCKIN' TIME YOU PUSH IT.
YO, I AIN'T INTA THAT SHIT, KNOWHUM-SAYIN'?
YOU WILL ALWAYS BE IN THE SHIT, LITTLE HUGHES...

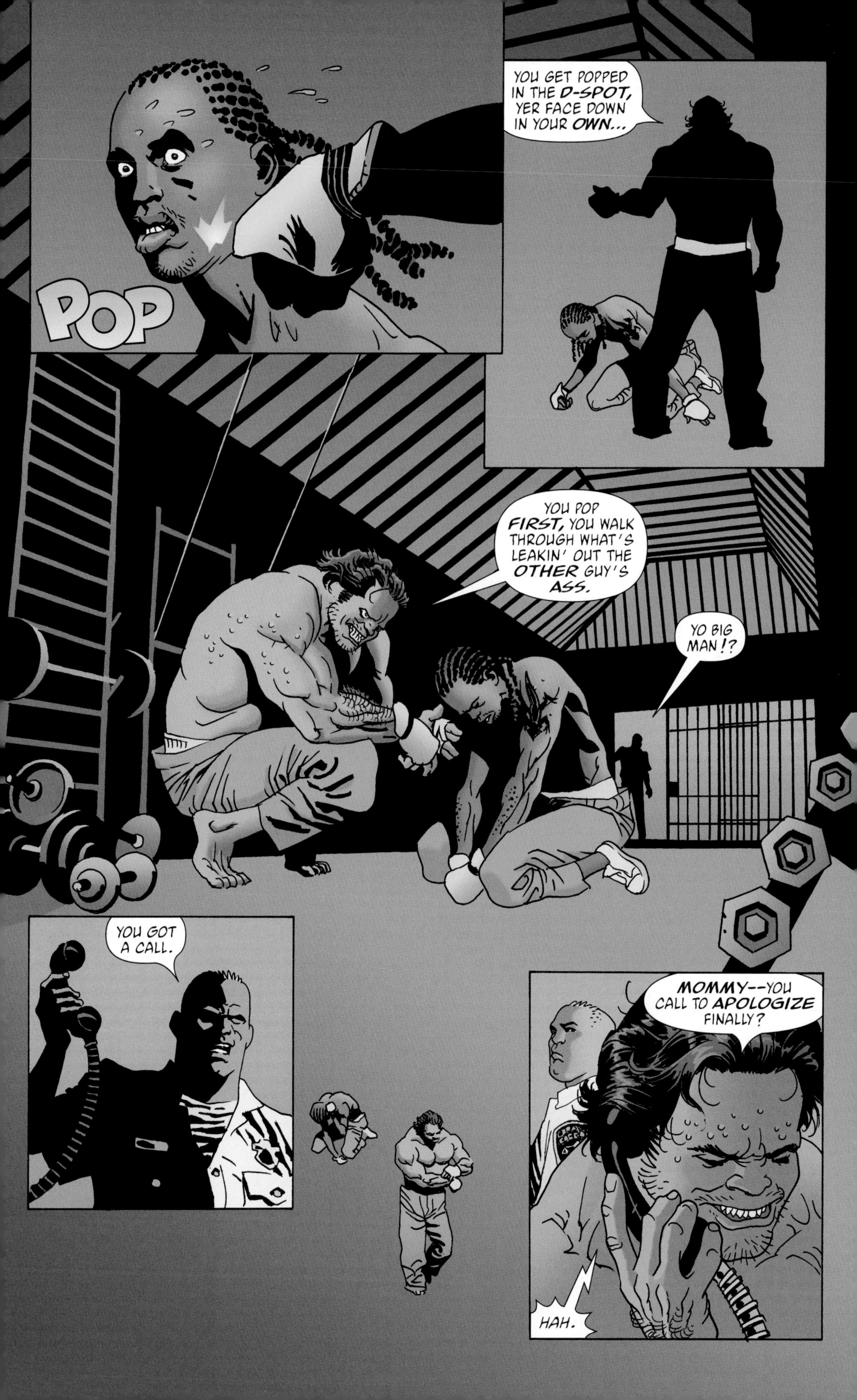
POP
YOU GET POPPED IN THE D-SPOT, YER FACE DOWN IN YOUR OWN...
YOU POP FIRST, YOU WALK THROUGH WHAT'S LEAKIN' OUT THE OTHER GUY'S ASS.
YO BIG MAN!?
YOU GOT A CALL.
MOMMY--YOU CALL TO APOLOGIZE FINALLY?
HAH.

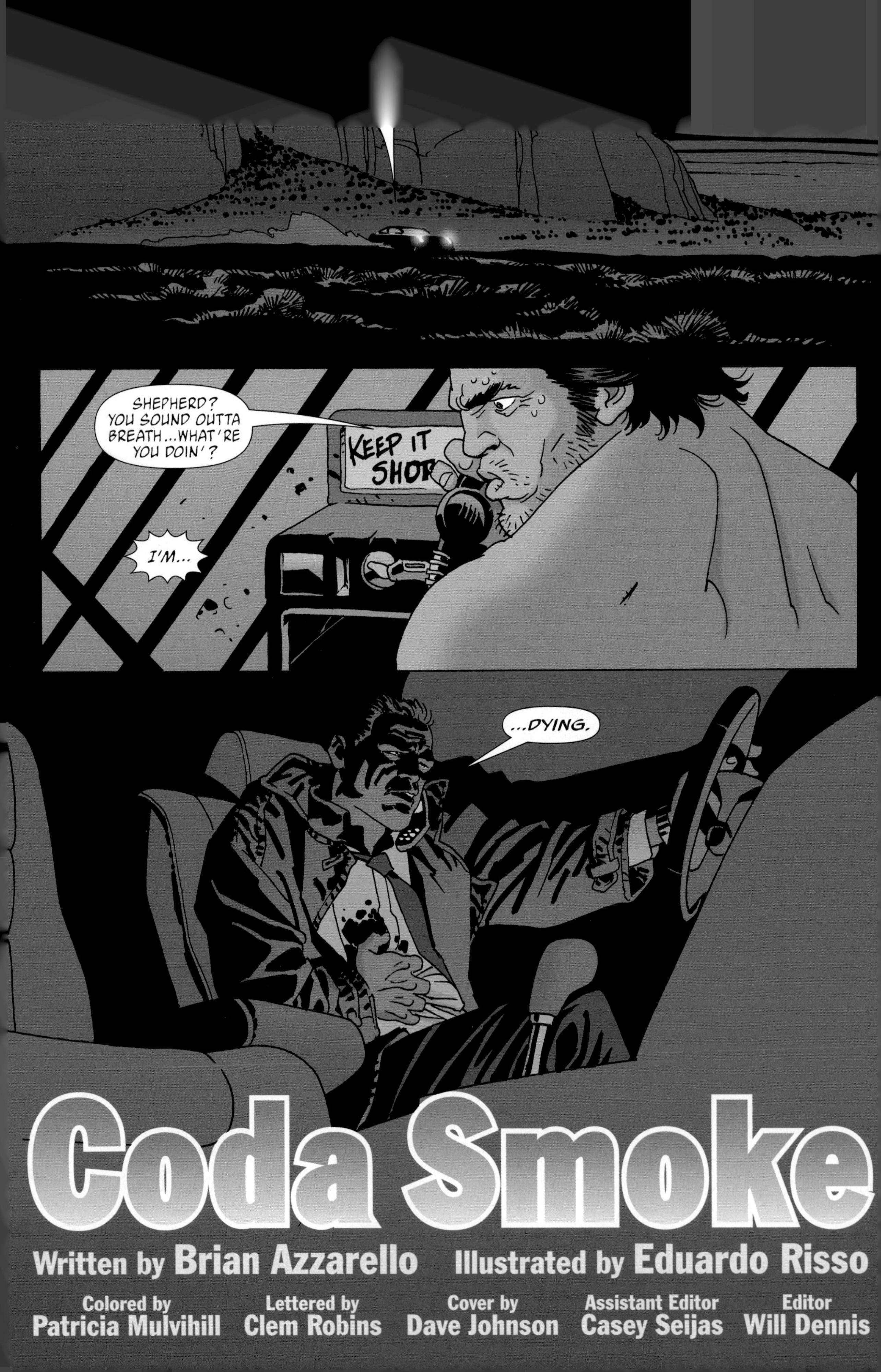

KEEP IT SHOR
SHEPHERD? YOU SOUND OUTTA BREATH...WHAT'RE YOU DOIN'?
I'M...
...DYING.

Coda Smoke

Written by Brian Azzarello Illustrated by Eduardo Risso

Colored by Patricia Mulvihill Lettered by Clem Robins Cover by Dave Johnson Assistant Editor Casey Seijas Editor Will Dennis

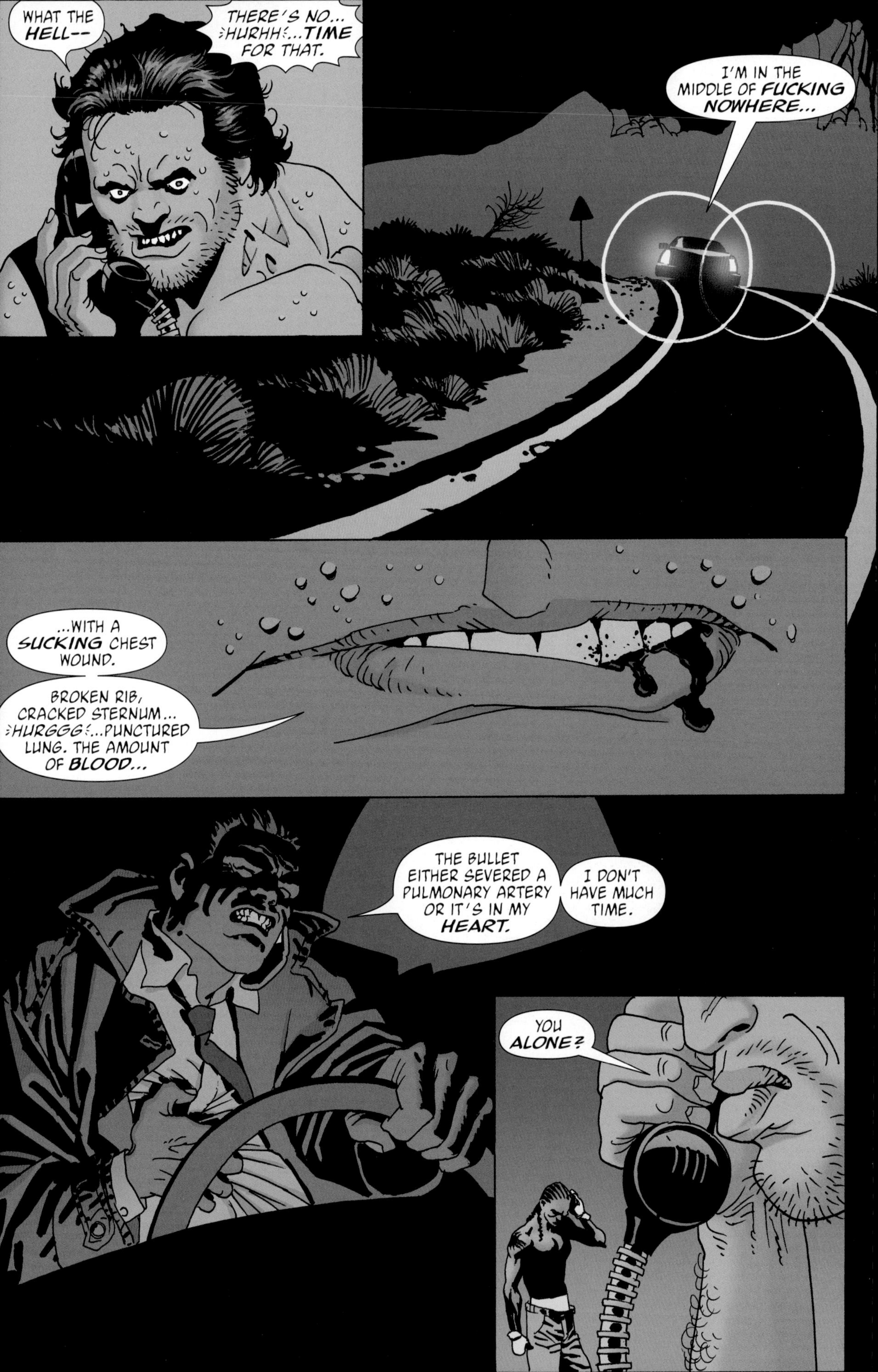
WHAT THE HELL--
THERE'S NO... HURHH ...TIME FOR THAT.
I'M IN THE MIDDLE OF FUCKING NOWHERE...
...WITH A SUCKING CHEST WOUND.
BROKEN RIB, CRACKED STERNUM... HURGGG ...PUNCTURED LUNG. THE AMOUNT OF BLOOD...
THE BULLET EITHER SEVERED A PULMONARY ARTERY OR IT'S IN MY HEART.
I DON'T HAVE MUCH TIME.
YOU ALONE?

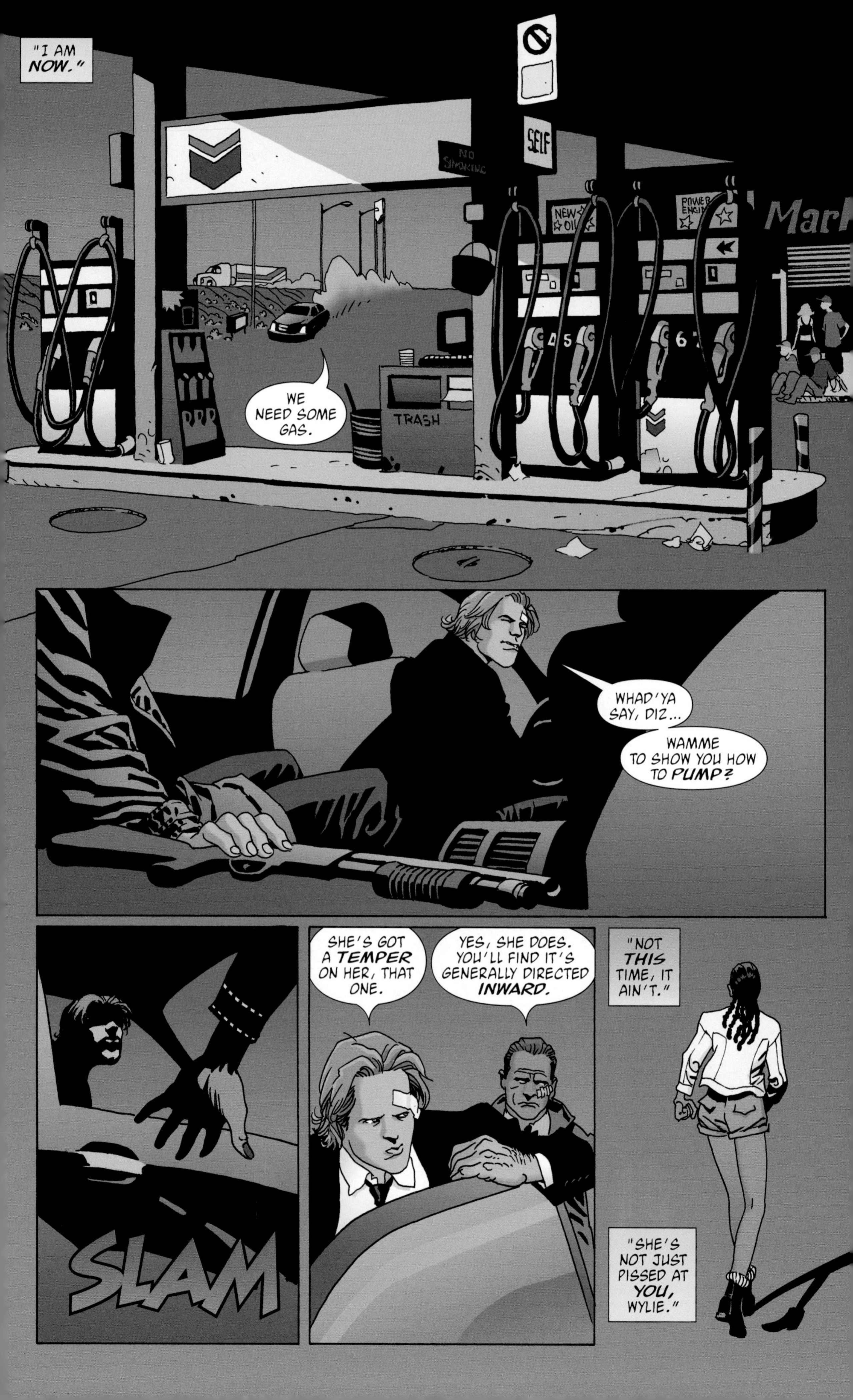
"I AM NOW."
NO SMOKING
SELF
NEW OIL
POWER ENGINE
TRASH
WE NEED SOME GAS.
WHAD'YA SAY, DIZ...
WAMME TO SHOW YOU HOW TO PUMP?
SLAM
SHE'S GOT A TEMPER ON HER, THAT ONE.
YES, SHE DOES. YOU'LL FIND IT'S GENERALLY DIRECTED INWARD.
"NOT THIS TIME, IT AIN'T."
"SHE'S NOT JUST PISSED AT YOU, WYLIE."

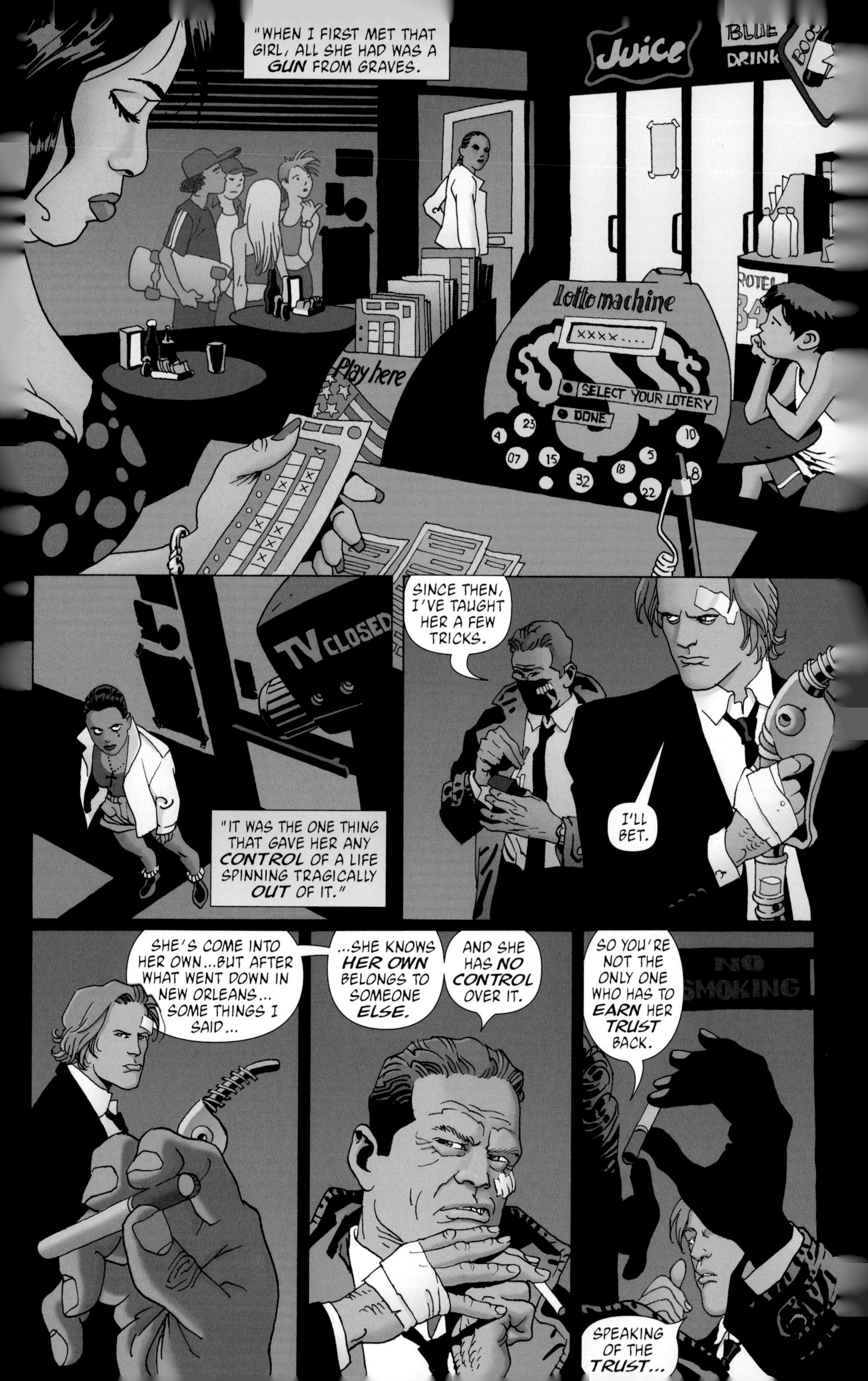
"WHEN I FIRST MET THAT GIRL, ALL SHE HAD WAS A GUN FROM GRAVES.
Juice
BLUE DRINK
Lotto machine
XXXX....
SELECT YOUR LOTERY
DONE
Play here
TV CLOSED
SINCE THEN, I'VE TAUGHT HER A FEW TRICKS.
"IT WAS THE ONE THING THAT GAVE HER ANY CONTROL OF A LIFE SPINNING TRAGICALLY OUT OF IT."
I'LL BET.
SHE'S COME INTO HER OWN...BUT AFTER WHAT WENT DOWN IN NEW ORLEANS... SOME THINGS I SAID...
...SHE KNOWS HER OWN BELONGS TO SOMEONE ELSE.
AND SHE HAS NO CONTROL OVER IT.
SO YOU'RE NOT THE ONLY ONE WHO HAS TO EARN HER TRUST BACK.
NO SMOKING
SPEAKING OF THE TRUST...

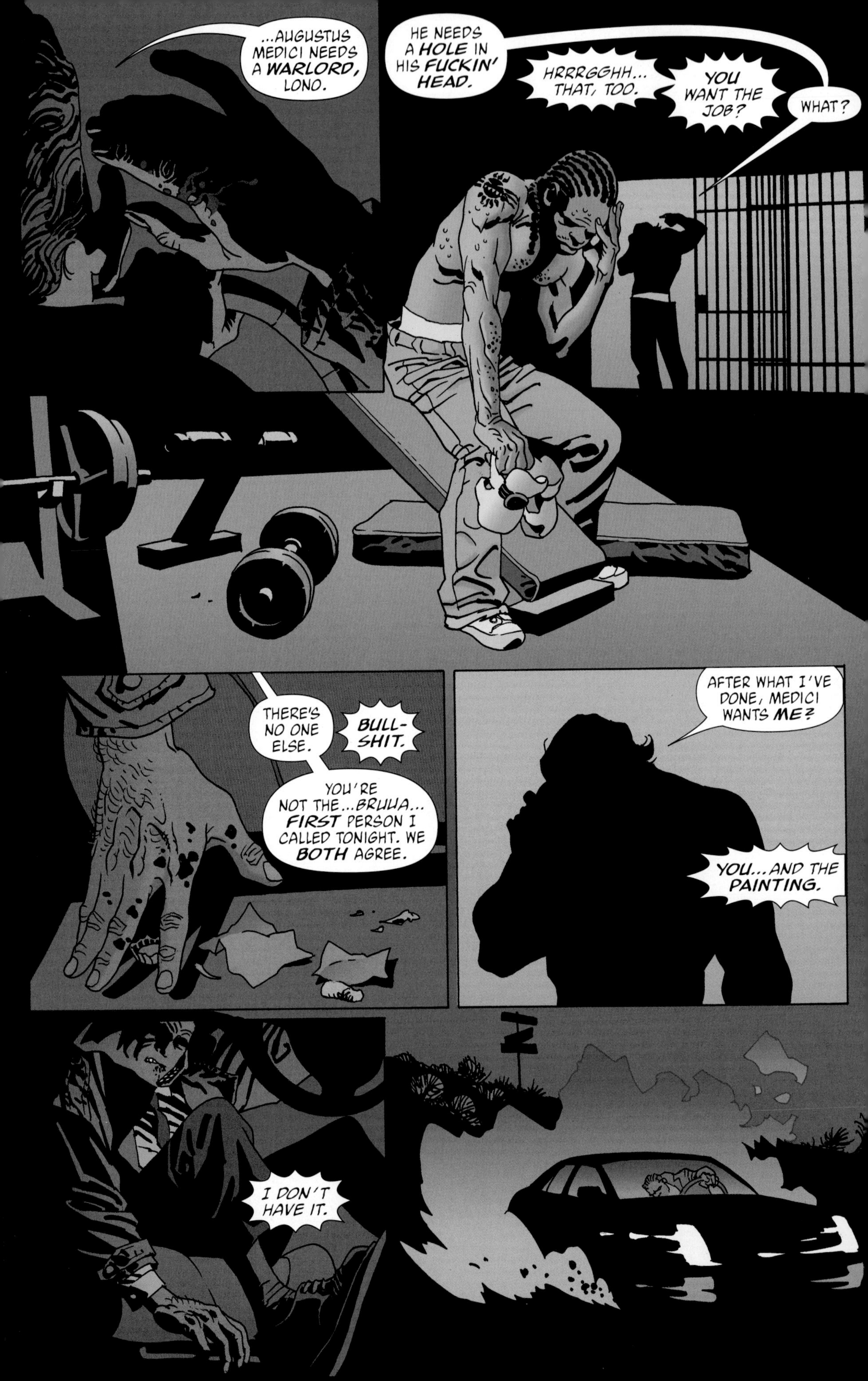
...AUGUSTUS MEDICI NEEDS A WARLORD, LONO.
HE NEEDS A HOLE IN HIS FUCKIN' HEAD.
HRRRGGHH... THAT, TOO.
YOU WANT THE JOB?
WHAT?
THERE'S NO ONE ELSE.
BULL-SHIT.
YOU'RE NOT THE...BRUUA... FIRST PERSON I CALLED TONIGHT. WE BOTH AGREE.
AFTER WHAT I'VE DONE, MEDICI WANTS ME?
YOU...AND THE PAINTING.
I DON'T HAVE IT.

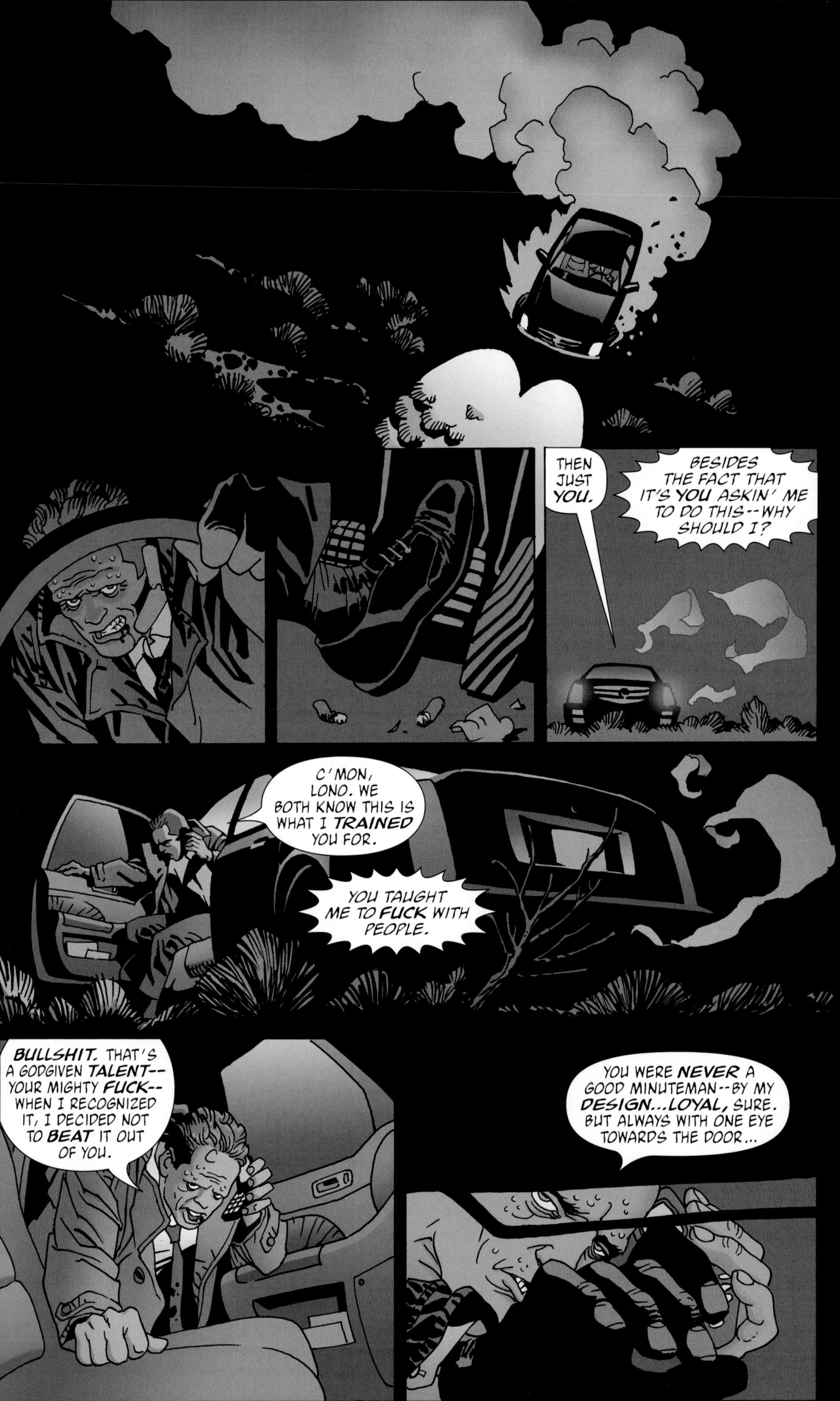
THEN JUST YOU.
BESIDES THE FACT THAT IT'S YOU ASKIN' ME TO DO THIS--WHY SHOULD I?
C'MON, LONO. WE BOTH KNOW THIS IS WHAT I TRAINED YOU FOR.
YOU TAUGHT ME TO FUCK WITH PEOPLE.
BULLSHIT. THAT'S A GODGIVEN TALENT-- YOUR MIGHTY FUCK-- WHEN I RECOGNIZED IT, I DECIDED NOT TO BEAT IT OUT OF YOU.
YOU WERE NEVER A GOOD MINUTEMAN--BY MY DESIGN...LOYAL, SURE. BUT ALWAYS WITH ONE EYE TOWARDS THE DOOR...

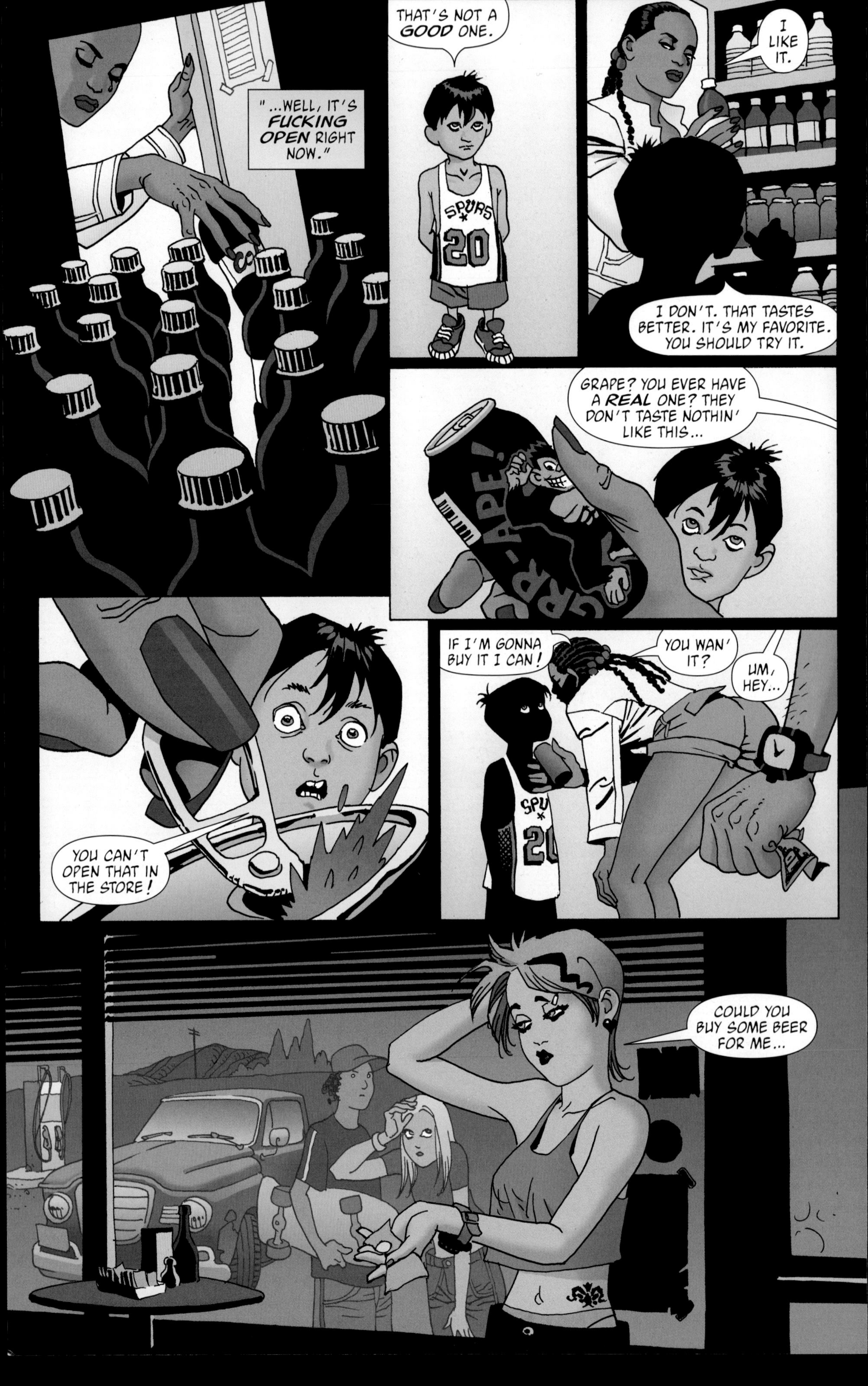
"...WELL, IT'S FUCKING OPEN RIGHT NOW."
THAT'S NOT A GOOD ONE.
I LIKE IT.
I DON'T. THAT TASTES BETTER. IT'S MY FAVORITE. YOU SHOULD TRY IT.
SPURS 20
GRAPE? YOU EVER HAVE A REAL ONE? THEY DON'T TASTE NOTHIN' LIKE THIS...
GRR-APE!
YOU CAN'T OPEN THAT IN THE STORE!
IF I'M GONNA BUY IT I CAN!
YOU WAN' IT?
UM, HEY...
COULD YOU BUY SOME BEER FOR ME...

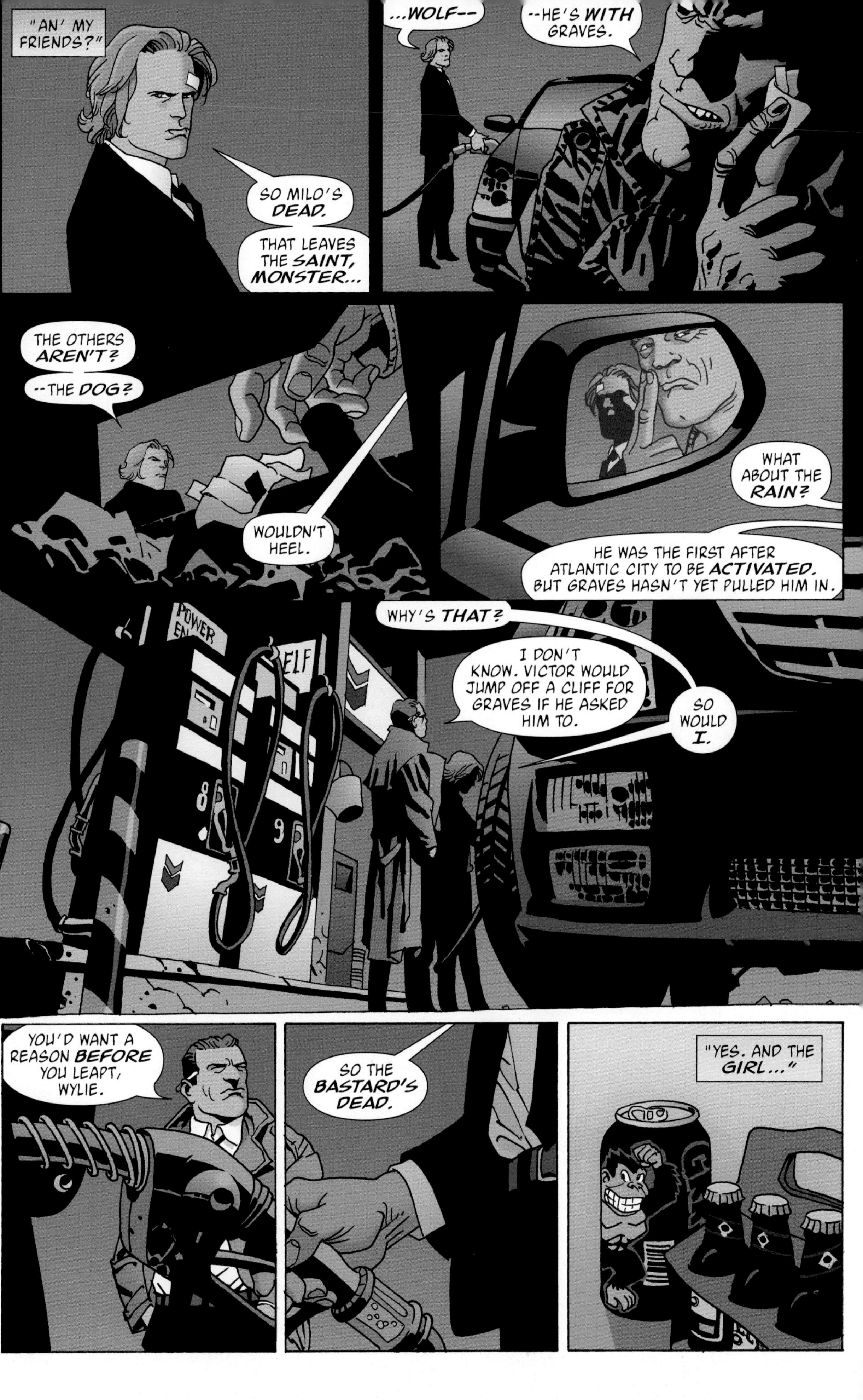
"AN' MY FRIENDS?"
SO MILO'S DEAD.
THAT LEAVES THE SAINT, MONSTER...
...WOLF--
--HE'S WITH GRAVES.
THE OTHERS AREN'T?
--THE DOG?
WOULDN'T HEEL.
WHAT ABOUT THE RAIN?
HE WAS THE FIRST AFTER ATLANTIC CITY TO BE ACTIVATED. BUT GRAVES HASN'T YET PULLED HIM IN.
WHY'S THAT?
I DON'T KNOW. VICTOR WOULD JUMP OFF A CLIFF FOR GRAVES IF HE ASKED HIM TO.
SO WOULD I.
YOU'D WANT A REASON BEFORE YOU LEAPT, WYLIE.
SO THE BASTARD'S DEAD.
"YES. AND THE GIRL..."

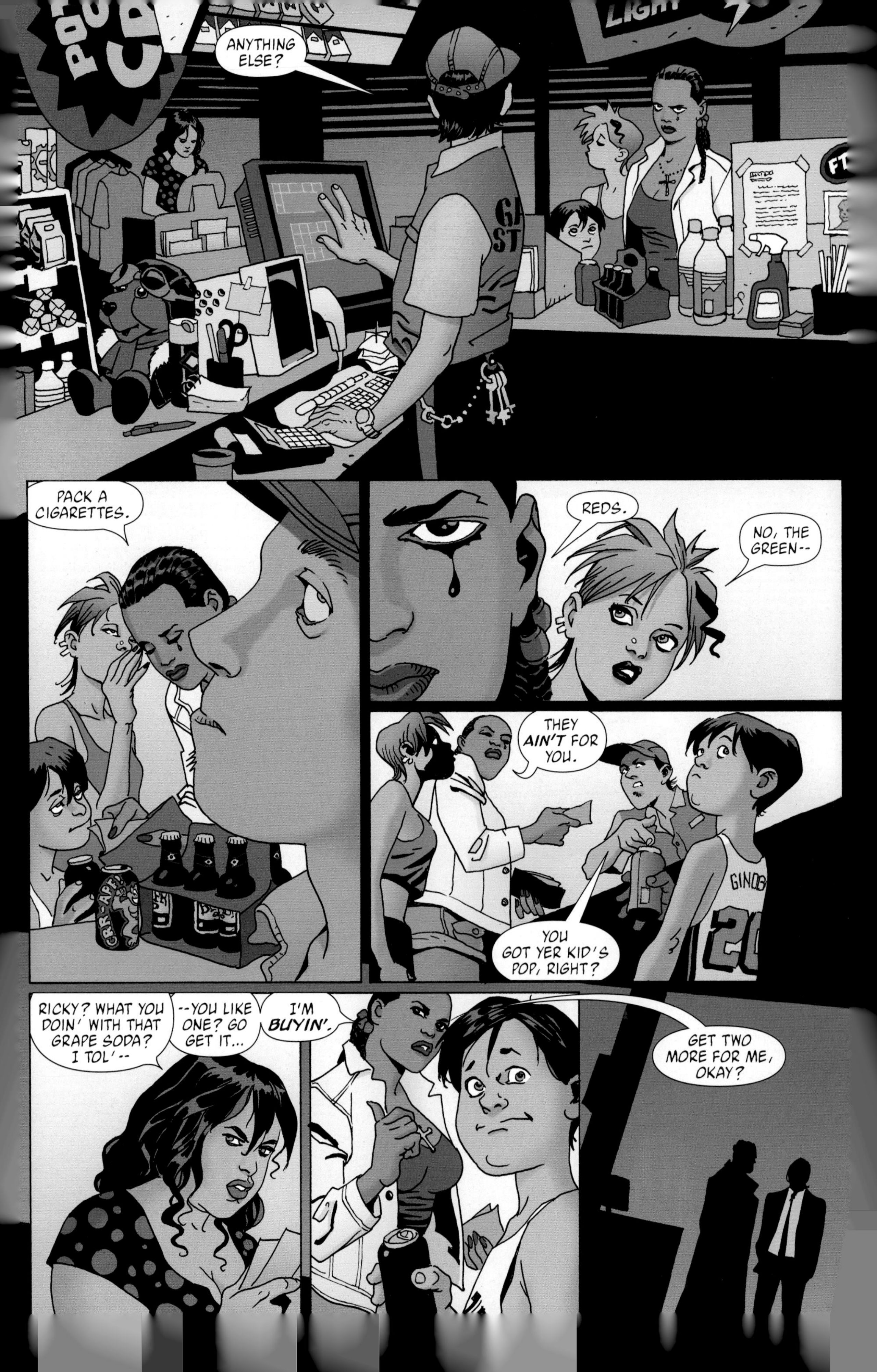
ANYTHING ELSE?
PACK A CIGARETTES.
REDS.
NO, THE GREEN--
THEY AIN'T FOR YOU.
YOU GOT YER KID'S POP, RIGHT?
RICKY? WHAT YOU DOIN' WITH THAT GRAPE SODA? I TOL'--
--YOU LIKE ONE? GO GET IT...
I'M BUYIN'.
GET TWO MORE FOR ME, OKAY?

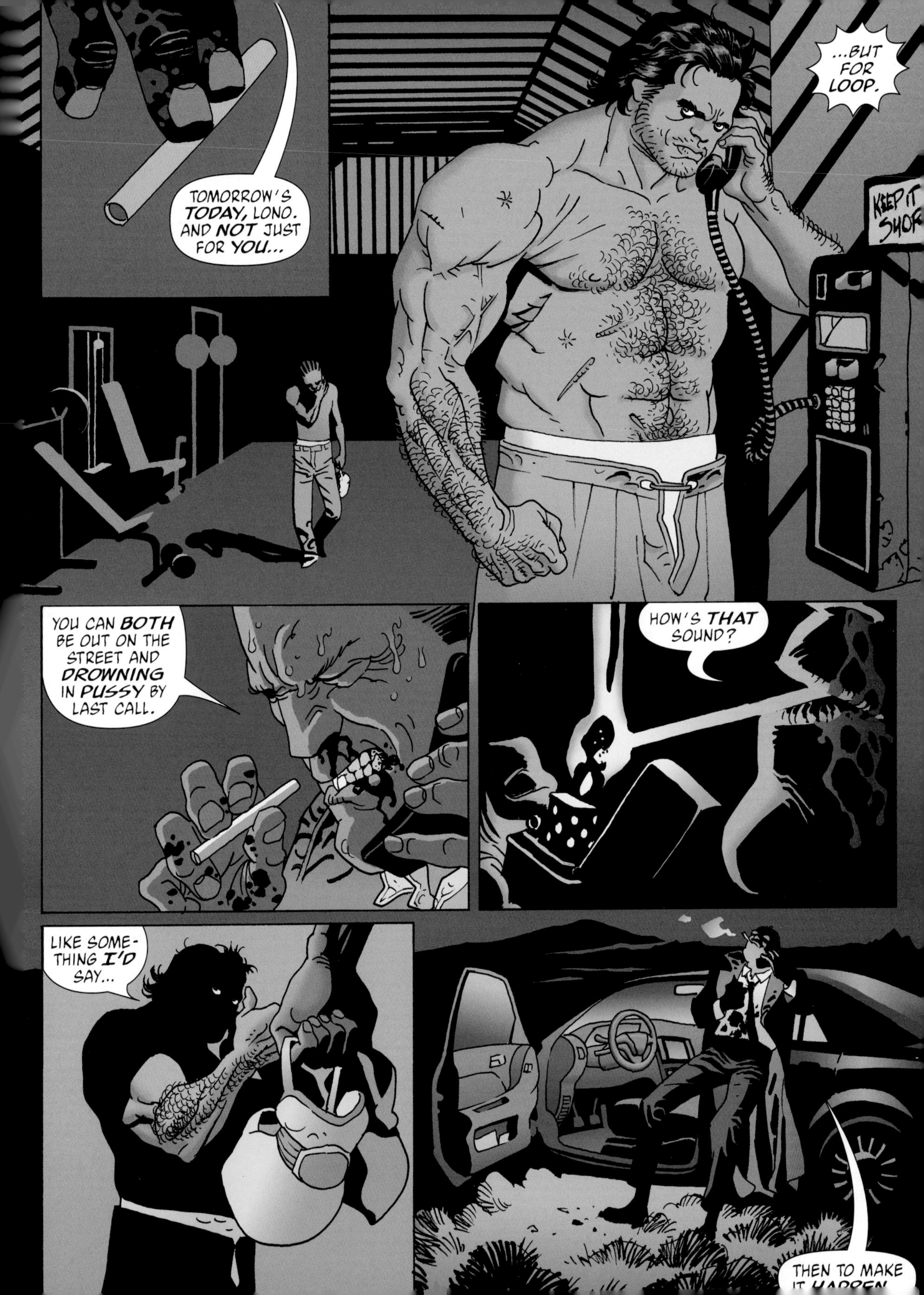
TOMORROW'S TODAY, LONO. AND NOT JUST FOR YOU...
...BUT FOR LOOP.
YOU CAN BOTH BE OUT ON THE STREET AND DROWNING IN PUSSY BY LAST CALL.
HOW'S THAT SOUND?
LIKE SOME-THING I'D SAY...
THEN TO MAKE

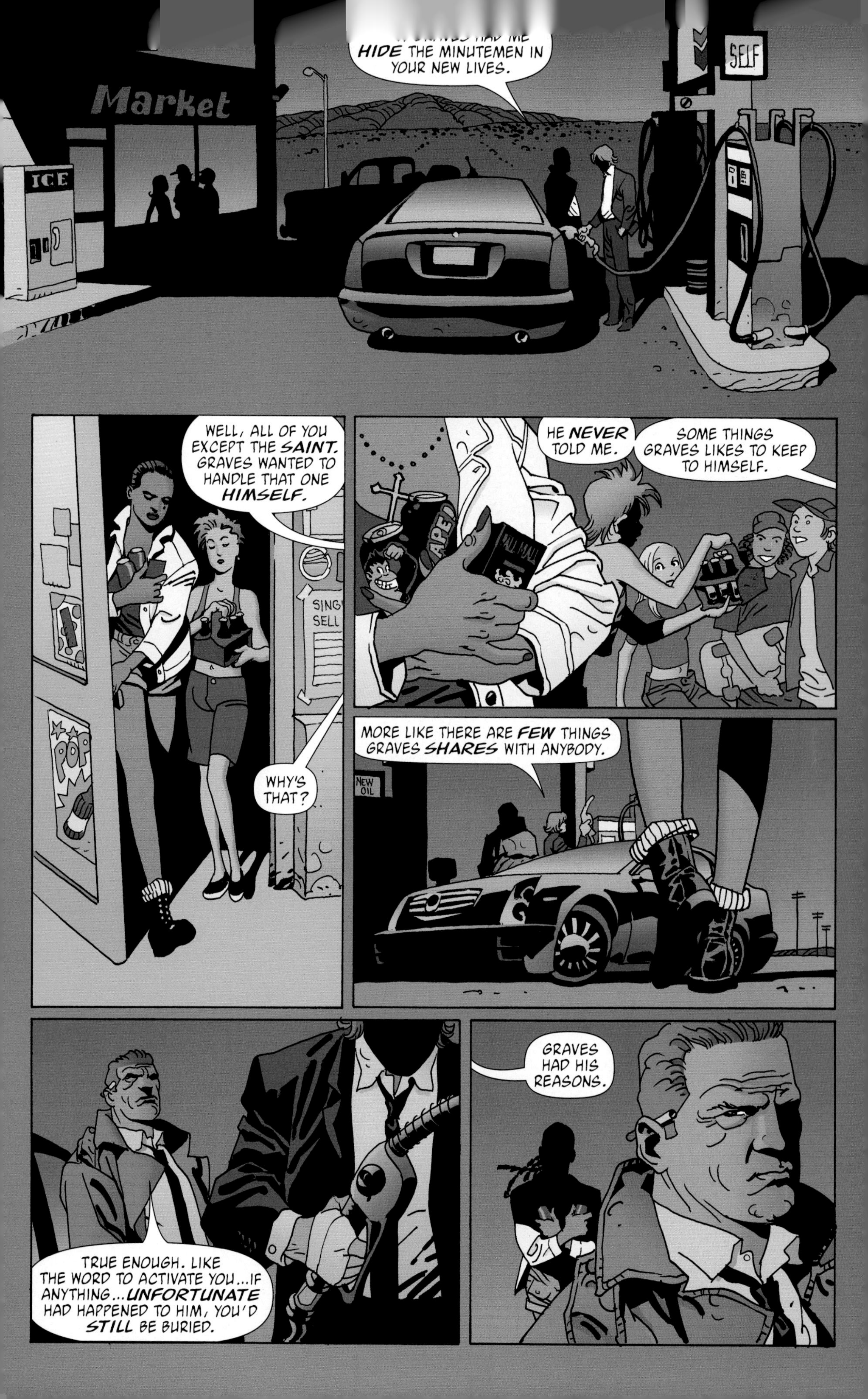

HIDE THE MINUTEMEN IN YOUR NEW LIVES.
Market
ICE
SELF
WELL, ALL OF YOU EXCEPT THE SAINT. GRAVES WANTED TO HANDLE THAT ONE HIMSELF.
WHY'S THAT?
HE NEVER TOLD ME.
SOME THINGS GRAVES LIKES TO KEEP TO HIMSELF.
POP
MORE LIKE THERE ARE FEW THINGS GRAVES SHARES WITH ANYBODY.
NEW OIL
TRUE ENOUGH. LIKE THE WORD TO ACTIVATE YOU...IF ANYTHING...UNFORTUNATE HAD HAPPENED TO HIM, YOU'D STILL BE BURIED.
GRAVES HAD HIS REASONS.

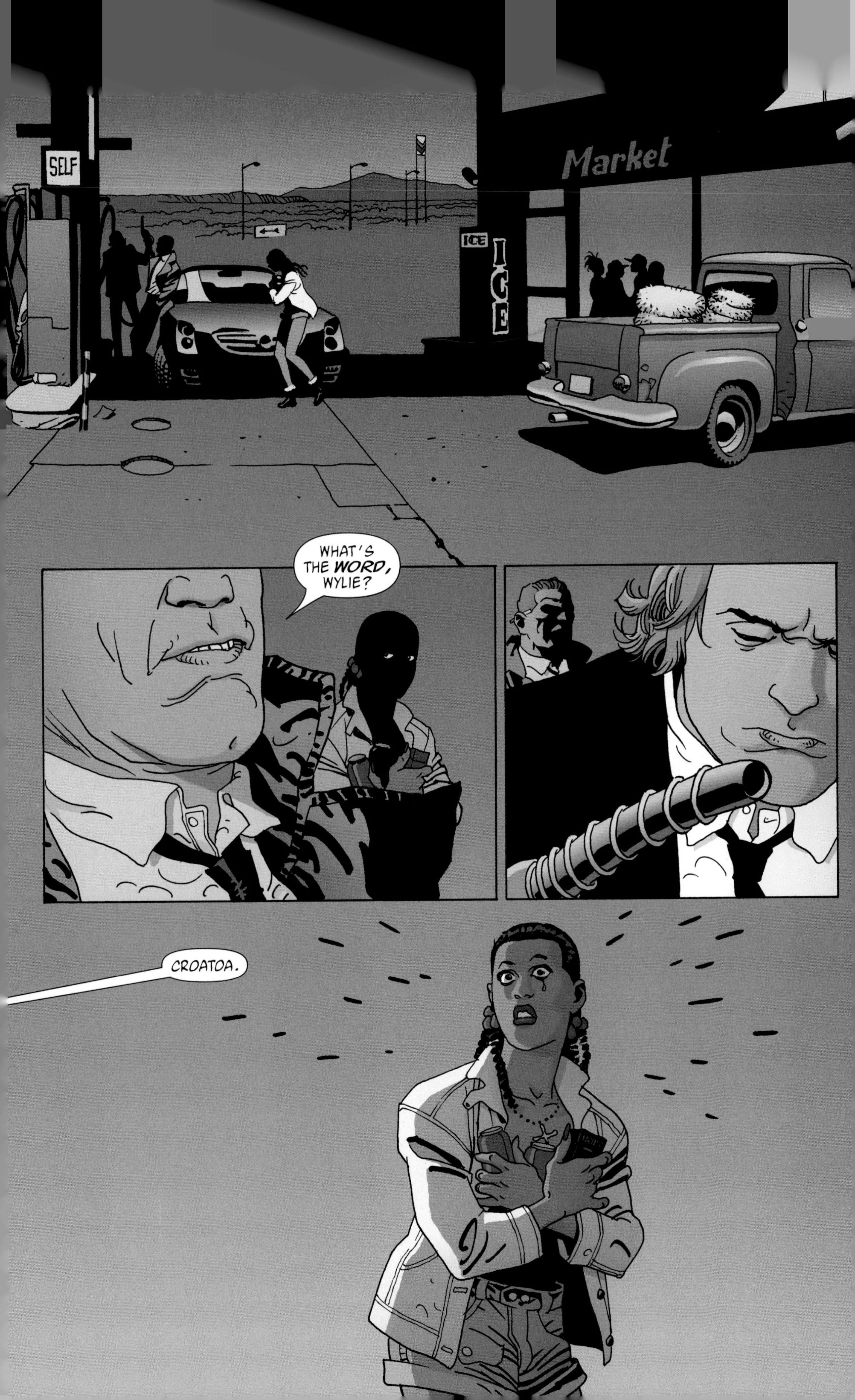
SELF
Market
ICE
ICE
WHAT'S THE WORD, WYLIE?
CROATOA.

SO WHAT'S THE **PLAN?**

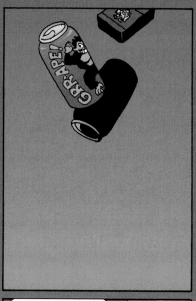

IN MY OPINION? FLAWED.

MAYBE EVEN BY **DESIGN.**

YOU BETTER THINK ABOUT WHAT YER SAYING, SHEPHERD.

GRAVES' PLAN IS TO PREVENT AUGUSTUS MEDICI FROM GRABBING **SOLE** CONTROL OF THE TRUST.

WHY THEN DOES EVERY MOVE WE MAKE HAND MEDICI **MORE** CONTROL?

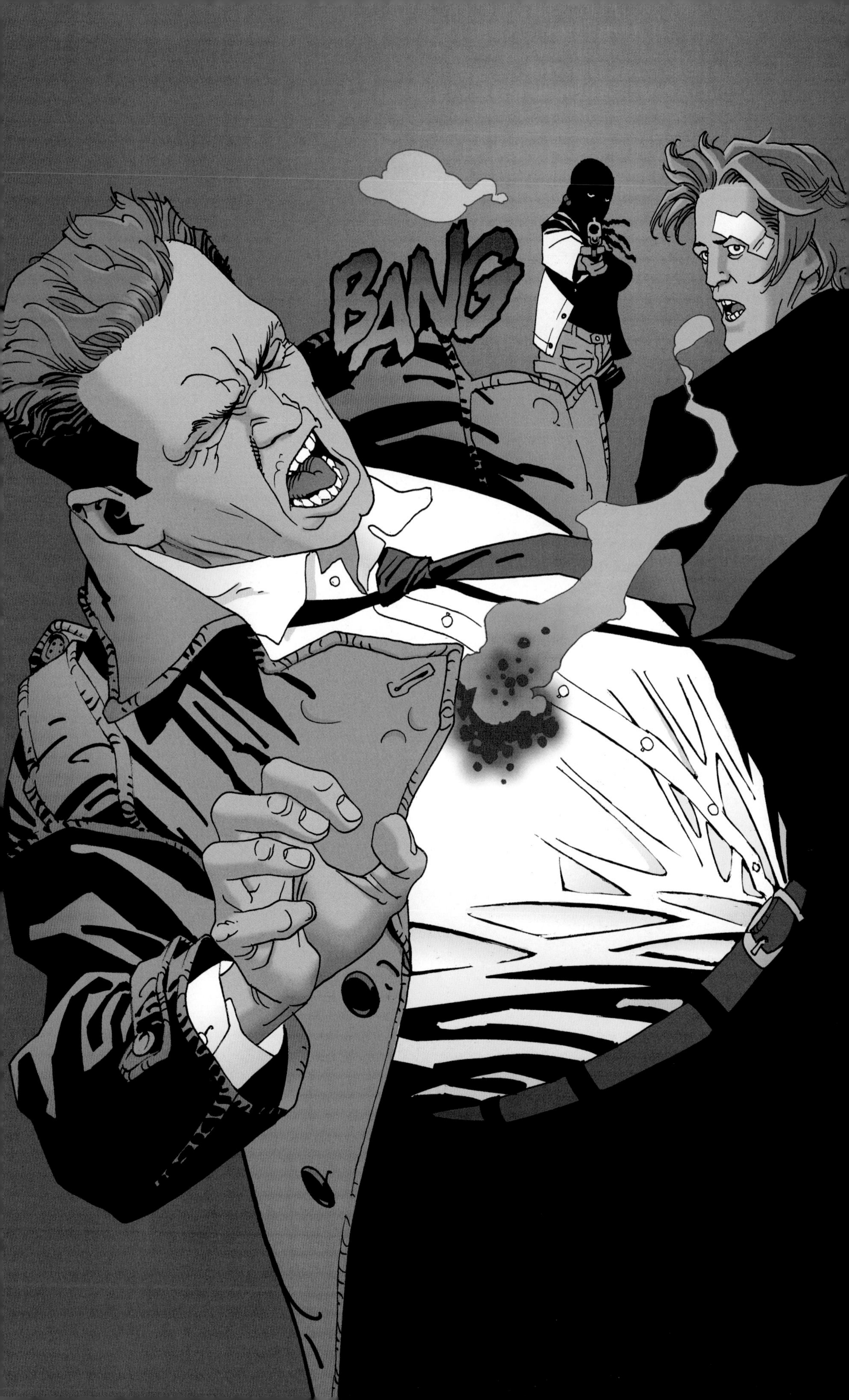
BANG

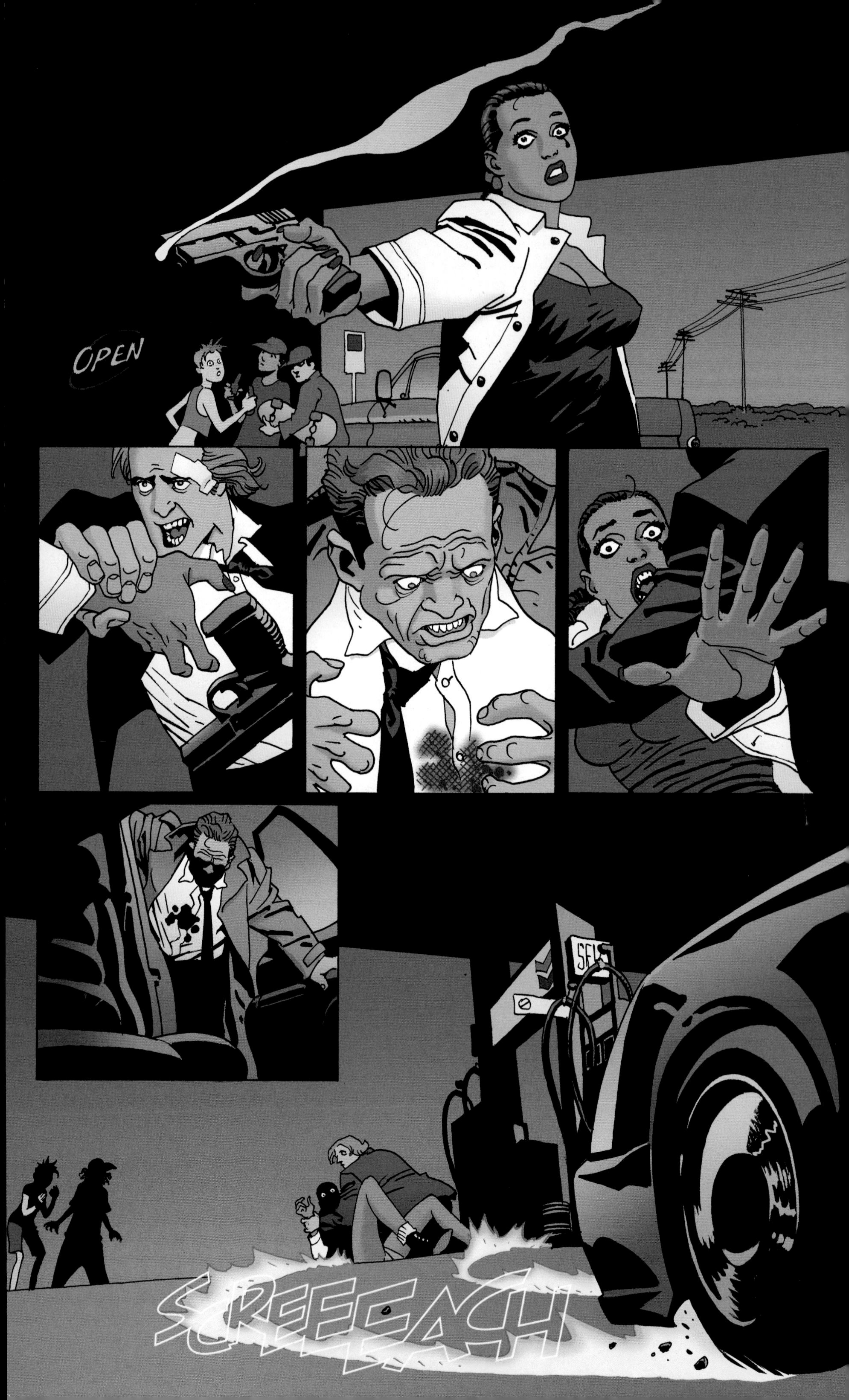
OPEN
SCREEEACH

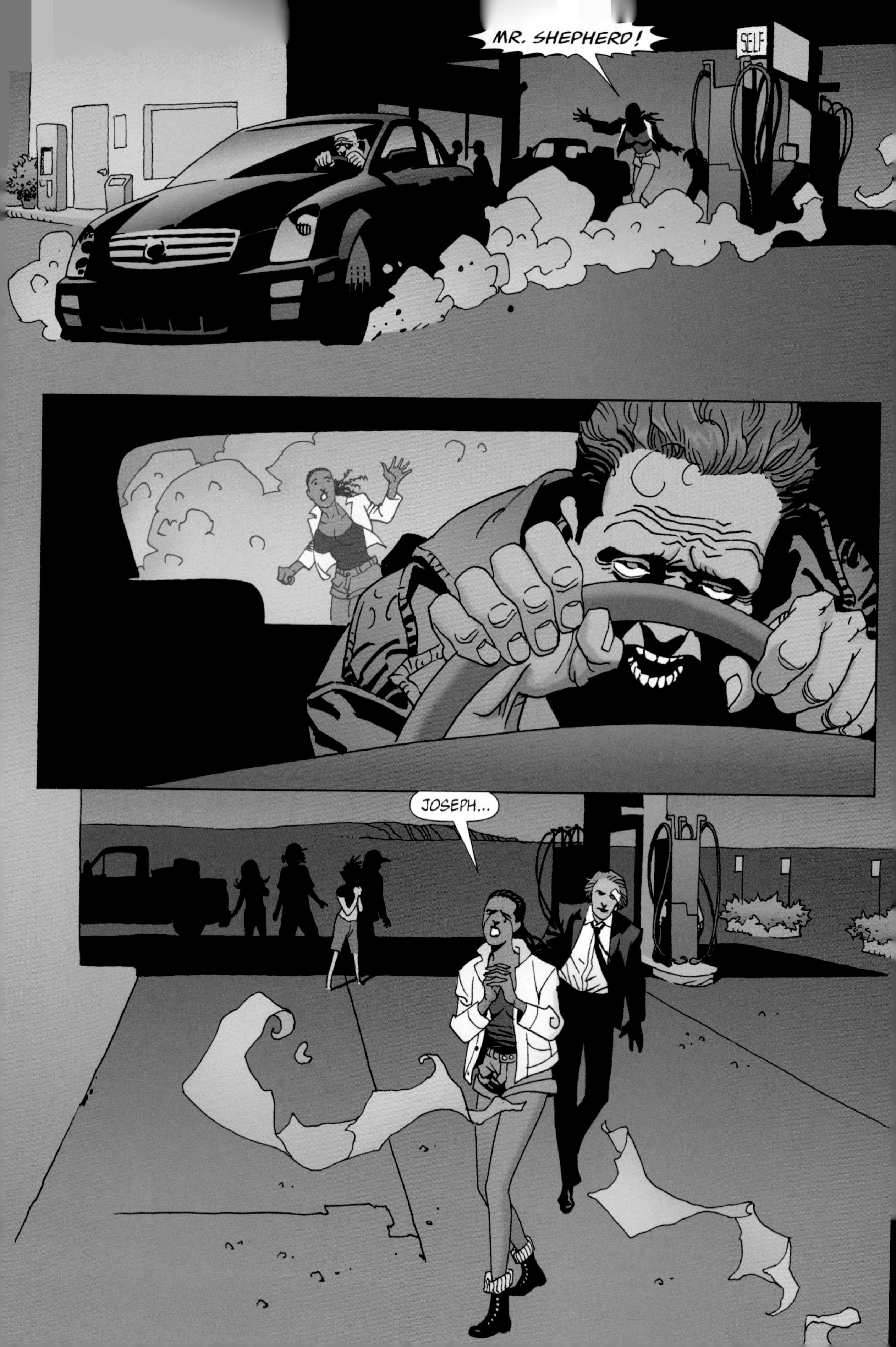
MR. SHEPHERD!
SELF
JOSEPH...

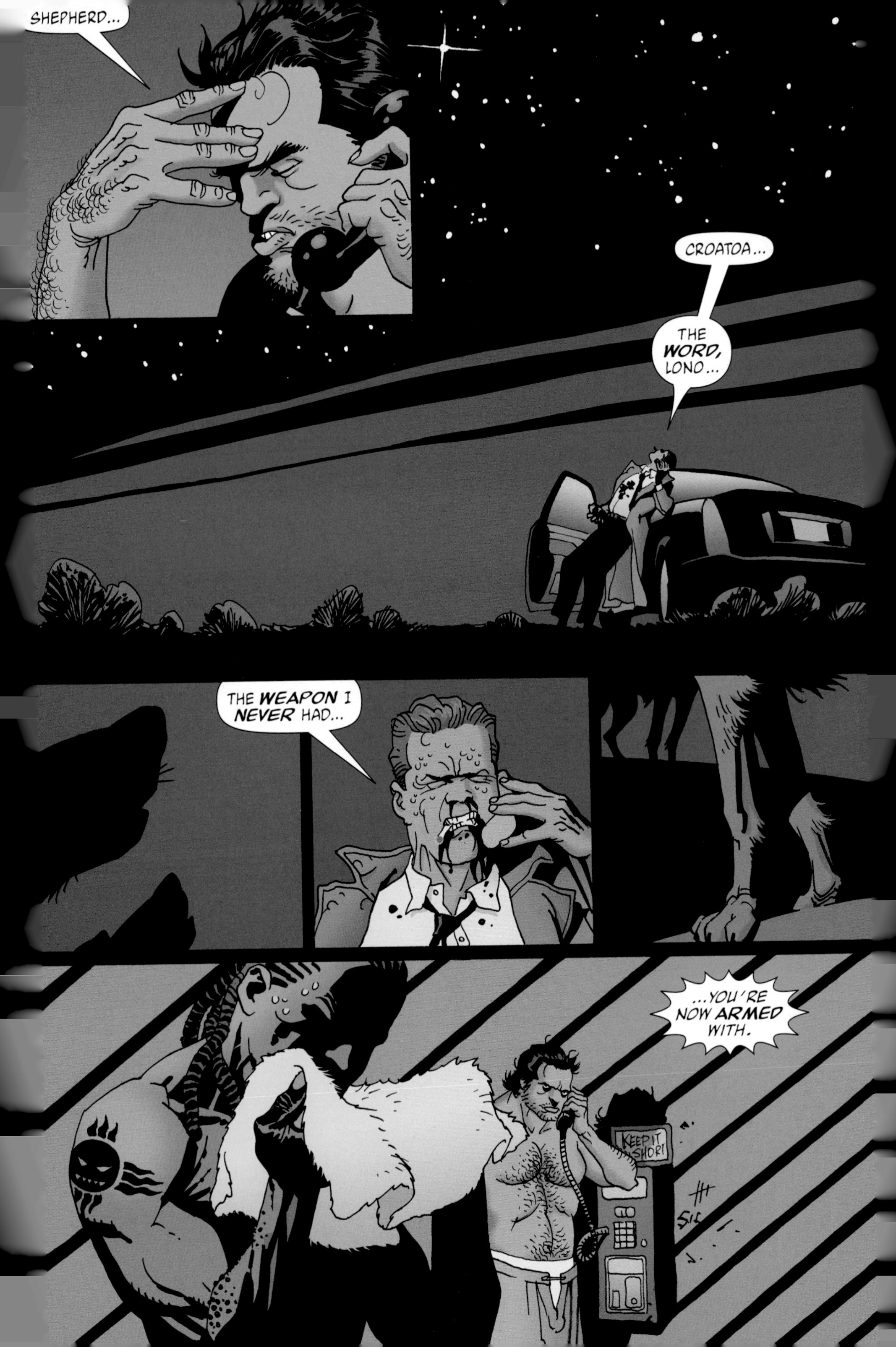
SHEPHERD...
CROATOA...
THE WORD, LONO...
THE WEAPON I NEVER HAD...
...YOU'RE NOW ARMED WITH.
KEEP IT SHORT

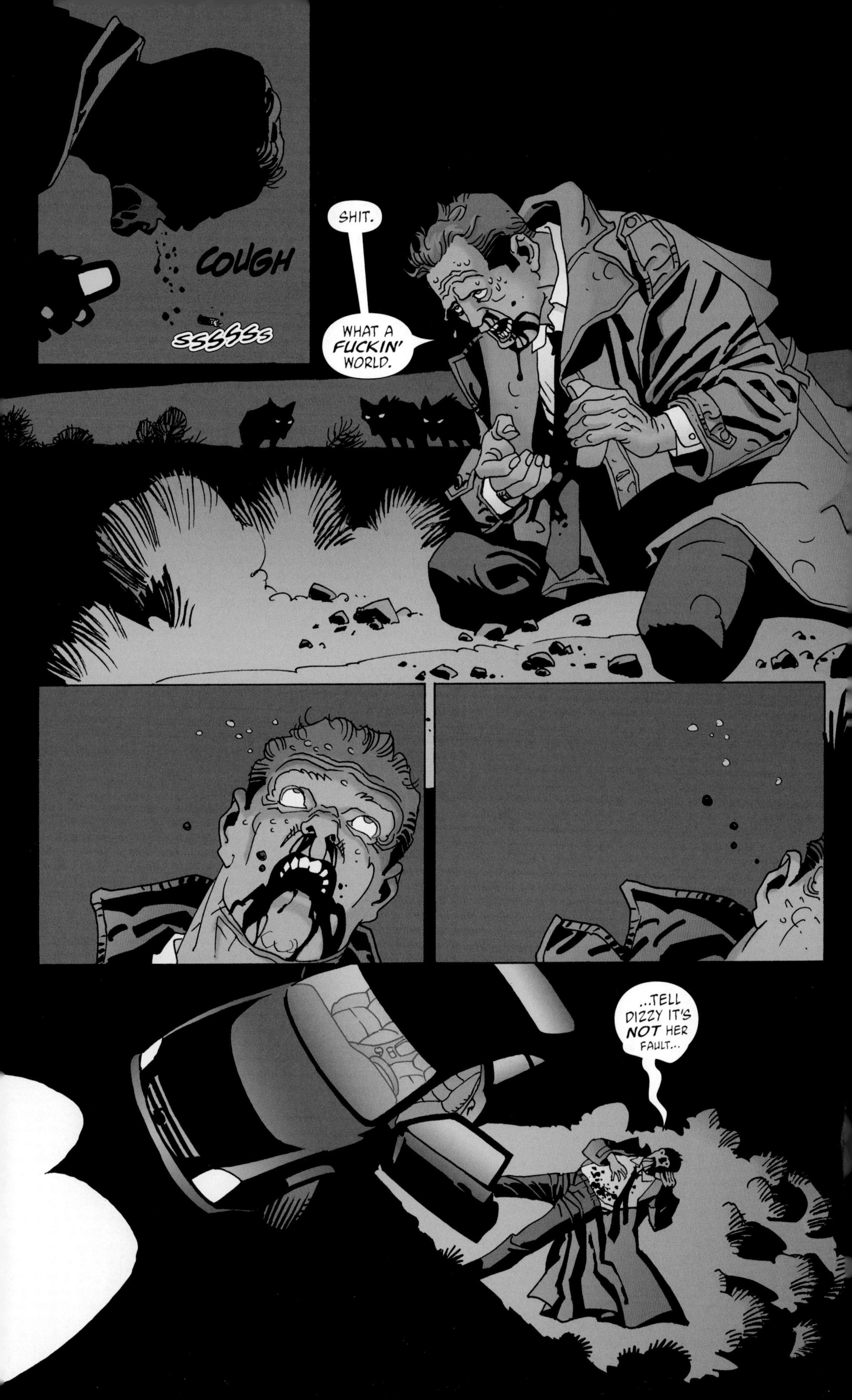
COUGH
SSSSSS
SHIT.
WHAT A FUCKIN' WORLD.
...TELL DIZZY IT'S NOT HER FAULT...

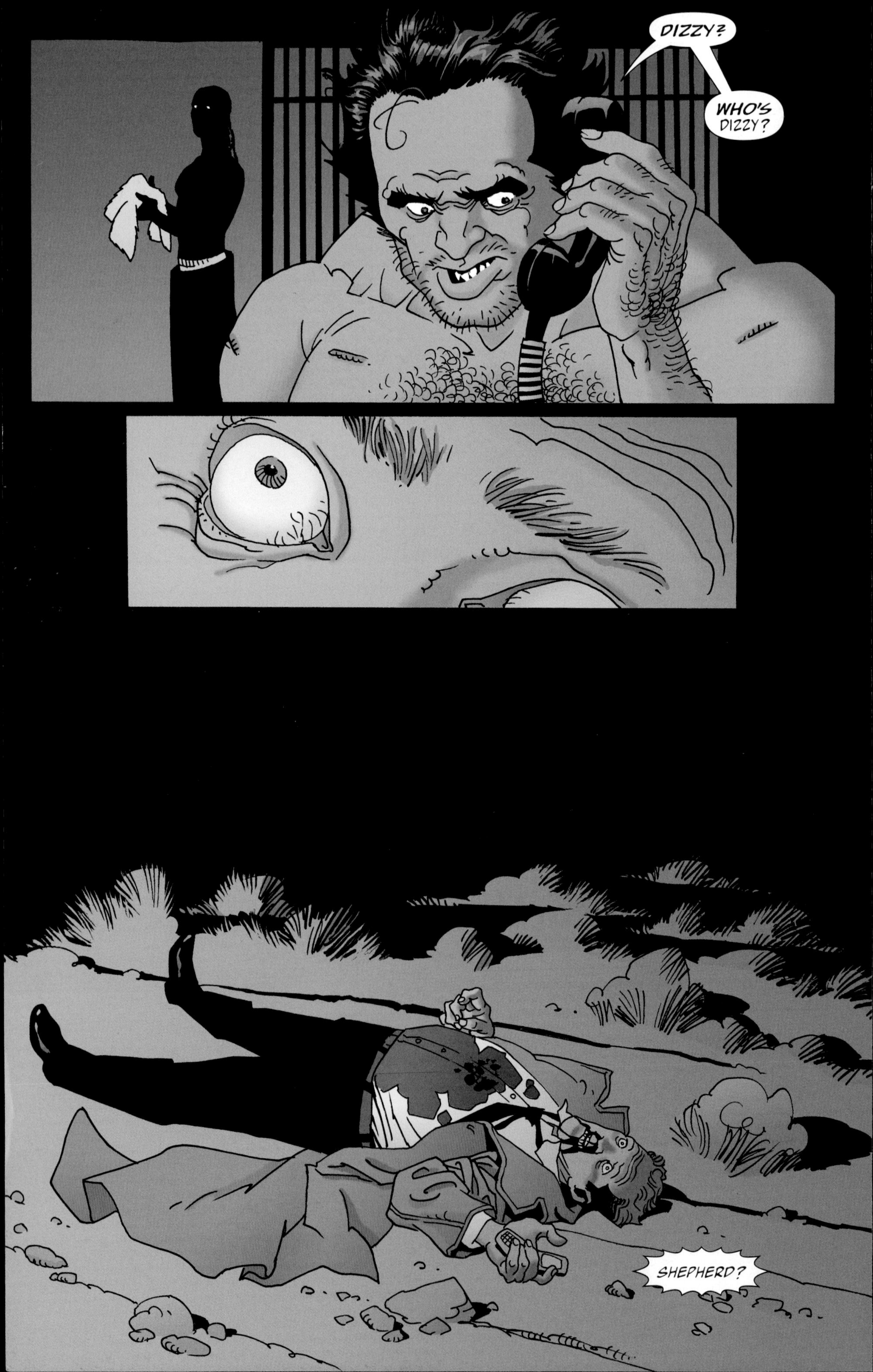
DIZZY?
WHO'S DIZZY?
SHEPHERD?

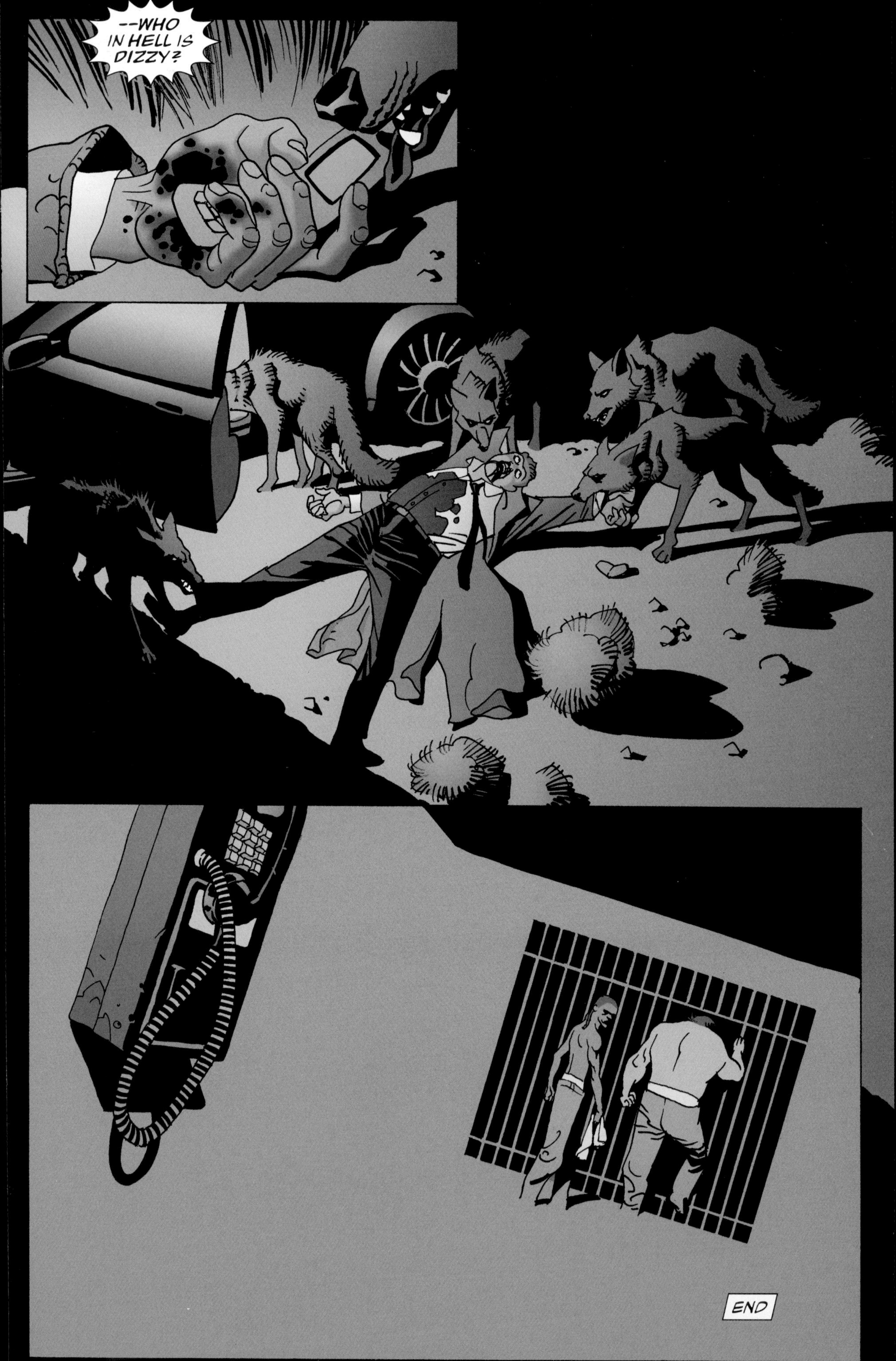
--WHO IN HELL IS DIZZY?
END

AVATARS

The Lost 100 BULLETS Video Game

During the original publication of 100 BULLETS, numerous offers for licensed products related to the series were considered by its creators and the Vertigo editorial team. One such proposal was a video game that would have featured new characters in its content. Though development on the project eventually stalled, Eduardo Risso did produce a series of model sheets for the characters, which are reproduced for the first time on the following pages.

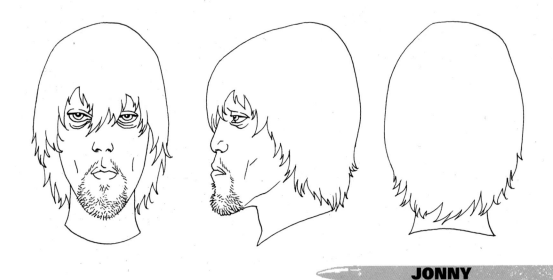

JONNY

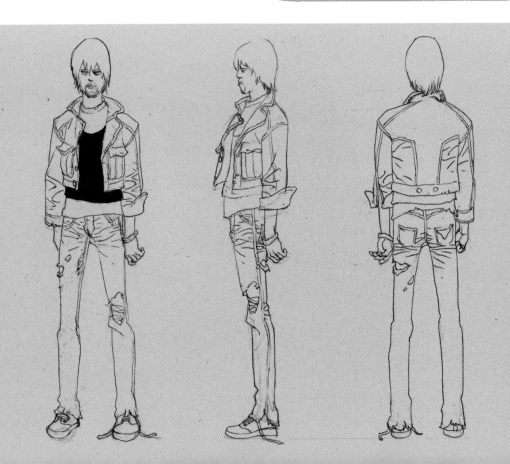

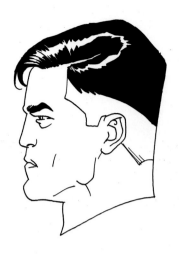

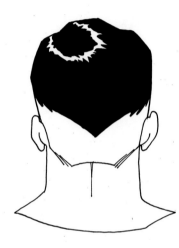

MARCUS

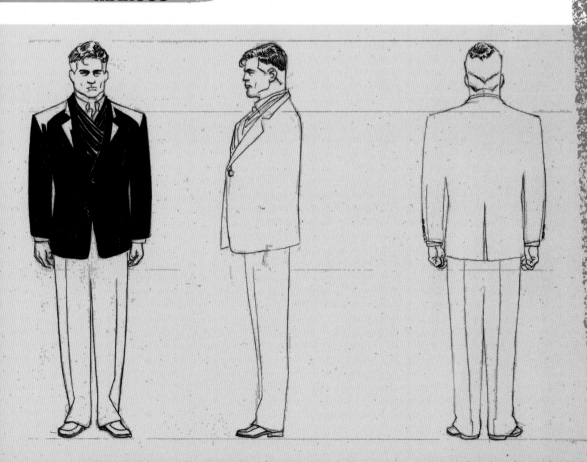

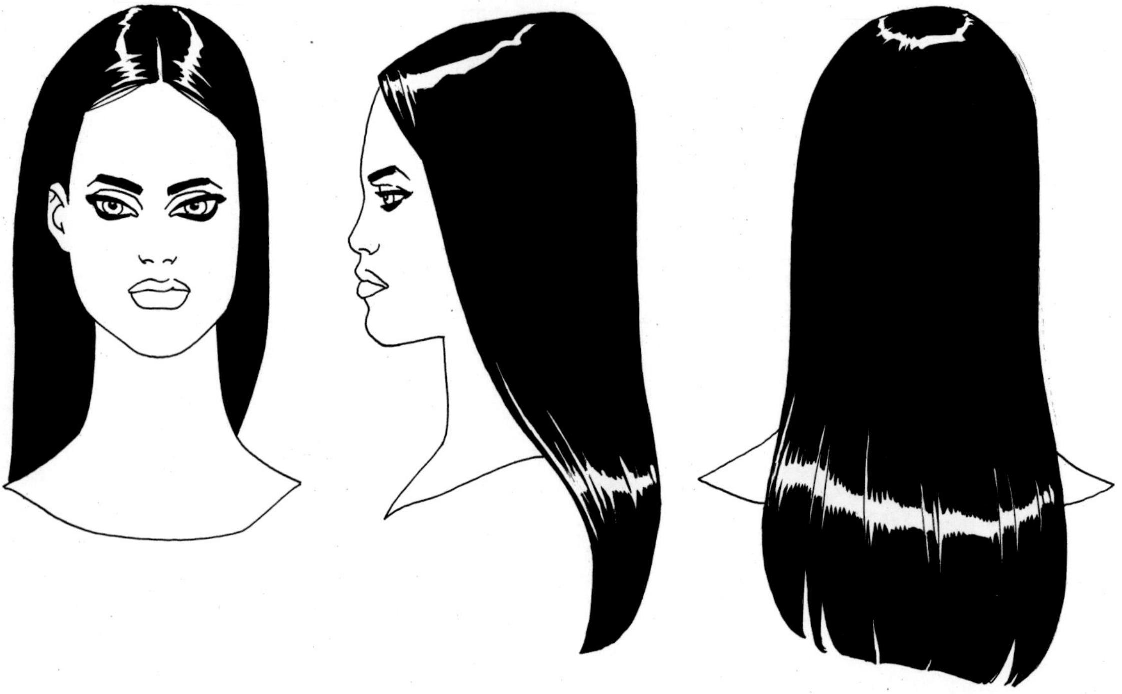

WINTER

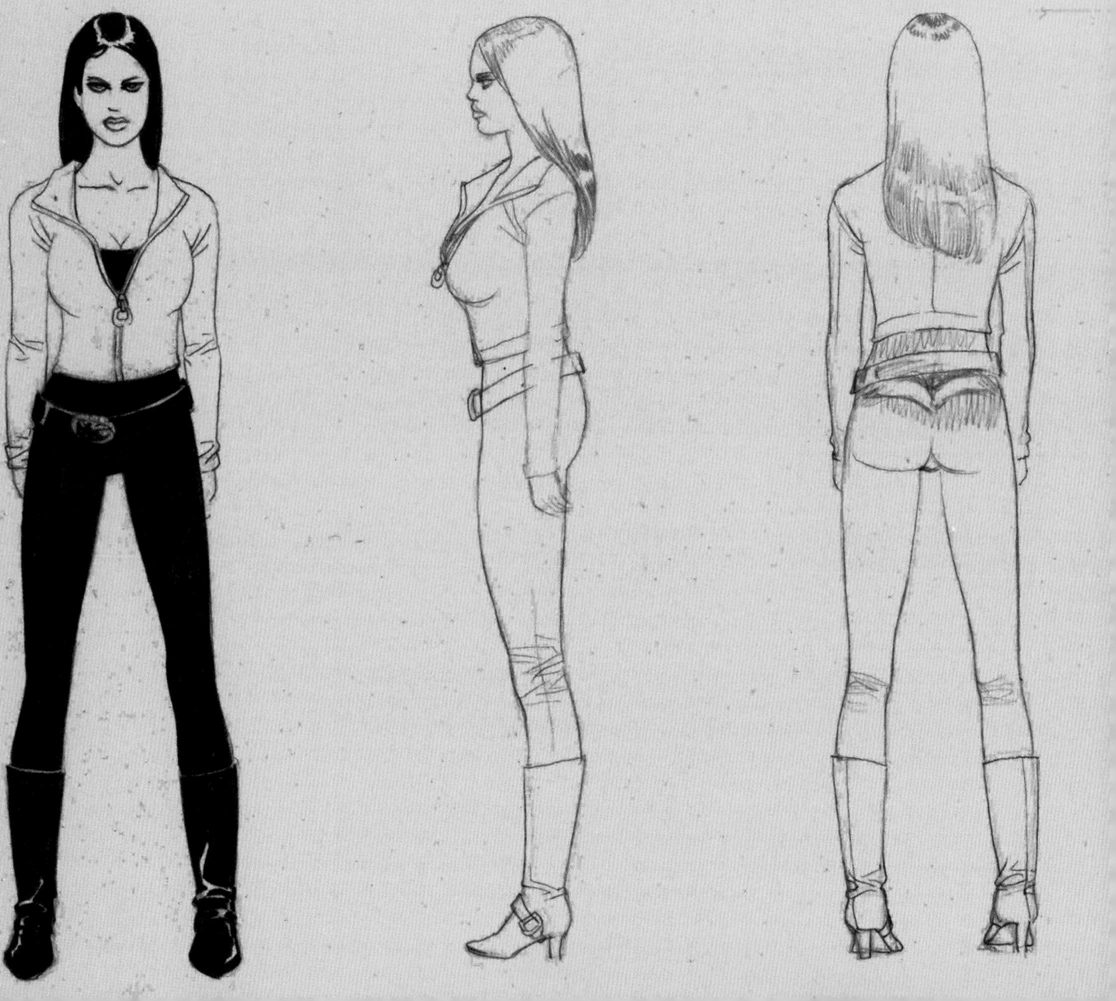

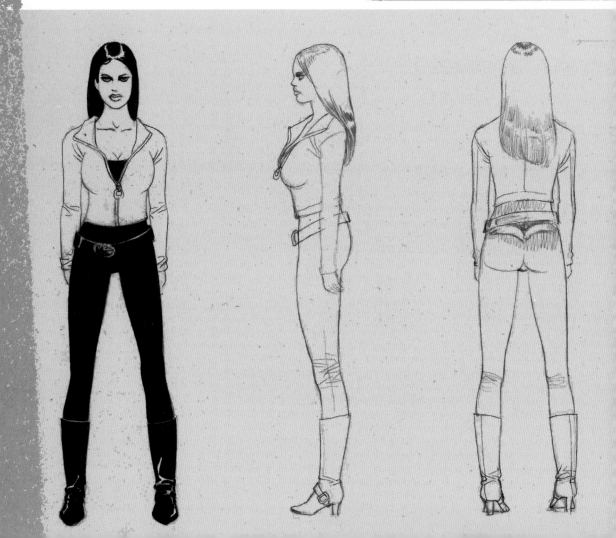

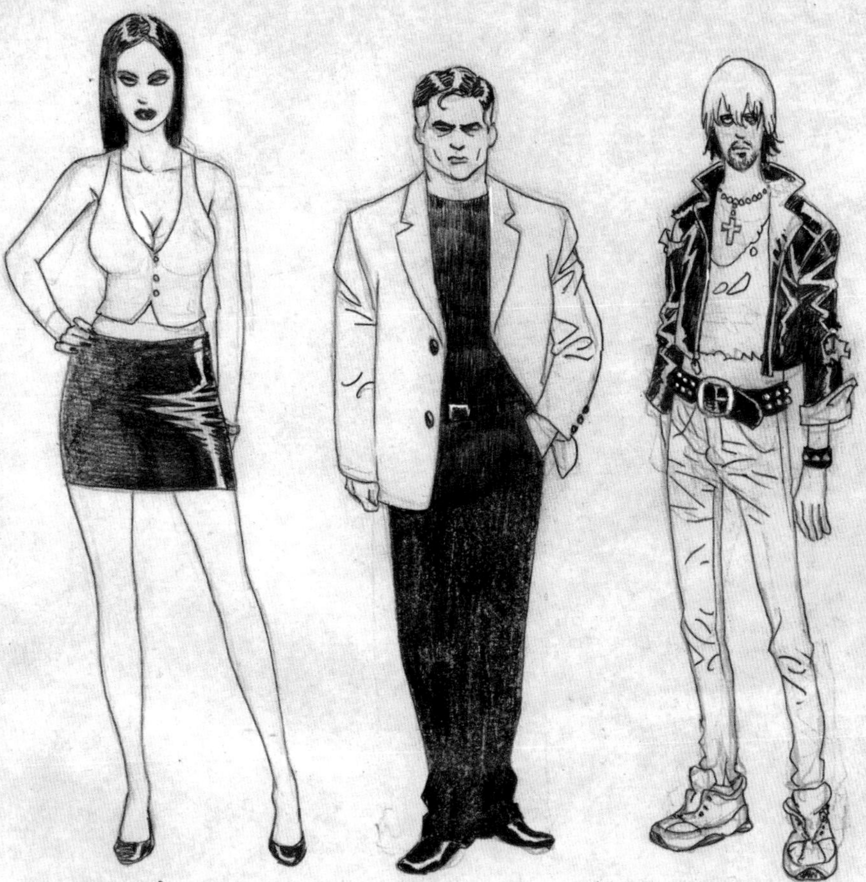

WINTER 1 MARCUS 1 JONNY 1

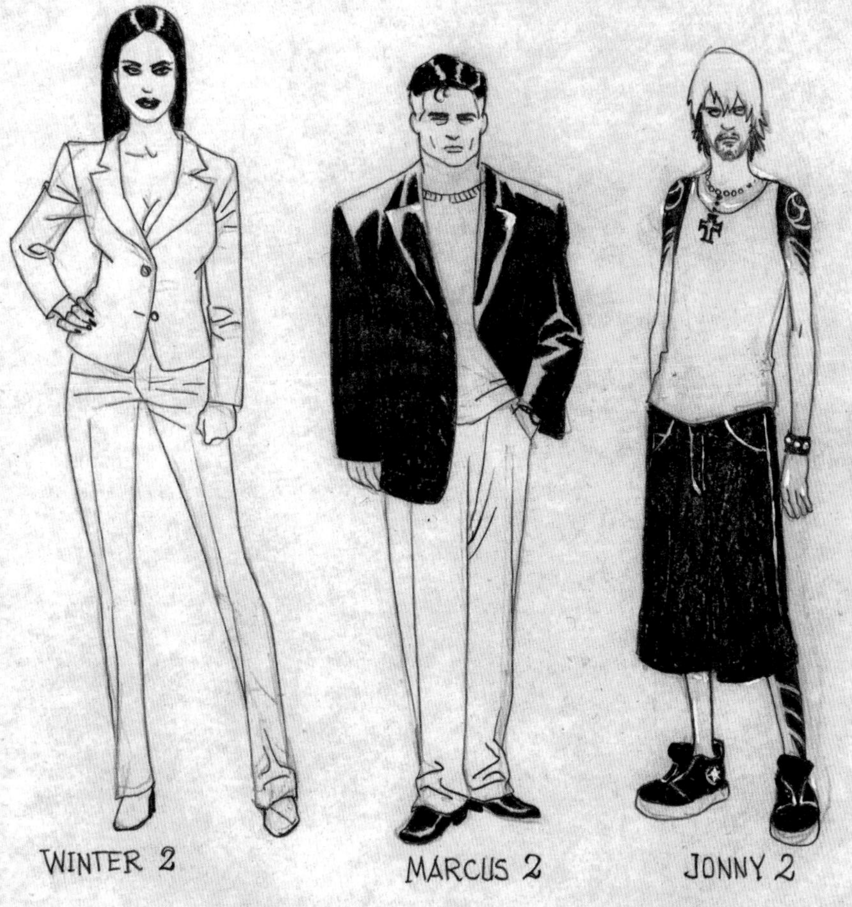

WINTER 2 MARCUS 2 JONNY 2

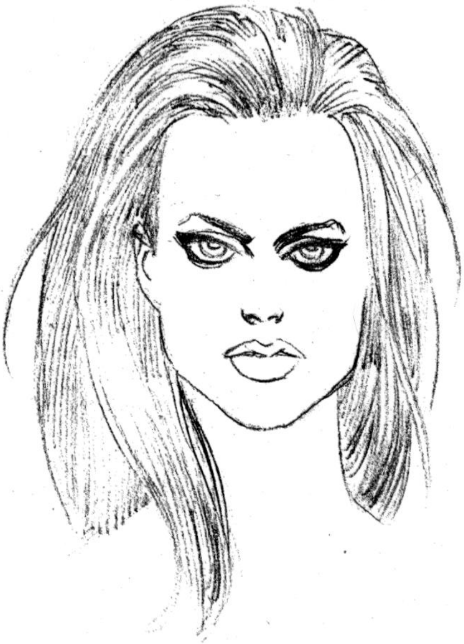

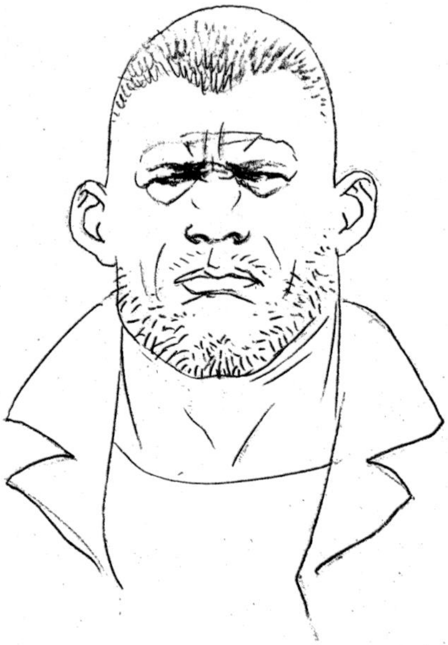

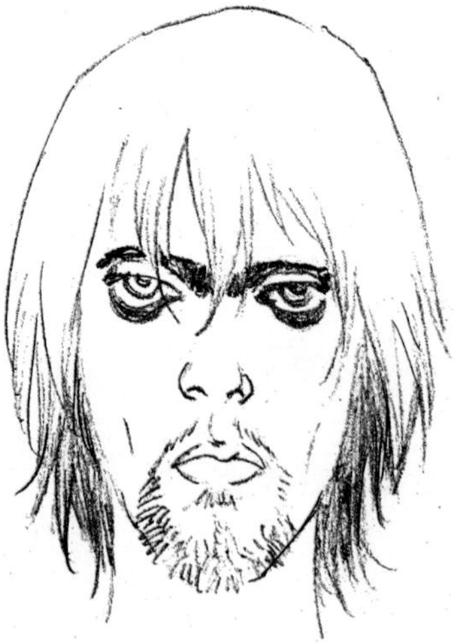